July 2019.

THE
EXPOSITOR'S
BIBLE
COMMENTARY

THE EXPOSITOR'S BIBLE COMMENTARY

in Thirteen Volumes

When complete, the Expositor's Bible Commentary will include the following volumes:

To see which titles are available, visit www.zondervan.com.

THE
EXPOSITOR'S
BIBLE
COMMENTARY

REVISED EDITION

Hebrews ~ Revelation

Tremper Longman III & David E. Garland

General Editors

GRAND RAPIDS, MICHIGAN 49530 USA

ZONDERVAN.COM/
AUTHOR**TRACKER**

ZONDERVAN

The Expositor's Bible Commentary: Hebrews–Revelation
Hebrews—Copyright © 2006 by R. T. France
James—Copyright © 2006 by George H. Guthrie
1, 2 Peter, Jude—Copyright ©by J. Daryl Charles
1, 2, 3 John—Copyright © by Tom Thatcher
Revelation—Copyright © by Alan F. Johnson

Requests for information should be addressed to:
Zondervan, *Grand Rapids, Michigan 49530*

Library of Congress Cataloging-in-Publication Data

The expositor's Bible commentary / [general editors], Tremper Longman III and David E. Garland.—Rev.
     p. cm.
    Includes bibliographical references.
    ISBN 978-0-310-26894-9 (hardcover)
    1. Bible. N.T.—Commentaries.   I. Longman, Tremper.   II. Garland, David E.
  BS2341.53.E96 2005
  220.7—dc22   2005006281

Interior design by Tracey Walker

Printed in the United States of America

09 10 11 12 13 14 15 16 17 18 19 20 • 27 26 25 24 23 22 21 20 19 18 17 16 15 14 13 12 11 10 9 8 7 6 5 4 3 2

CONTENTS

CONTRIBUTORS TO VOLUME THIRTEEN

Hebrews: **R. T. France** (Ph.D.) is an Anglican clergyman and New Testament scholar, now retired, whose appointments have included London Bible College and Wycliffe Hall.

James: **George H. Guthrie** (Ph.D., Southwestern Baptist Theological Seminary) is professor of Bible and chairman of the department of Christian studies at Union University in Jackson, Tennessee.

1, 2 Peter, Jude: **J. Daryl Charles** (Ph.D., Westminster Theological Seminary) is associate professor of religion and ethics at Union University in Jackson, Tennessee.

1, 2, 3 John: **Tom Thatcher** (Ph.D., Southern Baptist Theological Seminary) is associate professor of New Testament at Cincinnati Christian University in Ohio.

Revelation: **Alan F. Johnson** (Th.D., Dallas Theological Seminary) is emeritus professor of New Testament and Christian ethics and adjunct professor of theological ethics at Wheaton College and Graduate School in Illinois.

General editor: **Tremper Longman III** (Ph.D., Yale University) is professor of biblical studies at Westmont College in Santa Barbara, California.

General editor: **David E. Garland** (Ph.D., Southern Baptist Theological Seminary) is associate dean of academic affairs and William M. Hinson professor of Christian Scriptures at George W. Truett Seminary, Baylor University, in Waco, Texas.

PREFACE

Frank Gaebelein wrote the following in the preface to the original Expositor's Bible Commentary (which first appeared in 1979): "The title of this work defines its purpose. Written primarily by expositors for expositors, it aims to provide preachers, teachers, and students of the Bible with a new and comprehensive commentary on the books of the Old and New Testaments." Those volumes achieved that purpose admirably. The original EBC was exceptionally well received and had an enormous impact on the life of the church. It has served as the mainstay of countless pastors and students who could not afford an extensive library on each book of the Bible but who wanted solid guidance from scholars committed to the authority of the Holy Scriptures.

Gaebelein also wrote, "A commentary that will continue to be useful through the years should handle contemporary trends in biblical studies in such a way as to avoid becoming outdated when critical fashions change." This revision continues the EBC's exalted purpose and stands on the shoulders of the expositors of the first edition, but it seeks to maintain the usefulness of the commentary by interacting with new discoveries and academic discussions. While the primary goal of this commentary is to elucidate the text and not to provide a guide to the scholarly literature about the text, the commentators critically engage recent academic discussion and provide updated bibliographies so that pastors, teachers, and students can keep abreast of modern scholarship.

Some of the commentaries in the EBC have been revised by the original author or in conjunction with a younger colleague. In other cases, scholars have been commissioned to offer fresh commentaries because the original author had passed on or wanted to pass on the baton to the next generation of evangelical scholars. Today, with commentaries on a single book of the Old and New Testaments often extending into multiple volumes, the need for a comprehensive yet succinct commentary that guides one to the gist of the text's meaning is even more pressing. The new EBC seeks to fill this need.

The theological stance of this commentary series remains unchanged: the authors are committed to the divine inspiration, complete trustworthiness, and full authority of the Bible. The commentators have demonstrated proficiency in the biblical book that is their specialty, as well as commitment to the church and the pastoral dimension of biblical interpretation. They also represent the geographical and confessional diversity that characterized the first contributors.

The commentaries adhere to the same chief principle of grammatico-historical interpretation that drove the first edition. In the foreword to the inaugural issue of the journal *New Testament Studies* in 1954, Matthew Black warned that "the danger in the present is that theology, with its head too high in the clouds, may end by falling into the pit of an unhistorical and uncritical dogmatism. Into any new theological undertaking must be brought all that was best in the old ideal of sound learning, scrupulous attention to philology, text and history." The dangers that Black warned against over fifty years ago have not vanished. Indeed, new dangers arise in a secular, consumerist culture that finds it more acceptable to use God's name in exclamations than in prayer and that encourages insipid theologies that hang in the wind and shift to tickle the ears and to meet the latest fancy. Only a solid biblical foundation can fend off these fads.

The Bible was not written for our information but for our transformation. It is not a quarry to find stones with which to batter others but to find the rock on which to build the church. It does not invite us simply to speak of God but to hear God and to confess that his Son, Jesus Christ, is Lord to the glory of God the Father (Php 2:10). It also calls us to obey his commandments (Mt 28:20). It is not a self-interpreting text, however. Interpretation of the Holy Scriptures requires sound learning and regard for history, language, and text. Exegetes must interpret not only the primary documents but all that has a bearing, direct or indirect, on the grammar and syntax, historical context, transmission, and translation of these writings.

The translation used in this commentary remains the New International Version (North American edition), but all of the commentators work from the original languages (Hebrew and Greek) and draw on other translations when deemed useful. The format is also very similar to the original EBC, while the design is extensively updated with a view to enhanced ease of use for the reader. Each commentary section begins with an introduction (printed in a single-column format) that provides the reader with the background necessary to understand the Bible book. Almost all introductions include a short bibliography and an outline. The Bible text is divided into primary units that are often explained in an "Overview" section that precedes commentary on specific verses. The complete text of the New International Version is provided for quick reference, and an extensive "Commentary" section (printed in a double-column format) follows the reproducing of the text. When the Hebrew or Greek text is cited in the commentary section, a phonetic system of transliteration and translation is used. The "Notes" section (printed in a single-column format) provides a specialized discussion of key words or concepts, as well as helpful resource information. The original languages and their transliterations will appear in this section. Finally, on occasion, expanded thoughts can be found in a "Reflections" section (printed in a double-column format) that follows the Notes section.

One additional feature is worth mentioning. Throughout this volume, wherever specific biblical words are discussed, the Goodrick-Kohlenberger (GK) numbers have been added. These numbers, which appear in the *Strongest NIV Exhaustive Concordance* and other reference tools, are based on the numbering system developed by Edward Goodrick and John Kohlenberger III and provide a system similar but superior to the Strong's numbering system.

The editors wish to thank all of the contributors for their hard work and commitment to this project. We also deeply appreciate the labor and skill of the staff at Zondervan. It is a joy to work with them—in particular Jack Kuhatschek, Stan Gundry, Katya Covrett, and Dirk Buursma. In addition, we acknowledge with thanks the work of Connie Gundry Tappy as copy editor.

We all fervently desire that these commentaries will result not only in a deeper intellectual grasp of the Word of God but also in hearts that more profoundly love and obey the God who reveals himself to us in its pages.

David E. Garland, associate dean for academic affairs and professor of Christian Scriptures, George W. Truett Theological Seminary at Baylor University

Tremper Longman III, Robert H. Gundry professor of biblical studies, Westmont College

ABBREVIATIONS

Bible Texts, Versions, Etc.

ASV	American Standard Version	NET	New English Translation
CEV	Contemporary English Version	NIV	New International Version
CSB	Christian Standard Bible	NJB	New Jerusalem Bible
ESV	English Standard Version	NKJV	New King James Version
GNB	Good News Bible (see also TEV)	NLT	New Living Translation
GWT	God's Word Translation	NRSV	New Revised Standard Version
JB	Jerusalem Bible	NT	New Testament
KJV	King James Version	OT	Old Testament
LXX	Septuagint (the Greek OT)	Phillips	*New Testament in Modern English*,
MLB	Modern Language Bible		J. B. Phillips
MT	Masoretic Text of the OT	REB	Revised English Bible
NAB	New American Bible	RSV	Revised Standard Version
NASB	New American Standard Bible	TEV	Today's English Version
NCV	New Century Version	TNIV	Today's New International Version
NEB	New English Bible	UBS	United Bible Societies

Old Testament, New Testament, Apocrypha

Ge	Genesis	SS	Song of Songs
Ex	Exodus	Isa	Isaiah
Lev	Leviticus	Jer	Jeremiah
Nu	Numbers	La	Lamentations
Dt	Deuteronomy	Eze	Ezekiel
Jos	Joshua	Da	Daniel
Jdg	Judges	Hos	Hosea
Ru	Ruth	Joel	Joel
1–2Sa	1–2 Samuel	Am	Amos
1–2Ki	1–2 Kings	Ob	Obadiah
1–2Ch	1–2 Chronicles	Jnh	Jonah
Ezr	Ezra	Mic	Micah
Ne	Nehemiah	Na	Nahum
Est	Esther	Hab	Habakkuk
Job	Job	Zep	Zephaniah
Ps/Pss	Psalm/Psalms	Hag	Haggai
Pr	Proverbs	Zec	Zechariah
Ecc	Ecclesiastes	Mal	Malachi

Mt	Matthew	Jude	Jude
Mk	Mark	Rev	Revelation
Lk	Luke	Add Esth	Additions to Esther
Jn	John	Add Dan	Additions to Daniel
Ac	Acts	Bar	Baruch
Ro	Romans	Bel	Bel and the Dragon
1–2Co	1–2 Corinthians	Ep Jer	Epistle of Jeremiah
Gal	Galatians	1–2 Esd	1–2 Esdras
Eph	Ephesians	1–2 Macc	1–2 Maccabees
Php	Philippians	3–4 Macc	3–4 Maccabees
Col	Colossians	Jdt	Judith
1–2Th	1–2 Thessalonians	Pr Azar	Prayer of Azariah
1–2Ti	1–2 Timothy	Pr Man	Prayer of Manasseh
Tit	Titus	Ps 151	Psalm 151
Phm	Philemon	Sir	Sirach/Ecclesiasticus
Heb	Hebrews	Sus	Susanna
Jas	James	Tob	Tobit
1–2Pe	1–2 Peter	Wis	Wisdom of Solomon
1–2–3Jn	1–2–3 John		

Dead Sea Scrolls and Related Texts

1QapGen	*Genesis Apocryphon* (texts from Qumran)
1QIsa	Isaiah (texts from Qumran)
1QH	*Hôdāyōt* or *Thanksgiving Hymns* (texts from Qumran)
1QM	*Milḥāmāh* or *War Scroll* (texts from Qumran)
1QS	*Serek hayyaḥad* or *Rule of the Community* (texts from Qumran)
4QpNa	*Pesher Nahum* (texts from Qumran)
4QpPs	*Pesher Psalms* (texts from Qumran)
4Q44 (4QDt^q)	Deuteronomy (texts from Qumran)
4Q174	*Florilegium* (texts from Qumran)
4Q252	*Commentary on Genesis A*, formerly *Patriarchal Blessings* (texts from Qumran)
4Q400	*Songs of the Sabbath Sacrifice* (texts from Qumran)
4Q502	*Ritual of Marriage* (texts from Qumran)
11Q13	*Melchizedek* (texts from Qumran)

Other Ancient Texts

Abraham	*On the Life of Abraham* (Philo)	*An.*	*De anima* (Tertullian)
Aeth.	*Aethiopica* (Heliodorus)	*Ann.*	*Annales* (Tacitus)
Ag. Ap.	*Against Apion* (Josephus)	*Ant.*	*Jewish Antiquities* (Josephus)

Apos. Con.	Apostolic Constitutions	*Ep. Tra.*	Epistulae ad Trajanum (Pliny)
As. Mos.	Assumption of Moses	*Eth. nic.*	Ethica nichomachea (Aristotle)
Ascen. Isa.	Ascension of Isaiah	*Fam.*	Epistulae ad familares (Cicero)
Att.	Epistulae ad Atticum (Cicero)	*1 Apol.*	First Apology (Justin Martyr)
b. Ber.	Berakhot (Babylonian Talmud)	*2–4 Bar.*	2–4 Baruch
b. Sanh.	Sanhedrin (Babylonian Talmud)	*1–2 Clem.*	1–2 Clement
b. Šebu.	Shevuʾot (Babylonian Talmud)	*1–2 En.*	1–2 Enoch
Bapt.	De baptismo (Tertullian)	*Flacc.*	In Flaccum (Philo)
Barn.	Barnabas	*Flight*	On Flight and Finding (Philo)
Ben.	De beneficiis (Seneca)	*Fr. Prov.*	Fragmenta in Proverbia (Hippolytus)
Bibl.	Bibliotheca (Photius)	*Gen. Rab.*	Genesis Rabbah
Bibl. hist.	Bibliotheca historica (Diodorus Siculus)	*Geogr.*	Geographica (Strabo)
Bride	Advice to the Bride and Groom (Plutarch)	*Haer.*	Adversus Haereses (Irenaeus)
		Hell.	Hellenica (Xenophon)
Cels.	Contra Celsum (Origen)	*Hist.*	Historicus (Polybius, Cassius Dio, Thucydides)
Cic.	Cicero (Plutarch)	*Hist.*	Historiae (Herodotus)
Claud.	Divus Claudius (Suetonius)	*Hist. eccl.*	History of the Church (Eusebius)
Comm. Dan.	Commentarium in Danielem (Hippolytus)	*Hist. Rome*	The History of Rome (Livy)
Comm. Jo.	Commentarii in evangelium Joannis (Origen)	*Hom. 1 Tim.*	Homilies on 1 Timothy (John Chrysostom)
Comm. Matt.	Commentarium in evangelium Matthaei (Origen)	*Hom. 2 Tim.*	Homilies on 2 Timothy (John Chrysostom)
Corrept.	De correptione et gratia (Augustine)	*Hom. Josh.*	Homilies on Joshua (Origen)
Cyr.	Cyropaedia (Xenophon)	*Hom. Rom.*	Homilies on Romans (John Chrysostom)
Decal.	De decaloga (Philo)	*Hom. Tit.*	Homilies on Titus (John Chrysostom)
Def. orac.	De defectu oraculorum (Plutarch)		
Dial.	Dialogus cum Tryphone (Justin Martyr)	*Hypoth.*	Hypothetica (Philo)
		Jub.	Jubilees
Diatr.	Diatribai (Epictetus)	*J.W.*	Jewish War (Josephus)
Did.	Didache	*L.A.E.*	Life of Adam and Eve
Disc.	Discourses (Epictetus)	*Leg.*	Legum allegoriae (Philo)
Doctr. chr.	De doctrina christiana (Augustine)	*Let. Aris.*	Letter of Aristeas
Ebr.	De ebrietate (Philo)	*Lev. Rab.*	Leviticus Rabbah
Ench.	Enchiridion (Epictetus)	*Liv. Pro.*	Lives of the Prophets
Ep.	Epistulae morales (Seneca)	*m. ʾAbot*	Avot (Mishnah)
Eph.	To the Ephesians (Ignatius)	*m. Pesaḥ*	Pesahim (Mishnah)
Epist.	Epistulae (Jerome, Pliny, Hippocrates)	*m. Sanh.*	Sanhedrin (Mishnah)
		Magn.	To the Magnesians (Ignatius)

Mand.	Mandate (Shepherd of Hermas)	*Resp.*	Respublica (Plato)
Marc.	Adversus Marcionem (Tertullian)	*Rhet.*	Volumina rhetorica (Philodemus)
Mem.	Memorabilia (Xenophon)	*Rom.*	To the Romans (Ignatius)
Migr.	De migratione Abrahami (Philo)	*Rosc. com.*	Pro Roscio comoedo (Cicero)
Mor.	Moralia (Plutarch)	*Sera*	De sera numinis vindicta (Plutarch)
Moses	On the Life of Moses (Philo)	*Sib. Or.*	Sibylline Oracles
Nat.	Naturalis historia (Pliny)	*Sim.*	Similitudes (Shepherd of Hermas)
Onir.	Onirocritica (Artemidorus)	*Smyrn.*	To the Smyrnaeans (Ignatius)
Or.	Orationes (Demosthenes)	*Somn.*	De somniis (Philo)
Paed.	Paedagogus (Clement of Alexandria)	*Spec.*	De specialibus legibus (Philo)
		Stat.	Ad populum Antiochenum de statuis (John Chrysostom)
Phil.	To the Philippians (Polycarp)		
Plant.	De plantatione (Philo)	*Strom.*	Stromata (Clement of Alexandria)
Pol.	Politica (Aristotle)	*T. Ash.*	Testament of Asher
Pol.	To Polycarp (Ignatius)	*T. Jud.*	Testament of Judah
Posterity	On the Posterity of Cain (Origen)	*T. Levi*	Testament of Levi
Praescr.	De praescriptione haereticorum (Tertullian)	*T. Naph.*	Testament of Naphtali
		T. Reu.	Testament of Reuben
Princ.	De principiis (Origen)	*Tg. Ps.-J.*	Targum Pseudo-Jonathan
Pss. Sol.	Psalms of Solomon	*Theaet.*	Theaetetus (Plato)
Pud.	De pudicitia (Tertullian)	*Trall.*	To the Trallians (Ignatius)
Quaest. conv.	Quaestionum convivialum libri IX (Plutarch)	*Virt.*	De virtutibus (Philo)
		Vis.	Visions (Shepherd of Hermas)
Quint. fratr.	Epistulae ad Quintum fratrem (Cicero)		

Journals, Periodicals, Reference Works, Series

AB	Anchor Bible	*BA*	Biblical Archaeologist
ABRL	Anchor Bible Reference Library	BAGD	Bauer, Arndt, Gingrich, and Danker (2d ed). *Greek-English Lexicon of the New Testament and Other Early Christian Literature*
ACCS	Ancient Christian Commentary on Scripture		
ACNT	Augsburg Commentaries on the New Testament		
An.	De anima (Tertullian)	*BASOR*	Bulletin of the American Schools of Oriental Research
AnBib	Analecta biblica		
ANF	Ante-Nicene Fathers	*BBR*	Bulletin for Biblical Research
ANRW	Aufstieg und Niedergang der römischen Welt	BDAG	Bauer, Danker, Arndt, and Gingrich (3d ed). *Greek-English Lexicon of the New Testament and Other Early Christian Literature*
AThR	Anglican Theological Review		

BDB	Brown, Driver, and Briggs. *A Hebrew and English Lexicon of the Old Testament*	*EuroJTh*	*European Journal of Theology*
		EvQ	*Evangelical Quarterly*
		ExpTim	*Expository Times*
BDF	Blass, Debrunner, and Funk. *A Greek Grammar of the New Testament and Other Early Christian Literature*	*GNS*	*Good News Studies*
		GR	*Greece and Rome*
		GRBS	*Greek, Roman, and Byzantine Studies*
BECNT	Baker Exegetical Commentary on the New Testament	*HALOT*	Koehler, Baumgartner, and Stamm. *The Hebrew and Aramaic Lexicon of the Old Testament*
Bib	*Biblica*		
BibInt	*Biblical Interpretation*	*HBT*	*Horizons in Biblical Theology*
BibS(N)	Biblische Studien (Neukirchen)	Herm	Hermeneia commentary series
BJRL	*Bulletin of the John Rylands University Library of Manchester*	HNT	Handbuch zum Neuen Testament
		HNTC	Harper's New Testament Commentaries
BJS	Brown Judaic Studies		
BR	*Biblical Research*	*HTR*	*Harvard Theological Review*
BSac	*Bibliotheca sacra*	HTS	Harvard Theological Studies
BST	The Bible Speaks Today	*HUCA*	*Hebrew Union College Annual*
BT	*The Bible Translator*	ICC	International Critical Commentary
BTB	*Biblical Theology Bulletin*		
BZ	*Biblische Zeitschrift*	*IDB*	*Interpreter's Dictionary of the Bible*
BZAW	Beihefte zur Zeitschrift für die alttestamentliche Wissenschaft	*Int*	*Interpretation*
		IVPNTC	IVP New Testament Commentary
BZNW	Beihefte zur Zeitschrift für die neutestamentliche Wissenschaft	*JBMW*	*Journal for Biblical Manhood and Womanhood*
CBQ	*Catholic Biblical Quarterly*	*JBL*	*Journal of Biblical Literature*
CH	*Church History*	*JETS*	*Journal of the Evangelical Theological Society*
ChrT	*Christianity Today*		
CJT	*Canadian Journal of Theology*	*JSS*	*Journal of Semitic Studies*
CTJ	*Calvin Theological Journal*	*JTS*	*Journal of Theological Studies*
CTR	*Criswell Theological Review*	*JSNT*	*Journal for the Study of the New Testament*
DukeDivR	*Duke Divinity Review*		
EBC	Expositor's Bible Commentary	JSNTSup	JSNT Supplement Series
ECC	Eerdmans Critical Commentary	*JSOT*	*Journal for the Study of the Old Testament*
EcR	*Ecumenical Review*		
EGT	Expositor's Greek Testament	JSOTSup	JSOT Supplement Series
ESCJ	Etudes sur le christianisme et le judaisme (Studies in Christianity and Judaism)	KEK	Kritisch-exegetischer Kommentar über das Neue Testament
		LCC	Library of Christian Classics
ETS	Evangelical Theological Society	LEC	Library of Early Christianity

L&N	Louw and Nida. *Greek-English Lexicon of the New Testament: Based on Semantic Domains*	*PEGLMBS*	*Proceedings, Eastern Great Lakes and Midwest Bible Societies*
LCL	Loeb Classical Library	PG	Patrologia graeca
LSJ	Liddell, Scott, and Jones. *A Greek-English Lexicon*	PL	Patrologia latina
		PNTC	Pillar New Testament Commentary
MM	Moulton and Milligan. *The Vocabulary of the Greek Testament*	*Presb*	*Presbyterion*
		PresR	*Presbyterian Review*
		PTR	*Princeton Theological Review*
NAC	New American Commentary	*RBibLit*	*Review of Biblical Literature*
NCBC	New Century Bible Commentary	*RefJ*	*Reformed Journal*
Neot	*Neotestamentica*	*RelSRev*	*Religious Studies Review*
NewDocs	*New Documents Illustrating Early Christianity*	*ResQ*	*Restoration Quarterly*
		RevExp	*Review and Expositor*
NIBC	New International Biblical Commentary	SBB	Stuttgarter biblische Aufsatzbände
		SBJT	*Southern Baptist Journal of Theology*
NICNT	New International Commentary on the New Testament	SBLDS	Society of Biblical Literature Dissertation Series
NICOT	New International Commentary on the Old Testament	*SBLSP*	*Society of Biblical Literature Seminar Papers*
NIDNTT	*New International Dictionary of New Testament Theology*	SBT	Studies in Biblical Theology
		SE	*Studia evangelica*
NIDOTTE	*New International Dictionary of Old Testament Theology and Exegesis*	SEG	Supplementum epigraphicum graecum
NIGTC	New International Greek Testament Commentary	*SJT*	*Scottish Journal of Theology*
		SNT	Studien zum Neuen Testament
NIVAC	NIV Application Commentary	SNTSMS	Society for New Testament Studies Monograph Series
Notes	*Notes on Translation*		
NovT	*Novum Testamentum*	SP	Sacra Pagina
NovTSup	Novum Testamentum Supplements	STR-B	Strack, H.L., and P. Billerbeck. *Kommentar zum Neuen Testament aus Talmud und Midrasch*
NPNF	*Nicene and Post-Nicene Fathers*		
NTC	New Testament Commentary (Baker)	SUNT	Studien zur Umwelt des Neuen Testaments
NTD	Das Neue Testament Deutsch	*SVF*	*Stoicorum veterum fragmenta*
NTG	New Testament Guides	*TDNT*	Kittel and Friedrich. *Theological Dictionary of the New Testament*
NTS	*New Testament Studies*		
NTT	New Testament Theology	*TDOT*	Botterweck and Ringgren. *Theological Dictionary of the Old Testament*
OJRS	*Ohio Journal of Religious Studies*		

Them	*Themelios*	*TynBul*	*Tyndale Bulletin*
ThEv	*Theologia Evangelica*	*TZ*	*Theologische Zeitschrift*
THKNT	Theologischer Handkommentar zum Neuen Testament	*VE*	*Vox evangelica*
		WBC	Word Biblical Commentary
ThTo	*Theology Today*	WMANT	Wissenschaftliche Monographien zum Alten und Neuen Testament
TJ	*Trinity Journal*		
TLNT	*Theological Lexicon of the New Testament*	*WTJ*	*Westminster Theological Journal*
		WUNT	Wissenschaftliche Untersuchun-gen zum Neuen Testament
TNTC	Tyndale New Testament Commentaries		
		YCS	*Yale Classical Studies*
TOTC	Tyndale Old Testament Commentaries	*ZNW*	*Zeitschrift für die neutestamentliche Wissenschaft und die Kunde der älterern Kirche*
TS	*Theological Studies*		
TWOT	*Theological Wordbook of the Old Testament*	*ZPEB*	*Zondervan Pictorial Encyclopedia of the Bible*

General

AD	*anno Domini* (in the year of [our] Lord)	i.e.	*id est*, that is
		Lat.	Latin
BC	before Christ	lit.	literally
ca.	*circa* (around, about, approximately)	MS(S)	manuscript(s)
		n(n).	note(s)
cf.	*confer*, compare	NS	New Series
ch(s).	chapter(s)	p(p).	page(s)
d.	died	par.	parallel (indicates textual parallels)
diss.	dissertation	repr.	reprinted
ed(s).	editor(s), edited by, edition	rev.	revised
e.g.	*exempli gratia*, for example	s.v.	*sub verbo*, under the word
esp.	especially	trans.	translator, translated by
et al.	*et alii*, and others	vs.	versus
EV	English versions of the Bible	v(v).	verse(s)
f(f).	and the following one(s)		
frg.	fragment		
Gk.	Greek		
GK	Goodrick & Kohlenberger numbering system		
Heb.	Hebrew		
ibid.	*ibidem*, in the same place		

HEBREWS

R. T. FRANCE

Introduction

1. WHAT SORT OF WRITING?

Hebrews has traditionally been classified as a letter and is placed among the epistles of the NT,[1] yet its opening lacks all the normal marks of a NT letter[2]—the identification of author and recipients, the formal greeting, and prayer or thanksgiving. (In this it is paralleled in the NT only by 1 John.) Its sonorous opening sentence reminds us rather of the prologue of the gospel of John and suggests a philosophical or theological treatise. Yet its final chapter resembles the conclusions of Paul's letters, including not only exhortations and a request for prayer for the author and his ministry but also personal greetings and travel plans and a mention of Timothy, Paul's frequent companion. The contrast with the opening of the letter is so great that it has even been suggested that ch. 13 as a whole is a later addition intended to ensure the acceptance of Hebrews into the canon by turning it into a recognizable "epistle."[3]

But this is not a dispassionate academic treatise. It is a pastoral exhortation, interspersed with earnest appeals to the recipients to stand firm in their faith. Its "academic" arguments are deployed not for merely intellectual interest but as the essential basis for the author's appeal. He writes as a pastor closely aware of the specific situation of his readers, of their doubts and uncertainties, and of the issues that move them, and he writes looking for an existential response, not merely for intellectual assent. If his argument seems sometimes obscurely theological, caught up in matters of Jewish tradition and biblical exegesis that leave many

---

1. In the oldest surviving text, the Chester Beatty papyrus $\mathfrak{P}^{46}$ (ca. AD 200), Hebrews appears among the letters of Paul, between Romans and 1 Corinthians; it is probably placed there because of its length, this being the basis for the canonical order of Paul's letters. Several other early MSS place it after 2 Thessalonians, at the end of the letters to churches and before those to individuals.

2. The distinction often drawn between "letter" (a personal nonliterary communication) and "epistle" (a more formal literary document for wider circulation) is not a sharp one, especially in regard to the NT books from Romans to Jude; I shall use the more familiar term "letter" to describe them.

3. See G. W. Buchanan, *To the Hebrews* (AB 36; New York: Doubleday, 1972), 243–45; contra Buchanan and others who have doubted the authenticity of chapter 13, see W. L. Lane, *Hebrews 1–8* (WBC 47A; Waco, Tex.: Word, 1991), lxvii–lxviii.

modern readers cold, it is because he knows it is precisely in the understanding of these issues that his readers' problems begin, and as a good pastor he is scratching where they are itching. For all its "academic" content and sophisticated exegetical argument, this is essentially a "word of exhortation" (13:22).

Despite its rhetorical opening, therefore, Hebrews does seem to be rightly classified as a letter, in the sense of a written communication to a specific group of people for a specific purpose, rather than a pamphlet for general circulation. The author himself clearly so intends it when he uses the verb *epistellō* ("to send a letter," GK *2182*) to describe the form in which his "word of exhortation" has come to them (13:22). But it is certainly not like an ordinary business letter, ancient or modern. The other time the phrase "word of exhortation" occurs in the NT it denotes a synagogue sermon (Ac 13:15). Many have thus described Hebrews rather as a homily or sermon.[4] But perhaps the difference between a pastoral letter and a sermon was not so great in the ancient world as it might seem to us, since probably at least 80 percent of the average Christian congregation would be unable to read,[5] so that their access to Hebrews would not be by reading it quietly to themselves but by hearing it read in the congregation. (Cf. Ac 15:31, where a written communication read out in the churches is again described as a *paraklēsis*, "exhortation," GK *4155*.) Its combination of rhetorical sophistication and urgent pastoral appeal is well designed for this purpose. We should note especially the author's careful use of language about "speaking" (rather than writing) in such a way as to suggest he is actually present with them delivering the "sermon" (2:5; 5:11; 6:9; 8:1; 9:5; 11:32).

But if Hebrews functions as a "written sermon," we should not think of a stock homily retrieved from the author's filing system for this occasion; it is far too carefully customized to the specific problems of this particular Christian group for that. Rather, we are listening here to an experienced preacher who, whether in oral or written form, knows how to develop an argument relevant to the circumstances of a particular congregation and to apply it for their response. It may be that some of the arguments deployed in this letter would have formed part of his regular preaching ministry, but if so, they have been carefully adapted to this specific context.

I shall argue below (section 4) that the content of this letter is not that of a single "sermon" but of a whole series of expository studies and appeals, each developing a different scriptural theme and each adding its own new angle to the overall thrust of the letter. The author's method seems, then, to be one naturally employed by an experienced preacher to whom the exposition of OT texts is second nature, in order to present a powerful scriptural argument to a congregation in spiritual danger. Had he been personally present (as he would have preferred, 13:19, 23), he would no doubt have preached it. As it is, he speaks on paper in very much the same way in which he would have made his case orally and relies on the local reader to do justice to both his rhetorical skill and his pastoral concern.

2. AUTHOR, DESTINATION, AND DATE

We do not know who wrote Hebrews, or to whom, or when. In view of the considerable scholarly discussion on these issues, it is good to state this clearly at the outset. What follows is merely a summary of some of the considerations that have guided scholarly speculation, as well as an indication of my own (equally speculative) thoughts on the subject.

---

4. The issue is thoroughly discussed by Lane, *Hebrews 1–8*, lxix–lxxv.
5. See R. J. Bauckham, ed., *The Gospels for All Christians* (Edinburgh: T&T Clark, 1998), 66.

We have noted above the inclusion of Hebrews along with Paul's letters in the earliest surviving manuscript (ca. AD 200), and it came to be so regarded in later Christian thought, though never universally.[6] But many ancient writers had other ideas. Hebrews is not included in the Muratorian Canon (a list of NT books accepted for reading in the Roman church ca. AD 180), which carefully lists the thirteen letters of Paul but makes no mention of Hebrews. Photius (*Bibl.* 121) records that Irenaeus (second century) and Hippolytus (early third century) denied its Pauline authorship. At the beginning of the third century, Tertullian (*Pud.* 20) states, and apparently feels no need to argue the point, that it was written by Barnabas. Origen (early third century) observed that its style was clearly not that of Paul and suggested it might have been written by an unknown follower of Paul ("As to who wrote the epistle, God knows the truth"); he mentions that others have attributed it to Clement of Rome or to Luke (Eusebius, *Hist. eccl.* 6.25.11–14). Clement of Alexandria, also recognizing the difference in style, suggested it might have been written by Paul in Hebrew and translated by Luke into Greek (cf. Eusebius, *Hist. eccl.* 6.14.2–4). Eusebius (early fourth century) himself includes Hebrews as one of the "fourteen letters of Paul" but recognizes that others have followed the lead of the church of Rome in rejecting it as not by Paul (*Hist. eccl.* 3.3.4–5; 6.20.3).

The eventual inclusion of Hebrews among Paul's letters in the Western church (largely under the influence of Jerome and Augustine) was due not to literary conviction concerning its authorship (for few readers, especially of the letter in Greek, can fail to recognize this is not how Paul wrote) but to the need to find a suitable place in the canonical list for a book that had by then become widely accepted but did not name its author. Doubts about its authorship continued to be expressed, and its position in the received canon following Paul's shorter letters and preceding the other "general epistles" testifies to this continued uncertainty.[7] Speculation concerning its authorship continued in the Reformation period, the most important new suggestion being Luther's declaring that the author was Apollos, which remains perhaps the most widely favored view today.

From the letter itself we may glean that the author was (or wished to be seen as) male,[8] Jewish, very well schooled in the OT and in the sort of Jewish philosophical thinking that was dominant especially in Alexandria,[9]

---

6. Few if any modern scholars would argue that Paul wrote Hebrews. For a recent summary of the relevant data, see P. Ellingworth, *The Epistle to the Hebrews* (NIGTC; Grand Rapids: Eerdmans, 1993), 3–12. L. D. Hurst (*Hebrews and Hermeneutics* [SNTSM 36; Cambridge: Cambridge Univ. Press, 1979], 107–24) discusses the relationship between the thought of Hebrews and that of Paul and concludes that there may have been some Pauline influence on the author at the theological level but that there is no literary relationship.

7. The situation is well summarized by F. F. Bruce, *The Epistle to the Hebrews* (NICNT; Grand Rapids: Eerdmans, 1990), 14–17.

8. The participle *diēgoumenon* ("telling") in 11:32 is unambiguously male. The well-known suggestion of Adolf von Harnack that the author was Priscilla must assume this was either a deliberate self-concealment or a later alteration.

9. Scholarly views differ as to how closely the thought of Hebrews is related to that of Philo, the prolific Alexandrian Jewish writer of the early first century AD. One of the most thorough treatments is by R. Williamson, who finds the relationship less compelling than many others (notably C. Spicq [*L'épitre aux Hébreux*, 1.39–91], who regards Hebrews as the work of "a Philonist converted to Christianity"), in that while much of the vocabulary and ideas may be similar, Hebrews does not share the distinctive theological and hermeneutical stance of Philo. Cf. A. T. Hanson's conclusion (in D. A. Carson & H. G. M. Williamson, eds., *It Is Written: Scripture Citing Scripture* [Cambridge: Cambridge Univ. Press, 1988], 294) that "as far as exegesis of Scripture is concerned, Philo and our author have very little in common." See further Hurst, 7–42, concluding that Hebrews "developed certain OT ideas within the Jewish apocalyptic framework, while Philo developed the same themes within a Platonic framework. Both writers, in other words, probably go back independently to a common OT background." It is widely agreed that, even if there is no direct influence, both writers belong to the same strand of Alexandrian Judaism.

and an eloquent writer of sophisticated classical Greek,[10] and that he was associated with Timothy (13:23). All of these characteristics seem to fit well with Apollos, the "learned" Jew from Alexandria "with a thorough knowledge of the Scriptures" (Ac 18:24), who "vigorously refuted the Jews in public debate, proving from the Scriptures that Jesus was the Messiah" (18:28 TNIV). Apollos's eloquent advocacy of the claims of Christ in Ephesus and Corinth made him a serious rival to Paul himself in the leadership of the Corinthian church (1Co 1:12; 3:4–6, 22; 4:6) and may well explain Paul's sensitivity concerning "wisdom," "philosophy," and "eloquence" in the early chapters of 1 Corinthians. H. W. Montefiore,[11] following the commentary of C. Spicq, has assembled a strong argument that Hebrews was written by Apollos from Ephesus to the church in Corinth about AD 52–54, before Paul wrote 1 Corinthians. Montefiore offers a detailed and attractive reconstruction of the possible course of events involving Apollos, Paul, and the Corinthian church, drawing on the contents of Hebrews and 1 Corinthians. He may well be right, but his reconstruction, like the attribution to Apollos, remains speculative. There is no reason in principle why the author of this letter should be anyone whose name happens to be known to us from elsewhere. There must surely have been other well-schooled, eloquent Jewish pastors/theologians among the Christian congregations around the Mediterranean in the period around and following Paul's ministry—men (and women—remember Priscilla) not unlike Apollos. One of them wrote Hebrews, but we must settle for not knowing which.

Nor (contra Montefiore) can we know to whom he was writing. The traditional title "To the Hebrews"[12] is probably based on the nature of the letter itself and reflects the fact that its recipients must have been people who were firmly grounded in the OT and who identified themselves with the history and ideology of its people. There is wide (but not universal) agreement that the letter was written to Jewish Christians, or at least to Christians who, as former Jewish proselytes, had a deep knowledge of the OT.[13] But "To the Hebrews" might easily be taken to suggest a sort of encyclical to Jewish Christians everywhere, and that is certainly not the case. The target audience is a specific local group who are well known to the writer and with whose particular circumstances he is familiar. There is no reason to suppose them to be a large group; a sort of "house church" composed of converts from Judaism (and possibly former proselytes or "God fearers") would fit the nature of the letter well. There were Jewish communities all over the Mediterranean world, and such a group of Jewish Christians would probably be found in many of the cities of the eastern Roman Empire.

It is widely suggested that this particular group was in Rome and was perhaps part of the wider church made up of Jewish and Gentile members to which Paul wrote Romans. (Note that several house churches in Rome are mentioned in Ro 16:3–15.) The evidence for this suggestion is admittedly slender, the most

---

10. For an outline of the rhetorical characteristics of Hebrews in relation to classical Greek rhetoric, see H. W. Attridge, *The Epistle to the Hebrews* (Herm; Philadelphia: Fortress, 1989), 20–21.

11. H. W. Montefiore, *The Epistle to the Hebrews* (BNTC; London: A&C Black, 1964), 9–31.

12. The title is first attested in the Chester Beatty papyrus (ca. AD 200) and was apparently known to both Clement of Alexandria and Tertullian, around the same time.

13. The case is attractively presented by Bruce, 3–9; see also Lane, *Hebrews 1–8*, liv–lv. Ellingworth, 21–27, usefully discusses the arguments put forward for a Gentile readership and concludes that, while an exclusively Gentile readership is most unlikely, a mixed Jewish and Gentile church such as that at Rome might fit the evidence of the letter; in the end, however, Ellingworth prefers to speak of "a predominantly but not exclusively Jewish-Christian group."

significant pointer being the greetings sent by the writer from "those from Italy" (13:24), perhaps members of the group who have traveled away from home and are with the writer at the time. Another even less firm pointer is the comment that "you have not yet resisted to the point of shedding your blood" (12:4), which could suggest they were associated with others who had already faced martyrdom; if so, Rome is the only place we know in which Christians specifically were persecuted to death during the first century (under Nero in AD 64–65)—and it is possible that Jewish Christians in Rome were spared such persecution because their Jewish identity brought them within the Roman provisions for a "licensed religion," a protection Gentile Christians could not claim.[14] But all of this remains speculative. The fact that Clement of Rome knew the letter at the end of the first century (esp. *1 Clem.* 36:2–5) does not prove it was sent to Rome, though it would fit with that view. A group of Jewish Christians in Rome is an entirely plausible destination for the letter, but we cannot (and need not) be sure.[15]

As with most NT books, there is nothing in the letter that positively fixes the date of writing. The most significant argument is one from silence. The author's argument focuses on the theme of a new approach to God that replaces the old system of priesthood and its sacrifices. To such an argument the destruction of the temple in AD 70 would have provided an almost irresistible confirmation that the old system is finished, yet it is never mentioned. The most obvious explanation of this remarkable silence (comparable to Sherlock Holmes's dog that did not bark) is that the letter was written before AD 70. In particular, it would be very strange for a writer after AD 70 to say hypothetically of the animal sacrifices of the old covenant, "Would they not have stopped being offered?" (10:2), rather than pointing out that they had in fact already been stopped. This argument is perhaps weakened by the fact (which we shall discuss later) that the author of Hebrews never refers to the Jerusalem temple as such but rather to its wilderness predecessor, the tabernacle; but since he consistently describes its ritual in the present tense (another remarkable trait if the sacrificial system had now been brought to an end; see comments at 13:9–16), it seems likely he understands the present temple ritual as the successor to that of the tabernacle. All in all, a date before AD 70 seems more probable[16] and would accord with the possible context of the Neronian persecution mentioned above. Beyond that, we can only speculate.

3. BASIC THEME AND STRUCTURE

The Jewish Christians to whom this letter was sent were in the author's view in serious spiritual danger. He fears they may "drift away" by "ignoring such a great salvation" (2:1, 3), that they may "harden their hearts" and so "fall short" of the "rest" promised to the people of God (3:7–4:11), that by "falling away" they may "crucify the Son of God all over again" (6:4–6) and "trample the Son of God under foot" (10:29),

---

14. Cf. also the suggestion of Lane, *Hebrews 1–8*, lxiii–lxvi, that the earlier persecution referred to in 10:32–34 was associated with the expulsion of Jews from Rome under Claudius in AD 49.

15. Among other suggestions we may note the argument of Buchanan, 256–63, that the "coming to Mount Zion" in 12:22 is to be understood literally; he thus sees the recipients as a "very strict, communal, monastic sect" of people who had settled in Jerusalem after the time of Jesus' earthly ministry (2:3). Bruce, 10–14, sets out and discusses the various other destinations suggested.

16. See R. P. Gordon, *Hebrews* (Sheffield: Sheffield Academic Press, 2000), 29–33 (though Gordon seems surprisingly reluctant to draw the obvious conclusion from his argument); more fully, Buchanan, 256–63.

that by "refusing the one who speaks from heaven" they will not escape judgment (12:25–26). This striking sequence of "warning passages," combined with the repeated exhortations to them to "persevere" and not "shrink back," to "hold firmly till the end the confidence we had at first," to "enter in with confidence," to "make every effort" and to "hold unswervingly to the hope we profess" suggests their continued allegiance to Christ was in doubt, and the author was seriously worried they might give up their Christian profession altogether.

One reason for his concern was the suffering and persecution they had already faced and were likely to face again; this is the focus of much of his exhortation in 10:32–12:13, where he tries to help them see their suffering within the overall purpose of God and so not lose heart. But the bulk of his argument is on a different and more theological level, comparing and contrasting the key elements of OT religion with the "new and better covenant" they have entered into through faith in Jesus. It is this single-minded argument, deploying all the author's considerable scriptural erudition and rhetorical skill, which convinces most interpreters that the main threat to the continued Christian commitment of the recipients of the letter was not the persecutions they were facing but a more fundamental uncertainty as to whether their decision to follow Jesus had been a mistake.

It is hard for Gentile Christians to appreciate the force of this dilemma that faced many Jewish Christians in the first century (and in a different context still faces many Jewish Christians today). The initial excitement of discovering that Jesus was the Messiah in whom all God's dealings with his people since the days of Abraham had now found their fulfillment was soon challenged by continuing contact with fellow Jews who saw Jesus very differently. For them, Jesus had been a deceiver, and those who followed him had abandoned their ancestral heritage; they were traitors to the values and hopes of Israel, shamefully cutting themselves off from the community of God's covenant people through the ages. Subjected to such suspicion and hostility, Jewish Christians might well look over their shoulders and wonder whether they had taken the right step, and the more so when following Jesus seemed only to have brought greater suffering. The roots of one's cultural and religious inheritance are strong, and it must have been painful for these first Jewish Christians to find themselves isolated from their own people and at the same time involved in a new Christian community in which Gentiles, from whom they had hitherto been taught to keep themselves separate, were not only included as equals but also were increasingly calling the shots. In following Jesus, moreover, they had been taught to abandon the religious traditions of their ancestors, with their focus on the sacrificial cult, and consequently they may have begun to be aware of what R. P. Gordon suggestively describes as "cultic deprivation."[17] These were some of the factors that contributed to the "constant temptation to deemphasize, conceal, neglect, abandon, and thus in a crisis reject and deny the distinctively Christian dimension of their faith"[18] that the writer of this letter discerned in his readers' situation.

So the writer's argument from the opening salvo to the middle of ch. 10 consists of a series of comparative studies in each of which the glories of the OT religion are shown now to be succeeded by something "better" through the ultimate fulfillment that has come through "the Son." The prophets, angels, Moses

---

17. Gordon, 20–22.
18. Ellingworth, 80.

and Joshua, the OT priesthood, the covenant and the sanctuary through which it operated, together with the complex sacrificial system that had hitherto been the key to entering the presence of God—all these have now been superseded in the coming of Jesus, the Son, higher than the angels, superior to Moses and Joshua, our true and only high priest, the mediator of a new covenant and officiant in a new and heavenly sanctuary, and himself the one perfect sacrifice that forever renders all other sacrifices obsolete. As this panorama of fulfillment unfolds, with its listing of all that was the legitimate cause of Jewish pride in their religion and status as the people of God, the key word "better" (*kreittōn/kreissōn*, GK *3202/3201*) is heard again and again (1:4; 6:9; 7:7, 19, 22; 8:6; 9:23; 10:34; 11:16, 35, 40; 12:24). The writer's perspective is summed up in 8:6–13 as he shows how the coming of a new covenant has rendered the old one "obsolete." Surely there can be no going back to the old when the new is in every way "better." So the argument is summed up in 10:19–12:29 with an impassioned call to enter into their new heritage and to hold on in faith, whatever the cost, knowing that God has promised "better" things to those who run with perseverance the race in which Jesus has already gone before them.

The outline that follows this introduction attempts to set out the stages of this argument and appeal. In that outline I have picked out in bold type the sequence of "warning passages" that run through the letter, and in italics the expositions of key passages of Scripture around which much of the argument is focused. I shall say more about these "expositions" in the next section. As I see it, neither the warning passages nor the expositions in themselves form the structural backbone of the letter, though each in their own way (and especially the expositions) carry thes argument powerfully forward. No formal outline such as this can do justice to a living and moving text in which doctrinal argument is interwoven with pastoral exhortation and in which digressions, asides, and gradual transitions of thought defy neat analysis. But the main organizing principle of the letter up to 10:18 seems to me to be the "supersessionist" theme applied in turn to select key elements of OT religion.[19]

4. HEBREWS AS A BIBLICAL EXPOSITOR

Expository preaching, in which a text of Scripture is carefully explained and applied to the situation of a contemporary audience, holds an honored place in Christian tradition. But it is not a prominent feature of the NT. There are, of course, frequent references to the OT in most NT books but usually

---

19. While many interpreters have regarded some such "thematic" outline as the letter's basic structure, there are other approaches based more on its literary form than on its content. Most prominent has been the work of A. Vanhoye in *La structure littéraire de l'épître aux Hébreux* (Paris: Desclée de Brouwer, 1976) and many other works; cf. also L. Dussaut, *Synopse structurelle de l'épître aux Hébreux* (Paris: Cerf, 1981). It is interesting, however, that when these structuralist analyses are compared with a more traditionally thematic analysis such as that of F. F. Bruce, there are a significant number of points where they coincide in recognizing the turning points in the flow of the argument (so Ellingworth, 50–58). The same may be said of the independent structural scheme (though in significant ways dependent on Vanhoye) of Attridge, 17–19. L. Goppelt (*Theology of the New Testament* [Grand Rapids: Eerdmans, 1982], 2:240–42) suggests a thematic approach to the structure that, while superficially different from that here adopted, recognizes most of the same divisions of the text. For a careful discussion of differing approaches to the structure of Hebrews, see Steve Stanley, "The Structure of Hebrews from Three Perspectives," *TynBul* 45 (1994): 245–71; cf. also the chart by G. H. Guthrie (reproduced by Lane, *Hebrews 1–8*, lxxxix). Lane sets out and discusses Guthrie's own (now published) discourse-analysis of Hebrews (xc–xcviii).

in the form of passing citations or allusions in the course of developing a wider argument. Extended exposition of a single passage is rare. The one great exception is Hebrews. Here we meet an early Christian preacher for whom it seems to have been natural to select a significant text and not merely quote it and pass on but rather to stay with it, unpacking its significance and reminding the reader from time to time of its words in order to ensure that their understanding and response is properly grounded in Scripture.[20]

There are in Hebrews, as in the other NT books, plenty of references to the OT that are not developed in this special way, but there are also certain key texts (mostly from the Psalms) which have a more structural role in the development of his argument. The one that stands out most prominently is Psalm 110, referred to again and again throughout the letter, to the extent that G. W. Buchanan describes the whole of Hebrews 1–12 as "a homiletical midrash based on Psalm 110."[21] We shall see shortly how one verse of this psalm in particular (110:4) forms the basis for a central section of the argument, and I shall comment further in section 6 on the importance of Psalm 110 for the whole letter. But other texts come to the fore as the argument develops, each for a longer or shorter time occupying the stage while its implications are explored. This feature of Hebrews was helpfully noted in an article by G. B. Caird,[22] who noted four such "expositions," and developed by R. N. Longenecker,[23] who extended the number to five, all found within chs. 1–10. Others have followed their lead and noted other less extended expositions in the later chapters.[24] In the outline that follows this introduction, I have noted eight such "expositions," which may usefully be summarized here:

2:5–9	expounding Psalm 8:4–6
3:7–4:13	expounding Psalm 95:7–11
4:14–7:28	expounding Psalm 110:4
8:1–10:18	expounding Jeremiah 31:31–34
10:1–10	expounding Psalm 40:6–8
10:32–12:3	expounding Habakkuk 2:3–4
12:4–13	expounding Proverbs 3:11–12
12:18–29	expounding Exodus 19:10–23 and parallels

---

20. This section is based on my article "The Writer of Hebrews as a Biblical Expositor," *TynBul* 47 (1996): 245–76.

21. Buchanan, xix.

22. G. B. Caird, "The Exegetical Method of the Epistle to the Hebrews," *CJT* 5 (1959): 47–51. Caird's four expositions are the first four in the list that follows.

23. R. N. Longenecker, *Biblical Exegesis in the Apostolic Period* (Grand Rapids: Eerdmans, 1975), 175–85. The passage added by Longenecker to Caird's four is 1:3–2:4, which he describes as based on "a catena of verses drawn from the Psalms, II Sam. 7 and Deut. 32 (LXX)." Such a collection of texts, each of which is mentioned only once and with little or no individual expository comment, is in fact very different from the extended expositions in the other four passages, each based on a single text. Subsequent studies have not supported Longenecker's inclusion of 1:3–2:4 alongside the other expository sections.

24. For example, J. Walters (in an unpublished 1989 paper, referred to by Lane, *Hebrews 1–8*, cxiv–cxv); see also my "The Writer of Hebrews as a Biblical Expositor," 245–76; cf. Gordon, 23.

A glance at this list will immediately reveal that these expositions differ greatly in length and scale. Some provide the overarching basis for a long section of the argument, while others form only a small section within a greater theme. One (10:1–10) falls within a section (8:1–10:18) that as a whole revolves around a different text.[25] In some (notably 3:7–4:13) the words of the chosen text are repeated again and again, whereas in others the text is quoted only once, though its content governs the comments that follow. In several of these sections, other OT texts are interwoven with the main text to enrich the argument. The expository method I have noted is not therefore to be understood as a self-conscious and consistent literary technique around which the letter is deliberately structured but as a natural tendency in the author's thinking and communication that is deployed in quite varied ways as the argument requires. It is not a "technique" at all but rather an instinct to ground his arguments in Scripture and to work at a text until he has drawn out its full value for his audience. And each individual study makes its contribution within the single overarching argument of the letter, which we have noted above. The outline of the letter given below will show that the first four of the expository sections listed above correspond quite closely to the main thematic sections into which I have divided the argument of 1:1–10:18.

Comments on the author's treatment of the individual texts selected must wait until the commentary on each of these passages. But in general terms, it may be said that, however surprising our author's use of some OT texts may be (see next section), in the case of most of these to which he devotes more extended attention he generally understands the OT passage in its natural sense and in relation to its OT context and develops from it an argument a modern commentator would recognize as a legitimate (if not the only possible) conclusion from the text. There are exceptions in his use of Psalm 40, which is parenthetical to his main argument at that point in the letter and where his creative exploitation of the LXX word "body" (not in the Hebrew text) allows a specific application of the text a modern commentator might balk at, and in his argument from Psalm 8, which, while starting from a "correct" understanding of the meaning of the psalm, develops an argument from some aspects of its wording that goes far beyond what the text itself suggests. Such exegetical creativity is a feature of this letter elsewhere, but in his argument from the other key texts, we find the writer not so much exploiting Scripture as understanding and applying it with an exegetical responsibility of which a modern preacher might well be proud.

But this is not to say he merely repeats what the OT writer has said. The author of Hebrews reads the OT in the light of its fulfillment in Christ, and his object in selecting these texts is to show that they point beyond their own context to something "better" still to come. In so doing, he stands in company with most of the other NT writers and with Christians ever since who have understood the OT as a body of literature that points forward to something beyond its own horizons. It is the distinction of Hebrews that it develops this christological interpretation of the OT more consistently and more explicitly than most of the other NT books and so enables us to share the sense of discovery and of fulfillment that thrilled the first generations of Jewish Christians.

---

25. It was for this reason I did not include 10:1–10 in the list of expositions in my *Tyndale Bulletin* article, but on further reflection, it seems to me to have an "expository" character of its own within the wider section based on Jeremiah 31:31–34.

5. USE OF THE OLD TESTAMENT

The last two sections have given an overview of some of the ways in which the OT plays a part in the argument of Hebrews, but the argument from Scripture forms such a large part of the letter's agenda that it will be useful to say more now about the ways in which the writer reads and applies it.[26]

We should note first that our author (and presumably also his readers) belonged to that part of Judaism which naturally read the Hebrew Scriptures in the Alexandrian Greek version, which we call the Septuagint (LXX). His quotations are generally taken from that version (or versions—the textual history of the LXX is notoriously unclear, and the quotations in Hebrews reflect this diversity), sometimes drawing out features in it that are absent or not so explicit in the Hebrew text as we know it.[27]

He does not attribute his quotations to specific books or authors (except for the mention of David in 4:7), and his way of citing the OT is distinctive in that, unlike other NT writers, he does not use the formula "it is written," preferring to describe the texts as "speaking" or more usually to indicate that God or the Holy Spirit (or even occasionally Jesus himself: 2:11–13; 10:5–9) is the "speaker." The OT is for him not so much a historical record as the living voice of God to his people today, just as much as when it was first written down.

While he clearly has a special liking for the Psalms (nineteen of the thirty-nine explicit quotations in Hebrews are from the Psalms, with at least a further twenty-three clear allusions)[28] and draws the texts for several of his "expositions" from them, he also ranges widely across the Hebrew canon, its history and cultic provisions as well as its prophecy and poetry. He has a special interest in the pentateuchal descriptions of the tabernacle and its worship (and would have liked to say more on the subject if he could; 9:5). His preoccupation with the details of ritual (e.g., his list of the cultic equipment and structures in 9:1–7 and his discussion of the ritual significance of blood in 9:11–22) suggests to some that the author had himself been a priest but need reflect no more than the bookish interests of one who had long studied the Mosaic law. His exclusive interest in the tabernacle rather than its successor, the temple (which he never mentions), is remarkable, particularly since he speaks as though the worship of the tabernacle was still continuing in his day (note especially his description of contemporary Jewish priests as "those who minister at the tabernacle," 13:10); this feature has been variously explained as sheer antiquarianism or as revealing a hostility to the Jerusalem temple as such,[29] or on the other hand as implying that he saw no significant difference between the two successive centers of worship.

---

26. A detailed study by G. Hughes (*Hebrews and Hermeneutics* [SNTSMS 36; Cambridge: Cambridge Univ. Press, 1979], 3) aims to show that "the writer of Hebrews is the theologian who, more diligently and more successfully than any other of the NT writers, has worked at what we now describe as hermeneutics."

27. This point must be expressed with caution, since our present Hebrew text comes from a period long after the LXX was translated, so that where the latter differs from our Hebrew text, it may well reflect an earlier Hebrew version that was subsequently displaced. Hebrews 1:6 provides a classic example of this possibility in that the line there quoted from LXX Deuteronomy 32:43 is missing from our Hebrew text but has recently been found in Hebrew in a much earlier text of part of Deuteronomy 32 discovered at Qumran.

28. Statistics are taken from the listing of quotations and allusions in the back of the UBS *Greek New Testament*. R. N. Longenecker (*Biblical Exegesis*, 164–67) lists thirty-eight quotations and mentions "at least fifty-five" additional allusions to the OT. See Lane, *Hebrews 1–8*, cxv–cxvi, for various alternative figures.

29. On this basis some have suggested that the author represented, or was writing to those who represented, a strand of Judaism outside the mainstream, such as the Qumran community, which rejected the Jerusalem establishment. So, e.g.,

Many of the ways in which Hebrews argues from OT texts are, as we have noted in the last section, not unlike the way a modern preacher might operate, recognizing and giving full weight to the original author's intended meaning. There are, however, also places where his use of the OT surprises us. In such instances it is worth remembering that his interpretive methods, while less "scientific" than the exegesis expected in an academic commentary today, would have been quite familiar in the world of first-century Jewish interpretation, which was typically freer and more imaginative than what we are used to.[30] Thus his "deduction" from the silences of Genesis 14 to the effect that Melchizedek had no human family, birth, or death (7:3) is not so much a historical judgment as a literary observation that allows the author to make a theologically significant connection with the eternal Son of God; and his discovery of Jesus in the "son of man" mentioned in Psalm 8:4 (2:6–9) is drawing not on what the psalmist meant, nor even probably on what Hebrews thought he meant, but on a convenient form of words that allows a creative new understanding of the psalm. We shall meet other such instances as we work through the text. What leaves modern Western readers mystified may have been expected to appeal to Hebrews' original readers, who were used to a more creative approach to biblical interpretation.

But while our author's interpretive technique would probably have raised fewer eyebrows in his own day than it does in ours, a Jewish reader of his letter would immediately have noticed that his interpretations are governed by a distinctive underlying theological conviction. The key to his use of the OT is that it is in Jesus that it now finds its fulfillment, and therefore it is in the light of the coming of the Son that he now understands all that went before. In other words, what he is doing with the OT text is often not exegesis (in the sense of trying to draw out the original author's meaning) but christological interpretation. It is his understanding of the central place of Jesus in the unfolding revelation of God that governs and (in his view) legitimizes his use of the OT texts, even where it is clear the OT authors would not have recognized the meaning he discovers in their words.[31] He is writing for those who share this basic theological conviction, not to convince non-Christian Jews. Thus when he assumes without argument that OT references to "the Lord" are in fact talking about Jesus (see, e.g., on 1:6, 10–12), when in their OT context the reference is clearly to God the Creator, this is not sleight of hand but the natural result of a robust incarnational christology; and when in 2:9 (NASB) he interprets "a little lower than God" (Ps 8:5 NASB) as "for a little while lower than the angels,"[32] the key to his reading of the text is that he knows Jesus was "for a little while" brought down to our level through his incarnation. This may not be our way of expounding the OT, but if we are

---

P. E. Hughes, following Yigael Yadin, "The Dead Sea Scrolls and the Epistle to the Hebrews," in *Scripta Hierosolymitana*, vol. 4 (Jerusalem: Magnes, 1965), 36–55. See contra Lane, *Hebrews 1–8*, cviii; Ellingworth, 48–49. A full study by Hurst, 43–66, while recognizing several points of contact between features of Hebrews and ideas found in the Qumran texts, explains the similarities as the result of a common background of thought and of OT exegesis rather than indicating any direct contact with the Qumran community.

30. For a useful listing of ways in which Hebrews approximates to mainstream Jewish biblical interpretation of the period, see Lane, *Hebrews 1–8*, cxix–cxxiv, drawing heavily on D. Cohn-Sherbok's article on the subject ("Paul and Rabbinic Exegesis," *SJT* 35 [1982]: 117–32).

31. This issue is usefully explored and illustrated by G. Hughes, 57–63.

32. Note, however, that our author was not alone in understanding *ᵓĕlōhîm* in Psalm 8:5 as "angels" rather than "God"—see commentary at 2:5–9.

to appreciate Hebrews' argument, we must be prepared to recognize the way its christology is woven into the author's (and presumably also his readers') way of reading the OT, so that he looks back to the foreshadowing in the light of its fulfillment.[33]

6. THEOLOGY

The author of Hebrews has sometimes been listed with Paul and John as "the great theologians of the NT." While this is hardly fair to several of the other NT writers (not to mention Jesus himself!), it does testify to the important and distinctive theological contribution Hebrews is generally recognized to have made.[34] In this section we can merely highlight a few of the more distinctive features.[35]

The thought of Hebrews is often described as "dualistic," but two different and apparently competing forms of "dualism" are discerned (sometimes rather crudely described as, respectively, "vertical" and "horizontal" dualism). On the one hand, there is the contrast between the "shadows" of earth and the "realities" of heaven, a theme drawn out especially in chs. 8–9 in relation to the sanctuary and sacrifices of Christ's ministry as opposed to those of the OT. This perspective has often been rather simplistically described as "Platonic" and attributed to the author's familiarity with Alexandrian philosophy, especially that of Philo; we shall return to this issue in commenting on 8:1–5. On the other hand, there is the contrast familiar from other NT writing between the "present age" and the "age to come," between the "already" and the "not yet," so that the author is constantly urging his readers to press on toward the good things promised by God but not yet experienced. In the famous description of "faith" in 11:1 and in the examples of faith set out in the rest of ch. 11, we shall see these two "dualisms" brought together, as faith takes hold both of the reality of the invisible world and also of the certainty of God's promises. The supposed tension between "vertical" and "horizontal" dualism (and still less the simplistic idea that the former is Greek and the latter Jewish) seems not to have occurred to our author.[36]

A similar ability to hold in tension what are often seen as opposites may be seen in the christology of Hebrews. The twentieth-century theologian John Knox (not the Scottish Reformation leader of the same name!) once committed himself to the following provocative pronouncement: "We can have the humanity without the pre-existence and we can have the pre-existence without the humanity. There is absolutely no way of having both."[37] But not so in Hebrews, where perhaps more starkly than anywhere else in the

---

33. Buchanan, 249–51, sets out some of the main "typologies" the author finds in the OT. Buchanan goes on to suggest daringly that the title "To the Hebrews" may derive from the author himself, as he deliberately sets out a "comparison of the Hebrews in the wilderness with the Hebrews to whom this homily was addressed."

34. Lane, *Hebrews 1–8*, cxliv–cl, argues that much of the distinctiveness of Hebrews' theology derives from a background in the Hellenistic church, whose theology is expressed in the speech of Stephen recorded in Acts 7. Others have made the same connection, notably W. Manson, *The Epistle to the Hebrews* (London: Hodder & Stoughton, 1951). Hurst, 89–106, reviews Manson's argument sympathetically. A close affinity with the work of Luke more generally has also been posited (e.g., Goppelt, 265–66).

35. For a valuable brief account of the theology of Hebrews, see G. E. Ladd, *A Theology of the New Testament* (Grand Rapids: Eerdmans, 1993), 617–33; more fully, B. Lindars, *The Theology of the Letter to the Hebrews* (Cambridge: Cambridge Univ. Press, 1991).

36. The issue is helpfully discussed by Ladd, 618–23; more fully, Hurst, 7–42.

37. J. Knox, *The Humanity and Divinity of Christ* (Cambridge: Cambridge Univ. Press, 1968), 106.

NT, with the exception of the gospel of John, this logical paradox is boldly affirmed. On the one hand, Jesus is the eternal Son of God (a title Hebrews introduces dramatically in 1:2 and deploys throughout to emphasize Jesus' superiority to all other mediators), the agent of creation (1:2–3, 10–12), honored above even the angels (1:4–14), in whom God's essential nature is to be seen (1:3); in contrast with human priests he is sinless (4:15; 7:26–28) and eternal (7:3, 23–25) and exercises his ministry in heaven (4:14; 8:1–5). Yet, that same Jesus has been made lower than the angels (2:9), sharing our humanity (2:10–17; 5:1–3) and our suffering and temptation (2:18; 4:15; 12:2) as our elder brother (2:11–12); in a remarkable passage Hebrews describes graphically Jesus' "loud cries and tears to the one who could save him from death," his "reverent submission" and "learning obedience" through suffering so as to be "made perfect" as our savior (5:7–9). For Hebrews, if not for Knox, the pre-existence and the humanity stand side by side without embarrassment.

The description of Jesus as our high priest, already referred to, is the most distinctive christological contribution of Hebrews, introduced in 2:17 and 3:1 and developed in detail in the lengthy section 4:14–7:28, where Jesus is compared to the mysterious priest Melchizedek of Genesis 14:18–20, and contrasted with the merely human priests of the line of Aaron who in OT Israel held the monopoly in representing God's people in the temple cult. The key to this innovative theology of priesthood is found in Psalm 110:4, the only other reference to Melchizedek in the OT,[38] which promises that the Messiah will be a priest "in the order of Melchizedek." This remarkable verse, quoted or alluded to eight times between 5:6 and 7:28, makes two important contributions to Hebrews' christology: first it legitimizes a priesthood distinct from the Aaronic line (and, Hebrews will argue, superior to it), and second it is remarkable in the OT as almost the only place where kingship and priesthood, normally kept rigidly separate in ancient Israel, are brought together in one person (as they were in Melchizedek himself, both "king of Salem" and "priest of God Most High," 7:1). While Jesus himself (Mk 12:35–37; 14:62), and following his lead several of the other NT writers, drew on Psalm 110:1 as a pointer to his royal dignity as the Messiah, only the writer of Hebrews went on to note the significance of the fourth verse of that same psalm. His frequent use of the royal imagery of Psalm 110:1 (quoted in 1:13 and alluded to in 1:3; 8:1; 10:12–13; 12:2) is thus the springboard for a daring extension of the traditional concept of messiahship on the basis of that same psalm to include priesthood as well.

But Jesus, for Hebrews, is not only priest but also sacrifice: it is himself he offers in the heavenly sanctuary as the one sacrifice sufficient to take away all sin forever. Such language recurs repeatedly in the central part of the letter, but especially in 9:11–10:18, where the author shows how this sacrifice is "better" than, and renders obsolete, all the animal sacrifices that take up so large a part of the OT law codes. He pays particular attention to the ritual of the Day of Atonement[39] as the single annual sacrifice to remove sin that most clearly prefigured Christ's self-offering, no longer annual but once-for-all. For the modern reader to whom this is unfamiliar ground, the insistent focus on bloodshed in these verses is likely to be alienating rather than attractive, but to the original readers of Hebrews this was a vital and liberating message, and for the emerging Christian church it provided the essential basis for breaking away from the Jerusalem cult, so that Jews and Gentiles together, wherever they might be in the Roman

---

38. For Jewish interest in the figure of Melchizedek in the post-biblical period, see commentary at 7:1–10.

39. This aspect of Hebrews' theology is especially emphasized by Goppelt, 253–55.

world, could rejoice in the one perfect sacrifice that has made full salvation from sin available to all God's people forever. A symbol of this theology of atonement is the adverb *hapax* (GK *562*; or *ephapax*, GK *2384*), "once for all," which triumphantly echoes through these chapters to describe the self-sacrifice of Jesus (7:27; 9:12, 26, 28; 10:10). These days people tend to be more ambivalent about the sacrificial language in which the NT (and Hebrews most of all) explains how salvation could be achieved through Jesus' death, but unless we are willing to give full weight to the OT concept of sacrifice for sin, we shall never make sense of Hebrews.

One controversial outcome of this belief in the once-for-all efficacy of Jesus' atoning death is the corollary Hebrews draws with regard to those who once find this salvation but then "fall away." We have noted his repeated warnings to his readers of the dangers of turning back or drifting away from their new allegiance, but in two passages (6:4–8; 10:26–31) he is even more direct: for those who turn back there will be no second chance. Once the check has been cashed, as it were, there can be no further recourse to the bank of salvation. For those who have been brought up to believe in the total sovereignty of God and the ultimate triumph of grace, the prospect of final apostasy is not only pastorally but also theologically extremely uncomfortable. We shall discuss the issue more fully in the commentary on 6:4–8, but there is no doubt the issue of the ultimate security of the saved people of God is more sharply raised in Hebrews than anywhere else in the NT.

Another key word in Hebrews is "perfect,"[40] which is used not only of Jesus himself as our "perfect" high priest and savior (2:10; 5:9; 7:28) but also of the goal toward which we as his followers must aim (5:14–6:1). It was the failure of the OT system of sacrifice that it could never make people "perfect" (7:11, 19; 9:9; 10:1), but now we have a "perfect" high priest and a "perfect" sacrifice (10:14), and so Jesus can be relied on as the "perfecter" of our faith (12:2) and of the faith of those who have gone before (11:40; 12:23). We shall meet this theme frequently in the commentary. It is not to be understood in terms of the more limited later debate about the possibility of attaining "sinless perfection" in this life; this is a wide-ranging concept of the ultimate completion of God's saving purpose in Christ.

In section 3 we noted Hebrews' underlying conviction that, with the coming of Jesus, we have entered a decisive new phase in the story of God's dealings with his people. Not only does Jesus bring at every point something "better" than was available through the OT, but because the "better" has come, the old system has now ceased to be needed; it has been superseded. This theme is most clearly seen in Hebrews' argument from Jeremiah's prophecy of a new covenant, introduced in ch. 8 with the comment that a new covenant would not be needed if there were nothing wrong with the old (8:7), and the conclusion that therefore the old covenant is now "obsolete," soon to disappear (8:13). The most practical corollary of this belief in Hebrews is the declaration that now that we have a new and better high priest who has himself offered the one perfect sacrifice for sins forever, the whole ritual cult of the OT, with its priests and sacrifices, now has no further use. The earthly sanctuary and its cult are now to be seen merely as pointers to a heavenly sanctuary in which our great high priest now carries out his role, interceding for his people on the basis of the one great sacrifice already made in his death on the cross. This "supersessionist" theme is graphically summed up in the contrast drawn in 12:18–24

---

40. See the detailed study by D. Peterson, *Hebrews and Perfection* (SNTSMS 47; Cambridge: Cambridge Univ. Press, 1982).

between the two mountains that symbolize the two covenants: Sinai the mountain of fear, and Zion the mountain of joy.

Such overtly supersessionist language (which merely puts in more specific and vivid terms the theology of fulfillment that underlies many of the NT books, notably Matthew, John, and 1 Peter)[41] leaves many modern (post-Holocaust) readers uncomfortable. But it must be insisted that Hebrews is not in the least anti-Jewish. The author is a Jew writing to Jews. The OT remains his and their Scripture, the basis on which all truth must be decided.[42] It is not the OT itself that is left behind but those aspects of the religion and history it records that pointed forward to something "better" still to come and that now, in this era of fulfillment, may be left in honorable retirement. The issue is thus where the religion of the OT now finds its proper continuation, and for those Jews who accept that Jesus is the Messiah to whom the OT pointed forward, the answer is clear. Other Jews found a different way forward, itself no less "supersessionist" in its effect,[43] as the loss of the temple and its cult brought about the reassessment of religious principles we now know as rabbinic Judaism. Hebrews is perhaps the most clear-sighted representative of the Christian rather than the rabbinic form of supersessionism, but for the author, no less than for the rabbis, the new way was not so much the negation of the old as its appropriate rebirth for a new era of fulfillment, the "something better" to which the OT saints had looked forward and which it was the privilege of these first-century Christian Jews to enjoy, so that "together with us they would be made perfect" (11:39–40).

7. BIBLIOGRAPHY

The following is a selective list of commentaries and monographs on Hebrews available in English, confined for the most part to those referred to in the commentary (they will be referred to simply by the author's name [and initials only when necessary to distinguish two authors of the same surname]). References to other resources will carry full bibliographic details at the first mention and thereafter a short title.

Attridge, H. W. *The Epistle to the Hebrews.* Hermeneia. Philadelphia: Fortress, 1989.
Bruce, F. F. *The Epistle to the Hebrews.* New International Commentary on the New Testament. 2d ed. Grand Rapids: Eerdmans, 1990.
Buchanan, G. W. *To the Hebrews.* Anchor Bible 36. New York: Doubleday, 1972.
Ellingworth, P. *The Epistle to the Hebrews.* New International Greek Testament Commentary. Grand Rapids: Eerdmans, 1993.
Gordon, R. P. *Hebrews: Readings: A New Biblical Commentary.* Sheffield: Sheffield Academic Press, 2000.
Guthrie, D. *The Letter to the Hebrews.* Tyndale New Testament Commentaries. Grand Rapids: Eerdmans, 1983.
Hughes, G. *Hebrews and Hermeneutics: The Epistle to the Hebrews as a NT Example of Biblical Interpretation.* Society of New Testament Studies Monograph Series 36. Cambridge: Cambridge Univ. Press, 1979.
Hughes, P. E. *A Commentary on the Epistle to the Hebrews.* Grand Rapids: Eerdmans, 1977.

---

41. See Attridge, 30–31, for the view that 1 Peter is "the NT text with which [Hebrews] is most closely related." Hurst, 125–130, discusses the links and concludes that, whereas "1 Peter and Hebrews belong to the same general type of early Christian literature," there is no literary relationship, and the theological links with Paul are stronger than those with 1 Peter.
42. This point is rightly emphasized by R. McL. Wilson, *Hebrews* (NCBC; Grand Rapids: Eerdmans, 1987), 35–36.
43. I owe this insight to Gordon, 27–28.

Hurst, L. D. *The Epistle to the Hebrews: Its Background of Thought*. Society of New Testament Studies Monograph 65. Cambridge: Cambridge Univ. Press, 1990.

Lane, W. L. *Hebrews 1–8*. Word Biblical Commentary 47A. Dallas: Word, 1991.

———. *Hebrews 9–13*. Word Biblical Commentary 47B. Dallas: Word, 1991.

Lindars, B. *The Theology of the Letter to the Hebrews*. Cambridge: Cambridge Univ. Press, 1991.

Montefiore, H. W. *The Epistle to the Hebrews*. Black's NT Commentaries. London: A&C Black, 1964.

Peterson, D. *Hebrews and Perfection: An Examination of the Concept of Perfection in the "Epistle to the Hebrews."* Society of New Testament Studies Monograph Series 47. Cambridge: Cambridge Univ. Press, 1982.

Sowers, S. G. *The Hermeneutics of Philo and Hebrews: A Comparison of the Interpretation of the OT in Philo Judaeus and the Epistle to the Hebrews*. Richmond: John Knox, 1965.

Westcott, B. F. *The Epistle to the Hebrews*. New York: Macmillan, 1889.

Williamson, R. *Philo and the Epistle to the Hebrews*. Leiden: Brill, 1970.

Wilson, R. McL. *Hebrews*. New Century Bible Commentary. Grand Rapids: Eerdmans, 1987.

8. OUTLINE

The following outline sets out the sections into which I have divided the text for the purposes of commentary and attempts to highlight my understanding of the stages in which the argument develops. In particular, italics indicate the eight "expositions" I have outlined above, while bold print picks out the sequence of "warning passages."

But anyone who works on this letter soon discovers it is a flowing whole, not a succession of self-contained units. In particular, commentators often disagree as to just where the transition from one subject to the next occurs, and very often there is a "bridging passage" of a verse or more that belongs as clearly to what precedes as to what follows, so that its allocation into one section rather than the other is to some extent arbitrary. I shall comment on several such smooth transitions as we come to them. While such divisions are convenient for commentary, they must not be allowed to obscure the unity and cogency of the letter as a living whole.

   I. Better Than the Prophets (1:1–3)
  II. Better Than the Angels (1:4–2:18)
     A. The Greater Glory of the Son (1:4–14)
     B. **First Warning Passage** (2:1–4)
     C. Lower Than the Angels (*Exposition of Psalm 8:4–6*) (2:5–9)
     D. Able to Save (2:10–18)
  III. Better Than Moses and Joshua (3:1–4:13)
     A. The Servant and the Son (3:1–6)
     B. "Today, if you hear his voice" (**Second Warning Passage**; *Exposition of Psalm 95:7–11*) (3:7–4:13)
  IV. Better Than the OT Priesthood (*Exposition of Psalm 110:4*) (4:14–7:28)
     A. A Great High Priest (4:14–16)
     B. Qualifications for Priesthood (5:1–10)
     C. Digression: Toward Mature Understanding (Contains **Third Warning Passage**, 6:4–8) (5:11–6:12)
     D. God's Unchangeable Oath (6:13–20)
     E. The Priesthood of Melchizedek (7:1–10)
     F. A Better Order of Priesthood (7:11–19)
     G. Further Arguments for the Superiority of Jesus' Priesthood (7:20–25)
     H. Summary: The One True High Priest (7:26–28)
   V. Better Than the Old Covenant and Its Sacrifices (*Exposition of Jeremiah 31:31–34*) (8:1–10:18)
     A. A New Sanctuary (8:1–5)
     B. A New Covenant (8:6–13)
     C. The Worship of the Old Sanctuary (9:1–10)
     D. The One Effective Sacrifice (9:11–14)
     E. A New Covenant Requires a Death (9:15–22)
     F. A Single Sacrifice, Once for All (9:23–28)

NOTE: While the commentary is based on the NIV (1984), I have drawn attention at many points to the New Testament edition (2002) of *Today's New International Version* (TNIV).

Text and Exposition

I. BETTER THAN THE PROPHETS (1:1–3)

OVERVIEW

The first four verses of Hebrews form a single Greek sentence. By the end of the sentence, we have already been introduced to the theme of the superiority of the Son to angels, which will remain in focus throughout the rest of chs. 1–2. To impose a section break between vv.3 and 4 is therefore to favor a thematic analysis of the text over its grammatical form. My reason for doing so is that the contrast with the prophets with which the sentence opens (and which will not be made explicitly again in the rest of the letter) serves to set the scene more broadly than just in relation to angels and provides our author with the cue for his most powerful christological statement—indeed one of the three or four most striking accounts in the NT of the incarnate Son of God. The theme and indeed much of the language of vv.2–3 is closely parallel to what is said about the role of the Word/Son in creation and revelation in John 1:1–18 and especially Colossians 1:15–20.

> [1]In the past God spoke to our forefathers through the prophets at many times and in various ways, [2]but in these last days he has spoken to us by his Son, whom he appointed heir of all things, and through whom he made the universe. [3]The Son is the radiance of God's glory and the exact representation of his being, sustaining all things by his powerful word. After he had provided purification for sins, he sat down at the right hand of the Majesty in heaven.

COMMENTARY

1–2a One of the chief glories of OT religion was its prophetic tradition. Israel lived not by human insight but by divine revelation as God "spoke through the prophets." Our author has no wish to belittle this privilege, and he will quote from those same prophets later in the course of his argument. But now God has provided something even better. The prophets were many and varied, and their revelations came to the forefathers sporadically over a considerable period. But now their place has been taken by a single spokesman, whose message has been delivered once-for-all "in these last days" (lit., "at the end of these days," echoing the OT formula "in the end of the days," Ge 49:1; Isa 2:2; etc.). The period of preparation is over, and all that the prophets have looked forward to is now fulfilled in the single person of "a Son." (The lack of article does not indicate one son among many but rather the true nature and status of this new spokesman as against his predecessors the prophets.) This title, which will form the backbone of Hebrews' presentation of Jesus, is dramatically introduced in contrast with the mere messengers who have gone before and will immediately be filled out with a series of descriptive clauses that totally set him apart from all merely human representatives. Note that the name "Jesus" will not appear until 2:9, when the focus will be on the period of the human incarnation of the Son. In his essential nature he is better designated not by his human name but by a title that directly links him to God.

2b–3a Seven arresting statements now fill out the unique status of "the Son" and make it unmistakably clear he is much more than a passing historical figure like the prophets. The first five statements focus on his relationship to God and to the created universe in such a way as to place him outside the natural order as its originator and sustainer. Two further clauses in v.3b will then bring his historical work of redemption into focus, but first we are invited to contemplate the eternal glory of the Son since before the world was made.

Three clauses trace the role of the Son in relation to the universe, covering respectively its past, present, and future. It was "through" the Son that God made the universe in the past; in the present that same Son upholds everything "by his powerful word"; and the future destiny of the universe is understood also in relation to him who has been made the "heir of all things" (perhaps echoing Ps 2:8; cf. the quotation of Ps 2:7 that follows in v.5). This is the same threefold relation to the creation, embracing all eternity, which is succinctly expressed in Paul's formula in Romans 11:36: "from him and through him and to him are all things"; Paul was speaking there of God, not of Christ, but in Colossians 1:16–17 he says the same of Christ: "all things were created by him and for him . . . , and in him all things hold together." The author of Hebrews, like Paul (and John in 1:1–3), has no hesitation in saying of Jesus what in Jewish orthodoxy was reserved for God the Creator.

The double clause that opens v.3 describes the Son's relation to God more directly and even more unequivocally, not now in his creative role but in his essential nature: he is "the radiance of God's glory and the exact representation of his being." He is, in other words, as in John 1:14, 18, God made visible. To see what God is like we must look at the Son. "Radiance" (*apaugasma*, GK *575*) means literally the "outshining" (though it is sometimes also used of a "reflection") of the glory that is God's essential character, while "exact representation" translates the vivid Greek metaphor *charaktēr*, "imprint, stamp" (GK *5917*), used, for instance, of the impression made on a coin, which exactly reproduces the design on the die. (The idea is the same as the more familiar phrase "the image of God.") Again there is a close echo of Colossians 1:15, 19: "He is the image of the invisible God. . . . God was pleased to have all his fullness dwell in him."

3b The glory of the Son consists not only in his eternal nature but also in his role in bringing salvation to human beings. The two clauses that conclude the description of the Son take up this theme and thus introduce two of the most prominent themes of the letter as a whole. First, he has "provided purification for sins." The theme of the sacrificial work of Christ will come into focus especially in chs. 9–10 as the outworking of his office as our great high priest, where the author will emphasize that this work of purification is now fully complete. While at this point he does not yet spell out the means by which this "purification" has been achieved, his readers would be well aware that it must be through the shedding of blood (9:14, 22, etc.). The way is thus prepared for the paradoxical argument of ch. 2 that it is in his humiliation and death that the superior glory of the Son, as our perfect redeemer, is revealed.

But humiliation is followed by exaltation, and the author's first allusion to Psalm 110:1 introduces the language of "sitting at the right hand," which will echo through the letter (cf. 1:13; 8:1; 10:12; 12:2). The Son, his earthly work complete, now occupies in heaven the place of highest authority next to God himself.

Such is the nature of the Son, who has now added to his unique creative work by coming into the world he made in order to bring the final and perfect revelation of God by making the true nature of the invisible God visible on the canvas of a human life, and by his redeeming work has fulfilled God's purpose of salvation. "The Word became flesh and made his dwelling among us. We have seen his glory" (Jn 1:14). Here is a work of God on a different level altogether from what the prophets could offer.

NOTES

1 The opening words are carefully crafted for rhetorical effect. The writer begins not with the subject of the sentence but with two matching adverbs which, while easily understood, were not in normal use: πολυμερῶς, *polymerōs*, and πολυτρόπως, *polytropōs*, are effectively synonymous, literally "in many parts" and "in many ways." The sentence, having begun with two striking adverbs beginning with *p*, increases the effect with further alliteration: πολυμερῶς και πολυτροπως παλαι ο θεοσ λαλησας τοις πατρασιν εν τοισ προφηταις, *polymerōs kai polytropōs palai ho theos lalēsas tois patrasin en tois prophētais.*

2 "The universe" at the end of v.2 renders τοὺς αἰῶνας (*tous aiōnas*, GK *172*), which elsewhere more often means "the ages." In Jewish thought time was divided into two "ages," "the present age" and "the age to come" (see 6:5), so that "the ages" taken together represent the totality of time but by transference can also be used of the whole physical creation. See 11:3 for the same use of τοὺς αἰῶνας, *tous aiōnas*, with reference to the original creation of the universe; cf. the title "King of the Ages" used for God, e.g., in 1Ti 1:17. Paul speaks of this αἰών (*aiōn*) in parallel with this κόσμος (*kosmos*, "world," GK *3180*) in 1 Corinthians 1:20 and 3:18–19.

3 The first-century BC Alexandrian Jewish work, the Wisdom of Solomon, uses similar language in a poetic description of the divine Wisdom: she is "a pure emanation of the glory of the Almighty; . . . an outshining [ἀπαύγασμα, *apaugasma*, GK *575*] of eternal light, a spotless mirror of the working of God, and an image of his goodness" (Wis 7:25–26). Philo, also an Alexandrian Jew, spoke of the Logos (which he identifies with "Wisdom") as God's image, as the imprint on a seal. Early Christians delighted to claim for Jesus what Jewish thought attributed to Wisdom, who was also understood (following Pr 8:22–31) to have been God's agent in creation.

"Being" renders ὑπόστασις (*hypostasis*, lit., "substance," GK *5712*), a wide-ranging word Hebrews will use for the "reality" or "assurance" of future promises (11:1) and for Christian "confidence" (3:14), but which here must have its more basic meaning of "real nature, fundamental reality" (as opposed to outward appearance). We should not read back into Hebrews the later philosophical usage of Christian Trinitarian debate, which (rather confusingly) distinguished between God's essential οὐσία (*ousia*, "substance," GK *4045*) and the three ὑποστάσεις (*hypostaseis*, "persons") of Father, Son, and Spirit.

"The Majesty in heaven" is literally "the greatness in the heights" (ἡ μεγαλωσύνη ἐν ὑψηλοῖς, *hē megalōsynē en hypsēlois*). A similar use of ἡ μεγαλωσύνη, *hē megalōsynē* (GK *3488*), as a substitute for the name of God occurs in 8:1; it reflects Jewish reverential language, as when Jesus refers to God as "the Power," again in connection with sitting at his right hand (Mk 14:62). Not that Hebrews finds any difficulty in speaking directly of God in such a connection (10:12; 12:2), but this is part of the author's natural Jewish idiom.

II. BETTER THAN THE ANGELS (1:4–2:18)

OVERVIEW

Most of the argument of Hebrews will concern the superiority of Christ to the various human agents and institutions through which God related to his people in OT times, but first he takes a wider view by looking outside the human sphere. God also communicated with his people through angels, and surely they, as supernatural beings, must represent the highest power next to God himself. Yet even the angels, our author insists, cannot match the glory of the Son. He makes his point in two sharply contrasting ways.

First, in 1:4–14 he will prove from Scripture that the inherent dignity and authority of the Son is higher than that of angels; he is the one whom they serve and honor. But then (after a brief aside concerning the importance of a message conveyed to us not by angels but by the Son—the first "warning passage")—he turns to a quite different and strongly contrasting argument. The Son is superior to angels, paradoxically, in that for a time he was willing to be made lower than them through coming to earth as one of us. It was only through the temporary "humiliation" of becoming human that he could save human beings. No angel could do this; only the supernatural being, the Son, who has chosen to be identified with his human creation as our

"brother" (2:11–12), can be our perfect "author of salvation."

The substantial amount of space devoted to this dual argument for the superiority of the Son to the angels may surprise modern readers, for most of whom angels are little more than part of the romantic scenery of the Christian message, a matter of biblical tradition rather than of existential significance. But for the original readers of this letter they are likely to have had a much higher profile, as a careful study of the references to angels in the NT as well as in the OT will make clear. It was through angels that the Law was believed to have been given to Israel (see on 2:2). The writings from Qumran and other Jewish literature of the period (notably the apocalypses) show that interest in angels grew stronger after the OT period, and this preoccupation continued to develop into the *Merkabah* mysticism of later Judaism. Indeed there are hints in the NT that some Christians at that time were developing an unhealthy preoccupation with angels, according them a theological importance that threatened to usurp the place of Christ (Col 2:18; 1Pe 3:22; Rev 22:8–9). In the context of first-century Christianity a comprehensive argument for the supremacy of Christ that ignored the issue of the angels would have been inadequate.

A. The Greater Glory of the Son (1:4–14)

OVERVIEW

The theme of the Son's sitting at the right hand of God (1:3) provides the cue for a general statement of his superiority to the angels in v.4. In vv.5–13 the

author then quotes a total of seven OT texts to prove this point before summarizing in v.14 the less exalted status of angels in comparison with the Son.

The use of the OT in this section is unlike what we find in Hebrews as a whole. Each text is cited with only the very briefest of introduction and then left without further explanation. Texts follow one another in rapid succession, linked together not so much by any inherent connection between them (except in v.5), but by the theme the author has selected them to illustrate. This collection thus contrasts sharply with the more expository method of quotation, with extended discussion arising from the initial quotation of the text, which we have noted to be typical of this letter (see Introduction, pp. 25–27).

But there is one aspect of this series of quotations that is typical of our author's method more generally. While some of the quotations would have been generally recognized as messianic texts (vv.5a–b, 8–9, 13), so that a Christian reader would not be surprised to find them used of the Son, in two of them (vv.6 and 10–12) he simply takes what the OT text says about God and applies it to the Son without further ado. We have noted the breathtaking boldness of this line of argument in the introduction (p. 29). It depends not on exegesis of the original meaning of texts but on the theological assumption, which he clearly expected his readers to share, that what is true of God is necessarily true of his Son.

Of the seven texts selected for this little anthology (five of them drawn from the Psalms and one each from 2 Samuel and Deuteronomy), five simply underline the unique status and authority of the Son without specific reference to angels (vv.5 and 8–13). In between are two texts that refer to angels, one of them (v.6) envisaging the angels worshiping the Son, the other (v.7) defining their role as one of service, the point the author will take up in summarizing the implications of the chapter in v.14. All the texts thus contribute in their different ways to his argument for the superiority of the Son to the angels, but the readers are left to fit those contributions together for themselves.

Note that in these quotations, as generally in this letter, the words of Scripture are taken as spoken by God himself. In three of the quotations (vv.5a–b and 13) the words quoted are presented in the OT text as God's words, but in all the others the words are those of Moses or the psalmist speaking *about* God (or in vv.8–9 the king); yet all are quoted under the same rubric, expressed or understood, "he said/says." This feature of the author's hermeneutical method perhaps makes it easier for him in vv.6 and 10–12 to understand the OT words not as praise for God but as God's declaration about his Son.

[4]So he became as much superior to the angels as the name he has inherited is superior to theirs.
[5]For to which of the angels did God ever say,

"You are my Son;
today I have become your Father"?

Or again,

"I will be his Father,
and he will be my Son"?

[6]And again, when God brings his firstborn into the world, he says,

"Let all God's angels worship him."

⁷In speaking of the angels he says,

> "He makes his angels winds,
>> his servants flames of fire."

⁸But about the Son he says,

> "Your throne, O God, will last for ever and ever,
>> and righteousness will be the scepter of your kingdom.
> ⁹You have loved righteousness and hated wickedness;
>> therefore God, your God, has set you above your companions
>> by anointing you with the oil of joy."

¹⁰He also says,

> "In the beginning, O Lord, you laid the foundations of the earth,
>> and the heavens are the work of your hands.
> ¹¹They will perish, but you remain;
>> they will all wear out like a garment.
> ¹²You will roll them up like a robe;
>> like a garment they will be changed.
> But you remain the same,
>> and your years will never end."

¹³To which of the angels did God ever say,

> "Sit at my right hand
> until I make your enemies
>> a footstool for your feet"?

¹⁴Are not all angels ministering spirits sent to serve those who will inherit salvation?

COMMENTARY

4 This is a participial clause that concludes the opening sentence of the letter by showing how the exalted status of the Son set out in vv.2–3 entails the next point to be argued, his superiority to the angels. Note already the first use of the keynote word *kreittōn*, "better" (NIV, "superior," GK *3202*), backed up by the roughly synonymous *diaphorōteron*, "more excellent" (NIV, again "superior," GK *1427*), which Hebrews will use in 8:6 again to supplement *kreittōn*. The "superior name" is of course the title "Son," which has been introduced in v.2 and will be the explicit basis of the first two quotations that follow in v.5. It is because he is God's Son that he holds authority even over God's angels. The use of the verb "inherited" rather than simply "received" stresses that he holds this name not by favor but by right, as the Son who shares his Father's authority.

5 The rhetorical question that introduces the first quotations will be repeated in v.13 with the last, thus forming a framework for the set of seven quotations. The first two quotations form a tightly connected pair and were linked together in Jewish thinking about the Messiah (see note). The prophetic words of Nathan in 2 Samuel 7:14, even though uttered with immediate reference to Solomon, were the foundation of the developing hope of a descendant of David through whom God's purpose for his people would ultimately be fulfilled, and the words attributed to God in Psalm 2:7 drew on that earlier oracle as confirmation of the special relationship between God and David's son which would allow the latter to be called himself "God's son." Such a title clearly places him in a different category from the angels, who might sometimes be referred to collectively as "the sons of God" (Ge 6:2; Job 1:6; Ps 29:1) but none of whom was ever singled out for this special title, with its implication of a unique Father-Son relationship between God and his Messiah. Thus in citing these two linked verses the author provides a scriptural basis for his designation of Jesus as "the Son," and at the same time locates him firmly in the center of the fulfillment of the messianic hope of the OT.

6 The first quotation that explicitly mentions angels poses two problems. The first is the point we have noted above that the text quoted refers in its OT context (see note below) to the angels (or "gods") worshiping God himself, so that its relevance to the Son is a matter of creative reapplication rather than of strict exegesis. The second is that this is the only one of the quotations in this anthology that has a significant interpretive introduction, and it is not easy to see just how the author has reached the view that this text applies to the time "when God brings his firstborn into the world." As part of Moses' song in Deuteronomy 32 it relates in its

historical context to a time more than a thousand years before the incarnation of the Son in the person of Jesus of Nazareth, which is the most natural meaning of God's "bringing his firstborn into the world." It seems that our author, looking back in the light of what God has now done (and perhaps recalling the angelic worship of Lk 2:13–14), has found in Moses' words an appropriate call to other spiritual beings to acknowledge the divine status of the Son who becomes incarnate, even though the song refers to no figure other than the avenging and delivering God himself. Once again, this is not exegesis but the creative reuse of a text where the author discerns a theological parallel: the worship due to the God of Israel is due also to his incarnate Son. Hebrews does not elsewhere speak of Christ as *prōtotokos*, "firstborn" (GK *4758*), though the title sums up well the dignity of the Son who is God's "heir" (1:2, 4); cf. its use for David, chosen by God as supreme ruler, in Ps 89:27. (For *prōtotokos* as a christological title, cf. Ro 8:29; Col 1:15, 18; Rev 1:5.)

The point of the quotation in this context is that, once its applicability to the Son is granted, it unequivocally places him on a level of authority above the angels, whose place it is to offer him worship.

7 The other text that specifically mentions angels is no less problematic from the point of view of "scientific exegesis." The Hebrew words of Psalm 104:4 are normally (and surely rightly in terms of their context in the psalm) translated as in the NIV, "He makes winds his messengers, flames of fire his servants." (This is part of a long series of participial clauses describing the God whose praise is introduced in v.1; whether these clauses are rendered in the third person or, as in many versions, by continuing the second person from v.1 does not affect the sense.) It is a description of how God uses the natural elements to fulfill his purpose in the world. The objects of the verb "makes" are thus "winds" and "flames of fire," while "messengers" and "servants" are their descriptive complement. On this interpretation the verse makes no reference to angels. But two ambiguous words suggested a different interpretation: Hebrew *malʾak* and Greek *angelos* (GK 34) both have the double meaning "messenger" or "angel," and Hebrew *rûah* and Greek *pneuma* (GK 4460) both mean either "wind" or "spirit"; and in Greek religious usage the meanings "angel" and "spirit" are far more common. On this basis, the LXX version, used by Hebrews, has apparently reversed the syntax, so that "angels" and "servants" are understood as the object and "spirits" (so, rightly, TNIV) and "flames of fire" as the complement. Clearly this is how Hebrews interprets the text, since the author says it is "speaking of angels." Perhaps then he thought the verse described God's original creation of the angels as spiritual beings, though it is not clear what parallel sense he might find in "making his servants fire." But the value of the verse, so understood, for his argument is that the parallelism identifies the angels as merely servants (a point he will take up again in v.14), and therefore as on a lower level of authority than the God who made them such. And since his whole argument presupposes that the Son's authority is that of the Creator himself (see especially vv.10–12), the point is established that the Son is above the angels. It is not an argument that could have been made by anyone working from the Hebrew text of Psalm 104:4, but the LXX version has provided an opportunity our author has been glad to exploit.

8–9 In contrast with what "he says" about angels the author now sets what God says "about the Son" (or "to the Son"). The quotation this time is from Psalm 45:6–7, a psalm that celebrates the marriage of the king in such extravagant terms it was widely understood to be looking forward to the eschatological king, the Messiah. From the Christian point of view, then, there is no problem in describing this

as a psalm "about the Son," and the LXX version quoted is a quite close rendering of the Hebrew. As applied to a human king these words are extravagant almost to the point of blasphemy in that the first line not only declares him the sovereign of an everlasting empire but also apparently addresses him directly as "God." The second verse quoted, however, restores the balance by declaring that he has been anointed king by God, who is described as "your God." (This point would not be invalidated if, as is possible, the first "God" in v.9 is also taken as vocative, thus reading "therefore, O God, your God has set you . . . .") The combination of a second person address to the king as "God" with a third person reference to "God, your God" leaves the reader of the psalm with a teasing paradox, which our author has been glad to exploit in order to underline the divine status of the Messiah, who is nonetheless a human figure, God's anointed.

The end of the quotation similarly combines the superior status of this messianic king ("above your companions") with the recognition of his humanity, as one in solidarity with those he rules: they are *metochoi*, "companions," literally "sharers," a term that will be used again in 3:14 for the solidarity of Christ's people with their leader (and cf. 2:11–18 for the same theme, especially the use of *metechō*, "share," GK 3576, in v.14).

One thus addressed as "God," human though he is, is clearly on a level above the angels; his designation as God sitting on an eternal throne picks up the theme of Christ's sitting at God's right hand (1:3), the theme from which this whole argument began and with which the anthology of OT quotations will conclude (1:13).

10–12 Here again is a quotation (slightly adapted) from the LXX text of a psalm that corresponds quite closely to the Hebrew. Psalm 102 is titled "a prayer of an afflicted man" and contrasts the psalmist's own wretchedness with the eternal power of the Creator. Its concluding verses, quoted here, celebrate the eternity of God over against the transience of the created order. The choice of this text here identifies the Son with the eternal Creator over against the angels, who are themselves part of his creation. This identification was probably aided by the introduction in the LXX both of "he answered" in v.23 of the psalm, suggesting a change of speaker so that now it is God addressing someone else, and also of the address *Kyrie*, "Lord," in v.26 (in the Hebrew the addressee is identified as "my God" in v.24), *ho Kyrios*, "the Lord," being an established title of Christ. But v.6 has already shown us that our author is capable of applying to Christ what the OT says about God without any such prompt. It is a natural development from what he has said in vv.2–3 about the Son's agency in creation.

13 The final quotation in the anthology (with its introduction echoing that in v.5) provides the explicit scriptural basis for the language about sitting at God's right hand that the author has already introduced in v.3. Psalm 110, which plays a central role throughout the letter (see Introduction, pp. 26, 31), was understood by Christians (and by some Jews) as a messianic psalm (and had been used as such by Jesus himself: Mk 12:35–37; 14:62). The words here quoted are in the psalm spoken by "the Lord" to "my Lord," and this was generally understood to mean God addressing his Messiah. So the Son, his messianic work complete, sits at God's right hand awaiting the final establishment of his sovereignty over his enemies (cf. 10:12–13). While the angels are not to be numbered among those "enemies," none of them could be envisaged as receiving this unique honor and authority. The Son reigns supreme.

14 The quotations are finished, and the author sums up his argument with another comment specifically on the status of angels that picks up the language of v.7. They are "serving spirits," God's workforce in looking after his human subjects. The Son came to provide "salvation" for human beings (cf. "purification for sins," v.3), as ch. 2 will spell out further, and now that it has been made available it is for them to "inherit" what is now theirs (cf. the Son himself "inheriting" all creation and a supreme name as his by right, vv.2 and 4). Angels neither provide that salvation nor do they need it for themselves (2:16); their role is merely the subordinate function of looking after those who are to be saved.

NOTES

4 It has been suggested (e.g., Montefiore, 39–42) that the argument for the Son's superiority to the angels reflects a tendency on the part of some Christians to view Christ himself as an angelic figure, comparable with Michael. But while there is evidence (particularly from Qumran) that some Jews at this time entertained the idea of an angelic Messiah (sometimes associated with Melchizedek; see on 7:1–10), the idea is not clearly attested in first-century Christianity.

5 The two texts linked here were also cited together in the Qumran document (4Q174) which has come to be known as the Florilegium, a collection of OT texts relating to the Messiah. (The fragment breaks off in the middle of the quotation of Ps 2, before v.7 is reached, but the connection of the two passages suggests a similar thought to that of Hebrews here.)

The clause "Today I have begotten you" perhaps applied in the psalm's original context to the enthronement of the king, but here it cannot be so understood, since the Son has already been presented as an eternal divine being (1:2–3); our author probably understood it to refer to the Son's relationship with the Father before creation, not to a temporal beginning. The word "today" was not the focus of his interest in quoting this verse.

6 Some have suggested the reference is not to the incarnation but either to the parousia, construing πάλιν (*palin*, "again") with "brings" instead of, as generally in Hebrews (cf. 1:5; 2:13 [twice]; 4:5; 10:30), as the marker of an additional quotation, or to the ascension, which depends on taking οἰκουμένη (*oikoumenē*, GK *3876*) not in its normal sense of "the world" but in the very unnatural sense of "the heavenly realm"; this latter suggestion is supported only by 2:5, but there it is only the presence of the qualifier μέλλουσα (*mellousa*, "to come") that can be taken to suggest something other than the normal sense, and I shall argue that such a suggestion is misplaced there as well. Here there is no such indication.

The OT text quoted in this verse does not appear in the received Hebrew text of Deuteronomy 32:43, but the LXX has a longer text that includes the two clauses, "Let all the sons of God worship him," and, "Let all God's angels strengthen [? the verb is unusual] him." The exact wording quoted by Hebrews occurs also in the version of Moses' song, which appears as Ode 2 in the Odes that are appended to the Psalms in the LXX. This longer LXX version must represent an earlier form of the Hebrew text, since the same verse appears in Hebrew in a form longer than our received text on a small fragment of parchment found at Qumran (4Q44 [4QDtq]) that includes the clause, "Worship him, all you gods." (For the use of "angels" to translate the Hebrew ʾᵉlōhîm, "God" or "gods," see comments below on 2:6–8a. It occurs again in the similar text, Ps 97:7.)

8 The address to the (messianic) king as "God" is so surprising that other renderings of the Hebrew (and Greek) text of Psalm 45:6 have been suggested (described by Gordon, 43, as "face-saving alternatives"). As there is no expressed verb in v.6, it would be possible to take ʾᵉlōhîm, "God," not as a vocative but as the subject of a predicative sentence that would then mean, "God is your throne for ever and ever," and the LXX could be made to bear the same meaning. But this is a strange statement, especially when followed by reference to God as the one anointing the king. Other suggested renderings represent what it is thought the psalmist intended to say rather than any natural meaning of the actual Hebrew text: they include, "Your divine throne endures forever and ever" (RSV); "Your throne is like God's throne, eternal" (NEB); "The kingdom that God has given you will last for ever and ever" (GNB); "God has enthroned you for all eternity" (REB). These renderings have in common not only that they are not what the Hebrew says but also that they are not possible meanings of the LXX either. The rendering of NIV (and NRSV) is the only one that makes adequate sense both of the form of the Hebrew text and of its LXX version and agrees with ancient Jewish interpretation. (See further L. C. Allen, in *Christ the Lord*, ed. H. H. Rowdon [Leicester: Inter-Varsity, 1982], 220–42.) Gordon, 44, comments, "'Mighty god' as an appellation of a Davidic monarch in Isaiah 9.6 shows that Psalm 45.6, understood in its natural sense, is not a theological solecism within the OT."

12 While the rest of the quotation from Psalm 102:25–27 follows the LXX closely, here Hebrews has ἑλίξεις (*helixeis*, "you will roll up") instead of ἀλλάξεις (*allaxeis*, "you will change"), a similar-sounding verb that serves to make the metaphor more vivid and may well represent an alternative reading of the LXX. The author has also added a further reference to a garment to create balancing poetic lines (though some MSS restore the LXX text by omitting ὡς ἱμάτιον, *hōs himation*, "like a garment," in this verse).

14 The Greek λειτουργικός (*leitourgikos*, "ministering," GK *3312*) derives from a word that originally applied to public service in a wider secular sense but that in biblical Greek is used especially of religious service, whether in cultic matters (cf. our "liturgical") or more broadly. When the angels' role is further specified as διακονία (*diakonia*, "service," GK *1355*), a word often used of domestic and other practical help, it suggests that their function in relation to God's human people is understood in quite broad terms. Ellingworth, 133, advocates combining the two aspects of service in this paraphrase: "They live to worship God in heaven, and serve him by being sent on earthly missions for the benefit of those to whom God is to give salvation."

B. First Warning Passage (2:1–4)

OVERVIEW

In introducing the second main section of the argument of Hebrews (1:4–2:18), I described 2:1–4 as "a brief aside concerning the importance of a message conveyed to us not by angels but by the Son." It is an "aside" in that in these verses the argument for the superiority of the Son to angels is not further advanced, as it will be again from v.5 onward, but rather the author pauses to comment on the pastoral implications of the argument so far. It is the first of several passages where the author betrays his keen sense of the danger in which his readers find themselves; while he frequently pauses to call on them positively to press on in their faith,

in five passages (which I have highlighted in the outline of the letter as the "warning passages") he focuses more directly on the consequences of failing to do so. In this first such "shot across the bow" he highlights the danger of "drifting away," diplomatically using the first person plural even though it is their situation he is concerned about. This pastoral warning arises directly out of the argument of the first chapter, since it contrasts the punishment for violating the Law, which was "spoken through angels," with the far more serious (but as yet undefined) consequences of ignoring the fuller revelation that has now come through the Son.

¹We must pay more careful attention, therefore, to what we have heard, so that we do not drift away. ²For if the message spoken by angels was binding, and every violation and disobedience received its just punishment, ³how shall we escape if we ignore such a great salvation? This salvation, which was first announced by the Lord, was confirmed to us by those who heard him. ⁴God also testified to it by signs, wonders and various miracles, and gifts of the Holy Spirit distributed according to his will.

COMMENTARY

1 The danger is of "drifting away," an unusual word that means more literally, "to flow by," as of a river (or perhaps a drifting boat) effortlessly slipping past—not primarily doing something they should

not, so much as failing to take positive action and merely allowing things to slide. The antidote to such carelessness is to "pay more careful attention to what we have heard," which in vv.3–4 will be spelled out as the message of salvation. They have, of course, heard and responded to the Christian gospel, but that, our author implies, is not on its own enough to guarantee their salvation (a theme that will be more fully developed in the later warning passages); they must continue to take its demands seriously.

2 "The message spoken through angels" (TNIV; see Notes) is the OT law (cf. Gal 3:19; Ac 7:38, 53). While the first contrast drawn in this letter was between the Son and the prophets, from now on it will be the Law that is more in focus, by implication when Jesus is contrasted with the lawgiver, Moses (3:1-6), and more directly as his priesthood and its sacrificial provision is contrasted at length with the priesthood, sanctuary, and sacrifices of the Mosaic law (4:14-10:18). At this point it is introduced into the letter because of the belief, not found clearly in the OT but attested in Judaism of the NT period (see G. Hughes, 8), that one of the glories of the Law was that it had been brought to Moses by the agency of angels. Coming to Israel with such sanction, no wonder the Law was "binding" (lit., "firm, fixed"). The "just punishment" for breaking the Law may refer to the wide range of judicial sentences provided in the Mosaic law, but in this context it seems more likely that the author is thinking of the actions which God says he himself will take against his disobedient people, particularly the curses pronounced for various transgressions in Deuteronomy 28:15-68. The people of Israel knew from their experience throughout history (cf. 3:7-4:11) that the demands of their covenant with God were not to be taken lightly.

3-4 But that first covenant, for all its impressive sanctions, pales into insignificance beside God's latest and final word (see again 1:2). It is a word not so much of law as of "salvation," and when God offers such salvation it would be even more disastrous to "ignore" (lit., "not care about") it than it was for Israel to neglect the demands of the Law. The point is underlined by contrasting the angels who brought the Law with the far more impressive list of those through whom the new "salvation" was announced and brought into operation. It was first spoken "through the Lord," here meaning Jesus (as in 7:14; 13:20), even though the term is more often used in Hebrews for God, especially in OT quotations. Here its reference to Jesus is confirmed by the following mention of "those who heard him" (the original apostles) as the means by which the good news has come to the writer and his readers, and also by the subsequent mention of "God" as corroborating the message delivered through "the Lord." So over against the angels (and of course Moses, though he is not mentioned yet) we are to set the testimony of Jesus and his apostles and the confirmatory signs and wonders by which God has endorsed their message. Whereas the declaration of the good news in v.3 is by words, in v.4 we have a series of terms denoting not words but visible manifestations. In the light of the three preceding nouns, we should understand the "distributions of the Holy Spirit" also as focusing attention on the evidential value of charismatic phenomena, such as Paul describes in 1 Corinthians 14:22-25, and particularly perhaps the effect of the initial "distribution of the Holy Spirit" in Acts 2:1-13 (cf. Ac 2:43; 3:10; 5:12-16; "signs and wonders" is a regular term for such phenomena in Acts, as it is in the OT for the divine actions at the time of the exodus). But it is likely the author appeals not only to the reported experiences of the early church in Jerusalem but also to the readers' own experience of the Spirit's power since they decided to follow Christ (cf. Gal 3:5). Such an evidently supernatural undergirding of the Christian gospel leaves no room for doubt that the "salvation" so proclaimed is the authentic voice of God. The rhetorical question "How shall we escape?" with its implied reminder of what happened to disobedient Israel, vividly underlines the vital importance of taking such a salvation seriously.

NOTES

2 "By angels" is more literally, "through angels" (so TNIV), and so "spoken" is best taken as a "divine passive"—"spoken by God." The wording in v.3 is parallel: the message of salvation was spoken (by God) "through the Lord."

The belief that angels were intermediaries (not themselves the authors) in the giving of the Law may have been derived from God's coming from Sinai with "myriads of holy ones" (Dt 33:2, where the LXX specifies angels; cf. the "chariots" of Ps 68:17). The belief is reflected in rabbinic sources and in the Book of Jubilees and the writings of Philo, as well as in the NT texts mentioned above.

4 The phrase translated "gifts of the Holy Spirit distributed" is literally, "distributions of the Holy Spirit" (πνεύματος ἁγίου μερισμοῖς, *pneumatos hagiou merismois*), with the phrase "according to his will" qualifying the implied verb "God distributed." The Holy Spirit is thus here to be taken as the object rather than the subject of the implied verb (cf. the use of the cognate verb διαμερίζομαι, *diamerizomai*, GK *1374*, for the "distribution" of the tongues of fire in Ac 2:3); God "distributes the Holy Spirit" as he enables people to work by the Spirit's power. (Cf. Paul's insistence in 1Co 12:4–6 on the Trinitarian basis of what are often described simply as "gifts of the Spirit.")

C. Lower Than the Angels (2:5–9)

OVERVIEW

The argument for the Son's superiority to the angels now takes a surprising turn. Verse 5 indicates it is again a matter of his greater authority as the one to whom, unlike the angels, "the world to come" is subjected, and yet the means by which this subjection is achieved is that he is "made for a little while lower than the angels." By accepting the (subangelic) status of a human being, the Son has achieved the "glory and honor" God had decreed for humanity. The point will be developed more fully in vv.10–18 as the implications of the incarnation of the Son are explored. In particular, because he was willing to share our life, and even more to share our death, he is able to be the Savior we need; and that is an honor no angel could aspire to.

This argument is established by one of this author's most daring pieces of biblical interpretation, based on Psalm 8:4–6. Here, unlike the staccato series of proof texts in ch. 1, we have the first example of our author's delight in expounding a key text at some length, drawing out the implications of the OT wording for the new Christian situation. Psalm 8 speaks with wonder of the privilege of humanity, appointed by God to have dominion over the animal creation as his vicegerent and thus placed only a little below God himself. Our author understands it in that sense and builds his argument around the concept of vicegerency, but in so doing he exploits two features of the wording of the psalm that allow him to find in it a more direct reference to the story of Jesus than the psalmist could have intended.

The basic elements of the argument seem to be as follows: God has placed the "world to come" under the authority not of angels but of human beings (the same opposition will be repeated in v.16); but "at present we do not see everything subject" to them; Jesus, however, now fulfils that destiny on behalf of humanity; he can do so because his temporary humiliation "below the angels" has enabled him to identify with, and therefore to represent, humanity. The last point is not spelled out fully in these verses, but will be developed in vv.10–18. But to outline the steps of the argument in this way is to miss much of its innovative subtlety.

---

⁵It is not to angels that he has subjected the world to come, about which we are speaking. ⁶But there is a place where someone has testified:

"What is man that you are mindful of him,
   the son of man that you care for him?
⁷You made him a little lower than the angels;
   you crowned him with glory and honor
⁸and put everything under his feet."

In putting everything under him, God left nothing that is not subject to him. Yet at present we do not see everything subject to him. ⁹But we see Jesus, who was made a little lower than the angels, now crowned with glory and honor because he suffered death, so that by the grace of God he might taste death for everyone.

COMMENTARY

5 The idea of God's "subjecting the world" is drawn from the words of Psalm 8:6. But the psalm is speaking of the world as we know it, whereas Hebrews interprets it of the "world to come." This expression, unique in the NT, sounds to modern ears as though it means heaven, but that is not the author's intention (see note). He uses this unusual expression to mean *this* world, as God intended it to be and as it has now become through the salvation Christ has brought ("the new world-order inaugurated by the enthronement of Christ at the right hand of God," Bruce, 33). That, too, is an extension beyond what the psalmist envisaged, in that God's purpose for humanity in his world is understood as embracing the promised time of salvation, but it is one that makes better sense of the argument in this context: if the "subjection" refers to something necessarily wholly in the future, it is hardly surprising that "at present we do not see" it!

6–8a The strangely indefinite quotation formula (for what would have been understood to be a psalm of David) might suggest that the author's memory of his source is vague; but this is unlikely, since he is able to quote the LXX text verbatim and at length. Rather it reflects Hebrews' tendency not to mention the human authors of Scripture (see Introduction, p. 28). It introduces a full citation of LXX Psalm 8:4–6, except it is abbreviated by the omission of v.6a, the sense of which is repeated in v.6b. Two features of the LXX text are particularly important for our author's argument.

First, the second line contains the phrase "the son of man," translating a standard Hebrew term for "human beings" but more conspicuous when put literally into Greek, where it is not a natural idiom and therefore invites the attention of a Christian reader who is aware that this term was chosen by Jesus to describe himself in his messianic role. There is little doubt our author, with his excellent knowledge of the OT, recognized the meaning of the Hebrew idiom and therefore understood the psalm to be speaking of humanity in general (as indeed his argument requires), not of a messianic "Son of Man." But the presence of this phrase in the Greek version has given him a convenient basis for extrapolating from the generic sense of "humanity" to the specific "Son of Man," Jesus. This transfer is further aided by the fact that "everything under his feet" in Psalm 8:6 echoes the language of 110:1, which our author has already applied to the Son (1:13).

Second, the clause which in the Hebrew probably means "a little lower than God" appears in the LXX as "a little lower than the angels." We have already noted at 1:6 the tendency of ancient (and indeed some modern) interpreters sometimes to take the Hebrew plural term for God (ʾelōhîm) as referring to a plurality of spiritual beings, the angels; in Psalm 8:5 this translation occurs not only in the LXX but also in the surviving Aramaic and Syriac versions (cf. NIV's "the heavenly beings," with "God" as an alternative translation in the footnote). This translation therefore provides an immediate link with the author's argument about angels, but at the expense of making the "Son of Man" *lower* than the angels. But here another ambiguity comes to the rescue: the phrase "a little" can in Greek (and possibly in Hebrew; cf. Job 10:20) be understood to mean "for a little while." With that, the raw materials for our author's argument are complete.

8b–9 The first step in the argument is the simple observation that humanity's dominion over *everything* (and the comment that "God left nothing that is not subject to him" underlines the breadth of that statement) does not yet seem to be a reality. But

the occurrence of the phrase "the son of man" suggests the next step: what we *do* see is a "Son of Man" in whom this high destiny is achieved, Jesus. The first use in this letter of the "human" name, Jesus, thus appropriately links him with the humanity he has come to represent. (In the Greek word order the name Jesus appears emphatically after "the one who was made a little lower than the angels," specifying who it is who has come to share this human status.) The "glory and honor" for which humanity is destined is thus fulfilled in him who is the "heir of all things" (1:2) and who now sits at God's right hand (see on 1:3, 13) on our behalf.

The argument thus turns on Jesus' ability to represent us. The reality of his human nature and experience will be spelled out more fully in what follows (2:14–18; 4:15; 5:7–10), but here two grounds are stated for linking Jesus with the rest of humanity. First, his being made a little (for a little while) lower than the angels indicates his incarnation: the one who is the eternal Son, sharing with his Father a status far above the angels, has chosen to come down to our level. It was only "for a little while" (TNIV rightly gives this translation in v.9, where the author's interpretation of the phrase is clear), and now he is again "crowned with glory and honor," and the more so in the light of what he achieved during that time of temporary humiliation. For, second, he is worthy of that honor "because he suffered death," not as we must suffer it as our inevitable fate but because it was God's will that he should "taste death for everyone." The thought is reminiscent of Philippians 2:6–11: humiliation, becoming man, obedient even to death, and therefore now exalted to the highest place (Hurst, 114–19, interestingly compares the two passages). The phrase "by the grace of God" sets Jesus' death for everyone in the context of God's gracious purpose to provide salvation through the death of his Son. How that salvation was achieved will be explained in vv.10–18, and much more fully in chs. 9 and 10.

NOTES

5 "The world to come" translates the Greek τὴν οἰκουμένην τὴν μέλλουσαν, *tēn oikoumenēn tēn mellousan*. This phrase, which is not used elsewhere to mean heaven, should not be so understood here either for the following reasons: (1) The Greek οἰκουμένη, *oikoumenē*, literally, "that which is inhabited" (GK *3876*), regularly refers to the world as we know it especially with reference to its human inhabitants (as in 1:6). (2) That is clearly what Psalm 8, from which our author is arguing, is talking about. (3) "About which we are speaking" (the "we" is epistolary convention for the author alone), if it refers to the immediately preceding context, points us to this-worldly experience. What he has just been speaking of is the experience of salvation. The Greek μέλλουσαν, *mellousan*, "to come" or "intended (by God)" (GK *3516*), may thus be understood as a way of describing the situation in this world once God's intended purpose of salvation has been established. The idea is similar to that of the "age to come," a Jewish expression picked up in 6:5 (cf. Eph 1:21), though the term used there is ὁ αἰὼν ὁ μέλλων, *ho aiōn ho mellōn*; the use of οἰκουμένη, *oikoumenē*, here places the emphasis more explicitly on this world.

This verse may reflect the Jewish belief, based on Deuteronomy 32:8 (where the LXX has "according to the number of God's angels" at the end of the verse) and exemplified in Daniel 10:13, 20–21, that God originally placed the nations under angelic rulers or guardians. If so, that role was only temporary and was not intended to apply to the "world to come."

6 TNIV's decision to present the text of the psalm quotation here as it stands in the OT and therefore also to put "them" for "him" throughout v.8, while correctly translating the sense of the Hebrew text, means that (unless one notices what is in the footnote) the Greek phrase "the son of man," which was important for our author, is no longer visible as the basis for his transition from humanity in general to Jesus in particular.

9 The NIV has changed the order of the clauses by putting "because he suffered death" (lit., "through the suffering of death") after "crowned with glory and honor," thus separating the "crowning" from the following purpose clause and avoiding the apparent implication that the crowning was prior to his death. Lane, 42–43, avoids this implication by transferring the final clause to before both "through the suffering of death" and "crowned with glory and honor" in his translation (so also the GNB). The final purpose clause probably relates not specifically to the immediately preceding clause about crowning but rather to the whole complex of events just mentioned, namely, incarnation, death, and subsequent glory.

There is strong patristic evidence for an early alternative reading χωρὶς Θεοῦ, *chōris theou*, "apart from God," in place of χάριτι Θεοῦ, *chariti theou*, "by the grace of God," even though the latter is found in most surviving MSS. The reading with χωρίς, *chōris* (GK *6006*), possibly an allusion to Jesus' abandonment by God on the cross (Mk 15:34), appears so starkly and without explanation here that it might have been changed into χάριτι Θεοῦ, *chariti theou* (GK *5921*) to avoid embarrassment. But it is also possible it was a marginal comment on v.8 ("nothing not subject to him—except God"; the exception is made explicit in 1Co 15:27) that then found its way into the text by mistake.

The biblical idiom "taste death" means a full experience of death, not, as our idiom might suggest, a tentative "taste" without going through with it; see Mk 9:1 par.; Jn 8:52 (and cf. Ps 34:8; 1Pe 2:3). Cf. the parallel phrase, "the suffering of death," earlier in the verse. For "taste" see further on 6:4–5. Chrysostom's argument that the author uses "taste" because the resurrection cut short Jesus' experience of death is too subtle and does not fit the wider usage of the verb.

D. Able to Save (2:10–18)

OVERVIEW

I have divided 2:5–18 into two sections for convenience, but the argument continues without a break; it moves now from the exposition of Psalm 8 to consider some of the implications of the Son's being made "for a little while lower than the angels."

In v.10 we meet for the first time the language of "making perfect," which will be a prominent feature throughout the letter (see Introduction, p. 32; cf. Attridge, 83–87). It indicates the fulfillment of God's saving purpose and contrasts the complete efficacy of Christ's saving work with the inadequacy of what went before. Here the focus is on "salvation," and it is the purpose of these verses to explain how Jesus, through his incarnation and therefore his full sharing in our human condition, could be the "perfect" savior we need. These verses therefore provide us with one of the most emphatic accounts in the NT of the true humanity of Christ—a point that for most modern readers may seem a self-evident truth rather than a matter for debate but that, in the light of the strong emphasis on the divine glory of the Son in ch. 1, serves here as an appropriate reminder of the other side of the necessary paradox of a divine-human Jesus.

The contrast between the Son and the angels is not explicit for most of this section but is clearly implied as the author explains how only the one who came "lower than the angels" to share our humanity can be our savior; angels cannot aspire to this role, nor can they benefit from it, since "it is not angels he helps, but Abraham's descendants" (v.16).

[10]In bringing many sons to glory, it was fitting that God, for whom and through whom everything exists, should make the author of their salvation perfect through suffering. [11]Both the one who makes men holy and those who are made holy are of the same family. So Jesus is not ashamed to call them brothers. [12]He says,

"I will declare your name to my brothers;
    in the presence of the congregation I will sing your praises."

[13]And again,

"I will put my trust in him."

And again he says,

"Here am I, and the children God has given me."

¹⁴Since the children have flesh and blood, he too shared in their humanity so that by his death he might destroy him who holds the power of death — that is, the devil — ¹⁵and free those who all their lives were held in slavery by their fear of death. ¹⁶For surely it is not angels he helps, but Abraham's descendants. ¹⁷For this reason he had to be made like his brothers in every way, in order that he might become a merciful and faithful high priest in service to God, and that he might make atonement for the sins of the people. ¹⁸Because he himself suffered when he was tempted, he is able to help those who are being tempted.

COMMENTARY

10 We are first reminded of the purpose that underlies the whole divine plan: it is to "bring many sons to glory." (TNIV has correctly changed "sons" to "sons and daughters," since no one believes the author thought only males were to be saved; such changes are rightly made throughout the letter wherever masculine terms such as "sons," "brothers," and "men" are used in an inclusive sense, and I shall from now on take them for granted rather than draw attention to them individually.) "Many" is in contrast with the one Son through whom the many are brought to glory (rather than restricting the scope of "everyone" in v.9; cf. the "many" of Isa 53:11–12). The nature of that "glory" will be explained more fully later, for instance in terms of the heavenly "rest" (4:1–11) and the festivities of Mount Zion (12:22–24). Salvation is thus not merely a rescue mission but the positive fulfillment of the "glory and honor" for which humanity was created (Ps 8:5), sharing in the authority and glory of the living God, "for whom and through whom everything exists." (Note that this clause echoes closely what was said of the Son in 1:2.) And it is the role of the Son to be the "author" of that salvation; the term *archēgos* (GK 795) means both "leader" and "originator," and probably here as in 12:2 suggests not only the one who makes salvation possible but also

the one who has gone on ahead to prepare the way (cf. 6:20). Some versions helpfully translate *archēgos* as "pioneer." But his ability to fulfill that role depends on his first undergoing suffering on our behalf, so that it is "through what he suffered" (TNIV) that he becomes "perfect" as our savior. "Perfect" here, as always in Hebrews, is not a term for moral rectitude but speaks of the completion of God's purpose (see Introduction, p. 32); Peterson, 66–73, argues in detail for a "vocational" sense here. There is no suggestion Jesus was at some time "imperfect" in the moral sense (cf. 4:15; 7:26).

11 "Making holy" now takes the place of "bringing to glory" as a statement of God's saving purpose. The same term (sometimes translated "sanctify") will recur in 10:10, 14, 29; 13:12 (and cf. 12:10, "sharing in his holiness"), as our author contrasts the ritual "holiness" offered through the OT cult (9:13) with the true holiness of Christian salvation. Jesus is able to "make holy" because both he and we who are to be "made holy" belong to "the same family" (the Greek is simply "are from one," with some interpreters taking the "one" to be their "one Father," God, others taking it to refer to Adam and thus to their common humanity), so that he is able and willing to describe us as his "brothers and sisters" (as Jesus in fact did with his disciples: Mk 3:34–35; Mt 28:10; Jn 20:17). Of course in one sense the distance between the Son of God and mere human beings is immense, and that is why the author comments with grateful amazement that Jesus "is not ashamed" (cf. 11:16) to be identified with us in this way. But the effect of his incarnation is that that distance has vanished to nothing—we are "of one." While the NT testifies in numerous ways to the real humanity of the incarnate Son, there is an unparalleled boldness, mixed with awe, about Hebrews' portrayal of Jesus here as our elder brother. (Even Ro 8:29, "the first-born among many brothers and sisters," focuses more on our future relationship with Jesus than on his incarnate status.) He thus comes to us not as an alien being (as an angel would have been) but as one of us.

12–13 The family solidarity of Jesus with us is illustrated by two OT quotations (differing only very slightly from the LXX text), both of which are attributed to Jesus himself as speaker (as also in 10:5). In the case of the quotation from Psalm 22:22 (v.12) this attribution is easily understood, since this is the psalm that Jesus himself made his own on the cross (Mk 15:34) and that Christians quickly came to recognize as describing his passion. The words quoted are from the final section of the psalm, where the sufferer gives thanks to God for rescuing him. Its point here is that he (i.e., on the Christian interpretation of the psalm, Jesus) speaks of his fellow-worshipers as his brothers and sisters; the use of *ekklēsia*, "congregation" in the LXX helps our author in applying the text to Christian believers. More problematical is the second quotation. (The "and again" inserted between the two clauses in v.13 suggests two separate quotations, but in fact the two clauses quoted follow each other in the OT text; cf. 10:30, where the same phrase again links two parts of the same text.) The first clause, Isaiah 8:17c, has no obvious relevance to the context other than to introduce the second (v.18a), and in the latter the prophet speaks not of his brothers and sisters but of his children. That is still a family relationship, but not the one at issue here. Moreover, the speaker is Isaiah himself, who in the original context refers to his children in order to remind his hearers that their names are symbolic of God's purpose (as explained in Isa 7:3; 8:1–4). The second quotation can therefore be understood as establishing our author's argument only in the rather tangential way of illustrating a God-given family relationship between the prophet (assumed without argument to stand for Jesus) and "the children" of whom he speaks. That phrase, which in Isaiah 8 denotes literally the prophet's children, is picked up by our author in the next verse as a designation of humanity in general. From our modern exegetical point of view, the argument would have been stronger if he had confined himself to the quotation from Psalm 22 alone!

14 The NIV, while correctly interpreting the sense, rather underplays the strength of our author's emphasis on "sharing": since the children "share in blood and flesh" (lit.; Hebrews reverses the traditional order; cf. Eph 6:12), so "he also in just the same way has taken his share [a different Greek word, in the aorist tense, to denote a deliberate act and/or a particular time] in the same things" (i.e., flesh and blood). This emphatic statement of the reality of the incarnation (cf. "became flesh," Jn 1:14) paves the way for an equally striking statement of its purpose. Only by sharing our flesh and blood could Jesus die a real death, and it is through that death that he has set us free from the fear of death. The statement that the devil "holds the power of death" has no direct parallel in Scripture but is an extension of his role as the source of all evil. As the one who through his seduction of Eve first brought death into the world, and as the one who loves to destroy, the devil stands for death as God stands for life. But his "power of death" (like his designation as "ruler of this world" in Jn 12:31; 14:30; 16:11 NASB) is only temporary, until Christ's victory over him (Mk 3:27; Lk 11:21–22). Now Christ's own death has "broken his power" (TNIV rightly for "destroy" here; cf. Buchanan, "incapacitate," and Montefiore, "depose"; there is no suggestion the devil has ceased to exist); cf. the idea of Christ's triumphing over the principalities and powers through the cross (Col 2:14–15). So "death is swallowed up in victory" (1Co 15:54).

15 All this does not mean that now people will not need to die. It is not death itself that is the problem but the "fear of death." It is that which makes people "slaves" (as pastoral experience with the dying and the bereaved soon confirms) and enables the devil to wield his power over them, and it is from this that Christ's death has set us free. We might have expected our author here to mention the resurrection as the clear pointer to life beyond death, as Paul would surely have done. Perhaps in mentioning Christ's death he assumes the resurrection too, but the perspective of this letter is more focused on Jesus' death as the prelude to heavenly exaltation, and the resurrection is mentioned specifically only in 13:20. Just how the death of Jesus removes the fear of death is not yet explained, but the account of his role as both priest and sacrifice later in the letter will focus on his providing "purification for sins" (1:3) so as to open our way into the holy presence of God. Once that sacrificial work has been achieved there is nothing to fear, and the devil's power is broken.

16 This whole discussion arose out of the contrast between Jesus and angels, and so the author cannot resist a further comment on angels even though it is something of an aside (as *dēpou*, "of course," indicates) in relation to the discussion of the purpose of the incarnation. Why "flesh and blood"? Because it was flesh-and-blood people, not otherworldly angels, that Jesus came to "take hold of."

(The NIV's "help" is rather weak. *Epilambanomai* [GK *2138*] is to "take hold of" and so perhaps to "take up the cause of"; it may pick up the image in v.10 of the pioneer "grasping" his people to take them to glory.) In this whole amazing drama of incarnation and redemption, through which Jesus has come to be "crowned with glory and honor" above the angels, they have no place except as spectators. It is we, not they, who share in it with him. But why only "Abraham's descendants"? Did the author have no concept of the salvation of non-Jews? Perhaps his vision at this point extends no further than this necessary initial focus for the redeeming work of Christ (who in his incarnation became a "descendant of Abraham"), but perhaps he is aware of the ideology explained by Paul in Romans 4 whereby Abraham (the "ancestor of many nations," Ge 17:4–6) is the spiritual father of all who share in the faith of Christ. Our author may also be echoing LXX Isaiah 41:8–9: "you descendants of Abraham . . . I took . . ."

17 The assertion of Christ's sharing our condition is now taken to the furthest extent: as our "brother" he is like us "in every way" (though 4:15 will point out one necessary exception to this blanket statement); "the likeness is not a superficial, quasi-docetic one" (Attridge, 95). In explaining the need for this identification the author now introduces what will later become the central theme of his presentation of Christ, namely, Christ as our high priest (see Introduction, p. 31); he will return to pick up this theme in 4:14. As he will explain in 5:1–3, priests must be chosen from among the community they serve so that they can both represent them and empathize with their problems. So Jesus as our high priest can be "merciful," because he knows what it is like to be human (cf. 4:15–16; 7:25), and can faithfully represent us "in service to God" (lit., "toward God") as he makes atonement for his people's sins through his one perfect sacrifice. The two meanings of *pistos* (GK *4412*)— "faithful" and "trustworthy"—allow us both to remember the costly obedience this entailed on the part of Jesus (cf. 5:7–10; 10:5–10) and to be assured that this priest is one we may trust without reserve. All this will be spelled out at length in chs. 7–10, but even this brief summary is enough to explain why the real humanity of the Son was vital to our salvation.

18 This verse underlines the assertion that Jesus can be a "merciful" high priest because he (unlike the angels) has shared and therefore understands our human weakness. In the NT it is always difficult to know whether *peirazō* (GK *4279*) should be translated "tempt" or "test"; both senses are inherent in the verb, and both apply to the experience of Jesus, "tested" by his Father and "tempted" by Satan (Mt 4:1–11); his passion was the supreme "test" (12:2–3). In Hebrews the verb is used of the Israelites "testing" of God (3:9) and of God's "testing" of Abraham (11:17); but in 4:15, where it is used again specifically of Jesus, the qualification, "yet without sin," suggests temptation to do wrong. That Jesus shared our experience of temptation, though without succumbing to it, is one of the most profound indications of his real humanity—and our assurance of his understanding and effective help when we are tempted.

NOTES

10 There may be a deliberate play on the ἄγω, *agō*, element in the word ἀρχηγός, *archēgos*, and the verb ἄγω, *agō*, used for God's purpose of "bringing" sons to glory. Lane, 56–57, argues that ἀρχηγός, *archēgos*, designates Christ as "champion," comparing him with Hercules.

13 The quotation of Isaiah 8:17c does of course suggest Christ's faithfulness, which will become significant later (2:17; 3:6; 12:2), but that is not where the argument has reached at this point. It is sometimes suggested the author quotes Isaiah 8:17c to underline Christ's true humanity in that, like us, he had to trust God; and also that the "children" in v.18a include Isaiah's disciples (cf. v.16), so that this verse, as Psalm 22:22, includes the sense of the solidarity of the speaker with God's people. Neither suggestion is objectionable in itself, but both seem rather wide of the immediate context, with its focus on Jesus as our brother. Our author's choice of this text may derive from the fact that the LXX has inserted "he will say" at the beginning of v.17, so that what is in the Hebrew a declaration by the prophet himself now reads as a statement by an unidentified speaker in the future; the author assumes this person to be Christ.

17 "Make atonement for" represents the verb ἱλάσκομαι, *hilaskomai* (GK *2661*), which when it is followed by the direct object "sins" is more normally translated "expiate." The verb is used only here in Hebrews, while the probably related noun ἱλαστήριον, *hilastērion* (GK *2663*), occurs in 9:5 (see comments there) as the technical term for the "mercy seat" (NIV, "atonement cover") on the ark. The theological debate that has been generated by ἱλαστήριον, *hilastērion* in Romans 3:25 (and that prompted the NIV footnote here, wisely removed by TNIV) is scarcely relevant here, where the focus is on the priest's sacrificial role in dealing with sin. "The people" translates λαός, *laos* (GK *3295*), the term that in the LXX specially denotes the chosen people of God in distinction from other nations but that here (as with "Abraham's descendants," v.16) is applied to all those who benefit from the sacrifice of Christ (cf. 13:12).

III. BETTER THAN MOSES AND JOSHUA (3:1–4:13)

OVERVIEW

The argument moves on from Jesus' superiority to angels, a theme that transcends history, to the beginnings of Israel's corporate life as the people of God under their first two leaders, Moses and Joshua, and their prospect of life in the promised land. The points of comparison with the OT order, which will follow in chs. 5–10, will revolve around the institutions set up at that time (the priesthood, tabernacle, covenant, and sacrifices), which were the basis of Israel's experience as the people of God. The argument is thus not set out along a historical axis but rather focused on the one foundational period in the nation's history. That is why we move straight to Moses without at this stage considering the patriarchs. The "omission" will be remedied when we come to ch. 11, where the author does attempt, even if only incompletely, a historical survey of the great men and women of Israel.

This section of the letter is thus thematically a comparison of the Son with Israel's founding leaders, a comparison given added point by the fact that he shares the same human name, Jesus (the Greek form of Joshua), as Moses' great successor. It shows how the hope set before us in Christ is far superior to the hope of "rest" in the land of Canaan which beckoned to Israel's ancestors in the wilderness. In all this our author reflects the common Christian typology of the work of Christ and the foundation of his church as a new exodus, Sinai, and wilderness experience. But again our author is not able to set out the comparison in terms of cold logic; rather, he is moved by the thought of the promised "rest" to his longest and most elaborate "warning passage," which this time takes the form of an exposition of Psalm 95:7–11, in which exegetical comment (some of it typically innovative) is closely interwoven with pastoral exhortation.

A. The Servant and the Son (3:1–6)

OVERVIEW

Any attempt to demonstrate the superiority of Jesus to all that had gone before must reckon with Moses. Insofar as any human being could be regarded as the founder of Israel, it was Moses, the man who led a rabble of demoralized slaves out of Egypt and who at Sinai formed them into the people of God, with the covenant and laws that were to be the essential basis of their life as a nation under God. As a national hero and the architect of Israel's corporate life, Moses for a Jew stood above all

comparison. Our author therefore carefully sets up the comparison between Moses and Jesus not by disparaging Moses but by endorsing the verdict of Numbers 12:7 that Moses was "faithful in all God's house." At this point there is similarity rather than contrast in that Jesus, like Moses, was "faithful" (v.2), but the mention of the "house" prompts the further argument (vv.3–6) that, while in that house Moses was merely a "servant" (Nu 12:7), Jesus as the Son "has greater honor" in his Father's house.

¹Therefore, holy brothers, who share in the heavenly calling, fix your thoughts on Jesus, the apostle and high priest whom we confess. ²He was faithful to the one who appointed him, just as Moses was faithful in all God's house. ³Jesus has been found worthy of greater honor than Moses, just as the builder of a house has greater honor than the house itself. ⁴For every house is built by someone, but God is the builder of everything. ⁵Moses was faithful as a servant in all God's house, testifying to what would be said in the future. ⁶But Christ is faithful as a son over God's house. And we are his house, if we hold on to our courage and the hope of which we boast.

COMMENTARY

1 For the first time the author addresses his readers directly (though he will revert to his more typical first-person address in v.6). Picking up the significant term "brothers and sisters" from 2:11–12, 17, he enhances it by adding "holy," a term which here, as in 6:10 and 13:24, and as often in the NT, distinguishes this religious brotherhood, "made holy" by Christ (2:11), from mere earthly kinship. The reminder that they are called to heaven (the adjective "heavenly" characterizes Christian salvation also in 6:4; 8:5; 9:23; 11:16; 12:22) reinforces their special status and also prepares for the warning that follows in 3:7–4:13 concerning the danger of losing that heavenly goal.

His invitation to "fix your thoughts on" (*katanoeō*, perhaps better here "take notice of") Jesus alerts them that he is now about to explain another aspect of Jesus' special significance. He introduces him with a unique double title, "our apostle and high priest" (TNIV). This is the only time Jesus is described as "our apostle" in the NT. The title denotes the one sent by God (cf. 1:6a; 10:7–9) as his representative (Montefiore translates "envoy"), as when it was applied to the original disciples sent on mission. By this time, however, it was no doubt already familiar as a term for the founding leaders of the Christian movement and so might also convey

the same sort of idea as "pioneer" in 2:10 and 12:2. "High priest" echoes 2:17 and will be developed more fully as the letter proceeds; it attributes to Jesus a role that was allocated not to Moses but to his brother Aaron, despite Moses' evident role as intermediary and intercessor for the people. "Apostle" and "high priest" are thus two different aspects of the special authority Christians "acknowledge" (TNIV, for the NIV's "confess") in the one through whom they come to God.

2 Perhaps the highest praise accorded to Moses in the OT is in Numbers 12:6–8, where God rebukes Aaron and Miriam for their failure to respect Moses, and describes Moses as "my servant, faithful in [the Heb. perhaps means "entrusted with"] all my house," distinguished from all the prophets in that, while they receive God's word in dreams and visions, with Moses God speaks clearly "face to face." "Servant of God" (the term denotes a trusted domestic official, not a slave) is thus an honorable title (cf. Ex 14:31; Jos 1:2; etc.), and our author will start from this high point in order to show that Jesus exceeds even Moses in authority, since the Son is more than a "servant." But first he takes up Moses' attribute of faithfulness or trustworthiness and points out that Jesus too deserves that accolade as the "faithful high priest" (2:17) who has undertaken the task his Father assigned to him and fulfilled it despite all opposition (12:2).

3–4 Moses' status as "servant" will be taken up more directly in v.5, but first Jesus' superiority is demonstrated by a strangely oblique argument that focuses not on Moses but instead on the "house" in which his faithful service was performed. In the OT text, the "house" was probably understood as the nation of Israel, conceived as God's "household" or estate within which Moses acted as chief steward. "House" in both Hebrew and Greek carries this secondary meaning, as well as denoting the building in which one lives; it also became a recognized term for the temple as God's "house," and the two meanings are memorably exploited in 2 Samuel 7:11–16. So when our author points out that the "house" is of less consequence than the person who has made it and then adds the parenthetical comment that, while every house has a builder, behind them all lies God, the "founder" (the verb translated "built" and "builder" in vv.3–4 is *kataskeuazō*, "prepare," rather than *oikodomeō*, "build") of everything, it is not easy to be sure which sense of the word he intends. And how does this relate to Moses and Jesus? Perhaps his thought is that if Moses was the *servant* in the "house," the house takes priority over the one who serves in it, whereas the householder, God, takes priority over the house he has founded. But this still leaves Jesus out of the equation, and we have to wait until v.6 to be reminded of his kinship with the householder as his Son (though 1:2, 10–12 have also already attributed to him God's work of creation). We should probably not further complicate an already obscure argument by introducing the idea of the temple here, since our author elsewhere seems consistently to think not of the temple but of the tabernacle, which was certainly not a "house," and it is with the construction of the tabernacle, not of a "house," that Moses will be connected in 8:1–5.

5–6 The argument now picks up from the quotation in v.2 and draws the obvious conclusion that since Numbers 12:7 describes Moses as the "servant" *in* God's house he is not on the same level as the Son, who by his family status has authority *over* the house. Both servant and son have tasks to perform faithfully for the householder, but whereas the former will always be looking after someone else's property, the latter will one day own it. The point is developed by the observation that Moses' service was "bearing witness to what would be spoken by God in the future" (TNIV; cf. 1:1–2 for God's decisive "speaking" through his Son; also 2:3). Moses' ministry, no less than that of the prophets, was not complete in itself but looked forward to a coming time of fulfillment (cf. 10:1 where Moses' law is described as "a shadow of the good things that are coming"). He was looking after the house the Son was later to inherit.

And that "house" is now identified as "we"—the author and his readers and all the people of faith whom they represent—the household over which the Son holds authority. When Peter speaks of believers as a "spiritual house" (1Pe 2:5; cf. 1Co 3:16; Eph 2:19–22), he is using the imagery of the physical temple, but here, as we have noted above, it is more likely the "household" that is the basis of our author's metaphor (cf. 1Ti 3:15; 1Pe 4:17). But our status as that "household" is not automatic; rather, it depends on our keeping firm hold on our "confidence" (so TNIV, for the NIV's "courage") and "hope"; note the similar conditional clause in 3:14 and negatively in 10:26. This is a note that will be sounded repeatedly throughout the letter and leads the author directly into a lengthy warning on the danger of failing to keep hold of that hope. He fears that for his readers the Christian "confidence and hope," which should be their greatest boast, is in danger of becoming a matter of uncertainty and shame.

NOTES

1 The Greek phrase translated "the apostle and high priest of our confession" could be understood, as in TNIV, "whom we acknowledge as our apostle and high priest," or as, "the apostle and high priest of the faith we profess," taking the noun ὁμολογία, *homologia*, "confession" as denoting the content of Christian faith (as in 4:14; 10:23). The difference is not great.

2 Lane, 71, suggests the participial phrase πιστὸν ὄντα (*piston onta*, "being faithful") may better be translated not as a new sentence, as in the NIV, but as depending on κατανοήσατε (*katanoēsate*, "observe"): "observe *that* the apostle . . . Jesus was faithful."

6 The Greek is ambiguous as to whose "house" is in view. The NIV has put "God's" where the Greek simply says "his," and it is equally possible the author is making the point that because Jesus is the Son the house is really his. The second half of the verse would then describe Christians as *Jesus'* household (cf. "my church," Mt 16:18).

B. "Today, if you hear his voice" (3:7–4:13)

OVERVIEW

The author maintains his focus on the period of Moses and Joshua, but now it takes the form of an impassioned exhortation to his readers not to repeat the mistakes of Israel in the days of Moses. The historical background is the story that follows closely after the events of Numbers 12 on which the argument of vv. 1–6 has been based, namely, the account in Numbers 14 of what happened at Kadesh when Israel refused to trust God to bring them into the promised land after they had heard the adverse report of the scouts. As a result God swore they would wander in the wilderness for forty years until all the adult generation who had left Egypt had died except for faithful Caleb and Joshua, whose "minority report" was overruled at the time but who proved in the end to have been right. It was this incident that inspired Psalm 95:7–11, where the psalmist reflects on Israel's rebellion (including also their earlier turning against God's purpose for them at Massah/Meribah, Ex 17:1–7) and on the "rest" in the promised land they forfeited through unbelief,

and calls on his own contemporaries not to repeat their ancestors' mistake: "Today, if you hear his voice, do not harden your hearts."

The author of Hebrews finds in this psalm a message still relevant to his own readers, followers of one greater than Moses, and so proceeds to expound Psalm 95:7–11 at length. This is the most elaborate of his expositions of Scripture (see Introduction, pp. 25–27), in that nowhere else does he so insistently return to the words of his key text, citing them again and again and exploring both their historical background and their contemporary relevance. He finds particular significance in the word "rest," which in the psalm described the forfeited entry into the promised land, but which for our author is a model for the more ultimate heavenly "rest" promised to the people of God. If Israel's rebellion cost them the temporal "rest" of Canaan, how much more should his readers now take care that they do not lose their heavenly rest. Israel's fault was in not heeding the voice of God; and God continues to speak "today," another word our author dwells on, pointing out that "today" does not last forever. So let them not in their turn refuse to listen. As the stakes are now higher (the heavenly rest), so the imperative echoes more strongly, "Do not harden your hearts." The essential argument is similar to the typological application of the wilderness stories by Paul in 1 Corinthians 10:1–11 (note Paul's explicit statement of the typological principle in vv.6 and 11), but by using Psalm 95 as his vehicle, our author has produced a richer as well as considerably longer exposition.

While the focus of this whole long section is on the words of Psalm 95:7–11, it is typical of our author to notice verbal connections between familiar OT texts, and the mention of God's "rest" irresistibly draws him also to Genesis 2:2–3; a brief meditation on that text further enriches his appeal, extending the idea of "rest" to include the model of the Sabbath. In this he perhaps takes a step further than a modern preacher might feel justified in taking, but in his essential exposition of Psalm 95 he follows the same sort of principles as a modern expository preacher might be expected to use, considering the text in terms of its original intention, understood against its background in biblical history, and drawing out its contemporary implications. If there is an element of boldness in his assertion that the psalmist's "today" is to be understood in a contemporary sense, this is no more than to assert that the exhortations of Scripture can have a relevance beyond their own day. The parallel he draws between Israel under Moses and his own readers is no more extravagant than that which the psalmist himself had assumed when he too "contemporized" the wilderness experience for his own audience. The concluding comment on the penetrative power of the "word of God" (4:12–13) is justification enough for deploying the words of Scripture in this pastorally responsible way.

3:7So, as the Holy Spirit says:

"Today, if you hear his voice,
8   do not harden your hearts
as you did in the rebellion,
    during the time of testing in the desert,
9where your fathers tested and tried me
    and for forty years saw what I did.
10That is why I was angry with that generation,
    and I said, 'Their hearts are always going astray,
    and they have not known my ways.'
11So I declared on oath in my anger,
    'They shall never enter my rest.'"

12See to it, brothers, that none of you has a sinful, unbelieving heart that turns away from the living God. 13But encourage one another daily, as long as it is called Today, so that none of you may be hardened by sin's deceitfulness. 14We have come to share in Christ if we hold firmly till the end the confidence we had at first. 15As has just been said:

"Today, if you hear his voice,
> do not harden your hearts
as you did in the rebellion."

¹⁶Who were they who heard and rebelled? Were they not all those Moses led out of Egypt? ¹⁷And with whom was he angry for forty years? Was it not with those who sinned, whose bodies fell in the desert? ¹⁸And to whom did God swear that they would never enter his rest if not to those who disobeyed? ¹⁹So we see that they were not able to enter, because of their unbelief.

^{4:1}Therefore, since the promise of entering his rest still stands, let us be careful that none of you be found to have fallen short of it. ²For we also have had the gospel preached to us, just as they did; but the message they heard was of no value to them, because those who heard did not combine it with faith. ³Now we who have believed enter that rest, just as God has said,

"So I declared on oath in my anger,
> 'They shall never enter my rest.'"

And yet his work has been finished since the creation of the world. ⁴For somewhere he has spoken about the seventh day in these words: "And on the seventh day God rested from all his work." ⁵And again in the passage above he says, "They shall never enter my rest."

⁶It still remains that some will enter that rest, and those who formerly had the gospel preached to them did not go in, because of their disobedience. ⁷Therefore God again set a certain day, calling it Today, when a long time later he spoke through David, as was said before:

"Today, if you hear his voice,
> do not harden your hearts."

⁸For if Joshua had given them rest, God would not have spoken later about another day. ⁹There remains, then, a Sabbath-rest for the people of God; ¹⁰for anyone who enters God's rest also rests from his own work, just as God did from his. ¹¹Let us, therefore, make every effort to enter that rest, so that no one will fall by following their example of disobedience.

¹²For the word of God is living and active. Sharper than any double-edged sword, it penetrates even to dividing soul and spirit, joints and marrow; it judges the thoughts and attitudes of the heart. ¹³Nothing in all creation is hidden from God's sight. Everything is uncovered and laid bare before the eyes of him to whom we must give account.

COMMENTARY

7–11 For the Holy Spirit's "speaking" in Scripture (and note that he speaks in the present, not just in the past), cf. 10:15; 9:8; this conviction in no way negates human authorship, for David will also be named as the author in 4:7. The second part of Psalm 95 is quoted in full as the text for the following "sermon," in a slightly altered form of the LXX version. Echoing Exodus 17:7, the Hebrew names Meribah and Massah (which appear in v.8 of the psalm) are translated in the LXX not as proper names but as "rebellion" and "testing," so that the specific echo is lost. By using these names, the psalmist had linked the climactic rebellion of Numbers 14 with the original act of defiance in Exodus 17, but our author's use of the LXX, where that echo does not occur, has the effect of focusing attention only on the incident of Numbers 14, with its disastrous consequence in the loss of the "rest" in Canaan.

The full quotation of the text provides the basis for the exposition that follows. Not every line of it will be picked up for comment, but its overall message of the disastrous consequences of rejecting God's voice underlies the whole argument. Key lines will be repeated in 3:15; 4:3, 5, 7, while the words "today" and "rest" and the idea of hardening hearts (a standard OT term for stubborn refusal to obey) will recur throughout the discussion.

12 The general message of the quotation is summed up in a brief second-person exhortation in vv.12–13, picking up the imperative of Psalm 95:8; from v.14 the author will revert to his more normal first-person style of "pastoral inclusion" for the remainder of this section. He explains the "hardening of hearts" in the psalm as, literally, "an evil heart of unbelief," since he traces the failure of the wilderness generation to their refusal to trust God to bring them into the promised land (3:19; 4:2–3). The

nature of this unbelief was that they "turned away from" God (*apostēnai* [GK *695*], the root from which we get "apostasy" and which echoes the appeal of Caleb and Joshua to the people in Numbers 14:9 not to be *apostatai* from God). And the God they turned away from is no less than the "living God"; cf. Jos 3:10, where the successful crossing of the Jordan is proof to the succeeding generation that "the living God is among you." This powerful title is used sparingly in both the OT and NT, with only fifteen occurrences in each; but four of those are in Hebrews (cf. 9:14; 10:31; 12:22). It speaks of a God who, in contrast both with literal idols and with mere formal ritual, is active and dynamic, a God to be confidently relied on but also a dangerous enemy.

13 In v.12 the appeal was individualized ("that none of you has") and the same emphasis is now repeated (cf. also 4:1, 11). The author is aware that the spiritual health of the group depends on the attitude of each individual within it; the same focus on the potential danger for the group from the failure of the individual will recur in 10:24–25; 12:15–16. So they need to be concerned not only for themselves but also for each other, keeping each other up to the mark, reminding each other of the psalmist's warning. And they must do so every day (did this Hebrew Christian group meet daily?; see 10:25 and cf. Ac 2:46–47), for the psalmist's appeal is for "today." But the phrase "as long as it is called 'today'" draws out another lesson from the psalmist's word: "today" is not unending, and there will come a tomorrow when it is too late, as there did for the wilderness generation. Where there is spiritual danger, there is no room for procrastination. The phrase "sin's deceitfulness" (Lane, "deceitful attractiveness") perhaps echoes the serpent's "deception" through which sin first came (Ge 3:13) and warns them against being taken in by the attraction of the superficially easy way.

14–15 A repetition of the key exhortation from vv.7–8 of the psalm underlines the point just made and provides the text for the author to go on in vv.16–19 to explain the historical background to the "rebellion" mentioned in the psalm. But first in a typical parenthetical comment the author reminds his readers of what they stand to lose if they are not careful. We are "sharers," *metochoi* (GK *3581*), a favorite word of Hebrews (cf. 1:9; 3:1; 6:4; 12:8) to denote the privileges Christians have in common as opposed to those who have not found salvation in Christ. Here to be "sharers of Christ" could mean either to share *in* Christ himself (cf. Paul's language about the body of Christ and being "in Christ") or to be partners *with* Christ; the use of the word elsewhere in Hebrews favors the former. The term "Christ" is used here for Jesus perhaps with a special emphasis on its original titular sense, "sharers in the Messiah," as opposed to other Jews who have not yet discovered him. The phrase "have come to share" (lit., "have become sharers") indicates a decisive change of status. But as in 3:6 that sharing remains conditional on our continuing to "keep firm hold on" our confidence (TNIV, "conviction," not the same word as in 3:6 but that which will be used in 11:1 for the "*being sure of* what we hope for"). The contrast between the "beginning" (*archē*; NIV, "at first"; TNIV, "original") and the "end" poignantly reminds the readers that they are still running the race (cf. 12:1) and that it is not won until it is finished.

16–18 While other incidents from the exodus story might also be described as "the rebellion" (of Israel against God; e.g., Ex 17:1–7; Nu 20:2–13), the rebellion which determined that the exodus generation would die in the wilderness was that of Numbers 14. It was a rebellion in which all who left Egypt (except Moses himself, Caleb, and Joshua)

were implicated and as a result of which God declared that none except Caleb and Joshua would reach the promised land (14:21–35). By a series of questions and answers that draw on the language of Psalm 95:7–11, our author establishes the identity of those who were the objects of God's anger and of the "rest" they forfeited; all three questions and answers identify the same group of people. The statement that their "bodies fell in the desert" echoes God's verdict in Numbers 14:29, 32, where the same unusual term (lit., "limbs") is used for dead bodies in the LXX. The mention of a divine oath is drawn from Psalm 95:11, reflecting the fact that in Numbers 14:21, 28 God's declaration is introduced by "As I live"; in Deuteronomy 2:14, that same declaration is explicitly referred to as an oath.

19 The verb that concludes v.18 normally means "disobeyed," but in the NT it is sometimes used of "refusing to believe" the gospel (e.g., Ac 14:2; 19:9; Ro 15:31). Either sense would fit the OT story, since the disobedience of the people to God's call to go into Canaan stemmed from their not believing the assurance of his presence with them (note the reference to unbelief in Nu 14:11). Whether or not our author therefore intended the verb in the latter sense in v.18, now he makes it quite clear that unbelief was the essence of their failure, with the implied warning to his readers (picking up on his language in v.12) against similarly failing to take God at his word. There may also be a further reference to the Israelites' subsequent inability to enter Canaan when they tried to do so on their own initiative despite God's oath (Nu 14:39–45).

4:1 So much for history, but now it is time to apply the message to the readers of the letter, and again, as in vv.12–13, the focus is on each of them individually: "none of you." The fear ("let us be careful" is literally "let us be afraid"; cf. 10:27, 31) is that they may "fall short" of what God has promised; the verb *hystereō* (GK *5728*) can also mean to "be too late," and its use here may include a reminder of the limited period of God's grace (see on 3:13). The relevance of the text for the writer's own day is found in the fact that "the promise of entering his rest still stands," in that those to whom it was originally made failed to take it up. Insofar as the literal entry to Canaan is concerned, of course, the promise was in fact fulfilled to the following generation under Joshua, even if only gradually and painfully, but it will become clear as the argument proceeds that our author is thinking not of literal possession of territory but of a more ultimate "rest," of which God's promise in the wilderness was a foreshadowing. (Buchanan, 64–65, 72–74, stands alone among recent commentators in suggesting that in Hebrews, too, the goal is still literally "the promised heritage of the land of Canaan under the rule of the Messiah.") This is the first occurrence of the word "promise," which will appear repeatedly from now on as a focus of the author's argument: Christian faith is all about taking up God's "promises."

2 The typological parallel is now made explicit: both the Israelites in the wilderness and the readers of this letter have received "good news" (TNIV for the NIV's "the gospel," which hardly fits the OT context), in the one case the promise of Canaan (and more specifically the favorable account of it brought by the scouts), in the other the promise of a greater "rest." But the Israelites could not "cash in" the promise because the majority of them did not share the faith of Moses, Caleb, and Joshua that God was able to fulfill his word, and so for them the promise lapsed.

3–5 So the "rest" that they lost (and Ps 95:11 is repeated to remind us of how they forfeited it) remains for *us* to enter, since we, unlike them, "have believed." And indeed those who have believed are already entering it (the tense of the verb is present); their Christian life is a journey with that goal as its end. But what is that "rest"? The repetition of Psalm

95:11 reminds us that in that verse God spoke about "*my* rest." While this phrase in itself need mean no more than the rest that God gives, our author takes it more graphically of the rest God himself enjoys. So when does *God* rest? There can only be one answer to that question, and that is to recall the language of the creation story in Genesis 2:2–3 (for the apparently casual way in which even this well-known text is referred to, "somewhere he [God] has spoken," see above on 2:6): after the work of creation was complete, God "rested" on the seventh day. Ever since then, therefore, God has been resting, since "his work has been finished." *God's rest* is thus already a reality, not just a future hope, and it is that rest which he invites his people to share. Yet another citation of Psalm 95:11b in v.5 further underlines the striking concept of *God's* rest.

By this word association between the two texts, Psalm 95:11 and Genesis 2:2–3 (a method common in rabbinic writings, known as *gezerâ shawâ*), our author has imaginatively broadened the discussion and raised the stakes. The "rest" he is talking about is not a mere cessation from trouble in an earthly paradise but a sharing in the eternal rest of God himself, which began when creation was finished and will never end. (The idea of a heavenly "rest" is one that appears in several Jewish works of this period, notably those of Philo; see Attridge, 126–28.) It is this heavenly Sabbath which beckons to his Christian readers as the outcome of their belief and which they risk losing if they do not continue firm in that faith.

6–7 Another reminder that the Israelites' failure to take up God's promise has left it still open for others to benefit from (cf. vv.1–2) leads the author to reflect again on the word "today," with which his quotation from Psalm 95 began. The psalm, he points out, was spoken by God "through David" (note the author's conviction of the partnership of God and the human author in the production of Scripture), and David lived "a long time later" than the exodus events when God's declaration was originally made. Yet still at that later time God's promise remained valid, and that is why God could specify that it required the people's response "today." Of course, from the point of view of the first-century readers, David's "today" was also now a long way in the past, but the implication the author does not explicitly draw out at this point is presumably that what was postponed already for the centuries between the exodus and David could find a further contemporary application centuries later. The offer has not yet been withdrawn.

8 So God's later (i.e., through David) reference to "another day" proves the promise of "rest" was not finally fulfilled, even when the descendants of the wilderness rebels eventually did make their way into the promised land after the death of Moses. They entered Canaan indeed, which is what their ancestors had been promised, but both the incompleteness of the conquest and the frustrating precariousness of their hold on the land that followed in the period of the judges meant that under Joshua they still did not find the "rest" they had hoped for. The name in the Greek text is of course *Iēsous*, the Greek form of Joshua, and while the context allows no doubt the OT Joshua is intended, the mere fact that the names are the same invites us to compare the "Jesus" who brought his people into Canaan with the Jesus who now gives his people "rest" on a far higher level (though our author does not directly exploit the coincidence of names).

9–10 And picking up the reflections of vv. 3–5, that rest is now described as a "sabbath-rest." The term used is not the regular *sabbaton* but *sabbatismos*, a verbal noun used nowhere else in biblical literature but with the effect of focusing on the experience of "sabbathing" rather than merely on the day itself. Such an experience of enjoying sabbath "remains" for God's people in that it has not yet been fulfilled in history. It is boldly equated with

God's own experience of enjoying sabbath when he had finished his work of creation. So too God's faithful people (the evocative noun *laos* [GK *3295*], typically used in the LXX for Israel as God's chosen people, is here used for the people of faith), their earthly work of serving him duly completed, can look forward to joining him in his heavenly rest (cf. Rev 14:13). For the prospect of joy and security in heaven as an incentive for faithful service on earth, cf. 11:13–16; 12:22–24.

11 The lesson of Psalm 95 is rounded off by another direct appeal to make sure that each individual ("no one"; see on 3:13) remains faithful so as to achieve the ultimate rest rather than repeating the disastrous disobedience of the Israelites in the wilderness; "fall" (TNIV, "perish") echoes the verb used in 3:17 and Numbers 14:29, 32. The call to "make every effort" could also be translated "be zealous or eager." It is a matter of attitude as well as of activity. The author wants his readers to be in no doubt that this matter of "entering rest" must be their single most important concern. For if that rest is lost, everything else is lost as well. Their faith in Christ means they are on the road to heaven, but it is still possible to "fall" and to lose the prize.

12 The exposition of Psalm 95:7–11 is complete, but before moving on with his argument the author pauses to reflect in vv. 12–13 on the power of "the word of God," and the "for" shows this reflection is not a self-contained comment but a colorful and rhetorically powerful underlining of what has just been taught from the psalm. The psalm has focused on God's speaking, both in the "voice" that the people are exhorted to heed (95:7) and in the declaration on oath that sealed the fate of those who refused to listen (vv. 10–11). This could be all that our author refers to when he speaks of "the word of God," but he has also made it clear that he regards the whole message of the psalm as coming from the Holy Spirit (3:7) and from God (4:7), not just from

David, so that vv.12–13 are more likely to be understood in that wider sense. The whole text he has just been expounding is "the word of God" and as such cannot lightly be dismissed. To go further and find in these two verses a description of the whole of the OT goes beyond what the context requires but would be consonant with the authority our author clearly attributes to a wide variety of OT passages. Quite likely he also has in mind the "word of God" as it now comes through Christian preachers, of whom surely he himself was one (cf. 13:7, where the same phrase is used).

God's word, like its author (3:12), is "living" (TNIV, "alive"). It is also "at work" (*energēs*, "active, effective, powerful," GK *1921*); the thought is close to that of Isaiah 55:11, where God's word goes out from his mouth and accomplishes the purpose for which he sent it (cf. Ps 147:15, 18). Jeremiah conveyed this dynamic idea of God's word by describing it as like a fire and like a hammer smashing the rock (Jer 23:29). Our author goes for a different metaphor, that of a double-edged sword (one designed for stabbing rather than slashing like a cutlass), which conveys not so much its sheer power as its ability to cut through our human resistance. This dynamic understanding of the word of God is vividly symbolized in the picture of a "sharp, two-edged sword" coming out of the mouth of the risen Lord in Revelation 1:16 (cf. 19:15). In the context of his discussion of Psalm 95, our author may be thinking of Numbers 14:43, where even after God's oath some Israelites nonetheless tried to enter Canaan directly, only to be cut down by the sword of the Amalekites and Canaanites; God's word is sharper even than that.

The metaphor continues in the following description of the sword (literally) "going right through to the division of soul and spirit, of joints and marrow." The latter pair, "joints and marrow," refers to the literal body of flesh and bones, though it is not easy to see how joints can be "divided" from marrow; we may feel the effect of the metaphor without needing to inquire too closely how it might be envisaged physically. But with the former pair, "soul and spirit," we seem already to be moving beyond the literal picture of what a sword can do. Words such as "soul" (*psychē* [GK *6034*], sometimes better translated "life") and "spirit" (*pneuma* [GK *4460*], used for angels [1:7] and for the Holy Spirit as well as for people alive after death [12:23]) are notoriously slippery, and our author's use of the two words elsewhere does not suggest he thought of them as two separate "parts" of a person. As with joints and marrow, we probably do better to feel the force of the metaphor than to press pedantically for a literal explanation. Both terms denote our "real, innermost selves," and at that level, too, we are still open to the penetrative power of God's word.

The final description of the word of God as "judging the thoughts and attitudes of the heart" has left the metaphor of the sword behind. The unusual adjective *kritikos*, "judging" or "discerning" (GK *3217*), denotes its ability to break through pretense and confusion to expose the reality of our inmost being.

13 The last description of the word of God is now explained in more direct language: we cannot hide from God the Creator, who knows all about everything and everyone that he has made. "Uncovered and laid bare" translates a remarkably vivid phrase (Montefiore, "naked and prostrate"), in which the second term comes from wrestling and originally denoted "taken by the throat" or "with the neck twisted back," hence at the mercy of your opponent. (An alternative sense that might still reflect the imagery of the sword is that it pictures a sacrificial victim with its neck bared to the knife.) The sense is that of Psalm 139, with its insistent declaration that God knows everything about us and it is no good trying to escape him.

NOTES

3:7 The "if" in the Hebrew text may well express a wish: "If only you would." In that case the following line would begin a new sentence. But the LXX quoted by Hebrews does not suggest this understanding, and the "if" makes good sense as specifying the situation in which they are not to harden their hearts.

9–10 By inserting διό, *dio*, "therefore," before "for forty years," Hebrews has linked the latter phrase with the period of seeing God's works rather than the period of his anger, as it is in the psalm (Heb. and LXX); but the general sense is not affected, and in 3:17 he will speak of forty years as the period of God's anger.

10 For the LXX's "that generation," Hebrews has "this generation" (contra NIV). In the psalm context "that" is appropriate as God looks back on past history, but "this" (echoing the frequent condemnations of "this generation" in the gospels) enables the readers of Hebrews more easily to note its contemporary application.

11 "They shall never enter" is literally "if they shall enter." The LXX literally reproduces the regular Hebrew oath formula, whereby the thing threatened is expressed positively as a condition with the main clause ("may such and such happen to me") left unexpressed; e.g., Genesis 42:15, "you will not leave this place," is literally "if you leave this place." (See Ru 1:17; 2Ki 6:31 for examples where the main clause *is* expressed.) The same "if" form is used in Numbers 14:30: "Not one of you will enter." The only other use of this Semitic idiom in the NT is Mark 8:12, where "no sign will be given" is literally, "if a sign will be given."

14 The Greek ὑπόστασις, *hypostasis* (GK *5712*), here translated "confidence," more normally has a philosophical sense of "substance" or "reality" (see note on 1:3), and that meaning has been suggested here: they are to "hold onto reality" or to "the basic position we had at the beginning" (Lane). But the phrase "the beginning of the [our] ὑπόστασις [*hypostasis*]" makes this sense unlikely, and the parallel in 11:1 supports the sense of "conviction," or perhaps "resolve."

15–16 The LXX word translated "rebellion" and Hebrews' echoing verb "rebelled" are παραπικρασ-μός, παραπικραίνω, *parapikrasmos*, *parapikrainō*, derived from πικρός, *pikros*, "bitter" (GK *4395*). The LXX uses this word often for Israel's "provocations," which "embittered" their relationship with God. (Montefiore renders the noun "the Exasperation.") It will be echoed in 12:15, where a "bitter" root threatens the readers' spiritual status.

4:2 The unusual Greek wording of the "because" clause at the end of the verse has led to divergent readings, but the reading given in the NIV footnote, "because they did not share in the faith of those who obeyed," is better supported and has been put as the text in TNIV. "Those who obeyed" (or "heard") would then best be understood as Moses, Caleb, and Joshua, who stood out against the unbelief of the majority; alternatively it could look forward to "us" who have now heard and believed, taking the first clause of v.3 as explaining who "those who obeyed" are.

7 "Through David" is literally "in David." The Hebrew text of Psalm 95 has no heading ascribing it to David, but the LXX does. The general ascription of the psalms as a whole to David means that here "in David" need not indicate any more than that the text comes from the Psalter. Our author's argument does not depend on its actual authorship, so long as it is post-Mosaic.

10 While TNIV, understanding this verse to speak of believers in general, has rightly made the language inclusive by turning the first part of the verse into the plural, it should be noted that the singular form of the Greek ("he who enters . . . from his own work") also allows the possibility of a reference to Christ's "resting" after his work of salvation is complete; see, however, Ellingworth, 255–57, for a detailed argument against this interpretation.

12 For the imagery, cf. Wisdom of Solomon 18:14–15, where God's "all-powerful word" leaps from heaven to earth as a warrior carrying "the sharp sword of your command."

In the comments above it is assumed "soul and spirit" are a pair that the sword divides, and likewise "joints and marrow," and this is supported by the use of the particle τε, *te*, linking the second pair; but others have suggested the idea is of division within each of the four elements individually.

13 The last clause, πρὸς ὅν ἡμῖν ὁ λόγος, *pros hon hēmin ho logos*, could mean either "with whom we have a reckoning" (hence the NIV's "must give account") or "with regard to whom we are speaking," a rather ponderous literary way of referring to the God whose "word" is the subject of these verses, since the name "God" has not been used since the beginning of v.12. (the NIV's "God's" in v.13 is simply "his" in Greek.) The former requires a less common sense of λόγος, *logos* (GK *3364*), the latter a less common sense of πρὸς, *pros* (GK *4639*), though both are idiomatically possible.

IV. BETTER THAN THE OT PRIESTHOOD (4:14–7:28)

OVERVIEW

We have already twice seen Jesus referred to as "our high priest" (2:17; 3:1) but so far without further explanation of the title. Now the understanding of Jesus as high priest comes to the center of the writer's argument. This theologically rich theme will be explored from several different angles in the chapters that follow, culminating in the triumphant climax of 7:26–28; and the subsequent phases of the argument in chs. 8–10 concerning the new sanctuary, the new covenant, and the one perfect sacrifice will all depend on the priestly character of Christ's saving work, which is to be demonstrated in these central chapters of the letter.

We have already been shown how in Jesus God has provided something "better" than what came in OT times through the ministry of prophets and angels and through the founding leadership of Moses and Joshua. But for an OT Israelite concerned to maintain a healthy day-to-day relationship with God, it was none of these that would immediately come to mind but rather the regular ministry of the priests, the official intermediaries between God and his people. Their role had two main focuses: to represent God to the people by teaching his law, and to represent the people to God particularly through the unending round of sacrifice to atone for the people's sin. It is this sacrificial ministry that will concern us in this letter. A great deal of space is devoted in the OT to the careful prescription of sacrifices both on a regular basis and for special occasions, and the appointment of a large number of priests to carry out this ministry in the sanctuary was one of the distinctive features of Israel's corporate life. But among the thousands of ordinary priests the high priest stood out as the key figure in maintaining Israel's relationship with God, and the whole sacrificial system reached its annual climax in the ritual of the Day of Atonement, when the high priest alone was permitted to enter the inner sanctuary of the temple to make the blood offering for the sins of the people.

Other NT writers speak of Christ's saving work in sacrificial language, but only Hebrews goes so far as to cast him in the role of high priest, thus creating the bold imagery of the one man who is both the sacrifice and the priest who offers that sacrifice. In this section of the letter the author will demonstrate how Jesus replaces the old high-priesthood, both because his "appointment" is on a higher level of authority and also because he lives forever, and therefore there is no longer any need for the priest's term of office to be limited to the span of a human life. In chs. 9 and 10, he will further explain how the single perfect sacrifice offered by Jesus on the cross has now made any other offering superfluous. Here then is a carefully worked-out theology of atonement that, while it uses sacrificial imagery similar to that of Paul and the other NT writers, is explained in far more sophisticated detail and with a striking boldness of typology. At its heart is the role of Jesus as our "great high priest."

The whole argument centers around a single verse from Psalm 110, a verse no other NT writer has drawn attention to. Our author has already quoted Psalm 110:1 in 1:13 and drawn on its imagery in 1:3, and he will return to that enthronement imagery in 8:1; 10:12–13; 12:2. But the psalm goes on in v.4 to describe the king who sits at God's right hand as also "a priest forever, in the order of Melchizedek." It is this intriguing pronouncement that will be quoted in 5:6 and 7:17, 21, while the argument of chs. 5–7 as a whole will

revolve around its words, just as the argument of 3:7–4:13 has revolved around the words of Psalm 95:7–11. This, then, is the third and perhaps the most far-reaching of our author's extended expositions of a key OT text (see Introduction, pp. 25–27).

But why has he selected Psalm 110:4 for this treatment? It is a text other early Christian authors do not seem to have found particularly attractive, and one modern readers find unhelpfully obscure, with its reference to the mysterious figure of Melchizedek. We shall return to the significance of Melchizedek in the comments on 7:1–10. But here we should note that what is being talked about in Psalm 110:4 is an "order" of priesthood radically different from the sons of Aaron to whom the office was limited in the OT (and to whom Jesus, of the tribe of Judah, did not belong); here then was God's announcement of a new type of priesthood that would replace the old and that, unlike theirs, would be "forever." Moreover, Melchizedek was, according to Genesis 14:18, not only a priest but also a king. In OT Israel the two offices were kept strictly separate: priests were not kings, and kings who attempted to usurp the priestly office suffered for it. Those Jews who looked forward to a priestly Messiah expected him to be a different person from the royal Messiah (so in the Qumran writings and in the *Testaments of the Twelve Patriarchs*). Yet Psalm 110 looked to a future figure, "my lord," who would be not only the king enthroned at God's right hand but also a priest forever. And for that unique combination of roles there was only one OT precedent, the priest-king Melchizedek, who lived in the days before Israel's historical orders of priesthood and monarchy were set up. "You are a priest forever, in the order of Melchizedek"—here are words rich in potential for our author as he seeks to demonstrate that Jesus, the messianic king at God's right hand, is also the true and only high priest forever.

A. A Great High Priest (4:14–16)

OVERVIEW

This introductory paragraph sets out in a nutshell the significance of the theme we are about to explore and draws out its pastoral implications in a call to "hold firm" because our high priest is fully able to understand and meet our every need. A similar exhortation and encouragement will conclude the discussion of Jesus' priestly and sacrificial work in 10:19–23.

[14]Therefore, since we have a great high priest who has gone through the heavens, Jesus the Son of God, let us hold firmly to the faith we profess. [15]For we do not have a high priest who is unable to sympathize with our weaknesses, but we have one who has been tempted in every way, just as we are—yet was without sin. [16]Let us then approach the throne of grace with confidence, so that we may receive mercy and find grace to help us in our time of need.

COMMENTARY

14 As the full glory of our Savior is increasingly revealed, the author now suggestively brings together in the phrase "Jesus the Son of God" two titles that have so far occurred only separately (the divine title "Son [of God]" in 1:2, 5, 8; 3:6; the human name "Jesus" in 2:9; 3:1). The statement that Jesus has "gone through the heavens" may seem to suggest a temporary visit; TNIV has rightly substituted the less literal "ascended into heaven," since it is Jesus' penetration right into heaven itself that is emphasized by the choice of the verb "gone through"; cf. his "going through" the curtain into the inner sanctuary in 6:19–20 (and cf. also 9:11–12, 24). Perhaps our author already has in mind the ritual of the Day of Atonement, when the high priest penetrated behind the curtain into the Holy of Holies. By contrast, our high priest has gone right through into heaven itself, and that is where he is now enthroned at God's right hand.

15 But can such a great high priest in heaven also care about our human concerns? As we have seen in ch. 2, his greatness derives paradoxically from the fact that he has shared our human condition to the full, including its "weaknesses." As we noted at 2:18, those weaknesses include the experience of being "tested" or "tempted"; both are valid meanings of the verb *peirazō* (GK *4279*), but the further comment here that Jesus remained "without sin" suggests the author is thinking particularly of "temptation" to do wrong. It is part of being truly human to feel the attraction of that which is wrong, but the uniqueness of Jesus is shown in that he knew the power of temptation without giving way to it. While there is never any doubt of Jesus' full humanity, the NT writers express in a variety of ways the belief that he never actually sinned (7:26; Jn 8:46; 2Co 5:21; 1Pe 2:22; 1Jn 3:5; etc.). Peterson, 188–90, usefully discusses how sinlessness is compatible with fully sharing our human condition. "In every way, just as we are" is a very comprehensive statement, covering both the hard circumstances of Jesus' life and death and his experience of temptation throughout that period; our modern circumstances may be very different, but in principle we are assured Jesus has been here before. There is a great difference between an omniscient but detached awareness of what human beings face and a personal experience of the power of temptation. Only Jesus can "empathize" (TNIV) with us in that way.

16 Verses 14–15 have set side by side the two essentials for the perfect high priest: to be in the position of ultimate authority with God in heaven, and yet also to have a personal knowledge of our human condition. No earthly priest could offer the first, and no angel the second, but in Jesus we have both. So there can be no barrier to the *parrēsia* (GK *4244*),

"confidence" or lack of inhibition, with which we can approach God (cf. 10:19–22, where the same word *parrēsia* is used). In the OT, the priests alone were entitled to "approach" the sanctuary, but now through our great high priest all of us can fearlessly approach God himself. Of course we must not forget the absolute holiness and majesty of the God who "lives in unapproachable light" (1 Ti 6:16), but through Jesus we have come to know that the throne of majesty is also a "throne of grace," a place of welcome, not of rebuff, where "mercy" and "grace" are freely available through the high priest who has gone there to intercede for his people (7:25). This theme of access to the presence of God will be graphically developed in 12:18–24. And its relevance is not only to our ultimate acceptance before God when this earthly life is finished but also to the present crises of life on earth; in such "time of need," too, effective "help" is there for the asking.

NOTES

14 The phrase "gone through the heavens" may reflect the idea found in some Jewish and Gnostic circles of a succession of heavens leading up ultimately to the throne of God (sometimes described as the "seventh heaven" or the "heaven of heavens"); see, e.g., *Ascension of Isaiah* 7–9; cf. 2 Corinthians 12:2.

As in 3:1 (see note there) the Greek word translated "the faith we profess" could also be translated "our profession," meaning our allegiance to Christ, but the difference is not great. The faith professed is reflected in the phrase "Jesus the Son of God" (cf. Ac 9:20; 1Jn 4:15; 5:5).

16 The phrase "throne of grace" perhaps draws on the language of the Day of Atonement, when the high priest's offering was made at the "mercy seat" (cf. on 9:5) on the ark of the covenant, where God was understood to be present.

B. Qualifications for Priesthood (5:1–10)

OVERVIEW

Having introduced the theme of Jesus the great high priest in 4:14–16, the author now sets about constructing his argument to show how Jesus fits that

role. The earthly Jesus, of course, was not and could not be an officially appointed priest since he did not come from the priestly family of Aaron. (The point will be tackled directly in 7:11–19.) But both in his earthly experience and in his heavenly exaltation he, in fact, fulfills and far surpasses the role to which the OT priests were appointed. So in vv.1–4 our author first points out the two essential OT qualifications for priesthood: (1) the candidate must be "from among the people" (TNIV) whom he is to represent, and (2) he must be "called by God," not self-appointed. Then in vv.5–10, he goes on to show (in reverse order) how Jesus fulfills these two conditions.

In these verses, Psalm 110:4 already plays an essential role in the argument, and the author's summary of its implications in v.10 provides the launching pad for the exposition of that text which will continue through ch. 7, setting Jesus on a level far above the Aaronic priesthood of the OT. But first the argument will be interrupted at v.11 with a comment on the difficulty his readers are having in following his argument, and it will not be until 6:13 that the exposition is resumed.

¹Every high priest is selected from among men and is appointed to represent them in matters related to God, to offer gifts and sacrifices for sins. ²He is able to deal gently with those who are ignorant and are going astray, since he himself is subject to weakness. ³This is why he has to offer sacrifices for his own sins, as well as for the sins of the people.

⁴No one takes this honor upon himself; he must be called by God, just as Aaron was. ⁵So Christ also did not take upon himself the glory of becoming a high priest. But God said to him,

"You are my Son;
today I have become your Father."

⁶And he says in another place,

"You are a priest forever,
in the order of Melchizedek."

⁷During the days of Jesus' life on earth, he offered up prayers and petitions with loud cries and tears to the one who could save him from death, and he was heard because of his reverent submission. ⁸Although he was a son, he learned obedience from what he suffered ⁹and, once made perfect, he became the source of eternal salvation for all who obey him ¹⁰and was designated by God to be high priest in the order of Melchizedek.

COMMENTARY

1 A priest, including the high priest, is a representative, and if he is to represent the people he must himself be one of them. The emphatic repetition of *anthrōpos* ("human being," GK 476) in the Greek emphasizes the point: literally, "taken from among humans, appointed on behalf of humans." That representation is "in matters related to God," literally, "in the things toward God" (the same phrase is used in 2:17), and is defined more particularly in terms of the offering of sacrifices. We may perhaps understand the double phrase "gifts and sacrifices for sins" as covering the full range of the sacrifices prescribed in the OT—not only the atoning sacrifices specifically required to restore the relationship damaged by the people's sins but also the regular offering of "gifts" that were not specifically expiatory but simply expressions of the people's devotion. But it is the sacrifices for sin, particularly those of the Day of Atonement, that are our author's concern throughout these chapters on priesthood, and it is in that light he will interpret Christ's sacrificial death.

2 Picking up the point he made in 2:18 and 4:15 about Jesus, the author draws out the implications of this human solidarity. First, in this verse the priest's own human weakness enables him to empathize with, and thus to treat with understanding, the problems of people who are "ignorant and going astray": the choice of terms focuses on the helpless condition of human beings, apparently unable to discern and follow God's way, rather than on high-handed rebellion (see Nu 15:27–31 for the distinction); in 9:7 the point will be made that the sacrifice of the Day of Atonement was to cover sins of "ignorance." It is such weakness rather than deliberate defiance against God that merits the sympathetic treatment expressed in the unusual Greek verb *metriopathein* (GK *3584*), a philosophical term for moderating one's feelings [in this case, the emotion of anger against sin]); "deal gently" appropriately conveys its pastoral implications, but it is a less warm and positive term than was used for Jesus in 4:15 (*sympatheō*, "empathize," GK *5217*).

3 But a second consequence of this human solidarity is less positive. The priest not only understands human sin, he also shares in it, and so his offering must be on behalf of himself along with the people (cf. 9:7). This point will be the basis for a key element in the argument of Hebrews, namely, that Jesus, the only high priest who is not himself also sinful (see on 4:15), is the only one who can offer a

sacrifice that is solely for the benefit of others, not also for himself (cf. 7:26–28).

4 The second essential qualification for priesthood is a divine call. Aaron, the prototypical high priest (and ancestor of all the OT priests who followed him), was appointed not by his own choice or that of Moses but by God's direct instruction (Ex 28:1; cf. 29:44). The office of priest, and especially of high priest, is rightly described as an "honor," and its special status might tempt others to seek it for themselves (a point still relevant to the various forms of Christian ministry today!), but it is for God to choose those who will act for him. The story of Korah and his associates in Numbers 16 provides a cautionary tale about what could happen to those who made an unauthorized bid for a priestly role. As usual, the author's thought is focused only on the OT pattern, not on the more recent history of Israel, when the hereditary principle in the appointment of high priests had broken down, and powerful men did indeed "take this honor on themselves" or receive it as a political prize.

5–6 So also Christ's "office" as high priest derives not from any desire for status but from a divine call to which he was obedient (cf. 10:5–7). This call is traced to two psalms that have already been quoted to show the superior status of the Son in 1:5, 13 and that are understood to refer to God's Messiah, thus to Jesus. Psalm 2:7 does not directly speak of a priestly role but illustrates, as it did in 1:5, that the special status of the Son derives from God's own declaration. The two psalm verses therefore bring together the two key christological titles of Hebrews, Son and High Priest, as equally of divine origin. It is with Psalm 110 that the priestly appointment becomes explicit, and this time the quotation is not of v.1, with its royal language, but of v.4, where the same royal figure is also declared to be a priest. Each part of that verse will be subjected to careful study in the chapters that follow—not only the two elements explicit in the words quoted here ("a priest forever" and "in the order of Melchizedek") but also the introductory part of the verse, which attributes this status to an unalterable divine oath. It is those introductory words, "The Lord has sworn and will not change his mind" (which will be expounded in 6:13-20; 7:20-22), that give particular force to our author's point here: Jesus' divine appointment as a priest could hardly have been more emphatic.

7 Returning to the first qualification for priesthood, solidarity with those the priest represents, the author now illustrates, in one of the most remarkable expressions in the NT of what it meant for the Son of God to "become flesh," the reality of Jesus' human condition and experience by referring to his prayers. The language is deliberately strong and leaves no room for a "docetic" Jesus whose humanity was only skin-deep. His "prayers and petitions" were no sham. He prayed because he needed God to help him, and he prayed in anguish. The striking phrase "in the days of his flesh" (lit.; NIV, "Jesus' life on earth") underlines the reality of the incarnation, though at the same time it reminds us that those "days" were not the whole story of the one who was also eternally existent as the Son of God through whom the worlds were made (1:2-12) and who now, after the "days of his flesh," continues at God's right hand in heavenly glory.

That Jesus prayed to "the one who could save him from death" suggests the author is thinking especially of his prayer in Gethsemane, when he asked his Father if possible to take from him the cup of suffering, and this is certainly the most striking instance of Jesus' prayers recorded in the Gospels, though the broad phrase "during the days of his flesh" suggests the author did not regard Gethsemane as a unique experience of such anguished prayer. The crisis he faced was unique to him, but the "loud [TNIV, "fervent"] cries and tears" it provoked (cf. the emotional language of the Gethsemane

account, Mk 14:33-34) were such as all God's people can sometimes experience.

Insofar as there is a specific reference here to Jesus' prayer in Gethsemane rather than to his prayer life in general, the statement that he "was heard" seems strange. He was not "saved from death." But his "if possible" was followed by "not my will, but yours," and we should perhaps understand it was in response to that demonstration of his "reverent submission," rather than in granting his earlier natural desire to escape death, that he "was heard." More generally, of course, his resurrection and exaltation to God's right hand demonstrate that his offering of prayer, no less than his offering of himself on the cross, had been accepted.

8 The Greek sentence continues without a break to the end of v.10. Verse 7 consists of two participial clauses ("having offered up ... and having been heard"), which are now followed by an "although" clause before we reach the first main clause, "he learned ..." The learning of obedience is therefore directly linked with, and is the outcome of, the experience of prayer (and especially the prayer of Gethsemane). Jesus prayed to be spared if possible, but it was his reverent acceptance of God's will rather than his own that was heard, and thus he "learned obedience" through the suffering to which he then willingly submitted. It is important to understand this sequence of thought in order to avoid the misunderstanding to which the words of this verse alone might give rise, namely, that a previously disobedient Jesus had to be compelled to obey against his will by being made to suffer. In this context to "learn obedience" means, not to become obedient after having been disobedient, but to discover in personal experience what obedience—and obedience that involves suffering—really means; only by coming to share our human condition could the Son of God know this experience. Cf. the argument of 2:10-18 and the comments on being "made perfect through suffering" in 2:10.

Within this sequence of very human experiences, the opening clause of v.8, "Son though he was" (TNIV), reminds us of the other side of the truth about Jesus. This concessive clause relates primarily to the main clause that follows—even though he was the Son of God, he had to undergo this new experience of obedient suffering. But it also contrasts with the preceding mention of Jesus' "reverent submission," thus underlining the paradox that the one who as Son has all authority needed nonetheless to submit.

9 A further participle, "having been made perfect," leads into a second main clause, "he became . . . ," which balances that of v.8; his "learning [of] obedience" was thus not an end in itself but the means by which he was able to fulfill perfectly his saving mission. For "made perfect," see above on 2:10 and the introduction, p. 32; the reference is not to attaining moral perfection but to being perfectly equipped to fulfill his saving mission. The verb *teleioō*, "make perfect" (GK *5457*), has special resonance in this context as *teleioō cheiras*, "to perfect (or fill) the hands," is often used in the LXX for consecration to priestly service (e.g., Ex 29:9, 29, 33, 35; NIV, "ordain"). Peterson, 103, sums up a lengthy discussion (96–103) by endorsing the verdict of O. Michel that the "perfecting" of Christ here involves "his proving in temptation, his fulfillment of the priestly requirements and his exaltation as Redeemer of the heavenly world."

And just as Christ "learned obedience," so those who are to benefit from his saving work must also "obey" him. For them, he is the "source" (lit., "cause," the one responsible for) of salvation (cf. 2:10, "pioneer of their salvation"). Jesus in Gethsemane could not bypass physical death, and neither can we; but this is "eternal" salvation on a different level altogether from merely escaping death. Just how Jesus' obedience to a mission of suffering would bring about salvation for others is not yet spelled out, but the theme will be richly developed in chs. 9–10, and already there is a strong pointer in the fact that the issue under discussion here is priesthood, with its connotations of sacrifice. We will also read there why the solution that Jesus has provided for sin is not temporary, like the sacrifices of the OT priests, but "eternal," since it is secured by the one sacrifice offered once for all by the eternal Son.

10 A further participial clause ("having been designated . . ." [NIV, "and was designated . . ."] could be understood wrongly to speak of a *subsequent* designation rather than the prior calling the participle denotes) rounds off the sentence and grounds it again in the text from Psalm 110 that is the legitimation for Christ's priestly office. The reason it was appropriate for Jesus to undergo all this human suffering was because he had a role to play in fulfillment of the divine calling to be a high priest in the order of Melchizedek. Thus, the time is now ripe for our author to explain what this special order of priesthood is all about—but that explanation must first be postponed while the author's frustration with his readers finds expression in a remarkable digression.

NOTES

2 OT sin offerings were prescribed specifically for unwitting sins (Lev 4:2, 13, 22, 27; 5:15, 17; Nu 15:22–29), whereas deliberate sin could not be atoned for in the same way (Nu 15:30–31). Hebrews, too, will describe deliberate apostasy as beyond the scope of atonement or forgiveness: 6:4–8; 10:26–31.

3 The Day of Atonement ritual specifically required sacrifice first for the sins of the high priest himself and his family and then for those of the people (Lev 16:6–17).

7 "Offered up" is the same verb προσφέρω, *prosphero* (GK *4712*), as is used for the priest's sacrificial role in vv.1 and 3 and elsewhere in the letter, and also for Christ's own "offering" on the cross (7:27; 9:14; etc.). It is a characteristic word of Hebrews, with its special interest in priesthood and sacrifice. Christ's prayer is thus seen as part of his priestly role.

"Reverent submission" translates the noun εὐλαβεία, *eulabeia* (GK *2325*), which in secular usage denotes a prudent caution or fear but in the NT is used for the awe or fear that is the proper response to a holy God. (Cf. 12:28 and the cognate verb in 11:7, while the adjective εὐλαβής, *eulabes*, describes the "devout" or "godly," Lk 2:25; Ac 2:5; 8:2; 22:12.) Montefiore, 98–99, taking εὐλαβεία, *eulabeia*, in its secular sense, argues for the awkwardly elliptical sense "and being heard [was set free] from fear." (See Peterson, 89–92.)

8 The wordplay of ἔμαθεν ἀφ' ὧν ἔπαθεν, *emathen aph' hon epathen*, "he learned from what he suffered," is often found in other Greek writings that link learning with suffering. The theme will be explored in 12:4–11, where it is applied to the readers' own suffering.

C. Digression: Toward Mature Understanding (5:11–6:12)

OVERVIEW

I have labeled this section a "digression" not because it is unimportant; indeed, its warnings and encouragements are central to the author's pastoral purpose. Moreover, it contains in 6:4–8 one of the most hotly debated sections of the letter, and one that has significant and uncomfortable implications for constructing a Christian doctrine of salvation. These verses appear to speak directly against the assurance found in other parts of the NT that those who have once entered into the realm of salvation are safe forever and cannot be lost. We shall focus on this issue and on the ways that have been suggested to avoid the apparent meaning of Hebrews' warning when we come to these verses in the commentary.

But in terms of the development of the author's theme of Jesus as our great high priest, this whole section is a digression, a pastoral appeal that interrupts the expository argument, just as we have seen in 2:1–4 but now at greater length. The issue of priesthood drops out of sight for the time being until the exposition of Psalm 110:4 is resumed from

6:13. Instead, the author now turns directly to his readers to complain of their failure to grasp the truths he is trying to explain. His exhortation develops along the following lines:

1. A statement of their immaturity (5:11–14)
2. A call to move on from the basics to more mature understanding (6:1–3)
3. A warning about the danger of spiritual disaster (6:4–8)
4. An assurance that they are not yet in such a dire state, and encouragement to spiritual progress (6:9–12).

The very threatening language of 6:4–8 stands out as a surprising move in this sequence of thought. A lack of maturity is not in itself a sign of imminent apostasy, and the author is at pains, after setting out the catastrophic scenario of 6:4–8, to assure his readers he does not think it applies to them. But clearly he thinks it *might*, and he is taking no chances. The result is a sort of carrot-and-stick technique, alternating between dire warning and warm encouragement.

In 6:13 the direct appeal will be over and the author will resume where he left off in despair at 5:11. Does he think this intervening section will have been sufficient to shock his readers into a serious grappling with the issues such as at 5:11 he felt they lacked? Or is what follows in 6:13–7:28 something less "advanced" than he originally had in mind? Or is Bruce, 138, right that "their particular condition of immaturity is such that only an appreciation of what is involved in Christ's high priest-

hood will cure it. Their minds need to be stretched, and this will stretch them as nothing else can"? Unfortunately, we can hear only one end of the conversation, and we cannot know how the original readers coped with his argument. But if 6:13–7:28 is a scaled-down version of the exposition he originally intended, we may well wonder what the "solid food" would have been like! Perhaps Lane, 135–37, is right to insist that the depiction of the readers' infantile condition is more an ironical challenge than a literal description of what the author believes to be their actual state.

5:11 We have much to say about this, but it is hard to explain because you are slow to learn. 12 In fact, though by this time you ought to be teachers, you need someone to teach you the elementary truths of God's word all over again. You need milk, not solid food! 13 Anyone who lives on milk, being still an infant, is not acquainted with the teaching about righteousness. 14 But solid food is for the mature, who by constant use have trained themselves to distinguish good from evil.

6:1 Therefore let us leave the elementary teachings about Christ and go on to maturity, not laying again the foundation of repentance from acts that lead to death, and of faith in God, 2 instruction about baptisms, the laying on of hands, the resurrection of the dead, and eternal judgment. 3 And God permitting, we will do so.

4 It is impossible for those who have once been enlightened, who have tasted the heavenly gift, who have shared in the Holy Spirit, 5 who have tasted the goodness of the word of God and the powers of the coming age, 6 if they fall away, to be brought back to repentance, because to their loss they are crucifying the Son of God all over again and subjecting him to public disgrace.

7 Land that drinks in the rain often falling on it and that produces a crop useful to those for whom it is farmed receives the blessing of God. 8 But land that produces thorns and thistles is worthless and is in danger of being cursed. In the end it will be burned.

9 Even though we speak like this, dear friends, we are confident of better things in your case—things that accompany salvation. 10 God is not unjust; he will not forget your work and the love you have shown him as you have helped his people and continue to help them. 11 We want each of you to show this same diligence to the very end, in order to make your hope sure. 12 We do not want you to become lazy, but to imitate those who through faith and patience inherit what has been promised.

COMMENTARY

5:11 "About this" could equally be translated "about him," and in that case the "him" could be understood either as Melchizedek or as Christ, but on either understanding the general sense is the same. The author has embarked on quite a complex argument concerning Christ, the priest forever in the order of Melchizedek, which he now fears they are not going to be able to follow. The reason is stated in the perfect tense, literally, "you *have become* sluggish in hearing," which suggests a more recent development rather than an innate inability (Ellingworth, 301: "Not only have they stopped growing altogether: they have actually retrogressed") and perhaps indicates a problem of will rather than of intellectual capacity (as the NIV's "slow to learn" suggests). TNIV's rather free rendering "you no longer try to understand" gets the point well.

12 Maturity in discipleship is measured by the ability to teach others (cf. 2Ti 2:2), and by that measure they have failed dismally. They need to go back to kindergarten to learn their Christian ABC's. The "elementary truths of God's word" must include those that will be listed in 6:1–2, but the expression is quite general; they haven't grasped the basics, and so how can they hope to understand serious theology? Then, to make matters even more embarrassing, the author changes his metaphor from the kindergarten to the nursery: they are not even on solid food yet. Even worse, the perfect tense, "you have become in need of," may imply retrogression as in v.11: they have gone *back* to needing milk. The same imagery of milk is used in 1 Corinthians 3:1–3, again as a complaint at the readers' lack of maturity, but more positively in 1 Peter 2:2, where the readers' state as "newborn" Christians is encouraged rather than rebuked.

13 The nursery metaphor is further rubbed in with the addition now of the term "infant," contrasted with the "mature" in v.14 (cf. Eph 4:13–14; 1Co 3:1 for the same imagery). By remaining on a milk diet, they are missing out on "the teaching about righteousness," by which the author perhaps means that understanding of how to live a fully Christian life which only those who are relatively mature can master, as the next verse will explain.

14 "The mature" represents the same Greek root, *teleios* (GK *5455*), as is used for Christ's being "made perfect" as our Savior (2:10; 5:9; 7:28) but also for the goal of the "perfection" of human worshipers, which the OT law could not achieve (7:19; 9:9; 10:1) but which Christ alone can effect (10:14). As we noted in reference to 2:10, the focus of this language is not on moral rectitude but on the completion of God's purpose, whether for Christ or for those who follow him. (Cf. its use in 11:40; 12:23 for people eventually reaching their goal.) Here the nursery metaphor makes it clear it refers not to "sinless perfection" but to being "grown-up" Christians, those who have achieved, or are on the way to achieving, their potential instead of remaining in a state of spiritual infancy. "Have trained themselves" translates a phrase that is more literally "have their faculties [or perceptions] trained," and is a word that refers literally to physical exercise, gymnastics, and so adds yet another level of metaphor (cf. 12:11; 1Ti 4:7–8). The following phrase, "to distinguish good from evil," indicates it is their moral sensitivity that is particularly in view. ("Good and evil" could also be used more intellectually for truth and error, but the moral sense is the more normal, and "righteousness" in v.13 points that way.) Grown-up Christians, then, are those who have learned through experience to make well-judged moral decisions for themselves instead of needing, like children, to be told what to do. For "knowing good and evil" as a Jewish expression for responsible adulthood, see Buchanan, 102–3.

6:1a "The elementary teachings about Christ" is literally "the word of the beginning of Christ," an idiom similar to that in 5:12 (see Notes), but now with the specific mention that it is Christian teaching, not just OT Scripture, that is in view. The call to "leave" this basic teaching does not mean it is now to be discarded as something they have outgrown; TNIV rightly translates "move beyond." That basic teaching is the launching pad from which they ought now to "go on"; the verb means literally "to be carried," the passive probably implying God's agency rather than their "being borne along on the flood tide of the author's argument" (Montefiore, 104). The goal is "maturity" (the same word group as in 5:14) rather than "laying again the foundation," a metaphor that speaks for itself in that a foundation once laid is there to be relied on but does not need to be revisited.

1b–2 The "elementary teachings about Christ" are now summarized in three pairs of phrases that presumably would have been familiar enough to the original readers but that cause some surprise to us as a summary of the Christian basics. None of the phrases are exclusively Christian, and all could have been agreed to in some sense by most strands of first-century Judaism. In particular, they include no mention of Christ and of his saving role, which is, in fact, the main theme of this letter.

The first pair is the least surprising: repentance and faith. The two terms occur together elsewhere as a summary of the gospel imperative (Mk 1:15; Ac 20:21) and neatly express the twofold nature of Christian conversion, turning from the "acts that lead to death" or "useless rituals" (see note) and turning to God in faith.

The second pair of elements in the Christian "foundation" is less obvious. Later Christian sacramental usage suggests to many readers that the terms "baptisms" and "laying on of hands" refer to the Christian rituals of baptism and what would later be called either confirmation or ordination. But it is not likely such a technical sense of the latter phrase could have been assumed at this stage. And two peculiarities of the wording here point away from Christian baptism. First, the word here is "baptisms" (plural), and there is no other NT instance of baptism being referred to in the plural; indeed, its character as a single initiatory act makes such a usage very unlikely. Second, the Greek noun here is not *baptisma* (GK 967), which is used in the NT for Christian baptism (and for that of John the Baptist), but *baptismos* (GK 968), which is used elsewhere in the NT only for Jewish ritual washing of utensils (Mk 7:4; Heb 9:10; there may be a use for Christian baptism in Col 2:12, but the text is disputed). So despite the similarity of the Greek words, TNIV is right to avoid the loaded word "baptism" here and use instead "cleansing rites." Whether these "cleansing rites" were the same as those of Judaism or some Christian development from them (see comments at 10:22), and whether baptism itself may have been included among them, it is impossible to say. "Laying on of hands" is a broader term with many possible applications. In the OT, hands were laid on people as a mark of blessing or consecration, including commissioning for God's service (Nu 27:18–23), but also on sacrificial animals as a mark of identification (Lev 1:4; 16:21; etc.). In Christian circles, hands were laid on in connection with healing (Mk 6:5; Ac 9:17), commissioning (Ac 6:6; 13:3; 1Ti 4:14), and the gift of the Spirit (Ac 8:17; 19:6). Thus it seems the Christian basics our author assumes included some form of ritual either taken over from Judaism or developed as Christian equivalents to the Jewish rites. We have here, then, perhaps a glimpse into an early strand of "Messianic Judaism" that continued to accept as normal aspects of Jewish ritual or Christian substitutes for them for which we have no evidence in the Pauline churches of the NT.

81

The third pair of Christian basics introduces a more doctrinal note. The "resurrection" referred to is not that of Jesus but that of dead people more generally. And that resurrection leads to an "eternal judgment," which will be mentioned again in 9:27 as something all people must face. These beliefs, which occur together in Daniel 12:2, would have been shared by many Jews at that time, so that the readers may have already accepted them before they became Christians. But they remain an essential aspect of the Christian gospel, and the special role of Jesus as the judge (Mt 25:31–46; etc.) gives them added force.

The three pairs of "basics," therefore, strike us in different ways. The first pair would be in anyone's summary of what the Christian gospel is about; the second pair have little place in our understanding of faith as Gentile Christians; the third pair expresses an aspect of Christian (and some Jewish) belief that modern Christians would accept but perhaps might not have chosen for emphasis in such a short list of the basics. It is in this curious mixture of Jewish and Christian elements that the readers are still stuck; surely it is time to move on to a more distinctively Christian understanding.

3 It sounds as though the author would like to "go on to maturity" in his argument straight away. But first he feels it necessary to issue a severe warning to the immature, perhaps on the basis that safety in Christian discipleship, like riding a bicycle, depends on keeping moving forward. Their failure to move on from the basics leaves them in danger of "falling off" because of the lack of forward momentum.

4 Some such connection with what precedes seems required by "for" (not represented in the NIV), which begins this sentence. While this conjunction can sometimes be merely a stylistic addition, it indicates here that there is not a complete change of subject but that this warning arises in some way out of what the author has just said about

his readers. While he will hasten to reassure them in v.9 that his solemn words do not describe their present situation, he is sufficiently worried about them to feel the need to paint a worst-case scenario.

Four participial clauses in vv.4–5 describe in positive terms the situation of the people he is talking about. That they "have once been enlightened" picks up the common NT metaphor of Christian conversion as moving from darkness into light (Jn 8:12; Ac 26:18; Eph 5:8; 1Pe 2:9; 1Jn 2:8–11). The verb *phōtizō*, "enlighten" (GK *5894*), is used in 10:32 to describe the initial conversion experience of the readers (it came to be used of baptism after the NT period). This dawning of the light is a once-for-all experience (*hapax*, "once," GK *562*, for which see on 7:27; it does not mean "formerly," as the English "once" sometimes does; also cf. Paul's language in 2Co 4:6, where the cognate noun *phōtismos* is used).

The English use of "taste" for something less than a real eating or drinking may suggest that to "taste the heavenly gift" means merely a superficial acquaintance with the blessings of salvation, but in biblical language "taste" as a metaphor means to experience to the full. Christ's "tasting death" in 2:9 was certainly nothing less than fully dying, and the same sense is required in other Scriptures (e.g., Job 27:2; Ps 34:8; Mk 9:1; Jn 8:52; 1Pe 2:3). This familiar metaphorical use of "taste" (which recurs in the next verse) renders it unlikely here that the reference is to the literal eating of the Eucharist. The "heavenly gift" is a general term such as Paul uses in 2 Corinthians 9:15 for God's generosity experienced in Christian salvation. The "sharing in the Holy Spirit" is another aspect of this general Christian experience, and our author's use of *metochos*, "partaker" (GK *3581*), elsewhere again indicates a full participation (see on 3:14, and cf. 3:1; 12:8, and the verb *metechō* in 2:14).

5 A further mention of "tasting" reinforces what we have seen in v.4, that these are people of real

Christian experience. What they have experienced is here spelled out in two ways. "The word of God" probably covers both the OT Scriptures of which he has spoken in 4:12–13 and also the Christian message, which has brought them salvation. "The powers of the coming age" apparently describes actual miracles they have experienced since they began their Christian life, whether through their own or other Christians' agency (cf. 2:4). For "the coming age," cf. "the good things that are coming" in 10:1, which speaks of the time of fulfillment into which we as Christians have already entered; see also comments on "the world to come" at 2:5. Following on the mention of the Holy Spirit in v.4, this phrase, therefore, speaks of supernatural events experienced within the Christian community. Bruce, 147, suitably compares Simon Magus (Ac 8:9–24) as a person who shared in such experiences but then turned against apostolic Christianity (cf. also Mt 7:22–23).

It therefore seems clear that the people described in these verses are real Christians, not just interested people on the fringe. This is the clear implication of the language used in the light both of Hebrews' use of similar terms elsewhere and of general NT usage. If it were not for the difficulty many readers find in the concept of "real Christians" falling away, no one would ever have doubted this is what our author is talking about. We shall return to the broader question after v.8.

6 The four positive clauses that identify these people as real Christians are followed by a further participle that sets up the specific scenario with which our author is concerned. He is going to describe what follows if such people then "fall away." This is the only use of the verb *parapiptō*, "to fall aside" (GK *4178*), in the NT, but in the LXX it is used for those who "act faithlessly" and turn against God (Eze 15:8; 18:24; 20:27). From the comments that follow, it seems clear he is speaking,

not of the fact that Christians do continue to sin (and are then able to repent and be restored), but of those who deliberately abandon their Christian profession—what he described in 3:12 as "turning away from the living God."

The sentence began back in v.4 with "It is impossible." What is now declared impossible is, literally, "to renew them again into repentance." Repentance began their Christian experience (v.1), but for those who have repudiated that experience, there is no second start. The very "once-for-allness" of their initial enlightenment (v.4) means it cannot be repeated. The reason is spelled out in two present participles that characterize the position they have now reached (contrasting with the aorist participles that have described their previous experience in vv.4–6a): by now publicly rejecting the faith they once embraced, they are, literally, "recrucifying the Son of God" and "exposing him to shame" (a stronger version of the word used for Joseph's "shaming" Mary by a public scandal [Mt 1:19] and of Christ's "making a spectacle" of the evil powers on the cross [Col 2:15]). You can't do that sort of thing and then turn around and say you didn't mean it. Verse 26 of ch. 10 will add a further reason for the impossibility of a second start: the one sacrifice for sin has already been "used up." Perhaps the author also has in mind the rebellious wilderness generation, for whom there was no second chance of "entering rest" (3:7–4:11).

7–8 The two stages of this scenario are illustrated by an agricultural parable that recalls Jesus' parables of the sower and of the weeds. The author describes the land in strongly personal language (it "drinks," "gives birth," "receives blessing," but then becomes "disqualified" and "cursed") that makes its figurative function clear. At first the land benefits from the generous supply of rain and produces valuable crops, and so it shares in God's blessing; but then it changes and instead produces thorns and thistles (the echo of the curse of Ge 3:17–18 is significant). There is no future for such land. It is no longer worth cultivating and risks being written off and eventually burned. The moral is obvious and needs no spelling out.

4–8 The problem of these verses (and of the parallel passage in 10:26–31) is that they appear to presuppose as a real possibility that which other parts of the NT appear to rule out, namely, that a real Christian may eventually be lost. Jesus speaks, for instance, in John 10:27–29 of the security of his sheep who cannot be snatched out of his and his Father's hand, while Paul envisages no slippage between the beginning and the end of the process of salvation (Ro 8:29–30). Three suggested ways of resolving the problem may be mentioned.

(1) Some argue that those described here were never real Christians at all but merely interested fellow travelers who have "tasted" and observed without entering fully into Christian salvation. We have seen in the comments on vv.4–5 that this is not a plausible reading of the words the author uses. Moreover, the point of this passage in context is that it relates in some way to the author's concern for his readers, and the letter as a whole makes it clear he is writing to those who both in their own view and in his are genuine Christians, however immature and vulnerable. He is calling them not to initial conversion but to fuller discipleship.

(2) Others suggest he envisages a spiritual shipwreck, which is nonetheless not terminal (perhaps rather like Paul's concept of being saved "as if through fire" [1Co 3:15], though the focus there is not on personal security but on whether the results of a person's ministry will survive). The idea is appealing, but it must be admitted there is nothing in the language of Hebrews 6:4–8 and 10:26–31 to suggest it. To speak of no possibility of repentance, of recrucifying the Son of God, and of no more sacrifice for sins but only a fearful expectation

of judgment and destruction (10:26–27) could hardly sound more terminal.

(3) A third suggestion is that this is all purely hypothetical language describing a scenario that could never in fact occur. But what would be the point of that? It is true that the author does not think his readers are yet in this condition (6:9), but his fear is that they could be. This is no academic flight of fancy; he is seriously worried, warning them to turn back from the brink. Moreover, no early Christian with the example of Judas Iscariot fresh in the memory could doubt that final apostasy was not just a hypothesis; even Jesus' prayer in John 17:12 allows for that exception, and if there was one, might there not be others? (Cf. Jesus' words about an unforgivable sin in Mk 3:29 and the "sin that leads to death" in 1Jn 5:16.) The situation envisaged here may also be compared with the seed on the rocky ground in Jesus' parable of the sower: initial enthusiasm and visible growth, followed by collapse under pressure.

So despite well-intentioned efforts to square the logical circle, it remains the most natural exegesis that Hebrews envisages the possibility of a final apostasy, which John and Paul appear to rule out. Perhaps a more satisfying approach is to note the different pastoral purposes for which the passages concerned may have been written. There are Christians who are plagued by doubt and fear and who find it hard to relax in the confidence that God is in ultimate control, that "underneath are the everlasting arms" (Dt 33:27) For them the assurance of John 10:27–29 and Romans 8:28–39 is the most important teaching that could be given. It is support for the fainthearted. But there are others whose danger is not doubt but complacency. The "sluggishness" the author has perceived in his readers suggests a lack of serious spiritual concern. People who are drifting into such an attitude need to be pulled up sharp, and Hebrews 6:4–8 is such a pastoral warning. It is a shot across the bow of the careless. If such an approach does not make it any easier for us to draw up a systematic theology of salvation that does justice both to ultimate security and to final apostasy, it does attempt to do justice to the different intentions of the texts in their contexts.

9–10 After the stick, the carrot (note "dear friends," used here for the only time in this letter). They are not useless ground. The author's knowledge of them assures him of better things in their case. The "things that accompany salvation" (TNIV, "the things that have to do with salvation") are expounded in the next verse as he explains his confidence that they are truly God's people. Their behavior proves the reality of their salvation—not just good deeds as such, but work that springs from an obvious love for God (lit., "for his name") and that has in the past resulted in practical service to their fellow Christians (cf. 10:32–34). But past behavior alone is no guarantee that they still remain faithful to their calling, and so the author adds that they are continuing in this service (and so clearly have not "fallen away"). God, the just judge, knows this and will not forget. The point is not that their good deeds earn God's favor, but that God is well aware of the evidence which even to a human observer testifies to their spiritual genuineness.

11–12 But there is still the danger they might rest on their laurels. Instead they must make sure this same enthusiasm continues to characterize their lives. Only so can they be really sure they will stay the course and safely reach their goal. As in 3:12–13; 4:1, 11, he is concerned for "each of you" individually (see comments at 3:13). "To make your hope sure" is more literally "toward the certainty [or fullness] of hope," using the same form of expression as in 10:22, "full assurance of faith"; it was this Christian assurance he feared they might be losing through complacency and carelessness. "Lazy" is the same word he used for their being "sluggish" in hearing in 5:11. He perceives they are already losing enthusiasm and wants them to snap out of it. Instead, they must be like those who have gone before. In ch. 11, he will talk at length about these heroes of faith who trusted God's promises and were not let down (though 11:39–40 will qualify the extent to which they "inherited what was promised" in their lifetime). Chief among them will be Abraham, whose example will also introduce the next section (vv. 12–15). "Faith" and "patience" sum up the attitude of the true people of God in the interim period while the promises remain in the future and life gets hard.

NOTES

5:12 The NIV's "the elementary truths of God's word" represents a complex Greek phrase that is more literally "the elements of the beginning of the sayings of God." While the noun στοιχεῖα, *stoicheia*, "elements" (GK *5122*) sometimes has a cosmological or philosophical connotation (see Gal 4:3, 9; Col 2:8, 20), the controversy that surrounds the exegesis of those verses is not relevant here, where it is clearly used in an educational sense for "the basics"; it sometimes means quite literally the letters of the alphabet. The NIV takes "of the beginning" as an adjectival phrase qualifying "elements"; it could also be attached rather to the following phrase, so that "the beginning of the sayings of God" refers to the initial Christian teaching; but the overall effect is the same. The plural expression "the sayings of God" translates λόγια, *logia* (GK *3359*), which is used for divine utterances in Acts 7:38; Romans 3:2; and 1 Peter 4:11, and probably includes not only Scripture (i.e., the OT) but also Christian teaching and prophecy, as 6:1 will make clear.

6:1–2 A textual variant reads the noun rendered "instruction" not as a genitive parallel to all the other genitives that describe the six elements constituting the "foundation" but as an accusative parallel to "foundation." This reading, which has early but limited support, is preferred by most commentators. Its effect would be to divide the six items into two groups, the first two being the "foundation" and the other four the subjects of the instruction by which that foundation is established (so REB; Bruce, 137, 139; Lane, 132).

1 The phrase νεκρὰ ἔργα, *nekra erga*, "dead works," will recur in 9:14 to describe what is left behind when we begin to worship the "living God." In that context, Christ's perfect sacrifice is contrasted with the merely outward effect of the OT animal sacrifices (9:13), which are unable to take away sin (9:9–10; 10:1, 4, 11), so that it is appropriate to understand the "dead works" there as the "useless rituals" (NIV footnote) of animal sacrifice. But the NIV rendering, "acts that lead to death" (in both passages), takes the phrase in a more moral sense, and most commentators follow that interpretation. On this understanding, Christian repentance is not from merely external religious rituals but from a spiritually "fatal" sinful lifestyle (cf. Ro 6:21). This would be a sense more in keeping with general NT teaching on conversion, but it is not the most natural understanding of the phrase νεκρὰ ἔργα, *nekra erga* (νεκρός, *nekros* [GK 3738], means "dead," not "fatal"), and in the special circumstances of this letter it seems to me more appropriate to take it here in the ritual sense suggested by 9:14, namely, works that are unable to bring eternal life.

6 The opening participle, rendered by TNIV "and who have fallen away," completes the scenario set up by the series of participles that began in v.4; the NIV's use of "if" has the same effect in context and does not make the situation envisaged any less real.

In nonbiblical Greek, ἀνασταυρόω, *anastauroō*, means simply to "crucify," to put *up* (*ana*) on the cross. But early interpreters of this text took the ἀνα- to mean "again," as it does in some compound verbs (cf. ἀνακαινίζω, *anakainizō*, "to renew," also in this verse); the context here favors the idea of a second crucifixion, and this is the sense assumed by the NIV. If, however, the verb is taken in its regular sense, the emphasis must fall on ἑαυτοῖς, *heautois* ("for themselves"; NIV, "to their loss")—to "crucify the Son of God *for themselves*" would mean to add their own imprimatur to his original rejection. The meaning is not greatly different.

7–8 The continuation of the same subject through the two verses in the Greek text (obscured by the NIV's introduction of "land" again in v.8) indicates this is an account of a single field, which changes its character, rather than of two parallel fields, one good and one bad.

10–12 Note the traditional Christian triad of "faith, hope and love" (cf. 1Co 13:13; 1Th 1:3) expressed in these verses—the "love" already demonstrated (v.10), the "hope" (v.11) and "faith" (v.12) to be maintained to the end.

D. God's Unchangeable Oath (6:13–20)

OVERVIEW

I have described 5:11–6:12 as a digression after which the argument about Christ's priesthood is resumed. With 6:12, the direct appeal to the readers has come to an end, but it will not in fact be until 7:1 that the discussion of Melchizedek, which is the heart of that argument, is directly resumed. In this transitional section, however, the author moves us back into his discussion of Christ's priesthood by taking up the matter of God's oath, which in 5:4–6 he has shown to be the basis of that priesthood according to Psalm 110:4. On the basis of God's unchangeable oath, he will ground his confident assertion that our security is based on the heavenly ministry of the one who now fulfills that priestly role, and the repetition in v.20 of the scriptural credentials of our great high priest will then lead directly into the detailed explanation of the key text about Melchizedek. This is, therefore, a

bridging passage, like many in Hebrews: taking its cue from the pastoral exhortation of vv.11–12, with its reference to the faith of the patriarchs, it leads us back into the main stream of the argument, establishing in the process the important principle that God's word, and still more God's oath, is a firm foundation for Christian assurance. In a remarkable series of metaphors in vv.18–20, the author gives vivid expression to the security we have in Christ, a security that contrasts sharply with the terrible condition of the apostates, which he has set out in vv.4–8.

¹³When God made his promise to Abraham, since there was no one greater for him to swear by, he swore by himself, ¹⁴saying, "I will surely bless you and give you many descendants." ¹⁵And so after waiting patiently, Abraham received what was promised.

¹⁶Men swear by someone greater than themselves, and the oath confirms what is said and puts an end to all argument. ¹⁷Because God wanted to make the unchanging nature of his purpose very clear to the heirs of what was promised, he confirmed it with an oath. ¹⁸God did this so that, by two unchangeable things in which it is impossible for God to lie, we who have fled to take hold of the hope offered to us may be greatly encouraged. ¹⁹We have this hope as an anchor for the soul, firm and secure. It enters the inner sanctuary behind the curtain, ²⁰where Jesus, who went before us, has entered on our behalf. He has become a high priest forever, in the order of Melchizedek.

COMMENTARY

13–15 The "for" with which this sentence begins (not represented in the NIV) links it with the reference in v.12 to those who by faith and patience inherit what has been promised. The specific promise he had in mind was God's promise to Abraham in Genesis 22:17 after the "restoration" of Isaac (the child in whom the earlier promise of Ge 12:2–3; 15:4–5; 17:3–8 was being fulfilled), and that promise is now quoted in its LXX form slightly abbreviated. Abraham's faith and God's promise to him of innumerable descendants will be discussed

more fully in 11:8–19, including his extraordinary willingness to trust God's promise even when he was called on to sacrifice Isaac. Here his "patience" rather than his faith is emphasized, but the basis for that patience was his conviction that God's word could be trusted. Chapter 11 will point out ways in which the promises to Abraham remained unfulfilled (11:13, 39–40), but the focus here is on the promise of descendants, which Abraham saw beginning to be fulfilled both through the birth of Isaac and through his restoration in Genesis 22.

But the author draws our attention also to another feature of the account in Genesis 22, the fact that the promise was confirmed by God's oath: he puts into the third person the phrase "I swear by myself" from 22:16. While human oaths in the OT are normally sworn by God's name, God himself has no one greater to swear by, and so we find this formula, "I swear by myself" (Ex 32:13; Isa 45:23; Jer 22:5; Am 6:8); cf. "I swear by my great name" (Jer 44:26); "the Sovereign LORD has sworn by his holiness" (Am 4:2) and the frequent, "as I live, says the LORD." God's oath is a familiar feature of the OT stories, particularly his oath to give the land of Canaan to Abraham's descendants. We have been reminded also in 3:11 of his oath sworn against the wilderness generation (Nu 32:10–12; Dt 1:34–35; Ps 95:11). And this same OT motif is at the basis of our author's present argument, since it was by an unchangeable oath that God also declared that the Messiah would be a priest forever in the order of Melchizedek (Ps 110:4; see on 5:6 above). The significance of this oath will be expounded in ch. 7 (note especially 7:20–22, 28); here he will lay the groundwork for that discussion by establishing there can be no higher authority, and therefore no firmer ground of assurance, than God's own oath.

16–17 A real oath (as opposed to a flippant ejaculation) depends on a sanction greater than the authority of the person swearing, and in that case it is accepted as the most reliable and binding form of human assurance (the terms used for "oath," "confirm," and "argument" often have legal connotations; see note on v.17 for further legal language). But how, then, can God, who has no higher authority to appeal to, convince his people that his word is to be trusted and that his purpose is unchanging (*ametatheton*, "nonnegotiable," GK *292*)? Verse 13 has explained that he did so by an oath, as human beings do, but that God's oath is on a higher level than ours since it is sworn "by himself" as the final court of appeal. No greater sanction could be provided.

18 The result is that our confidence in God's promise is based not just on a mere word but on "two unchangeable things in which it is impossible for God to lie." Most interpreters take the "two unchangeable things" to be the promise and the oath that confirms it, but it is also possible to find here a reference to a second oath, the oath to Abraham being succeeded by the oath of Psalm 110:4 by which the Messiah is made a priest in the order of Melchizedek (and which is explicitly said to be unchangeable—God "will not change his mind"). Since the succeeding argument will focus on the oath of Psalm 110:4 (not that to Abraham), it is tempting to understand the "two unchangeable things" in this sense of the two oaths on which our security as God's people now depends. But the language is allusive rather than explicit. The essential point is that God does not lie, and if he has declared something on oath, we may be even more certain he will keep his word. This confidence is a "powerful encouragement" to us who as refugees from sin and failure (or as Bruce, 154, puts it, "refugees from the sinking ship of the present world-order, so soon to disappear") have seized "the hope set before us" (TNIV; NIV, "offered to us") by God's promise. As always in the NT, "hope" does not have the tentative sense the English word conveys, since "faith is being sure of what we hope for" (11:1), and this certainty is founded on God's unchangeable oath.

19 The metaphors now pile up in rich confusion. Already in v.18, we are "refugees" who "take hold of" the hope set before us (perhaps the language of claiming sanctuary; cf. 1Ki 1:50; 2:28, taking hold of the horns of the altar). Now this same hope becomes an anchor that "enters the inner sanctuary behind the curtain." (Grammatically it could be the "hope" rather than the "anchor" that enters, but since the anchor represents the hope, this makes little difference to the boldness of the imagery.) There is no need to try to visualize the bizarre picture of refugees holding on to an anchor as it goes through a curtain; the metaphorical sense is clear enough. It is about finding security in the safest place of all, and that place is described in the language of the inner shrine of the OT tabernacle. The anchor is "safe and sound"—it will not slip. And it provides security for the "soul," a term we have considered at 4:12, where I suggested it may best be taken to refer to "our real, innermost selves." Here it makes clear that the purpose of all of these physical metaphors is to describe our spiritual security.

20 The metaphor of the inner sanctuary of the tabernacle leads to a further extension of the imagery, and this time one that brings us right back to the main theme of Christ as our high priest. The sanctuary is not just the place where the "anchor" is fixed but also the place where our high priest has gone in "on our behalf," as the OT high priest went in each year on the Day of Atonement on behalf of the rest of the people to make atonement for their sins. He is identified again by his human name, Jesus,

as he was also in 3:1 and 4:14 when his high priestly office was introduced (and cf. the language of "going through" into heaven in 4:14). But unlike the OT high priests, whose privilege of entering the sanctuary was shared with no one else, our high priest has gone in as the "forerunner" (so rightly TNIV; NIV, "who went before us"), a term not used elsewhere in the NT but used in secular Greek especially for the advance guard of an army; it picks up the theme of the "pioneer" in 2:10, and especially as it will be developed in 12:2, where Jesus has run the race ahead of us. Where Jesus has gone, he prepares the way for his people to follow (cf. Jn 14:2–3); and in 10:19–20, we will be exhorted to do so. And his right to enter the sanctuary derives from his status, declared by God's oath, as a "high priest forever in the order of Melchizedek." Thus we are brought right back into the "difficult" argument begun at 4:14 and abandoned at 5:10, and this time the author will have no hesitation in developing his thesis from Psalm 110:4. It all hinges on the mysterious figure of Melchizedek.

NOTES

17 For Christians as "heirs" of God's salvation see 1:14; 6:12; 9:15–17, and the "inheritances" of the people of God in the OT, 11:7, 8; 12:17. "Confirmed" represents μεσιτεύω, *mesiteuō*, "to mediate" (GK *3541*); the language, like that of inheritance, has a legal tone, as when Christ is described as the "mediator" of the new covenant (8:6; 9:15; 12:24). Cf. the legal terms used in v.16. To "mediate" with an oath is to establish trust between the two parties to an agreement or, in this case, a promise; Lane suggests the legal sense— "to furnish a guarantee."

18 "Fled" translates καταφεύγω, *katapheugō*, to "take refuge" (GK *2966*), the term used in the LXX for the fugitive seeking sanctuary in the cities of refuge set up in OT Israel (Nu 35:25–26; Dt 4:41–43). The following words, "to take hold of the hope," can be understood as dependent either on "fled," as in the NIV and REB, or on "a powerful encouragement" (which precedes "we who have fled" in the Greek), as in the GNB and NRSV; but the general sense is not affected.

19 Exodus 26:31–37 shows there were curtains both at the entrance to the outer sanctuary, the "Holy Place," and between the Holy Place and the Holy of Holies, but the development of the imagery in the next verse makes it clear it is the latter curtain that is here in view; "enter the inner sanctuary behind the curtain" is the expression used of Aaron in Leviticus 16:2 with reference to the Day of Atonement.

E. The Priesthood of Melchizedek (7:1–10)

OVERVIEW

Melchizedek was first introduced through the quotation of Psalm 110:4 in 5:6, and the allusion to that verse in 6:20 has now brought him back to our attention. Since our author has chosen to establish his claim for Christ's superior priesthood by means of Psalm 110:4 (for reasons we have discussed in the introductory comments to section IV of the letter), he needs to fill in some of the background to this mysterious figure. He does so now from the only biblical source available to him, the story of Abraham's meeting with Melchizedek in Genesis 14:18–20, which is the only other place in the OT where Melchizedek is mentioned.

Our author was not the only Jewish thinker to be intrigued by Melchizedek. Some (e.g., Josephus and the Qumran *Genesis Apocryphon*) referred to him merely as a historical figure, and the Samaritans apparently looked back to this first priest to be mentioned in Scripture as the originator of their own line of priesthood. But others saw him as a figure of the future as well. In a recently discovered document from Qumran (11Q13), Melchizedek appears (insofar as the fragmentary text can be confidently deciphered) as a messianic figure who will bring liberty and atonement for God's people and will execute judgment on Belial and his followers, thus ushering in a time of joy and plenty in Zion, a time referred to as "the acceptable year of Melchizedek." Melchizedek appears here to be a superhuman or angelic figure who executes God's judgment, and most interpreters read the text as actually referring to Melchizedek himself as ʾelōhîm ("God" or "supernatural being"). Other Jewish apocalyptic thought identified him with the archangel Michael or another angel, but his priestly role was also

remembered when he was cast in the role of the high priest of the messianic age. Some Gnostics also saw Melchizedek as an angelic power, while others looked for his coming as the miraculously born messianic priest-king. Philo saw him as an allegory of "the right Logos."

So the readers of this letter may have had more awareness of and interest in Melchizedek than we might expect from his minimal appearance in the OT. Indeed, some interpreters suggest that, far from having to introduce Melchizedek to them for the first time, our author is engaged in damping down an unhealthy preoccupation with Melchizedek in favor of the true Messiah, Jesus. But this is probably to go too far, since it is remarkable that, whereas Hebrews sets other OT figures against Christ as his inferiors, there is no argument for the superiority of Christ to Melchizedek; rather, he is Melchizedek's successor, in his "order." Melchizedek's role in the argument of the letter is thus to legitimate the higher order of priesthood to which Christ belongs, after which he fades from the argument while Jesus is contrasted not with him but with the Aaronic priests.

In this paragraph the main argument drawn from Genesis 14 is to the effect that Melchizedek, as the one who pronounces a blessing on Abraham and to whom Abraham offers "tribute," is superior to Abraham and thus also superior to Levi, Abraham's descendant, from whom the official OT priesthood was descended. The purpose of this demonstration is clearly to establish that therefore also Christ, as a priest of Melchizedek's "order," shares this superior status, but this development of the argument is not yet explicit. Indeed, the only mention of Christ in this paragraph is in v.3, where the author notes

Melchizedek's apparent immortality (and "forever" in Ps 110:4) as a pointer to the eternity of the Son of God.

The underlying argument of this section is thus more complex than we have seen so far in the letter. Instead of a straight comparison between Jesus and an OT figure (prophets, angels, Moses, Joshua), we now have an argument in two layers, with Melchizedek coming in as the middle figure. It is the superiority of Melchizedek (not Jesus) to Abraham that is explicitly at issue, though the purpose of establishing this is so the author can go on to transfer this status to Jesus as the new Melchizedek. Nor is it the status of Abraham himself that is the author's ultimate concern but rather that of the OT priests who are descended from his great-grandson Levi. There are thus now four members in this comparison: Melchizedek the priest is superior to Abraham, and thus also to Abraham's descendants, the Levitical priests; and therefore Jesus, the priest "according to the order of Melchizedek," also exercises a priesthood superior to theirs. That is where this argument is ultimately designed to lead.

[1]This Melchizedek was king of Salem and priest of God Most High. He met Abraham returning from the defeat of the kings and blessed him, [2]and Abraham gave him a tenth of everything. First, his name means "king of righteousness"; then also, "king of Salem" means "king of peace." [3]Without father or mother, without genealogy, without beginning of days or end of life, like the Son of God he remains a priest forever.

[4]Just think how great he was: Even the patriarch Abraham gave him a tenth of the plunder! [5]Now the law requires the descendants of Levi who become priests to collect a tenth from the people—that is, their brothers—even though their brothers are descended from Abraham. [6]This man, however, did not trace his descent from Levi, yet he collected a tenth from Abraham and blessed him who had the promises. [7]And without doubt the lesser person is blessed by the greater. [8]In the one case, the tenth is collected by men who die; but in the other case, by him who is declared to be living. [9]One might even say that Levi, who collects the tenth, paid the tenth through Abraham, [10]because when Melchizedek met Abraham, Levi was still in the body of his ancestor.

COMMENTARY

1–2a First we are reminded, in a compilation of words from LXX Genesis 14:17–20, of the essence of the brief episode that follows from the story of Abraham's defeat of the four Mesopotamian kings who had invaded the Jordan valley and captured Lot. (Hebrews consistently uses the longer name "Abraham" even for events preceding Ge 17, when his name was changed from Abram.) Salem is generally understood to have been an alternative name for Jerusalem (Ps 76:2), at that stage a Jebusite city, and "God Most High" was the name of a Canaanite god—though it also came to be used for Israel's God, and Abraham identifies this "God Most High" with Yahweh in Genesis 14:22. Melchizedek thus represents a non-Israelite regime in Jerusalem earlier than that of the Levitical priests who operated there during OT times. The abbreviation of the Genesis account has the effect of placing side by side the two aspects of Melchizedek's unique dual role as both king and priest (see introductory comments at 4:14–7:28).

2b–3 Before going on to the implications of Abraham's meeting with Melchizedek, our author pauses to draw some interesting conclusions about Melchizedek himself from the very meager information provided in Genesis 14:18–20, drawing first on the meaning of the names and then on the significance of what Genesis does *not* say. His etymology of the names Melchizedek ("king of righteousness") and Salem ("peace") draws on obvious verbal similarities in Hebrew, though in neither case is it necessarily the actual origin of the name; the latter is supported, however, by the LXX's use of *eirēnē*, "peace," to translate Salem in Psalm 76:2, and both interpretations are paralleled in Philo. The author may have expected his readers to draw theological or devotional significance from these names, but if so, he gives them no further help in doing so. Instead he focuses on the silences of the Genesis text.

In Genesis 14, Melchizedek is introduced out of the blue and disappears as quickly, his brief appearance interrupting a narrative that deals with the king of Sodom (vv.17, 21–24). We know his name and office but nothing of his family or his previous or subsequent history. In terms of the biblical narrative, he is thus "without father or mother, without genealogy, without beginning of days or end of life." His literary persona therefore suggests to our author a parallel with the Son of God, who is in very fact "without beginning of days or end of life," and the psalm, which speaks of "a priest *forever* in the order of Melchizedek," reinforces this thought. It is not a historical argument—nothing in the OT suggests Melchizedek historically had no parents, was not born, and did not die, and our

author's argument does not necessarily show that he thought this to be the case (though v.8 may point that way). It is rather an argument from literary silence, setting Melchizedek up as a literary model for the eternal Son of God. In his very rootlessness and timelessness, he forms a suitable model for the one who was to come, the Son (not of any man but) of God, who shares God's eternal existence and can thus uniquely exercise that eternal priesthood Psalm 110:4 has claimed to be the prerogative of the "order of Melchizedek." To our historically tuned minds, this may seem a bizarre conclusion to draw from silence, but it is an argument from the text, not from history, following the well-attested Jewish hermeneutical principle (found both in rabbinic and in Alexandrian writings) that what is not mentioned in the Torah does not exist. The comparison serves to underline the eternity of our true high priest in contrast with the transience of the OT priests, a theme that will be developed in vv.23–25.

4–6a Abraham, the founding father of the Jewish people, stood on a level above ordinary people; only Moses and David were held in anything like the same veneration. Yet here is someone superior even to Abraham. The point is established by two arguments from the Genesis text. First, in these verses Abraham handed over a part of the spoils of war ("perhaps as tariff for crossing his land," Buchanan, 117–18). This in itself is a significant act, suggesting the tribute offered by a lesser figure to his social superior, and the author underlines its paradoxical significance by placing the title "the patriarch" emphatically at the end of the sentence. But our author finds significance particularly in the fact that the portion handed over was a tenth—the same proportion the Law required Israelites to give to the Levites, who in turn gave a tenth of it to those of them who were appointed priests (Nu 18:20–32). Both the priests (as descendants of Levi) and those who give them the tithes belong to the descendants of Abraham; but here we see Abraham himself, the ancestor of the nation within which this sacred tithe is collected, making the same level of payment to someone outside his own family. And the verb in v.6a, *dedekatōken* ("collected a tenth from"), suggests Melchizedek took this share by right, just as the Levitical priests "collect a tenth from" their fellow Israelites.

6b–7 The second argument drawn from the Genesis text depends on the statement that Melchizedek blessed Abraham (and indeed Ge 14 gives the wording of the blessing in full). Blessing was, of course, one of the central functions of the Levitical priests (Nu 6:22–27). It is axiomatic (lit., "without any contradiction") that the one giving the blessing is the superior. Yet the one who received this blessing was no less than the one to whom God had made his momentous promises, discussed already in 6:13–15. (The promise actually quoted in 6:13–14 comes from a later chapter of Genesis, but it derives from the initial promise of Ge 12:2–3, which had already set Abraham apart before the incident of ch. 14; cf. also 13:14–17.) How great, then, must be the person who can presume to pronounce a blessing on God's chosen patriarch!

8 The superiority of Melchizedek to Abraham has thus been established. Two further arguments follow. First, in this verse we find a comparison between Melchizedek and the OT priests, who later also received tithes. The latter were ordinary mortals, but Melchizedek is different in that he "is declared to be living" (i.e., presumably, to be immortal). No such declaration is made in the OT text (unless it be by inference from the "forever" of Ps 110:4), but the author is here drawing again on his observation in v.3 that, as presented in the Genesis story, Melchizedek was "without beginning of days or end of life"; his wording here perhaps goes further than v.3 toward reflecting the fairly widespread view (see introductory comments on this section) of Melchizedek as an angelic being, not just a figure in human history. Clearly such a priest is superior to mere mortals.

9–10 The second argument develops the observations made in vv.4–6a about tithes. When Abraham gave the tithe to Melchizedek, it was in principle Levi, the as yet unborn ancestor of the priestly tribe, who made the payment through his great-grandfather. (The phrase "one might even say" recognizes that the author is indulging his imagination a little here!) And so we have the satisfyingly paradoxical situation of the tithe-exactor himself paying the tithe. The argument has thus reached its intended conclusion: the OT Levitical priesthood is manifestly inferior to that of Melchizedek—and therefore to that of anyone who belongs to Melchizedek's "order."

With that, Melchizedek has served his purpose in this letter and will not appear again, except in further references to the "order of Melchizedek," which Psalm 110:4 envisages. If this "order" shares the status of Melchizedek, it must be on a far higher level than the priesthood of the OT (the "order of Aaron," v.11), superior even to the original ancestor of Israel himself and therefore to all his descendants, whether priestly or not. There is thus no need to raise the question of the relative importance of Jesus and Melchizedek, and he can exit as mysteriously as he came in and leave his successor-priest, Jesus, in possession of the stage.

NOTES

1–10 The account given above of Jewish views of Melchizedek is incomplete. A less eschatological interest is found also both in the Sadducean legitimation of the Hasmonean priest-kings on the model of

Melchizedek and in the corresponding Pharisaic disparagement of Melchizedek in favor of Abraham; a striking lacuna at the relevant point in *Jubilees* also suggests a deliberate suppression of the story of Melchizedek. He is sometimes identified with Shem. For a fuller account, see, e.g., B. A. Demarest, *A History of Interpretation of Hebrews 7, 1–10* (Tübingen: Mohr, 1976); F. L. Horton, *The Melchizedek Tradition* (Cambridge: Cambridge Univ. Press, 1976); R. N. Longenecker, in R. A. Guelich, ed., *Unity and Diversity in the NT* (Grand Rapids: Eerdmans, 1978), 161–85; Attridge 192–95.

1 The abbreviated account of the Genesis story omits Melchizedek's provision of bread and wine. As Bruce, 158, remarks, "Few typologists of early Christian or more recent days could have resisted so tempting an opportunity of drawing a eucharistic inference from these words!"—particularly when the subject is priesthood.

3 The terms ἀπάτωρ, ἀμήτωρ, *apatōr, amētōr*, "without father or mother," are found in both pagan and Jewish writings to describe divine beings.

"Like" (TNIV, "resembling") represents ἀφωμοιωμένος, *aphōmoiōmenos*, literally, "having been made like" (GK *926*), which could be understood either in terms of an actual resemblance or as a literary comparison. The wording gives no support to the quaint patristic idea that the Melchizedek of Genesis 14 is to be understood as a preincarnate appearance of Christ.

6 "Did not trace his descent" translates μὴ γενεαλογούμενος, *mē genealogoumenos*, which echoes ἀγενεαλόγητος, *agenealogētos*, "without genealogy" (a word apparently coined by our author) in v.3. This pointed terminology underlines the irony that it is the very lack of the pedigree that was the glory and the authority of the Levitical priests (Nu 3:10; 18:1, 7) which is the basis for this extraordinary priest's superior status, outside and above the family of Abraham. (For the problem faced by would-be priests within Israel who could not produce a recorded genealogy, see Ne 7:63–65.)

F. A Better Order of Priesthood (7:11–19)

OVERVIEW

As often in Hebrews, interpreters vary as to how they divide this chapter into sections for comment. Such divisions are more for the commentator's convenience than representing actual "sections" intended by the author. The argument flows throughout this chapter, leading from the OT story of Melchizedek to the conclusion that in Jesus we have the perfect high priest forever "in the order of Melchizedek," and within the chapter, themes recur and interweave in a way that defies neat analysis.

I have separated off vv.11–19, because here the argument is centered on the issue of what is involved in speaking of another "order of priesthood," as Psalm

110:4 does. This is a crucial question for the author's exegesis of his psalm text, and it has the effect of focusing attention in these verses on the inadequacy of the OT priesthood, which made it necessary for it to be replaced by something "better." That key word of Hebrews' argument (see Introduction, pp. 24–25) now begins to be deployed more insistently, as the author speaks of a "better hope" (v.19), a "better covenant" (v.22; 8:6), and "better promises" (8:6), which are made available to us through the unique ministry of a priest of the order of Melchizedek.

The issue is tackled in these verses in more general terms. There is indeed specific reference to Jesus as the priest of the new order (though not yet by name) in the comments on his non-Levitical ancestry (vv.13–14) and his "indestructible life" (v.16), but the focus of this phase of the argument is on the inadequacy of the old order of priesthood. From v.20 on, the spotlight will fall more directly on Jesus and on the positive evidence for his superiority.

The ultimate failure of the old order is asserted on the basis that it could never bring about "perfection" in the worshipers, the two uses of *teleiōsis/teleioō* (GK *5459/5457*; vv.11, 19) forming a sort of framework around these verses. We have already noted the importance of this wide-ranging term for Hebrews, especially for Jesus' "perfect" qualification to be our savior (see Introduction, p. 32, and comments at 2:10; 5:9, 14). Its use in this more cultic context (and cf. its repetition in 9:9; 10:1, 14) refers to the aim of the sacrificial system to restore people's relationship with God. The worshiper comes to sacrifice with a consciousness of sin and failure and hopes thereby to find a new and unbroken relationship with God; but every time these hopes of a "perfect" resolution to the problem of sin have been disappointed, and the round of sacrifice must be endlessly repeated. It is only when the "perfect" high priest comes to offer the one "perfect" sacrifice that it is possible for his people to be "made perfect forever" (10:14). The positive side of this argument is still to come; here our author's concern is with the negative, the inability of the old order to deliver "perfection" (though Bruce, 169, goes a little too far in asserting that "the whole apparatus of worship ... *was calculated* rather to keep people at a distance from God than to bring them near" [italics added]).

---

[11]If perfection could have been attained through the Levitical priesthood (for on the basis of it the law was given to the people), why was there still need for another priest to come—one in the order of Melchizedek, not in the order of Aaron? [12]For when there is a change of the priesthood, there must also be a change of the law. [13]He of whom these things are said belonged to a different tribe, and no one from that tribe has ever served at the altar. [14]For it is clear that our Lord descended from Judah, and in regard to that tribe Moses said nothing about priests. [15]And what we have said is even more clear if another priest like Melchizedek appears, [16]one who has become a priest not on the basis of a regulation as to his ancestry but on the basis of the power of an indestructible life. [17]For it is declared:

"You are a priest forever,
    in the order of Melchizedek."

[18]The former regulation is set aside because it was weak and useless [19](for the law made nothing perfect), and a better hope is introduced, by which we draw near to God.

COMMENTARY

11 The essential argument is that you only replace something if it is faulty. So when in Psalm 110:4 God announces a different order of priesthood, this must indicate the existing (Levitical) order is not working. A closely parallel argument will be presented in 8:7–13: God's promise of a new covenant through the prophecy of Jeremiah shows that the old covenant has failed. Here the argument depends on the psalm statement. This may account for the unexpected presence of the verb *legesthai* (unrepresented in the NIV) at the end of the verse; literally it probably means "and not *to be described as* in the order of Aaron," reflecting on the fact that the psalm explicitly designates this priest as belonging to an order other than the official one. The way in which the OT priesthood ("the order of Aaron"—see note) has failed to deliver "perfection" will be spelled out in 10:1–4.

The thrust of the obscure parenthesis rather literally translated by the NIV "for on the basis of it the law was given to the people" is perhaps not that suggested by the free TNIV rendering "and indeed the law given to the people established that priesthood," but rather that the Levitical priesthood was fundamental to the Law. The point is that it was the Levitical priesthood (not that of Melchizedek) that was legally established as the heart of Israel's cultic system, even though it proved not to meet their religious need. That is why the Law needed to be changed (v.12) if perfection was to be achieved.

12 Hebrews does not directly set Jesus and his ministry over against the OT law as such, as Paul does in Romans 10:4 and Galatians 3:24–25. The author tends to talk about various personages, institutions, or regulations in the Law rather than about the Law itself. Even when Jesus was explicitly contrasted with Moses (3:1–6), Moses' law was not directly mentioned. But he often mentions that the OT practices now superseded were "according to the law" (7:5; 8:4; 9:19, 22; 10:8), and when he speaks in 8:7–13 of the "obsolescence" of the old covenant (itself based on the Law, 8:10), he gets close to saying the Law itself is due for replacement. The Law was, after all, only a "shadow of the good things that are coming" (10:1). So it follows that if the Aaronic priesthood was set up by the Mosaic law, a change of priesthood requires a change of law, since priesthood and law are

inextricably bound together (v.11). He does not spell out what this new law is, but as far as the present argument is concerned, he was probably thinking of the divine declaration on oath in Psalm 110:4 as the "legal" basis of the new order of priesthood.

13–14 "He of whom these things are said" ("these things" being the pronouncement of Ps 110:4) is Jesus, as becomes explicit in v.14. "Our Lord" is not used elsewhere in the letter simply as a title of Jesus except in 13:20, with the name "Jesus" added, and *kyrios*, "Lord," is normally used for God, especially in OT quotations; but the context here makes the reference unambiguous (and cf. 2:3). The same point would of course have been equally true of Melchizedek, who was not even from Israel, let alone the tribe of Levi. As long as the Mosaic law remained in force, only Levites could "serve at the altar," and by that ruling, Jesus, of the royal tribe of Judah, is automatically excluded from priesthood (indeed in the OT the priesthood was jealously guarded from royal interference). That is why the author must establish a new and different legal basis for Jesus' priesthood. The priesthood "in the order of Melchizedek" (both priest and king) gives him the basis to do so. The statement that "Moses said nothing about priests" in relation to Judah may be simply a reference to the Pentateuch in general but perhaps more likely reflects specifically on Deuteronomy 33:7, where Moses' brief blessing of Judah stands in contrast with the fuller account of Levi's priestly function, which follows in vv.8–11.

15–17 "What we have said" is the whole argument about the need for a change in the Law so that a new order of priesthood can take the place of that of Aaron. This is "even more clear" because we are talking not about a theoretical possibility but about an actual event. A new priest *has* appeared who traces his legitimacy not from the pedigree established by the Law but from the non-Levitical order of Melchizedek. Nor is it simply a matter of claiming an alternative priestly dynasty, for the key verse from Psalm 110 (quoted yet again in v.17 to clinch the argument) speaks of a priesthood different in essence from that of the OT priests, since it is a priesthood "forever." And this is what characterizes this new priest: he comes in the power of an "indestructible life." Here again is the point alluded to in v.3 in relation to Melchizedek's "eternity"—the new priest is no less than the eternal Son of God, alive forever and therefore able to carry to its full extent the priestly ideal that the mortal priests of the OT could only imperfectly embody. (See further below on vv.23–24.)

The phrase "a regulation as to his ancestry" (NIV) is literally "the law of a fleshly commandment," and the word "fleshly" (*sarkinos*) is probably intended to convey not only the content of the regulation, governing physical descent, but also its inferior status as a merely "mortal" provision. The phrases "the law of a fleshly commandment" and "the power of an indestructible life" thus vividly contrast the different levels of legitimation that govern the two types of priesthood, with each member of the balancing phrases sharply offsetting its counterpart— "law" against "power," "commandment" against "life," and "fleshly" against "indestructible." If it is

the latter phrase that describes our high priest's legitimation, what can the mere "fleshly regulation" of the Levitical office matter?

18–19 A classical *men ... de* construction sets up the two sides of a sharp contrast: on the one hand, the discarding of the "former regulation" in all its inadequacy, but on the other hand, the introduction of a "better hope." The focus of the contrast is not so much on the nature of the two dispensations in themselves but on their different effects (not only "weak" but also "useless"). On the one hand, the old system could not "make perfect" (see further on 10:1–4), while on the other hand, the "better hope" enables us to "draw near to God." So it is made clear that the "perfection" the old system sought and failed to find was the relationship of "nearness" to God, and it will be this theme of approaching God that will in 10:19– 23 form the author's triumphant conclusion to his exposition of the salvation Christ has now provided. If the "former regulation" could not offer that, then it is time for it to go. Notice that in his parenthetical comment in v.19, the author gets as close as he will ever get to declaring that "the law" itself is no longer worth preserving (see comments at v.12 above), not just that a specific "regulation" has been set aside.

NOTES

11 The noun τάξις, *taxis*, "order" (GK *5423*) is used for many sorts of organization or ranking of things or of people, such as military "ranks." It is not a regular LXX term for the structure within which priests operated (though see LXX 1 Esd 1:5, 15; and cf. its use in Lk 1:8 for the tour of duty of a priestly division), but our author has understood it in Psalm 110:4 as a new priestly "dynasty," and so naturally he speaks of an "order of Aaron" to parallel that of Melchizedek. (See Josephus, *Ant.* 20:224ff., for the theory and history of the Aaronic succession of high priests.) The new "order" is described as "different": ἕτερος, *heteros* (GK *2283*), often implies "another of a different kind" as opposed to ἄλλος, *allos*, "another of the same kind" (GK *257*), and is also used for the "different tribe" in v.13.

14 "Descended from Judah" is literally "has arisen out of Judah"; the verb ἀνατέλλω, *anatellō*, "arise" (GK *422*), is normally used of the rising of the sun or of a star and may be intended here to echo Balaam's prophecy in Numbers 24:17, "a star will come [LXX ἀνατέλλω, *anatellō*] out of Jacob"; cf. also the messianic prophecy of a "branch" (ἀνατολή, *anatolē*) to "arise" (ἀνατέλλω, *anatellō*) in Zechariah 6:12 (cf. Jer 23:5).

That Jesus belonged to the tribe of Judah follows from his title "son of David," a title which Hebrews does not take up but which was an established tenet of early Christian belief (Ac 13:22–23; Ro 1:3; 2Ti 2:8; and cf. the genealogy of Mt 1:1–17 with its focus on David and the adoption of Jesus by Joseph "son of David" in Mt 1:20–25). Both Matthew and Luke record Jesus' birth in the Judean town of Bethlehem, and both gospel genealogies necessarily include Judah, the ancestor of David (Mt 1:2–3; Lk 3:33). There is no trace here of the later patristic argument that Jesus was of Levitical descent through his mother, whose relative Elizabeth was "a descendant of Aaron" (Lk 1:5).

18 The ἀθέτησις, *athetēsis*, "setting aside" (GK *120*; sometimes a technical legal term for annulment or cancellation) of the legal prescription, here sets up an interesting formal contradiction with 10:28, where the author assumes that someone who had "set aside" (ἀθετήσας, *athetēsas*) the law of Moses was rightly punished. In the latter case, however, he is talking about a rebellious Israelite under the old covenant who despised God's law, not about a Christian who has found the fulfillment of that law in Jesus.

G. Further Arguments for the Superiority of Jesus' Priesthood (7:20–25)

OVERVIEW

The preceding section has established that the old priesthood in the "order of Aaron" has failed to meet its purpose and must be replaced. The argument continues by showing more directly how it is in Jesus (mentioned by name in v.22 for the first time in this chapter, the name being emphasized by coming last in the Greek sentence) that the "better hope" signaled in v.19 is to be found. Two further arguments are deployed. The first (vv.20–22), again based directly on the wording of Psalm 110:4, concerns the divine oath that is the basis of Jesus' priestly office (a theme already adumbrated in 6:13–20; the verbal links between the two passages are helpfully set out by G. Hughes, 21). The second (vv.23–25) takes up again the theme of Jesus' "indestructible life" (v.16; cf. also v.3), and by an explicit contrast with the mortality of all other priests shows how this makes Jesus a complete savior and so also a pastorally effective high priest. The section thus ends in v.25 with a brief but important pointer to an aspect of Jesus' priestly work—his unending intercession for his people—which is not taken up explicitly elsewhere in the letter (but cf. the emphasis on his sympathy with and help for his people's condition in 2:17–18; 4:15–16), since our author's main interest is in the sacrificial aspect of his priesthood.

²⁰And it was not without an oath! Others became priests without any oath, ²¹but he became a priest with an oath when God said to him:

"The Lord has sworn
  and will not change his mind:
'You are a priest forever.'"

²²Because of this oath, Jesus has become the guarantee of a better covenant.

²³Now there have been many of those priests, since death prevented them from continuing in office; ²⁴but because Jesus lives forever, he has a permanent priesthood. ²⁵Therefore he is able to save completely those who come to God through him, because he always lives to intercede for them.

COMMENTARY

20–22 In 6:13–20, we have noted the importance of God's oath as a guarantee that what he has promised will not be changed. We now return to that other divine oath, which I suggested was already in mind at that point, and Psalm 110:4 is again quoted, with the focus this time on the first part of the verse, where God's oath is recorded as the basis of Christ's eternal priesthood in the order of Melchizedek and is emphatically declared to be unchangeable. There can therefore be no doubt about the validity of his priesthood or about his qualification for fulfilling that office; it is on the soundest possible foundation. All of this is in contrast with other priests who, as v.20b points out, are appointed with no such divine affirmation. That is why Jesus is "by so much" (see note) a more effective priest.

But the climax of this argument in v.22 is expressed not in terms of priesthood as such but of Jesus as the "guarantee [TNIV more correctly, "guarantor"] of a better covenant." *Engyos*, "guarantor" (GK *1583*), is a legal term used for those who stand as surety for a monetary or other agreement. While God surely needs no one to "guarantee" his covenantal promise, he has chosen to appoint on oath his Son Jesus to assure us of its security. "He is a guarantee to those who believe God's promise, and know that it has been accomplished in Christ, though they do not yet see its fulfillment" (O. Becker, *NIDNTT* 1.372). If there is also the thought that Jesus guarantees his people's adherence to the covenant, this is not brought out in the discussion.

The author has thus slipped in for the first time a word that will become central to his argument in chs. 8–10. It was God's "covenant" with Israel at Sinai that constituted them as his people (and obliged them to keep his law). But that covenant has since proved unable to maintain the special relationship, and God has promised to replace it with a new covenant. This theme will be expounded at length in 8:6–13 and will recur several times in the following chapters, where it will become clear that the new covenant has now been established through the sacrificial death of Christ. In that capacity he will be described as the "mediator" of the covenant (8:6; 9:15; 12:24), and this idea underlies this preliminary hint of a key theme still to be unfolded.

"Guarantor of the covenant" is not a natural way to describe the office of a priest: the Levitical priests might perhaps be said to have "mediated" God's covenant with his people by acting for the people toward God and by teaching God's law to the people, but it is hard to see how they could be described as "guarantors." So while the overall theme of the passage remains that of Christ's priesthood, at this point our author seems to have moved onto a higher level that transcends the functional comparison of Jesus with the office of the Levitical priests.

23–24 The appointment of a single "priest forever" signals a completely new concept, since the "many" previous priests have been mortal (cf. v.8), so that no single priest could continue in office, but each must pass on the office to a successor. (For the contrast of the "many" with the one, cf. 1:1–2: many prophets, one Son.) It is only with the appointment of a priest "on the basis of the power of an indestructible life" (v.16) that the declaration of Psalm 110:4 could be fulfilled. The eternal life of Jesus, noted already at v.3, is more explicitly stated here and in the next verse ("he always lives"). The author does not explain whether he is thinking specifically of Jesus' resurrection (which is directly stated in this letter only at 13:20 but may be implied by the use of "indestructible" in v.16) or more generally of the eternity inherent in the supernatural character of the Son (ch. 1); it is not likely he would have seen any need to distinguish the two. The result is that his priesthood, unlike all who have gone before him, is "permanent": the unusual term *aparabaton* (which etymologically could suggest "not moving beyond"; GK 563) is perhaps chosen to emphasize that the office will not pass to a successor, though in secular usage it normally means simply "unchangeable."

25 It is Jesus' eternity that makes him the perfect Savior. "Completely" translates the phrase *eis to panteles*, which can be taken either of degree ("wholly, totally") or of time ("forever"). In this discussion of mortality and immortality, the latter sense would clearly be appropriate, but since a "total" salvation must be one that is "for all time," the two senses are not in competition. The nature of that salvation is succinctly summed up in the phrase "come to God through him." The Christian privilege of entering the presence of God, for which Paul uses

the evocative term *prosagōgē*, "access" (Ro 5:2; Eph 2:18; 3:12), is expressed equally powerfully by our author with the simple term "to come to" God, which recurs in 4:16; 10:1, 22; 11:6 and will be vividly illustrated by the imagery of "coming to" the two mountains in 12:18, 22 (cf. "draw near to God," v.19). But just as the OT priests acted as intermediaries for the people, so we too need the services of a priest to introduce us to the divine presence; we come to God "through him."

As the argument develops, it will become clear that the primary sense in which we come to God "through Jesus" is that he has offered on our behalf the perfect sacrifice. But the priests in the OT had also another function, not so often mentioned—the role of intercession for the people before God (perhaps best exemplified by Moses, Ex 32:11–14, 30–32, but also symbolized in the high priest's "bearing the names of the sons of Israel over his heart . . . as a continuing memorial before the LORD," Ex 28:29), and that role too is fulfilled by our high priest. Whereas his sacrifice was offered once for all, his intercession continues, and that is why we need a high priest who "always lives." While he was on earth, Jesus prayed for his people (Lk 22:32; Jn 17), and Paul speaks in Romans 8 not only of the Spirit pleading on our behalf but also of Jesus interceding for us at God's right hand (Ro 8:26, 34; cf. also 1Jn 2:1). The theme may not be frequently mentioned, but it is a vital source of pastoral assurance and one without which the process of our salvation would be incomplete (cf. 9:24).

NOTES

20–22 These three verses form a complex Greek sentence in which καθ' ὅσον, *kath' hoson*, "inasmuch as" (v.20a) prepares for κατὰ τοσοῦτο, *kata tosouto*, "to that extent" (v.22), with vv.20b–21 sandwiched between the two parts of the main sentence as an explanatory aside. The NIV simplifies the structure by eliminating καθ' ὅσον, *kath' hoson*, and instead indicates the logical connection by the phrase "because of this oath" in v.22—a device which, though rightly conveying that Jesus' effectiveness as covenant guarantor depends on the oath described in vv.20–21, rather flattens the rhetoric which declares that the new covenant is "by so much the better" than a covenant established without such divine authority.

20 "Oath" here and in vv.21, 28 translates a more formally legal term, ὁρκωμοσία, *horkōmosia* (GK *3993*), which designates the ceremony of "oath taking" rather than the oath (ὅρκος, *horkos*) itself.

H. Summary: The One True High Priest (7:26–28)

OVERVIEW

While these verses add a number of new strands to the argument, they serve also to round off with a flourish the discussion of the priesthood of Jesus in the order of Melchizedek, as the unique quality of our high priest is celebrated. We are invited to consider first his character (v.26), second his efficacy (v.27), and third his eternity (v.28). He is God's final provision of all that the priesthood had been intended to accomplish but had hitherto been unable to deliver. As such, he, and he alone, is "perfect forever."

When the theme of Jesus' priesthood was first introduced in 2:17; 3:1; 4:14, 15; 5:5, 10; 6:20, he was described not as "priest" (the term was used only in 5:6 when quoting Ps 110:4) but specifically as "high priest," though in this chapter the term "priest" has been used consistently and frequently up to this point. This is because the argument has been developed from the figure of Melchizedek, who is described simply as "priest"

in Genesis 14:18, as is his successor in Psalm 110:4. The discussion has been of the office of priest in itself rather than of the specific role of the (Levitical) high priest. But it is in the light of this role that in the end our author wants Jesus to be understood, and now at the end of the chapter, as he paints a concluding portrait of the special character of Jesus' priesthood, the term "high priest" is reintroduced. From this point on it will again be the dominant term used for Jesus, except surprisingly in the climactic 10:21, though there the addition of the adjective "great" perhaps serves the same function. In the "order of Melchizedek" there is only one priest to be considered, so that the issue of hierarchy as such does not arise; but clearly no lesser term can be used for this one perfect priest who supersedes all others, and it will be the distinctive role of the high priest on the Day of Atonement that will be the special focus of the discussion of sacrifice that follows in chs. 9–10.

²⁶Such a high priest meets our need—one who is holy, blameless, pure, set apart from sinners, exalted above the heavens. ²⁷Unlike the other high priests, he does not need to offer sacrifices day after day, first for his own sins, and then for the sins of the people. He sacrificed for their sins once for all when he offered himself. ²⁸For the law appoints as high priests men who are weak; but the oath, which came after the law, appointed the Son, who has been made perfect forever.

COMMENTARY

26 "Meets our need" is literally "was appropriate/right for us" (using the same verb to describe the divine plan as was translated "it was fitting" in 2:10), and the author goes on to spell out the "job specification" that Jesus, and Jesus alone, so fully satisfies. "Holy," "blameless," and "pure" are related ideas, which together indicate Jesus' total goodness and godliness. The focus, as the following phrases will show, is on Jesus in his exalted state, though the words could equally well describe his moral character on earth. The OT law required a priest to be "unblemished" in the physical sense (Lev 21:16–23) and "pure" in the sense of avoiding ritual defilement (Lev 21:1–15); his moral purity seems to have been taken for granted, but the OT knows instances of priests who were moral failures (1Sa 2:12–17). Our author here is primarily concerned with moral purity. Both "holy" and "pure" might be understood in a ritual as well as a moral sense, though a ritual concept of holiness would normally be indicated by *hagios* (GK *41*) rather than by *hosios*, "godly, devout" (GK *4008*), which is used here. But "blameless" (lit., "without evil") clearly again asserts Jesus' sinlessness (see on 4:15), which will be shown in the next verse to be essential to his saving role. The passive participle "set apart from sinners" again asserts Jesus' sinlessness but especially draws attention to the fact that he is now exalted, as the next clause will make clear. The phrase emphasizes his unique character rather than suggesting aloofness and must be read in conjunction with the emphatic declaration earlier in the letter that Jesus is one of us and has shared our human weakness (2:10–18) and that he continues to be concerned for our salvation (2:17–18; 4:15–16; 5:9; 7:25). It is the combination of his humanness and his sinlessness that makes him uniquely qualified to be the Savior of humanity ("he must be humanly perfect as well as perfectly

human," Montefiore, 129). For "exalted above the heavens," see on 4:14; "above" is not used here literally to suggest that Jesus is now above God—this is evocative language to describe the one who, unlike earthly priests, is high above all earthly limitations and shares the throne of God himself.

27 Because our high priest is perfect, his ministry can be on a different level from that of the fallible human priests appointed by the Law. First, his sacrifice is not, as it were, dissipated by the need to atone for his own sins, as well as for those of the people he represents (see 5:2–3 for a similar observation), since he has no sins of his own to atone for; his offering can therefore be entirely for their benefit. Second, whereas repeated sin on the part of both priest and people made it necessary for the OT sacrifices to be constantly repeated so that the job was never finished, the sacrifice of Christ is "once for all." It is, moreover, a sacrifice not of an unwitting animal, however physically unblemished, but of "himself," the morally sinless Son of God. Here for the first time our author indicates explicitly that the sacrifice Jesus offered was his own life; the point will be developed in 9:12–15, 25–28; 10:5–10. This, therefore, is priestly ministry on a new level altogether, a ministry that needs, indeed allows, no repetition.

The term *ephapax*, "once for all" (GK *2384*), here occurs for the first time but will be a recurrent emphasis throughout the next few chapters as the efficacy of Christ's sacrificial work is set out. There is no significant difference in Hebrews' usage between the simple *hapax*, "once" (GK *562*; 9:26, 28) and *ephapax* (7:27; 9:12; 10:10), though the latter is more emphatic in form. Whereas the OT high priest made the Day of Atonement sacrifice "once" each year (9:7), our high priest has made atonement "once" for all time. The OT system failed to provide for its worshipers cleansing "once for all" (10:2), but

Jesus has now achieved this, and no further sacrifice can ever be needed again. In an interesting comparison in 9:27–28, our author will show how that single sacrifice correlates to the "once and once only" human experience of death and judgment. "Once for all" lies at the heart of our author's theology of atonement and of salvation.

28 TNIV has changed "men who are weak" to "men in all their weakness" in order to avoid the absurd suggestion that the Law deliberately picked out "men who are weak" *in preference to* any other sort of human being! The fact is that there is no other sort. (The Greek term is *anthrōpos*, "human being" [GK 476], not *anēr*, "male" [GK 467]; in fact, under the OT system only males were appointed, but that is not the issue here.) But in contrast to those weak and mortal high priests, we have one who is both "forever" and "made perfect" (see above on 2:10; 5:9 for

the meaning of the term in this sort of context), in virtue of his being not just a human being but "the Son [of God]."

The difference in quality between the Levitical priesthood and that of Jesus is further underlined by the contrast between "the law," which appointed the former, and "the word of the oath taking" (lit.; see note on v.20), by virtue of which Jesus serves as high priest. For a divine oath as the ultimate sanction, see 6:16–18; here we have a further argument for the superiority of the oath to the Law in that the oath (declared in Ps 110, assumed to be from David) came later than the Law and thus represents God's last word, which supersedes the old order set up under the Law. (This argument is interestingly opposite to that of Paul in Gal 3:17–18 that the Law cannot set aside God's promise, which *preceded* it!)

NOTES

26 The plural "the heavens" is normal Greek idiom for "heaven," and all references to "heaven" in Hebrews use the plural form except 9:24; 11:12; 12:26 (see note there). But for the possibility the author may have shared the Jewish concept of multiple heavens, see note on 4:14.

27 Leviticus 16:6–14 prescribes the high priest's preliminary sacrifice for himself and his family on the Day of Atonement, a sacrifice that took place only once a year. There is no specific OT law providing for such sacrifice on a daily basis, though Leviticus 4:3 provides for sacrifice for the priest's own sin on other occasions. This may be in our author's mind, or he may be inferring that the daily sacrifices (which are not described specifically as sin offerings [Ex 29:38–42; Nu 28:2–8]) necessarily included atonement for the priests' own sins. While the OT does not say that the high priest was personally required to offer sacrifice every day, this is assumed by Ben Sira 45:14 and Philo.

V. BETTER THAN THE OLD COVENANT AND ITS SACRIFICES (8:1–10:18)

OVERVIEW

There is a natural progression from the previous section of the letter into this one, in that having

established Christ's status as high priest the author now considers aspects of the priestly ministry that follow from this status, the new and heavenly sanctuary in which he ministers, the new covenant under which he operates, and especially the one perfect sacrifice that replaces the sacrificial ministry at the heart of OT priesthood.

But it is appropriate to designate 8:1–10:18 as a new section. The previous section has reached its climax in the summarizing peroration of 7:26–28 with its fine portrait of "such a high priest" (7:26), and so we are now ready to consider what follows if, as is in fact the case, we do have "such a high priest" (8:1). This consideration of the outworking of Christ's priesthood thus brings us into a new, though connected, subject area. And we now enter a new phase of the author's biblical exposition, in that whereas 4:14–7:28 was an extended exposition of Psalm 110:4, that text has now served its purpose and will not be further referred to; in its place Jeremiah's great prophecy of a new covenant will now be the expository focus of the argument. Jeremiah 31:31–34 is quoted at length in 8:8–12 and more briefly again at 10:16–17 to round off the exposition, while all that falls between these two quotations serves to explore the implications of a new covenant and its replacement of the old order.

A. A New Sanctuary (8:1–5)

OVERVIEW

As usual in Hebrews, neat paragraph divisions and headings do not do justice to the interwoven nature of the author's argument. Verse 6 of chapter 8 will not be a new beginning but will conclude the contrast between Jesus and the OT priests begun in v.3, and indeed v.6 is rightly punctuated in the UBS text as a continuation of the same sentence. But the introduction of the theme of the new covenant in v.6 also launches the theme that will occupy the rest of ch. 8. Meanwhile, the contrast between earthly and heavenly sanctuaries has not been forgotten and will be resumed when the earthly sanctuary described in 9:1–10 is contrasted with the "greater and more perfect tabernacle" of Jesus' ministry in 9:11 and again in 9:23–24.

The "true tabernacle" is three times (8:2; 9:11, 24) described as not made by human hands, a suggestive echo of Jesus' own alleged claim that he would destroy the temple "made with human hands" and replace it with another "not made with hands" (Mk 14:58 TNIV), itself picked up also in Stephen's declaration that "the Most High does not live in houses made by human hands" (Ac 7:48 TNIV). It is questionable whether our author wishes to go as far as Stephen, whose attack was apparently on the very concept of an earthly sanctuary at all. Here there is no suggestion that the tabernacle should not have been made; indeed it was made on God's direct instructions (v.5). But like all the institutions of the OT our author is passing in review, it was not God's final purpose. It served its temporary purpose but all the time was pointing forward to a "greater and more perfect tabernacle" (9:11), and this new sanctuary is distinguished by the fact that it is in heaven, not on earth. As such it represents the true God-given reality of which the earthly tabernacle, made by human hands, was merely a "copy and shadow" (v.5).

This language of heavenly reality and earthly copy has inevitably been compared with the widely influential philosophy of Plato, which understood all earthly things as "copies" of the true "forms" in heaven. Such influence is not in itself unlikely if the letter comes from an Alexandrian

Jewish background, since Philo gives clear evidence of Platonic influence there. But while the language may be similar, Hebrews is not simply repeating a Platonic worldview. When our author speaks elsewhere of shadows and reality (10:1; cf. in different language 9:8–9), he is thinking not primarily in "vertical" terms of earth copying heaven but "horizontally" of the progression in time from promise to fulfillment (see Introduction, p. 30). And when he speaks of the tabernacle and its ceremonies as "copies" in v.5 and 9:23, 24, the concept is explained not from Plato but from the language of Exodus 25:40, which he takes to mean that on Mount Sinai Moses was shown a divine "blueprint" for the making of the sanctuary. Later Jewish writings make it clear that many Jews envisioned heaven in terms of the tabernacle/temple structure, as does the book of Revelation. It is this background of thought rather than Platonic philosophy that best explains Hebrews' language.

As we have noted in the introduction (p. 28), the sanctuary our author speaks of is the tabernacle in the wilderness as described in Exodus, not its successor, the temple in Jerusalem. His interest is apparently in the pattern originally laid down in the Mosaic law rather than in its contemporary manifestation. But the tabernacle, no less than the temple of whose dissolution Jesus and Stephen spoke, was a man-made shrine, even though Moses erected it according to God's instructions. It therefore shares the imperfection and the obsolescence of all human institutions. (That the author here makes no mention of the Roman destruction of the temple in Jerusalem, which would surely have been relevant to his argument, suggests the letter was written before that event took place in AD 70; cf. also comments at 10:2.)

[1]The point of what we are saying is this: We do have such a high priest, who sat down at the right hand of the throne of the Majesty in heaven, [2]and who serves in the sanctuary, the true tabernacle set up by the Lord, not by man.

[3]Every high priest is appointed to offer both gifts and sacrifices, and so it was necessary for this one also to have something to offer. [4]If he were on earth, he would not be a priest, for there are already men who offer the gifts prescribed by the law. [5]They serve at a sanctuary that is a copy and shadow of what is in heaven. This is why Moses was warned when he was about to build the tabernacle: "See to it that you make everything according to the pattern shown you on the mountain."

COMMENTARY

1 TNIV appropriately captures the force of the opening words: "Now the main point of what we are saying is this." He is drawing out the implications of the argument so far, and the verbal echo "such a high priest" links this verse closely with the conclusion of the preceding chapter, as Ellingworth, 393, neatly explains: "The relation between the two passages is simply: (1) we need such a high priest (7:26–28); (2) we have such a high priest (8:1f.)." "Sat down at the right hand of the throne of the Majesty in heaven" clearly echoes 1:3, itself based on Psalm 110:1. It is on the basis of Psalm 110:4 that our author has just established Jesus' priesthood, and now he links this theme with the other main contribution of Psalm 110 to his argument, namely, the declaration that this same person is the "lord" enthroned at God's right hand. He is thus the heavenly priest-king to whom the priest-king Melchizedek pointed forward. That is what has been established by the argument so far.

2 "Serves in the sanctuary" is literally "a minister of the holy things [or places]." Since "the true tabernacle" is preceded by *kai*, "and" (not translated in the NIV on the assumption that it here means "that is" rather than conveying its normal sense), "the holy places" may refer to the Holy of Holies (see note on 9:2), while "the tabernacle" refers to the whole complex; but the distinction is not important here. A priest needs a sanctuary in which to carry out his ministry, and our high priest serves not in the earthly tabernacle, a tent pitched by Moses, "a mere human being" (TNIV), but in the true tent that God has "set up" (the verb used is the normal term for pitching a tent, possibly echoing LXX Nu 24:6), which v.5 and 9:24 will explicitly locate in heaven (cf. 4:14). We have already had a hint of the author's vision of Christ's heavenly ministry in terms of the earthly tabernacle and its curtain separating off the Holy of Holies (6:19–20), and in the next chapter this typology will be more fully worked out.

3 A sanctuary requires appropriate sacrifices, and so the groundwork is now laid for the full discussion of Christ's sacrificial work in chs. 9–10: he, too, must have had a sacrifice to offer (the aorist tense implies a single offering in contrast to the repeated offerings of the OT priests), and we will later be told it was a sacrifice that so transcended all earlier ones that it made them all obsolete. But for the moment all our author needs to establish is that Jesus is a true sacrificing priest; the nature of the sacrifice, already hinted at in 7:27, will be explained in 9:11–14 and in the following paragraphs. The sacrifice itself did of course take place

on earth but not in the official sanctuary (a point that will be emphasized in 13:12); the priestly ministry that results from it is in heaven.

4 Our high priest needs a different kind of sanctuary because as a non-Levite he was not qualified to serve in the earthly one, as has been explained in 7:13–14. That place has, as it were, already been filled, and there is no vacancy. The priestly ministry established there was "prescribed by law," and under that law Jesus had no access to priesthood. (Note the change here from "high priest" to "priest." He could not be even a priest, let alone high priest.) But of course we have already been told (7:28) that the Law has now been superseded by a new divine dispensation under which Jesus, and he alone, is established as a "priest forever."

5 In any case, there would be no point in Jesus' serving in that earthly sanctuary, since it was not the real thing but only a "copy and shadow" ("a shadowy suggestion," Lane) of the true sanctuary in heaven. "Shadow" vividly conveys the idea of something insubstantial and passing, showing the "shape" of the real thing but lacking its substance. Cf. 10:1 where the Law is contrasted with the time of salvation as shadow to reality. "Copy" is explained from Exodus 25:40, according to which Moses received at Sinai a "pattern" (*typos* [GK *5596*], the term from which "typology" is derived; but see on 9:24 for Hebrews' distinctive use of such terms) of the tabernacle God wanted him to construct on earth. But our author's word *hypodeigma* (GK *5682*; "preliminary sketch" rather than "copy"; see note) relates this earthly tabernacle not so much back to the original blueprint as forward to the true heavenly sanctuary it inadequately represents.

Exodus 25:40 in its OT context probably means God explained verbally to Moses what was to be the design of the tabernacle (the details of which take up most of Ex 25–30), but the LXX wording, which our author echoes here (and even more the Hebrew, which here and in Ex 25:9 speaks of Moses' "seeing" a *tabnit*, "plan" [GK 9322], or perhaps more likely "model"), allows him to think that on the mountain Moses actually saw the "real thing" as a blueprint; and since on the mountain he was meeting with God, that which he saw belonged to heaven rather than to earth. So there is a "real" tabernacle in heaven to which the earthly one was intended to correspond and to which it points forward.

NOTES

2 "True" represents ἀληθινός, *alēthinos* (GK *240*), which here and in 9:24 distinguishes the "real" from the "shadow." (Cf. its use in John for the spiritual reality to which an earthly metaphor points: Jn 1:9; 6:32; 15:1.)

5 "Copy" translates ὑπόδειγμα, *hypodeigma* (GK *5682*), which normally (like the more common παράδειγμα, *paradeigma*, "paradigm") means a pattern or example to be followed or avoided (as in 4:11), with much the same meaning as τύπος, *typos* (GK *5596*), which is correctly translated "pattern" in the LXX quotation from Exodus that follows; in LXX Ezekiel 42:15, ὑπόδειγμα, *hypodeigma*, is used for the "plan" of the new temple revealed to Ezekiel. Here and in 9:23, however, Hebrews is often understood to use it from the opposite perspective, i.e., not of the original pattern but of the resultant copy, a sense not attested elsewhere; so most modern translations, but see Hurst, 13–17, for the proposal that it should be understood here as a "preliminary sketch" to be filled in later (see further on 9:23–24).

Philo (*Moses* 2.74–75) also draws on this text in Exodus to show that Moses "saw with the soul's eye the immaterial forms of the material objects about to be made," which "had to be reproduced in copies perceived by the senses, taken . . . from patterns conceived in the mind." This sounds more immaterial and more Platonic than Hebrews' more "concrete" interpretation of the heavenly "model."

B. A New Covenant (8:6–13)

OVERVIEW

As we noted in the Overview at vv. 1–5, there is no break here, and indeed v.6 completes the contrast between Jesus and former high priests that began at v.3. But the contrast is concluded with a new feature of Jesus' special high priesthood, previously hinted at in 7:22, which once introduced in v.6 becomes the focus for the argument until v.13. The focus of these verses therefore is the theme of covenant.

Ancient rulers made covenants with their subject peoples, i.e., legally binding agreements regulating the relationships between them. The idea of covenant provided a fruitful metaphor for the OT

writers to explain the commitment of God to his people and their obligations to him. We hear of God's covenant with Noah (and thus with all surviving humanity) in Genesis 9:1–17 and with Abraham (and thus with the Hebrew people) in Genesis 15 and 17. But the word is especially associated with Mount Sinai, where God took a refugee rabble to be his own people and gave them his laws as a basis for their special relationship, which was summed up in the covenant formula "I will be your God and you shall be my people" (e.g., Lev 26:12; Jer 7:23; cf. v.10c for the same formula expressing the essence of the new covenant). This covenant was established with a solemn ceremony in Exodus 24:4–8 (which will be referred to in 9:18–20), and similar ceremonies marked the reaffirmation of the covenant at key moments in Israel's history (Jos 24:1–27; 2Ki 23:1–3). It was the covenant that made Israel the people of God.

So when Jeremiah proclaimed that the existing covenant had failed in its purpose and announced a new covenant between God and his people (Jer 31:31–34), this was a far-reaching, and for his hearers no doubt a profoundly shocking, message of a radical new beginning. At the Last Supper, Jesus had alluded to Jeremiah's bold language (Mk 14:24; Lk 22:20; 1Co 11:25). It is that same prophecy that dominates the present section and forms the basis for the whole discussion of Christ's priestly ministry, which will run through to 10:16–17 where it will be quoted again.

Like the other aspects of the OT so far discussed, the covenant was a good thing, instituted by God. The argument here is not that it was not good but that it must now give way to something better. Like the old priesthood and the old sanctuary it has served its purpose, but it could never deliver "perfection" because of the fallibility of the people who were a party to it. So this section begins by celebrating the "better" relationship with God that is now ours in Christ and ends with the declaration of 8:13, which does not so much repudiate the old covenant as consign it to an honorable retirement.

---

⁶But the ministry Jesus has received is as superior to theirs as the covenant of which he is mediator is superior to the old one, and it is founded on better promises.

⁷For if there had been nothing wrong with that first covenant, no place would have been sought for another. ⁸But God found fault with the people and said:

"The time is coming, declares the Lord,
    when I will make a new covenant
with the house of Israel
    and with the house of Judah.
⁹It will not be like the covenant
    I made with their forefathers
when I took them by the hand
    to lead them out of Egypt,
because they did not remain faithful to my covenant,
    and I turned away from them,
                    declares the Lord.
¹⁰This is the covenant I will make with the house of Israel
    after that time, declares the Lord.
I will put my laws in their minds
    and write them on their hearts.
I will be their God,
    and they will be my people.

> [11] No longer will a man teach his neighbor,
>   or a man his brother, saying, 'Know the Lord,'
>   because they will all know me,
>   from the least of them to the greatest.
> [12] For I will forgive their wickedness
>   and will remember their sins no more."
>
> [13] By calling this covenant "new," he has made the first one obsolete; and what is obsolete and aging will soon disappear.

COMMENTARY

6 The language of superiority stacks up in this verse, with two uses of *kreittōn*, "better" (GK *3202*), and one of *diaphorōteras*, "superior" (GK *1427*), as in 1:4. The comparison is phrased like that of 1:4: "by so much superior ... as ..."; the measure of how much superior Jesus' ministry is to that of the OT priests is the "betterness" both of the covenant he represents and of the promises that are its legal basis. "Founded" (TNIV, "established") is literally "legislated," the word used for the "law given to the people" in 7:11. To find such legal terminology used in relation to God's promise may surprise us in light of Paul's contrasting of law and promise (Ro 4:13–16; Gal 3:16–18), but our author is speaking of the covenant, itself a "legal" agreement, which derived from God's sovereign initiative of blessing on his people (his "promises"), to which their legal obligations were the appropriate response. The nature of the "better promises" in Christ will be spelled out partly in the language of Jeremiah's prophecy about to be quoted—especially the themes of the knowledge of God and the forgiveness of sin (vv.11–12)—but more fully in the whole argument of the letter as to the "great salvation" Jesus has won for us, with its prospect of heavenly rest (4:1–11). The theme of promise will be explored more fully in ch. 11.

In 7:22 we heard of Jesus as the "guarantor" of the new covenant. "Mediator" here and in 9:15; 12:24 is a related idea of a third party between God and his people. The OT priests had an intermediary role under the old covenant, teaching God's law to the people and representing the people before God especially in sacrifice. But in Jesus we have a far more effective mediator in that he actually belongs to both sides of the covenant. As the Son of God he represents God to us, and as our "brother" (2:11–13) he represents us to God. And while Moses was God's spokesman in establishing the old covenant (Paul calls him "mediator" in Gal 3:19), Jesus has a more central role in establishing the new, in that it is he who through his priestly sacrifice has made it possible for us to "draw near to God" (7:19).

7–8a Just as the announcement of a new priesthood in Psalm 110 revealed the inadequacy of the old priesthood (7:11–19), so the proclamation of a new covenant through Jeremiah's prophecy shows that God was not satisfied with the old covenant. But it is noteworthy that our author does not say God found fault with the covenant itself but rather with the people. The reason it failed to achieve its purpose was not any fault inherent in the covenant's provisions but the inability or unwillingness of the people to "remain faithful to my covenant" (v.9). The essence of Jeremiah's prophecy is, therefore, that God will provide a new basis for the people's response, not now by an externally written law they could not or would not keep, but by a law "written on their hearts," so that they know God for themselves.

8b–12 Jeremiah 31:31–34 is quoted in full in the LXX version with only very minor variations. It is remarkable that this, the longest OT quotation in the NT, is left by our author to convey its own impact. He makes no attempt to explain it clause by clause and does not single out specific expressions for emphasis, as he has done in his expositions of Psalms 95 and 110. He draws only the broadest general conclusion in v.13, and it is clearly this general point rather than the details of Jeremiah's vision that he needs to establish his argument at this point.

The discussion of Jesus' priestly ministry, which separates this quotation from his abbreviated resumption of the text in 10:16–17, will, however, be based on the concept of the new covenant (9:15–22) and on the effective forgiveness and removal of sins as its basis (9:14, 15, 22, 26; 10:3, 12). Thus the full quotation of the Jeremiah pericope here provides the basis for the following exposition (as we shall note from time to time in the commentary), even though its words will not be explicitly appealed to again before 10:16–17, unless there is an oblique reference to it when he speaks of being "set free from the sins committed under the first covenant" (9:15). Full consideration of the wording of Jeremiah's stirring prophecy may therefore best be left to commentaries on Jeremiah. Here our author is content to let it speak for itself, and we may appropriately do likewise.

13 The one word in the OT text the author does single out for comment is the word "new," which, as he has already pointed out in vv.7–8a, implies the replacement of what went before. It

needs to be replaced because it is old and worn-out. The "he" is God, who has been understood in v.8 to be the person who uttered the prophecy; by using such language, God has "made old" (or "treated as old"; for the NIV's "made obsolete," see the following comments) the previous covenant. Three vivid terms make the point: the former covenant is "old" (twice), "aging," and (literally) "close to disappearance." TNIV's "obsolete and outdated" is misleading, however, in that the Greek terms are present participles that more literally mean "getting old and aging." (The former verb is used for things [as in 1:11; Lk 12:33], the latter normally for people [as in Jn 21:18].) Neither term, therefore, says the former covenant has actually ceased to be in force (as "obsolete" implies), and similarly "close to disappearance" carefully avoids this implication. The image is rather that it is still just barely hanging on but cannot last much longer. The author is well aware that people continue to try to serve God under the old covenant, but he is serving warning that its time is up (Gordon, 94, graphically speaks of its "superannuation"). When the new has already come, there can be no justification for keeping the old.

This stance has a clear relevance to the position of Judaism in the last few years before the practice of the old system of sacrifice and priesthood was brought to an end with the Roman destruction of the temple, which was its physical focus. If, as I have suggested, the letter was written during that period, the author may have been reflecting on Jesus' prediction of the fall of the temple (Mk 13:2 par.). But his perspective is wider than merely the end of the Jerusalem sanctuary. His point is theological rather than political: Jesus' once-for-all sacrifice and superior priesthood had already rendered the old system superfluous, even while it still remained physically possible. The new covenant had already been established.

NOTES

6 The significance of the term διαθήκη, *diathēkē*, "covenant" (GK *1347*), in Hebrews and the variety of language this author uses in relation to it are helpfully discussed and tabulated by Ellingworth, 386–88.

8 Lane proposes the translation "God finds fault when he says to them" on the basis of an alternative reading αὐτοῖς, *autois*, for αὐτούς, *autous*, which allows (though it does not require) the interpretation that the covenant itself is the object of "finds fault." This reading is less well supported, and since the object of μέμφομαι, *memphomai*, "find fault," can be expressed in either the accusative or dative, it does not necessarily differ in meaning; the word order does not support Lane's proposal.

9 The LXX, followed by our author, differs from the Hebrew in the final clause of this verse. A difference of one Hebrew letter *bāʿaltî/gāʿaltî* would change "though I was a husband [or master] to them" to "and I rejected [or loathed] them"; the latter seems to underlie both the LXX and Syriac and may well be the original reading (see NIV footnote at Jer 31:32), expressing the disastrous outcome of Israel's disobedience.

C. The Worship of the Old Sanctuary (9:1–10)

OVERVIEW

The tabernacle set up by Moses on God's instructions was intended as a "copy and shadow" of the true heavenly sanctuary (8:5). It follows, therefore, that a study of the "copy" can be expected to yield by analogy a better understanding of the heavenly ministry of our great high priest. Our author therefore now launches into an account first of the structure and furnishings of the tabernacle and then of the worship that took place in it, with special reference to the ritual of the Day of Atonement. All of this, to the end of v.7, is purely descriptive of the OT situation, as we know it from the Mosaic laws. Only in vv.8–10 does the author explain why he is spending time on this historical study: the provisions for worship under the old covenant were the Holy Spirit's way of preparing us for something better to come and as such were not in themselves adequate to meet the needs of the worshipers. They did not provide access to the presence of God (v.8) and dealt only with external purification, not with the sinner's conscience (vv.9–10). The ground is thus prepared for the explanation of the "new order" (v.10) brought about by the superior sacrifice of Christ, which will be the theme of the letter from 9:11 to 10:18.

¹Now the first covenant had regulations for worship and also an earthly sanctuary. ²A tabernacle was set up. In its first room were the lampstand, the table and the consecrated bread; this was called the Holy Place. ³Behind the second curtain was a room called the Most Holy Place, ⁴which had the golden altar of incense and the gold-covered ark of the covenant. This ark contained the gold jar of manna, Aaron's staff that had budded, and the

stone tablets of the covenant. [5]Above the ark were the cherubim of the Glory, overshadowing the atonement cover. But we cannot discuss these things in detail now.

[6]When everything had been arranged like this, the priests entered regularly into the outer room to carry on their ministry. [7]But only the high priest entered the inner room, and that only once a year, and never without blood, which he offered for himself and for the sins the people had committed in ignorance. [8]The Holy Spirit was showing by this that the way into the Most Holy Place had not yet been disclosed as long as the first tabernacle was still standing. [9]This is an illustration for the present time, indicating that the gifts and sacrifices being offered were not able to clear the conscience of the worshiper. [10]They are only a matter of food and drink and various ceremonial washings—external regulations applying until the time of the new order.

COMMENTARY

1 This introductory verse summarizes what follows—the "regulations for worship" in vv.6–7 and the "earthly sanctuary" (as contrasted with the heavenly sanctuary, cf. 8:2, 5) in vv.2–5. The word for "sanctuary" here is the singular "holy (place)," referring to the tabernacle in general; the plural will be used in a more specific sense in the next verse.

2–3 The NIV captures the sense of the opening statement, which is, however, more literally "The first tent was set up, in which were . . ." Unusually, "tent" is used here and in v.6 not for the whole mobile sanctuary but for its main chamber, so that the "second curtain" (v.3) is understood to separate off a second, inner "tent" (the NIV's "room" in vv.3 and 6 translates the same word as "tent" or "tabernacle"), even though it was in fact a second chamber, part of the same structure. The construction of the "first tent" (the outer sanctuary) is described in detail in Exodus 26:1–30, and the seven-branched lampstand and the table for the consecrated bread in 25:23–40. The bread itself (mentioned in the Exodus account but not actually described until Lev 24:5–9) is listed here as a separate item (lit., "and the setting out of the loaves"), but since the table was provided specifically for the display of the bread, TNIV has appropriately linked them together ("the table with its consecrated bread"). For the title "the Holy Place," see note.

For the "second curtain," see the note on 6:19. There the context suggested that the curtain intended was the one separating off the inner sanctuary; here the addition of "second" and the mention of the "Most Holy Place" make that explicit. This curtain and its function are described in Exodus 26:31–35. For the "Most Holy Place," see also the note below. It will be this inner part of the tabernacle, and the high priest's annual entry into it, that will be the focus of the author's interest.

4–5 Both the author's phrasing ("which had") and the natural progression of the description would suggest the "golden altar of incense" (for which see Ex 30:1–10) was inside the inner sanctuary, as were the other items mentioned in vv.4–5. But the Exodus account indicates the incense altar was, in fact, in the "Holy Place" outside the "second curtain" and associated with the lamps already mentioned in v.2. While it featured in the annual atonement ceremony when the high priest went behind the curtain (Ex 30:10), it was also to be used twice every day (30:7–8), and no one was allowed behind the curtain on any other day of the year. The incense altar stood directly in front of the curtain, so that the high priest had to pass it (and sprinkle it, like the mercy seat, with blood) as he went inside, and in that sense it can be described (functionally if not physically) as "belonging to the inner sanctuary" of Solomon's temple (1Ki 6:22, but omitted by the LXX). This may have influenced our author's description, though his words seem to place the altar in the same room as the ark (Attridge, 234–38, adduces evidence that other Jews also shared this idea).

For the ark and its "atonement cover" surmounted by cherubim (symbolic winged creatures, probably sphinxlike), see Exodus 25:10–22, and for the contents of the ark, see Exodus 16:31–34; 25:16; Numbers 17:8–11; Deuteronomy 10:3–5. The jar of manna and Aaron's staff were apparently placed in front of the ark rather than in it (see 1Ki 8:9). Our author describes these items, which were the only contents of the inner sanctuary, with some emphasis on their splendor: "cherubim of glory" suggests something magnificent (though the NIV may well be right in rendering it "cherubim of the Glory," i.e., of the *shekinah* of God's presence, which they symbolized; cf. the GNB's "the winged creatures representing God's presence"), and gold is mentioned three times. The phrase translated "gold-covered" in the NIV is literally "covered all over with gold" (cf. Ex 25:11, "both inside and out"). The author does not feel this is the place to go into detailed explanation, but there is a note of wistfulness about the concluding clause, which suggests he would very much have liked to do so!

He uses two words that deserve some comment. The word "covenant" twice in these verses ("ark of the covenant" and "tablets of the covenant") reproduces traditional OT terminology, but in this context, the reappearance of the word must remind us of the preceding section of the letter. Perhaps we are invited to reflect that if the old covenant deserved all this splendor, the new must be even more wonderful. And the "atonement cover" (Gk. *hilastērion*,

traditionally rendered "mercy seat") reminds us of our great high priest's work of "making atonement for [*hilaskomai*; see note on 2:17] the sins of the people" (2:17) and of our privilege of "approaching the throne of grace" (see note on 4:16) in a way the people of the old covenant were not allowed to. Perhaps these were some of the issues our author would have liked to explore "in detail" if he could. He might also have been tempted to contrast the temporary satisfaction of the manna with the new spiritual food his readers have "tasted" (6:4–5); Aaron's authenticating staff with the divine appointment of our high priest (5:4–6; 7:20–22); and the stone tablets of the old covenant with the law "written on hearts" (8:10) in the new. But we shall never know!

6 Having described the "earthly sanctuary," the author now goes on to its "regulations for worship" (v.1). A general statement of the regular sacrificial duties in the outer sanctuary (v.6) is followed by a more specific mention of the annual ceremony in the inner sanctuary (v.7). The "regular" ministry performed by the priests (not just the high priest) inside the Holy Place included the twice daily offerings on the incense altar, the tending of the continuously burning lamps, and the weekly changing of the consecrated bread; it did not include animal sacrifices, which took place at the altar of burnt offering outside the sanctuary.

7 Whereas there was regular activity in the Holy Place, it was only once a year on the Day of Atonement, and only under the "protection" (see Lev 16:13) of incense and atoning blood, that the high priest alone was allowed to go through the curtain into the Holy of Holies, or "Most Holy Place." The ritual is spelled out in detail in Leviticus 16. It was "not without blood," as it included the sacrifice on the main altar of a bull as a sin offering "for himself and his house" and a goat as a sin offering "for the people" (see above on 5:3; 7:27 for this dual focus of sacrifice); the high priest then took the blood of each animal inside the sanctuary and sprinkled it on both the mercy seat and the ground in front of it. (The importance of blood will be further spelled out in vv.12–14, 18–22.) Leviticus 16:16, 30 says that this atoning provision was for "all their sins," but our author assumes this can cover only sins committed "in ignorance," since "high-handed" deliberate sin could not be atoned for by a sin offering (see note on 5:2).

8 So far in this chapter we have simply been reminded of what was described in the OT law, but now it is time to consider what it all means. Far from regarding the OT accounts as valueless, our author recognizes them as deriving from the Holy Spirit and therefore as a means of divine revelation. But what the Holy Spirit reveals through these details is not something for the time they were originally instituted (except in the negative sense that they show that the way was not yet open), but rather a message for the future, when the "way into the Most Holy Place" would at last be "disclosed." The Day of Atonement ceremony spoke of exclusion, of access to the presence of God only on the most stringent conditions and for one person alone. But the day was to come when the way would be open for all God's people to enter in with confidence (4:16; 7:19; 10:19–22).

The way was to be "disclosed" by the recognition that our great high priest has now entered the heavenly sanctuary on our behalf (6:19–20), and the fact that he is our "forerunner" (6:20) shows we too may follow him there. But perhaps the author also has in mind the tradition recorded in Mark 15:38 that at the time of Jesus' death on the cross, the temple curtain (presumably the "second curtain" of v.3) was torn, visibly opening the way into the sanctuary (see further on 10:20). But the way could not be open as long as the "first tabernacle" was still "functioning" (TNIV, for the NIV's "standing"). The tabernacle proper of course ceased to function when Solomon built the temple, but as usual our author treats the Jerusalem temple as though it were still the wilderness tabernacle. Historically speaking, there was a

period (probably that during which this letter was written) when the temple continued to function, even after its curtain had been torn, and Jesus' sacrifice had made its rituals superfluous, but like the old covenant (8:13), the temple was, in our author's view, already "close to disappearance"; even if still standing, to him it was not still "functioning" in any meaningful way.

9 The feminine gender of "this" indicates it refers to the "first tabernacle," which serves as "an illustration for the present time," as type points forward to antitype (cf. 10:1). Its pattern of access to God is a model to help us understand the new way Jesus has now opened for us. The Greek word *parabolē* (GK *4130*), here translated "illustration," covers a variety of kinds of figurative or nonliteral language, not just what we now call "parables," and is well suited to convey the sense of a typological foreshadowing. Yet typology does not postulate an exact correspondence between type and antitype but rather a progression onto a higher level, so that it operates as much by contrast as by comparison. So here we are reminded that the "illustration" serves negatively to show what could *not* be achieved under that system and thereby points forward to a new and different way by which it would at last be achieved. What the old system could not do was to "clear the conscience of the worshiper." The verb is our old friend *teleioō* (GK *5457*), previously translated "make perfect" (2:10; 5:9; 7:19, 28), and our author is reminding us again of the point he made in 7:11, 19 about the inability of the priesthood and the Law to "make perfect" the people's relationship with God. By speaking of "conscience," he focuses on the worshiper's own inner condition, and especially the awareness of sin that separates us from God (cf. 9:14; 10:2, 22, where the same idea is developed).

10 The scope of the argument extends beyond the Day of Atonement, and indeed beyond the sacrificial system altogether, to take in the laws of purity, though a link may be found in that some uncleanness was expiated by sacrifice (see 9:13). The reason the old system could not really work was that it remained at that "external" ceremonial level, not changing the person within (cf. 8:9–10 for the need for a new covenant that applied directly to the "minds" and "hearts"). These "external regulations" (lit., "regulations of the flesh"; the author probably refers to the food laws of Lev 11 and the numerous ceremonial washing rituals already mentioned in 6:2) belong to the old order, and point forward to a better "new order" to come (and which has now come through the work of Christ). "New order" translates

diorthōsis (GK 1481), a word not used elsewhere in the NT but which essentially means a "putting right" and so a "reformation" (Bruce); it encapsulates the essence of Jeremiah's prophecy (8:8–12).

Three significant expressions in vv.8–10 thus reveal much about our author's view of how the new covenant relates to the old. Negatively the old system shows the way "not yet disclosed" (v.8); positively it is an "illustration for the present time" (v.9), and the present time is one of "setting right" (v.10 NRSV) what was inadequate in the old order, thus at last opening the way to "perfection."

NOTES

2–3 The titles "the Holy Place" (τὸ ἅγιον, *to hagion*, GK *41*) and "the Most Holy Place" (τὸ ἅγιον τῶν ἁγίων, *to hagion tōn hagiōn*; English versions often reproduce the Hebrew idiom literally as "the Holy of Holies"), drawn from LXX Exodus 26:33–34, were used as technical terms for the two sections of the tent shrine. Hebrews uses the two terms in their technical LXX senses here in vv.2–3 (though in the plural, τὰ ἅγια, *ta hagia*; ἅγια ἁγίων, *hagia hagiōn*) but elsewhere uses the plural τὰ ἅγια, *ta hagia*, more broadly for the sanctuary as a whole (8:2; 9:24; 10:19), sometimes clearly using it for what he here calls "the Most Holy Place," the inner sanctuary (9:12, 25; 13:11, in all of which the NIV has translated it as "the Most Holy Place"; LXX Lev 16 similarly refers to the inner sanctuary simply as τό ἅγιον, *to hagion*); our author does not use ἅγια ἁγίων, *hagia hagiōn*, elsewhere.

4 "Altar of incense" translates θυμιατήριον, *thymiatērion* (GK *2593*), which in LXX usually means a "censer," while this altar is described as θυσιαστήριον θυμιάματος, *thysiastērion thymiamatos* (the term used in Lk 1:11). But Hebrews' use of the shorter form to mean the altar, not a portable censer, conforms to the later usage of Philo and Josephus.

7 The second goat, which was not killed (the "scapegoat"), is not mentioned by our author since his interest is focused on sacrifice and on what happened inside the sanctuary.

8 "The first tabernacle" translates ἡ πρώτη σκηνή, *hē prōtē skēne*, the same phrase that in vv.2 and 6 was translated "the first [or outer] room." Some interpreters (e.g., Lane, 223–24) take it in that special sense here: as long as the first chamber of the tabernacle kept the worshiper away from the inner sanctuary, the way was not open. But this separate significance attributed to the outer sanctuary, as though it had cultic status independently of that of the whole tabernacle, fits awkwardly into the author's argument, especially as it leads Lane to conclude that the outer sanctuary was symbolic of the old covenant regime (see note on v.9 for "the present time"), while the inner symbolized the new. It seems more straightforward to take σκηνή, *skēne*, here again in its more normal sense to denote the whole sanctuary (cf. 8:2, 5; 9:11, 21; 13:10); "first" then indicates the former earthly sanctuary as opposed to its heavenly replacement, just as the "first" covenant (8:7, 13; 9:1, 15, 18) designates the one now being replaced. See further Hurst, 26–27.

9 "The present time" is a stronger expression than the English suggests. "Time" is καιρός, *kairos* (GK *2789*), which is used especially of a specific and significant time or event (as in v.10 for the "time of the new order"), not of the passage of time in general; "present" is ἐνεστηκώς, *enestēkos*, "having now arrived" (as opposed to μέλλων, *mellōn*, "to come," cf. 10:1). The phrase thus emphasizes that the future hope of the OT has now decisively arrived. It is thus quite unsuited to the interpretation of Lane (see note on v.8; cf. the KJV's "the time then present"), who takes it to mean the period *before* the "time (καιρός, *kairos*) of the new order" in v.10; for our author that period is now past, not ἐνεστηκώς, *enestēkos*, and the "new order" has already come with Christ.

10 "A matter of food and drink" might be understood to refer not to the sources of impurity (drink as such is not mentioned in this context except tangentially in Lev 11:34), but to offerings consisting of food and drink (Ex 29:39–41; etc.), but this would combine less naturally with "ceremonial washings."

D. The One Effective Sacrifice (9:11–14)

OVERVIEW

The argument from 8:1 has so far been primarily negative in tone, focusing on the inadequacy and failure of the old covenant and of the old sanctuary and its worship. But the promise of a new covenant and the author's conviction that the earthly sanctuary is merely a "copy and shadow" of the true heavenly one have prepared us for a positive counterpart, and vv.8–10 have reinforced that expectation of a "time of putting right." Now in this short paragraph we come to the heart of this section of the letter, with the declaration of the one perfect sacrifice that has taken the place of the whole ritual pattern of the old covenant.

In 8:1–9:10 our great high priest has not been named (the last occurrence was the name "Jesus" in 7:22; it is not in the Greek at 8:6), but now the title "Christ" is emphatically reintroduced as the first Greek word of v.11. The explanation of his perfect sacrifice is still in contrast with what has gone before, but the emphasis now is on its positive efficacy, and the phrase "once for all" in v.12 signals what will be the main focus of the remainder of this section. Verses 11–12 draw a direct contrast between the role of the Levitical high priest on the Day of Atonement and the atoning work of Christ, while vv.13–14 make a more general statement on the efficacy of the blood of Christ compared with that of the OT sacrifices.

[11]When Christ came as high priest of the good things that are already here, he went through the greater and more perfect tabernacle that is not man-made, that is to say, not a part of this creation. [12]He did not enter by means of the blood of goats and calves; but he entered the Most Holy Place once for all by his own blood, having obtained eternal redemption. [13]The blood of goats and bulls and the ashes of a heifer sprinkled on those who are ceremonially unclean sanctify them so that they are outwardly clean. [14]How much more, then, will the blood of Christ, who through the eternal Spirit offered himself unblemished to God, cleanse our consciences from acts that lead to death, so that we may serve the living God!

COMMENTARY

11 "Christ" in this emphatic position is not simply a personal designation but highlights his messianic office. His high priesthood belongs not to the old Levitical order but to "the good things that are now already here" (TNIV). What from the OT point of view were "the good things to come" (10:1) from the Christian perspective have already arrived, in that Christ's saving work has been accomplished and the way into the sanctuary now stands open. The main clause of the single Greek sentence that makes up vv.11–12 is "he entered the Most Holy Place" (see note on vv.2–3). It is qualified by two long prepositional phrases both introduced by *dia*, but in different senses. The word is translated "through" in v.11 and "by means of" and "by" in v.12. The first *dia* clause describes the route he took into the inner sanctuary, making his way "through" the tabernacle to its inner chamber, as the high priest did on the Day of Atonement (cf. "gone through the heavens," 4:14). "Greater and more perfect" and "not made with human hands" (TNIV) take up a theme already familiar to us from 8:2–6, namely, the contrast between earthly and heavenly sanctuaries, and the additional explanation "that is to say, not a part of this creation" underlines its heavenly character. This is the only time Hebrews uses the *teleio* word group ("perfect") of a thing rather than of people; it emphasizes that in this (metaphorical) sanctuary, God's saving purpose foreshadowed in the earthly cultic ritual now finds its intended completion.

12 The second *dia* clause is a double one, stating both negatively ("not by means of") and positively ("but by") the nature of the sacrifice that enabled Christ to enter the inner sanctuary. The ritual of Leviticus 16 required the OT high priest to take with him into the inner sanctuary the blood of a bull and of a goat he had slaughtered, but the blood that

authorized Jesus' entry was his own, shed in his death on the cross. (Note that the author does not speak of Christ as presenting his blood as an offering.) The brief mention in 7:27 that he "offered himself" (cf. also 9:14) is now filled out by the specific mention of Christ's blood, by which he "obtained eternal redemption," and "blood" will remain a key term throughout this chapter. *Lytrōsis*, "redemption" (GK *3391*), and its variant *apolytrōsis* (GK *667*; translated "a ransom to set them free" in v.15) feature significantly in NT explanations of Christ's death, drawing on his own statement that he was to give his life as a "ransom" (*lytron*, GK *3389*) for many (Mk 10:45). The root idea is that of liberation at a price, and the price is the blood (death) of Jesus. When the OT speaks of God as "redeeming" his people, the focus of the metaphor is on the freedom won rather than the means by which it is achieved, but the NT linkage of this language with the sacrifice of a life gives it greater depth. Why Christ's redemption is "eternal" in contrast with that provided annually under the old covenant will be explained in the following verses. What he has done can never be repeated, and there is no more to be done. For "once for all," see on 7:27.

13 This whole verse is an "if" clause in Greek, leading up to the "How much more" of v.14. The author is assuming for the sake of argument that there was some value in the OT sacrifices, but he points out that this value was at the relatively insignificant level of outward ceremonial purification, which left a person's spiritual relationship with God untouched (cf. 7:18–19; 9:9–10). In contrast, the sacrifice of Christ goes to the heart of the matter. Along with the Day of Atonement sacrifices (bull and goat) alluded to in v.12, he now introduces another quite separate OT sin offering, the ritual of the "red heifer" (for which see Nu 19), which was for regular, not just annual, use; the heifer's ashes mixed with water provided a "water of cleansing" that was sprinkled on those who had contracted ceremonial defilement in order to restore them to ritual purity. For our author, this provision illustrates the essentially "external" nature of the OT system, resulting only in (literally) "cleanness of the flesh."

14 With Christ all is different. This is no unwilling animal but rather the voluntary self-offering of the Son of God; his offering is not according to human routine but "through the eternal Spirit"; whereas OT sacrifices had to be physically "unblemished" (e.g., the red heifer, Nu 19:2), Christ was spiritually perfect, without sin (4:15; 7:26); and whereas OT sacrifices cleansed the flesh, this one cleanses the conscience and sets us free from a round of "dead works" to serve the living God.

The mention of the Holy Spirit in connection with Christ's self-offering serves to locate it in the spiritual realm as opposed to that of earthly ritual, and in the process affords one of those intriguing NT pointers toward the doctrine of the Trinity, in that all three Persons are involved in the work of atonement. "Conscience" recalls the comment in v.9 that the OT sacrifices were unable to "perfect the conscience"; but Christ's offering can cleanse the conscience from "dead works." This is the same phrase as in 6:1 (see note there), and here, as there, it may be understood either morally as "works that bring death" (so the NIV and many commentators) or religiously as "useless rituals" (NIV footnote), which therefore cannot bring eternal life. Here the latter sense seems to me not only the natural sense of the Greek phrase but also more relevant to the immediate context. The "dead works" here stand over against the worship of "the living God" (see on 3:12), and the sense of "lifeless" (rather than "fatal") makes a more appropriate contrast with "living": it is when we are set free from the round of ineffective sacrifices offering only external cleansing that we can offer the spiritual service appropriate to the living God.

NOTES

11 Many manuscripts, especially later ones, have "the good things to come" (see NIV footnote), which is probably a scribal correction to make this verse agree with 10:1. But the perspective in 10:1 is different, as we shall see.

12–13 The change from μόσχοι, *moschoi*, "calves" (v.12, also in v.19), to ταῦροι, *tauroi*, "bulls" (v.13, also in 10:4) is merely stylistic. The noun μόσχος, *moschos*, is the LXX term for what is normally called a "bull" in English versions of Leviticus 16; it denotes a young bull or bullock but does not emphasize immaturity, as "calf" does for us.

14 "Through" is the same preposition we saw used in vv.11–12 both for the route through the tabernacle and the blood "through" which it was taken. The phrase is literally "through eternal spirit," and some have suggested the reference is to Christ's own spirit ("in his eternal nature," Montefiore), but this would be an unusual usage for Hebrews, and "the eternal Spirit" would be a natural term for the Holy Spirit, who belongs to the divine as opposed to the human realm. The role of the Spirit is not elsewhere in the NT mentioned in connection with Christ's death (but see Ro 1:4; 1Pe 3:18 for the Spirit's role in his resurrection) but is perhaps to be understood in the light of the descent of the Spirit at Jesus' baptism as his divine empowerment for messianic mission. Bruce, 217, traces the link to the endowment of the Servant of Yahweh with God's Spirit (Isa 42:1).

E. A New Covenant Requires a Death (9:15–22)

OVERVIEW

We have already been reminded of the importance of blood (and the death that produces it) in the OT sacrificial system (vv.7, 12, 13), and the author has alerted us to the fact that the sacrifice of Christ also involves the shedding of blood—his own (9:12, 14). In these verses he explores the theological significance of blood and death in this sacrificial context, leading up to the conclusion that "without the shedding of blood there is no forgiveness." As usual, he writes with a specific OT model in mind, the sacrifice Moses offered at Sinai to inaugurate the old covenant (Ex 24:3–8). The sacrificial blood, splashed not only on the altar but also on the people, sealed their commitment. So

also, our author argues, the new covenant must be sealed with blood.

The analogy is helped by the fact that the same Greek word, *diathēkē* (GK *1347*), means both "covenant" and "will" (as in "last will and testament"; there is a similar ambiguity in the old English use of "testament"; cf. Gal 3:15–17 for a similar wordplay). The author exploits this verbal coincidence to argue that a *diathēkē* requires a death, so that it was only through Christ's blood that the new covenant could be established. The wordplay is hard to reproduce in English, but the argument depends on our remembering the two meanings of the word.

---

¹⁵For this reason Christ is the mediator of a new covenant, that those who are called may receive the promised eternal inheritance—now that he has died as a ransom to set them free from the sins committed under the first covenant.

¹⁶In the case of a will, it is necessary to prove the death of the one who made it, ¹⁷because a will is in force only when somebody has died; it never takes effect while the one who made it is living. ¹⁸This is why even the first covenant was not put into effect without blood. ¹⁹When Moses had proclaimed every commandment of the law to all the people, he took the blood of calves, together with water, scarlet wool and branches of hyssop, and sprinkled the scroll and all the people. ²⁰He said, "This is the blood of the covenant, which God has commanded you to keep." ²¹In the same way, he sprinkled with the blood both the tabernacle and everything used in its ceremonies. ²²In fact, the law requires that nearly everything be cleansed with blood, and without the shedding of blood there is no forgiveness.

COMMENTARY

15 This complex sentence (simplified in the NIV by being divided into two parts with a dash) sets out a basic understanding of what it means for

Jesus to be the "mediator of a new covenant" (see on 8:6 for the phrase and cf. also "guarantor" in 7:22); it states both the purpose and the means of that mediation. The purpose is "that those who are called may receive the promised eternal inheritance." In 6:12, 17 we have heard of the promises that Abraham "inherited" and that are a model for all those who after him will also become "heirs," and in 1:14 God's people have been described as "those who will inherit salvation." The theme of receiving God's promises by faith will be developed more fully in ch. 11. The phrase thus speaks of all the good things God has in store for his people (cf. also the "heavenly rest" of 4:1–11). It was the purpose of the covenant that they should receive these blessings, and under the new covenant they have been more fully spelled out as the knowledge of God and the forgiveness of sins (8:10–12). Hebrews has spoken of our "heavenly calling" in 3:1 and so here can describe Christians as "those who are called" (cf. Ro 1:6–7; 8:30; 1Pe 5:10; etc.; and also "chosen," Ro 8:33; etc.).

We have considered the theme of "mediator" in 8:6 and noted that Jesus not only "stands between" God and his people but is also by his sacrifice the one who has made the relationship possible. Moses offered a blood sacrifice to effect the old covenant (see vv.18–21), but Jesus' mediation has gone still further—he *is* the sacrifice. His death is a "ransom to set them free" (*apolytrōsis*, see on v.12), thus making possible the forgiveness of sins that is at the heart of Jeremiah's vision of the new covenant (8:12). "Sins" here is not the usual word but *parabasis*, "transgression" (GK *4126*), which is particularly appropriate to the breaking of laws, and the added phrase "under the first covenant" suggests our author is thinking again of Jeremiah's complaint that Israel failed to keep the provisions of the old covenant (8:9). It was these "transgressions" that the old sacrificial system failed to deal with adequately (7:11, 18–19; 9:9); only the perfect sacrifice of Christ can achieve this (v.14). But while the words used focus especially on the breaking of the Mosaic laws, as the argument proceeds it will be clear that it is not only from sins "under the first covenant" that we can be set free by Jesus.

16–17 The mention of death as the basis of the new covenant ("he has died" in v.15 is literally "a death has occurred"), together with the idea of "inheritance," leads the author into his wordplay on *diathēkē* (GK *1347*). A will (*diathēkē*) does not take practical effect until the testator has died, as these verses explain at rather repetitious length; "inheritance" comes only as the result of a death. The switch to the second sense of *diathēkē* (an "obvious rhetorical conceit," Attridge, 254) should not be pressed too far, since the death involved with regard to the new covenant is not that of the one who made the *diathēkē* (namely, God) but of his Son as a third party ("mediator"). The promise of a new *diathēkē* does not demand the death of God! Our author's point is merely that *diathēkē* and death belong together.

18 So the Sinaitic covenant necessarily involved blood, as the ceremony carried out by Moses in Exodus 24:3–8 shows. It was a ceremony of dedication: *enkainizō*, "put into effect," derives from *kainos*, "new" (GK *2785*), and is used sometimes for renewal but especially for the dedication of that which is new, e.g., Solomon's temple, 1 Kings 8:63 (cf. Dt 20:5). Thus we are reminded that the "old covenant" was itself once new. Now a "new" covenant requires a new dedication offering. For the rhetorically emphatic phrase "not without blood," cf. v.7 and for "not without an oath," 7:20.

19–21 The ceremony that followed the initial proclamation and writing down of the "Book of the Covenant" (Ex 20–23) is now described, following and expanding the account in Exodus 24:3–8. The author adds ritual details that are not in the Exodus account: "water, scarlet wool and branches of hyssop," which belong to the regulations for the sacrifice of the red heifer mentioned in v.13 (Nu 19:6,

17–18) and for the cleansing of a leper (Lev 14:4–6). Apparently our author assumes these features would also have been included on this occasion of "cleansing." (Wilson, 163, rightly points out that to "check every statement in his sources" was "a much more difficult thing to do before the days of concordances and chapter and verse divisions.") According to Exodus 24:6, 8, the blood was sprinkled on the altar and on the people but not also, as our author assumes, on the scroll from which Moses read. And the further sprinkling on the tabernacle and its implements (v.21) goes far beyond the occasion in Exodus 24, since these had not yet been made at that stage! Indeed the later dedication of "the tabernacle and everything in it" was done with oil, not blood (Ex 40:9–11; Lev 8:10), though Josephus (*Ant.* 3.206) mentions blood in this connection as well. Our author is thus expanding the Sinai event with a broad-brush mention of later aspects of OT ritual to produce a more comprehensive account of the importance of blood. But it is the words of Moses in Exodus 24:8 (quoted in a form slightly different from the LXX) that provide him with the key text for this principle: it is "the blood of the covenant," the phrase Jesus himself also adopted to explain his sacrifice at the Last Supper (Mk 14:24; the change from "Behold" in Ex 24:8 to "This is" may reflect the eucharistic allusion).

22 A summary comment draws out the point of the expanded account of the Sinai ritual just given. The phrase "nearly everything" acknowledges a degree of exaggeration, in that cleansing of "things" in the OT law was not always by blood but sometimes by water or fire. Even the details he has listed in vv.19 and 21 go significantly beyond what the OT text says. But the fact that he goes on to speak of "forgiveness" rather than ritual purity suggests he intends "everything" to include people as well as objects, and in that case the prominence of blood sacrifices in restoring and maintaining people's relationship with God in the Mosaic law justifies his comment.

The concluding remark that "without the shedding of blood there is no forgiveness" is sometimes treated as an independent aphorism, but in fact it is part of the same sentence that sets out the situation "according to the law." The Levitical laws are based on the belief that sin cannot simply be brushed aside and forgotten but that it needs to be atoned for, and the prescribed method of atonement is by the shedding of (animal) blood; see especially Leviticus 4–5. According to Leviticus 17:11, blood represents life, and its shedding thus represents life poured out; when an animal dies in a person's place its poured-out life is accepted in place of the death earned by the person's sins. It is this basic OT principle to which our author appeals to explain why the final, perfect sacrifice made by Jesus on our behalf also needed to be a blood sacrifice; anything less would not be taking the problem of sin seriously. This is why a new covenant that has at its heart the promise "I will forgive their wickedness and will remember their sins no more" (8:12) must be established by the death of its "mediator."

NOTES

15 The idea that Christ's death provides redemption from "sins committed under the first covenant" suggests a retrospective efficacy such as Paul hints at in Romans 3:25, "the sins committed beforehand," referring probably to the salvation of God's people in OT times. The thought is not developed here, but cf. 11:40, where the "making perfect" of the OT saints had to wait to be achieved "together with us."

16–17 Unlike most recent commentators, Lane, 231, 242–43 (depending on J. J. Hughes, "Hebrews ix 15ff and Galatians iii 15ff.: A Study in Covenant Practice and Procedure," *NovT* 21 [1979]: 27–96) argues that διαθήκη, *diathēkē*, means "covenant" in these verses and that they refer not to a will but to "the procedure for the ratification of a covenant." This entails the improbable suggestion that "the one who made it" means the sacrificial animal whose blood "ratified" the covenant.

16 The NIV's "to *prove* the death" translates φέρεσθαι, *pheresthai*, "to be brought" (GK *5770*). For a death "to be brought" need mean no more than for it to take place, to come into the picture, but the word was sometimes used of a formal announcement or deposition; hence the translation "established" (REB, NRSV).

19 Most manuscripts add "and goats" after "the blood of calves," but there is strong evidence for an original text without the addition, which echoes the double mention of animals elsewhere in 9:12, 13; 10:4. Such an addition is more likely than that a scribe removed the goats (but not the water, wool, and hyssop and the sprinkling of the scroll) because they were not mentioned in the Exodus account.

The red wool was probably used to tie together the sprigs of hyssop with which the blood was sprinkled (cf. Ps 51:7), and the water would serve to keep the blood liquid for the purpose.

22 The previously unattested word αἱματεκχυσία, *haimatekchysia*, "outpouring of blood," may be intended as a further echo (cf. v.20) of Jesus' words at the Last Supper, "my blood . . . poured out for many" (Mk 14:24).

Lane's proposal (Lane, 232–33) that ἄφεσις, *aphesis* (GK *912*), means not "forgiveness" but "decisive purgation" in a cultic sense runs counter to general NT usage and does not do justice to the importance for this argument of Jeremiah's prophecy of forgiveness under the new covenant (in connection with which the word will occur again in 10:18).

F. A Single Sacrifice, Once for All (9:23–28)

OVERVIEW

Having established the importance of blood and death in the OT covenant, the author goes on to apply this principle to the sacrifice of Christ. The analogy of the new covenant means that what was needed for the old is no less necessary for the new, but as with all such typological comparisons, the emphasis is not so much on repetition as on fulfillment on a higher level that transcends the imperfections of the old system. The old sacrifices related to an earthly sanctuary, but the sacrifice of Christ to a heavenly one. And whereas the OT sacrifices—even the climactic sacrifice on the Day of Atonement—had to be constantly repeated, the sacrifice of Jesus is one perfect offering, once for all, after which there is no more atonement to be made.

In these verses, then, we revisit several of the themes already developed in the discussion of Christ's priestly ministry, but with increased emphasis on the "once for all" finality of this culminating point in God's unfolding purpose for the redemption of his people. In that context, there is also a rare (for Hebrews) reference to Christ's second coming as the event in which the process of salvation will be rounded off.

²³It was necessary, then, for the copies of the heavenly things to be purified with these sacrifices, but the heavenly things themselves with better sacrifices than these. ²⁴For Christ did not enter a man-made sanctuary that was only a copy of the true one; he entered heaven itself, now to appear for us in God's presence. ²⁵Nor did he enter heaven to offer himself again and again, the way the high priest enters the Most Holy Place every year with blood that is not his own. ²⁶Then Christ would have had to suffer many times since the creation of the world. But now he has appeared once for all at the end of the ages to do away with sin by the sacrifice of himself. ²⁷Just as man is destined to die once, and after that to face judgment, ²⁸so Christ was sacrificed once to take away the sins of many people; and he will appear a second time, not to bear sin, but to bring salvation to those who are waiting for him.

COMMENTARY

23–24 For the two sanctuaries, see above on 8:1–5 and 9:11. "Copies" in v.23 translates the same word, *hypodeigma* (GK *5682*), as was used in 8:5 (see note there), but "copy" in v.24 represents *antitypon* (GK *531*), the correlative to *typos*, "pattern," which in 8:5 denotes the original to which the earthly sanctuary is to correspond. This use of the terms by Hebrews is not that of modern typological language (or of Ro 5:14; 1Co 10:6, 11; 1Pe 3:21), in which the "type" is the preliminary (earthly) model and the "antitype" its later and greater fulfillment; but the thought here operates on a different principle, not the "horizontal" trajectory of historical progression but the "vertical" comparison of heaven and earth. As the true (*alēthinos*, GK *240*; see note on 8:2) heavenly sanctuary surpasses its earthly "copy," so the sacrifices by which the latter is "purified" (as we have seen in vv.21–22) must be superseded by something "better" (the key word again). To ask why heaven needs to be "purified" is probably to press the analogical nature of the argument too far. If the author has any specific "purification" in mind (rather than a general sense of consecration or dedication), it is probably that of God's people

(cf. the "cleansing" of our conscience, 9:14, using the same verb) so they can take their place with their "pioneer" in the heavenly sanctuary, which but for his sacrifice they would have polluted by their sinfulness. Cf. 3:6 for the idea that "we" are God's house or temple.

There is no need to spell out what the "better sacrifices" consist of, as this has already been explained in vv.11–14. The surprising plural (in that the whole point of the argument is to emphasize Christ's *one* sacrifice) is a literary device to establish the comparison with the plurality of sacrifices that have gone before; the following verses will show why the "better sacrifices" must in fact consist of only one. The suggestion by Wilson, 165–66, that the author is thinking also of the "sacrifices" of praise and good works that God's people are to offer (13:15–16) seems unlikely in this context, where all the emphasis falls on the uniqueness of Christ's sacrifice.

Christ's entry into heaven as high priest into his true sanctuary has already been declared in 4:14; 6:19–20; 8:1–2; 9:11–12. But his single sacrifice was made not in heaven but on earth, on the cross. So his priestly role in heaven cannot be to offer sacrifice; he entered the heavenly sanctuary "by" his blood, not in order to shed it, since he had already "obtained eternal redemption" (9:12). Verse 24 therefore explains his priestly role in heaven as "to appear for us in God's presence." The language reminds us of a legal advocate "appearing for" a client, and that may be the metaphor intended. The same verb is used in Acts 24:1; 25:2 for Paul's accusers "appearing before" the governor to accuse him, but Christ is a witness for our defense. But the verb is passive here, which is perhaps more naturally interpreted simply as an expression for his presence rather than as a deliberate legal metaphor. Even so, however, the sense of representation is clear in the phrase "for us" (on our behalf), and the idea echoes that of 7:25, "to intercede for them." Our high priest in heaven pleads for us on the basis of his sacrifice already offered on earth.

25 The contrast between Christ's sacrifice and the Day of Atonement ritual continues with two further points already raised in 7:27 and 9:12: Christ's single sacrifice as compared with the annual repetition, and his offering of himself as compared with the offering of animal blood ("not his own"). The point is thus further underlined that Christ's heavenly ministry is not, like that of an earthly high priest, one of offering sacrifice. That has already been done, and no more is needed.

26 The author dismisses any idea that Christ's sacrifice might need to be repeated (and the following "but now," "but as a matter of fact" [Lane], shows this was not a real possibility) by pointing out that this would have entailed multiple sufferings (which in this context means death, and v.27 will point out that death cannot be repeated) "since the creation of the world." In using this phrase, the author is perhaps again hinting at the retrospective

effect of the cross. It is because the single sacrifice of the cross covers all sin for all time, including those committed "under the first covenant" (see on v.15), that there has been no need for other such sacrifices "since the creation of the world." The fact that historically Jesus died only once thus shows that no additional sacrifices were needed.

That whole period of history "since the creation of the world" is contrasted with the climactic moment of Christ's once-for-all (see on 7:27) "appearing," the "end [TNIV "culmination"] of the ages." For a similar contrast between the long time of preparation and the decisive time of fulfillment, see 1:1–2, and for the phrase, see Paul's description of Christians as those "on whom the fulfillment of the ages has come" (1Co 10:11, using a related word for "end"; cf. also 1Pe 1:20). "Appeared" (*phaneroōmai*, GK *5746*; a different word from that in v.24) is used of Christ's coming as a revelation also in 1 Timothy 3:16; 2 Timothy 1:10; 1 Peter 1:20; and 1 John 1:2 (and for similar imagery of the dawning of the light, see Jn 1:1–18; 2Co 4:6). But he was revealed specifically to offer the sacrifice of himself, which would "do away with sin." *Athetēsis*, "removal" (GK *120*), is the same term used in 7:18 for the "setting aside" of the old order of priesthood. It goes further than merely forgiveness and implies the total removal of sin; cf. "I will remember no more" in 8:12. This is God's final solution.

27–28 The once-for-allness of Christ's sacrifice is further emphasized by a comparison with human experience: just as we die only once, and after that judgment follows, so too the sacrifice that enables us to survive that judgment (by "taking away the sins of many") is needed only once. The reference to our death and judgment thus serves in context as the minor element in a comparison designed to emphasize the uniqueness of

Christ's sacrifice. The once-for-allness of human death and judgment is simply stated as an agreed fact and is not itself made the subject of an argument. Later Christian discussions about what happens after death (the nature of resurrection and judgment, purgatory, etc.) are far from the author's mind. He will have more to say about judgment in 10:27–31; 12:18–24.

But if Christ's sacrifice was a single event in the past, that does not mean his role in our salvation finished then. Just as our death is followed by judgment, after Christ has died, "he will appear a second time" (yet another Greek word for "appear" [see on vv.24, 26]; this verb means simply "be seen"). The parousia is not directly mentioned elsewhere in Hebrews, though it is probably alluded to in the author's adaptation of Habakkuk 2:3 to speak of "the coming one" (10:37). Here it is simply taken for granted as part of Christian truth, the necessary sequel to Jesus' first coming and death. The Greek clause is compact and reads literally "a second time

without sin he will be seen to (by) those who are awaiting him for salvation" or, less naturally, "be seen for salvation to those who are awaiting him." The phrasing allows various permutations in translation, but it seems clear the author understands the purpose of the parousia to be the (completion of the) salvation of Christ's faithful followers. ("Await" is a strong verb suggesting eager expectation.) If the comparison with our death and judgment suggests the parousia should be seen as a time of judgment, this thought is not developed, and the emphasis falls instead on salvation. The phrase "without sin" is the same as in 4:15, where it spoke of Christ's own sinlessness, and that sense is possible here: even though he "bore sin" on the cross, when he comes again, it will be "without sin." But most interpreters agree with the NIV ("not to bear sin") in understanding this observation in regard to the purpose of the second coming: sin has been dealt with in the first coming and will not enter into the picture at the second.

NOTES

23–24 Hurst, 13–19, arguing that ὑπόδειγμα, *hypodeigma* (GK *5682*), means not "copy" but "preliminary sketch" (see note on 8:5), takes ἀντίτυπος, *antitypos* (GK *531*), here as "prefiguration." The earthly sanctuary, while in one sense a "copy" of what Moses was shown (8:5), at the same time serves as a "prefiguration" of the true sanctuary in heaven.

24 In addition to the legal sense mentioned above, to "appear before the presence [lit., face] of God" is a term suited to service in the sanctuary (1Sa 1:22) as well as to worship (Ex 23:17; etc.).

28 "Many" is used to emphasize the contrast between the single sacrifice of the one and its plural effect (cf. 2:10). In the context, it is inappropriate to draw attention to the use of "many" rather than "all"; cf. Ro 5:15–19, where Paul alternates "many" and "all" in a similar context. In all such references to the effect of Christ's death, the term "many" echoes Jesus' own words in Mark 10:45; 14:24 with their background in the repeated "many" of Isaiah 53:11–12. The same OT background also accounts for the use here of ἀναφέρω, *anapherō* (GK *429*), here translated "to take away" (elsewhere in Hebrews it means "to offer"), since this is the verb used twice in LXX Isaiah 53:11–12 for "bearing" sins. It might therefore be better translated here "to bear" (on himself), as in 1 Peter 2:24, though the purpose of such "bearing" of sins is, of course, to take them away.

G. Christ's Self-offering (10:1–10)

OVERVIEW

The death of Jesus has already twice been described as his "offering [of] himself" (7:27; 9:14) as a sacrifice, and the theme has been explored from various angles in 9:11–28. The focus of these verses remains on the same theme, but now with the added confirmation of a passage from Psalm 40:6–8, which our author takes to be concerned with Christ's "coming into the world" for the purpose of offering his body as the perfect sacrifice. A brief exposition of that passage from the psalm takes up vv.5–10, but since in vv.15–17 the author will return to his main text from Jeremiah 31, this short section constitutes an exposition within an exposition (cf. the inclusion of a supplementary study of Ge 2:2 within the exposition of Ps 95:7–11 in 4:4–10; see Introduction, pp. 26–27). It is not one of his more elaborate expositions and focuses directly on the main point of the psalm text, namely, that God is more interested in sincere obedience than in animal sacrifices; but the occurrence in his LXX version of the word "body" (which is not in our Hebrew text) allows him to

find in it a more specific application to the offering of Christ's "body" on the cross than the psalmist could have envisaged.

In order to prepare for the psalmist's contrast between the sacrifice of animals and that of the body of Christ, the author states once again in vv.1–4 the problem of the sacrificial system established by the Law, that it could never "make perfect" the worshipers (cf. 7:11, 18–19; 9:9–10), and more specifically that it could not "take away sins" as he has argued Christ's offering has done (9:11–15, 26, 28). God's purpose in establishing the old system was therefore not as an end in itself but to point forward to "the good things to come," to the reality, which would make the inadequate foreshadowing redundant (cf. 9:8–10 and the theme of the earthly and heavenly sanctuaries in 8:2–5, 9:11–12). In this section, therefore, we do not have a new stage in the argument but a reinforcement of points already developed, focused now in a biblical exposition that sums up the essential contrast and thus the superiority of Christ's sacrifice.

¹The law is only a shadow of the good things that are coming—not the realities themselves. For this reason it can never, by the same sacrifices repeated endlessly year after year, make perfect those who draw near to worship. ²If it could, would they not have stopped being offered? For the worshipers would have been cleansed once for all, and would no longer have felt guilty for their sins. ³But those sacrifices are an annual reminder of sins, ⁴because it is impossible for the blood of bulls and goats to take away sins.
⁵Therefore, when Christ came into the world, he said:

"Sacrifice and offering you did not desire,
    but a body you prepared for me;
⁶with burnt offerings and sin offerings
    you were not pleased.

7 Then I said, 'Here I am—it is written about me in the scroll—
I have come to do your will, O God.'"

8 First he said, "Sacrifices and offerings, burnt offerings and sin offerings you did not desire, nor were you pleased with them" (although the law required them to be made). 9 Then he said, "Here I am, I have come to do your will." He sets aside the first to establish the second. 10 And by that will, we have been made holy through the sacrifice of the body of Jesus Christ once for all.

COMMENTARY

1 Here is another strong statement of the typological principle that has undergirded much of the last two chapters. Just as the wilderness tabernacle was only a "shadow" of the heavenly one, so the Sinai law itself is (the Greek says "has") also only a "shadow" of "the good things to come." See on 9:11, where these good things were rightly described as "now already here" (since they have come with the coming of Christ), but from the point of view of the Law, they must be described here as still "to come." (The NIV's "that are coming" wrongly suggests they are still future at the time of writing.) In Colossians 2:17, Paul similarly speaks of legal regulations as "a shadow of the things that were to come." "Year after year" suggests the author is still thinking primarily of the sacrifices of the Day of Atonement, but even that very special occasion comes under the dismissive description of "the same sacrifices repeated endlessly," picking up the theme of 9:25–26. "Endlessly" is not in itself pejorative, as the same phrase is translated "forever" or "for all time" in 7:3 and 10:12, 14, where it refers to Christ's priesthood and the effect of his one sacrifice. What is dismissed here is the repetition "forever" of sacrifices that never achieve that effect, whereas one single true sacrifice would secure it "forever." The accusation that the Law cannot "make perfect" echoes that of 7:11, 19; 9:9. For "drawing near" to

God in worship, see on 7:25 (and cf. 4:16; 10:22; 11:6, all using the same verb).

2 The mere fact of repetition proves that the old sacrifices provided no lasting solution. The need for sacrifice presupposes a sense of guilt, and this sense of guilt arises from the knowledge of sin that has not been "cleansed." Only a "once for all" cleansing (which only a "once for all" sacrifice can provide) can break the vicious circle and set the conscience free. Once that has occurred, there is no place for the repetition of sacrifices.

The bold rhetorical question "Would they not have stopped being offered?" is the most telling pointer yet to the date when the letter was written; after AD 70 they had "stopped being offered," and the question would have been pointless (see Introduction, p. 23, and comments at 8:1–5).

3–4 There is a sharp irony in describing the sacrifices as merely "an annual reminder of sins" when the OT worshipers' hope was that they would actually deal with the problem. But any limited value sacrifices may have (see 9:13) falls far short of the actual removal of sin, which alone could "make perfect" those who wished to be truly God's people and which was the essential basis of the new relationship with God set out in Jeremiah's vision (8:12, where "remember no more" contrasts sharply with "reminder" here). Another reference to "the blood of bulls and goats" (cf. 9:12, 13, 19) reminds us that the only truly effective sacrifice is not of animals but of the Son of God, and the blunt and radical denial of the efficacy of such offerings (more uncompromising than in 9:10, 13, where a limited value was acknowledged) prepares us for the psalmist's devaluing of animal sacrifice in the quotation to follow.

5–7 If the readers thought the author was being unduly negative about the value of sacrifice, he now reminds them that he is not the first person to take this line, and that it has good scriptural precedent. The passage quoted is from Psalm 40:6–8a in the LXX version, slightly altered. It is a psalm of personal devotion deriving from the experience of God's deliverance: in the light of such experience, the merely outward worship of sacrifice (the four terms used in the psalm together represent the main types of offerings prescribed in Leviticus) is inadequate to express the psalmist's praise and gratitude. Indeed, he expresses himself even more negatively: God does not want such sacrifices. Several prophetic texts make a similarly radical comment (Isa 1:11–17; Jer 7:21–23; Hos 6:6; Am 5:21–27; Mic 6:6–8; cf. also 1Sa 15:22; Ps 51:16–17), but in each case, as in Psalm 40, the sacrifices are set in contrast with living in obedience to God's will; such OT protests aim not so much to abolish sacrifice as to put it in its place by stressing the uselessness of a *merely* ceremonial approach to God.

In contrast with such outward ceremony, the psalmist sets his "open ear" (obedient listening) and inward delight in God's will and bases his self-offering to God's service on what is written about him "in the scroll of the book" (lit.). This last phrase need mean no more than that his obedience is based on God's demands written in the Law (as is suggested also by the following clause in the psalm, "your law is within my heart"), but the LXX phrase "about me" (the Hebrew could be taken simply as "for me") lends itself to our author's deduction that the reference is to a specific personal role rather than to the

obedience required of all God's people. And the LXX reading "you have prepared me a body," in place of our Hebrew reading "you have opened my ear" (see Notes), then allows him to find in this text a prophecy specifically of Christ, who through his incarnation was given a "body" to offer (v.10). It was in this unique way that he was to "do God's will." A slight modification of the LXX wording enables the psalm to say not only that he "desired" to do God's will but more emphatically that he "came to" do it.

The argument depends not only on the different reading of the LXX (which as usual our author has adopted without betraying any awareness that it differs from the Hebrew) but also on his assumption that the speaker is Christ himself. In the psalm the speaker is clearly the same throughout—the writer who thanks God for his deliverance and expresses his trust in God's continuing protection. But we have already seen evidence of our author's assumption that the "real" speaker in all Scripture is God (1:6, 7, 8, 10; 3:7; 8:8); here, where the speaker addresses God, it is not difficult for him to discern the voice of the Messiah, as he did in the words of the psalmist and of Isaiah quoted in 2:12–13. The clause "Look, I have come" further leads him to think of the time "when he came into the world" (cf. 1:6, and comments there) especially as the quotation speaks of a body prepared for him (in his incarnation). As a result, our author is able to draw from the psalm not only the essential sense that ritual sacrifices must give way to self-offering but more specifically that the one special offering of the body of Christ has now replaced them.

8–9 The expository comment is simple and to the point. Two types of devotion are contrasted in the text: the multiple sacrifices, which God declares he does not want (listed in an abbreviated paraphrase of v.6 of the psalm that emphasizes their multiplicity), and the "coming to do God's will," which takes their place. The former are therefore "set aside" in favor of the latter. "Set aside" is a rather weak translation for *anaireō*, "remove, destroy" (GK *359*), which is more often used for killing a person; here it denotes the abolition of the old system. This is bold language to use about regulations that God's own law had laid down, as the parenthesis at the end of v.8 acknowledges (TNIV, "though they were offered in accordance with the law"). But the whole argument of the letter is increasingly underlining that the provisions of the old covenant were of only temporary validity. Now that their replacement has come, it is indeed time for them to be "removed"; they have no further practical role.

10 Three key words from the psalm quotation—"offering," "body," and "will"—are now woven into a summary statement that ties in the author's discussion of the psalm with the overall thrust of his argument. It was in fulfillment of God's declared "will" that Jesus Christ "offered" his "body" on the cross, thus providing the one perfect sacrifice that has achieved what no quantity of animal sacrifices ever could. By it "we have been made holy," the perfect tense pointing to our already achieved standing before God rather than to existential holiness of behavior. See on 2:11 for "make holy" as one of our author's varied expressions for the nature of Christian salvation (and cf. 10:14, 29); in this context it poignantly contrasts with the superficial "holiness" sought through animal sacrifice (9:13). And this saving work of Jesus Christ (there is a tone of creedal formality in this first use of the two names together in Hebrews), we are reminded yet again, has now taken place "once for all," that key term standing emphatically at the end of the paragraph.

NOTES

1 "The realities themselves" is literally "the image itself of the things"; εἰκών, *eikōn*, "image" (GK *1635*), is normally used for that which represents or reproduces something else (as in Mk 12:16 of the image on the coin, or when humanity is described as the image of God) but here denotes the true form as opposed to the shadow; cf. Paul's use of εἰκών, *eikōn*, for the "true pattern" to which believers are to be conformed (Ro 8:29) and also for the "visible reality" of God in Christ (Col 1:15). In a similar context, Paul uses σῶμα, *sōma*, "body" (GK *5393*), in contrast to "shadow" (Col 2:17).

The Greek word order allows the possibility of taking εἰς τὸ διηνεκές, *eis to diēnekes*, here translated "endlessly," not as further describing the annual sacrifices but with the following clause and thus in its more usual positive sense: "bring the worshipers to perfection *for all time*" (Montefiore; ditto NEB, but corrected by REB). But this is a less natural reading of the word order.

5 The unusual Hebrew phrase (lit.) "ears you have dug for me" was probably intended to be understood as making him able to hear and obey. The LXX σῶμα, *sōma*, "body," has been explained as an accidental misreading of ὠτία, *ōtia*, "ears," together with the concluding ς of the preceding word, but is more likely a deliberate attempt to give concrete meaning to the unusual and awkward Hebrew imagery. There is no other evidence for an alternative Hebrew text. (The NIV footnote at Ps 40:6 is misleading: both Symmachus and Theodotion have corrected σῶμα, *sōma*, to ὠτία, *ōtia*.)

7 As the author does not make any comment on the clause "it is written about me in the scroll of the book," it is impossible to be sure whether he thought that, as applied to Christ, it referred to a particular scriptural text or prophecy or more generally denoted God's expressed will (or perhaps a heavenly "book of destiny," cf. Ps 139:16). The singular "scroll of a book" would not be a natural description of the OT as a whole, which consisted of at least twenty scrolls; even the Law alone consisted of five scrolls.

H. No More Sacrifice for Sin (10:11–18)

OVERVIEW

With these verses we reach the end of the more directly "doctrinal" part of the letter, with its sustained demonstration of the superiority of the salvation God has provided for us in Christ, after which the focus will fall more on drawing out the pastoral and ethical implications of this carefully drawn theological argument and applying them more specifically to the situation in which the author understands his readers to be. More particularly, these verses bring to a ringing climax the argument begun in 8:1 concerning the effective priestly ministry of Christ in contrast to the inadequacies of the Levitical system and its sacrifices.

Typically of our author, the climax is reached with a reminder of two of the key OT texts that have undergirded the discussion in these chapters. In 8:1 our high priest was portrayed not only as serving in the order of Melchizedek according to Psalm

110:4 but also in the terms of the first verse of that psalm as seated in the place of supreme power at God's right hand. This imagery from Psalm 110:1, which recurs throughout the letter (see also 1:3, 13; 12:2), is triumphantly recalled now in vv. 12–13 to show the successful completion of the priestly task.

And in ch. 8 we were also first introduced to Jeremiah's great prophecy of the new covenant. Its vision, especially of the inward knowledge of God and his law, and the forgiving and forgetting of sin, has been repeatedly echoed since then, though without further explicit quotation. But now those key elements of the prophecy are quoted again in vv. 16–17 to round off the author's detailed exposition of how Christ has established Jeremiah's new covenant through his sacrificial self-offering. Once that has been achieved, sacrifice for sin is no longer necessary.

[11]Day after day every priest stands and performs his religious duties; again and again he offers the same sacrifices, which can never take away sins. [12]But when this priest had offered for all time one sacrifice for sins, he sat down at the right hand of God. [13]Since that time he waits for his enemies to be made his footstool, [14]because by one sacrifice he has made perfect forever those who are being made holy.

[15]The Holy Spirit also testifies to us about this. First he says:

[16]"This is the covenant I will make with them
    after that time, says the Lord.
I will put my laws in their hearts,
    and I will write them on their minds."

[17]Then he adds:

"Their sins and lawless acts
    I will remember no more."

[18]And where these have been forgiven, there is no longer any sacrifice for sin.

COMMENTARY

11 We are reminded again of two related aspects of the old system, the unending repetition of the Levitical sacrifices ("day after day," "the same," "again and again"; cf. 7:27; 9:25–26; 10:1–3), and the author's conviction that they are unable to "take away sins" (cf. 9:9; 10:1, 4), which is why they must always be repeated. The general statement of this verse takes in not only the ministry of the high priest on the Day of Atonement but also that of all the priests on a daily basis. The Greek sentence structure sharply contrasts the routine functions of "every priest" (under the old regime) with "this one" (v.12). The apparently unnecessary detail that the priest "stands" to perform his sacrificial duties sets up a suggestive contrast with "sat down" in v.12—an important feature derived from Psalm 110:1.

12–13 "One sacrifice for sins for all time" sums up the argument of chs. 9–10 so far, contrasting the "one" (a term not used hitherto in this connection, but cf. the frequent "once for all") with the many and emphasizing its permanent effect. "For all time" (the same phrase will recur in v.14) repeats the characterization of Melchizedek's priesthood as "forever" in 7:3; see note on 10:1 for its use in a rather different way.

The remainder of vv.12–13 is a close paraphrase of Psalm 110:1. The invitation there issued by "the LORD" to "my lord" is now realized, and our high priest, his earthly work complete (so that he no longer needs to "stand" as earthly priests must, v.11), has already taken his seat beside the throne of God (cf. 1:3, where this sitting is similarly said to follow his "providing purification for sins"). This is the place of supreme authority, and yet the victory is still not complete, for the psalm speaks of a period of waiting "until." So our author must picture the heavenly priest as still "waiting" for the final subjugation of his enemies. No indication is given here,

any more than it was in 1:13, as to who these "enemies" may be; the term is provided by the psalm, but it is not part of our author's purpose to explore it. He is content to repeat the psalmist's vision of a victory already won but not yet finally worked out. This tension between the reality of Christ's triumph already and the need to wait for its full implementation runs throughout the NT (note the parallel use of Ps 110:1 in 1Co 15:24–28) and was of pastoral importance to Christians who could see only too clearly that not everything was yet under divine control (cf. 2:8). But it is only a matter of "waiting"; the victory is already won.

14 The terms used in v.12 ("one sacrifice," "forever") are repeated again, but the tenses of the verbs suggestively reflect the tension just noted in vv.12–13. On the one hand, he "has made perfect" (perfect tense, for an act completed, "a definitive consecration of man to God in the present" [Peterson, 153]), but on the other hand, the beneficiaries of his sacrifice are "those who are being made holy" (present tense, of an ongoing process). In v.10 the author could declare that through Christ's sacrifice we "have been made holy" in the sense that the vital transaction has been completed. But in our actual experience it remains to be fully implemented, just as Christ's decisive victory still leaves room for a period of "waiting." If this perspective seems logically untidy, it is pastorally essential; to focus (as some Christian groups have been prone to do) on the once-for-all "perfection" without recognizing the reality of our continuing struggle with sin is a recipe for frustration and disillusionment.

15–17 In returning to the key text of this section, the author does not feel the need to quote it in full, as he did in 8:8–12, but singles out what are for him the salient points in an abbreviated quotation (with some further variation in the wording) from Jeremiah 31:33–34. He signals his abbreviation by separating v.33 (quoted in v.16) from v.34c (in v.17) by his introductory formulae, which are literally (and awkwardly) "For after saying" and simply "and." He seems to have lost track of the grammatical structure of his quotation formulae, with the result that there is in fact no main verb; but most English versions (and several later Greek manuscripts and versions) have helped him out by supplying one (or even two, as in the NIV's "First he says. . . . Then he adds"!).

In 8:8 the quotation was introduced simply by "he says," and we were left to assume (as the repeated "declares the Lord" within the quotation confirms) that the speaker was understood to be God. Here the author is more explicit, attributing this prophecy to the Holy Spirit, as he did with both Psalm 95 (3:7) and the Day of Atonement regulations (9:8). We noted in regard to the quotations in ch. 1 (see comments at Overview, 1:4–14; see also Introduction, p. 28), and have been reminded several times since, that our author regards God (or the Holy Spirit; it does not seem to matter which) as the real author of all Scripture, whether recorded as a divine utterance or not. In this case, that assumption is supported by the prophetic character of the passage and by the formula "says the Lord." The words of Scripture are, as usual, spoken of not merely as a past revelation but as the continuing witness of the Spirit "to us" in the present.

The point of reintroducing Jeremiah's prophecy here is to underline the nature of the "perfection" and "holiness" achieved by Christ's unique sacrifice. The final solution for the problem of human sin, which had eluded the sacrificial system under which the old covenant operated, is in the inward transformation of God's people and in a cleansing from sin that leaves them not merely "outwardly clean" (9:13) but inwardly restored to fellowship with God by having their sins not only forgiven but also forgotten, and thus finally "taken away" (v.11).

18 The simple words of this verse thus sum up the whole thrust of the argument: If Christ has done what the Levitical sacrifices could not do, and has thus brought in Jeremiah's new covenant, "sacrifice for sin is no longer necessary" (TNIV, suitably supplying the sense of the verbless Greek clause "no longer sacrifice for sin").

NOTES

11 The NIV's "take away" represents three different Greek verbs in 9:28; 10:4; 10:11. Whereas in 9:28 the verb gave an indication of how sin could actually be removed through the sacrifice of Christ (see note there), in the latter two cases the verbs (which differ little in meaning) simply indicate the complete removal, which animal sacrifices could not achieve.

12 As in v.1 (see note there), the Greek word order allows εἰς τὸ διηνεκές, *eis to diēnekes*, "for all time," to be taken with the following clause, "he sat down at the right hand of God," rather than as describing the permanent effect of the one sacrifice. This reading would bring in an echo of Psalm 110:4 to complement the allusion to v.1. But in view of the author's constantly repeated stress on the once-for-allness of Christ's sacrifice, it is more likely the phrase serves that function here too. It thus supplies the basis for the resumptive echo in v.14, where the same phrase again characterizes the effect of the sacrifice.

16 An alternative solution to the problem of the missing second part of the quotation formula is to find it within the quotation itself, namely, in the words "says the Lord." Thus the NJB takes these words out of the quotation and prints them as the author's quotation formula, "the Lord says," picking up from "for after saying" in v.15. But the fact that in 8:10 the same words were clearly understood to be part of Jeremiah's text makes this construction very unlikely. Attridge, 281, supporting this understanding, speaks of it as the author's deliberate "manipulation" of the text but does not make clear what such manipulation might be intended to achieve.

VI. A CALL TO FOLLOW JESUS IN FAITHFULNESS AND ENDURANCE (10:19–12:29)

OVERVIEW

Any attempt to divide this letter into neatly defined sections quickly runs into problems. The author's thought is too fluid and his style too subtle to allow that. There is therefore some artificiality in designating 10:18 as a major turning point in the progress of the letter, and this hesitation is intensified by the suspicion that this division is foisting a typical Pauline structure (theological exposition followed by ethical and pastoral implications) on a non-Pauline letter. There is nothing inevitable about such a division; indeed, not even all of Paul's letters can be so neatly divided in any case (notably 1 and 2 Corinthians).

But the widespread perception that with 10:19 the author moves from sustained theological exposition to pastoral application is in fact soundly based on what we find in the text. It is not that the letter so far has been devoid of pastoral application. Three of what are usually described as the five "warning passages" have already been included (2:1–4; 3:7–4:13; 6:4–8), and the author's demonstration of the superiority of the salvation we have in Christ has from time to time already led him to issue a more direct appeal to his readers to enter fully into this heritage with faith and confidence (3:1, 6; 4:14–16; 6:9–12). But whereas hitherto such appeals have been brief conclusions drawn in the course of a carefully structured, ongoing theological argument, now this argument is fully in place, and it is time to draw

out its existential implications at greater length. From here on, there will be no further elements added to the demonstration of the superiority of Christ, and the biblical expositions will focus not so much on the contrast between the old and the new as on the appropriate attitudes of the people of God in their response both to God's promises and to the experience of suffering as his people.

What we find from 10:19 on then is not a complete change of subject but the natural movement of the letter from the doctrinal demonstration, which needed to be presented first as the essential basis of the author's appeal, to the more direct call for the response of faith and endurance, which he as a pastor understands to be their current need. The "therefore" that introduces this section in 10:19 thus functions very similarly to the "therefore" that introduces Paul's "ethical sections" at Romans 12:1 and Ephesians 4:1. The doctrinal complexities of the earlier chapters are not forgotten but are now subsumed into the confident, overall assumption that the salvation we have received in Christ is the one supremely wonderful and indispensable basis for his people's life and hope. If the readers have followed his argument thus far, it is surely inconceivable that they should slacken in their resolve to follow Jesus, whatever the cost, still less that they might contemplate giving up altogether.

From 10:19 to 12:29, therefore, the author explores the dimensions of the life of faith in the context of a persecuted church, partly negatively in two further warnings of the danger of turning back (10:26–31; 12:25–29) but much more through a positive appeal to follow the examples of those who have triumphantly lived the life of faith, and supremely of Jesus, "the author and perfecter of our faith."

A. Confidence to Enter the Sanctuary (10:19–25)

OVERVIEW

The theme of entering the sanctuary, drawing on the model of the high priest's annual entry on the Day of Atonement, has recurred several times in the preceding argument (6:19–20; 8:1–2; 9:11–12, 24–25), but the focus in these passages has been on the unique ministry of Jesus, our great high priest. In 6:19–20, however, there was a strong hint of another and even more radical dimension to our author's imagery: Jesus has gone into the heavenly sanctuary "on our behalf" as our "forerunner," with the astonishing implication that we are to follow him there. Under the OT law, no one could go into the inner sanctuary except the high priest; he went on the people's behalf, but they remained outside. Now Jesus has opened the way into the presence of God, and all his people may go in too. So the author exhorts his readers not to remain outside, like the Jewish worshipers waiting outside the tabernacle for their high priest to emerge again, but to "draw near" without fear to enjoy the unheard-of privilege he has won for them.

And in light of that privileged access, he further appeals to them to remain true to their Christian profession and not to give up. In particular, he is acutely aware of the danger posed by some individuals within their community whose commitment is now in doubt and reminds them of their mutual responsibility as they strengthen each other's resolve within their corporate commitment as God's holy people.

Verses 19–25 constitute a single complex Greek sentence, the main structure of which begins with the participle "having," which has two objects ("confidence to enter," v.19, and "a great priest," v.21), followed by three parallel exhortations ("let us draw near," v.22; "let us hold," v.23; "let us consider . . . one another," v.24), the last of which is then unpacked in v.25 by two further participles, "not giving up" and "encouraging."

---

[19]Therefore, brothers, since we have confidence to enter the Most Holy Place by the blood of Jesus, [20]by a new and living way opened for us through the curtain, that is, his body, [21]and since we have a great priest over the house of God, [22]let us draw near to God with a sincere heart in full assurance of faith, having our hearts sprinkled to cleanse us from a guilty conscience and having our bodies washed with pure water. [23]Let us hold unswervingly to the hope we profess, for he who promised is faithful. [24]And let us consider how we may spur one another on toward love and good deeds. [25]Let us not give up meeting together, as some are in the habit of doing, but let us encourage one another—and all the more as you see the Day approaching.

COMMENTARY

19 Our author does not use "brothers and sisters" (TNIV) as often as Paul does to address his readers, but here, as in 3:1, 12, it underlines his pastoral appeal to those who with him "share in the heavenly calling" (3:1), which his argument so far has been explaining. It is a defining mark of such people to enjoy "confidence" before God (cf. 3:6; 4:16; 10:35). The word echoes closely his appeal in 4:16 (see comments there); its meaning contains both subjective and objective elements, both confidence and freedom of access, and thus contrasts with both the fear and the formal exclusion that kept people out of God's presence under the old covenant. Now they are free to enter (lit.) "the holy things," but *ta hagia* (GK *41*) here probably again denotes the inner sanctuary of the tabernacle (see note on 9:2–3, and cf. 9:12, 25; 13:11 for the same usage), which symbolizes the very presence of God. The sanctity of the inner sanctuary meant that the OT high priest could enter it only "by means of the blood of goats and calves" (9:12), but since Jesus has entered it "by his own blood" (9:12), his people can now do the same, relying on the cleansing which this blood has provided.

20 The old way into the sanctuary was through a curtain (9:3). In 9:8 we have been reminded that under the old covenant that "way" remained closed, but now Jesus has "opened" it for us (the verb is the same as was used for the "inauguration" of the old covenant in 9:18, where we noted that it is used especially for the dedication of something new). So it is "new and living," not now a matter of an ancient physical shrine but on a different level altogether; it is new not only in time but in quality, "appropriate to the new age and the new covenant" (Lindars, 102). A "living" way is needed for access to the living God (3:12; 9:14; 12:22). For the combination of "way" and "life," cf. John 14:6. The "curtain" through which we may now enter is imaginatively (and

rather awkwardly, since Jesus also went through it [6:19–20]) identified as Jesus' "body" (lit., "flesh," that "flesh" which he took when he became one of us [2:14; cf. 5:7]). The imagery is perhaps again suggested by the tradition that the temple curtain was torn apart at the moment when Jesus' "fleshly" life came to an end on the cross (Mk 15:38; cf. above on 9:8). The open way into God's presence symbolized by that event is now ours through the sacrifice of Jesus' "flesh." (Gordon, 117, helpfully discusses the link between the curtain and the flesh.)

21 The references to Jesus' "blood" (v.19) and "flesh" (v.20) remind us that it is by his death that the way has been cleared. But by a glorious paradox, when his people make their way in through his death, they find he has gone there before them, alive forever, as their "great priest" (not Hebrews' usual term for "high priest," *archiereus*, but the normal LXX term, which is a literal translation of the Hebrew term for that office: the "great priest"; cf. 4:14, where both terms were used together: "a great high priest"). As such, he is not just in the house of God but "over" it, as the Levitical high priest presided over the worship of the earthly tabernacle. The phrase "house of God" might thus be understood to refer to the heavenly sanctuary (though Hebrews does not elsewhere use "house" in that connection and prefers the imagery of the "tent"), but see on 3:3–6 for the idea that it is the people of God rather than any building who constitute his true "house" or "household" over which the Son has authority; the counterpart of the tabernacle is therefore to be found not so much in a heavenly place of worship as in the people of God, who now constitute his true sanctuary (cf. also on 9:23–24).

22 For "drawing near" to God as the ultimate goal of our salvation, see on 7:25 (cf. 4:16; 10:1). Just as Psalm 15 spells out the qualifications of those who may live on God's "holy hill" (cf. Ps 24:3–6), so here four phrases set out the features that should characterize those who are privileged to come to God. The first two, "a sincere heart" and "full assurance of faith," speak of an open, transparent genuineness toward God and a robust trust in his promises. We shall hear much more of what "faith" implies in ch. 11, but linked with *plērophoria*, "full assurance" (GK *4443*; rendered in 6:11 as the "making sure" of hope), it indicates a confident reliance on God that is a far more sturdy quality than "faith" conveys to some today. For such faith as an essential qualification for approaching God, cf. 11:6.

The second pair of phrases balances one another, both speaking of cleansing but focused respectively on the heart and the body. The author has spoken of "sprinkling" to achieve ritual purity with blood (9:19, 21) and with the "water of cleansing" containing the ashes of the red heifer (9:13), and in 12:24 he will extend the imagery to "sprinkling" with the blood of Jesus. Here he does not specify what is sprinkled, but probably the same idea is in mind. The effect of this sprinkling is to provide purification from a "guilty [lit., just "bad"] conscience," which we were told in v.2 could not be cleansed by the old sacrifices (cf. also 9:9, 14, all using the same term *syneidēsis*, "conscience," GK *5287*). It is no surprise to see such cleansing of the "heart" through the sacrifice of Christ among the qualifications for drawing near to God, but there is also a balancing phrase—"our bodies washed with pure water." The balancing construction setting "bodies" over against "hearts" makes it unlikely this washing with water is intended in a purely metaphorical sense, as in Ezekiel 36:25, though that passage may well be in the author's mind. In the light of 6:2 (see comments there), it is possible he is speaking of regular ritual ablution as still appropriate for those who worship God (as it was under the old covenant [Ex 29:4; Lev 16:4]), but it is more

likely he is referring to Christian baptism as the outward counterpart of the inward "sprinkling" of the heart. The outward and inward aspects of baptism are explicitly contrasted in 1 Peter 3:21, but our author regards them as complementary, with no indication that the physical is of less importance. (Both John the Baptist and Jesus linked baptism in water and in spirit [Mk 1:8; Jn 1:33; 3:5].)

23 The call to "draw near" to God is supplemented by two further exhortations in vv.23 and 24–25 respectively. This verse repeats the appeal expressed in 4:14; 6:11–12 and implied in 3:6 (and spelled out more fully in the warning passages 2:1–4; 3:7–4:13; 6:4–8) to remain true to their Christian commitment. For the noun *homologia*, "confession" (GK *3934*), see notes on 3:1 and 4:14; in its three uses in Hebrews, the object of our "confession" is respectively "Jesus," "faith," and "hope." "Hope" has been used several times to express the essence of our Christian salvation and security (3:6; 6:11, 18; 7:19). It is not mere wishful thinking, because it is based on the promises (a key word in this letter; see esp. 6:12–18; 8:6; 9:15) of a God who is "faithful" in that he can be trusted to keep his promises, as 6:13–18 has demonstrated and as ch. 11 will illustrate at length (note esp. the similar language of 11:11). Because our hope is so firmly founded, it can and must be held "unswervingly"—a graphic term for not leaning over or wobbling, as the author clearly felt his readers were liable to do.

24–25 Verse 23 appealed to the readers corporately to stand firm, but in these verses the author takes up a theme he has already hinted at: the danger that some within the group might lose their commitment and thus endanger the others. We noted in 3:12–13; 4:1, 11; 6:11 that his concern for the whole group was more specifically focused on the need for "each of [them]" individually to maintain their stand, and the same individual focus will become even more prominent in 12:15–17. Here he indicates the basis of this concern in that some are apparently already in the habit of absenting themselves from the church's meetings—perhaps under pressure from non-Christian Jews, perhaps through their own disillusionment and uncertainty. We do not know whether this particular group still tried to maintain the early Christian practice of daily meeting (Ac 2:42–47; Heb 3:13 might suggest this) or whether the Sunday gathering (Ac 20:7; 1Co 16:2) had by now become the normal focus, but whatever the frequency, our author clearly understands regularly meeting together to be vital to their spiritual health.

So it is essential they "consider one another." The verb is the same as "fix your thoughts on" in 3:1, where I suggested it might better be translated "take notice of"; perhaps here "keep an eye on one another" would get the sense. The purpose of this mutual concern is not negative, looking out for failings to criticize, but rather to "spur one another on toward love and good deeds" and to "encourage one another" in the recognition that all are fallible and that therefore each needs the support of the rest. "Spur on" translates the vivid noun *paroxysmos* (GK 4237), used of the "sharp disagreement" that separated Barnabas from Paul in Acts 15:39; here it has a more positive connotation, but it certainly shows that the author expected the "encouragement" to

be bracing and even confrontational rather than merely comforting. For the sort of "love and good deeds" he may have had in mind, cf. vv.32–34.

The last clause of v.25 introduces a note that has not been prominent in Hebrews but that runs through most of the NT, namely, the sense of eschatological urgency. "The Day" is probably a technical term (shorthand for "the Day of the Lord"), as it seems to be also in 1 Corinthians 3:13 and 1 Thessalonians 5:4. There has so far been a single mention of Christ's second coming to complete the work of salvation (9:28), but the quotation of Habakkuk 2:3–4, which follows in 10:37–39, will focus on the expectation of "the coming one," and the two remaining warning passages (10:26–31; 12:25–29) will speak also of a coming time of judgment and of the "shaking" of earth and heaven. Whether their expectation of "the Day" was focused more on the element of salvation or on that of judgment, its approach was a clear incentive for the readers to take their discipleship seriously and to guard carefully their corporate hope. We do not know how soon the author expected "the Day" to come or in what way his readers might be expected to "see it approaching," but the tone of this clause suggests that the early Christian expectation of an imminent parousia was still very much alive.

NOTES

19 While it is true that παρρησία, *parrēsia*, "confidence" (GK 4244), here implies an (objective) "right" to enter the sanctuary, to translate it formally as "authorization" (Lane) is unnecessarily to lose the subjective sense of "uninhibited confidence" that dominates the usage of this richly suggestive word.

20 Gordon, 116, suggests that "living" may be intended to contrast the new way with the constant fear of death that surrounded access to God's presence under the old covenant (Ex 28:35, 43; Lev 10:6–9; 16:2).

Some interpreters take "that is, his body" as qualifying the "new and living way" rather than the curtain (hence the NEB's "the way of his flesh"), but this is a more awkward reading of the Greek, in which the genitive σαρκός, *sarkos*, "flesh," more naturally stands in apposition to καταπετάσματος, *katapetasmatos*, "curtain," rather than qualifying the accusative "way" farther back in the sentence. It would also be out of keeping with the style of Hebrews, which frequently uses "that is" for explanatory descriptions in apposition (2:14; 7:5; 9:11; 11:16; 13:15).

22–24 Many commentators note the presence in these verses of the traditional Christian triad of "faith," "hope," and "love," but their wide separation in the text makes it unlikely there was a conscious intention to emphasize them as a group of three.

B. Fourth Warning Passage (10:26–31)

OVERVIEW

After the warm confidence of the preceding verses, this passage comes as an unwelcome contrast, but it is not a non sequitur (in Greek it is introduced by "for"; cf. a similar "for" in 6:4). If there is now a "new and living way" into God's presence, then there are bound to be serious consequences if it is rejected. And the mention in v.25 of members of the church who were beginning to detach themselves raises the serious question of what might happen to them if they persist in this course. The concluding mention of the imminence of "the Day" adds further urgency to the issue of possible apostasy. The result is a warning as serious and as uncomfortable for traditional theology as was 6:4–8; the essential thrust of the two passages is the same.

As in ch. 6, the author here describes the possibility of apostasy objectively without suggesting that what he says is actually true of any of his readers, and following this passage he will again, as he did in 6:9–12, give reasons for confidence that they are not yet in such a state. But here, as there, there would be no point in setting out a purely hypothetical scenario; this is a warning of what *could* happen if they are not careful. We considered in the comments on 6:4–8 the problem of reconciling such a possibility with a strong doctrine of Christian assurance, and since the same issues in principle arise here, I trust this earlier discussion will suffice to set this passage too in its wider scriptural context. The following

comments will therefore focus only on the specific terminology of this second assertion that deliberate apostasy is irrevocable.

The opening words may give the impression the author is speaking here not of the final sin of apostasy but of any and every sin committed after "receiving the knowledge of the truth." In that case, he would be expressing a rigorism far in excess of anything else in Scripture and impossible to reconcile with pastoral experience. (See Bruce, 262–64, for the debates in the second-century church on the problem of "post-baptismal sin.") People do sometimes sin after their initial Christian commitment, and the consistent witness of Scripture is that in such cases there is forgiveness (1Jn 2:1–2; etc.); our author implies as much in his references to our high priest's continuing ministry of intercession for his people (7:25; 9:24; cf. also his sympathy with his people's weakness in 2:17–18; 4:15–16). But the words used suggest he is not in fact speaking here of any and every sin. In v.26 the sin described is deliberate and continuing, and the extreme language of v.29 recalls that of 6:6 in portraying a decisive reversal of their Christian allegiance and a contemptuous repudiation of the faith (and the Savior) they had once embraced. The subject is again, as in 6:4–8, not just sin but apostasy.

The logic of the argument depends on the preceding account of Christ's once-for-all sacrifice. That account concluded with the reassurance that "sacrifice for sin is no longer necessary" (10:18 TNIV). But the sobering reverse side of this conclusion is that once that unique sacrifice has been appropriated, while it is sufficient for all sins for all time, it is not repeatable. If it is repudiated, there can be no other. If final salvation is achieved only through Christ's sacrifice, then to reject that salvation leaves only final judgment.

---

²⁶If we deliberately keep on sinning after we have received the knowledge of the truth, no sacrifice for sins is left, ²⁷but only a fearful expectation of judgment and of raging fire that will consume the enemies of God. ²⁸Anyone who rejected the law of Moses died without mercy on the testimony of two or three witnesses. ²⁹How much more severely do you think a man deserves to be punished who has trampled the Son of God under foot, who has treated as an unholy thing the blood of the covenant that sanctified him, and who has insulted the Spirit of grace? ³⁰For we know him who said, "It is mine to avenge; I will repay," and again, "The Lord will judge his people." ³¹It is a dreadful thing to fall into the hands of the living God.

COMMENTARY

26 "Deliberately" is placed first in the Greek sentence to emphasize that the subject is not inadvertent sin or human fallibility under pressure but what Numbers 15:30 called "high-handed" (NIV, "defiant") sins (see on 5:2; 9:7). Most interpreters understand the present tense of the verb to indicate not an uncharacteristic lapse but a settled course of deliberate sin (REB/NRSV, "deliberately/willfully persist in sin"; GNB, "purposely go on sinning"; the NJB, however, translates more broadly "deliberately commit any sins"). Unlike in 6:4–8, the author introduces this scenario in the first person, associating himself with his readers as those who theoretically might take this course, and thereby making it clear he is talking again of those who are already real Christians, not some hypothetical fellow travelers.

"Receive the knowledge of the truth" is not used elsewhere in this letter to describe the initial Christian commitment but is similar to "enlightenment" in 6:4; 10:32. The phrase does not denote baptism as such, so that to describe this passage as concerned with "post-baptismal sin" is too specific and derives more from the debates of the second-century church than from Hebrews. Its focus is not on baptism but on the embracing of Christ's sacrifice for salvation. It is this once-for-all acceptance that leaves no further sacrifice for sins still available—nor is any needed, if the Christian commitment is maintained.

27 The alternative to salvation is expressed in extreme terms. Instead of the joyful "waiting" for salvation at Christ's return (9:28), there is a "waiting for" (a related term) judgment. The expectation itself is described as "fearful" (*phoberos*, "terrifying" [GK *5928*], a word used in the NT only in Hebrews; cf. 10:31; 12:21) because of the nature of the judgment involved. The imagery of fire for divine judgment is common in the NT, but it gains extra force by the vivid phrase that translates literally "a zeal of fire" (echoing the language of Isa 26:11; cf. Zep 1:18), picturing "the fire of judgment which, with its blazing flames, appears like a living being intent on devouring God's adversaries" (BDAG, 427). The idea of the fire "eating" God's enemies (again drawn from Isa 26:11) is equally violent in its imagery. Those "enemies," we are left to assume, include those who deliberately persist in sin.

There is no explicit statement of when this judgment may be expected. In the light of 9:27–28, we might reasonably link it either with the judgment that necessarily follows a person's death (9:27) or with the expected return of Christ (9:28). The author does not feel it necessary to specify; it is enough that it is a reality that must be expected to follow the act of rebellion and that cannot be evaded.

28 Another "how much more" argument like that of 2:2–4 (cf. also 12:25) underlines the fearsome nature of this judgment by comparison with its OT counterpart. If there was no mercy for those who rejected the Mosaic law, itself only a shadow of what was to come (10:1), how much more serious is the rejection of the reality itself? Not all infringements of Mosaic laws carried the death penalty, of course, but the author speaks here of "rejecting" the Law itself, which was tantamount to rejecting the authority of God. It is true that he has himself spoken of the Law as now due to be "set aside" (7:18, using the same verbal root) with the coming of the new covenant, but God's replacement of his own law is a very different matter from its rejection by those who were under its authority. "The testimony of two or three witnesses" was the standard criterion for conviction under the Mosaic law; here the author is referring to Deuteronomy 17:6, where that testimony was the basis of the death penalty for someone who had violated God's covenant by worshiping other gods. For "without mercy," cf. also Deut 13:8, again concerned with incitement to worship other gods.

29 The rhetorical question (cf. 2:2–4) is no less emphatic, and perhaps more psychologically effec-

tive, than the blunt "it is impossible" of 6:4–6. The greater seriousness of Christian apostasy is spelled out in three clauses that describe in lurid terms what the apostate's action amounts to. To "trample under foot" the Son of God recalls the imagery of "recrucifying" him in 6:6, but this new and graphic metaphor intensifies the note of contempt (cf. the pigs trampling the pearls in Mt 7:6); here, as in 6:6, the title "the Son of God" underlines the heinousness of the offense. To "treat as an unholy thing" (the same terminology as is used for "ceremonially unclean" in 9:13) the blood of the covenant (cf. 9:20, citing Ex 24:8 and also recalling the eucharistic words of Mk 14:24) is to despise and repudiate the whole "new covenant" salvation symbolized by that blood. The specific comment that this is the blood by which the apostate has been sanctified (cf. vv.10, 14) sets up a poignant contrast with treating it as "unholy." It also makes it clear that this potential apostate is a person who has already benefited from Christ's saving work. To "insult the Spirit of grace" recalls Jesus' solemn words about the unforgivable sin of blasphemy against the Holy Spirit (Mk 3:29), and the contrast between the arrogant contempt (*enybrizō*, to treat with hubris) of the apostate and the "grace" of the Spirit compounds the offense. The language of the three clauses could hardly be more shockingly chosen to highlight both the offensiveness and the finality of deliberate apostasy.

30 Two quotations from the song of Moses in Deuteronomy 32 remind the readers that God is not to be trifled with. The first, quoted in an identical form in Romans 12:19, is from Deuteronomy 32:35 in a version that follows the probable Hebrew text (and that of the Aramaic targums) where the LXX is different, though using the LXX verb for "repay." The second quotation comes from a few lines later (Dt 32:36, this time in exact agreement with the

LXX; it occurs again in the same form in Ps 135:14). As in 2:13b two clauses from the same text are separated by the author's "and again," which here is the more appropriate since the two lines are not consecutive in the original. (In 1:5 and 2:13a the same formula separates quotations from different sources.) The first line quoted is indeed about God's punitive judgment on his enemies, but the verb "judge" in the second (and in its parallel in Ps 135:14) refers in context to God's giving judgment *in favor of* his oppressed people. In the latter case, the author of Hebrews seems to have founded his application more on the normal meaning of the verb "judge" itself than on its meaning in this OT context; read in that way it suits his purpose well, as the judgment he is speaking of does indeed fall on God's own people if they have turned against him.

31 The point of the dual quotation, as our author understands it, is summed up in a pithy and startling epigram. Elsewhere in Hebrews, "the living God" is one to be served with joyful confidence (9:14; 12:22). But to "turn away from the living God" (3:12) is to make a dangerous enemy (cf. the equally threatening uses of the phrase in 1Sa 17:26, 36; 2Ki 19:4, 16; Jer 10:10; cf. also Dt 5:26). Precisely because he is "living," he is not to be trifled with. For "fall into the hands of," contrast 2 Samuel 24:14, where David preferred to fall into God's hands than into human hands, "for his mercy is great"; for Hebrews there is a limit to that mercy. The same God who is a loving Father is also a "consuming fire" (12:29).

NOTES

29 TNIV has justifiably changed the generic singular subject ("a man . . . him") into the plural so as to avoid the specifically masculine language that might otherwise suggest that women are not capable of apostasy. The reference is not to a specific person but to anyone who takes this disastrous course.

The unusual phrase "the Spirit of grace" echoes LXX Zechariah 12:10, where God will pour out "a spirit of grace" on his people. The reference there is primarily to their attitude of repentance rather than to the Spirit viewed personally, but the passage goes on to speak of them mourning for "the one they have pierced" and of a fountain of cleansing (Zec 13:1), and its imagery was important for the early Christian understanding of salvation.

C. Faithfulness under Pressure (10:32–12:3)

OVERVIEW

As I shall be dividing this section of the text into nine subsections for the purpose of commentary, I need first to defend my decision (which other commentaries do not share) to treat it as a single unit of the argument. At its heart is the great celebration of "faith," which takes up ch. 11 and is often treated as though it were a self-contained unit. I disagree with that isolation of ch. 11 with regard both to the text that follows the chapter and to that which precedes it.

The former point is perhaps the more commonly noted, namely, that 12:1–3 is in fact the conclusion to the survey of faith in action. First, it picks up the heroes of ch. 11 in their new role as "witnesses" of the continuing race of faith that the readers must now run. But second, it presents Jesus not just as the "perfecter" of our faith but also as himself taking his place as the last in the illustrious line of examples of living by faith surveyed in ch. 11, and thus as the immediate "pioneer" of the readers of the letter who must follow in their footsteps.

Yet neither is 11:1 a new beginning that introduces a new subject into the argument. The language of "faith" has already been introduced through the quotation of Habakkuk 2:3–4 in 10:37–38, together with the expository comment that follows it in 10:39. The purpose of ch. 11 is then to illustrate the nature of the faith to which the author is summoning his readers and which he will declare in 12:1–3 to be now their responsibility. Verses 37–39 of chapter 10 focus on the contrast between "faith" and "shrinking back." It is such "shrinking back" the author most fears in his readers, and the gallery of OT heroes in ch. 11 consists of those who had every reason to "shrink back" but who refused the easy option. The whole chapter serves then to fill out the appeal the author bases on Habakkuk 2:3–4. This is why I have described not just 10:37–39 but the whole of 10:37–12:3 as an "exposition" of Habakkuk 2:3–4. It is all about what it means to press on in "faith" and not to "shrink back."

And in fact 10:37 is not the beginning of the appeal; rather, it introduces the key OT text to back up the appeal already issued in vv. 32–36 as the author reminds them of their past faithfulness and urges them to carry it forward. Only so can they hope to "receive what God has promised," as ch. 11 will illustrate over and over again. The whole of 10:32–12:3, therefore, constitutes an extended appeal not to shrink back (thus balanc-

ing the warning just issued in 10:26–31)—an appeal which, typically of our author, is grounded in a key OT text. If most of the words of Habakkuk 2:3–4 are not again quoted in the rest of the section, its key term, "faith," is repeated and explored throughout, and in that way the message of Habakkuk for the author's readers is memorably expounded and applied.

As usual in Hebrews, section divisions are to some extent arbitrary. The extended discussion of faith takes further both the appeal and the warning of 10:19–25 and 10:26–31, and there is again no clear break at 12:4 but rather a series of further exhortations to perseverance. But inasmuch as the direct discussion of the nature of "faith" is focused in 10:32–12:3, and from 12:4 a new text (Pr 3:11–12) takes over from Habakkuk 2:3–4 as the expository basis of the argument, it seems appropriate to end this main section at 12:3.

Throughout this section it is important to remember that the range of meaning of the Greek word *pistis* (GK *4411*) is not the same as our "faith." "Faith" (or "the faith") can be used in English for the content of belief, and there is perhaps a trace of that meaning in Hebrews' use of *pisteuō* (GK *4409*) in 11:6 for "believing *that*." But overwhelmingly our author uses this language not for intellectual acceptance but for an attitude of commitment and existential trust in a God who is real and who keeps his word. Such an attitude shades over into what we would call "faithfulness," equally a part of the meaning of *pistis*, and indeed the heroes of ch. 11 are not only those who trusted God but who themselves proved trustworthy as they lived out their lives in loyalty to his will. In Habakkuk 2:4, this sense of "faithfulness," of patient endurance as opposed to "shrinking back," is predominant, and it is important in reading ch. 11 to remember that *pistis* is not just a feeling but a way of life.

1. Faithfulness Past and Future (10:32–36)

OVERVIEW

The call to stand firm in the face of discouragement and persecution is not anything new to the readers. The author is asking them only to maintain the faithfulness they have already displayed. After going through so much for the sake of the gospel, surely they cannot now think of throwing it all away and losing the promised reward (as vv.26–31 have been warning them).

The author's brief description of their previous experience does not allow us to reconstruct a full picture of what had happened to them since they were first "enlightened." Imprisonment and the loss of property (v.34) suggest some measure of official suppression, and the implication seems to be that this came to them specifically because of their Christian commitment. The only official persecution of Christians as such for which we have clear historical evidence in the first century is that by Nero in AD 64–65, which was apparently limited to Rome, and

it is tempting to link these comments with that unsettled period (if the letter was written to a group in the capital, as many believe); the comment in 12:4 that they have not yet had to shed their blood might then be in comparison with the large number of Roman Christians who were in fact martyred at that time (Tacitus, *Ann.* 15.44). But the author is apparently speaking here of a time soon after their original conversion, and this is likely to have been earlier than the sixties. In any case, our historical information is limited, and other local acts of persecution probably took place from time to time, not at the official imperial level, but involving local officials and a hostile population; cf. the frequent attacks on Paul from non-Christian Jews recorded in Acts. In the uneasy period of the church's gradual separation from Judaism, it would be surprising if groups of Jewish Christians did not sometimes have to face such hostility and sometimes violence.

³²Remember those earlier days after you had received the light, when you stood your ground in a great contest in the face of suffering. ³³Sometimes you were publicly exposed to insult and persecution; at other times you stood side by side with those who were so treated. ³⁴You sympathized with those in prison and joyfully accepted the confiscation of your property, because you knew that you yourselves had better and lasting possessions.

³⁵So do not throw away your confidence; it will be richly rewarded. ³⁶You need to persevere so that when you have done the will of God, you will receive what he has promised.

COMMENTARY

32 For "receiving the light," see comments at 6:4; together with "earlier days" it speaks of the time when they first became Christians. The term "contest"

(TNIV, "conflict") uses a strong physical metaphor from wrestling or athletics, and the following verses will show that this "prize fight of sufferings" (lit.) involved not just adverse circumstances but the hostility of other people. The verb "stood your ground" (TNIV, "endured") indicates the readers were the victims rather than the perpetrators of the violence. "Endurance" is a key theme of these later chapters (esp. 10:36; 12:1–3, 7).

33 "Publicly exposed" is another vivid metaphor, this time from the theater (cf. 1Co 4:9 for the same metaphor), while "insult" and "persecution" suggest respectively verbal and physical abuse. (Cf. 1Pe 3:14–16; 4:3–4, 12–17 for the sort of abuse some early Christians had to face.) To be forced to endure such treatment oneself is hard enough, but the author reminds them that they were willing also to stand alongside (lit., "become sharers with") their fellow Christians when they faced it. The important NT idea of *koinōnia* (GK *3126*) is significantly applied here not to the sharing of spiritual and material blessings but, as in 2 Corinthians 1:7 and 1 Peter 4:13, to the sharing of sufferings. In their ordeal the readers have discovered what it means to be members of the body of Christ, in which "if one part suffers, every part suffers with it" (1Co 12:26).

34 "Sympathize" translates a Greek verb which more literally means "suffer along with" (TNIV). While it need have no more than the emotional sense of our "sympathize," here it picks up the "sharing" of v.33 and suggests an active involvement with imprisoned fellow Christians (cf. 13:3). Prisoners in the ancient world depended on the active help of friends and family for the necessities of life, not just for supportive visits. Such open identification with those in prison might put them at risk of the same punishment.

The loss of possessions (a very general term not limited to real estate, as our use of "property" tends to be) is expressed using a strong word ("seizing, plunder"), which implies strong-arm tactics and victimization, perhaps in this context looting, rather than the official action suggested by the NIV's "confiscation." The phrase translated by the NIV as "better possessions" is in fact singular, and while the noun can be used in a collective sense, it is possible the author uses it to indicate the one single great "possession" (NASB) that outweighs all the (plural) possessions (a related term) they have lost. The term "better," so often used in this letter for the nature of Christian salvation in contrast to its OT antecedents, here points to something on a different level from those earthly possessions, and the phrase "and a lasting one," added prominently at the end of the sentence (NASB), underlines the contrast with the temporary advantage of earthly wealth. The whole verse therefore portrays the true riches of their heavenly calling (3:1), and ch. 11 will go on to illustrate repeatedly how faith puts such wealth before earthly security (11:8–10, 13–16, 24–26). For "joy" in such circumstances, cf. Luke 6:22–23.

35–36 The opening "So" shows the link with vv.32–34: their past record is the basis for the author's appeal for continuing faithfulness. Having come so far so well, they must not think of giving up now. In these verses, three terms express the demands of the present (their "confidence," "persevering," and "doing the will of God"), while two speak of what lies ahead (a "rich reward" and God's "promise"). For "confidence," see on v.19; here too the more objective sense of their standing before God underlies their subjective assurance or boldness. "Reward" represents a compound term peculiar to Hebrews in the NT (cf. 11:6, 26 and, in a negative sense, "punishment" in 2:2), not essentially different in meaning from the simpler term used by other writers but conveying more vividly the sense of full recompense. The "promise" is here unspecified, but by now the theme is familiar (cf. 4:1; 6:12; 8:6; 9:15; 10:23). The promised reward is reserved only for those who have remained faithful in "doing the will of God." To turn back now would be to lose it all, as vv.26–31 have spelled out.

NOTES

32–34 Bruce, 268–70, argues that the persecution referred to may be associated with the expulsion of Jews from Rome by Claudius in AD 49 (cf. Ac 18:2). There is no evidence that this affected Christians as such (despite the persistent but unsupported assumption that Suetonius's mention in this connection of a certain "Chrestus" points to anti-Christian riots), but Bruce offers a plausible reconstruction of a possible scenario; cf. Lane, lxiii–lxvi.

2. Living by Faith: Habakkuk 2:3–4 (10:37–39)

OVERVIEW

The appeal just made in vv.35–36 is now grounded in the key text that will be the basis for the extended exploration of "faith" and "faithfulness" in 11:1–12:3. The passage from Habakkuk 2:3–4 is one Paul liked to quote in relation to "justification by faith," but his interest seems to have been focused on the single clause "the righteous will live by faith" (quoted in Ro 1:17; Gal 3:11). Hebrews, on the other hand, quotes the passage at greater length, and by applying the text existentially to how God's people should live, he is closer to its original sense than Paul, who develops his theology of justification by faith on other grounds and uses this text only as a convenient "slogan." But our author, while basing his discussion on the original sense of the passage, handles the text quite freely, and his exposition depends in part on the distinctive rendering of the LXX.

---

[37]For in just a very little while,

"He who is coming will come and will not delay.
[38]   But my righteous one will live by faith.
And if he shrinks back,
     I will not be pleased with him."

[39]But we are not of those who shrink back and are destroyed, but of those who believe and are saved.

COMMENTARY

37–38 The first line, "In just a very little while" (which TNIV has rightly included within the quotation), comes not from Habakkuk but from an unusual idiom found in LXX Isaiah 26:20 (= Ode 5:20 in the LXX), where it describes the "little while" God's people must hide until he has punished his enemies. Its context is thus similar to Habakkuk's impatient waiting atop his watchtower until God reveals how he will judge the wicked, and our author seems to have used a memorable phrase from one prophetic eschatological oracle to introduce another related one. Such combined quotations are frequent in the NT, though not typical of the style of Hebrews elsewhere.

The remainder of the quotation is taken from LXX Habakkuk 2:3–4, which differs substantially from the Hebrew in that (1) the Hebrew idiom "coming it will come" (meaning "it will certainly come") has been woodenly translated with the masculine participle "coming," which suggests a personal subject, whereas in the Hebrew what is coming is "the revelation"; (2) LXX has "my faith(fulness)" for "his faith"; (3) the first line of 2:4 is quite different, with the Hebrew "See, he is puffed up [or will fail]; his desires are not upright" becoming in the LXX "if he shrinks back, my soul is not pleased with him." Our author has reproduced the LXX but with three significant changes: (1) he has added a definite article before "coming" so as to make it more clearly personal—"the coming one"; (2) he has reversed the two lines of 2:4 so that the "shrinking back" follows the "faith" and thus becomes a hypothetical action of "the righteous," whereas in the LXX its subject was perhaps the "coming one," though the sequence is unclear; (3) he has attached the LXX "my" to "righteous one" instead of to "faith," leaving it to be understood that the "faith" is (as in the Hebrew) that of the righteous rather than God's "faithfulness." (Paul has no possessive in his two quotations of the text, which allows him to take "by faith" as qualifying "righteous," whereas in both the Hebrew and the LXX it depends on "live.") The resultant text speaks of the imminent arrival of the "coming one" and distinguishes in that light two possible courses to be

taken by "my righteous one": first that of "faith," by which he will live, and second that of "shrinking back," which would forfeit God's favor.

Surprisingly, in view of the considerable freedom exercised by both the LXX and our author, the overall effect remains relatively close to the meaning of the Hebrew text in that in a time of waiting those who are described as "righteous" will endure and survive by their faith(fulness). The added contrast with "shrinking back," which results from our author's manipulation of the order of clauses in the LXX, serves as a negative reinforcement of this message rather than introducing a new point. But the additional idea of the imminent arrival of "the coming one" (unidentified, but we are left to assume it is the returning Jesus of 9:28) reminds the readers also of the note of urgency introduced in v.25, and the added words from Isaiah 26:20 enhance the sense of imminence.

39 The immediate pastoral application of the text (note the "we" again, assuring the readers that despite 10:26–31 the author does not in fact think of them as apostates) simply contrasts the two options the (amended) text from Habakkuk has set out, namely, the ways of "shrinking back" and "faith(fulness)." The former results in "destruction" (as 10:26–31 has explained) but the latter in "possession of life" (lit.; NIV, "are saved"). The first noun in this phrase implies taking possession of that which is rightly one's own (it can also mean "keeping safe"), while the second (translated "soul" in 4:12; 6:19) here emphasizes being truly (spiritually) alive as opposed to "destruction."

It still remains to be explored, however, just what "faith(fulness)" means as a way of life.

NOTES

38 One early manuscript and most later ones omit "my," but this is best understood as an attempt to conform the text both to its OT form and to Paul's quotations of it. It is very unlikely copyists would introduce "my" under the influence of the LXX and yet place it differently in the sentence. (Some LXX manuscripts place it with "righteous one," but this is probably due to the influence of Hebrews.)

3. The Essence of Faith (11:1)

¹Now faith is being sure of what we hope for and certain of what we do not see.

COMMENTARY

1 These famous words are not so much a "definition" of faith as a declaration of the dual perspective from which our author intends to explain how the life of faith commended by Habakkuk 2:4 is to work out in practice. This verse thus gives us a framework within which to read the long series of examples of living by faith that he is now going to draw from the OT.

In the first clause, the NIV phrase "being sure of" represents the noun *hypostasis* (GK *5712*), which we have already met in 1:3 and 3:14, where the NIV respectively translates the word as "being" and "confidence." The note on 1:3 refers to its "more basic meaning of 'real nature, fundamental reality' (as opposed to outward appearance)," and that sense underlies its meaning here: faith is being sure that what is hoped for will in fact take place, that however discouraging present appearances may be, there is a solid reality underlying them—the reality of God's utterly reliable promises. Faith, in other words, relies on what God has said and acts on the basis of this firm hope, even when circumstances are against it.

The second clause could be understood in the same sense, the things "we do not see" being again those promised blessings still in the future. But whereas "what we hope for" is explicitly about the future, "what we do not see" covers the present as well. The author's two balancing clauses are there-fore probably designed to convey two different (though closely related) aspects of faith. "What we do not see" includes also the unseen reality of the presence of God, indeed the whole spiritual dimension of life as opposed to the merely material. Faith takes the invisible world as seriously as the visible and, in particular, reckons on the reality of a God who cannot be proved by merely empirical observation. The NIV's "[being] certain of" again represents a Greek noun, *elenchos*, "proof" or "conviction" (GK *1793*), that belongs especially to the law court. What the eye cannot see, and therefore a materialistic worldview would deny, is in fact "proved" by the experience of faith.

So "faith" has a dual perspective that could be simply summed up as *looking forward* (to the fulfillment of God's promises) and *looking up* (to the unseen reality of God's presence). These twin dimensions enable people of faith to overcome the discouragements and obstacles of the "seen" world and its often hostile circumstances and to press on as the people of God to inherit all that he has prepared for them. As this chapter trawls through some of the more striking examples of men and women of God in the OT, all of them will in their own ways illustrate one or both of these twin qualities—as he will from time to time explicitly point out (see, e.g., vv.6, 7, 10, 11, 13–16, 26, 27). Most of the OT accounts he draws on do not use the actual words "faith" or "believe"; he is not engaged in a word study but in a much broader survey of true men and women of God, whose characteristic attitudes he has chosen to classify under what he calls "faith."

This "faith" by which they overcame all opposition is what the readers need if they too are to fulfill the model of Habakkuk 2:3–4, to stand firm and not to "shrink back."

NOTES

1 Comparable lists of the great and the good occur in various Jewish sources, the most famous being Ben Sira 44–50 ("Let us now praise famous men . . ."). See also 1 Maccabees 2:51–68; Wisdom of Solomon 10 (curiously anonymous throughout); and the historical surveys of Psalms 78 and 136 (without the same focus on individual heroes) and of Acts 7.

The translator must choose between the "objective" and "subjective" senses of ὑπόστασις, *hypostasis*, "substance/reality" ("groundwork," Buchanan), or "confidence/assurance" (GK *5712*), but it is likely the author's choice of this suggestive word had both aspects in mind; see note on 1:3. A legal sense, "title deed" or "guarantee," has also been suggested on the basis of usage in later papyri, but this is not supported by first-century evidence.

4. Examples of Faith: Creation to Abraham (11:2–12)

OVERVIEW

The series of illustrations works through the OT in chronological order, beginning right at the beginning with the work of creation and continuing with selected major figures as far as the entry to the promised land under Joshua (vv.30–31), after which the author finds it necessary to cover the remaining twelve centuries or so in a tightly packed summary (vv.32–38). Within the period covered two figures stand out, Abraham (vv.8–19) and Moses (vv.23–29). Abraham's faith in God's promises has already been singled out for mention in 6:13–15, just as he was for Paul the prototype of saving faith (Ro 4; Gal 3:6–9). For our author, his costly obedience to God's commands provided a particularly telling example of faith in action, and so he not only recalls several aspects of Abraham's experiences but also interrupts his running commentary with a lyrical passage (vv.13–16) in which he draws out the special relationship Abraham

and his family had with God and its promised outcome. That "interlude" provides us with a convenient division for our study of the chapter, though of course there is no break in the flow of the exposition.

In vv.2–12, therefore, we have the first stage of our author's OT survey. It begins with a general summary (v.2) and then works through the early chapters of Genesis, picking out as key figures Abel, Enoch, Noah, Abraham, and Sarah. The surprise in this list is Sarah, whose reaction to God's promise as described in Genesis 18:10–15 does not sound like "faith." As we shall see, v.11 has caused sufficient discomfort to have produced a significant textual variation and an alternative exegetical proposal (represented by the NIV) which keeps Abraham as the subject throughout vv.8–12, but this commentary will argue that, against all the odds, Sarah did find her (admittedly minor) place in the gallery of faith.

Within this first section, two verses do not quite conform to the general pattern of the chapter. Verse 3 is a statement not about an OT character's faith but about our faith as we read the OT; the comments below will discuss how this fits into the author's purpose. Verse 6 is a general summary of the demands of faith arising out of the account of Enoch but not limited to him; it amounts to a reaffirmation, in other words, of the dual perspective set out in v.1.

²This is what the ancients were commended for.

³By faith we understand that the universe was formed at God's command, so that what is seen was not made out of what was visible. ⁴By faith Abel offered God a better sacrifice than Cain did. By faith he was commended as a righteous man, when God spoke well of his offerings. And by faith he still speaks, even though he is dead.

⁵By faith Enoch was taken from this life, so that he did not experience death; he could not be found, because God had taken him away. For before he was taken, he was commended as one who pleased God. ⁶And without faith it is impossible to please God, because anyone who comes to him must believe that he exists and that he rewards those who earnestly seek him.

⁷By faith Noah, when warned about things not yet seen, in holy fear built an ark to save his family. By his faith he condemned the world and became heir of the righteousness that comes by faith.

⁸By faith Abraham, when called to go to a place he would later receive as his inheritance, obeyed and went, even though he did not know where he was going. ⁹By faith he made his home in the promised land like a stranger in a foreign country; he lived in tents, as did Isaac and Jacob, who were heirs with him of the same promise. ¹⁰For he was looking forward to the city with foundations, whose architect and builder is God.

¹¹By faith Abraham, even though he was past age—and Sarah herself was barren—was enabled to become a father because he considered him faithful who had made the promise. ¹²And so from this one man, and he as good as dead, came descendants as numerous as the stars in the sky and as countless as the sand on the seashore.

COMMENTARY

2 "The ancients" translates *hoi presbyteroi* (GK *4565*), which in other contexts would normally be rendered "the elders" (in an ecclesiastical sense) but here must clearly be used in its more original sense of "the older ones." We are embarking on a lesson from ancient history, and from that point of view, all the people in this chapter, even the most recent heroes whose exploits are summarized in vv.32–38, are "ancients." "Were commended" is more literally "were testified to," the reference being to the testimony of Scripture (cf. the same verb in 7:8, 17; 10:15) from which the following accounts of faith will be drawn. The verb *martyreō*, "testify" or "bear witness" (GK *3455*), is prominent in this chapter ("commended," vv.2, 4, 5, 39; "spoke well of," v.4), marking God's approval of these people's faith conveyed to us through Scripture; and as a result they too become *martyres*, "witnesses," in 12:1.

3 "Faith" cannot be found in the normal way in the creation story, since there were no human beings there to exercise it (except Adam and Eve, who are conspicuously and understandably not included in the list!). The opening "by faith" cannot therefore have here the biographical focus it has throughout the rest of the chapter. It might then seem an unnecessary and inconvenient decision to include Genesis 1–2 in the catalogue at all: did the author really have to start at the *very* beginning? But in fact, different as this example must be, it contributes something important to the chapter, a telling example of "being certain of what we do not see." People can look at the created universe and see it as a self-contained reality—many scientists and ordinary people do so today, as they always have. It is only "by faith" that we, guided by the scriptural account, are able to see behind the scenes, to find in the visible world a testimony to "what we do not see," the God who made it. The point is important. When all the philosophical arguments have been rehearsed and refined, it remains in the end a matter of faith. There will always be those who cannot see beyond the surface level, and argument alone will not persuade them. This is the realm of faith.

"What is seen was not made out of what was visible" (or "was made out of what was not visible"— the Greek allows either rendering) makes the point emphatically. Behind the sequence of matter begetting matter there lies a beginning, when the material world was made not out of preexisting matter but by the creative word of the invisible God. "What was visible" translates the Greek word *phainomena*— phenomenology is not the whole story! For "the universe," see note on 1:2.

4 The first human being in the Genesis story who is "commended" is not Adam or Eve (who represent rebellion rather than faith) but Abel (Ge 4:2–8). As the first victim of murder, he would form a suitable model for those who faced the possibility of martyrdom at the hands of their faithless "brothers." The Genesis account does not explain why Abel's animal sacrifice was more acceptable to God than Cain's vegetable offering, but for our author, the fact is enough. His character as a true worshiper of God is demonstrated from the title "righteous" (used of Abel also in Mt 23:25; 1Jn 3:12—and based on God's words in Ge 4:7, which imply that Abel, unlike Cain, did "what is right"), from the fact that God approved his sacrifice (Ge 4:4), and from his continued "speaking" even after his murder. This last point is an inference from Genesis 4:10, where God tells Cain that his dead brother's blood "cries out to me from the ground"; it will be mentioned again at 12:24. From this admittedly limited evidence, our author concludes that what distinguished Abel from Cain was his "faith," a healthy and living relationship with the God whom he worshiped.

5 Among the human ancestors listed before the flood, Enoch stands out as special. The very brief account of him (Ge 5:21–24) includes twice over the statement that he "walked with God," an accolade he shares only with Noah (Ge 6:9). He is also distinguished by the relatively short span of his life (365 years compared with an average of some 900 before the flood), which is explained by the enigmatic phrase "he was not, for God took him," the LXX version of which our author quotes: "He could not be found, because God had taken him away" (TNIV rightly puts these words in quotation marks). In Jewish tradition, this was taken to mean he bypassed death, as did Elijah (2Ki 2:11) and (according to tradition, though not according to Dt 34:5–7) Moses. As one who was taken alive to heaven, Enoch became a significant figure in Jewish thought, and a rich variety of late Jewish apocalyptic material is presented as Enoch's accounts of his visions. (There are three lengthy apocryphal "Books of Enoch," the first of which consists of material probably originating between 200 BC and AD 100.) Our author explains this special privilege of Enoch by the fact that he is twice said to have "pleased God" (the LXX version of "walked with God"). In this case too, therefore, "faith" consists in a close relationship with God that linked earth with heaven in a single continuum.

6 The LXX phrase "pleased God" prompts our author to comment on the essential basis for such a good relationship with God. It is "faith" as described in verse 1: believing that God exists is what we there called "looking up," while believing that he rewards is "looking forward." Without this firm conviction of the reality of God (cf. Hebrews' favored phrase "the living God") and the reliability of his promises, there is no basis for the sort of "walking with God" Enoch enjoyed. That is why Enoch, even though the Genesis account does not mention his "faith," finds his proper place in this chapter. A further call to take God seriously is contained in the rider that God's rewards are for those who "earnestly seek him," where the intensive form of the verb "seek" implies not a passing interest but going right through with it. (The same intensified verb is used in 12:17 for Esau's agonized but unavailing attempt to regain his lost blessing.)

7 From Enoch we turn to the other Genesis character who "walked with God." Noah's building of the ark when there was as yet no sign of a flood was a supreme example of faith triumphing over appearances. He did it not because he could *see* the need but because God told him what was coming. (*Chrēmatizō* [GK *5976*], here translated "warned," is used especially of divine communications to guide God's people; cf. 8:5; Mt 2:12, 22; Lk 2:26; Ac 10:22.) By describing the flood as "things not yet seen," the author again reminds us of faith's grasp on "what we do not see" (v.1). Noah's response to God's apparently bizarre command was one of "holy fear" (the same word as "reverent submission" in 5:7 and "reverence" in 12:28) in that he took God's word more seriously than the

evidence of his eyes. In this he "condemned the world" (REB, "put the whole world in the wrong") in that his faith contrasted with their skepticism; the mockery of Noah by his contemporaries for building a huge boat on dry land, while not mentioned in the Genesis account, became a standard feature in the retelling of the flood story, as did Noah's preaching in vain to them to repent (cf. 2Pe 2:5; *1 Clem.* 7:6; and, e.g., *Sib. Or.* 1:125–199; Josephus, *Ant.* 1.74).

The NIV's phrase "the righteousness that comes by faith" sounds like Paul's language about justification, making Noah, like Abraham after him, a prototype of Christian salvation. But our author's terminology is different, using a phrase Paul never uses and more correctly rendered by TNIV as "the righteousness that is in keeping with faith." Faith is not so much its origin as the context in which it is found. The phrase in itself could then simply mean the righteous behavior of a man of faith (Ge 6:9: Noah was "righteous" and "blameless"). But "became heir of" hardly fits such a meaning and suggests a status resulting from Noah's response to God, namely, justification rather than righteous behavior (cf. Ge 7:1: God "found [Noah] righteous"). The meaning may not then be very far from Paul's, though the terminology is different. Noah believed God and acted on that belief, and as a result he is counted among the "righteous" who, like him, live by faith, as Habakkuk 2:4 requires (see 10:38).

8 The first part of the account of Abraham (Hebrews never mentions his earlier name, Abram) will focus on God's twin promises to him of land (vv.8–10) and of a family (vv.11–12). Like Noah, Abraham acted on the basis of a divine command against all the dictates of human wisdom. His "going out" (from Haran, Ge 12:1–4; the NIV's "go" and "went" lose the significant element of going *out*, which is in the Greek; cf. the Christian's "going out" in 13:11–14) meant leaving security on the basis of a mere word of God; indeed, in the Genesis account even the promise of possession of the land is not given until Abraham arrives there (Ge 12:7). He did not even know his destination, only that God would show it to him (Ge 12:1).

9 The author clearly finds a poignant significance in the concept of Abraham together with Isaac and Jacob (to whom the same promise was made [Ge 26:3; 28:13], hence their description here as his "joint heirs") living in their own promised land as nomadic aliens (as does Stephen, Ac 7:4–5); he will take up the theme of temporary residence (*paroikia*, GK *4229*; cf. 1Pe 1:17; 2:11; the word echoes Abraham's self-description in LXX Ge 23:4) more fully in vv. 13–16. Their very "tents" were a continuing reminder that they were not yet at home. For the time being, heirs though they were, they had the promise without the reality. That is what faith means for our author—to look to the promised future rather than at the unsatisfactory present.

10 For the true nomad, a city is anathema, but our author writes as a city dweller for whom the nomadic life can never be more than a temporary arrangement. The settled life of the city, which Abraham had known in Haran (though Isaac and Jacob never had), was, he assumes, implicit in the promise of the land to which they looked forward. In v. 16 and in 12:22; 13:14, he will repeat the vision of the "city" as the ideal future, as it will be filled out by John in Revelation 21. Modern city dwellers whose chief aim is to escape to the supposed tranquillity of the countryside need to recognize a cultural change here: the city in the Bible represents not noise, violence, and squalor but security, stability, and the good life. The "foundations" speak of its stability in contrast with tents erected on the bare ground and quickly moved again. But the Greek is literally "which has *the* foundations," indicating not just any city but one specially characterized by its foundations (cf. Rev 21:14, 19–20). When our author goes on to speak of God as the "architect and builder" of this city, it is thus

clear that his thought has moved from the nomadic patriarchs and the literal settlement in Canaan to the heavenly city and the "rest" it symbolizes for the continuing people of God; see 4:1–11 for the typology of "rest" in the promised land.

11 These comments will follow TNIV, which has, rightly in my view, placed in the text what in the NIV was given as a footnote (see note below for the textual issue). As we noted above, the inclusion of Sarah within the account of Abraham's faith is a surprise, especially when she is not only listed as an example of "faith" but is said to have "considered him faithful who had made the promise." In Genesis 18:10–15, Sarah hears the promise she will have a son and laughs, not with pleasure, but out of cynicism, and is rebuked for her unbelief. When eventually her son is born, the laughter of unbelief gives way to the laughter of joy, from which Isaac gets his name (Ge 21:6–7), but there has been no indication in the narrative that the change was the result of faith rather than of the undeniable evidence of pregnancy. It is not surprising, therefore, that the verse was found difficult and that variants arose which attributed the faith to Abraham rather than to Sarah. But our author has apparently judged Sarah by her whole experience rather than by the specific incident recorded in Genesis 18:10–15. For a hitherto barren woman of ninety (Ge 17:17) to bear a child was a remarkable instance of God's overruling of circumstances, and the woman at the heart of the story, even if initially unable to believe it, must have been a woman who took God seriously, though at first she had to lean on Abraham's faith rather than her own. Thus, despite her initial unbelief, "even Sarah" (the phrase reveals the author's own awareness of the boldness of his claim) finds herself, along with Moses' mother (v. 23) and Rahab the prostitute (v. 31), representing the women of the OT in our author's gallery, just as in 1 Peter 3:5–6 she stands as a representative godly wife for Christian wives to imitate.

12 The inclusion of Sarah's "faith" was a sort of footnote to the main focus of this passage, namely, the faith of Abraham. If Sarah was old, Abraham was still older (Ge 17:17), though "as good as dead" (cf. Ro 4:19) rather exaggerates the point in view of his subsequent exploits and eventual death seventy-five years later (Ge 25:7)! Unlike Sarah, Abraham believed God's promise from the first (Ge 15:6), and it was to be abundantly fulfilled, as our author reminds his readers by echoing God's subsequent promise to Abraham in Genesis 22:17 (to which he rather prosaically adds the explanatory adjective "uncountable," drawing on the wording of the earlier promise in Ge 15:5).

NOTES

6 For "comes to," see on 7:25, and cf. 4:16; 10:1, 22. The reference is not to an individual act of worship but to that total relationship with God which is the goal of Christian salvation. For an interesting discussion of how this verse may relate to the story of Cain and Abel, see Gordon, 130–31.

7 For the role of faith in Hebrews as compared with Paul, see Lindars, 109–10.

10 Buchanan, 188–89, unnecessarily argues that "the city with the foundations" means the earthly Jerusalem of the future. Hebrews' identification of the heavenly city as Jerusalem (12:22) suggests otherwise.

11 A text such as that represented in the NIV, including the word στεῖρα, *steira*, "barren" (GK 5096), which I will call the "Abraham text," has wide attestation. Reasons for preferring the equally widely attested shorter reading given in the NIV footnote (the "Sarah text") include the following: (1) the apparent conflict with the Genesis account would make the Sarah text an obvious target for emendation; (2) the structuring of the opening of the verse irresistibly points to Sarah as the subject; Abraham is not mentioned; (3) the Abraham text involves reading the phrase "and Sarah herself barren" as a "nominative absolute," an extremely harsh construction in any Greek and quite out of keeping with the sophisticated style of Hebrews, or, alternatively, turning it into the dative, for which there is no textual warrant; (4) there are significant variations in the wording of MSS that support the Abraham text, which look like further attempts to "tidy up" the text. Apart from the issue of conformity with the Genesis account, the main argument ("the one firm argument," according to Bruce, 295, even though he supports the Abraham text) in favor of the Abraham text has been that καταβολὴ σπέρματος, *katabolē spermatos*, which the Sarah text seems to require to mean "to bear children," normally indicates the male part in procreation. But the more literal translation "received power for [or with regard to] the deposition of seed" suggests that the "deposition" is not necessarily what Sarah herself did but rather that she "received power" for her part in the process, namely, that of receiving the "deposited seed." See more fully J. H. Greenlee, "Hebrews 11:11: Sarah's Faith or Abraham's?" *Notes* 4 (1990): 37–42.

5. Summary of the Life of Faith: The Patriarchs (11:13–16)

OVERVIEW

The account of Abraham's faith is interrupted by a more extended meditation on what living by faith meant for him and his family. The nomadic life of the patriarchs between Abraham's migration from

Haran and Jacob's move to Egypt provides a literal illustration of the theme of "not being at home," which in a less literal sense must characterize all God's true people as they pass through this visible world. Its poignancy derives not only from the sense of temporary residence but also from the fact that all this time the very land where they were living had been promised to them by God but was not yet theirs. So the life of faith is one of looking forward, knowing that God has something better in store. The present reality is insecurity and unfulfillment, but the goal is the city (see on v.10), and the "better country" they looked forward to is explicitly interpreted as a "heavenly" one. The imagery resembles again that of ch. 4, where the "rest" of Canaan stands for the ultimate heavenly rest for God's people.

> [13] All these people were still living by faith when they died. They did not receive the things promised; they only saw them and welcomed them from a distance. And they admitted that they were aliens and strangers on earth. [14] People who say such things show that they are looking for a country of their own. [15] If they had been thinking of the country they had left, they would have had opportunity to return. [16] Instead, they were longing for a better country—a heavenly one. Therefore God is not ashamed to be called their God, for he has prepared a city for them.

COMMENTARY

13 "All these people" does not extend back to the beginning of the chapter, since the following comments do not fit the experiences of Abel, Enoch, and Noah, but rather covers those mentioned in vv.8–12, namely, Abraham and Sarah with Isaac and Jacob. Their "dying in faith" is equated with their not yet having received what was promised, because our author understands that faith is in essence forward-looking and so excludes present possession. Verses 39–40 will further develop the essentially forward-looking character of OT faith.

There is a formal tension between the statement that the patriarchs "saw" what was promised and the general emphasis of this chapter on faith's dealing in things "not seen"; but the seeing here is "from a distance" and relates to the eye of faith, not to present experience (like Moses' "seeing the invisible" in v.27). They "saw" that God would fulfill his promises to their descendants, even though they themselves were not to share that experience. It is true that, according to the Genesis account, Abraham began the process of acquiring land in Canaan (Ge 23) and that Isaac and Jacob were able to settle down to the extent of growing crops and becoming respected residents in the region. But there was always a sense of impermanence and insecurity, until at last famine forced them out of Canaan altogether. In contrast with Lot, who settled in the cities of the plain, Abraham, continuing in his tents on the hills (Ge 13), remained a potent image for the character of patriarchal life.

"Aliens [TNIV, foreigners] and strangers on earth" is a recurrent NT view of the Christian situation (cf. 13:14; Php 3:20; 1Pe 1:1, 17; 2:11–12). The latter term (Gk. *parepidēmos*, GK *4215*) denotes a temporary resident, one on the way through to somewhere else. The related concept of the *paroikos* (GK *4230*) supplied the verb for Abraham's settling in Canaan "like a stranger in a foreign country" (v.9). Here, "on earth" could be translated "in the land" (of Canaan) as in v.9, which was of course the literal situation of the patriarchs, but the way the author will go on to expound the idea makes it clear that for him this is a model of the situation of all God's people as "citizens of heaven" on their way home and therefore always "aliens" on earth.

14 "People who say such things" refers initially to the patriarchs, who willingly confessed their "alien" status (Ge 23:4; 28:4; 47:9), but the author is clearly thinking on a broader front of all those who look beyond this world for their true home. "A country of their own" translates Greek *patris*, "homeland" (GK *4258*; or "hometown" as in Mk 6:1; etc.), normally the place where you were born and the place where you really belong and are recognized as family.

15 With the concept of *patris*, the author's thought has moved beyond the literal situation of Abraham and his family, since Abraham himself was born in Ur, while both Isaac and Jacob were born as "aliens" in Canaan. So what *patris* were they aspiring to? The author recognizes the problem by pointing out that the option of returning to Abraham's literal *patris* in Mesopotamia, "the country they had left," remained open to them but had no attraction for them (cf. Ge 24:2–8, where Abraham insists there can be no going back to live in Haran). So he must be thinking of some other sort of *patris*.

16 Here the ambiguity is resolved as the author makes it clear he is not talking about an earthly settlement. What the patriarchs were in fact looking forward to as a matter of history was the eventual possession of Canaan, as God had promised them, not a new location but a new status within it. But they have become for our author models of the Christian pilgrim whose true home is not on earth at all. So "they" (in context the patriarchs but in intention all those whom they represent) are pictured as longing for a "better" (*kreittōn* [GK *3202*], the key word of Hebrews' argument; see Introduction, pp. 32–33) *patris*, a true home beyond this temporary world, and now he states explicitly that what he has in view is "heaven."

So central is the patriarchs' faith to biblical religion that God is willing to be identified as "the God of Abraham, Isaac and Jacob" (cf. Jesus' also being "not ashamed" to acknowledge his people as his brothers and sisters in 2:11). He is thus bound up in their family history, and it follows that their earthly story, which finishes with their still awaiting the fulfillment of his promises, cannot be the end of the matter (cf. Jesus' argument in Mk 12:26–27 for God's continuing involvement with the patriarchs on the basis of the title "the God of Abraham, Isaac and Jacob," concluding that therefore they are still alive with him). Their faith is to be rewarded by a "city" (see on v.10), and the city the author has in mind is here, as in 12:22–24, the heavenly Zion. It is there rather than in the earthly Canaan that they will ultimately be at home—and with them all those who share their faith and their looking forward.

NOTES

13 The opening clause is literally "According to faith all these died." The opening κατὰ πίστιν, *kata pistin* (rather than the regular πίστει, *pistei*, "by faith"), which introduces each new item in the series, shows that this paragraph is not introducing a new subject but reflecting on the preceding verses.

15 When he speaks of an "opportunity to return," the author may well intend his readers to reflect on their own temptation to "go back" from their decision to follow Christ and return to their previous condition.

6. Examples of Faith: Abraham to Jericho (11:17–31)

OVERVIEW

Another "by faith" signals our return to the sequence of OT examples that began in 11:3 and will now continue without further intermission until we reach the point (v.32) where the author decides he must resort to summary rather than continuing to list each case separately. We return to the period of the patriarchs and progress through the Egyptian period to the exodus and the beginning of the Israelite conquest of Canaan, the point at which God's territorial promise to Abraham began to be fulfilled.

Within this period two names naturally stand out—those of Abraham (again) and Moses. The author's return to Abraham (and also briefly to Isaac and Jacob) after his general comment on the faith of the patriarchs may seem unnecessary, but he is concerned not only with a general perspective but also with specific examples of faith in action that his readers can relate to as models. In vv.8–12 we considered in general terms God's promises to Abraham of land and descendants, and vv.13–16 have dwelt on the first of those promises, but in vv.17–19 we are reminded of the single most memorable example of the testing of Abraham's faith, this time in relation to the promise of descendants. Even after that promise had begun to be fulfilled in the birth of Isaac, it was called into question by God's extraordinary command to sacrifice Isaac; even then, Abraham's faith rose to the test.

Isaac, Jacob, and Joseph are dealt with more briefly (vv.20–22), the author selecting just one episode for each. In all three cases, the focus is on their vision of the future, which demonstrates their faith in the fulfillment of God's promises.

Before Moses himself comes on the scene, there is a brief mention of his parents (v.23), whose willingness to defy the immediate threat of Pharaoh's decree testifies to their determination to put God first (thus anticipating their son's defiance of Pharaoh because he gave greater priority to "him who is invisible," v.27). Then Moses' story is summarized (vv.24–28), successive episodes being introduced with the "by faith" formula. This in turn shades into the faith of the people as a whole in the exodus and the conquest of Jericho (vv.29–30), though in each case, no doubt, much depended on the lead given by the faith of Moses and Joshua respectively.

Perhaps the most surprising character to be included in the list (rather than merely in the following summary) is Rahab the prostitute of Jericho (v.31). Though hardly a main character in the OT story, Rahab made a deliberate break with her own people to take the side of the invading Israelites, and her action not only contributed to the fulfillment of God's purpose for his people but also illustrates the openness to God's future despite present appearances (for the conquest had not yet begun) that is the essence of faith.

The emphasis falls throughout, as vv.1 and 6 have led us to expect, on faith as confidence in God's promises (and action deriving from that confidence), even when circumstances point the other way, and as a conviction of the reality of the unseen God that is stronger than the more tangible threat of human opposition. With such faith the readers of the letter will have the inner resources to stand firm in their commitment as Christ's people, even though their present circumstances may seem bleak and the opposition overwhelming.

The story of Abraham and Isaac brings into focus a theme that recurs throughout the chapter: faith even in the face of death. Death is mentioned in vv.4–5, 12–13, 19, 21–22, 28–29, 34–35, 37. Sometimes faith results in escape from what appears to be imminent death, but not always. More important is the fact that faith looks *beyond* death, so that those who, like the patriarchs, "die in faith" (v.13) know that this is not the end and that God's promises are not frustrated by death. The sacrifice of Isaac illustrates this aspect of faith. In that case death was in fact averted, but Abraham's faith was equal even to the prospect of his son's death, because he "reasoned that God could raise the dead" (v.19). Death was apparently at least a potential threat to the readers of the letter (12:4), but their faith must be sufficient to reckon that even death, whether it was to be literally averted or transcended by resurrection, could not thwart the purposes of God.

---

¹⁷By faith Abraham, when God tested him, offered Isaac as a sacrifice. He who had received the promises was about to sacrifice his one and only son, ¹⁸even though God had said to him, "It is through Isaac that your offspring will be reckoned." ¹⁹Abraham reasoned that God could raise the dead, and figuratively speaking, he did receive Isaac back from death.

²⁰By faith Isaac blessed Jacob and Esau in regard to their future.

²¹By faith Jacob, when he was dying, blessed each of Joseph's sons, and worshiped as he leaned on the top of his staff.

²²By faith Joseph, when his end was near, spoke about the exodus of the Israelites from Egypt and gave instructions about his bones.

²³By faith Moses' parents hid him for three months after he was born, because they saw he was no ordinary child, and they were not afraid of the king's edict.

²⁴By faith Moses, when he had grown up, refused to be known as the son of Pharaoh's daughter. ²⁵He chose to be mistreated along with the people of God rather than to enjoy the pleasures of sin for a short time. ²⁶He regarded disgrace for the sake of Christ as of greater value than the treasures of Egypt, because he was looking ahead to his reward. ²⁷By faith he left Egypt, not fearing the king's anger; he persevered because he saw him who is invisible. ²⁸By faith he kept the Passover and the sprinkling of blood, so that the destroyer of the firstborn would not touch the firstborn of Israel.

²⁹By faith the people passed through the Red Sea as on dry land; but when the Egyptians tried to do so, they were drowned.

³⁰By faith the walls of Jericho fell, after the people had marched around them for seven days.

³¹By faith the prostitute Rahab, because she welcomed the spies, was not killed with those who were disobedient.

COMMENTARY

17–18 The sacrifice (or rather near-sacrifice) of Isaac in Genesis 22:1–14 made a deep impression on Jewish thought. In rabbinic theology the focus was often on Isaac's willing self-offering, which came to be regarded as a meritorious act with a vicarious value to provide atonement for Israel as a whole. It is questionable, however, how widespread this *Aqedah* doctrine was by the first century AD, and certainly our author here shows no awareness of it. His interest is only in the faith of Abraham. In Genesis, this story is specifically described as a "test" for Abraham (Ge 22:1), and our author's quotation from LXX Genesis 21:12 underlines the nature and severity of that test, since God's demand appeared to run directly counter to his promise. Abraham already had another son, Ishmael, but it was Isaac, his only son through Sarah, who had been the subject of God's promise and was explicitly designated as the ancestor of what was to become the chosen people. In that sense (rather than in strict biology) he was "his one and only son," a point emphasized in Genesis 22:2. But it is interesting that our author does not use the LXX adjective *agapētos*, "beloved" (GK *28*; perhaps echoed in God's designation of Jesus in Mk 1:11) but rather *monogenēs* (GK *3666*), which is also the special Johannine designation of Jesus as God's "one and only" Son (Jn 1:14, 18; 3:16, 18; 1Jn 4:9). It is tempting to speculate whether our author was aware of this usage and intended to provoke reflection on the parallel between Abraham and God, who also offered his "one and only Son," but he may simply be substituting a closer Greek translation of the Hebrew *yāḥîd*, "unique" (GK 3495), used especially of an only child.

James 2:21–23 also takes this episode as a model of faith, with his distinctive emphasis that it was the deed which demonstrated and "completed" the faith; see on v.31 for James's parallel use also of the story of Rahab. Hebrews 11 thus includes both the specific OT examples cited by James to prove that "faith without works is dead," a view amply supported by our author's survey of faith in action.

19 The Genesis story does not say what Abraham expected to happen after the sacrifice, but our author attributes to him a belief "that God could even raise the dead" (TNIV rightly adds "even"), not perhaps in the sense of a general resurrection but of God's way of dealing with this specific problem. Is there a

hint of such a hope in the remarkable plural of Genesis 22:5, "*we* will come back"? No such resurrection was in fact needed, but the author rather whimsically (NIV, "figuratively speaking"; TNIV, "in a manner of speaking") finds a "resurrection" in the fact that, having given his son up for dead, Abraham was given him back. His point is that for people of faith, even death is no obstacle to the fulfillment of God's purposes—a truth that was to be supremely exemplified when God gave up his own Son to the cross but then raised him from death. For the importance of this perspective in ch. 11 as a whole, see above, pp. 156–57.

20–22 Patriarchal blessings (on the deathbed or in old age) feature prominently in Genesis and provide in these verses a series of examples of faith in that the patriarch in each case looked forward to the future events through which God's promises were to be fulfilled. In the first instance, the author single-mindedly ignores Jacob's trickery, which for us is the most memorable aspect of the story, and focuses only on the blessing that illustrates Isaac's faith. The "blessings" given by Isaac to Jacob and Esau (Ge 27:1–40; 28:1–9) were very different, but the largely negative "blessing" of Esau (see 12:17) serves as a foil to emphasize God's sovereign choice, which despite Esau's greater strength and prior claim would continue the promised line through Jacob.

Jacob in turn blessed his grandsons Ephraim and Manasseh (Ge 48:1–20), again putting the younger before the older, as his father had done for him; faith, in the perception of God's sovereign purpose, again took priority over primogeniture. The author adds the visual image of the aged Jacob leaning on his staff (LXX Ge 47:13; Heb. probably "his bed," though the consonants are the same), which immediately precedes the account of the blessing of Joseph's sons and thus also recalls the earlier occasion when Jacob gave his final instructions to Joseph himself and insisted on being buried back in Canaan.

Finally in the patriarchal period, Joseph, too, looked forward to future events, specifically the exodus (which would restore the Israelites to their promised land after he had brought them for temporary survival into Egypt). He also had a sense of being in an "alien" situation, and like his father (Ge 47:29–31, alluded to in v.21) gave instructions for the eventual burial of his bones in Canaan when at last God's promise to his family would be fulfilled (Ge 50:24–25; for the carrying out of his instructions, see Ex 13:19; Jos 24:32). The forward vision of the patriarchs thus carries us through the centuries of Egyptian exile to the point where the next great hero of faith can take up the story.

It is a mark of our author's single-minded approach that he is able to pass over all Joseph's extraordinary achievements, which modern readers find so appealing, and mention him only in relation to the faith he displayed on his deathbed.

23 The NIV suggests that Moses' parents, like Sarah, have their own "by faith" introduction, but in fact the subject of the Greek sentence is Moses ("By faith Moses, having been born, was hidden for three months by his parents . . ."). But it is, of course, their faith, not his, that is in view here. Without their act of defiance against Pharaoh's policy of "ethnic cleansing," there would have been no Moses to lead the exodus and to be the founder of Israel's national life. Their hiding of Moses is recorded in Exodus 2:1–2, where the only motive given is that he was a "fine child." There is no suggestion in the biblical account that they saw him as the future deliverer, though the NIV has smuggled in such an idea by the phrase "no ordinary child." The Greek term, however, is simply *asteion* (GK *842*), which here, as in LXX Exodus 2:2 from which it is derived, simply means a good-looking child—a reference to parental pride rather than to any prophetic insight. Our author may have been aware of the later Jewish tradition that Moses' parents knew their child

was to be the deliverer (see note), and it may be for this reason that he is prepared to classify them as exemplars of "faith," but his words, drawn directly from the exodus account, do not spell this out.

24–26 The first example we are given of Moses' own faith is his refusal, "when he had grown up" (an echo of LXX Ex 2:11), to benefit from his privileged upbringing (see Ex 2:11–15 for the events that sealed this decision). In this, a more drastic renunciation even than that of Abraham when he left Haran (vv.8–10), he shows the true faith perspective, which puts ultimate realities before present advantage. The ultimate reality in this case is to belong to "the people of God," which the author anachronistically equates in v.26 with belonging to "Christ." The latter term could of course here be translated "the Messiah," but that idea would be equally anachronistic at the time of Moses unless the author is supposing Moses to have a prophetic vision of the future Messiah. He does not say that (though there may be a hint of such an idea in 3:5), and it seems more likely that here, as often, our author sees the OT stories in the light of their typological fulfillment in the NT, so that the two perspectives merge and historical verisimilitude gives way to a sense of the wholeness of the total continuity of the people of God in both the OT and NT (hence, perhaps, his use of "the people of God" in v.25 rather than the more specific "the sons of Israel" used in Ex 2:11; see Ac 7:23 NASB).

What Moses forfeited is described in terms of status (being "known as the son of Pharaoh's daughter"), enjoyment ("the pleasures of sin"), and material affluence ("the treasures of Egypt"). These categories sum up many people's ambitions, but the author is careful to qualify them with negative comments. "The fleeting pleasures of sin" (TNIV) speaks both of their transience and of their incompatibility with living as the people of God, while the treasures of Egypt are outweighed by a "greater wealth" (lit.; NIV, "of greater value"). With sharp paradox he describes this "greater wealth" as "being mistreated along with the people of God" and as (lit.) "the reproach of Christ" (lit.; cf. 13:13 for the same idea applied directly to the readers), the social stigma of belonging to an unpopular minority movement. By casting in his lot with the oppressed slave nation of Israel, Moses ensured himself a hard life and the loss of worldly status and security, but he knew that in God's purpose he was choosing the winning side— he was "looking ahead to his reward." (For the theme of "reward" in Hebrews, cf. 10:35; 11:6.) In all this, then, Moses splendidly illustrates the faith that is so "sure of what we hope for" (v.1) that it can endure present deprivation and suffering.

27 If vv.24–26 illustrate one of the twin perspectives of faith set out in v.1 ("being sure of what we hope for"), this verse illustrates the other, "being certain of what we do not see." Moses' "leaving Egypt" might refer to his escape to Midian when Pharaoh wanted to kill him (Ex 2:15), but in that passage, unlike here, Moses is explicitly said to have acted in fear (2:14), and in view of the sequel, it seems more natural to take it of the more famous "leaving" in the exodus against Pharaoh's determined opposition; v.28 then narrows the focus to the climactic event that precipitated this "leaving." What was only too visible to Moses as he negotiated for the liberation of the Israelites was "the king's anger," but he also "saw" (with the same sort of sight by which the patriarchs could transcend their current circumstances, v.13) the invisible God; the Greek *hōs*, "as," not represented in the NIV, acknowledges the metaphorical nature of the "seeing." The exodus, and with it the whole future of God's people, depended on his willingness to give priority to the invisible over the visible and so, like his parents, to defy the displeasure of the most powerful man on earth.

28 The climax of Moses' defiance of Pharaoh was reached in the killing of the Egyptian firstborn. To announce such a drastic miraculous intervention (Ex

11:4–8) required strong faith, but our author focuses not on the killing itself but on the action God commanded of Moses so that Israel might be exempted from the slaughter (Ex 12:1–13). To kill lambs and smear their blood on Israelite doorposts (the NIV's "sprinkling" does not easily describe the action of "painting" the blood around the door with a stem of hyssop [Ex 12:22]; TNIV has changed it to "application") would seem from a human perspective no more sensible than Noah's building of a boat on dry land, but Moses was prepared to take God at his word.

29 The parting of the Red Sea (the LXX term for what in Hebrew is the Sea of Reeds) was another equally implausible command from God, to which Moses' faith was also equal. While the subject of this sentence is not Moses but all the people who went through the sea (since the action was taken by them all), the faith is again primarily that of Moses. Indeed, the exodus account (Ex 14:9–31) contrasts his confidence in God's power with the panic of the people (vv.10–14), though after the event they came to share his faith (v.31). The Israelites shared vicariously in the deliverance that resulted from Moses' faith, but the Egyptians had no such faith to rely on, and the sea closed back over them, again because Moses obeyed God's command (Ex 14:26–27). Faith, it seems, is not only a blessing to those who have it but also a danger to those who do not.

30 The forty years in the wilderness have already been commented on in 3:7–4:13 and are conspicuously not an example of faith. Instead we move on to the end of that period and the entry into the promised land, and to a third equally implausible event: the command to march around the walls of Jericho for seven days blowing trumpets (Jos 6:1–5). This time there is no personal subject in the sentence, and Joshua, the key figure in the story, remains surprisingly unnamed (while even so minor a character as Rahab finds her place in the list). Is the author reluctant to use the Greek name, which might invite confusion with his greater namesake (see on 4:8)? But it was Joshua's unquestioning obedience to a bizarre command from God, like that of Moses by the Red Sea, that led to the miraculous fall of the walls of Jericho. This time the biblical account does not drive a wedge between leader and people, and we are left to assume that all the Israelites shared Joshua's confidence in God's power—though experience of human nature might suggest the historical reality was otherwise!

31 The final example in the list is set in the same historical context of the fall of Jericho but with the focus now on one humble individual (the mention of her trade emphasizes her ordinariness), and she not even an Israelite. Rahab the Canaanite prostitute joins Sarah (v.11) and Moses' mother (v.23) as the only women in the roll call of faith. Her faith was shown by her unpatriotic willingness to protect the Israelite scouts (Jos 2:1–21) because she recognized the superior power of their God as "God in heaven above and on the earth below" (Jos 2:9–11) and was rewarded by the preservation of herself and her household (Jos 6:22–25). By contrast the other inhabitants of Jericho were "unbelieving" (see note). James 2:25 uses Rahab's action as an example of the "works" that result from true faith (see on vv. 17–18).

NOTES

17 The NIV's "was about to sacrifice" represents the Greek imperfect tense "was sacrificing," which can have the sense of setting out to do what was not in fact completed. The tenses carefully reflect the OT story in which Abraham "offered" his son (perfect tense of the same verb) but was not allowed to go through with the sacrifice.

19 The Greek phrase ἐν παραβολῇ, *en parabolē*, "figuratively speaking" (GK *4130*), may be intended to convey not just that the language is nonliteral but more specifically that the author is thinking typologically (cf. his use of παραβολή, *parabolē*, in 9:9) of Isaac's binding for sacrifice and restoration as pointing forward to the crucifixion and resurrection of Christ—a typological link that the NT does not develop but that was exploited in early Christian writing.

23 Josephus (*Ant.* 2.205–6; 215–16) tells of a revelation of the birth of the deliverer to Pharaoh (cf. *Tg. Ps.-J.* Ex 1:15) and adds a specific revelation to Amram that it was to be his child. Note, however, that Philo (*Moses* 1.8–11) and *Jubilees* 47:1–4 show no knowledge of such a tradition. In Pseduo-Philo 9:10 a similar revelation is given to Moses' older sister Miriam, but her parents refuse to believe her. Clearly the details of the popular expansion of the story were still evolving in the first century.

26 "The reproach of Christ" is often taken to be an echo of LXX Psalm 89:51, where the psalmist tells how the other nations "mock your anointed one [Israel]," but it is unlikely our author could expect his readers to understand the familiar name "Christ" in this corporate sense, particularly as he will again use the phrase "his [Christ's] reproach" in 13:13.

"Looking ahead" translates ἀποβλέπω, *apoblepō*, literally, "look away" (GK *611*); cf. 12:2 where the readers are exhorted to "look away" to Jesus (ἀφοράω, *aphoraō* [GK *927*], a related verb), a metaphor that equally suggests setting this world's experiences in a wider perspective.

27 Some have taken Moses' "seeing the invisible" as a reference to the burning bush (Ex 3:1–6), where Moses saw the bush but not the God who spoke from it. But the argument does not require such a specific allusion.

28 "Kept" (lit., "did") is in the perfect tense, perhaps to indicate an act that was the precursor to what has since continued as an annual reenactment. "The destroyer" echoes LXX Exodus 12:23. The passage as a whole speaks of God himself as killing the firstborn (Ex 12:12–13, 23a, 27, 29), but in v.23b God will restrain "the destroyer," perhaps envisaged as an angelic agent, as in 2 Samuel 24:16–17 and 2 Kings 19:35.

31 "Unbelieving" (NIV footnote) is perhaps a more likely rendering of ἀπειθέω, *apitheō* (GK 578), than "disobedient" in this context, where it describes the Canaanites who did not share Rahab's "religious conversion"; when the same verb is used in 3:18, the following verse identifies it with unbelief.

7. Examples of Faith: Summary of Later Periods (11:32–38)

OVERVIEW

We have reached the period of the conquest of Canaan. The remaining stretch of OT and later Jewish history down to the author's day—some 1,300 years—is covered not with individual examples introduced by the "by faith" formula but by a summary containing first a list of six names (which still take us only down to about 1000 BC), together with the more general phrase "the prophets," and then a succession of cameos of what faith achieved or endured, without specific attribution to named individuals. Some of these are expressed so generally that they could apply to many of the known figures of the OT, while others are so specific that there is little doubt whom the author had in mind. These cameos fall roughly into two groups; the first set (vv.33–35a) are what one might call success stories, the great exploits and deliverances of faith, while the rest (vv.35b–38) list the sufferings endured by people of faith, with no indication they were rescued from them in this world and indeed with a focus on martyrdom, though with the prospect for them all of a "better resurrection" (v.35b). These who appear as losers in the world's eyes are thus ultimately winners with God, and their pilgrim orientation is memorably summed up in the verdict "the world was not worthy of them" (v.38).

The author's decision to resort to summary at this point is no doubt mainly because, as he suggests (v.32), to continue through a further thousand or more years at the same level of detail would become tedious. But his OT survey accelerates toward its end perhaps also because he has now covered the period that interested him most—the period of the patriarchs, exodus, and conquest, with its recurrent focus on God's promises to Abraham and his descendants and the ways in which they at least began to be fulfilled. Once Israel became a settled people in their promised land, the pilgrim life which for our author so powerfully summarizes what it means to live by faith would no longer apply to them in the same way. Faith remained the key, but it would be exercised and exemplified in a much wider variety of ways, which the summary treatment of these verses appropriately captures.

The summary continues to draw its material from the OT narratives, including the stories of Maccabean times (which being in the LXX were part of the author's OT), though it is quite possible that some unidentified items in the list also relate to figures beyond the OT period proper, just as some of the data concerning OT figures is drawn from post-biblical traditions (see on v.37).

³²And what more shall I say? I do not have time to tell about Gideon, Barak, Samson, Jephthah, David, Samuel and the prophets, ³³who through faith conquered kingdoms, administered justice, and gained what was promised; who shut the mouths of lions, ³⁴quenched the fury of the flames, and escaped the edge of the sword; whose weakness was turned to strength; and who became powerful in battle and routed foreign armies. ³⁵Women received back their dead, raised to life again. Others were tortured and refused to be released, so that they might gain a better resurrection. ³⁶Some faced jeers and flogging, while still others were chained and put in prison. ³⁷They were stoned; they were sawed in two; they were put to death by the sword. They went about in sheepskins and goatskins, destitute, persecuted and mistreated—³⁸the world was not worthy of them. They wandered in deserts and mountains, and in caves and holes in the ground.

COMMENTARY

32 The author's shortage of "time" (a standard rhetorical comment) perhaps suggests an oral delivery of this material, though the expression would not be out of place for a writer who fears a longer list will place unacceptable demands both on his own time for composition and on the reader's patience.

The six names only begin the process of summarizing the later periods and do not include several of those whose stories are clearly alluded to in the following verses. The first four names are the four judges whose stories are told at greatest length (not "a random sampling," so Lane, 383) in the period following the entry into Canaan, all of them involved in the struggle to establish Israel's foothold among the hostile peoples of the area (though the most prominent woman, Deborah, is surprisingly not mentioned alongside or instead of Barak, whose mentor she was). Then comes Samuel, the transitional figure from the judges to the monarchy, and his protégé David, the greatest (if not quite the first) of the kings. The order in which the names are listed is curious: three

chronologically successive pairs appear, but with the order reversed within each pair. Perhaps the author deliberately grouped them in pairs but then in each case put the better-known name before the lesser-known. The position of Samuel at the end allows a smooth transition to "the prophets" who succeeded him.

"The prophets" then broadly indicates the centuries that followed and thus opens the door for many more people to be included anonymously, even though not all the people whose exploits are alluded to in the following verses were recognized as prophets.

33 "Through faith" (a different formulation both from the "by faith" formula and from the "according to faith" of v.13) stands at the head of the series of cameos to cover them all. "Conquered kingdoms" would apply to several of those listed in v.32 but most conspicuously to David, whose conquests established the greatest extent that Israel's empire ever reached (2Sa 8). "Administered justice" perhaps refers to Solomon, though the earlier judges, especially Samuel, and David were also remembered for this. "Gained what was promised" perhaps refers (in light of the emphasis earlier in the chapter on God's promise to Abraham of the land of Canaan) especially to the judges and later kings who consolidated Joshua's conquest of the promised land. But with "shut the mouths of lions" we jump forward many centuries to Daniel in the Persian court (Da 6:22).

34 "Quenched the fury of the flames" keeps us in the same period, with the ordeal of Shadrach, Meshach, and Abednego (Da 3:21–27), but all the remaining clauses in this verse are too general to allow any specific identification with confidence. Any reader with a good knowledge of the OT would be able to recall suitable stories of Israel's great military heroes from the judges to the Maccabees to fit these descriptions. "Whose weakness was turned to strength" would well describe the story of the reluctant hero Gideon (Jdg 6:11–7:25) and possibly also that of Samson's final victory in Gaza (Jdg 16:21–30).

35a The final item in the series of "success story" cameos is a little different. Here the earlier reference to "the prophets" is directly relevant, as we recall how both Elijah and Elisha restored to life the son of a female supporter (1Ki 17:17–24; 2Ki 4:18–37). By making the women (rather than the prophets) the subject of the sentence, the author emphasizes that there was faith on both sides, even though it is only after the event that the first woman declares her faith (1Ki 17:24); the second showed her faith by her determination to enlist the help of the man of God (2Ki 4:21–22, 30). For the recurrent theme of faith in the face of death, see pp. 156–57; here a specific mention of "resurrection" (cf. v.19) reinforces the connection, even though in these cases what was involved was resuscitation to life on earth rather than "resurrection" in the sense of life beyond this world. But in the second half of this verse that "better resurrection" will indeed be envisaged.

35b So far we have been reminded of stories of earthly achievement and earthly survival in the face of death. But now a different perspective takes over—that of the people of faith who were not vindicated in this life and for whom faith did not mean they escaped suffering and death. In vv.36–38 their tribulations and martyrdoms will be listed without further comment on what might lie beyond, but in the first of these cameos here in v.35b, we have a key statement which illuminates all that follows. The specific reference is most probably to the famous story in 2 Maccabees 7 of the seven brothers and their mother commanded by Antiochus Epiphanes to eat pork as the condition for "being released" and their heroic refusal, which resulted in death through gruesome tortures graphically described. Their clear conviction of a resurrection to everlasting life is repeatedly expressed in the chapter (2 Macc 7:9, 11, 14, 29, 36). The resurrection they expected was "better" than mere resuscitation, as in v.35a, but, more important, "better" than all the sufferings and inducements that could be offered by God's enemies. Their explicit conviction thus forms a suitable introduction to the list of other oppressed and martyred people of God who, even though their stories may not include so explicit a confession of faith, may be assumed to have been sustained by the same conviction that God does not ultimately let his people down.

36–37a These verses recall especially the stories of OT prophets, several of whom found themselves in trouble for speaking God's word faithfully. The terms used in v.36 echo the experiences of Jeremiah (Jer 20:2, 7; 37:15; etc.). Second Chronicles 24:21 tells of the prophet Zechariah's being "stoned" to death, and Jewish tradition ascribed the same fate to Jeremiah (*Liv. Pro.* 2:1). According to tradition, Isaiah was executed by King Manasseh by being "sawn in two" (*Ascen. Isa.* 5). Uriah was "put to death by the sword" (Jer 26:23), as were numerous prophets in the time of Elijah (1Ki 19:10).

37b–38 Whereas the preceding clauses concerned persecution and especially martyrdom, the concluding series deals with the material conditions in which some of the people of God have had to live their lives. Persecution is again mentioned, but the focus is on material deprivation. It is hard, and probably unnecessary, to recognize specific allusions to OT characters here. Elijah was noted for his "garment of hair" (2Ki 1:8) and at least once slept in a cave (1Ki 19:9), though neither OT account suggests special deprivation—a cave was better than the open air. First Kings 18:4 talks of the hundred prophets who had to hide in caves to avoid Jezebel's purge. The terms used also recall the experiences of the freedom fighters in Maccabean times who had to resort to a rough life in the mountains (1 Macc 2:29–31; 2 Macc 5:27; 10:6). But these clauses speak rather in more general terms of the situation of the faithful, who find no security and comfort on earth and, like the patriarchs, look forward to the end of their pilgrimage.

The poignant aside "the world was not worthy of them" sums up much of the perspective of this chapter, in which people of faith have been seen at odds with "the world." The word *kosmos* (GK *3180*) has been used a few times in this letter of the created world in a neutral sense (4:3; 9:26; 10:5), but in v.7 it denoted the sinful human "world" that was destroyed when Noah's faith kept him safe, and here again it carries something like the Johannine sense of people in general seen as standing over against God and his people. Our author's expression is heavily ironical: the world saw such people as misfits, and so they were, but not because of *their* "unworthiness" but rather that of the world itself, which is no fit place for God's people, even though it must be the place of their pilgrimage toward heaven. To readers who felt themselves uncomfortably ostracized by "the world," this revised perspective is important.

NOTES

32 "To tell" translates the masculine participle διηγούμενον, *diēgoumenon*. Those who argue for a female author for Hebrews must assume either that she deliberately concealed her sex or that an originally feminine participle was subsequently altered (for which there is no evidence).

34 The word for "armies" often still has its original sense of "camps" and may especially recall Gideon's famous rout of the Midianite camp in Judges 7.

35 "Tortured" is literally "put on the rack," which was the actual form of execution endured by Eleazar, whose story precedes that of the seven brothers (2 Macc 6:19, 28). He is probably also in mind here, though in his case there is no explicit hope of resurrection.

36 See Ellingworth, 629–30, for suggestions for identifying these experiences, as with those of v.35b, in the Maccabean period.

37 Many MSS add "were tested" before or after "were sawn in two." The verbs look similar, and the addition could be accidental, but "were tested" could well be a deliberate substitute for the unusual and shocking verb "to saw" applied to a person. "Were tested" would be oddly out of place in the middle of a list of violent forms of death.

8. The Privilege of the Christian (11:39–40)

³⁹These were all commended for their faith, yet none of them received what had been promised. ⁴⁰God had planned something better for us so that only together with us would they be made perfect.

COMMENTARY

39–40 This general comment looks back over the whole list of heroes of faith and puts them all, even men of the stature of Abraham and Moses, into perspective within the whole scope of God's plan of salvation. None of them had reached the ultimate goal to which they were looking forward, whether consciously or not. They may have received the fulfillment of many "promises" (see vv.11–12, 17, 33; 6:15) and seen God's power spectacularly at work in their behalf, but there still remained "the promise" (singular; NIV, "what had been promised"), which for our author denotes something beyond all these temporary blessings: the ultimate fulfillment of God's purpose for his people. So he now generalizes the point he made in v.13 about the patriarchs, their awareness of something "better" still in the future, and applies it to all who lived as the people of God during the time of the old covenant. Their faith, exemplary as it was, could not yet be fully rewarded until "these last days" (1:2), when all the shadows of the old dispensation were to give way to the full light of the gospel of God's Son.

40 It is only with "us" (emphatically repeated in v.40) that God's purpose has reached its ultimate goal. The author and his readers represent the generation of fulfillment, the final piece of the jigsaw. Even the giants of OT faith, Abraham and Moses, stand on a lower level, not in terms of their personal qualities or their status as the people of God,

but in terms of the situation within which their faith had to flourish. For them the best was yet to be; for us it is already here. That is why in their own lifetime they could never be "made perfect" (see Introduction, p. 32, and comments at 2:10; 5:14); there was always more to come. It is only now that God has sent his Son so that they and we can enjoy the fullness of salvation (cf. 7:11, 19; 9:9; 10:1, 14 for the inability of the old system to deliver "perfection").

This theological perspective on God's plan of salvation has important implications for our understanding of the relationship between the OT and the NT and the issue of the status of those who lived before the time of Christ but are now joined "together with us" in the enjoyment of God's "perfect" salvation. It also has obvious pastoral implications for the readers. If all the great men and women of this chapter could provide such shining examples of faith in action, even though they lived in the time of unfulfillment, how much more should those who have now experienced the culmination of God's saving purpose stand firm as his people. Not only have they witnessed the coming of "something better," but they have now in their great high priest a helper beyond any the OT saints could know. Verses 1–3 of chapter 12, therefore, go on to drive home this moral imperative for those who, unlike Abraham, Moses, and the rest, can now "fix their eyes on Jesus." The function of these verses is thus not only to round off the story of faith in the OT period but equally to lead into the final item in the list, in which at last the hopes that sustained the OT saints find their fulfillment.

9. The Supreme Example of Faith: Jesus (12:1–3)

OVERVIEW

The last two verses of ch. 11 have moved the spotlight from the historical figures who have filled that chapter to the readers ("us"), whose turn it now is to take their place in the continuing "race" of faith. But they do not run alone, for the stands are filled with a great "cloud of witnesses"—the heroes of ch. 11, who, their own race having finished, now stand to cheer on those who have taken their place and to encourage them with their own hard-won perspective of faith: "It's all worthwhile." And more than that, they have before them a more recent and even more illustrious example of the faith that defies circumstances and wins—that of Jesus himself. With such a model

before them, they have every incentive to press on in faith and not to "grow weary and lose heart." Moreover, Jesus is not only an example. As they "fix their eyes" on him, they will find him also to be the "perfecter" of their faith—"perfect" in the same sense of bringing to maturity and fulfillment we have found so prominently throughout the letter. The perceived inadequacy of their faith is to be corrected not only by the example of Jesus but also by his power at work within them. In these three verses, then, we have not only a stirring climax to the great panorama of faith in action but also a concise guide to the successful completion of the Christian "race."

¹Therefore, since we are surrounded by such a great cloud of witnesses, let us throw off everything that hinders and the sin that so easily entangles, and let us run with perseverance the race marked out for us. ²Let us fix our eyes on Jesus, the author and perfecter of our faith, who for the joy set before him endured the cross, scorning its shame, and sat down at the right hand of the throne of God. ³Consider him who endured such opposition from sinful men, so that you will not grow weary and lose heart.

COMMENTARY

1 The intimate connection of these verses with ch. 11 appears in the unusually emphatic "therefore" (*toigaroun*) that opens this verse. It is immediately followed by *kai hēmeis*, "we too"; "we" are not only part of the same race but also, as 11:39–40 has explained, the culmination of it, so that all the previous runners are looking to "us" to finish off what

they have begun so well. The striking visual metaphor of a "cloud" (*nephos*) of witnesses ("fig. of a compact, numberless throng" [BDAG, 670]) surrounding the runners further emphasizes the solidarity of the Christian with God's faithful people through the ages. They are "witnesses" (*martyres*) because their lives (and in some cases their deaths) witnessed to the unconquerable faith in God for which they were "commended" (11:2, 4, 5, 39—the verb is *martyreō*, GK *3455*), but they are also, as those who trusted God and whose faith has been vindicated, witnesses to the reliability of God's promises. Moreover, the presence of these "witnesses" (the secondary sense "spectators," while not the main point, fits the metaphor well) means that to fail to complete the race would be not just a personal disappointment but a public disgrace.

The NT contains several references to the Christian life under the metaphor of an athletic contest (notably 1Co 9:24–27; Gal 2:2; 5:7; 1Ti 6:12; 2Ti 4:7; in this letter already in 10:32); here it is specifically a long-distance footrace for which they are entered. Such a race, run in a very public arena, requires not only maximum concentration but also the removal of all that could reduce performance, pictured in terms of the athletic metaphor as "weights" (NIV, "everything that hinders"; the word could cover excess bodily weight as well as things carried or worn), but then also specified nonmetaphorically as entangling "sin" (in general, not just specific sins). The author coins a graphic term that probably means "easily ensnaring or obstructing," picturing something, perhaps a flowing garment, that clings around the runners' legs. Instead, the runners need "perseverance," the determination to keep going even when it hurts. In 10:32, the author has commended them for this quality in the past and in 10:36 has singled it out as the essential basis for their continuing as God's faithful people in the difficult situation they now face.

2 As we noted at 11:26, where a similar verb was used of Moses, "fix our eyes on" is more literally "look away to." It thus denotes both the deliberate ignoring of present circumstances and a reference point beyond them, in the person of Jesus, perhaps envisaged as standing at the finishing line. At 2:10 we considered the range of possible meanings of

archēgos (GK *793*) as both "originator" and "leader" or "pioneer." Both senses would be appropriate here—"pioneer" in that he has run the race before us (cf. "forerunner," 6:20), as the last and greatest example of faith in action, but also "author" in that it is from him that faith (the Greek does not specify "our" faith, though this would be included in the sense) derives, just as it is in him that it will be completed ("perfecter"; notice the contrast with the "uncompleted" faith of the OT heroes, 11:40). While the focus of these verses is on Jesus as the supreme example of faith in action, he is also much more. Our faith begins and ends in him, and his seat of authority at God's right hand assures us he will not let us down.

The story of Jesus closely matches the pattern of faith established in ch. 11. His earthly experience was of suffering and death ("a cross"; there is no article in the Greek), and of ostracism from human society ("shame"), but he was willing to "endure" all this (the same word as in 10:32, 36; 12:1, "persevere") because he could see beyond it to the future "joy." As a result, he now enjoys the fulfillment of God's promises in that he is seated "at the right hand of the throne of God" (cf. 1:3, 13; 8:1; 10:12), his victory won and his eternal authority secure. Here writ large is the perspective of faith, which is "sure of what we hope for" (11:1), however improbable it may seem in light of present circumstances.

3 By taking Jesus as their model ("consider" translates *analogizomai*, GK *382*, from which we get "analogy"), the readers can also find the strength to "endure" (or persevere, the same verb as in v.2) the "opposition of sinners." (TNIV has rightly removed the NIV's "men"; the Greek is not gender-specific.) Their "sin" is seen not so much in wrong acts as in their rejection of God and his people (cf. "the world" in 11:38).

With such a model before them, the readers must not allow themselves to be discouraged by their adverse circumstances. The language of weariness and fainting (the same verb is used for those who do not have the stamina for a journey, Mk 8:3) recalls again the athletic metaphor and prepares us for the following exposition of Proverbs 3:1–12, which calls on the reader not to "faint" (the same verb, v.5) under the experience of suffering. Verses 12–13 will conclude this exposition with a more graphic image to the same effect, picking up again the metaphor of the long-distance race.

NOTES

1 The "entangling sin" may be intended not so much to specify what is meant by "weight" as rather to add a further encumbrance, so that the "weights" would then be things that are not in themselves sinful but that get in the way of effective discipleship. Lane, 398–99, argues in favor of a reading found in one ancient MS which has "easily distracting" instead of the unique word "easily entangling," but most commentators think it more likely the rarity of the latter word caused the former to be substituted.

2 Buchanan suggests an alternative translation: "having despised the cross of shame, endured [it]." The Greek would allow this, but the resultant meaning is not significantly different. The phrase "for the joy set before him" might also be translated "in place of the joy that was open to him" (REB meaning; so also Lane), indicating what he gave up in order to go to the cross, but it is not obvious what this forfeited "joy" might be, and most interpreters find the NIV interpretation more appropriate in context.

3 "Opposition" is ἀντιλογία, *antilogia* (GK 517), which was translated "argument" in 6:16 and "doubt" in 7:7. It focuses not so much on physical abuse as on an attitude of hostility and rejection. The NIV omits a phrase meaning "against himself," which would underline this sense of hostility; but the text is disputed, many earlier MSS reading "against themselves," which is not easy to make sense of in context. (Montefiore and Ellingworth suggest "sinners against themselves" could be an echo of the description of Korah and his associates in Nu 16:38 [LXX 17:3]; Lane, 400, 416–17, rejects the OT allusion and suggests instead an analogy with 6:6, "crucifying the Son of God *to their loss*.")

D. A Christian View of Suffering (12:4–13)

OVERVIEW

As usual in Hebrews, our paragraph break marks not so much a change of subject as a further development of the argument. A prime cause for the readers' tendency to "shrink back" (10:35–39) rather than to persevere in the faith that 11:1–12:3 has called for is their experience of suffering (10:32–34), and the author now turns directly to this subject in order to offer a theological perspective on what it means to suffer as a follower of Jesus. His argument is based on a new text from the OT, Proverbs 3:11–12, which now takes over from Habakkuk 2:3–4 as the basis of his exposition.

The subject is one of perennial importance in Christian apologetics and pastoral care. A definitive and universal answer to "the problem of suffering" is something every Christian pastor would dearly love to discover. In these verses are some important ingredients for any answer, but it would be a dangerous mistake to take the author's "educative" understanding of suffering as solving all pastoral problems. There are many examples of suffering in which it is impossible to discern any educative value, and the suggestion that God deliberately wills all suffering in order to educate his people would be grossly insensitive. It is important, therefore, to recognize the limitations of this discussion if we are not to turn it into a mere Pollyanna platitude. First, the author is speaking only of the suffering of those who are God's "children" in a covenantal relationship, not of suffering in general, whether through natural disaster, illness, or human causation. Second, he is addressing specifically the situation of his readers (as already outlined in 10:32–34) and calling them to a pastorally healthy response to those experiences, not offering a philosophical explanation of the problem of evil. Here, then, are some expository thoughts on the problem of Christian suffering that may help the believer locate his or her experiences within the loving purpose of God rather than a blanket "solution" to why bad things happen in God's world.

At the heart of this paragraph is the understanding of God as "Father." The book of Proverbs reflects a culture that took for granted the father's disciplinary role. Its frequent references to "the rod" are not popular in our society, which has adopted a different understanding of the educational process and in which the relationship of parents with their children is often far from the authority and respect this discussion is able to presuppose. Here, even more than in other NT language about God as Father, it is important not to read our cultural experiences and expectations into the biblical imagery but rather to start from the biblical understanding of the authoritative discipline that was the unquestioned role of a loving and responsible father.

Another feature, both of the Proverbs text and of our author's discussion of it, that is alien to much modern thought is the assumption that suffering comes directly from God's hand. Biblical writers tend to ignore second causes. Their robust sense of God's sovereignty leads them to speak of God himself as imposing discipline, where we might be more comfortable speaking of human or natural agencies that operate under a general divine providence. This biblical perspective gives a sharper focus to the parent-child relationship in the light of which our author understands the experience of suffering.

⁴In your struggle against sin, you have not yet resisted to the point of shedding your blood. ⁵And you have forgotten that word of encouragement that addresses you as sons:

"My son, do not make light of the Lord's discipline,
    and do not lose heart when he rebukes you,
⁶because the Lord disciplines those he loves,
    and he punishes everyone he accepts as a son."

⁷Endure hardship as discipline; God is treating you as sons. For what son is not disciplined by his father? ⁸If you are not disciplined (and everyone undergoes discipline), then you are illegitimate children and not true sons. ⁹Moreover, we have all had human fathers who disciplined us and we respected them for it. How much more should we submit to the Father of our spirits and live! ¹⁰Our fathers disciplined us for a little while as they thought best; but God disciplines us for our good, that we may share in his holiness.

> [11]No discipline seems pleasant at the time, but painful. Later on, however, it produces a harvest of righteousness and peace for those who have been trained by it.
>
> [12]Therefore, strengthen your feeble arms and weak knees. [13]"Make level paths for your feet," so that the lame may not be disabled, but rather healed.

COMMENTARY

4 This verse establishes the readers' situation as the basis for the exhortation that will follow. Their suffering is characterized as a "struggle against sin" (using the athletic metaphor again but now with the focus more on wrestling or boxing than on running), which picks up the memory of the "opposition of sinners" that Jesus endured (v.3). The author is thus probably referring here not so much to the "entangling sin" that impedes their Christian race (v.1) but to the more active hostility that they, as God's people, have endured from those outside the Christian circle (10:32–34). Their struggle, unlike that of Jesus, has been "not yet as far as blood" (lit.), as was the case for many of the heroes of ch. 11; perhaps this implies that other Christians have already suffered the martyrdom which so far has not come to them, a situation that would fit well if the letter was written to Rome in the mid-sixties (see Introduction, pp. 22–23).

5–6 TNIV repunctuates these verses as a question: "And have you completely forgotten this word . . . ?" The syntax could be read either way (and Greek manuscripts had no punctuation marks), but the gently scolding interrogative perhaps better suits the stronger form of the verb "forget" chosen by the author. It is typical of our author that the words of Proverbs 3:11–12, in which the OT author addresses his own son, are taken as an exhortation addressed directly to the readers as God's children (just as this letter is itself an "exhortation," the same word, 13:22), though this time it is Scripture itself rather than God or the Spirit that is understood to be speaking.

The quotation as usual follows the LXX, which by adding the verb "punishes" (TNIV "chastens"; lit., "flogs") in the last line has sharpened and made more unambiguously physical the nature of the parental "discipline." There are two opposite but equally wrong ways to respond to discipline: to "make light of" it by refusing to learn from it, or to be so oppressed by it as to "lose heart." The LXX verb "lose heart" or "faint" picks up the language of v.3 and so focuses the readers' attention on how these words fit their own situation. But the key word for our author's purpose is "discipline" (Gk. *paideia*, GK 4082), which will be repeated six times in vv.7–11 as the text is expounded. It is the normal Greek term for education or upbringing, but, like its Hebrew counterpart *mûsār* (GK 4592), it denotes much more than a merely intellectual process. It is instruction for living, as much concerned with morality and resolve as with mental stimulation and information. And in the process of turning a child into a responsible adult, the ancient world took it for granted that corrective "rebuke" would play an important role at the physical as well as the verbal level. For a similar use of this OT theme, see Revelation 3:19.

7–8 If, as the Proverbs text indicates, suffering is to be understood in the context of *paideia*, then it is to be seen not as a negative experience but as an essential part of the parent-child relationship and therefore as a sign that those who undergo it are truly God's children (even God's Son Jesus had to learn through suffering, 5:8). Just as discipline is an inevitable part of being brought up in a human family, so it is in God's family, and our author presses the point rather daringly to the conclusion that anyone who does not undergo it cannot be a true child of God. The experience of "discipline" is thus a measure of our Father's love and care.

9 Taking the analogy further, he reminds his readers that, whatever the immediate reaction (see v. 11), children come to appreciate their parents' motives and to respect them for the discipline they may have resented at the time it was given. How much more, then, should we accept the good purpose of God when he disciplines us? For God is "the Father of spirits" (so TNIV, rightly removing the NIV's "our," which is not in the Greek; for the phrase "God of spirits," cf. Nu 16:22; 27:16), a spiritual and therefore perfectly reliable Father as opposed to fallible human parents. The goal of his discipline is not mere adulthood but *life*.

10 The comparison is now made explicit. Human parents exercise discipline "as they think best" (RSV, "at their pleasure," retaining an unfortunate KJV phrase, wrongly suggests a sadistic motivation), but their assessment of the situation may be at fault and may indeed be quite arbitrary. God, on the other hand, knows what is really "for our good." Parental discipline is only for the "little while" of our childhood, but God's discipline continues throughout our earthly life. And its goal is not mere human maturity but that we may "share in his holiness" (cf. 2:11; 10:10, 14, 29 for holiness as the goal of Christian salvation). God's children are to become like him, just as human children grow to be like their parents.

11 No one enjoys being "flogged." It is in hindsight that we appreciate the value of the experiences we have resented at the time. For the result is a "harvest of righteousness and peace" (cf. Jas 3:17–18), a growth in godly character and living that would not otherwise have been achieved. In describing the experience as "training," the author again uses the language of athletics, reminding his readers of the painful regimen of physical exercise and disciplined lifestyle that athletes are willing to endure in order to reach their best performance.

The emphasis on hindsight is pastorally important. It may be impossible in the middle of suffering to see what good outcome it might have, and to talk blandly about the "educative" value of suffering to someone in that situation is likely to be counterproductive. But the perspective our author here offers calls at least for a willingness to suspend our negative reaction until we are able to see it in perspective. For the present we are called to recognize in our experiences the hand of God, who alone knows the whole picture and whom we can trust as our utterly reliable Father.

12–13 Returning to the athletic metaphor of vv. 1–2, the author now rounds off his explanation of suffering with a pastoral exhortation, using vivid physical imagery drawn from Isaiah 35:3 to reinforce the call of Proverbs 3:11 not to "lose heart" (v. 5). The "feeble arms and weak knees" describe the marathon runner whose strength is exhausted toward the end of the race, but they must be "strengthened" ("straightened up," "restored"; the term is echoed in the "level" paths of v. 13) for the final sprint. The imagery of the race reminds the author also of another phrase from Proverbs 4:26, where the sage's instruction to his son on living a single-minded and purposeful life includes the call to "make level" or, better, "straight" the paths he follows (NIV, following the LXX; TNIV, "give careful thought to," reads it as a different Hebrew verb); the Christian runner cannot afford to get off the beaten track. The danger of going off course into rough ground is that "the lame may be disabled." This enigmatic phrase probably refers to the runner's own "weak knees," which must not be allowed to succumb to the strain. To be disabled in this way would be to be put out of the race, but if the threatened limbs are "healed," they will yet reach the finish line.

NOTES

4 If the imagery is of a boxing match, the "blood" could refer to the fact that boxers (wearing spiked gloves) regularly drew blood; the point would then be that they had not yet entered into serious conflict. But a reference to "blood" just after the reminder of Jesus' violent death is more likely to convey martyrdom.

7 The Greek ὑπομένετε, *hypomenete*, "endure," could be read either as imperative (so the NIV) or indicative, in which case the sentence would read, "It is for discipline that you endure hardship"; the imperative sharpens the exhortatory focus, but the resultant sense is not very different.

13 "Disabled" in the NIV translates ἐκτρέπω, *ektrepō* (GK *1762*), which more normally means "to turn away." It could therefore be understood of someone else in the race who is liable to be "knocked off course" by a fellow runner who stumbles. But the fact that "the lame" is neuter plus the following mention of "healing" suggest that here the verb has its occasional sense as a medical term for the dislocation of a joint and thus refers to the runner's own limb rather than to another runner. Ellingworth, 657, however, interprets the whole of vv.12–13 as exhorting "the strong members of the community to encourage the weak" (the latter symbolized by the feeble arms and weak knees).

E. Call to Holiness (12:14–17)

OVERVIEW

Moving on from the metaphor of the race, the author now spells out directly the qualities that will enable his readers to fulfill their Christian calling and the vices that would hinder them. A series of cultic-sounding terms ("holy/holiness," "defile," "godless/profane") shows the author's concern for his readers to live as the people of God. Verses 14–16 are a single sentence, with the imperative call to peace and holiness in v.14 as the leading motif, and vv.15–16 as a participial clause warning against three negative qualities that would negate that calling ("seeing to it that . . . that . . . that . . ."). The third of these negative qualities is illustrated by the example of Esau, and v.17 is then added to spell out the consequences of Esau's failure. The overall effect is a powerful summons to take both the positive and the negative demands of discipleship seriously, with Esau held out as a graphic warning of what can happen to those who do not do so.

> [14]Make every effort to live in peace with all men and to be holy; without holiness no one will see the Lord. [15]See to it that no one misses the grace of God and that no bitter root grows up to cause trouble and defile many. [16]See that no one is sexually immoral, or is godless like Esau, who for a single meal sold his inheritance rights as the oldest son. [17]Afterward, as you know, when he wanted to inherit this blessing, he was rejected. He could bring about no change of mind, though he sought the blessing with tears.

COMMENTARY

14 The imperative "pursue" (NIV, "make every effort") suitably links with the race metaphor: these are the "straight paths" they are to follow. "Peace" is in relation to other people (cf. Ro 12:18), and "holiness" in relation to God. To "pursue peace with everyone" (an echo of Ps 34:14) is a more active goal than merely avoiding conflict; it echoes Jesus' saying, "Blessed are the peace*makers*." While the context of mutual concern within the community might suggest the reference is especially to relations with fellow Christians, no such restriction is explicit here, any more than it was in Jesus' beatitude.

The goal of Christian salvation is to be "made holy" like God (2:11; 10:14), but we are reminded here that this passive verb does not negate the disciple's own responsibility positively to "pursue" holiness. Holiness is God's own character, and it is only those who share it (v.10) who can "see" him. God is, of course, literally invisible (11:27), which gives the greater force to the biblical use of "seeing" God as a metaphor for enjoying personal fellowship with him (e.g., Ps 27:4; Mt 5:8; Rev 22:4).

15 The phrasing of vv.15–16 suggests more than concern for one's own holiness. "See to it" is *episkopeō* (GK *2174*), the verb from which we get *episkopos*, "bishop, overseer," and the three following clauses begin "lest any[one]." Just as in 10:24–25 the readers were expected to assume responsibility for each member of the group, so here they (he does not restrict his instruction to the leaders) are to keep an eye on each other so that no individual may go off course.

The first "lest anyone" clause concerns "missing" (TNIV, more lit., "fall short of"; cf. 4:1) God's grace, probably in the drastic sense of ultimately losing salvation, as has been envisaged in 3:7–4:11; 6:4–8; and 10:26–31. They are to look out for any member of the group who shows signs of giving up the Christian race.

The second clause speaks not of "anyone" but of any "bitter root," but the metaphor, drawn from Deuteronomy 29:18, refers to a person who is a source of "bitterness" within the community. (For "bitter" as a term for an ungodly attitude, cf. Ac 8:23; Eph 4:31; Jas 3:14; in Dt 29:18 a "root that produces bitter poison" describes the effect of an idolater on the community.) So our author's verbs, "cause trouble and defile many," point to the destructive effect of even one ungodly person within the group. Their "bitterness" is contagious, just as one neglected root of nettle will quickly grow and in time overrun the whole garden.

16 The third "lest anyone" clause combines two different vices, namely, sexual immorality (lit., "a fornicator") and godlessness (the word is the opposite of "holy" and is used of desecrated places and profane people). Since Esau, who is cited as an example, is not known in the OT (as he is in some later Jewish tradition) for sexual misbehavior (unless marrying two Hittite wives counts as such [Ge 26:34–35]), it is possible our author is here using *pornos* ("fornicator," GK *4521*) as a metaphor for idolatry, as the prophets often do; this would also fit the preceding allusion to Deuteronomy 29:18. Lane actually translates *pornos* here as "apostate." But its literal sense would also be appropriate to a group the author will feel it necessary to warn against such sins again in 13:4.

Esau's "godlessness" is shown by his disregard for his God-given position as Isaac's heir and thus the heir of God's covenantal promises (Ge 25:29–34; note the concluding clause "So Esau despised his birthright"). More broadly, his willingness to give up his whole inheritance in return for a single meal illustrates the shortsightedness of those readers who might be tempted to give up their heavenly calling for the sake of temporary relief.

17 The author drives home the point by reminding the readers of Esau's subsequent remorse on a second occasion ("afterward") when the same issue was taken to its logical conclusion. The "tears" refer to Genesis 27:34, 38, when Jacob has again stolen a march over Esau by appropriating the first-born's blessing (to which, he might have claimed, the transaction of 25:29–34 had entitled him).

The phrase *topos metanoias*, "a place of repen-tance/change of mind," has sometimes been inter-preted not of Esau's inability (or lack of opportunity) to repent but of his failure to change his father's (or God's?) decision (so apparently the NIV). The latter is not a likely reading of *metanoia* (GK *3567*), which in 6:1, 6 clearly denote a person's response to God; the idea of "no place for *metanoia*" particularly echoes the language of 6:6. TNIV's "he could not change what he had done" captures less literally the force of the OT narrative. The point is not that Esau was psychologi-cally unable to repent (indeed his tears show he did feel remorse at least), but that his tears came too late to change his earlier decision to barter away his inher-itance rights; there was now no way back, no room for second thoughts. The possibility of reaching a point of no return is one of our author's most telling pastoral weapons (3:7–4:11; 6:4–6; 10:26–27).

NOTES

15 "Root of bitterness growing up causes trouble," ῥίζα πικρίας ἄνω φύουσα ἐνοχλῆ, *rhiza pikrias anō phyousa enochlē*, clearly echoes LXX Deuteronomy 29:17 (EV v.18) ῥίζα ἄνω φύουσα ἐν χολῆ καὶ πικρίᾳ, *rhiza anō phyousa en cholē kai pikria*, "a root growing up in gall and bitterness." Hebrews may have used a Greek text in which ἐνοχλῆ, *enochlē*, "causes trouble," stood in place of ἐν χολῆ, *en cholē*, "in gall" (as it does in some MSS of the LXX, probably as a result of assimilation to the Hebrews quotation), but it is also possible our author deliberately played on the similarity of the Greek words.

16–17 Gordon, 155, suggests that the choice of Esau as a warning example is linked to the author's view that his Christian readers are now the true Israel: "to go back to their ancestral faith would not mean a return to 'Jacob-Israel' but an identifying with Esau."

F. The Mountain of Fear and the Mountain of Joy (12:18–24)

OVERVIEW

The choice confronting the readers has eternal consequences, as the example of Esau has just reminded them. The author now reinforces the point with a graphic "tale of two mountains"—Mount Sinai, the mountain of fear, which represents the old covenant and all they have left behind, and Mount Zion, the mountain of joy, which represents the heav-enly city, the new era of salvation through Christ (cf. Gal 4:24–29 for a similar argument concerning Mount Sinai as representing the old covenant and "the Jerusalem that is above" representing the new). Even within the OT, Sinai represented only "a staging-post on the way to a destination, namely Canaan, and ulti-mately the holy city of Jerusalem" (Gordon, 157); but for our author the contrast is greater still, since the Zion he speaks of is in heaven, not on earth.

The basis for this striking contrast is the account (Ex 19:10–23; 20:18–21; cf. Dt 4:10–12; 5:22–27) of the fear of the Israelites when they stood before Mount Sinai at the time when the old covenant was enacted, when the fire and storm symbolized the seriousness of the new relationship they were about to enter with God. The imagery of Exodus 19 will be further explored in the warning passage that follows in vv.25–29, which draws on the "trembling" of Mount Sinai and the fear it inspired and sums it up in the memorable words "Our God is a consuming fire." But God's ultimate purpose was not that his people should live in perpetual fear, and our author's exposition of the Exodus account consists not only of a reminder of that terrible occasion but also of an imaginative contrast with a different type of mountain. As he lists the features of the heavenly Mount Zion and the people whom the readers are to meet there, there is a warm sense of confidence and security. The earlier references to a future "city" (11:10, 16) are now filled out into a joyful celebration of salvation that points forward to the lyrical account of the new Jerusalem, which will bring the NT to its triumphant climax in Revelation 21–22.

The imagery of the two mountains presents in pictorial form the theology of salvation that Paul summed up in the words "The Spirit you received does not make you slaves, so that you live in fear again; rather, the Spirit you received brought about your adoption to sonship. And by him we cry, '*Abba*, Father'" (Ro 8:15 TNIV).

---

[18] You have not come to a mountain that can be touched and that is burning with fire; to darkness, gloom and storm; [19] to a trumpet blast or to such a voice speaking words that those who heard it begged that no further word be spoken to them, [20] because they could not bear what was commanded: "If even an animal touches the mountain, it must be stoned." [21] The sight was so terrifying that Moses said, "I am trembling with fear."

[22] But you have come to Mount Zion, to the heavenly Jerusalem, the city of the living God. You have come to thousands upon thousands of angels in joyful assembly, [23] to the church of the firstborn, whose names are written in heaven. You have come to God, the judge of all men, to the spirits of righteous men made perfect, [24] to Jesus the mediator of a new covenant, and to the sprinkled blood that speaks a better word than the blood of Abel.

COMMENTARY

18–19 The features of the description of Mount Sinai (not named here, as it is in Gal 4:24) are drawn from Exodus 19–20, which describes what sounds like a volcanic eruption. The oddly elliptical opening phrase "something that can be touched" (see Notes) prepares for the contrast between this physical mountain and the heavenly reality with which it will be contrasted in v.22, though v.20 will remind us that the Israelites were in fact forbidden to touch this "tangible" mountain (Ex 19:12–13). For the fire, darkness, storm, and trumpet blast, see Exodus 19:16–19; 20:18 (cf. Dt 4:11), and for God's voice coming from the mountain, see Exodus 19:19 and Deuteronomy 4:12. The terrified people's request that God not speak directly to them is in Exodus 20:19.

20–21 Their fear arose from God's initial command in Exodus 19:12–13 (summarized rather than directly quoted in the words "if even an animal touches the mountain, it must be stoned"), which isolated the mountain temporarily as a sacred area to which only Moses and Aaron were admitted. As a result, the Ten Commandments and the laws of the covenant were given to Moses to transmit to the people, who kept their distance so that they should not hear God's voice and die (Ex 20:18–21; cf. Dt 5:23–27). Even Moses, who was granted privileged access to the mountain, was not immune to the terror of the occasion, according to our author, though the words quoted, "I am trembling with fear," echo Deuteronomy 9:19. There Moses recalls not his initial approach to God at Sinai but his return to plead for the people after their idolatry with the golden calf, when the main cause of his fear was the Lord's anger at what the people had done rather than the frightening physical phenomena.

The story of Sinai and of the establishment of Israel's covenant with Yahweh thus symbolizes for our author a religion of fear and separation, which is the very opposite of the confident approach to God that Christ has won for his people (10:19–23). The following verses speak of a religion where the worshiper is no longer kept at arm's length but welcomed and included.

22–24 These verses form one long sentence, which begins with the strongly contrasting clause "But you have come to ..." and continues with a series of nine descriptive phrases identifying the place and the people that represent the Christian's true destination. For "come to" as a term for the relationship with God that results from Christ's saving work, see on 4:16; 7:25, and cf. 10:22; 11:6. It is important to note that the author speaks not merely of a future hope (as he did when speaking of the patriarchs in 11:10, 13–16) but of a salvation already achieved—"you *have* come"; those who belong to Christ are already citizens of Mount Zion. The author is calling them not to a new status but to appreciate and enjoy what is already theirs.

In the Greek, each of the nine phrases is introduced by "and" except for "the heavenly Jerusalem," which stands in apposition to "the city of the living God." The first three phrases identify the place, while the remainder speak of its inhabitants. A brief comment on each phrase follows.

"Mount Zion" echoes a frequent OT name for Jerusalem (especially the temple hill), which is also used for the people of God whose life and worship is centered on his city; the name therefore has strong covenantal associations. In the NT it is used elsewhere only in OT quotations except for Revelation 14:1, where the Lamb is seen standing on Mount Zion among his redeemed people. Its use here in contrast with Mount Sinai reminds us that, despite the "obsolescence" of the old covenant, the people of God redeemed by Christ are in continuity with those of the OT.

"The city of the living God" is rightly restored by TNIV to its place after "Mount Zion"; it is another way of describing the same place. We have heard in 11:10, 16 of the "city" promised to the wandering patriarchs, and the same vision is set before Christian believers in 13:14. The presence of "the living God" (see on 3:12) sets this city apart from all its earthly foreshadowings. The phrase has special force here, following the account of the Sinai theophany, since the people's fear there derived from their hearing the voice of "the living God" (Dt 5:26).

For "the heavenly Jerusalem," cf. "the Jerusalem above" (Gal 4:26) and "the new Jerusalem" (Rev 3:12; 21:2, 10). The adjective "heavenly" ensures that the reader cannot think of the earthly city; cf. the use of "heavenly" in 11:16 for the "better country" and in 8:5; 9:23 to distinguish the true sanctuary from its earthly counterpart. The first three phrases together, then, direct the readers' attention away from earthly circumstances to the ultimate fulfillment of God's purpose for his people. But of that heavenly city they are already citizens.

"Thousands upon thousands of angels in joyful assembly" reminds us of the great tableau of the worship of the angelic host in Rev 4 and 5 (cf. also the myriads of angels in Dt 33:2; Da 7:10), but the addition of "in joyful assembly" (see note) adds a note of festivity and celebration—the term was used for great celebratory gatherings, both religious and secular. The angels, whom we have seen in ch. 1 to be under the authority of the Son, are gathered in heaven to celebrate his triumph.

"The church of the firstborn, whose names are written in heaven" again reminds us of Revelation, where in ch. 7 the worship of the angels is swelled by the uncountable throng of the redeemed from all nations. (For the "names written in heaven," cf. Rev 3:5; 13:8; 17:8; 21:27.) Elsewhere in the NT, "firstborn" is used as a title of Christ himself (see in this letter 1:6), not of his people, but it recalls the OT description of Israel collectively as God's "firstborn son" (Ex 4:22; Jer 31:9). Here it may well be intended to include God's true people of both OT and NT eras. The firstborn is the heir, the most precious child, and the church (or "assembly"—*ekklēsia*, GK *1711*; it need not carry here its developed Christian sense; cf. 2:12, its only other use in this letter) consists of those whom God has appointed as his heirs (1:14; 6:12, 17) and who have not, like Esau, bartered away their birthright (vv. 16–17).

It is surprising that "God, the judge of all" comes so late in the list, but perhaps the author is working his way from the periphery of the heavenly scene to its center.

The reference to God as judge then prompts a second mention of the redeemed, now described as "the spirits of the righteous made perfect"—a phrase probably to be understood especially (but not exclusively) of the OT saints we saw to be still awaiting their "perfection" in 11:39–40. "Spirits" is an unusual term in the NT for redeemed human beings in heaven (though it is so used in some Jewish literature of the period), but the following words confirm this meaning here. They have been "made perfect" in the sense that we have so often seen in this letter (see Introduction, p. 32, for the concept of "perfection"), in that their salvation is now complete.

The list reaches its climax with the one who made it all possible, "Jesus the mediator of a new covenant" (see on 8:6 for the phrase). By his redeeming death he has opened the way to heaven, and now he is there to welcome his people and share its joys with them.

"The sprinkled blood" is hardly another component in the festive assembly but rather an extension of the description of Jesus' role as mediator, and one that further underlines the contrast with Sinai, where the old covenant was ratified in sprinkled blood (Ex 24:8). The reason Christ's people are able to be on Mount Zion is that blood has again been shed (see esp. 9:15–22), fulfilling the model of the ceremonial "sprinklings" of blood in the OT (9:13, 19, 21). But not all bloodshed is beneficial, as we are reminded by a further reference to the first bloodshed of the Bible (cf. 11:4). Abel's blood cried out with a message of condemnation (Ge 4:10), but the message of Jesus' blood is far "better" (the last use of this pregnant term in Hebrews).

NOTES

18 Translations such as "something that can be touched" (NRSV) represent the most probable text, in which the word "mountain" does not occur in this verse, but the familiar Exodus imagery and especially the quotation in v.20 leave no doubt this was the intended reference. Later MSS added the word ὄρει, *orei*, "mountain" (from the parallel in v.22).

22 G. Hughes, 67, refers to the perfect tense "you have come" as "strangely daring"; he goes on to discuss helpfully "the dialectic, or rather the bipolarity, of Christian eschatological existence" (71), the tension between "already" and "not yet" as we encounter it in Hebrews.

The word πανηγύρει, *panēgyrei*, "in joyful assembly" (which occurs nowhere else in the NT), stands between the clauses about the angels and the church of the firstborn and is sometimes taken either as a separate item on its own ("a national assembly," Buchanan) or with the following clause, "to the full concourse and assembly of the firstborn" (REB). But the NIV reading is preferable, since a one-word item would not fit the style of the list, and καί, *kai*, "and," which introduces each new item in the list, follows πανηγύρει, *panēgyrei* rather than precedes it.

23 Some commentators understand the "assembly of the firstborn" as a further description of the angels (who were created before human beings), but the term is not elsewhere used of angels (and indeed is used in this letter to describe Christ specifically in distinction from the angels, 1:6), and "names written in heaven" is a familiar idiom for God's redeemed people (cf. Lk 10:20; Php 4:3).

G. Fifth Warning Passage (12:25–29)

OVERVIEW

As so often in this letter, the author balances warm encouragement with stern warning. The terrors of Sinai set out in vv. 18–21 serve not only as a foil to the joy of Mount Zion but also now as the basis for a warning that the God who spoke in such awesome power then is still speaking to his people, and his voice cannot be ignored with impunity. This last solemn warning passage thus picks up the themes of the earlier ones, and especially of the second in 3:7–4:13: "Today, if you hear his voice, do not harden your hearts."

So the exposition of the Sinai story now continues as our author picks out an aspect of the Sinai theophany he did not mention in vv. 18–21—the earthquake: "The whole mountain trembled violently" (Ex 19:18). Terrifying as that "shaking" was, it points forward to a yet more violent "shaking" of the earth and even heaven itself, which our author finds promised in the words of Haggai 2:6 and which he takes to be still in the future. That being so, the only safe course for the readers is to ensure they are securely enrolled in the heavenly "kingdom that cannot be shaken," so that they experience the God of Sinai as their Savior rather than as "a consuming fire."

²⁵See to it that you do not refuse him who speaks. If they did not escape when they refused him who warned them on earth, how much less will we, if we turn away from him who warns us from heaven? ²⁶At that time his voice shook the earth, but now he has promised, "Once more I will shake not only the earth but also the heavens." ²⁷The words "once more" indicate the removing of what can be shaken—that is, created things—so that what cannot be shaken may remain.

> 28Therefore, since we are receiving a kingdom that cannot be shaken, let us be thankful, and so worship God acceptably with reverence and awe, 29for our "God is a consuming fire."

COMMENTARY

25 The link with vv.18–21 is clearer in Greek than most English versions have been able to convey, in that "refuse" here translates the same Greek word as "begged that no . . ." in v.19. "Refuse him who speaks" is thus a direct echo of the Sinai story; the readers are urged not to shrink away in fear from the speaking God, as their Hebrew ancestors once did. The God who spoke then is still speaking and requires a response. (The readers might also infer that God "speaks" today through the "speaking" of Jesus' blood [v.24]; but the reference to Sinai is primary.)

For the "how much less/more" argument from OT precedents, cf. explicitly 2:2–3; 10:28–29; the whole of 3:7–4:13 is an implicit argument of the same type. It is not immediately obvious in what way those who refused to listen to God at Sinai "did not escape." The author may be thinking of the punishment that fell on some of them soon after as a result of worshiping the golden calf (Ex 32:27–28, 35), or of the later, more comprehensive punishment that resulted from their refusal to obey God's call to enter Canaan (see 3:7–4:13). At Sinai God's voice came in the earthly setting of the sacred mountain, but now in the NT era he speaks "from heaven." That last phrase recalls that it is the heavenly Mount Zion, not the earthly Sinai, which is the true home of "God, the judge of all" (vv.22–23), though the author does not explain how his heavenly voice can now be heard by those on earth in a way different from the revelation through Moses at Sinai. The verb *chrēmatizō*, "warn" (see on 11:7), could suggest direct supernatural communication, but it is unlikely the author was thinking

only of this relatively uncommon mode of hearing the voice of God. We have been reminded in 1:2 that God's speaking is now especially "by his Son."

26 The earth/heaven contrast remains in focus, as the author now contrasts the earthly "shaking" of Sinai with God's warning in Haggai 2:6 (cf. 2:21) that he will shake "the heavens and the earth, the sea and the dry land." Our author does not quote the LXX directly but has singled out the two elements he is interested in (heaven and earth), and by reversing them and adding "not only . . . but also . . . ," he has achieved the contrast he intends. The LXX phrase "once more" (*eti hapax*; see on 7:27 for the significance of *[ep]hapax* in Hebrews) indicates to him not just one further event in a series but a single climactic event, the eschatological "shaking" of the created universe. It is in light of this ultimate catastrophe that the readers must be sure their security is founded in the one place that cannot be "shaken."

Haggai does not seem to have had quite so ultimate a scenario in mind. The prophecy in 2:6 concerns the future glory of Jerusalem and its temple, and the "shaking" of earth, sky, and sea is in order to bring in "what is desired by all nations" (TNIV) in order to beautify the temple (the earthly Zion) with silver and gold, thus inaugurating not the end of the world but a new era of glory and peace. In 2:21, the "shaking" leads to the overthrow of kingdoms and armies and the establishment of Zerubbabel's power. But our author has read a more eschatological sense into the prophet's words, and other early Jewish interpreters of the text take it in the same way.

27 The author explains his eschatological interpretation of *eti hapax* as indicating the end of the physical creation (for "removal" in this ultimate sense, cf. 7:12; 11:5, where the same word is translated "change" and "take away" respectively). This is no ordinary earthquake but the final dissolution of all that "can be shaken" (i.e., of all that is physical), including Mount Sinai itself, leaving only the "unshakable," nonphysical reality of the heavenly Mount Zion. (Cf. Ps 102:25–27, quoted in 1:10–12, according to which when heaven and earth are destroyed God himself "remains the same" forever.)

28 In using the word "kingdom," the author is perhaps reflecting Jesus' teaching about the coming "kingdom of God," of which his true followers are now members; the idiom is in any case appropriate after speaking of Zion (the royal city) as the place where God is the judge of all (cf. the frequent references to Jesus sitting at the right hand of the throne of God). There may also be an echo of Daniel 7:14, the "indestructible kingdom" of the Son of Man. It is to this "unshakable kingdom" (in contrast to the "shaken" kingdoms of Hag 2:21–22) that the readers, together with all God's people of the old and new covenants, have come (vv.22–23). The present participle in this verse ("we are receiving") maintains the typical NT tension between the assured future and the contingency of the present: it is theirs already, and yet its possession is not finally assured as long as they remain in this "shakable" world. So they must live even now as citizens of heaven, and that life is spelled out in terms of giving thanks (the Greek words could also be translated "have grace," but "give thanks" is the normal sense of the idiom) and acceptable worship, which is characterized by reverence and fear (not the usual NT word but a more formal classical term for fear or awe), words that especially recall the attitude of Jesus himself during his time on earth (see note on 5:7). Such reverent submission to the will of God is the very opposite of "refusing him who speaks." Only so can they be sure that when the final "shaking" comes, they will be kept safe.

29 The overall message of our author's reflections on the Sinai story is now summed up in words drawn from the LXX of Deuteronomy 4:24, where Moses warns the Israelites in the wilderness of the danger of incurring God's anger, since he is "a consuming fire, a jealous God." In Deuteronomy 9:3 he uses the same formula for the effect of Yahweh on Israel's enemies if Israel obeys him. God is a powerful friend but a dangerous enemy. To serve him faithfully is to enjoy his unshakable kingdom on Mount Zion, but to turn against him is to face the terrifying fires of Sinai. They have been warned.

NOTES

25 Some interpreters take the one "who warned them on earth" to be Moses, but χρηματίζω, *chrēmatizō*, "warn" (GK *5976*), is regularly used of God's communication rather than of his human spokesperson (cf. 8:5; 11:7), and it was specifically God's voice, not Moses', that they begged not to hear at Sinai. There is only one speaker throughout this verse. All throughout the letter it is God who speaks and whose voice must be obeyed.

26 The shaking of the earth at Sinai may not be derived from Exodus 19:18, since in the LXX (which our author normally uses) it is the people who tremble, not the mountain. But the tradition of an earthquake at Sinai is well established elsewhere in the OT (see Jdg 5:4–5; Pss 68:8; 114:1–7).

"Heaven" or "the heavens" can denote both the upper part of the created universe, which can be "shaken" and destroyed, and (as in vv.22–23) the unseen spiritual realm, which cannot. "Heaven [singular] and earth" here, and in Haggai 2:6, has the former meaning (cf. also 1:10–12), in contrast with Hebrews' use of "heaven" (normally in the plural) elsewhere for the spiritual realm where God dwells eternally—the meaning in v.25 (where "heaven" is plural).

VII. CONCLUDING EXHORTATIONS AND GREETINGS (13:1–25)

OVERVIEW

The more piecemeal character of this final chapter gives it the feeling of an appendix. From 13:18 to the end, the first-person address and the personal character of the messages, together with the impressive doxology, remind us of the end of a typical Pauline letter; and the collection of ethical and pastoral exhortations that make up the earlier part of the chapter are in marked contrast to the more structured theological argument that has characterized the letter as a whole, even though it has been interspersed with pastoral appeals.

Some have therefore suggested that this chapter was added subsequent to the original writing of the treatise that ends in 12:29, in order to turn it into something more nearly approaching the standard NT letter form. But most interpreters, while recognizing the change of tone as the letter draws to its end, accept ch. 13 as an integral part of the original writing. In particular, vv.9–16 have close links with the preceding argument and take up again several of its prominent themes, as we shall see. In the following comments we shall also note other such links elsewhere in the chapter. And the content of this chapter as a whole is very much in keeping with the pastoral tone of the author's repeated appeals to his readers within the main body of the letter and especially with the personal knowledge of his readers' circumstances, which has emerged in 5:11–14; 6:9–12; 10:24–25, 32–34. The main argument has been completed, but our author still has a number of issues he wishes to raise with his readers before he signs off.

A. Living as the People of God (13:1–8)

OVERVIEW

Verses 1–4 present a series of ethical imperatives centered around the theme of relationships in community and family. While the logical linkage between some of the elements in these verses is not obvious, the dominant demand is for a spirit of generosity, expressed in hospitality to those in need, rather than a selfish concern about financial security. The latter point then leads the author to reflect on the greater security that comes from a confident trust in God's promise of support, on the good example of the first leaders of the church, and on the unchanging reliability of Jesus.

¹Keep on loving each other as brothers. ²Do not forget to entertain strangers, for by so doing some people have entertained angels without knowing it. ³Remember those in prison as if you were their fellow prisoners, and those who are mistreated as if you yourselves were suffering.

⁴Marriage should be honored by all, and the marriage bed kept pure, for God will judge the adulterer and all the sexually immoral. ⁵Keep your lives free from the love of money and be content with what you have, because God has said,

"Never will I leave you;
never will I forsake you."

⁶So we say with confidence,

"The Lord is my helper; I will not be afraid.
What can man do to me?"

⁷Remember your leaders, who spoke the word of God to you. Consider the outcome of their way of life and imitate their faith. ⁸Jesus Christ is the same yesterday and today and forever.

COMMENTARY

1 These three Greek words (lit., "let brotherly love remain") provide the essential basis for the exhortations that follow. It is a NT commonplace to speak of "love" as the basic Christian virtue; however, the word used here is not *agapē* but the more family-oriented term *philadelphia*, "brotherly love" (GK *5789*), which emphasizes that the members of the church have a special responsibility to each other as fellow members of the family of God (see Ro 12:10; 1Th 4:9–10). This sense of family was brought out especially in the description of Jesus as our "elder brother" in 2:11–13. The readers have already shown such mutual concern (6:10; 10:32–34), but it must not be allowed to fade. The verb "remain" here echoes 12:27, which spoke of the unshakable things that will remain. Love is one of them.

2 "Do not forget" (and "remember" in v.3) again indicates this is no new proposal but a reinforcement of the generous concern for others they have already shown. The second part of v.2 suggests that the "entertaining" here envisaged (TNIV, "show hospitality to") is not directed toward members of their own group but toward strangers. But both the "brotherly love" of v.1 and the reference to "angels" probably indicate that visiting Christians are especially in mind. *Didache* 11–13 provides a vivid picture of the demands traveling Christian workers might make on the resources of church members not long after this letter was written, and our author is perhaps concerned about the natural fear of exploitation that might inhibit hospitality toward genuine Christian travelers. If this church was located in Rome, the problem is likely to have been especially acute.

The possibility of "entertaining angels without knowing it" reflects the experience of Abraham in Genesis 18, where the three travelers turned out to be apparently "two angels" (Ge 19:1) and the Lord himself (cf. the well-known Greek story of Philemon and Baucis, a poor old couple who entertained two strangers who turned out to be Zeus and Hermes in disguise). Even if their visitors are no more than human, however, there may be unexpected blessings from their visits. (Cf. Jesus' words about serving him incognito in the person of his "little brothers and sisters" [Mt 25:34–40]).

3 In 10:34 we heard of how the readers have a record already of "suffering along with" (TNIV) prisoners. They are to continue in this good work, identifying with the prisoners' experience. Similarly, they are to identify with those who are "mistreated," the reference probably being again to the sort of persecution we heard of in 10:32–34. Following on the very practical emphasis of v.2, the "remembering" is surely to be understood in terms of active help, not just sympathy.

The last clause is literally "as being also yourselves in the body." This could mean merely that they sympathize as fellow human beings, but in that case the "as" would not correspond to the one in the previous clause, "as if you were their fellow prisoners," since the latter involves imaginative identification, whereas "being in the body" is a fact for the readers as well as the victims, not a matter of mental projection. The NIV has therefore taken "mistreated" to be elliptically understood also in the "as if" clause, making it a parallel imaginative identification to that with the prisoners: they may not themselves be suffering mistreatment "in the body" currently, but they know what it is like.

4 This very brief but uncompromising affirmation of the Christian code of sexual ethics does not give us any details of the problem being addressed, but here is another way in which the family relationship of the people of God may be threatened. (Cf. Paul's description of sexual misbehavior as "wronging or taking advantage of a brother or sister" in 1Th 4:6.) The threats to the "honor" and "purity" of marriage are literally "fornicators and adulterers," which in the normal sense of the terms means those who have illicit sexual relations, whether or not they or their partners are already married. Such activity, in ancient society and in ours as well, may be permissible under the secular law, but the Christian is under a higher authority: *God* will judge them (see also comments at 12:16).

5–6 Materialism and acquisitiveness are the enemies of the sort of caring love commended in vv.1–3. The call to be content with what we have echoes the famous advice of 1 Timothy 6:6–10, where "godliness with contentment" is set over against "the love of money." This would have had particular force for the readers if they were still, as previously (10:34), suffering material deprivation on account of their faith. The basis for this call is not the Stoic ideology of self-sufficiency but an active trust in God instead of in possessions.

The point is made by two OT quotations, which correspond to one another as promise and response. The first most closely echoes Moses' farewell reassurance to Israel in LXX Deuteronomy 31:6, 8, though the first-person form reflects the similar reassurance issued by God himself to Joshua in Joshua 1:5 (and cf. the promise to Jacob in Ge 28:15; in all cases the "you" is singular, as here); the speaker is not identified in the Greek formula "he himself has said," but as usual in Hebrews, the words of Scripture are understood to be the words of God. The second quotation comes from Psalm 118:6 in the LXX (which translates the Hebrew "with me" or "for me" more specifically as "my helper"), expressing the confidence of the psalmist, traditionally David, that results from his experience of God's active deliverance from danger. For the person who knows God's protective power, human opposition is put in perspective. What was true for these OT saints is equally true for all who trust God, and in that case there is no need to put material security before Christian generosity. Fear gives way to joyful confidence.

7 A comment on the example of Christian leaders comes rather awkwardly between statements on the reliability of God himself (v.6) and of Jesus (v.8), but it provides a further incentive to selfless Christian service. The leaders are described as having spoken the word of God to them in the past (aorist tense, implying they are no longer doing so), and to speak of the "outcome" of their lives suggests they are no longer alive. (*Ekbasis* [GK *1676*] may mean either "going out," i.e., the ending of their lives, or "result, achievement"; while the latter is probably intended here, such achievement is best seen at the end of a person's life.) While these earlier leaders are not specifically identified as the founders of this particular church (cf. 2:3), this is a likely inference from the language (as opposed to their current leaders, mentioned in vv.17, 24). We do not know who they were, but apparently it was recently enough for them to be still remembered by the current church members. To recollect how they lived (and perhaps also how they died, the "outcome") will provide a model for imitation not only of their behavior but of the

faith (in the same sense as in 10:37–12:3) that inspired it.

8 This famous verse has neither verb nor immediate link with what precedes and follows to clarify what is its intention in context. Probably it is to be understood as summing up the faith of the church's founders (its epigrammatic form suggests a well-memorized creedal "motto"), which the readers are now called to imitate. Following the mention of the "outcome" of these earlier leaders' lives, it serves to reassure the readers that, whereas their founding fathers may have died, Jesus remains and always will remain a secure foundation for their faith. The unexpected word order that separates the first two time references from the last—"Jesus Christ yesterday and today the same, and forever"—is perhaps intended to emphasize that the fact that he has proved unchanged so far ("yesterday and today") assures us he will remain the same for the future. Following the assurance of vv.5–6, this verse thus locates the reliability of our unfailing God more specifically in the unchangeability of Jesus—and thus, as so often in this letter, places Jesus alongside God without distinction. (Cf. 1:12, where our author has quoted the description of God's unchangeability in Ps 102:27 [using the same phrase "the same"] as though speaking of the Son; for the threefold division of time, cf. the doxologies of Rev 1:4, 8; 4:8.)

NOTES

1–25 The presence in this chapter of a number of typically Pauline words and motifs has suggested to some either that it is a deliberate imitation of a Pauline letter conclusion or even that it is a bit of genuine Paul that somehow got attached to a non-Pauline letter. But the "Pauline" features noted are not statistically significant and are outweighed by the clear links with the rest of Hebrews noted in the commentary. (See further Lane, *Hebrews 1–8*, lxvi–iii; *Hebrews 9–13*, 495–97.)

4 As there is no verb in the first half of the verse, it could be translated not as an imperative but as a statement defending marriage: "Marriage is honored among all people [or in every way], and the marriage bed is not defiled." This could then be understood as an attack on an ascetic doctrine of the superiority of celibacy (cf. 1Ti 4:3). But the preceding verses are imperative, and v.5 begins with a parallel verbless construction ("Life free from the love of money"), which is clearly also imperative.

B. Serving Jesus "Outside the Camp" (13:9–16)

OVERVIEW

Many commentators prefer to place a section division after v.6, treating vv.7–17 (or 7–19) as a unit. One reason for this is a supposed *inclusio* (an overworked concept in recent commentaries on Hebrews!) between the "leaders" of v.7 and those of v.17. But the two verses do not refer to the same group of leaders, while v.24, which does refer to the same "leaders" as v.17, is not given the same structural weight.

Though here, as elsewhere in the letter, the sectional divisions imposed on the text by commentators are to a large extent arbitrary, I prefer to keep vv.1–8 as a unit, first so as not to separate the related grounds of confidence in the faithfulness of God (vv.5–6) and the unchangeability of Jesus (v.8), and second because there seems to me to be a recognizable unity of theme through vv.9–16 that is not shared with vv.7–8 and 17.

That theme is focused on the imagery of going to Jesus "outside the camp." In the Pentateuchal regulations, those parts of certain sin offerings that were not required on the altar were to be burned outside the camp. The author draws a parallel between this practice and the fact that Jesus was executed "outside the city gate." In that case, the readers must be prepared to go out to join him there, whatever the shame involved; they have no further place inside that city, since they now belong (as 12:22–24 has shown) to a different and far better city.

The alienation that now exists between the readers and non-Christian Jewish society is explained in vv.9–10 by the "strange teachings" and ineffectual ritual practices of the old regime, as compared with the Christian "altar" to which those who "minister at the tabernacle" have no right of access. Instead of continuing to hanker for the old ways, the readers must devote themselves to the sorts of sacrifices God really does desire, those of praise and good living (vv.15–16).

These verses therefore graphically illustrate the author's conviction that there can now be no accommodation between the Christian community and non-Christian Judaism. Those readers who may still have been trying to keep a foot in both camps must accept that there is now no place for them in the old city, from which their Lord was thrown out in disgrace; like the patriarchs of 11:13–16 they must recognize that they do not now belong in the old world but are citizens of "the city that is to come."

In these verses, then, the "supersessionist" convictions of the author (see Introduction, pp. 32–33) come very clearly to the surface, the more remarkably for being simply assumed, without any need to argue the case. And this new perspective is not just a theological tenet but a whole way of life, for here and eternity. (Note, too, that the argument assumes throughout that the old covenant rituals are still being enacted—a further pointer to a date for the letter before the destruction of the temple in Jerusalem and the consequent end of the sacrificial system.)

The references to "foods," to eating from an "altar," and to a "sacrifice of praise" in these verses lead many commentators to assume the author is especially referring to the Christian Eucharist as the counterpart of the sacrificial meals of the old covenant, which are "of no benefit." If so, his language is very cryptic, and the lack of clear eucharistic allusions in the rest of the letter suggests this was not a major concern of the author. The whole section can be understood without any eucharistic background, though there is no inherent improbability in such a reference.

⁹Do not be carried away by all kinds of strange teachings. It is good for our hearts to be strengthened by grace, not by ceremonial foods, which are of no value to those who eat them. ¹⁰We have an altar from which those who minister at the tabernacle have no right to eat.

¹¹The high priest carries the blood of animals into the Most Holy Place as a sin offering, but the bodies are burned outside the camp. ¹²And so Jesus also suffered outside the city gate to make the people holy through his own blood. ¹³Let us, then, go to him outside the camp, bearing the disgrace he bore. ¹⁴For here we do not have an enduring city, but we are looking for the city that is to come.

¹⁵Through Jesus, therefore, let us continually offer to God a sacrifice of praise—the fruit of lips that confess his name. ¹⁶And do not forget to do good and to share with others, for with such sacrifices God is pleased.

COMMENTARY

9 Despite my preferred section division, there is, of course, a link between vv.8 and 9 in the contrast between the reliability of the one unchanging Jesus, the object of the readers' faith, and the variety of "strange" and unhelpful teachings around them. If he is referring to the ritual practices of non-Christian Judaism, the term "strange" (lit., "foreign") is surprising, since Jewish ritual teaching was neither new nor unfamiliar to the readers, who had, it seems, been brought up on it. It would, however, be "foreign" to the Christian faith they now hold, which depends on the conviction that Jesus' sacrifice has rendered animal sacrifices obsolete, so that to be attracted back to it would be to be "carried away" from their Christian moorings. The reference to "foods" (see note) may, however, indicate that the pressure is coming now not so much from traditional Judaism but from a legalistic Christian movement attempting to reinstate Jewish food laws.

The antithesis between "grace" and "foods" as the basis for strengthening the heart (perhaps reflecting the language of Ps 104:15 [NRSV], "bread to strengthen the human heart") suggests a contrast between the spiritual and the physical, but the focus on "foods" is unexpected, since the letter so far has focused on the sacrificial system rather than on the food laws of the OT (apart from a passing mention in 9:10). But we know from the rest of the NT that the question of "unclean" food, so sharply raised by Jesus himself (Mk 7:14–23), became a serious issue in the early churches, even when they were still predominantly Jewish in composition, and the more so as Gentile members were added. It is therefore possible that a dispute like that of Colossians 2:16, 20–23 lies behind this warning, with members of the church insisting on a code of ritual purity for food the author feels to be now obsolete and therefore can dismiss as "of no value" (TNIV, "of no benefit") to those who "observe such rituals" (TNIV; lit., "walk in them [the foods]," a rather awkward application of "walk" in the Pauline sense of "manner of life"). Some interpreters suggest that some were promoting ceremonial meals within a Jewish cultic setting as a positive means of grace for Christians (so Lane, 534–36). But we have no data beyond these verses to enable us to reconstruct the situation with

187

confidence; see Attridge, 394–96, for a survey of different conjectural reconstructions. The fact that the "foods" are contrasted with "grace," not with a different kind of meal, suggests caution in finding a eucharistic reference at this point.

10 The themes of food and sacrifice come together in the OT provisions for sacrificial meat to be eaten by priests and worshipers (Ex 29:26, 31–33; Lev 6:16–18; 7:6, 15–18, 31–34; etc.). Deuteronomy 12:7, 17–18 envisages the Israelites gathering at the sanctuary not only to offer sacrifice but also to eat and rejoice together. But the Christians (who, if they do not observe the Levitical food laws, are ritually excluded from the Jewish altar) have a different sanctuary as the basis for their celebration, and one the worshipers at the old tabernacle have no right to approach. "It is a bold reversal of positions to suggest that it is the adherents of temple and sacrifice who are now cultically debarred" (Gordon, 167).

Among many different ways of understanding the Christian "altar" here, two may be singled out. One is that the author is thinking of the heavenly sanctuary he has spoken of in 8:1–6; 9:11, 23–24. But he has not hitherto mentioned it has an "altar"—indeed strictly speaking it should not have one, since there are no further sacrifices to be offered. On this interpretation there would be no special significance in the choice of the term, since it serves here simply to make the contrast with the earthly altar (mentioned in 7:13) rather than to say something specifically about the nature of its heavenly counterpart: worshipers under the old covenant ate from the altar (cf. 1Co 9:13; 10:18), but Christians find their spiritual sustenance in a different milieu. A spiritual "altar" fits well with the spiritual sacrifices that now constitute true Christian worship (vv. 15–16).

Other interpreters argue, however, that the Christian "altar" refers not to the heavenly sanctuary but to the historical event of Golgotha, where the one final sin offering was made—a sacrifice whose benefits are only for those who follow Jesus. This sacrifice will be further referred to in v.12 under the imagery of the sin offering of the Day of Atonement, which, unlike most other offerings, was not allowed to be eaten even by the priests; Christians, however, do receive its benefits.

Ellingworth, 711–12, may be right to conclude that there is "a certain ambivalence in the text itself, not only in our understanding of it"; he goes on to refer to the author's "language which blurs the dividing line between earth and heaven." In view of the range of exegetical possibilities, it is hazardous to draw any theological conclusions from the author's use of "altar" in a Christian context (the only such use in the NT), especially with reference to Christian understandings of the Eucharist; most recent commentators conclude that the author was not here thinking of the Eucharist, so that any relevance of this passage to eucharistic doctrine is at best indirect. It was not until the third century that "altar" became a recognized term for the Communion table (Westcott, 453–61).

11 The author describes concisely an aspect of the ritual for certain sin offerings spelled out in Exodus 29:14 and Leviticus 4:12, 21: after the blood and some of the internal organs with the fat had been offered at the altar, the rest of the carcass was burned in a ceremonially clean place outside the camp. (The author continues to think in terms of the wilderness and the tabernacle, not the settled life of Jerusalem.) On the Day of Atonement (whose ritual is described in the first half of this verse, following Lev 16:11–16), this procedure was followed, and the man responsible for the burning was then required to undergo a ritual ablution before being allowed back inside the camp (Lev 16:27–28). The implication is that, as sin offerings, the carcasses were now unclean (these offerings, unlike others, were not to be eaten by priests or people) and that uncleanness must be kept away from the purified people of God.

12 There is therefore a daring symbolism in the author's observation that Jesus' death took place "outside the city gate" (an aspect of the gospel story [e.g., Jn 19:20] he assumes to be well known). He went out as a sin offering, rejected as unclean by the religious establishment. In making this connection, the author makes clear his understanding, already implicit in his earlier use of Day of Atonement imagery (9:11–12, 23–25, etc.), that Jesus' once-for-all sacrifice was specifically a sin offering. It is only by the removal of sin that his people can truly be "made holy" (cf. 2:11; 10:10, 14). It was to achieve this effective removal of sin, not just a symbolic gesture, that it was necessary for him to present "his own blood" rather than, like the high priest, merely the blood of animals (9:12, 25; 10:3–4). But whereas the OT sacrifices were killed inside the camp and burned outside, Jesus was killed outside the city; his blood therefore has efficacy only for those who also are "outside."

13 The readers cannot be involved in the sacrifice, which has already been offered once for all, but they can and must identify with the ostracism and shame their high priest has undergone for them. To follow him is to find themselves also "outside the camp," treated as unclean by the Jewish religious establishment of their day. (Blasphemers and Sabbath breakers were also taken "outside the camp" to be stoned [Lev 24:14, 23; Nu 15:35].) The readers have known persecution for their faith already (10:32–34; 12:4), and the author offers them no hope that it will prove temporary; rather, they must embrace the "disgrace" (the same word as "insult" in 10:33; cf. also 11:26, "disgrace for the sake of Christ") as a part of their calling, since they share it with their Lord. This verse expresses in different imagery Jesus' call to take up the cross and follow him (Mk 8:34).

14 Their true home is elsewhere. It has been glowingly described in 12:22–24, but whereas there the author spoke of their already "having come" to Mount Zion (since their salvation has already been achieved), here he recognizes that in actual experience its enjoyment remains in the future. They, like the patriarchs in 11:13–16, are not yet at home but are still looking forward to a secure city (cf. the "city with foundations" in 11:10). Thus the "already/not yet" dialectic we noted at 12:28 (cf. also note on 12:22) remains in play, as it does throughout the NT. In one sense the forward-looking faith of the OT saints has now reached its "perfection" (11:39–40), and the people of the new covenant have a "better" and assured place in God's saving purpose, but even for them there is still a "not yet." As long as we remain in this physical, transient world ("no enduring city"), we are away from home; life on earth must always be a life of looking forward. For other imagery for the Christian's ultimate destination, cf. 3:7–4:11 ("rest"); 9:15 ("eternal inheritance"); 12:28 ("unshakable kingdom").

15–16 In this interim period, the readers' allegiance to Jesus must be shown by sacrifices of a different kind from his own self-offering and from the rituals of the old covenant. The obsolete sacrifice for sin is now replaced by the Christian "sacrifice of praise"; the phrase occurs several times in the LXX, but the author may be thinking especially of Psalm 50:14, 23, where it denotes the type of sacrifice God requires, in contrast to animal sacrifice (vv.8–13). Such a sacrifice must be "continual," *dia pantos* ("always, constantly"), a term often used in the LXX for the regular animal sacrifices; Jesus' once-for-all sacrifice makes further animal sacrifices unnecessary, but the regular sacrifice of praise must take their place. It is offered "to God" and "through Jesus"; in view of the virtual equation of Jesus with God elsewhere in the letter, the distinction may not be very important, but the NT often speaks of prayer and praise *to* God *through* Jesus (e.g., Jn 15:16; Col 3:17; 1Pe 2:5), even though sometimes it is Jesus himself who is the direct object of praise and prayer.

The sacrifice of praise is further defined as "the fruit of lips praising his name." *Homologeō* (GK 3933), which usually means "confess," is here followed by a dative of object and in such cases means to "praise," though the author's choice of this verb may also be intended to recall the noun *homologia*, which in 3:1; 4:14; 10:23 denotes the Christian's open commitment to Jesus (see notes on 3:1; 4:14). When in praise we declare God's greatness and express our commitment to him, this is the verbal equivalent of the OT offerings of produce, "the fruit of lips" (echoing LXX Hos 14:2).

But true worship is not only verbal; God also requires the sacrifices of practical service to others.

"Do not forget" echoes v.2, and "doing good" and "sharing" sum up the sort of lifestyle vv.1–3 called for. *Koinōnia* (GK 3126), here translated "to share with others," is normally used in the NT for the special "sharing" that takes place within the Christian family (often in a practical, financial sense), and in 10:33 the author used the cognate noun for active support for (NIV, "stood side by side with") imprisoned fellow Christians. But neither of the words used here in itself demands that the practical service be confined to fellow Christians.

In describing praise and practical service as the sort of "sacrifices" God is pleased with (cf. 1Pe 2:5, 9, and also the "acceptable worship" of 12:28), the author again underlines his view that the old regime of cultic sacrifice is finished. God is looking now for a different kind of worship.

NOTES

9 The NIV's adjective "ceremonial" is not in the Greek but is added to suggest a preferred interpretation of βρώματα, *brōmata* (GK 1109), which means simply "foods." The only other use of βρώματα, *brōmata*, in Hebrews is at 9:10, where it clearly refers to matters of ritual observance, "external regulations applying until the time of the new order"; a similar meaning seems likely here.

13 The call to "go out of the camp" may also recall Exodus 33:7, where, after the "pollution" of the Israelite camp by the idolatry of the golden calf, Moses set up the "tent of meeting" outside the camp, so that anyone wishing to meet with God had to go out to it.

C. Personal Appeal (13:17–19)

OVERVIEW

Before the closing prayer and doxology, the author issues a personal appeal, both on his own behalf and on behalf of the leaders of the church to which he is writing. The fact that he is hoping to "be restored to you soon" indicates he himself had some role in the leadership of the church, and the plural language of v.18 may be intended to link him with the leaders of v.17; but the letter does not allow

us to work out just what that relationship was. One plausible scenario is that those he is writing to are a dissident group of people who have been causing problems for the leaders of the larger church body, and that the latter have appealed to him (one of their number who is temporarily away from home), as someone known to enjoy the confidence of the dissidents, to "intervene in the crisis" (so Lindars, 7–8).

> ¹⁷Obey your leaders and submit to their authority. They keep watch over you as men who must give an account. Obey them so that their work will be a joy, not a burden, for that would be of no advantage to you.
> ¹⁸Pray for us. We are sure that we have a clear conscience and desire to live honorably in every way. ¹⁹I particularly urge you to pray so that I may be restored to you soon.

COMMENTARY

17 In contrast with the past "leaders" of v.7, the "leaders" referred to here and in v.24 are currently responsible for the church. The lack of any more specific title of office ("elder," "deacon," etc.) is surprising in view of the fact that Paul's churches had such designated officers from an early period (Ac 14:23; Php 1:1), but this need not indicate a different type of church structure; rather, the author has no need to be specific in issuing what is a very general appeal for compliance with the leadership. Any attempt to discover a particular problem of insubordination behind this local appeal must be purely speculative.

"Obey" represents not the normal term for obedience, but literally "be persuaded," implying a willing acceptance of their leadership; cf. TNIV's "have confidence in." (The second "obey them" of the NIV ["do this," TNIV] is not in the Greek but is added to break up the sentence.) "Submit to their authority" translates *hypeikō* (lit., "yield to"), which is not used elsewhere in the NT but apparently carries much the same sense as Paul's frequent injunction to "be in submission" (*hypotassomai*, GK 5718). This attitude of willing compliance and support is the appropriate response to the leaders' own service as those who, like stewards, must "give an account" to their employer. Their particular role is to "keep watch over you," a strong verb that often means simply to "stay awake" and implies the unflagging vigilance of the shepherd (and possibly losing sleep?

Bruce, 385). "Over you" is more literally "on behalf of your souls." While *psychē* (GK 6034) often means simply "life," and thus a "living person," in Hebrews it tends to focus attention on the "real, innermost self" and on spiritual life rather than mere existence (see comments at 4:12; 6:19; 10:39); here, then, the focus is on responsible spiritual oversight rather than organizational office.

The following comment could profitably be written large over many a congregation and church meeting! The NIV loses something of the vividness of the Greek: "that they may do this with joy and not groaning." "Groaning" leaders are not only unhappy in themselves but are "of no advantage" to those they lead. The way to a happy and successful church is a healthy relationship of responsible oversight on the part of the leaders and willing compliance and support from those they serve.

18–19 Here the language is close to that of several of Paul's letter endings. The request for their prayer support in v.18 is in general terms and expressed in the plural, perhaps to include the leaders of v.17 along with the author (though the plural could be read as merely stylistic, as in other first-person comments in the letter [5:11; 6:9; etc.]). Then in v.19 the singular verbs narrow it down to the prayer that he (the author) may be "restored to" them soon. The verb implies he is normally part of the group but is unavoidably absent for the present. We can only speculate as to why he is away and why prayer is needed to enable him to return, but v.23 speaks as though he (unlike Timothy) is free to make his own travel plans, so that the constraint on him would seem to be that of other responsibilities rather than imprisonment or other duress.

Particularly in his dealings with the Corinthians, Paul sometimes found it necessary to defend his own conduct and motivation. Our author strikes a similar note when he speaks of his (and the other leaders'?) "clear conscience" as a basis for their prayer support. Again we cannot know what lies behind this defensive note, but perhaps the alternation of scolding and pleading especially in 5:11–6:12 indicates a rather uneasy relationship with the church for which he feels responsible; v.22 also shows some uncertainty over how his letter would be received. Was there an element of "groaning" in his own leadership of the church as well?

D. Closing Prayer (13:20–21)

OVERVIEW

These two verses form the magnificent climax to the letter, followed only by a brief postscript of personal messages. The prayer proper in v.21a is preceded by a memorable description of the God to whom the prayer is offered and followed by a brief but telling doxology. The whole form is that followed by the traditional "collects" of Western Christendom (Bruce, 387).

20May the God of peace, who through the blood of the eternal covenant brought back from the dead our Lord Jesus, that great Shepherd of the sheep, 21equip you with everything good for doing his will, and may he work in us what is pleasing to him, through Jesus Christ, to whom be glory for ever and ever. Amen.

COMMENTARY

20 "Peace" (cf. Heb. *shalom*) was a standard formula in opening and closing letters, but here it is traced to its true source in "the God of peace" (cf. Ro 15:33; 1Th 5:23). But the feature of this God that is picked out for comment is his power shown in the resurrection of Jesus. The idea of resurrection has appeared so far in this letter with reference to the experience of the people of God (see Overview at 11:17–31 and comments at 11:19, 35; also 6:2), not that of Jesus. The resurrection of Jesus as such has not been mentioned at all, and the argument has focused rather on his ascension to heaven and sitting at God's right hand; but it has been assumed in the constant perspective of his death leading to triumph and exaltation, while his "indestructible life" has been noted in 7:3, 16, 24–25. Even here, where Jesus' resurrection is clearly in view, the author does not use one of the regular NT verbs for "raise" but speaks of God as "bringing up" (the NIV's "brought back" is a possible but less basic meaning of the verb) Jesus from the dead (cf. the same phrase in Ro 10:7), a term that better suits his emphasis on Christ's exaltation to heaven. But while the focus of our author's thought may differ from that of Paul or of the early Christian preaching in Acts, the fact that Jesus was "brought up from the dead" underlies his faith as much as theirs. The imagery of the shepherd and his flock is another frequent feature of NT writing that does not occur elsewhere in this letter (though it may be implied in the sleepless watching of the leaders, v.17); its purpose here may be to reassure the readers that in his resurrection theirs, too, is assured.

"The blood of the eternal covenant" more naturally relates to Jesus' death (9:15–22) than to his resurrection. In the Greek word order, the phrase comes between the titles "the great Shepherd of the sheep" and "our Lord Jesus," so that it may be understood as defining Jesus' role as the shepherd who gives his life for the sheep rather than (as the NIV suggests) specifying the "means" of his resurrection. The words "blood" and "covenant" remind us of the heart of the author's atonement theology in chs. 9 and 10; the resurrection of Jesus is an essential step in the working out of that covenantal promise.

21 The prayer in v.21a is a "wish prayer" expressed by an optative verb (as in 1Th 3:11–13; 5:23; 2Th 2:16–17; 3:16). It remarkably avoids using the author's favorite term "perfect," but that is what it is about; indeed, the verb translated

"equip" implies making good what was previously imperfect. The purpose of being "equipped with everything good" (later manuscripts specified "every good *work*," but the original text was more general) is not for the readers' own benefit but to enable them to "do his will." In this clause we see the typical NT dialectic between human responsibility to serve God and the divine grace that alone makes it possible, neither of which excludes the other (cf. Php 2:12–13). The second clause of the prayer makes the point even more explicit: what is "pleasing to him" is what he himself "works in us."

"Through Jesus Christ" (note the full title in this more formal expression, as in the "creedal" statements of v.8 and 10:10) serves both to specify the channel through which God's grace flows to us and also to state the basis of the prayer ("through Jesus, to God," as in v.15). The fact that the phrase occurs at the end of the prayer makes it more natural to read the following doxology as an ascription of praise to Jesus, even though the terms ("glory for ever and ever") are those traditionally used in praise of God (Ro 11:36; 16:27; Gal 1:5; etc.; in some other NT doxologies, Jesus is associated with God [as in Eph 3:21; Rev 5:13], while in others [e.g., 1Pe 4:11] the syntax leaves it unclear whether God or Jesus is the subject). A doxology specifically to Jesus (cf. 2Pe 3:18; Rev 1:6) suits our author's virtual equation of the Son with God (see on 1:8, 10–12).

NOTES

20 There may be a deliberate echo here of LXX Isaiah 63:11, "he who brought up from the earth/land [Heb. "sea"] the shepherd of the sheep," where the "shepherd" is Moses; in that case the author's addition of "great" would mark Jesus out as the greater Moses, brought up not merely from Egypt but from death. The phrase "in the blood of the covenant" corresponds to LXX Zechariah 9:11, where the "in" denotes the theological basis of the deliverance achieved through the messianic king.

E. More Personal Messages (13:22–25)

OVERVIEW

A personal appeal (v.22), a brief "news flash" (v.23), greetings (v.24), and a final benediction (v.25) form a personal postscript to a letter that has already reached its climax in vv.20–21. If the author followed Paul's practice of having the body of the letter written by a secretary, this might be the point where he takes the pen to sign off in his own hand.

> ²²Brothers, I urge you to bear with my word of exhortation, for I have written you only a short letter.
> ²³I want you to know that our brother Timothy has been released. If he arrives soon, I will come with him to see you.
> ²⁴Greet all your leaders and all God's people. Those from Italy send you their greetings.
> ²⁵Grace be with you all.

COMMENTARY

22 *Paraklēsis* ("exhortation," GK *4155*) carries the sense of encouragement as well as demand. If the readers may feel a little bruised by the repeated calls to reform, implied rebukes, and severe warnings of this lengthy "word," he wants his "brothers and sisters" to take it all in the pastoral spirit in which it is intended. See above on vv.17–19 for the delicate situation that might have made his letter unwelcome to the readers. There is no need to see "bear with" as ironical: Lane, 566, suggests "listen willingly" (cf. Ac 18:14; 2Ti 4:3); cf. the NJB's "take kindly." His comment that his missive has been "short" may have evoked a wry smile or perhaps relief that he could not indulge himself further! But 1 Peter 5:12 (also concluding a letter of "encouragement") suggests this may be a conventional deprecatory comment (see Lane, 568–69, for further examples).

23 This is probably the same Timothy we meet so often in association with Paul's mission. It may be that after Paul's death (or indeed during Paul's imprisonment) Timothy continued his work in association with the author, who may have been linked with members of the wider Pauline circle listed (e.g., in 2Ti 4:10–13, 19–21). But we do not know the background, nor do we have any further information on Timothy's imprisonment (which is the most natural, though not the only possible, implication of "release," and in view of Paul's experiences is not at all unlikely). It seems our author was himself free to travel, and it may have been natural for him and Timothy to make a joint pastoral visit to the readers.

24 It may be inappropriate to read too much detail out of such a conventional-sounding formula, but the wording suggests the addressees are not among the local church's leadership and are also distinguished from the wider body of "God's people" where they live. This lends weight to the possibility that they were a (possibly dissident) subgroup or house church within a wider church body (see introduction to 13:17–19); in that case the greetings are not purely conventional but are intended to help to reintegrate the local Christian community. But in addition to the greetings they are asked to pass on to others, there are greetings for themselves, too, from "those from Italy." As noted in the introduction, if the letter is sent to Rome, these could be former members of the Roman church now away from home and associated with the author (people like Aquila and Priscilla [Ac 18:2]), but other possibilities can of course be suggested, such as that the writer is himself in Italy and sending greetings from his associates there to some other area.

25 The author signs off with a benediction like those that conclude Paul's letters, brief and to the point.

JAMES

GEORGE H. GUTHRIE

Introduction

1. AUTHORSHIP

The name "James" has a rich biblical history that is not immediately apparent to readers of English. The earliest English translators of the NT took the form of the name from earlier European translations, such as Spanish (in which *Jaime* was used) or Old French (*Gemmes*), which in turn were based on the Latin *Jacobus*, itself based on the Greek form *Iakōbos*. The Greek more readily reflects its Hebrew origin, *Ya͑aqōb*, normally translated into English as "Jacob." Given the importance of the patriarch Jacob, whose name was changed to "Israel" (Ge 32:28), it is not surprising that the name was very popular among Jews of the first century AD (Shanks and Witherington, 56, 97; Johnson, 92–93). Thus the writer of our book bore the name of the patriarch Jacob, father of the twelve tribes of Israel.

Roughly a half dozen people in the NT are called by the name "James." These include two of the original disciples of Jesus—James son of Zebedee and James son of Alphaeus (Mk 3:16–19)—"James the younger," whom some identify with the son of Alphaeus (Mk 15:40; 16:1), James the father of Judas (not Iscariot; Lk 6:16; Ac 1:13), and James the brother of Jude (Jude 1), who may be one and the same as James the brother of Jesus (Mt 13:55; see Martin, xxxi). Jesus' brother James probably was named after his grandfather "Jacob" (Mt 1:15–16).

Only two of these, the son of Zebedee and the brother of Jesus, have been considered prime candidates for the authorship of the letter of James. Although James son of Zebedee was a member of Jesus' inner circle of disciples, along with Peter and John (Mk 5:37; 9:2; 10:35; 13:3), he died a martyr's death at the hands of Herod Agrippa I in AD 44 (Ac 12:2). This date seems too early for some of the concerns in the book (especially the tension over faith and works in 2:14–26). In any case, James the brother of the Lord, who became the prominent leader of the Jerusalem church, eclipsed the son of Zebedee in terms of early church influence, and the book matches admirably what we know of Jesus' brother from early Christian literature (e.g., Ac 15:13–29; 21:17–26; Hegesippus, in Eusebius's *Hist. eccl.* 2:23). Of the known NT candidates who lived long enough to write the book, only Jesus' brother, without further identification, could have attached his name to the letter before us and could have exerted widespread authority among the churches addressed (Moo, 10).

Further, there are striking similarities between the wording of the book and the speech by James recorded in Acts 15:13–21,[1] and James's ministry, primarily to Jewish Christians in a poor economic situation, seems to fit the concerns addressed by the letter of James. For these and other reasons, that James the brother of the Lord wrote the letter has been the dominant opinion on the authorship of James in the history of the church.

Yet this view has had its challengers.[2] For instance, some suggest that if the brother of the Lord had written the book, he would have identified himself in terms of that relationship; yet, as already noted, the simplicity and self-effacing manner by which James attaches his name to the letter can actually be seen as supporting the traditional position. James the Just, as he came to be called, did not need to bolster his authority in this way (if his posture as reflected in the NT is to be trusted), while a pseudonymous author may have been more inclined to emphasize the relationship between Jesus and James.

A weightier challenge concerns the Greek used by the author of James and aspects of the book's cultural background. The Greek of the book is very good, with literary flourishes at points, and it is "less idiosyncratic than the Greek of Paul and far more polished than that of John" (Johnson, 7). Further, some scholars suggest that the author seems familiar with writings popular in broader Hellenistic Judaism, such as the book of Sirach and the writings of Philo, and that he borrows from the Greek philosophers. Critics of the traditional view on authorship suggest this book could not be the product of a Palestinian carpenter's son (e.g., Ropes, 50).

Yet this argument is not as weighty as it first appears (Johnson, 7; Moo, 14). James rose to be the leader of a Jerusalem church that had a broad constituency of both Palestinian Jews and Jews of the Diaspora, so he certainly had extensive exposure to people of a wide variety of cultural backgrounds and levels of education (Acts 6). Moreover, research of the past few decades has demonstrated decisively that Greek was spoken fluently by many Jews in Palestine, and Galilee in particular, and many Jewish communities in the area had

---

1. See esp. J. B. Mayor, *The Epistle of St. James* (2d ed.; London: Macmillan, 1897), iii–iv. Also, on the nature of the speech in Acts, see Richard Bauckham, "James and the Gentiles (Acts 15.13–21)," in *History, Literature, and Society in the Book of Acts*, ed. Ben Witherington (Cambridge: Cambridge Univ. Press, 1996), 154–84. Bauckham, 184, concludes that "the probability that the substance of James's speech derives from a source close to James himself is high."

2. For a full discussion of the authorship of James, see esp. Peter H. Davids, *The Epistle of James* (NIGTC; Grand Rapids: Eerdmans, 1982), 2–22 (note the helpful table, p. 4); see also Ralph P. Martin, *James* (WBC; Waco, Tex.: Word, 1988), lxi–lxxvii; Luke Timothy Johnson, *The Letter of James* (AB; New York: Doubleday, 1995), 108–21. Other than the traditional view, two other views are notable. Based on the Jewish nature of the epistle and the lack of overt references to Jesus' life and teaching, some have held that James is really a Jewish document to which was attached a thin Christian veneer. On this view, the references to Jesus at 1:1 and 2:1 are simple interpolations added to make the book seem Christian in orientation. However, the extensive work done in recent years on James's use of traditional material from the Synoptic Gospels (esp. the Sermon on the Mount) makes this view implausible. A second position that continues to exert considerable influence among NT scholars is that the book was written pseudonymously. Some read the book as based on the teachings of James himself and perhaps assembled by one or a group of his disciples. Martin, for instance, believes the book was based on James's teachings in the early sixties, which were then carried to Syria and published there. Davids, 12–13, also holds to a two-stage approach but says that James could have been the author of both stages, with an amanuensis polishing the finished work.

been deeply influenced by the broader Hellenistic culture (Davids, 11–12; Moo, 14–15).[3] Also, much recent research has shown that the background of the book's material is most readily explained in terms of Jewish traditions rather than demonstrating much dependence on Greek literature (e.g., Davids, "Palestinian Traditions"). Finally, for such a letter, sent to Jews of the Diaspora, James could have used an amanuensis (or secretary, as did Paul on a number of occasions), who perhaps crafted and polished the final product. In short, James could have written the book, and as we will see, many of the book's features point to a Jewish, Palestinian context and to an author deeply committed to traditional Jewish teachings, as well as to the teachings of James's brother Jesus.

In recent years James the brother of Jesus, or James "the Just" as he was called by the early church, has garnered a good deal of scholarly attention.[4] James was an amazing person. The eldest of Jesus' four brothers, he became the most prominent leader of the Jerusalem church and thus one of the most important leaders of the early Christian movement, being ranked with Peter and Paul (Ac 15:13–21; 21:18–25; Gal 2:12; Jude 1). He seems to have played a mediating role, at once sensitive to the need to stay oriented to Scripture and God's commands to the Jewish people and also to the powerful work of God among the Gentiles. James was remembered in the early church as faithful to the Law and devoted to prayer, and he seems to have garnered respect even from the broader Jewish community of Jerusalem, according to Josephus.

2. DATE

Many factors point to an early date for James, including its thoroughly Jewish orientation, the dynamics and structure of the Christian churches it addresses, and its seeming lack of reference to the Gentiles or the Judaizing controversy (though, admittedly, this is an argument from silence). For many modern believers primarily oriented to Paul, the book has the pleasing, musty smell of something old and rich and culturally unfamiliar.

If James the brother of the Lord is the author, the latest possible date of writing is just prior to his martyrdom in AD 62 at the instigation of a rash, new high priest named Ananus (Josephus, *Ant.* 20.199–203). Yet those who hold to the traditional position on authorship are divided between those who place the book very early (in the forties, making it perhaps the earliest NT book written) and those who place it in the last decade of James's life. Creatively, Ben Witherington dates the book to around AD 52, after the Jerusalem Council, understanding it as a Jewish letter corresponding to the letter sent by that council to the Gentiles (Shanks and Witherington, 146). But this does not seem to fit the content of the letter, which is geared to the problem of social fractiousness in the communities addressed. Rather, it may be suggested that the book of James reflects a time prior to the Jerusalem Council, for 2:14–26 reflects a situation in which the detailed arguments of the council, reflected in Acts 15, have yet to be aired widely. However, it

---

3. See esp. Martin Hengel, *Judaism and Hellenism* (2 vols.; Philadelphia: Fortress, 1974); J. N. Sevenster, *Do You Know Greek? How Much Greek Could the First Jewish Christians Have Known?* (NovTSup; Leiden: Brill, 1968).

4. For recent research on James the brother of Jesus, see Richard Bauckham, *James* (New York: Routledge, 1999); John Painter, *Just James* (Columbia: Univ. of South Carolina Press, 1997); Bruce Chilton and Jacob Neusner, eds., *The Brother of Jesus* (Louisville, Ky.: Westminster, 2001); Bruce Chilton and Craig A. Evans, eds., *James the Just* (NovTSup 98; Leiden: Brill, 1999).

also seems obvious from James that misunderstandings of the teachings characteristic to the ministry of Paul and Barnabas concerning the centrality of faith for salvation have begun to surface.[5] It may be that a period *after* the beginning of Paul and Barnabas's ministry in Antioch (Ac 11:19–26) but *prior* to the Jerusalem Council is not far off the mark. Thus we date the book roughly in the mid- to late-forties.

3. DESTINATION AND OCCASION

Traditionally, James has been labeled a "general," or "catholic" (i.e., universal), letter, along with 1 and 2 Peter; 1, 2, and 3 John; and Jude, due to its general address "To the twelve tribes scattered among the nations." The phrase translated "scattered among the nations" (*en tē diaspora*, GK 1402) refers to the "dispersion" of Jewish people from Palestine throughout the Mesopotamian and Mediterranean worlds beginning in the eighth century BC. Although some have read the address "twelve tribes" as a symbolic way of referring to Christians generally, it is better taken as a reference to Jews, and in the context of James's commitment to Jesus (1:1; 2:1), specifically Jews who are followers of the Messiah (Nystrom, 17–19). Yet Bauckham, 16, reminds us that the early Jewish followers of Jesus did not think of themselves as a separate category of Jew but as the heart of, and a movement of renewal from within, true Judaism; consequently, "What James addresses in practice to those Jews who already confess the Messiah Jesus, he addresses in principle to all Israel." It is also clear from the reference to the dispersion that the letter originated from Israel, and most probably from Jerusalem, the center of early Jewish Christianity. So James seems to have been written from Jerusalem to Jewish Christians of the Diaspora.

Occasion

One of the most striking themes of James, and one that weaves its way through the book, has to do with dynamics related to poverty and wealth (1:9–11, 27; 2:1–11, 14–26; 4:13–5:6). Tensions arising from these dynamics may also explain interpersonal, attitudinal problems in the communities James addresses (e.g., 3:1–12, 13–14:4; 5:7–11) and the "trials" that figure prominently in the book (e.g., 1:2–4, 12; 5:7–11). The primary group addressed is the "pious poor" who were to be rich in faith toward God by fulfilling the love command in spite of oppression. Yet there are those in the Christian communities who have material resources and are challenged to share those resources with their less fortunate brothers and sisters (2:14–26) and to shun the values of the world (e.g., 4:13–17; see Wacob, 195–97). In short, these are communities under stress, materially and relationally, both through external pressure by the wicked rich (5:1–6) and internal pressure from the demands of their relational circumstances (Davids, 85).

---

5. Since the time of Martin Luther, who in 1522 pegged James an "epistle of straw" for its lack of emphasis on "the gospel," many have sought to set James, especially 2:14–26, over against Paul's doctrine of salvation by faith through grace. Yet, as a number of commentators have pointed out, their apparent differences stem from two very different "problem groups" they address. Paul is concerned with Judaizers, who suggest that salvation cannot be had apart from certain religious practices, while James writes concerning supposed Christians who do not have the fruits of salvation (see Johnson, 58–64; Davids, 20–21; James H. Ropes, *A Critical and Exegetical Commentary on the Epistle of St. James* (ICC; Edinburgh: T&T Clark, 1916), 35; and Bauckham, 135–40, who suggests that James and Paul, though having their differences, were "on common ground").

This situation matches what certainly must have been the experience of Jewish believers, "scattered" (*diesparēsan*, GK *1401*) from Jerusalem in the early years of the church first to broader Judea and Samaria (Ac 8:1) and then beyond to Phoenicia, Cyprus, and Antioch (Ac 11:19). They would have had no extended help from a Jerusalem church that itself was burdened with poverty (Ac 11:29; Ro 15:22–29; 2Co 8–9; Gal 2:10). Perhaps forced to work as day laborers, many would have struggled in an eastern Mediterranean social context in which the poor too often were exploited by the rich and the oppressiveness of the situation only intensified during times of famine (Ac 11:27–30; Jas 5:17–18). James seems to have in mind what would have been common situations of those in churches in which a majority of poor and a minority of economically stable persons were thrown together and forced to deal with pressures, both from a larger social context dominated by the wealthy outside the church and from their interpersonal relationships. James challenges both the poor and those with material resources in the church to handle their situations from the perspective of God's righteous wisdom (1:5–8; 3:13–18), found especially in the OT and the teachings of Jesus.

4. STRUCTURE AND MAIN THEMES

The letter of James represents a paraenetic, encyclical letter, i.e., one built around exhortation and meant to circulate among numerous churches (Bauckham, 11–13). As will become plain in the commentary, to accomplish his purpose James draws from a number of traditions, the most important of which are Leviticus 19, aspects of Jewish Wisdom literature, and the teachings of James's brother Jesus (Johnson, 29–48, 55–58). Yet the author does not piece these traditions together in a somewhat disconnected string of thoughts, as Dibelius, 2, suggested by saying that "the entire document lacks continuity in thought." Rather, James has carefully crafted the structure of the book to highlight his primary concerns and move his hearers to desired actions.

Just as a modern author uses subheadings to mark sections of an article or book, the ancients often marked sections of their works with literary devices so that the reader or hearer was notified of various stages of a discourse. For instance, James uses sophisticated transition techniques, including "hook words" (words that occur at the end of a unit that then are repeated at the beginning of the next unit) to effect a smooth transition from one unit to the next (see George H. Guthrie, *The Structure of Hebrews* (Grand Rapids: Baker, 1998), 12–14; Dibelius, 6–7). He also uses *inclusio*, by which an author employs the same or similar words or phrases at the beginning and end (or near the end) of sections to mark those sections as distinct (Guthrie, 15, 76–77). Finally, Taylor, 115, has demonstrated the importance of key transitional passages, worded as proverbial expressions, at 1:12; 1:26–27; 2:12–13; 3:13–18; 4:11–12; and 5:12—and these figure prominently into our assessment of James's structure.

More recent studies of the very difficult structure of James have taken these and other dynamics into consideration, yet nothing close to a consensus on the book's outline has been reached (Taylor, 50–51; Penner, 128). The proposal that follows draws from the tradition of Herman Cladder, F. O. Francis, and Peter Davids (Taylor, 21–29), all of whom see a chiastic structure to the book, but it understands the development of that structure differently at numerous points. Space does not allow a detailed analysis of all the intricate dynamics of the book's development, so general patterns will be the focus here.

An explanation of the book's development is as follows.[6] The letter of James is comprised of three primary movements: an epistolary opening and a double introduction (1:1–27); the body of the letter, which is focused on "Living the Law of Liberty" (2:1–5:6); and a conclusion (5:7–20). Following an epistolary opening, James introduces the book with a double introduction (Taylor, 24–29; Davids, 25, 27; Francis, 111–18), a literary convention that F. O. Francis has demonstrated was used in letters of the period. James uses his double introduction to address the programmatic theme for the whole letter, "Living by Righteous Wisdom." The first half of this double introduction explores the topic "Handling Trials with Righteous Wisdom" (1:2–11), and has three primary subunits addressing "The Spiritual Benefit of Trials" (1:2–4), "The Need for Righteous Wisdom" (1:5–8), and "Wise Attitudes for the Rich and Poor" (1:9–11). The section is bracketed by an inclusio that opens at 1:2 and closes at 1:12, crafted with the theme "endurance under trial" (Taylor, 88). Notice that at the center of 1:2–11 stands the need to ask for wisdom (1:5–8).

Yet v. 12 also forms the opening of an inclusio marking the beginning of the second half of the double introduction and closing at 1:25 (Taylor, 86–89). The inclusio is formed by the "blessed person" theme at 1:12 and 1:25. Therefore, v. 12 forms a unique type of transition, which may be referred to as "overlapping" since it overlaps the end of the double introduction's first half and the beginning of the second half (Guthrie, 102–3; Taylor, 114). In v. 12, the author both reiterates the theme of perseverance under trials from 1:2–4 and leads into the discussion of temptation's true nature.[7] In a sense, then, v. 12 belongs exclusively neither to the first half of the introduction nor to the second but stitches the two together.

The second half of the double introduction actually extends from 1:13 to 1:27 and is given thematic cohesion by the recurring theme of self-deception (1:16, 22, 26). I agree with Peter Davids that the second half of the double introduction echoes the three movements of the first half, but we differ as to how this is accomplished. My understanding of the relationship is as follows:

1:2–11	1:13–27
The Spiritual Benefit of Trials (1:2–4)	Don't Be Deceived Regarding Temptation (1:13–16)
The Need for Righteous Wisdom (1:5–8)	Don't Be Deceived Regarding Righteous Living (1:17–25)
Wise Attitudes for the Rich and Poor (1:9–11)	Don't Be Deceived Regarding Religious Practice (1:26–27)

6. My analysis of the structure has been greatly aided by the extensive analysis and synthesis of recent research on the structure of James by Mark Taylor in his dissertation (see bibliography). I have gained insights both as an external reader on that project and as a continuing dialogue partner concerning the book's structure. Taylor focused the dissertation on analysis of past work and synthesis of key insights. Consequently, he did not present his own depiction of the structure of James. The final analysis of the structure presented here is my own, but it was arrived at, in part, with help from the synthesis and a number of insights presented in Taylor's work.

7. The term translated "trial" at 1:12 (*peirasmos*) is cognate to the verb form of the word translated "tempted" at 1:13 (*peirazō*).

Yet these parallels do not do justice to the complexity of 1:13–27 or to the vital relationship of 1:13–27 to the rest of the discourse. This complexity is due to two factors. First, the four subunits running from 1:13 to 1:25 are woven in the following way:

1:13–16	Temptation's True Nature: Do Not Be Deceived
1:17–19a	GOD'S TRUE NATURE: HE GIVES THE WORD
1:19b–21	RIGHTEOUS LIVING THROUGH THE WORD
1:22–25	Do Not Be Deceived: Be Doers of the Word (the Law of Liberty)

James 1:13–16 addresses the peril of misjudging temptation. Appropriately, this unit ends with the exhortation "Don't be deceived, my dear brothers." The second unit (1:17–19a) provides a mirrored picture of the first, addressing what God, who is not the source of temptation, *does* give—his wise word of truth. It ends with "My dear brothers, take note of this," referring to what has just been said. Thus 1:17–19a ends with "my dear brothers," as did 1:13–16, the two units having parallel conclusions. The third unit begins similarly to the second, the "everyone" (*pas anthrōpos*) providing a parallel introduction to "every good and perfect gift" (*pasa . . . pan*) of 1:17. This third unit continues the theme of the "word," which is to be accepted, begun in the second unit. Finally, the fourth unit, 1:22–25, begins as the first unit ended with a warning about being deceived. This unit balances the "righteous living through the word" theme of 1:19b–21 by showing how wise living must be accomplished, that is, by doing the word. Consequently, these four units are interwoven and resist a simple analysis of their structure. Units one and two mirror each other, as do units three and four; yet units two and three also have a distinct relationship, and units one and four both carry the deception theme.

Second, 1:26–27, the third main subdivision of 1:13–27, both concludes the book's double introduction, rounding out the theme of self-deception, and makes what commentators have correctly judged as a dynamic transition to the body of the book. This transition introduces the topics "The Importance of Right Speaking" (1:26) and "The Importance of Right Actions" (toward the poor and in living righteously; 1:27), which then are dealt with in inverted order in the letter's body: "Wrong Actions toward the Poor" (2:14–26) and Wrong Speaking toward One Another in Principle" (3:1–12; in part similar to Motyer, 13).

The body of James is symmetrical and develops the themes of right actions and right speech introduced in 1:26–27. This symmetrical development is accomplished in an extended reflection on the "law of liberty" (Lev 19:18), which is foreshadowed at 1:25, is reiterated strongly in the body's introduction (2:1–11), and forms the central thought of two summary statements that bracket the body's heart, 2:12–13 and 4:11–12 (Taylor, 92–93).

> Speak and act as those who are going to be judged by the law that gives freedom, because judgment without mercy will be show to anyone who has not been merciful. Mercy triumphs over judgment!
>
> James 2:12–13

> Brothers, do not slander one another. Anyone who speaks against his brother or judges him speaks against the law and judges it. When you judge the law, you are not keeping it, but sitting in judgment on it. There is only one Lawgiver and Judge, the one who is able to save and destroy. But you—who are you to judge your neighbor?
>
> James 4:11–12

With these twin exhortations at the heart of the author's intentions, the symmetrical structure of the letter's body may be depicted as follows':

A   2:1–11 Violating the Royal Law through Judging the Poor: Wrong Speaking and Acting in Community

   B 2:12–13 *So Speak and So Act as One Being Judged by the Law of Liberty*

      C 2:14–26 Wrong Actions toward the Poor (Need for an Active Faith)

         D 3:1–12 Wrong Speaking toward One Another in Principle

            E 3:13–18 RIGHTEOUS VS. WORLDLY WISDOM

         D' 4:1–5 Wrong Actions and Speaking toward One Another in Practice

      C' 4:6–10 A Call to Humility and Repentance

   B' 4:11–12 *Do the Law, Do Not Judge It*

A'   4:13–5:6 Twin Calls to the Arrogant Rich

              4:13–17 A Rebuke of Arrogant Presumption

              5:1–6 A Statement of Judgment on the Wicked Rich

James 2:1–11 introduces the body of the letter by addressing the violation of the "royal law" through judging the poor. This involves both wrong speech and wrong actions in the community of faith. James 2:14–26 clearly is concerned with an active faith, and this unit flows from and has numerous connections with 2:1–11. James 2:12–13, on the other hand, stands between these two units, at once forming a climactic statement on 2:1–11 and playing a key role, in tandem with 4:11–12, in marking the heart of the letter's main body as shown in the outline above.

James 3:1–12 continues the development of the book by addressing the problem of "wrong speaking" to one another in the community. In our outline, we have added the words "in principle" because of the highly "theoretical" nature of 3:1–12. In this passage, James does not address specific problems in the communities, which he will take up in 4:1–5, but rather offers a teaching on the destructiveness of the tongue by presenting a series of graphic illustrations and principles. It may be that he specifically has teachers of the communities in mind at this point, given his statement about the ministry of teaching in 3:1. As noted above, this theme of "wrong speaking" had been "announced" at 1:26.

Standing at the midpoint of the chiastic structure of the book, James 3:13–18 contrasts righteous wisdom with worldly wisdom, reaching back, via a number of lexical parallels, to both 1:5–8 and 1:17–21 (Taylor, 153), each of which stands at the center of their respective halves of the double introduction. This clear call to live out God's righteous wisdom forms a fitting climax to the first half of the body, addressing the need for righteous actions and attitudes that promote right relationships in the communities of faith. At the same time, its emphasis on humility over against arrogance anticipates the primary theme of 4:6–5:6. James 3:13–18 also stands as a key transition between 3:1–12 and 4:1–5, moving the discourse from the destructiveness of the tongue to general patterns of relational destructiveness in the communities of faith. Furthermore, James 4:1–5 has a number of parallels with 3:1–12, giving balance to that unit by addressing "Wrong Actions and Speaking toward One Another in Practice." In effect, it sums up and provides a scathing rebuke of the serious relational problems in the communities stemming from failure to "speak and act" in accordance with the law of love.

James 4:6–5:6, a sustained call to humility, is bracketed by an inclusio constructed with the "opposition" theme at 4:6 and 5:6 (Taylor, 96). At 4:6, in the words of Proverbs 3:34, God is said to be opposed to the proud, and this leads into a general call for repentance (4:6–10). James 5:1–6, on the other hand, concludes with a scathing statement of judgment on the wealthy landowners, proclaiming that the righteous, innocent person does not "oppose" (or resist) them. Structurally, the call to humility in 4:6–10 gives balance to the wrong actions toward the poor in 2:14–26, and the twin treatments of the rich, which have parallel introductions at 4:13 and 5:1, balance 2:1–11, in which favoritism is shown by honoring the rich over the poor.

The conclusion of the book, 5:7–20, also has two movements, and these mirror the double introduction of the book, exhibiting extensive lexical parallels with the introduction (Taylor, 98–100). The first movement of the conclusion, "The Need for Patient Endurance" (5:7–11), roughly parallels the first half of the introduction (1:2–12), and the second, "The Need for Righteous Words in Community" (5:12–20), demonstrates extensive connections to 1:12–25.

Thus James, with extensive use of literary devices, sophisticated theme development, and generous amounts of exhortation, constitutes a complex and dynamically developing letter. The book's beauty and practicality are woven in a masterpiece, blending elements of style, pieces of Jewish and Christian tradition, and the author's own reflections on appropriate application. In this manner, James calls the first readers and all Christian readers since to a life of righteous living as an embodiment of God's righteous wisdom.

5. BIBLIOGRAPHY

The following is a selective list of commentaries and monographs on James available in English, confined for the most part to those referred to in the commentary (they will be referred to simply by the author's name [and initials only when necessary to distinguish two authors of the same surname]). References to other resources will carry full bibliographic details at the first mention and thereafter a short title.

Adamson, James B. *The Epistle of James*. New International Commentary on the New Testament. Grand Rapids: Eerdmans, 1976.

Bauckham, Richard. *James: Wisdom of James, Disciple of Jesus the Sage*. New Testament Readings. New York: Routledge, 1999.

———. "James and the Gentiles (Acts 15.13–21)." Pages 154–84 in *History Literature, and Society in the Book of Acts*. Edited by Ben Witherington III. Cambridge: Cambridge Univ. Press, 1996.

Bray, Gerald, ed. *James, 1–2 Peter, 1–3 John, Jude*. Ancient Christian Commentary on Scripture. Downers Grove, Ill.: InterVarsity, 2000.

Chilton, Bruce, and Jacob Neusner, eds. *The Brother of Jesus: James the Just and His Mission*. Louisville Ky.: Westminster John Knox, 2001.

Chilton, Bruce, and Craig A. Evans, eds. *James the Just and Christian Origins*. Novum Testamentum Supplements 98. Leiden: Brill, 1999.

Davids, Peter H. *The Epistle of James: A Commentary on the Greek Text*. New International Greek Testament Commentary. Grand Rapids, Mich.: Eerdmans, 1982.

———. "Palestinian Traditions in the Epistle of James." In *James the Just and Christian Origins*. Edited by Bruce Chilton and Craig A. Evans. Novum Testament Supplements. Leiden: Brill, 1999.

Dibelius, Martin, and Heinrich Greeven. *James*. Hermeneia. Translated by M. A. Williams. Philadelphia: Fortress Press, 1975.

Edgar, David H. *Has Not God Chosen the Poor? Social Setting of the Epistle of James*. Journal for the Study of the New Testament: Supplement Series 206. Sheffield: Sheffield Academic Press, 2001.

Francis, F. O. "The Form and Function of the Opening and Closing Paragraphs of James and 1 John." *Zeitschrift für die neutestamentliche Wissenschaft und die Kunde der älteren Kirche* 61 (1970): 110–26.

Johnson, Luke Timothy. *The Letter of James: A New Translation with Introduction and Commentary*. Anchor Bible. New York: Doubleday, 1995.

————. "The Use of Leviticus 19 in the Letter of James." *Journal of Biblical Literature* 101 (1982): 391–401.

Laws, Sophie. *The Epistle of James*. Black's New Testament Commentaries. Peabody, Mass.: Hendrickson, 1980.

Martin, Ralph P. *James*. Word Biblical Commentary 48. Waco, Tex.: Word, 1988.

Moo, Douglas J. *The Letter of James*. Pillar New Testament Commentary. Grand Rapids: Eerdmans, 2000.

Motyer, J. A. *The Message of James: The Test of Faith*. The Bible Speaks Today. Downers Grove, Ill.: InterVarsity, 1985.

Neusner, Jacob, and William Scott Green, eds. *Dictionary of Judaism in the Biblical Period: 450 B.C.E. to 600 C.E.* Peabody, Mass.: Hendrickson, 1999.

Nystrom, David P. *James*. NIV Application Commentary. Grand Rapids: Zondervan, 1997.

Penner, Todd C. *The Epistle of James and Eschatology: Re-reading an Ancient Christian Letter*. Journal for the Study of the New Testament: Supplement Series 121. Sheffield: Sheffield Academic Press, 1996.

Ropes, James H. *A Critical and Exegetical Commentary on the Epistle of St. James*. International Critical Commentary. Edinburgh: T&T Clark, 1916.

Ryken, Leland et al., eds. *Dictionary of Biblical Imagery*. Downers Grove, Ill.: InterVarsity, 1998.

Shanks, Hershel, and Ben Witherington III. *The Brother of Jesus: The Dramatic Story and Meaning of the First Archaeological Link to Jesus and His Family*. New York: HarperCollins, 2003.

Taylor, Mark Edward. "A Textlinguistic Investigation into the Discourse Structure of James." Ph.D. diss., Southwestern Baptist Theological Seminary, 2001.

Wacob, Wesley Hiram. *The Voice of Jesus in the Social Rhetoric of James*. Society of New Testament Studies. Cambridge: Cambridge Univ. Press, 2000.

6. OUTLINE

Text and Exposition

I. THE OPENING OF THE LETTER (1:1)

OVERVIEW

In general, letters of the ancient world followed a standard form that included the author's self-identification, those to whom the letter was addressed, and a greeting, and James uses this pattern to open his work. The NT letters in particular, however, often carry interesting overtones hinting at nuances in how the author regarded himself and the recipients of his work, and as seen in v.1, James includes such overtones.

---

¹James, a servant of God and of the Lord Jesus Christ,

To the twelve tribes scattered among the nations:

Greetings.

COMMENTARY

1 Our author, as already discussed in the introduction, probably is James, brother of the Lord and leader of the Jerusalem church in the mid-first century (e.g., Ac 15:13–21). However, James does not appeal to his familial relationship with Jesus as a basis for authority. Rather, he calls himself "a servant of God and of the Lord Jesus Christ" (the NASB reads "a bond-servant"). The term translated "servant" is *doulos* (GK *1528*), a word used of various kinds of slavery or servanthood in the ancient world. A specific use of the word to emphasize leadership as service to the Lord, both in the OT and other Jewish writings, is probably in the immediate backdrop here. For instance, both Moses and David were referred to as God's servants, and the Servant of Isaiah obviously carries the title. In these cases the servant of God is God's humble representative, who comes not with an arrogant posture in his own authority but rather to carry out work or ministry as one called by God. Didymus the Blind, a writer of the fourth century, remarked that those of the world who wish to glorify themselves play up their qualifications when they write letters, but by contrast the apostles begin their letters by noting "that they are slaves of God and Christ" (cited in Bray, 2). Thus the designation combines the softness of humility and the strength of authority in an integrated vision of leadership under the lordship of God.

Further, James is a servant of "the Lord Jesus Christ." Commentators have pointed out that the construction rendered "of God and of the Lord Jesus Christ" by the NIV is awkward in Greek. It is possible to translate the construction as "of [our] God and Lord Jesus Christ," but it is more likely the NIV has it right in this case. James witnesses to the fact that servanthood to God and his Messiah, Jesus, is a package deal. Jesus, whom God "made both Lord and Christ," the second member of the Trinity, is one to whom James owes his allegiance. In Christianity, to be the servant of God necessitates being the servant of the Lord, God's Messiah, and to follow Messiah implies service to God.

The "greetings" (*chairein*, GK *5897*), a very common form of salutation in ancient letters of the time, is addressed "To the twelve tribes scattered among the nations." In the wake of the destruction of the northern kingdom by Assyria (722 BC; see 2Ki 17:5–6) and the exile brought against the southern kingdom by the Babylonians (587–538 BC; see 2Ki 25:1–12), the Jewish people were "dispersed" among the nations. The term *diaspora* (GK *1402*) could variously refer to the *place* to

which the Jews had been scattered, the scattered people themselves, or the *state of being dispersed* abroad. As noted in the introduction, although some have read the address "twelve tribes" as a symbolic way of referring to Christians generally, it is better taken as a reference to Christian Jews (1:1; 2:1), who did not see themselves as adherents to a religion different from broader Judaism (Nystrom, 17–19; Bauckham, 16). One of the promises concerning Messiah is that he would bring the twelve tribes back together again in a cohesive nation (Isa 11:11–16; Jer 31:8; Eze 37:15–22). Indeed, this promise was seen by the early Christian community as fulfilled in their existence as reconstituted Israel, the new people of God bought by his salvation through Christ (e.g., Ro 9:24–26; see Laws, 47–48). Yet here the designation should be taken as racial and geographical.

II. DOUBLE INTRODUCTION: LIVING BY RIGHTEOUS WISDOM (1:2–27)

A. Introduction Part I: Handling Trials with Righteous Wisdom (1:2–11)

OVERVIEW

At first blush, the subunits of James 1:2–12 appear somewhat disjointed. Yet the first and last verses of this introductory movement of the book may be taken as marking the beginning and end of a cohesive unit. Placed in the context of the whole book, we see that the themes of trials, wisdom, and wealth recur over and again and, when understood in light of James's overall program, make sense in relation to one another. It may be, as suggested in the introduction, that the specific trial of dealing with rich oppressors is in the forefront of applications

the author has in mind. Thus these are people struggling to keep attitudes and actions in line with God's ways, and they need perspective on how such trials, though difficult, work for the believer's benefit and can be approached with righteous wisdom. James 1:2–4 gives "The Spiritual Benefit of Trials"; 1:5–8 introduces "The Need for Righteous Wisdom" when confronted by trials; and 1:9–11 points to a specific application—the attitudinal difficulties involved in the polar material experiences of being either rich or poor. All three units cohere around the need for wise perspective in approaching life.

As noted in the introduction, v.12 forms a special transition that both concludes the introduction's first main movement and introduces the introduction's second main movement. Thus, v.12 will be considered separately below.

1. The Spiritual Benefit of Trials (1:2–4)

[2]Consider it pure joy, my brothers, whenever you face trials of many kinds, [3]because you know that the testing of your faith develops perseverance. [4]Perseverance must finish its work so that you may be mature and complete, not lacking anything.

COMMENTARY

2 James likes to speak to his readers as "brothers" (1:16, 19; 2:1, 5, 14; 3:1, 10, 12; 4:11; 5:7, 9–10, 12, 19), an address commonly used in the ancient world for both men and women with whom one shared a religious affiliation. The word connotes intimacy of relationship and places the exhortations of the book squarely in the context of community. James does not challenge them as a remote authority but rather as an intimate member of the group.

His challenge to recognize the benefit of their trials has twin main thrusts, expressed in the passage's two main clauses: "Consider it pure joy," and "Perseverance must finish its work" (more appropriately rendered as an exhortation by the NASB with "Let endurance have [its] perfect result"). The life circumstance in mind here is "whenever you face trials of many kinds." The term translated "trials" (peirasmois, GK 4280) could be used to connote "difficulties" or periods of "testing" in life (e.g., Ac 20:19; 1Pe 1:6, 4:12), such as when a believer experiences persecution of some kind. It could also be used of temptation, or enticement to sin (e.g., 1Ti 6:9). Although James uses the verbal form of the word (peirazō, GK 4279) in 1:13–14 with this latter meaning, the NIV and NASB correctly translate it as "trials" here. The general logic of the passage parallels other NT passages (e.g., Ro 5:2–5; 1Pe 1:6–7) that encourage believers to endure under difficulties of various kinds because of the spiritual payoff of such trials.

If the broader context of James is an indication, the trials in mind here may have to do primarily with the oppression suffered under wealthy landowners (5:1–11). Nevertheless, James describes the trials as "of many kinds," broadening the exhortation to hit a wide spectrum of challenges brought on by life. When we "face" (NASB, "encounter") the various difficulties of life, the experience often is unexpected. This term rendered "face" by the NIV (peripiptō, GK 4346) could be used, for instance, of a traveler suddenly coming upon robbers, as in the story of the good Samaritan (Lk 10:30), or a ship suddenly hitting a reef. Most trials don't "call ahead" to announce themselves. Their sudden presence in our lives demands a ready spiritual response.

That response is to "consider it pure joy." The verb translated "consider" is in the imperative form and could mean "to think," "to regard," or "to consider"; it calls for the readers to look at their circumstances from an unexpected vantage point. As human beings, our natural response to difficulties is to read them as negative interlopers that detract from our well-being. James challenges his readers to shift their perspectives and consider their trials from a different angle, an angle that sees in the pain of tribulation a reason for "pure joy." The description of the joy as "pure" intensifies the idea—every bit of the trial can be redeemed by God for a good use, so the joy is not a trumped-up face put on a deeper melancholy. Rather, this is *real* or *genuine* joy that flows from a changed perspective.

3 This change of perspective, the basis on which we can see trials from the vantage point of genuine joy, is "because you know that the testing of your faith produces endurance." Jewish literature contained a rich heritage concerning the positive effect of trials. For example, the Lord tests the hearts of his people like gold and silver is tested in a crucible (Pr 17:3), and his remnant will be purified through their difficulties (Isa 48:10–11). In many of the OT passages, the people are tested in fires of their own building with the fuel of disobedience (Eze 22:17–22). Yet God is a redeemer who can carry his people through the water and fire of troubles and bring them out to a place of abundance (Ps 66:12). The productivity of faith under fire can be seen in great figures of the OT such as Abraham, Job, and Joseph, who, resolute in their trust in God and commitment to walking in his ways despite opposition, received the spiritual dividends of the experience.

Thus the testing of faith is productive, and James states that it produces "endurance" (*hypomonē*, GK *5705*), or the ability to hold up under the stress of difficult circumstances with a right spiritual posture. As a diamond is formed in the grip of extreme pressure, so the valuable character trait of endurance is crafted in the crucible of trials (see 2Co 6:4; 1Th 1:3; Rev 1:9; 2:2; 14:12).

4 In 1:4 James describes this aspect of Christian character as the ultimate purpose for enduring under difficulties: "And let endurance have [its] perfect result, so that you may be perfect and complete, lacking in nothing" (NASB). It is certainly a temptation to jettison endurance, to attempt to escape the path of difficulty. James, however, exhorts the reader to remain in the posture of endurance until the "perfect result" is attained. Perfection here, rather than speaking simply of a sinless state, refers to a maturity of character, "a full-blown character of stable righteousness," which "is the virtue of the righteous man" (Davids, 70). Through endurance under trials, therefore, we "pick up" those aspects of Christian character that can be had through no other means, and we gain a stability spiritually that can withstand the storms of life.

Therefore, James 1:2–4 challenges believers undergoing trials to consider their difficulties from the vantage point of the spiritual payoff of the experience. Such trials may be embraced with joy, therefore, not by relishing the trial itself but rather by seeing the greater effect as one learns to endure in such circumstances. Neither is the act of enduring in and of itself the ultimate goal. Instead, the path of endurance leads to a place of well-rounded Christian character, a place where we do not lack the necessary equipment for facing the variety of difficulties we are bound to experience in this life.

2. The Need for Righteous Wisdom (1:5–8)

⁵If any of you lacks wisdom, he should ask God, who gives generously to all without finding fault, and it will be given to him. ⁶But when he asks, he must believe and not doubt, because he who doubts is like a wave of the sea, blown and tossed by the wind. ⁷That man should not think he will receive anything from the Lord; ⁸he is a double-minded man, unstable in all he does.

COMMENTARY

5 In v.4, James has just provided a portrait of fully developed Christian character. The fully mature believer is one who is "lacking in nothing." Yet alas, most of us are still on the path, not having arrived at that level of maturity. Therefore, James makes a transition to this next passage by pointing to a possible need among his readers: "If any of you lacks wisdom . . ." It is vital to grasp what James means by "wisdom." Wisdom here connotes an understanding of the ways of God and a readiness to act according to those ways. This close connection between wisdom and righteousness can be seen in James 3:13–18:

> ¹³ Who is wise and understanding among you? Let him show it by his good life, by deeds done in the humility that comes from wisdom. ¹⁴ But if you harbor bitter envy and selfish ambition in your hearts, do not boast about it or deny the truth. ¹⁵ Such "wisdom" does not come down from heaven but is earthly, unspiritual, of the devil. ¹⁶ For where you have envy and selfish ambition, there you find disorder and every evil practice. ¹⁷ But the wisdom that comes from heaven is first of all pure; then peace-loving, considerate, submissive, full of mercy and good fruit, impartial and sincere. ¹⁸ Peacemakers who sow in peace raise a harvest of righteousness.

Thus, true wisdom issues forth in living according to the ways of the Lord, and if anyone lacks this understanding of and commitment to the ways of God, God himself—wisdom's true and only source who gives "to all"—may be approached. In other words, God has shown himself to have issued an open invitation to people to come and find in him the wisdom they need to approach life righteously. This thought echoes Wisdom passages in Proverbs, such as the following (Pr 2:1–7):

> ¹ My son, if you accept my words and store up my commands within you, ² turning your ear to wisdom and applying your heart to understanding, ³ and if you call out for insight and cry aloud for understanding, ⁴ and if you look for it as for silver and search for it as for hidden treasure, ⁵ then you will understand the fear of the LORD and find the knowledge of God. ⁶ For the LORD gives wisdom, and from his mouth come knowledge and understanding. ⁷ He holds victory in store for the upright, he is a shield to those whose walk is blameless.

Furthermore, James expresses the manner in which God gives wisdom as "generously" and "without finding fault." The first suggests that God is not stingy with wisdom but rather eager to provide guidance for how life should be approached.

That he gives "without finding fault" means he does not insult or put down those who come to him with their deficiency. Unlike the father who slaps the hand of a child reaching up for a desired item, God eagerly gives wisdom to the person desiring his perspective on life.

6–7 This generous act of giving, however, is not without qualifications, for the seeker "must believe and not doubt, because he who doubts is like a wave of the sea, blown and tossed by the wind." The Greek phrase the NIV renders as "must believe" is in reality a prepositional phrase more accurately translated "in faith," as by the NASB. "Faith" is a prominent theme in James, with forms of the word *pistis* (GK *4411*) or its cognate verb occurring fourteen times (1:3, 6; 2:1, 5, 14–26; 5:15). Most of these congregate in the famous "faith and works" passage, 2:14–26. For James, faith seems to involve a strong commitment to act on what is right. Faith is not simply a state of mind but rather a posture of trust in God that expresses itself in action. The antithesis of this posture of active trust is "doubting," which the one asking from God must avoid. The admonishment here might be rendered better with the translation "not hesitating," for when in the middle voice the term can connote "disputing with oneself" (Moo, 60). Thus a person who fails to take a solid stance of active trust in the Lord correspondingly hesitates in spiritual commitments.

This lack of trust in the Lord, which finds a person hesitating between a firm commitment to God's way of wisdom and the way of unrighteous fools, leads to a striking state of spiritual instability. Therefore, the vacillator is shilly-shally like a wave in the sea that swishes first one way, then the next, depending on which way the wind blows and swirls around it. James suggests such a person by no means should expect a positive answer from the Lord because he is "double-minded" and "unstable in all he does."

8 To be double-minded means to be of a divided heart or commitment, to be a person whose allegiances at best are not clear and at worst struggle in profound conflict. In the OT the idea was expressed as being double-tongued or "two-faced," or having two hearts rather than a single heart of integrity (Nystrom, 53; e.g., Ps 12:2; Dt 26:16). Such a person is "unstable" (*akatastatos*, GK *190*), a term also used in 3:8 to speak of the restlessness or uncontrollable nature of the tongue. The final phrase of 1:8, "in all he does," places emphasis squarely in the realm of actions. It is not merely that such a person struggles with inner conflict. Rather, the emphasis here is on the outer manner of life that is profoundly affected by inner spiritual conflicts. The foolish person, never able to marshal resolute commitment to God, lives foolishly and, thus, is out of sync with God's ways.

In James 1:5–8 we are given a gracious offer. God freely and eagerly supplies wisdom—a right understanding of and commitment to righteous living—to those who come to him in a posture of active trust, a readiness to live out God's ways. Yet one must come with a firm, prior commitment to obedience, not hesitating between the way of wisdom and the way of fools. Such a person James characterizes as a spiritual vacillator who, due to a divided inner life, cannot expect God's gift of wisdom.

It may be that James is concerned especially with those among his readers who, caught up in trials and conflicts (1:2–4), are needing to respond in endurance but are not sure how to live out such endurance. If indeed the backdrop here involves the specific trials stemming from social conflicts in the church, then the need for wisdom involves a need to understand what might constitute a righteous response to the conflicts at hand. This brings us to the third unit in this section and to a consideration of the "Wise Attitudes for Rich and Poor."

3. Wise Attitudes for the Rich and Poor (1:9-11)

OVERVIEW

Perhaps one of the universal, perennial issues for human beings generally is our relationship to material resources and how the possession or lack of such resources shapes us, our attitudes, and our relationships with others. It is not surprising, therefore, that the Scriptures would have a great deal to say about how our economic state affects us spiritually, and James 1:9–11 addresses two levels at which temptation related to one's economic status manifests itself.

This passage may seem at first blush to sit awkwardly in the first chapter's flow of thought. However, as mentioned above, there is logic to the topic being raised at this point. The author has given us hints that, while vv.9–11 constitute a distinct unit of thought, the thought flows from what has gone before (Davids, 75). Specifically, 1:9–11 may be taken as a wise approach (1:5–8) to one of the "various

trials" (NASB) mentioned previously (1:2–4). In line with the earlier exhortation on life's difficulties, the verb *kauchasthō* (GK *3016*, v.9), which the NIV appropriately renders "take pride in" and the NASB "to glory," if not semantically corresponding to the "consider it pure joy" of v.2, at least suggests a positive attitude in the situation (Motyer, 42).

As to the structure of the passage itself, the author begins with twin contrasting exhortations to have proper perspective—"to glory" in one's position—whether one is poor or rich (vv.9–10a). He continues with an analogy to the rich person's situation, likening it to the fleeting nature of a wildflower's existence, followed with a description of the flower's demise (vv.10b–11a). He then closes with a truism concerning the tentative nature of the rich man himself (v.11b). This structure of the passage (NASB) may be depicted as follows:

Exhortations: But the brother of humble circumstances
                             is to glory in his high position;
                                    and

contrast ⟶ the rich man *is to glory* in his humiliation,

Analogy/reason: because
                                  like flowering grass he will pass away.

Description: For
                        ┌ the sun rises with a scorching wind
                        │   and
progression │ withers the grass;
                        │   and
                        │ its flower falls off
                        │   and
                        └ the beauty of its appearance is destroyed;

Truism: so too the rich man in the midst of his pursuits will fade away.

⁹The brother in humble circumstances ought to take pride in his high position. ¹⁰But the one who is rich should take pride in his low position, because he will pass away like a wild flower. ¹¹For the sun rises with scorching heat and withers the plant; its blossom falls and its beauty is destroyed. In the same way, the rich man will fade away even while he goes about his business.

COMMENTARY

9 The first exhortation is addressed to "the brother" of "humble circumstances." The use of *adelphos* ("brother," GK *81*) makes it clear a fellow believer is in view. The term translated "humble circumstances" (*ho tapeinos*, GK *5424*) can refer to a person's status, resources, opportunities, or attitude and often is rendered as "humble" or "lowly." Here the situation of being poor materially seems to be in view, because this brother is contrasted with "the rich" in the next verse. In the biblical literature, the "lowly" or "poor" person is of special concern to God (Johnson, 184–85; e.g., LXX Pss 9:39; 17:28; 33:19; 81:3; 101:18; Isa 11:4; 14:32), and James, here and with the quotation of Proverbs 3:34 in 4:6, picks up on this biblical theme. This affirmation of the person who struggles with a humble situation in life also connects very directly to the teachings of Jesus, in which there often is a reversal of status—the exalted are brought lower and the lowly are raised up (Edgar, 68–70; e.g., Mt 23:12/Lk 14:11; Lk 6:24–25; 12:16–21; 16:19–31; 18:4).

So the humble brother "ought to take pride in his high position." The special favor of God makes for a situation in which "boasting" is appropriate. The term rendered "take pride in" (*kauchasthō*, GK *3016*) by the NIV can be used to speak of boasting or glorying in something or someone and in the wisdom tradition of the OT is often seen as a very appropriate action, the basis of the boasting being

the key (Johnson, 185). The concept in the NT is especially found in Paul's writings. Paul can speak, for instance, of boasting in God (Ro 2:17), in the Lord (2Co 10:17), or in Christ Jesus (Php 3:3), but he can also speak of taking pride in weaknesses (2Co 12:9) and in afflictions (Ro 5:3) because these have spiritual value in God's economy. So James exhorts the poor Christian to "take pride in his high position," that is his high status as a member of the community of God's people. Here again we are challenged to see our experiences from the perspective of God's values rather than those of the world.

10 Commentators are fairly evenly divided as to whether the "rich" person of v.10 is also a Christian brother or one of the rich oppressors outside the church, and it is difficult to come to a firm conclusion. Those who hold the latter position take the exhortation as highly ironic, since an unbeliever would not "take pride in" his humiliation. Elsewhere in James (e.g., 2:7; 5:1–6) the "rich" seem clearly to be unbelievers, and in strands of Jewish tradition the rich are set in contrast to the "poor" people of God. Further, the rich person of 1:10–11 is offered no future hope, so it is difficult to conceive of this person being a believer (Davids, 77; Laws, 63–64; Martin, 23; Dibelius, 87).

On the other hand, those who understand the rich person here as a Christian brother point out that grammatically both the subject and verb must be supplied to the main clause at the beginning of v.10, and these flow naturally from the previous verse. The verb in v.9, translated "to take pride in," carries over to this clause, and so should the subject, "the brother" (*ho adelphos*, GK *81*). The parallelism between the two clauses strengthens this conclusion. Further, these commentators suggest, the irony required by the "unbeliever" position is excessive. The exhortation for a rich Christian to glory in the tentative nature of his economic strength makes more sense (Nystrom, 54; Adamson, 61; Motyer, 43).

It may be pointed out also that the Christian communities to whom James writes seem to have the wealthy in their midst (2:1–2), and the exhortation of 4:13–17 can be understood to be addressed to Christians involved in business. The thought of the latter passage parallels our passage under consideration. It is not difficult to imagine a situation in which the "trials" of dealing with the rich come on various levels for the church. On one level, navigating the relationships between the poor and rich within the congregation is challenging. On another, the poor would struggle with the oppression of the rich outside the church, and the brother of financial resources would struggle against falling into the cultural patterns of rich unbelievers with whom they would have had some association. On balance, therefore, that here we are dealing with a rich believer may have the upper hand, though the case is far from clear.

What is clear is the principle encapsulated in the balance of v.10 and v.11. Oecumenius asserts, "James calls the rich man both proud and humble at the same time, because what puffs him up also brings him down" (cited in Bray, 10). The impermanent, fleeting nature of material possessions should be a cause for pause for the rich and should spur the wealthy person to glory in the "low position"

of being spiritually dependent on God. The proverbial analogy that the rich person's passing away is like a wildflower is taken from Isaiah 40:7 (LXX): "All flesh is grass, and all the glory of man as the flower of grass. The grass withers, and the flower falls off, but the word of our God remains forever" (1Pe 1:24; cf. Ps 103:15–16). In Palestine were wildflowers, such as the anemone and the cyclamen, that wither before the burning heat of the sun (Davids, 77).

11 A description of the progression of the wildflower's demise follows in v.11: the sun rises with its scorching heat, the plant withers before it, the flower falls off, destroying the flower's beauty. The term rendered "scorching heat" by the NIV could also refer to the sirocco, a seasonal, burning "wind" (NASB) that blows for three or four days in the fall and spring, and this is a common use of the word in the LXX (e.g., Hos 12:2; 13:15; Isa 49:10; Jer 18:17). Yet that wind blows day and night, not being directly related to the rising of the sun (Davids, 78). It is better, therefore, with the NIV, to understand the reference here to the blazing heat of the sun.

James ends with a truism, "In the same way, the rich man will fade away even while he goes about his business." The word translated "fade away" can connote the drying up of plants as well as the dying of a person, and the term rendered "business" variously refers to patterns of life or journeys. Thus the rich person is reminded that in the process of pursuing business activities, he or she will suddenly die one day. Here lies the weighty basis for the exhortation. The rich person's "glory" is misplaced if placed in his riches, for all patterns of earthly life will come to a sudden termination (cf. 5:1–6).

James 1:9–11 reminds us that one's economic situation can be an occasion for spiritual reflection. For the poor believer, humble circumstances are no excuse for bitter attitudes, since that person can take pride in the high status afforded him in God's eyes. The rich person, on the other hand, must avoid the temptation to draw a sense of worth, to glory in, an exalted earthly status based on material resources, which are provisional in nature. Rather,

the wealthy should take pride in a posture of humility that stems from proper reflection on the reality of things—the glory of earthly possessions fades quickly, like a withering flower before the rising sun.

NOTES

1–11 As noted in the introduction under our discussion of structure, authors during this time period did not use subheadings to mark the various movements of a letter or discourse. In fact, they didn't even use spaces between their words, and chapter and verse divisions would not come on the scene for another one and a half millennia. Rather, they often used a device called *inclusio*, the repeating of a similar statement or phrase at the beginning and end of a section. By doing so, the author signals to the reader or hearer that the section was coming to an end.

5 James uses a device here known as a *hook word*, a form of transition by which a term at the end of one section is used again at the beginning of the next.

B. Overlapping Transition: Blessings for Those Who Persevere Under Trial (1:12)

[12]Blessed is the man who perseveres under trial, because when he has stood the test, he will receive the crown of life that God has promised to those who love him.

COMMENTARY

12 This verse plays a vitally important role in the book's double introduction. As noted in the introduction to this commentary, it forms both the conclusion to 1:2–12 and the introduction to 1:12–27, the author crafting it as an "overlapping transition." The reference to endurance under trial reaches back to 1:2–4, while the "blessed" person theme reaches forward to 1:25, where the author begins to draw the introduction to a close. He also uses v.12 to lead into the discussion of temptation's true nature in vv.13–16.

The word translated "Blessed" (*makarios*, GK *3421*) calls to mind Jesus' teachings, especially the

Beatitudes (Mt 5:3–11; 11:6; 13:16; 16:17; 24:46; Lk 6:20–22; 7:23; 11:27–28; Jn 13:17; 20:29), which hark back to Jewish tradition embodied, for instance, in the Psalms (e.g., Pss 1:1–2:12; 31:1; 39:5; 83:5; 111:1; 143:15). "Blessedness" has to do with well-being in life that flows from the favorable position in which one is rightly related to God (Johnson, 187). Here the blessing is for the person who endures a trial. The absence of the Greek article probably indicates that no specific trial is in view, and the earlier passage, 1:2–4, has noted that trials are "various" (NASB). James, then, is interested in giving his readers encouragement in the face of discouraging and difficult experiences in general.

The basis for this proclamation of blessing and, therefore, the source of encouragement follows: "because when he has stood the test, he will receive the crown of life." In Jewish literature, the concept of being "tested" is almost ubiquitous, being found wherever God relates to his people. The most famous story in Jewish tradition is the testing of Abraham through the offering of Isaac (Ge 22). Jacob, Ruth, David, Daniel, and many other biblical exemplars face tests of various kinds, and the tests reveal the character of the one tested.

Thus for the believer, it is when one has been "approved" (NASB) that the crown of life is gained. In the OT "crowning," in a general sense, can symbolize the blessings of God, as in Proverbs 10:6 or Isaiah 35:10 (Ryken, 185). Yet crowns in the ancient Mediterranean world were of various kinds and, therefore, could symbolize various dynamics. The winner of a battle or athletic competition was, at times, honored with a bay or olive wreath; royalty wore crowns representing their authority; and a flower garland, worn during a time of celebration such as a wedding or festival, represented joy (Laws, 68). It may be that the first of these images is in mind here. In the NT the athletic imagery is, at points, overt (1Co 9:25; 2Ti 2:5), and in line with such imagery, "the crown" is given, as here in James, to those who faithfully endure various difficulties associated with living for God (2Ti 4:8; 1Pe 5:4; Rev 3:11). That it is the crown "of life" (Rev 2:10) can be understood epexegetically as meaning "the crown that is life." In other words, those who endure are honored with the full realization of eternal life in the presence of God. Accordingly, this crown is reserved for those who, through their faithful perseverance under trial, through an embracing of God's way of wisdom in the world, have demonstrated that they love God.

NOTES

12 The earliest manuscripts (e.g., 𝔓²³, ℵ, A, B) have the term ἐπηγγείλατο, *epēngeilato*, without a supplied subject. Later scribes felt compelled to add κύριος, *kyrios*, or ὁ θεός, *ho theos*, to make clear who has promised the crown of life to faithful believers. Yet as pointed out by Bruce Metzger (*A Textual Commentary on the Greek New Testament* [2d ed.; Stuttgart: German Bible Society, 1994]), the omission is very much in keeping with the Jewish practice of allowing God's name to be supplied mentally.

C. Introduction Part II: The Perils of Self-Deception (1:13–27)

OVERVIEW

Having made a critical transition via v.12, the section running from 1:13 to 1:27 is marked by the triple encouragement not to deceive oneself (1:16, 22, 26) and parallels 1:2–11 by addressing temptation, wisdom, and wealth, but from another vantage point—the potential for self-deception. The first two subunits in this section exhort us not to fall to false views of God in the heat of temptation (1:13–16) but rather to adopt a true view of God (1:17–19a). The second pair of subunits involves being a wise person who understands righteous living (1:19b–21) and then lives by the law of liberty, not merely being a listener to it (1:22–25). The final movement of the section (1:26–27) is transitional but begins to put the application of God's perfect law in concrete terms, addressing control of the tongue, caring for the destitute, and keeping oneself unsullied by the world.

1. Temptation's True Nature: Do Not Be Deceived (1:13–16)

¹³When tempted, no one should say, "God is tempting me." For God cannot be tempted by evil, nor does he tempt anyone; ¹⁴but each one is tempted when, by his own evil desire, he is dragged away and enticed. ¹⁵Then, after desire has conceived, it gives birth to sin; and sin, when it is full-grown, gives birth to death. ¹⁶Don't be deceived, my dear brothers.

COMMENTARY

13 The noun translated "trial(s)" in 1:2, 12 (*peirasmos*, GK *4280*) has a verbal form (*peirazō*, GK *4279*) used in vv.13–14, and both the noun and the verb can connote testing through trial, as in 1:2, 12, or more specifically temptation to sin. As Moo points out, the latter should not be separated too sharply from the former, since temptation, while distinct from our difficult situations of life, often occurs in relation to our experience of trials (Moo, 72). In vv.13–14, however, a transition to the topic of temptation clearly is in view, the concept being associated with evil, lust, and sin. Luke Timothy Johnson, 191, highlights the transitional nature of v.13 by translating the first part as "let no one when tested say, 'I am being tempted by God.'" So the general trials or testing of 1:2, 12 now come to focus in the difficulty of temptation at 1:13–18.

One of the natural responses to difficult situations that test us—and temptation is no exception—is to ask "Why is this happening?" and if we are not careful, we can slide into the false thought that God is the author of our temptation. When God asks whether Adam has eaten of the forbidden tree,

Adam responds, "The woman *you put here with me*—she gave me some fruit from the tree, and I ate it." In his response, the first man points the finger at Eve but also implicates God himself (Nystrom, 73; cf. Pr 19:3, "A man's own folly ruins his life, yet his heart rages against the LORD").

James counters such an inappropriate assignment of blame with the exhortation "Let no one say when he is tempted, 'I am being tempted by God.'" He points out that there are two reasons such a response to temptation is wrongheaded theologically. First, evil cannot tempt God. The word translated "cannot be tempted" is an adjective meaning "without temptation," and the context makes the author's intention clear: God experiences no effects from evil's enticements.

Second, neither is God himself the author of temptation. It is clear biblically that God is the author of some tests, such as when he tested Abraham and the wilderness generation (Ge 22:1; Dt 8:2). Yet this type of testing should be distinguished from temptation to sin. The writer of Sirach (15:11–15, 20 NRSV), a Jewish work of the intertestamental period, made it clear that God is not the author of temptations, but rather that sin results from wrong choices by people:

> Do not say, "It was the Lord's doing that I fell away"; for he does not do what he hates. Do not say, "It was he who led me astray"; for he has no need of the sinful. The Lord hates all abominations; such things are not loved by those who fear him. It was he who created humankind in the beginning, and he left them in the power of their own free choice. If you choose, you can keep the commandments, and to act faithfully is a matter of your own choice. . . . He has not commanded anyone to be wicked, and he has not given anyone permission to sin.

Speaking of the passage at hand, Augustine clarified that God "tests" the believer for his good and God's greater purpose, but as the church father points out, James is here speaking of evil intention that involves deception and bondage to sin (cf. Bray, 11). Accordingly, God's tests have nothing to do with enticement to sin. The sum of the thought in this passage, in fact, is that God has nothing whatsoever to do with evil; neither does he experience its draw, nor is he the encourager of it. Consequently, our temptations do not come from him.

14 However, temptations do have an identifiable source: "But each one is tempted when he is carried away and enticed by his own lust" (NASB). The word rendered "lust" (*epithymia*, GK *2123*) can refer to the desire for good things, such as Paul's desire to depart and be with Christ in Philippians 1:23, but in the NT it is normally used in the negative sense of wicked desire (e.g., Mk 4:19; Ro 1:24; 6:12; Gal 5:24; Col 3:5) and often has sexual overtones. This darker, edgier connotation of craving something inappropriate is in view here,

and the background of James's thought may derive from the Jewish concept of the evil *yēṣer*, which at points is associated with adultery (Davids, 84). In Jewish theology of the day, every person had two inclinations—one to do evil and the other to do good. When the former gains the upper hand, a person sins (Neusner and Green, 312).

The participles, translated by the NIV as "dragged away and enticed," are graphic. The first can speak of physically dragging someone off against his will, but it can also have the figurative sense of being drawn out, or away, by some desire. The second term at times was used of fishing, meaning to lure with the use of bait. Given the context, however, the image of lust as a wicked temptress comes to mind. Like a temptress, lust drags a person away from God's right path, luring with false promises of pleasure. This constitutes the true nature of temptation, capturing both temptation's attractiveness and destructiveness.

15 Once lust is embraced, destructive, progressive dynamics are set in motion. Perhaps playing off the sexual associations with "lust," James focuses his figurative imagery on the processes inherent to pregnancy and birth in order to describe that progression. The two parts of this verse are perfectly balanced. First, James personifies the wicked temptress, lust, as becoming pregnant (Johnson, 194). In her perversion of desire, she draws a person into her embrace, and the result is tragic. As a physical pregnancy ends with the mother giving birth to a baby, so lust, once conception has taken place, ultimately gives birth to her child, sin. The second part of the verse focuses on the effect of sin. Having been born of lust, sin, "when it is full-grown" (NIV) or "accomplished" (NASB), itself gives birth to death. Thus the ultimate result of giving in to temptation is death, the "grandchild" of lust.

16 Now comes the exhortation warning of self-deception: "Don't be deceived, my dear brothers." The peril of getting off track theologically, and therefore morally, is of paramount importance in the NT (e.g., 1Co 6:9; Gal 6:7; 1Jn 1:8). So James strongly warns against wrong thinking that ultimately would result in wrong living. Again he puts this exhortation to his hearers, calling them "brothers"—an address James likes to use (1:2, 19; 2:1, 5, 14; 3:1, 10, 12; 4:11; 5:7, 9–10, 12, 19) and one commonly used in the ancient world of both men and women in a religious group. Moreover, here, as in 1:19 and 2:5, he adds the affectionate "dear" or "beloved" (*agapētos*, GK *28*). Thus he exhorts them from the standpoint of community relationships.

2. God's True Nature: He Gives the Word (1:17–19a)

¹⁷Every good and perfect gift is from above, coming down from the Father of the heavenly lights, who does not change like shifting shadows. ¹⁸He chose to give us birth through the word of truth, that we might be a kind of firstfruits of all he created.
¹⁹My dear brothers, take note of this:

COMMENTARY

17 The contrast between the insidious nature of evil desire and the picture James now paints of God's nature could not be more stark. As in 1:5, James portrays God as a generous giver—a giver of "every good and perfect gift" (NIV). The author crafts the sentence in Greek poetically (*pasa dosis agathē . . . pan dōrēma teleion*), and the NASB maintains the balance of the wording better than the NIV with "every good thing bestowed and every perfect gift." Commentators point out that James may have adapted a common proverb, something along the lines of "every gift is good and every present perfect," roughly equivalent in meaning to "don't look a gift horse in the mouth" (Davids, 86). Whether the wording is his own or not, James's confession is clear: God's gifts are good, not evil. Whereas temptation—an evil force that leads to sin and death—has its source in human lust, good gifts have God as their source.

These good and perfect gifts "come down from the Father of lights." James has in mind here the heavenly bodies—sun, moon, and stars—and they are seen as part of God's good creation (Ge 1:14–18). Further, he tells us that, unlike these heavenly bodies he has created, God's character does not involve "variation or shifting shadow" (NASB). These words are used only here in the NT, but in the literature of the period they could be used in astrological discussions. The first word means "change," or, as the NASB presents it, "variation." The second was used as a technical term in astronomy for the movement, or change of position, of the heavenly bodies and can be translated "turning." So the "shadow" is caused by the movement, or turning, of the heavenly lights. In both Greek and Jewish literature the heavenly bodies represent the always changing nature of existence. Yet God's nature is different. He does not shift and move with reference to issues of good or evil; rather, he is immovable in that sense (Dibelius, 102; Johnson 196–97).

18 To counteract the devastating effect of pregnant lust's birthing of sin, which leads to death, God exercised his will in giving us one of his good gifts. He "chose to give us birth", which could be a reference to God's creation of human beings in the beginning (Laws, 75–78) but is more likely a reference to redemption (Moo, 79; Martin, 40). "God's will" is a common biblical idea speaking of God's sovereign choice rooted in his own determination (Job 23:13; Ps 113:11). This "birthing" is how God determined to express his grace to us.

The means of this birth experience is "the word of truth." Whereas deception is possible in this fallen world, God's word is true and has the wonderful spiritual effect of establishing our relationship with God (2Co 6:7; Eph 1:13; Col 1:5; 2Ti 2:15).

The reason God has acted this way toward us is "that we might be a kind of firstfruits of all he created." "Firstfruits" is a designator variously used of believers in the NT (Ro 16:5; 1Co 16:15; 2Th 2:13; Rev 14:4), and in the OT the concept carries several connotations. It, of course, refers to the first ripening of a harvest or first offspring of an animal, which was offered to God in acknowledgment that he owns everything already (Ex 23:16–19; Lev 27:26; Nu 18:15–18; Dt 14:22–23).

Thus the firstfruits were considered sacred, set apart for God. More closely related to James's usage, it also referred to the firstborn among sons (Ex 34:20) and was used to speak of Israel as God's firstborn, or chosen, people (Ex 4:22; Dt 7:6; Jer 2:3). So we are set apart as God's special people for the destiny to which God has birthed us and designated us.

19a The first part of v.19 presents us with several difficulties. For instance, the form of *iste* can be understood either as an imperative ("know this") or an indicative ("you know this"). The NIV takes the former position ("My dear brothers, take note of this") and the NASB the latter ("This you know, my beloved brethren"). Since in the vast majority of the cases in James where the author addresses his readers as "brothers" the imperative form is used (e.g., 1:2, 16; 2:1, 5; 3:1; 4:11; 5:7, 9–10, 12), the NIV probably has it right in this case (Martin, 38, 41; Nystrom, 89; contra Johnson, 198–99). Also, there is a question whether this exhortation sums up what goes before (vv.16–18; so Martin, 38, 41; Johnson, 198–99) or introduces what follows (vv.19b–21; so Dibelius, 109; Nystrom, 89). The position taken in this commentary is that the exhortation forms a parallel conclusion with 16a, the conclusion of the previous unit, and should be translated "remember this, my dear brothers," or, with the NIV, "take note of this."

NOTES

17 These words have caused a great deal of discussion and have a number of variants in the earliest manuscripts. For the discussion, see Davids, 87–88.

19a Some ancient manuscripts have the word ὥστε, *hōste* ("so that," or "therefore"), which is much smoother than ἴστε, *iste* ("you know"). Most commentators understand the latter to be the correct reading. In textual criticism the more difficult reading is seen as more likely, since an ancient scribe would have been more likely to "smooth out" a reading than make it more difficult.

3. Righteous Living through the Word (1:19b–21)

Everyone should be quick to listen, slow to speak and slow to become angry, [20]for man's anger does not bring about the righteous life that God desires. [21]Therefore, get rid of all moral filth and the evil that is so prevalent and humbly accept the word planted in you, which can save you.

COMMENTARY

19b The triple exhortation "be quick to listen, slow to speak and slow to become angry" is proverbial in nature. The virtue of being a ready listener who knows how to control the tongue, and the corresponding moral danger of being a hothead, hasty talker, are widespread in both Hellenistic and Jewish literature. Davids, 92, suggests that *pas anthrōpos* (GK *476*), translated as "everyone" by the NIV, points to a Jewish background, and passages such as Proverbs 13:3 immediately come to mind: "He who guards his lips guards his life, but he who speaks rashly will come to ruin" (see also Pr 15:1; 29:20; Ecc 7:9). Yet this triple challenge also brings to the surface James's deep concern over the divisiveness among the people he addresses. Time and again James deals with the proper use of the tongue in the community, which is a hallmark of one walking according to God's way of wisdom (e.g., 2:12; 3:1–12; 4:1–3, 11–12; 5:9).

20 James then offers a basis for the exhortation: "for the anger of man does not achieve the righteousness of God" (NASB). Passionate outbursts of anger do not "achieve" or "bring about" or "carry out" God's righteousness. The verb has to do with work or effort of some kind. However, what does he mean when he speaks of "the righteousness of God," for at least four interpretations are possible. The phrase could refer to God's character as righteous, his justification, his eschatological justice (cf. 5:7), or his standard of right living (Laws, 81; Davids, 93). Of

these the final option is to be preferred, since it is only in living according to God's standard that human beings can "accomplish" or "work" his righteousness (Moo, 84). Consequently, the idea here is that when we allow anger to control us, spewing out poisonous emotional garbage onto our fellow believers, this falls far short of what God has designed for our relationships in the community of faith.

21 The "Therefore" (*dio*) at the beginning of v.21 is very strong and shows that what this author is about to say is inferred from the previous statement. James is saying, "Based on this need to live up to God's standard by being self-controlled in our interactions with one another, here's what you need to do," and he follows first with what needs to be put aside and then with what needs to be embraced. The word translated "get rid of" (NIV) is, in reality, a participle, which the NASB translates more accurately with "putting aside." This term was used at times in the ancient world to refer to taking off clothes, but it occurs in the NT in a figurative sense of "laying aside" something spiritually bad, such as lying (Eph 4:25), malice, deceit, hypocrisy, envy, slander (1Pe 2:1), or anything that would hold us back from following Christ fully (Heb 12:1). Accordingly, "moral filth" (*rhyparia*, GK *4864*) translates the figurative sense of a term that literally refers to dirt or filth. In its figurative uses it can connote bad behavior, moral uncleanness, greed, or sordid attitudes or actions. The "evil that is so prevalent," which is also to be laid aside, Laws, 81, translates pointedly with "the great mass of malice" and refers to the malicious and vulgar wagging of the tongue with which the author is concerned (3:1–12; cf. 1Pe 2:1; Davids, 94). These community-corroding attitudes and actions must be done away with, for they are out of line with God's righteous standard and, therefore, inappropriate for his community.

On the other hand, we are to replace these filthy rags of wickedness with something: "humbly accept the word planted in you, which can save you." The term rendered "humbly" connotes a posture of gentleness or meekness, as opposed to an aggressive haughtiness that forces its opinion and desires on others. Given the context and James's emphasis on community dynamics, the term as used here might carry the nuanced sense of courtesy or being considerate of others. In its one other use in the book, the word is contrasted with envy and selfishness, which bring about evil and disorder (3:13). Thus in

James's putting forth of this concept, it has to do with living life well relationally in the community of faith, which is a manifestation of God's wisdom.

It is not surprising that James integrates humility with receptiveness to God's word. In v.18, James has already pointed out that we were "birthed" by the word of truth. He now challenges us to an attitude of ready openness to the "word planted in you." The term rendered "planted in you" is an adjective modifying "word" (*logos*, GK *3364*) and can also carry the idea of "inborn," which fits with the imagery of v.18. The word God used to give us birth is now a part of who we are as people (cf. Jer 31:31–34). Although Davids, 95, asserts that "inborn" is unrelated to receiving, the same could be said of something already "implanted." What James has in mind here is a heart that the dictates of God's wise word may influence. This word "can save," alluding to the future aspect of our salvation. The word is able to bring us all the way to the consummation of our salvation at the end of the age.

4. Do Not Be Deceived: Be Doers of the Word (the Law of Liberty) (1:22–25)

22Do not merely listen to the word, and so deceive yourselves. Do what it says. 23Anyone who listens to the word but does not do what it says is like a man who looks at his face in a mirror 24and, after looking at himself, goes away and immediately forgets what he looks like. 25But the man who looks intently into the perfect law that gives freedom, and continues to do this, not forgetting what he has heard, but doing it—he will be blessed in what he does.

COMMENTARY

22 In 1:22–25 James comes to the heart of a major problem among those he addresses (see 2:14–26) and a point eminently relevant to the church of any age. There are, of course, various ways a person can interact with the word of God. Yet here James asserts that listening to the word without actively applying it to life is deficient interaction. Thus he exhorts his

readers to become doers of the word, not only hearers. His concern is strikingly similar to Paul's concern in Romans 2:13: "it is not the hearers of the Law who are just before God, but the doers of the Law will be justified" (NASB). The point is clear. If one merely listens to the word taught and takes no action to incorporate it into the patterns of life, this does not constitute true receptiveness. God's word should change behavior, not just stimulate the mind. The concept of doing the word is Semitic and anticipates the discussion of "faith and works" in 2:14–26.

In fact, those who hear the word without acting on it "deceive themselves" (*paralogizomenoi* [GK *4165*] *heautous*). The word translated "deceive" can carry the meaning "cheat" or "defraud," but based on the analogy to which we will turn momentarily (1:23–24), deception, or the idea of misleading, clearly is in view. Paul uses this term in Colossians 2:4 of being deceived by persuasive arguments. So the sense of James's assertion is comparable to one saying, "If you think it is OK to listen to the word without acting on it, *you are fooling yourself!*"

23–24 James now offers an analogy as an explanation for why hearing without doing is unacceptable: "Anyone who listens to the word but does not do what it says is like a man who looks at his face in a mirror." The "face" is, more literally, the "face of his birth," or the "face with which he was born," and what James has in mind is what the person *really* looks like. Looking in a mirror, he sees his own face as it really is. Yet "after looking at himself, [he] goes away and immediately forgets what he looks like." In other words, when he gets away from the mirror, which provided a point of reference for a true evaluation, that true picture of his own face fades in his memory. What is inferred is that, in light of the face given him at birth, this person has a higher opinion of his own appearance than is warranted!

Thus he deceives himself, because the truth does not stay with him to change his perspective.

25 Now the contrast. The "doer" "looks intently into the perfect law that gives freedom, and continues to do this." In contrast with the man who looks in a mirror briefly and then walks away, the person who is actively engaged in applying the word to life stays focused on the perfect law. The term translated "looks intently" can be rendered "look into," or "bend down to look," and has the figurative meaning of investigation. Thus it is more than a mere glance, and both the NASB and NIV capture the note of effort by adding the word "intently." The "perfect law of liberty" is a key concept for the book, governing the structure of the body with reference to it at 2:8 as "the royal law" and at 2:12–13 and 4:11–12. This law of liberty is the OT Scriptures epitomized in Leviticus 19:18, "love your neighbor as yourself" (2:8), which was emphasized to James through the teaching of Jesus (Moo, 94; Davids, 99–100). It is a law of liberty because it brings freedom to the one who lives by it.

The "doer" not only has this practice of investigating God's law but stays with it. In other words, the law becomes a frame of reference for living. With the law ever before the eyes of the heart, this person lives out the law instead of forgetting it. This is the path of blessing. One thinks of passages such as Psalm 1:1–3: The person is blessed whose delight in the Lord's law is manifested by a constant meditation on it. Such a person is like a tree planted by streams of water.

5. Transition: Self–Deception Regarding Speaking and Acting (1:26–27)

OVERVIEW

The general principle of vv.22–25 the author now applies in concrete terms, pulling together several themes of great import in the book. On the one hand, vv.26–27 conclude the theme of self-deception that has knitted all of vv.13–27 together. Also the admonitions to right use of the tongue, care for the disadvantaged, and keeping oneself unstained by the world are the fitting crescendo for the treatment of true wisdom begun in v.17. Specifically, the importance of keeping tight control over the tongue echoes the admonition to be "slow to speak and slow to become angry" in v.19, and "to keep oneself from being polluted by the world" matches the challenge to "get rid of all moral filth" in v.21. Finally, vv.26–27 not only look back, drawing together these important themes of the first chapter, but also foreshadow what is to come. The author treats appropriate concern for the disadvantaged in the whole of ch. 2—the stimulating discussion of faith and works in 2:14–26 being an extension of this general theme—and thoughts on the power of the tongue follow in 3:1–12.

a. Do Not Be Deceived: The Importance of Right Speaking (1:26)

26If anyone considers himself religious and yet does not keep a tight rein on his tongue, he deceives himself and his religion is worthless.

COMMENTARY

26 The word translated "religious" (*thrēskos*, GK *2580*) is rare and unknown in Greek prior to this occurrence in James. The related and much more common word *thrēskeia* (GK *2579*), which James uses at the end of v.26 and again at the beginning of v.27, has to do with religious ritual but could also imply the internal piety of the worshiper (*TLNT* 2:200–203). James clearly uses both terms to speak of service to God via right attitudes of the heart and righteous living (see 1:20). In line with the previous passage, true religion does not participate simply in forms of worship (i.e., hearing the word spoken or read) but must extend to a transformation of life that has implications for how one interacts in community.

Specifically, if a person thinks of himself as religious and cannot keep control of his tongue, he is self-deceived. The word translated "considers himself" does not have the pronoun attached to it in Greek, and the term *dokeō* also can communicate the idea of reputation, or "to seem." Thus it might be better to translate the clause, "If anyone seems to be religious," or, "If anyone has the reputation of being religious." Yet what seems to be is not really true, for this person uses words destructively in the community. Both the NIV and NASB reflect that the term for "control" (*chalinagōgeō*, GK *5902*) was used literally of a horse's bridle, which is the main means of controlling the horse; hence the figurative meaning of "keep under control." If the tongue is not kept in check, two conclusions may be drawn. The person deceives his own heart, and he has a worthless religion. The heart was seen variously as the seat of the physical, emotional, mental, and spiritual life of a person. In its figurative use, it represented, among other things, the inner self where moral decisions were made. James's emphasis here is that we can trick ourselves into thinking ourselves religious when the clear evidence indicates otherwise. If the tongue is not under control, the supposed religion is "worthless," a word connoting that it is useless, fruitless, powerless, or even lacking truth.

b. The Importance of Right Actions (1:27)

> ²⁷Religion that God our Father accepts as pure and faultless is this: to look after orphans and widows in their distress and to keep oneself from being polluted by the world.

COMMENTARY

27 By contrast, what then is "religion that God our Father accepts as pure and faultless"? The term "pure" has a wide range of meanings and could refer to being clean from dirt, guiltless in terms of morality, or, in terms of religious ritual, something fit for offering to God (cf. Lev 18:22–27). The other adjective, translated by the NASB as "undefiled" and the NIV as "faultless," is a synonym used elsewhere in the NT only in three places. Hebrews 7:26 speaks of Christ's character as a perfect high priest; in Hebrews 13:4 the author stresses the importance of sexual purity in marriage; and the Christian's inheritance is said to be "undefiled" in 1 Peter 1:4. Thus the religion James has in mind is not corrupted by the sin of neglecting the disadvantaged, nor by enmeshing oneself in the world's immorality.

The admonition to care for widows and orphans expresses a widely held virtue of Jewish piety.

God's concern for the poor and distressed, his taking their cause of justice and basic sustenance as his own, must extend to the person who is God's follower in the world. Widows and orphans especially had little means of provision for basic needs other than the care and generosity of their broader communities. Thus the person who claims to be religious in the best sense must seek to address the plight of the poor and most vulnerable (Isa 1:17). Further, true religion takes morality seriously. Here James may be echoing his exhortation of 1:21, which, as we have already suggested, probably refers to malice and conflict with others in the community. This form of wickedness and its contrast with wise living receive generous treatment in James (3:1–12; esp. 3:13–18; 4:1–12; 5:7–12). Thus James concludes his introduction with exhortations that lead into critical concerns in the letter's main body.

NOTES

26–27 In his important work on the structure of Hebrews, Albert Vanhoye labeled this literary device as "announcement of the subject." See *La structure littéraire de l'Épître aux Hébreux* (2d ed.; Paris: Desclée de Brouwer, 1976), 37.

III. LIVING THE "LAW OF LIBERTY" (2:1–5:6)

A. Violating the Royal Law through Judging the Poor: Wrong Speaking and Acting in Community (2:1–11)

OVERVIEW

As suggested in our study of James 1, that first chapter served as an extended, two-part introduction to the book and presented key themes unpacked in the remaining chapters. With 2:1–11, we now move into the letter's main body, the author picking up the theme of right action toward the poor as a key to fulfilling God's righteousness. The author seems to have in mind one of two possible situations in the church, and in the light of details in the passage, it is difficult to decide which should be given the interpretive nod (Moo, 99–100). First, it may be that James is thinking of a typical worship service at which people from a variety of socioeconomic contexts are in attendance. In that case, he is concerned with giving the rich social honors and denying the poor due respect. Second, given the language used in the passage and texts from the broader Jewish context, it is possible that in view here is a church court setting in which leaders of the Christian community are trying a dispute of some kind (so Johnson, 223; Davids, 109; Martin, 57–58; see Mt 18:15–20; 1Co 5:3–5; 6:1–8; 1Ti 5:19–24). In light of the facts that (1) James uses language often tapped in legal contexts; (2) there exist rabbinic texts that describe this situation exactly (see R. B. Ward, "Partiality in the Assembly: James 2:2–4," *HTR* 62

(1969): 87–97; e.g., *b. Šebu.* 31a reads, "How do we know that, if two come to court, one clothed in rags and the other in fine raiment worth a hundred *manehs*, they should say to him, 'Either dress like him, or dress him like you'. . . . When they would come before Raba son of R. Huna, he would say to them, 'Remove your fine shoes, and come down for your case.'"); and (3) Leviticus 19:9–18, a text that forms the backdrop for several themes in James and this passage particularly, deals directly with justice in judicial decisions, the latter interpretation perhaps has the edge.

This first movement of ch. 2, combined with the vitally important transition passage at 2:12–13, has an intricate logic that we would do well to think through before getting to the details of our study. Both this section and 2:14–26 are similar to a form of argument in the Greco-Roman world (a "diatribe"), a brief ethical speech put in the form of a running dialogue. In such a dialogue, the writer, as James does here, addresses an implied listener and uses rhetorical questions and hypothetical situations, warnings, comparisons from real-life situations, quotations with which the audience would be familiar, and a conversational tone. The logical development of these first thirteen verses we depict as follows:

2:1	A Personal Exhortation: "Don't show favoritism to the rich!"
2:2–4	A Hypothetical Situation and Assessment
2:5–6a	An Appeal to Principle: "God has chosen the poor," and the Contrast with Wrong Actions: "but you have dishonored the poor man"

230

Notice that the structure of this section is very balanced, forming a chiastic pattern of A–B–C–C'–B'–A'. Exhortations begin and end the section. The hypothetical situation of 2:2–4 is balanced with the hypothetically stated appeal to the royal law and the importance of keeping that law. The two center units concern, respectively, God's favor on the poor (2:5–6a) and the wickedness of the rich (2:6b–7). Through this highly stylized and structured approach, James confronts his readers with a critical aspect of living as God's people in community: according to the royal law of love, we must not make distinctions between people based on economic status.

1. A Personal Exhortation: "Don't show favoritism to the rich!" (2:1)

1My brothers, as believers in our glorious Lord Jesus Christ, don't show favoritism.

COMMENTARY

1 Once again James addresses his readers as "brothers" (1:2, 16, 19; 2:5, 14; 3:1, 10, 12; 4:11; 5:7, 9–10, 12, 19; see discussion at 1:2) and exhorts them, as followers of Christ, not to show favoritism. The NIV's translation "as believers in our glorious Lord Jesus Christ, don't show favoritism" the NASB renders more literally with "do not hold your faith in our glorious Lord Jesus Christ with an attitude of personal favoritism." The idea of "holding the faith" has to do with a public posture of identifying oneself as a follower of Christ, and thus the NIV's "as believers" serves the author's intention. That Christ is "glorious" points to his manifestation of the presence of God, as seen in the *shekinah* glory of the OT (e.g., Ex 14:17–18; Ps 96:3; Isa 60:1–2), and passages in the NT relating to his exaltation and eschatological salvation. Consequently, James may use the qualifier here to point to Christ as the exalted Judge, "whose glory will be fully revealed in eschatological judgment" (so Davids, 107).

Therefore, one must not hold faith in him "with favoritism" (*en prosōpolēmpsiais*, GK 4721). The word translated "favoritism" speaks of the attitude of partiality by which one person is shown favor, or special consideration, over another. In the OT the concept often refers to unjust judgment against the vulnerable on the part of those in power (e.g., Ps 82:2; Pr 18:5; 24:23; 28:21; Mal 2:9–10; so Martin, 59; Nystrom, 114). Such an attitude is contrary to God's way of dealing with people when he judges them (Ro 2:11; Eph 6:9; Col 3:25) and, therefore, inappropriate for his people. In the broader context of Leviticus 19:18, to which James turns momentarily (2:8), the law states, "Do not show partiality to the poor or favoritism to the great, but judge your neighbor fairly" (Lev 19:15). By his exhortation in 2:1, James implies that a public commitment to Christ, the Lord of glory, is incompatible with an attitude that degrades a fellow believer or puts the person at a disadvantage, for such an attitude runs contrary to God's law.

NOTES

1 Johnson reads the genitive forms here as subjective (i.e., "faith of Jesus Christ") rather than objective (i.e., "faith in Jesus Christ"), but most commentators have followed the latter route. Johnson has a point that Jesus' teaching lies behind parts of James, and so James could be emphasizing the practice of faith as embodied in Jesus. However, that he is the "glorious Lord" (see comment) places an emphasis on his identification with God and perhaps his exaltation. Therefore, Johnson, 220, oversteps when he suggests, "The Christology of the letter is not such as to make 'faith in Christ' natural."

The construction of ἔχω, echō, plus the preposition ἐν, en, could speak of having an attitude of some sort.

2. A Hypothetical Situation and Assessment (2:2–4)

²Suppose a man comes into your meeting wearing a gold ring and fine clothes, and a poor man in shabby clothes also comes in. ³If you show special attention to the man wearing fine clothes and say, "Here's a good seat for you," but say to the poor man, "You stand there" or "Sit on the floor by my feet," ⁴have you not discriminated among yourselves and become judges with evil thoughts?

COMMENTARY

2–3 James now presents a hypothetical situation. Although hypothetical, given the graphic nature of the illustration, James probably has in mind real-life situations he has seen or heard of. Suppose two people come to a meeting of believers, one poor and in nasty rags and the other marked by expensive, shining clothing and a ring, which could be a symbol of status, power, and even arrogance (Johnson, 221). It is interesting that here James uses the term *synagōgē* (GK *5252*), and if it refers to the gathering of the church, this is its only such use in the NT. It could, of course, refer to a building, but most take it to refer to a meeting of believers (Martin, 61). Furthermore, suppose that, because of their respective social situations, those in attendance treat these two individuals differently, honoring the rich person with a place of prominence and degrading the poor person with a lowly position. The wealthy person is invited to sit comfortably in a place reserved for one of status; by contrast, the poor person is made either to stand up or sit in a position of subordination. In his description of the hypothetical situation, James presents a perfect illustration of the breaking of Leviticus 19:15, quoted above.

4 Here James assesses such a situation: "have you not discriminated among yourselves and become judges with evil thoughts?" The term "discriminated" could be used in a legal context for passing judgment, and, as mentioned above, some understand this to be the context James has in mind. If so, it means the outcome of the case has already been predisposed in the favor of the wealthy person (see v.6). In any case, the term can connote "to differentiate by separating," or to show a distinction by the way something is arranged. If this is the nuance intended here, in placing wealthy and poor persons in the room according to their respective economic positions, a value judgment has been made that suggests the poor do not deserve equal treatment, as shown by where they are placed physically in the community. Thus those present have become "judges with evil thoughts." The OT backdrop of judging with evil motives is extensive (Ps 82:2; Pr 18:5; 24:23; 28:21; Mal 2:9–10) and proclaims in no uncertain terms God's great displeasure at such situations.

3. An Appeal to Principle (2:5–6a)

⁵Listen, my dear brothers: Has not God chosen those who are poor in the eyes of the world to be rich in faith and to inherit the kingdom he promised those who love him? ⁶But you have insulted the poor.

COMMENTARY

5–6a The renewal of his address to the hearers with "listen, my dear brothers" intensifies James's dialogue and signals the introduction of a new approach in his exhortation. In 2:5–6a he appeals to a theological principle and then places the dishonoring of the poor in stark contrast with that principle. The theological principle, given in the form of a question anticipating an affirmative answer (the *ou* construction), asserts that God has "chosen those who are poor to be rich in faith and to inherit the kingdom." In biblical theology, God is a God who chooses (e.g., Nu 16:5; Dt 4:37; 7:7; 14:2; Isa 14:1; 43:10), and his choosing to put special favor on the poor is grounded in his care for their plight (Dt 16:3; 26:7). In the OT, as well as in broader Jewish literature, poverty and piety became closely associated. This association forms the backdrop for Jesus' teaching in Luke 6:20,

"Blessed are you who are poor, for yours is the kingdom of God," and Jesus' teaching certainly is in the background of James's comment here (Davids, 111). The poor are more disposed to recognize their need for God. Their poverty (and God's choice) has made them rich "in faith." It is not that they have a greater quantity of faith but that, from the perspective of God's view of things, they are indeed wealthy (1:9; see Ropes, 194).

Further, they are heirs of the kingdom of God. In the Greco-Roman world, the concept of inheritance was very important, though the exact laws of inheritance varied from the fifth century BC to the second century AD. Normally, sons were the heirs in earlier times, but later, in certain circumstances, wives, daughters, and even mistresses could be heirs. Generally speaking, in the ancient Mediterranean world an heir is one with the authority to utilize or administer some possession or possessions. In biblical literature specifically, the Lord gave the land as an inheritance to Israel (Ge 28:4; Dt 1:8; 2:12; 4:1), and in Psalms the Lord himself is spoken of as a person's inheritance (Ps 16:5) and gives an inheritance that will last forever (Ps 37:18). Moreover, believers are called heirs in Paul (Ro 8:17; Gal 3:29; 4:7; Eph 1:14, 18; Tit 3:7), and here in James, in the topsy-turvy values of God's economy, the poor, who are defined as such by how little they own, are destined to inherit God's kingdom (Johnson, 225). This is a promise to those who love God. Thus it is not

poverty per se that is affirmed here. Rather, James is reflecting on a poor person, part of the community of faith, and asserting that this person shares the high privileges and status of the kingdom, which is a kingdom that puts down the proud and lifts up the needy.

This is what makes favoritism in the church so odious; it runs counter to God's countercultural assessments! So, in line with 2:6a, believers are dishonoring poor fellow believers, whom God has honored with spiritual riches and inheritance. This contrast shows a conflict of values that is unacceptable.

4. An Appeal to Personal Experience (2:6b–7)

Is it not the rich who are exploiting you? Are they not the ones who are dragging you into court? 7Are they not the ones who are slandering the noble name of him to whom you belong?

COMMENTARY

6b–7 Next, James appeals to the hearers' personal experience with the rich, pointing to three items of evidence: "Is it not the rich who are exploiting you? Are they not the ones who are dragging you into court? Are they not the ones who are slandering the noble name of him to whom you belong?" First, the rich are characterized as exploitative. The term "exploit" means to oppress or dominate someone (cf. the one other use in the NT in Ac 10:38) and is used in the Greek translation of the OT, for instance, of the rich oppressing the poor (Am 4:1; Zec 7:10; Jer 7:6; Eze 18:12). Here the term reflects a continued harsh reality of socioeconomic strata in the ancient Mediterranean world. Because of their power and wealth, rich landowners were able to buy up more and more land, forcing the poor to work

for them and in the process taking advantage of them (Moo, 108; Martin, 66; Johnson, 225–26).

Second, and this thought is closely associated with the one just addressed, the rich are characterized as dragging members of the church into court. How the rich handled the debts, rent payments, and wages of the poor, as well as abuse of the legal system of the day by the rich, are probably in mind. The wealthy landowner could use a poor person's debt to take land or possessions, charge unreasonably high interest rates, and withhold pay for spurious reasons, all of which were common practices. To make matters worse, their money and social status often enabled the rich to buy off the court system. Thus they could drag the poor before the courts and systematically abuse them.

Third, the rich are characterized by blaspheming the name of Christ with which believers are associated. Generally, the term *blasphēmeō* (GK 1059) referred to slander or insult, especially in a religious context, where a deity is denigrated in some way. Thus, for instance, the evil blaspheme God's name

(Ro 2:24; 1Ti 6:1), his Spirit (Mk 3:29; Lk 12:10), Christ (Mt 27:39; Mk 15:29; Lk 23:39), angels (2Pe 2:10), or things associated with believers (Ro 14:16; Tit 2:5; 2Pe 2:2). What seems to be in view here is verbal abuse hurled at believers, which disparages their religion and the Lord they claim to follow.

5. Two Courses of Action, Hypothetically Stated (2:8–11)

OVERVIEW

The author now confronts his hearers with two courses of action that James places in stark contrast: "living by the royal law" or living in the sin of

partiality. Once again he states these hypothetically, because the decision lies before the community and their course of action is, as yet, undetermined.

⁸If you really keep the royal law found in Scripture, "Love your neighbor as yourself," you are doing right. ⁹But if you show favoritism, you sin and are convicted by the law as lawbreakers. ¹⁰For whoever keeps the whole law and yet stumbles at just one point is guilty of breaking all of it. ¹¹For he who said, "Do not commit adultery," also said, "Do not murder." If you do not commit adultery but do commit murder, you have become a lawbreaker.

COMMENTARY

8–9 James first appeals to Scripture by quoting Leviticus 19:18, "you shall love your neighbor as yourself," and asserts that they are doing well if they are fulfilling this command. The term translated by the NASB as "however" (*mentoi*) has a note of contrast in it, setting v.8 over against the dishonor given the poor in v.6a. (That is, favoritism dishonors the poor person, though a better course, fulfilling the royal law, is there for the taking.) This law of love is "royal" because it is foundational for how people treat each other in the kingdom of God, under the rule of the king. The fact that Leviticus 19:18 occurs at Matthew 5:43; 19:19; 22:39; Mark 12:31–33; Luke 10:27;

Romans 13:9; and Galatians 5:14 witnesses to its importance as an ethical standard for those who would follow Christ. Indeed, Christ proclaimed that the whole of the Law finds its focus in this law and the law to love God.

Moreover, it is clear from the broader context of Leviticus 19:18 that partiality is tacitly a violation of the commandment to love one's neighbor. Among other points, this broader context (Lev 19:9–18) addresses a number of themes that parallel concerns in James, including concern shown to the poor and alien by leaving parts of a harvest, not profaning the Lord's name, not defrauding a neighbor, and not holding back the wages of a hired person. Leviticus 19:15 commands not to show partiality to the poor or favoritism to the great (or rich). James is especially interested in the latter. James makes clear in v. 9 his point by quoting Leviticus 19:18: the person who shows favoritism is breaking God's law, and that person stands convicted.

10–11 To drive home the point, James stresses there are no small parts of the Law that can be treated lightly. Modern biblical scholars speak of the danger of having "a canon within a canon," meaning an elevation of the parts of Scripture as more important than other parts. By their actions, those whom James addresses were not taking this part of the Law seriously. So James states plainly that to "stumble" on this one law constitutes being guilty. The word rendered "stumble" (*ptaiō*, GK *4760*), which could also be translated "trip," was used figuratively to speak of sin (e.g., Ro 11:11; Jas 3:2).

Jewish teachers of the era emphasized the unity of God's law. For example, in 4 Maccabees 5:19–21 Eleazar, upon being commanded by the pagan king to eat unclean food, replies that there are no small sins, for to break the Law in small matters or great is equally serious. Paul also reflects this sentiment in Galatians 5:3, where he writes, "Again I declare to every man who lets himself be circumcised that he is obligated to obey the whole law" (see Moo, 114). For James and those of his day, the importance of the whole Law, and the Law's unity, was grounded in the authority of God, who gave the Law. The same God who gave the command not to commit adultery also gave the command not to commit murder. Thus these laws are linked by the action and authority of the Giver. Consequently, if a person does not commit adultery and yet does commit murder, the Law has been broken, since one point of the Law has been violated.

B. So Speak and So Act as One Being Judged by the Law of Liberty (2:12–13)

¹²Speak and act as those who are going to be judged by the law that gives freedom, ¹³because judgment without mercy will be shown to anyone who has not been merciful. Mercy triumphs over judgment!

COMMENTARY

12–13 James concludes the unit, as he started it, with an exhortation: "Speak and act as those who are going to be judged by the law that gives freedom." Yet at the same time, 2:12–13 forms another key transition in the structure of the book and works with the reference to the law and judging at 4:11–12 to bracket the heart of the letter. Here James highlights that the law of love involves both right speaking and right acting. This twin approach

to righteous living, speaking and acting, is seen in Leviticus 19:9–18, which, as already noted, has a significant influence on James, as well as on the teaching of Jesus (see, e.g., Mt 5:21–48; 25:31–45). If interpersonal relationships within the community of faith are to be healthy, right speaking and right acting must be embraced. The law of freedom, as noted at 1:25, is the divine ethic of love, taken up and reaffirmed by Jesus, as central to a life lived effectively for God. It is, therefore, God's law that sets the standard by which the actions of all individuals will be assessed. Therefore, the one who breaks God's law (such as that delineated in Lev 19:9–18), demonstrating a lack of love and mercy, will be judged mercilessly, perhaps echoing the implication of Jesus' words, "Blessed are the merciful, for

they will be shown mercy" (Mt 5:7). Earlier in the passage James has shown favoritism to be a form of evil judgment (v.4). Thus the tables are turned, the judges standing before God as Judge! The concluding statement, "mercy triumphs over judgment," perhaps means that a life of mercy diffuses such a judgment.

NOTES

12–13 Johnson, "Use of Leviticus 19," points to allusions here in v.9 and in 4:11; 5:4, 9, 12, 20.

C. Wrong Actions toward the Poor (2:14–26)

OVERVIEW

At least since 1:22 James has been concerned about the practical dichotomy, evident in the lives of some professed believers, between "belief" in God and the working out of that belief in living according to God's righteousness. Now the matter comes to bold expression in his treatment of the

relationship between faith and works. A number of commentators have noted the relationship between our passage at hand and the first half of ch. 2. For instance, Martin, 77, who marks 2:14–26 as the theological heart of James, has noted the following correspondences between the two passages:

My brothers . . . faith (2:1)	My brothers . . . faith (2:14)
The poor person in filthy clothes (2:2)	A brother or sister ill-clad and lacking in daily sustenance (2:15)
The poor . . . wealthy in faith (who) love God (2:5)	Faith . . . works [two terms in association 10x in 13 vv.]
You are right (*kalōs poieite*) (2:8)	Excellent! (*kalōs poieis*) (2:19)
The fine name by which you have been *called* (2:7)	(Abraham) was *called* God's friend (2:23)

In general, both passages address the problem of a professed faith characterized by inattention to the poor (Martin, 79), but that inattention is shown in vv.14–26 to have a deeper, sinister cause—an inadequate understanding of faith's implications.

Further, G. M. Burge ("'And Threw Them Thus on Paper': Recovering the Poetic Form of James 2:14–26," *SBT* 7 [1977]: 31–45) has noted that our passage at hand is highly structured, having two parallel parts of two stanzas each. James 2:14–17 and

2:18–20 make up part 1; 2:21–24 and 2:25–26 form part 2. At the end of each of the four stanzas is a reiteration of the inadequacy of a faith not expressed in works:

v.17   "faith by itself, if it is not accompanied by action, is dead"

v.20   "faith without deeds is useless"

v.24   "not by faith alone"

v.26   "faith without deeds is dead"

Thus James drives home his point.

The author's argument is as follows. In the first movement of part 1 (2:14–17), James begins (v.14) with his main thesis in the form of two rhetorical questions, proclaiming that a professed faith that is a workless faith is a non-saving faith. He illustrates the "works" he has in mind (vv.15–16) by providing another hypothetical situation. If a brother or sister does not have proper clothing or food for the day, and a person merely gives them the empty "gift" of verbal encouragement, their interaction has no useful end. "Faith" that is not expressed by works is a "dead" faith (v.17). In the second movement of part 1 (2:18–20), James moves to a dialogue with an imaginary objector who says, "You have faith and I have works," and immediately shows up this statement of the dichotomy between faith and works to be false also, suggesting rather that the only way true faith can be demonstrated is via righteous living (v.18). Those who simply give mental assent to God's reality (v.19) obviously do not have saving faith, for even the demons believe in this sense and tremble. So faith apart from righteous living is not effective (v.20).

In the second part of the passage (2:21–26), the writer finishes off his treatment of the matter with parallel illustrations of Abraham (vv.21–24) and Rahab (vv.25–26), showing that each expressed their faith in action and were accordingly justified. He closes by reiterating that faith without works is dead, being like a body that has no spirit (v.26).

14What good is it, my brothers, if a man claims to have faith but has no deeds? Can such faith save him? 15Suppose a brother or sister is without clothes and daily food. 16If one of you says to him, "Go, I wish you well; keep warm and well fed," but does nothing about his physical needs, what good is it? 17In the same way, faith by itself, if it is not accompanied by action, is dead.

18But someone will say, "You have faith; I have deeds."

Show me your faith without deeds, and I will show you my faith by what I do. 19You believe that there is one God. Good! Even the demons believe that—and shudder.

20You foolish man, do you want evidence that faith without deeds is useless? 21Was not our ancestor Abraham considered righteous for what he did when he offered his son Isaac on the altar? 22You see that his faith and his actions were working together, and his faith was made complete by what he did. 23And the scripture was fulfilled that says, "Abraham believed God, and it was credited to him as righteousness," and he was called God's friend. 24You see that a person is justified by what he does and not by faith alone.

25In the same way, was not even Rahab the prostitute considered righteous for what she did when she gave lodging to the spies and sent them off in a different direction? 26As the body without the spirit is dead, so faith without deeds is dead.

COMMENTARY

14 Here James uses a couplet of rhetorical questions to put forth his basic thesis: a confessed faith that does not manifest righteous works is not saving faith. He begins by asking, "What good is it, my brothers, if a man claims to have faith but has no deeds?" The term *ophelos* (GK *4055*), rendered "good" by the NIV and "use" by the NASB, connotes the idea of benefit or advantage (cf. 1Co 15:32). James's rhetorical question anticipates a negative answer—"there is no benefit." The situation he has in mind concerns a person who talks "faith talk" but does not walk in the "works" associated with true faith. The word "claims" is very important at this point. To claim that one has faith does not mean that true faith is at hand. In fact, a confessed faith is marked as inadequate if the person "has no deeds." The NIV's "deeds" (*ergon*, GK *2240*) helps to make a distinction between what James has in mind here and Paul's focus on religious practices such as circumcision (see the discussion on James and Paul below). As is clear from the hypothetical situation that follows in vv.15–16, James's concern is that faith is manifested in practical acts of piety, such as caring for the poor. The "works" he has in mind, therefore, are quite distinct from Paul's rebuke of those who would depend on "works" (i.e., religious rituals) for salvation. Consequently, for James, a person who gives mere lip service to faith but does not live righteously lives in a religious posture that has no advantage or benefit. In fact, he asks, "Can such faith save him?" James is not suggesting that faith cannot save but rather that the type of faith just described cannot save. Further, the salvation in mind is the salvation of the soul, mentioned also at 1:21; 4:12; and 5:20—i.e., deliverance from God's righteous judgment (2:12–13) at the end of the age (Moo, 123–24).

15–17 James continues with an illustration, specifically a hypothetical situation, which illustrates the emptiness of such subpar "faith." If a brother or sister in Christ is desperately poor, not having basic necessities such as adequate clothing or sustenance for the day, and all they receive from the professed believer is the verbal encouragement "Go in peace; may you be warm and full of food!" it is, in fact, an empty, insubstantial nonaction. The NASB's "what is necessary" (*epitēdeios*, GK *2201*) could be used in the ancient world to speak of what was "appropriate" or "fit" or called for in a given situation. James clearly has in mind basic physical needs, for food and clothing are the most basic necessities "for their body" (NASB). To provide for the poor the necessities of life, such as clothing and daily food, was a most fundamental requirement of Jewish piety (Isa 58:7). It is the wicked who "cause the poor to go about naked without clothing, and . . . take away the sheaves from the hungry" (Job 24:10 NASB; see Nystrom, 149). In effect, by not contributing food and clothing to a brother or sister in need, when these are readily available, a person demonstrates a substandard "faith" that has no life to it. In fact, such an expression of so-called "faith" is dead—it just sits alone, powerless and ineffective, the term "dead" (*nekros*, GK *3738*) being used here to speak of something that is so deficient spiritually as to call into question its reality.

18 Now comes the counterargument in v.18. As detailed by Johnson, and given the lack of punctuation in the original Greek text, there are many ways we might read the brief dialogue with "someone" found in the first part of v.18 (Johnson, 240). If with the NASB we read the statement as "You have faith and I have works," James seems to be placing his own position in the mouth of his opponent, who then would be emphasizing his own works! Ropes, 209, and Dibelius, 156, followed by Davids, 123, Laws, 122–24, and Johnson, 240, have followed a different and perhaps the best interpretation, however, pointing to the juxtaposition of "you" (*sy*) and "I" (*egō*) in this manner as indicating a sharp division between the two concepts in view. In other words, the gist of the dialogue partner's statement is, "One person has faith and the other person has righteous works." James immediately answers this fallacious dichotomy by insisting the two must go together. A faith without works is not demonstrable and, therefore, cannot be defended. Rather, works of righteousness are the expressions of real faith.

19–20 Mental assent to God's reality is not enough, as James asserts in v.19. The confession that God is One was the most basic confession of Judaism, found in the Shema and taken up into earliest Christianity (Mk 12:29). James does not intend to contradict this proposition but rather suggests that mere mental assent is inadequate (Martin, 89–90). The demons, being monotheists, hold to that form of belief, the reality of which, rather than being a comfort, causes them to tremble! If one confesses God's reality, he or she must come to grips with God's requirements of righteous living, recognizing that a workless faith is no good. Not to recognize this basic truth is to be "foolish," or an empty-headed person, whose lack of understanding has led to a lack of right living. Bede the Venerable pointedly wrote, "There are many evil people around who . . . believe that God means what he says, and they are quite prepared to accept that he exists. But it takes someone who is not just a nominal Christian but who is one in deed and in living to love God and to do what he commands. Faith with love is Christian, but faith without love is demonic" (cited in Bray, 30).

21–24 The balance of the passage takes up two illustrations from the OT. The first is Abraham (vv.21–24), who by offering up Isaac on the altar was justified by this expression of faith. The concept of "justification" here is different from that put forth by Paul at a number of points (although see Ro 2:13). James follows a more traditional use of the concept as found, for instance, in the LXX. In the traditional use of the concept, justification was an affirmation by God based on a person's righteous actions. In other words, God proclaimed a person just based on his or her actions. But Paul sometimes used the term "justified" to speak of a right standing conferred on the basis of Christ's work on the cross (Ro 3:24; 5:1).

In Abraham's action, faith and works coalesced, faith being brought to its mature end by action (v.22). Thus Genesis 15:6, "Abraham believed the LORD, and he credited it to him as righteousness," spoken years before the offering of Isaac, was brought to full expression. Abraham's reverence of God found full demonstration by his action of not holding back the most precious Isaac from sacrifice. The result was that Abraham was called God's friend. Abraham was a man of faith, and that faith was evidenced in Abraham the man of action.

25–26 Rahab, whom James bluntly identifies as "the prostitute," provides a corresponding, though in some ways a starkly contrastive, illustration to holy Abraham. He was a man, a patriarch, and great exemplar of the faith; she was a woman and a minor character of the Scriptures. Yet she made the good confession "the LORD your God is God in heaven above and on the earth below" (Jos 2:11), and believing that God was with the Israelites, she acted, taking in the messengers, hiding them, and seeing that they got away safely. Her belief combined with action is what brought her salvation from the destruction at hand. James infers that if she had done nothing to put feet to her faith, that "faith" would have been empty and in vain. Thus he concludes by reiterating that faith which is not expressed by righteous deeds is as dead as a lifeless body.

EPILOGUE

JAMES AND PAUL

Our passage under consideration has caused a great deal of agitation and discussion in the history of interpretation, Martin Luther even calling James a letter of straw! Based on a surface reading of 2:14–26, it is easy to understand why James has been placed over against Paul and his resounding proclamations of justification by faith alone, apart from works (Ro 4:1–25; Gal 5:1–6). What makes the situation more striking is that both Paul and James appeal to Abraham as an exemplar and quote Genesis 15:6 in support of their positions! As explained by Peter Davids ("James and Paul," in *The Dictionary of Paul and His Letters*, ed. G. Hawthorne and R. P. Martin [Downers Grove, Ill: InterVarsity, 1993], 457–61), there have been at least four views of how the matter is to be resolved.

Some have suggested that Paul and James were ministering and thinking independently, and that their writings reflect no interaction one with the other. Yet we know from Galatians and Acts (Gal 1:19; 2:9; Ac 15; 21:17–26) that they had significant interaction. This, along with their use of the same terminology—although their uses of the terms vary from one another—makes this position unlikely. Second, others have suggested that Paul is correcting James or a skewed version of James's teaching. A third possibility, some propose, is that James, perhaps having read some of Paul's writings, is attempting to counteract Paul's position on justification. Finally, still others suggest that James is reacting to a distortion of Paul's teaching.

Of the four, this last one seems the most likely. In his writings, Paul himself is concerned about those who misunderstand his teachings, and he strongly denied that his doctrine of justification meant one need not be concerned about righteous living (Ro 3:8; 6:1; 1Co 6:12). On close scrutiny, "What becomes clear is that James is not attacking any actual belief of Paul's, and that Paul could endorse everything James wrote" (Davids, "James and Paul," 460).

How, then, can we place their teachings in perspective? The key to understanding the relationship between Paul and James is to consider each against the backdrop of the false teachings with which they were concerned. As we have shown in our study of the passage, James addresses a very specific problem in the churches. There are those among his readers who profess to have faith (i.e., they claim to be in right relationship with God already), yet this profession seems to consist of mere mental assent and is not reflected in righteous living. James categorically points out that such a "faith" is questionable, since biblical faith *always* finds its full expression in righteous actions. Correspondingly, James's use of the term "justified" (2:21, 24) is more in line with the Septuagint's understanding of the term, i.e., a righteousness that is lived out and therefore affirmed by God. His proclamation of the truth looks something like this:

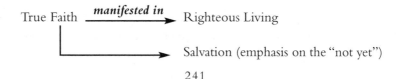

True Faith   *manifested in*   Righteous Living

Salvation (emphasis on the "not yet")

241

So James's emphasis in the passage under consideration is on the relationship between true faith and the righteous works expressed by such a faith.

Paul's primary nemeses, on the other hand, were those who held up certain religious practices, such as circumcision and food observances, as mandatory for Gentiles entering the new covenant. He combats this error by stating in no uncertain terms that entrance to the new covenant is by faith in Christ, through God's grace alone. Those who wish to add religious practices to the mix suggest that grace is not sufficient. Paul's proclamation of the truth, therefore, we depict as follows:

By God's Grace, Faith in Christ ⟶ Salvation (now and not yet)

An aspect of salvation is being "justified," in the sense of being placed in right standing with God (Ro 4:25; 5:18). It is by God's grace through faith in Christ that salvation comes to an individual, and salvation is multidimensional, beginning at the point of entrance to the covenant and being consummated when the Lord returns. Thus for Paul, by God's grace, only faith gains us entrance to right relationship with God. However, in Paul we also find James's concern for righteous manifestation of true faith. For instance, in Philippians 2:12–13 Paul exhorts the Philippians to work out the salvation that God has worked into their lives, for God is at work in them both to will and to act in accordance with God's purpose. Colossians 2:6–7 says that as Christ has been accepted as Lord, this acceptance demands a life of obedience. Therefore, our diagram on Paul's thought could be augmented as follows:

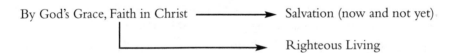

By God's Grace, Faith in Christ ⟶ Salvation (now and not yet)
⟶ Righteous Living

The difference between James and Paul is a matter of emphases, given the specific problems on which each is focusing. They should not be placed over against each other theologically. It may be that James is addressing some who have taken a skewed form of Paul's teaching to an ill-conceived conclusion, but James and Paul appear to agree that true faith is manifested in righteous living.

This emphasis on the relationship between faith and righteous living is one greatly needed in the modern church. In America especially, the important emphasis on grace (inherited from the Reformation), and in some quarters the focus particularly on one dimension of salvation (i.e., conversion) apart from ongoing transformation and righteous living, has resulted in large portions of the church tragically illustrating a vapid, inadequate faith. In response to James, we must again emphasize that one part of what it means to follow Christ faithfully is to live for him righteously in this world. This righteous living does not earn entrance to the covenant but rather manifests that the new covenant life is present. Those who simply give mental assent, failing especially to take up the tasks of practical ministry in the body (e.g., meeting the needs of the poor), must be called into question as to the validity of their faith. May God grant us the grace to understand and live out the true relationship between faith and works in the years to come.

D. Wrong Speaking toward One Another in Principle (3:1–12)

OVERVIEW

In our overview of the structure of James, we suggested that themes introduced in the twin introductions to the book (ch. 1) are developed systematically in the following chapters. James 2, as we have seen, addresses issues surrounding the rich and poor. In James 3:1–12, the author picks up the topic of the tongue. At a number of points in the book thus far, James has been concerned with right speech, or the impact of wrong speech in one form or another (1:13, 19–20, 26; 2:3, 12, 16). He especially is extending his exhortation of 1:19 to be "slow to speak" and the assertion of 1:26 "If anyone considers himself religious and yet does not keep a tight rein on his tongue, he deceives himself and his religion is worthless" (cf. Johnson, 254). Now these concerns find full force in a brief, well-crafted discourse full of striking, colorful illustrations and figures of speech that address the problem of divisive bickering and verbal war in a community.

James begins in 3:1–2 by introducing the gravity with which one should approach the tongue's use, noting that teachers are judged strictly, for teaching offers plenty of opportunities to stumble, and speech is the most difficult aspect of life to control. James continues in vv.3–5a with twin illustrations in which something small governs a much larger thing to which it is attached. The small bit directs the whole horse. A small rudder steers the whole ship. So also the tongue is small but has a big impact. In vv.5b–6 he continues this line of thought by comparing the tongue to a flame, but here he begins to address the tongue's destructiveness as well. The tongue is like a small flame that sets a whole forest on fire. James 3:6 specifically uses metaphor, associating the tongue with fire; the whole body, even the whole of life, burns up by the lick of this hellish flame called the tongue.

The imagery shifts in vv.7–8, where the author now compares the tongue to a wild animal. Whereas humanity has learned to tame the animals of the world—the beasts, birds, reptiles, and sea creatures—the tongue defies taming, being both restless and poisonous. Finally, in 3:9–12 James focuses on the incongruity of both praising and cursing coming from the same mouth. He again illustrates the point, noting that fountains do not produce two types of water, and fruit trees and vines do not produce fruit inconsistent with their nature; also, fresh water does not come from salt water. Thus the person who claims to be part of the community of faith should not produce cursing. From this overview we see that the whole of James 3:1–12 drives home this point: the tongue is powerfully destructive and difficult to control, but the Christian must master it.

[1]Not many of you should presume to be teachers, my brothers, because you know that we who teach will be judged more strictly. [2]We all stumble in many ways. If anyone is never at fault in what he says, he is a perfect man, able to keep his whole body in check. [3]When we put bits into the mouths of horses to make them obey us, we can turn the whole animal. [4]Or take ships as an example. Although they are so large and are driven by

strong winds, they are steered by a very small rudder wherever the pilot wants to go. [5]Likewise the tongue is a small part of the body, but it makes great boasts. Consider what a great forest is set on fire by a small spark. [6]The tongue also is a fire, a world of evil among the parts of the body. It corrupts the whole person, sets the whole course of his life on fire, and is itself set on fire by hell.

[7]All kinds of animals, birds, reptiles and creatures of the sea are being tamed and have been tamed by man, [8]but no man can tame the tongue. It is a restless evil, full of deadly poison.

[9]With the tongue we praise our Lord and Father, and with it we curse men, who have been made in God's likeness. [10]Out of the same mouth come praise and cursing. My brothers, this should not be. [11]Can both fresh water and salt water flow from the same spring? [12]My brothers, can a fig tree bear olives, or a grapevine bear figs? Neither can a salt spring produce fresh water.

COMMENTARY

1–12 These verses provide a sobering picture of the tongue's power, destructiveness, and instability. Behind James's treatment of this small member of the body is a theology that much human evil resides in the use of the mouth and, more specifically, the widespread divisions caused by slander and cursing in the churches he addresses. Through one graphic illustration after another, James crafts a picture of the tongue that is meant to arrest attention, the descriptions being stated in the strongest of terms. His treatment is a sober reminder that, to a great extent, the health of any church depends in part on the discipline with which the members are able to subdue this wildest of beasts.

1–2 Again addressing his audience as "my brothers" (1:2, 16, 19; 2:1, 5, 14; 3:1, 12; 5:12, 19), James exhorts them, "Not many of you should presume to be teachers" (NIV), and thus sets the context for his treatment of the tongue in the following verses. The NASB translates the sense of the verse a bit more clearly, since the term rendered "not" (*mē*), plus the present tense form of the word "become" (*ginomai*),

communicates more than a mere suggestion; rather, James intends a prohibition: "Let not many of you become teachers." As was the case with teachers in broader Judaism, the role of teacher was highly valued in the early church (e.g., Mt 13:52; Ac 13:1; 1Co 12:28). The status afforded the role, therefore, led unfit people to seek it, and the church had to deal with the problem of false or immoral teachers (1Ti 6:3; 2Ti 4:3; 1Pe 2:1; 1Jn 3; cf. Davids, 136–37; Laws, 140–44). James's prohibition implies that an abundance of people aspiring to be teachers is not healthy for the church.

The basis for the prohibition follows: teachers will be judged more strictly than others in the church. The term rendered "stricter" and "more strictly" by the NASB and the NIV, respectively, is a comparative form of the word we normally translate as "great," and here communicates an intensity to the judgment (*krima*, GK *3210*) received by the teachers. In Jesus' teaching he proclaimed that the teachers of the Law would be held to greater account than others (Mk 12:40; Lk 20:47), and as our present passage indicates, this principle seems to be present in the context of earliest Christianity as well. Why James begins here in addressing the challenges associated with the tongue becomes clearer with v.2.

2 The "for" at the beginning of 3:2 is explanatory, indicating that James is about to provide the reason for his prohibition in v.1. Why should many not seek the role of teacher? Because of a general principle: "We all stumble in many ways" (and especially through what we say!). To "stumble" was a common figure of speech referring to sin or to making mistakes (Ro 11:11). Sin trips us up, in a sense, keeping us from walking well according to God's ways. Further, the ways in which we stumble are many. The various dimensions of life, such as our thoughts, the things at which we look, what we do with our hands, and where we go with our feet, provide ample opportunities for sinning against God. Taking moral tumbles by violating God's ways, moreover, is the experience of every person, without exception, the term for "all" here (*hapas*) being intensive and meaning "absolutely everybody."

James now moves from the general principle to his specific concern. Although stumbling is the problem faced by every person, the tongue presents a special challenge: "If anyone is never at fault in what he says, he is a perfect man, able to keep his whole body in check." If a person is able to keep from stumbling in what he says, this fact indicates he has reached a certain level of spiritual maturity. The idea was widespread both in Jewish wisdom and Hellenistic moral philosophy. In a close parallel to James, the Jewish writer Philo (*Posterity*, 88) said it well: "But if a man succeeded, as if handling a lyre, in bringing all the notes of the thing that is good into tune, bringing speech into harmony with intent, and intent with deed, such an one would be considered perfect and of a truly harmonious character." The term "perfect" here does not mean

"completely without sin" but rather has to do with a state of maturity, being fully developed in character. James goes on to argue from a most difficult situation to a less difficult one, suggesting that a person with such a high level of self-control will be able to control the fleshly whims of the rest of the body.

It seems that James is concerned about destructive speech among those who are aspiring to the role of teacher in the communities of faith. Since that role was held in high esteem, many probably sought it who were not morally qualified (Davids, 136). James's point is that to stand before other believers and attempt to teach the truths of God carries a grave responsibility. When such a role, in which the tongue has full vent, combines with unrighteous relational dynamics, destruction ravages a community. Consequently, the role of teacher demands a concurrent commitment to being disciplined in what one says—and this demand is not easily fulfilled.

3-5a James now addresses the power of the tongue, which though small has a very large effect. This the author illustrates in parallel by pointing to the bits in horses' mouths (v.3) and the rudder that turns a ship (v.4), images used widely in ancient literature as pictures of control (Dibelius, 185-90; Ropes, 231). Horses are large animals, and the point of riding a horse is to get it to go where you want it to go. The rider of a horse puts a bit in its mouth in order that the horse will obediently go in the right direction. Using the bit, the rider can move the whole body of the horse. That which is small sets the direction for something much greater in size. Specifically, references to the horse's mouth and "body" (*sōma*, GK *5393*) prepare for a fitting analogy to the tongue as a part of the human body in v.5 (Moo, 153).

In the same way, ships are very large and driven along by very strong or violent winds. Travel by ship was common in the first century (e.g., Ac 13:4;

18:21; 27:1), so the imagery of v. 4 would have been quite familiar. The pilot of a ship is able to direct such a great vessel, which powerful, natural forces drive along, by using a relatively small rudder. That which is small sets the direction for something much greater in size.

Now comes the point. In the same way, the tongue is a relatively small part of the body. Yet its impact is far out of proportion to its size. Both the NIV and NASB indicate that the tongue's effect has to do with its boasting or bragging (*aucheō*, GK 902) about great things. From the broader context of James, the author makes it clear he has in mind an evil boasting born of arrogance: "But as it is, you boast in your arrogance; all such boasting is evil" (4:16 NASB). Thus he highlights an arrogance associated with the use of the tongue, and this may be related directly to those teachers causing strife in the community. The tongue, though small, is the member of the body that manifests our arrogant presumption that we are "big," or more important than others in the church.

5b–6 The author adds yet another vivid word picture to describe how something so small can cause a great effect, but now the emphasis moves toward the destructive nature of that effect: "Consider what a great forest is set on fire by a small spark." Forest fires occurred in the ancient world, as they do today, and the devastation was striking for the ancients. Again, James reiterates the principle: something relatively small has a profound impact on something much larger. Yet in v. 6 James focuses our attention on the insidious power of the tongue by using metaphorical language. "The tongue also is a fire." When metaphor is used, we need to grasp the analogies intended, and James's point is that just as fire is horribly destructive, so the tongue can be devastatingly destructive. The image of the tongue as a fire is found both in Jewish wisdom writings (e.g., Pr 16:27; 26:20–21), and Greek literature (see Johnson, 258–59).

James explains that the tongue is "the very world of iniquity" (NASB). The phrase rendered "world of evil" by the NIV is notoriously difficult to interpret—perhaps the most difficult in the whole book. (For a detailed discussion of the options, see Davids, 141–43; Johnson, 259.) It clearly refers to the "wicked, evil world," according to Dibelius (194; but he thinks part of the text is a gloss, i.e., not an original part of the book but a later addition). The author refers to the "world" as a system opposed to God at 1:27 and 4:4, and these verses have other connections with 3:6. The former verse states that part of authentic religion is "to keep oneself unstained [*aspilos*, GK 834] by the world" (NASB). In 3:6 the tongue is established among the members of the body as that part which "corrupts" (*spiloō*, GK 5071) or stains the whole body. Further, 4:4 speaks of person's being established (*kathistēmi*, GK 2770) as God's enemy, and the same term is used in 3:6 of the tongue's being established among the members of the body. The idea is that the tongue serves as the arch representative of the evil world. All kinds of unrighteousness are imported to life via the tongue.

Further, the tongue is set among the members of the body as that which defiles, or pollutes, the whole. Though a different Greek verb is used, this point brings to mind the teaching of Jesus that what comes out of a person defiles the person (Mk 7:20). James's statement drives home one of the striking difficulties of dealing with the tongue—this world of unrighteousness, as a member of the body, is part of us, and the consequences of its presence are great! When uncontrolled, the tongue is an agent of spiritual and moral pollution that corrupts the entire body.

He now returns to the tongue as a flame of fire. It sets on fire "the wheel of existence," a phrase found in common use in extrabiblical literature and appropriately translated by the NIV as referring to the course of a person's life. The consequences of misusing the tongue can have far-reaching and devastating effects in a life. The reason for this is that the fire of the tongue, its destructive nature, originates in "hell." The term for hell here is *Gehenna*. *Gê Hinnōm* was a ravine south of Jerusalem, and its association with burning was twofold. First, it had been a site of pagan sacrifices by fire in the OT era (2Ki 23:10; Jer 7:31), and second, it came to be the garbage dump of Jerusalem, a place of perpetual burning. By the NT era *Gehenna* was used of the place of eternal, fiery punishment and corruption (*Laws*, 151–52). Thus the out-of-control tongue, as a "fire," receives its impetus from hell. It stands in direct contrast to righteous living, which has its origin in God (3:17–18).

7–8 James's discussion of the tongue's destructiveness continues by comparing it to the wildest of animals. James notes that every species of animal, bird, reptile, and sea creature is being tamed and has been tamed by human beings. "Tamed" can also mean "controlled" or "subdued." The point is that, in relation to the other species of the earth, humans are distinct. In the creation of people and animals on the sixth day (Ge 1:24–28) God stated this distinction explicitly. He proclaimed in Genesis 1:26, "Let us make man in our image, in our likeness, and let them rule over the fish of the sea and the birds of the air, over the livestock, over all the earth, and over all the creatures that move along the ground." James's point is that the creation mandate of ruling over the lesser beasts had been carried out. Animals, birds, reptiles, and sea creatures are subdued. One must not think here of "tamed" as in a circus; rather, James has in mind humans as dominant.

Yet, irony of ironies, that small beast, the tongue, defies subjugation. James states plainly, "but no man can tame the tongue." He probably speaks hyperbolically in v.8, since his appeal is that those of the congregations do just that. Yet the two descriptions at the end of the verse leave no room for doubt concerning the seriousness with which the tongue

must be taken. Like a wild animal pacing about, attack and tearing in its every thought, the tongue is a "restless evil." The word "restless" (*akatastatos*, GK 190) also connotes the concept of being "unstable" and occurs in James's description of the double-minded person of 1:8. In one ancient work, slander is personified as a "restless demon" (Shepherd of Hermas, *Mand.* 2:3). Moreover, this wild animal is full of death-dealing poison. The thought parallels Paul's quote of Psalm 140:3 at Romans 3:13. There the apostle conflates a number of OT passages to speak of the comprehensive nature of human sin, pointing out that sin is often associated with the "mouth" (i.e., speech). He includes the quotation from Psalm 140:3, a psalm that describes wicked people of violence who devise evil plans and slander with their poisonous tongues: "The poison of vipers is on their lips." So too James points out that the tongue is like a wild, poisonous animal that kills with its blows.

9–10 In Paul's treatment of sin in Romans 3, he follows the quotation of Psalm 140:3 with a quotation of Psalm 10:7 (Ro 3:14), "Their mouths are full of cursing and bitterness," and in the same way, James moves from talk of the poison tongue to the topic of cursing. His special concern in vv.9–12 is the incongruity of the tongue's mix of praising God with cursing people, "who have been made in God's likeness." The worth of other human beings, formed in the image of God, demands a carefulness in the speech used to address them. Yet members of the church are violating this principle. The same tongue produces both praise and cursing, and James states categorically, "My brothers, this should not be."

11–12 The final two verses in the unit offer illustrations from nature to support James's assertion that the mix of praise and cursing is wrong. In the first, he points out that two incompatible products cannot come from the same source, and the rhetorical questions with which he begins expect a negative answer.

When water is gushing out of a hole in a spring or fountain, both sweet and bitter water do not come out. Most towns in Palestine were located near a spring of good water, apart from which they could not exist (Moo, 165). As was the case when the Israelites came to Mara, bitter water was not fit for drinking (Ex 15:23). The NIV translates the term "sweet" (*glykys*, GK *1184*) as "fresh" and "bitter" (*pikros*, GK *4395*) as "salt," but it may be better at this point to see the contrast as between good water fit for drinking and that which, for whatever reason, is not potable. In v.14 the term "bitter" will be used again to speak of the bitterness of jealousy, and as found in earlier Jewish texts it could describe corrupt speech (e.g., Ps 64:3; Pr 5:4). James's point is that sweet and bitter water do not mix, being incompatible in nature, and the same is true for praise and cursing.

Incompatibility in nature also constitutes the theme of v.12. A fig tree does not bear olives; neither does a grapevine bear figs, since fruits bear according to their nature. The fruit analogy calls to mind Jesus' teachings, though he speaks of good and bad fruit (Mt 7:16–20; 12:33–35). Yet Jesus' point is that plants bear fruit according to their nature, and this is close to James's intent (Davids, 148).

Neither does salt water produce fresh. Whereas the illustration of v.11 has to do with two types of water coming from the same source, the final statement of v.12, in line with his agricultural analogies, suggests that salt water by its nature cannot produce fresh water. The analogy between these illustrations and the tongue is clear. When the tongue praises God and curses other people, a base incongruity exists.

NOTES

1–12 I have given this unit the title "Wrong Speaking toward One Another in Principle" because it has been shown to have significant lexical links to 4:1–6, which constitutes the "practice" of wrong actions and speaking in the Christian communities to which James writes. These links are as follows: μέλεσιν, *melesin* (3:5–6/4:1); the forms of δύναμαι, *dunamai*, at 3:8/4:2; the use of κακός/κακῶς, *kakos/kakōs*, at 3:8/4:3; the use of κόσμος, *kosmos*, and forms of καθίστημι, *kathistēmi*, at 3:6/4:4; the use of μεῖζον, *meizon*, and μείζονα, *meizona*, at 3:1/4:6. See Taylor, 128.

E. Righteous vs. Worldly Wisdom (3:13–18)

OVERVIEW

We now come to a focal passage for the whole of James. As noted in our treatment of James 1:5–8, true wisdom, the wisdom that comes as a gift of God, is closely associated with righteous living. This truth he embodies clearly in the passage at hand. James begins by asking a rhetorical question, "Who is wise and understanding among you?" and then answers by wedding wisdom with good conduct (v.13). He then sets this teaching in bold relief by contrasting this godly wisdom with a lifestyle of relational discord due to jealousy and selfishness (v.14). Rather than coming from heaven, this so-called "wisdom" has the demonic as its source, being earthly and unspiritual (v.15), for jealousy and selfishness are associated with a lack of order and the practice of evil (v.16). Such a pattern of relating to others stands in direct contrast to the pattern of heaven's wisdom, which issues forth in righteous living (vv.17–18).

---

¹³Who is wise and understanding among you? Let him show it by his good life, by deeds done in the humility that comes from wisdom. ¹⁴But if you harbor bitter envy and selfish ambition in your hearts, do not boast about it or deny the truth. ¹⁵Such "wisdom" does not come down from heaven but is earthly, unspiritual, of the devil. ¹⁶For where you have envy and selfish ambition, there you find disorder and every evil practice.

¹⁷But the wisdom that comes from heaven is first of all pure; then peace-loving, considerate, submissive, full of mercy and good fruit, impartial and sincere. ¹⁸Peacemakers who sow in peace raise a harvest of righteousness.

COMMENTARY

13 In the ancient world, to be "wise" (*sophos*, GK 5055) could refer to being skilled or experienced (e.g., 1Co 3:10); but most often in biblical literature, the word communicates an understanding that results in right attitudes and right living, for God himself is wise (Ro 16:27; 1Co 1:25) and therefore is the source of divine wisdom. James wants his audience to consider such godly wisdom, for he asks rhetorically, "Who is wise and understanding among you?" The term translated "understanding" (*epistē-mōn*, GK 2184) has to do with being knowledgeable or expert in some area of life. It may be that there were strong personalities in the churches James addresses—people who boasted of their great learning and "wisdom," insisting that their perspectives on certain matters be given the highest consideration. Yet James issues a reminder that true wisdom "speaks" loudest in one primary way: a life lived well and with an attitude of humility. Thus one must "show," or demonstrate (*deiknymi*, GK 1259), "deeds" (*ta erga*, GK 2240) associated with a righteous pattern of life. This "good life" (*tēs kalēs ana-strophēs*, GK 2819, 419) constitutes high moral quality and excellence of conduct (Gal 1:13; Eph 4:22; Heb 13:7; 1Pe 3:2). Further, true wisdom is the source of humility, so the "showing" of good deeds, which really stems from divine wisdom, will manifest itself in a humbleness of spirit rather than stimulating a boastful attitude. The word rendered "humility" (*prautēs*, GK 4559) by the NIV and "gentleness" by the NASB can also carry the meaning "courtesy" or "considerateness," and, given the relational conflicts addressed in the passage, these nuances may be in line with James's intention.

14 Now comes the contrast, expressed in the little conjunction translated "but" (*de*). If rather than this righteous pattern of living, which manifests true wisdom, a person holds to bitter jealousy and rank selfishness, another kind of "wisdom" is in evidence. The term rendered "envy" by the NIV and "jealousy" by the NASB could be used positively in the ancient world for a desire to emulate another person or for an intense interest in something (e.g., 2Co 9:2; Php 3:6). However, the context here—especially the addition of the word "bitter" (*pikros*, GK 4395)—makes it clear that James has a vice in mind. So used, jealousy refers to an intense, inappropriate sorrow over another person's achievements or possessions (Johnson, 271). "Selfish ambition," on the other hand, probably refers to some parts of the church setting themselves over against others and advancing their agendas (see Martin, 130). In contrast to true wisdom's humility, inappropriate boasting characterizes a this-worldly approach to relationships. Although there is no object of the verb "boast" (*katakauchaomai*, GK 2878) in the Greek text, based on the context wisdom probably is the understood object. These jealous, ambitious people were bragging about their "wisdom." Such attitudes constitute a lie against the truth, since true wisdom manifests humility and healthy relationships (Moo, 172).

15 Moreover, to find the source of this corrupt so-called "wisdom," one must look somewhere other than "above," i.e., the heavenly realm where God dwells. In 1:5 James proclaims that God is the one to ask for true wisdom, for he is a generous giver of such. Indeed, "Every good thing given and every perfect gift is from above" (1:17 NASB). Yet the "wisdom" of which James speaks in 3:15 is neither good nor perfect and has its source elsewhere. First, it is "earthly" (*epigeios*, GK 2103). This term could be used of what is typical of earth in contrast to that which is characteristic of heaven. Paul uses the word in this way at 2 Corinthians 5:1, for instance, to speak of the "earthly tent," the physical body (see also Jn 3:12). Yet James uses the word more in line with Philippians 3:19, where Paul speaks of the immoral pattern of life followed by the "enemies of the cross of Christ." So this "wisdom" has a twisted nature, an immoral bent. Second, it is "unspiritual" (*pseuchikos*, GK 6035). Originally having to do with the soul, the word at points came to connote worldliness, as it does in Jude 19, for instance, where the "worldly" people are those who cause divisions in the church and are devoid of the

Spirit. Paul uses it in his description of the "unspiritual" person who, in contrast to the person of the Spirit, does not understand the Spirit's wisdom (1Co 2:14). Finally, this earthly, unspiritual "wisdom" James describes as "demonic" (*daimoniōdēs*, GK 1229), originating from the realm of demons.

16 The next verse rounds off James's description of this earthly wisdom by describing its fruit. The "jealousy" and "ambition" already mentioned in v.14, and which are so characteristic of a this-worldly pattern of thinking and living, are concomitant with "disorder and every evil practice." The word rendered "disorder" (*akatastasia*, GK 189) speaks of disturbances (Lk 21:9) and at points of an unruliness that challenges authority (see 2Co 12:20). The "evil" (*phaulos*, GK 5765) practice has to do with bad or morally base actions, and the word "every" (*pan*) added to the description indicates that the earthly wisdom is the source for all actions and activities out of line with God's righteousness. In other words, the earthly wisdom, characterized as it is by jealousy and ambition, is associated with disrupted and dysfunctional community that does not walk in God's righteousness.

17–18 James now contrasts the worldly wisdom with God's wisdom "from above," describing it in detail as "pure; then peace-loving, considerate, submissive, full of mercy and good fruit, impartial and sincere." The term translated "pure" (*hagnos*, GK 54) could mean "holy" or "innocent" and in the context stands in contrast to "every evil practice" in the previous verse. That it is "peace-loving" (*eirēnikos*, GK 1646) marks this wisdom as conducive to healthy relationships and again places it in contrast to the earthly wisdom that spawns disorder (v.16). Accordingly, God's wisdom also is "considerate" (*epieikēs*, GK 2117), or gentle and kind when dealing with others; and it is "submissive" (*eupeithēs*, GK 2340), an interesting word that occurs only here in biblical literature. Josephus (*J.W.* 2.577) uses the term of troops under the control of a commander, and the first-century philosopher Epictetus of a person who is persuadable. Rather than connoting a passive obedience, the word as used in the first century "implies good will and mutual understanding; it refers . . . to an inclination to accept suggestions and conform to them willingly" (*TLNT* 2:129–30). Thus the NLT renders it "willing to yield to others." True wisdom manifests healthy interpersonal skills and attitudes. That this wisdom is "full of mercy" (*meste eleous*, GK *1799*) means it is characterized consistently by compassion or kindness toward someone who has a need. Jesus' words come to mind as we read that godly wisdom is also full of "good fruit" (plural): "By their fruit you will recognize them" (Mt 7:16, 20). The close association of the people of Palestine with agriculture made the concept of "fruit" a ready figure for the result, outcome, or product of one's pattern of life (e.g., Mt 3:8; 21:43; Gal 5:22; Eph 5:9; Php 1:11). Therefore, James proclaims that the product of a life characterized by God's wisdom is "good." This wisdom is also "impartial" (*adiakritos*, GK *88*), a better translation than the NASB's "unwavering," given the orientation to healthy relationships in James's list of 3:17. The term has to do with not being judgmental of others, being free from prejudice (cf. 2:1–11; 4:11–12). Finally, this wisdom from above is "sincere" (*anypokritos*, GK *537*) or genuine, being without pretense (Ro 12:9). This sincerity is the antithesis of hypocrisy, and elsewhere in the NT it is used of a genuine, nonhypocritical love (2Co 6:6; 1Pe 1:22) or faith (1Ti 1:5; 2Ti 1:5).

James rounds off the unit with v.18, elaborating the figure of "fruit" and putting forth the high value of peace in the community: "Peacemakers who sow in peace raise a harvest of righteousness." Divisiveness and disorder, products of earthly ways in interpersonal relationships, have their counterpoint in peace, in a community that is unified and harmonious because it lives according to God's wise patterns of interaction. Earlier in the chapter (v.12), the author made the point that plants naturally bear fruit according to their nature. Having more to do with the conditions in which a crop of righteousness is planted, James insists that peacemakers must sow this crop (*karpos*, GK *2843*) in the soil of peace. In other words, a righteous community grows only in a context of healthy relationships where a high premium is placed on peace (Eph 2:15; 4:3; 2Ti 2:22; 1Pe 3:11).

NOTES

14 The term ἐριθείαν (*eritheian*, "selfish ambition," GK *2121*) is very rare, and its meaning is somewhat uncertain. See the discussion in BDAG, 392, and in Martin, 130.

F. Wrong Actions and Speaking toward One Another in Practice (4:1–5)

OVERVIEW

Whereas James 3:13–18 presents a general theological treatise contrasting wise living with a false, demonic "wisdom" that causes disorder in the communities, the author now directly confronts the disorder and strife that are quite evident among his readers. This unit forms a natural extension of the previous one, yet as shown in the introduction, it also has significant lexical connections to 3:1–12. James 4:1–5 is confrontational, its language as harsh as at any point in the book, as the author reflects on conflict in the communities to which he addresses the letter. He diagnoses their spiritual problem as originating in their pleasures (vv.1, 3), which place members of the communities at odds with one another by spawning fights and quarrels. James offers a prophetic assessment of their condition, labeling the hearers "adulterous people" who have situated themselves as God's enemies by embracing friendship with the world and its ways (v.4). Supporting his exhortation with an allusion to the OT (v.5), he drives home the point that God also has desires—he desires the spirit who lives in us, and this desire is depicted in terms of "jealousy" (*phthonos*, GK *5784*). He does not sit idly by as our affections are drawn elsewhere.

> ¹What causes fights and quarrels among you? Don't they come from your desires that battle within you? ²You want something but don't get it. You kill and covet, but you cannot have what you want. You quarrel and fight. You do not have, because you do not ask God. ³When you ask, you do not receive, because you ask with wrong motives, that you may spend what you get on your pleasures.
>
> ⁴You adulterous people, don't you know that friendship with the world is hatred toward God? Anyone who chooses to be a friend of the world becomes an enemy of God. ⁵Or do you think Scripture says without reason that the spirit he caused to live in us envies intensely?

COMMENTARY

1 As with 3:13, James begins with a rhetorical question, and puts its answer also in the form of a question: "What causes fights and quarrels among you? Don't they come from your desires that battle within you?" The double use of *pothen* ("from where?") signals impassioned preaching at this point (Davids, 156). The term for "fights" (*polemos*, GK *4483*) could refer to literal wars or battles (e.g., Mt 24:6; Lk 14:31), but it also had a figurative meaning, as it does here, that spoke of relational antagonism or conflict. "Quarrels" (*machē*, GK *3480*) is roughly synonymous to the previous term, although *machē* can connote disputes or arguments (2Co 7:5; 2Ti 2:23; Tit 3:9), and this repetition of similar ideas may indicate a high level of intensity in the situation. The word for "not" (*ouk*) at the beginning of the second sentence anticipates a positive answer. Thus the rhetorical question implies that fighting and quarreling characterize the communities being addressed, so the question provides us a clarifying peek at the relational discord that seems to be an underlying concern of the book (Ropes, 252). The fragmentation of these communities had reached serious levels, and James confronts the discord quite directly and forcefully.

He answers his own question by pinpointing their "desires" (*hēdonē*, GK *2454*), or "pleasures," as the stimulating factor behind the infighting among these believers. Although the term could be used in the ancient world to speak of enjoyment or pleasantness, here, as elsewhere in the NT, it refers to evil pleasures that have a negative spiritual effect (Lk 8:14; Tit 3:3; 2Pe 2:13). In fact, the "fights" and "quarrels" in the churches are symptomatic of a deeper condition, since the internal conflicting desires resident in each person are in a state of "battle" (*strateuō*, GK *5129*). The word translated "battle" could mean "to serve as a soldier" (1Co 9:7; 2Ti 2:4) but here refers figuratively to some type of fight or conflict (cf. 2Co 10:3; 1Ti 1:18; 1Pe 2:11). Thus the phrase translated "within you" (NIV), or "in your members" (NASB), refers to the evil desires inside these people rather than merely desires played out in conflicted community relationships (Laws, 168; Davids, 157).

2 In v.1 the author used a rhetorical question and its answer to demonstrate the cause-and-effect relationship between inappropriate desires and the resulting fights and quarrels among those in the church. Utilizing a rapid-fire series of clauses in v.2, James reiterates the problem and its cause by strongly asserting that their lust and envy are leading to relational breakdown. The NIV and NASB represent two different ways of understanding the organization of this series of clauses. The NIV translates the bulk of the verse with a three-part structure:

> You want something but don't get it.
> You kill and covet, but you cannot have what you
> want.
> You quarrel and fight.

The problem with this approach is that it does not make clear the obvious parallelism in the verse. Much better is the NASB's translation, which suggests that James presents wrong desire, failure to obtain the desire, and the resulting sin in parallel fashion (Moo, 182):

> You lust and do not have; so you commit murder.
> You are envious and cannot obtain; so you fight
> and quarrel.

James has already explained the role of lust as a temptress that gives birth to sin and death (1:14–15). It is a power that promises much and delivers nothing good. Consequently, those James addresses are coming up empty in actually fulfilling their desires. Out of frustration, then, they "kill" or "murder"

(*phoneuō*, GK *5839*). Johnson, 276–77, has shown that "envy" and "murder" go together in literary treatments of envy in the ancient world, the latter being a logical extension of the former. Although James could have literal murder in mind (cf. 5:6), his brief treatment of it makes this unlikely. A figurative understanding of "killing" as doing people harm verbally or socially may be suggested on two bases. First, we have seen that Jesus' teaching at points lies behind James's thought, and Jesus used the concept of "murder" in the figurative sense of being horribly angry with someone (Mt 5:21–26). Also, the failure to care for the needs of the poor was referred to as murder in some strands of Jewish tradition and is seen in James 2:11 and 5:6 (Davids, 159). Second, in the parallelism depicted above, lust parallels envy, "do not have" parallels "cannot obtain," and "you commit murder" parallels "you fight and quarrel." Their fights and quarrels seem to be utmost in the author's mind, since he started the unit by addressing these problems. Thus the parallelism within the verse supports the figurative meaning, and yet the figure itself indicates the intensity of the conflict in the communities.

When James says, "You do not have, because you do not ask God," he points to their general prayerlessness as another indicator of their spiritual condition. They have intense desires that are promoting relational havoc in the church, and yet the desires find no answer because they have ceased to go to the source of real fulfillment—God himself.

3 James continues with what seems to be a contradictory statement to the one just made: "When you ask, you do not receive, because you ask with wrong motives, that you may spend what you get on your pleasures." He now says that indeed they have asked, but the assertion should be understood as a qualification rather than a contradiction (Laws, 172). James has already noted that prayer will not be answered for a person waffling in commitment to God (1:5–8). Now he emphasizes another reason that prayer, at times, is not answered. Prayer prayed out of wrong motives (lit., "badly," *kakōs*), from a lustful heart, falls on deaf ears. The term translated "pleasures" spoke generally of enjoyment or something that was pleasant, but here, as in v.1, it refers to evil pleasures. Furthermore, in v.1 James has already pointed out that their pleasures are the source of the warring spirit, the quarrels and fighting tearing the communities apart. For God, then, to feed those evil pleasures with answered prayer would in effect be for God to promote discord among his people, which is antithetical to his nature. Consequently, in terms of effect, the prayer prayed from a twisted heart is comparable to the prayer never prayed at all.

4 In prophetic style, James calls his hearers "adulterous." The image of an adulteress for people who, turning away from the true God, give themselves to other "gods" has a rich background in the OT, where it is the most common image for apostasy. Israel is like a wandering, faithless wife who turns away from Yahweh, her husband, to go after other gods (e.g., Jer 2:1–3; 5:7; Eze 6:9; 16:1–63; Hos 1:2–3). In the NT Jesus calls those who reject his ministry and teaching an "evil and adulterous generation" (Mt 12:39; 16:4; cf. Mk 8:38). Both the OT's use of the image and Jesus' use of it speak of those who, consumed in their own interests, have turned away from faithful love of God. The image is extended to false teachers in 2 Peter 2:14, which asserts that evil, false prophets have "eyes full of adultery," and the book of Revelation uses the image (in the form of Jezebel) of false teaching as well (2:20–22).

James seizes on the image to speak of divided loyalty, asking, "Don't you know that friendship with the world is hatred toward God?" He then reiterates, "Anyone who chooses to be a friend of the world becomes an enemy of God." To embrace the world in friendship is "hatred" (*echthra*, GK *2397*) or "enmity" toward God. The term speaks of being the enemy of someone, or hostile to them, such as when Pilate and Herod were enemies (Lk 23:12), and such relational

hatred is one of the deeds of the flesh (Gal 5:20). Christ, on the other hand, breaks down such hostility (Eph 2:14, 16). Most egregious of all is to have a posture of hostility toward God himself (Ro 8:7), as James describes here. Yet the choice of the world and its ways over God and his wisdom constitutes just such a posture, and a choice, either for God or the world, must be made. One cannot have it both ways.

5 Now an allusion to Scripture is brought to bear: "He jealously desires the Spirit which He has made to dwell in us" (NASB). Two questions must be answered in relation to v.5. First, how should this allusion be translated? The NIV reads, "The spirit he caused to live in us envies intensely," reading "spirit" as a reference to the human spirit and "envy" as an immoral attitude. The NASB, on the other hand, understands "Spirit" as a reference to the Holy Spirit and "jealousy" as God's jealousy in the face of our adultery. To the point of jealousy (*pros phthonon*, GK *5784*) he "desires" (*epipotheō*, GK *2160*) the Spirit in us. The term rendered "desires" by the NASB speaks of a strong desire or longing (2Co 9:14; 1Pe 2:2), but is it our human spirit that desires, or is it God who desires? Of the two, the latter probably is the better interpretation, given the context. That those addressed are "adulterous," putting themselves in a posture as God's enemies, recalls the message of prophets like Hosea. As a jealous husband, God desires for his people to be in right relationship with himself (Moo, 189–90; Nystrom, 227–28). Their sinful jealousy (3:16) is prompting God to righteous jealousy. Correspondingly, it probably is not the Holy Spirit that God desires, but rather the human spirit he has placed in people (Davids, 164).

Second, though James refers to the allusion as "Scripture," the exact passage(s) to which he alludes is not clear. The allusion in general terms may be to the Pentateuch, specifically passages such as Exodus 20:4 and 34:14, where God prohibits idolatry even as he proclaims his jealousy. If this is the case, it means that in the face of his people's friendship with the world, God does not sit by idly. He has made us for

relationship with himself, and he will not passively let us embrace the world in an adulterous relationship.

G. A Call to Humility and Repentance (4:6–10)

OVERVIEW

In James 4:6–10, we learn that grace is available to those who humble themselves. We must not equate grace here with forgiveness, for grace has its demands on those who would be its recipients. Grace forms even while it forgives. Thus James gives

a series of exhortations: submit to God, resist the devil, come near to God, wash yourselves, mourn, and humble yourselves. These are the paths to exaltation in God's presence.

⁶But he gives us more grace. That is why Scripture says:

"God opposes the proud
but gives grace to the humble."

⁷Submit yourselves, then, to God. Resist the devil, and he will flee from you. ⁸Come near to God and he will come near to you. Wash your hands, you sinners, and purify your hearts, you double-minded. ⁹Grieve, mourn and wail. Change your laughter to mourning and your joy to gloom. ¹⁰Humble yourselves before the Lord, and he will lift you up.

COMMENTARY

6 James 4:6–10 develops from and balances 4:1–5 by providing an answer for the spiritual problem leading to relational fragmentation in the communities to which James writes, and that answer is humble repentance. The remedy for spiritual adultery, manifested in blatant self-centeredness, is grace, and the grace God gives is, as rendered in the NASB, "greater" (*meizona*, GK *3505*), or "extraordinary." As the Scripture says, "God opposes the proud but gives grace to the humble." The quote is taken from LXX Proverbs 3:34, which expresses succinctly a prominent biblical value. The "mighty" of the earth, who because of status, wealth, or power have an inflated view of their significance in the

world, are opposed by God. In other words, he resists or works against them and their agendas. By contrast, he gives grace to the "humble," an attitude already highlighted by James as important (1:9–10).

7 What, then, is an appropriate response to Proverbs 3:34? In a series of exhortations, James describes the path of humility. First, we are to "submit ... to God." In the NT the term "submit" (*hypotassō*, GK *5718*) is quite common. The act connotes yielding to the perspective or position of another and is basic to Christian practice. Believers are to submit to one another (1Co 16:16; Eph 5:21), and in that broader framework wives are to submit to husbands (Eph 5:24; Col 3:18; Tit 2:5; 1Pe 3:1, 5), the young to the old (1Pe 5:5), slaves to masters (Eph 6:5; Tit 2:9; 1Pe 2:18), and Christ-followers to the government (Ro 13:1). As here in James 4:7, God's people are to submit to God (1Co 15:28; Heb 12:9) and further to the law of God (Ro 8:7). Whereas worldly wisdom draws us away from God and out of line with his ways, submission begins the process of drawing us back, for submission is an act of humility to which God responds.

Second, we are to "resist the devil." Whereas God "opposes" (*antitassō*, GK *530*) the proud (v.6), we are to "resist" or "oppose" (*anthistēmi*, GK *468*) the devil. The two Greek terms are roughly synonymous (see the use of both in Ro 13:2). To resist means to place oneself on the opposite side of someone or something, as when Elymas the magician opposed Paul and Barnabas (Ac 13:8) and when Paul opposed Cephas to his face (Gal 2:11). At points in the NT the term involves resisting in the sense of standing one's ground (Eph 6:13; 1Pe 5:9). In the context here, James probably has in mind resisting taking part in the devil's work of discord in the communities. If the devil is resisted, "he will flee from you" (see Davids, 166).

8 By contrast, James exhorts his hearers to "come near to God," an action that has its own result: "and he will come near to you." The concept of drawing near to God occurs in relation to approaching God in priestly service (e.g., Ex 19:22; 40:46; Lev 10:3), and new covenant believers can draw near because they have a better hope through Christ's sacrifice (Heb 7:19). To draw near to God means to approach him in prayer, to turn toward him and not away from him. The result will be that God himself will respond by approaching the one who approaches him. In other words, a healthy relationship will be reestablished. As was the case in the old covenant system of worship, part of the process of drawing near to God involves cleansing, which James states in parallel fashion: "Wash your hands, you sinners,

and purify your hearts, you double-minded." The images here, of course, are figurative and represent repentance from sin. The author has already mentioned the "double-minded" person in 1:8, and, as in that context, the double-minded people James has in mind are those with a divided commitment and questionable loyalties and therefore those who are unstable spiritually. These are "sinners" because they have not been committed resolutely to the ways of the Lord. Thus repentance is needed.

9 Next the author exhorts, "Grieve, mourn and wail. Change your laughter to mourning and your joy to gloom." To "grieve" (*talaipōreō*, GK *5415*), a word that occurs only here in the NT, means to have deep sorrow or to feel miserable, and C. Spicq (*TLNT* 3:367–68) notes that the term, along with its cognate noun and adjective, is used to reflect the cry of a broken heart. Paul uses the related adjective when he cries out, "What a wretched man I am!" (Ro 7:24). The deep sorrow expressed by the use of the verb in v.9 is over sin. Mourning and weeping are appropriate responses in the face of God's impending judgment and express repentance (2Sa 19:1; Ne 8:9; Ac 18:11, 15, 19). Correspondingly, mourning and weeping mean the putting away of a happy, carefree attitude. Laughter and joy are to be exchanged for mourning and "gloom" (*katēpheia*, GK *2993*) or "grief" (Am 8:10; Pr 14:13). The thought recalls the words of Jesus, who said, "Woe to you who are well fed now, for you will go hungry. Woe to you who laugh now, for you will mourn and weep" (Lk 6:25). Rather than experience mourning at the judgment, sinners should mourn now in true repentance so that they will not have to mourn then (Davids, 167–68).

10 James wraps up the unit by reiterating the call for humility reflected earlier (v.6) in his quote of Proverbs 3:34: "Humble yourselves before the Lord, and he will lift you up." The value of humility as the right path to exaltation is widely published in the OT, but the most immediate backdrop for James is the teaching of Jesus, who said, "For everyone who exalts himself will be humbled, and he who humbles himself will be exalted" (Lk 14:11; cf. Mt 23:12; Lk 18:14). The thought is echoed in the writings of the early church (e.g., 1Pe 5:6; see Moo, 196), due in no small measure to the example of the Lord himself, who lived a life of perfect submission to the Father in the face of suffering and was exalted as a result (Heb 2:9; Php 2:5–11). This forms a cornerstone of the Lord's upside-down value system, which governs the kingdom. The way "up" is "down"; the path of freedom is submission; the road to joy is walked in mourning and with tears. Yet the end result is grace. The Lord lifts those who, recognizing their sin, repent, bowing before him in submission.

H. Do the Law, Do Not Judge It (4:11–12)

OVERVIEW

Luke Timothy Johnson, 291–92, notes the considerable difficulty of defining the role played by James 4:11–12 in the development of the book. Is the unit primarily to be understood to stand alone, the opening of a series of units running from 4:11 to 5:6, as Johnson and others suggest, or as the conclusion of what has gone before? The whole of 3:1–4:12 deals with forms of intercommunity conflict and reflects on this conflict in the light of key biblical principles, especially the concern over controlling what one says and the effect of the tongue's misuse in spreading relational discord (3:1–12, 14; 4:1–3, 11–12). James 4:11–12, therefore, continues the theme of the tongue's misuse begun in 3:1–12. At the same time, the emphasis on "judging" points in two directions. First, it anticipates the theme "A Statement of Judgment on the Wicked Rich" in 5:1–6, and the rich are judged in part because of their unjust judgment of the righteous (5:6). So

4:11–12 may be understood as transitional, pointing back to the previous three units and ahead to God's judgment on the wicked. Second, as explained in the introduction, 4:11–12, with its emphases on "judging the law" and being a "doer of the law," echoes the very important transition at 2:12–13 and, along with that passage, brackets the heart of the letter's main body. In effect, 2:12–13 challenges the reader to "speak and act" as one who will be judged by the law of liberty, and 4:11–12 exhorts not to judge the law by speaking against a brother but rather to do the law, to act on it. It may be suggested that the reason 4:11–12 has caused such difficulties as to its role at this point in the book is that it is transitional, and it plays a significant role in structuring the broader discourse. In other words, its concerns include but are broader than the topics of the units by which it is sandwiched.

11Brothers, do not slander one another. Anyone who speaks against his brother or judges him speaks against the law and judges it. When you judge the law, you are not keeping it, but sitting in judgment on it. 12There is only one Lawgiver and Judge, the one who is able to save and destroy. But you—who are you to judge your neighbor?

COMMENTARY

11–12 James begins this small concluding unit with yet another admonition to the "brothers"— "Do not slander one another"—and then immediately describes a slanderer as one who "speaks against his brother or judges him." The word *katalaleō* (GK *2895*) means "to speak in a harmful manner" about someone or "to defame." In biblical literature, one who is in a close relationship with God "does not slander with his tongue" (Ps 15:3 NASB), and the slanderer is called "a fool" (Pr 10:18). Slander is an evil tool of the wicked person, a tool used to destroy the person who is in dire straits (Isa 32:7). Finally, it is the action of evil people who speak against those who are walking in the ways of God (1Pe 2:12; 3:16). In the communities to which James writes, there are those who are destroying the lives of others through slander.

Yet James states that anyone who slanders a fellow believer actually slanders the law and sits in judgment on it. What might this mean? We have already seen that Leviticus 19 plays a significant role in the development of James's thought, and Leviticus 19:16 reads, "Do not go about spreading slander among your people." Therefore, if we slander a person, treating such a clear statement of God's will as though it is meaningless, we have actually passed judgment on the law itself and have spoken against it. In short, the utter disregard of the law slanders the law as beneath consideration. James states that when we set ourselves up as critics of the law in this way, we obviously are not engaged in "keeping it," in living it out. We have moved from a place of submissive obedience to God's law to trampling that law under our feet.

The utter presumptuousness of such a posture is striking. God is the one who has given the law and therefore is the only one who can sit in judgment. He alone is "able to save and destroy." God alone can bring salvation or eschatological judgment (5:1–6). By contrast, in judging a neighbor, a person takes on a role for which no human being is suited or appointed.

NOTES

11–12 LXX Leviticus 19:16 uses the phrase οὐ πορεύσῃ δόλῳ (*ou poreusē dolō*, "do not go about in a cunning manner"), and the Hebrew text uses the term *rakîl* ("slander").

I. Twin Calls to the Arrogant Rich (4:13–5:6)

1. A Rebuke of Arrogant Presumption (4:13–17)

OVERVIEW

Early in James, the author confronts the rich with their need for spiritual humility. The basis for his exhortation has to do with the transitory nature of life (1:10–11). He now addresses the sin of presumptuousness that causes the businessperson to "boast and brag" about where they are about to go, how long they will stay there, and the financial profit they are going to make in their business deals. Again James appeals to the uncertainty of life, which is a mere mist that dissipates suddenly. The proper posture is to say, "If it is the Lord's will, we will live and do this or that," for to brag about the future as though our plans for it are certain puts us in the place of God and, therefore, is evil. As suggested in the introduction, James 4:13–17 has a similar structure to 5:1–6, which also carries an address to the rich, and the two units form twin mini-discourses on the peril of riches.

> [13]Now listen, you who say, "Today or tomorrow we will go to this or that city, spend a year there, carry on business and make money." [14]Why, you do not even know what will happen tomorrow. What is your life? You are a mist that appears for a little while and then vanishes. [15]Instead, you ought to say, "If it is the Lord's will, we will live and do this or that." [16]As it is, you boast and brag. All such boasting is evil. [17]Anyone, then, who knows the good he ought to do and doesn't do it, sins.

COMMENTARY

13 The opening challenge, rendered "Now listen" (*age nyn*), is found in the NT only here and at 5:1 but is common in broader Greek literature (Davids, 171). It was used simply as a way to get someone's attention. James addresses these businesspeople very generally as "you who say" (*hoi legontes*), so he may be pointing to a common attitude among a subgroup in the communities but more likely to a general attitude of a group outside the church. Laws, 189–90, suggests they are major movers and shakers of the business world of the day rather than small-scale merchants who could afford to move their operations from one major city to another in order to establish trade between centers of commerce and take advantage of market trends. The plans of these rich businesspeople involve timing ("today or tomorrow"), destination ("we will go to this or that city"), duration of stay ("spend a year there"), and activities ("carry on business and make money").

14 The key concern for James is the presumptuousness inherent in the boast. They brag about the future, over which they have no control, and in effect place themselves in the seat of God. James expresses

the presumption with, "Why, you do not even know what will happen tomorrow." Only God knows what each day will hold. He further challenges this presumption with a common biblical word picture for the brevity and uncertainty of life: "What is your life? You are a mist that appears for a little while and then vanishes." The businessperson who feels at the top of the world, who sees himself as a mover whose significance is measured by the scale of his enterprises, has lost perspective on the limited nature of human existence. Rather than a being of grand significance, the braggart is but a mist, a vapor that hangs for a moment in the air before vanishing.

15 The corrective for this attitude of presumption is found in v.15: "Instead, you ought to say, 'If it is the Lord's will, we will live and do this or that." In the Scriptures, "the Lord's will" is either revealed or hidden. The revealed will of God primarily has to do with mandates for righteous living or events that have already taken place. The future, as in our passage under consideration, is a part of the hidden will of God. The condition "if it is the Lord's will" implies that a veil lies over the future and that the Lord himself will determine one's actions and the outcomes of those actions. Further, God himself will determine whether an individual will even be alive. Notice that the thought "we will live" (*zaō*) is assumed in the travel plans of v.13, but James points out that living another day is not guaranteed but is subject to the Lord's will. The appropriate response to the veiled nature of the future is humble submission—an attitude implicit in the conditional clause "if it is the Lord's will."

16–17 Their current posture, however, is reflected in the presumptuous pomposity of these businesspeople. They "boast and brag," which might better be translated "boast in your arrogance" (NASB) or "boast in your pretensions," the word meaning "pretensions" (*alazoneia*, GK *224*) being plural. James states tacitly that "all such boasting is evil," which he has already made clear in 3:14. In the broader Greco-Roman culture, the "braggart" who spews forth a vapid arrogance was the subject of much moral discourse, and this denigrated character is also treated in Jewish Wisdom literature as an object of scorn (e.g., Pr 21:24; cf. Johnson, 297).

James concludes with, "Anyone, then, who knows the good he ought to do and doesn't do it, sins," and many commentators have noted the awkwardness of this addition to the end of the unit addressing the rich merchants. Moo is right to reject Laws's suggestion that here we have an echo of Proverbs 3:27, which admonishes not to withhold good to a neighbor when it is in your power to perform it (Laws, 194; Moo, 207–8). Moo opts rather to read v.17 in the light of v.15, i.e., the exhortation to take God into consideration in everything one does. Thus the sin of omission here refers to not reckoning God into one's plans. Yet it is also possible James alludes back to his emphases in 1:22–25 and 2:14–26 on being a doer of the word. The unit immediately preceding the one under consideration, 4:11–12, has already drawn the hearer's attention back to that earlier context in the book. If we are correct that the twin calls to the rich in 4:13–17 and 5:1–6 structurally mirror 2:1–11, then perhaps James is placing the rich merchant's arrogant posture over against the practice of the "royal law" toward one's neighbor (cf. 2:7–9).

2. A Statement of Judgment on the Wicked Rich (5:1–6)

OVERVIEW

In terms of both form and content, James 5:1–6 has much in common with 4:13–17 (Moo, 9–10). Both passages deal with a blinding materialism that leads the rich and powerful to disregard the will of God, and both begin with a challenge, "Now listen" (*age nyn*), common in broader Hellenistic literature, though rare in the NT (only here and at 4:13). Although some commentators insist these parallels demonstrate that the author addresses the same people in each passage (either both are read as addressing believers, or both as addressing nonbelievers), there are also dissimilarities between the

passages that must be considered. James 4:13–17 is in the style of a diatribe, and those addressed are believers of the merchant class exhorted to take an appropriate posture toward their business endeavors by saying, "If it is the Lord's will ..." James 5:1–6, on the other hand, is in the form of an OT prophetic pronouncement and concerns the dire consequences for the wicked rich who have abused their wealth (Martin, 172–73). This latter form is also echoed in the words of Jesus (Lk 6:24–26) and is yet another link between James and the teachings of his brother. Thus it is possible to read the two passages as related in form and subject but distinct in exact concerns, the former passage addressing Christian merchants who are in danger of placing too much trust in their material circumstances, and the latter wealthy landowners who have no part in the church (Davids, 174–75).

If we have read 2:1–13 correctly, James has already shown concern for justice in legal situations. In the passage at hand, the common first-century socioeconomic situation in which the wealthy normally came out on top in legal disputes is turned on its head. The rich instead find themselves standing before God as judge, and James calls them to account, placing before them extensive evidence of their guilt. In short, they stand condemned by the very riches in which they place their confidence.

The structure of the passage can be understood as a call to account (v.1) followed by a series of assertions mingled with overt statements of impending judgment (vv.2–6). The transient nature of their material possessions (vv.2–3), the pay that they have robbed from the laborers in their employ (v.4), their

indulgence (v.5), and their unjust condemnation, indeed their murder, of the righteous (v.6), all bear witness against them, sealing their doom. Certainly Leviticus 19:13, part of that broader passage of OT law that seems to be driving James at a number of points, lies behind this harshest of proclamations in the book. That verse reads, "You shall not oppress your neighbor, nor rob him. The wages of a hired man are not to remain with you all night until morning" (NASB), and James seems to be reading it in conjunction with Deuteronomy 24:14–15 (NASB):

> You shall not oppress a hired servant who is poor and needy, whether he is one of your countrymen or one of your aliens who is in your land in your towns. You shall give him his wages on his day before the sun sets, for he is poor and sets his heart on it; so that he will not cry against you to the LORD and it become sin in you.

Therefore, we read the passage as a pronouncement of judgment on the wicked rich, which in turn serves as a word of encouragement to the righteous poor who are enduring mistreatment in the world.

---

¹Now listen, you rich people, weep and wail because of the misery that is coming upon you. ²Your wealth has rotted, and moths have eaten your clothes. ³Your gold and silver are corroded. Their corrosion will testify against you and eat your flesh like fire. You have hoarded wealth in the last days. ⁴Look! The wages you failed to pay the workmen who mowed your fields are crying out against you. The cries of the harvesters have reached the ears of the Lord Almighty. ⁵You have lived on earth in luxury and self-indulgence. You have fattened yourselves in the day of slaughter. ⁶You have condemned and murdered innocent men, who were not opposing you.

COMMENTARY

1 As in 4:13, James begins by calling the rich to account. He uses a construction only found in the NT at these two places in James, translated by the NIV as "now listen," and by the NASB as "come

now." The "rich people" about whom he is concerned are wealthy landowners who in their grab for wealth are using the poor egregiously. The social and economic distance between these two classes in the first century contributed to widespread abuse of the latter by the former.

The balance of the verse presents an exhortation, followed by the manner in which that exhortation is to be carried out and, finally, the basis for the exhortation. The exhortation is for the rich to "weep," a response in biblical literature to deep grief and remorse over some tragedy (e.g., Isa 15:2–3; Jer 9:1; 13:17; La 1:1–2; see Nystrom, 269). The manner in which they are to weep is by "wailing" or "howling" (*ololuzō*, GK *3909*), an onomatopoeic term in the form of a participle. Here is no quiet, solemn crying from a repentant heart but rather the howl of anguish over lost opportunities and misplaced priorities. Further, James gives the reason for such anguish: "because of the misery that is coming upon you." The term translated "miseries" by the NASB is, again, a rare word in the NT found only here and at Romans 3:16; yet it is very common in the Greek OT and connotes calamity, ravaging, pillaging, and other forms of devastation (Isa 59:7; Am 3:10; Joel 1:15; Hab 2:17; cf. *TLNT* 3:366). Though the NIV translates the word as singular, it is in fact plural and, therefore, perhaps speaks of multifarious forms of trouble awaiting those under judgment. The rich, who have placed so much hope in their riches and have pillaged others, are about to face their own forms of devastation.

2–3 The first witness against the rich concerns their disintegrated possessions, which via three graphic descriptions are presented as both temporal and useless. The perfect tense is used in all three and, rather than a prophetic anticipation of future judgment, speaks of the vapid nature of material possessions before God (so Laws, 198). It is not that their riches will become useless in the future. Rather, from a spiritual perspective these riches hold no value now and thus condemn the rich who trust in them. First, their "wealth has rotted." The word "wealth" (*ploutos*, GK *4458*) is general and may serve as an

inclusive heading for the "clothes" and "gold and silver" that follow. This wealth "has rotted" (*sēpō*, GK *4960*), or spoiled, fallen prey to a corrupting decay. Second, their clothes, which constitute one of the marks of a wealthy person (see 2:2), have become eaten by moths (*sētobrōtos*, GK *4963*), a term found only here in the NT. Though the language here is rare, the image is widely used in the Scriptures (e.g., Pr 25:20; Isa 33:1; 50:9; 51:8; Mt 6:20; see Davids, 176). Third, the condition of their gold and silver is described as "rusted" (NASB) or "corroded" (NIV; *katioō*, GK *2995*), also only found here in the NT. Of course, gold and silver do not rust, but what may be described as scientifically impossible is proverbially powerful, speaking to the absolute uselessness of gold and silver horded by the rich. Such treasures on earth should be used, instead, to help the poor and to build spiritual treasures. In this regard James echoes Jesus, who in Matthew 6:20 exhorts his followers, "But store up for yourselves treasures in heaven, where moth and rust do not destroy. . . ."

The rich, moreover, are condemned by the corrosion of their most prized possessions (so Laws, 199; Johnson, 300; Adamson, 184–85). The imagery is striking since the wealthy were notorious for being able to buy off the courts of their day. Yet here they stand condemned in God's court, and their own tarnished possessions personified have taken the stand against them. Further, the rust on these precious metals will "eat [their] flesh like fire." The term for "corrosion" (*ios*, GK *2675*) has already been used of "poison" in 3:8, and James may be crafting a play on his images. Nevertheless, the image clearly speaks of destruction, extended from the possessions to the person. The tragedy of horded wealth is not in the loss of the wealth alone but in the ultimate destruction of the person who has served it. Thus the corrosion eats them up like the fire of God's judgment.

Ironically, the rich have "hoarded wealth" only to have that wealth turn on them in the "last days," the time of God's judgment (Isa 2:2; Jer 23:20; Da 2:28; Hos 3:5; Jn 6:39–44; Ac 2:17; Heb 1:2; 1Pe 1:5, 20; Jude 18). Instead of storing up riches for earthly comfort and pleasure in their latter years, they have stored up the wrath of God's consuming fury (Mt 25:41; 2Pe 3:7; Rev 20:9; see Johnson, 301).

4 Whereas decaying possessions serve as the first witness to take the stand against the rich (vv.2–3), the author now calls due wages stolen and the resulting cries of the harvesters in witness to the flagrant injustice perpetrated by these wealthy landowners. As elsewhere in the book, he uses the word translated "look" (*idou*, GK *2627*) to rivet the readers' attention (3:4–5; 5:7, 9, 11), and their attention is drawn to a blatant form of unfairness—pay that is due a laborer for an honest day's work. The farmworkers have harvested grain for their employers with the expectation of being paid for their labor. In contrast to the rich landowners, who hoarded great surpluses of wealth, many common laborers lived day-to-day and depended on their meager wages for the basic necessities of life. To be deprived of what one had rightly earned could constitute a threat to life itself (Moo, 216; Laws, 201–2).

Thus two cries are raised against these crooked landowners, the first by the wages themselves. James defines the wages with a perfect passive participle meaning "having been stolen" (*apostereō*, GK *691*). Biblical literature bears witness eloquently concerning the consequences for those who take advantage of common laborers in this way (e.g., Lev 19:13; Job 7:1–2; Jer 22:13; Mal 3:5; Mt 20:8). As mentioned above, James seems to have in mind both Leviticus 19:13 and Deuteronomy 24:14–15. The latter passage points to special responsibility toward the poor: "Pay him his wages each day before sunset, because he is poor and is counting on it."

Moreover, these wages "are crying out" in demand of justice. The prepositional phrase *aph' hymōn* can be read in two ways. If understood as associated with the adjectival participle immediately before it, James is stressing the idea of agency: "the wages stolen *by you*." This use of *apo* is rare, though James does employ it at 1:13 in asserting that temptation does not originate with God. However, the phrase also could be read as belonging to the verb that follows, with *apo* having the more characteristic sense of source. In this case, James confronts the rich with the cries emanating from the money they have stolen, proclaiming that these stolen wages cry out *from* their very moneybags.

Second, condemning cries go up from the workers themselves, rising up to "the Lord Almighty." In the Bible, the Lord's concern for his people is, at times, expressed as his hearing their cries, such as the cry of Abel's blood from the ground and the cries of the Israelites in bondage, or simply the cry of the righteous person for help (e.g., Ge 4:10; Ex 2:23; Ps 17:7). With his reference to "the ears of the Lord Almighty," James seems to be alluding to the Greek translation of Isaiah 5:9, a verse offered as part of a scathing judgment against the wealthy of the land. The term *sabaōth* (GK *4877*) is a favorite of Isaiah, used in the book some sixty times, and refers to God's awesome power (Johnson, 302–3; Davids, 177–78). That power descends in judgment on all oppressors of God's people.

5 Their luxurious lifestyle of indulgence constitutes a third witness against the rich landowners. The first descriptor, "you have lived ... in luxury" (*tryphaō*, GK *5587*), suggests a life lived in the hot pursuit of pleasure. This self-indulgent lifestyle has been lived out "on earth" (NIV, NASB, ESV, NLT) or, perhaps more appropriately to the context, "on the land" (Martin, 179), and it is lived with blatant disregard to the poverty of others. The second term, translated by the NASB with "led a life of wanton pleasure" (*spatalaō*, GK *5059*; see 1Ti 5:6), James uses similarly to describe a life lived extravagantly, outside the bounds of decency. As sheep fed very, very well for the fateful meeting with the butcher, the rich, in living out the demands of their lusts, simply have been fattening their hearts "in a day of slaughter" (NASB), the day of God's judgment (Ps 22:29; Isa 30:33; Jer 46:10; Eze 39:17; Rev 19:17–21; see Davids, 178–79).

6 The last in this graphic series of witnesses against the rich is their condemning to death innocent righteous people. This theme of the wealthy using their power unjustly to destroy the lives of the poor finds wide expression in both biblical and broader Jewish literature (e.g., Ps 37:14, 32; Pr 1:10–19; Am 8:4). A legal setting may be in view in which the rich buy the courts to have the poor taken out

of the way, or perhaps the result of starvation resulting from unpaid wages is in mind. However, the statements of condemnation and murder serve to show the extremes to which wickedness will go. Justice is turned on its head. The innocent are condemned. The honest worker, who should have the basics by which to live, is murdered.

The final statement could be read as a rhetorical question proclaiming God's opposition to the wicked rich: "Does he not oppose you?" However, given the context, the NIV and NASB appropriately reflect this part of the verse as a simple statement speaking to the helplessness of the poor righteous person (Laws, 207).

NOTES

2–3 Some manuscripts (e.g., $\aleph^2$, A, P) add the phrase ὁ ἰός, *ho ios*, evidently to make clear the connection back to the previous clause. As commentators have pointed out, the question of punctuation in relation to the phrase ὡς πῦρ, *hōs pur*, constitutes the more critical issue. Does the phrase modify the effect of the corrosion, or does it belong with the ἐθησαυρίσατε, *ethēsaurisate*, that follows? My judgment is that the better case has been made for the former (Johnson, 300; Laws, 200; Dibelius, 237; contra Ropes, 287).

4 A variant supported by $\aleph$ and B* reads ἀφυστερημένος, *aphysterēmenos*, "withhold," and this reading is followed by the NASB. However, given the strong admonitions against defrauding the poor in biblical literature, the variant ἀπεστερημένος, *apesterēmenos*, followed by most, is to be preferred.

IV. CONCLUSION: ENDURING IN RIGHTEOUS LIVING IN COMMUNITY (5:7–20)

A. The Need for Patient Endurance (5:7–11)

OVERVIEW

Having offered one form of encouragement to beleaguered believers of the dispersion—the wrath of God and looming doom hang over the wicked rich, who are condemned by numerous witnesses (5:1–6)—James now offers another form, challenging them to "be patient" (5:7, 8). It may be suggested that 5:7–11 forms a hinge for, or unique transition from, the material that has preceded it (4:11–5:6) and the section to follow (5:12–20; see Johnson, 311–12). It continues the theme of judgment and the admonition not to speak against brothers in Christ in the previous section, but it also takes up the positive, community-oriented exhortations that follow in vv.12–20.

Furthermore, the author crafts 5:7–11 with the following structure:

exhortation:	"Be patient" (7a)
duration:	"until the Lord's coming"
illustration:	the farmer waits for the seasonal rains (7b)
reiteration and expansion of the exhortation:	"Be patient" "Stand firm"; "Strengthen your hearts," NASB (8a)
basis:	"the Lord's coming is near"(8b)
exhortation:	"Don't grumble against each other" (9a)
basis:	"or you will be judged"
	"The Judge is standing at the door!" (9b)
illustrations:	the example of the prophets (10) the example of Job (11)

The initial exhortation to be patient and the reiteration and expansion of that exhortation (vv.7a, 8a) are one and the same, cut from the same cloth, as the parallel references to the Lord's coming (vv.7a, 8b) demonstrate. Sandwiched between these exhortations is the agricultural illustration of the autumn and spring rains. The third exhortation, which speaks against grumbling, continues to give insight into James's concern for the interpersonal relationships in the Christian communities addressed, highlighting, perhaps, one effect that external pressure was having on those relationships. When emotions are strained, we tend to stray from the love command. Finally, James offers two illustrations of patient endurance: the collective example of the prophets, who spoke patiently as representatives of the Lord in the face of suffering, and Job, perhaps the exemplar par excellence of patient endurance.

> [7]Be patient, then, brothers, until the Lord's coming. See how the farmer waits for the land to yield its valuable crop and how patient he is for the autumn and spring rains. [8]You too, be patient and stand firm, because the Lord's coming is near. [9]Don't grumble against each other, brothers, or you will be judged. The Judge is standing at the door!
>
> [10]Brothers, as an example of patience in the face of suffering, take the prophets who spoke in the name of the Lord. [11]As you know, we consider blessed those who have persevered. You have heard of Job's perseverance and have seen what the Lord finally brought about. The Lord is full of compassion and mercy.

COMMENTARY

7–8 The passage at hand is connected to the previous unit on the guilt of the wicked wealthy (5:1–6) by the word "therefore" (NASB; *oun*), indicating that judgment on the rich serves as a basis for encouragement to the righteous. On this basis they are to "be patient" (*makrothymeō*, GK *3428*), a term connoting enduring under provocation or waiting with a right attitude (1Co 13:4; 1Th 5:14; Heb 6:15; 2Pe 3:9). It is almost synonymous with *hypomonē* (GK *5705*), used in both its verbal and nominal forms in v.11. It may be that life's hardships in general are in mind (Ropes, 293), but James specifically ties the exhortation back to 5:1–6 and thus seems to have patience under injustice or oppression in view. That patience involves waiting is further highlighted by the *duration*: they are to be patient "until the Lord's coming." Behind the "coming" (*parousia*, GK *4242*) motif lies both the day of the Lord in broader Jewish thought (although the term itself is not used of the Messiah in the Greek OT), as well as the Christian hope of Christ's return (Mt 24:3, 37, 39; 1Co 15:23; 1Th 3:13; 4:15; 5:23; 2Pe 1:16; 3:4). That day will be a day of judgment on the enemies of God, as well as a day of vindication for God's true people. The difficulty for the believer under trial is that the day has yet to arrive and thus constitutes a future hope that must be anticipated and waited for.

To encourage his readers to patience, James uses an agricultural illustration. A farmer does not receive his valuable crop shortly after planting. Rather, the maturation of the crop is seasonal, receiving both the "early" rains (NASB), which could refer to rains either in late October and early November or in November and December, and the "late" rains (NASB) in March and April (Neusner and Green, 519). This identification of these two seasons of rain locates James and his audience along the eastern coast of the Mediterranean Sea. The reference to the two rains also parallels the LXX (Jer 5:24; Hos 6:3; Joel 2:23; Zec 10:1), including a reference in the Shema, the daily confession (Dt 11:14), which of course would have been very familiar in Jewish circles (Dibelius, 243–44). The early rains got the crop started, allowing the seed to sprout and experience initial growth. The late rains enabled the filling out of the grain. James's point is that the full cycle of a mature and productive crop is something for which the farmer had to wait with patient endurance. In the same way, the believer must wait for the Lord's coming with patient endurance.

Therefore, in v.8 James reiterates the exhortation with which he started the unit, saying, "You too, be patient," and then goes on to add, "Strengthen your hearts" (NASB). The heart was understood as the seat of all aspects of the inner life—the will, emotions, reason, and moral understanding. To strengthen the heart, then, is to encourage oneself, setting one's resolve to "stand firm" (NIV) in the faith (Ps 111:8; 1Th 3:13) in the light of the Lord's coming, which James describes as "near." Here he points to the belief in the imminence of Christ's return as an aspect of Christian posture in the world. Believers are to live in expectation of that day.

9 Further, James's readers are exhorted as "brothers" with, "Don't grumble against each other." He uses the address "brothers" (*adelphos*, GK *81*) throughout the book to address fellow Christians (2:1, 5, 14; 3:1, 10, 12; 4:11; 5:12, 19) and in the present passage in three places (5:7, 9, 10). The term translated "grumble" (*stenazō*, GK *5100*) could mean to complain but also could connote to sigh or groan. The word is used at Hebrews 13:17 of the antithesis of joy, suggesting that embattled leaders, who are not blessed with ready followers, are provoked to groaning. In light of the phrase "against each other" (*kat' allēlōn*), here the idea of complaining or grumbling seems clearly in view and picks up on the theme of infighting in the Christian community covered earlier (3:16; 4:1–4, 11–12). Those who grumble against others in the church face God's judgment, a possible allusion to the words of Jesus against harsh speaking against a brother (Mt 7:1; see Davids, 185). "The Judge is standing at the door" serves as a graphic image of immanence with God depicted as just on the other side of the door of the courtroom, hand on the door, poised to enter and pronounce judgment.

10–11 James now offers two illustrations or examples of patient endurance under adverse circumstances. In the rhetoric of the Greco-Roman world, including the Jewish subcultures, exemplars were often used both positively and negatively, either to encourage people to right action or discourage them from wrong action. Here James wishes to exhort his listeners to follow biblical examples who form part of their spiritual heritage. First, the prophets carried out their ministries, speaking "in the name of the Lord," often in very difficult circumstances. They demonstrate "patience in the face of suffering." For example, the prophets Isaiah, Jeremiah, Ezekiel, and Daniel are worthy of mention in this regard (Heb 11:32–38). How should believers think of such prophets? James proclaims, "We consider blessed those who have persevered" (v.11). To be "blessed" was a common Jewish description connoting wholeness of life and again echoes Jesus' teaching on the upside-down reality

in God's kingdom—those who suffer now should be counted as blessed (Mt 5:11–12). The path to blessing, therefore, is patient endurance. Consequently, those in James's Christian communities should look to such prophets so they might find encouragement for their own difficult situations, persevere, and be blessed.

Finally, James points to the preeminent example of patient endurance, Job. Of course, as those very familiar with the Jewish Scriptures and Jewish traditions, they "have heard of Job's perseverance." Job demonstrated tremendous patience, refusing to curse God in the face of overwhelming loss and suffering, both physical and emotional (1:20–22; 2:9–10; 13:15; 19:25–27). What one sees from the Job account, moreover, is "what the Lord finally brought about. The Lord is full of compassion and mercy." The phrase translated "what the Lord finally brought about" (lit., "the end of the Lord") refers to the good conclusion of Job's story (Dibelius, 246). That story climaxes with Job's recognition of his own limitations in the light of God's awesomeness (40:1–2; 42:1–6). Then God restores Job's fortune and family (42:10–17). In short, Job is faithful to the end, despite an intense struggle in the face of personal devastation, and God expresses his "compassion and mercy." The point for James's readers is that God's blessings await those who endure. Just as the Lord dealt with Job in a way that had a happy result, so he will deal with his people who endure suffering patiently as they await the coming of the Lord.

NOTES

7 The text based on 𝔓⁷⁴ and B has only the terms πρόϊμον καὶ ὄψιμον, *proimon kai opsimon*; NIV, "autumn and spring rains." The word ὑετόν, *hyeton*, "rain," is added in A, P, Ψ and many other manuscripts, and in its place καρπόν, *karpon*, "fruit," in still others. Dibelius, 243, is probably right that the text with the two adjectives apart from a stated noun is to be preferred. The adjectives, however, are certainly to be understood as technical terms for the early and late rains.

B. The Need for Righteous Words in Community (5:12–20)

OVERVIEW

James 5:12–20 serves as the final movement of the book, offering a challenge to reverse negative patterns of action (especially wrong speech) in the communities by choosing the way of righteous wisdom. In rapid-fire succession James challenges his readers not to swear but rather to practice plain speaking (v.12); to pray (v.13a) or sing (v.13b), depending on the circumstance; to call for the church elders if sick so they can pray and anoint with oil (v.14–15); and to confess sins to one another and pray for one another (v.16–18). These exhortations have attached to them at points the means by which (e.g., v.12b, "not by heaven …") or manner in which (e.g., v.14c, "anoint him with oil") the exhortation is to be followed. Further, James gives the reason for following the exhortation (e.g., v.12d NASB, "so that you may not fall under judgment") or the results of following it (e.g., v.15), or he provides an illustration, as in the case of Elijah (vv.17–18). Finally, once again prompted by Leviticus 19, James concludes with the importance of righteous rebuke of persons in one's community who have strayed into sin (vv.19–20).

[12]Above all, my brothers, do not swear—not by heaven or by earth or by anything else. Let your "Yes" be yes, and your "No," no, or you will be condemned.
[13]Is any one of you in trouble? He should pray. Is anyone happy? Let him sing songs of praise. [14]Is any one of you sick? He should call the elders of the church to pray over him and anoint him with oil in the name of the Lord. [15]And the prayer offered in faith will make the sick person well; the Lord will raise him up. If he has sinned, he will be forgiven.
[16]Therefore confess your sins to each other and pray for each other so that you may be healed. The prayer of a righteous man is powerful and effective.
[17]Elijah was a man just like us. He prayed earnestly that it would not rain, and it did not rain on the land for three and a half years. [18]Again he prayed, and the heavens gave rain, and the earth produced its crops. [19]My brothers, if one of you should wander from the truth and someone should bring him back, [20]remember this: Whoever turns a sinner from the error of his way will save him from death and cover over a multitude of sins.

COMMENTARY

12 This verse begins with the phrase "above all," marking the beginning of the letter's closing remarks (Davids, 189; Laws, 220; Martin, 203), as the author transitions to a focus on important ways believers are to use their words wisely in community. James again uses the address "brothers," repeated here for the fourth time since the beginning of v.7, and continues giving attention to the obligations of living in Christian community (5:7, 9–10).

The exhortation "do not swear" once again echoes a basic teaching of Jesus from the Sermon on the Mount (5:33–37). James 5:12 serves to remind believers that integrity lies close to the heart of kingdom life and ethics. James is not speaking against vulgar language but rather against using oaths to shore up one's word to make it more believable. Oaths in and of themselves were not prohibited in the OT, and even God used oaths as a form of guarantee (see esp. Heb 6:13–18; 7:21). Leviticus 19:12, however, located in a passage from which James draws throughout the book, forbids swearing falsely by God's name, for that is profaning the name. Jesus goes even farther in Matthew 5:34–37, which certainly lies behind James's words at this point (contra Laws, 223), the two passages paralleling each other in great detail. There Jesus commands, "Do not swear at all" (Moo, 232–33).

The verb, in the present imperative and preceded by *mē*, can be translated as a command to end a certain course of action ("stop swearing"), and this view finds some support in the failure to control the tongue in the communities addressed by James (3:1–12; 4:1–4). However, the same construction is used to communicate a general precept or guideline for life, regardless of whether or not the action has started, and this is the approach taken by both the NIV and NASB: "do not swear." The means by which the exhortation is to be lived out is stated both negatively and positively. Negatively, believers should not swear—"not by heaven or by earth or by anything else." James means the triple prohibition to be all-inclusive, covering the gamut of possible orientations used to strengthen an oath.

Positively, Christ-followers are to speak plainly, saying "yes" when they mean "yes" and "no" when they mean "no." If a person's word is true, and she is known as a person of integrity who reflects the values of God's kingdom, such basic words as "yes" and "no" do not need strengthening with an oath, for they are infused with the power of an honest character. John Chrysostom wrote, "Now the person who has heard the blessings of God and who has prepared himself as Christ has commanded will never claim any need to do anything of the kind, for he is respected and honored by all. What is needed beyond a simple yes and no? An oath adds nothing to these" (cited in Bray, 59). The reason one should not swear concerns the danger of falling "under judgment" (NASB), which is James's restatement of Jesus' teaching that "anything beyond this comes from the evil one" (Mt 5:37).

13 With this verse James shifts the focus to prayer, a focus he will maintain through v.18 and one with which many of the NT books move to their conclusions (e.g., Ro 15:30–32; Eph 6:18–20; Php 4:6; Col 4:2–4; 1Th 5:16–18, 25; Phm 22; Heb 13:18–19; Jude 20). In this verse he addresses two common conditions of life. The first, expressed with the verb *kakopatheō* (the nominal form of which is used of the prophets in 5:10; GK *2802*), can mean to experience the distress of various difficulties (2Ti 2:9) or, on the other hand, to endure in the face of such suffering (2Ti 4:5; cf. *TLNT* 2:238–40). Given that the word is set over against *euthymeō* (GK *2313*), which means to be cheerful, the former meaning perhaps gets the nod. James has been concerned with appropriate Christian responses to trials from the very beginning (1:2–4), and here he emphasizes that difficulties are to be addressed with prayer. Perhaps, given the broader context, in which James has focused on oppression of the poor at the hands of the rich (5:1–6), he counters our natural human tendency to respond with hatred and even violence. Rather, we should respond with the godly posture of prayer, trusting God for justice and vindication (Davids, 192).

The other life experience, then, is to be "cheerful" (NASB) or joyful. The term could also mean to be encouraged (Ac 27:22, 25, 36). Here is a picture of one who presently feels positive about life (Johnson, 329). Such joy should prompt the believer to "sing songs of praise" (see Ro 15:9; Eph 5:19). Consequently, whether one's life feels laden with trouble or buoyed with joy, the right response is to turn to God, praying in the face of the former and praising in face of the latter.

14 James mentions another common life experience, that of sickness. Although it is true that the term *astheneō* (GK *820*) can refer to weakness, need, or personal limitations in general, the context, which details the role of the elders, the use of oil, and the results of the prayer offered in faith, clearly indicates that illness is in mind. "Elders" (*presbyteros*, GK *4565*) is one of four designations for the primary local church leadership role in the NT, the other three being "overseers," "pastors," and "leaders." When used of this role, the last of these terms is only found in the NT at Hebrews 13:7, 17 (although it is used adjectivally at Ac 15:22), and "pastors," referring to the position, only occurs as a noun at Ephesians 4:11. The words for "elders" and "overseers," given their use in Acts 20:17, 28 and Titus 1:5–7, are synonymous, and these leaders are instructed by Paul to "be shepherds of," or "pastor" (*poimainō*, GK *4477*) God's people (Ac 20:28). Consequently, the elders were the overseers or pastors of the church.

That the elders are to be called for indicates that the illness in mind is of a more serious nature, since evidently the person could not go to them (Davids, 192). They are to pray over the person, and the manner in which they are to do so is "anoint him with oil in the name of the Lord." Oil had a variety of practical purposes in the ancient world, including lighting, cooking, skin conditioning, application in sporting events, and medicinal uses (e.g., Isa 1:6; Jer 8:22; Mk 6:13; Lk 10:34). It was also used in religious and ceremonial practices, such as the anointing of the Hebrew kings, priests, and prophets in the OT (e.g., 1Sa 10:1; 1Ki 19:15–16; Heb 1:8–9). The act of praying over a person combined with anointing with oil was common, though the action could be understood in a variety of ways: as purely medicinal, as a means of pastoral encouragement, as sacramental, or as symbolic. Moo, 238–40, who has a clear discussion of various interpretations of the act, may offer the best argument by suggesting that James has in mind "a physical action symbolizing consecration."

The "name of the Lord" was used in healings and exorcisms in the early church (Mk 9:38; Lk 10:17; Ac 3:6), as well as in baptism (Ac 2:38; 8:16; 10:48; 19:5) and even merely gathering in Christian community (1Co 5:4); the Lord's name communicated the authority by which an action was carried out. Invoking Jesus' name in this way—for he certainly is the "Lord" James has in mind—was a means of calling on his power (Johnson, 331).

15 James now reflects on three results of the elders' prayer introduced in the previous verse. The term for prayer in v.15 (*euchē*, GK *2376*) is used in the NT only three times—here and twice in Acts (18:18; 21:23), where it refers to a solemn promise or vow. Yet here it carries its other meaning of a petition directed to God and is the nominal form of the verb for prayer (*euchomai*, GK *2377*) in v.16. The phrase "offered in faith" translates *tēs pisteōs* (GK *4411*), more literally "of faith," read as a descriptive genitive. Thus it is prayer offered as an expression of the elders' trust in God and his power to work supernaturally on the sick person's behalf.

The first result of this type of prayer is that it will "restore the one who is sick" (NASB) or "make the sick person well" (NIV). The verb *sōzō* (GK *5392*) has a broad range of theological meanings in the NT, including "to save from harm" or "rescue" from natural or physical phenomena on the one hand and from a transcendent or eternal destruction on the other. The latter use, found often in the NT to speak of the salvation of believers, occurs in the immediate context at 5:20, and some commentators have read spiritual salvation into the use at hand as well (see Martin, 209). However, it seems that salvation from a physical illness is in mind, the related terms *astheneō* (GK *820*, v.14; "is sick") and *kamnō* (GK *2827*; "the sick person") more naturally referring to physical illness (Moo, 184). Thus the prayer of faith is able to "make the sick person well" (Mt 9:21–22; Mk 5:23, 28; Lk 8:36; Ac 4:9; 14:9).

Second, "the Lord will raise him up," the physical manifestation of the person being healed, as with the paralytic of Mark 2:1–12 and other healings performed by Jesus (e.g., Mk 3:3; 5:41; 10:49; Lk 7:14; 8:54). The person gets up from the sickbed and rejoins the normal activities of the well.

Third, "If he has sinned, he will be forgiven." This, too, recalls Jesus' healing of the paralytic, for Jesus healed the man with the words, "Your sins are forgiven" (Mk 2:5). That physical illness could be related to a person's sins has a rich backdrop in Jewish thought: in the "blessings" and "curses" that stem from the people's response to God's commands in Deuteronomy (Dt 28:1–68; 30:1–19), in principles from the wisdom tradition (e.g., Pr 3:28–35; 13:13–23; 19:15–16), in the teachings of the rabbis, and in the NT at 1 Corinthians 11:29–30, where Paul suggests that eating and drinking the Lord's Supper inappropriately had led to sickness and even death among the Corinthians. In using a conditional clause, James implies that sickness does not necessarily stem from sin. Yet he also implies that an illness may be related profoundly to sin, which suggests a more holistic vision of human personhood in which sin affects numerous aspects of life, including the physical (Johnson, 333).

16 Clearly building on the thought of the previous verse, with its mention of sins, prayer, and healing, the author transitions to exhort those in the Christian communities to mutual confession of sins and prayer. The use of "Therefore" (*oun*) followed by two present imperative verbs facilitates the transition. The first exhortation is to "confess your sins to each other." Ropes, 309, understands the confession to be by the sick persons, who then are prayed for by the well, resulting in physical healing, but James seems to move from the specific situation of a seriously sick person in v.15 to the general principle concerning the need for mutual confession and prayer in v.16. On this interpretation, it is difficult to see the confession as preventative (as with Davids, 195), since the healing follows sickness in the verse, but the connection between sin in a community and physical illness seems clear nonetheless. Confession, a public acknowledgment of one's guilt, may be by an individual or as a community, and in many cases in biblical literature, confession is connected to physical healing or some general form of salvation (Davids, 195–96; Johnson, 334). Johnson especially has shown the connection between physical healing and social restoration. This dynamic is prominent in the ministry of Jesus (e.g., Lk 5:17; 6:18–19) and reiterated in Acts (4:22, 30; 28:27; see Johnson, 335). Thus James, dealing with communities in which there was a good bit of social strife, points to vital Christian remedies for fractured relationships—open confession of sin and mutual prayer, which are actions that promote transparency, support, and unity. Consequently, the exhortations to confession and prayer are followed by "so that" (*hopōs*), a marker showing the purpose for something, and that purpose in the present case is expressed as "you may be healed." The healing in mind is physical but points to a deeper spiritual healing of sin and broken relationships.

Whereas the first part of v.16 consists of exhortations, the second makes a theological assertion concerning the effectiveness of prayer. In this case, the NASB reflects more accurately than the NIV the structure of the Greek text: "The effective prayer of a righteous man can accomplish much." First, the prayer under discussion is that of a righteous person. In 1:5–8 and 4:3–4, James has already noted that a sinful lifestyle hinders prayer, and he now expresses the flip side of that fact. In 5:17–18, he follows by offering Elijah as a prime example of such a person. Second, the prayer is "effective" (*energeō*, GK *1919*), expressed with an adjectival participle meaning "to work," "to be active," or "to be operative." Thus the prayer in mind is prayer put into action, or made operative. Finally, this prayer is able to "accomplish much." James uses a verb (*ischyō*, GK *2710*) that connotes having the resources or power to bring something about, and what prayer is able to accomplish is "much."

17–18 James now turns to an illustration of the assertion given at the end of 5:16 concerning the prayer of a righteous person. James alludes to an event from the life of Elijah found in 1 Kings 17:1; 18:1–46. When Ahab came to power as king over Israel, he was horribly evil, marrying the Sidonian Jezebel, worshiping Baal, and erecting an Asherah pole (1Ki 16:29–33). Elijah made a pronouncement to Ahab, proclaiming there would be neither rain nor dew unless he gave the word permitting them (1Ki 17:1). The Lord's word came to Elijah in the third year, after the drought had become very severe, telling him he would send rain, and following a showdown with the prophets of Baal on Mount Carmel, God did send rain in response to Elijah's prayer (1Ki 18:41–46).

James calls Elijah "a man just like us," pointing to the fact that he was human rather than superhuman in nature. James's readers would need a reminder that the prayer power available to Elijah was available to God's people generally, since the prophet was revered greatly in Judaism of the day both for his grand miracles and his powerful prophetic voice against the corrupt powers of his time (Moo, 247).

The logic of the illustration is simple: Elijah prayed earnestly, and it did not rain; he prayed again, and it rained. His prayer is described as being prayed "earnestly," reflecting a Semitic construction (lit., "he prayed with prayer"). The conclusion to be drawn is that prayer works and should be a common aspect of Christian community.

19–20 James concludes the book with a reflection on the importance of lovingly rebuking one who has fallen into a pattern of sin. Once again he uses his common address "brothers," referring to all the believers, male and female, in the communities to which he writes. Verse 19 is crafted with a compound conditional clause, with the indefinite pronoun *tis*, translated "one" and "someone," as the subject of each aorist subjunctive verb. The first part of this generalized condition is "if one of you should wander from the truth ..." James has already used the verb "wanders" (*planaō*, GK *4414*) to exhort his readers not to be deceived (1:16), but here the verb is used figuratively of wandering from the path of truth (*alētheia*, GK *237*). God is a God of truth, and he has used "the word of truth" as his instrument to effect believers' spiritual birth (1:17–18). Thus the truth does connote right belief concerning the gospel, but for James, of course, the truth is something that is ultimately manifested in right living (3:14). In the NT, the figurative use of "wandering" as wandering from right thinking and, therefore, into deeper levels of wrong living occurs at numerous points (Mt 22:29; 2Ti 3:13; Tit 3:3; 2Pe 2:15). So James speaks of wandering from the truth as a wandering into sin (Moo, 249; Johnson, 337).

As the second part of the condition, James writes, "and someone should bring him back." The verb *epistrephō* (GK *2188*) means to "turn around" or "go back" and can be used figuratively to speak of turning from one spiritual path to another, either from God's way (e.g., Gal 4:9; 2Pe 2:21) or to God in repentance (e.g., Ac 9:35; 2Co 3:16; 1Th 1:9).

The call to turn people back to the ways of God was common to the prophet's role in the OT (e.g., Joel 2:12; Am 4:16; Zec 1:3) and characterized John the Baptist's ministry (Lk 1:16–17). Here the action of bringing a person back to God's path communicates an interpersonal responsibility as believers relate to one another in community. James does not describe specifically how this is to be done, but the loving confrontation of a person embracing a pattern of sin certainly is in mind (Mt 18:15; Gal 6:1).

The "let him know" (NASB) of v.20 refers to the one who has returned the erring fellow believer back to the way of the Lord. The statement of this verse constitutes a word of encouragement for those who take up their spiritual responsibility to turn "a sinner from the error of his way." To "know" in this case refers to being aware of the spiritual benefits inherent to the difficult action of holding another person accountable. Two are noted. First, whoever does this "will save him from death" (lit. "will save his soul from death," NASB). Biblically, sin leads to death—physical death, yes, but ultimately eternal death as a result of God's judgment (Dt 30:19; Ps 1:6; 2:12; Pr 2:18; Jer 23:12; Jude 23; see Moo, 250),

as James has already proclaimed (1:15; see Davids, 199–200).

Second, alluding to Proverbs 10:12 (cf. 1Pe 4:8), he "will . . . cover over a multitude of sins." A number of commentators understand the person saved to be the sinner, and the person whose sins are covered to be either the one who turns the sinner back or both the one offering loving rebuke and the sinner (Laws, 240–41; Ropes, 315–16; Dibelius, 258–60). However, James more likely uses parallelism to speak of two effects on the sinner (Martin, 220; Davids, 201; Johnson, 339; Moo, 250–51). The covering of sins can be read simply as speaking of forgiveness (Ps 32:1; 85:2), but Johnson, 339, suggests it has more to do with suppression or prevention of sins yet to be committed.

James thus concludes his letter with a series of exhortations on the proper use of one's words wisely in community. The specific appeal for mutual accountability to live in the ways of the Lord, both for health in the community and for personal, spiritual health, serves as a fitting conclusion to a letter oriented to the effects of wise, righteous living in Christian community.

NOTES

12 Some of the traditional wisdom on the use of prohibitions in the Greek NT has now been overturned by recent research. See Daniel Wallace, *Greek Grammar Beyond the Basics* (Grand Rapids: Zondervan, 1996), 714–25.

16 The word here for "pray," εὔχεσθε, *euchesthe* (GK *2377*), is fairly rare, only occurring in the NT six times. The early manuscripts A and B have forms of the more common word for prayer, προσεύχομαι, *proseuchomai* (GK *4667*), which occurs eighty-five times in the NT. However, Metzger (*Textual Commentary*, 614–15) explains that the UBS committee followed ℵ, K, P, and other manuscripts, reasoning that A and B introduced the more common word for praying based on common Christian usage.

1 PETER

J. DARYL CHARLES

Introduction

1. HISTORY OF INTERPRETATION: AUTHORSHIP, ATTESTATION, DATING

The author of this letter identifies himself as "Peter, an apostle of Jesus Christ" (1:1), "fellow elder" (5:1), and "witness of Christ's sufferings" (5:1). Personal references to "Silvanus" (5:12 NASB; cf. Ac 15:22; 2Co 1:19; 1Th 1:1; 2Th 1:1) and "my son Mark" (5:13; cf. Ac 12:12),[1] as well as allusion in 2 Peter 3:1 to "my second letter," further buttress the case for apostolic authorship and strengthen the belief, existing among the Fathers, that the second gospel was commissioned by Peter.[2] On evaluating the letter, the reader becomes aware of the author's personal and intimate identification with both his audience and the sufferings of Christ. This very tendency and tone have the effect of lending authority. Correlatively, as one might expect, the teaching and admonition being set forth in the letter are in full accord with and reminiscent of that of Jesus. The letter's strong Christology, coupled with the related ethical implications, is precisely what one would expect from the apostle who had walked with Jesus, failed his master, and subsequently been entrusted with shepherding the flock of God.

If we assume the writer to be an eyewitness of Jesus' life and ministry, much of the material in 1 Peter indeed seems to corroborate Jesus' teaching recorded in the gospel narratives—for example, salvation through Christ being prophesied (1:10–12); salvation as ransom through the blood of Christ (1:18–19); the command to love one another (1:22); being born again (1:23); good deeds that glorify God (2:12); the admonition to submit to the authorities (2:13–15) and not retaliate (3:9); being blessed because of persecution and Christ's

---

1. It is plausible that 2 Peter 1:15 is a reference to the gospel of Mark.

2. Irenaeus (late second century) ascribes the letter to the apostle Peter (*Haer.* 3.1.1; 4.9.2; 4:16.5; 5.7.2). Michaels, xxxiii, adroitly observes the importance of geography: "The testimony of Irenaeus is significant because Irenaeus was active not only in Asia Minor but also in the West." Eusebius (*Hist. eccl.* 3.25.2) acknowledges that the letter is one of the undisputed books (see further illuminating comments by Eusebius [2.15 and 6.25.8]). See also Oecumenius and Andreas (cited in Bray, 126–27), each of whom attests to the letter's authenticity.

name (3:13–17); allusion to the days of Noah (3:20); refusing to lord it over others (5:3); and not being anxious (5:7).[3]

A major obstacle for some (e.g., Beare, 28–30, and Craddock, 12) in accepting 1 Peter as genuinely Petrine is the stylistic polish and eloquence of the letter. This eloquence extends to vocabulary, syntax, acquaintance with the LXX, and the use of metaphors and rhetorical devices. According to this objection, the Peter depicted in Acts 4:13—wherein Peter and John are described as *anthrōpoi agrammatoi kai idiōtai* [GK 2626], literally, "men [who are] illiterate and unlearned"[4]—was not capable of a literary product such as 1 Peter. In response to this objection, others have argued that, following Peter's conversion, thirty years of running a fishing business in a cosmopolitan port such as Bethsaida would virtually guarantee that Peter was bilingual, albeit with a thick accent (Mt 26:73), and thus be sufficient to overcome the stereotype of an illiterate and unlearned fisherman (so Hillyer, 2, and Grudem, 27–31). While this response is possible, it is not sufficiently plausible. The more plausible explanation is lodged within the text itself: "Through Silvanus, . . . I have written to you briefly" (5:12 NASB). As one commentator has remarked, these words indicate that "he [Silvanus] was more than merely Peter's stenographer" (so Barclay, 43).

This Silvanus is doubtless the "Silvanus" of Paul's letters (1Th 1:1; 2Th 1:1 NASB) and the "Silas" of the book of Acts (15:37–40; 16:16–40; 17:10–15; 18:5–17). Silvanus must have been a significant figure in the early church, not only because he was a ministry companion to Paul, but also because he possessed Roman citizenship (Ac 16:37). We may infer from this that, in comparison to Peter, he was a well-educated and cultured individual.[5] Hence the thought belongs to Peter, while the writing in all probability belongs to Silvanus.[6]

---

3. Examining the theological and linguistic parallels between 1 Peter and the gospel tradition is the thrust of Robert Gundry's essays ("'*Verba Christi*' in 1 Peter: Their Implications Concerning the Authorship of 1 Peter and the Authenticity of the Gospel Tradition," *NTS* 13 [1966/67]: 336–50; "Further *Verba* on *Verba Christi* in 1 Peter," *Bib* 55 [1974]: 211–32). E. Best ("1 Peter and the Gospel Tradition," *NTS* 16 [1970]: 95–113) has done the same, although he adopts a different approach. While Gundry assumes authenticity of the gospel passages, Best ascribes any similarities to the early church's catechetical material. Similarly, Hillyer, 1–2, has helpfully noted material and themes common to 1 Peter and the Gospels and Acts, while Michaels, xl–xlii, considers the writer's use of the OT and the gospel tradition.

4. Guthrie, 763–64, maintains that the more likely meaning of *agrammatos* (GK 63) is "not formally trained" rather than "illiterate."

5. Neither is the language of the letter a problem, nor is it necessary to say in an inflated way with Beare, 28, that the use of a secretary in 1 Peter is "a device of desperation," nor can one, based on the ancient evidence, say with Achtemeier, 8, that *dia Silouanou* "in fact . . . probably cannot" mean secretarial assistance. On the peculiarities and distinctiveness of vocabulary and style in 1 Peter, see Elliott, 41–68. One need not argue, as Michaels, lxii, 306–7, and E. R. Richards ("Silvanus Was Not Peter's Secretary: Theological Bias in Interpreting *dia Silouanou . . . egrapsa* in 1 Peter 5:12," *JETS* 43/3 [2000]: 417–32), that the phrase "through Silvanus" more likely indicates the *bearer* of the letter. The role of a "co-sender" is anything but clear. Moreover, the reference to Silvanus in 5:12 naturally suggests secretarial help. Contra Michaels, 307, who writes that "if Silvanus had even a small part in writing the letter, it is more plausible that his name would have been linked with Peter's at the outset," Paul's use of Tertius as a secretary appears at the *end*, not the beginning, of Romans (16:22). And Richards, 432, after attempting to build a case that Silvanus did *not* write 1 Peter, in the end is left to concede that "Silvanus certainly *could* have been the secretary" (emphasis his). Finally, it is a breathtaking overstatement to assert, as F. W. Danker does ("1 Peter 1,24–2,17: A Consolatory Pericope," *ZNW* 58 [1967]: 102), that "Silvanus's role as midwife [is] largely irrelevant, and pseudonymous authorship [is] beyond the need of further demonstration."

6. Evidence of the use of professionally trained scribes or secretaries (Lat., *amanuenses*) abounds in the literature of antiquity. In Greco-Roman culture, those who were educated were trained in dictation, a practice that remained part of the

Whereas the authenticity of the second letter bearing the apostle's name has been doubted, throughout church history 1 Peter has been viewed as genuinely apostolic. Only more recently has this been called into question. The arguments against authenticity, in the main, tend to proceed from objections along literary/stylistic and historical lines. Further response to those objections can be found in section 6 below.

In the end, what is striking is the relative absence of any credible voices that dissent from Petrine scholarship. With few exceptions, the Fathers held 1 Peter to be genuine. These witnesses include Irenaeus (*Haer.* 4.9.2; 5.7.2; 4.16.5); Clement of Alexandria (*Paed.* 3.11–12; 4.18–20; Clement is said by Eusebius [*Hist .eccl.* 6.25.8] to have offered commentary on all the "Catholic Epistles"); Eusebius (*Hist. eccl.* 3.3); Didymus (PG 39:1755); Augustine (*Doctr. chr.* 2.12); Oecumenius (PG 119:513); and possibly *1 Clement*[7] as well as Papias.[8] Several commentators (e.g., Kelly, 2; Michaels, xxxii; Guthrie, 760) find clear evidence of familiarity with 1 Peter in a letter from Polycarp of Smyrna to the believers in Philippi (early second century). Unlike 2 Peter, 1 Peter is not considered by Eusebius (*Hist. eccl.* 3.3; 6.25) to be one of the *antilegomena*, the disputed books.[9] Several of the Fathers (e.g., Didymus the Blind; Oecumenius) recognized that the letter has close affinities to the letter of James and that both men were apostles, though Peter concentrated more on those living outside Palestine.[10] In the final analysis, attestation for 1 Peter's authenticity appears as strong as any NT document.[11]

Western educational tradition until relatively recently (thus J. Murphy-O'Connor, *Paul the Letter-Writer* [GNS 41; Collegeville, Minn.: Liturgical Press, 1995], 8). These scribes would have been employed by both the relatively illiterate and those of the upper class, such as public officials and businessmen, for letter writing, providing documentation, and maintaining records. The role of the amanuensis, couched as the sender's coworker, combined with the sender's apostolic authority to lend the letters of the NT an official character. This would be all the more important in the provincial and somewhat cosmopolitan surroundings of Asia Minor.

While Paul composed letters both independently and in collaboration with others, he did not always write them out. Such an example is his letter to the Romans, dictated to and written by Tertius: "I, Tertius, who wrote down this letter, greet you in the Lord" (Ro 16:22). Other remarks by Paul regarding his own handwriting reveal the possible presence of a secretary (e.g., 1Co 16:21; Gal 6:11; Col 4:18; 2Th 3:17; Phm 19). In the end, the problem of eloquence in 1 Peter is no real problem.

7. Bigg, 7–9, attempts to identify close parallels between *1 Clement* (late first century) and 1 Peter. J. B. Mayor (*The Epistle of St. Jude and the Second Epistle of St. Peter* [New York: Macmillan, 1907], cxx) and Wand, 9, believe that Clement's use of 1 Peter is notable. Numerous correspondences between *1 Clement* and 1 Peter are also noted by Kelly, 12.

8. We learn of Papias through Eusebius (*Hist. eccl.* 3.39.17), who writes that Papias had cited 1 Peter.

9. At the same time, Eusebius draws attention to several "spurious" and "questioned" Petrine works—among these are the *Gospel of Peter*, the *Acts of Peter*, the *Apocalypse of Peter*, and the *Doctrine of Peter*.

10. A patristic consensus is outlined in Bray, 65. Didymus the Blind writes, "Why does Peter, an apostle to the Jews, write to those who are scattered in the dispersion, when most of them were still living in Judea at the time? To understand his meaning, we have to compare what he says with texts like [Ps 39:12], 'I am a pilgrim and stranger on earth, as were all my forefathers.'"

11. Thus the claim of Elliott, 124—it is "virtually certain that 1 Peter is a pseudonymous letter"—needs attenuation. Similarly, R. P. Martin's assertion (Chester and Martin, 92) that "the question of authorship remains unresolved" is an overstatement, while his remark that "the traditional view which accepts the claims of the epistle to be apostolic is more reasonable than any alternative hypothesis" is understated. And while Craddock, 13, states what may be factually correct—"Arguing for or against Petrine authorship has lost its importance for most students of this letter"—his rationale will be unsatisfactory for many: "This letter represents the teaching and preaching of Simon Peter and extends that ministry into Asia Minor, whether or not Simon penned it, dictated it, or was the source of the content used by a follower of his." Most assuredly, the early church did not share this view of authorship.

The dating of 1 Peter is linked both to questions of authorship and the manner in which persecution as it is mirrored in the letter is understood. If the letter is genuinely Petrine, it is generally assumed to be dated in the mid-sixties AD. The author gives the impression that he is presently "in Babylon" (5:13), most probably a cryptic reference to Rome. Although we lack sufficient evidence to be conclusive about the persecutions mentioned in the letter, traditional scholarship has assumed a date for 1 Peter in the early- to mid-sixties, either immediately preceding or concurrent with the early stages of Neronic persecution. If Neronic persecution is in advanced stages, however, the reference in 2:13–15 to the political authorities is problematic at best,[12] and the rhetorical question posed in 3:13 seems nonsensical.[13] For the minority of interpreters who assign the epistle a late dating, similarities between 1 Peter and the persecutions of Domitian[14] or Trajan—as reflected, for example, in the letters to the emperor Trajan from Pliny, governor of the province of Bithynia (Pliny, *Ep. Tra.* 96, 97)—are typically adduced (of which Beare, 41–43, is representative).

What is the precise nature of the persecution to which the readers are subjected? And how are the sufferings on display in 1 Peter to be interpreted? A reading of the epistle suggests that the readers' suffering is of a generic variety, that is, it is probably more with *discrimination* than with persecution per se that they have to contend.[15] The readers are said to "suffer for what is right" (*dia dikaiosynē paschō* [GK 4248], 3:14) and be "insulted because of the name of Christ" (*oneidizesthe* [GK 3943] *en onomati Christou*, 4:14); they endure "all kinds of trials" (*poikiloi peirasmoi* [GK 4280], 1:6) and "sufferings of Christ" (*eis Christon pathēmata* [GK 4077], 1:11).

Their social situation further suggests itself through the admonition "Live such good lives among the pagans that . . . they may see your good deeds . . ." (2:12). This state of affairs is unchanging, even in the face of misunderstanding, alienation, and slander. Being misunderstood, alienated, and slandered are realities that accompany normative Christian living—realities that are described in the context of the household code (2:13–3:7), which speaks to normal social relationships. This impression is further supported by the letter's opening admonition (1:13–16). The tone of this exhortation is decidedly ethical.

---

12. To "honor" the emperor in the midst of Nero's mid–64 campaign against Christians strikes the reader as perverse. First Peter 2:13–15 is written in the same spirit as Romans 13:1–10. The book of Revelation is the only NT book where the emperor is demonized. At the other extreme, to honor the emperor in the face of second-century persecution, if one presupposes a late date for the letter, also strikes the reader as incredible. It is precisely this language—the language of respect toward political authorities—that constitutes evidence of an early dating of 1 Peter for J. H. L. Dijkman ("1 Peter: A Later Pastoral Stratum?" *NTS* 33 [1987]: 265–71).

13. W. M. Ramsay (*The Church in the Roman Empire Before A.D. 70* [3d ed.; London: Hodder & Stoughton, 1894], 282–88) challenges the broadly accepted idea that Peter was martyred during Neronic rule by arguing that the letter is Petrine but dated at about AD 80. Church tradition regarding Peter's martyrdom largely rests on the statements of Eusebius and *1 Clement* that Peter was in Rome at the end of his life and that he died a martyr's death, with precisely where and when remaining speculative. Grudem, 36, sees some leeway here, arguing that Peter was in Rome *near* the end but not necessarily *at* the very end of his life.

14. Reicke, 72, asks where the writer's instructions on confronting sacrifices to the emperor are if 1 Peter is mirroring Domitian persecution. W. H. C. Frend (*Martyrdom and Persecution in the Early Church* [New York: Oxford Univ. Press, 1965], 217) downplays the level of persecution during Domitian's reign: "In Rome the persecution of Domitian does not appear to have amounted to very much."

15. Goppelt, 36–45, has perhaps best summarized the social setting facing the readers.

Moreover, the sufferings in the body to which the readers are exposed are described in the context of being "done with sin" (*pepautai hamartias*, 4:1) and no longer living according to the flesh (*en sarki*, GK *4922*), as the pagans live (4:2–3)—i.e., those who are surprised "that you do not plunge with them" into the same carnal excesses (4:4). The impression here is one of normative Christian living in pagan culture, a social context in which Christian discipleship stands in marked contrast. Significantly, the "purification" that the readers are undergoing (*hagnizō*, 1:22) is one for which *they themselves* are responsible, not the Lord.[16]

Thus, given (1) the generic character of persecution being depicted in the epistle, (2) the social context that was normative for Christians throughout the Roman Empire, (3) the distinction throughout the empire between *religiones licitae* and *religiones illicitae*, and (4) the relative restraint of the writer when describing the governing authorities (esp. when compared to the book of Revelation), imperial persecution may be less of a factor in interpreting 1 Peter than some commentators are willing to grant.[17] It is reasonable to maintain that persecution of Christians could have occurred during the reign of any emperor from the middle of the first century onward. Furthermore, local outbreaks of persecution throughout the empire would vary greatly. Finally, against the supposition that 1 Peter reflects the period of Domitian or Trajan, it should be kept in mind that Eusebius (*Hist. eccl.* 2.25.2–5) writes that Peter is succeeded as bishop of the church in Rome in the year 66.

Though secondary to the issues of authorship and persecution, a further hint informing the question of dating issues out of the writer's approach to church organization. Significantly, there is no allusion in 1 Peter to the offices of bishop (*episkopos*, GK *2176*) or deacon (*diakonos*, GK *1356*) that one might expect at the turn of the century or in the early second century; there is only mention of elders (5:1).[18]

---

16. Perhaps the primary reason for the supposition that 1 Peter is addressing a fiercer, concentrated sort of persecution induced by the state is the allusion in 4:12 to the "painful trial" that is testing the readers. The command "do not be surprised" (*mē xenizesthe*, GK *3826*) is already used in 4:4 to describe the reaction of pagans who wonder why the Christians are not indulging in excesses. The sense of the imperative appears to be moderate wonder—"Don't entertain the thought"—rather than a response to catastrophic paralysis—"Be faithful unto death." The former is hardly the language one would expect if political terror resulting in execution were afoot.

17. See, e.g., D. Warden, "Imperial Persecution and the Dating of 1 Peter and Revelation," *JETS* 34/2 (1991): 203–12. Unquestionably, assessing the character of imperial persecution toward the Christian church, difficult as it is, requires an examination of practices in the provinces, where tensions vary considerably. The imperial cult, e.g., would appear to be notably entrenched in Ephesus, Pergamum, and Smyrna (cf. in this regard Rev 2:8–17), though not universally so. Consider the exhortation to the church in Smyrna: "Do not be afraid of what you are about to suffer. I tell you, the devil will put some of you in prison to test you, and you will suffer persecution for ten days. Be faithful, even to the point of death, and I will give you the crown of life" (Rev 2:10). In the end, we can only guess at the degree to which impending persecution in its concentrated form is present.

18. Selwyn, 56–63; U. Holmer (*Die Briefe des Petrus und der Brief des Judas* [Wuppertal: Brockhaus, 1976], 14–15); Barclay, 165; and E. Schweizer (*Der erste Petrusbrief* [3d ed.; Zürich: Theologischer Verlag, 1973], 11) all point to an early date based simply on church organization, since there is no mention in 1 Peter of bishops or deacons. Elliott ("Rehabilitation of an Exegetical Step-Child," 254) holds a middle-of-the-road position, i.e., between AD 70 and 90, based on certain form-critical considerations (e.g., the reworking of material in Christian circles).

On the basis of both internal and external evidence, then, the most likely scenario is that 1 Peter was written from Rome, with persecution imminent or building, in the mid-sixties, though Eusebius places Peter's death later.[19]

2. READERSHIP

The recipients of the letter are addressed as "God's elect strangers" who are scattered throughout the provinces of Pontus, Galatia, Cappadocia, Asia, and Bithynia (1:1), which together constitute the northern region of Asia Minor.[20] Whether these are new believers is difficult to ascertain, although the contrast of "before" and "after" is prominent throughout the epistle (1:14–15, 18, 22; 4:1–5), indicating a predominately Gentile (though racially mixed) population. Given the governing metaphor of Diaspora or "sojourning,"[21] the social location of the readers is Gentile and pagan, even when a sizable number of Jews inhabited parts of Asia Minor and Galatia in particular (cf. Ac 16:1–5). The greeting is consonant with the picture of the early church we find in the NT; thus Goppelt, 5, is justified in maintaining that 1 Peter presupposes and mirrors the spread of Christian faith. Already in the fifties, Ephesus, in addition to Galatia, had become a Christian center as a result of Paul's ministry. Colossians 4:12–16, moreover, creates the impression that the door to Pontus and Bithynia would be open by the sixties. Additionally, the order in which the provinces are listed is largely assumed to be the route traveled by the messenger in the delivery of this circular or encyclical letter (so Hort, 157–84, C. J. Hemer, "The Address of 1 Peter," *ExpTim* 89 [1977/78]: 239–43, while Kelly, 42, adduces Josephus, *Ant.* 16.21–23, as evidences of such an ordered route).

Such a picture coincides with our prior argument that the discrimination/persecution and suffering being mirrored in 1 Peter is of a generic variety and not a result of state-induced policy (cf. 2:12). What we can reconstruct about the recipients from the epistle's text is that they are of varied socioeconomic standing,[22] and most likely predominately Gentile, given (1) the allusions to the preconversion state (e.g., 1:14, 18; 2:9; 4:3–4), (2) the relational duties expressed through the household code (2:13–3:12), and (3) the admonition toward civic duty over against the ruling authorities (2:13–17).

There is no evidence to suggest that either Peter (cf. 1:12) or the apostle Paul had worked in these provinces (cf. Ac 16:6–7), although people from "Cappadocia, Pontus and Asia" were present at Jerusalem on the day of Pentecost (Ac 2:9). Nevertheless, if we suppose that Paul is dead, it would not be unnatural "for the surviving senior apostle to send a message of encouragement to Gentile churches if the apostle to

---

19. Those who hold 1 Peter to be pseudonymous tend to link the epistle with the persecutions under Domitian (late first century) or Trajan (second decade of the second century). Michaels (lvii-lxi) goes to great lengths to relativize supposed allusions to Peter's martyrdom, whether from the fourth gospel (e.g., John 21) or from pseudepigraphal sources (e.g., *Epistle of Clement to James*). While it is impossible to be conclusive about Peter's death, the warning of Michaels, lxi, "against linking the question of the authorship of 1 Peter too closely to the question of date" is perhaps overstated. Indeed the two are intertwined, even when precision eludes us as to when Peter died, based on church tradition.

20. The exception is Galatia, which also extends southward.

21. Contra Elliott, *Home for the Homeless*, 142–43, whose position is maintained in his commentary (*1 Peter*, 94–97, 476–83), we take the "Diaspora" allusion in 1:1 to be metaphorical and not literal. For an evaluation of Elliott's argument, which deserves serious consideration, see section 3 below.

22. Best, 17, points to 2:18–3:7 as evidence of this diversity. Specifically, 2:13–17 may be addressed to freemen, a group probably including wealthy individuals.

the Gentiles was no longer alive" (thus Guthrie, 773). A plausible explanation for the listing of the provinces as we find it in 1:1 is that it represented the route by which the encyclical was to be delivered (see section 4 below). It goes without saying that intense, state-directed persecution (were we to presuppose this element in the letter as in the book of Revelation) would have precluded such activity. To the contrary, the discrimination that the readers are suffering is described as worldwide (5:9).

First Peter combines features of private correspondence—e.g., terms of endearment (1:14; 2:11; 4:12), personal instructions (5:1–4), personal greetings (5:12–14), and a personal understanding of the readers' plight (1:6; 3:13–15)—with those of a public encyclical, which is to circulate among various Christian communities in a wider geographical area. The writer's appropriation of OT language and concepts, which are both direct and indirect, might inform us more about the theological orientation of the writer than the actual recipients themselves. Thus it is to the matter of literary composition we must now turn.

3. COMPOSITION AND LITERARY INTEGRITY

A merely casual reading of the epistle shows the writer's acquaintance with and dependence on the OT, both in his indirect allusion—by means of language, images, and theological understanding—and in direct citation.[23] Chester and Martin, 88, contend that, with the possible exception of Romans and Hebrews, "no NT book ... is so permeated with OT hints and ideas" as 1 Peter. Indeed, it might be reasonably argued that 1 Peter *exceeds* both Romans and Hebrews in its dependence on the OT; a strong case could surely be made for this claim.[24] Reliance on OT tradition material is mirrored in the following:

- use of the "sojourning"/Diaspora metaphor (1:1, 17; 2:11)
- the designation of the readers as "elect," or "chosen" (1:1; 2:4; 5:13)
- the foreknowledge of God (1:2)
- allusion to the sprinkling of blood (1:2)
- reflections of Malachi 3:3 (1:7)
- allusion to the prophets of old (1:10–12)
- admonition to be holy because the Lord is holy (1:16)
- reflections of Exodus 12:5; Leviticus 22:19–21; Deuteronomy 17:1 (1:19)
- citation of Isaiah 40:6–8 (1:24–25)
- citation of Psalm 34:8 (2:3)
- reminiscences of Psalm 118:22 (2:4)
- reflections of Isaiah 56:7 (2:5)
- reflections of Exodus 19:5–6 (2:4–5, 9)

---

23. See in this regard E. G. Selwyn, "Eschatology in 1 Peter," in *The Background of the New Testament and Its Eschatology*, ed. W. D. Davies and D. Daube (Cambridge: Cambridge Univ. Press, 1956), 394–401. Schutter, 5–43, believes that half of the epistle consists of OT material. Two attempts to illuminate the hermeneutic employed in 1 Peter are D. E. Johnson, "Fire in God's House: Imagery from Malachi 3 in Peter's Theology of Suffering (1 Peter 4:12–19)," *JETS* 29/3 [1986]: 285–94; and W. L. Schutter, "1 Peter 4:17, Ezekiel 9:6 and Apocalyptic Hermeneutics," *SBLSP* 26 (Atlanta: Scholars Press, 1987), 276–84.

24. Goppelt, 30–31, conveniently supplies a list of notable similarities between 1 Peter and James, as does Hillyer, 8–9.

- allusion to the offering of sacrifices (2:5)
- citation of Isaiah 28:16 (2:6)
- citation of Psalm 118:22 and reflections of Isaiah 8:14 (2:7–8)
- allusion to a chosen people (2:9)
- allusion to a holy nation (2:9)
- allusion to a people belonging to God (2:9)
- reflections of Isaiah 42:16 (2:9)
- allusion to Hosea 1:6, 9, 10; 2:23 (2:10)
- allusion to the day of visitation (2:12)
- reflections of Isaiah 53:4–5, 7, 9, 11 (2:22–24)
- use of the sheep/shepherd metaphor (2:25; 5:2, 4)
- allusion to Sarah and Abraham (3:6)
- citation of Psalm 34:12–16 (3:10)
- allusion to Noah (3:20)
- reflections of Psalm 110:1–2 (3:22)
- allusion to grumbling (4:9)
- allusion to judgment (4:17)
- reminiscences of Proverbs 11:31 (4:17–18)
- reflections of Psalm 31:5 (4:19)
- use of the Babylon metaphor (5:13)

The writer is particularly adept at taking OT concepts and images and weaving them together into important themes (e.g., the "stone" passages and the people/priesthood/nation passages).[25] These strands, while they are the object of further discussion in section 7 below, require some comment at this point.

It is an understatement to say that the recent history of the interpretation of 1 Peter has been characterized by diverse exegetical approaches. Part of the reason for this is the epistle's literary character, which is thought to complicate the exegetical task. In what is perhaps the most extensive examination of Petrine scholarship over the last one hundred years, Troy Martin, in *Metaphor and Composition in 1 Peter*, identifies numerous interpretive approaches that have emerged.[26] Some scholars believe 1 Peter to be comprised of two different letters.[27] Some regard the letter as a baptismal homily in its entirety, while others allege that

---

25. Davids, 211, has listed not only direct citations but also perceived allusions to the OT, some of which I have noted and others of which, though likely, are more difficult to assess. On the matter of varying hermeneutical approaches to Jewish tradition-material and the degree to which such material is "borrowed," particularly as it is on display in the General Epistles, see my articles "Noncanonical Citations in the General Epistles," and "The Old Testament in the General Epistles," in *Dictionary of the Later New Testament and Its Developments*, ed. R. P. Martin and P. H. Davids (Downers Grove, Ill.: InterVarsity, 1997), 814–19, 834–41.

26. Martin's volume is devoted to an analysis of the letter's structural integrity. In his survey of scholarship, Martin identifies six general explanations for the composition of 1 Peter. More recently, S. C. Pearson (see bibliography) identifies five: (1) epistle, (2) baptismal homily, (3) baptismal liturgy, (4) apologetic tract, and (5) homiletic midrash.

27. So, e.g., Hort, 3; Wand, 1–2; C. F. D. Moule, "The Nature and Purpose of 1 Peter," *NTS* 3 (1956/57): 1–11.

a baptismal sermon has been spliced into the letter.[28] Yet others take an opposite approach, viewing the original as the sermon with a letter simply appended.[29] A variation of these is the view that 1 Peter is a letter containing two baptismal homilies.[30] Another variation is that 1 Peter represents a paschal liturgy.[31] Those who see no rhyme or reason to the structure of 1 Peter tend to view the letter as a series of exhortations.[32] Still others detect in the epistle several unrelated themes.[33]

Most—though by no means all—commentaries take note of the variations on the baptismal theme. In the end, attempts to read a baptismal or liturgical context into 1 Peter provide an inadequate—though intriguing—method of examining the letter. At the most rudimentary level, there is only one reference to baptism that surfaces in the entire epistle.

As we consider the question of composition, one influential study worthy of note is J. H. Elliott's *A Home for the Homeless*.[34] Herein Elliott takes a central metaphor employed by the writer—"strangers," or "aliens" (1:1)—and interprets it literally in a sociopolitical sense to mean people who are disenfranchised, those living on the margins of society. The identification of this imagery is without question important to the letter's interpretation; nevertheless, Elliott's understanding of the metaphor, while useful, needs modification.[35] The proper way to interpret this controlling metaphor of the Diaspora (1:1)—the counterpart of which is "Babylon," utilized at the end of the letter (5:13)—is metaphorically.[36] Indeed the epistle of James utilizes the same imagery (1:1), with its greeting extended to the twelve tribes in the Diaspora.

---

28. So, e.g., H. Gunkel, *Der erste Brief des Petrus* (SNT 2; Göttingen: Vandenhoeck & Ruprecht, 1906), 530; Reicke, 74; O. S. Brooks, "1 Peter 3:21—The Clue to the Literary Structure of the Epistle," *NovT* 16 (1974): 290–305; and more recently, Schutter, 35–43.

29. So, e.g., A. von Harnack, *Geschichte der altchristlichen Literatur bis Eusebius—Vol. 1* (Leipzig: Hinrich, 1897), 451; R. Perdelwitz, *Die Mysterienreligion and das Problem des I. Petrusbriefes* (Giessen: Töpelmann, 1911), 12–15; W. Bornemann, "Der erste Petrusbrief: Eine Taufrede des Silvanus?" *ZNW* 19 (1920): 161; H. Windisch, *Die katholischen Briefe* (HNT 4/2, 2d ed.; Tübingen: Mohr, 1930), 46–47; Beare, 8; Leaney, 8.

30. So R. P. Martin, "The Composition of 1 Peter in Recent Study," in *Vox Evangelica: Biblical and Historical Essays*, ed. R. P. Martin (London: Epworth, 1962), 40.

31. So Cross, 20. The position of R. P. Martin (see previous note) resembles to a certain degree that of Cross: 1 Peter is an epistle that incorporates catechetical and liturgical material.

32. So, e.g., Cranfield, 122; W. C. van Unnik, "First Letter of Peter," in *IDB* 3:759–68; W. Schrage, *Die "katholischen" Briefe* (NTD 10; Göttingen: Vandenhoeck & Ruprecht, 1973), 64–65.

33. So, e.g., Goppelt, 8–12; Elliott, *A Home for the Homeless*, 284; Balch, *Let Wives Be Submissive*, 124.

34. See also, more recently, Elliott's *1 Peter* in the Anchor Bible series.

35. To his credit, Elliott (*A Home for the Homeless*, 13–14) demonstrates a willingness and ability to bring insights from a variety of disciplines to bear on exegesis. His approach seeks to direct attention to the "total constellation of factors" (ecological, economic, political, social, and cultural, including religious) that shape the context in which a text is produced.

36. D. L. Balch ("Hellenization/Acculturation in 1 Peter," in *Perspectives on First Peter*, ed. C. H. Talbert [Macon, Ga.: Mercer Univ. Press, 1986], 79) wisely cautions against Elliott's literal understanding of Diaspora: "Sociological theory should be suggestive rather than generative," illustrative but not determinative. Satisfactory responses to Elliott's argument have been offered by a number of scholars—among them Balch; Talbert, 141–51; T. Martin, 144–46; Achtemeier, 55–58, 173–76. Michaels, xlvi–xlix, 310–11, concurs, though his identification of the genre of 1 Peter as an "apocalyptic Diaspora letter to 'Israel'" needs some qualification. While noting parallels between 1 Peter and *2 Baruch* 78–87, Michaels, lxvii, concedes in the end that the "formal features" of apocalyptic literature are absent from 1 Peter.

A proper construal of this metaphor has important implications for our interpretation of 1 Peter. The depiction of the readers as "Diaspora," as Kelly, 4, rightly notes, is a representative instance of the early church's habit of "transferring to itself, as the new Israel, the language appropriate to the experience of the old." Danker ("Consolatory Pericope," 99) concurs, emphasizing that the new community is an *extension* of Israel, even when a crucial difference exists: in the OT, Israel suffered due to disobedience. This is by no means the case in 1 Peter, however. The images that appear in the epistle can be understood as corollaries, then, of the Diaspora metaphor—for example, sojourning, a holy nation, a chosen people, and the household/temple of God (all of which appear in 1:14–2:10), in addition to righteous suffering (2:11–3:12 and 3:13–5:12).[37] In contrast to the wildly divergent attempts to understand 1 Peter's literary structure already noted, most of which result in disunity, this interpretive scheme renders unitary—and intelligible—the epistle of 1 Peter.

4. FORM ANALYSIS

The epistle as a generic form, writes Klaus Berger, is "not only an external transmission form of written communication, but it is also essentially a major genre with constitutive characteristics."[38] First Peter follows the standard form of the Greek private letter, with its introduction, greeting (*chairō*, GK *5897*), body proper, and conclusion,[39] and falls somewhere between public and private correspondence.[40] The typical letter opens with identification of the sender and the address to the receiver, followed by a greeting. On occasion the sender's identity is expanded; on occasion that of the recipient is amplified. In 1 Peter a modified greeting, "grace and peace" (standard in most Pauline epistles), is used. As to its specific character, 1 Peter may be understood as something of an encyclical,[41] given the geographical distribution of the addressees and the needs being addressed.

The epistle not only constitutes its own genre; it also serves as a "framing" mechanism for other genres. In his important monograph on 1 Peter, Troy Martin, 85, has called attention to the presence in the epistle

---

37. In fact, the "servants" in 2:18–25 are *oiketai* ("household servants," GK *3860*), in keeping with the family vocabulary used throughout the letter. The household image, write Osiek and Balch, 190, "provides an anchor of identity in a sea of strangerhood," given that the saints are *oiketai* (1:17; 2:11) and *parepidēmoi*, GK *4215* (1:1; 2:11). See the extensive commentary on this cluster of associated images in T. Martin, 161–267, as well as the helpful overview of the language and thought-world of 1 Peter found in Achtemeier, 3–23.

38. K. Berger, "Hellenistische Gattungen im Neuen Testament," in *ANRW* II.25.2, ed. H. Temporini and W. Haase (Berlin: de Gruyter, 1984), 1338 (my translation).

39. On epistolary content and structure, see S. K. Stowers, *Letter Writing in Greco-Roman Antiquity* (LEC; Philadelphia: Westminster, 1986), W. G. Doty, *Letters in Primitive Christianity*. More recently, in *Paul the Letter-Writer*, Murphy-O'Connor has examined at length the role of letter writing in the apostle Paul's life.

40. So Craddock, 12. That is, 1 Peter is "public" insofar as it is to be read in Christian communities extending throughout several provinces of Asia Minor, and it is "private" to the extent that it addresses a specific readership on a specific issue.

41. This assumption derives from Hort, 157–84. It finds further support in Ramsay, *The Church in the Roman Empire*, 279–95; Ramsay, *The Letters to the Seven Churches* (London: Hodder & Stoughton, 1904), 183–96; and Hemer, "Address of 1 Peter," 239–43, even when explanations of the traffic routes in Asia Minor vary. Most commentators describe the epistle in terms of a "circular" or encyclical. So, e.g., Kelly, 3; Goppelt (in *Der erste Petrusbrief*, ed. F. Hahn [KEK 12/1; Göttingen: Vandenhoeck & Ruprecht, 1978], 44–45), who describes 1 Peter in terms of a *Rundbrief*; Michaels, 9; Chester and Martin, 98.

of an inordinate number of imperatives, beginning with 1:13 and extending to 5:12.[42] Admonitions and prescriptives are the language of paraenesis, i.e., hortatory literature. While paraenesis (the *logos parainētikos*; cf. Ac 27:9, 22), or moral exhortation, is found in virtually every NT epistle, the Christian paraenetic tradition is perhaps most richly on display in the General Epistles.[43] In these letters, ethics and pastoral theology rather than theological formulations of doctrine per se are accentuated.[44] Paraenesis has as its goal the presentation of a standard for conduct, and it is this ethical trajectory that characterizes 1 Peter.[45] Accordingly, paraenesis typically incorporates the elements of regulatory rules of conduct, ethical proscriptions, ethical justification, warnings, and catalogs of virtue and/or vice.[46]

---

42. Martin cites J. H. Moulton's *Grammar of New Testament Greek*, which counts twenty-eight imperatives in this portion of the letter.

43. Both L. G. Perdue ("Paraenesis and the Epistle of James," *ZNW* 72 [1981]: 241–56) and R. W. Wall ("James as Apocalyptic Paraenesis." *ResQ* 32 [1990]: 11–22) have called attention to the role of paraenesis in James; I have noted elsewhere the paraenetic character of Jude and 2 Peter (*Literary Strategy in the Epistle of Jude* [Scranton, Pa.: Univ. of Scranton Press, 1993], 72ff., and *Virtue amidst Vice: The Catalog of Virtues in 2 Peter 1* [JSNTSup 150; Sheffield: Sheffield Academic Press, 1997], 37–43 [implicit in 84–98]); Lauri Thurén (*Argument and Theology of 1 Peter: The Origins of Christian Paraenesis* [JSNTSup 114; Sheffield: Sheffield Academic Press, 1995]) and T. Martin, 85–121, argue for its guiding presence in 1 Peter.

44. Another feature common to paraenetic literature that goes hand in hand with imperative language is the use of moral typology. Not infrequently, the ethical standard being advocated is illustrated through either historical or legendary models that belong to popular tradition. We see this practice vividly on display in Jude (unbelieving Israel, the fallen angels, Sodom and Gomorrah, Cain, Balaam, and Korah), 2 Peter (the fallen angels, Noah and his contemporaries, Sodom, Lot, and Balaam's ass), and James (Abraham, Rahab, Job, and Elijah), where moral paradigms are marshaled for the purpose of admonishing or warning the readers. In 1 Peter fewer models are presented, and yet the hortatory language is equally strong when compared to the other General Epistles. Moral paradigms in 1 Peter include Christ (2:21–25; 3:18–22; 4:1–2), Sarah (3:1–6), and even the author himself (5:1–5). On the hermeneutical tendencies and use of moral typology in the General Epistles, see my "Interpreting the General Epistles," in *Interpreting the New Testament: Essays on Methods and Issues*, ed. D. A. Black and D. S. Dockery (Nashville: Broadman and Holman, 2001), 433–56.

45. Those who proceed from the assumption that 1 Peter is paraenesis include Selwyn; Balch, *Let Wives Be Submissive*; D. Hill, "'To Offer Spiritual Sacrifices . . .' (1 Peter 2:5): Liturgical Formulations and Christian Paraenesis in 1 Peter," *NTS* 16 (1982): 45–63; T. Martin, 85–134.

46. On the paraenetic tradition in general, see Berger, "Hellenistische Gattungen," 1075–77; A. J. Malherbe, *Moral Exhortation: A Greco-Roman Sourcebook* (LEC; Philadelphia: Westminster, 1986), 124–29. Identification of the letter as paraenesis is further supported by several conspicuous lexical phenomena—in particular, the abundance of imperatives and related participles. Throughout 1 Peter the readers are admonished toward particular behavior in innumerable ways—see, e.g., 1:13, 15, 22; 2:1, 2, 5, 11, 13, 17; 3:14; 4:1, 7, 12–13, 15, 16; 5:2, 5, 6, 8. Correlatively, literary-rhetorical features such as ethical catalogs (i.e., vice and virtue lists), contrast or antithesis, and household codes are defining (though not universally appearing) characteristics of paraenetic literature. The ethical catalog abounds as a teaching device in Stoic ethical discourse, both in literary and oral tradition, and is readily imported into Christian literature. Numerous examples of virtue lists and vice lists are employed by the NT writers, perhaps the most conspicuous example being 2 Peter 1:5–7 (see commentary on 2 Peter). Four ethical catalogs occur in 1 Peter—one virtue list (3:8) and three vice lists (2:1; 4:3; 4:14). A further element in paraenesis frequently linked to the use of moral paradigms is contrast or antithesis. More often than not, this involves setting positive and negative behavior in opposition. First Peter exhibits this feature prominently: 1:14–15 and 2:1–2 contrast the believers' former and present life; believers and unbelievers are compared in 2:7–9 and 4:4–5; 2:20 contrasts misconduct with right conduct; 3:3–4 compares a woman's inner disposition and outward appearance; 3:9 places insulting and blessing in contrast; 4:15–16 compares suffering justly and unjustly; while 5:1–3 sets against one another proper and improper ways of leading.

Compositional considerations, noted in the previous section, combine with lexical peculiarities, literary-rhetorical devices, and the social context of the readers to inform us of the literary genre of 1 Peter, which we have identified as paraenesis. The presence of each of these elements in this epistle deserves comment.

A peculiar feature of 1 Peter to which a considerable amount of literature has been devoted is the so-called household or station code.[47] The purpose of this device can be detected in its content and the relative uniformity of its form. Household codes appearing in antiquity reiterate the duties and obligations that encompass the family circle—typically men, women, children, masters, and slaves. For example, husbands and wives demonstrate reciprocal love and respect, while children are to show obedience. Four of these constitutive elements are found in 1 Peter—slaves and masters (2:18–20), wives (3:1–6), and husbands (3:7)—while children are absent. Yet a fifth—"all of you" (3:8–9; 5:5)—might be added to this list of obligations in the letter (so T. Martin, 126), based on the writer's exhortation toward subordination, which undergirds the purpose of the household code in its generic sense.

It is often the case that the social situation behind paraenesis dictates a relationship of the author to his readers which is that of a father figure to a son or mentor to a disciple, the effect of which is to lend moral authority to his accompanying exhortations (so Berger, "Hellenistische Gattungen," 1076). Such a relationship is certainly mirrored in the manner by which the writer addresses his audience. In 1 Peter he utilizes terms of endearment (1:11; 4:12), empathizes with his readers (5:1–5), reaffirms what they already know, and reminds them that they have a model to follow (3:13–14, 18–22), all of which have the effect of facilitating moral persuasion or dissuasion.

5. LITERARY RELATIONSHIP TO 2 PETER

It is broadly assumed by NT scholarship that the two Petrine letters do not issue from the same individual. Reasons for this are doctrinal and linguistic, as well as historical. Unlike 1 Peter, with its rich Christology (cross and atonement, resurrection, ascension and session, baptism), 2 Peter is thought to be devoid of theological affirmation aside from its eschatological outlook. Indeed, 1 Peter is universally praised for the exalted theological perspective it advocates. Chester and Martin, 104, are representative:

> Probably no document in the New Testament is so theologically oriented as 1 Peter, if the description is taken in the strict sense of teaching about God. The epistle is theocentric through and through, and its author has a robust faith in God which he seeks to impart to the readers. The author's mind is filled with the centrality of the divine plan and purpose in both human and cosmic affairs, from the opening exultation . . . to the closing affirmation and appeal.

While 1 Peter, when contrasted with 2 Peter, strikes the reader as theologically richer, this may be the result of pastoral need rather than the writer's own theological orientation. Linguistically, the two epistles, while both exhibiting an elevated use of the Greek, have their distinct features. Furthermore, their

---

47. Two helpful examinations of the household code and related literature are the book by D. C. Verner (*The Household of God* [SBLDS 71; Chico, Calif.: Scholars Press, 1983]) and the essay by Balch, "Household Codes," 25–50. On the use of the household code in 1 Peter, thorough and helpful discussions are found in T. Martin, 124–30, and Goppelt, 162–228. Further discussion of the household code is found in the exposition of 2:13–17.

appropriation of Jewish tradition-material—both biblical and extrabiblical—would seem to differ in methodology. For example, whereas 2 Peter does not utilize any direct citations, 1 Peter engages Jewish sources in both direct and indirect ways. Both, however, make paraenetic use of their sources, creatively marshaling typology and metaphor for the purpose of moral exhortation. In the end, both epistles address a readership that finds itself in a pervasively Gentile social environment, even when the specific needs in the community appear to be different.

On closer examination, 1 and 2 Peter exhibit numerous points of resemblance that are striking in and of themselves.[48] These similarities, which are theological, lexical, and rhetorical in nature, are deserving of mention:

1. Christ's second coming is a major focus of both letters (1:7, 13; 4:13; 5:4//1:16; 3:12).
2. Correlatively, the theme of judgment surfaces in both (1:17; 2:21; 4:5–6, 17//2:3–4, 9, 11; 3:6–7).
3. Much of the material in both is devoted to the presentation of a distinctive Christian social ethic (1:13–17, 22; 2:1, 11–20; 3:1–17; 4:1–19; 5:1–11//1:5–15; 2:4–22; 3:1–7, 11–18).
4. Divine "foreknowledge" (epignōsis, GK 2106) in both letters establishes the basis on which the saints can interpret the dealings of God (1:2//1:2–3, 8; 2:20).
5. An important subtheme in both letters is divine election, the cornerstone of the ethical life (1:1, 15; 2:4, 6, 9, 21; 3:6, 9; 5:10, 13 [syneklektos, GK 5293]//1:3, 10 [eklogē, GK 1724]).
6. Correlatively, the language of "reserving," or "keeping/holding" (tēreō, GK 5498), is employed in both letters (1:4//2:4, 9, 17; 3:7).
7. In both letters, grace and peace are multiplied to the readers (1:2//1:2).
8. Divine glory (doxa, GK 1518) and the glory of Christ feature prominently in both letters (1:7, 11, 21, 24; 4:11, 13–14; 5:1, 4, 10–11//1:3, 17; 2:10; 3:18).
9. Being holy (hagios, GK 41) is an important subtheme in both letters (1:12, 15–16; 2:5, 9; 3:5//1:18, 21; 2:21; 3:2, 11).
10. Correlatively, the saints as "righteous" (dikaios, GK 1465) and "righteousness" (dikaiosynē, GK 1466) are prominent in both letters (2:24; 3:12, 14, 18; 4:18//1:1, 13; 2:5, 7–8, 21; 3:13).
11. Being "without blemish" (amōmos, aspilos, GK 320, 834), whether denoting Christ or the saints, is important in both letters (1:19//3:14).
12. One's "way of life," or "behavior" (anastrophē, GK 419) is of utmost importance in both letters (1:15, 18; 2:12; 3:1–2, 16//2:7; 3:11).
13. The triune God—the Father, Christ the Son, and the Spirit—is presented in both letters (1:2–3, 11–13, 17, 19; 2:5, 21; 3:4, 15–16, 18–19, 21; 4:1, 6, 11, 13–14; 5:1, 10, 14//1:1, 8, 11, 14, 16–17; 21; 2:20; 3:4, 18).
14. Prophets, prophesying, and prophecy occur in both letters (1:10//1:21; 2:1, 16, 19; 3:2).
15. Correlatively, the "word(s) of the Lord/prophets" (1:23, 25; 2:8; 3:1//1:19; 3:2, 5, 7) figures prominently in both.

48. Contra W. Marxsen (Introduction to the New Testament, trans. G. Buswell [Philadelphia: Fortress, 1970], 236), who asserts that "the contents [of 1 Peter] do not reveal a 'Petrine character' in any way," thus making it "unlikely for a number of reasons" that Peter was the author of this work.

16. Both letters conclude with an exhortation to grow or stand fast in the grace of God (5:12//3:18), which is an important concept for both writers (1:2, 10, 13; 2:19–20; 3:7; 4:10; 5:5, 10, 12//1:2; 3:18).

17. Both letters employ moral paradigms in the service of promoting Christian ethics (2:21–25; 3:5–6; 3:18–20; 5:1//2:4–10, 15–16).

18. Noah appears in both letters as a model of faithfulness (3:20//2:5).

19. The reality of the angelic realm, both in facilitating and resisting the divine purpose, is mirrored in both letters (1:12; 3:19, 22; 5:8//2:4).

20. The fallen angels are depicted as imprisoned in both letters (3:19//2:4).

21. The flood is mentioned in both letters (3:20//2:5; 3:5–6).

22. Correlatively, the disobedient are described as "unrighteous" (3:18//2:9).

23. "Salvation" (*sōtēria*, GK *5401*) from the Lord appears in both letters (1:5, 9–10//3:15).

24. Virtue, i.e., "moral excellence, praises, goodness" (*aretē*, GK *746*), appears in the Petrine letters three of the four times it is found in the NT (2:9//1:3, 5).

25. Brotherly affection (*philadelphia*, GK *5789*) is commended in both letters (1:22; 3:8//1:7).

26. God "provides/supplies in abundance" (*epichorēgeō, chorēgeō*, GK *2220, 5961*) for the saints as described in both letters (4:11//1:5, 11).

27. The writer of both letters addresses his readers as "dear friends" (2:11; 4:12//3:14).

28. Both letters utilize the metaphor of redemption drawn from the slave market (1:18//2:1),

29. thereby reminding the readers of their spiritual freedom (*eleutheria*, GK *1800*) (2:16//2:19).

30. Both letters appeal to the patience (*makrothymia*, GK *3429*) of God (3:20//3:9, 15).

31. Correlatively, this knowledge spawns greater endurance (*hypomonē*, GK *5705*) in both letters (2:20//1:6).

32. Both letters condemn the licentiousness (*aselgeia*, GK *816*) of surrounding pagan culture (4:3//2:2).

33. Both letters warn the readers to abstain from fleshly lusts (*epithymia*, GK *2123*) (1:14; 2:11; 4:2–3//1:4; 2:10, 18; 3:3).

34. Both letters appropriate an eschatological perspective that links present living with future promise (1:5, 7, 20–21; 4:13//2:3–4, 9, 11; 3:3, 6–7).

35. In both letters the world "perishes" (*apollymi*, GK *660*; 1:7//3:6, 9).

36. The only occurrences of the word "eyewitness" in the NT are in the Petrine letters, in its verbal form ("see," *epopteuō*, GK *2227*) and nominal form (*epoptēs*, GK *2228*) respectively (2:12; 3:2//1:16).

37. The intended result of both letters is that the saints be "established" (*stērizō*, GK *5114*) in their faith (5:10//1:12).

38. This being "established" stands in direct relation to the saints' "knowing" (*eidotes* [GK *3857*], *eidotas*; 5:9//1:12).

39. In both letters the writer's self-designation is an "apostle of Jesus Christ" (1:1//1:1).

40. Personal apostolic reminiscences are employed in both letters (5:1//1:14, 16–18).

41. Both letters contain similar doxological praise (4:11//3:18).

6. TRENDS IN PETRINE SCHOLARSHIP

Critical scholarship of the last fifty years has sought to probe authorship, purpose, and literary form in 1 Peter. More recent Petrine scholarship has concerned itself both with literary structure and sociological perspectives. Even when the assessments of critical scholars such as Stephen Neill (1 Peter represents the "storm center of NT studies"; *The Interpretation of the New Testament, 1861–1961* [London: Oxford Univ. Press, 1966], 343) and Elliott (the letter is an "exegetical step-child" of NT studies; "Rehabilitation of an Exegetical Step-Child," 243–54) may seem somewhat extreme, the sheer volume of recent commentary on 1 Peter has presented us with fresh interpretive perspectives.[49] Much of the recent work in 1 Peter has heightened our appreciation for the writer's deft use of tradition-material that informs his literary-rhetorical strategy as well as the epistle's literary unity.[50] That scholars have searched for an appropriate hermeneutical key using wildly divergent methods is not to consign the letter to the status of an enigma, even when it has caused some to remark that the study of 1 Peter is "at a crossroads" (so J. D. McCaughey, "On Rereading 1 Peter," *AThR* 10 [1983]: 41–49; Pearson, 2).

Questions have been raised by mid- and late-twentieth-century scholarship as to the letter's authenticity. This argument consists of several planks that have already been noted—among them the dating and precise nature of persecution being mirrored in the letter, the apostle's prior contact with churches in Asia Minor, the elegance of the Greek employed by the writer, and questions surrounding the role of "Silvanus [Silas]."[51]

---

49. For a bibliography of 1 Peter scholarship up to ca. 1982, see D. Sylva, "A 1 Peter Bibliography," *JETS* (1982): 75–89 (reproduced in Talbert, *Perspectives on First Peter*, 17–36). Detailed bibliographies of ancient, medieval, early modern, and modern sources on the epistle can be found in T. Martin, 289–338; Goppelt, xxi–xlii; Elliott, 155–227.

50. In his important study on the composition of 1 Peter, Schutter, 43, identifies six variations of hermeneutical method: (1) telescoping an OT text, (2) uniting a catena of texts through a single idea, (3) conflating multiple texts, (4) utilization of a "text-plot," (5) associating a text with a known exegetical tradition, and (6) utilizing florilegia (i.e., numerous texts strung together).

51. Although not widely held, the view that 1 Peter is pseudonymous has several variations. One school of thought, presupposing a late date, detects in the epistle what Guthrie, 778, calls "pseudepigraphal machinery"—i.e.,, fictitious material that might generate "authority," such as the apostolic pedigree in 1:1, references to "Silvanus" and "my son Mark" in 5:12–13, and the cryptic allusion to "Babylon" in 5:13. The most prominent representative of this position is Norbert Brox ("Zur pseudepigraphischen Rahmung des ersten Petrusbriefes," *BZ* 19 [1975]: 78–96; "Tendenz und Pseudepigraphie im ersten Petrusbrief," *Kairós* 20 [1978], 110–20). Another school of thought, perhaps wishing to circumvent the ethical problems normally associated with pseudonymity, prefers to speak of a "Petrine school" or "Petrine community" (thus, e.g., Best, 63; M. L. Soards, "The Letter of 1 Peter: An Account of Research," *ANRW* II.25.5 [Berlin: de Gruyter, 1988], 3827–49; P. J. Achtemeier, "Newborn Babes and Living Stones: Literal and Figurative in 1 Peter," in *To Touch the Text*, ed. M. P. Horgan and P. J. Kobelski [New York: Crossroads, 1989], 207–36). In this way, it is suggested, the early church "was affirming the leader's abiding presence and valuing the legacy of his continuing influence," thereby "appealing to what the apostle might have said if he had survived to a later decade" (so Chester and Martin, 91). Advocates of this position tend to opt for an intermediate date, usually between the years 75 and 85. As already noted, the church historically has accepted the letter as apostolic. Evidence has already been put forward to demonstrate that any challenges to Petrine authorship are less than persuasive. No irrefutable obstacles arise externally from the church's tradition or internally from the text of the epistle itself. The judicious observation of A. F. Walls (*The First Epistle General of Peter* [TNTC; Grand Rapids: Eerdmans, 1959], 22) remains unchallenged: the references to "Peter" in the letter are quite restrained—the very opposite tendency of pseudepigraphal writings.

In the previous section we observed the tendency of some scholarship—both past and recent—to associate 1 Peter with a baptismal homily or liturgy. While parts of the letter present credible evidence for this theory, this approach in its variations is not without weaknesses in explaining the epistle's literary unity and overall purpose.[52] Nevertheless, these variations on the baptism theme, in their sheer number and diversity, are compelling and thus are to be taken seriously. Is baptism primary or secondary in our interpretation of 1 Peter? In offering a comprehensive compositional analysis of 1 Peter, we will have to contextualize baptism against the backdrop of the letter's purpose and dominant themes.

7. PURPOSE AND PROMINENT THEMES

It can be rightly argued that the significance of 1 Peter is disproportionate to its length. Thus, Waltner, 17, observes that "its potential significance for contemporary church life and ethics . . . is larger than the brevity of the letter suggests." Indeed Martin Luther (*Luther's Works* 12.260) would agree, having declared that 1 Peter was "one of the most significant and convicting works of the New Testament." And how could it be otherwise? Its universal appeal is guaranteed by the themes it addresses—suffering, hope, promise, and divine care.

Several catchwords hold a prominent place in the letter and assist the reader in identifying crucial themes. Initially, the saints are depicted as "called" or "chosen"/"elect" multiple times throughout the epistle. In fact, the language of "calling" (*kaleō*, GK *2813*, used six times [1:15; 2:9; 2:21; 3:6; 3:9; 5:10]; *eklektos*, GK *1723*, used four times [1:1; 2:4; 2:6; 2:9]) forms something of an inclusio in the letter's opening and closing (1:1; 5:10).[53] In addition, the language of "suffering" is pervasive. It is a suffering, moreover, that has two sides: both the saints and Christ "suffer" innocently;[54] indeed, the saints share in the "sufferings"[55] and "testing"[56] of Christ.

Most commentary recognizes the theme of suffering in 1 Peter, though as we have noted there is great diversity of opinion as to the epistle's literary composition and form-critical considerations. Furthermore, there is a wide divergence of opinion as to the precise nature of the readers' suffering and, consequently, as to the writer's use of relevant sources. Nevertheless, innocent suffering is assumed or acknowledged by all commentators, regardless of their views on literary composition.

---

52. T. G. C. Thornton ("1 Peter: A Paschal Liturgy?" *JTS* 12 NS [1961], 14–26) has raised much-needed criticisms in the light of the proposed baptismal liturgy theory.

53. Significantly, the language of calling is buttressed by the "stone" passage (2:4–8), which borrows the stone metaphor from Isaiah 28:16 (the selected, precious cornerstone), Psalm 118:22 (the stone the builders rejected), and Isaiah 8:14 (the stone of stumbling). This strong emphasis of divine purpose—revealed in part to the prophets of old and fully realized in the crucified, risen, and ascended Lord who now sits in power, ruling over the cosmos—is important for the readers in the light of a second dominant theme.

54. The verb *paschō*, "suffer," GK *4248*, occurs twelve times (2:19, 20, 21, 23; 3:14, 17, 18; 4:1 [twice], 15, 19; 5:10), with the verb *hypomenō*, "endure," GK *5702*, appearing twice in 2:20. The link between the saints who suffer and Christ, the paschal lamb who suffered, is immediate: in the epistolary opening the readers are linked to "the sprinkling by [Christ's] blood" (1:2; cf. also the reference to Christ as "a lamb without blemish or defect," 1:19).

55. See 1 Peter 1:11; 4:13; 5:1; 5:9. Significantly, the generic word for "distress, affliction," *thlipsis*, GK *2568*, does not occur in the letter. "Suffering" is conceived of in 1 Peter primarily in terms of *pathēma*, GK *4077*, and *paschō*.

56. The "testing" or "trial" (*peirasmos*, GK *4280*) they encounter (1:6; 4:12) is reminiscent of that which Christ endured.

For the purposes of thematic unity, a brief review is in order. Elliott (*A Home for the Homeless*, 48, 129) sees in 1 Peter "resident aliens," people who are sociologically marginalized. Schutter, 108, believes 1 Peter is a homily on righteous suffering, specifically a suffering that leads to glory. Michaels, 295, likewise sees the theme of humiliation leading to exaltation as a prominent motif in 1 Peter, with a basis in the OT, the gospel narratives, and elsewhere in Christian literature. Hillyer, 4, maintains that the emphasis of 1 Peter is hope, given the grace of God that enables the readers to overcome trial and tribulation; for Clowney, 24, as well, bearing witness to the grace of God is the letter's burden. Goppelt, 19, identifies the letter's central theme as living in a non-Christian society and overcoming hardship. Similarly, Krodel, 42, understands the epistle to communicate encouragement and consolation on the basis of divine grace to believers under duress. Mounce, 5, believes the letter is intended to extend hope to those enduring hardships as a result of their Christian commitment, while Donelson, 71, sees 1 Peter as a reflection of alienation due to Christians' moral rigor.[57] And Waltner, 18, holds that the burden of the letter is aimed at *how* the readers respond to their experience of suffering, with Christ as their model.

Attentive to the role of suffering in the epistle, T. Martin, 273, calls attention to the role played in 1 Peter by "the overarching and controlling metaphor of the Diaspora." From the opening verse to the letter's end, "images and concepts from the Jewish Diaspora dominate the material. The Diaspora provides the author with an image contributor that allows him to describe his readers' ontological status as well as the morality ensuing from that status." This leitmotif may be understood to have two purposes: (1) to encourage the readers to engage the course of life in terms of a journey, and (2) to admonish them not to grow faint in heart when they encounter trials and opposition to the faith, even grief—all of which arise in the context of their pagan social location.

In light of this dual function of the governing "Diaspora" metaphor, baptism may be understood to ground once for all the saints in those realities they have confessed—Christ's atonement and salvation, resurrection, ascension, and rule by session. In this sense, baptism "saves" (3:21), for in the context of suffering the saints are promised rescue by God, just as the water saved Noah.

The epistle's thematic structure proceeds from the readers' very identification in the greeting. The saints are simultaneously "chosen according to the foreknowledge of God the Father" and "strangers in the world, scattered . . ." (1:1–2). Thus the major blocks of material in 1 Peter are devoted to—and issue out of—these themes: the readers are (1) a called and holy people (1:13–2:10); (2) strangers and sojourners in this world (2:11–3:12); and (3) sufferers whose righteous suffering will ultimately be vindicated (3:13–5:11). Chester and Martin, 114, summarize the message of 1 Peter well: "1 Peter is designed to inculcate that our lives are not at the mercy of ruthless forces outside [our] control, and that the beneficent power called God has entered our human experience of suffering and distress—and triumphed."

8. BIBLIOGRAPHY

The following is a selective list of commentaries and monographs on 1 Peter available in English, confined for the most part to those referred to in the commentary (they will be referred to simply by the

---

57. The reflections of Donelson, 69–86, on suffering constitute one of the most thoughtful and nuanced discussions that can be found. See also Davids, 30–44.

author's name [and initials only when necessary to distinguish two authors of the same surname]). References to other resources will carry full bibliographic details at the first mention and thereafter a short title.

Achtemeier, P. J. *1 Peter*. Hermeneia. Minneapolis: Fortress, 1996.

Balch, D. L. "Household Codes." Pages 25–50 in *Greco-Roman Literature and the New Testament*. Edited by D. E. Aune. Society of Biblical Literature Sources for Biblical Study 21. Atlanta: Scholars, 1988.

———. *Let Wives Be Submissive: The Domestic Code in 1 Peter*. Society of Biblical Literature Monograph Series 26. Chico, Calif.: Scholars, 1981.

Barclay, W. *The Letters of James and Peter*. Daily Study Bible. 2d ed. Edinburgh: The Saint Andrew Press, 1958.

Beare, F. W. *The First Epistle of Peter*. 3d ed. Oxford: Basil Blackwell, 1970.

Best, E. *1 Peter*. New Century Bible. London: Oliphants, 1971.

Bigg, C. *A Critical and Exegetical Commentary on the Epistles of St. Peter and St. Jude*. International Critical Commentary. Edinburgh: T&T Clark, 1901.

Bray, G., ed. *James, 1–2 Peter, 1–3 John, Jude*. Ancient Christian Commentary on Scripture 11. Downers Grove, Ill.: InterVarsity, 2000.

Chester, A., and R. P. Martin. *The Theology of the Letters of James, Peter, and Jude*. New Testament Theology. Cambridge: Cambridge Univ. Press, 1994.

Clowney, E. P. *The Message of 1 Peter: The Way of the Cross*. Bible Speaks Today. Downers Grove, Ill.: InterVarsity, 1988.

Craddock, F. B. *First and Second Peter and Jude*. Westminster Bible Companion. Louisville, Ky.: Westminster John Knox, 1995.

Cranfield, C. E. B. *1 and 2 Peter and Jude*. Torch Bible Commentaries. London: SCM, 1960.

Cross, F. L. *1 Peter, A Paschal Liturgy*. 2d ed. London: Mowbray, 1957.

Dalton, W. J. *Christ's Proclamation to the Spirits: A Study of 1 Peter 3:18–4:16*. Analecta biblica 23. Rome: Pontifical Biblical Institute, 1965.

Davids, P. H. *The First Epistle of Peter*. New International Commentary on the New Testament. Grand Rapids: Eerdmans, 1990.

Donelson, L. R. *From Hebrews to Revelation: A Theological Introduction*. Louisville, Ky.: Westminster John Knox, 2001.

Doty, W. G. *Letters in Primitive Christianity*. Philadelphia: Fortress, 1973.

Elliott, J. H. *A Home for the Homeless: A Sociological Exegesis of 1 Peter, Its Situation and Strategy*. Philadelphia: Fortress, 1981.

———. "The Rehabilitation of an Exegetical Step-Child: 1 Peter in Recent Research." *Journal of Biblical Literature* 95 (1976): 243–54.

———. *1 Peter: A New Translation with Introduction and Commentary*. Anchor Bible 37B. New York: Doubleday, 2000.

Goppelt, L. *A Commentary on 1 Peter*. Edited by F. Hahn. Translated by J. E. Alsup. Grand Rapids: Eerdmans, 1993.

Grudem, W. *The First Epistle of Peter*. Tyndale New Testament Commentaries. Grand Rapids: Eerdmans, 1988.

Guthrie, D. *New Testament Introduction*. 4th ed. Downers Grove, Ill.: InterVarsity, 1990.

Hillyer, N. *1 and 2 Peter, Jude*. New International Biblical Commentary on the New Testament. Peabody, Mass.: Hendrickson, 1992.

Hort, F. J. A. *The First Epistle of St. Peter*. Edited by B. F. Dunelm. London: Macmillan, 1989.

Kelly, J. N. D. *A Commentary on the Epistles of Peter and Jude*. London: Adam and Charles Black, 1969.

Krodel, G. "1 Peter." Pages 42–83 in *The General Letters: Hebrews, James, 1–2 Peter, Jude, 1–2–3 John*. Rev. ed. Edited by G. Krodel. Minneapolis: Fortress, 1995.

Leaney, A. R. C. *The Letters of Peter and Jude*. Cambridge Bible Commentary. Cambridge: Cambridge Univ. Press, 1967.

Lohse, E. "Paraenesis and Kerygma in 1 Peter." Pages 37–59 in *Perspectives on First Peter*. Edited by C. H. Talbert. Macon, Ga.: Mercer Univ. Press, 1986.

Marshall, I. H. *1 Peter*. IVP New Testament Commentary. Downers Grove, Ill.: InterVarsity, 1991.

Martin, T. W. *Metaphor and Composition in 1 Peter*. Society of Biblical Literature Dissertation Series 131. Atlanta: Scholars Press, 1992.

Michaels, J. R. *1 Peter*. Word Biblical Commentary 49. Waco, Tex.: Word, 1988.

Mounce, R. H. *Born Anew to a Living Hope: A Commentary on 1 and 2 Peter*. Grand Rapids: Eerdmans, 1982.

Osiek, C., and D. L. Balch. *Families in the New Testament World*. Louisville, Ky.: Westminster John Knox, 1997.

Pearson, S. C. *The Christological and Rhetorical Properties of 1 Peter.* Studies in Bible and Early Christianity 45. Lewiston, N.Y.: Mellen, 2001.

Reicke, B. *The Epistles of James, Peter, and Jude.* Anchor Bible. Garden City, N.Y.: Doubleday, 1964.

Schutter, W. L. *Hermeneutic and Composition in 1 Peter.* Wissenschaftliche Untersuchungen zum Neuen Testament 2/30. Tübingen: Mohr, 1989.

Selwyn, E. G. *The First Epistle of St. Peter.* London: Macmillan, 1946.

Senior, D. *1 & 2 Peter.* New Testament Message 20. Wilmington, Del.: Glazier, 1980.

Talbert, C. H. "Once Again: The Plan of 1 Peter." Pages 141–51 in *Perspectives on First Peter.* Edited by C. H. Talbert. Macon, Ga.: Mercer Univ. Press, 1986.

Talbert, C. H., ed. *Perspectives on First Peter.* Macon, Ga.: Mercer Univ. Press, 1986.

Waltner, E., and J. D. Charles. *1 and 2 Peter, Jude.* Believers Church Bible Commentary. Scottdale, Pa.: Herald, 1999.

Wand, J. W. C. *The General Epistles of St. Peter and St. Jude.* Westminster Commentaries. London: Methuen, 1934.

9. OUTLINE

I. Letter Opening (1:1–2)

II. Letter Body (1:3–5:11)

  A. Theological Prolegomena on Christian Hope (1:3–12)

    1. The Basis for Hope (1:3–5)

    2. The Benefits of Hope (1:6–9)

    3. The Privilege of Hope (1:10–12)

  B. Christian Identity as the New Diaspora Community (1:13–2:10)

    1. The New Community's Lifestyle (1:13–2:3)

      a. The Lifestyle of Holiness (1:13–16)

      b. The Lifestyle of Reverence (1:17–21)

      c. The Lifestyle of Love (1:22–25)

      d. The Lifestyle of Transformation (2:1–3)

    2. The New Community's Identity (2:4–10)

      a. The Paradox of Election and Rejection (2:4–8)

      b. God's People as God's Chosen (2:9–10)

  C. Christian Witness as a Diaspora Community (2:11–3:12)

    1. The Necessity of Good Deeds (2:11–12)

    2. The Necessity of Ordered Relationships (2:13–3:12)

      a. A Christian View of Authority (2:13–17)

      b. A Christian View of Unjust Treatment (2:18–25)

      c. A Christian View of Marriage (3:1–7)

      d. A Christian Response to Unjust Treatment (3:8–12)

  D. Christian Suffering Due to Righteous Living (3:13–5:11)

    1. A Christian Perspective on Suffering (3:13–4:6)

      a. Preparing a Christian Response to Suffering (3:13–17)

      b. Christ's Suffering and Vindication (3:18–22)

      c. Christ's Example as Motivation for Living (4:1–6)

    2. Eschatology and Christian Ethics (4:7–19)

      a. Eschatology and Christian Relationships (4:7–11)

      b. Eschatology and Christian Suffering (4:12–19)

    3. Christian Leadership in the New Diaspora Community (5:1–11)

      a. Challenge to the Elders (5:1–4)

      b. Challenge to the Young Men (5:5a)

      c. Challenge to All (5:5b–9)

      d. Benediction and Doxology (5:10–11)

III. Letter Closing (5:12–14)

  A. Acknowledgment of Silvanus's Assistance (5:12a)

  B. Purpose of the Letter (5:12b)

  C. Greetings (5:13–14)

Text and Exposition

I. LETTER OPENING (1:1–2)

¹Peter, an apostle of Jesus Christ,

To God's elect, strangers in the world, scattered throughout Pontus, Galatia, Cappadocia, Asia and Bithynia, ²who have been chosen according to the foreknowledge of God the Father, through the sanctifying work of the Spirit, for obedience to Jesus Christ and sprinkling by his blood:

Grace and peace be yours in abundance.

COMMENTARY

1 Peter begins with the standard private epistolary form of sender-recipient-greeting that characterizes letters of antiquity. The writer identifies himself as "Peter, an apostle of Jesus Christ." Here he uses his nickname ("Blessed are you, Simon son of Jonah," Mt 16:17; "You are Simon son of Jonah. You will be called Cephas [which, when translated, is Peter]," Jn 1:42) by which the NT writers typically identify him. As "an apostle of Jesus Christ" he joins the inner circle of those providentially called and "sent out" (*apostellō*, GK *690*) to witness to the life, death, resurrection, and lordship of Jesus Christ.

Writing as an apostle, then, Peter addresses his intended readers with inherent authority; his letter is therefore to be received as wholly inspired and authoritative. But this authority is also one that has been tried and tempered by deep maturity. Gone is the impetuous, impulsive nature of earlier years. Moreover, the Peter who presently writes is a "fellow elder" and "witness of Christ's sufferings" (5:1), a man of deepened humility (hence the call to a humble attitude in

5:5–6). Finally, the writer conveys the sense of a father figure, one who views Mark as a "son" (5:13).

The recipients of the letter are described in a twofold manner: they are "dispersed people" or "exiles" (NIV, "strangers . . . scattered"; *diaspora*, GK *1402*, from which we derive the noun "Diaspora"; for the Christian community elsewhere in the NT as a new Diaspora, see Heb 13:14 and Php 3:20), and they are "elect" (*eklektos*, GK *1723*, from *eklegomai*, GK *1721*). These two designations inform the very substructure of the epistle, from which the major themes derive and in which 1 Peter coheres. As exiles or sojourners, the readers are said to be scattered in various provinces of Asia Minor. Five provinces are named: Pontus, Galatia, Cappadocia, Asia, and Bithynia. Together these territories constitute all of Asia Minor (present-day Turkey) north of the Taurus mountain range. The province of Asia, bordering the Aegean Sea, included the cities of the seven churches mentioned in Revelation. Furthermore, Paul had ministered in several of these regions; among those noted by Luke, for example, is southern Galatia (Ac 16:1–5). The order in which the provinces are listed is largely assumed to be the route traveled by the messenger in the delivery of this circular or encyclical letter.

But precisely who are these "sojourners"? Is the language of "Diaspora" to be interpreted literally or metaphorically? And why are the readers scattered or dispersed? An intriguing answer has been put forth by J. H. Elliott in his work *A Home for the Homeless*, which has animated 1 Peter commentary for the last two decades. Elliott interprets the allusion to *parepidēmoi* (GK *4215*; cf. *TDNT* 2:64–65) in 1:1 and 2:11 and *paroikoi* (GK *4230*; cf. *TDNT* 5:841–53) in 2:11 (*paroikia* in 1:17) literally, understanding the readers to be "resident aliens," i.e., those who have been marginalized in a socially and politically hostile environment.

While the merits of Elliott's argument have already been considered in section 3 of the introduction, it should be observed that his interpretive rubric is simultaneously a help and a hindrance. Elliott's attentiveness to the sociological implications of a document such as 1 Peter provides fresh insights into the epistle that have invigorated the present generation of commentators. At the same time, he does not take into sufficient account the hermeneutical method employed by virtually all the NT writers themselves, which is to take language, images, concepts, and metaphors that applied to the covenantal people of Israel—the chosen—and apply them to the new covenant community—the church. Indeed, Jesus predicted that the inheritance of Israel would be taken from them and given to others (Mt 21:41; Mk 12:9; Lk 20:16), thereby establishing the Christian community as the chosen, the true Israel of God. Not insignificantly, this is one of the important subthemes of 1 Peter.

From the perspective of the new covenant, the real "Diaspora" is not the Jewish people; it is the community of Christian saints scattered throughout the world. These are "exiles" who are called to be *in*

but not *of* this world. Rightly understood, exile is not withdrawal or isolation; rather, it is the awareness that we are not *fully* at home, given the fact that our allegiance is to something beyond this world. That allegiance is our touchstone and guide for conduct.

2 The theme of exile and sojourning, i.e., Diaspora, is incomplete, however, unless it is tethered to another familiar theme in the history of the Jewish people—one that reflects transcendence. The saints are not merely exiles; they are also (and more importantly) the elect of God (*eklektoi*), chosen by God as his own people (also 2:9; cf. Dt 4:37; 7:8; 10:15; 1Ch 16:13; Pss 33:12; 105:6; Isa 45:4; Am 3:2). The "choosing" of the saints results from the predetermination of the divine purpose; God moves all things toward a goal, a *telos* (GK *5465*, 1:9). Special status as well as special responsibilities inhere in the reality of divine election. In order for the readers of 1 Peter to fulfill their responsibilities—to persevere in the face of adversity and cultural hostility—they must be anchored in an awareness that they are the elect of God, the recipients of noteworthy grace (1:2; 5:12). In the words of Waltner, 26, "More significant than their ethnic background, social status or place of residence is their relationship to God."

Exploiting the OT language of election, Peter calls his readers to ethical transformation by means of a Trinitarian formula. He reminds them that they are called "according to the foreknowledge of God the Father," that this is done "through the sanctifying work of the Spirit," and that such has as its goal "obedience to Jesus Christ and sprinkling by his blood." The saints' election is rooted in the mystery of divine foreknowledge (*prognōsis*, GK *4590*) and thus in God's eternal purpose (Ac 2:23; Ro 8:29–30; 11:2; Eph 1:4–6, 11–14; 2Th 2:13). In times that try one's faith, an awareness of this mysterious reality is reassuring.

The church, then, is no mere voluntary association of like-minded individuals; nor does its origin lie in the will of the flesh. It owes its very being to the eternal counsel of God the Father, who creates and sustains his own creation. God's fatherhood in 1 Peter is highly qualified: the Father is sovereign (1:2), merciful (1:3; 2:10), creative (1:3; 2:23), holy (1:15–16), impartial (1:17), just (2:23), sustaining (2:23), patient (3:20), faithful (4:19), and gracious (4:10; 5:12).

The second part of the Trinitarian formula calls attention to the sanctifying work of the Holy Spirit. Among other things, 1 Peter is an emphatic call to be holy, to be set apart (1:14–16; 2:9) in the world. This calling, it goes without saying, is critical both to Christian self-understanding and Christian morality. The divine command "Be holy, for I am holy" (1:16; cf. Lev 11:44; 19:2) is fulfillable only to the extent that believers appropriate and submit to the Spirit's dynamic. It is the Spirit who is the operative agent in conforming the believer to the image of Christ, for he awakens within the desire for holiness, brings conviction of impediments to holiness, supplies empowerment to attain holiness, and gives assurance that God is, in fact, making us holy.

The third and christological affirmation within the Trinitarian formula underscores God's purpose revealed through the Spirit: *obedience to Jesus*. The metaphor of "sprinkling by blood," borrowed from Israel's cultic life, bespeaks cleansing and consecration. It is fitting for the readers to be reminded that Jesus' blood, whether in the cultic ritual of the OT or the once-for-all sacrifice that ratifies the NT, is "precious" (1:19), i.e., costly in terms of the price of redemption. Through the sacrifice of Christ, these two realities are actualized in the believer's life: sins have been cleansed and forgiven, and one is pledged to a life of obedience. Hillyer, 26, summarizes the work of the triune God in the believer's life: "the Father purposes; the Spirit sanctifies; [and] the Son brings believers into a right relationship with himself."

The wish extended to the recipients of 1 Peter, following the theologically rich address, is the standard Christian formula appearing in all the Pauline epistles (Ro 1:7; 1Co 1:3; 2Co 1:2; Gal 1:3; Eph 1:2; Php 1:2; Col 1:2; 1Th 1:1; 2Th 1:2; 1Ti 1:2 [with "mercy" added]; 2Ti 1:2 [with "mercy" added]; Tit 1:4; and Phm 3), as well as in 2 Peter and 2 John (*1 Clem.* has the same salutation as 1 Peter: *charis hymin kai eirēnē plēthyntheiē*). Peter wishes them "grace and peace" and that both be theirs "in abundance" (*plēthynō*, GK *4437*, also in 2Pe 1:2; Jude 2). The tandem of grace and peace in all likelihood is an echo of early Christian worship and derives from Jewish liturgy, a practice rooted in the priestly blessing recorded in Numbers 6:24–26: "The LORD . . . be gracious to you; . . . and give you peace."

NOTES

1 To be an apostle in the narrow, restricted sense, according to Peter, was to be "one of the men who have been with us the whole time the Lord Jesus went in and out among us" (Ac 1:21). Moreover, the apostolic office required being "a witness with us of his resurrection" (Ac 1:22). It is this narrow scope of high privilege that the apostles themselves rehearsed as they met in the upper room to find a replacement for Judas Iscariot (Ac 1:12–26). In witnessing to Christ's ministry, death, and resurrection, the apostles by virtue of their authority were the guarantors of the Christian (i.e., apostolic) tradition that would be passed on to others. For this reason, along with the prophets, the apostles are described in the NT as the "foundation" of the church, "with Christ Jesus himself as the chief cornerstone" (Eph 2:20).

Not all the NT writers are "apostolic" in the technical sense. And to a certain extent, the one individual who plays the greatest role in developing Christian theology in the early church—Paul, the "apostle to the Gentiles"—did not meet this technical requirement until his personal encounter with the risen Lord on the Damascus Road (Ac 9). Therefore, when Paul states in one of his letters, "I am the least of the apostles" (1Co 15:9), this is not merely rhetorical flourish. Paul is, in fact, keenly aware that he was not "one of the men" who "went in and out among us." Only through sovereign appointment by the Lord himself was Paul made an apostle, and the qualifying element was being a witness to the resurrected Christ—hence his rhetorical question to the Corinthians (some of whom were questioning his authority), "Have I not seen Jesus our Lord?" (1Co 9:1).

2 On the Jewish practice of doxology and benediction inherited by the early church, see R. Deichgräber, *Gotteshymnus und Christushymnus in der frühen Christenheit* (SUNT 5; Göttingen: Vandenhoeck & Ruprecht, 1967).

II. LETTER BODY (1:3–5:11)

A. Theological Prolegomena on Christian Hope (1:3–12)

1. Basis for Hope (1:3–5)

³Praise be to the God and Father of our Lord Jesus Christ! In his great mercy he has given us new birth into a living hope through the resurrection of Jesus Christ from the dead, ⁴and into an inheritance that can never perish, spoil or fade–kept in heaven for you, ⁵who through faith are shielded by God's power until the coming of the salvation that is ready to be revealed in the last time.

COMMENTARY

3–4 Hymnic praise to God begins the writer's description of the grounds for Christian hope. This hymn of praise is identical to that utilized by Paul in 2 Corinthians 1:13 and Ephesians 1:13 and was likely a pattern of earliest Christian confession (see Ro 10:9; 1Co 12:3; and Php 2:11). The ground for Christian hope is mercy—indeed, "great mercy" (*poly eleos*) that results in the person's new birth spiritually (cf. Tit 3:5 and Eph 2:4–5). The assurance for Christian hope is rooted in "the resurrection of Jesus Christ from the dead." A realization of the basis of

their hope will affect both how the saints embrace the suffering that comes their way and their standard of conduct before a watching world.

Hope is integral to the message of 1 Peter (1:3, 13, 21; 3:15). In a climate of hostility and spiritual opposition, the sojourner is inclined to despair and will not persevere. The salvation that infuses the believer with hope is not only evidenced by the new birth that lies in the past; it is also an inheritance (*klēronomia*, GK *3100*) that is future in scope—an inheritance that is "reserved" (NIV, "kept"; *tēreō*, GK *5498*) in heaven, imperishable, undefiled, and unfading in nature. "Reservation"/"preservation" is an important concept in the Petrine epistles (1Pe 1:4; 3:19 [*phylakē*, GK *5871*]; 4:19 [implied]; 2Pe 2:4–5 [*phylassō*], 9, 17; 3:7) and strengthens the readers' future-orientation. It is important to be future-oriented when sojourning, for in this world there will be misunderstanding, slander, and persecution for one's faith. Hence Peter can speak of a "living hope" that the believer possesses.

At the heart of the Christian gospel is "the resurrection of Jesus Christ." This event establishes, historically and for all time, the validity of both the Christian experience—"it [baptism] saves you by the resurrection of Jesus Christ" (3:21)—and the authority of Christian truth-claims. We have already noted that being a witness to the resurrection was requisite for apostolic authority. In the same way it constitutes the grounds for ongoing witness by the church in the world (3:15): the believer, on being tested and examined, is admonished toward a particular mind-set, namely, "always be prepared to give an answer [*apologia*, GK *665*] . . . for the hope that you have." And what is the basis for this hope? It is the fact that Jesus has been raised from the dead and now sits "at God's right hand, with angels, authorities and powers in submission to him" (3:22). If even death is subject to Christ, the Christian lives with hope and has nothing to fear ("Do not fear what they fear [i.e., those who insult you]; do not be frightened" [3:14]).

Thus the resurrection not only validates Christian experience and proclamation, it is also assur-

ance of the inheritance that lies in the future—an assurance the writer will reiterate (3:9; 4:13; 5:4). Michaels, 21, and others note the rhetorical effect created by the alliteration of the three terms *aphthartos* (GK *915*), *amiantos* (GK *299*), and *amarantos* (GK *278*), used in succession to describe this inheritance: it is free from death, impurity, and decay. What is more, it is an inheritance that is being "kept [*tēreō*] in heaven." No one can remove, undermine, or destroy this promise; it is in safe custody.

5 Salvation, whether in its past, present, or future manifestation, is a core Petrine concept (*sōzō*, GK *5392*, 3:21; 4:18; *diasōzō*, GK *1407*, 3:20; *sōteria*, GK *5401*, 1:5, 9–10; 2:2). While it entails the individual, it does not emphasize the individual over the community. The salvation that comes from God, furthermore, has both temporal as well as eschatological dimensions.

This multi-perspectival view of salvation and inheritance, it should be noted, fits the theme of sojourning and pilgrimage. In the OT, the chief means of typologizing the believer's inheritance was Canaan, the promised possession (e.g., Lev 20:24; Dt 15:4; 19:10; 20:15), though the Lord himself is the occasional object of such language (e.g., Dt 10:9; Pss 16:5; 73:26). The promised "land" only had meaning, however, against the background of Israel's wandering in the desert and exile in Babylon. Salvation for Israel was past (i.e., deliverance from Egyptian bondage), present (in its "exilic wandering"), and future (blessings predicated on obedience to divine commands), and it retains these multiple dimensions in the new covenant for the chosen people of God.

NOTES

3 The parallels between the early Christian emphasis on "new birth" and that contained in mystery religions are fascinating, especially given the fact that 1 Peter is addressed to Christians scattered throughout Asia Minor, where mystery cults proliferated. Moreover, the verb ἐποπτεύω, *epopteuō* (GK *2227*, "to be a witness"), and its nominal form ἐπόπτης, *epoptēs* (GK *2228*), appearing in the NT only in Petrine literature (1Pe 2:12; 3:2; 2Pe 1:16), are employed in a technical sense to describe those individuals who have been initiated into the mystery rituals (*TDNT* 5:374). Nevertheless, resemblances in 1 Peter remain at the level of speculation.

5 On the nature of salvation, Waltner, 37, writes, "Regeneration is thus perceived as initiation into salvation; the spiritual growth that follows moves them toward its fullness," i.e., the Petrine understanding of salvation is both "process and possession." It is already experienced (1:22–23; 3:21), and it is yet to be revealed (1:5, 13; 4:13; 5:4). The expression "in the last time" mirrors the eschatological dimension of salvation that is foundational to the world of NT thought. Jewish theology divided time into the present age—an age dominated by evil powers—and the age to come. In between lay the "last days," the "day of the Lord," and divine judgment. The early Christians clearly believed they were already living in the last time, and not infrequently warnings were attached to this concept (e.g., 2Th 2:1–2; 2Ti 3:1; 1Jn 2:18; Jude 18). Nevertheless, this notion is expanded somewhat through divine revelation (e.g., Ac 2:17; Heb 1:2), so that the early church must persevere and wrestle with the "already/not yet" eschatological tension and its attendant implications. This inherent ambiguity is lodged in Jesus' parables, which stress both *imminence* and *occupying*.

2. Benefits of Hope (1:6–9)

⁶In this you greatly rejoice, though now for a little while you may have had to suffer grief in all kinds of trials. ⁷These have come so that your faith–of greater worth than gold, which perishes even though refined by fire–may be proved genuine and may result in praise, glory and honor when Jesus Christ is revealed. ⁸Though you have not seen him, you love him; and even though you do not see him now, you believe in him and are filled with an inexpressible and glorious joy, ⁹for you are receiving the goal of your faith, the salvation of your souls.

COMMENTARY

6–7 From his reiteration of the basis for Christian hope Peter moves to its effects in the believer's experience, hereby mirroring the readers' actual situation. The saints are able to "greatly rejoice" (*agalliazō*, GK *22*, also in 1:8; 4:13; *chairō*, GK *5897*, is used only in 4:13; cf. Jude 24), despite the fact that it has been "necessary" to "suffer grief" in the context of "various trials" (cf. Ac 5:41). Peter does not offer any description of the precise nature of those trials. Rather, his emphasis is twofold: that they are diverse and varied (*poikilos*, GK *4476*), giving the impression of being highly generic in nature, and that they are to be expected (based on the *ei deon* ["it is of necessity"] construction). The suffering and trials are neither ascribed directly to God nor viewed as detrimental to one's faith. And yet the language of trial being employed here makes it clear that the writer is not minimizing the readers' experience of hardship; theirs is an agonizing ordeal.

The present trials, nevertheless, are said to serve a purpose (as expressed through the *hina* clause), namely, "so that the genuineness of your faith [*hina to dokimion hymōn tēs pisteōs*] . . . may be proved . . . ." The suffering and trials the readers currently encounter are compared to the process of metal refinement ("of greater worth than gold, which perishes"). Through the refining process the value of the object increases, since the object becomes purer, more genuine.

And so it is with a believer's faith. Having gone through sundry trials, the saints are encouraged to recognize the purifying effect that these have had on their faith. Indeed, purification is an important subtheme that laces its way throughout the epistle—1:2 (sprinkling as a medium); 1:7 (faith as refined by fire); 1:15 (holiness as imperative); 1:19 (Christ as without blemish); 1:22 (obedience as a medium); 2:1 (exhortation to "rid yourselves"); 2:2 (milk as pure); 3:2 (purity and reverence); 3:4 (genuine beauty as an inner quality); 3:16 (keeping a clear conscience); and 3:21 (baptism as symbolic of cleansing). It is impossible, humanly speaking, to perceive the divine intention in the midst of refinement itself; for this reason, the believer needs perspective and reassurance that the testing lasts "now for a little while" (v.6). The refinement must be understood as both temporal and temporary.

In sum, the result of their testing—a result that is enduring, indeed eternal—is twofold: (1) one's faith is stronger and more valuable, and (2) the believer garners "praise, glory and honor" at the appearance (*apokalypsis*, GK *637*, lit., the "unveiling") of Jesus Christ. The saints are thus vindicated and rewarded in Christ's return to take his own.

But such endurance, though rigorous and disciplined, does not depend on self-effort. Not insignificantly, the same adjective that is used to describe trials, *poikilos* ("all kinds of"), also modifies the grace of God later in the epistle (4:10, "various forms"). Our afflictions may be varied, but so is the nature of divine grace. For every trial there stands accessible to the believer an appropriate and corresponding grace (a promise also reiterated by Paul, 1Co 10:13). No trial exists without an available source of the grace of God.

8-9 Based on the material that follows, the character of the trials confronting the readers appears to be related to hostility that issues out of the tension between culture and Christian faith. The message of 1 Peter is consonant with that of the entire NT: believers are to rejoice when they are persecuted for their faith insofar as this persecution arises out of their identification with "the name of Christ" (4:14; cf. Mt 5:11–12; Lk 6:22–23; Jn 15:18–25; Ac 5:40–42; Ro 8:18, 35–39; 2Co 6:4–10; 1Th 1:6; 2Th 3:12; Heb 10:32–39). On the eve of his crucifixion, Jesus accents this reality with sobering clarity: "If the world hates you, keep in mind that it hated me first. If you belonged to the world, it would love you as its own. As it is, you do not belong to the world, but I have chosen you out of the world. That is why the world hates you. Remember the words I spoke to you: 'No servant is greater than his master.' If they persecuted me, they will persecute you also" (Jn 15:18–20).

It is difficult not to see in 1:8–9 the writer's personal reflections on being an apostle. Peter the apostle was privileged to have been called and commissioned by the Lord Jesus (Mt 16:13–20; Jn 1:40–42; Ac 10:39). Indeed, kings and prophets would have wished to witness what Peter and the apostles witnessed, yet did not (Mt 13:16–17; Lk 10:23–24; Heb 1:1–2). In time the realization of this commissioning would grow, both in terms of privilege and responsibility for shepherding God's flock (Ac 1:15–26; Eph 2:20; 4:11–16); hence the language of shepherding in 1 Peter is significant: "For you were like sheep going astray, but now you have returned to the Shepherd and Overseer of your souls" (2:25); "Be shepherds of God's flock that is under your care, serving as overseers" (5:2); "And when the Chief Shepherd appears, you will receive the crown of glory that will never fade away" (5:4); "Your enemy the devil prowls around like a roaring lion, looking for someone to devour" (5:8).

The writer of 1 Peter is not the impetuous hot-head he once was. He has been tempered and seasoned by the sufferings that accompany both "the name" (5:1; 4:14) and the apostolic office (1Co 4:9–13; 2Co 6:4–10). But as an apostle he commends the readers who believe—and suffer—even though they have not had the privilege of personal contact with the Lord Jesus. This lack of physical contact is not, however, the source of faith. The message of the NT is this: "we live by faith, not by sight" (2Co 5:7), for faith is "being sure of what we hope for and certain of what we do not see" (Heb 11:1). Jesus himself was adamant about this very point: "Blessed are those who have not seen and yet have believed" (Jn 20:29). And yet, despite never having seen Christ, the saints are intimately united with him. The relationship, as depicted in 1 Peter, is one of love and radiant, inexpressible joy.

The result, goal, or destiny (telos) of such faith—a faith that is established (cf. 5:10) though without sight—is "the salvation of your souls." The modern reader must resist the temptation to interpret "soul" in the narrower sense of psychē, or fallen nature. Rather, as Waltner, 39–40, has well emphasized, salvation in 1 Peter concerns the total person, as confirmed by its use in 2:11 and the allusion to salvation in 3:20. Furthermore, the living hope that is a subtheme of 1 Peter is for the whole person, confirmed by and anchored in Christ's resurrection (1:3; 3:18).

NOTES

6–9 Occurring frequently in Scripture (e.g., 1Ch 29:17; Job 14:4; 18:15; 22:23–25; 23:10; 31:6; Pss 26:2; 119:27; 139:23; Pr 8:10; 17:3; 27:21; Jer 9:7; Zec 13:9; Mal 3:3; Ro 5:3–5; 2Co 4:17; Jas 1:2–3; Rev 2:18; 3:18), the refinement imagery on display in these verses is understandably conspicuous in the book of Job, which features a man for whom the process of refinement has taken agonizing turns (see esp. 22:23, 25; 23:10; 28:15; 31:6).

7 One can withstand pain, hardship, and deprivation if there is a goal—and subsequent motivation—impelling one onward. Such is poignantly demonstrated by the athlete, who will endure (at least, to the average person) indescribable hardship—both physically and psychologically—for the sake of the prize, the reward, the crown, the trophy. For this reason, the readers are reminded of the goal of persevering faith and the reward that awaits: that it "result in praise, glory and honor when Jesus Christ is revealed." The verb "result," εὑρίσκω, heuriskō (GK 2351), hints at judgment, i.e., a day of moral reckoning, and therefore gives an early hint in the letter of vindication for the righteous. (Note Paul's use of the athletic metaphor in 1 Corinthians 9:24–27, where he speaks of beating his body for the sake of the prize that lies ahead; cf. also Ac 20:24; Gal 2:2; Php 2:16; 3:14; 1Ti 1:18; 2Ti 2:5; 4:7. For the apostle, the athletic metaphor has crucial parallels to Christian living, without an understanding of which the believer risks disqualification.)

REFLECTIONS

In both the introductory remarks to this commentary and the commentary itself, the position has been taken that 1 Peter does not yet mirror persecution of an official (i.e., state-induced) character but rather is mirroring what much of the NT promises: "everyone who wants to live a godly life in Christ Jesus will be persecuted" (2Ti 3:12). This position needs some qualification. There are two perspectives to be avoided as we seek to interpret suffering in 1 Peter. One is the viewpoint that minimizes the specific or local variety of trial facing the readers. As already noted, the imperial cult varied greatly in strength and allegiance throughout Asia Minor. Thus, some of the congregations in the five provinces listed in 1:1 may have had to endure persecution of a particularly intense degree, whereas others may not. Moreover, it is quite probable that Peter is writing on the eve of an outbreak of persecution in Rome and thus is acutely sensitive to the sufferings of Christians elsewhere throughout the empire. The other viewpoint to be avoided is one that only sees in 1 Peter state-sanctioned persecution such as is displayed in Revelation. This reading is inclined to minimize the reality of the normal, day-to-day hostility with which early Christians throughout the world (5:9) had to deal. Either of these ill-advised readings has the potential to rob the letter of its value and relevance to contemporary Christians.

3. The Privilege of Hope (1:10–12)

¹⁰Concerning this salvation, the prophets, who spoke of the grace that was to come to you, searched intently and with the greatest care, ¹¹trying to find out the time and circumstances to which the Spirit of Christ in them was pointing when he predicted the sufferings of Christ and the glories that would follow. ¹²It was revealed to them that they were not serving themselves but you, when they spoke of the things that have now been told you by those who have preached the gospel to you by the Holy Spirit sent from heaven. Even angels long to look into these things.

COMMENTARY

10–11 An additional reason for rejoicing is suggested by the writer besides reflecting on the basis and benefits of Christian hope. Gratitude for the high privilege of identification with Christ will serve as a healthy antidote to the discouragement or despondency that might be the inclination of those encountering persistent trials. The readers are reminded of the progressive nature of divine revelation and salvation—a salvation that was typologized and previewed in the old covenant and is now fully realized in Christ. In the old scheme, the prophets of God spoke under the inspiration of the Spirit and even predicted in various ways the coming and passion (cf. Lk 24:25–27) of the Messiah. They were granted partial, incomplete insight into the purposes of God. By contrast, every saint who partakes of the new covenant is far better off by virtue of possessing greater revelation than the prophets. Such is the meaning of Jesus' astounding commendation of John the Baptist's ministry (Mt 11:11, 13). This Petrine

understanding of OT revelation and the divine economy is vividly on display in the apostle's sermon at
Pentecost (Ac 2:14–36), in which the present is
explained solely in terms of prophetic speech from
the past. Primary sources cited in this sermon are Joel
and Davidic psalms (cf. also Ro 15:4; Heb 1:1–2).

Two nuances in this intriguing passage invite our
consideration. One is the writer's indication,
revealed in the language of vv. 10–11, that much
speculation among Jews attended the advent of the
messianic age—its time, its nature, its manner, and
its embodiment. This certainly squares with the picture we find in the Gospels, particularly in John 1,
where numerous messianic notions are mirrored.
The second concerns Peter's description of the
object of the prophetic inquiry. The prophets are
said to have been guided by the Spirit in a twofold
direction: they foretold Messiah's "sufferings" as well
as his "glories that would follow." Mention of both
is important because of the writer's identification
with his readership. Christ is presented in 1 Peter as
a model, and his example beckons the readers in
two fundamental ways: (1) he suffered, *like them*
(1:18–19; 2:21–24), and thus "entrusted himself to
him who judges justly" (2:23); and (2) he was vindicated, *like they will be*, having been raised and now
exalted "at God's right hand—with angels, authorities and powers in submission to him" (3:22).

12 The particular revelation of the old covenant,
incomplete as it was, is said by Peter to have foreseen
both aspects of Christ's ministry—suffering and
glorification. From the standpoint of the sufferer,
this is good news and a necessary consolation—
suffering is not an end in itself; it leads to ultimate
vindication ("glory") over one's enemies. Moreover,
the reader should take courage all the more to know
that the prophets, who indicated these two aspects
of divine purpose, "were not serving themselves but
you." And this is precisely the message the readers
have received from those "who have preached the
gospel to you by the Holy Spirit sent from heaven,"
of which Pentecost was a dramatic demonstration.

But Peter does not end with the prophets.
As though to pique the readers' fascination (and
gratitude) further, he adds somewhat cryptically that
"even angels long to look into these things," i.e., the
nature and embodiment of salvation to which only
humans have been made privy. The double verb used
to described angelic inquiry, *epithymeō* ("to long,"
GK *2121*) and *parakypsai* ("to lean the head side-
ways," GK *4160*) is intended to accent the sense of
curiosity and fascination. Since this remark about
angels occurs only in passing, it resists any attempt on
the part of the reader to develop a full-blown
"Petrine angelology." The point of emphasis is simply
that angels, who as part of creation are limited in
knowledge and authority (cf. also a similar statement
in Heb 2:16), are curious about salvation. Such agrees
with the Pauline statement that the "manifold wisdom of God" was "made known to the rulers and
authorities in the heavenly realms" (Eph 3:10; cf.
1Co 6:3). Salvation, then, is a high privilege that
humans alone can appreciate, especially if even angels
themselves are denied personal understanding of the
crucial event of salvation history—as well as its effects
in the believer's life.

NOTES

10–11 While the role of the OT prophets was both to "forthtell" and foretell, Kelly's caution, 59, has
some merit: "In their historical setting the prophets were not so much concerned to peer into the future
as to announce God's verdict on the world in which they lived." Indeed, salvation for the prophets was first
and foremost *this-worldly*: geopolitical events inevitably were a mirror of divine activity in the world.

12 The fact that the remark by the writer that the angelic realm "longs to look into" the things of salvation is made in passing is not to say that the angelic realm is unimportant. Rather, it is to emphasize that the angels are limited in knowledge and authority. Indeed, Petrine angelology (1:12; 3:18–22; cf. 2Pe 2:4) confirms the utter glory and purposes of God. Kelly, 63, sees in 1:12 a parallel to *1 Enoch* 9:1, which depicts four archangels looking down from heaven at events on earth. Given the quasi-Enoch imagery in 3:18–22 (see commentary), this is plausible.

B. Christian Identity as the New Diaspora Community (1:13–2:10)

1. The New Community's Lifestyle (1:13–2:3)

a. The Lifestyle of Holiness (1:13–16)

OVERVIEW

Having established a theologically rich basis for faith and hope—entities that are predicated on God's revelation through Christ—the writer is now ready ("Therefore . . .") to exhort his readers on how to conduct themselves. They are simultaneously *elected* by God and *rejected* by the world, and thus must come to terms, ethically speaking, with their identity as the new, universalized "Diaspora." High privilege entails unique responsibilities that will alienate. In this light, how are they to conduct themselves? How are they to resolve the tension of being *in* the world but not *of* it? How are they to reconcile the dual responsibilities of earthly *and* heavenly citizenship? And by what qualities will the distinctly Christian ethic be characterized?

The Christian lifestyle, according to Peter, takes on a conspicuous shape: it will be mentally prepared, self-controlled, anchored in divine grace, obedient and not conforming to the desires associated with the former life, and, most important, exhibiting of the divine character of holiness. In a word, it will be countercultural. Each of the aforementioned traits is organically related to the others. Each has a notable ethical quality about it.

> ¹³Therefore, prepare your minds for action; be self-controlled; set your hope fully on the grace to be given you when Jesus Christ is revealed. ¹⁴As obedient children, do not conform to the evil desires you had when you lived in ignorance. ¹⁵But just as he who called you is holy, so be holy in all you do; ¹⁶for it is written: "Be holy, because I am holy."

COMMENTARY

13 The first attitude comes to vivid expression in the Greek by means of a metaphor—literally, "Gird up your mind"—that connotes a sense of readiness or alertness. It does so by calling to mind a person tightening a garment or robe with a belt around the waist for maximum freedom of movement, so as not to be hindered, impeded, or distracted in the task (thus Barclay, 183: to roll up one's sleeves or take off one's jacket). The idea being conveyed is the need to be prepared for *whatever* may come.

The second disposition called for is to be sober-minded or self-controlled. The verb used here, *nēphō* (GK *3768*), also occurs in 4:7, where it is applied to prayer, and in 5:8, where alertness to the wiles of the devil is enjoined. Mental alertness will lead to sobriety and a disciplined life. This stands in stark contrast, it goes without saying, to surrounding society, which is given to excess, carnality, indiscretion, and faddishness. Not surprisingly, the Christian community is called again and again in the NT to exhibit the virtue of self-discipline (e.g., 1Th 5:6; 2Ti 1:7; Tit 1:8; 2Pe 1:5); indeed, as a character trait it is virtually synonymous with wisdom (e.g., Ps 94:12; Pr 3:11; 5:12, 23; 12:1; cf. Heb 12:11). It is the sign that one is under the control and inspiration of another master when one lives the disciplined life.

The imperative that follows is to "set your hope fully [*teleiōs*, GK *5458*, lit., "perfectly" or "absolutely"] on the grace to be given you when Jesus Christ is revealed." Herein the readers are reminded that ethics is eschatologically motivated, i.e., that it has one eye on the future so as not to get bogged down in the present. Hope is rooted in one's expectation of future reward; therefore, one can persevere and live a prepared, disciplined life. To endure hardship or rigor is to be motivated by future anticipations; both the musician and the athlete serve to demonstrate an awareness of this important connection. But 1 Peter simultaneously assures the reader that the disciplined life does not consist merely of sheer willpower, such as the Stoic moralist might envision. Rather, the Christian draws from the wellspring of divine grace. Whereas secular ethics is self-originating and self-directed, Christian ethics is rooted in a grace-filled conception of living. The Christian's

confidence lies not in his or her ability to be self-sufficient; it is tethered to grace, which is constant and available, regardless of the situation (cf. 1Co 10:13).

14 Peter further exhorts his readers, as "obedient children," not to conform (*syschēmatizomai*, GK *5372*, from which we derive "schema," or "pattern") to former desires (*epithymia*, GK *2123*, appearing frequently in the Petrine epistles; also 2:11; 4:2, 3; 2Pe 1:4; 2:10,18; 3:3) that typified the previous life of "ignorance." Obedience is an important Petrine concept. It is obedience to Jesus that is God's purpose (1:2); obedience to the truth results in purification (1:22); and Sarah's obedience to Abraham is considered paradigmatic for godly women (3:6). To take obedience seriously, according to 1 Peter, is to resist conformity to the world (cf. Ro 12:1–2), which characterizes life *before* the new birth. It is both the privilege and responsibility of the Christian to live a life that is qualitatively different.

15–16 If nonconformity expresses the negative duty of obedience, the positive side is to emulate the very Lord himself, who is moral perfection; for "just as he who called you is holy, so be holy in all you do." To this end, scriptural admonition is cited from the Torah: "Be holy, because I am holy" (Lev 11:44, 45). The reader's *conduct* (*anastrophē*, GK *419*, occurring six times in the letter, with the verbal form appearing once) is of utmost importance to Peter. To be holy is to be set apart or consecrated *to* something, and that something is the Lord himself. Just as there are negative and positive ingredients to obedience, i.e., nonconformity and holiness, holiness itself has both positive and negative coordinates. Holiness is incomplete if it *only* consists of avoiding the world or certain patterns of behavior. It must first and foremost be directed *to* an object—and for the Christian that object is transcendence that in its essence is moral perfection. Peter, of course, will have much more to say about being a holy people.

NOTES

13–14 The linkage of faith leading to self-control and perseverance is also present in the catalog of virtues found in 2 Peter 1:5–7. Faith generates virtue (ἀρετή, *aretē*, GK *746*, i.e., moral excellence), which generates knowledge, which generates self-control, which generates perseverance, which generates godliness, which generates brotherly affection, which generates and ultimately expresses itself in love (ἀγάπη, *agapē*, GK *27*). On the moral progression suggested in this catalog of virtues and its function within the epistle, see my "The Language and Logic of Virtue in 2 Peter 1:5–7," *BBR* 8 (1998): 55–73; a fuller discussion of the catalog is found in my *Virtue amidst Vice*, 128–52.

Paul, in his Areopagus address in Athens, also speaks to the issue of pagan "ignorance" (ἄγνοια, *agnoia*, GK *53*) in the context of announcing that the Creator-God calls people everywhere to repent (Ac 17:30). Of interest is his particular use of ἄγνοια, *agnoia*, which appears to be part of a skillfully crafted wordplay on "knowledge" (γνῶσις, *gnōsis*, GK *1194*), a subtheme in his address (17:22–33) and in Luke's summary recounting of Paul's work in Athens (17:16–21). In the brief narrative of 17:16–33, "knowledge" derivatives occur in vv.19–20, 23 (twice), and 30 (cf. my "Paul before the Areopagus," *Philosophia Christi* 7 [2005]: 134–35).

Clues to the readers' former life, hinted at in v.14 and scattered throughout the epistle, suggest themselves as the following: lusts (1:14; 2:11; 4:2–3); the combination of malice, deceit, hypocrisy, envy, and slander (2:1); disobedience (2:8); darkness (2:9); ignorant speech (2:15); license (2:16); an improper view of authority (2:16–18); disordered relationships (3:1–8); retaliation (3:9); guilty consciences (3:16, 21); the combination of pagan debauchery, drunkenness, sexual immorality, and idolatry (4:3); greed (5:2); self-service (5:2–3); and pride (5:6).

b. The Lifestyle of Reverence (1:17–21)

[17]Since you call on a Father who judges each man's work impartially, live your lives as strangers here in reverent fear. [18]For you know that it was not with perishable things such as silver or gold that you were redeemed from the empty way of life handed down to you from your forefathers, [19]but with the precious blood of Christ, a lamb without blemish or defect. [20]He was chosen before the creation of the world, but was revealed in these last times for your sake. [21]Through him you believe in God, who raised him from the dead and glorified him, and so your faith and hope are in God.

COMMENTARY

17 Following the exhortation to holiness, Peter extends the sojourning theme with which the epistle is opened. He appeals to God the Father, who is an impartial judge, as ethical motivation for the reader: "live your lives [*anastrephō*, GK *418*] as strangers [*paroikia*, GK *4229*] here in reverent fear." A significant amount of material in 1 Peter (material bridging chs. 2 and 3) is devoted to ordered relationships—e.g., servants and masters, husbands and wives, even the emperor and God. It is noteworthy that, in the context of differing levels of authority, Peter writes, "Show proper respect for everyone: Love the brotherhood of believers, fear God, honor the king [emperor]" (2:17). While all people are to be respected, including the governing authorities, only God is to be feared reverentially.

18–20 In Petrine theology there is no tension between divine judgment and divine mercy. Having already offered praise to God for his great mercy and the believers' living hope (1:3–5), Peter rehearses by means of standard paraenetic language (*eidote*) the marvel of redemption and the purchase price for that redemption—the blood of Christ. The metaphor of the slave market occurs frequently in the NT (e.g., Mk 10:45; Ro 6:15–23; 8:15; Gal 4:1–7; 1Pe 1:18–19; 2:16; 2Pe 2:19–22) and is critical to a proper understanding of the nature of salvation. It speaks to the condition of bondage caused by sin, to the beneficence of the one buying the slave, to the costly nature of the redemptive transaction, and to the state of freedom (i.e., the household) into which the redeemed is brought. From the Petrine perspective, reverential fear is heightened by the believers' grateful awareness of the high cost of ransom. This cost, sacrificial blood, greatly exceeds the value of silver or gold used in the business transaction, either of which is perishable (cf. 1:4). The result is that the believer is brought into a marvelous spiritual freedom (2:16). Reverence acknowledges that the ransom price was indeed high.

This costly transaction, however, is presented in 1 Peter as no second thought or "plan B" in the counsel of God (cf. Ro 16:25–27; 1Co 2:7–10; Eph 3:1–6; Col 1:26–27; Tit 1:1–3). Rather, the ransom, it is emphasized, was in the purpose of God "before the creation of the world," even though it has been fully "revealed in these last times" for the sake of the saints. Once again, as in the letter's opening, Peter appropriates the language of sovereign election: Christ, the unblemished sacrificial lamb (cf. the language of Ex 12:5 and Isa 52:13–53:12 and its resemblance to 1 Peter), was "chosen" or, more precisely, "foreknown" (*proginōskō*, GK *4589*). Peter's confession of Christ's role in salvation history is a remarkable and compelling witness to the preexistence of the second person of the Trinity (on which cf. Jn 1:1–3; 17:5, 13, 18, 24; 8:16, 58; Php 2:6–11).

21 The believer's faith, mediated through Christ, is in God, "who raised him [Jesus] from the dead and glorified him." This confession, thought by Kelly, 77, and others to contain elements of an established early hymn, is crucial for the readers who struggle to put their suffering in proper perspective. It is a declaration that Jesus, having suffered on the cross, was vindicated (lit., "given glory") by God. The same pattern is repeated in 3:18–22, which depicts Christ's triumph over evil and extends to the saints themselves. Thus their "faith and hope are in God," who will vindicate them as well.

NOTES

17 The fear of the Lord, while by no means confined to the OT, is nonetheless a prominent theme in the OT. Reverential fear, rightly conceived, is the appropriate response of human beings to God's holiness. Reverence is the characteristic disposition of a person who consciously lives in the presence of Almighty God. The failure to realize this truth is the lesson of tragedies such as those that befell Nadab and Abihu (Lev 10:1–3; Nu 3:4). What is recorded of the Lord's response to "unauthorized" attempts at an offering is instructive. "Among those who approach me I will show myself holy . . . I will be honored" (Lev 10:3) is the divine response to Aaron's sons, who offer "unauthorized fire before [the LORD]."

On various occasions Luke records that great "fear" came upon the church throughout the book of Acts at the manifestation of the Lord's work (e.g., Ac 2:43; 5:5, 11; 9:3, 31; 19:17). Paul observes that holiness is, literally, "brought to completion [ἐπιτελέω, *epiteleō*, GK *2200*] in the fear of the Lord" (2Co 7:1). Peter simultaneously admonishes the church to *fear* God (1Pe 1:17) and *not to fear* the terror of those persecuting them (3:14). The clear suggestion is that there is a legitimate and illegitimate fear. The former is anchored in a proper reverence. This reverence, it should be added, while it does not disengage or cancel out the subject's love and affection (1:8), does proceed from the awe that properly recognizes the Lord as holy (v.16) and as judge (v.17)—thus Paul's observation in Romans 11:22: "Consider therefore the kindness and sternness of God." The Christian lives with the awareness of a day of moral reckoning; for this reason, the fear of the Lord should compel the saints toward moral earnestness.

c. The Lifestyle of Love (1:22–25)

²²Now that you have purified yourselves by obeying the truth so that you have sincere love for your brothers, love one another deeply, from the heart. ²³For you have been born again, not of perishable seed, but of imperishable, through the living and enduring word of God. ²⁴For,

"All men are like grass,
   and all their glory is like the flowers of the field;
the grass withers and the flowers fall,
²⁵   but the word of the Lord stands forever."

And this is the word that was preached to you.

COMMENTARY

22 Obedience and purification, two important subthemes in the letter, as we noted earlier, arc said by the writer to result in a *brotherly love* (*philadelphia*, GK *5789*) that is "sincere": "Now that you have purified [*hagnizō*, GK *49*, as opposed to *hagiazō*, "sanctify," GK *39*, suggesting the need for *cleansing*] yourselves by obeying the truth . . ." Love that is "sincere" (*anypokritos*, GK *537*)—i.e., unfeigned or unhypocritical—is hearty and affectionate among the saints. To love one another "deeply" and "from the heart" is particularly important in a social climate of hostility, wherein mutual encouragement, affection, and support would be indispensable to be able to withstand persecution. As Hillyer, 53, and John Piper ("Hope as the Motivation for Love: 1 Peter 3:9–12," *NTS* 26 [1980]: 212–31) fittingly observe, a community of love will produce and necessarily preserve a community of hope.

23–25 Reinforcement of the enduring nature of love, which undergirds communal bonds, is found in Isaiah 40:6–8. This citation follows Peter's reiteration of abiding, imperishable seed (*spora*, GK *5078*) of the new birth, i.e., the regenerative and living "word of God" (cf. Mt 4:4; 13:1–23; Mk 4:1–20; Lk 8:1–15; Heb 4:12). The link between community and new birth is not to be lost on the readers. Mutual love cannot exist in unadulterated, unfeigned fashion without the element of purification that only comes by way of a new (i.e., spiritual) birth.

But the citation from Isaiah 40 is important for another reason. Its historical context concerns the experience of exile foreseen by the prophet. The prophetic word of God "comforts" the people of God (40:1) in the midst of sojourning as resident aliens. The message is intended to encourage Israel,

to offer hope at a time of social hostility in her exilic experience. This point of contact with Peter's audience is readily recognized. The purposes of Almighty God stand, and he has not forgotten his Diaspora people, even though their sufferings would seem to suggest such. "The word of the Lord stands forever," Peter recalls, and *this word*, furthermore, is that which was "preached to you." This preached word, let it be remembered, is "good news" (cf. Isa 40:9). And the good news remains: the Sovereign Lord comes with power, and his arm rules for him (40:10). His care for his people, declared by the prophet Isaiah, is never far from the mind of Peter (2:25; 5:2): "He tends his flock like a shepherd: He gathers the lambs in his arms and carries them close to his heart; he gently leads those that have young" (Isa 40:11).

NOTES

22 Contra Waltner, 64, the intention behind these admonitions is not to contrast φιλαδέλφια (*philadelphia*) and ἀγάπη (*agapē*, GK *27*), nor is it to show the deficiencies of the former and the qualitative superiority of the latter. As the catalog of virtues in 2 Peter 1:5–7 makes clear, the two coexist, are necessary, and emphasize a different quality in the way humans relate to one another. In the Petrine epistles, one does not have priority over the other.

d. The Lifestyle of Transformation (2:1–3)

¹Therefore, rid yourselves of all malice and all deceit, hypocrisy, envy, and slander of every kind. ²Like newborn babies, crave pure spiritual milk, so that by it you may grow up in your salvation, ³now that you have tasted that the Lord is good.

COMMENTARY

1 Peter recapitulates at this point. The sum total of the imperatives of holiness, reverence, and love irreversibly point, "therefore," to transformation, i.e., a changed life. Theirs is to be an ethical standard that stands in marked contrast to its pagan counterpart, characteristics of which are said to be malice, deceit, hypocrisy, envy, and slander—what one commentator describes as a "comprehensive list of the ills to which the human heart is host" (so Hillyer, 56). Because of the corrosive effect of these practices on the Christian community and Christian fellowship in general, Peter calls his readers in no uncertain terms to action: "rid yourselves" (*apotithēmi*, "to discard or strip off as a garment," GK *700*) of them *all* (three times the word *pan*, "all," "every," is used for emphasis). This catalog of vices—an ethical-rhetorical device that occurs frequently in the NT (e.g., Ro 1:29; 1Co 6:9-10; 2Co 10:20; Eph 4:31; Col 3:8; Gal 5:19-21; 1Ti 1:9-10)—closely resembles its secular counterpart commonly employed by Stoic moralists of the day. These vices constitute behavior that is patently opposed to and incompatible with *philadelphia* (1:22). The ethic of transformation, however, is not rooted in self-sufficiency, as pagan Stoic moralists might contend. As we have already seen, it is anchored in grace (1:13)—a grace that allows the believer to grow progressively in the salvation that is already a present reality.

2 Growth in any area of human existence is progressive, incremental. This growth, it goes without saying, is dependent on food as nourishment. Having noted the enduring character of the word of God, Peter depicts this "word" as being the means by which nourishment comes to the Christian. This food, in contradistinction to the vices just enumerated, is "pure" (*adolos*, GK *100*); it is free from mixture, containing not the slightest trace of impurity. Peter describes the word as a kind of "pure spiritual milk," conjuring an image of life sustenance in its basic form. The believer is to "crave" (*epipotheō*, GK *2160*) the milk of the word, just as a baby craves its milk (the imagery of infants and milk also occurs in 1Co 3:2; 1Th 2:7; Heb 5:12). While it is natural for commentators to see in this image the idea of spiritual immaturity (a notion reinforced by the context in which milk is used in Heb 5:12-13), or to view the readers as young in the faith (so, e.g., Beare, 114, and Kelly, 84), the main point of the imagery—illustrated by the verb "crave"—is to stress the idea of

hunger and focused pursuit. Peter wishes foremost to convey motivation for growth, not to suggest immaturity on the part of the readers (thus Grudem, 94).

3 With a focus on the readers' *experience* of Christian faith, Peter employs a partial citation from Psalm 34:8, writing, "now that you have tasted that the Lord is good." While at first glance, the writer's borrowing from this Davidic psalm may seem arbitrary, very much the opposite is the case. Psalm 34 extols the Lord in the context of affliction (v.2), deliverance from fears (vv.4, 7), and salvation from difficulties (v.6). The psalmist therefore enthuses, "The angel of the LORD encamps around those who fear him [cf. 1Pe 1:17], and he delivers them" (v.7), which leads into the subsequent declaration (vv. 8-9): "Taste and see that the Lord is good; blessed is the man who takes refuge in him. Fear the LORD, you saints, for those who fear him lack nothing."

The points of contact between Psalm 34 and 1 Peter become immediately apparent: trials and difficulties, affliction, deliverance from fear, salvation, and a pronounced reverential fear and trust in the Lord. The remainder of the psalm confesses divine nearness: "the eyes of the LORD are on the righteous" (v.15); "the LORD is close to the brokenhearted and saves those who are crushed in spirit" (v.18); "a righteous man may have many troubles, but the LORD delivers him from them all" (v.19); and "the foes of the righteous will be condemned" (v.21). The psalm concludes with the reassuring proclamation that "the LORD redeems his servants" and that "no one will be condemned who takes refuge in him" (v.22).

Sensitive to his readers' situation, Peter appropriately enlists the "word of God," spoken in a similar situation, in order to encourage and strengthen his audience. Indeed, Psalm 34 is of such relevance to the readers that Peter will cite verbatim from it later in the epistle (3:10-12). Peter's reminder is ethical in trajectory. To the extent that the readers experience ("taste and see") the Lord as good, they move progressively forward in the continuum of salvation.

NOTES

1–3 On the use of ethical catalogs in the NT, see B. S. Easton, "New Testament Lists," *JBL* 51 (1932) 1–12; N. J. McEleney, "The Vice Lists of the Pastoral Epistles," *CBQ* 36 (1974): 203–19; my "Vice and Virtue Lists," in *Dictionary of New Testament Background*, ed. C. A. Evans and S. E. Porter (Downers Grove, Ill.: InterVarsity, 2000), 1252–57; my *Virtue amidst Vice*, 112–27. In addition to 1 Peter 2:3, other verbal parallels to Psalm 34 in the NT include Hebrews 6:4–5 (34:8); Luke 1:53 (34:10); and John 19:36 (34:20).

2. The New Community's Identity (2:4–10)

a. The Paradox of Election and Rejection (2:4–8)

OVERVIEW

After a rehearsal of Christian conduct (holiness, reverence, love, transformation), attention is now directed toward a fuller understanding of the church's identity as the new Diaspora community, the leitmotif of 1 Peter that was introduced in the opening of the letter. In the present section, Peter is wholly reliant on OT themes and images. Unless the saints have an accurate understanding of their identity and place in this world, they will not be sufficient to the task of mirroring a distinctly Christian ethic, more generally speaking, or of enduring persecution and hardship in the narrower sense. Orthopraxis, i.e., right conduct, is rooted in orthodoxy, right belief. Something of an enduring nature is lodged in the OT image of Israel as God's chosen covenantal people. It is the teaching of the NT that the church has been grafted into Israel (Ro 11:11–24) and now represents the new Diaspora community in its universalized expression.

Numerous metaphors are used by the writers of the NT to depict the nature and function of the church. More often than not, the NT writer is dependent on OT images—a bride, an army, a flock, a temple, a people, etc. Several of these "types" appear in 1 Peter. Typology is a chief means by which NT writers show that peoples, institutions, and events of the old covenant find their ultimate fulfillment in the new. The language of typology is critical to an understanding of the Petrine hermeneutic—e.g., the sacrificial lamb and Christ, the suffering of the righteous, vindication of the righteous, Israel and the church as God's elect, Israel and the church as a Diaspora community, the temple and the church as God's habitation, the Levitical priesthood and the church in offering acceptable sacrifice. Typology underscores the sovereign purposes of Almighty God, for what has been determined in the divine counsel goes into fulfillment not only as a preordained result but also at the appointed time through the appointed means. If Christ the lamb is chosen before the foundations of the world to redeem humanity, then the church—the new community—has a privileged place in mediating that redemption to the world in which it has been placed. Several perspectives on the church's nature and function are accented in 1 Peter.

Most commentary on 1 Peter assumes on the part of the writer a "midrashic" reworking of Jewish tradition-material. This creative reinterpretation and contemporizing of OT texts in the early church mirrors an exegetical practice employed within mainstream Judaism concurrent with the advent of Christ. This practice can be seen in Peter's appropriation and application of selected OT "stone passages." Several of these are marshaled to symbolize both the cornerstone, Christ, as "the living stone," and believers as "living stones" that constitute a new temple, a dwelling place of God's presence. Midrashic application to the new covenant of the stone metaphor, however, does not begin with Peter. Referring to himself, Jesus declares, "The stone the builders rejected has become the capstone," citing Psalm 118:22 (Mt 21:42; Mk 12:10; Lk 20:17). Peter also freely cites Psalm 118 when he and John are interrogated by Jewish leaders (Ac 4:11), as he does twice in this epistle (2:4 and 2:7). The stone metaphor contains a paradox that applies to Christ as well as to his disciples. Both were elected by God; both are rejected by humans. Lest the saints despair because of their rejection by the world, they are reassured of their election in the divine purpose. God considers them "chosen" and "precious." Thus the new Diaspora community can rest in the fact that it will be vindicated, as Christ their model in fact was (1:21; 3:18–22).

Two other OT references using the stone symbolism are utilized with persuasive rhetorical effect. Cited is the word of the prophet Isaiah at a time of national apostasy and geopolitical intrigue: "See, I lay a stone in Zion, a tested stone, a precious cornerstone for a sure foundation" (Isa 28:16). While this passage is not messianic, it nevertheless depicts Yahweh's faithfulness to his people—a covenantal faithfulness that ultimately leads to the messianic advent. The other citation depicts the Lord as "a stone that causes men to stumble," although the offense applies to Israel herself (Isa 8:14). The emphasis of being "chosen" *and* "precious" resonates with the readers, particularly if they struggle with a sense of social shame arising out of cultural hostility.

It is indeed fitting that among the NT writers it is Peter who develops a homiletical midrash using the stone metaphor. After all, it is Simon Peter, "the Rock," who makes the important messianic confession for which he is commended by means of a wordplay: "And I tell you that you are Peter, and on this rock I will build my church" (Mt 16:18). And it is the same Peter to whom Jesus forcefully declares, "Get behind me, Satan! You are a stumbling block to me" (16:23).

⁴As you come to him, the living Stone—rejected by men but chosen by God and precious to him—⁵you also, like living stones, are being built into a spiritual house to be a holy priesthood, offering spiritual sacrifices acceptable to God through Jesus Christ. ⁶For in Scripture it says:

"See, I lay a stone in Zion,
    a chosen and precious cornerstone,
and the one who trusts in him
    will never be put to shame."

⁷Now to you who believe, this stone is precious. But to those who do not believe,

"The stone the builders rejected
    has become the capstone,"

8and,

"A stone that causes men to stumble
    and a rock that makes them fall."

They stumble because they disobey the message–which is also what they were destined for.

COMMENTARY

4–5 There exists in the mind of the writer a natural extension of the stone metaphor that allows him to conceive of the Christian community as "a spiritual house" whose architect is God himself: "You also, like living stones, are being built into a spiritual house." The notion of God's people as a house, building, or temple is one of the prominent reapplications of OT imagery by the writers of the NT (e.g., Ac 7:48; 1Co 3:9–17; 2Co 6:16; Eph 2:21–22; 1Ti 3:15; Heb 3:6; Rev 21:3). A reinterpretation of the time-honored temple, in fact, is traceable to Jesus himself in his previewing of sacrifice (Mt 26:59–61; Mk 14:55–59; 15:29; Jn 2:19)—words that are offensive to Jewish leaders—and in his commendation of Peter for the latter's messianic confession (Mt 16:18).

With the sealing of believers with the Holy Spirit in the new covenant (Eph 1:13–14; 2Co 1:21–22), the saints collectively constitute the temple of God, a spiritual habitation for God that is continuously "being built," i.e., under construction. Thus it is fitting that Peter begins this material, "As you come to him" (2:4); it is reminiscent of the language in Psalm 34:5, and it is consistent with the temple image as well. Individual believers fulfill their true calling and assume their true position *only* to the extent that they allow themselves to be built into the edifice that is the church, the Christian community. Barclay, 195–96, writes, "Individualistic Christianity is an absurdity; Christianity is community within the fellowship of the church."

Not only is the notion of the temple, the house of God, extended here (as elsewhere in the NT) but also the concept of a consecrated or "holy priesthood." This second image is of necessity an extension of the first: the duties of the Levitical order as required in the OT now belong to all the saints. All have access to God and bring others to God while offering spiritual sacrifices that are acceptable to God, whether in worship, praise, or petition. This occurs through the mediation of the great High Priest, Jesus Christ (cf. Heb 4:14–5:10).

7–8 Peter interjects application of the stone passages: "Now to you who believe, this stone [which was rejected] is precious" (v.7). To the believer, God's chosen agent of redemption (1:18–21) is "precious" (*timē*, GK *5507*), honored, and respected. To those who do not believe, writes Peter, there is only rejection and stumbling: "They stumble because they disobey the message." The consequence of disobedience, Peter adds, is that for which "they were destined" (*tithēmi*, GK *5502*, used in a similar way and bespeaking appointment in Mt 22:44; Lk 12:46; Jn 15:16; 2 Ti 1:11; and Heb 1:2). The language of condemnation here is not unlike that of Jude, who writes that the condemnation of some was "written about long ago" (v.4).

These verses are not teaching that people are without moral agency. The language of predestination, rather, underscores the certainty of divine retribution for those who disobey. In Scripture, divine sovereignty and human freedom coexist.

Such balance is notably on display in 1 Peter, which encourages the saints with the language of sovereignty and election while simultaneously exhorting them via paraenesis to moral earnestness.

The paradox of selection and rejection is part of the writer's arsenal to address the tension that arises from faith encountering culture. Cognizant of their own election, the saints can cope with the shame and stigma arising from the world's rejection. Otherwise, they will be tempted to capitulate. But as Christ, the rejected one, was vindicated, they too await the same reward.

NOTES

4–8 On the nature of typology, the best resource remains L. Goppelt, *Typos: The Typological Interpretation of the Old Testament in the New* (Grand Rapids: Eerdmans, 1982). See also G. W. H. Lampe and K. J. Woollcombe, *Essays on Typology* (Napierville, Ill.: Allenson, 1957).

When biblical scholars employ the term "midrash," they are referring, in the wider sense, to the tendency of the writer to interpret an OT passage in the light of contemporary circumstances. Such a hermeneutic usually has the character of a paraphrase, prophecy, or parable (thus J. Neusner, *What Is Midrash?* [Philadelphia: Fortress, 1987] 25). On the nature of midrashic exegesis, see M. Gertner, "Midrashim in the New Testament," *JSS* 7 (1962): 267–92; A. G. Wright, "The Literary Genre Midrash," *CBQ* 28 (1966): 118–38. On its application in the General Epistles, see I. Jacobs, "The Midrashic Background for James ii.21–23," *NTS* 22 (1976): 457–64; P. H. Davids, "Tradition and Citation in the Epistle of James," in *Scripture, Tradition, and Interpretation*, ed. W. W. Gasque and W. S. LaSor (Grand Rapids: Eerdmans, 1978) 113–26; R. J. Bauckham, "James, 1 and 2 Peter, Jude," in *It Is Written: Scripture Citing Scripture*, ed. D. A. Carson and H. G. M. Williamson (Cambridge: Cambridge Univ. Press, 1988), 303–17; my *Literary Strategy in the Epistle of Jude*, 31–33, 73–74; my *Virtue amidst Vice*, 84–95; my "On Angels and Asses: The Moral Paradigm in 2 Peter 2," *PEGLMBS* 21 (2001): 1–12.

That Paul also cites the same two texts from Isaiah suggests they had a prominent place in the preaching of the early church. Selwyn, 268–77, believes that vv.6–8 of 1 Peter 2:1–10 constitute a partial hymn that is appropriated by both Peter and Paul (Ro 9:33). This suggestion is plausible, though inconclusive. On the use of the "stone" passages in the NT in general, see C. D. F. Moule, "Some Reflections on the 'Stone Testimonia' in Relation to the Name Peter," *NTS* 2 (1955): 56–59; L. W. Barnard, "The Testimonium Concerning the Stone in the NT and in the Epistle of Barnabas," *SE* 3 (1964): 306–13; N. Hillyer, "Rock-Stone Imagery in 1 Peter," *TynBul* 22 (1971): 58–81; P. S. Minear, "The House of Living Stones: A Study of 1 Peter 2:4–12," *EcR* 34 (1982): 238–48.

b. God's People as God's Chosen (2:9–10)

⁹But you are a chosen people, a royal priesthood, a holy nation, a people belonging to God, that you may declare the praises of him who called you out of darkness into his wonderful light. ¹⁰Once you were not a people, but now you are the people of God; once you had not received mercy, but now you have received mercy.

COMMENTARY

9 Here Peter recapitulates, stringing together OT metaphors that remind the saints of God's covenantal faithfulness and their basic identity. The saints are a "chosen people," a "royal priesthood," "a holy nation," and a "people belonging to God" (cf. Ex 19:5–6; Dt 7:6; 10:15; 1Sa 12:22; Isa 43:21; 62:2). As God's "chosen" people, believers are reminded of and encouraged by the notion of covenant. The fact that God has entered into covenant with his people entails both privilege and obedience/obligation; the two go hand in hand.

A "royal priesthood" is best understood in the light of the LXX's translation of Exodus 19:6, rendered "a kingdom of priests" in most versions. Michaels, 109, and Achtemeier, 165, understand this phrase as a priesthood that belongs to and acts in the service of the king. For Kelly, 96, the community is royal because the king dwells in her midst. Not insignificantly, in Revelation the saints are a "kingdom and priests" (1:6; 5:10), where "they will reign"; i.e., the saints are *vindicated*.

As a "holy nation," the readers are reminded again that they are consecrated to God and thus set apart, in the sense of being different, from the world. They will resist conformity to the world because of their ultimate allegiance. Also, they are "a people belonging to God" and, consequently, have great value. Precisely why is it important to affirm basic Christian identity? What is the goal of the Christian community? It is "that you may declare the praises of him who called you out of darkness into his wonderful light." The church's mission, simply put, is to witness to the splendor of moral transformation.

10 The remarkable nature of this transformation—before and after—is illustrated by yet another interpretive use of the OT (Hos 1:6, 9–2:1, 23), wherein the prophet had drawn parallels between his unfaithful wife and Israel. By the creative, restorative mercy of God, those who were formerly "not a people" were now made "the people of God." Just as divine compassion and mercy were available to restore Israel, despite her unfaithfulness, pagans as well, who had no former claim on God's mercy, were candidates (and recipients) thereof. The saints are simultaneously called out of something—spiritual darkness—and to something far greater—spiritual illumination leading to moral transformation.

NOTES

9 The light-darkness dualism is pronounced in the NT (see, e.g., Mt 4:16; Lk 1:78–79; Jn 1:5; 3:19; 8:12; 12:35; Ro 2:19; 13:12; 2Co 4:6; 6:14; Eph 5:8; Col 1:12–13; 1Th 5:4–5; 2Pe 1:19; 1Jn 1:5).

C. Christian Witness as a Diaspora Community (2:11–3:12)

OVERVIEW

In order to persevere in the face of social hostility and rejection by the world, the pilgrim community must be firmly anchored in the awareness of its identity, hence, the precision and care with which Peter has developed the material in 1:3–2:10. This protracted section of the epistle is no mere academic exercise; rather, it is a thoroughly necessary theological prolegomena. In order to bear up under the world's rejection, the saints must be secure in their sense of divine election. Only on this foundation can they endure hardship.

1. The Necessity of Good Deeds (2:11–12)

[11]Dear friends, I urge you, as aliens and strangers in the world, to abstain from sinful desires, which war against your soul. [12]Live such good lives among the pagans that, though they accuse you of doing wrong, they may see your good deeds and glorify God on the day he visits us.

COMMENTARY

11 Following the writer's opening rehearsal of the divine purpose and reaffirmation of the new community's basic identity—both of which are well-calculated, theologically rich, and immersed in OT concepts—Peter is able to get to the (pastoral) point at hand. The ethical implications of the saints' privileged status must now be stressed. His admonition is twofold, containing a negative and positive dimension. Verse 11 begins the writer's *logos pareinetikos*, his word of exhortation, as from a father to a son ("Dear friends," 2:11 and 4:12): as "aliens [*paroikoi*, GK *4230*; also in 1:17 and 2:11] and sojourners [NIV, "strangers"; *parepidemoi*, GK *4215*; also in 1:1 and 2:11] in the world" (cf. Lev 25:23), they are "to abstain from sinful desires, which war against [the] soul." In this paraenesis, Peter blends a military image (cf. Ro 7:23; 2Co 10:3; Eph 6:12; Jas 4:1) with the letter's controlling Diaspora metaphor.

12 The readers are further charged: "Live such good lives among the pagans that, though they accuse you of doing wrong, they may see your good deeds and glorify God on the day he visits us." If any in the Christian community misconstrue being the new Diaspora—i.e., "aliens and strangers"—to mean escapism or isolation, Peter dispels that illusion. In truth, responsible earthly citizenship struggles with how most effectively to "advertise" or bear witness to the transcendent values of the kingdom of God. The veracity of Christian truth-claims, one may infer from Petrine teaching, is demonstrated to the extent, and only to the extent, that the Christian lifestyle is *ethically viable*. This will entail translating Christian ethics in relevant ways to the pagan mind-set—ways suggested in the material that immediately follows (2:13–3:7).

The implication is this: Christian witness will be upheld by the quality of "goodness" unbelievers observe in the Christian community. Whether or not pagans convert to the Christian faith is in God's hands, but this is not Peter's immediate concern. Rather, he insists that, even if pagans malign or accuse believers wrongly, on the day of moral reckoning—literally, on "the day of overseeing" (*hemera episkopes*)—they themselves will have to acknowledge the qualitative difference among Christians, thereby "glorifying" God.

One might legitimately argue that doing good deeds that glorify God was the heart of Jesus' teaching, based on Matthew's representation (5:16): "Let your light shine before men, that they may see your good deeds and praise your Father in heaven." Peter, at least late in life, seems to concur: the essence of the Christian lifestyle is leading a virtuous life, demonstrating the Christian ethic in a manner that shows it to be qualitatively different.

REFLECTIONS

We have just observed a core assumption in Petrine thinking: The Christian ethic must translate itself in ways that are relevant to the pagan mind-set. This is the essence of good citizenship. Goodness, as the reader discovers, is a major concern to the writer (see W. C. van Unnik, "The Teaching of Good Works in 1 Peter," *NTS* 1 [1954/55]: 92–110). The frequent appearance in 1 Peter of *agathos* (GK *19*) and cognate forms (*agathos*, 2:18; 3:10, 11, 13, 16 [twice], 21; *agathopoios*, 2:14; *agathopoia*, 4:19; *agathopoieō*, 2:15, 20; 3:6, 17; *kalos*, twice in 2:12) confirms this emphasis and reveals an operating assumption on the part of the writer: *agathopoieō*, doing good (GK *16*), is the basis for Christian credibility, since it is a standard acknowledged even by pagan unbelievers themselves.

Goodness is not merely "Jewish" or "Mosaic" or "Christian" in the narrow sense; rather, it is responsible conduct that is universally recognized. Perhaps there are those present in the community whose eschatological outlook is such that the only way of expressing Christian hope is to cling to an imminent return of the Lord; and indeed the writer himself states later on in the letter that "the end of all things is near" (4:7). While this statement in its context is taken up later in the present commentary, several remarks are presently in order. One is that the early church continually lived with the expectation of the Lord's return. And yet it must also be said that every generation since has struggled with this very tension: how does one live in the light of "the end of all things"? The bulk of the NT's teaching—and that of Jesus ("Occupy until I come")—is directed not toward passively awaiting the Lord's return but *active occupation until the end*. And so it is in 1 Peter.

Inevitably, this creative approach to responsible "occupation" affects how we relate to people. Indeed, one measurement of the distinctiveness of the Christian ethic is the manner in which Christians conduct their social lives. How do they relate to the employers? To governing authorities? To established social conventions? How are their marriages? Their families? Are they isolationist? Subversivist? Conformist? Such will be the test of whether, in the end, the Christian message is to be believed in a pagan context, in accordance with its claim, or whether it is just another sect with its strange notions of deity, sexuality, and afterlife. Throughout the empire, and certainly in Asia Minor, these are the kinds of questions that would be asked of the Christian community. The Christian witness, then, has an inevitable *social* dimension by which it is judged. It is to this social dimension we now turn.

2. The Necessity of Ordered Relationships (2:13–3:12)

OVERVIEW

For Peter, the social dimension of Christian witness consists of several crucial realms. In each realm particular duties are the norm for established culture. One central element that as a thread unites all of these spheres is that of *authority*. If the Christian community is going to demonstrate both coherence and relevance in a pagan context, faith will show itself viable in the way it understands and responds to authority—a point argued convincingly by C. F. Sleeper ("Political Responsibility According to

1 Peter," *NovT* 10 [1968]: 270–86). Christians, above all social groupings, will be responsible in their attitude toward varying forms of authority. In the end, social responsibility will authenticate Christian witness.

Without question, Jesus' exhortation to "give to Caesar what is Caesar's, and to God what is God's" (Mt 22:21) is as radical—and timeless—today as it was in the first century. This admonition, of course, cuts both ways. To those who are only concerned about religious duty, the first half of this command seems untenable. To those, however, who are beholden to earthly cares, the second half tends to desacralize.

Doubtless for the first-century Christian the issue of authority was a delicate subject, given the pervasive nature of Roman *imperium* as well as the varying approaches to rule by the provincial governors. As a Jew living in Galilee for most of his life, Peter is under no illusions: Christians must live their lives against the backdrop of authorities that at best tolerate their faith and at worst persecute them for their faith. But not even the apostles believed that citizenship was passive in nature; according to Paul, Christians are called to intercede "for kings and all those in authority" (1Ti 2:2).

NT scholarship has recognized in 2:13–3:7 a standard code of duties governing social relations that has been called a household or station code. These obligations range from civic duty to familial obligations at various "stations" of life and had become popularized in Stoic notions of morality (e.g., Epictetus, *Diatr.* 2.14.8; 2.17.31; Seneca, *Ep.* 94.1) and find their way into the NT (Eph 5:21–6:9; Col 3:18–4:1; 1Ti 2:8–15; Tit 2:1–10; cf. *Did.* 4.9–11; *1 Clem.* 1:3; 21:6–9; *Barn.* 19:5–7).

It is only natural that the early Christians would adopt this feature into their writings. The thread that unites each part of the material in 2:13–3:7 is the attitude of respect that must be rendered in several common social contexts. In 1 Peter this attitude of respect is mirrored in five specific areas: governing authorities (2:13–17), slaves with masters (2:18–25), wives toward husbands (3:1–6), husbands toward wives (3:7), and everyone in the Christian community (3:8–12). Despite modernity's quandary over the vocabulary, the fact that admonitions to three of these five groups contain the verb *hypotassō* ("submit," GK *5718*) reflects the Greco-Roman primacy of respect for order (*taxis*, GK *5423*), as Goppelt, 175, and Elliott, 498, have sought to emphasize. Hierarchical harmony and domestic order were thought by Hellenistic culture to produce stability and order in the city-state (thus Aristotle, *Pol.* 1 [1253b]; *Eth. nic.* 8 [1160a–1161a]). Moreover, Roman philosophers, governors, and emperors viewed the household code as useful in an attempt to *maintain order* in an aggressively expanding empire (so Balch, *Let Wives Be Submissive*, 65–80). To "submit" is a form of honor and respect, and Peter's concern is that Christians be motivated by respect at every level (a reading confirmed by 5:5). Balch ("Household Codes," 29 n. 234) sees in the household code a virtual "apologetic" function, to the extent that it serves to deflect outside criticism of the Christian community. Why? Because the household code promotes integration rather than isolation, allowing Christians a "selective acculturation" as they struggle with the tension between faith and culture. A divided (and disrespectful) "house," then, is understood by the writer to undermine Christian witness.

In the first sphere (2:13–17), the believers are admonished, "Submit [*hypotassō*] yourselves . . . to every authority instituted among men," and this "for the Lord's sake." In the second section (2:18–25), slaves are admonished to submit to their masters, both to the kind and the harsh. Wives and husbands are further and specific objects of exhortation; wives are to be submissive to their husbands as a demonstration of Christian witness (3:1–6), while husbands "in the same way" are to be considerate of and show understanding toward their wives, treating them with respect (3:7). Lastly, Peter appeals to all in the community to be mindful of and sympathetic toward one another (3:8–12).

a. A Christian View of Authority (2:13–17)

¹³Submit yourselves for the Lord's sake to every authority instituted among men: whether to the king, as the supreme authority, ¹⁴or to governors, who are sent by him to punish those who do wrong and to commend those who do right. ¹⁵For it is God's will that by doing good you should silence the ignorant talk of foolish men. ¹⁶Live as free men, but do not use your freedom as a cover-up for evil; live as servants of God. ¹⁷Show proper respect to everyone: Love the brotherhood of believers, fear God, honor the king.

COMMENTARY

13–14 Case illustration number one calls for subordination to "every authority instituted among men." Some disagreement among interpreters exists as to how to translate *ktisis*. The NRSV renders *ktisis hypotassō* as "accept the authority," a reading that has both strengths and weaknesses. To be commended in this reading is the extent to which "accept" entails the notion of *recognition*. The recognition underscored by Peter and reiterated by Paul in Romans 13 is that authority in its generic form derives from the Creator. The recognition that all authority is owing to God is not qualified in either Peter or Paul by those who exercise the authority, whether just or unjust. The prophetic viewpoint of the OT reminded Israel again and again that the Lord accomplishes his purposes through the existing powers (cf. Pr 21:1; Jer 25:9; 27:6; 43:10; Da 4:17). The reading of "accept" is weak to the extent that it does not do full justice to the nuances of the verb *hypotassō*. Lest the reader view Peter's prescription as unquestioning obedience or spiritual compromise (a major concern of Achtemeier, 182; Michaels, 121; Waltner, 87), Peter's exhortation is framed in terms of doing wrong and doing right. The context is guided by the issue of

punishment for wrongdoing (cf. Ro 13:3–4). Thus this has to do with criminal justice.

14–15 The Petrine understanding, consistent with Paul's, is that governing authorities are appointed by God for sociomoral order; 1 Peter 2:13–17, therefore, cannot be misconstrued as a call to uncritical subservience. The primary responsibility of the "king" (vv. 13, 17; elsewhere in the NT at Jn 19:15; Ac 17:2; Rev 17:12) and the "governors" (v. 14, *hēgemōn*, GK *2450*; cf. Mt 10:18; Mk 13:9; Lk 21:12) is to preserve the social order. Part of this entails "commending those who do right," and Peter believes that good deeds will "silence" (*phimoō*, "to muzzle," GK *5821*) the mouths of ignorant people—people who might falsely accuse Christians. Moreover, both 1 Peter and Romans frame social obligation in terms of conscience, *syneidēsis* (GK *5287*, 1Pe 3:21; Ro 13:5), and subordination, *hypotagē* (GK *5717*, 1Pe 2:13, 18; 3:1; Ro 13:5). That governing authorities are listed first in the household code suggests the consistent presence of both the Roman *imperium* and governors in the lives of the saints.

16–17 Several practical words of advice follow, with the writer keenly aware of class and social distinctions: "Live as free men," regardless of worldly or social status; "do not use your freedom as a cover-up for evil," rather "act as free men" who are "servants of God," since freedom is conditioned by responsibility; and "show proper respect to everyone." Three examples of respect are listed— "love the brotherhood of believers, fear God, honor the king"—each of which has decidedly practical ramifications. Brotherly affection (cf.

1:22) among Christians will not only be a needed encouragement in a socially hostile climate, it will also validate Christian witness. While the emperor is the supreme political authority, the exhortation toward "respect" and "honor" simultaneously desacralizes the emperor in status and addresses an attitude of disrespect toward political authority that some Christians—perhaps "Zealot" types— might harbor.

NOTES

13–17 The expression "station code" comes from the German *Ständetafel*. T. Martin, 138, attributes the origin of the term to Hans von Campenhausen, *Polykarp von Smyrna und die Pastoralbriefe* (Heidelberg: Winter, 1951). See Balch ("Household Codes," 25–50) for a survey of research on the household code up to ca. 1988; cf. Martin, 124–30. With some justification, Goppelt, 165, laments that the designation "household code" in the end is inadequate, since "station" better reflects the social institutions to which one is assigned in God's providence.

b. A Christian View of Unjust Treatment (2:18–25)

OVERVIEW

Barclay, 210, has estimated that there were as many as sixty million slaves in the Roman Empire at the time Peter was writing. Given their sheer numbers and their lack of legal rights (thus Aristotle, *Eth. nic.* 10.8 [1134b]), it would be quite natural, though misleading, to think they were consigned to mere menial tasks. Indeed they served as teachers, musicians, tutors, physicians, and secretaries. It is important to note that the term Peter uses for slaves is not *douloi* (GK *1528*), typically rendered "slaves," but *oiketai* (GK *3860*), i.e., household or domestic servants. Thus we have to do with a household code in 2:18–25. Treatment of household *oiketai* varied greatly; some were treated harshly, while some were treated with respect and considered members of the family. Peter's admonition mirrors both scenarios.

The early Christian community offered a radical contrast to society, since it collapsed social barriers such as slave and free (1Co 12:13; Gal 3:28; Col 3:11). Understandably, not a few slaves were members of the Christian community. Most likely, it is for this reason that the NT devotes considerable advice to them (e.g., 1Co 7:21; Eph 6:5–8; 2Pe 2:19. Correlatively, masters are addressed in Matthew 6:24; Luke 16:13; Ephesians 6:9; and Colossians 4:1. The introduction of Christian faith into a slave's life—or a master's for that matter— would raise new and perhaps baffling tensions. Certainly the question "Does faith eradicate social distinctions or conventions?" is one many would have pondered. Whatever the tensions, Peter wishes to emphasize the Christian element in the relationship, choosing not to editorialize on the ethical viability of master-slave relationships. He acknowledges that some slaves will incur "good and considerate" (*epieikēs*, GK *2117*) masters, while others will have "harsh" (*skolios*, GK *5021*) ones. For the latter, day-to-day bearing up under such conditions is an enormous ethical challenge.

> [18]Slaves, submit yourselves to your masters with all respect, not only to those who are good and considerate, but also to those who are harsh. [19]For it is commendable if a man bears up under the pain of unjust suffering because he is conscious of God. [20]But how is it to your credit if you receive a beating for doing wrong and endure it? But if you suffer for doing good and you endure it, this is commendable before God. [21]To this you were called, because Christ suffered for you, leaving you an example, that you should follow in his steps.
>
> [22]"He committed no sin,
> and no deceit was found in his mouth."
>
> [23]When they hurled their insults at him, he did not retaliate; when he suffered, he made no threats. Instead, he entrusted himself to him who judges justly. [24]He himself bore our sins in his body on the tree, so that we might die to sins and live for righteousness; by his wounds you have been healed. [25]For you were like sheep going astray, but now you have returned to the Shepherd and Overseer of your souls.

COMMENTARY

18–20 In the context of master-slave relationships, Peter wishes to emphasize respect that issues out of redemption. His admonition to "submit," and to do so "with all respect," has two goals: to engender respect but also to preview vindication. Indeed, "fear" (NIV, "respect"; *phobos*, GK *5828*) cuts both ways. Peter observes further that it is "grace" (NIV, "commendable"; *charis*, GK *5921*) before God, i.e., evidence that grace is operative in our lives, when a person "bears up under the pain of unjust suffering"—doubtless an approach to suffering radically different from what comes naturally. It is in such a crucible that the Christian distinctive is evidenced. There is, of course, no merit to suffering for wrongdoing, as is accentuated through the rhetorical question "But how is it to your credit . . . ?"; after all, such is deserved. But the consequence of being a

Christian, i.e., being "insulted because of the name of Christ" (4:14), is that a person will suffer unjust treatment, given the conflict that exists between two different standards of conduct and the fact that the Christian is "conscious of God" (cf. 1:17). But one endures hardship, it must be stressed, not out of Stoic indifference or Stoic self-sufficiency, but out of "conscience before God" (NIV, "conscious"; *dia syneidēsin theou*, v.19).

21–22 While a revolutionary call to undermine the social structure is not Peter's emphasis, Jesus' attitude toward suffering and unjust treatment is. To facilitate this model, the "suffering servant" song of Isaiah 53 is utilized, of which Jesus' attitudes are reminiscent (cf. also its use by Philip, Ac 8:26–40). This establishes an immediate and obvious link to the readers' situation—committing no sin, no deceit being found in his mouth, refusal to respond in kind, and not threatening under the heat of suffering but entrusting himself to God. After all, Christians constitute the "community of the cross" (so Davids, 106–8).

Peter is by no means fatalistic about persecution for the sake of Christ, but once more he enlists the language of election: "To this [i.e., suffering for good] you were called [*eklēthēte*, GK *1721*]" (cf. up to this point 1:1; 2:4, 9). The Petrine perspective on suffering is that Christians endure hardship for the sake of Christ precisely because he suffered, as an example (*hypogrammos*, GK *5681*), for us. The words "To this you were called" are a reiteration of the conditions of basic Christian discipleship, and the call of Jesus is to "take up the cross" and "follow" him (Mt 10:38; 16:24; Mk 8:34; Lk 9:23; 14:27). For this reason, the saints are called to "follow in his steps." In recalling Jesus' penetrating post-resurrection challenge to Peter to "follow" (Jn 21:19), Peter's failure earlier in his life to do precisely this doubtless imbues his present exhortation to "follow in his steps" with deep meaning.

24 Peter returns here to the notion of sacrifice (cf. 1:19), which provides a thematic link to Isaiah 53, making application to all in describing Christ's willingness to "bear our sins in his body on the tree" (cf. Isa 53:4, 12). That Christ did so "in his body" accents his identification with the human situation as vicarious sufferer; Jesus is representative through his suffering. The sins of all humanity were being borne, "so that we might die to sins and live for righteousness." Christ, therefore, redeems our plight. Suffering, thus seen, has a redemptive element: "by his wounds you have been healed" (cf. Isa 53:5). Sin-sick humanity is restored, and Christian "freedom" is predicated on the bedrock of redemption (as already suggested in 1:18–21).

25 Rhetorically speaking, Peter finds it necessary to remind his readers that, formerly, "you were like sheep going astray" (cf. Isa 53:6), as he has already

suggested earlier in the letter (1:14, 18; 2:10). But "now you have returned [*epestraphēte*, GK *2188*]." Doubtless his own returning is in the back of the writer's mind; he knows what it means to be restored ("when you have turned back [*epistrepsas*], strengthen your brothers," Lk 22:32).

Given the delicate nature of the themes being addressed (unjust suffering, mistreatment, showing respect to all, confidently entrusting ourselves to God who vindicates), it is fitting that this section concludes with the sheep/shepherd metaphor, reminiscent once more of Isaiah 53:6–7. The shepherd tends the flock, and in so doing he selflessly cares for the sheep, recovering those who stray. He alone is aware of dangers lurking that threaten the flock's welfare. Christ's example is compelling for several reasons. Not only did his vicarious suffering bring about redemption and not only did he not respond in kind, but through his own suffering he also established *solidarity* with the saints. Because "we do not have a high priest who is unable to sympathize with our weaknesses, but . . .who has been tempted in every way—yet was without sin" (Heb 4:15), the saints can "approach the throne of grace with confidence." It is there that they "receive mercy and find grace to help [them] in [their] time of need" (4:16).

Christ is here depicted as both "Shepherd" and "Overseer of your souls." The designation "Overseer" (*episkopos*, GK *2176*, hence the English "bishop") is not intended to denote an ecclesiastical title (and thereby suggest a later date for the epistle, as some commentary assumes). In a secular milieu, *episkopoi* are governors or administrators who supervise law and maintain public safety; thus, rich in what it suggests, the term reinforces the fact that Christ is concerned for—and superintends—the saints' welfare. He guards them in a multifaceted way. Not incidentally, Paul addresses the elders of Ephesus in very similar terms. He calls them both to "be shepherds of the church of God" and be "overseers" thereof, which was "bought with his own blood" (Ac 20:28). These attributes, which Christ himself exhibits toward the church and which inhere in the sheep/shepherd metaphor, are emphasized again later in the epistle's concluding exhortations (5:2–4); the elders are to demonstrate the same qualities as they shepherd the flock of God.

REFLECTIONS

What is disturbing to the modern mind-set is that the NT writers do not call slaves to leave their households and masters. Peter and Paul share the common conviction that Christian faith transforms relationships, in the process transcending the existing social differences—hence Paul's instructions to Onesimus not to run away from Philemon but to respond as a brother in Christ (Phm 16). The social scheme, flawed as it was, was not to be bypassed or jettisoned; rather, transforming the social scheme was the intended goal.

Peter, it should be said, is not calling his readers passively to embrace abuse. For both him and the apostle Paul, social status is neither an advantage nor a disadvantage in Christian discipleship. For both, Christians are to resist taking justice into their own hands (cf. Ro 12:17–21). A negative exhortation—refraining from these actions—is matched by a positive obligation, predicated again on the Master himself: "he entrusted himself to him who judges justly" (cf. 1:17)—an injunction Peter repeats later in the epistle (4:19). The Lord himself judges all men; he is all-seeing and all-knowing. Ultimately there will be a day of moral reckoning, at which time the saints can expect vindication.

Great confusion exists within the Christian community in our present day and age regarding peace, peacemaking, forgiveness, and nonviolence. One noted confusion advocates a "peace" ethic that conflates personal forgiveness with political responsibilities to the social order. Biblical revelation witnesses to the governing authorities' appointment by God to execute justice—and thus maintain social order—commensurate with Romans 13:1–7 and 1 Peter 2:13–17. The magistrate, therefore, is not held accountable by God to "forgive," as is mistakenly suggested by Waltner, 116–18, who draws from the arguments of Richard Hays, *The Moral Vision of the New Testament* (San Francisco: HarperSanFrancisco, 1996), and L. Gregory Jones, *Embodying Forgiveness: A Theological Analysis* (Grand Rapids: Eerdmans, 1995). While individuals privately are commanded in Scripture not to harbor bitterness, resentment, or hatred, forgiveness in the technical sense may not be granted where *repentance* has not first occurred—a spiritual reality implicit in teaching as diverse as Matthew 18:15–18 (reconciling a brother) and Leviticus 16:1–34 (the Day of Atonement). For a thorough discussion of forgiveness that is both faithful to biblical revelation and sensitive to interpersonal psychology, see A. Clendenen and T. W. Martin, *Forgiveness: Finding Freedom Through Reconciliation* (New York: Crossroads, 2002).

c. A Christian View of Marriage (3:1–7)

¹Wives, in the same way be submissive to your husbands so that, if any of them do not believe the word, they may be won over without words by the behavior of their wives, ²when they see the purity and reverence of your lives. ³Your beauty should not come from outward adornment, such as braided hair and the wearing of gold jewelry and fine clothes. ⁴Instead, it should be that of your inner self, the unfading beauty of a gentle and

quiet spirit, which is of great worth in God's sight. [5]For this is the way the holy women of the past who put their hope in God used to make themselves beautiful. They were submissive to their own husbands, [6]like Sarah, who obeyed Abraham and called him her master. You are her daughters if you do what is right and do not give way to fear.

[7]Husbands, in the same way be considerate as you live with your wives, and treat them with respect as the weaker partner and as heirs with you of the gracious gift of life, so that nothing will hinder your prayers.

COMMENTARY

1–2 Peter maintains his focus on domestic relationships (*homoiōs gynaikes*, "Wives, in the same way") and considers the tensions that might arise within the marriage as a result of Christian faith. His advice is directed toward both husbands and wives, with the latter addressed initially. The exhortations to wives strongly suggest that Peter envisions marriage in which one partner has become a believer. In keeping with the letter's theme of hardship, Peter insinuates that the marital relationship might emit strain in the case of a "mixed" marriage. Accordingly, husbands "who do not believe [*apeitheō*, GK *578*] the word" will be "won over" or "gained" (*kerdainō*, GK *3045*). Precisely how are unbelieving husbands won over? According to Peter, it is the wife's "behavior" (*anastrophē*, GK *419*, twice in vv. 1–2; also in 1:15, 18; 2:12; 3:16) that is strangely effective. Because of the power of purity and reverence in their conduct, as confirmed by parallels in ancient literature (e.g., Seneca, *Ben.* 7.9; Philo, *Virt.* 39; *Moses* 2.243; Plutarch, *Mor* 1, 141), Peter can exhort wives to subordinate themselves (*hypotassō*) to their husbands; such serene behavior has the ability to change the husband (on which, see Osiek and Balch, 148).

At first glance, the modern reader may wonder why the instructions to wives are significantly longer than those directed to husbands. This may well reflect the fact that the wife's position,

especially following conversion to the Christian faith, was much more precarious. Barclay, 218, writes, "If a husband became a Christian, he would automatically bring his wife with him into the Church and there would be no problem. But if a wife became a Christian while her husband did not, she was taking a step which was unprecedented and which produced the acutest problems [given the absence of any rights for women in antiquity and the absolute obedience to the husband that was expected]."

Curiously, however, despite these potential challenges Peter does not counsel such women to leave their husbands. Nor are they encouraged to undermine existing social distinctions—something that may strike the modern reader as scandalous. Since submission of the wife to the husband was the social custom, in a mixed marriage a lack of submission would undermine the gospel. For this reason a wife who has become a Christian must be judicious with her freedom. Seen in this light, Peter's advice is to underscore how powerful and immensely attractive—a woman's lifestyle can be. Such purity and reverence, he observes, can "win over" the husband. Moreover, this "conversion" is predicated on the wife's behavior "without words." Hereby, Peter may be speaking to or countering the temptation toward being argumentative, nagging, or manipulative toward the unbelieving husband, which might be counterproductive.

3–6 A woman's attractiveness is magnified in Peter's argument by means of a contrast between inner and outer beauty. To the pagan, virtue is praiseworthy. Believing wives have a model in this regard—Sarah in her relationship to Abraham—and should thus aspire to be "her daughters" in doing "what is right." In contrast to an "outward adornment" that is characterized, for example, by "braided hair" (cf. 1 Ti 2:9), "the wearing of gold jewelry," and donning "fine clothes," authentic beauty subsists in the attractiveness of the "inner self"—in a beauty that is "unfading" (*aphthartos*, GK *915*, also used in 1:4 regarding the saints' inheritance and 1:23 denoting the word of God). This inner beauty, it is pointed out, shows itself in "a gentle and quiet spirit," which is said to be "of great worth in God's sight."

Just as Peter has alluded to Jesus as a model of not returning evil for evil, so he cites "holy women" of the OT as an example to follow (v.5). They are exemplary because they "put their hope in God" and were accustomed to adorning themselves by being "submissive toward their husbands." Sarah is singled out as one such model or type (v.6). It is specifically noted of Sarah that she "obeyed Abraham and called him her master," an allusion to Genesis 18:12 and Sarah's response to childbearing in spite of her age. While nothing in the Genesis narrative suggests exemplary obedience, rabbinic tradition developed the idea of Sarah's obedience and submission to Abraham. Peter appears to be borrowing from extrabiblical tradition in his weaving together of several important subthemes in the letter—holiness (1:2, 5, 19, 22; 2:5), hope (1:3, 21; 3:15), and respect undergirded by humility (2:13–3:12). Sarah is useful in weaving these strands together.

Christian wives who model Sarah's attitude become "her daughters" to the extent that they "do what is right" and "do not give way to fear." This image of Sarah seems a counterpart to Abraham, who is a model (cf. Ro 4:12). Doing right and not being governed by fear constitute a call to be active, constructive, and hopeful in the married relationship rather than being passively acquiescent, to which many might be inclined. From the Genesis narrative it can be reasonably asserted that Sarah was "forced" to trust the Lord; i.e., the path on which the Lord was directing her was *not of her own choosing*; nevertheless, it was a path she ultimately embraced by faith (Heb 11:11). Further, Peter's admonitions to wives resist modern interpreters' attempts to read into the text the notion that 1 Peter is oppressive. The writer is attuned to the difficulties women would have experienced in the domestic context, particularly in a mixed marriage.

7 Following his exhortations to wives, the writer addresses husbands. Four requirements are noted. The first of the four is strikingly suggestive, with the text literally reading, "living together according to knowledge" (*synoikountes kata gnōsin*), hence, "being considerate." In the context of day-to-day marital relations, this imperative is sweeping. Living with a woman "according to knowledge" stands in marked contrast to living with a woman out of "sheer thoughtlessness" (so Barclay, 223). Waltner, 99, encompasses the full range of female needs when he writes that this exhortation "constitutes a call to respect the full personhood of the woman in a marriage relationship."

Second, husbands are to "treat [their wives] with respect as the weaker partner" (*hōs asthenesterō skeuei tō gynaikeiō*). How the woman is "weaker" is the subject of varied—and fancied—explanation by commentators. Whether *asthenēs* ("weak," GK *822*) has physical, psychological, or emotional application is debatable but beside the point. Marshall, 103–4, strikes a reasonable balance: husbands, cognizant of the wives' situation, are to treat them with courtesy; given their station, they are more vulnerable. Christian faith has a revolutionary effect not only on the way men treat women but also on how they view them. What is incontestable about the plight of married women in the ancient world is that they possessed no authority and influence beside their husbands. Hence, Christian husbands are doubly sensitive to this "weakness," consequently treating them with *timē*, "honor" (NIV, "respect"; GK *5507*). This social reality also explains why the verb *hypotassō* ("submit," GK *5718*), appearing in 2:13; 2:18; 3:1 (and later in 3:22; 5:5), is not used in 3:7, since husbands already exercise a natural social authority over their wives. This authority, in the Petrine scheme, must be accompanied by deference and courtesy. Husbands are to honor rather than exploit, since exploitation likely is the norm.

Third, husbands are to keep in mind that their wives are "heirs with [them] of the gracious gift of life" (*synklēronomois charitos zōēs*). If indeed wives, in the social scheme of antiquity, were without rights and considered of inferior status, Christian faith elevated the status of women, so that in Christ male and female are coequal (1Co 12:13; Gal 3:28). The full

blessing, peace, and welfare that arise from Christian faith are shared by both husband and wife. They are partners in the riches and benefits of the gospel (similarly, 2Pe 1:1). There exist equality and complementarity within the social scheme of things.

The fourth quality issues out of the prior three. A husband who is inattentive to his wife, failing to show her consideration, honor, and respect, finds that a barrier is erected between him and his God. For this reason, husbands are to be attentive to the needs of their wives, "so that nothing will hinder your prayers." Advice of a similar nature is given by Paul to the Corinthians in the sphere of marital relations (cf. 1Co 7:4–5). Harmony in the relationship is predicated on a principle enunciated by Jesus: if our relationships are not right, we are to "leave [the] gift there in front of the altar" (Mt 5:24; cf. also 18:15) until the block has been removed. This is all the more applicable in marital union and is likely the principal rationale for calling men "everywhere to lift up holy hands in prayer" (1Ti 2:8; cf. 1Co 11:29).

NOTES

1–7 Lohse, 37–59, and Marshall, 83–84, have clearly and concisely framed the issue of honor and respect as it touches the role of husbands and their wives. That husbands do not submit to their wives, given the existing social scheme in the first century, would have been understood. That "all of you"—the final group addressed by Peter (v.8)—are admonished toward unity, sympathy, and humility suggests a sort of "mutual submission" at work within the community.

REFLECTIONS

The extent to which Christian faith dignified the status of women of antiquity is mirrored in the pages of the NT. Women figure prominently in the ministry of the fledgling church (e.g., Ac 16:11–15; 18:1–4, 18–28) and in the ministry of the apostle Paul (e.g., Ro 16:1–16; 1Co 1:11; 16:19; 2Ti 4:19–21). Indeed, within the church, social distinctions that existed in surrounding society fell away

(e.g., Ro 11:17–21; 1Co 12:13; Gal 3:28). By contrast, women to whom Paul was writing were without legal rights and protection according to Roman law. Marriage merely moved a woman from the authority of the father (*patria potestas*) to that of a husband, to whom she was now absolutely subject. Given the social restrictions on women fully apart from religion, it is exceedingly difficult for the modern reader—at least in many parts of the world—to visualize and empathize with a woman's problems if she became a Christian and thereby refused her husband's loyalties, religious or otherwise. Without any rights in the technical sense, life for Christian wives of unbelieving husbands may have seemed unbearable.

While the amount of instruction directed at wives might give the impression of unevenness on the part of the writer, appearances are deceiving. In relatively little space the writer has much to say to admonish husbands, who "in the same way"—i.e., reciprocally—have important obligations toward their wives. Respect, the thread linking each constitutive element in the household code with the others, is measured by Peter for husbands in four tangible ways: showing understanding, showing deference to the "weaker" partner, treating her as a joint heir in the faith, and acting in such a way that one's prayers are not hindered. It becomes immediately apparent to the reader that Peter maintains equality within the existing social conventions.

d. A Christian Response to Unjust Treatment (3:8–12)

[8]Finally, all of you, live in harmony with one another; be sympathetic, love as brothers, be compassionate and humble. [9]Do not repay evil with evil or insult with insult, but with blessing, because to this you were called so that you may inherit a blessing. [10]For,

"Whoever would love life
   and see good days
must keep his tongue from evil
   and his lips from deceitful speech.
[11]He must turn from evil and do good;
   he must seek peace and pursue it.
[12]For the eyes of the Lord are on the righteous
   and his ears are attentive to their prayer,
but the face of the Lord is against those who do evil."

COMMENTARY

8 Peter signals the conclusion of the household code admonitions with "finally, all of you." The concluding exhortation is addressed to everyone in the community. What applies specifically to individual groups regarding respect and harmony applies to the community. The Christian ethic will exhibit unity, sympathy, brotherly affection, compassion, humility, and nonretaliation. Together these six qualities possess a corporate character that will strengthen the Christian community's witness to society.

To be of the same mind (*homophrōn*, GK *3939*; NIV, "live in harmony with") is to be on guard against divisions that would hinder Christian unity. Because of the imperative of unity as witness to the world, Jesus prays, on the eve of his crucifixion, for his disciples to realize a degree of unity that he and the Father have shared in eternity (Jn 17:1–5). Jesus' prayer is "that all of them may be one . . . so that the world may believe that you have sent me" (Jn 17:21). The accent on Christian unity is found throughout the NT (e.g., Ac 4:32; Ro 12:4–5, 16; 1Co 1:2, 10; 3:5–9, 21–23; 10:17; 12:4–7, 12–13; 2Co 13:11; Eph 4:4–6; Php 1:27; 2:2; 4:2). Unity does not require uniformity; being of the same mind is not predicated on simple agreement with others. It is, however, founded on a common Lord, a common confession, and a common goal of witness to the world. No Christian can live the Christian life in isolation, but only as he or she is joined, with one mind, to other members of God's church, living stones that together comprise one building. The church is not church if there is no inherent, manifested unity. If the readers are encountering hostility from society around them, Christian unity is no luxury; it is critical for survival.

A related attitude is that of being sympathetic (*sympatheis*, GK *5218*). It is the essential nature of the human body to be "sympathetic" (cf. 1Co 12:26), to which Peter calls his readers. Sympathy, as Barclay, 227, reminds us, is the opposite of self-absorption, the ability to identify with the sufferings and pains of others. To share in the sufferings of others is both the cause and effect of Christian unity. The believers' model once again is Christ, the high priest, who sympathizes with [*sympathēsai*] our weaknesses (Heb 4:15). Significantly, sympathy is not merely a Christian virtue; it was also held in high esteem by Hellenistic moralists (e.g., Plutarch, *Mor.* 432; Strabo, *Geogr.* 6.3.3). Like unity, sympathy strengthens Christians in the world.

Furthermore, being "affectionate" (NIV, "love as brothers"; *philadelphos*, GK *5789*), "compassionate" (*eusplanchnos*, GK *2359*), and "humble" (*tapeinophrones*, GK *5426*) all stand in direct relation to sympathy and Christian unity. Moreover, all are vital to the community's survival in a hostile environment. Brotherly affection is also included in the catalog of virtues appearing in 1 Peter 1:5–7, where it is related to—

though distinct from—love (*agapē*, GK *27*). While the distinction should not be pressed too far, the former is a virtue valued by pagans, appearing frequently in Stoic virtue lists, for example. A practical test in any cultural context is whether the Christian will love his fellow human. Moreover, a hearty affection for one's brothers and sisters in the community will attest to the vibrancy of the community's faith. *Philadelphia* has a notably *social* trajectory.

The word rendered "compassionate," *eusplanchnos*, vividly conveys feeling and emotion. Deriving from *splanchna* (GK *5073*), one's inner organs, the term by extension conveys deep, intense emotion. Its only other NT occurrence is in Ephesians 4:32, contextualized in Pauline admonitions toward tenderheartedness, though the verb form is found in the Synoptic Gospels, notably in depicting the Good Samaritan (Lk 10:33), who "took pity," and the father of the prodigal (Lk 15:20), who on seeing his son returning home "was filled with compassion." And it finds its fullest expression in Jesus himself (Mk 1:41), who is said by the evangelist, when approached by a leper, to have been "filled with compassion."

Among secular Hellenistic moralists, to be "humble" was not considered a virtue, given the primacy of self-sufficiency (*autarkeia*, GK *894*). Hence it is a peculiarly Christian ethical distinctive. The Christian ethic reorients and transforms one's outlook. Humility springs in part from an awareness of our creatureliness and thus of our utter dependence on the Creator. But this contrast is not intended to be demeaning, provided that the creature draws on divine provision (i.e., grace). Humility that acknowledges and appropriates grace is a humility that does not humiliate; rather, it is buoyed by gratitude (cf. 1:6–9, 18–21) and results in attitudes and actions that are active rather than passive.

9 As it pertains to the readers' situation, being humble will lead to an active and redemptive response toward the wrong being directed toward

Christians. It will result in "not repaying evil with evil or insult [*loidoria*, GK *3367*] with insult." The true test of character—and Christian faith—is how the believer responds when treated with contempt, since out of instinct humans tend to retaliate (cf. Mt 5:39–42). Mounce, 48, cogently identifies the rub, since repaying insult with insult, evil with evil, is fundamental to human nature: "But isn't that the essence of Christian conduct—acting contrary to our old and fallen nature?"

Rather than a response of insult or retaliation, the Christian is admonished, on the contrary, toward "blessing" (*eulogeō*, GK *2328*) others, i.e., acting graciously toward them. This advice is strikingly reminiscent of that given by Paul, who writes in a similar context, "Bless those who persecute you; bless and do not curse" (Ro 12:14). Indeed, Peter writes that Christians have been "called" (*eklegomai*, GK *1721*; note again the language of election, as in 1:1, 15; 2:4, 9, 21; 3:9; 5:10) to extend goodwill, even to those who oppose or mistreat them. Why? Peter's rationale is that the saints themselves have been recipients of divine mercy; therefore, it is within them to extend the same to fellow human beings—teaching that lies at the heart of the Christian gospel (e.g., Mt 5:38–48; Lk 6:27). Jesus'

instructions concerning prayer are guided by a similar principle (cf. Mt 6:12, 14–15).

Peter's further rationale for dealing graciously with others is pragmatic: "so that you may inherit a blessing." Earlier, Peter had reminded his readers of the incorruptible, undefiled, and unfading inheritance (*klēronomia*, GK *3100*) that was theirs through the new birth (1:3–5). Peter here uses the verbal form, *klēronomēsēte*, to encourage them: if they bless, they will inherit a blessing.

10–12 As he has done throughout the letter, Peter buttresses his paraenetic teaching by citation, and once more he appropriates Psalm 34, adapting it for his present purposes. Important points of contact between the psalm and the readers' situation are worth noting: keeping the tongue from evil and the lips from deceitful speech, turning from evil and doing good, seeking and pursuing peace, as well as divine omniscience and attentiveness to their cares (thus G. L. Green, "The Use of the Old Testament for Christian Ethics in 1 Peter," *TynBul* 41/2 [1990]: 278–82). The citation from Psalm 34 has the effect of instilling the fear of the Lord in the reader, with its concluding reminder that the Lord's face is set against anyone who does evil. Thus the Christian is compelled to pursue good.

REFLECTIONS

The biblical understanding of authority is that all earthly forms of power inhere in and derive from a heavenly source. This is evidenced in the OT, whether through Pharaoh (e.g., Ex 7:3; 14:17–18; cf. Ro 9:17) or Nebuchadnezzar (e.g., Jer 28:14; 25:8–11; 27:6–7; 43:10–13) or Cyrus (e.g., Isa 44:28; 45:1). One exceedingly exemplary member of the OT Diaspora community reveals his own understanding of authority as follows: "Praise be to the name of God for ever and ever, wisdom and power are his. He changes times and seasons; he sets up kings and deposes them" (Da 2:20–22).

The same understanding of authority is found in the NT. The apostle Paul writes to the Christians living in the imperial seat of Rome to reassure them that the governing authorities are appointed by God himself and possess no authority apart from what is granted to them (Ro 13:1–7). On the eve of his crucifixion, Jesus confesses this very reality. When Pilate reminds him that he has the authority to release or crucify Jesus, Jesus' response is telling: "You would have no power over me if it were not given to you from above" (Jn 19:11). The Great Commission, recorded at the end of Matthew's gospel, leaves no room for uncertainty: "All authority in heaven and on earth has been given to [Jesus]" (Mt 28:18). This absolute authority cannot be "given" unless it resides already in the Father, the sovereign Lord.

It is exceedingly difficult for the modern reader to read the social obligations enumerated in 2:13–3:12 without raising a multitude of questions. At the very least, the political and social structures of life in the twenty-first century appear so radically different from those of the first century that we are tempted to impose modern presuppositions on the text. One interpretive approach to be avoided is to assume that the NT writers are naive or indifferent to political, social, and familial relationships and, consequently, impose contemporary values and categories on the biblical text. Another mistaken interpretive approach is to marshal 1 Peter in support of contemporary values. Thus this epistle should not be made to support totalitarian or oppressive authority, but neither should it be made to explain away or ignore the implications of *hypotassō* (GK 5718). To illustrate: thoroughly unacceptable is Barclay's claim, 206, contextualized in his comparison of democracy and dictatorship, that "submission"

only has to do with the authoritative state that demands "absolute obedience." Distortions of this kind have more to do with faulty notions of what constitutes submission than with different types of government. It is my position that no interpreter comes to the text in a "neutral" fashion, but also that the text must be permitted to speak in its political, social, and cultural context, thereby forcing the modern reader to scrutinize certain cherished assumptions. The perspective of 1 Peter is that faith works through—rather than invalidating—social conventions. Moreover, submission on an earthly level, while voluntary, is rooted in a submission to the heavenly Master and balanced by a strong emphasis on God's authority, judgment, and providential care. Properly conceived, submission is a sign of respect, not servility (so Senior, 49, 58). Further, "submission" is within the bounds of what God wills, requires, and commands; hence the language of *submission to divine authority* that laces its way throughout the household code: e.g., "for the Lord's sake" (2:13); "God's will" (2:15); using freedom as "servants of God" (2:16); "fear God" (2:17); "because he is conscious of God" (2:19); "commendable before God" (2:20); "in God's sight" (3:4).

D. Christian Suffering Due to Righteous Living (3:13–5:11)

1. A Christian Perspective on Suffering (3:13–4:6)

a. Preparing a Christian Response to Suffering (3:13–17)

OVERVIEW

There is a shift in the writer's focus beginning with 3:13. It is not a shift from the theoretical to the practical; Peter has very practically illustrated that Christian witness and transformation work its way through existing social conventions. Rather, it is a shift to address the theme of suffering head-on and expressly exhort the readers in the midst of their

hardships. (While the household code of 2:13–3:7 does not address suffering directly, it is nevertheless in the background, as J. L. de Villiers, "Joy in Suffering in 1 Peter," *Neot* 9 [1975]: 65, observes.) Consistent with the rest of the letter, Peter does not engage in a "theology of suffering" per se. Neither does he wrestle with the nagging question of *why* the righteous suffer or *why* a good and loving God can permit it. From this point forward, the emphasis is essentially threefold: (1) to be prepared for it, (2) to look once more to Jesus as our model, and (3) to entrust oneself into the hands of a just God, who will both vindicate and judge. In the material that follows, these three strands are effectively interwoven.

---

[13]Who is going to harm you if you are eager to do good? [14]But even if you should suffer for what is right, you are blessed. "Do not fear what they fear; do not be frightened." [15]But in your hearts set apart Christ as Lord. Always be prepared to give an answer to everyone who asks you to give the reason for the hope that you have. But do this with gentleness and respect, [16]keeping a clear conscience, so that those who speak maliciously against your good behavior in Christ may be ashamed of their slander. [17]It is better, if it is God's will, to suffer for doing good than for doing evil.

COMMENTARY

13 Peter opens with a rhetorical question intended to cause reflection: Who among those accosting (*ho kakōsōn*, in most translations rendered "harming" or "doing evil," GK *2808*) the saints succeeds "if you are eager to do good"? The immediate answer, "No one," based on Peter's previous argument of eternal perspective (i.e., the past, present, and future), is that nothing can detract from their inheritance that is imperishable, undefiled, and unfading (1:3–9). Peter's focus, however, remains the same as before: *doing good*. While it is possible to be passionate or misguided about the wrong things, being zealots of the good cannot be faulted. Peter's admonition has the ring of Paul, who describes Christians as a people "zealous for good deeds" (*zē-lōtēn kalōn ergōn*, Tit 2:14 NASB). Moral integrity, in the end, cannot be impugned.

14 But in cases where Christians indeed do "suffer for what is right" (*paschō dia dikaiosynēn*), they are declared, as Jesus announced, to be "blessed." This suffering, it should be emphasized, is not some hypothetical situation, as some commentators have assumed; rather, we can presume that the readers are, in reality, suffering in their present situation, a situation already intimated in 1:6. Peter's response to suffering "for what is right" is to reiterate the words of his master: "Blessed are those who are persecuted because of righteousness, for theirs is the kingdom of heaven" (Mt 5:10). In taking up Christian discipleship, one learns that persecution is unavoidable, as Jesus states without ambiguity (Mt 10:34–39; Jn 15:18–22).

14–16 Peter forthrightly tells his readers that awareness of one's status before God (*makarios*, GK *3421*) does not guarantee an absence of intimidation and fear of consequence. His exhortation consists of four elements—two parts negative and two parts positive. "Do not fear what they fear; do not be frightened [or intimidated]" are the two negative requirements, while "set apart Christ as Lord" and "always be prepared to give an answer" are the positive rejoinders. In the heat of conflict, it is impossible for human nature, apart from divine grace, to respond redemptively and with self-composure to evil intentions; fear and intimidation are natural. As before on multiple occasions, Peter marshals support for his paraenesis from the OT—this time from Isaiah 8:12, the context of which finds Judah discouraged as it faces an impending Assyrian invasion. In extracting this citation, Peter is not merely casting about for OT promises; he is identifying with a persecuted community in the old covenant, and concerned moreover to transfer honor and lordship to Christ. "But in your hearts set apart Christ as Lord," furthermore, is not merely a call to pious devotion; it is intended to underscore the *public* ramifications of Christ's rule—a rule, as the writer will accent, that culminates in his exaltation, "with angels, authorities and powers in submission to him" (3:22).

Accordingly, the awareness of the cosmic dimension of Christ's rule/lordship allows the believer—indeed, frees the believer—to be ready with an apologetic for "everyone who asks you to give the reason for the hope that you have." That is to say, a mind-set rooted in Christ's uncontested lordship produces *boldness*—boldness both to resist intimidation and to offer an apologetic. Carrying over certain elements of the legal term *apologia* (GK *665*), Peter (as Paul in Php 1:7, 16) exhorts his readers toward readiness in laying out a formal defense of their faith, whenever and wherever it might occur. Significantly, the apologetic is described by Peter as a defense of Christian hope, consistent with what has been an important leitmotif throughout the epistle (1:3, 13, 21; 3:5). Only because they are hopeful can the readers face and overcome persecution. Those commentators who view this admonition as referring to a general posture rather than a particular crisis situation correctly grasp the thrust of this paraenesis. Michaels, 188, expresses it this way: "Peter sees his readers as being 'on trial' every day as they live for Christ in a pagan society." The defense, moreover, is one that is reasonable, sustained, accessible, and well articulated, as any courtroom presentation would have to be in order for it to be credible.

A reasonable defense of Christian hope, however, while anchored in a boldness that alone finds its source in Christ's cosmic lordship, nevertheless must be done "with gentleness and respect" (Barclay, 231, "with winsomeness and love"). Note again that the attitude of human *respect*—the attitude that undergirds each element of the household code—is the Christian's baseline motivation. Hillyer, 109, aptly notes that a quiet dignity is far more effective than argument and belligerence. Christians must learn to supply a defense of the faith without being "defensive" in the way they present themselves. This is especially important in dialogue with pagans, who will tend to be suspicious of the Christian community. The Christian defense, moreover, is to issue out of a "clear conscience" (the second such appeal to conscience in the letter; also in 2:19; 3:21). That conscience is related to right conduct and personal integrity, as most commentators observe, is certainly true, but the present context relates conscience to the Christians' response to abuse and reviling (vv. 9, 16). The sense in which "clear conscience" is applicable appears similar to what Peter had in mind earlier: seeing your goodness the pagan will "glorify God" on the judgment day (2:12) and be "silenced" in shame (2:15). Peter's reasoning ("so that") here—"those who speak maliciously against your good behavior in Christ may be ashamed [*kataischynō*, GK *2875*, also used in 2:6] of their slander"—follows his earlier line of reasoning that doing good would "silence the ignorant talk" of foolish people (2:15).

17 But what if the abusers do not have a change of heart? What about unjust suffering? After all, there is no guarantee that the believer's integrity under trial will "silence" or stop the offender. In such cases, then, "it is better . . . to suffer for doing good than for doing evil." This advice is precisely the same as that given earlier to slaves who encounter abusive masters (2:20–21). Given the alternatives before the believer in such situations, one can either respond by "doing evil"—and suffer the (just) consequences—or respond by doing good—in which case Peter has already said that the offended, like Christ, is to entrust himself "to him who judges justly" (2:23).

NOTES

13–17 It is difficult at this juncture not to read into Peter's admonition regarding "readiness" the possibility that in the back of his mind is lodged his own failure years earlier. The fourth gospel captures with a sense of tragic irony this failure on the part of the impetuous disciple to offer up a defense: upon following Jesus after Jesus' betrayal and arrest, Peter wholly disavows his Lord (Jn 18:15–18). This occurs, it will be remembered, despite his vigorous assertion made only hours before that he would be willing to die for his Master (Mt 26:30–35; Mk 14:26–31; Lk 22:31–34). Doubtless, a lifetime could not erase such a bitter memory (Lk 22:62).

REFLECTIONS

The writer's full rationale for *not* responding in kind to abusers has yet to be developed. In the material that follows (3:18–4:19), suffering as a Christian (i.e., suffering for "doing right") is qualified with an important eschatological reality: those who endure unjust suffering can expect vindication. This vindication is as sure as *Christ's* vindication (3:18–22) and as sure as the fact that God is a God of judgment (4:1–19). To be fully convinced of future vindication and not lapse into despair, one must lay hold of an eschatological perspective that is firmly anchored; neither emotional experience nor religious feelings will hold in the heat of persecution. Reassuring his readers that vindication in fact *does* await the innocent sufferer is the task at hand. Once more, the writer points to the example of Christ, whose destiny should encourage the disconsolate.

b. Christ's Suffering and Vindication (3:18–22)

OVERVIEW

In all the NT, 1 Peter 3:18–22 is considered one of the most difficult and enigmatic passages to interpret. Martin Luther's perplexity was thusly expressed: "This is as strange a text and enigmatic a saying as there is anywhere in the New Testament, so that I do not yet know exactly what St. Peter means" (*Luther's Works* 12.367). The history of its interpretation is characterized by wildly divergent assumptions and understandings of what it purports to teach. These complexities notwithstanding, 3:18–22 represents something of a climax in the unfolding of the Petrine case regarding suffering. For this reason, our determination of both its function in the epistle and its teaching for the church cannot be overemphasized. We must therefore attempt to arrive at a basic understanding of the text by paying careful attention to its place in the Petrine argument. The judicious words of Dalton, 7–9, from whose thorough investigation of these verses any student of the NT would benefit, are worth repeating: "The difficulty of the text lies not in the thought of the author, which is neither odd nor fantastic, but in our ignorance of his background and field of reference. . . . Studies in later

Jewish apocryphal writings and in early Jewish-Christian literature reveal a whole world of ideas which was powerfully at work, all the more so because simply taken for granted, in the writers of the New Testament."

In these verses we pass from Christ's suffering, a central theme of the letter, to Christ's triumph, both of which relate to his saving work. In 3:8–17 the author had traced the psychology of the believer's suffering for Christ in a pagan and hostile world. Now he views the effects of Christ's work in terms of its results, for Jesus goes into heaven and is enthroned at the right hand of God, with all powers subject to his rule. The writer wishes to comfort his audience with the reassurance that (1) Christ is their "captain," the one who went before them and also suffered, and (2) there is nothing in the cosmos that remains outside the conquest and reign of Christ. Insofar as 4:1 resumes discussion of the prior theme ("Therefore, since Christ suffered in his body . . ."), 3:18–22 may be viewed as a parenthesis. In this parenthetical thought, the writer wishes to inform the readers that not everything that Christ's death entails meets the eye. Those who henceforth take refuge in Christ, the Victorious One, come through the flood of divine retribution.

Structurally, the declarations contained in 3:18–22, as evidenced by their symmetry and hymnic form, are generally assumed by commentators to mirror the early church's creedal affirmation. The symmetry takes on an ABA'B' design: Christ died, Christ rose, Christ descended, and Christ ascended:

A   He was put to death in the body.
B   He was made alive by the Spirit.
A' He descended and preached to the spirits.
B' He ascended and rules over the spirits.

Indeed, one might go a step farther, as S. E. Johnson did ("The Preaching to the Dead [1 Peter 3.18–22]," *JBL* 79]1960]: 48–51), in detecting in the structure of this "hymn" a chiastic or reversed symmetry:

A   He suffered and was put to death.
B   He was made alive and went and preached to the spirits
C   who were disobedient
D   in the building of the ark, in which a few were saved.
D' This pattern corresponds to baptism that now saves you,
C' not a washing of dirt from the body, but a stipulation toward God of a good conscience
B' through the resurrection of Jesus Christ, who has gone into heaven—with angels, authorities and powers in submission to him.
A' Therefore, since Christ suffered . . .

[18]For Christ died for sins once for all, the righteous for the unrighteous, to bring you to God. He was put to death in the body but made alive by the Spirit, [19]through whom also he went and preached to the spirits in prison [20]who disobeyed long ago when God waited patiently in the days of Noah while the ark was being built. In it only a few people, eight in all, were saved through water, [21]and this water symbolizes baptism that now saves you also–not the removal of dirt from the body but the pledge of a good conscience toward God. It saves you by the resurrection of Jesus Christ, [22]who has gone into heaven and is at God's right hand–with angels, authorities and powers in submission to him.

COMMENTARY

18 Immediately preceding this verse, the writer stresses the Christian response to persecution. Believers are thus to look to their Lord: "For Christ suffered . . ." (NIV, "died"; *paschō*, GK *4248*, used twelve times in 1 Peter, roughly one-third of all its occurrences in the NT). This suffering, moreover, was vicarious, for the sins of others; it was substitutionary atonement—"the righteous for the unrighteous," unique and once-for-all (*hapax*, GK *562*) in character (Heb 7:27; 9:28; 10:11–12; cf. Jude 5). This was done, writes Peter, "to bring [*prosagō*, GK *4642*] you to God." Accessibility to the divine throne, where Peter ends in this parenthetical insertion (3:22), is of critical importance to the readers psychologically if they are enduring considerable hardship in the present cultural context.

That Christ was "put to death [*thanatoō*, GK *2506*] in the body" establishes immediate and crucial identification with the readers. Both share a common existential experience (lit.) "in the flesh": both suffer. But this is not the end; the story progresses. While Christ was put to death in the flesh, on the one hand, he was also and subsequently "made alive by the Spirit" (*zōopoieō pneumati*). This flesh-Spirit contrast serves several purposes. At one level, it counters any divorce or dichotomizing of the two that would have typified Hellenistic thinking (cf. 1Jn 4:2). The scandal of the early church's preaching was its Christology: Jesus Christ is fully human and fully divine (cf. Col 1:19). At another level, it reminds the audience that, while "the body is weak," indeed, the Spirit is willing (cf. Mt 26:41). The same Spirit who sanctifies (1:2), grants revelation (1:11), makes us holy (1:15–16), and raised Jesus from the dead (3:18) also quickens the believer. The Spirit helps us transcend our earthly limitations.

19–22 In the realm of the Spirit, according to Peter, Christ "went and preached to the spirits in prison." Two problems surface in this somewhat cryptic declaration: the identity of "spirits in prison" (*en phylakē pneumasin*) and the identity of the message "preached" (*kēryssō*, GK *3062*). Two prominent interpretations of "imprisoned spirits," enjoying support both in the patristic period as well as today, vie for our consideration. One is that these are contemporaries of Noah, a reading that seems plausible in light of v.20. The second alternative is that this a reference to OT saints, i.e., righteous persons who died before Christ.

Several remarks about both possibilities—"spirits" as deceased humans—are in order. Among the arguments cited in support of rendering *pneumata* in 3:19 as human souls are: (1) the occurrence in v.18 of *pneumati* and in v.19 *pneumasin*; (2) the low probability that Peter's readers, who are scattered through Asia Minor, would understand any allusion to a Jewish pseudepigraphal work such as *1 Enoch*; (3) "preaching" that is addressed to humans in 4:6; (4) a similar *sarx/pneuma* (GK *4922, 4460*) dualism found in 4:6; (5) reconciling the time and place of preaching to fallen angels with the clause "when God waited patiently in the days of Noah while the ark was being built"; (6) the emphasis in Genesis 6 on human disobedience as the cause of divine judgment; and (7) the emphasis in 1 Peter on *human*, not demonic, sources of persecution.

According to the first view, Christ in his preexistent state is said to preach through Noah to Noah's generation, which was "imprisoned" by spiritual blindness. Despite the allusions to Noah and to disobedience that follow in the text, it is not clear from the context why only the generation of Noah would be singled out by Peter. The most that can be said about this reading is that Noah's contemporaries are paradigmatic. "Prison" and "spirits" in this interpretation, then, must be understood metaphorically. Also and more importantly, this view fails to do justice to the contextual link extending to v.22, at which point Christ is said to rule over the angelic, and specifically the demonic, realm. Finally, Christ's preaching through Noah evaporates any notion of a "descent."

The second interpretation, that "spirits" represent OT saints before Christ, suffers from similar weaknesses. It violates the contextual flow and represents something of a digression in the writer's argument. Thus when Tertullian (*An.* 55.2) writes that "Christ descended into hell in order to acquaint the patriarchs and prophets with his redeeming mission," he does so with total disregard for the contextual and thematic development of 1 Peter's argument. Further, it does not accord with the sense of "imprisonment"—that is, forced restraint and confinement—that *phylakē* suggests.

On the whole, both views fail to give account of the fact that *pneumata* in the NT normally designates angelic beings (e.g., Mt 8:16; 10:1; 12:45; Mk 1:27; 3:11; 5:13; 6:7; Lk 4:36; 6:16; 7:21; 8:2; 10:20; 11:26; Ac 5:16; 8:7; 19:12–13; 23:8–9; 1Ti 4:1; Heb 1:7,14; 12:9; 1Jn 4:1; Rev 1:4; 3:1; 4:5; 5:6; 16:13–14).

Even though an understanding of "spirits" as demonic angels probably would have been taken for granted in the first century due to its prominence in Jewish apocalyptic literature, the view that the "spirits" were humans, whether deceased righteous ones or contemporaries of Noah, seems to have prevailed among many church fathers. One wonders whether the human interpretation of "spirits" among them owed to the same reason documents such as 2 Peter and Jude encountered difficulties in being accepted in some parts of the church, namely, due to an increasing wariness of apocalyptic and pseudepigraphal writings. Such works, particularly those in the mold of *1 Enoch,*

are fantastic and fanciful to the extreme in their depiction of the demonic realm and its interaction with the material world.

In identifying the "spirits," we have already suggested that a proper interpretation of 3:18–22 must be in accordance with—and not violate—the contextual flow of the writer's thought. That the work of Christ touches the *angelic world* is by no means tangential to the epistle. The holy angels curiously long to peer into the mysteries that surround redemption (1:12). Moreover, the result of Christ's work is that angelic powers, not mere mortals, are in submission to Christ (3:22). Finally, readers are admonished to be alert, since "your enemy the devil," the prince of demons, desires their ruin.

Although biblical literature contains no systematic explanation of the spirit world, the language of "imprisoned spirits" appears elsewhere in the NT. Jude 6 and 2 Peter 2:4 afford a tantalizing—albeit cryptic—glimpse at the demonic realm. Both texts incorporate the fallen angels in a catalog of disobedient, wicked paradigms that were befallen by divine judgment. Similarly, the apocalyptic visions contained in Revelation 18 and 20 help clarify the identity of "imprisoned spirits." Neither text describes a place of departed souls; rather, both visions depict punishment and banishment. "Babylon" in 18:2 is referred to as "a home for demons and a haunt for every evil spirit," while 20:1–3 depicts an angel coming down out of heaven with a key to the "Abyss," wherein Satan is "bound," "thrown," and "sealed." An "Abyss" is also mentioned in Luke 8:31; Romans 10:7; Revelation 9:1–2, 11; 11:17; and 17:8. In each of these contexts, it connotes demonic confinement, in stark contrast to "Abraham's side" (Lk 16:22) and "paradise" (Lk 23:43). The similarity of imagery in 1 Peter 3 to Jude 6, 2 Peter 2:4, Revelation 18:2; and 20:1–3 suggests, at minimum, a common religious thought-world.

Yet another important text that supplements our understanding of "imprisoned spirits" is found in Colossians. The apostle notes that God through Christ cancelled the debt of sins that stood against us, "nailing it to the cross." Thereby, he "disarmed the powers and authorities" and "made a public spectacle of them, triumphing over them by the cross" (Col 2:14–15). Two images are combined in this text, ever so briefly, to illustrate the extent of Christ's work: a legal metaphor and a military metaphor. The latter concerns the effects of Christ's sacrifice in the spirit world—effects illustrated by means of the image of a Roman triumphal procession. This picture, immediately transparent to the readers, finds a transferring of the military conquest by Rome and subsequent public humiliation of the vanquished throughout the streets of the city to the work of Christ and his foes in the spirit realm. Christ is conqueror and parades the vanquished foes—demonic powers—before the onlooking universe (cf. 1Co 15:24–27; Php 2:10).

The vocabulary of the unseen world utilized by Paul comports precisely with that used in 1 Peter 3:22, which describes Christ as having subjugated every *angelos* (GK *34*), *exousia* (GK *2026*), and *dynamis* (GK *1539*). Elsewhere Paul alludes to the consummation of all things by declaring that "at the name of Jesus every knee should bow, in heaven and on earth and under the earth" (Php 2:10). The description "under the earth" is a reference to the demonic realm.

Closely related to the objects of Christ's preaching is the message being preached. That the verb *euangelizomai* ("to preach the gospel," GK *2294*) is not used here, as it is in 4:6, is instructive. Rather, Peter uses the verb *kēryssō* (GK *3062*); i.e., Christ announces his triumph over the powers of evil. Scripture never depicts Christ as "evangelizing"— or redeeming—the spirit world. The burden of

1 Peter, it should be reiterated, is the endurance of Christians, not the salvation of "spirits" (however one might define them).

The point of Christ's preaching to the spirits, then, the notion of which reaches a climax in v.22, is to show that Jesus has triumphed over and exposed *the very powers of evil themselves*—forces that are hostile to Christ and Christ's disciples. More to the point, Jesus Christ, the innocent sufferer, was vindicated. If our interpretation is correct, the idea that Christ—the new Enoch, the Son of Man, the Messiah, the Righteous One—triumphed over the powers should serve to *greatly* encourage the readers. This message of encouragement represents a "crystallization of various Jewish traditions" (so Pearson, 198)—traditions corroborated by other important NT texts—and reminds Peter's audience of the utter conquest of evil.

If 1 Peter is depicting Christ as an "end-time" Enoch who has proclaimed judgment over the fallen spirits, a similar literary strategy is applied by using Noah, who in Jewish apocalyptic tradition is the type par excellence of a righteous man (e.g., *1 En.* 10:1–4; 67:1; *2 En.* 35:1; *Jub.* 5:19; 7:20–39; 8:10–11; 10:1–13; 39:24; Wis 10:4; Sir 44:17–18; 2 Esd 3:11; 4 Macc 15:31; *T. Naph.* 3:5; Josephus, *Ant.* 1.3.2). The early church appears to have had keen interest in Noah and the flood narrative. Its mention in Matthew 24:37–39; Luke 17:26–27; Hebrews 11:7; 2 Peter 2:5; and 3:5–9 would suggest it was the subject of much midrashic interpretation in the Christian community—an element doubtless inherited from the early Christians' Jewish forebears. The clause "when God waited patiently in the days of Noah while the ark was being built" is normally understood to mean *contemporary with* Noah. However, it could also be construed to mean, as Mounce, 57, suggests, that the angels were still in a state of disobedience when the men of Noah's era were testing God (even though

340

the angels fell long before Noah). The words *en hē-merais Nōe* ("in the days of Noah") would be considered representative, since the flood was *the* great judgment of the ancient world. The very wording used here—"when God . . . in the days of Noah"—is illuminated by the language of Enochic literature, even when the NT writers do not import Enochic theology.

In these verses, a parallel exists between the age of the flood and the present, expressed by the words "God waited patiently" (cf. Ge 6:3a). Both the fallen angels and the flood typology are analogous to the situation being addressed by 1 Peter. Both are types of final judgment (hence, the "preaching" of v.19 cannot be salvific). Noah's contemporaries refused to repent during the period of the construction of the ark, and those persecuting the Christians in 1 Peter refuse to believe (*apeitheō*, GK 578). The parallel that "a few people . . . were saved" also has clear implications for Peter's audience. Perhaps they feel a sense of inadequacy, the sense that they are a mere "eight in all" amidst a sea of scornful onlookers. They can take courage that, in fact, the few righteous indeed "were saved through water." Hence for them the "antitype" of baptism is significant: the waters of the flood were a preview, a prefiguring, a type of reality to come—water symbolizes baptism.

But how is the somewhat problematic statement that baptism "now saves you" to be understood? Can Peter be interpreted as advancing baptismal regeneration? A twofold qualification follows: (1) baptism as an antitype expresses an inner state of conscience before God, and (2) this transformation is realized through union with the resurrected Christ. Just as the cleansing properties of water pertain to removal of dirt but not to a pure heart, by the same token identification with the crucified and risen Christ is the substance of salvation (cf. 1Co 15:14, 17). The "good conscience toward God"

(*eperōtēma eis theon*) does not express mere removal of dirt from the physical body; rather, it cleanses internally by means of one's being united with the resurrected Christ. The baptismal "pledge" marks the faithful; it elicits utter loyalty to God and constitutes a very real and intensely relevant assurance of salvation to a persecuted minority. Baptism, therefore, "saves" insofar as it *declares* publicly Christ's uncontested lordship. The link between baptism and suffering is that baptism is "the sign of voluntary self-commitment to the Christian way" (so D. Hill, "On Suffering and Baptism in 1 Peter," *NovT* 18 [1976]: 184–85). At baptism, the consequences of Christian discipleship are acknowledged, including a willingness to suffer.

In addition to the parallels in the text that result from typology at several levels—Christ and Enoch, Noah and the church, the flood and baptism—a further instance of parallelism is to be noted. Jesus' "going" (*poreutheis*, GK 4513), expressed as descent in v.19, is completed in v.22: Christ, who has suffered and was raised, now "has gone into heaven," where he rules over all angelic powers. This is the language—and imagery—of vindication. "With angels, authorities and powers in submission to him," Christ's example serves to encourage the readers greatly. Because he is their captain, they will experience vindication as well. Vindication expresses itself in the form of judgment, and it is the eschatological outlook that must now be stressed.

Verses 18–22, then, constitute something of a climax in the thought of the writer. The creedal community is thereby declaring the full effects of its salvation, the basis of which is described in 1:3–12. The new identity of God's people is spelled out in 1:13–2:10, with 3:13–22 enhancing the role of Christ, who is present with the readers in their suffering and who, as innocent sufferer, has been vindicated for all the cosmos to behold.

NOTES

18–22 The hymnic character of 3:18–22 is fairly well acknowledged. See, e.g., Cross, 156–68; Lohse, 37–59; Dalton, 96–102; Johnson, "Preaching to the Dead," 48–51; Brooks, "1 Peter 3:21," 290–305.

The history of interpretation of these verses shows no clear consensus regarding the identity of the imprisoned spirits. And it must be conceded that serious exegetes have supported one or the other "human" explanation—among them, C. E. B. Cranfield, "The Interpretation of 1 Peter iii.19 and iv.6," *ExpTim* 69 (1957/58): 369–72; J. S. Feinberg, "1 Peter 3:18–20, Ancient Mythology, and the Intermediate State," *WTJ* 48 (1986): 303–36; W. Grudem, "Christ Preaching through Noah: 1 Peter 3:19–20 in the Light of Dominant Themes in Jewish Literature," *TJ* 7 (1986): 3–31.

REFLECTIONS

Intriguing parallels in Jewish apocalyptic literature, albeit fantastic, are worth mentioning, while needing some qualification. They are significant, not because the NT writers adopt their theological assumptions—indeed, they reject the apocalyptic framework in favor of a *prophetic* perspective—but rather because they mirror a common religious thought-world, one vividly on display in documents such as Jude, 2 Peter, and Revelation. Imprisoned fallen angels are a favorite theme of Jewish apocalyptic. One exemplary work, *1 Enoch* (first century BC–AD first century?), deserves mention, since at least one NT writer, Jude, indicates close familiarity with its traditions (cf. Jude 14–15, a near-verbatim citation of *1 En.* 1:9), while 1 Peter displays notable features that are standard for apocalyptic literature (enumerated by Davids, 15–17). Relating to our text is the description in *1 Enoch* 12–14 of the imprisonment of the fallen angels and the commission given to Enoch to go and preach to them. The modern reader would also do well to note that in Jewish tradition, two paradigms of righteousness stand out: Enoch and Noah. On the Noah paradigm in Jewish tradition-material, see J. P. Lewis, *A Study of the Interpretation of Noah and the Flood in Jewish and Christian Literature* (Leiden: Brill, 1968), as well as the essay by James VanderKam ("The Righteousness of Noah," in *Ideal Figures in Ancient Judaism: Profiles and Paradigms*, ed. J. J. Collins and G. W. E. Nickelsburg [Chico, Calif.: Scholars Press, 1980], 13–32).

c. Christ's Example as Motivation for Living (4:1–6)

[1]Therefore, since Christ suffered in his body, arm yourselves also with the same attitude, because he who has suffered in his body is done with sin. [2]As a result, he does not live the rest of his earthly life for evil human desires, but rather for the will of God. [3]For you have spent enough time in the past doing what pagans choose to do—living in debauchery, lust, drunkenness, orgies, carousing and detestable idolatry. [4]They think it strange that you do not plunge with them into the same flood of dissipation, and they heap abuse on you. [5]But they will have to give account to him who is ready to judge the living and the dead. [6]For this is the reason the gospel was preached even to those who are now dead, so that they might be judged according to men in regard to the body, but live according to God in regard to the spirit.

COMMENTARY

1 The material in 3:18–22 may strike the reader as "an unusually complicated digression" (so Mounce, 61) into unusually complex theological speculation. Indeed, 3:18 ("[Christ] suffered [NIV, was put to death"] in the body") and 4:1 ("Christ suffered in his body") appear to be bookends in a theologically intriguing—but unnecessary—excursus! But for the writer, this perspective should arm the readers with knowledge, while it strengthens their courage. And the purpose of this knowledge? It is that we might not "live the rest of [our] earthly life for evil human desires, but rather for the will of God." How one lived in the past, which is to say, how pagans conduct themselves, is illustrated through a catalog of vices that follows (v.3).

As applied to the readers' particular situation, there is a peculiar theological reality at work: the person who suffers in the flesh "is done with sin." The notion that suffering purifies, perhaps offensive to the rationalist, materialist mind, is amply supported throughout both OT and NT. "Blessed is the man you disciple, O LORD," writes the psalmist (94:12). The writer of Hebrews endorses this view: "The Lord disciplines those he loves" (12:6). A parallel of limited proportions is part of Peter's thought: Christ suffered "once for all" for sins (cf. 3:18) to put an end to sin; thus the readers are to have the same mentality and put away sin (cf. 2:1). As the sinless one, Christ took upon himself our sins (2:22, 24). Whereas he had no need of purging, suffering has in the believer the effect of purification, which is important to the development of the writer's overall argument (1:2, 7, 22; 2:1; 3:21).

3–4 The material in this passage offers strong evidence of the readers' social situation and serves as a reminder of their former life—a life characterized by a litany of vices—"debauchery" (*aselgeia*, GK *816*, also in 2Pe 2:2, 7, 18), "lust" (*epithymia*, GK *2123*, also in 1:14; 2:11), "drunkenness" (*oinophlygiai*, GK *3886*, from *oinos*, "wine," plus *phlyō*, "to bubble up"), "orgies" (*kōmoi*, GK *3269*, also in the lists of Ro 13:13 and Gal 5:19), "carousing" (*potoi*, GK *4542*), and "detestable idolatry" (*athemitoi eidēlolatriai*, GK *116, 1630*).

This catalog of vices has the rhetorical effect of producing shame and highlighting the contrast between Christian and pagan conduct. To the same end, Peter's choice of words heightens this contrast: he speaks of "what pagans choose to do" (*boulēma* [GK *1088*] *tōn ethnōn*) on the one hand (v.3) and the "will of God" (*thelēmati* [GK *2525*] *theou*) on the other (v.2). The ethical standards could not be more opposite. What is conspicuous is this: the pagan lifestyle revolves around indulging one's appetites, "a flood of dissipation" (*asōtias anachysin*, GK *861, 431*), so that pagans "think it strange that you do not plunge with them . . ." The Christian ethic, in notable contrast, is characterized by bridled passions (1:14; 2:11), purity (1:22), and a good conscience (3:21). That the surrounding pagans are said to "think it strange" (*xenizō*, "to astonish," GK *3826*) conveys more than mere amazement or wonder. As evidenced by their response, "they heap abuse" (*blasphēmeō*, GK *1059*), which is to say, they are expressing *outrage and resentment* (cf. 2:12, "they accuse you of doing wrong"; also 3:16, "they speak maliciously"). Part of the experience of normative Christian suffering is to be vilified for not participating in the hedonistic lifestyle of pagan culture; not to participate is to provoke resentment.

5 But this is not the last word. Peter wishes in the next breath to remind his readers that those who so abuse them "will have to give account to him who is ready to judge [both] the living and the dead." As he has reminded them before in the letter (1:17; 2:12), now he does so again, but more forcefully: this will be a day of moral reckoning. God stands "ready" (hetoimōs) as an impartial judge (cf. 1:17), knows all (1:2), and cares for those who have entrusted themselves to him (2:23, 25; 4:19). The phrase "the living and the dead," moreover, expresses the universal scope of the coming judgment, so that, past or present, none can evade that fearful reality. Interestingly, Peter uses the same expression (krinai zōntas kai nekrous) to describe judgment when he preached God's counsel to Cornelius at the home of Simon the tanner (Ac 10:42).

6 But what about the dead? Peter has mentioned that Jesus died (3:18), and he speaks of judgment that touches the living and the dead (4:5). How is death to be put in perspective? Many explanations of this verse fall short of being satisfactory, and, like the difficult verses that precede it, 4:6 has been the subject of varied interpretation. "For this is the reason the gospel was preached even to those who are now dead" raises important questions. Initially it is important to note that, unlike 3:19, here the verb euangelizomai, not kēryssō, is employed, with the implication that Peter is returning to the human from the angelic sphere. But how is "preaching the gospel" to be understood? Does it modify the statements preceding it or statements that follow? If the former, does it refer to the judgment of v.5 or the reality of a changed life in vv.1–5? If we interpret the preaching of the gospel as the "reason" for judgment, the sense is that judgment exists as a basis for the gospel, but this seems to place the cart before the horse. Theologically speaking, the teaching of the NT is that judgment is predicated on the gospel, not vice versa—i.e., people will be judged according to how they responded to the gospel, the "good news," of Christ.

If we interpret v.6 as pointing forward, i.e., referring to material that follows, we find a point of contact with the reference to judgment in 4:17–18. However, what immediately follows (vv.7–16) would then appear to be a digression in the writer's thought—material devoted to the saints' corporate life (vv.7–11) and recapitulating thoughts on suffering (vv.12–16). Contextually, the most natural link unites 4:6 with material that preceded (vv.1–5), namely, the reality of a changed lifestyle. "For this is the reason" can be understood in the sense of "For the purpose of a transformed life." Moreover, Peter wishes to affirm that all the righteous—those alive and those deceased—will be vindicated. As Achtemeier, 291, puts it, death has overtaken no one. The rhetorical and theological emphasis is this: just as there is vindication at the spiritual level (3:22), there is also vindication at the human level (4:6).

Thus, just as the message being preached in 4:6 stands in contrast to that of 3:19, its audience differs as well: the "living and dead" are humans who will "give account." The question of identifying precisely who are the "dead" who are "quickened according to the Spirit [NIV, live according to God in regard to the spirit]" remains. Alternative explanations present themselves. One view is that all people, in the end, are reconciled to God. This view, however, fails to make any distinction between the righteous and the unrighteous on the judgment day (Mt 25:31–45; Rev 20:11–16). A second possibility is that these are dead in a spiritual or figurative sense. But this interpretation fails to the extent that Peter is not resorting to allegory anywhere in the letter. Those who are "dead" are so en sarki, "according to the flesh [NIV, in the body]," which has established the context since 3:18. Death in 4:6 is physical and literal. Yet a third view might seem plausible, i.e., that the physical "dead" are righteous saints through the ages, those whose faith in God commended them (e.g., Heb 11:4–40). But the NT makes clear that OT saints were justified by faith (Ro 4; Gal 4:21–31; Heb 11); therefore, there is no further need for justifying them as though they wait in a sort of spiritual limbo.

Hence a fourth view is to be preferred: v.6 refers to converts to Christ who have died since hearing and embracing the gospel. Indeed, Paul's first letter to the Thessalonians presents strong evidence that the question of those who die before Christ's return was a quandary for the early church (1Th 4:13–14; cf. Ac 1:9–11). Most commentators, in observing the symmetry of the verse—being "judged according to the flesh like men" and being "quickened according to the Spirit before God"—believe this represents an early unit of Christian creedal confession. Indeed, evidence from the NT itself seems to support this; thus Paul's hymnic declaration to Timothy on the "mystery of godliness" (1Ti 3:16) displays some similarity to 1 Peter 3:18–22. Peter's teaching is simply this: whereas all humans are destined to taste death and face judgment, those who are found righteous will be vindicated for their faithfulness.

2. Eschatology and Christian Ethics (4:7–19)

a. Eschatology and Christian Relationships (4:7–11)

OVERVIEW

In this section, numerous admonitions are listed that corroborate the quality of relationships for which the Christian community is to be known. These collective duties are to be motivated by an eschatological conviction that "the end of all things is near." Present in the teaching of Jesus and in the literature of the NT is evidence of the belief, pervasive in the early church, that the consummation (*telos*) of all things was imminent (e.g., Jn 9:4; Ro 13:11–12; Php 4:5; Heb 10:25; Jas 5:8; 1Jn 2:18; Rev 22:20).

Doubtless the disciples, on witnessing Christ's ascension, developed the expectation, based on the angels' testimony (Ac 1:10–11), that they would personally witness the return of the Lord in their lifetime. Indeed, every generation since then has entertained the same expectation. In considering the exhortations toward watchfulness and readiness that were a part of Jesus' teaching (e.g., Mt 24:45–25:13; Mk 13:33–37), one is struck by the sheer force this eschatological outlook (in this case, a sense of immediacy) exercises on ethics. And certainly in 1 Peter, eschatology motivates ethics (1:4–5, 8–9; 2:12; 4:5, 17–18). It goes without saying that Peter's emphasis on vindication (3:18–22) and judgment (4:5–6) would induce his readers to think about "the end."

While the eschatological question of the Lord's return—and the "end of all things"—intrigues and perplexes every generation, we are left to confess that we can only "see through a glass darkly." To some "early Catholic" theologians who reflected on the return of the Lord, the early church was mistaken in its expectation. A more plausible explanation of the tension that arises out of imminence-yet-delay is that human beings' understanding of the temporal element is fallible and limited. Second Peter 3:9 serves as a reminder in this regard for those who await judgment as vindication, for the "delay" in the second advent is ascribed to divine forbearance (NIV, "patience"; *makrothymia, GK 3429*).

> ⁷The end of all things is near. Therefore be clear minded and self-controlled so that you can pray. ⁸Above all, love each other deeply, because love covers over a multitude of sins. ⁹Offer hospitality to one another without grumbling. ¹⁰Each one should use whatever gift he has received to serve others, faithfully administering God's grace in its various forms. ¹¹If anyone speaks, he should do it as one speaking the very words of God. If anyone serves, he should do it with the strength God provides, so that in all things God may be praised through Jesus Christ. To him be the glory and the power for ever and ever. Amen.

COMMENTARY

7 What may be said, then, as we reflect on the eschatological tensions inherent in the statement "The end of all things is near" is the very thing Peter seems to presuppose throughout the entire letter: believers are to live with a heightened sense of eternal values.

What qualities will be on display as a result of this heightened sense of eternal perspective that Peter wishes to inculcate? In the light of future realities ("Therefore"), for Peter, how one thinks, how one acts, and specifically how one serves others are essential to the Christian social ethic. Every admonition contained in 4:7b–11 is accompanied either by a justification or a qualification.

Two qualities mirror a Christian mind-set. Believers are to "be clear minded" (*sōphroneō*, GK 5404) and "self-controlled" (*nēphō*, GK 3768, also in 1:13). To think in a sober and self-controlled manner is to adopt precisely the opposite mind-set that characterizes surrounding society, i.e., irrationality and frivolity. Spiritual reality makes us alert to the fact that the human flesh wars against the spirit (Ro 7:21–25; 8:1–17). To the unbeliever, spiritual things are foolishness, since they are spiritually discerned (1Co 2:14–15). Thus the human need is for the Spirit to reign over the flesh (Ro 8:1–17), for as a person thinks, so he or she truly is. An important reason for this alertness is offered: "so

that you can pray." This appears to reiterate the principle noted earlier: husbands possess the ability to have their prayers "hindered" (1Pe 3:7), and this specifically through the attitudes of insensitivity and lack of respect toward their wives.

8 In the mind of Peter, proper thinking will lead to proper action, and a distinctly Christian social ethic is the embodiment of love. Love for others, "above all," is to characterize the Christian community, and such love is to be tenacious, full-bodied, intense, deep (*ektenēs*, GK 1756). If the NT teaches anything, it teaches the primacy of love in accord with the teaching of Jesus (Mk 12:31; Lk 10:27; Jn 13:34–35; 15:12; 1Co 13:1–13; Eph 5:1–2; Php 2:2; Jas 2:8; 1Jn 2:10; 4:7–11, 19–21). Moreover, in the face of extreme social hostility, love will be necessary for spiritual survival. For Peter the primacy of love is accompanied by a qualification, and this qualification is a partial citation of Proverbs 10:12 similar to James 5:20—"love covers over a multitude of sins," rather than magnifying the faults of others. After all, love is patient and doesn't keep a record of wrongs (1Co 13:4, 5).

9 A related admonition concerns hospitality, a trait that would validate the Christian community's faith claims. Early Christians were known for their hospitality (Ro 12:13; 1Ti 5:10; Heb 13:2), and it is doubtless for this reason that the gospel spread with such rapidity in the church's formative years. Missionary preachers, evangelists, and house churches (Ro 1:5; 1Co 16:19; Tit 1:8; Phm 2) were dependent on hospitality, and unquestionably the early Christians took to heart the words of Jesus himself: "I was a stranger and you invited me in" (Mt 25:35). Ultimately, hospitality might be thought of as the best bridge between believer and unbeliever. Peter's qualification that no "grumbling" should accompany hospitality reminds them that love will be attentive to the needs of others, even though such may entail inconvenience on our part.

10–11 Hospitality is a vehicle of *service* to others, and it is a serving attitude that undergirds the exhortations that follow. Serving, of course, is predicated on the notion of stewardship—stewardship of divine grace—i.e., the Christian has received mercy and grace and therefore is entrusted with passing that on to others. Peter is in agreement with Paul in observing that Christians are stewards, "household managers" (in keeping with the theme of *oikos* [2:18–3:7]) of the grace of God. Grace, of course, is imparted in "various forms" (cf. Ro 12:3–8; 1Co 12:4–11), two examples of which are delineated in 1 Peter: speaking "as one speaking the very words of God," and serving "with the strength God provides." The manner in which God provides is suggested vividly by the Greek term *chorēgeō* (GK *5961*; see commentary at 2Pe 1:5, 11).

Although 4:7–11 resembles the language and logic of 1 Corinthians 12 and Romans 12, causing most commentators to assume that the reference to *charisma* (GK *5922*) in v.10 concerns corporate congregational life, this is not required of the text. Spiritual gifts, which are intended to serve others, may be more broadly understood as applying to Christians *as a community* (as opposed to an assembly in worship). Thus the language may simply be an extension of the household theme, with stewardship providing the link. Hospitality, Christians' relationships, and their service one to another are critical components of community if they are to survive in the context of their social location.

These qualities, when they are manifest, are said to glorify God through Jesus Christ in all respects, just as it was expressed earlier that doing good glorifies God (2:12). Here Peter reiterates not merely that these things are necessary for Christian witness but also that they bring glory to God. Fittingly, this block of exhortations concludes with doxological praise: "To him be the glory and the power for ever and ever. Amen" (cf. Ro 16:27; Jude 25). While to some commentators the insertion of doxological praise here rather than at the end of the letter seems unnatural, Kelly, 182, is correct to suggest that such is an expression of the author's "awe and devotion" in the face of God's majesty.

NOTES

7–11 Admonitions toward mental-spiritual alertness occur in the Pauline letters, e.g., Col 3:1–4 (setting one's mind on "things above, not on earthly things") and Eph 4:17–32 (esp. vv.22–23), the structure of which resembles Peter's argument (putting off the old self and putting on the new). Evidence exists elsewhere in the NT that actions and attitudes are capable of hindering prayer. An example is Paul's admonition to men in the congregation to "lift up holy hands" in worship (1Ti 2:8), with the suggestion that "anger and disputing" serve to impede their prayers. This principle represents "practical theology" at its best: one's prayer life is directly related to one's thought life and actions.

REFLECTIONS

From the divine perspective, God is long-suffering in terms of his relationship to fallen humanity. Seen humanly, the divine purpose must run to its appointed *telos*, the timing and nature of which remain to us every bit the mystery. Each generation that confesses creedally the return of Christ wrestles with the tension of present-future realities—the "already and not yet" of God's kingdom. In this sense every generation lives like the first generation of Christians, cognizant that the NT calls us simultaneously to watchfulness as well as to occupation. Two extremes are to be avoided. On the one hand, if we focus *solely* on Christ's return and fail to wrestle with the present complexities of engaging culture, we make the mistake of withdrawal and isolation from society, resulting in the creation of a religious subculture divorced from the cultural mainstream. Such breeds a severe attenuation of Christian witness, of which Peter would not approve; cut off from society, Christian faith lacks any public demonstration of relevance. The other extreme, toward which the contemporary church is perhaps more inclined as we navigate the twenty-first century, altogether relaxes the tension between faith and culture. The result is a capitulation to and absorption into culture, so that the church loses any prophetic presence in its social location; of this danger Peter is fully aware.

b. Eschatology and Christian Suffering (4:12–19)

OVERVIEW

In this final exhortation on suffering, Peter recapitulates by bringing together each of his perspectives on suffering that surfaced earlier in the letter. The readers are reminded (1) of their union with Christ (1:6–9; 2:21–25; 3:18–22); (2) of the coming revelation of Christ's glory (1:7–8; 5:4); (3) that they are blessed if they suffer for the name of Christ (3:9, 14); (4) that suffering for Christ glorifies God (2:12); (5) that they are not to suffer for doing wrong (2:12, 20; 3:17); (6) that they should not be ashamed of suffering for Christ (2:6); and (7) that those who suffer are to commit themselves to the care of their faithful Lord while continuing to do good (2:23, 25). This summarizing of Petrine perspectives on suffering concludes with a reiteration of a future day of moral reckoning—one that touches both believer and unbeliever. The promise of judgment serves as a promise of vindication. Knowing that God the Judge is the "great leveler" should encourage the saints who suffer so that in the end they can entrust themselves to God. The reiteration of Petrine perspectives invites reconsideration on the part of the reader.

> [12]Dear friends, do not be surprised at the painful trial you are suffering, as though something strange were happening to you. [13]But rejoice that you participate in the sufferings of Christ, so that you may be overjoyed when his glory is revealed. [14]If you are insulted because of the name of Christ, you are blessed, for the Spirit of glory and of God rests on you. [15]If you suffer, it should not be as a murderer or thief or any other kind of criminal, or even as a meddler. [16]However, if you suffer as a Christian, do not be ashamed,

but praise God that you bear that name. ¹⁷For it is time for judgment to begin with the family of God; and if it begins with us, what will the outcome be for those who do not obey the gospel of God? ¹⁸And,

"If it is hard for the righteous to be saved,
    what will become of the ungodly and the sinner?"

¹⁹So then, those who suffer according to God's will should commit themselves to their faithful Creator and continue to do good.

COMMENTARY

12 In what follows, the writer returns to the theme of suffering with a final admonition regarding his readers' particular situation. Herewith he addresses them affectionately and intimately (*agapē-toi*, GK *28*) as a father figure. His concern is to adjust their perspective on suffering: "do not be surprised [*xenizō*, GK *3826*; also in 4:5] . . . as though something strange were happening." After all, the human inclination is to question the "necessity" of suffering. "Where are you, God? Why is this happening to me?" But despite the tendency to question—or rebel against—suffering, Christians are not to be "surprised" when, in the form of hostility, ostracizing, and persecution, suffering visits. Jesus himself promised as much: "If they persecuted me, they will persecute you also" (Jn 15:20). For this reason, John can affirm: "Do not be surprised . . . if the world hates you" (1Jn 3:13). In the end, persecution will reveal whether our faith is genuine.

But even when the writer understands suffering as "normative" in the Christian life, he does not belittle its impact on the lives of Christians; suffering is very real, as suggested by the vocabulary—"suffering" (*pathēmata*, GK *4077*), "painful trial" (*pyrōsei pros peirasmon*, GK *4796, 4280*, lit., "a purifying by fire"). Suffering in any context is painful, and the pain endured by the readers in their present situation is very real and not to be diminished.

13 Rather than be shocked or surprised at suffering, the readers are told to rejoice. The writer is not hereby glibly suggesting that one rejoices in suffering qua suffering. It is rather "in the Lord" (Php 4:4) that one rejoices. Believers "participate in the sufferings of Christ" (cf. Php 3:10, which speaks of "the fellowship of sharing in his sufferings"), based on the believer's union with Christ, and therefore can emit a response of "rejoicing." The believer is *united* with Christ in his death as well as his resurrection (Ro 6:5–14), not in the sense of paying for our sins, as only the Son of God could do, but in the sense that "our old self was crucified with him . . . that we should no longer be slaves to sin . . . but alive to God" (Ro 6:6, 11). Rejoicing and shock stand at opposite ends, and a deep awareness of our union with Christ—and all that it entails—preserves the Christian from surprise that metastasizes into disenchantment and disillusionment. To expect suffering, it should be emphasized, is not to welcome it in some blindly fatalistic way; it is, however, to be realistic about our union with Christ.

The attitude of rejoicing in the context of suffering is further magnified by the cognizance of the coming revelation of Christ's glory. Peter writes, "so that you may be overjoyed [lit., 'that you may rejoice exultingly'] when his glory is revealed," using the same strengthened form of "rejoice" (*agalliaō*, GK *22*) as earlier (1:6, 8), and in the same context (Christ's return). His theological rationale squares with that of Paul: "if indeed we share in his sufferings in order that we may also share in his glory" (Ro 8:17); "if we endure, we will also reign with him" (2Ti 2:12). Suffering for Christ is a privilege and not a penalty (so Barclay, 258). In Petrine thinking, eschatology informs Christian ethics.

14 Peter further reminds his readers that they are "blessed" if they are "insulted [*oneidizō*, GK *3943*; used of Jesus' experience on the cross, Mk 15:32] because of the name of Christ." His assertion is expanded with the somewhat strange statement that "the Spirit of glory and of God rests on you." This language is frequently used in the book of Exodus to describe the glory of the Lord as it descended on Mount Sinai (24:16), in the desert (16:10), on the tabernacle (29:43; 40:34) and ark (Lev 16:2), or when it filled the temple (2Ch 7:3). Indeed Paul resorts to similar language and imagery in describing the glory of the new covenant (2Co 3:7–18). Significantly, Stephen's countenance is depicted in this way in Luke's account of his martyrdom (Ac 7:55; cf. 6:15). Peter would seem to be suggesting that the presence of God is particularly notable in those times when the saints are being persecuted. The Spirit glorifies Jesus (Jn 16:14); therefore, as believers experience persecution on account of Christ, they are filled with the Spirit's presence, and in so doing they are glorifying God.

15 Earlier in the letter, Peter intimated that not all suffering is because of Christ; it is possible to suffer because of wrongdoing (2:14, 20; 3:17). For this reason the believer is called to self-examination, in order that no one suffers "as a murderer or thief or any other kind of criminal, or even as a meddler." Three of the four categories of wrongdoing are specific, but, more important, the list moves from heinous crime to common fault, i.e., "meddling" (*allotriepiskopos*, GK *258)* in the affairs of others.

Suggested in this descending order is the fact that we all can easily become open to criticism by actions or attitudes that undermine our faith—criticism that in fact is deserving.

16 Nevertheless, some instances of suffering are undeserved, such as our identification with the name of Christ. In such cases, that person should not "be ashamed, but praise [i.e., glorify] God that you bear that name." And among the early disciples, it is Peter who knows—agonizingly so—the truth of this fact: there is *honor* in the name. The painful memories, though lying many years in the past, serve to motivate the Christian elder statesman: do not be ashamed (as I was as a young man), but glorify God in the present context. Believers will need to be reminded that persecution, as Goppelt, 322, has pointed out, is due not so much to particular behaviors per se as to faith and character.

17–18 The link between eschatology and ethics in 1 Peter reaches a climax in the writer's summary exhortation: "It is time for judgment to begin" (v.17; cf. Eze 9:6; Mal 3:1–3). It begins, says Peter, with the "household [NIV, "family"; *oikos*] of God." Herewith Peter utilizes a further variation of the household cluster of images (*oikos* in 2:5; 4:17; *oikonomos* in 4:10; *diakoneō* in 1:12; 4:10–11) that has been extremely effective up to this point. Peter compares the judgment of God's elect with that of the ungodly, borrowing from Proverbs 11:31. This contrast, framed in the form of a rhetorical question, is intended not to say that the righteous will scarcely be saved but rather that judgment will be indescribably cataclysmic for the unbeliever. For this reason persecution, which purifies, will result in the saints' vindication, sparing them the awesome fate that awaits those who carry out the persecuting.

19 In conclusion, the readers are once more admonished ("So then") to "commit themselves to their faithful Creator and continue to do good." Entrusting oneself into divine care has been a crucial subtheme of 1 Peter (2:23; 4:19; 5:7), as has doing good (2:12, 20; 3:13, 17; 4:19). It is fitting that the two should interlock at this point. Moreover, the one to whom the saints commit themselves is "faithful," able to be trusted by those who "cast all [their] anxiety," since "he cares for [them]" (5:7). What is more, Peter is quite conscious that the readers' hardships are not arbitrary; rather, they are part of God's overall plan, hence his framing of both suffering and doing good in terms of "God's will" (2:15; 3:17;

4:2, 19)—a conviction that presses to the fore throughout the entire letter.

Mounce, 78–79, summarizes this closing advice well: "Committing oneself to God is not passive submission. It involves active well-doing. While believers will certainly endure hostility of an unbelieving world, there is no place for a martyrdom mentality. Suffer in silence but get on with the job of living an active life of good deeds. Christians should be known for what they do, not for what they suffer. Fixation upon the difficulties of life robs the believer of the opportunity to display his concern for the welfare of others."

3. Christian Leadership in the New Diaspora Community (5:1–11)

OVERVIEW

Having finished his comments on Christian suffering, the writer concludes with remarks directed at the several specific groups: (1) those with oversight of the community, to whom most of his comments are addressed; (2) those who are younger in the community; and then (3) all members of the community.

Most commentators observe in this division a pattern similar to that of the household code appropriated earlier. This pattern once again mirrors the writer's conviction that relationships within the Christian community must be ordered and respectful; otherwise the witness of Christians will be weakened.

a. Challenge to the Elders (5:1–4)

[1]To the elders among you, I appeal as a fellow elder, a witness of Christ's sufferings and one who also will share in the glory to be revealed: [2]Be shepherds of God's flock that is under your care, serving as overseers—not because you must, but because you are willing, as God wants you to be; not greedy for money, but eager to serve; [3]not lording it over those entrusted to you, but being examples to the flock. [4]And when the Chief Shepherd appears, you will receive the crown of glory that will never fade away.

COMMENTARY

1 The first of the three groups, the elders, receives the bulk of instruction, and fittingly so,

since spiritual oversight of a church called to suffer requires sensitivity, selflessness, and leadership by example. In appealing to them, however, Peter establishes common ground in several important ways. He appeals to them as a "fellow elder" (*sympresbyteros*, GK *5236*), as "a witness of Christ's sufferings," and "one who also will share in the glory to be revealed."

As a "fellow elder," Peter takes seriously and shares in the responsibility of pastoral care. His own pastoral sensitivities doubtless are piqued by memories of Jesus' sober, poignant, and penetrating challenge to him, in the context of being called anew to "follow" Christ (Jn 21:15–19). As a "witness of Christ's sufferings," Peter is in a position to supply moving eyewitness testimony to Jesus' passion. This includes his own inability to "watch and pray" during Jesus' trial in the garden (Mt 26:37–46; Mk 14:32–42; Lk 22:39–46), his cutting off the guard's ear in the garden (Mt 26:47–54; Mk 14:47; Lk 22:47–53; Jn 18:26), and his following (at bay) a condemned Jesus, who was led away to interrogation by the high priest (Mt 26:57–75; Mk 14:53–72; Lk 22:54–62). The latter episode is particularly agonizing in the Lukan narrative, where immediately after Peter's third denial, "the Lord turned and looked straight at Peter." As a result, Peter "went outside and wept bitterly" (Lk 22:61, 62). Doubtless the "look" of Jesus still pierced Peter's heart as an older man. Yet to be an eyewitness is no mere sentimental reality; it also conveys authority—authority that inheres in the apostolic office.

Peter's third qualification is that he, too, shares in the glory yet to be revealed. This self-designation is important for several reasons. The coming revelation of Christ's glory has been a subtheme throughout the letter (alluded to in 1:5, 7; 4:13; 5:1, 4). It is a theological reality that anchors Peter's eschatology as well as his ethic. The reality of Christ's reign is "already and not yet"—a present reality, though not fully consummated. But another reason impels the writer, and once more it is deeply personal. Along with James and John, Peter was privileged to witness an "inbreaking," as it were, of Christ's glory on the Mount of Transfiguration (Mt 17:1–13; Mk 9:1–8; Lk 9:28–36; cf. 2Pe 1:16–18). Of all people it is Peter, James, and John who are granted the high privilege of beholding the transcendent glory of the second Person of the Trinity as he spoke with Moses and Elijah. Moreover, just as Christ suffered and was glorified (1:21; 3:18–22), so it is with those who follow in his steps: for "when the Chief Shepherd appears, you will receive the crown of glory that will never fade away" (5:4).

2–3 Peter's exhortation to those entrusted with spiritual leadership in the community is marked by great care and pastoral sensitivity. He is careful to emphasize *how* the elders exercise their oversight. He does this in a manner consistent with the sheep/shepherd imagery appropriated earlier (1:19; 2:22–25) and so frequently used in the OT to depict the relationship between God and his people (e.g., Ge 48:15; 1Ki 22:17; Pss 23:1–6; 80:1; 100:3; 119:176; Jer 3:15; 23:1–4; 31:10; 50:6; Eze 34:2, 11; Mic 5:4; Zec 9:16; 10:2). Peter's charge is, "Be shepherd of God's flock that is under your care"—language reminiscent of Paul's charge to the Ephesian elders (Ac 20:28). Implicit in the shepherding metaphor is a concern for the flock's total well-being, constitutive elements of which are feeding, watering, protecting, and guiding. Such attentiveness to the flock's needs is by no means arbitrary, for the flock belongs to God. Hence they have been entrusted by the Lord himself; in the end, shepherds are accountable stewards (cf. 4:11). And certainly an extra measure of passion lies behind Peter's directive to shepherd the flock, given Jesus' post-resurrection charge to him: "Feed my lambs. . . . Take care of my sheep. . . . Feed my sheep" (Jn 21:15–17).

How precisely are the elders to "serve as over-seers"? Three qualifications follow, each consisting of a negative and positive exhortation to form a contrast: (1) not by compulsion, but willingly (cf. 1Ti 3:1); (2) not for dishonest gain, but eagerly (cf. 1Ti 3:8; 6:6–10; Tit 1:7; cf. 1Co 9:7–11); and (3) not lording it over others, but as examples (cf. Mk 10:35–45; Php 3:17; 2Th 3:9; 1Ti 4:12; Tit 2:7).

All three speak to the issue of personal motivation. All three strike at the essence of human nature. The exercise of authority, given the human predicament, tends to be coercive, self-centered, and domineering. Jesus' warning to the disciples at a crucial point in his ministry is poignant: "Not so with you" (Mk 10:43). Rather, Jesus' prescription is that the true leader "must be your servant." And this is the spirit of Peter's admonition. By overseeing in this manner, the elders will be examples (*typoi*, "types," GK *5596*) to all. One leads not by asserting but by serving the needs of others. A self-serving shepherd is a contradiction in terms.

4 Furthermore, in so leading they will "receive the crown of glory that will never fade away" when "the Chief Shepherd appears." Whereas in 2:25 Christ is "Shepherd," in 5:4 he is "Chief Shepherd" (*archipoimēn*, GK *799*). By virtue of his rule, he will dispense rewards appropriate to one's service. Although there are many shepherds, there is one "Chief Shepherd"—the very idea expressed in Hebrews 13:20, which calls Jesus "that great Shepherd of the sheep." The idea of a crown as reward saturates the NT (e.g., Jn 19:2, 5; 1Co 9:25; 2Ti 2:5; 4:8; Heb 2:7; Jas 1:12; Rev 2:10; 3:11; 4:4; cf. Isa 28:5; Jer 13:18), mirroring Hellenistic culture's practice of bestowing honor on citizens for distinguished public service as well as on victorious athletes. According to Peter, this "crown," as the inheritance described in 1:4, will never "fade away" (*amarantinos*, GK *277*), unlike victory wreaths that were made of ivy, flowers, or vines. And consistent with the stress in 1 Peter on accountability, this is part of divine *vindication* as well.

b. Challenge to the Young Men (5:5a)

> ⁵Young men, in the same way be submissive to those who are older.

COMMENTARY

5a Peter then turns away from "elders" and addresses "young men" (*neōteroi*). This designation in the Greek text is somewhat ambiguous. Who precisely are these young men? Are they potential leaders or simply the younger people in the community? Peter admonishes these individuals to "be submissive" to older people "in the same way." But in what way? Given the earlier pattern in the household code, which calls for submission at several levels (cf. the admonition to wives, "in the same way be submissive" [3:1]), a natural interpretation of 5:5a is that younger people in the community must order themselves after the older out of respect for them. Mounce, 85, captures the spirit of this admonition: "The point is that submission to those who are older (and presumably wiser) is socially appropriate for young men."

c. Challenge to All (5:5b–9)

All of you, clothe yourselves with humility toward one another, because,

"God opposes the proud
but gives grace to the humble."

[6]Humble yourselves, therefore, under God's mighty hand, that he may lift you up in due time. [7]Cast all your anxiety on him because he cares for you.

[8]Be self-controlled and alert. Your enemy the devil prowls around like a roaring lion looking for someone to devour. [9]Resist him, standing firm in the faith, because you know that your brothers throughout the world are undergoing the same kind of sufferings.

COMMENTARY

5b Following the words of instruction to elders and young men, a call to humility is presented to everyone in the community. As has been his custom throughout the epistle, Peter supports this exhortation with a citation from the OT; here he borrows from Proverbs 3:34: "God opposes the proud but gives grace to the humble." One is justified in calling humility the "law of the community," as Barclay, 258, does. The admonition to "clothe yourselves with humility" is vivid, for it calls to mind the servant putting on an apron, such as Jesus, in fact, did as an example to the disciples (Jn 13:4–5, 14–15).

6–7 Humility, however, is not mere self-effacement; it is an awareness of the greatness of God in comparison, as well as the realization that the humble one day will be exalted: "Humble yourselves, therefore, under God's mighty hand, that he may lift you up in due time." James, also drawing inspiration from Proverbs 3:34, makes similar application; the common elements in both letters are (1) divine resistance to pride, (2) the bestowal of grace, (3) submission to God, and (4) the acknowledgment of a spiritual enemy (cf. Jas 4:6–7). The attitude of humility before Almighty God allows those who

face hardship and hostility to cast all anxiety on him because he indeed cares for them.

Peter's language in v. 7 is remarkably similar to Psalm 55:22: "Cast your cares on the LORD and he will sustain you" (ESV). Psalm 55, it should be noted, is devoted to the complaint of the righteous and the cry of deliverance. In submission, one genuinely is set free from fear and anxiety; to be in the arms of God is to know divine provision and care. The psychological release that comes from "casting" (*epiriptō*, GK *2166*, a strengthened form of *riptō*, "to cast down" or "throw") our cares on the Lord is admirably described by Mounce, 87: "Anxiety follows when we forget that God is the One who cares for us. We are not left adrift on the sea of chance facing shipwreck on the shoals of an impersonal destiny. We are under the care of a sovereign God who controls the course of history and is intricately involved in the everyday life of each of his children."

8 To entrust oneself fully to divine care is not to conclude that we have no role to play. Peter continues, "Be self-controlled and alert." The reason for this is "your enemy the devil prowls around like a roaring lion, looking for someone to devour." While the profile of "Satan" in the OT is (relatively speaking) low, in 1 Chronicles 21:1; Job 1:6–12; 2:1–8; and Zechariah 3:1–2, he manifests the character of an accuser (*diaballō*, "to press charges" or "accuse," GK *1330*) and provoker—a role amplified in the NT (Mt 4:10; 13:37; 16:23; Jn 6:70; 1Co 7:5; 2Co 11:14; 12:7; Eph 4:27; 6:11; 1Ti 3:7; 1Jn 3:8; Rev 12:9; 20:2, 7, 10). Vigilance is being accented by Peter as he prepares to conclude his letter—and with good reason, for he no doubt agonizes over the *lack* of it at a critical time leading up to the crucifixion of his Lord (Mt 26:38–46; Mk 14:32–42; Lk 2:39–46).

Often in the OT, persecutors are compared to a crouching lion waiting to attack and devour (e.g., Ps 7:2; 10:8–10; Jer 4:7; Eze 19:6; Na 2:11–13). Because in Scripture the image of a devouring lion is not infrequently associated with the persecutor, this image is effective in the thought of Peter.

9 The readers, however, are not called to fear the devil; they are called to opposition. Peter's response is simple: "Resist him"—a strategy also found in James (4:7; cf. also Eph 6:10–13), remaining "firm in the faith, because you know that your brothers [and sisters] throughout the world are undergoing the same kind of sufferings." Solidarity with those whose experience is the same creates an extraordinary bond and motivation to persevere. Whether people share suffering or joy, this common fellowship (what the NT calls *koinōnia* [GK *3126*] breeds uncommon motivation.

d. Benediction and Doxology (5:10–11)

[10]And the God of all grace, who called you to his eternal glory in Christ, after you have suffered a little while, will himself restore you and make you strong, firm and steadfast. [11]To him be the power for ever and ever. Amen.

COMMENTARY

10 Peter understands well the bonds of koinonia that encourage perseverance in the faith. And the end of the matter, after the saints "have suffered a little while," is that the Lord, "the God of all grace," the one "who called [*kaleō*, GK *2813*, also in 1:15; 2:9, 21; 3:6, 9] you to his eternal glory in Christ," will respond in four ways: he will "restore" (*katartizō*, GK *2936*), he will "make firm" or establish (*stērizō*, GK *5114*), he will "make strong" (*sthenoō*, GK *4964*), and he will "make steadfast [like a foundation]" (*themelioō*, GK *2530*). That is, the Lord himself will make things right, he will place them squarely on their feet, he will impart new strength and firmness, and he will settle their hearts and lives, freeing them from anxiety and allowing them to persevere. This is his promise.

11 It is only fitting that this rousing and passionate confession of the Lord's provision conclude with a second outburst of doxological praise: "To him be the power for ever and ever. Amen." God's promises rest on his mighty power (*kratos*, GK *3197*); hence his title in Scripture—*ho pantokratōr*, "the Almighty." Confession of the Lord as *pantokratōr* is critically important for those who go through severe hardship.

III. LETTER CLOSING (5:12–14)

¹²With the help of Silas, whom I regard as a faithful brother, I have written to you briefly, encouraging you and testifying that this is the true grace of God. Stand fast in it. ¹³She who is in Babylon, chosen together with you, sends you her greetings, and so does my son Mark. ¹⁴Greet one another with a kiss of love.
Peace to all of you who are in Christ.

COMMENTARY

12 Peter concludes his letter by indicating that the "faithful" Silvanus (NIV, Silas) has played a part in the epistle: *Dia Silouanou hymin . . . oligōn egrapsa.* The role that Silvanus/Silas plays has already been discussed at length in the introduction to the commentary. Peter's final word of exhortation and encouragement is to testify or declare emphatically (*epimartyreō*, GK *2148*) that "this is the true grace of God. Stand fast in it." He has exhorted and admonished, aroused and encouraged. The rest is up to them. God's grace (mentioned ten times in the letter) is, in the end, sufficient.

13 The letter's conclusion contains two greetings and two exhortations. The greetings issue, somewhat cryptically, from a party designated "she who is in Babylon, chosen [*syneklektē*, GK *5293*] together with you" and from "my son Mark." It is widely believed that the second gospel narrative was compiled by Mark and based largely on Peter's reconstruction of the ministry of Jesus. The reference to Babylon, generally understood to mean Rome, is likely intended to encourage the readers insofar as all Christians are exiles in this world.

14 The admonition to "greet one another with a holy kiss [NIV, kiss of love]" (also in Ro 16:16; 1Co 16:20; 2Co 13:12; 1Th 5:26) mirrors a practice common in Near Eastern culture and certainly common among early believers when assembled. The epistle ends as it opened (1:2)—with the wish that the readers be rooted in the peace of God.

2 PETER

J. DARYL CHARLES

Introduction

1. HISTORY OF INTERPRETATION: DATING AND COMPOSITION

Apart from the epistle of Jude, described by one NT scholar as "the most neglected book in the New Testament" (D. J. Rowston, "The Most Neglected Book in the New Testament," *NTS* 21 [1974-75]: 554–63), one might legitimately argue that 2 Peter has perhaps suffered more misunderstanding—not to mention its own share of neglect—than any other NT document. Traditional commentary on 2 Peter tends to be highly derivative in character and unified in its belief that the letter is not authentically Petrine. This is for several reasons: (1) the letter's struggle to achieve canonical status in the early church; (2) the obvious literary relationship to Jude; (3) the letter's relationship to 1 Peter and our difficulty in reconciling the language and style of 2 Peter with the NT portrait of the apostle; and (4) the predominance of an "early Catholic" reading of the epistle, with its governing historical-theological assumptions.

For roughly a century and a half the governing presupposition of NT scholarship has been that in 2 Peter (and Jude) a second-century church at war with the forces of Gnosticism is on display. A perusal of most standard introductions to the NT quickly identifies prevailing assumptions regarding this document. Willi Marxsen resolutely states what is a *sine qua non* for critical scholarship:

> So long as we assume the traditional idea of canonicity and accept as permanently normative only what derives from the apostles or the disciples of the apostles, as did the early Church, "not genuine" is a serious charge to make. . . . But if we admit its pseudonymity we are far more likely to place the letter in its particular historical context and to be able to understand it. Whether we draw the line [of composition] at the beginning of the second century or earlier is simply a matter of choice. If we make the cut at the beginning of the second century, we are faced with a relatively compact body of literature. We could perhaps exchange 2 Peter for the *Didache* and Jude for *1 Clement*, but this is of no significance as far as basic [interpretive] principles are concerned, and we should therefore not make it a problem.[1]

In 1958 Marxsen published a seminal work on early Catholicism in the New Testament, this at a time when Marxsen joined other influential NT scholars such as Ernst Käsemann in training an emerging

---

1. Willi Marxsen, *Introduction to the New Testament* (Philadelphia: Fortress, 1968), 12–13.

generation of theologians and exegetes who would influence NT interpretation up to the present day. In describing the life-setting of 2 Peter, Marxsen writes the following:

> This document gives us a glimpse of the situation of the Church at a relatively late period. The eschatology which looks to an imminent End has fallen into the background, and one has to adjust oneself to living in the world (cf. esp. the Pastorals). The Church is in the process of becoming an institution. . . . In the post-Pauline period—long after Paul, in fact, for he has already become a "literary entity" belonging to the past—the futurist eschatology of the Church is attacked by the Gnostics. "Where is the promise of his coming? For from the day that the fathers fell asleep, all things continue as they were from the beginning of the creation" (iii.4). Though far removed from the beginnings of the Church, the author is seeking to remain in continuity with these beginnings and sets out an "apologia for the primitive Christian eschatology" in its apocalyptic form.[2]

While an "early Catholic" reading of the NT is by no means confined to 2 Peter, it is here that it is applied in its most concentrated form. The epistle is almost universally assumed to be the latest of the NT writings,[3] mirroring second-century developments in the life of the church. Ferdinand Hahn summarizes the underlying assumption of most commentators in approaching 2 Peter: "Even though the implications might not yet be clearly seen, there is a practical awareness that the apostolic era is surely closed and that the immediate postapostolic period is soon ending. Hence, now the present tradition-material must be preserved in its basic meaning and form."[4] K.-H. Schelkle's verdict is unequivocal: "The letters [2 Peter and Jude] say themselves that the generations of the church are past. . . . The Apostolic era is closed and lies behind."[5]

The term "early Catholicism" is understood to represent the period of transition from earliest Christianity to the postapostolic church—a transition completed with the disappearance of the imminent expectation of the parousia, or second advent; a growing institutionalization of the church and need for a teaching office (which replaces the charismatic work of the Spirit); the codification of beliefs into creedal confessions for the purposes of defending the faith against Gnostic heresy; and the increasing dichotomy of priests and laity. Because 2 Peter, in the words of James D. G. Dunn, is "a reaction to the repeated disappointment of apocalyptic hopes [in Christ's return]," it "is a prime example of early Catholicism."[6]

It is inevitable for NT scholarship that the presence of "early Catholic" phenomena undermines the notion that 2 Peter can be authentically Petrine. Thus Käsemann, 156–57, can describe the epistle as "dubious" and displaying irreconcilable theological contradictions, while Gunter Klein thinks it

---

2. Willi Marxsen, *Der 'Frühkatholizismus' im Neuen Testament* (BibS(N) 21; Neukirchen: Neukirchener Verlag, 1958), 244.

3. Critical scholarship in the main tends to favor a dating of the epistle that ranges from the late first or early second century (e.g., Bauckham, 157–62), and thus roughly a generation removed from the apostles, to the late second century (e.g., A. Vögtle, "Die Schriftwerdung der apostolischen Paradosis nach 2. Petr 1,12–15," in *Neues Testament und Geschichte* [Zürich/Tübingen: Theologischer Verlag/Mohr, 1972], 297–305), during which time the NT canon was taking shape. There exists a virtually unanimous consensus among NT scholars that the epistle is postapostolic. Notable exceptions include E. M. B. Green, *2 Peter and Jude* and *2 Peter Reconsidered*; Guthrie, 805–58; Hillyer, 9–12; Charles, 11–75.

4. F. Hahn, "Randbemerkungen zum Judasbrief," *TZ* 37 (1981): 209–10 (my translation).

5. K.-H. Schelkle, "Spätapostolische Briefe als frühkatholisches Zeugnis," in *Neutestamentliche Aufsätze für J. Schmid*, ed. J. Blinzer et al. (Regensburg: Pustet, 1963), 225 (my translation).

6. J. D. G. Dunn, *Unity and Diversity in the New Testament: An Inquiry into the Earliest Character of Christianity* (Philadelphia: Westminster, 1977), 351.

inconceivable that 2 Peter is authentic and in the same league as the epistles of Paul: "This writer could not have dreamt that his own letter would join—and in fact follow—in the same canonical collection the letters of Paul, whose writings he held to be suspect.... For this reason, the clearly inescapable question puts our assurance of faith to the test, namely, whether we can ultimately consider the epistle of 2 Peter, with its conceptualization of canon, to be canonical."[7]

The effect of an "early Catholic" reading of 2 Peter (and other NT documents) has been to create a "canon within the canon," i.e., to view certain writings of the NT as authentic reflections of the early church's identity (e.g., the genuinely Pauline epistles), and thus of highest theological import, and other NT documents against the background of this supposed authenticity. Because writings such as 2 Peter judged less than authentic nevertheless have been retained in the NT canon by the church, assessments such as the following are not atypical, even when rather remarkable:

> The author ... wants to restore the fragile doctrine of last things to a new credibility, but he is only able to destroy it yet further. In spite of how vigorously he asserts himself, he is basically helpless.... The defender of Christian hope has had his feet pulled out from under him.... The dubious manner with which he treats his subject is a clear reflection of the writer's own lack of self-assurance.[8]

> Even when the epistle [2 Peter] is lacking in theological depth and spiritual energy ... it is not simply worthless. Above all, it mediates historical insights into the church's crisis resulting from second-century heresy.[9]

> I would want to insist that in not a few compositions Martin Luther and John Wesley, for example, were as, if not more inspired, than the author of II Peter.[10]

Given this half-embrace by biblical scholarship, it goes without saying that writings such as 2 Peter and Jude have labored under a heavy load. Thus, any initial attempt to interpret 2 Peter must begin with an assessment of the "early Catholic" thesis. It should be stressed that the problem with "early Catholicism" is not in its observation of second-century ecclesiastical phenomena. That these developments emerge in the subapostolic era is indisputable. Nor can it be denied that the NT contains foreshadows of "early Catholic" theological tendencies that come to full bloom in the second and third centuries. Rather, the problem lies with its starting point. "Early Catholicism" begins with the assumption that apostolic authorship presents an "obstacle" to NT exegesis.[11] Being presupposed, as we have seen, is that (1) the writer is far removed from the beginnings of the church; (2) pseudonymity allows us for the first time to grasp the full meaning of the letter; and (3) writings such as the *Didache* or *1 Clement* or *Barnabas*, with no theological significance, can be substituted in the canon for 2 Peter or Jude. In the end, what this means for 2 Peter is that we can say, along with James D. G. Dunn, that Luther's insights are at times more "inspired" than those of our epistle.

7. G. Klein, "Der zweite Petrusbrief und der neutestamentliche Kanon," in *Ärgernisse: Konfrontationen mit dem Neuen Testament* (Munich: Chr. Kaiser Verlag, 1970), 112 (my translation).

8. Ibid., 111–12.

9. H. Balz and W. Schrage, *Die katholischen Briefe* (NTD 10; Göttingen: Vandenhoeck & Ruprecht, 1973), 123 (my translation).

10. Dunn, *Unity and Diversity*, 374–86.

11. Alignment with the church's historical consensus constitutes a major stumbling block for many historical-critical scholars. For evangelicals, it is a necessary precommitment in the exegetical task and something they are prepared to do. To defer to the church's consensual exegesis historically is not to be obscurantist; rather, it is to acknowledge the limitations of both the interpretive community and the exegete.

An important step in helping correct the distortion of the historical situation being mirrored in 2 Peter was the 1983 publication of Richard Bauckham's rich commentary on Jude and 2 Peter. Bauckham, 8, was moved to observe, "The whole concept of 'early Catholicism' as New Testament scholars have used it to illuminate the history of first-century Christianity is ripe for radical reexamination. It has undoubtedly promoted too simple a picture of the development of Christianity."

What is it in the "early Catholic" reading of 2 Peter that necessitates a "radical reexamination"? As to the "early Catholic" assumption that the church has abandoned the hope of the parousia, quite the opposite would seem to be on display in 2 Peter. The writer avows with great earnestness that the eschatological day of reckoning is *certain*. That a pastorally sensitive explanation for the "delay" is given (3:8–13) cannot legitimately be construed to mean that hope for the parousia is fading; rather, the author attributes this delay to divine long-suffering: "The Lord is not slow in keeping his promise, as some understand slowness. He is patient with you, not wanting anyone to perish, but everyone to come to repentance" (3:9). Moreover, to the false teacher, the false prophet, and the moral skeptic, the second advent is not a hope but a *threat*.[12]

But if, for the sake of the argument, the NT does give evidence of an "early Catholic" church evacuating hope in an imminent parousia, a more serious issue emerges. Given Jesus' confident assertions about a possible imminent return, the church surely would have been tempted to abandon its allegiance to him after the "cardinal error" had been exposed. If Jesus was speaking only apocalyptically with a temporal nearness in mind for the purposes of encouraging his flock, his expedience leads to quite delusory—and pastorally deleterious—results.[13] Not infrequently, critical scholarship's reconstruction of the so-called "early Catholic" scenario tends to cast the church as spiritually dull and undiscerning.

Witnesses as diverse as I. Howard Marshall ("Is Apocalyptic the Mother of Christian Theology?" in *Tradition and Interpretation in the New Testament*, ed. G. F. Hawthorne and O. Betz [Grand Rapids: Eerdmans, 1987]) and Jaroslav Pelikan (*The Christian Tradition: The Emergence of the Catholic Tradition (100–600)* [Chicago: Univ. of Chicago Press, 1971], 1:123–24, 130–31) have written that, while the imminence of the second advent was indeed part of Jesus' teaching, it is not what "early Catholic" proponents have made it out to be. With regard to succeeding generations, Pelikan believes it is more accurate to speak of a *shift within the polarity* of the "already/not yet" tension inherent in the Christian message; a renewed appreciation for ethical imperatives that address the church's relationship to the world is being realized.

---

12. Thus Green, *2 Peter and Jude*, 27. The primary issue, from the standpoint of the writer, is not *timing* but the *fact* of a day of reckoning. Those who would ascribe to 2 Peter a late date due to a "fading parousia hope" fail to note that the earliest NT letters we possess—1 and 2 Thessalonians, address this issue. Both early and later NT documents mirror the same eschatological tension—e.g., Heb 10:36–39; Jas 5:8; 1Pe 4:7; 2Pe 3:1–10; Rev 22:20. Even in subapostolic writings, this is still the case—e.g., *Did.* 10:6; *1 Clem.* 23:5; *2 Clem.* 12:1, 6; *Barn.* 4:3; Herm. *Vis.* 3:8, 9.

13. So Ernst Käsemann: "We have to state clearly and without evasion that this hope proved to be a delusion and that with it there collapsed at the same time the whole theological framework of apocalyptic" (*New Testament Questions of Today* [Philadelphia: Fortress, 1969], 106). Franz Mussner ("Die Ablösung des Apostolischen durch das nachapostolische Zeitalter und ihre Konsequenzen," in *Wort Gottes in der Zeit* [Düsseldorf: Patmos, 1967], 169–70, translation mine) concurs: "The detachment [from the apostolic period] represents a vacuum in the church's history that almost gives the impression of a 'fracture'. . . . One must imagine oneself in that situation, with the burning question that confronted them: The apostles are dead. What now?"

Our reconsideration of the NT's eschatological perspective leads us to rethink basic "early Catholic" assumptions. Does "early Catholicism"—with its supposed "delay" in the parousia hope and second-century reconstruction—imply *a priori* a wrong exegetical or theological starting point, an interpretation that is *imposed on* rather than *drawn from* the text?

In 2 Peter, as in Jude, no reference to church officeholders appears—required if the letter is mirroring second-century developments. To the contrary, the flock is admonished to guard itself. The readers are exhorted to "make every effort" to strengthen the ethical underpinnings of their faith (1:5–9). Whereas it is assumed by "early Catholic" proponents that doctrine is being guarded by an office or institution, a more plausible explanation—and one that issues out of the text itself—is that the audience, planted in a Gentile and broadly pagan cultural environment, is struggling with the ethical requirements that betoken vital Christian faith. Second Peter is a call for the community to guard itself.

Similarly, the assumed need for ecclesiastical control over doctrine does not manifest itself in 2 Peter in the way that "early Catholic" exegetes have maintained. In fact, it is the silence of the ecclesiastical voice that strikes the reader. Not an institution, not an office, but the inspiration of the Holy Spirit is at work in the people of God (1:21b). Rightly understood, 1:20–21 has nothing to do with scriptural interpretation, the church's official teaching office, or a primitive type of church magisterium; the issue at hand, supported by the letter's contextual flow, is *prophetic and authoritative speech*. The author, who is claiming to be an eyewitness of the transfiguration (1:16–18), is vigorous in his assertion: "And we have the word of the prophets made more certain" (1:19), for which a better translation might be, "Thus we have the prophetic message attested." It is the inspiration of the Spirit that is said to convey authority.[14]

If we are to assume, along with proponents of the "early Catholic" thesis and mainstream critical scholarship, a late dating of the epistle (i.e., one that is generations removed from the apostles),[15] then it follows that the author and readers would long have had access to all of Paul's letters, in which case the statement in 3:15–16 makes less sense if penned by a pseudepigrapher. Michael Green's observation, 158–59, in this regard is worth repeating. To "Peter," Paul is a "beloved brother"; to Polycarp, several generations removed, he is "the blessed and glorious Paul." In the second century one tended to view Paul either as an archvillain (given the maturity of heretical teachings) or as the apostle par excellence; it is, however, highly dubious that Paul would have been referred to as a "dear brother" by later generations.

2. CANONICAL CONSIDERATIONS

Of the seven canonical documents denominated "catholic," or general, epistles, only 1 Peter and 1 John were not considered to be "disputed writings" by the early church. Yet, in his compendium of early church history, Eusebius (*Hist. eccl.* 3.25) informs the reader that, even when the other five were disputed (James, 2 Peter, Jude, 2 John, and 3 John), they were not unknown but were recognized by many. Of the seven

---

14. This interpretation is confirmed when we consider the basic motifs and solutions to the church's threat mounted by Ignatius, Clement, and the Shepherd of Hermas in the postapostolic period, e.g., calling the bishop, through whom Christ's authority is necessarily channeled; securing the church's authority by doing everything according to the proper order; and proclaiming penance and rationed forms of grace.

15. J. A. T. Robinson (*Redating the New Testament* [London: SCM, 1976], 327–35) believes that 2 Peter may have been cited in *1 Clement*, which has been dated as early as AD 95.

general epistles, 2 Peter appears to have had the greatest difficulty being accepted, for reasons explained by Eusebius (*Hist. eccl.* 3.3), who writes that, though many have thought it valuable and have honored it alongside the other Scriptures, much of the church has been taught to regard it as noncanonical. In the case of other writings attributed to the apostle (e.g., *The Acts of Peter*, *The Apocalypse of Peter*, and the gospel carrying his name), we have no reason whatsoever, according to Eusebius, to include them among the traditional, and nowhere in the church are they cited.

Eusebius further acknowledges that Clement of Alexandria (late second century) offered commentary on all the catholic epistles (*Hist. eccl.* 6.14). Other early witnesses paint an incomplete picture. Origen writes of one "acknowledged" letter of Peter and mentions a second that is "doubted" (*Comm. Jo.* 5.3), yet he himself accepts it as one of Peter's "twin epistles" (*Hom. Josh.* 7.1). Didymus the Blind (PL 39.1742, 1811–18) comments on all seven general epistles but considers 2 Peter to be a forged document (*esse falsatum*). Didymus of Alexandria, by contrast, several centuries later cites 2 Peter as authentic and thus authoritative.[16] The authors of the spurious *Apocalypse of Peter* and *Acts of Peter*, both second-century documents, show evidence of having known of 2 Peter's existence. That resistance to an acceptance of 2 Peter was greater in some areas—among Syrian churches, for example—may be related to the fact that the spurious pseudepigraphal works bearing the apostle's name were in circulation in these parts. This would reasonably explain why early patristic evidence supporting 2 Peter is scant. Second Peter nevertheless was recognized as canonical by the late fourth century.[17]

One of the challenges facing those who consider 2 Peter to be authentically Petrine is that its language, imagery, and tone differ markedly from that of 1 Peter. Given the acknowledgment in 1 Peter that the apostle is using a secretary (5:12), one solution is to suggest a different secretary, or amanuensis, at work, such as Jerome posited (*Epist.* 120.11). Nonetheless, modern scholarship has broadly rejected the epistle as authentic, even when all would concede that it is worlds removed from the spurious writings of the second century that bear Peter's name; thus, Bray observes the following in his overview of the early Fathers' attitudes:

> The Fathers all recognized that there are great differences between the first and second letters attributed to Peter, but they explained these variations in different ways. Some of them rejected the authenticity of the second letter and refused to accept it as part of the canon, but the majority were unwilling to go that far. They recognized that although there were many differences between the two letters, they were not as great as the differences between the letters, on the one hand, and other writings attributed to Peter that were known to be spurious, on the other.[18]

Indeed, although 2 Peter is the least well-attested book in the NT, its attestation far exceeds that of any of the noncanonical books.

---

16. See the textual evidence in B. M. Metzger, *The Canon of the New Testament* (Oxford: Clarendon, 1987), 213. An extensive summary of early patristic awareness of 2 Peter can be found in Bigg, 204–10, and Mayor, cxv–cxxiii.

17. Thus Augustine (Doctr. chr. 2.12). Cyril of Jerusalem and Athanasius include 2 Peter in their catalogs of catholic epistles. Significantly, the fourth-century councils of Hippo, Laodicea, and Carthage, while accepting 2 Peter, reject the letters of Clement of Rome and Barnabas, both of which previously had been held in high esteem. Mayor, cxv-cxxiii, painstakingly examines possible allusions to 2 Peter in the writings of the early Fathers.

18. G. Bray, ed, *James, 1–2 Peter, 1–3 John, Jude* (ACCS 11; Downers Grove, Ill.: InterVarsity, 2000), 129.

Robert Picirilli's extensive study of possible allusions in early patristic literature ("Allusions to 2 Peter in the Apostolic Fathers," *JSNT* 33 [1987]: 57–83) concludes that the epistle is *probably* being alluded to, though without decisive proof. He names twenty-two possible sources, including *1 Clement, Barnabas*, and *Shepherd of Hermas*. At the very least, what NT scholarship *cannot* dogmatically contend is that there are unquestionably no references to 2 Peter in the apostolic fathers. Authenticity, therefore, will have to be debated on grounds other than whether postapostolic fathers knew and used the epistle.[19]

The argument for 2 Peter's authenticity is further buttressed by several features. One is the notably personal style, evidenced by the opening salutation in which the author reverts to his original name, Simon, as though the author finds it necessary to verify his "signature" as one of the inner circle of apostles. Not insignificantly, it is "Simon Peter" who recognizes and confesses Jesus in his messianic fullness (Mt 16:13–20; cf. Jn 1:42). Hence the author's personal reminiscence, recorded in 2 Peter 1:16–18, is all the more deceptive if, as most commentators assume, the writer is pseudonymous. How does 2 Peter withstand the test of authenticity? Can one hold to the view that the NT writings are divinely inspired and sacred yet inauthentic?[20]

3. EPISTOLARY DESTINATION, AUTHORSHIP, AND THE QUESTION OF PSEUDONYMITY

The absence of names and places renders it difficult to be conclusive about the identity of the recipients of 2 Peter and the context out of which the letter arose. While the provenance and destination of the letter elude any certainty, numerous textual indicators point to a particular social location in which the readership finds itself, making it likely that the letter is addressed to Christians in Greece or Asia Minor, where Paul's letters had already circulated (3:15–16).[21]

In contrast to Jude, which reflects a distinctly Palestinian Jewish-Christian milieu, 2 Peter suggests an audience in pagan Gentile surroundings. Among such indicators are the allusion to equality (1:1), an important political virtue to the Hellenistic mind; the mystical-philosophical language of partaking in the "divine nature" (1:4); employment of a catalog of virtues (1:5–7), a common rhetorical device among Stoic moral philosophers; frequent paraenesis (moral exhortation) in the face of apparent ethical lapse (e.g., 1:12–15); use of the term "eyewitnesses" (1:16), a technical term in classical Greek used to describe those who had achieved the highest degree of Eleusinian mystery-religion experience; a reference to "hell" (Gk. *Tartarus*;

19. In a fascinating essay, F. W. Farrar ("The Second Epistle of St. Peter and Josephus," *ExpTim* 3.8 [1888]: 58–69) argued over a century ago that "an isolated Christian tract" such as 2 Peter could well have gained the notice of Josephus, particularly one written with such stylistic and rhetorical force.

20. While Erasmus rejected the epistle, Calvin and Luther reflect misgivings about 2 Peter, but for reasons different from those of modern scholars. For Luther, the epistle was not sufficiently christological and thus of an inferior quality. But the same essential bias in Luther extended to James and Jude as well, serving as a precursor to the unfortunate designation in modern historical-critical inquiry of a "canon within a canon." Calvin's assessment (and the Reformer was not uncritical regarding the matter of Petrine authorship) was that "if 2 Peter be received as canonical, we must allow Peter to be the author," and this based on (1) the name attached and (2) the testimony of personal experience with Christ. Calvin, 363, did allow for a disciple of Peter to do the writing, though not one removed from the apostle himself.

21. If one assumes 2 Peter to be authentic, it is likely to have been written from Rome shortly before the apostle's death (1:15).

2:4), the subterranean abyss and place of punishment in Greek mythology; the allusion to Noah's generation (2:5); comparison to Lot's predicament in Sodom (2:6); use of Balaam typology (2:15–16), which suggests apostasy and moral decay; common and pagan proverbial images to depict apostasy (2:20–22); a moral apologetic against radical relativists (3:3–7); and multiple allusions to the Hellenistic virtue of "godliness," or piety (1:3, 6, 7; 3:11).

Although the epistle carries the name of "Simon Peter," critical scholarship, with its "early Catholic" reading and assumed postapostolic dating, is virtually unanimous that Peter himself was not the author. Bauckham, 146–47, 161, while calling for a much-needed "reexamination" of the "early Catholic" thesis, nevertheless believes that 2 Peter is "fictionally represented as written shortly before Peter's death" and is most probably an emanation of a Petrine "circle" of Christian leaders in Rome. Indicative of most critical scholars, Bauckham, 158, believes that "language alone . . . makes it improbable that Peter could have written 2 Peter." The "fictional" character of the epistle, which according to Bauckham, 134, is "entirely *transparent*," is "decisively reinforced" by its literary quality. In the end, evidence that 2 Peter is not authentic is conclusive for Bauckham, 159 (emphasis his): "The evidence which really rules out composition *during Peter's lifetime* is that of literary genre . . . and that of date. . . . Either of these might be fatal for any degree of Petrine authorship. Together they must be regarded as entirely conclusive against Petrine authorship."[22]

But is the evidence in fact "entirely conclusive"? Neyrey, 118–20, suggests otherwise. He makes the observation that the unusual vocabulary of 2 Peter that is so problematic for many commentators may stem from the sources used by the writer and need not be adduced as "proof" that the epistle is not Petrine.[23]

In addition to dating and linguistic considerations, evidence of the "fictionality" of 2 Peter is thought to be further compounded by the author's use of the literary convention of a last will or testament (1:12–15).[24] Hereby it is understood that the name and influence of significant leaders in the church were perpetuated by their circle of disciples, and a posthumously published "farewell address" constitutes an appropriate way of transmitting the apostle's vision. Moreover, writing in the name of a leader is assumed to pose "no ethical problem for the ancients, and especially in farewell addresses" (so Craddock, 92). Thus one is left to conclude that the literary genre to which 2 Peter belongs makes it abundantly clear—to its initial readers and to contemporary readers—that the letter was pseudepigraphal. Green, 34–35, has adopted this critical stance regarding 2 Peter, seeing it as "both a letter and also an example of the type of work we meet in the *Testaments of the Twelve Patriarchs*." He goes on to make these observations:

> The author's aim was to defend apostolic Christianity in a subapostolic situation, and this he does, not by having recourse to his own authority, but by faithfully mirroring apostolic teaching which he adapts and interprets for his own day. "Peter's testament" formed the ideal literary vehicle for his plans. . . . Nobody

---

22. In response to Bauckham, Brevard Childs (*The New Testament as Canon* [Valley Forge, Pa.: Trinity, 1994], 467–68) argues that (1) there is no clear evidence 2 Peter was intended to be fiction and (2) Bauckham does not do justice to the problems and inconsistencies of pseudonymity theory.

23. Bauckham, 135–36, notes the high percentage of *hapax legomena* in 2 Peter. Unusual vocabulary, however, might issue out of specific sources used, or an amanuensis, and not simply the author's formal education or a high degree of literacy. Neyrey, 120, considers the author of 2 Peter to be of "solid, but by no means aristocratic . . . eloquence."

24. Jewish exemplars of such include the *Testament of Job*, the *Testament of Moses*, the *Testament of Adam*, and the *Testament of the Twelve Patriarchs*.

ever imagined it came from Peter himself. The literary convention of the testament was too well known. Such is the theory.

Because "the testamental function of the farewell speech in no way proceeds from the [apostolic] witness and guarantor of [apostolic] tradition himself,"[25] the genre of the farewell speech or testament is understood to reveal an attempt by later generations to "guarantee" the apostolic tradition faithfully.[26] What is assumed by critical scholarship is that the authors of pseudepigraphal testaments, who are chronologically removed from the apostles, nevertheless take a necessary (though secondary) place alongside the apostles and prophets (cf. Eph 2:20) in guarding and transmitting the apostolic tradition to the subapostolic church. In the words of Frederick Danker ("2 Peter," in *The General Letters*, ed. G. Krodel [Minneapolis: Augsburg, 1995], 84), "In most cases there was no attempt to deceive the public, but to say, 'If N.N. were living, this is what N.N. would say to us.'"

But such a verdict, with its necessary supporting assumptions, is open to challenge. How can it be so confidently asserted that 2 Peter was intended to be entirely transparent fiction, as mainstream scholarship has done? And are later generations in fact "guaranteeing" the apostolic tradition? While a thorough treatment of pseudepigraphy cannot be undertaken in the present discussion, the testamental thesis in 2 Peter, because of biblical scholarship's commitment to this hypothesis, requires some comment.[27]

To state the heart of the matter bluntly, as Michael Green has done, proponents of pseudepigraphy in 2 Peter—and the testament in particular—adduce evidence for the existence of a phenomenon in Christian literature that has never been shown to have existed.[28] While the amount of literature devoted to the question of Christian pseudepigraphy is massive,[29] discussion frequently falls short of satisfying answers to questions such as those posed by Bruce Metzger ("Literary Forgeries and Canonical Pseudepigrapha," in *New Testament Studies—Philological, Versional and Patristic* [Leiden: Brill, 1980], 1–22):

From an ethical point of view, is a pseudepigraphon compatible with honesty and candor, whether by ancient or modern moral standards? From a psychological point of view, how should one estimate an author who impersonates an ancient worthy . . . ? Should we take him seriously, and, if we do, how does

---

25. Thus O. Knoch, *Die "Testamente" des Petrus und Paulus* (SBB 62; Stuttgart: KBW, 1973), 28 (my translation).

26. On the genre of the testament in the NT, see Kurz, *Farewell Addresses*.

27. Reicke, 146–47, appears to have been the first to posit the testamental hypothesis for 2 Peter. Commentary since has assumed this starting point; thus, e.g., Bauckham, 131–35; Watson, 327–28; and more recently, Kraftchick, 73–76.

28. Green's argument is developed in both *2 Peter Reconsidered* and *2 Peter and Jude*. See also D. Guthrie, "The Development of the Idea of Canonical Pseudepigrapha in New Testament Criticism," in *Vox evangelica I*, ed. R. P. Martin (London: Epworth, 1962), 43–59.

29. A comprehensive bibliography of literature up to 1965 is found in W. Speyer, *Die literarische Fälschung im heidnischen und christlichen Altertum* (Munich: Beck, 1971). A more recent survey of the literature is found in J. D. Charles, *Literary Strategy in the Epistle of Jude* (Scranton: Univ. of Scranton Press, 1993), 81–90. For a more recent attempt to justify the use of pseudepigraphy in the NT, see D. G. Meade, *Pseudonymity and Canon: An Investigation into the Relationship of Authorship and Authority in Jewish and Earliest Christian Tradition* (WUNT 39; Tübingen: Mohr, 1986). A helpful response to Meade's position can be found in Ellis, 212–24.; T. D. Lea, "Pseudonymity and the New Testament," in *New Testament Criticism and Interpretation*, ed. D. A. Black and D. S. Dockery (Grand Rapids: Zondervan, 1991), 535–59; T. L. Wilder, "Pseudonymity and the New Testament," in *Interpreting the New Testament*, ed. D. A. Black and D. S. Dockery (Nashville: Broadman and Holman, 2001), 296–335; in addition to the earlier arguments set forth by Green and Guthrie that are yet to be answered plausibly.

this bear on the question of his sanity? From a theological point of view, should a work that involves a fraud, whether pious or not, be regarded as incompatible with the character of a message from God?

In addition, one of the broader methodological problems associated with the testamental hypothesis—and pseudepigraphy in general—is the open-ended and rather hopeless task of reconciling the fictive with the *real* occasion.[30] Ultimately, the problems affiliated with a testamental hypothesis in the case of 2 Peter are not easily dispelled, since both the identity of the author and the social location of the audience must be reconciled to the text of the epistle itself.[31] To what extent is the testamental hypothesis imposed on, as opposed to *leading from*, the text?

Standard testamental or "valedictory" address is thought to contain notice of one's imminent death, paraenesis or moral exhortation, eschatological predictions mediated through dreams or visions, an historical overview, a transfer of authority, and blessings or curses.[32] Examples of farewell speeches recorded in Scripture (notably Dt 34:1–4; Lk 22:24–30; Jn 13–17; Ac 20:17–37) on examination would seem to borrow from but not be confined to this pattern.

But how does 2 Peter conform to the pattern of testamental literature? More broadly, it must be stated that 2 Peter is free of legendary and apocryphal elements that characterize spurious documents—e.g., Jewish apocalyptic testaments as well as Petrine pseudepigrapha of the second century. With regard to particulars, the contrast is equally telling. Wholly absent from 2 Peter are apocalyptic dreams or visions and the element of blessings or curses, both of which are salient features of the standard testamental genre. The stamp of the epistle, by contrast, is decidedly and explicitly *prophetic*—"we have the word of the prophets made more certain" (1:19a)—rather than apocalyptic. Also absent is the characteristic transfer of authority, which Kurz, 50, calls the "primary function" of the biblical farewell address to "describe and promote transition from original religious leaders . . . to their successors." Second Peter, moreover, begins with substantial didactic material, which tends *not* to be a part of pseudepigraphal farewell speeches. Finally and significantly, the allusion in 2 Peter to the writer's death (1:14) is not immediate, neither is it prominent; rather, it is injected only parenthetically *after* the substantial paraenetic and didactic portions of the letter—and this only in a veiled manner. The special appeal of the farewell address, it should be remembered, is the relationship of the audience to the one standing before death (as Jn 13–17 well illustrates).

Furthermore, rather than transfer authority, 2 Peter contains testimony to the author's own authority, given the urgency of community's present needs. The writer's presence on the holy mountain is not some "cleverly invented story" for the purpose of deceiving others;[33] rather, it serves as an apostolic imprint that

---

30. In fact, Meade, 127, has argued that if indeed pseudonymity exists in the NT, then it is a "double pseudonymity"; i.e., we are confronted with the dilemma of both pseudonymous *author* and *audience.*

31. We cannot assume, along with Fornberg, 10–11, that 2 Peter was written "when the church became aware of the distance to the first Christian generation, and therefore wished to hold fast to the leading personalities of the first generation in order to solve problems of her own time." This assumption, originating outside the text and not required by the text itself, is insufficiently free of restraints imposed on the text by an "early Catholic" reading.

32. See Kurz, 48–52; Knoch, *Die "Testamente" des Petrus und Paulus*, 28–31.

33. Consider the apostle Paul's own words in this regard, as though attune to the possibility of apostolic imitation, that his readers are "not to become easily unsettled or alarmed by some prophecy, report or letter supposed to have come from us, saying that the day of the Lord has already come. Don't let anyone deceive you in any way" (2Th 2:2–3a).

is left behind for the sake of the church: "We were eyewitnesses of his majesty. . . . We ourselves heard this voice" (1:16, 18).[34]

The absence of one stylistically exemplary sample from antiquity of qualified testamental writing, coupled with the aforementioned difficulties, places the testamental hypothesis on shaky ground. Moreover, it should be emphasized, as Ellis, 220, has done, that early Christian writers knew how to transmit the teachings of an authority figure without engaging in pseudipigraphy. The writer of 2 Peter, if the epistle is a pseudepigraphon, clearly shows evidence of a deceptive intent, given the emphatic language being employed: "We did not follow cleverly invented stories . . . , but we were eyewitnesses" (1:16); "We ourselves heard this voice . . . when we were with him" (1:18); "Dear friends, this is now my second letter to you" (3:1).

In the end, the broadly accepted assumption that "Second Peter bears so many marks of the testament genre . . . that readers familiar with the genre must have expected it to be fictional" (Bauckham, 134) requires some moderation. In truth, several significant qualifying marks are absent. As a result of his exhaustive study of the language of 2 Peter, Starr, 4, is led to observe that "2 Peter is often described as belonging to the tradition of Jewish 'testaments,' but these at best exhibit only a tenuous similarity of genre to 2 Peter."[35]

The ethical dilemma of why the church would sanction the use of pseudepigraphy in the service of advancing Christian orthodoxy does not evaporate as readily as critical scholarship might contend, given the apostles' role in the church's foundation (Eph 2:20; 3:5). The function of the apostolate was in fact *dynamic*, *authoritative*, and *binding* in nature; "friends of the apostle," including next-generation disciples, were not accorded apostolic authority. Apostolic witness is not merely personal testimony that accords with what the apostle himself would have said. It is, rather, "infallibly authoritative, legally binding deposition, the kind that stands up in a law court. Accordingly, that witness embodies a canonical principle; it provides the matrix for a new canon, the emergence of a new body of revelation to stand alongside the covenantal revelation of the Old Testament."[36]

The implication of apostolicity as it relates to the possibility of pseudonymity in the NT is this: strictly speaking, "apostolic pseudepigrapha" is a contradiction in terms, since not even well-intended literary motives expressed under the name of an apostle warrant apostolic authority.[37] Given the role of the apostle in the early church, Ellis, 224, has argued that "scholars cannot have it both ways. They cannot identify

---

34. The reminiscence of the transfiguration experience, frequently thought by commentators to render the epistle inauthentic due to its differing from the Synoptic version, serves two purposes. First, it establishes a thematic link to the parousia in chapter 3. It is a foreshadow not only for the apostles but for all believers of "the power and coming of our Lord Jesus Christ" (1:16; cf. 3:4, 8–10). Second, and more immediately, it testifies to the writer's own authority.

35. Paul's "valedictory" speech to the elders of the church at Ephesus (Ac 20:17–37) may serve to illustrate that a farewell speech may adopt characteristics of a "last will" or "testament" without being restricted to the pseudepigraphal genre.

36. Thus R. B. Gaffin Jr., "The New Testament as Canon," in *Inerrancy and Hermeneutic: A Tradition, A Challenge, A Debate*, ed. H. M. Conn (Grand Rapids: Baker, 1988), 176.

37. A postbiblical source of no less stature than Tertullian (Bapt. 17) informs us that the writer of the pseudepigraphal work The Acts of Paul and Thecla, regardless of the best of intentions in seeking to pass off his work under the name of the apostle Paul, was punished as a forger by being defrocked as a presbyter.

apostolic letters as pseudepigrapha and at the same time declare them to be innocent products with a right to a place in the canon."[38]

However, *that* an epistle such as 2 Peter might issue from the apostle in the historical setting illuminated from within the text is not to say *how* it might issue from him. At some point the question must be addressed as to whether 2 Peter suggests (or even *allows for* the remote possibility of) some sort of scribal help via an amanuensis. E. I. Robson ("Composition and Dictation in New Testament Books," *JTS* 18 [1917]: 296) invites modern readers to make allowances for dictation in the NT, for "when an ancient writer wanted to write, his one anxiety seems to have been how he could best avoid writing; and the convenience of the slave-amanuensis enabled him so to avoid it, by allowing him to declaim, talk, even babble garrulously, at will, hardly feeling that he was making any special literary effort."

This neglected perspective, which would account for significant differences between the language and style of 1 and 2 Peter, is amplified by G. J. Bahr, "Paul and Letter Writing in the First Century," *CBQ* 28 (1966): 475–76: "The influence of the secretary would be even greater if he were left to compose the letter himself along general lines laid down by the author. The result would be that the letter might represent the basic thought of the author, but not necessarily his terminology or style.... It may be that the discrepancy between what Paul wrote and what he spoke was due to the abilities of a secretary who was expert in the composition of letters."

Given the secretary's freedom to insert a salutation or postscript, do his own revising of material, or add stylistic and literary artifice, the modern reader might do well to allow greater room for the work of an amanuensis in the NT epistles than we might customarily allow.[39] The differences in vocabulary and style between 1 and 2 Peter reasonably suggest the use of different secretaries.

An underlying presupposition of all pseudonymity theory is that, because a work ultimately found acceptance by the church as canonical, pseudonymity in the end is accepted. Any authority the writer possesses—whether he is a member of a "Petrine school," a "Petrine agent," or some individual several generations removed from the apostle—inheres in the fact that he is "faithfully interpreting" the apostolic tradition. We are asked to believe that because a work was "orthodox" and the writer's motives were noble, the work was accepted by the church. In his evaluation of Jewish and Hellenistic attitudes toward literary pseudepigraphy, Roger Beckwith (*The Old Testament Canon of the New Testament Church* [Grand Rapids: Eerdmans, 1985], 274–433) gently chides biblical scholarship for hypotheses propounded in order to avoid drawing the conclusion that Jews and Christians did not reckon pseudepigraphy as an

---

38. It is not at all unreasonable to conclude with Guthrie, 821, regarding 2 Peter, "It did not require much foresight for an old man to suggest that his end was not far away. Moreover, a pseudepigraphist writing this would not appear to add anything to the information contained in the canonical sources, in spite of writing after the event."

39. In the view of Bauckham, 158, the language alone "makes it improbable that the apostle could have written 2 Peter." By contrast, for Jerome (Epist. 120.9) the difference in style and expression between 1 and 2 Peter could be accounted for on the basis of different amanuenses. Antedating the Pauline epistles by a century, Cicero (Fam. 3.6; Att. 2.23; 7:138.12; 13.9; 14.21; 16.15) frequently at the end of his letters—and occasionally in the middle—offers explanations for writing with his own hand or dictating. Similarly, the apostle Paul shows evidence of both practices in his letter writing. His epistles are stated to have been written with his own hand (especially as he came to the end of his letters) as well as dictated (Ro 16:22; 1Co 16:21; Gal 6:11; Col 4:18; 2Th 3:17; Phm 19).

acceptable literary device.[40] It is precisely the concern for pseudonymity that seems to underlie Paul's exhortation to the Thessalonians not to be shaken "by some prophecy, report or letter supposed to have come from us" (2Th 2:2). The implication is that others were not averse to using his apostolic pedigree.

While it is true, as Chester and Martin, 147, write, that the status of 2 Peter "as part of the New Testament canon with normative value is both an ancient and a modern challenge," this challenge should not be overstated. One of the unfortunate by-products of contemporary scholarly thinking about 2 Peter is that the epistle has been marginalized in mainstream biblical studies, thus joining Jude's "most neglected" status.

J. Ramsey Michaels ("Second Peter and Jude—Royal Promises," in *The New Testament Speaks*, ed. G. W. Barker et al. [New York: Harper and Row, 1969], 351) is correct to note that the case against authenticity in 2 Peter has been overstated; and he is correct in his observation that "most of its content is perfectly credible as early tradition, oriented primarily to the apostle's own lifetime." In the end, the pseudepigraphal hypothesis, when scrutinized, asks far too much of us.[41] And in the end, the pseudepigraphal hypothesis, even when applied with noble intentions, would seem to have contributed significantly toward 2 Peter's marginalization.

4. LITERARY RELATIONSHIP OF 2 PETER TO JUDE

In addition to the question of 2 Peter's authenticity, its literary relationship to Jude has tended to dominate historical-critical examination of the letter. Starr, 7, has stated the matter well: "Scholarly research on 2 Peter has more than anything else been an investigation of parallels." The notable lexical and conceptual similarities in Jude and 2 Peter—of the twenty-five verses in Jude, parts or all of nineteen verses are found in 2 Peter—have led scholars to posit four options regarding literary dependence: (1) Jude borrows from 2 Peter;[42] (2) 2 Peter borrows from Jude;[43] (3) both 2 Peter and Jude borrow from a common third source;[44] or (4) 2 Peter and Jude stem from one and the same author.[45] The question of literary dependence involves arguments that are both external and internal to the text. External factors—e.g., the "early Catholic" hypothesis—arise from attempts by scholars to identify the historical and theological scenario behind 2 Peter. Internal factors would include indicators such as borrowed tradition-material, vocabulary, rhetorical technique, or prevailing verbal tense.

Regarding the problem of literary dependence, Neyrey, 122, issues a helpful cautionary note: although NT scholarship has weighed in regarding the above four possibilities (and Neyrey himself joins an impressive list

---

40. The resiliency and unrelenting character of pseudonymity theory has prompted J. A. T. Robinson (*Redating the New Testament*, 186) to remark that among biblical scholars "there is an appetite for pseudonymity that grows by what it feeds on."

41. It is entirely fair to say that neither the protracted treatment of external evidence in support of 2 Peter's authenticity (e.g., Guthrie, 805–38) nor the extensive examination of the evidence undertaken by Green (*2 Peter Reconsidered*) has yet been satisfactorily challenged by proponents of pseudonymity theory; see also more recently my *Virtue amidst Vice*, 49–83.

42. So Bigg, 216–23; T. Zahn, *Introduction to the New Testament* (Edinburgh: T&T Clark, 1909), 2.250–51.

43. So Mayor, i–xxv; Sidebottom, 95; Fornberg, ch. 3; Bauckham, 142; Neyrey, 122; Chester and Martin, 139.

44. So E. I. Robson, *Studies in the Second Epistle of St. Peter* (Cambridge: Cambridge Univ. Press, 1915); Reicke, 189–90; Hillyer, 13.

45. So Robinson, *Redating the New Testament*, 192–95.

of scholars who prefer the priority of Jude), none of the aforementioned options are conclusive. Redactive interests differ in 2 Peter and Jude, and it may be the differences rather than similarities that in the end serve as our most useful clue as to who borrowed from whom. But any certainty regarding the matter eludes us.

Certainly the parallels between the two epistles, both in vocabulary and in concept and imagery, are striking:

- Both authors describe themselves as "servants" of Jesus Christ (1:1; Jude 1).
- Grace and peace are to be multiplied to the readers (1:2; Jude 2).
- The readers have a received faith (1:1; Jude 3).
- Both epistles understand Christian faith in terms of a divine "call" (1:3, 10; Jude 1).
- The opponents deny Christ's lordship (2:1; Jude 4).
- Destructive heresies have been secretly brought in (2:1; Jude 4).
- The opponents are licentious in their ways (2:2; Jude 4).
- The opponents' condemnation has been declared long ago (2:3; Jude 4).
- The fallen angels serve as a moral paradigm (2:4; Jude 6).
- The fallen angels are held in darkness for judgment (2:4; cf. Jude 6).
- Sodom and Gomorrah serve as a moral paradigm (2:6; Jude 7).
- The opponents walk according to the flesh, indulge in their lusts, and do not hesitate to despise authority (2:10; Jude 8, 18).
- God's angels exhibit restraint in contrast to the opponents (2:11; Jude 9).
- The opponents are compared to brute beasts, irrational by nature (2:12; Jude 10).
- Balaam serves as a moral type (2:15–16; Jude 11).
- The opponents are portrayed as blots or blemishes (2:13; Jude 12).
- The opponents have erred, forsaking the right way (2:15; Jude 11).
- The opponents are compared to clouds (2:17; Jude 12).
- Blackest darkness has been reserved for the opponents (2:17; Jude 13).
- The opponents are boastful, lustful, and seductive (2:18; Jude 16).
- The apostasy of the opponents has been predicted (3:2–7; Jude 17–19).
- Scoffers in the last days were predicted (3:3; Jude 18).
- Jewish-Christian eschatological thinking is present (3:5–10; Jude 14–15).
- The readers are admonished to be without spot or fault (3:14; Jude 24).
- The readers are admonished toward stability (3:17; Jude 24).
- For the readers to fail to persevere is described in terms of "falling" (1:10; Jude 24).
- God is understood as "Savior" (2:7, 9; Jude 25).
- Doxological praise is ascribed to Jesus Christ as both Lord and Savior, now and forever (3:18; Jude 25).

Paying attention to the unique redactive interests of each writer, however, will reveal a unique literary-rhetorical strategy at work in each work. Thus it is helpful to observe the dissimilarities in the two epistles.

- The author of 2 Peter claims apostleship, whereas Jude identifies himself as a brother of James.
- Jude's language and imagery reflect a Palestinian Jewish-Christian milieu, whereas 2 Peter mirrors a more pervasively Gentile social environment.

- Jude exhibits a rampant use of triplets, a pattern not conspicuous in 2 Peter.
- Whereas Jude plunges immediately into theological controversy, in 2 Peter the controversy is reserved for later in the epistle.
- 2 Peter uses the moral paradigms to emphasize both deliverance and judgment, whereas in Jude the paradigms categorically announce judgment.
- Paradigms and tradition-material are employed in Jude that would be meaningful to readers with a Jewish background (e.g., the archangel Michael, the *Assumption of Moses*, *1 Enoch*, Cain, and Korah), whereas tradition-material utilized in 2 Peter is more meaningful for an audience surrounded by Gentiles.
- Jude speaks of the fallen angels as being kept in chains in darkness, whereas in 2 Peter they are said to have been cast into hell (Gk. *Tartarus*).
- Jude cites verbatim an extrabiblical text (*1 En.* 1:9), whereas no direct citations are utilized in 2 Peter.
- 2 Peter is a tract consisting primarily of exhortations toward virtuous living, spelling out the contours of Christian ethics; Jude is a tract announcing condemnation.
- The reference to Sodom and Gomorrah in Jude is unqualified, whereas in 2 Peter the emphasis is on Lot's struggle with surrounding wickedness.
- 2 Peter shows evidences of both a personal relationship to the readers and challenges to the author's authority.
- 2 Peter contains an expanded Balaam typology.
- 2 Peter suggests future developments among the apostate, whereas Jude suggests that these developments are present and matured.
- "Knowledge" and "godliness" are important catchwords in 2 Peter.
- 2 Peter mirrors possible circulating arguments that deny moral accountability and thus proffers a moral "apologetic" by incorporating eschatological typology.
- The author of 2 Peter gives the impression of personal relationship to the apostle Paul, reflecting on Pauline epistles that have been circulating.[46]

What might be gleaned from these nuances? Despite the obvious literary relationship between the two epistles, one encounters cumulative evidence of a unique social setting in both letters. This distinctiveness deserves our careful attention. Material is chosen and structured as literary "brick and mortar" for the purpose of addressing the needs of the community according to the peculiar social context. The *mode* of the Christian message is indivisible from its *content* and is informed by the pastoral needs in the community. Hereby we begin to appreciate the distinctiveness of the two epistles.

5. RECENT PETRINE SCHOLARSHIP

The publication in 1977 of Tord Fornberg's *An Early Church in a Pluralistic Society* was significant inasmuch as it challenged the exegetical starting point of traditional commentary on 2 Peter. Fornberg's work

---

46. See the first three chapters in Mayor for a nearly exhaustive discussion of literary convergence and divergence in the two epistles.

attempted to reconstruct the social location of the epistle's readership by paying attention to the numerous social indicators lodged within the text. He argued that the readers were immersed in a pervasively pagan social environment—perhaps in Asia Minor, Syria, or even Rome—in contradistinction to the conspicuously Jewish audience being mirrored in Jude. The effect of this study, which focused on textual markers rather than external theological presuppositions, was to call into question the prevailing assumptions of "early Catholicism," namely, that 2 Peter mirrors the church's battle against Gnosticism in the second century.

Following the publication of Fornberg's study, J. H. Neyrey ("The Form and Background of the Polemic in 2 Peter," *JBL* 99 [1980]: 407–31) also dared to question the operating assumptions of the "early Catholic" hypothesis. Responding to the criticisms of Käsemann, 194–95, that parts of 2 Peter were disconnected and "embarrassing," Neyrey, 407, contended that these criticisms were misplaced because Käsemann's analysis "did not attempt to understand 2 Peter in its proper historical context." By presenting fresh comparative materials dating roughly contemporary with emergent Christianity, Neyrey contributed toward the furnishing of a new starting point by which to reassess 2 Peter—a contribution richly on display in Neyrey's fine Anchor Bible commentary (see bibliography).[47]

In addition to Neyrey's work, three other essays deserve mention—two in particular because they move the discussion of ethics and eschatology in 2 Peter in a helpful direction by calling attention to similar apologetic parallels from pagan literature. Rainer Riesner ("Der zweite Petrusbrief und die Eschatologie," in *Zukunftserwartung in biblischer Sicht*, ed. G. Maier [Basel: Brunnen-Verlag, 1984], 124–43) compares the description in 2 Peter 3 of cosmic conflagration with the Stoic doctrine of the same (*ekpyrōsis*). Herein a fundamental difference in worldviews is apparent: there is a radical discontinuity between Judeo-Christian understanding of the cosmos and its Stoic counterpart, even when the former is depicted in Stoic categories.[48] Employing a similar interpretive trajectory, C. P. Thiede ("A Pagan Reader of 2 Peter: Cosmic Conflagration in 2 Peter 3 and the OCTAVIUS of Minucius Felix," *JSNT* 26 [1986]: 79–96) supplies further evidence from both pagan literature and the early church fathers to suggest that on display in 2 Peter is argumentation that mirrors contemporary pagan-Christian philosophical debates over cosmology and cosmic conflagration. E. Lövestam ("Eschatologie und Tradition im 2. Petrusbrief," in *The New Testament Age: Essays in Honor of B. Reicke*, ed. W. C. Weinrich [Macon, Ga.: Mercer Univ. Press, 1984], 2:287–300) also concerns himself with the eschatological question in 2 Peter. The focus of his study is the Jewish model of flood typology as an apologetic response; also considered are parallels from intertestamental literature, rabbinic literature, the Synoptics, and Jude.[49]

---

47. Neyrey furnishes parallels between 2 Peter and Plutarch (Sera), who purportedly mirrors an Epicurean polemic against divine providence with its denial of afterlife and, by extension, divine judgment. There is much in Neyrey's argument to commend. Indeed, 2 Peter contains many evidences of being an apologetic response designed to counter strains of Epicurean worldview that might have been adopted by some. The danger in their view is that they assume freedom from moral accountability; Christian theism cuts to the heart of Epicurean detachment from a moral universe.

48. Significantly, Riesner suggests a dating for 2 Peter that might fall within the apostle Peter's lifetime.

49. What is missing from Lövestam's treatment of eschatology and ethics is a discussion of the literary, social, and theological distinctives that set 2 Peter apart from Jude. In what specific ways does the polemic in 2 Peter distinguish itself from that of Jude?

The 1983 publication of Richard Bauckham's highly acclaimed commentary on Jude and 2 Peter brought welcome attention to these two neglected NT books. Moreover, it suggested the inadequacy of the "early Catholic" rubric being imposed on the text. After all, Bauckham, 8, cautioned us by citing Martin Hengel: "If we want to, we can find 'early Catholic traits' even in Jesus and Paul." Bauckham correctly noted the absence in Jude and 2 Peter of early Catholicism's primary distinguishing features—e.g., a fading of hope for the parousia, the increasing institutionalization of the early church, and a crystallizing of faith into set forms or formulas.[50]

The last fifteen years have witnessed marked interest in literary-rhetorical structures of the NT. Duane Watson's rhetorical criticism of 2 Peter and Jude (*Invention, Arrangement, and Style: Rhetorical Criticism of Jude and 2 Peter* [SBLDS 104; Atlanta: Scholars Press, 1988]) seeks to apply the canons of ancient rhetorical practice to these two documents. The strength of Watson's work is its premise that the writings of the NT did not occur in a cultural vacuum; rather, theological truth is clothed in literary arguments of the day.[51] More recent work in 2 Peter has assumed or made necessary refinements in Watson's rhetorical-critical study of the epistle.

My *Virtue amidst Vice* sought to extend and probe the line of thinking begun by Fornberg's *An Early Church in a Pluralistic Society*, namely, that in 2 Peter literary strategy mirrors a pervasively pagan, Gentile context. Therein I have attempted a critical reassessment of the reigning assumptions of "early Catholicism," while at the same time identifying a literary strategy at work in the epistle that sets it apart from Jude. It is the book's thesis that 2 Peter offers a window into the moral world and philosophical discourse of Greco-Roman paganism—a world in which moral relativism and moral skepticism, consummating in a denial of moral accountability, are on display.

In my book, I argue that a key element in 2 Peter's hortatory strategy consists in the application of Christian paraenesis by borrowing contemporary Hellenistic moral ideals and categories. At the heart of this strategy of moral persuasion is the writer's adaptation of a catalog of virtues (1:5–7), which is intended to counter ethical lapse in the community. The fact that the believer has been a recipient of divinely imputed righteousness (1:1) and a full knowledge of God (1:2)—indeed, of "everything we need for life and godliness" (1:3)—constitutes no guarantee of a moral life. The challenge set before the community is to validate its profession with virtuous living—this amidst a cultural climate that can only encourage vice. Thus I contend in the book that the burden of the writer of 2 Peter is less doctrine (presupposed by the "early Catholic" hypothesis) than *ethics* and *virtuous living*.[52]

---

50. And as we have contended, to Bauckham's argument can also be added a cardinal assumption made by "early Catholic" exegesis: presumption that the Spirit's charismatic work resides in an office. Both 2 Peter and Jude mirror quite the opposite: in 2 Peter the Spirit inspires prophetic utterance (1:21); in Jude the Spirit inspires persons (v.19) and prayer (v.20), distinguishing authentic from inauthentic believers (v.19).

51. The weakness of Watson's volume is that it makes no attempt to tie literary-rhetorical, sociological, and theological perspectives together for the sake of the overall interpretive enterprise. Starr, 53–58, provides a helpful, even-handed, nuanced, and highly qualified evaluation of Watson's rhetorical analysis.

52. I also advance this argument in two essays—"The Language and Logic of Virtue in 2 Peter 1:5–7," *BBR* 8 (1998): 55–73; "On Angels and Asses: The Moral Paradigm in 2 Peter 2," *PEGLMBS* 21 (2001): 1–12. See also my comments on 2 Peter in Waltner and Charles, *1–2 Peter, Jude*.

One further monograph deserving mention is likely to receive limited attention in the United States because it originated in Sweden. James Starr's *Sharers in Divine Nature: 2 Peter 1:4 in Its Hellenistic Context* (see bibliography) provides the reader (in English!) a rich treasure of background information by which to appreciate the linguistic and philosophical concepts that surface in 2 Peter. The book's title is a bit misleading, insofar as its contents extend well beyond the limits of one verse. It may well be the best resource for placing 2 Peter in its Hellenistic milieu. Furthermore, it is sensitive to theological as well as historical and cultural threads that must converge in responsible NT interpretation, unlike much commentary on 2 Peter. In the end, Starr's book interacts sufficiently with mainstream biblical scholarship and yet is blessedly free of methodological constraints that impinge on the text of 2 Peter. Starr, 50, correctly notes that this letter is concerned to "shape the events of the present in view of the inevitable future judgment of the individual's character," while calling to the reader's attention the "ever-present danger in the narrative structure of 2 Peter . . . the possibility of moral collapse."[53]

6. PURPOSE AND PROMINENT THEMES

The traditional "early Catholic" reading of 2 Peter proceeds on the assumption that the church is having to counter the forces of Gnosticism as they emerge in the second century; thus, Kelly, 231: "We are . . . justified in overhearing in these letters the opening shots in the fated struggle between the Church and Gnosticism which was to feature large in the second century."[54] Consequently, historical-critical scholarship has assumed that doctrine—and specifically false doctrine—is the chief burden of the writer.

Probing a literary-rhetorical strategy at work in 2 Peter that distinguishes the epistle from Jude requires a sharpening of our focus. What is the intent behind the writer's choice of literary "brick and mortar"? Why the use of language, image, and concepts that would appeal to a more Gentile audience? Why the sustained use of paraenetic language and ethical categories, particularly in the early part of the letter? And precisely what is it that should be so urgently recalled by the readers (1:12–15)?

The writer's burden is that his readers cultivate an ethos that offers proof of a virtuous lifestyle—proof both to the one who has provided abundant resources for life and godliness (1:3–4) and to the moral skeptic (3:3–7). *What kind of people ought you to be in terms of holy conduct and piety?* (3:11) is the ringing question the leaders are left to ponder.

Following the epistolary greeting, the accent of which is received righteousness and grace, a catalog of virtues (1:5–7) is introduced by means of philosophic and conspicuously pagan religious formulations (1:3–4). This catalog, which outlines the contours of Christian "life and godliness" and contains standard features of Stoic ethical lists, is designed to compel the readers toward moral progress.[55] To possess these virtues is to prevent an ineffective and unfruitful life (1:8–9); to lack them, conversely, is analogous to blindness resulting from a neglect of truth. At issue is moral self-responsibility.

---

53. While monographs on 2 Peter remain few and far between, the last decade has witnessed a number of commentaries on the epistle (see bibliography), including Neyrey (1993), Perkins (1995), Lucas and Green (1995), Knight (1995), Craddock (1995), Moo (1996), Watson (1998), Charles (1999), Kraftchick (2002), and Schreiner (2003).

54. More recently, Chester and Martin, 146, have identified the error as "Gnosticizing" in character, though with some qualification.

55. For a fuller discussion of the contrast between Christian and Stoic ethics, see my *Virtue amidst Vice*, 99–111.

This emphasis is abundantly clear in the language of paraenesis throughout 2 Peter 1—"for this very reason" (v.5); "if you possess these qualities" (v.8); "if anyone does not have them" (v.9); "if you do these things" (v.10); "so I will always remind you of these things (v.12); "I think it is right to refresh your memory" (v.13); "remember these things" (v.15). The rhetorical effect of this language, though easily lost on the modern reader, would have been unmistakable to its intended audience. Theirs is not a faith void of the moral life; rather, the distinctly Christian ethic is to shine forth in bold contrast to surrounding culture. Tragically, in the view of the author, some have disregarded the divine "promises" (1:4; implied in 1:9, 12, 15) and as a result of their intercourse with surrounding culture have "forgotten that [they have] been cleansed from [their] past sins" (1:9). Worse yet, some are even aggressively propagating that there is *no moral authority* before which they must give account (2:1; 3:3–5).

Moral typology and a detailed sketch of the opponents are prominently featured in 2 Peter 2. The allusion to "false prophets" and "false teachers" in connection with "heresies" in 2:1–3 is a sure indication for most exegetes that 2 Peter was written for the purpose of combating heresy, i.e., false (Gnostic) doctrine. While I discuss this choice of terms in detail elsewhere,[56] the writer's extensive ethical vocabulary exhibited throughout 2 Peter 1 and 2 indicates the nature of the pastoral problem being addressed. This vocabulary strongly suggests that the problem is not first and foremost *doctrinal*:[57] "reveling in their pleasures," "shameful ways," "slaves of depravity," "corrupt desire of the sinful nature," "despise authority," "bold and arrogant," "brute beasts," "lustful desires," "eyes full of adultery," "experts in greed," "springs without water," "returning to its vomit," and "wallowing in the mud." Alas, on closer inspection 2 Peter appears to be a textbook for Christian ethics.[58]

Three prominent motifs can be detected throughout 2 Peter 1. The first of these relates to a godly lifestyle and virtuous character (1:3–11). The author, by way of introduction, places notable emphasis on the fact that divine resources are available to the Christian for living a godly life. Divine power and promises have been provided so that the readers might escape moral corruption in the world around them. This demarcation, the writer takes great pains to point out, depends not merely on the promises themselves (great as they are) but on the ethical response of the Christian. To this end, the author employs a Hellenistic rhetorical device, a catalog of virtues, to exhort his readers to a higher ethical plane. Verses 3–7 have been said to constitute a page out of "current pagan textbook morality," as Kelly, 306, puts it. The net effect of the catalog, which suggests moral progress, should not be lost on the reader: human cooperation with God, while it does not *cause* righteousness, nevertheless "confirms" or validates the believer's "calling and election" (1:10). "Godliness," one of the important catchwords in 2 Peter (1:3, 6–7; 2:9), expresses generic "reverence" and occurs in both religious and nonreligious contexts. The NT seems to carry both Christian and

---

56. See ibid., 37–43.

57. The priority of ethics over doctrine in 2 Peter does not minimize the relationship between belief and practice, which is one of organic unity. It is rather a question of emphasis.

58. On display in 2 Peter is an ethical concern and not metaphysical/doctrinal dualism. The implications of a wrong exegetical trajectory, whereby doctrine and not ethics is the focal point, are significant and extremely unfortunate. The lack of attention among biblical scholars, theologians, and laypeople to ethics in 2 Peter is to be lamented precisely because of the contribution 2 Peter can make to the subject of NT ethics. The tragic nature of this omission can be seen at the textbook level, where there is a curious absence of 2 Peter in virtually all discussions of NT ethics.

broader Hellenistic connotations: the term serves to accent a particular way of life and behavior that is worthy of praise. The soul of religion, after all, is its practice. In 2 Peter, piety stands in direct and conspicuous opposition to moral "corruption" (*phthora*, GK 5785; 1:4; 2:12 [twice; NIV, "destroyed," "perish"]; 2:19 [NIV, "depravity"]) and "evil [corrupt, lustful] desires" (1:4; 2:10, 18; 3:3).

A second motif expressing itself through pastoral concern is seen in the surplus of "reminder" terminology (1:12–15) as well as in the use of the catchword "knowledge" with related verbal forms (*epignōsis*, *gnōsis*, GK 2106, 1194 [1:2–3, 5–6, 8, 16, 20]).[59] The writer intends "to always remind [them] of these things," even though the readers already "know them and are firmly established in the truth [they] now have." He deems it necessary to "refresh [the] memory" of his audience and seeks to "make every effort" in admonishing them "to remember these things." Knowledge—and specifically, the knowledge of God (1:2–3; 3:18)—is important to the writer. Not insignificantly, knowledge and grace both open and conclude the epistle, forming something of an inclusio for rhetorical effect.[60]

The third emphasis in ch. 1 is the accent on the writer's own moral authority. If it is assumed from the outset that the letter is from someone other than the apostle, 2 Peter is then read with a view of ferreting out evidence that would support the notion of pseudepigraphy. The result is, among other things, that the self-referential allusions such as one finds in 1:1 ("Simon Peter, . . . apostle") and 1:16–18 (eyewitness testimony of the transfiguration event) are to be viewed as literary hubris at best and forgery at worst. In the end, one is left with the majority of NT scholars to hypothesize about postapostolic scenarios and make inferences about a theologically inferior NT document.

If, on the other hand, the writer is defending himself and the integrity of the Christian gospel (as Paul was forced to do on occasion),[61] his own authority rests on nothing less than his historical relationship to Jesus. That (1) the writer seems not to be dependent on the Synoptic accounts of the transfiguration and (2) the pseudepigraphal *Apocalypse of Peter* makes use of 2 Peter together have been interpreted as casting doubt on 2 Peter's authenticity. Despite the overwhelming consensus of biblical scholarship in rejecting Petrine authorship, satisfactory explanations of the "eyewitness" language in these verses have yet to be offered. Green, 93, calls attention to "the apostolic 'we'" in "we were eyewitnesses"—indeed, a necessary accent *if* Christian truth is being undermined (cf. 1Co 15:3–8, 12–34; 1Jn 4:1–3). It is supremely difficult to envision moral authority resting in the literary product of one who, even though well intentioned, must resort to specious statements such as "we were there with him on the holy mountain." Such requires too much from the reader.

Whereas the use of moral typology in Jude is designed to underscore categorical judgment alone, in 2 Peter 2 it has a dual function—namely, to underscore both judgment *and* salvation. In Jude, God is Judge; in 2 Peter, however, he is both Judge and Savior.[62] Both epistles, to be sure, express the reality of coming judgment in terms and imagery that strike the reader as fierce and unrelenting. In 2 Peter 2 the judgment

---

59. "Knowledge" and "knowing" receive particular emphasis in 2 Peter 1 not because of a purported second-century Gnostic threat (contra Moffatt, 361–63, and others) but because of the grace the Christian believer has *already received* (1:1–4).

60. A second set of subthemes—life and godliness (1:3; 3:11)—enhances the rhetorical effect of this inclusio.

61. First Corinthians 4 is one such striking example.

62. Apocalyptic eschatology is utilized in both Jude and 2 Peter, though in the latter it functions as part of a moral apologetic directed at the radical moral skeptic whose worldview is pagan.

theme initially appears as a condemnation of the opponents. It is then substantiated in the author's reciting of historical types. But whereas in Jude moral typology functions to announce only judgment, in 2 Peter it also reminds the readers of the reality of divine mercy. Hence, Noah and Lot—not mentioned in Jude— are depicted as righteous amidst their contemporaries (2:5–9a). In addition, Balaam typology, abbreviated in Jude, is expanded in 2 Peter to illustrate the moral accountability that accompanies abandoning the knowledge of God (2:15–16). To abandon knowledge of the truth, i.e., apostasy, is not foremost a doctrinal issue; rather, it is ethical.[63] The knowledge motif is reiterated in 2 Peter 2 by means of two proverbial images—a dog returning to its vomit and a pig returning to the mud. To have had knowledge of the truth and then to deny that truth is depicted in rather severe terms (2:20–22).

In 2 Peter 3 the motifs of virtue, judgment, and the knowledge of God surface in the writer's apocalyptic exhortation to the moral skeptic (3:3–7) and in the concluding admonitions toward perseverance and virtuous living (3:8–18). Insofar as the ethical life has been the burden of the writer, thus shaping his literary-rhetorical strategy on display in 1:3–2:22, it remains for him to expose and critique those individuals who by reason of moral license and moral skepticism actually call into question the very existence of a created moral order.

Given the dominance of the "early Catholic" thesis and the presumption that Gnosticism is being combated, traditional commentary broadly assumes a doctrinal-eschatological argument in 2 Peter 3 that purports to counter a "parousia delay." Closer attention to literary strategy, however, suggests that the material belongs to a foremost ethical argument and qualifies as a type of "moral apologetic."

Logically, apostasy breeds the necessity of returning to cosmological "first things." Carried to its end, apostasy manifests itself in wholesale denial of all authority—local as well as universal. It is the latter, the more fundamental denial, that would appear to lie behind the caricature of the moral skeptic in 3:3–7. This process entails an eventual—and calculated—denial of divine intervention in history (3:5–6).

The effects of the moral skeptic on the believing community are by no means benign. Given the chance, they undermine one's faith and expectation in the Lord, one's ability to live righteously, and one's capacity properly to discern divine judgment (3:8–10). Cosmic catastrophe in the past serves as a foreshadow of moral reckoning to come. Moreover, it indicates that there are divine limits as to what the Creator and Judge of the whole earth, morally speaking, will permit. Bauckham, 302, expresses it in this way: "The final phrase [the exhortation contained in 3:7] reveals that although in this passage the author is certainly concerned with catastrophic upheavals in the physical world, which amount to the destruction and creation of worlds, he is not concerned with these for the sake of mere cosmology, but with their interpretation in a worldview which sees them as occurring by the sovereign decree of God as instruments of his judgment on humanity."

The apocalyptic flavor of the material in 2 Peter 3 serves to rebut the assumption of the moral skeptic that there is no judgment, no moral accountability, in the temporal order. It is designed to counter the individual advancing a pagan view of life, according to which one should seek pleasure (2:18b) and "freedom" (2:19) in the present life, with no permanent consequences for one's actions. Having been reminded that God indeed does judge the unrighteous, the readers are admonished to live a life that is worthy of their calling as they await the final day of moral reckoning.

---

63. Here I am making a distinction between "apostasy," i.e., the departure from what one knows to be true, and "heresy," which is false or errant teaching based on doctrinal distortions.

7. BIBLIOGRAPHY

See also the bibliography listed in 1 Peter (pp. 294–95).

The following is a selective list of commentaries and monographs on 2 Peter available in English, confined for the most part to those referred to in the commentary (they will be referred to simply by the author's name [and initials only when necessary to distinguish two authors of the same surname]). References to other resources will carry full bibliographic details at the first mention and thereafter a short title.

Bauckham, R. J. *Jude, 2 Peter.* Word Biblical Commentary 50. Waco, Tex.: Word, 1983.

Bigg, C. *A Critical and Exegetical Commentary on the Epistles of St. Peter and St. Jude.* International Critical Commentary. Edinburgh: T&T Clark, 1901.

Calvin, J. *Commentaries on the Catholic Epistles.* Translated by J. Owen. Grand Rapids: Eerdmans, 1959.

Charles, J. D. *Virtue amidst Vice: The Catalog of Virtues in 2 Peter 1.* Journal for the Study of the New Testament: Supplement Series 150. Sheffield: Sheffield Academic Press, 1997.

Chester, A., and R. P. Martin. *The Theology of the Letters of James, Peter, and Jude.* New Testament Theology. Cambridge: Cambridge Univ. Press, 1994.

Craddock, F. B. *First and Second Peter and Jude.* Westminster Bible Companion. Louisville, Ky.: Westminster John Knox, 1995.

Cranfield, C. E. B. *1 and 2 Peter and Jude.* Torch Bible Commentaries. London: SCM, 1960.

Ellis, E. E. "Pseudonymity and Canonicity of New Testament Documents." Pages 212–24 in *Worship, Theology and Ministry in the Early Church.* Edited by M. J. Wilkins and T. Paige. Journal for the Study of the New Testament: Supplement Series 87. Sheffield: JSOT, 1992.

Fornberg, T. *An Early Church in a Pluralistic Society: A Study of 2 Peter.* Coniectanea Biblica: New Testament Series 9. Lund: C. W. K. Gleerup, 1977.

Green, M. (E. M. B.). *2 Peter and Jude.* Tyndale New Testament Commentaries 18. 2d ed. Grand Rapids: Eerdmans, 1987.

———. *2 Peter Reconsidered.* London: Tyndale, 1961.

Guthrie, D. *New Testament Introduction.* 4th ed. Downers Grove, Ill.: InterVarsity, 1990.

Hillyer, N. *1 and 2 Peter, Jude.* New International Biblical Commentary on the New Testament. Peabody, Mass.: Hendrickson, 1992.

Käsemann, E. "An Apologia for Primitive Christian Eschatology." Pages 135–57 in *Essays on New Testament Themes.* London: SCM, 1964.

Kelly, J. N. D. *A Commentary on the Epistles of Peter and Jude.* Black's New Testament Commentaries. London: Adam & Charles Black, 1969.

Knight, J. *2 Peter and Jude.* New Testament Guides. Sheffield: Sheffield Academic Press, 1995.

Kraftchick, S. J. *Jude, 2 Peter.* Abingdon New Testament Commentaries. Nashville: Abingdon, 2002.

Kurz, W. S. *Farewell Addresses in the New Testament.* Collegeville, Minn.: Liturgical, 1990.

Lucas, D., and C. Green. *The Message of 2 Peter & Jude.* The Bible Speaks Today. Downers Grove, Ill.: InterVarsity, 1995.

Mayor, J. B. *The Epistle of St. Jude and the Second Epistle of St. Peter.* New York: Macmillan, 1907.

Moffatt, J. *The General Epistles: James, Peter and Judas.* Moffatt New Testament Commentary. London: Hodder and Stoughton, 1928.

Moo, D. J. *2 Peter, Jude.* NIV Application Commentary. Grand Rapids: Zondervan, 1996.

Neyrey, J. H. *2 Peter, Jude: A New Translation with Introduction and Commentary.* Anchor Bible 37C. Garden City, N.Y.: Doubleday, 1993.

Perkins, P. *First and Second Peter, James, and Jude.* Interpretation. Louisville, Ky.: Westminster John Knox, 1995.

Reicke, B. *The Epistles of James, Peter, and Jude.* Anchor Bible 37. New York: Doubleday, 1964.

Schreiner, T. R. *1, 2 Peter, Jude.* New American Commentary 37. Nashville: Broadman and Holman. 2003.

Sidebottom, E. M. *James, Jude and 2 Peter.* New Century Bible. London: Thomas Nelson, 1967.

Starr, J. M. *Sharers in Divine Nature: 2 Peter 1:4 in Its Hellenistic Context.* Coniectanea Biblica: New Testament Series 33. Stockholm: Almquist & Wiksell, 2000.

Waltner, E. and J. D. Charles. *1–2 Peter, Jude.* Believers Church Bible Commentary. Scottdale, Pa. Herald, 1999.

Watson, D. F. "The Second Letter of Peter." Pages 323–61 in *The New Interpreter's Bible* 12. Nashville: Abingdon, 1998.

8. OUTLINE

I. The Writer and His Audience (1:1–2)

II. Purpose for Writing and Authority (1:3–21)

    A. Resources Available for the Ethical Life (1:3–4)

    B. Catalog of Virtues (1:5–7)

    C. Admonition to Confirm an Ethical Calling (1:8–11)

    D. Prophetic Reminder to Recall (1:12–15)

    E. Prophetic Testimony Regarding Moral Authority (1:16–18)

    F. Nature of Prophetic Authority (1:19–21)

III. Profile of Apostasy (2:1–22)

    A. Prophetic Denunciation of the Apostate (2:1–3)

    B. Moral Paradigms (2:4–10a)

    C. Portrait of the Apostate (2:10b–18)

    D. Profile of Apostasy (2:19–22)

IV. Exhortation to the Faithful (3:1–18)

    A. Exhortation to Recall (3:1–2)

    B. Caricature of the Moral Skeptic (3:3–7)

    C. Promise of Universal Moral Accountability (3:8–13)

    D. Final Exhortation and Doxology (3:14–18)

Text and Exposition

I. THE WRITER AND HIS AUDIENCE (1:1–2)

OVERVIEW

The epistle opens with what is a typical form for NT letters ("A to B . . . grace"), though without the formal thanksgiving prayer that characterizes many of the Pauline epistles. Both the epistolary and homiletical character strike the reader. The epistolary opening contains several key words or ideas that, thematically, are developed more fully in the writer's stated purpose for writing (1:3–11) as well as throughout the letter—e.g., equality or impartiality, righteousness, knowledge of God, and deliverance. As in 1 Peter, the author of 2 Peter identifies himself as the apostle. Moreover, the author also expresses the same wish for his readers, namely, that "grace and peace be multiplied to you" (NIV, "be yours in abundance"; *charis hymin eirēnē plēthyntheiē*). The two letters differ, however, in their opening address to the extent that 1 Peter names a geographically specific group of believers, whereas the addressees in 2 Peter are undesignated—"To those who . . . have received a faith as precious as ours."

Although the origin and destination elude certainty, it is plausible that this letter was written in Rome shortly before the apostle's martyrdom. This lack of concrete evidence, however, stands in sharp contrast with the character of the epistle, which contains clear indications of a concrete local situation in which pastoral needs are present. The letter is clearly addressed to a particular congregation or community where serious problems are already established. In this sense, then, the designation "general epistle" for 2 Peter, which by definition is broader or "catholic" in scope, is misleading.

> ¹Simon Peter, a servant and apostle of Jesus Christ,
>
> To those who through the righteousness of our God and Savior Jesus Christ have received a faith as precious as ours:
>
> ²Grace and peace be yours in abundance through the knowledge of God and of Jesus our Lord.

COMMENTARY

1 The use of *Symeōn* (Simon), appearing with the nickname "Peter," is reminiscent of the gospel narratives (e.g., Mt 16:16; Lk 22:31) and Acts 15:14, both of which suggest a Palestinian setting. Here, however, it strikes the reader as unexpected. Commentators who hold 2 Peter to be inauthentic are inclined to regard the allusion to *Symeōn* as a "deliberate archaizing touch by a pseudonymous writer" (so Bauckham, 166–67) who is seeking the mark of authenticity. Admittedly, one would expect an opening similar to that of 1 Peter 1:1: "Peter, an apostle of Jesus Christ." Rejecting Petrine authorship, Bauckham, 167, suggests that *Symeōn* may reflect a writer who was part of a "Petrine circle" in Rome that included Mark and Silvanus (Silas; cf. 1Pe 5:12–13) as well as other Jewish-Christian leaders.

A more plausible explanation, assuming the writer to be the apostle and not an imposter or a "Petrine agent," lies with a first-century pastoral situation that requires denunciation, rebuke, and correspondingly strong exhortations, not unlike the scenario one encounters in Jude. The writer is thus in a position of having to "present his credentials" (so Green, 67). *Symeōn* was involved in the formal process of the Jerusalem Council (Ac 15), a situation that required the church's authoritative voice. Here he is at another point in his life when apostolic authority must be brought to bear on the Christian community—in this case both apostolically and prophetically (1:16–21) and not merely as a pastorally minded elder (cf. 1Pe 5:1). The double name would remind his readers of both past and present; a transformation has occurred in the life of this "elder statesman" of the Christian community.

The present letter, it must be emphasized, gives *precise* credentials. The writer is said to be a "servant and apostle of Jesus Christ." This twofold self-description very much resembles the introduction of Jude, in which passionate denunciation of the ungodly and affirmation of the faithful stand side by side. The strong nature of the prophetic word in 2 Peter, as the rest of the epistle indicates, mirrors a local situation calling for a vigorous application of spiritual authority rooted in the apostolic office. Yet, significantly, in both 2 Peter and Jude deep humility clothes the one who speaks with prophetic force. As a "servant" or "bond slave" (*doulos*, GK *1528*) of Jesus Christ, the writer shows evidence of being a seasoned man of God tempered by divine dealings, much as one finds in 1 Peter: "All of you, clothe yourselves with humility toward one another, because, 'God opposes the proud but gives grace to the humble'" (1Pe 5:5). It is

also possible that the twofold designation "servant and apostle" might be a faint recollection of Jesus' words to Peter during the Last Supper (so Hillyer, 158), given the latter's rather impetuous reactions to Jesus' servanthood (Jn 13:6–19, esp. v.16).

The readers are described as those "of equal [*isotimos*] standing who have received faith [NIV, "a faith as precious as ours"]." Some commentators (e.g., Mayor, 81) see in this formula a Jewish-Gentile factor—i.e., a faith that is equally accessible to both groups. However, a closer reading of 2 Peter 1 suggests that the issue of equality is not one of ethnic inclusion; nor is this opening concept designed "to communicate the apostle's teaching to a postapostolic generation" (contra Bauckham, 167). Instead, stress is laid on the fact that God's grace is open and accessible to all, which is to say to apostles and nonapostles. This reading is confirmed by what follows: "His divine power has given us everything we need....Through these he has given us his very great and precious promises" (1:3–4). This common provision, available to all, has been made on the basis of the righteousness of God (1:1); accordingly, no impartiality exists in the salvation issuing from the Savior, Jesus Christ. Divine righteousness secures the believers' equal standing.

The phrase "the righteousness of our God and Savior Jesus Christ" might be understood in one of two ways. Taken together with the doxology to Jesus Christ in 3:18, the two statements serve as an inclusio, i.e., a set of bookends for the epistle, in depicting the exalted status of Christ. Viewed another way, the expression may simply be intended to identify Jesus as the full manifestation of God's saving righteousness; coupled with 1:2, God and Jesus "our Lord" are together the content and the focus of the believer's *knowledge*.

2 The salutation "grace and peace be yours in abundance," similar to the greeting in 1 Peter 1:2, is not "in fact copied from 1 Peter" (contra Kelly, 298). Rather, it is one of the numerous points of contact between the two epistles. In 2 Peter, the key ingredient in receiving God's grace is the *full knowledge of God and Christ*. There is room for speculating with Green, 70, that "knowledge," a catchword in the letter, has something of a rhetorically polemical edge (see also my *Virtue amidst Vice*, 132–34). The author is likely reclaiming the word to oppose those who misuse it. As employed by the author, "full knowledge" (*epignōsis*, GK *2106*) reflects an understanding of the grace of God at work in the believer's life. Armed with this knowledge, the Christian community is kept from moral lapse and, ultimately, apostasy. With all believers having equal access to this grace through knowledge of Christ, all are on equal footing and therefore without excuse.

NOTES

1–2 W. G. Doty (*Letters in Primitive Christianity* [Philadelphia: Fortress, 1973], 4–8) notes the variety of epistles that circulated in the first century—business, official, public, fictitious/pseudonymous, and discursive. On ancient letter writing in general, see J. L. White, *The Body of the Greek Letter* (SBLDS 2; Missoula, Mont.: Scholars Press, 1972); J. L. White, *Light from Ancient Letters* (Philadelphia: Fortress, 1986).

II. PURPOSE FOR WRITING AND AUTHORITY (1:3–21)

A. Resources Available for the Ethical Life (1:3–4)

OVERVIEW

The writer's intent is to call the Christian community to a higher ethical plane. Rhetorically, the strategy consists initially of a review of the provisions available for Christian living (1:3–4), followed by exhortation to ethical rejuvenation through the use of a catalog of virtues (1:5–7). It concludes with the reassurance that these promises are sufficient for the ethical life (1:8–11). The Petrine formula for this provision is rooted in the "knowledge" of God (1:2). This full knowledge of him who has called us through his own moral excellence is the total sufficiency for a godly life (1:3). The result is, stated negatively, that the readers might escape "the corruption in the world caused by evil desires," and stated positively, that they might "participate in the divine nature" (1:4).

³His divine power has given us everything we need for life and godliness through our knowledge of him who called us by his own glory and goodness. ⁴Through these he has given us his very great and precious promises, so that through them you may participate in the divine nature and escape the corruption in the world caused by evil desires.

COMMENTARY

4 It is not uncommon in ancient literature for writers to use the language of union with God and divine immortality. Although commentators differ as to the precise function of *theias koinōnoi physeōs*, the language of divine union occurs in Hellenistic mystical philosophy and is particularly pronounced in pagan mystery religions, whose initiates understood themselves as being absorbed gradually into deity. Given its currency in the religious-philosophical thought of the day (e.g., Philo, *Somn.* 1.28; *Abraham* 107: *logikēs koinōnoi physeōs*), the author's language is calculated and suggestive of his readers' social location.

In what sense, then, does the Christian believer "participate in the divine nature"? The reference is not intended to be primarily eschatological (contra Bauckham, 182), since it is contextually qualified by the believer's behavior in the *present world*. Rather, in 2 Peter the concept is markedly temporal and christocentric: our union with Christ, based on grace, enables us to resist worldly corruption and live lives that are reverent and morally excellent. The "divine nature," then, in which believers are to participate, corresponds to qualities associated with Christ's nature (thus Starr, 45; Green, 74; Moo, 44).

NOTES

3–4 Use of similar metaphysical language ranges from 4 Maccabees 18:3 to Josephus (*Ant.* 8.107; *Ag. Ap.* 1.232) and Philo (*Decal.* 104; *Abraham* 144) to Plutarch (*Def. orac.* 10). The most comprehensive study of this notion as found in both Hellenistic and Jewish sources is J. M. Starr's *Sharers in Divine Nature* (see bibliography). Starr, 47, captures the proper sense of 2 Peter 1:4: "At length . . . 2 Peter makes plain that the flight from the world's corruption is *not* accomplished *in death nor in the parousia*, but in the Christ-believer's *past*" (emphasis mine). Eschatology in 2 Peter 3 is designed to bear on the present: "What kind of people ought you to be? You ought to live holy and godly lives" (3:11).

REFLECTIONS

The author's appeal in ch. 1 is above all a call, a decree, to holy living. The admonition is based on both the divine provision ("His divine power has given us everything we need . . .") and human cooperation ("so that through them you may . . . escape the corruption"). In the epistle there is no overemphasis on a predestination that circumvents human moral agency. Neither is there a doctrine of human perfectibility divorced from grace. Both the gracious promises of God as benefactor *and* human moral responsibility are part of the ethical equation. On the one hand, the divine provision covers every conceivable contingency for the purpose of moral growth; on the other hand, development of moral character is contingent on one's willingness to grow. In 2 Peter, the emphasis is clearly placed on the side of our responsibility, as summarized by Starr, 50: "Second Peter is concerned to shape the events of the present in view of the inevitable future judgment of the individual's moral character, as . . . noted in 1:1–11. . . . The ever-present danger in the narrative structure of 2 Peter is the possibility of moral collapse, which will lead to the believer's fall and the loss of his call (1:9–10; 2:14, 18–20; 3:17)."

B. Catalog of Virtues (1:5–7)

OVERVIEW

Having established the accessibility of divine resources, the writer wishes to accent moral self-responsibility. For this reason, the readers are to apply themselves fully, "making every effort" (*spoudazō*, GK *5079*) to respond to the ethical task at hand (1:5a). That this verb appears three times in 2 Peter 1 (vv.5, 10, 15) is highly instructive. It reflects the seriousness of the community's situation as well as the pastoral strategy in addressing the readers. Theirs is the challenge of exhibiting moral character amidst pagan amoral culture. This requires willingness and determination, both of which at the present may be lacking.

A catalog or listing of particular virtues shows the contours of the moral effort the readers are to make.

The significance of the ethical catalog lies in its rhetorical effect and mirrors a discussion of virtues commonplace among Hellenistic—and specifically Stoic—moral philosophers (so G. Kidd, "Moral Actions and Rules in Stoic Ethics," in *The Stoics*, ed J. M. Rist [Berkeley: Univ. of California Press, 1978], 247–58); my *Virtue amidst Vice*, 99–148). The ethical catalog reproduced in 1:5–7 shows notable affinities to contemporary secular usage—similar to the Stoic *prokopē*, or scheme of moral development—with the notable exception of *agapē* ("love") and a qualified use of *pistis* ("faith"), the bookends of the Petrine catalog.

If 2 Peter is addressed to the Christian community in a Gentile social setting, the concepts of virtue, faith, and love would be an appropriate means of countering immorality or amorality in a skeptical environment. In fact, borrowing from the Stoic view that virtue is a corollary of knowledge (a corollary that some in the community are flatly negating), the writer is able to "sanctify" the foundations of pagan ethical thought and appropriate them for his own purposes. Viewed in this way, an ethical list or catalog would be a fitting way of countering a deterioration of the moral life in the community, given its relevance in popular usage.

The Christian ethical distinctive is that one's faith is a response to divine grace and the reception of that grace. Hence, one's motivation is in the direction of demonstrating through one's works a lifestyle of gratitude that pleases God. That 2 Peter 1 is not promoting a "works righteousness" is made clear by the epistle's very introduction: the letter is addressed to "those who through the righteousness of our God and Savior Jesus Christ have received a faith ..." (1:1). Righteousness has been *received*; it is a gift imparted by God through Christ. The important Petrine theme of *righteousness* (1Pe 2:24; 3:12, 14, 18; 4:18; 2Pe 1:1; 2:5, 7–8 [twice], 21; 3:13) is foundational to a proper understanding of Christian ethics. The secular ethic, by contrast, wholly misses this fundamental understanding of righteous faith. On this foundation believers are to supply a repository of confirming virtues, thereby manifesting a virtuous life.

Hence the picture presented in 2 Peter is pregnant with meaning and implication: God, in his infinite glory and kindness, has covered, through his Son, the cost of provisions necessary for a life of holiness. On the basis of this exceeding generosity, the readers are to build, ethically speaking. In corresponding fashion, the readers are to be lavish in the way they invest themselves in the development of moral character, striving to offer the world the best window for viewing God's grace. As Hillyer, 165, observes, this approach to the Christian life is far removed from the cynicism that views the Christian experience as "an initial spasm followed by chronic inertia."

⁵For this very reason, make every effort to add to your faith goodness; and to goodness, knowledge; ⁶and to knowledge, self-control; and to self-control, perseverance; and to perseverance, godliness; ⁷and to godliness, brotherly kindness; and to brotherly kindness, love.

COMMENTARY

5 The supply of virtue, couched in an ethical catalog, is presented to the reader of 2 Peter in language that is evocative and adds much color to our reading of the text, even though the richness of the picture is lost in its translation. The verb translated "add" is *epichorēgeō* (GK *2220*), a strengthened form of *chorēgeō* ("to add, supply, supplement," GK *5961*). Originally, *chorēgeō* possessed the sense of "to lead a chorus"; in time it came to denote "defraying the expenses of something" (BDAG, 1087; cf. Josephus, *J.W.* 1.625). Typically, Greek theater proceeded on the generosity of a wealthy local benefactor, the *chorēgos*, who saw to it that actors, musicians, and dancers were paid. The relative extravagance attached to these productions is conveyed by the verb *chorēgeō*. The readers are not merely to "add" or "supply"; they are to *contribute extravagantly* to their own moral development, and this based on extravagant resources already provided by God, the wealthy Benefactor.

In contrast to the *pistis* ("faith," GK *4411*) that normally conveys trust or loyalty in common (secular) parlance, in 2 Peter it is subjective trust placed in the gospel, a faith produced *en dikaiosynē tou theou hēmōn kai sōtēros Iēsou Christou* ("through the righteousness of our God and Savior Jesus Christ"). This faith, in the Petrine scheme of things, results in *virtue* (NIV, "goodness"; *aretē*, GK *746*), i.e., moral excellence. In its earlier, classical usage, *aretē* denotes excellence or renown. Over time it was applied to the sphere of ethics, to which it became more or less restricted. Commonly employed in Stoic ethical lists, virtue is *the* quality of life, and not surprisingly the centerpiece of classic pagan morality. It is moral goodness toward which all humanity strives. For the Christian, virtue is tangible evidence of the reality of saving faith.

Moral excellence, in turn, supplies *knowledge* (*gnōsis*, GK *1194*). Knowledge frequently begins or concludes pagan ethical lists. Its placement in the catalog following virtue reflects the Stoic belief, confirmed in Christian thought, that there is an organic and indivisible link between the two qualities (to the Stoic, all vice is rooted in ignorance). Where Christian and Stoic views differ is that the former strips knowledge of its technical nuance so that *it is not a goal in and of itself* (1Co 8:1–4); hence, it is proper to speak of a chastened knowledge. In contrast with speculative philosophy, by which *gnōsis* underpins the acquisition of all virtues, in the Petrine progression it is an extension and not the *sole basis* for one's faith and virtue. Hereby, with some qualification, the intellectual element of belief is affirmed. A knowledge that is perceptive and desirous to know wisdom and truth can never harm the true seeker. For the Christian, knowledge perceives the proper and indivisible relationship between faith and virtue.

6 By the logic of virtue, knowledge motivates and moves the individual toward *self-control* (*enkrateia*, GK *1602*). A quality highly prized (and thus "cardinal") among Greek moral philosophers, *enkrateia* knows an organic connection to *gnōsis* that is not incidental; both elements go together just as their opposites, ignorance (*agnoia*, GK *53*) and lust (NIV, "evil desires"; *epithymia*, GK *2123*), find an irrepressible linkage, both in pagan ethics and the NT (1Pe 1:14; cf. *TDNT* 1:339–42). As a pagan virtue, knowledge is equated with mastery over one's lusts and appetites. True knowledge, therefore, leads not to license but to self-mastery. Herein an expressly Christian faith distinguishes itself: A system of belief divorcing content from ethics and severing belief from practice demonstrates itself as wrong teaching, and hence inauthentic. True knowledge, by contrast, will tend toward self-restraint, not libertinism. This is especially important for the fledgling Christian community dispersed throughout Hellenistic culture.

Self-control, in turn, supplies *perseverance* or endurance. Self-mastery and discipline have the effect of producing the ability to endure, literally to be patient under the weight of adversity. In its classical usage, *hypomonē* (GK *5705*) denotes brave resistance, in this way bringing honor (Plato, *Theaet.* 117b; cf. *TDNT* 4:581–88). Thus endurance, rightly understood, is active rather than passive. It is the mark of maturity (Jas 1:3–4), since superficial faith will not endure. Moreover, it has two sides: it expresses itself toward the world and toward God. Far from being the exercise of mere willpower, by which the Stoic deadened his sensibilities, endurance for the Christian issues out of a deep awareness of and confidence in God's sovereignty (so Paul, "Love always perseveres" [1Co 13:7]; also, Calvin, 363). In this way a Christian understanding of endurance distinguishes itself from its pagan counterpart insofar as it is not fatalistic or cynical. Because of this deep-rooted awareness, it can hold out, persisting in adverse circumstances (cf. 2Pe 3:9, 15).

The connection between self-control, endurance, and *godliness* or piety (*eusebeia*, GK *2354*)—the next link in the Petrine catena—is transparent and logical in the Christian ethical progression. Given the common occurrence of *eusebeia* in pagan ethical lists, it is best to interpret the term in its broadest sense. Godliness entails both vertical and horizontal duties. It is simultaneously reverence toward deity and a sense of duty toward people. In late Hellenism it expresses reverence in this general sense and occurs in both religious and nonreligious contexts—e.g., in the sense of reverence toward the gods, toward family, and toward tradition and the social order (cf. *TDNT* 7:175–85; also Starr, 42). Not insignificantly, all the occurrences of *eusebeia* in the NT are confined to the Pastoral Epistles (ten times) and 2 Peter (1:3, 6–7; 3:11). *Eusebeia* comes to expression most completely in the Christian community.

7 In the Petrine progression, piety leads in the direction of *philadelphia* (GK *5789*), mutual or brotherly affection. That is, godliness expresses itself in our relationships with others—particularly with those of the Christian community. Behind the term *philadelphia* stands the Greek ideal of friendship, suggesting duties that attend our filial and familial relationships. For the household of faith, however, it acquires a special meaning, though it can be taken for granted. It constantly needs to be refined by the work of the Spirit (e.g., Ro 12:9–10; Eph 4:1–3; Php 4:2, 5; Col 3:12–15; 1Th 4:9; Heb 13:1; 1Pe 1:22; 1Jn 5:1).

The catalog achieves its climax in *agapē* (GK *27*), which distinguishes the Christian ethos and without which it would be incomplete. Thus it is fitting to speak of *agapē* ("love") as the "crown" of moral development (so Green, 80; Bauckham, 187), i.e., in Christian terms, the ultimate expression of Christian belief (1Co 13:3) and the fruit of genuine faith (Gal 5:6; Jas 2:14–26). Christian morality is distinctly the morality of charity, whereby one demonstrates gratitude through actions for the experience of divine grace. Inasmuch as *agapē* is the fount and the goal of Christian virtue, therein lies the difference between the Christian and pagan ethos.

While vice and virtue lists in the NT are not of the same compositional variety, one peculiar feature absent from pagan catalogs is the occasional movement toward crescendo or decrescendo. Second Peter 1:5–7 features an ethical progression that builds toward a climax in *agapē*. The virtues do not stand in random or unrelated juxtaposition.

Together they represent the fruit of the life of faith, whereby each facilitates the next, though all comprise an organic unity. Mayor, 93, aptly summarizes the progression and interconnectedness of the virtues: "Faith is the gift of God already received; to this must be added (1) moral strength which enables a man to do what he knows to be right; (2) spiritual discernment; (3) self-control by which a man resists temptation; (4) endurance by which he bears up under persecution or adversity; (5) right . . . behavior toward God [godliness]; (6) toward the brethren [brotherly kindness]; [and (7)] toward all [love]."

NOTES

5–7 On the secular usage of the ethical catalog, see my *Virtue amidst Vice*, 112–27 (for a discussion of its rhetorical function, see ch. 5 ["The Ethical Catalog as a Pedagogical Device"]). The use of the ethical catalog by NT writers is considerable and derives from its function in Hellenistic and Hellenistic-Jewish literature. In the NT, both strands—Hellenistic form and Jewish theological assumptions—merge in the Christian paraenetic or ethical tradition. See, in its NT usage, B. S. Easton, "New Testament Ethical Lists," *JBL* 51 (1932): 1–12; N. J. McEleney, "The Vice Lists of the Pastoral Epistles," *CBQ* 36 (1974): 203–19.

Because the ethical contours of Christian thought were molded against the backdrop of Greco-Roman moral-social conditions, points of contact between Stoic discourse and the NT are numerous and to be expected. While the two systems differ radically in the way they perceive the *means* to the ethical life, they share common ethical categories. It is in the broader context of Paul's "natural theology" in Romans 1, for example, that a stereotyping of pagan moral depravity and an ethical catalog are employed. The vice list in 1:29–31—the lengthiest in the NT—is intended both to encompass every stereotype of human corruption possible and to mirror conditions in the imperial seat. There are no theoretical components to Paul's discussion of ethics in Romans. It is flatly assumed that all people "know" (ἐπιγινώσκω, *epiginōskō* [GK *2105*], 1:28, 32) the truth; the result is that all are guilty.

The Stoic view of moral actions and moral progress stands in contrast to its Christian counterpart. Pagan ethics knows nothing of the conceptual realities of sin, guilt, and redemption. To the extent that wisdom, temperance, prudence, justice, and courage are lauded, they are understood as the extension of a naturalistic ethic and rational reflection. They presuppose human autonomy and self-sufficiency, whereas the Christian ethic is rooted in divine grace propelling human action (see my *Virtue amidst Vice*, 99–127).

One unusually striking parallel to 2 Peter 1:5–7 comes from a first-century Asia Minor inscription in honor of Herostratus son of Dorcalion. Listed in this catalog, respectively, are πίστις, *pistis* (faith); ἀρετή, *aretē* (virtue, or goodness); δικαιοσύνη, *dikaiosynē* (righteousness, GK *1466*); ευσεβεια, *eusebeia* (piety, or godliness, GK *2354*); and σπουδή, *spoudē* (diligence, or effort, GK *5082*). Given the underlying Stoic belief that moral excellence was the result of human achievement (as opposed to righteousness and obedience through the Torah), without any consequence for the afterlife, the occurrence of ἀρετή, *aretē*, in the LXX is understandably rare, even when it does occur in literature reflecting a more Hellenistic Judaism (e.g., in Philo, Wisdom of Solomon, and 4 Maccabees).

Contra Bauckham, 184–85; and Moo, 45, the progression of the eight virtues listed in 2 Peter 1:5–7 is not "largely random" or "haphazard," wherein "only two virtues have a clearly intelligible place in the list." Escalation can also be detected in Romans 5:1–5, where the trajectory of grace moves from suffering to hope. Similarly, the list of hardships encountered by Paul recorded in 2 Corinthians 6:6 moves from general (afflictions and hardships) to specific (sleepless nights and hunger).

C. Admonition to Confirm an Ethical Calling (1:8–11)

[8] For if you possess these qualities in increasing measure, they will keep you from being ineffective and unproductive in your knowledge of our Lord Jesus Christ. [9] But if anyone does not have them, he is nearsighted and blind, and has forgotten that he has been cleansed from his past sins.

[10] Therefore, my brothers, be all the more eager to make your calling and election sure. For if you do these things, you will never fall, [11] and you will receive a rich welcome into the eternal kingdom of our Lord and Savior Jesus Christ.

COMMENTARY

8 The context of bearing fruit ethically "in [the] knowledge of our Lord Jesus Christ" by means of a virtuous lifestyle stands in contrast to the ineffectual life, which is described in terms of nearsightedness, blindness, and forgetfulness. The presence of the catalog of virtues leads to the following conclusion: "For if you possess these qualities in increasing measure, they will keep you from being ineffective and unproductive in your knowledge of our Lord Jesus Christ." In short, to be ineffective and unproductive is to cause a Christian scandal. The scandal consists in the fact that extraordinary provisions have been granted by God himself for the ethical task at hand. Faith received, far from being passive in nature, requires of the believer active cooperation with God's grace. The scandal is further caused by the coex-

istence of futility and fruitlessness alongside *epignōsis*, the knowledge of God; such is a blatant contradiction (cf. Col 1:10).

9 The metaphor of blindness is simple yet striking and coincides with the images of 2 Peter 2— slavery, a dog returning to its vomit, and a pig returning to the mud (2:19, 22). The blindness metaphor is an integral part of the Christian paraenetic tradition (Mt 15:14; 23:16; Jn 9:40–41; Rev 3:17–18) and is reminiscent of the imagery used in Revelation 3:14, 17–18 of the Laodicean church. While a flat translation of *typhlos estin myōpazōn* ("blind and short-sighted") loses its force, the more nuanced rendering of *myōpazo* (lit., "to close the eye"; GK *3697*) by Mayor (lxii) and followed by Green, 82, captures the correct sense, namely, that of willful blindness. The emphasis here is on moral self-responsibility. Some have shut their eyes to the truth, resulting in a blindness that is not inherited but cultivated. In 2 Peter the blindness is characterized by denial (2:1), deception (v.3), boldness and willfulness (v.10b), a lust for sin (v.14a), and seduction (vv.14b, 18). Those individuals possessing these traits are cast as antitypes of Balaam (vv.15–16), who was seduced by pagans with a view to lead the Israelites astray.

Astonishingly, some in the community have "forgotten" that they were forgiven and cleansed of their past. The text literally reads, "having received forgetfulness" (*lēthēn labōn*), which offers the faint suggestion of a voluntary acceptance of their deceived and darkened condition. Indeed, forgetting one's cleansing from past sins is the beginning of all apostasy (so Green, 82).

10 This moral reasoning is followed by a strengthened conclusion: "Therefore, . . . be all the more eager [*dio mallon spoudasate*] to make your calling and election sure." Hillyer, 170, captures the urgency contained in this imperative: "Determine to put in all the more effort." Repetition is important at this point, inasmuch as *spoudē* (GK 5082) appeared in the context of moral progression in 1:5. The tone has now intensified from teaching to exhortation, from didactics to warning.

The notion of confirming one's calling and election is a prominent feature of the Pauline epistles. To confirm one's calling is to offer proof—or disproof—of one's profession. As Calvin, 377, aptly

puts it, "Purity of life is not improperly called the evidence and proof of election, by which the faithful may not only testify to others that they are the children of God, but also confirm themselves in this confidence." Moreover, the ethical tension contained in the phrase "make your calling and election sure" illustrates the way in which 2 Peter blends sovereignty and moral agency, divine grace and human cooperation, even when emphasis is given to one side of the equation. While unmerited grace has been extended to the believer through Christ's righteousness, the believer must show evidence of this reality by means of virtuous living. On the one hand, great and precious promises have been provided to the believer—indeed, all the possible resources necessary for a life of godliness (1:3); on the other hand, the believer is to supply ("add") a calculated response that is measured over time in terms of ethical quality (1:5–7). The burden clearly rests on the shoulders of the readers to hold up their end of the covenantal agreement. If they are *willing*, they will never stumble. The guarantee is not that they will not sin, only that they will not *fall*.

11 The final "promise" extended by the gracious Lord and Savior is to "lavishly provide" (NIV, "receive"; once more, *epichorēgeō*) entrance into his eternal kingdom. This reward awaits those who have confirmed their calling through a virtuous life worthy of the divine name. Entrance is not earned, lest the Petrine ethic be misconstrued; rather, it is predicated on grace, all grace, lavishly provided by the divine Benefactor.

NOTES

10 The theological conundrum of whether election and apostasy are compatible is not taken up in 2 Peter. The emphasis of this letter is human effort and the cultivation of a virtuous life. Note, in this regard, the use of the middle voice, ποιεῖσθαι, *poieisthai* (GK 4472), as the readers are to make sure for themselves.

REFLECTIONS

F. W. Danker ("2 Peter 1: A Solemn Decree." *CBQ* 40 [1978]: 64–82) and Neyrey, 145–46, 151, see in 1:3–11 the language of a decree of honor, whereby it was customary for civic officials to pass special resolutions in honor of the said benefactor or patron. This language is applied here to God. God's "clients" are exhorted to honor God as patron with virtuous lives and piety. The glorious nature of divine promises bestowed invites a response of confirmation rather than forgetfulness.

D. Prophetic Reminder to Recall (1:12–15)

OVERVIEW

Much like Jude, 2 Peter uses a conspicuous "reminder terminology." Rhetorically speaking, repetition serves an important function. Mindful of both his apostolic duties and limited time yet to live, the writer reemphasizes the basics; hereby the purpose of the letter is clarified.

Frequently, the role of the Christian teacher or preacher is to remind the audience of what they already know, to exhort them in the truth they already possess. The metaphor of the body as tabernacle (cf. 2Co 5:1–4), used in the context of the writer's personal reflections, speaks of the transitory nature of life for Israel of old and the readers in the present. The readers of 2 Peter, like Israel of old, need to be reminded that they are pilgrims on a journey.

¹²So I will always remind you of these things, even though you know them and are firmly established in the truth you now have. ¹³I think it is right to refresh your memory as long as I live in the tent of this body, ¹⁴because I know that I will soon put it aside, as our Lord Jesus Christ has made clear to me. ¹⁵And I will make every effort to see that after my departure you will always be able to remember these things.

COMMENTARY

12–15 Two interpretive options present themselves here, as the earlier discussion of authorship has shown. Either the apostle Peter is reflecting on his approaching death, borrowing elements from the literary convention called a "farewell speech" or "testament," or the "farewell speech" as a pseudepigraphic convention is being employed in the postapostolic period.

For most commentators, the testamental character of the epistle is one of the clearest indications of its post-Petrine setting. The language used here, however, is reflective; it is that of an eyewitness of the Lord, not one writing a generation or generations removed from the apostolic era. The writer recalls the striking prophecy of Jesus years earlier (Jn 21:18–19; cf. Jn 13:36). Concerning Peter's death, the drama contained in the admonition of 2 Peter 1:12–15 is captured by Green, 87–88: "There may be something poignant in his use of the word *established* to describe his hesitant and wavering readers. For that is the word which Jesus used of him on one memorable occasion when, although so fickle, he was sure that he was established in the truth and could not possibly apostatize (Lk 22:32). It seems to have become a favorite word of this turbulent man who now really was established. He uses it in his final prayer at the end of 1 Peter (5:10), and a similar word occurs in a significant context in 2 Peter 3:17."

Painfully aware of what it means to waver in the faith and disown the Lord, the apostle reminds his audience with great earnestness of Christian "first things." Inasmuch as they are presently "established in the truth," apostasy—i.e., ethical lapse and denial of the faith—is the present danger, not heresy or wrong teaching per se.

E. Prophetic Testimony Regarding Moral Authority (1:16–18)

[16]We did not follow cleverly invented stories when we told you about the power and coming of our Lord Jesus Christ, but we were eyewitnesses of his majesty. [17]For he received honor and glory from God the Father when the voice came to him from the Majestic Glory, saying, "This is my Son, whom I love; with him I am well pleased." [18]We ourselves heard this voice that came from heaven when we were with him on the sacred mountain.

COMMENTARY

16–18 The issue of authority presses to the fore as the author's focus is sharpened. The clash, in the mind of the writer, is nothing less than between error—"cleverly invented stories"—and truth— "we told you about the power and coming of our Lord Jesus Christ, [and] we were eyewitnesses of his majesty." That the author can make these declarations validates the assertion that he indeed is one of the apostles.

Particular developments in the Christian community that demand a prophetic-pastoral response require that the writer exert his authority. This is achieved by his testimony as an "eyewitness" (*epoptēs*, GK 2228) of the Lord's glory. The use of *epoptēs* here is the sole appearance of the word in the NT. It normally designates those who had been initiated into the highest grade of mysteries in Hellenistic mystery cults (BDAG, 388; cf. Col 2:18). The most memorable, transforming event in Peter's life, a theophany described in the Synoptic Gospels, was on the Mount of Transfiguration.

The revelation and resulting perception of honor and glory bestowed by God the Father on Jesus doubtless left a permanent mark on Peter and remains etched in his memory throughout his life. In this revelatory moment, the eyewitnesses on the mountain were made to understand the unique relationship between the Father and the Son: "This is my Son, whom I love; with him I am well pleased. Listen to him!" (Mt 17:5). Of the disciples assembled on the mountain, it was especially for Peter's sake that the command "Listen to him!" was given.

Peter, it will be remembered, had rebuked Jesus for his teachings that the Son of Man must suffer and be killed and then rise again (Mt 16:22).

18 The language of self-witness in 1:12–18 (esp. vv.16–18) is both earnest and emphatic. It heightens the personal nature of the writer's testimony: "We ourselves heard this voice … when we were with him on the sacred mountain" The significance of this autobiographical witness should not be lost

on the readers. It reinforces his authority before he proceeds to censure the morally corrupt and offer a moral apologetic.

With this mark of apostolicity, the writer understands the prophetic message to be abundantly verified. More immediately, the writer wishes to stress solidarity between the prophetic message of the past and that of the present. In the present it is a message carried by the apostles.

NOTES

16–18 Neyrey, 175, understands the allusion to "stories" or "myths" in terms of rationalist rejection of punishment. While this may well apply to the material in 2 Peter 3, the immediate context suggests that the issue in question is one of *authority*. It is the solemn character of statements recorded in 1:16–18 that pseudepigraphy hypotheses fail to address adequately. To take seriously the writer's testimony, which is intended to be autobiographical, and yet claim that "Petrine authorship was intended to be entirely *transparent* fiction," as Bauckham, 134 (emphasis his), asserts, simply asks too much of the reader. The author claims authority to speak precisely *because of firsthand knowledge*, and not second- or thirdhand knowledge or reporting. "We heard" and "we saw" cannot legitimately be said by a "Petrine agent" or pseudepigrapher.

REFLECTIONS

The writer appears to be keenly aware of the uniqueness of apostolic authority. Apostolic preaching, i.e., proclamation issuing from eyewitness testimony of the resurrected Lord that initially brings the reader to the place of faith, is rooted in and flows out of historical events. Specifically, it is grounded in one's relation to Jesus and one's witness to the resurrection. This experience qualified an individual to preach the Christian message firsthand, thereby bestowing "apostolic authority."

F. Nature of Prophetic Authority (1:19–21)

OVERVIEW

Most discussions of vv.19–21, especially conservative commentary on v.19, assume an overarching thesis of correct interpretation of the Scriptures. Commentators read into this text a scenario in which the Scriptures are being read amiss, apart from illumination of the Holy Spirit. This reading, however, ignores the contextual flow of the material preceding and following. The fact that authority is being asserted in vv.12–18 strongly suggests that it is being denied by some. What was received from the prophets of old was taken to be the authoritative word of God. This same norm, confirmed by apostolic witness, is to continue to be the Christian's guide.

The true sense of these verses has to do with authentication of the prophetic voice, not interpretation of the Scriptures, as many commentators think (Green, 101, being one of the few to discern the correct sense). We may assume a background to 2 Peter in which Peter's apostolic authority is being denied, or at least being called into question. His response, which serves as a necessary introduction to chs. 2 and 3, is that prophetic speech originates

with God, even when spoken by human agents. The OT Scriptures are inspired and prophetic; thus they come to the reader as the "word of God." Presently, the writer wants his readers to know that he *speaks from God.*

Needed in the present situation is the application of apostolic authority for the purposes of countering certain influences injurious to the Christian community: doubt, hostility, mockery, hardness to truth, and consequent moral decrepitude. Perhaps Christian truth-claims are being derided; perhaps the apostle himself is being ridiculed. In essence, the writer is saying that to deny Simon Peter's apostolic authority is to deny the OT and the prophets themselves.

---

¹⁹And we have the word of the prophets made more certain, and you will do well to pay attention to it, as to a light shining in a dark place, until the day dawns and the morning star rises in your hearts. ²⁰Above all, you must understand that no prophecy of Scripture came about by the prophet's own interpretation. ²¹For prophecy never had its origin in the will of man, but men spoke from God as they were carried along by the Holy Spirit.

COMMENTARY

19 For the second time in ch. 1 the writer uses the term *bebaios* ("firm, sure, certain, well established," GK *1010*). In 1:10 it occurs in connection with confirming one's call (make "sure"); here, used comparatively, it describes the confirming—i.e., infallible and thus authoritative—character of the prophetic word (made more "certain").

The references to light shining in a dark place and the "morning star" rising are intriguing and defy any precise interpretation. The context suggests that the prophetic word is a torch that lights

our way in a dark environment; for the readers this may well be a continuation of the exhortation to persevere morally. The Greek term *phōsphoros*, "light-bearer," is rendered "morning star" and finds expression in both pagan and Christian contexts. In the book of Revelation, Jesus is hailed as the "Offspring of David" as well as the "bright Morning Star" (Rev 22:16; cf. Nu 24:17), which seems to combine both popular and religious notions. In 2 Peter the readers are admonished to persevere in the awareness that full light and revelation will be revealed eschatologically.

III. PROFILE OF APOSTASY (2:1–22)

A. Prophetic Denunciation of the Apostate (2:1–3)

OVERVIEW

Second Peter 2 continues the allusion to the OT introduced in 1:20–21. Central to the OT story are both true and false prophets, those who uphold the truth and those who actively suppress the truth. With this transition, the writer shifts the focus to his adversaries.

Commentators disagree on the identity of Peter's opponents. Kelly, 229–231, and Cranfield, 183, are among those who see here doctrinal shortcomings and ethical libertinism of second-century Gnostics, given the combative tone of much of the epistle and use of the catchword "knowledge." Such a reading, however, proceeds more from the assumption of a late dating imposed on the text than from the text itself. A closer reading of 2 Peter

suggests that an ethical rather than doctrinal departure lies at the root of the opponents' behavior (cf. M. Desjardins, "The Portrayal of the Dissidents in 2 Peter and Jude," *JSNT* 30 [1987]: 89–92). Consider the typical pattern when religious beliefs are rejected: (1) apostasy manifests itself via behavior that demonstrates a rejection of the truth; (2) thereupon follows heresy, i.e., doctrinal error, which has the effect of justifying one's actions. Peter's opponents are, first and foremost, sexual libertarians, as confirmed by the portrait that follows (2:2, 6–7, 10, 14, 18–20, 22) and the previous accent on moral virtue and self-control (1:5–7). The danger confronting the Christian community is one of being molded by the outside world.

¹But there were also false prophets among the people, just as there will be false teachers among you. They will secretly introduce destructive heresies, even denying the sovereign Lord who bought them—bringing swift destruction on themselves. ²Many will follow their shameful ways and will bring the way of truth into disrepute. ³In their greed these teachers will exploit you with stories they have made up. Their condemnation has long been hanging over them, and their destruction has not been sleeping.

COMMENTARY

1 In the present argument, the writer does not designate his adversaries as "false prophets"; rather, the term *pseudoprophētai* (GK *6021*) is applied to deceivers who arose "among the people," i.e., Israel of old. What the text does say is that "there will be

false teachers among you." The verbal tense is important, for it suggests that the Christian community will need to be on guard *in the future*.

Against the tendency of traditional scholarship to locate 2 Peter in the early or mid-second century, this description fits well in a mid-sixties scenario in the first century. Ethical lapse has visited the church as it seeks to take root in Gentile culture. Such occurs long before the noted (Gnostic) heretical schools of the second century are established. The appearance her of the term *haireseis* (GK *146*), from which we derive the word "heresy," has further fed the misconception that 2 Peter mirrors a late date— a date in which heresy is already widespread. However, Paul, writing in about the year AD 55, also uses the term in the sense of "factions" or "divisions" (1Co 11:18). The phrase "destructive heresies" can be understood in the sense that the opinions or teachings of Peter's opponents lead ultimately to their own ruin (so Bauckham, 239–40).

The slave-market metaphor, also in 2:19, is employed in v.1: "even denying the sovereign Lord who bought them" (cf. Jude 4, where the same language is used of Jude's opponents). What sort of denial might this be? As with Jude's adversaries, these people have apparently made a confession of faith at one time and now have departed from the faith. The denial, as Green, 107, observes, is primarily ethical and not intellectual in nature. The slave metaphor, reappearing in 2:19, confirms this suspicion.

2 Tragically, these individuals appear to be apostate former believers who have disowned their Lord. Not doctrine but the fact of their "shameful ways" and entrenched immorality constitutes the root of their apostasy and subsequent judgment. Moral skepticism and a resulting lapse into pagan ways have solidified into apostasy. The charge that because of these "the way of truth" will be brought "into disrepute" is reminiscent of Paul's condemnation in Romans 1:18–32, where sexual immorality is rooted in a suppression of the truth, and in Romans 2:24. Such an indictment is nothing short of scandalous. Sexual immorality gives Christianity a bad name in surrounding culture. Given the hostility of pagans toward Christians to begin with, this ethical scandal is all the more reprehensible.

3 The writer states further that the opponents are deceptive in their use of "stories they have made up." His response is several-fold: he announces that their condemnation "has long been hanging over them" (*to krima ekpalai ouk argei*) and that their "destruction has not been sleeping" (*hē apōleia autōn ou nystazei*). This declaration serves two purposes. It displays the language of foreknowledge and predestination so characteristic of the Jewish-Christian mind-set, and it may serve as a flat rebuke of the opponents' skepticism toward divine judgment (so Neyrey, "Form and Background of the Polemic," 415–16; Bauckham, 247).

NOTES

1–3 Cf. esp. Jude 4, 14, 17, where the same language is used. A feature not uncommon to OT and apocalyptic literature is the notion of names written in heavenly books (see, e.g., Ex 32:32–33; Pss 40:4; 56:8; 69:28; 139:16; Rev 3:5; 5:1–5, 7–8; 10:8–11; 20:12; *1 En.* 81:1–2; 89:62; 90:14; 104:7; 108:3, 7; *Jub.* 5:13; 6:31; 16:9; 23:32; 28:6; 30:9; 32:21; *2 Bar.* 24:1). These books reflect a religious self-understanding fundamental to Jewish thought, namely, that the divine purpose, though hidden from human view, is predetermined and revealed in history. See commentary at Jude 4.

REFLECTIONS

The nature of apostasy is such that it works covertly, negates Christ's lordship, is characterized by ethical lapse, denies the truth, and inevitably exploits others. Because of apostasy's cumulative negative effect on the body of Christ, the condemnation of the faithless is announced in no uncertain terms. At the same time, a righteous remnant is promised preservation.

B. Moral Paradigms (2:4–10a)

⁴For if God did not spare angels when they sinned, but sent them to hell, putting them into gloomy dungeons to be held for judgment; ⁵if he did not spare the ancient world when he brought the flood on its ungodly people, but protected Noah, a preacher of righteousness, and seven others; ⁶if he condemned the cities of Sodom and Gomorrah by burning them to ashes, and made them an example of what is going to happen to the ungodly; ⁷and if he rescued Lot, a righteous man, who was distressed by the filthy lives of lawless men ⁸(for that righteous man, living among them day after day, was tormented in his righteous soul by the lawless deeds he saw and heard)—⁹if this is so, then the Lord knows how to rescue godly men from trials and to hold the unrighteous for the day of judgment, while continuing their punishment. ¹⁰This is especially true of those who follow the corrupt desire of the sinful nature and despise authority.

COMMENTARY

4 The allusion to the fallen angels in 2 Peter, as in Jude, is somewhat veiled. Yet subtle nuances in language are worth noting and reflect in minor ways on the pastoral need in the community and thus on the purpose of the letter. Whereas Jude notes that they "did not keep their positions of authority but abandoned their own home" (v.6), the emphasis in 2 Peter is placed on the fact that God "did not spare angels when they sinned." Already in the first of three moral types, the tension between judgment and deliverance begins to emerge.

The Petrine allusion to the angels is further distinguished by reference to "hell" (Gk. *Tartarus*), the subterranean abyss and place of punishment in classical Greek mythology. The writer is sensitive to the social environment of the readers and borrows imagery without endorsing Greek mythology itself. Jude, by contrast, seems to presuppose a Palestinian social setting.

Second Peter, like Jude, does not identify the precise sin of the angels, only that they sinned and have consequently been reserved for judgment. The shocking nature of this illustration is not to be lost on the readers: the exalted ranks of angels themselves were not immune to rebellion and its eternal consequences. Even the angels God "did not spare" (*ouk epheisato*).

5 A second precedent of not having been spared is cited, a precedent curiously absent from Jude. This illustration of catastrophic judgment, unlike the first, exhibits an important bifurcation. The writer states that while God "did not spare the ancient world when he brought the flood," God did rescue "Noah, a preacher of righteousness, and seven others." (Although the OT does not explicitly state that Noah preached to his generation, he is accorded this role by diverse strands of Jewish tradition; see J. P. Lewis, *A Study of the Interpretation of Noah and the*

Flood in Jewish and Christian Literature [Leiden: Brill, 1968]). The generation with which this righteous preacher is compared is depicted in Genesis 6; Noah, by contrast, is portrayed as a "righteous man, blameless among the people of his time" (Ge 6:9). In Ezekiel 14:12–23 Noah stands alongside Daniel and Job as a paradigm of faithfulness amidst a generation facing inescapable judgment.

Similarly, the days of Noah are alluded to in Jesus' teaching on watchfulness (Mt 24:36–44; Lk 17:22–27), where Noah's generation teaches a moral lesson as a model of contemporary skepticism. Hebrews 11, another catalog of historical examples, salutes Noah as one of eight persons saved in the ark in the context of divine judgment. By heeding the divine warning to build the ark, Noah thus "condemned the world and became heir of the righteousness that comes by faith" (Heb 11:7). In 1 Peter 3:18–22 the days of Noah are described as a time when "God waited patiently," at the end of which eight persons "were saved through water." The biblical account is unified in its portrait of Noah as a model of righteousness and faithfulness.

In 2 Peter, attention is drawn both to judgment befalling the world of the ungodly and to the salvation of Noah and his family. This dual emphasis resonates with the readers, encouraging them to remain faithful in the midst of their own seemingly overwhelming social challenges. Thus Noah serves as a symbol to the Christian community of faithfulness in spite of overwhelming obstacles. In this epistle, attention is drawn twice (2:4–5; 3:3–7) to the flood God brought on the world as well as to the deliverance of a righteous remnant. The pastoral implications are clear: the readers are admonished to remain faithful in their present situation in spite of difficult cultural circumstances.

6–8 The third example also incorporates motifs of both judgment and salvation. It is instructive insofar as it exploits comparison for a notably pastoral effect. Because God reduced the cities of the plain to ashes, "making them an example of what is going to happen to the ungodly," punishment for Peter's opponents is certain. What is striking, however, about Peter's contrast is that Lot, depicted in Genesis 19 as morally tainted, is called "righteous" (*dikaios*) three times. He is cast as a victim of surrounding cultural licentiousness, one whose righteous soul was tormented day after day "by the lawless deeds he saw and heard." Thus Lot is righteous not by example, as Genesis 19 makes clear, but by comparison to surrounding debauchery. The clause "if God rescued Lot" confirms this comparative picture: Peter's audience should take heart in the throes of their present social context. If they find it difficult confronting pagan immorality, Lot had it even harder.

NOTES

4 Two of Jude's examples of judgment appear in 2 Peter. One of these, the fallen angels, is depicted in notably similar terms. Lists of historical paradigms depicting hard-heartedness appear in Jewish literature—both apocryphal/pseudepigraphal as well as rabbinic—with relative frequency (e.g., 3 Macc 3:7; Sir 16:5–15; *1 En.* 1–36; *T. Naph.* 2:8–4:9; *Jub.* 20:2–7). Among the most commonly cited in these lists are apostate Israel, Sodomites, Assyria, the giants, the generation of the flood, Korah, the Canaanites, and the fallen angels. Both 2 Peter and Jude borrow from this common exegetical tradition and enlist the use of moral paradigms for typological purposes (see my "Noncanonical Writings, Citations in the General Epistles," and "Old Testament in the General Epistles," in *Dictionary of the Later New Testament*, ed. R. P. Martin and P. H. Davids [Downers Grove, Ill.: InterVarsity, 1997], 814–19, 834–41).

4–5 Surely it is not coincidental that in this epistle Noah and the fallen angels appear together in the same context. In apocalyptic literature, the flood is bound together with the elaborate story of the fall of "the Watchers," i.e., the fallen angels (e.g., *T. Naph.* 3:5). Significantly, too, the reference to the days of Noah in 2 Peter has a notable and fascinating parallel in 1 Peter (3:18–20), where the demon hosts are subjugated to the rule of Christ (3:22). The allusion to Noah in both 1 and 2 Peter has a similar effect: it is intended to promise retribution and to comfort the righteous remnant.

5–9 The flood typology, conspicuously absent from Jude, joins fire typology in 2 Peter 2 and is intended to be prototypical of eschatological judgment. Noah and Lot become types of faithful Christians who, despite enormous social obstacles, expect God to bring deliverance (ῥύομαι, *rhyomai*, GK *4861*; 2:7, 9). The catchword "savior," occurring five times in the epistle (1:1, 11; 2:20; 3:2, 18), has more than a christological thrust; God *saves* a righteous remnant. The theme of righteous rescue, introduced in the second moral paradigm, is magnified in the third.

REFLECTIONS

Noah and Lot are instructive in the writer's thinking. They illustrate the fact that God is not indifferent toward the moral challenges of his people. Particularly for those living in a pluralistic Hellenistic environment, this reminder is crucial. Although Noah and Lot are worlds apart in terms of their personal ethical example, both are objects of God's redeeming and unmerited favor. Given the fact that Lot's character, based on the Genesis narrative, leaves much to be desired, the readers of 2 Peter can take courage. Sensuality and skepticism conspire against their faith as well. Yet, despite his weaknesses, Lot was the object of divine rescue, in this way joining the fellowship of Noah.

The message of 2 Peter, unlike Jude, is not mere condemnation. Instead, it is the assurance from the midst of the cultural "furnace" to the righteous who exhibit faith. Important points of contact exist between the social environment of the readers and the days of Noah. Hillyer, 188–89, captures the sense of these verses: "Peter thus maintains his pastoral purpose of encouraging his readers to keep faith with God in their own situation. Such a loyal stand will neither go unnoticed nor fail to attract a similar divine protection from the consequences of sin of the godless . . . , so the same God will protect believers who remain faithful to him in later generations."

C. Portrait of the Apostate (2:10b–18)

OVERVIEW

Structurally and stylistically, these verses bear notable similarity to Jude—down to minute detail. The obvious literary relationship has occupied NT scholarship considerably, as noted previously. In both letters, a portrait of the ungodly contains a litany of descriptions and accusations and follows the writer's use of historical paradigms. The present focus is on moral character. The individuals under indictment are initially compared with the angels.

Bold and arrogant, these men are not afraid to slander celestial beings; ¹¹yet even angels, although they are stronger and more powerful, do not bring slanderous accusations against such beings in the presence of the Lord. ¹²But these men blaspheme in matters they do not understand. They are like brute beasts, creatures of instinct, born only to be caught and destroyed, and like beasts they too will perish.

¹³They will be paid back with harm for the harm they have done. Their idea of pleasure is to carouse in broad daylight. They are blots and blemishes, reveling in their pleasures while they feast with you. ¹⁴With eyes full of adultery, they never stop sinning; they seduce the unstable; they are experts in greed—an accursed brood! ¹⁵They have left the straight way and wandered off to follow the way of Balaam son of Beor, who loved the wages of wickedness. ¹⁶But he was rebuked for his wrongdoing by a donkey—a beast without speech—who spoke with a man's voice and restrained the prophet's madness.

¹⁷These men are springs without water and mists driven by a storm. Blackest darkness is reserved for them. ¹⁸For they mouth empty, boastful words and, by appealing to the lustful desires of sinful human nature, they entice people who are just escaping from those who live in error.

COMMENTARY

10b–12 Whereas angels, "although they are stronger and more powerful, do not bring slanderous accusations against such beings in the presence of the Lord," these persons, in their boldness and blasphemy, "are not afraid to slander celestial beings," the fallen, evil angels. This statement by the author, a probable reference to a lost ending of the Jewish apocryphal work *Assumption of Moses* (see Jude), is less a theological assertion about angels than it is a simple and startling comparison that presupposes knowledge familiar to the readers: the apostate have no reverential fear that inhibits them; they "blaspheme" what "they do not understand." Moreover, these people are "brute beasts, creatures of instinct, born only to be caught and destroyed."

13–16 The description of the adversaries, while containing significant parallels to Jude, is differentiated by an expansion of the Balaam typology.

The moral corrosion that characterizes these individuals is breathtaking. They act as irrational beasts, they slander, they revel in their corruption. They are boastful, lustful, irreverent, disobedient, full of greed, and scornful. They are adulterous and insatiable in their appetite for sin; they actively seduce others. As apostates, they "have left the straight way and wandered off" and are reminiscent of Balaam, who "loved the wages of wickedness." Indeed, so entrenched in a moral stupor was Balaam, so overcome by "madness," that he had to be restrained by a donkey speaking with a human voice.

Only a brief standardization of this typology appears in Jude ("Balaam's error," v.11). However, in 2 Peter these individuals are more fully developed as a model. The language of "abandoning," "wandering off," and "loving wickedness" is the language of apostasy, and Balaam is the prototype of this mold. In Revelation, Balaam's name is associated with idolatry and sexual immorality (Rev 2:14). In Jewish tradition, Balaam becomes a paradigm of self-seeking and greed; for this reason Jezebel and Balaam, given the character of related OT narratives, are symbols for apostasy in the early church. According to 2 Peter, Balaam is prototypical of some in the community. Along with Balaam, these individuals are said to "love the wages of wickedness."

16 The point of emphasis here is that it took an ordinary, dumb (i.e., speechless) beast, Balaam's donkey, speaking "with a man's voice," to "restrain the prophet's madness" (compare the language to 2:12, which depicts the adversaries as "brute beasts" and "creatures of instinct").

NOTES

15 Some commentators see in "Balaam son of Beor" (Gk. *Bosor*) a play on words: the Hebrew *baśar* denotes "flesh"; in effect, Balaam is called "son of the flesh" (so Bauckham, 267–68).

On the variations of the Balaam tradition in Jewish and early Christian exegesis, see M. S. Moore, *The Balaam Traditions: Their Character and Development* (SBLDS 113; Atlanta: Scholars Press, 1990); J. T. Greene, *Balaam and His Interpreters: A Hermeneutical History of the Balaam Tradition* (Atlanta: Scholars Press, 1992).

15–16 Two strains of tradition exist in the OT concerning the Midianite prophet who led Israel astray. On the one hand, he is viewed as a villain, corrupt and seductive. On the other hand, he is depicted as a tragic hero. The narrative in Numbers 22–24 offers a mixed review. Most of the related OT texts tend to portray him as a strictly negative memorial, as a self-seeking practitioner of divination who was hired to curse and lead Israel astray (e.g., Nu 31:15–16; Dt 23:4–6; Jos 13:22; Ne 13:2).

REFLECTIONS

The downfall of a prophet of God is a singular phenomenon and one that is highly instructive. Over time, Balaam became ethically divorced from the message that he bore. The psychology and character of apostasy are such that moral skepticism and cynicism lead one to be indifferent to, if not loathe, what was formerly embraced. In the end, one "loves the wages of wickedness." Such a tragic case is a possibility that can befall the individual; it is also a cancer that threatens everything around it.

D. Profile of Apostasy (2:19–22)

OVERVIEW

One recurring description of Peter's opponents is that they deceive, entice, or seduce others (1:16; 2:1, 3, 14, 18). It is moral depravity that afflicts the community. False doctrine or heresy is no doubt present, but the fact that some "deny the sovereign Lord who bought them" (2:1), coupled with the language of moral reasoning that pervades the entire epistle, points foremost to an ethical dilemma affecting the community. What's more, the opponents are not content merely to apostatize; they seek to seduce and take others with them. Central to the apostates' rhetorical strategy is the promise of liberation. Yet they themselves are "slaves of depravity" (2:19).

> ¹⁹They promise them freedom, while they themselves are slaves of depravity—for a man is a slave to whatever has mastered him. ²⁰If they have escaped the corruption of the world by knowing our Lord and Savior Jesus Christ and are again entangled in it and overcome, they are worse off at the end than they were at the beginning. ²¹It would have been better for them not to have known the way of righteousness, than to have known it and then to turn their backs on the sacred command that was passed on to them. ²²Of them the proverbs are true: "A dog returns to its vomit," and, "A sow that is washed goes back to her wallowing in the mud."

COMMENTARY

19 Ultimately, as proverbial wisdom shows (cf. Jn 8:34; Ro 6:16), people are slaves to whatever rules them, even to their own bombastic nonsense (cf. 2Pe 2:18). The slave imagery was suggested already in 2:1. These persons apparently utilize the catchword "freedom," with all of its seductive attraction. Their error is first and foremost ethical; they insist on "freedom"—a freedom from moral restraint (1:4; 2:12 [twice]; 2:19) and divine activity (3:1–7).

20 Two vivid pictures from the natural realm sum up the state of the apostate, i.e., those who in the past "escaped the corruption of the world" but had become "entangled in it and overcome." Both images communicate actions that fit "brute beasts" and "creatures of instinct" (2:12). Common though these images are, they have the effect of shocking the readers when applied to the realm of faith. If people return to the world's defilement after rescue through knowledge of Jesus Christ, they enter a state said to be worse for them than the first. It would have been better, the writer declares, that they had never known the truth to begin with than to disavow what they knew (cf. Mt 12:43–45). In relative terms, ignorance of "the way of righteousness," at least accord-

ing to the apostle's logic, is better than apostasy from it. Disavowing the truth is serious business.

21 Green, 131, perceptively concludes from the text that the initial stage of apostasy is the rejection of the category of law, given the allusion to "the sacred command." Moreover, by using "command" in the singular (*entolē*, GK *1953*), the writer demonstrates that he is contending for the general function of the law (which is to restrain sin) and not the detailed prescriptions of pentateuchal law. Because God is holy, he commands that his people be holy as well (Lev 11:44–45; 19:2; 20:26; 1Pe 1:16). Orthopraxy (right action) flows out of orthodoxy (right belief); ethical living must validate one's religious convictions. Bold, willful, presumptuous, and blasphemous, the apostate intuitively seeks to be released from the moral constraints of law. Lawless deeds (2:8) characterize the spirit that prides itself in being beyond moral authority. Rejection of God's law, then, can be seen as the initial and necessary step in rejecting God's authority.

22 The common proverbial imagery depicting two unclean animals is in continuity with the previous "bestial" imagery and mirrors the sobering fact that God gives us over to that which we choose (cf. Ro 1:18–32): the dog returning to its vomit (cf. Mt 7:6; Rev 22:15, wherein dogs stand in association with idolaters and the sexually immoral) and the pig to its mud. The writer draws attention to two disgusting habits of these creatures, one of which finds its parallel in the OT. The fool in Proverbs is likened to a dog that returns to its vomit (Pr 26:11). This dog, moreover, is the *kyōn* (GK *3264*), the wild scavenger of the streets, not the *kynarion*, the house dog (Mt 15:26–27). Similarly, the proverb of the pig finds its analogue in the Egyptian pseudepigraphal work *Ahiqar:* "My son, you were to me like a pig which

had been in a hot bath . . . and when it came out and saw a filthy pool went down and wallowed in it."

The rhetorical effect of the imagery is to jolt the readers into seeing the folly of reverting to the moral squalor of pagan culture from where they came and were washed. The proverbs serve a dual purpose. They cinch the earlier argument that the opponents are "brute beasts" (2Pe 2:12), not unlike the prophet gone mad (2:16). And they further suggest that the opponents have formerly been "washed" and were clean. The combined effect is to sober the audience into seeing the utterly tragic nature of apostasy, which is a willful departure from revealed truth.

IV. EXHORTATION TO THE FAITHFUL (3:1–18)

A. Exhortation to Recall (3:1–2)

OVERVIEW

The material of 2 Peter 2 focuses sharply on the apostate. Now the writer returns to the faithful, who are in the throes of a dilemma and in need of a reminder. From the beginning of their spiritual sojourn they have been forewarned of the perilous nature of moral skepticism. The writer now blends pastoral insight and apologetic force in an attempt to exhort the faithful as they struggle to reconcile God's seeming indifference to their lot with the challenges of living in a radically skeptical environment.

Most commentators, in their interpretation of 2 Peter 3, are predisposed to view the material as a theological treatise on eschatology. While the escha-

tological element is present, the focus is not eschatology but ethics. The eschatological serves to reinforce the ethical; hence the material in ch. 3 is to be read in continuity with the material in chs. 1 and 2.

The readers are here urged to recall foundational Christian teaching; in fact, this is said to be the second such letter written by the apostle. Whether we have here a reference to 1 Peter or another unknown writing is unclear (cf. 1Co 5:9). What is certain is that the author is writing again, reiterating the apostolic basics. In the present context, this is meant to invoke authority for the purpose of drawing out the moral implications of Christian faith.

¹Dear friends, this is now my second letter to you. I have written both of them as reminders to stimulate you to wholesome thinking. ²I want you to recall the words spoken in the past by the holy prophets and the command given by our Lord and Savior through your apostles.

COMMENTARY

1–2 The material in ch. 3 finds the writer revisiting his reason for writing. He must remind his readers of the apostolic "first things." The language here is strongly motivational: "I have written . . . as reminders to stimulate you to wholesome thinking." It is a call to moral purity, to be unmixed and untainted. This exhortation follows on the heels of a stern warning (2:1–22). Like Noah and Lot, the readers are challenged to remain uncontaminated.

2 Once more, as in 1:19–21, the writer states that there is continuity between the OT prophets, who prefigured Christian discipleship, and the apostles who have spoken "the command given by our Lord and Savior." This view accords with the Pauline statements that the apostles and prophets constitute the foundation of the church (Eph 2:20) and that the mystery of the gospel has been revealed to and imparted through the apostles and prophets (Eph 3:5–6). They are the ones to whom the gospel message has been entrusted. One cannot speak of an authoritative "word of God" apart from the concept of apostolicity and the apostolic tradition (1Co 15:3–7). The apostle is authoritative inasmuch as he stands in direct relation to Jesus and thus is a deputized representative (cf. the close link between Peter's confession [Mt 16:13–20] and his experience of Jesus' transfiguration [2Pe 1:18]). The implications of the apostolic office are weighty.

One need not regard, with Kelly, 354, the reference to "your apostles" as something that "inadvertently betrays that the writer belongs to an age when the apostles have been elevated to a venerated group who mediate Christ's teaching authoritatively to the whole Church." Rather than suggesting a setting one or more generations removed from the apostles, as is broadly assumed by critical scholarship, "your apostles" may be understood as "the apostles whom you ought to trust" (so Bigg, 290), with a present and not a future emphasis. The author speaks of "your apostles" through whom the Lord has spoken. Set in contradistinction to the apostate, the apostles are those "who preach the gospel to you and founded the churches in your area" (Green, 137). Apostolic leadership preserves the community; when truth is being sacrificed, apostolic authority is needed to redirect the local situation. Second Peter offers strong evidence that precisely such a situation exists, with the corresponding need for authority to be exercised.

NOTES

1–2 Michael Green's analysis of the similarities and differences between 1 and 2 Peter—both in language and thought—is one of the more useful treatments of the subject (*2 Peter Reconsidered*, 14–23; *2 Peter and Jude*, 17–23). For an examination of the similarities between the two letters, see Mayor, lxviii–cv.

Considerable speculation characterizes traditional scholarship as to the identity of the "second letter." While this allusion naturally suggests 1 Peter as its predecessor, those who view 2 Peter as the work of a later writer using Peter's name dismiss 1 Peter as the intended reference. Accordingly, they take 2 Peter 3:1–2 as a transparent mark of forgery. Kelly, 353, states that this reference is "only another prop in the apparatus of pseudonymity." The contents and style of 2 Peter make it at least quite possible that 3:1–2 is an allusion to another, unknown epistle.

B. Caricature of the Moral Skeptic (3:3–7)

³First of all, you must understand that in the last days scoffers will come, scoffing and following their own evil desires. ⁴They will say, "Where is this 'coming' he promised? Ever since our fathers died, everything goes on as it has since the beginning of creation." ⁵But they deliberately forget that long ago by God's word the heavens existed and the earth was formed out of water and by water. ⁶By these waters also the world of that time was deluged and destroyed. ⁷By the same word the present heavens and earth are reserved for fire, being kept for the day of judgment and destruction of ungodly men.

COMMENTARY

3 The reference to "the last days" is intended to reflect on the local situation, characterized by scoffing, indulging in lust, and moral skepticism. The readers are to understand both the rationale of the hardened moral skeptic and the end of such hardened thinking. Cynical, carnal, and law-mocking individuals provide a justification for moral corruption. Their denial of what is true is what sets them apart and makes them dangerous. Self-indulgence, rooted in nihilistic hedonism, undercuts moral absolutes at the most basic level.

4 Contained within the apologetic that unfolds in ch. 3 is the caricature of the moral skeptic who denies a universe with moral accountability. Consider the method of reasoning employed by radical moral skeptics: They say, "Where is this 'coming' he promised? Ever since our fathers died, everything goes on as it has since the beginning of creation." Peter's opponents, in essence, are denying any divine intervention in human affairs.

5–7 To this assertion of moral relativity, the apostle responds with a cosmological argument—an argument based on the creation of a moral universe. And it incorporates the Jewish-Christian eschatological perspective by marshaling flood typology and fire typology. The lesson of the flood is above all a moral lesson. Water was the means by which judgment came initially (cf. 1Pe 3:19–20); fire and not water is the means by which eschatological judgment will proceed (cf. Ge 8:22).

NOTES

3–7 Neyrey ("Form and Background of the Polemic") considers parallels between 2 Peter and an Epicurean polemic against divine providence (Plutarch, *Sera*). The polemic is examined according to four constituent parts—cosmology, freedom, unfulfilled prophecy, and injustice—which function as sub-themes in 2 Peter. Neyrey's reconstruction is helpful, insofar as the four pillars of Plutarchian apologetic fit naturally into the schema of 2 Peter without causing the reader to become overly speculative. For example, "freedom" is promised by Peter's opponents—a freedom that is nothing short of a new slavery (2:19). For more on the Epicurean polemic, see Introduction, p. 374 n.47.

7 Touchpoints between ch. 3 and Stoic cosmology make an alternative interpretation plausible. Destruction of the cosmos by fire, alluded to here in v.7 and again in vv.10–13, mirrors quite possibly the Stoic belief that the universe underwent periodic renewal by means of burning. This restoration was understood to take place over and over. Without endorsing Stoic cosmology, the writer may be borrowing Stoic ideas and vocabulary for the sake of his argument. This would be relevant particularly if his opponents are challenging the very stability and moral order of the universe. A helpful discussion of the nature and origins of Stoic cosmology is found in D. E. Hahm, *The Origins of Stoic Cosmology* (Columbus: Ohio State Univ. Press, 1977), esp. 200–215.

REFLECTIONS

A main premise of traditional commentary on 2 Peter is that doctrine—specifically, false doctrine—represents the chief burden of the writer. The material in ch. 3 has been thought to support this argument. Accordingly, the opponents are said to have promulgated an eschatological viewpoint that must rationalize the "embarrassment" of a parousia that has been delayed (so Käsemann, 170). This delay is typically accompanied by the assumption that the writer is removed from the apostolic era. If one assumes that 2 Peter is a second-century tract to bolster the morale of the church, then the "problem" of the epistle takes on a decidedly doctrinal cast. If, however, it is written to counter first-century moral skepticism and ethical lapse, it becomes less a tract to affirm doctrinal orthodoxy than a passionate exhortation toward virtuous living. The burden of 2 Peter is not the timing of the Lord's coming or chronology per se; it is the fact of the Lord's coming as a *day of moral reckoning*.

C. Promise of Universal Moral Accountability (3:8–13)

OVERVIEW

At this point the writer shifts focus. He follows the counterargument that judgment foreshadowed by the past is being reserved for the ungodly by interjecting pastorally sensitive admonition. The faithful may be perplexed, however, by the delay in divine judgment and vindication of the righteous. Surfacing here are points of contact with Noah's and Lot's circumstances (cf. also 1Pe 3:20, where the patience of God is associated with the flood.) A delay in God's action calls for reassurance that the faithful have not been forgotten, even when it appears from the human standpoint that God is not intervening in human affairs. For this reason it is necessary to address the readers once more as "dear friends" (*agapētoi*, GK *28*; 3:1, 8).

⁸But do not forget this one thing, dear friends: With the Lord a day is like a thousand years, and a thousand years are like a day. ⁹The Lord is not slow in keeping his promise, as some understand slowness. He is patient with you, not wanting anyone to perish, but everyone to come to repentance.

> [10]But the day of the Lord will come like a thief. The heavens will disappear with a roar; the elements will be destroyed by fire, and the earth and everything in it will be laid bare. [11]Since everything will be destroyed in this way, what kind of people ought you to be? You ought to live holy and godly lives [12]as you look forward to the day of God and speed its coming. That day will bring about the destruction of the heavens by fire, and the elements will melt in the heat. [13]But in keeping with his promise we are looking forward to a new heaven and a new earth, the home of righteousness.

COMMENTARY

8–9 In stressing both the relativity and significance of time, the author appeals to the character of God. One aspect of the Godhead that distinguishes the divine from human nature is the attribute of forbearance, or patience. In reality, the Lord is "not slow in keeping his promise," even though it may seem that way. Instead, at the heart of the issue of "delay" is divine patience (*makrothymia*, GK *3429*; v.9). The object of this patience is people; *all* persons are given the opportunity to bow the knee and make room for "repentance" (cf. also 1Ti 1:16). Here again a central motif of 2 Peter—human moral agency—is emphasized. While a day of judgment is reserved for the ungodly (3:7), it is not God's will that they perish; rather, these have brought condemnation on themselves. Divine sovereignty does not cancel out human freedom to make moral decisions or the need to cultivate the moral life. It should be emphasized that 2 Peter eludes both Calvinist and Arminian attempts to systematize and isolate divine and human action.

10 This patience, however, should not be misconstrued as divine indifference. Mercy and not impotence is the reason for the delay. Delay in no way suggests nonfulfillment (cf. Mt 24:42–44; Lk 12:39; 1Th 5:2, 4; Rev 3:3; 16:15). Fulfillment, however, will come "like a thief" in the night. With this coming, the ungodly will be judged, with full disclosure of the deeds committed by humans.

To counter any distortions about the ultimate nature of divine judgment, the writer expresses the day of the Lord in cataclysmic terms. It is sudden, decisive, cosmic, and final in its nature. The "thief" motif underscores the fact that (relatively) few will be prepared for this event; it will be unexpected and without warning, like a thief breaking into a house. Destruction of the cosmos by fire (*pyroomai*, "to melt with fire," GK *4792*), alluded to in vv.10–13 (cf. v.7), may be thought to utilize language related to the Stoic doctrine of cosmic conflagration (*ekpyrōsis*), by which a reconstituted cosmos was anticipated (cf. *SVF* 2.617), and to coincide with the OT depiction of the coming of the day of the Lord. It would appear that in 2 Peter the writer engages the Hellenistic outlook on immortality and moral accountability. Epicureans wholly rejected the notion of an afterlife, while Stoics viewed human life as eventually reabsorbed into the cosmos. Regardless of the precise version of paganized cosmology he is mirroring, the writer adjusts this with the Jewish-Christian apocalyptic, eschatological framework (cf. Mal 3:2–5; 4:1; 2Th 1:8; Heb 10:27). And here eschatology is not in the service of theology proper, as commentators are inclined to interpret it; rather, eschatology in 2 Peter 3 is in the service of ethics.

11 In the teaching of 2 Peter, eschatology and ethics are indivisible. The certainty of judgment and the inevitability of "that day" (thus, e.g., Ob 1:8; Joel 2; Mic 4; and Zep 1) of moral reckoning prod believers on to holy living. Christians by nature are future-oriented rather than being fixed solely on the present. Creation and all of life point to a climax in the purposes of God. Outside the community of faith, from the perspective of nihilism and self-indulgent living, there is nothing ultimately to live for. Therefore, it matters how the readers of 2 Peter orient their lives.

13 From the Christian perspective, the passing of everything in this age unveils the reality of the coming age, all in accordance with God's promise. The writer closes out his eschatological exhortation, just as he introduced his letter, with the catchword "righteousness" (cf. 1:1; 13; 2:5, 7–8, 21): the new home (cf. Isa 65:17 and 66:22) to be anticipated is one "where righteousness dwells." The goal is transformation.

REFLECTIONS

While skeptics mock the fundamental notion of being called to account for their deeds, the faithful are to reflect on the ways of God in the past as he touched human affairs. For the readers, a proper perspective toward God's dealings is crucial. This entails the realization that God's purposes are a mystery. Many of the psalms articulate the agony of the human perspective: Why do the wicked prosper? And how long must the righteous endure suffering? Why does God refuse to act? Why is God lax concerning his promises?

If believers are to persevere in faith amidst social decay and moral skepticism, they need to recognize the difference between the human and divine perspectives. The plight of human beings, as least from an earthly perspective, is framed vividly by the psalmist in Psalm 13:1–2:

How long, O Lord? Will you forget me forever?
  How long will you hide your face from me?
How long must I wrestle with my thoughts
  and every day have sorrow in my heart?
  How long will my enemy triumph over me?

The apostolic wisdom applied to this vexing quandary is rooted in an adjusted perspective—the divine perspective. To the Lord, a day is like a millennium, and a millennium like a day. This language, reminiscent of Psalm 90:4 and surfacing in several intertestamental Jewish texts, is not chronological but comparative in its function. A prayer ascribed to Moses, Psalm 90 is a meditative reflection on the transient nature of our days: "they quickly pass, and we fly away" (90:10c). This contrasts with the Lord's dwelling in eternity: "from everlasting to everlasting you are God" (90:2b).

Significantly, not only the relativity of time but also its importance are integral parts of Psalm 90. This may be why 2 Peter 3:8 restates Psalm 90:4: "With the Lord a day is like a thousand years, and a thousand years are like a day." After the psalmist observes that our days pass quickly and we fly away, he offers this prayer: "Teach us to number our days aright, that we may gain a heart of wisdom" (Ps 90:12).

D. Final Exhortation and Doxology (3:14–18)

[14]So then, dear friends, since you are looking forward to this, make every effort to be found spotless, blameless and at peace with him. [15]Bear in mind that our Lord's patience means salvation, just as our dear brother Paul also wrote you with the wisdom that God gave him. [16]He writes the same way in all his letters, speaking in them of these matters. His

letters contain some things that are hard to understand, which ignorant and unstable people distort, as they do the other Scriptures, to their own destruction.

[17]Therefore, dear friends, since you already know this, be on your guard so that you may not be carried away by the error of lawless men and fall from your secure position. [18]But grow in the grace and knowledge of our Lord and Savior Jesus Christ. To him be glory both now and forever! Amen.

COMMENTARY

14–16 In the saints' present struggle to discern God's timing and patience, Peter's audience is to "make every effort" (*spoudazō*, also in 1:10, 15; GK *5079*) in striving toward three aims: (1) being spotless and blameless (cf. Jude 24); (2) being at peace with the Lord; and (3) viewing God's long-suffering as leading to the salvation of others. While the reader may not automatically see a connection between these three imperatives, they hinge on one another.

The first priority is foundational and affects one's ability to realize the other two. The saints are called to—and remain in—an impure, vulgar world. In spite of seemingly overwhelming cultural obstacles facing the Christian community, everything for life and godliness has already been provided, based on God's grace (1:3–4). The resources are there; what remains to be determined is the saints' willingness.

It is no coincidence that the same language employed earlier in the epistle to characterize those troubling the community occurs again. Those following their corrupt desires and despising authority (2:10a) are portrayed as "blots and blemishes" (2:13). Peter's concluding exhortation is that the faithful, in contrast, be without blot or blemish (3:14; cf. 1Pe 1:19). Christian truth-claims are only as authoritative as the vessels bearing them.

The second and third priorities relate to the first. The human tendency is to question God: "Where are you, God? How long, Lord?" Hence

at the heart of the ethical imperative lies the challenge of finding the place of God's peace, bearing in mind that others' salvation is lodged within the heart of God. The Lord, after all, does not want anyone to perish (3:9). The day of the Lord is a day of both justice and vindication. Yet, since God's timing and purpose are beyond human comprehension, believers are challenged to find the place of rest and peace as they await his activity and struggle with the mystery of divine purpose.

Meanwhile, this will entail enduring hardship as disciples of Christ, and this in a world at cross-purposes with its Creator. To endure is to manifest Christian virtue, to be godly in character (1:6). Human perseverance is born out of the deep conviction that God perseveres on our behalf: the Lord wants none to perish. God takes into account human freedom and does not restrict it.

Here it is not Peter the theologian who is speaking; it is rather Peter the pastor and apostle. Paul was the acknowledged theologian: "just as our dear brother Paul also wrote you with the wisdom that God gave him ... speaking in [all his letters] of these matters—i.e., about the nature of salvation (*sōtēr* [GK *5400*], a key word in the letter: 1:1, 11; 2:20; 3:2, 18) and the long-suffering of God. It is true, Peter grants, that these mysteries are "hard to understand," causing some to distort and pervert them for their own purposes.

17 The faithful, however, stand in bold contrast; they are prepared for these distortions and in steadfastness refuse to be carried away by the error of the wicked. As he concludes his letter, Peter reminds his readers once more that indeed it is possible for them to be affected by the lawless and thereby "fall from [their] secure position." If the angels, who were exposed to incomparable glory, fell from that exalted position (2:4), then the lesson is clear: the community must take moral agency seriously and be vigilant. They are responsible and accountable; therefore, they are to "be on [their] guard" (*phylasso*, GK *5785*).

It is possible to be exposed to the truth, as Peter had this utmost privilege years earlier (1:16–18; cf. Mt 17:1–8; Mk 9:2–8; Lk 9:28–36), and yet negate that truth, as Peter is personally and painfully aware (Mt 26:69–75; Mk 14:66–72; Lk 22:54–62). This denial of the truth may happen through fear, self-centeredness, or immorality. The man writing knows whereof he speaks; his is a poignant, lifelong memory of confession followed by denial (cf. Mt 16:13–20; 26:69–75). Thus the Petrine admonition has a decided ring of authority, an authority fashioned out of painfully difficult experience through the years: "Be on your guard so that you may not be carried away . . . and fall from your secure position."

18 Fittingly, the antidote to this possibility is repeated in the letter's concluding statement, just as it had appeared in the greeting (1:2): the readers are to grow in the "grace and knowledge" of their Lord and Savior Jesus Christ. The epistolary conclusion reveals a double inclusio: "making every effort" (1:5//3:14) and "grace and knowledge" of the Lord (1:2//3:18). The letter ends somewhat abruptly and without the customary epistolary features one might expect to find—personal wishes, greetings, instructions, requests, and so forth. The doxology "to him be glory both now and forever!" is ascribed to Christ alone and is thought unusual when contrasted with other NT doxologies.

NOTES

17 The use of φυλάσσω, *phylasso* (GK *5875*), applies to a soldier, while its nominal form, φυλακή, *phylakē* (GK *5871*), is the generic term for "prison." Most commentary that assumes 2 Peter not to be authentically Petrine fails to take seriously the personal and autobiographical element in the epistle, and 3:17 ("be on your guard") is an example. The writer's authority (and passion) issues out of the agony he himself has carried his whole life since his denial that he knew Jesus.

The term "secure position" (στηριγμός, *stērigmos* [GK *5113*] is the antithesis of the opponents, who are described as "unstable" (ἀστήρικτος, *astēriktos* [2:14; 3:16]). In Luke 22:32, the verb στηρίζω, *stērizō* (GK *5114*), is applied to Peter himself by Jesus: "When you have turned back, strengthen your brothers."

18 For Hillyer, 226–27, the concluding doxology is an indication of an early rather than late date for the letter: "If the letter had been written later than Peter's lifetime, a more stereotyped liturgical doxology would have been expected. . . . Before the end of the first century, stereotyped formulas to round off doxologies were commonplace, so Peter's unusual expressions . . . offer evidence for its authenticity."

1 JOHN

TOM THATCHER

Introduction

1. OPENING COMMENTS

The three epistles of John preserve the history and beliefs of Johannine Christianity, a distinct branch of the early church. While 1–2–3 John bear many similarities to Acts and the Pauline letters, they reveal a community with a unique experience and a unique perspective on Christian life and teaching. This community struggled with a number of serious difficulties arising from both external pressures and internal problems. As a result, Johannine thought often challenges the perspective of modern Christians who have grown comfortable in their faith.

The Johannine literature (the fourth gospel and 1–2–3 John) is perhaps the most loved and least understood section of the NT. Passages such as John 3:16, the "Good Shepherd" (Jn 10), and "God is love" (1Jn 4:8) have become slogans for the contemporary portrait of Christianity as a religion of charity and benevolence. Ironically, the warm universalism implied in these verses contradicts the main thrust of Johannine thought. While John is obsessed with God's love and the need for Christians to show love, he is also careful to distinguish those who should receive this love from those who should not. For this reason, the perspective of the Johannine letters is harder and more skeptical than that of Paul, being fueled by a dualism that rigorously discriminates between truth and falsehood. Because John believes that only true believers should enjoy the love of God and the fellowship of the church, 1–2–3 John are dominated by the themes of true faith and discipleship.

The author of 1–2–3 John hopes to guide believers to true faith and to protect them from falsehood. All three letters offer objective tests that Christians can apply to distinguish true believers from the rest of the world. True Christians, in John's view, can be identified by what they "know," which in these letters includes both doctrine and lifestyle. Following the adage "by their fruits you will know them," John suggests that true believers will adhere to certain confessional statements and will live in accordance with the implications of those statements. This produces a discussion that focuses heavily on obedience and offers grace only to those who think and walk within prescribed boundaries.

While it is always necessary to consider the historical background of a book before proceeding to exegesis, such considerations are particularly important to the analysis of 1–2–3 John. A careful introductory study of the historical setting of these letters will simplify many interpretive problems.

415

2. AUTHOR OF 1–2–3 JOHN

Like Hebrews, 1 John does not name its author and audience, and the author of 2 and 3 John refers to himself only as "the Elder." The authorship of these books must therefore be deduced from the limited internal evidence offered by the letters themselves, along with the testimony of the church fathers.

It is clear that the author of 1–2–3 John wishes to maintain a pastoral relationship with his audience. John refers to his readers as "[my] children" (*teknia*, GK *5451*, or *paidia*, GK *4086*) seven times (1Jn 2:12, 18, 28; 3:7, 18; 4:4; 5:21) and "beloved" (*agapētoi*, GK *28*; NIV, "dear friends") six times (2:7; 3:2, 21; 4:1, 7, 11). In 1 John 3:13 he calls them "brothers" (*adelphoi*, GK *81*), the term used throughout the letter to characterize the relationship between all Christians (cf. 2:9–11; 4:10–17). This familial terminology emphasizes the author's love for the audience but also, as elsewhere in the NT, implies an expectation of their loyalty (cf. Phm 1, 20; 1Ti 1:1–2; 2Ti 1:1–2, 2:1; Tit 1:4; 2Pe 3:1–14). This is particularly evident in 3 John, where the Elder refers to his addressee, Gaius, as "dear friend" ("beloved") before each exhortation (vv. 2, 5, 11) and says that he is pleased with reports of Gaius's obedience because he is always glad to hear that "my children are walking in the truth" (v. 4). The pastoral authority claimed by the Elder seems to be transcongregational, extending to many individual churches and their leaders. He feels confident to command both "the chosen lady" and Gaius, apparently leaders of their respective churches, to reject certain teachers and accept others (2Jn 10–11; 3Jn 12), and plans to take disciplinary action against another leader, Diotrephes, who has not followed his instructions (3Jn 9–10). The Elder also claims the right to visit individual churches to instruct and encourage them (2Jn 12; 3Jn 14). In exchange for his loving patronage, then, the author expects to enjoy the audience's obedience.

a. The Traditional View of Authorship

Beyond this very general profile based on internal data, the only other ancient evidence for the authorship of 1–2–3 John comes from the church fathers. Because the author of these letters, or at least of 1 John, was apparently also involved in the composition of the fourth gospel, ancient testimony concerning that book is helpful here also. It is clear that these writings were associated with the apostle John, a member of the "inner circle" of Jesus' disciples (Mk 5:37; 9:2; 14:33), by the end of the second century AD. The editors of the Muratorian Canon (1.34–35; ca. AD 200), a list of books considered sacred and authoritative by the church in Rome, associated 1 John with the fourth gospel and said both were written by the apostle John:

> When his fellow-disciples and bishops urged him [to write a gospel, John] said: "Fast with me from today for three days, and what will be revealed to each one [of us] let us relate to one another." In the same night it was revealed to Andrew, one of the apostles, that, whilst all were to go over [the gospel], John in his own name should write everything down. . . . What wonder then if John . . . adduces particular points in his epistles also, where . . . he confesses (himself) not merely an eye and ear witness [1Jn 1:1–3], but also a writer of all the marvels of the Lord in order.

Further support is offered by Irenaeus, the bishop of Lyons. In a treatise written about AD 180, Irenaeus relates the apparently widespread belief that "John, the disciple of the Lord, who also leaned upon his breast [Jn 13:23], did himself publish a Gospel during his residence at Ephesus." Later in the same work, Irenaeus quotes both 1 and 2 John and attributes these letters to John the apostle as well (*Haer.* 3.1.1; 3.16.5, 8). At about the same time, Clement of Alexandria (AD 190s), Origen's teacher, offered the theory, still popular today, that John the apostle wrote a "spiritual Gospel" as a theological supplement to the Synoptics (cited in Eusebius, *Hist. eccl.* 6.14.7). By the end of the second century, then, the Johannine letters were widely associated with the fourth gospel under the common authorship of John the apostle. This position may therefore be referred to as the "traditional view" of the authorship of 1–2–3 John.

While the early testimony supports the apostolic authorship of 1–2–3 John, one major variation of the traditional view, also based on patristic evidence, should be mentioned. The debate centers on an obscure statement by Papias, one of the earliest postapostolic sources available. According to early Christian tradition, Papias was a disciple of the apostle John in Ephesus at the end of the first century. The "Anti-Marcionite Prologues," introductory notes to a mid-second century canon, even suggest that Papias wrote the fourth gospel for the apostle John by dictation. Unfortunately, Papias's writings no longer exist, but several quotations from his work were preserved by the church historian Eusebius (AD 320s). Eusebius (*Hist. eccl.* 3.39.2–6) did not accept the popular legends about Papias and attempted to disprove them from Papias's own writings (the quotation from Papias appears in italics below):

> Papias himself, according to the preface of his treatises, makes plain that he had in no way been a hearer and eyewitness of the sacred apostles but teaches that he had received the articles of the faith from those who had known them [i.e., from disciples of the apostles], for he speaks as follows: *"And I shall not hesitate to append to the interpretations all that I ever learnt well from the presbyters and remember well, for of their truth I am confident. For unlike most I did not rejoice in them who say much, but in them who teach the truth, nor in them who recount the commandments of others, but in them who repeated those given to the faith by the Lord and derived from truth itself; but if ever anyone came who had followed the presbyters, I inquired into the words of the presbyters, what Andrew or Philip or Peter or Thomas or James or John or Matthew, or any other of the Lord's disciples, had said, and what Aristion and the presbyter John, the Lord's disciples, were saying. For I did not suppose that information from books would help me so much as the word from a living and surviving voice."* It is here worth noting that he twice counts the name of "John," and reckons the first "John" with Peter and James and Matthew and the other Apostles, clearly meaning the evangelist, but by changing his statement places the second ["John"] with the others outside the number of the Apostles, putting Aristion before him and clearly calling him a "presbyter."

In its original context, Papias's statement was intended to stress the validity of his own teaching (which included comments on 1 John and Revelation) on the basis that his doctrine had been shaped by people with a close connection to Jesus. His wording, however, is obviously unclear and seems to include two distinct lists of people whose teaching he solicited: "the Lord's disciples," people such as Andrew and Peter, and "the presbyters," people such as Aristion. Both lists include a "John." Since Papias's Christian training occurred in Ephesus, this raises the possibility that there were two early Christian leaders in Ephesus named "John," one the apostle and one the presbyter or "Elder."

Several modern scholars have developed this possibility that there were two "Johns" associated with Ephesus. Commenting on the passage cited above, Martin Hengel (*The Johannine Question* [Philadelphia: Trinity, 1989], 28–31) argues that "whereas the first group of seven well-known names [mentioned by Papias] belongs in the rather distant past [i.e., before Papias's time], the two disciples of the second group [Aristion and John] come from the time of the author." Stressing this distinction, Hengel argues that the second John, the Elder, was the one known to Papias. It is this person, in Hengel's view, who wrote the gospel of John and the Johannine letters, which explains why he refers to himself as "the Elder" in the introductions to 2 and 3 John. This variation of the traditional view, then, suggests that the Johannine letters were written by John the Elder of Ephesus, who may have been a disciple of Jesus or possibly a disciple of one of the apostles but who was not himself an apostle.

b. The "School" Approach of Authorship

The traditional view has been challenged in recent years by those who see the Johannine literature as the product of a group of unknown teachers. These scholars prefer to think of a "Johannine school" rather than a single author. This "school" consisted of the founder of the Johannine community ("John") and his disciples, who helped promote and develop his teaching. The identity of the founder of this school, perhaps the "Beloved Disciple" of the fourth gospel, cannot now be determined, but he probably died before the epistles were written (cf. Jn 21:20–23). The notion of a Johannine school has received significant support from the "developmental approach" to the composition of the Johannine literature. Advocates of the developmental approach believe that the fourth gospel was gradually "developed" through a series of revisions by "John," and later by his disciples, to keep its material relevant to immediate community concerns. 1–2–3 John were written sometime during or just after the gospel's development in response to a specific doctrinal crisis in the Johannine community. Most advocates of this position insist that the actual author(s) of 1–2–3 John was not a disciple of Jesus, although some believe that the founder of the community ("John") may have had some contact with the historical Jesus. Most recent commentaries adopt some version of the Johannine school approach to explain the authorship of 1–2–3 John.[1]

c. Conclusion on Authorship

A key passage in the debate between the traditional view and the school approach is 1 John 1:1–3. There the author says that the orthodox Christian witness about Jesus concerns that "which we have heard, which we have seen with our eyes, which we have looked at and our hands have touched . . . which was with the Father and has appeared to us." Proponents of the school approach believe that the word "we" in these verses refers to a group of Johannine teachers who claimed to preserve the true and authoritative doctrine promoted by their dead founder. Since none of these teachers were actual disciples of the historical Jesus, the apparent references to a physical experience are simply intended to stress the authority of this "corporate tradition." As Rensberger, 47, puts it, the author of 1 John uses these references to stress that he "or the group [of teachers] that he represents, is a link in the chain of testimony extending from the events of the revelation of eternal life in Jesus to the readers of 1 John." Further, the emphasis on physical experience—"heard," "seen," "touched"—is intended to stress the human physicality of Jesus against a heretical devaluation of his humanity and a denial that the Christ came in the flesh (cf. Brown, 159–61; Lieu, 23–27; Johnson, 26–27). From this perspective, the prologue to 1 John accomplishes two things at once: stressing the authority of the author's doctrine while staging his attack on heretical Christology.

---

1. Current versions of the developmental approach originate with J. Louis Martyn's *History and Theology in the Fourth Gospel* (Nashville: Abingdon, 1968), which provided the interpretive rationale for the theory. Many scholars who currently adopt this position avoid the term "school" due to uncertainties about the nature of philosophical and religious schools in the ancient world.

While this interpretation is reasonable, three pieces of evidence must be weighed against it. First, the author of 1 John uses verbs that refer to a physical experience of Jesus seven times in 1:1–3, all in the first person ("we"). His "testimony" (*martyreō*, GK *3455*) and "proclamation" (*apangellō*, GK *550*) are connected to verbs of sight and hearing in vv.2–3, and his authority is based on the claim that he has "heard," "seen," and "touched" something concerning "the Word of life." Second, as will be seen below, it is clear that the author's authority has been challenged by rival teachers with a different view of Christ. These other teachers, whom the author calls Antichrists, seem to disagree with him on key points of the Johannine Jesus tradition and have apparently persuaded some Johannine Christians to accept their position. Third, most scholars would agree that the Johannine Jesus tradition was still in a fluid state at the time the epistles were written. Whether or not the writing of the fourth gospel was complete by this time, the letters reflect a setting in which oral teaching about Jesus was still seen as equally authoritative to written gospels. In light of these three considerations, 1 John 1:1–3 seems to be a claim that the author is an actual witness to the life of the historical Jesus. Authority in oral cultures is established by age and experience, and it would be natural for the Elder to validate his version of the gospel by claiming to have been an actual eyewitness to the major points of the story. He therefore stresses that his information about "the Word of life" is firsthand, because he has heard, seen, and touched the historical Jesus who is at the core of the tradition.

While these considerations lend credence to the view that 1–2–3 John were written by a person who claimed to be a disciple of Jesus, they do not prove or even suggest that this person was the Beloved Disciple—the apostle John—or John the Elder of Ephesus. They also do not discount the many indications from the letters themselves that numerous teachers were at work in the Johannine churches. The view adopted here therefore combines elements of the traditional view and the school approach.

Behind the Johannine literature, there seems to have been a group of teachers united by common adherence to the founder of the Johannine community. The authority of the founder, the Elder, was based on his claim to be a disciple of the historical Jesus, and this person was probably the source, if not the author, of the material in the fourth gospel. The absence of any specific identification within the letters themselves and the uncertainties surrounding the evidence from the early church make it impossible to reach a dogmatic conclusion on the Elder's identity. The ancient evidence points to John the apostle. If John is not the author, his name was probably attached to these letters in the mid-second century to enhance their prestige during the early debates over canonicity. For convenience, the author of 1–2–3 John will be referred to as "John" or "the Elder" throughout this introduction and commentary.

3. HISTORICAL SETTING OF 1–2–3 JOHN

The audience of 1–2–3 John seems to have been members of a group of house churches with local independent leaders who look to the author as their superior and patron. Several of these local leaders—Gaius (3Jn 1), the "chosen lady" (2Jn 1), and the rebellious Diotrephes (3Jn 9–10)—are mentioned in the letters. Similar to the Pauline system of administration, this network of churches was managed by a group of John's disciples, including Demetrius and "the brothers" mentioned at 3 John 5–6, 12. From ancient times, scholars have situated these churches in western Asia Minor, with John's headquarters in Ephesus (Irenaeus, *Haer.* 3.3.4; Eusebius, *Hist. eccl.* 3.1.1; 3.23.3–4; 3.39.6; Hengel, *Johannine Question*, 30–31). Recent scholarship has focused on the experiences of these churches as keys to the tone and content of 1–2–3 John.

a. "The World" and "the Jews"

The Johannine literature promotes a dualistic worldview. "Dualism" may be loosely defined as the belief that there are two forces at work in the universe, one "good" and the other "evil." These forces are absolute and completely opposed, so that no person or thing can participate in both at the same time. The dualistic perspective often expresses itself in the use of labels that imply polar oppositions: "good/evil," "light/dark," "white/black," "true/false," and "love/hate." A convenient illustration of Johannine dualism appears at John 3:16–21. This section opens with the famous statement that "God so loved the world that he gave his one and only Son," implying that God intends to bring salvation to everyone. Indeed, "God did not send the Son into the world to condemn the world, but to save the world through him." But Jesus immediately clarifies that "whoever does not believe stands condemned already," for such people "love darkness instead of light." "Light/dark," "love/hate," and "saved/condemned" are key oppositions in Johannine dualism, ways of labeling people to clarify their place in the cosmic scheme of things. Jesus is the "light" and all those who believe in him "walk in the light" and enjoy forgiveness of sins (1Jn 1:7), while those who do not believe are lost in a satanic darkness. There are no innocent bystanders in this battle between light and darkness, for all people either "love" the light and "hate" the darkness or "love" the darkness and "hate" the light. Such language indicates a dualistic worldview.

From this dualistic perspective John sees that there are two types of people. The first group, those on the side of God and light, are the "children of God" who have been "born again" (Jn 1:12; 3:3–5; 1Jn 4:7). Logically one would expect John to call the second group "children of the devil," but instead he refers to those who reject Jesus as "the world." Although God loves the world, this love is unrequited, for the world hates Jesus and rejoices over his death (Jn 7:7; 16:20). Because the disciples are "not of the world," Jesus warns them that the world will hate them also (Jn 15:18–19; 17:14–16). There is hope for believers, however, for Jesus has overcome the world (Jn 16:33), and they may also overcome the world by keeping their faith in him (1Jn 5:4–5). In John's view, every person in "the world" operates in willful rejection of, and open hostility toward, all that Jesus represents. While it is impossible to know for certain why John felt this way, it is reasonable to conclude that he had experienced persecution at some point from nonbelievers, making him suspicious of "the world" and suggesting that all those in "the world" are enemies of Christ and the church.

The key to this experience of suffering may lie in another dualistic label that appears frequently in the gospel of John, namely, "the Jews." It is clear that John does not use the term "Jews" in the obvious sense to describe people of a specific ethnic or religious background. For example, in John 5:15, the man whom Jesus heals at Bethesda "told the Jews that it was Jesus who had made him well," and in 13:33 Jesus tells his disciples, "as I told the Jews, so I tell you now: Where I am going, you cannot come." In both cases "the Jews" are in a separate category from Jesus and the disciples, despite the fact that both Jesus and the disciples are Jewish by race and religious heritage. Similarly, John's Jesus several times refers to the OT as "your own Law" when debating with "the Jews" (Jn 8:17; 10:34), even though Jesus, as God incarnate (1:1–4), presumably authored the Scriptures.

This distinction between "Jews" and disciples does not mark a friendly coexistence. The disciples are "born of God" (Jn 1:12–13; 1Jn 3:1; 4:7), while the Jews are children of the devil, who is a "murderer" and "liar" (Jn 8:44). Not surprisingly the Jews constantly seek to do the devil's work of harassing those who might accept Jesus (Jn 9:22; 19:38–39). In John's vocabulary, "the Jews" seem to be Jewish people who reject Jesus and subsequently abuse his disciples. Because they reject Jesus, all "Jews" are also members of the world.

The Johannine presentation of the Jews probably derives from John's own experience of persecution from Jewish people who refused to accept the gospel. Jesus warns his disciples that they will be outcasts from the synagogue (Jn 16:1–4), perhaps alluding to an excommunication John and his audience had already experienced by the time 1–2–3 John were written. Removed from the relative safety of the Jewish community, the Johannine Christians would be left alone to face a hostile and unbelieving world on their own, without enjoying the rights and privileges granted to Jews in the Roman Empire.

b. The "Antichrists"

John's division of all people into two groups—"disciples" versus "the world/the Jews"—suggests that the Johannine churches faced persecution and alienation from outsiders. Many passages from 1–2–3 John suggest that another danger was lurking within the Christian community itself. These texts relate to a group of people whom John calls "Antichrists" (1Jn 2:18). While John reveals very little about this group, many theories on the nature of their doctrine and origins have been suggested. It will be helpful to examine the limited internal evidence from the letters before reaching a conclusion about the identity of John's rivals.

The Antichrists are first mentioned at 1 John 2:18, where the Elder warns his "children" that "as you have heard that the Antichrist is coming, even now many Antichrists have come." The name John gives them reveals his major contention with them. The Greek prefix *anti-* can mean both "against" and "in place of," so that an Antichrist is apparently a person who advocates another doctrine of Christ "in place of" the doctrine John teaches. The Antichrists disagreed with John about the relationship between the human and divine aspects of Jesus' nature. In John's view the divine Christ was incarnate in the human Jesus (Jn 1:14), so that the divine Christ, "who came by water and blood" (1Jn 5:6), could be seen and touched (1Jn 1:1–2). Jesus was, then, both fully human and fully divine at the same time. The Antichrists, however, held that the human Jesus and the divine Christ must be kept separate, with primary emphasis being placed on his divine nature. They therefore disputed John's claim that "Jesus [the human being] is the [spiritual] Christ" and that "Jesus [the] Christ has come in the flesh" (1Jn 2:22; 4:3; 2Jn 7). Because they did not accept his "witness," John refers to the Antichrists as liars and deceivers (1Jn 2:22; 2Jn 7).

Despite John's polemical protests, it is clear that the Antichrists, unlike "the world" and "the Jews," were an *internal* threat to the community. John's admission that "they went out from us" (1Jn 2:19) indicates that even he considered them Christian at one time, and it seems that Diotrephes, a congregational leader, prefers their doctrine over that of John (3Jn 9–10). The Antichrists were probably former disciples of John, Christian teachers who departed from the traditional Christology. Because they were known to and accepted by members of John's churches, it was easy for them to secure a following. The Elder therefore goes to pains to specify that true believers must accept the orthodox view, for "no one who denies the Son [Jesus] has the Father [God] also" (1Jn 2:23).

The Antichrists' distinction between the human Jesus and the spiritual Christ has led many to conclude that they were Gnostics. The theory that John wrote in response to a Gnostic heresy originates with the church fathers. Irenaeus (*Haer.* 1.26.1; 3.3.4) records an encounter between the apostle John and Cerinthus, an early teacher associated with the Gnostic movement. Cerinthus seems to have taught that "the Christ," a divine spiritual being, descended on the human Jesus at his baptism and "possessed" him until his crucifixion, departing from Jesus just before his death.

The Antichrists have also been associated with another early branch of Gnosticism called "Docetism." Docetists, from the Greek *dokeō* ("to seem," GK *1506*), believed that "the Christ" was a purely spiritual being who only "seemed" to have a human body (Jesus), thus denying the incarnation. The writings of Ignatius (AD 115; *Trall.* 9–10; *Smyrn.* 2–7) indicate that Docetists were active in western Asia Minor not long after the Johannine literature was produced. Although the suggestion that the Antichrists were Gnostics offers a quick and convenient historical backdrop for the Johannine letters, it is important to stress that "while striking parallels can be adduced between early known heresies and the epistles of John, none of these heresies perfectly mirrors the false teachings of 1 and 2 John" (Thompson, 18; cf. Rensberger, 22–24). The origins and development of Gnostic thought are far from certain, and the available evidence suggests that the Gnostic movement was composed of a large number of independent teachers whose views were similar but distinct. The label "Gnostic" is therefore not especially helpful and can, in fact, be detrimental to analysis of 1–2–3 John, especially since the Antichrists' doctrine does not seem to bear all the characteristics of Gnostic thought.

Whether or not the Antichrists were Gnostics or part of a larger "incipient Gnosticism," two questions must be answered. First, why did the Antichrists distinguish between the spiritual Christ and the human Jesus? Second, on what basis could the Antichrists successfully dispute the Elder's authority, especially since the Elder's position on Jesus seems to represent the established beliefs of the community? The answer to both questions may lie in John's own teaching about Jesus.

Most scholars today believe that the major points of the Johannine Jesus tradition, and perhaps of the fourth gospel, had been thoroughly established before the writing of 1–2–3 John (see R. Brown, *The Community of the Beloved Disciple* [New York: Paulist, 1979], 106–7, 138–44; Smalley, xxvi–xxvii; von Wahlde, 114–22; Rensberger, 24). According to this established tradition, Jesus made a number of specific promises to the disciples during the Last Supper concerning the coming of the Holy Spirit, or "Paraclete." It is clear from these "Paraclete Sayings," preserved now in the fourth gospel's farewell address (Jn 13–17), that the Johannine Christians understood the Spirit to be Jesus' living presence in the community and also understood that the Spirit would continue to offer the teaching and guidance provided by the human Jesus. Indeed, Jesus himself would "come to you" in the form of the "Spirit of truth," who would "live with you" and "be in you" (Jn 14:16–18). As such, the Paraclete would "teach you all things" (14:26) and "guide you into all truth," speaking not his own words but the words given to him by Jesus (16:13).

These passages suggest that every individual Christian receives the Spirit and enjoys the continuing presence of Jesus through the Spirit's work. For this reason, the author of 1 John can assure his audience that "we know that he lives in us . . . by the Spirit he gave us" (3:24) and can remind them that the Spirit testifies to Jesus as the Son of God (5:7). In fact, even the message of the Antichrists originates in the spirit realm, although the spirit that guides them, the "spirit of falsehood," is "from the world" (1Jn 4:1–6; cf. 1Co 12:1–3). It seems, then, that the Johannine community believed strongly in the continuing work of Jesus through the Holy Spirit and in the work of other "spirits" that led people to oppose God and truth.

From John's perspective, this teaching about the Paraclete establishes a close connection between the human Jesus of the past and the divine Spirit of God who continues to operate in the community after Jesus' death. But it seems that the Antichrists interpreted Jesus' words about the Spirit in a different way: if the resurrected Lord, through the Spirit, continues to speak and act in the church, there is little need to worry about the life and teachings of the human Jesus. In fact, if the same divine Word that appeared incarnate in the human Jesus continues to speak through believers, there is really not so much difference between Christians and Jesus himself.

From this perspective, there would be no point in stressing that "Jesus [the man] is the [spiritual] Christ," for every believer possesses the spiritual Christ in the form of the Paraclete. Further, from the Antichrists' perspective, anything that the Spirit seems to be saying *now* would be just as authoritative as anything the human Jesus said *then*. Following this principle, the Antichrists could freely modify or reinterpret the established Jesus tradition in the light of new revelations. Rensberger, 24, notes, "If the opponents claimed that their ideas were inspired by the Spirit . . . , they would not hesitate to offer *new* concepts built up from their basic interpretation of the tradition" (cf. Brown, *Community of the Beloved Disciple*, 138–42; Gary Burge, *The Anointed Community* [Grand Rapids: Eerdmans, 1987], 218–19). These new concepts, of course, would be of equal authority with the Elder's teachings.

This reconstruction of the Antichrists' position answers both questions raised above. Their own experience of the Spirit made it unnecessary for them to differentiate between the human Jesus and the spiritual Christ, who continued to speak and act as the Paraclete. To defend this position, they could interpret the tradition now preserved in John 14:18 to mean that Jesus' human body was only a temporary abode for the Word of God, who now dwelt within all believers. This first conclusion would naturally answer the second question, for those who are guided by the Spirit of God would have no need to submit to the Elder or anyone else in regard to their judgments about life and faith. For this reason the Antichrists posed a serious threat to John's authority and to the orthodox understanding of Jesus' life and teaching.

4. STRUCTURE

While 2 and 3 John follow standard epistolary formats, the genre of 1 John is difficult to determine. Although 1 John seems to address the needs of a specific group of believers, it lacks the formal introduction and conclusion typical of ancient letters, and its structure does not follow a standard epistolary outline. First John has therefore been variously described as "an essay or sermon or enchiridion or church order" (Rensberger, 30), and one commentator compares it to "a musical reprise" (Johnson, 15).

Whether or not 1 John can be ascribed to a specific genre, it seems likely that the book was a circular intended to be read aloud in meetings of the various house churches under John's jurisdiction. It was probably delivered to the various churches by John's disciples, "the brothers" mentioned in 3 John 5–8. To help local leaders distinguish between "the brothers" and the Antichrists, the Elder presumably sent letters of recommendation with his official envoys. Third John is probably one such letter. The bearers of these recommendations most likely read 1 John to the gathered churches and explained its implications to them.

First John breaks down into two major sections, reflecting the two major conflicts John faced. After a brief prologue that introduces the christological issue and establishes the need to create boundaries (1:1–4), the first major section (1:5–2:17) distinguishes those who are "in the world" from those who have "overcome the world." The second major section (2:18–5:21) further distinguishes true disciples from Antichrists. Within each section, John presents a series of tests that will help the audience determine who is "in" and who is, or who should be, "out" of true fellowship with God. These "tests" take the form of the oft-discussed "slogans" of 1 John, statements that sort individuals into absolute dualistic categories based on their beliefs or behaviors. Both 2 and 3 John present warnings and encouragement, while stressing the Elder's desire to maintain fellowship with the recipients.

5. SUMMARY

1–2–3 John were written to a church facing external and internal pressures. Forces outside the community—"the world" and "the Jews"—brought the threat of persecution, challenging believers to abandon the faith. In the face of this hostility, the leadership of the group had fragmented. The founder of the community, John, was being opposed by some of his former disciples. These opponents, claiming the Spirit's guidance, had reinterpreted the community's Jesus tradition and created a new Christology, which focused on the divinity of Christ while rejecting his humanity. 1–2–3 John are intended to encourage Christians to endure the persecution and to discourage them from accepting the doctrines of the Antichrists. In the process, John must reassert his own authority as a witness to the Jesus tradition and restate in the strongest possible terms the marks of true Christianity.

6. BIBLIOGRAPHY

The following is a selective list of commentaries and monographs on 1–2–3 John available in English, confined for the most part to those referred to in the commentary (they will be referred to simply by the author's name [and initials only when necessary to distinguish two authors of the same surname]). References to other resources will carry full bibliographic details at the first mention and thereafter a short title.

Barker, Glenn. *1–2–3 John*. Expositor's Bible Commentary. Grand Rapids: Zondervan, 1976.

Brown, Raymond. *The Epistles of John*. Anchor Bible. Garden City, N.Y.: Doubleday, 1982.

Bruce, F. F. *The Epistles of John: Introduction, Exposition, and Notes*. Grand Rapids: Eerdmans, 1970.

Bultmann, Rudolf. *The Johannine Epistles*. Translated by R. Philip O'Hara, Lane C. McGaughy, and Robert Funk. Hermeneia. Philadelphia: Fortress, 1973.

Culpepper, R. Alan. *1 John, 2 John, 3 John*. Knox Preaching Guides. Atlanta: John Knox, 1985.

Dodd, C. H. *The Johannine Epistles*. Moffatt New Testament Commentary. New York: Harper, 1946.

Grayston, Kenneth. *The Johannine Epistles*. New Century Bible Commentary. Grand Rapids: Eerdmans, 1984.

Houlden, J. L. *A Commentary on the Johannine Epistles*. Harper's New Testament Commentaries. New York: Harper and Row, 1973.

Johnson, Thomas F. *1, 2, and 3 John*. New International Bible Commentary. Peabody, Mass.: Hendrickson, 1993.

Lieu, Judith M. *The Theology of the Johannine Epistles*. Cambridge: Cambridge Univ. Press, 1991.

Malatesta, Edward. *Interiority and Covenant*. Rome: Biblical Institute, 1978.

Marshall, I. Howard. *The Epistles of John*. New International Commentary on the New Testament. Grand Rapids: Eerdmans, 1978.

Plummer, Alfred. *The Epistles of St. John*. 1886. Reprint. Grand Rapids: Baker, 1980.

Rensberger, David. *1 John, 2 John, 3 John*. Abingdon New Testament Commentaries. Nashville: Abingdon, 1997.

Schnackenburg, Rudolf. *The Johannine Epistles: Introduction and Commentary*. Translated by Reginald Fuller and Ilse Fuller. New York: Crossroad, 1992.

Smalley, Stephen. *1, 2, 3 John*. Word Biblical Commentary 51. Waco, Tex.: Word, 1984.

Stott, John R. W. *The Letters of John*. Revised Edition. Tyndale New Testament Commentaries. Grand Rapids: Eerdmans, 1988.

Thompson, Marianne Meye. *1–3 John*. IVP New Testament Commentary. Downers Grove, Ill.: InterVarsity, 1992.

von Wahlde, Urban. *The Johannine Commandments: 1 John and the Struggle for the Johannine Tradition*. New York: Paulist, 1990.

7. OUTLINE OF 1 JOHN

   I. Prologue: Setting the Boundaries (1:1–4)

  II. Tests to Distinguish True Disciples from the World (1:5–2:17)

      A. Test #1: Walking in the Light (1:5–10)

      B. Test #2: Keeping His Commands (2:1–6)

      C. Test #3: Loving Your Brothers (2:7–11)

      D. Test #4: Loving the World (2:12–17)

 III. Tests to Distinguish True Disciples from Antichrists (2:18–5:21)

      A. Test #5: The True Confession (2:18–27)

      B. Test #6: Living without Sin (2:28–3:24)

      C. Test #7: The True Spirit (4:1–6)

      D. Test #8: Perfect Love (4:7–21)

      E. Test #9: True Faith (5:1–13)

      F. Test #10: Sin That Leads to Death (5:14–21)

Text and Exposition

I. PROLOGUE: SETTING THE BOUNDARIES (1:1–4)

OVERVIEW

The prologue to 1 John draws a boundary between the author's group and his enemies—"the world" and the Antichrists. This boundary is ideological, categorizing people on the basis of whether or not they accept John's teaching—"the Word of Life." People in John's group enjoy a fellowship with God and Jesus that brings joy, and those who wish to enter this fellowship of joy must accept John's testimony unconditionally. Consistent with Johannine dualism, there is no compromise position: the reader must choose fellowship with John *or* fellowship with the world and must accept the consequences of that choice.

¹That which was from the beginning, which we have heard, which we have seen with our eyes, which we have looked at and our hands have touched—this we proclaim concerning the Word of life. ²The life appeared; we have seen it and testify to it, and we proclaim to you the eternal life, which was with the Father and has appeared to us. ³We proclaim to you what we have seen and heard, so that you also may have fellowship with us. And our fellowship is with the Father and with his Son, Jesus Christ. ⁴We write this to make our joy complete.

COMMENTARY

1 As in the gospel of John, the opening sentence of 1 John is based on Genesis 1:1, but with a slightly different application. John 1:1 emphasizes the deity of Jesus by placing him at the "beginning" (*archē*, GK *794*) of time, when God's creative Word spoke the universe into being. First John 1:1, however, emphasizes the humanity of Jesus by stressing that the one who existed from the "beginning" (*archē*) of time more recently appeared in human form. This focus is evident in the emphasis on the Word's empirical existence. Four verbs referring to sensory experience are used here to emphasize that the "Word of Life" is not only mystical and spiritual but also physical and tangible. This dual emphasis immediately distinguishes John's teaching from that of the Antichrists. While the Antichrists would argue that the church is guided by a mystical experience of the Holy Spirit, John insists that faith is founded on objective realities from a real moment in human history.

The Greek of 1:1–3 is notoriously complicated. One major set of problems concerns the meaning of *tou logou tēs zōēs* ("the Word of life") at the end of v.1. It is difficult, first of all, to determine whether *logos* ("word," GK *3364*) refers to Jesus personally or to John's message about Jesus. Since John elsewhere uses *logos* as a title for Christ (Jn 1:1–4; 14:6), many commentators understand "the Word" at

426

1 John 1:1 to be Jesus himself, the one who has been heard, seen, and touched. On the other hand, since the opening sentence includes the verb *apangellō* ("we proclaim," GK *550*, v.3), it may be that *logos* refers more generally to "the message" that "we proclaim," i.e., the gospel. Since John is stressing the validity of his own teaching, and since Jesus is clearly referred to as "the Life" in v.2, it seems most likely that "the Word" in v.1 is John's message about Jesus.

In what sense, then, is this a message "of life"? The genitive *tēs zōēs* (GK *2437*) may be translated "the word *which is life*" (appositive genitive), "the *life-giving* word" or "the *living* word" (descriptive genitive), or "the word *about life*" (objective genitive). John is probably using the term in the third sense to describe the substance of his message. The "word" that he proclaims is about "the Life," which was revealed in the specific form of the human Jesus. In John's view, the "word" of the Antichrists is wrong because it fails to recognize that this Life could be heard, seen, and touched.

2 Before finishing the thought of v.1, John pauses to elaborate the subject of his preaching, "the Life" (*hē zōē*, GK *2437*). "Life" is a key term in Johannine thought, appearing thirty-six times in the fourth gospel and thirteen times in 1–2–3 John. In the fourth gospel, *zōē* is an aspect of Christ's divine identity that he shares with the Father (Jn 1:4; 6:57; 14:6). As such, *zōē* has an eternal quality (Jn 3:16–17) that distinguishes it from *psychē* (GK *6034*), biological life. While all living things have *psychē*, Jesus has come into the world so that human beings may have *zōē*, divine life, as well (John 3:16; 11:25–26). Hence Jesus will "lay down his [physical] life [*psychē*]" so that his sheep may have spiritual "life [*zōē*] ... to the full" (Jn 10:10–11). This abundant life is available to those who "know God," i.e., those who accept Jesus as the one whom God has sent (Jn 17:3). The offer of life continues in the true Christian preaching, which proclaims the signs of Jesus'

deity so that all those who "believe that Jesus is the Christ, the Son of God ... may have life in his name" (Jn 20:31).

The emphasis on "life" in the fourth gospel may have contributed to the problem John is addressing in 1 John. The Antichrists could easily interpret these references to mean that the physical body of Jesus was expendable, a temporary inconvenience that had to be eliminated before he could share true spiritual life with his people. John affirms the fourth gospel's teaching, while countering the Antichrists' argument, by stressing that "life" is not a subjective experience but rather the person of Jesus himself. Although the Life was "with the Father," John states twice in v.2 that "it has appeared to us" (*phaneroō*, GK *5746*), so that it was "seen" in the form of the human Jesus. In John's view, the church's witness and testimony are based on the fact of this manifestation. The eternal life that Christians enjoy originates in the physical life of Jesus and cannot be separated from it.

3 It is clear that John wishes to create a sense of solidarity with the reader at the beginning of the letter by differentiating between two groups—"us" and "them." The boundary between the two groups is the message ("word," v.1) that John proclaims. Only those who accept John's teaching that Life manifested itself in the human Jesus "may have fellowship with us." As noted in the introduction, there has been considerable debate over the identity of the "we" in 1:1–4. These verses include eleven first-person-plural verbs ("we do x") and seven occurrences of the pronoun *hēmeis* ("we/us"). Some scholars interpret "we" here to be the entire Johannine community or a group of orthodox teachers within the community, making these verses a rallying cry to defend the "corporate tradition" against the Antichrists (see Introduction). This view does not, however, adequately account for fact that the pronoun "you" (*hymeis*) is also used four times in these verses to distinguish the reader from the author. Since "1 John is probably not a missionary tract for unbelievers but a communication with those who belong to the church" (R. A. Culpepper, *The Gospel and the Letters of John* [Nashville: Abingdon, 1998], 255), "we" (the author) and "you" (the audience) must be co-members of the Christian community who are different in some way. The point of difference seems to be that "we" have heard, seen, touched, and witnessed Jesus, while "you" have not. "We" must therefore refer to the collective group of witnesses to the life of Jesus, of whom John claims to be a member. This witness puts John in a special category with those whose testimony cannot be refuted, a status the Antichrists do not enjoy. Only those Christians among "you" who accept John's witness may remain in fellowship with him.

3a The Greek word *koinōnia* (GK *3126*) is translated "fellowship" in the NIV. While the English word "fellowship" is used to describe everything from a deep friendship to a potluck dinner, *koinōnia* refers to a bond of partnership in a common enterprise or experience. Luke uses this term to refer to the sharing of possessions in the early church (Ac 2:44; 4:30), and Paul speaks of the *koinōnia* he enjoys with the Philippians due to their common commitment to the gospel (Php 1:5). To have *koinōnia* with someone means to share a sense of community with that person. Brown, 170, therefore refers to *koinōnia* as "both the dynamic *esprit de corps* that brings people together and the togetherness that is produced by that spirit." John hopes that his audience will be united with him on the basis of their common faith in Jesus.

3b The second half of 1:3 elevates the basic distinction between "us" and "them" to absolute terms with ultimate consequences. John's word gives him fellowship "with the Father and with his Son, Jesus Christ"; logically, those who refuse to accept John's witness put themselves out of fellowship with

Christ and God and therefore render themselves ineligible for eternal life. Ironically, the Antichrists, by focusing too much on their present experience of Christ through the Spirit and rejecting John's witness about Jesus' past, have placed themselves out of fellowship with God.

4 Following the adamant exclusivism of vv. 1–3, John suddenly adopts a pastoral tone. This shift highlights an apparent paradox in 1 John. Marshall, 105, notes, "At first sight he [John] appears [in the prologue] to be addressing them [the readers] as if they were not Christians . . . yet later on in the writing it is quite certain that he is writing to Christian believers." John's wavering posture toward his audience is probably the result of his recent experience. Though most of his audience have been loyal in the past, the doctrinal crisis presented by the Antichrists and the desertion of leaders such as Diotrephes seem to have left John uncertain of his audience's loyalties. While John demands that his audience choose either to stay with him or to leave, he holds on to the hope that they will remain. Indeed, their fellowship would increase the joy he receives from his own fellowship with the Father. But it is probably too much to say that "even the author's fellowship with God is not fully satisfactory without the reader's incorporation" (Rensberger, 47). In Johannine thought, "joy" is a gift from God that transcends the difficulties of life in the world, because it recognizes God's continuing love in the face of the world's hatred (Jn 15:11; 16:20–22). Jesus therefore prays that his disciples "may have the full measure of my joy within them," despite the fact that he is sending them into a hateful world (Jn 17:13). In this sense, John's joy will continue, whether or not the audience makes the right decision, but their positive response would "fulfill" (*plēroō*, GK *4444*; NIV, "make complete") his joy by granting him the satisfaction of success as a witness.

II. TESTS TO DISTINGUISH TRUE DISCIPLES FROM THE WORLD (1:5–2:17)

OVERVIEW

In a context of divisions and conflicting loyalties, John calls on Christians to reassert their faith in the true Word and to examine their lives. Those who wish to remain in fellowship with "us," the true believers, must distinguish themselves from enemies without, "the world," and enemies within, the Antichrists. But in light of the doctrinal confusion brought on by the Antichrists, how can believers tell who is in which group? After establishing

the basic boundaries and his own credentials in the prologue, John proceeds to offer a series of tests that will distinguish the true children of God from the world and the Antichrists. The logic of each test follows an "if x, then y" format, wherein the "if" clause describes particular beliefs or actions a person might exhibit, and the "then" clause describes the necessary conclusion to be drawn from these observations.

A. Test #1: Walking in the Light (1:5–10)

⁵This is the message we have heard from him and declare to you: God is light; in him there is no darkness at all. ⁶If we claim to have fellowship with him yet walk in the darkness, we lie and do not live by the truth. ⁷But if we walk in the light, as he is in the light, we have fellowship with one another, and the blood of Jesus, his Son, purifies us from all sin.

⁸If we claim to be without sin, we deceive ourselves and the truth is not in us. ⁹If we confess our sins, he is faithful and just and will forgive us our sins and purify us from all unrighteousness. ¹⁰If we claim we have not sinned, we make him out to be a liar and his word has no place in our lives.

COMMENTARY

5 John opens the first series of tests with a foundational principle: "God is light; in him there is no darkness at all." This being the case, those whose lives are filled with darkness cannot be in fellowship with God. The means by which one identifies a life full of darkness are indicated in vv.6–10.

John assumes that this theological principle ("God is light") cannot be denied because it comes "from him," apparently the living Jesus of whom

John is a witness. The statement "God is light" is introduced in the Greek text by *hoti*, which would seem to indicate that John is directly quoting something Jesus said ("God is light"). But no such statement appears in the fourth gospel, and although the Johannine Jesus refers to himself as "light" on several occasions (Jn 3:19; 8:12; 9:5; 12:35, 46; see also 1:4–5), he never speaks of God in this way. This apparent discrepancy has led many scholars to suggest that the *hoti* introducing "God is light" indicates indirect discourse ("we declare to you *that* God is light"), meaning that the statement in some way summarizes Jesus' teaching about God's moral nature (so NIV, NAB, NEB, NRSV, NKJV). Some scholars who take this view, noting the above references to Jesus as "the light" in John's gospel, suggest that John is not referring to Jesus' verbal teaching, but to the actions of Jesus that revealed God as light to the world. From this perspective, "God is light" summarizes "what they learned [about God] from Jesus from observation of his life" (Johnson, 29). This would be consistent with John's insistence that he proclaims what he has "seen" Jesus do (1Jn 1:1–3). Other scholars who take this view suggest that John has combined a number of traditional statements and concepts into a composite saying (so Brown, 227–29; Rensberger, 51). This is a reasonable proposition, especially since the Johannine tradition seems to have been preserved primarily in the form of the oral testimony of teachers in the community at this time. In such a setting, it would be easy for John to summarize several ideas from the accepted Jesus tradition into one creedal statement supporting his argument.

While the above solutions are reasonable, the formula that introduces "God is light" suggests that John thinks of the statement as a saying of Jesus. He refers to it as the "message" (*angelia*, GK *32*) that "we heard from him," and he uses *anangellō* (GK *334*; "we declare") to describe his current proclamation of the same message "to you." While John has previously insisted that he saw and touched the Life (1:1–3), the terms in 1:5 all refer to hearing and speaking, even though it would be more logical to refer to "seeing" that "God is light." In this context it seems most likely that the *hoti* at 1:5 indicates direct discourse ("And this is the message we heard from him and declare to you: 'God is Light.'"). In support of this conclusion it should be noted that,

while the fourth gospel gives no evidence that Jesus spoke of God as "light," the underlying structure of the argument at 1 John 1:5–10 is formally similar to passages in the fourth gospel where Jesus is attempting to prove a point. In any case, even if John has combined several traditional sayings or motifs into one creed, he seems to be presenting the statement here from the platform of his authoritative witness to Jesus.

6–7 The first test in the first series of tests builds directly on the statement that "God is light." The Greek word *koinōnia* ("fellowship") is used again, suggesting that two parties "have something in common" (Marshall, 105). This being the case, *if* anyone walks in darkness, *then* that person cannot be in fellowship with the God in whom "there is no darkness at all" (1:5). Those who claim to have fellowship with God but "walk in darkness" are therefore liars who cannot be members of John's group because they do not enjoy the same fellowship with God that John does (1:3). The positive converse is stated as a second test at verse 7: *If* someone "walks in the light," *then* that person has fellowship with God and John because, again, God is "in the light."

These two tests follow a pattern that will continue throughout 1 John. First, all the tests John offers are objective and observable, designed to reveal a person's true intentions apart from verbal claims. Deeds are the test for words, and while words can be false John seems to believe that a person's actions reveal his or her true nature. Second, many of John's tests follow the "if . . . [but] . . . then" pattern evident here, giving them an absolute quality consistent with his dualistic stance. This presentation effectively eliminates any gray area, for a single premise ("if") always leads to a single conclusion ("then"), irrespective of any contingent circumstances ("but"). Here, "if" one claims to have fellowship with God "but" walks in the darkness, "then" he is a liar; on the other hand, "if" one walks in the light, "then" her sins are forgiven, granting fellowship with God. There are no exceptions.

What does it mean, then, to "walk in the light" or to "walk in the darkness"? Since vv.8–10 stress the need to acknowledge sin, it is reasonable to understand vv.6–7 in ethical terms. Marshall, 110, observes that "to live in the darkness means to live without the benefit of divine illumination and guidance and so to live in sin." Similarly, Brown, 230–31, is surprised that "the first overt attack on dangerous ideas [in 1 John] is in the moral sphere. One might have expected the author to begin with the Christological errors that are so much on his mind." It may be, however, that Brown's expectation is more accurate than his conclusion. While vv.8–10 clearly address the problem of sin, "walking in the darkness" is not typically used in this way in the fourth gospel. In John 8:12, for example, Jesus says, "I am the light of the world. Whoever follows me will never walk in darkness, but will have the light of life." During his final public appeal in Jerusalem, Jesus urges the Jews to believe in him and "walk while you have the light, before darkness overtakes you. The man who walks in the dark does not know where he is going" (Jn 12:35; cf. 11:9–10). Each time Jesus refers to "walking in darkness," he does so in the context of a claim that God's "light" is available, and 1 John 1:5–7 also explicitly contrasts "walking in the darkness" with the claim that "God is light." These texts suggest that "walking in the darkness" refers to a failure to accept the revelation of God through Jesus. To "walk in the light" presumably means to accept John's teaching about Jesus, which is why he and such people "have fellowship with one another." This fellowship is based on a common experience of forgiveness of sins, which in John's view only true Christians enjoy.

The question remains as to whom John wishes to distinguish with this first set of tests (1Jn 1:5–10).

Many scholars believe that his remarks are aimed at the Antichrists, whose life and doctrines indicate that they "walk in the darkness." Most who hold this position detect echoes of the Antichrists' teaching in the tests John offers, suggesting that they used slogans, such as "we have communion with him" (v.6) and "we do not have sin" (v.8), which John wishes to refute (so Marshall, 110–13; Brown, 231–32; Culpepper, 16–18; Johnson, 29–32; Rensberger, 49–50). While this is certainly the case later on in the letter (2:22; 4:1–3), there is no way to tell whether or not the Antichrists advocated the doctrines mentioned here. It is clear that they did not share John's view of the human nature of Jesus, but this belief would not inherently lead to the conclusion that Christians have no sin or that people who "walk in the darkness" can have communion with God.

On the other hand, John states on numerous occasions that "the world" is guilty of unrepentant sin and that those who are of the world, particularly the Jews, have serious misconceptions about their relationship with God. The world does not recognize Jesus (Jn 1:10; 12:47–49; 14:31; 17:25) and rejects him because his "light" exposes their evil deeds (Jn 3:19–20; 7:7; 16:8–11), and the Jews, who "do not have the love of God in [their] hearts" (Jn 5:42), have misunderstood Jesus and thereby rejected God (cf. Jn 1:5, 11; 5:39–47; 6:26, 36; 7:28–29; 8:14–15; 10:25–26, 34–38). The Jews, in fact, continue to cling to the false notion that salvation may be found in the Scriptures, Moses, and their lineage from Abraham, even after witnessing Jesus' signs (Jn 5:39, 45–46; 6:32–33; 8:31–44). It seems more likely that John is speaking of these people rather than the Antichrists when he refers to those who "walk in the darkness." Christians can easily distinguish themselves from such people on the basis of their faith in Jesus. Those who do not have faith—the world and the Jews—cannot be in good fellowship with God because their sins are not cleansed by Jesus' blood.

8–9 John has just mentioned at the end of v.7 that those who have fellowship with God are cleansed of sin by Jesus' blood. He now offers another test that further distinguishes those who receive this cleansing from those who do not. The new test follows the same formula as that in 1:6: "*If* we claim to be without sin, [*then*] we deceive ourselves and the truth is not in us." Verse 9 restates this test from a positive perspective: "*If* we confess our sins, [*then*] he . . . will purify us from all unrighteousness." The latter test is again undergirded with an undeniable principle about God's nature. Not only is God "light," he is also "faithful and just" and will therefore respond to our admission of guilt by forgiving our sins.

There is an important shift from the singular *hamartia* ("sin," GK *281*) to the plural *hamartias* ("sins") between vv.8 and 9. The singular "sin" appears in v.8 with *ouk echomen*, "we have no sin" (NIV, "we claim to be without sin"). John elsewhere uses the phrase "to have sin" to emphasize the guilt that is accrued by committing sinful acts (cf. Jn 9:41, where the NIV translates *hamartia* as "guilt"; 15:22–24, where the NIV translates "not have sin" as "not be guilty of sin"; 19:11, where the NIV translates "has greater sin" as "is guilty of a greater sin"). Rensberger, 53, notes that John always uses this phrase of "people hostile to Jesus." While many scholars would again suggest that John is addressing a doctrine of the Antichrists, it seems more likely he is referring to the world's disregard for Jesus' proclamation. Both Jesus and the Spirit insist that the world is guilty of sin (Jn 12:47–48; 15:22–24; 16:8–11), but the world, by refusing to accept Jesus, denies this claim. Jesus has very low regard for such people and tells the Pharisees on one occasion that "if you were blind, you would not be guilty of sin [lit., would have no sin]; but now that you claim you can see, your guilt [lit., sin] remains" (Jn 9:41).

The same complex of ideas underlies 1 John 1:8–9. While John is a dualist, he is not a perfectionist. All people—the world, the Jews, and believers—are guilty of sin. Christians are different from the rest in that they acknowledge this fact and receive forgiveness, but those who deny their guilt only deceive themselves. John seems to be thinking here of the initial experience of Christian conversion, when those in the world admit their sin, accept Jesus, and subsequently receive "the right to become children of God" (Jn 1:12).

John's dualistic perspective is evident in the promise that those who confess their sins will be "cleansed" (*katharizō*, GK *2751*; NIV, " purify"). John has already used this term in v.7 to indicate that those who walk in the light are "cleansed" by Jesus' blood. The Greek *katharizō* reinforces the language of "light" and "darkness" by distinguishing people as "clean" or "unclean." Those who do not confess their sins are unclean and alienated from God, whereas those who do confess are made pure, thereby allowing fellowship with him. Cleansing is necessary because, in a further dualistic distinction, God is "just" (*dikaios*, GK *1465*) while sinners are "unjust" (*adikos*, GK *94*; NIV, "unrighteous"). This injustice is eliminated only through the mercy of a just God.

It is interesting to note that John associates God's forgiveness with his justice (*dikaios*) rather than his mercy (*eleos*, GK *1799*) or grace (*charis*, GK *5921*). The terms "faithful and just" echo OT covenantal language, stressing that God keeps his promises (cf. Dt 7:9; 32:4; Ps 145:13; Mic 7:18–20). The promise John has in mind seems to be connected with God's sending his Son into the world to take away sins—an act that allows us to "rely on the love God has for us" (1Jn 4:16; cf. Jn 3:16–17). This act of love should give Christians comfort and confidence about their salvation and their unique relationship with God (1Jn 5:13–15).

10 John now offers a test that logically extends vv.8–9. Verse 8 addressed the person who claims to have no sin, i.e., who claims not to be guilty of sin before God. Verse 9 spoke of the person whose guilt is removed through the confession and forgiveness of individual "sins." To complete his argument, John offers a test to distinguish those who falsely claim that they are not guilty of "sin" because they have never committed individual "sins." The "if" clause in this case is comprehensive, using the perfect tense of *hamartanō* ("we have never sinned") to characterize a certain lifestyle: "*If* we say we are not sinners . . ." Many scholars again see this as a veiled reference to the teachings of the Antichrists (so Marshall, 114; Brown, 211–12; Culpepper, 19; Johnson, 33), but it seems more likely that John is condemning the moral indifference of the world. Those who deny their sinfulness and refuse to accept their sinful guilt show they have no fellowship with God.

Those who refuse to acknowledge their sinfulness "make him out to be a liar" and prove that "his word is not in them" (NIV, "his word has no place in our lives"). This terminology implies that such a claim is incompatible with something God has said. Culpepper, 19–20, suggests that John is thinking of the "word of God" revealed in OT texts on sin such as 1 Kings 8:46 and Proverbs 20:9. Others point to the general Christian proclamation that all people are sinners in need of redemption through Christ (so Dodd, 23; Marshall, 114–15; Johnson, 33–34). While the OT texts Culpepper mentions may be in the background, the latter interpretation seems more likely. John opened this first series of tests by citing a traditional saying (1:5) and now closes it by making another appeal to his Jesus tradition. Here again it is unclear what specific teaching John has in mind. The Johannine Jesus has very little to say about "sins" beyond the major sin of rejecting his revelation of God (cf. Jn 15:22–24; 16:8–11). Further, the formula for introducing the teaching at 1 John 1:10 is much less specific than that at 1:5, suggesting that John is now referring to a general theme in Jesus' teaching: all people are sinners in need of divine redemption. Perhaps John is thinking of statements such as John 8:24, where Jesus tells the Jews that unless they accept him, "you will indeed die in your sins," or 8:34, where Jesus says that "everyone who sins is a slave to sin." In John's view this teaching is not subject to reinterpretation. Those who refuse to accept it portray God as a "liar" because they deny the truth of what Jesus has clearly said.

NOTES

5 In certain passages in the fourth gospel, Jesus makes a definitive statement about God and then uses that statement as a "given" to support his argument. For example, in his discussion with the Samaritan woman on the proper place of worship Jesus first states the principle "God is spirit" to support the conclusion that "his worshipers must worship in spirit and in truth" (Jn 4:24). In John 10:34–36, Jesus defends his right to be called "God" by first citing the word of God in Psalm 82:6, a Scripture that "cannot be broken" and that therefore functions as an indisputable premise in his argument. Similarly, 1 John 1:5 states the principle that "God is light" to undergird the tests of fellowship introduced in the following verses.

5 "Light" was a common metaphor for deity in ancient religions. The Johannine usage probably builds on the OT, where God is associated with light to stress his guidance and redemption (Pss 27:1; 36:9; Isa 9:1–2; 60:1–2) or his perfection and holiness (Ps 104:2). The fourth gospel usually applies the metaphor to Jesus in the former sense, stressing the revelation of God available through him (Jn 1:4–5; 8:12; 12:35). Ironically, this light resulted in both redemption and judgment, for many who saw the light did not recognize him (Jn 1:5; 3:19).

6–7 The understanding that vv.6–7 refer to a doctrinal rather than an ethical test of fellowship is consistent with John's dualistic presentation (see Introduction). The dualistic perspective generally associates "light" and "darkness" with the inner nature of the person rather than with his or her visible behavior. This perspective is evident in the Dead Sea Scrolls, which categorize individuals either as "children of light" or "children of darkness" (see 1QS 3–4). Similarly, John can refer to all those who reject Christ as "the darkness" without commenting on their ethical behavior (Jn 1:5) and can differentiate people's behavior from their "love of darkness" or "love of light" (Jn 3:19–21). "Walking in the darkness" refers not so much to what people *do* as to what they *are* by nature, which is revealed, in John's view, by whether or not they accept Jesus. Those who do not accept him deceive themselves if they claim to have fellowship with God.

8–9 Many scholars believe that the doctrine of the Antichrists included a radical revision of orthodox Johannine ethics. Thompson, 15, provides a convenient summary of this view, with supporting texts from 1 John. She argues that the Antichrists "held the view that those who were the 'children of God' (3:1–2) attained a spiritual status by being 'born of God' (3:9–10) that not only delivered them from the guilt and power of sin but actually rendered them sinless. They claimed to be without sin and to have attained a state of perfect righteousness (1:8, 10)" (cf. Dodd, 21–22; Brown, 80–83, 233–34; F. Segovia, *Love Relationships in the Johannine Tradition* [SBLDS 58; Chico, Calif.: Scholars Press, 1982], 77–79; Culpepper, 17–18; Johnson, 32; Rensberger, 25, 53). This hypothesis, while intriguing, relies on a number of passages from 1 John that touch on Christian ethics without specifically mentioning the Antichrists. The ethical teachings of John's rivals are therefore difficult to reconstruct.

REFLECTIONS

John's first group of tests has identified those whose beliefs do not coincide with key teachings of Jesus on the relationship between God and the world. Jesus teaches that God is light, making "liars" of those who claim fellowship with God while walking in darkness. Jesus teaches that all people sin and bear the guilt of sin, making those who are morally indifferent to be enemies of God. Such people are not cleansed by Jesus' blood and therefore cannot be in fellowship with John and his community. These tests thereby distinguish believers from "the world." It is difficult to overlook the exclusive tone of John's remarks. In his view there is no hope of salvation apart from faith in Jesus and participation in the true community of God's people.

B. Test #2: Keeping His Commands (2:1–6)

OVERVIEW

Now that John has established the basic *doctrinal* difference between believers and the world, he turns to tests that will distinguish the *behavior* of believers from outsiders. While the first set of tests focused on nonbelievers, John now highlights the life of the Christian. Consistent with the emphasis on tradition in ch. 1, believers are distinct because they "obey his commands" (2:3), i.e., they live by the teachings of the historical Jesus.

> [1]My dear children, I write this to you so that you will not sin. But if anybody does sin, we have one who speaks to the Father in our defense—Jesus Christ, the Righteous One. [2]He is the atoning sacrifice for our sins, and not only for ours but also for the sins of the whole world.
>
> [3]We know that we have come to know him if we obey his commands. [4]The man who says, "I know him," but does not do what he commands is a liar, and the truth is not in him. [5]But if anyone obeys his word, God's love is truly made complete in him. This is how we know we are in him: [6]Whoever claims to live in him must walk as Jesus did.

COMMENTARY

1 John has just stressed that all people have sinned and bear the guilt of this sin, and he has told believers that God will cleanse them if they confess their sins (1:8–10). Lest this be taken as a license to sin, John immediately clarifies that he is writing "so that you will not sin." Recognition of God's grace and forgiveness should lead to obedience, not to further sinning.

Continuing the thought of vv.8–10, John introduces Jesus as the advocate (*paraklētos*, GK *4156*) of Christians who sin. The term *paraklētos*, which appears in the NT only in the Johannine literature, is used in the fourth gospel exclusively in reference to the Holy Spirit. *Paraklētos* literally means "one called alongside" to help someone, highlighting the Spirit's ministry of teaching and guiding the disciples (Jn 14:26; 16:13), empowering their testimony (15:26), and vindicating Jesus' self-revelation (16:8–11). Even in the fourth gospel, however, there is a close connection between Jesus and the Paraclete, for the Spirit is the form in which Jesus will come to the disciples and remain with them (14:16–18). For this reason Jesus refers to the Spirit as *allos paraklētos*, "another Paraclete" (NIV, "another Counselor"), like himself. The Greek *allos* means "another" of the same type or category, emphasiz-

ing the continuity between Jesus and the Spirit. John prefers this term over the Greek *heteros*, which would indicate "another" helper of a different kind.

2 John's discussion of Jesus' relationship with sinners suddenly shifts from a legal motif to a sacrificial motif. The word translated "atoning sacrifice" is *hilasmos* (GK *2662*; KJV, "propitiation"). Considerable debate surrounds this term and its theological significance (cf. Marshall, 117–18; Brown, 218–22). While *hilasmos* is rare in the NT, it was commonly used in pagan literature to refer to a sacrifice made to appease the wrath of an angry deity. Some have therefore concluded that this verse means that Jesus' death as "the Righteous One" expends the anger God feels toward those who confess their sin (so Marshall, 118). Those who take this view focus on God's wrath and the need for Christ to take action that will quench this wrath. Dodd, 25–27, has challenged this view, arguing that *hilasmos* refers not to the propitiation of God's wrath but to the "expiation" of the believer's sin. In some contexts, the verbal form of *hilasmos* means "to perform an act by which defilement [ritual or moral] is removed" from a person. If this is the meaning at v.2, John is arguing that Jesus, as our advocate, restores our relationship with God by removing our sin and defilement.

Those who take this view focus on the believer's sin and Christ's action to remove that sin.

The issue is difficult because both interpretations of *hilasmos* fit the context of v.2. On one hand, believers have, by their own admission, sinned against God and bear the consequent guilt of that sin (1:8–9). This guilt is removed by the blood of Jesus (1:7), stressing his sacrificial death to appease God's wrath. On the other hand, John describes the removal of sin as "cleansing" twice at 1:7–9, suggesting that the believer's impurity is the primary obstacle to her relationship with God. Forgiveness is granted not because God's wrath is appeased but because he is "faithful and just," keeping his promises to pardon those who are penitent (1:9). It may also be that John has both meanings of *hilasmos* in mind. The NIV reflects this possibility by translating *hilasmos* as "atoning sacrifice." "Atonement" focuses on the removal of impurity and the restoration of our relationship with God, while "sacrifice" highlights the death of Jesus in place of believers to absorb God's wrath toward sin. Both are critical aspects of Jesus' work as advocate.

John's reference to Jesus as the "atoning sacrifice" for the sins of *the whole world* seems "remarkably inclusive . . . for the otherwise often closed and world-rejecting 1 John" (Rensberger, 57). It may be, though, that John is still thinking in exclusive terms. Although Jesus did die on behalf of the world, John has already established that the world walks in darkness, refusing to confess sins so as to receive forgiveness (1:5–10; cf. Jn 3:16–20). Consequently, no person can hope for atonement while remaining in the world. All people must come to Jesus in order to appease God's wrath, but most will never do so, and there is no other way to experience redemption. First John 2:2 thereby eliminates any possible hope of salvation for the vast majority of human beings by insisting that Jesus is the single, universal sacrifice for sins.

3 John now introduces the principle that supports the two tests (vv.4–5) in this section: "We know that we have come to know him if we obey his commands." In John's view, "knowing God" is not only a confession or a mystical experience but also a lifestyle that follows the teachings ("commands") of the historical Jesus. Forgiveness does not negate the real need for obedience. Christians are distinct from the world in that their sins are forgiven, but they are also to be distinct from the world in that they avoid sin in the first place.

The idea that true believers may be identified by what they "know" pervades 1 John. Special knowledge distinguishes those who "walk in the light" from those who "walk in the darkness," ignorant of God and their own true nature. According to John, Christians "know":

- "that we have come to know him" if we obey his commands (2:3)
- "him who is from the beginning" (2:13–14)
- "the truth," that "Jesus is the Christ," and that anyone who says otherwise is an Antichrist (2:20, 22)
- "that everyone who does what is right has been born of [God]" (2:29)
- that when Jesus appears, we will be like him (3:2)
- that Jesus came to take away sins (3:5)
- that "we have passed from death to life" (3:14)
- that if we believe that Jesus is the Son, we have eternal life (5:13)
- that God hears our prayers (5:15)
- that Jesus keeps those "born of God" from sin, that believers are "of God" while the world belongs to Satan, and that Jesus came so we could understand the true God (5:18–20)

As will be seen, many of these knowledge statements are connected to specific tests. For example, because Christians know "the truth," they should be able to distinguish Antichrists from true believers (2:20–22); and because Christians know that Jesus "appeared so that he might take away sins," they should realize that no one who keeps on sinning "lives in him" (3:5–6).

4–5 John now offers two tests that will obliterate any claim that "knowing God" is a purely intellectual activity. The first test is negative: *If* someone says, "I know him," *but* "does not do what he commands," *then* one must conclude that this person is a liar. The reference to such people as liars echoes the language of 1:6, 10. Like 1:10, this test seems to compare something that someone might say to something Jesus has said—a "command." John is probably thinking of sayings such as John 14:15, 21–24 ("if you love me, you will obey what I command"). Since Jesus said these things and since his word is truth, anyone who would dispute such teaching is a "liar."

The positive counterpart to the negative test at v.5 has notoriously complex grammar, making it difficult to determine whether the phrase "this is how we know we are in him" goes with the statement that precedes it or with the one that follows. The NIV places this phrase with v.6, but it seems more likely it properly belongs with the test in v.5 (so KJV; cf. Brown, 258; Culpepper 24; Johnson, 40). The grammatical confusion in this case results from the fact that John draws two conclusions from one condition: "*If* anyone obeys his word" [= obeys the teaching of Jesus], *then* (1) "God's love is truly made complete in her," and (2) "we know we are in [Jesus]."

The statement that "God's love is truly made complete" in the person who obeys his word has generated considerable controversy. The genitive *tou theou* ("the love *of God*") could be objective or subjective. If subjective, the phrase would mean that God's love *for us* becomes complete when we obey him, perhaps because the barrier of sin is removed; if objective, it would mean that our love *for God* becomes complete when we obey him, stressing that faith must be combined with action. The con-

text suggests that the genitive here is objective: John is thinking of our love for God as that love which expresses itself in obedience. Love of God is thus parallel to knowledge of God in v.3, the two terms reflecting different aspects of a single Christian experience. The verb *teleioō* (NIV, "made complete") suggests that the goal of this experience is a life of obedience. The Johannine Jesus utters this word with his dying breath to indicate that he has finished everything God sent him to accomplish (Jn 19:30).

6 While the language of this verse is grammatically similar to that of v.4, it seems John is now offering a maxim to validate the two tests in vv.4–5. While v.3 focused on the need to obey Jesus' teaching, v.6 emphasizes the need to live by his example. The person who claims to remain in Jesus "ought to walk just as he walked" (NIV, "must walk as Jesus did"), meaning that the true believer's life will be patterned after the example of Jesus.

The maxim in v.6 describes the person who "claims to live in him." The Greek word *menō* (NIV, "live"; GK *3531*) is a key term in Johannine thought. *Menō* literally means "remain," "stay," or "abide," and John sometimes uses the term in this general sense to imply endurance or durability (cf. Rensberger, 62–63). He warns believers, for example, to "see that what you have heard from the beginning remains in you" in the face of the threat of the Antichrists (2:24) and tells the "chosen lady" that "the truth which remains in us will be with us forever" (2Jn 2; NIV, "the truth, which *lives* in us . . .").

Other passages indicate that *menō* is a codeword for several key points in Johannine theology. It is frequently used in the fourth gospel to describe "the relationship of mutual indwelling of the Father, the Son, and the believer" (W. L. Kynes, "Abiding," in *Dictionary of Jesus and the Gospels*, ed. Joel Green et al. [Downers Grove, Ill.: InterVarsity, 1992], 2). The Father abides in Jesus, empowering his work (Jn 14:10), and will also abide in those who love Jesus and obey his teaching (14:23). The disciples, in turn, must abide in Jesus, apparently meaning that they must live by his word in order to maintain their relationship with him. It is through this process of mutual indwelling that Jesus gives believers life and power to accomplish his work (15:4–9). This special relationship gives an eschatological dimension to Christian experience. Those who remain with Jesus faithfully throughout their lives will "abide [NIV, live] forever" because they have escaped from the world and its desires (1Jn 2:17). First John 2:6 highlights the ethical obligation that follows from this relationship: if we truly abide in Jesus, this will be evident in the way we live our lives. All those who do not live this way "abide in death" (1Jn 3:14; NIV, "remain in death").

NOTES

1 While there is some debate over the precise historical background of "Paraclete" in the fourth gospel, "in the present context [1 Jn 2] the word undoubtedly signifies an 'advocate' or 'counsel for the defense' in a legal context" (Marshall, 116; cf. Dodd, 24–25; Brown, 215–17; Culpepper, 20; Rensberger, 56). The reference to Jesus as the παράκλητος (paraklētos; NIV, "one who speaks in our defense") follows from the legal terminology introduced in the preceding section. Thinking of the divine courtroom, John contrasts the person who pleads "not guilty" to charges of sin (1:8) with the person who confesses (ὁμολογέω, homologeō, GK 3933) his sins before the God who is "just" (δίκαιος, dikaios; 1:9). While the former person is found to have no truth in himself, the latter has his injustice (ἀδικία, adikia) cleansed. Those who confess also enjoy the intercession of Jesus as their advocate (παράκλητος, paraklētos), who is able to appeal to a just God because he himself is also just (2:1).

3 John's emphasis on knowledge might suggest that the primary distinction between Christians and nonbelievers is intellectual. Several of the knowledge statements in 1 John obviously refer to the cognitive aspect of faith, representing the believer's consent to certain creeds (2:20–22; 3:5; 5:13). But the Greek γνῶσις, gnōsis ("knowledge"; GK 1194), and its cognates have both intellectual and experiential components, and it is clear John has both types of knowledge in mind. For example, the statement that believers know "him who is from the beginning" (2:13, 14) clearly refers to an experience that goes beyond intellectual assent to a proposition about God's existence. Other knowledge statements in 1 John clearly refer to subjective points of faith: that God hears our prayers (5:15); that we will be like Jesus when he appears (3:2); that believers have eternal life (5:13). To have "knowledge" in 1 John summarizes a wide range of Christian experiences. It seems that John thinks the believer starts with cognitive knowledge of the proper doctrinal abstracts, moves on to a faith experience of God, and then gives evidence of that experience in her behavior. All three aspects of Christian knowledge are evident in 2:3: "We know [cognitive awareness] that we have come to know him [have had an experience of God] if we obey his commands [behavior]." Lifestyle thus becomes the test of knowledge.

6 This second set of tests (2:1–6) seeks to weed out pseudo-Christians within the community. This is evident from the language of v.6. While μένω, menō, is a key term in Johannine thought, John's usage is "virtually unique . . . not only in the New Testament but in Hellenistic religious literature in general" (Rensberger, 62). Presumably, then, only a Christian would "claim to abide [live] in him." Those who make this claim but do not live by it are, in John's view, "liars" who belong in the same category as the world.

REFLECTIONS

Prior to 1 John 2:6, John's remarks have focused exclusively on Jesus' teaching as the measure of faith. Verse 6 stresses that the traditions about Jesus' life are also essential to Christian ethics. This sudden change in emphasis is somewhat surprising, for the fourth gospel does not present Jesus as a moral example. While the Synoptic Gospels highlight Jesus' imitable qualities, such as kindness, mercy, compassion, and freedom from greed, the works of Jesus in John's gospel highlight ways in which human beings *cannot* imitate Jesus by revealing his divine identity (e.g., Jn 5:36; 10:25–26). Since the ethics of 1 John center on the need for believers to love and serve one another, John may be thinking here of episodes from Jesus' life such as the footwashing (Jn 13:1–17), where the disciples are specifically commanded to follow Jesus' example, and Jesus' general portrait of his death as a sacrificial act for those he loves (Jn 10:11; 12:23–27; 1Jn 3:16). True believers are distinct from the world in that they live the same life of sacrificial service that Jesus lived.

C. Test #3: Loving Your Brothers (2:7–11)

OVERVIEW

John's first set of tests (1:5–10) distinguished true Christians from the world on the basis of their faith and confession. The second set of tests (2:1–6) narrowed the field further by eliminating those who claim to have faith but do not live by the teaching and example of Jesus. The third set of tests specifies which teachings of Jesus John has in mind. In John's view, Jesus' ethical teaching is centered around the love command (Jn 13:34). True Christians are distinct in that they show true love for one another.

> [7]Dear friends, I am not writing you a new command but an old one, which you have had since the beginning. This old command is the message you have heard. [8]Yet I am writing you a new command; its truth is seen in him and you, because the darkness is passing and the true light is already shining.
>
> [9]Anyone who claims to be in the light but hates his brother is still in the darkness. [10]Whoever loves his brother lives in the light, and there is nothing in him to make him stumble. [11]But whoever hates his brother is in the darkness and walks around in the darkness; he does not know where he is going, because the darkness has blinded him.

COMMENTARY

7 Before offering a new test, John insists that there is nothing innovative in what he is about to say. His doctrine is consistent with "the message you have heard" "since the beginning" and should therefore only be a rehearsal of what believers already know to be true. Because the tests in this section focus on love among believers (vv.9–10), it seems that John is referring to John 13:34, where Jesus informs the disciples that he is giving them a "new command" to "love one another." While this command was "new" when Jesus delivered it, it is not "new" to John's audience, but rather the same "old" message they have heard before. Indeed they have "had [it] since the beginning." The word for "beginning" here is *archē*, which refers, as in 1:1 (see comment there), to the beginning of the Jesus tradition. John thus asserts that his remarks are in complete accord with the teachings of Jesus and therefore cannot be disputed.

8 This verse is notoriously difficult, for John seems to be contradicting what he has just said. The sentence opens with *palin*, which normally means "again" but here probably functions as a conjunction. The NIV translates it, "*Yet* I am writing you a new command." Does John intend to repeat an old command (v.7) or write a new one? And if he only intends to repeat the love command, how can it be both "old" and "new" at the same time?

Most scholars believe that John is still thinking here of the love command from v.7. If this is the case, his words carry a note of irony. The audience should be well aware of Jesus' command to love, but their lack of concern for one another makes it seem as though they have never heard it before. If so, John may be commenting on the doctrinal divisions that had arisen in his churches in conjunction with the Antichrists. Most commentators, however, pointing to the statement that "the darkness is passing and the true light is already shining," detect an eschatological tone in John's remarks. The command to love is "old" (*palaia*, GK *4094*, v.8) in the sense that it goes all the way back to Jesus, but it is "new" (*kainē*, GK *2785*) in the sense that it describes life in the new age of the Messiah (cf. Dodd, 34–35; Marshall, 129–39; Brown, 266–67, 286–87; Culpepper, 29–30; Johnson, 43; Rensberger, 64).

While this interpretation is reasonable, it may be that John is actually indicating he is about to say something new in v.8—something different from the love command, which his audience already knows. Brown, 287, notes that the fourth gospel suggests the Spirit will both remind the disciples of what Jesus had said and "tell you what is yet to come" by speaking what he continues to hear from Jesus (Jn 14:26; 16:13–15). It may be, then, that John wishes to distinguish what he is about to say from the community's established Jesus tradition. Paul uses a similar device to distinguish his own remarks from the words of Jesus at 1 Corinthians 7:10, 12, 17, 25. While the "old command" is apparently the love command, the "new command" would be the statement in v.8 introduced by *hoti* (NIV, "because"): "The darkness is passing . . ." This statement is a "command" in the sense that John is delivering it by the Paraclete's authority but is "new" in the sense that it did not originate with Jesus.

John's new teaching is "true in [Jesus] and you." The phrase "which is true in him" (NIV, "its truth is seen in him") cannot refer directly to the "command" itself, for the Greek word *entolē* ("command," GK *1953*) is feminine in gender, while the phrase "which is true" (*ho estin alēthes*) is neuter. Rensberger, 65, notes that this probably means "the *content* of the commandment is true." In what sense, then, is the statement that "the darkness is passing" "true in him and you"? It is "true in him" in the sense that Jesus' incarnation marked the opening of a new age in which "a true light shone forth on the earth offering people a choice between light and darkness" (Brown, 287). It is "true in you" in that those who live by the love command are already living as "children of light" in a dark age (Jn 12:36). Jesus' advent proved that a new age was dawning—a fact verified by those who follow the command to love one another.

9 Now that John has situated the love command in his broader dualistic system, he offers two tests to distinguish true believers from those who do not walk as Jesus walked (v.6). As before, the negative test is stated first: *If* someone "claims to be in the light" *but* also "hates his brother," *then* that person "is still in the darkness," irrespective of any claims he may make to the contrary. The word "still" translates the Greek phrase *heōs arti*, which literally means "until now" but which here has the force of "all along." The person who confesses Jesus and follows most of his ethical teachings but does not obey the love command has actually been in the darkness "all along," deceiving herself and others about her true nature (cf. 1:8).

10 The positive counterpart to this test appears here: *If* someone "loves his brother," *then* that person "lives in the light." There is a notable difference in the formulation of the "if" statements in these two tests. The first test considers a person who *says* something (*ho legōn en tō phōti einai*, "claims to be in the light"), while the second considers a person who *does* something (*ho agapōn ton adelphon*, "loves

his brother"). This reflects John's position that true love expresses itself in actions, not words (3:18).

11 John closes this brief section with another maxim (cf. 2:6), which restates the test at v.9 in stronger terms. The one who hates his brother "walks around in the darkness," meaning that John classifies that person with people of the world (see comments at 1:5–6). This principle is a logical extension of John's view that the world hates believers (1Jn 3:13; see Introduction). Since the world hates and persecutes believers, and since Jesus says that Christians are to love one another, it must be the case that those who claim to be Christians but do not love their fellow believers are deceiving themselves. John therefore says that such a person "does not know where he is going." The darkness of hatred has blinded such people to reality, making them believe that they can continue in God's favor while breaking his commands. Jesus uses similar imagery in the fourth gospel to describe those whose wickedness prevents them from accepting his claims (Jn 9:39–41).

NOTES

8 John's "new" teaching situates the love command in the dualistic framework he has been developing to differentiate believers from the world: "The darkness is passing and the true light is already shining." Love, like truth and purity, is a distinguishing characteristic of those who walk in the light.

8 Although this teaching is "new" in the sense that it is not a direct quotation of Jesus, it faintly echoes a number of statements from the fourth gospel in which Jesus speaks of "day" as the sphere in which he and his people operate (Jn 8:12; 9:4–5; 11:9–10; 12:35–36, 46).

10 John's emphasis on love for one's "brother" has faint echoes of the second commandment of the Synoptics: "Love your neighbor as yourself" (Mk 12:31 and parallels). It is clear, however, that John uses "brother" in a much more exclusive sense than the Synoptics' "neighbor." While popular contemporary theology appeals to the universal "brotherhood of humanity," John's "brothers" are those Christians who are in good fellowship with him (cf. 3Jn 5–8). Culpepper, 31, notes that "1 John does not extend the duty of love to one's enemies or to all human beings; it focuses narrowly on the new commandment, that Christians love one another. They are *brothers* in the sense that they are now all children of God through faith . . . (see Jn 1:12; 20:17; 21:23)." John does not expect cordial relations between believers and the world. He does, however, expect those who claim to be Christians to treat other Christians as Jesus commanded.

D. Test #4: Loving the World (2:12–17)

OVERVIEW

This section concludes the first part of 1 John by offering a final broad test to identify true Christians. John challenges believers to recognize the distinction between themselves and the world and to ally themselves with God. The challenge is undergirded by a rallying cry of slogans and traditional sayings (vv. 12–14) that remind believers of their past faithfulness.

> ¹²I write to you, dear children,
>   because your sins have been forgiven on account of his name.
> ¹³I write to you, fathers,
>   because you have known him who is from the beginning.
> I write to you, young men,
>   because you have overcome the evil one.
> I write to you, dear children,
>   because you have known the Father.
> ¹⁴I write to you, fathers,
>   because you have known him who is from the beginning.
> I write to you, young men,
>   because you are strong,
>   and the word of God lives in you,
>   and you have overcome the evil one.
>
> ¹⁵Do not love the world or anything in the world. If anyone loves the world, the love of the Father is not in him. ¹⁶For everything in the world—the cravings of sinful man, the lust of his eyes and the boasting of what he has and does—comes not from the Father but from the world. ¹⁷The world and its desires pass away, but the man who does the will of God lives forever.

COMMENTARY

12–14 These verses are based on a tight grammatical formula, which is reflected by the poetic format in the NIV. John makes six parallel statements, each of which opens with *graphō* ("I write," GK 1211), followed by *hymin* ("to you") plus a term of address ("children," "fathers," "young men"), then *hoti* (NIV, "because"), then a descriptive phrase. Two general questions must be answered before the particular details of each verse can be considered. First, what is the function of *hoti* in this formula? Is it causal ("because you . . ."), or does it introduce indirect discourse ("that you . . .") or direct discourse (quotation: "you are . . .")? Second, what is the significance of the various terms of address John uses? Four such terms appear in these verses: *teknia* (GK *5448*, v.12; NIV, "dear children"); *pateres* (GK *4252*, vv.13–14; NIV, "fathers"); *neaniskoi* (GK *3734*, vv.13–14; NIV, "young men"); and *paidia* (GK *4086*, v.13; NIV, "dear children" ["I write to you, dear children" in v.13 of the NIV appears in v.14 in the Greek New Testament (UBS, 4th ed.); the NIV citation will be used throughout this discussion]). Are these general references to all believers, or does each represent a specific group within the church?

On the first question, some commentators believe that *hoti* has causal force in this section ("because you"). Marshall, 136, concludes that "John is writing the Epistle *because* certain things are true of his readers; consequently, they need the further instruction and are capable of obeying the injunctions which he is giving them" (emphasis added; cf. Westcott, 58; Rensberger, 71; so NIV, NASB, NEB, NRSV, NKJV). Others believe that *hoti* has declarative force in this section, introducing indirect discourse ("I write to you *that* you …"). Culpepper, 34, for example, feels that this reading is more consistent with the historical setting of 1 John: "The Elder is not writing to the community *because* these things are true; he writes to assure them in the face of opposition *that* they are indeed the ones who have been forgiven, who know the Christ, and who have overcome the evil one."

As a third possibility, *hoti* may be used here to introduce direct discourse, a series of quotations ("children, 'You are …'"). This position is supported by three pieces of evidence. First, John has already used *hoti* six times to introduce direct discourse (1:5, 6, 8, 10; 2:4, 6; see comments at 1:5), and nothing in the present context suggests that a different usage is intended. Second, up to this point John's arguments have depended heavily on direct and indirect allusions to his community's Jesus tradition (1:1–3, 5, 10; 2:7–8); it is logical he would use a similar technique here to introduce the test at 2:15, which distinguishes believers from the world once and for all. A concentrated citation of familiar sayings and

slogans would function as a rallying cry for group loyalty and solidarity. Third, as is often observed, the *hoti* statements at 2:12–14 largely summarize points John has already made. That believers' "sins have been forgiven" was established at 1:9; that they "have known him who is from the beginning" was established at 2:3; that "the word of God lives in" believers reflects the language of 1:10 and 2:5. John seems to be summarizing these points and stressing their validity by attaching them to traditional sayings and slogans. It seems, then, that 2:12–14 includes five traditional sayings or slogans that undergird John's final, comprehensive test to distinguish believers from the world (2:15). Malatesta, 166, thus refers to this section as "a strong declaration of the content of the author's message."

But to whom are these slogans addressed? Two of the four groups, *teknia* and *paidia*, are clearly synonymous, so that the NIV translates both as "dear children" (2:12, 13). John tells this group that their "sins have been forgiven on account of his name" and that they "have known the Father." "Fathers" (*pateres*) are reminded that they "have known him who is from the beginning." John has somewhat more to say to the "young men" (*neaniskoi*): they "are strong," "the word of God lives" in them, and they "have overcome the evil one."

While these terms might seem to divide the audience into three age groups, John typically uses "children" as a general designation for his entire audience (see Introduction). Commentators are therefore generally agreed that *teknia/paidia* refers to "the whole Johannine Community that is in *koinōnia* [fellowship] with the author" (Brown, 298; cf. Culpepper, 34–35; Rensberger, 70). But who are the "fathers" and "young men"? Dodd, 38–39, sees no distinction, arguing that all three terms represent various facets of a single Christian experience: "all Christians are (by grace, not nature) *children* in innocence and dependence on the heavenly Father, *young men* in strength, and *fathers* in experience." It seems more likely, however, that John uses "fathers" and "young men" to divide the larger Christian community into two groups on the basis of age. Brown notes that John's reminder that older believers "have known him who is from the beginning" is more appropriate for people who "have been Christians a long time," and even Dodd admits that "it is natural enough that young men should be congratulated because they are strong" (see discussion in Brown, 300; Dodd, 38; Culpepper, 35; Houlden, 70–71 [who offers the novel thesis that "fathers" and "young men" represent two church offices in the Johannine community equivalent to the Pauline "elders" and "deacons"]). The same basic division of God's people into two age groups appears in the OT and the Pauline literature. In any case, while John probably does have a broad age distinction in mind, the slogans he addresses to "fathers" and "young men" reflect general Christian qualities that should characterize members of both groups.

12 The first of John's five slogans/sayings, addressed to his "children," recalls the theme of 1:9–2:2: "your sins have been forgiven on account of his name." Because this is clearly a comment on the salvific work of Jesus, and because it refers to Jesus in the third person, John is most likely citing a community slogan rather than a saying of Jesus (some have suggested this slogan is cited from an ancient baptismal formula; so Brown, 302–3, 320–21; Culpepper, 35; Rensberger, 71–72).

While 1–2–3 John and the fourth gospel have surprisingly little to say about forgiveness (cf. Jn 20:23; 1Jn 1:9–2:2), the "name" of Jesus is an important point of Johannine thought. Jesus' "name" represents his divine identity and power, so that "belief in his name" means acceptance of John's claim that Jesus came from God (Jn 1:12; 3:18; 1Jn 3:23; 5:13). Those who act in Jesus' name enjoy various benefits, including the expectation that the Father will answer their prayers (Jn 16:23–26), the hope of eternal life

(Jn 20:31), and (here at 1Jn 2:12) forgiveness of sins. Marshall, 139, notes that John may be reminding his readers of the forgiveness they received when they first accepted the name of Jesus at conversion. The perfect tense of *aphiēmi* (GK *918*; NIV, "your sins *have been* forgiven") focuses on the continuing effect of a past event (Johnson, 49). The experience of forgiveness should motivate them to remain faithful.

13a John's second statement is another slogan that affirms the community's common faith: "you have known him who is from the beginning." The language here reflects both John 1:1 and 1 John 1:1, suggesting that "him" refers to Jesus, who existed from the beginning of time and whose life and death mark the beginning of Christian faith. The "fathers" "know" Jesus in the sense that they have accepted John's witness and are now enjoying a relationship with God. By reminding his audience that their experience of Jesus is real and authentic, John hopes to encourage them to keep themselves distinct from the world.

13b, 14 John next reminds the "young men" that they "have overcome the evil one." The language of this statement is somewhat surprising, for the Johannine literature has notoriously little to say about Satan. When the Johannine Jesus does speak of Satan, he refers to him as "the devil" (*ho diabolos*, GK *1333*), who is a "murderer" and a "liar" (Jn 8:44), or "the prince of this world" (Jn 12:31; 14:30; 16:11). John himself also calls Satan "the devil" (Jn 13:2) but refers to him as "the evil one" (*ho ponēros*, GK *4505*) when associating him with murder (1Jn 3:12) or describing his rule (5:18–19). The language of 2:13, then, seems to be closer to that of John than Jesus, suggesting that this statement is another community slogan. This slogan affirms that believers achieve victory over the devil through their faith.

But what does it mean to "overcome [*nikaō*, GK *3771*] the evil one"? A clue is offered at v.14, where John repeats this slogan but connects it to another slogan—"the word of God lives in you"—and conditions both statements by assuring the "young men" that "you are strong." The "word of God" refers to the demands God makes of believers, which are encapsulated in the teachings of Jesus (see 1:10). This teaching "abides" (*menō*; NIV, "lives") in them, suggesting that it empowers believers, making them "strong" (*ischyros*, GK *2708*) so that they may overcome sin. While this language of spiritual victory has eschatological overtones, John is probably focusing on the "moral effects" of Christian experience (cf. Malatesta, 168–70, who attempts to minimize the ethical implication; Brown, 305–6, suggests that John is thinking primarily of the ethical demands of the love command). Believers share in Jesus' victory over the devil when they, like Jesus, avoid temptation and obey the Father's word (Jn 4:34; 5:19; 8:28–29; 17:4).

13c The last *hoti* statement in this section appears at the end of v.13. Not only have believers known Jesus, they have also "known the Father." From John's perspective, these are synonymous concepts, for "anyone who has seen [Jesus] has seen the Father" (Jn 14:9). Why, then, does John differentiate between "knowing the Father" and "knowing him who is from the beginning"? The distinction may be stylistic, especially if John is already thinking of the "fathers" he is about to address in the next line. It may also be that John is here citing a traditional saying of Jesus rather than a community slogan. The Johannine Jesus frequently makes statements that closely parallel 1 John 2:13. For example, after declaring himself "the light of the world," Jesus says to the Pharisees, "If you knew me, you would know my Father also" (Jn 8:19); later he tells the disciples, "If you really knew me, you would know my Father as well. From now on, you do know him" (Jn 14:7; cf. 7:28–29; 8:54–55). John clearly believes that Jesus referred to true disciples as those who "know the Father" and by quoting such a saying seems to be reminding his readers that they enjoy this status.

15 John prefaces his fourth test with a comprehensive admonition. Again following his dualistic framework, John draws a boundary between God's people and everyone else: "*If* anyone loves the world, [*then*] the love of the Father is not in him." Love "of the Father" here seems to be, as at 2:5, an objective genitive (love "for the Father"). As John 3:16 indicates, God loves everyone, including the world, but those who are of the world and those who love the world do not love him.

16 John has just referred to "loving the world" and to the fact that Christians must not do this. Does this mean Christians are to take a hostile posture toward nonbelievers and isolate themselves from them? And if such is the case, how could John's remarks be consistent with the teaching of Jesus at John 3:16? To clarify his point, John now specifies the things "of the world" that Christians must avoid. Two issues must be addressed in considering this verse. First, what is the function of the *hoti* that introduces John's statement? The NIV, in an effort to remain neutral, translates *hoti* as "For": "*For* everything in the world . . ." Is this the most natural reading? Second, what does John mean by "the world" here? Is he referring to people, to things, or to something else?

On the first question, the NKJV and NEB treat *hoti* as an insignificant connective particle, omitting the word in English translation. The NIV, NASB, and NRSV suggest that *hoti* has causal force, so that the test at v.15 is valid *because* nothing in the world is from the Father. It seems, however, that John is once again using *hoti* to introduce direct discourse, reminding his audience of a familiar slogan about the world. In the light of John's general posture toward the world, it is reasonable to conclude that slogans similar to the one in v.16 were used by Johannine preachers to encourage believers to keep themselves separate from worldly things.

What, then, does this slogan suggest about "the world"? Elsewhere in the Johannine literature "the world" clearly refers to people who do not accept Jesus (see Introduction). The description of "the world or anything in the world" offered here, however, suggests that John is thinking of the lifestyle of those who are guided by their instincts rather than the Spirit. He characterizes this lifestyle with three broad statements (translated rather loosely in the NIV): "the lust [*epithymia*, GK *2123*] of the flesh" (NIV, "the cravings of sinful man"); "the lust of the eyes" (NIV, "the lust of his eyes"); and "the pride of life" (NIV, "the boasting of what he has and does"). It seems clear that John is now switching from the objective genitive of v.15 to the subjective genitive, nominating three sources of "lust" and "boasting" (flesh, eyes, and pride). The "lust *of the flesh*" is thus "lust which *comes from* the flesh" or originates with the flesh, i.e., physical desire. The "lust *of the eyes*" (Rensberger, 74, calls it "an unusual phrase, not clearly related to biblical, Jewish, or general Hellenistic moral teaching") seems to refer here to a faulty spiritual perception. In a similar way the Johannine Jesus says that the Pharisees are "blind" because they do not accept him (Jn 9:39–41; see also 12:40), and the Synoptic Jesus occasionally uses sight as a metaphor for spiritual judgment (Mt 5:29; 6:22–23; 7:3–5; Lk 11:34). Combined with "lust of the flesh," "lust of the eyes" describes the faulty moral perception arising from a value system that is not centered on the revelation of God in Jesus. The "pride *of life*" uses *bios* (GK *1050*) instead of the more typically Johannine *zōē* (GK *2437*), referring specifically to biological life

rather than spiritual life (see comment at 1Jn 1:2). The term *bios* can also have connotations of material wealth (i.e., "making a living," "living the good life"), so that the NIV translates the same word as "material possessions" at 3:17. Those who take pride in such things, placing their confidence either in social position or money, are not motivated by the Father's commands.

Brown, 326, notes that "not the sinful but an absence of the otherworldly is what characterizes the three factors" mentioned here. John expects believers to distinguish themselves from the world, and he concludes that those who are not sufficiently distinct are "not from the Father." Those whose lives are directed by such lusts cannot truly have love for God within themselves (v.15). John here touches on a theme, common in the teachings of Jesus, that Christian ethics often contradict natural human intuition.

17 John closes the first section of the book with a word of encouragement for believers who pass the tests. Because the things of the world do not originate with God, they are, like the darkness (2:8), "passing away," while those who do God's will "abide [NIV, live] forever." The Greek *menō* ("abide") emphasizes the permanence of the believer's relationship with God, extending from this world into the next. The nominal form of *menō* (*monē*) is used in John 14:2 to describe the many dwelling places (NIV, "rooms"; KJV, "mansions") Jesus has prepared for his followers in heaven. Those who keep his word will have a place with him forever, long after the world has faded away into oblivion.

NOTES

12–13 The first three statements here use the present tense of γράφω, *graphō*, while the last three use the aorist ἔγραψα, *egrapsa*. The variation seems to be purely stylistic, with ἔγραψα, *egrapsa*, functioning as an epistolary aorist, referring to what John has been saying up to this point in the letter in a summary fashion. John uses the epistolary aorist in similar fashion at 2:21, 26; 5:13. Because the epistolary aorist is synonymous with the present tense, the NIV translates all six usages as "I write to you."

16 Intense debate has centered on the meaning of the term "flesh" (σάρξ, *sarx*, GK *4922*) in the NT. The NIV reflects the view that σάρξ, *sarx*, refers to a natural inclination to sin, indicated by the translation here "sinful man" (cf. Ro 7:5; Gal 5:13; Col 2:11; Marshall, 144–45). Whether or not this is the true Pauline sense of the term, σάρξ, *sarx*, clearly has a more neutral connotation in the Johannine literature. John is adamant that Christ came in σάρξ, *sarx* (see Jn 1:14; 1Jn 4:2; 2Jn 7, where the NIV translates it "flesh"), apparently referring simply to his physical humanity. The phrase "lust of the flesh" here touches on the broader Johannine dualism. John divides the universe into two realms—"above" and "below," where "above" refers to the realm of God and "below" to the realm of weak humanity (Jn 8:23). Jesus therefore tells Nicodemus that those who wish to enter the kingdom must be born "from above" (ἄνωθεν, *anōthen*; NIV, "again"; Jn 3:3–13). Highlighting such references, Brown, 326, concludes that "'flesh' is not a sinful principle in John or a synonym for sex; rather, . . . it is human nature incapable of attaining to God unless it is re-created by His Spirit." The "lust of the flesh" refers, then, to all human desires that originate from a worldly perspective without regard for God's commands.

III. TESTS TO DISTINGUISH TRUE DISCIPLES FROM ANTICHRISTS (2:18–5:21)

OVERVIEW

As I noted in the introduction, the audience of 1–2–3 John was caught between a rock and a hard place. Persecution and hostility from "the world" and "the Jews" challenged believers to abandon the faith. John responds to this threat by offering the series of tests in 1:5–2:17. These external threats were accompanied by internal tensions that were dividing, or had already divided, John's churches. The second major section of 1 John (2:18–5:21) addresses this problem. John offers a series of tests that distinguish true believers from Antichrists, people who do not accept John's witness about Jesus (see Introduction). The beliefs and actions of the Antichrists are explored, along with the consequences of such beliefs. John's hope is that believers will separate themselves from both the world and the Antichrists so that they may have fellowship with him and with God.

A. Test #5: The True Confession (2:18–27)

¹⁸Dear children, this is the last hour; and as you have heard that the antichrist is coming, even now many antichrists have come. This is how we know it is the last hour. ¹⁹They went out from us, but they did not really belong to us. For if they had belonged to us, they would have remained with us; but their going showed that none of them belonged to us.

²⁰But you have an anointing from the Holy One, and all of you know the truth. ²¹I do not write to you because you do not know the truth, but because you do know it and because no lie comes from the truth. ²²Who is the liar? It is the man who denies that Jesus is the

Christ. Such a man is the antichrist—he denies the Father and the Son. ²³No one who denies the Son has the Father; whoever acknowledges the Son has the Father also.

²⁴See that what you have heard from the beginning remains in you. If it does, you also will remain in the Son and in the Father. ²⁵And this is what he promised us—even eternal life.

²⁶I am writing these things to you about those who are trying to lead you astray. ²⁷As for you, the anointing you received from him remains in you, and you do not need anyone to teach you. But as his anointing teaches you about all things and as that anointing is real, not counterfeit—just as it has taught you, remain in him.

COMMENTARY

18 John immediately stresses the urgency of the situation by bringing the doctrinal conflict to an eschatological arena. He labels his opponents Antichrists and says that their appearance coincides with "the last hour." Both terms seem to be drawn from a community slogan, which John has split in order to create a chiasm. The two halves of the slogan are indicated by the repetition of *hoti*, which again introduces direct discourse: "you have heard, 'Antichrist is coming'"; "we know 'it is the last hour.'"

In the last hour	Antichrist is coming
[now] many Antichrists	[therefore]
have come	it is the last hour.

The original form of the slogan epitomized what must have been a more extensive eschatological doctrine: "In the last hour Antichrist is coming." John applies it to the present situation to demonize his opponents.

While the terms "last hour" and "Antichrists" seem to be drawn from a community slogan, their precise meaning is unclear. Neither term appears outside 1 and 2 John, and despite the tendency for eschatological labels to intermingle in popular Christian thought (i.e., "last hour" = "last days" = end times; "Antichrist" = "Man of Sin" [1Th 2] = "the Beast/666" [Rev 13]), it is not clear whether any real synonyms may be found. Barker, 323–24,

draws a parallel between "the last hour" and the more frequent "the last days/times." The NT authors sometimes use "last days" to refer to "the new age that they associated with the advent of Jesus," says Barker, and so he concludes that "the last hour" is a general reference to "the fulfillment of time, the time of redemption and salvation," inaugurated by Jesus' death and continuing to the present. The motives for this conclusion are, however, clearly apologetic. Barker admits that "last days" is also commonly used "to designate the last days before Christ's return," but he refuses to see this meaning in 1 John 2 because it leads to the conclusion "that the author was mistaken," since Jesus did not return in the wake of the Antichrists' activity (cf. Stott, 107–9). Most commentators, however, agree that "the last hour" "must be taken in its obvious sense: the end of time is at hand" (so Rensberger, 77; cf. Dodd, 48–49; Brown, 330–32, 364–65; Culpepper, 44).

The Johannine Jesus uses "the last day" on several occasions to refer to the end of time, when the dead will be resurrected to enjoy eternal life or suffer judgment (Jn 6:39–44, 54; 12:48; cf. 11:24; 5:24–30). Does this mean John was mistaken in his estimate of the divine plan? The NT writers make no pretense to special knowledge about the time of Christ's return, consistently emphasizing that human beings are not privy to God's eschatological timetable (cf. Mt 24:36; 1Th 5:1–3; 2Pe 3:8–10). Looking at his situation, it seemed to John that the world was going from bad to worse, with godless people and heretics gaining ground on all sides. In light of the general ancient view that the forces of evil would gather at the end of time to make a final stand against God's people, John could reasonably conclude that "the last hour" was at hand. The focus is not on a timeline but on the urgency of a situation in which Christians must fight to preserve their identity.

John's proof that "the last hour" has come is provided by the Antichrists. As noted in the introduction, in 1–2–3 John this title functions as a technical term for the Elder's opponents. The plural "Antichrists" (antichristoi, GK 532) is an extension of the original community slogan, where the term apparently appeared in the singular (antichristos; hence the NIV, "the Antichrist"). While "Antichrist" literally means "against Christ" or "in place of Christ," its precise nuance is difficult to determine; Rensberger, 78, notes that "the notion of Antichrist . . . is not found at all in Jewish literature, nor in Christian literature except where it is dependent on 1 and 2 John." While the OT and other Jewish writings do occasionally anticipate the appearance of a leader of evil at the end of time, this figure is always set in opposition to God, not the Messiah (see Brown, 332–36, for a survey of possible backgrounds for the concept of Antichrist). In any case, John clearly expects his audience to be familiar with an eschatological figure who would oppose God and Christ, and he associates his opponents with this figure to highlight their treachery. The teachings of these people are, in fact, inspired by "the spirit of the Antichrist" (4:3), suggesting that they promote a substitute Savior distinct from the Jesus proclaimed by the community. Believers must therefore urgently resist such people and separate them from Christian fellowship.

19 The Greek text of this verse consists of three statements that reveal John's feelings toward the Antichrists and indicate that he no longer considers them to be in fellowship with him. But what were the Antichrists' feelings toward John? Each statement can be read in two ways, depending on the Antichrists' posture toward the Elder at the time 1–2–3 John was written. Because this issue is significant in reconstructing the historical setting of the letters, both readings will be explored before a conclusion is reached.

The first statement—"they went out from us, but they did not really belong to us"—is difficult in the Greek. A more literal reading highlights the apparent paradox of John's words: "from us they went out but they were not from us." The genitive ex hēmōn ("from us") appears twice, apparently with ablative force both times to indicate source or point of origin. The first phrase, "from us they went out," indicates that the Antichrists were once members of John's circle and were apparently in good standing with him. The second phrase, however, seems to deny this by insisting that the Antichrists "were not from us." This apparent discrepancy arises from John's dualistic perspective. In John's view, all people are by nature either "of light" or "of darkness" (see comment at 1Jn 1:5–6), and each person's true identity is revealed by her actions (1:9–10; 3:17–18; 5:2; Jn 8:39–47). Although the Antichrists once appeared to be genuine Christians, their subsequent behavior has revealed that they were actually full of darkness all along. The NIV reflects this perspective by translating the second phrase, "they did not really belong to us," suggesting that they were never really genuine Christians.

John's use of the ablative or "genitive of source" ("from us") raises two possibilities about the motives of the Antichrists. It may be that they returned John's hostile feelings. Perhaps his rejection of their views led to a doctrinal conflict, which they resolved by rejecting John and leaving his community. If this is the case the phrase "they went out from us" is equivalent to "they stopped coming to my church," perhaps seeking the fellowship of Christian leaders like Diotrephes who were more tolerant of their views (3Jn 9–10). As a second possibility, it may be that the Antichrists were a group of the Elder's protégés who "went out" on a preaching tour to the Johannine congregations but who began teaching things John did not accept. If this is the case, their "going out" would not necessarily imply any hostility toward the Elder. They may have considered themselves to be in good fellowship with John and presented themselves as his disciples to the churches they visited. This would make the Antichrists especially dangerous because it would seem that they came with the Elder's authority, thus explaining the urgency of his rebuttal.

The second and third statements in 2:19 are consistent with either interpretation of the Antichrists' motives. To prove that the Antichrists were false brothers all along, John points out that "if they had belonged to us, they would have remained with us." "Remain" here is *menō*, which carries the sense of constancy and permanence (see comments at 1Jn 2:5–6, 14). If John is thinking of the Antichrists as a hostile group who left his church in anger, this second statement reemphasizes the first: the fact that they did not remain in John's fellowship shows that they were never really dedicated to the community in the first place. If John is thinking of the Antichrists as a group of itinerant teachers who still consider themselves faithful, their failure to "abide" relates more specifically to their doctrine. Even if the Antichrists thought they were helping John, the fact that their teachings did not "remain" within the confines of John's witness shows that they were ignorant of the truth in the first place.

The third statement here is much stronger in the Greek text than the NIV suggests. John now attaches a purpose clause with *hina* to *exēlthan* from the first statement to explain the reason why the

Antichrists "went out": "so that it should be manifest . . ." (NIV, "their going showed . . ."). "Manifest" (*phaneroō*, GK *5746*) is followed here by *hoti*, which seems to introduce a slogan John has developed in the course of the Antichrist conflict: "not everyone is from us," or "not everyone is one of us" (NIV, "none of them belonged to us"). The fact that the Antichrists did not "remain" with John makes the truth of this slogan "manifest," validating in his mind the view that some who call themselves "Christian" are not to be trusted. If John is thinking of the Antichrists as a group who left his churches, this slogan supports the exclusivism engendered in the tests in the first section of the book. Christians must be tested to separate the true from the false, because not everyone who claims to "abide in him" actually does. If John is thinking of the Antichrists as a group of itinerant teachers, the slogan stresses the need for such people to have proper credentials, because not everyone who "goes out from us" is really "one of us" (see 2Jn 7–10).

While any conclusion about the Antichrists must remain speculative, a combination of the two views creates the most likely hypothesis. It seems that the doctrinal conflict envisioned in 1–2–3 John was in its initial stages when these letters were written. A group of teachers had left on a preaching tour of John's churches with his authorization, but after they departed, John learned that their doctrines did not "remain" within orthodox boundaries. This created confusion and division in the churches, which John attempts to rectify by writing 1–2–3 John. By this time the Antichrists may have recognized their differences with John but continued to seek converts to their position, winning over leaders such as Diotrephes (3Jn 9–10). John interprets this, perhaps correctly, as a hostile act and accuses his opponents of violating the love command, stressing that their treachery shows they were never loyal to him. The tests he offers in the remainder of 1 John are intended to draw clear lines between these traitors and true members of the community.

20 John now introduces the key term in this section—*chrisma* ("anointing," GK *5984*). True believers are different from Antichrists because they have a special anointing from God that gives them "knowledge." The contrast is highlighted in the Greek text by a wordplay that cannot be translated. The Antichrists (*antichristoi*) claim to know the truth about Jesus, whereas it is actually believers who have an anointing (*chrisma*) that gives them true knowledge. Both terms derive from the verb *chriō*, which means to rub or smear with oil. By opposing Christ (*christos*, "the Anointed One"), the Antichrists lose the anointing (*chrisma*) that would grant true knowledge.

In the light of John 14:26 and 16:13, many commentators have concluded that the "anointing" to which John refers is the Holy Spirit, "who guides you into all truth" (so Brown, 345–47, 370; Culpepper, 147; Johnson, 57–58; Rensberger, 79–80). Dodd, 61–63, however, argues that the *chrisma* "is the Gospel, or the revelation of God in Christ, as communicated in the [Johannine] rule of faith to catechumens" (cf. Lieu, 28–31). The broader context suggests that Dodd's reading is more accurate, making *chrisma* ("anointing") and *oidate* ("you know," GK *3857*) in v.20 synonymous. In support of this conclusion, it may first be noted that the Paraclete sayings (Jn 14:26; 16:13) suggest that *all* Christians receive special instruction from the Spirit. It would therefore do John little good to argue that Christians are guided into truth by the Spirit, for the Antichrists could make the same claim to justify their own views and perhaps did so (see Introduction; von Wahlde, 126–27). The Antichrists could not, however, claim that their revelations from the Spirit were consistent with John's witness—a point stressed at 1 John 4:1–6. Here as elsewhere John's point is "not that doctrine must be tested by inspiration, but that

inspiration must be tested by the Gospel" (Dodd, 62). Whether or not they possess the Spirit, the Antichrists do not pass the doctrinal test.

21 Further evidence that the "anointing" of v.20 refers to established tradition rather than the Spirit's guidance appears in vv.21, 24, and 27. Returning to the formula of 2:12–14, John uses *hoti* here to cite a sarcastic reversal of John 8:32. Jesus did not say, "You *do not* know the truth"; rather, he said, "You *do* know it [the truth]." A second *hoti* introduces a maxim that extends the application of this saying in dualistic terms (cf. 1Jn 2:7–8): "no lie comes from the truth." Since both Jesus and the Spirit are "truth" (Jn 14:6, 16–17), anyone who contradicts what John has witnessed about Jesus through the Spirit's power must be a liar.

At v.24, John again stresses that "what you heard from the beginning," the true teaching about Jesus, must "remain in you" if you wish to "remain in the Son and in the Father." The anointing also "remains in you" and "teaches you about all things" (v.27). Since both "the anointing" and "what you heard" are to "remain in you," it is reasonable to suggest that the anointing and the tradition are synonymous in this context. John therefore associates the anointing with an ongoing catechetical process, using *didaskō* ("teach," GK *1438*) three times in v.27 to stress that those who already know the truth about Jesus need not learn anything more.

22 Verse 22 offers the first test to distinguish true believers from Antichrists. The point of all such tests is to demonstrate that the Antichrists do not have the anointing, i.e., they do not adhere to orthodox teaching about Jesus. John uses *hoti* to introduce a central christological tenet and then draws two conclusions about those who reject this creed: *If someone denies that "Jesus is the Christ," then* that person (1) is a "liar" and (2) "denies the Father and the Son." "Deny" here is *arneomai* (GK *766*), used elsewhere in the NT to describe formal rejection of

Jesus and willful apostasy from the Christian faith (see Lk 12:9; 2Pe 2:1; Jude 4). The Johannine Jesus uses this term in reference to Peter's denial on the night of the arrest (Jn 13:38). The belief that "[the human] Jesus is [also] the [divine] Christ" is, in John's mind, a core issue of Christian faith that is not subject to debate. Those who do not accept this principle have effectively removed themselves from Christian fellowship, whether they realize it or not.

23 While John has already established that those who reject his witness are "liars" (1:6; 2:4), the claim that those who deny that "Jesus is the Christ" also "deny the Father" requires explanation. Verse 23 elaborates the logic of this statement by offering two maxims based on traditional sayings that stress the unity of God and Jesus (see Jn 5:19–20; 7:28–29; 8:19, 29, 38, 42; 10:30, 36; 14:9–11; 17:5). Since Jesus and the Father are one, "no one who denies the Son has the Father"; on the other hand, "whoever acknowledges the Son has the Father." The Father and Son come together in a single package, so that those who refuse John's witness about Jesus cannot have a proper view of God. The Antichrists are therefore no better than pagans (see comment at 3Jn 7).

24–25 After exhorting the audience to allow what they "heard from the beginning" to "remain in [them]," John presents the positive version of the test of v.23: *If* "what you have heard from the beginning remains in you," *then* "you also will remain in the Son and in the Father." Similar language is used in the farewell section of the fourth gospel, where "remaining" in Jesus and the Father has the idea of maintaining a permanent relationship with them (Jn 14:23; 15:4–9). The tests in 1 John 2:18–27 make this relationship contingent on a creedal confession: those who do not accept John's orthodox teaching cannot be in fellowship with the Father. The benefit for those who do hold to this confession is mentioned in v.25, namely, "eternal life" (see comment at 1Jn 1:2).

26–27 These verses encourage believers to pass the test and cling to the rule of faith so that they are not "[led] astray." Everything they need to know has been provided by the "anointing," the true gospel they have already received, which teaches them "all things." Those who suggest that they have something to offer beyond this teaching are therefore deceivers. Of course, the Antichrists did not think of themselves in this way, and John is probably referring to their doctrine rather than their motives. They would insist that their views are a legitimate extension of what John taught. John therefore emphasizes that the anointing is "real, not counterfeit"; nothing can be true that is not consistent with it. Orthodox tradition must be the standard for measuring new revelations and personal spiritual experience.

NOTES

18 Rensberger, 78, sees a possible parallel between the Johannine Antichrist and Jesus' warning about "false christs" at Mark 13:21–22, suggesting that John may be thinking of a false Messiah who would appear at the end of time (cf. Marshall, 150–51). If this is the case, John must be using the same concept with a very different nuance. The "false christs" of Mark 13 and Matthew 24 seem to be political figures, messianic pretenders associated with events leading up to the fall of Jerusalem in AD 70. It is not clear whether the term "Christ" is ever used in the Johannine literature with this sort of political implication, even in passages that reflect the views of nonbelievers (cf., e.g., Lk 23:2 with Jn 18:33 and 19:12).

19 Both views of the Antichrists' motives can be supported from the language of v.19. Most commentators conclude that the Antichrists were secessionists who were openly hostile toward John. For example,

Marshall, 151–52, says they "had once been members or adherents of the church, but had now departed from it, presumably to set up their own group. . . . It is a case of the voluntary departure of those who held views opposed to those of John." These people had previously accepted John's witness but "were now openly campaigning against it," attempting to increase their number by proselytizing in John's churches, persuading the faithful to join them (cf. Malatesta, 201; Brown, 338–39, 366–67; Smalley, 101–3; Culpepper, 45; Thompson, 75–76; Johnson, 56–57; Rensberger, 78–79). Because the Antichrists abandoned the fellowship rather than staying and working out the doctrinal differences, John makes failure to love other Christians the ultimate test of faith (1Jn 3:10–18; 4:7–12, 19–21). This position assumes that the conflict with the Antichrists is some time past, with the battle lines clearly drawn before the writing of 1 John.

The second position—that the Antichrists considered themselves to be in good fellowship with John and his churches—is less popular. This position assumes the conflict with the Antichrists is in progress or just beginning, with many Christians (including possibly the Antichrists themselves) still unaware of the problem. This view's most notable proponent is Rudolf Bultmann, 36, whose position is supported by several pieces of evidence from 1–2–3 John. First, John's statement that the Antichrists "went out from us" does not necessarily imply a hostile parting. Parallel with 1 John 2:19, ἐξέρχομαι, *exerchomai* ("go out," GK *2002*), is used at 2 John 7 of the "deceivers" John wishes the church to avoid. But at 3 John 7 the same word is used of "the brothers," associates of the Elder, who left on a preaching tour with his blessing and who may have delivered 1 John to the churches. The Johannine Jesus also uses ἐξέρχομαι, *exerchomai*, on several occasions to describe his departure from the Father ("I came from God"; Jn 8:42; 16:27–28; 17:8). It seems, then, that "went out" is a neutral term in John's vocabulary that refers to the process of embarking on a mission. Second, it is clear from the letters that many Christians were not yet aware of the conflict. At least two Christian leaders, Gaius (3Jn 1) and the "chosen lady" (2Jn 1), need to be told which teachers they ought to receive, suggesting that the doctrinal crisis is still in the initial stages, when reports are beginning to circulate and party lines are just developing. Third, the fact that the Elder needs to stress the distinction between true believers and Antichrists in 1 John, and to demand that all of his churches recognize this distinction in 2 and 3 John, suggests that the Antichrists still enjoyed access to John's churches. This is most easily explained if they claimed to be John's envoys preaching under his authorization.

20 The words "the truth" in the NIV do not appear in the Greek text, which literally reads, "You have an anointing from the Holy One and you all know." The translators have attempted to stress that believers know what is true, i.e., what is consistent with John's witness, while the teaching of the Antichrists is false.

REFLECTIONS

Culpepper, 52, rightly characterizes John's debate with the Antichrists as an expression of "the tension . . . between the conservative principle and the liberal, the need to preserve and the need to adapt." The Antichrists took the position that the gospel was plastic and subject to expansion under the Spirit's guidance. John, however, insists that Christians are identified by their adherence to core creeds about Christ. The tests he offers in this section make acceptance of these central tenets essential to a genuine relationship with God.

B. Test #6: Living without Sin (2:28–3:24)

OVERVIEW

Like the Antichrists, true believers live and act in an eschatological age. Cognates of *phaneroō* are used four times at 1 John 2:28–3:10 to situate Christian experience between Jesus' first "appearing" in flesh and his second "appearing" at the end of time. Believers face many hardships during this interim period, but God knows his children and will distinguish them from the world and the Antichrists when he comes to judge. In the meanwhile, true Christians can be identified by the fact that they do not sin.

John's teaching on "sin" (*hamartia*, GK *281*) is notoriously difficult, and it will be helpful to establish the general thrust of his argument before proceeding. On several occasions John makes extreme statements about sin that seem to contradict one another, sometimes even within the same passage. At times he seems to advocate a rigorous ethical perfectionism, arguing that true Christians do not sin at all (3:9–10), while elsewhere he insists that everyone sins and that anyone who denies this fact is a liar (1:8–10). Urgent ethical admonitions appear alongside gentle pastoral assurances that those who confess their sins enjoy Christ's advocacy (2:1–2, 12; 2:28–3:3). This tension between obedience and grace is epitomized at 5:16–18, where John says that Christians should pray for "brothers" who sin but then immediately emphasizes that no one "born of God" (presumably a "brother") sins (NIV, "continues to sin"). Many theories have been offered to explain the apparent paradoxes in John's discussion of sin, and it will be helpful to survey several before analyzing 2:28–3:24 (commentators rarely adhere to a single approach, making it difficult to categorize the major views; cf. Smalley, 159–62; Marshall, 178–81;

Brown, 411–16). As will be seen, the debate centers around two verses from this section, 3:6 and 3:9.

One popular interpretation, generally associated with the Wesleyan tradition, understands 3:6, 9 in the most literal, moral sense. From this perspective, Christians can reach a point in their faith experience where they no longer "sin," i.e., they no longer commit acts that violate God's commands. Ethical perfection is achieved, however, only after an existential experience of sanctification, in which the Holy Spirit forcefully reorients the inner moral compass of the believer. Those who are "wholly sanctified" lose their desire to sin, wishing only to obey God's will. It should be stressed that proponents of this view do *not* claim that those who are sanctified never violate God's moral law. They would, however, suggest that the sins of the sanctified person are committed unwillingly, originating not in the believer's will but in the power of sin itself (Ro 7:13–23). John therefore stresses that even sanctified believers must confess their sinful acts and receive forgiveness (1Jn 1:8–2:2). The historical origins of this view are reviewed in I. Howard Marshall, "Sanctification in the Teaching of John Wesley and John Calvin," *EvQ* 34 (1962): 75–82.

A second major interpretation of these two verses is reflected in the NIV. John's extreme statements on sin in these verses contain present-tense Greek verbs. If John is using the present tense to imply continuing action, he may be arguing that the Christian *lifestyle* is not characterized by willful disobedience. The NIV thus translates the phrase "no one who is born of God does sin [*hamartian ou poiei*]," at 3:9 as "no one who is born of God will *continue to* sin . . .; he cannot *go on* sinning" (emphasis added). By contrast, at 2:1 John uses the aorist tense, implying completed past action, to assure his audience that Christians who occasionally violate God's commands have Christ as their advocate (NIV, "if anybody does [commit a] sin, we have one who speaks to the Father"). From this perspective, then, John acknowledges that Christians sin from time to time, but he insists that they cannot continue in a lifestyle of habitual sinning (cf. Stott, 35–36; Johnson, 74–75).

A third interpretation, closely related to the second, explains John's view of sin by analogy with Paul's teaching. John, like Paul, believes that Christians commit sins but does not believe they are "sinners" in God's eyes, because they enjoy grace through Christ. While John focuses on the implications of grace for Christian lifestyle, Paul focuses on the status believers enjoy before God. Smalley, 164, who notes parallels between John and Paul and cites Luther's maxim that the believer is *simul justus et peccator* ("at once innocent and guilty"), states that "it is the potential state of sinfulness which John has in view throughout the present passage [1Jn 3]; and the actual occasions of sinfulness which he treats in chapters 1 and 2." These two views explain the tension in John's remarks by highlighting the paradox of grace: Christians are expected to abide by God's commands, but John realizes that they will break them from time to time, compelling them to appeal to Christ for help.

A fourth approach is provided by those commentators who focus on the rhetorical function of 3:6, 9 within the broader historical setting of 1 John. These scholars contend that the Antichrists advocated a doctrine of moral indifference, teaching that Christians, by their nature as God's children (3:1–2, 9; Jn 1:12), are unable to sin, regardless of their behavior. Brown, 431, suggests that the Antichrists saw "divine childhood [as] a once-for-all gift and not [as] a life that has to express itself in the behavior of the Christian" (cf. Brown, 81–83, 430–31; Dodd, 79–81; Culpepper, 63–64). Some who support this interpretation associate the Antichrists' position with the material dualism of later Gnostic thought: since the human body is material, evil, and unredeemable, ethics are irrelevant to the believer (so Barker, 331–32). To counter such teaching, John insists in the strongest terms that even God's children are subject to regulations for ethical purity. Passages such as 1 John 3:6, 9 are thus taken as hyperbole, with the more moderate statements on confession and forgiveness representing John's true perspective.

A fifth major interpretation situates 3:6, 9 in the broader context of John's eschatological dualism. Advocates of this position may focus on the *spatial* (here versus there) or *temporal* (now versus then) dimensions of John's dualistic thought. Those who focus on the spatial dimension stress John's distinction between "us" and "them," between his community and the hostile world. In John's view, the world is under the sway of "sin," an abstract cosmic power that controls the thoughts and motives of those who walk in darkness. Those who enter the community and experience rebirth as God's children are freed from this power, enabling them to truly obey God (Jn 1:5, 12–13; 3:3–6; 8:34–36). Christians thus "belong to the sphere where sin has no place"; they may, however, still choose to violate God's commands, even though such acts go against their new nature (Lieu, 36).

Those who focus on the temporal dimension see John's teaching on sin as the outworking of a realized eschatology. For example, Thompson, 91–92, highlights 1 John 3:1–3, noting that these verses stress that, although believers are truly God's children now, our transformation will not be complete until "he appears," for only then will we "be like him." When John describes Christians as those who "do not sin," he is imposing this future status on our present experience to highlight the goal of Christian life. Thompson writes, "In speaking of the present reality, John anticipates the promised transformation. . . . The power that is at work in the children of God in the present is the same power that shall transform them at the return of Christ." The believer's present obedience is thus a foretaste of the impending eschatological renewal. For this reason, John can speak of Christian perfection despite our ethical failures. Brown, 431, who adopts a version of this position, believes that John is thinking of a process of spiritual maturation: "The divine seed abides and continues to transform the child of God into the image of God's Son . . . until at the final revelation we are like God himself. The more that this divine seed transforms the Christian, the more impossible it is for the Christian to sin."

While all of these interpretations are reasonable, none are entirely satisfactory. Any attempt to soften John's doctrine of sin runs aground on the hard language of 3:6, 9. Verse 6 literally reads, "Everyone who remains in [Christ] does not sin; everyone who sins has not seen him or known him." Verse 9 is even stronger, insisting that the Christian "is not able (*ou dynatai*, GK *1538*) to sin, because she has been born of God." How is it, then, that John elsewhere says that anyone who denies his sin is a "liar"? It has already been noted that 1:8–10 most likely refers to the nonbeliever who refuses to confess his sins and enter the church (see comment), but this does not resolve the dilemma, for 5:16–18 clearly speaks of the "brother" who sins and needs prayer.

It seems most likely that John is using the term "sin" in a narrower sense at 3:6–10 than at 1:8–10, and that this narrower usage is related to the immediate context. The Greek *hamartia* ("sin") literally means "to miss the mark," to fall short of a standard God has set. As 1:8–10 indicates, no human being can claim moral perfection, for every person has fallen short of at least one divine command in some way. But not every person has broken God's law at every point, and 3:6–10 highlights a particular point in which true believers *never* violate God's law. This point is the love command (Jn 13:34), which was introduced at 2:9–11 as a test of Christian identity and is forcefully restated at 3:10–11. True Christians do not "sin" against the command to love their brothers.

This reading resolves the apparent tension between 3:6, 9 and 1:8–10. From John's perspective, all people sin in various ways, but those who are true Christians *never* sin against the love command. Disobeying the command to love is, in other words, not among the sins that believers must confess. John uses the same logic in 5:16, 18, where he urges believers to pray for the "brother" who sins and then insists that no one born of God sins. Christians can commit certain sins that need forgiveness, while other sins indicate that one is not a Christian in the first place. John can therefore distinguish between sins that should be prayed for and the "sin leading to death." Those who are "born of God" do not commit the "sin that leads to death" (5:16), even though a "brother" may need help with his moral failings. Similarly, only a person of the world or an Antichrist would need to confess to hating the brothers, for a true Christian perfectly obeys the love command. It seems, then, that in the context of 2:28–3:24, *hamartia* ("sin") and its cognates are used exclusively to refer to violations of the love command.

²⁸And now, dear children, continue in him, so that when he appears we may be confident and unashamed before him at his coming.

²⁹If you know that he is righteous, you know that everyone who does what is right has been born of him.

³:¹How great is the love the Father has lavished on us, that we should be called children of God! And that is what we are! The reason the world does not know us is that it did not know him. ²Dear friends, now we are children of God, and what we will be has not yet been made known. But we know that when he appears, we shall be like him, for we shall see him as he is. ³Everyone who has this hope in him purifies himself, just as he is pure.

⁴Everyone who sins breaks the law; in fact, sin is lawlessness. ⁵But you know that he appeared so that he might take away our sins. And in him is no sin. ⁶No one who lives in him keeps on sinning. No one who continues to sin has either seen him or known him.

⁷Dear children, do not let anyone lead you astray. He who does what is right is righteous, just as he is righteous. ⁸He who does what is sinful is of the devil, because the devil has been sinning from the beginning. The reason the Son of God appeared was to destroy the devil's work. ⁹No one who is born of God will continue to sin, because God's seed remains in him; he cannot go on sinning, because he has been born of God. ¹⁰This is how we know who the children of God are and who the children of the devil are: Anyone who does not do what is right is not a child of God; nor is anyone who does not love his brother.

¹¹This is the message you heard from the beginning: We should love one another. ¹²Do not be like Cain, who belonged to the evil one and murdered his brother. And why did he murder him? Because his own actions were evil and his brother's were righteous. ¹³Do not be surprised, my brothers, if the world hates you. ¹⁴We know that we have passed from death to life, because we love our brothers. Anyone who does not love remains in death. ¹⁵Anyone who hates his brother is a murderer, and you know that no murderer has eternal life in him.

¹⁶This is how we know what love is: Jesus Christ laid down his life for us. And we ought to lay down our lives for our brothers. ¹⁷If anyone has material possessions and sees his brother in need but has no pity on him, how can the love of God be in him? ¹⁸Dear children, let us not love with words or tongue but with actions and in truth. ¹⁹This then is how we know that we belong to the truth, and how we set our hearts at rest in his presence ²⁰whenever our hearts condemn us. For God is greater than our hearts, and he knows everything.

²¹Dear friends, if our hearts do not condemn us, we have confidence before God ²²and receive from him anything we ask, because we obey his commands and do what pleases him. ²³And this is his command: to believe in the name of his Son, Jesus Christ, and to love one another as he commanded us. ²⁴Those who obey his commands live in him, and he in them. And this is how we know that he lives in us: We know it by the Spirit he gave us.

COMMENTARY

2:28 John restates the admonition to "continue [*menō*] in him" and now situates it in an eschatological context. As in 2:19, *menō* refers to faithfulness to the orthodox view of Jesus and his teaching. Those who live by this teaching will not be ashamed at Jesus' *parousia* ("coming," GK *4242*), a common NT word for the second coming that highlights the implications of being in Christ's "presence." Those who deserve judgment fear the presence of the judge, while the innocent may approach the judge boldly. The Greek *schōmen parrēsian*, translated "be confident" in the NIV, is literally "to have plainness/boldness." In the fourth gospel, *parrēsia* refers to language that is clear and direct (Jn 16:25–30). True believers, who have obeyed Jesus' commands, will speak to Jesus this way at the second coming because they have nothing to hide.

29 Here John weaves together two community slogans, each introduced by *hoti*, to create the first test in this section: "*If* you know 'He is righteous [*dikaios*],'" *then* you also know, "'Everyone who does what is right [*dikaiosynē*] has been born of him.'" The logic of this test is based on the Johannine maxim that "the child imitates the parent" (Rensberger, 93). If God is indeed righteous—a premise John considers indisputable—then any person who is truly his child will act righteously.

It is clear, however, that John is using *dikaiosynē* in a highly nuanced way, related to the special meaning of *hamartia* ("sin") discussed above. Since "righteousness" is the logical opposite of "sin" (note the contrast at 3:7–8), and since "sin" refers in this context to failure to love one's brother, "righteousness" must refer to loving one's brother in obedience to the love command. John has already hinted at this usage at 1:9, stressing that God forgives sinners because he is "faithful and just [*dikaios*]," and at 3:10 he specifically associates godly righteousness with love for one's

brothers. The righteous person, then, is the one who loves other believers the way God loves them.

3:1 The first three verses of ch. 3 elaborate the status of the person who passes the test of love at 2:29. Childhood has both disadvantages and eschatological benefits. The disadvantages are explored at 3:1 in language that echoes several passages from the fourth gospel, most notably the prologue (Jn 1:1–18) and the farewell (Jn 13–17). Jesus came to his own, but the world did not "know him" (Jn 1:10; 1Jn 3:1) and does not know his disciples either. Because of this ignorance the world hates God and Jesus and will also hate anyone born of God (Jn 15:18–16:4; 17:14–15). The difficulties this creates for believers are, however, far outweighed by the eschatological benefits of childhood, which John explores in vv.2–3.

2 Many commentators have been struck by the language here, for at first glance it seems more Pauline than Johannine. Paul frequently speaks of the believer's transformation at the second coming (1Co 13:12; 15:35–53; Php 3:20–21; 1Th 4:13–17), but the fourth gospel stresses that Christians have already been reborn to eternal life (Jn 1:13; 3:3–8; 5:24–26; 6:53–57; 14:23). Indeed, the Johannine Jesus has almost nothing to say about his return except that he will come to his disciples in the form of the Paraclete (cf. Jn 14:18–23 with Mk 13 and Mt 24–25). Rensberger, 89, therefore concludes that 1 John 3:2 is "closer to non-Johannine forms of early Christian eschatology" than to the fourth gospel (cf. Barker, 330–31; Marshall, 171–73; Johnson, 68). Going a step further, Stott, 119, attempts to harmonize John's position with Paul's, positing a threefold sequence of events: "he will appear; we shall see him as he really is; we shall be like him." But the order of the two slogans at 3:2 suggests that John has not shifted from the realized eschatology of the fourth gospel.

Contra Stott's outline, John actually says that believers "shall be like him" *before* referring to their vision of Jesus. Believers will not be like Jesus because they will see him; rather, believers will see Jesus because they have been like him. As God's children, true Christians are already "like him," and Christ's appearing will only confirm this established fact. Rather than shifting from the "realized eschatology" of the fourth gospel, then, 3:2 asserts that the second coming will only clarify what believers already know to be true about God and themselves.

3 While childhood has benefits, it also carries responsibilities. These are summarized, again in eschatological terms, at v.3. All those who hope to see Jesus must "purify" themselves because Jesus is "pure." The Antichrists, who are "impure," are not like Jesus now, and this will be clearly revealed when he appears. At 1:7–9 John used purity language to describe the state of those whose sins have been forgiven. Since the primary sin under consideration in ch. 3 is violation of the love command, "purifying oneself" seems to refer to eliminating hatred from one's heart. The word "hope" (*elpis*, GK *1828*) here should not be taken in the modern English sense of uncertainty or wishful thinking but rather as a confident expectation about a future reality. There is no question that believers will "see him as he is" (v.2); the question is whether or not they will look like him. Those who love their brothers will look like him, while those who hate will not.

4–6 The second test in this section appears in v.6 and is supported by the assertions in vv.4–5. John first establishes a direct correlation between "sin" (*hamartia*) and "lawlessness" (*anomia*, GK *490*). Although v.4 is apparently John's own formulation rather than a communal creed (as indicated by the absence of *hoti*), he clearly expects his audience to appreciate the significance of this association. As a result, *anomia* is left undefined and unclear to modern readers. "Sin" and "lawlessness" are used synonymously in the LXX, but John seems to feel that the terms carry different nuances, so that "lawlessness" can be used to emphasize the seriousness of sin (cf. Brown, 398–99). Dodd, 72–73, suggests that John refers to sin as "lawlessness" to stress that "he is speaking of actual infraction of the moral law," keeping the discussion strictly within the confines of ethical behavior and away from claims based on spiritual experience. Our status as "children of God" does not change the basic definition of sin, nor does it alleviate our moral responsibility. Sin is always "lawlessness," whether committed by a child of God or anyone else. Other scholars believe that *anomia* derives from the broader eschatological thrust of 2:18 and 2:28–3:24. Several NT passages anticipate an outbreak of intense evil in the last days before Christ's return (e.g., Mt 13:41; 24:11–12). Since John has already cited a slogan about the coming of the Antichrist, it is relevant to note that Paul refers to another eschatological figure as "the Lawless One" (2Th 2:3–10). Brown, 400, therefore concludes that "the author [of 1 John] is again appropriating the apocalyptic expectations of the final time to describe his opponents," the lawless ones.

Both interpretations of *anomia* are reasonable, and perhaps both are correct. John clearly wishes to stress the eschatological urgency of the situation but perhaps also fears that his audience may be too lax in their attitude about sin. Since John is using "sin" to refer to a lack of love, he may need to stress that violation of the love command is of the same category as other, more concrete ethical violations (murder, lying, etc.). There are no degrees of sin, and love is not optional. In the eschatological scheme of things, those who do not keep the love command are enemies of God.

5 After battling the Antichrists in the eschatological arena, John now suddenly shifts the venue back to Jesus' first appearing. Apparently citing a community slogan (*hoti*), John reminds his audience that Jesus appeared for the purpose of taking away sins, not for the purpose of allowing his children to revel in lawlessness. Verse 5 epitomizes John's unique perspective on Jesus' sacrificial work. While Paul would associate the removal of sins specifically with Jesus' death or resurrection (Ro 4:25; 5:6–10; 1Co 15:17; Gal 1:4; Eph 5:1–2; Col 1:21–23; 1Th 5:9–10), John's view is broader, highlighting the salvific significance of the whole incarnation. John can therefore say, with Paul, that Jesus' blood cleanses the sinner (1Jn 1:7), but he can also say more generally that Jesus' very incarnation took sins away. Further, while other NT authors would specify that Jesus was able to die as a sacrifice only because he was morally perfect (Heb 7:26–28), John does not stress this point—perhaps he sees it as self-evident. The NIV therefore correctly treats the phrase here, "And in him is no sin," as a distinct thought. Taken together, the two sentences in v.5 emphasize the logic that underlies the test at v.6: Jesus has never had anything to do with sin—not then and not now. Since John is thinking of the love command, he may be touching on sayings such as John 15:9–13, which stress the purity and constancy of Jesus' love for his disciples.

6 The test at v.6 parallels that offered at 2:29. This time the positive scenario is stated first: *If* someone "lives [*menō*] in him," *then* that person does not sin (NIV, does not "keep on sinning"). This is the logical implication of John's earlier remarks, for if Jesus has no sin in himself, those who abide in him will be sinless also. As noted earlier, John recognizes the impossibility of this statement in a moral sense, but he clearly expects true believers to be perfect in their love for one another. The negative version of this test therefore suggests that, *If* anyone sins (NIV, "continues to sin"), *then* that person has not "seen him or known him." The idea that such a person has "not seen him" builds on the language of 1:1–3. Because John has, in fact, both seen and heard the

teaching of Jesus firsthand, he challenges any claims to knowledge of Jesus that overlook the love command. To make this test inclusive of every contingency, John introduces each scenario with the Greek *pas* ("all"). Every person who fails to love thereby proves she does not abide in Jesus, with no exceptions.

7–8 John continues the thought of vv.4–6 with two more tests at vv.7–8. These will prevent believers from being "led astray" by those who take a different view of the importance of love in the community. Since John has already identified the deceivers as the Antichrists (2:26), the tests may counter the Antichrists' belief that they could remain in good fellowship with God (and John?) after abandoning John's witness. First, *If* someone "does what is right," *then* that person is righteous, just as God is righteous. In this context, John means that those who love the brothers the way God does are "righteous." On the other hand, *If* anyone "does sin" (NIV, "does what is sinful"), *then* that person is "of the devil," which means that those who do not show love are enemies of God.

8 Realizing the harsh tone of this condemnation, John attempts to defend it by appealing to a traditional saying, "The devil has sinned [NIV, has been sinning] from the beginning." The fourth gospel situates a complex of similar sayings in the dialogue between Jesus and the Jews at the Feast of Tabernacles in John 8. As in 1 John 3, Jesus deduces that the Jews are children of the devil because they, like the devil, are guilty of the sin of hating him. Notably, whereas 3:8 says that the devil has sinned "from the beginning," Jesus specifies that the devil was *a murderer* "from the beginning" (Jn 8:44). As 1 John 3:11–12 will indicate, to hate and murder one's brother is the ultimate sin, for it obliterates the love command.

John's dualism comes through strongly here in the absolute contrasts between God/Satan, righteousness/sin, and love/hate. There can be no friendly differences or agreements to disagree. The Antichrists, by leaving John's doctrinal boundaries and stepping outside his fellowship, show themselves to be children of the devil. Indeed, if "the reason the Son of God appeared was to destroy the devil's work," how could God's children peacefully coexist with the devil's children?

9 John introduces his next test (v.10) with two premises supported by traditional statements. The first premise, that the person who is born of God does not sin, is supported by the slogan "God's seed remains in him." The second premise, that the believer is not able to sin (NIV, "go on sinning"), is supported by the statement "he has been born of God."

The first slogan, "his seed remains in him," has generated considerable controversy. The grammar of this statement is obscure and the thought is unique, with no direct NT parallels. One major difficulty relates to the intended reference of the pronoun *en autō* ("in him"). Most scholars prefer the NIV's understanding that *en autō* means "in the believer," so that God's "seed" (*sperma*, GK 5065) is a genetic principle or quality that remains in those who are his children, following the metaphor of biological birth. Some scholars who hold this view understand God's *sperma* to be the Holy Spirit, who regenerates believers at the point of conversion and remains in them to empower them not to sin (so Culpepper, 62–63; Johnson, 94–95; Rensberger, 91–92).

While this is consistent with John's view of the Paraclete, it is relevant to note here other passages in which John says that something "remains in" believers. At 1 John 2:14, John says that "the word of God" remains in believers; at 2:24, Christians are exhorted to allow what they "heard from the beginning" to remain in them; at 2:27, the true "anointing," a metaphor for the orthodox gospel (see comment), remains in believers; finally, at 2 John 2, "the truth," later defined as the love command (2Jn 5–6),

remains "in us and will be with us forever." These references suggest that God's "seed" is the tradition John has passed on to believers, a tradition that protects them from sin by teaching them what is right (cf. Dodd, 77–78; Malatesta, 247–50). Perhaps it is more important to stress what John does *not* mean here: God's "seed" is clearly not a reference to a New Age or Gnostic "divine spark" in human beings. In this context, John has been speaking of the need for believers to obey the love command perfectly, and v.9 simply stresses that God's true children are well acquainted with that teaching.

10 John has already highlighted the differences between the devil's children and God's children, and in v.10 he offers an absolute test to identify members of each group: *If* anyone does not do what is right, *then* that person is not from God. The next statement defines "doing right." Unfortunately, the NIV has translated the *kai* ("and") that connects these phrases as "nor," implying that John is thinking of two types of people: those who do not do what is right and those who do not love. More likely, John is specifying that the sin he has in mind throughout this section is failure to love. The person who does not love his brother cannot be from God, because God is love (5:16).

11–17 The test at v.10 is followed by two examples, one the audience should emulate and one they will hopefully reject. The good example, Jesus (vv.16–17), represents the behavior of those who pass the test and are found to be God's children. The bad example, Cain (vv.11–15), represents those who fail the test and show themselves to be children of the devil by hating their brothers. The language of the Cain illustration builds on the encounter between Jesus and the Jews in John 8:12–59, which is based, in turn, on the story of the first murder in Genesis 4. A brief review of both episodes will clarify John's understanding of the difference between Christians and Antichrists.

Genesis 4:1–16 narrates a single incident involving an offering to the Lord. Abel brings God an animal sacrifice from "the firstborn of his flock," whereas Cain brings "some of the fruits of the soil." For unspecified reasons God accepts Abel's offering but rejects Cain's, advising Cain to bring a proper sacrifice and to control his anger. Instead Cain ambushes and murders Abel, bringing God's curse on himself. The paucity of information here creates an aura of mystery, which allowed Cain to become a general symbol of evil in ancient Jewish and Christian writings (cf. Brown, 442–43). The early Christians apparently believed that Cain killed his brother out of envy, coveting the approval Abel had received from God, and allegorized the story to explain the Christian experience of persecution. Jesus says that those who harm his followers will be held responsible for all "the righteous blood that has been shed on earth, from the blood of righteous Abel to the blood of Zechariah" (Mt 23:35). The author of Hebrews alludes to Cain twice, the first time commending Abel because he won God's approval by offering "a better sacrifice than Cain did" (11:4), the second time comparing the blood of Abel to the covenantal blood of Jesus (12:22–24). Jude, in his tirade against heretics, says such people "have taken the way of Cain" because they "speak abusively against whatever they do not understand," resisting those who teach the truth rather than repenting (10–11). These examples suggest that the story of Cain and Abel was used in early Christian rhetoric for apologetic purposes to explain why true believers suffer. Persecution occurs because the wicked (Cain) recognize that God has rejected them for their evil deeds and envy those who have won God's approval through obedience (Abel).

The early Christian allegorization of Cain and Abel was well suited to John's dualistic thinking. Within a matrix of absolute contrasts, Johannine Christians could easily associate the children of light with Abel and the children of darkness with Cain, portraying the conflict between Christians and the world in terms of Genesis 4. One clear example of this rhetorical strategy appears in an encounter between Jesus and the Jews. Jesus portrays himself as "the light of the world," who "stands with the Father" because he is "not of this world" (Jn 8:12, 16, 23). Like Abel, Jesus does not glorify himself but instead receives glory because God approves of his deeds (Jn 8:29, 54). The Jews, however, have been overpowered by sin, like Cain (Ge 4:7; Jn 8:34–35). They therefore resist Jesus' claims and seek to kill him for telling the truth (Jn 8:37, 59), just as Cain killed Abel for offering the appropriate sacrifice. Because John variously refers to this same group of people as "Jews," "Cain," and "children of the devil" (1Jn 3:8–10), and because Cain is notorious as the first murderer, the Johannine Jesus can make the strange assertion that the devil (= Cain) "was a murderer from the beginning" (Jn 8:44) and can also portray the Jews' rejection of his claims as an intent to murder him long before they actually express any interest in killing him (Jn 8:37, 40, 44, 59). It seems, then, that the Johannine Christians occasionally used images and terms from the story of Cain and Abel to describe the conflict between Jesus and those who rejected him.

11 John's allegorization of Genesis 4 brings the extreme statements of 1 John 3:11–16 into focus. The section opens with a restatement of the love command (Jn 13:34), which they have "heard from the beginning" in the sense that it originates with Jesus.

12 From John's dualistic perspective, those who do not "love" believers must "hate" them the way Cain hated Abel, leading him to murder his own brother. In the context of 1 John 3, Cain's act of murder symbolizes the Antichrists' departure from John's fellowship. Of course, the Antichrists would dispute this association, either because they still consider John to be in their good fellowship or because they would blame John for severing the relationship. To counter such claims, John extends the analogy in dualistic terms, insisting that the Antichrists did not leave due to doctrinal disagreements but rather out of envy. They realized that John's deeds, like those of Abel, were "righteous" (*dikaios*, GK *1465*) and therefore godlike (1Jn 1:9; 2:29; 3:7, 10), while their own were "evil" (*ponēra*, GK *4505*), like Cain's, because they originated with the "evil one" (*ho ponēros*; cf. Jn 3:20). Further, in order to stress the treachery of their departure John describes Cain's act of murder by using the word *sphazō* ("murder," GK *5377*), which emphasizes the violence of Abel's death and the hostility of the Antichrists' actions.

13 Yet John is not surprised that the Antichrists would behave this way toward him, for Christians should expect the world to hate them. Verse 13, along with the comment at 2:19 that the Antichrists "did not really belong to us," indicates that John has separated the Antichrists from his fellowship and now considers them no different from other members of the world.

14 This verse contains the first of two tests to identify those who possess the spirit of Cain. The test at v.14 is based on two *hoti* phrases, the first of which introduces a community slogan and the second of which is causal, establishing the condition under which the slogan is true: If (*hoti*) we love the brothers, *then* we know "we have passed from death to life." Those who fail this test "remain in death," a gruesome image that serves as a logical counterpart to the Johannine emphasis on "abiding" (*menō*) in God and God's word. The perfect tense of *metabainō* (GK *3553*; NIV, "have passed") is synonymous with John's frequent use of the passive of *gennaō* ("to be born," GK *1164*), describing Christian conversion as a transformation of one's nature. In John's view, all people start out in the world alienated from God.

Those who truly accept Jesus' claims are transformed into God's children (Jn 1:12–13), passing "from death to life" (see comment at 1Jn 1:2). Jesus discusses the same transition at John 5:24, indicating that this occurs when someone "hears my word and believes him who sent me." In that context, emphasis is placed on accepting Jesus' self-revelation, but in 1 John 3 "my word" becomes the love command. Verse 14 thus specifies that true spiritual renewal does not occur at the point of faith but rather at the point of love for other believers. Christians are distinct from the world on the basis of their faith and distinct from Antichrists on the basis of their mutual love (cf. Jn 13:35; 17:21). Anyone who does not love the brothers, irrespective of her doctrinal claims, is not welcome in John's fellowship.

15 Realizing that some might object to such a narrow view of salvation, John returns to the Cain analogy with a second test at v.15. The all-inclusive proposition (*pas*; NIV, "anyone") is undergirded by a condition: If anyone "hates [*miseō*, GK *3631*] his brother," *then* that person "is a murderer." The significance of this conclusion is indicated by the next phrase, a slogan stating the apparently general belief that "no murderer has eternal life in him" (cf. Ro 1:28–32). Although perhaps extreme, the equation of hatred with murder is consistent with John's dualistic disposition toward "reducing an ethical issue to its most basic form" (Rensberger, 99). Because hatred is the root of murder (cf. Dt 19:11), those who hate are in the same category as Cain. The possible origins of the slogan John cites to make this point are intriguing. While "having life" is a typically Johannine moniker for salvation (e.g., Jn 3:16; 10:10), no such teaching on hatred appears in the fourth gospel, and many commentators have noted the remarkable similarity between 1 John 3:15 and Matthew 5:21–22. There Jesus, commenting on the sixth commandment (Ex 20:13), states that "anyone who is angry with his brother will be subject to judgment." It seems unlikely, however, that John is appealing to the tradition that underlies Matthew 5, for Matthew's wording is different from John's, and Matthew focuses on the need to control one's tongue rather than the salvific status of believers who hate other Christians. John's slogan more likely derives from the Cain allegory than from any specific teaching of Jesus. Matthew would, however, support John's basic assertion that hatred and murder are cut from the same cloth. The Antichrists are thereby placed outside not only the sphere of John's community but also the sphere of salvation.

16 Having vilified the Antichrists by analogy with Cain, John offers a positive example of true love: Jesus. The NIV's colon renders the Greek *hoti*, which here introduces a paraphrase of John 15:13—"Greater love has no one than this, that he lay down his life for his friends" (cf. Jn 10:11–18). "Lay down his life [*psychē*, GK *6034*]" is a uniquely Johannine way of describing Jesus' voluntary self-sacrifice, an act that represents the highest possible expression of love (Jn 15:13). The citation at 1 John 3:16 is introduced with the perfect tense of *ginōskō* ("we have known," GK *1182*), which probably refers both to mental awareness and emotional experience (see comment at 2:2). True believers "have known" of Jesus' love not only in the sense that they have accepted John's witness about Jesus but also in the sense that they have experienced divine love and forgiveness. Such an experience should motivate them to act in the same self-sacrificing way toward other believers.

John's dualistic mind-set is evident in his narrow and absolute definition of love (*agapē*). There are no degrees of love: those who sacrifice themselves, like Jesus, show love; those who do not act this way show hate. The NIV reflects this emphasis with the translation "This is how we know what love is." Since there is only one kind of love, and since this one kind was modeled by Jesus, Christians, like Jesus, "ought to lay down our lives for our brothers." In the

historical setting of 1–2–3 John (see Introduction), this might mean that some Johannine Christians had literally suffered martyrdom for the community, but the application of the principle in v.17 suggests that John is thinking of one's material possessions. The person who does not sacrifice herself and her wealth for her brothers is no different from the Antichrists and Cain. If it seems too much to ask for this sort of love, John could point out that Jesus laid down his life not only for his friends (Jn 15:13) but even for the hostile world (Jn 6:51). Surely, then, Christians can at least love other Christians.

17 Up to this point, John's discussion of love and hate has been rather abstract, focusing on vague generalities. Here he offers a direct and practical test that will identify selfless love. John states this test in the form of a sarcastic rhetorical question. The Greek text of the verse consists of four phrases loosely arranged in a brief narrative:

1. *If* someone has "the life of the world" (NIV, "material possessions"), and
2. *If* that person "sees his brother having need," and (*kai*; NIV, "but")
3. *If* that person "closes his heart to" (NIV, "has no pity on") the needy brother,
4. *then* the love of God does not remain in him.

The opening statement in John's illustration is considerably stronger in the Greek text than in the NIV. While the NIV translates *ton bion tou kosmou* ("the life of the world"; cf. Marshall, 194 n. 20) with the somewhat neutral "material possessions," both *bios* and *kosmos* (GK *3180*) have negative implications in Johannine thought. First John 2:16 refers to material wealth as the "pride of life [*bios*]," associating it with "the lust of the flesh" and "the lust of the eyes," which do not proceed from the Father. The true origin of such things is indicated here in 3:17: they are "from the *kosmos*," the hostile world that is alienated from God and hates Jesus (see Introduction). While modern Western Christians might be uncomfortable with the association, John suggests that material wealth is inherently worldly, making it almost unnatural for a believer to be possessed of excess resources. This being the case, Christians should have no difficulty relieving themselves of money whenever a need arises.

Phrase 2 introduces the second character in John's scenario. The contrast between this person and the first person hinges on the repetition of *echō*, "has." While the first person "has life," the second person "has need." John uses *theōreō* ("sees," GK *2555*), to describe the first person's realization of the second person's need. While poverty may indeed manifest itself visibly in the appearance of its victims, John probably wishes to stress that the person in question has firsthand information about his brother's need. In such a situation, the example of Jesus would call the wealthy brother to divest himself of his worldly goods and help the person who is less fortunate.

The plot of John's story, however, takes a tragic turn, for phrase 3 indicates that the wealthy brother has gone the way of Cain. The NIV dilutes the treachery of the wealthy man's deed by saying that he "has no pity," suggesting only a passive indifference toward the brother's need. In fact, John portrays the wealthy brother as one who actively distances himself from the situation by "closing his heart" to his brother. "Heart" here is *splanchna* ("the bowels," GK *5073*), which the ancient Greeks saw as the seat of the emotions. The unusual image of "closing" (*kleiō*, GK *3091*) one's affections probably builds on *theōreō* from phrase 2. The wealthy man's eye is open to his brother's need, but his heart is closed so he takes no action. He has failed the test.

Phrase 4 offers the conclusion that must be drawn in such a case. "Love of God" uses the objective genitive ("love for God") to stress a point that echoes a number of sayings in both the Synoptics and the

fourth gospel: those who do not love their brothers do not love God either. Jesus set the standard for self-sacrifice, and those who disregard that standard cannot legitimately claim to love him (Mt 25:31–45; Mk 10:45). The Johannine Jesus stresses this point in the final moments with his disciples in the upper room. After washing their feet, Jesus tells them, "You should do [for each other] as I have done for you" (Jn 13:14–15). Shortly thereafter Jesus gives the disciples the "new command," that they must "love each other as I have loved you" (13:34; 15:12). Since Jesus commanded believers to treat one another in this way, and since only those who obey Jesus' commands remain in his love (15:9–14), John concludes that those who disobey the command to love are not friends of Jesus, meaning that they do not truly love God. Caring for one's brothers becomes, then, a visible test of one's relationship with God. Those who fail this test remain in the world with Cain.

While the general ethical implications of this test are obvious (if painful), John's sudden emphasis on Christian benevolence, a subject he has not previously mentioned, seems abrupt. In what way does this test apply to the Antichrist situation, and how does it distinguish the children of God from the children of the devil (v.10)? The answer may lie in the distinction John makes between Gaius and Diotrephes in 3 John. Both 2 and 3 John suggest that the Johannine churches were held together by a network of itinerant teachers, protégés of John who spoke and acted on his behalf (see Introduction; comment at 1Jn 2:19). Second John 10–11 and 3 John 5–8 indicate that John's representatives relied on the support and hospitality of local congregations to finance their travels. The test at 1 John 3:17 may be aimed at people such as Diotrephes, an apparent ally of the Antichrists, who "refuses to welcome the brothers [and] also stops those who want to do so" (3Jn 10). In such a setting, the wealthy person would represent the kind of inhospitable people (e.g., Diotrephes) who show hatred for their righteous brothers (John's representatives) by ignoring their needs and refusing to support them. Such hostile behavior proves in John's mind that Diotrephes and others like him do not truly love God. On the other hand, Christian leaders such as Gaius, who has shown hospitality to John's associates and has "sent them on their way in a manner worthy of God" (3Jn 6), prove their love for God by obeying the love command.

18 After blasting the Antichrists John suddenly shifts to a more pastoral tone to encourage his "children" (*teknion*), those who pass the test of love. Verse 18 summarizes vv.11–17 and also John's general view of Christian duty. Love does not express itself "with words or tongue" but rather "in deeds and truth" (NIV, "with actions and in truth"). This statement parallels John 4:24, where Jesus tells the Samaritan woman that true worshipers must approach the Father "in spirit and in truth." "In truth" has a doctrinal orientation, referring to a correct view of Jesus. Just as real worship depends on a proper recognition of Jesus' identity, genuine Christian ethics must also be based on John's orthodox witness. This verse epitomizes John's belief that all aspects of Christian life are grounded in Christology.

19–20 These verses discuss the benefits enjoyed by those who express their love "in deeds and truth." The Greek text of these verses is difficult, being one long, convoluted statement that the NIV tries to clarify by breaking into two shorter sentences. At least three points of translation, all of which carry significant implications for exegesis, must be addressed. First, John uses *hoti* three times in these two verses. The first usage (v.19), clearly seems to introduce direct or indirect discourse (NIV, "*that* we belong . . ."), but the function of the other two usages is far from certain. Second, the verb *peithō* (NIV, "set at rest," GK *4275*) permits of two possible translations, both of which are reasonable in this context. Third, the word "heart" (*kardia*, GK *2840*),

which also appears three times in these verses, carries a slightly different connotation in Greek than in English. Any exegesis of these verses must account for these difficulties and their implications.

The easiest of the three problems concerns the value of the Greek term *kardia*. The NIV translates the word literally as "heart," but the English "heart" suggests a complex of ideas that are alien to John's thinking. Popular English generally uses "heart" to represent the emotions, particularly the more tender feelings (love, compassion, grief, etc.). The NIV's "we set our hearts at rest" suggests to the modern reader that John is speaking of freedom from feelings of guilt. But John has just used *splachna*, not *kardia*, in v.17 to refer to the feelings, and, as Marshall, 198 n.5, observes, "In Hebrew thought the heart is tantamount to the conscience." John is thus not speaking about an emotional burden but rather about an objective self-evaluation of one's moral standing. Neither John nor any other NT author suggests that Christians should respond to moral failure by plaguing themselves with feelings of guilt.

In what sense, then, do the consciences of true believers "condemn" (*kataginōskō*, GK *2861*) them, so that they need to know that "God is greater than our hearts" (v.20)? At first glance the warm reassurance of vv.19–20 seems to contradict the apparent moral perfectionism of vv.4–10. After apparently insisting that Christians do not sin, John now seems to assume that Christians will violate their consciences and proceeds to assure them that God's grace is greater than our sense of imperfection. The tension between these two passages may be resolved by stressing once again that "sin" in 2:28–3:24 refers exclusively to violation of the love command. The love command is in John's view the core of the Christian life, making it an absolute test of faith: those who do not love the brothers are not Christians in the first place. No true Christian, then, can have a bad conscience about the love command, for all who fail to love are not true believers. But true believers may commit other sins, and their consciences may rightly conclude that these actions are unacceptable in God's sight. It is these sins John has in mind when he says that "God is greater than our hearts." God knows that true believers desire to do what is right, and he forgives them when they fail to do so. But God's grace cannot cover the sin of breaking the love command, for grace is limited to true believers, and no true believer fails to love. While this may seem harsh, it is relevant to note that John's view is consistent with that of Matthew. The Matthean Jesus also limits the boundaries of grace ("Forgive us our debts, as we also have forgiven our debtors") and assures those who refuse to forgive that God will not forgive them either (Mt 6:9–15; 18:21–35). Similarly, John insists that God can overcome every violation of conscience except a failure to show love to others. In fact, John's view is somewhat more lenient than that of Matthew, for while Matthew's Jesus insists that his disciples must love even their enemies and, going far beyond John, "pray for those who persecute you" (Mt 5:44), John demands only that Christians love one another. Those who do not love have little hope of forgiveness, while those who do can rest assured that all other sins are swept away.

The next difficulty in the Greek text of 1 John 3:19–20 relates to the proper translation of *peithō*. The NIV, consistent with the notion that "heart" refers to the emotions, translates the term, "we *set* our hearts *at rest*," suggesting that our fears and feelings of guilt are assuaged by our knowledge of God's greater grace (cf. Marshall, 197 n. 2; Johnson, 87–88). Brown, 455, however, notes that *peithō* normally means "'to convince, persuade, win over,' usually with the implication of persuading people to do something toward which they would not naturally be inclined, or of convincing them of something

that is not obvious." While there is only a slight shade of difference between the two readings, the context suggests that Brown's understanding is technically more accurate. Since "heart" here refers to the conscience, and since the conscience is the moral prosecutor of each person's behavior, it seems that *peithō* builds on *kataginōskō* ("condemn") in v.20. Whenever the conscience reels under moral failure, our recognition of God's grace "persuades" our conscience that all is well. Again, this persuasion comes only to those who pass the love test at v.18.

Perhaps the most significant difficulty in the Greek text of vv.19–20 derives from the triple use of *hoti*. The NIV interprets the first *hoti* (v.19) as an introduction to indirect discourse: "This then is how we know *that* we belong to the truth" (Dodd, 92; Brown, 439; Smalley, 199–200; Johnson, 87–88; Rensberger, 103). Against this view, it should be noted that John generally combines *hoti* with verbs of "knowing" to introduce traditional sayings or community slogans (see comments at 1Jn 2:3–4, 5, 29; 3:2, 5, 14, 15, 16). The same appears to be the case here. The slogan "we are of the truth" builds on the title "children of God" in v.10 via John's belief that Jesus is "the truth" (Jn 14:6) and his insistence that the orthodox Christian proclamation is true (1Jn 2:20–22, 27). In the light of v.18, "we are of the truth" asserts that those who obey the love command show themselves to be in line with John's true witness, which gives them confidence "in [God's] presence." The sudden reference to God's presence probably draws on the eschatological imagery John has been using throughout this section (cf. 2:28; 3:2; 4:17). The verbs *ginōskō* ("we know") and *peithō* ("set at rest") at v.19 are both future tense, indicating that our confidence awaits its final fulfillment. At the judgment, those whose beliefs and deeds are correct will have nothing to fear (cf. 3:1–3).

The value of the second *hoti* at the beginning of v.20 is more difficult to ascertain. Some commentators suggest that the Greek text, which reads *hoti ean kataginōskē*, should be corrected to *ho ti an kata-ginōskē*, understanding *hoti* as the neuter of the relative pronoun *hostis* ("who"/"which"). This gives the phrase the flavor of an indefinite condition, as reflected in the NIV: "we set our hearts at rest in his presence *whenever* [lit., *in whatever*] our hearts condemn us" (cf. Marshall, 196–97; Smalley, 200). Other scholars suggest that *hoti* introduces a parenthetical statement that continues the thought of v. 19 by indicating the conditions under which our consciences would need to be persuaded. This makes the first *hoti* in v. 20 a punctuation mark that does not translate into English: "we shall convince our heart that, if our heart condemns us, God is greater . . ." (so Brown, 439, 456; Rensberger, 103–4). As a third possibility, *hoti* may be used here in a causal sense, indicating the reason we may convince our hearts. If this is the case, the phrase "whenever our hearts condemn us" is an interruption of John's main line of thought, which is resumed by repeating *hoti* a third time, making the third *hoti* a punctuation mark. The NKJV takes this approach with the reading "by this we know that we are of the truth, and shall assure our hearts before Him. *For if* our heart condemns us, God is greater . . ." Although all three translations produce similar readings, in this context the third interpretation seems most likely. John has just indicated that Christians may have confidence in God's presence and now explains that they enjoy this assurance "because" God's knowledge overcomes our self-condemnation.

The third *hoti* in these verses introduces the statement "God is greater than our hearts, and he knows everything." The creedal nature of this statement suggests that John is citing a community slogan, so that *hoti* in this case introduces direct discourse. The slogan is reminiscent of the story of Peter's restoration. The resurrected Jesus questions Peter three times about the sincerity of his love in light of Peter's failure to confess Jesus in the

moment of trial (Jn 21:15–17; cf. Jn 18:15–18, 25–27). Peter realizes his treacherous actions have challenged his claim to loyalty, and he appeals in desperation to Jesus' omniscience: "Lord, you know all things; you know that I love you" (21:17). Similarly, the slogan at 1 John 3:20 reminds true believers that God is aware of their good intentions, allowing him to treat us more graciously than we treat ourselves.

21–22 These verses explore the condition of those who consciences do not condemn them—true believers who recognize that God's penetrating knowledge overcomes their moral failures. Such people "have *parrēsia*" ("have confidence") before God, which allows them to "receive from him anything we ask." *Parrēsia* is a particularly appropriate term here, for in the fourth gospel it refers to language that is forward and direct (Jn 16:25–30; see comment at 1Jn 2:28). Those whose consciences are clear may make requests with confidence because they have nothing to hide from God. The two reasons for this confidence are introduced by a *hoti* that carries, as the NIV indicates, causal force: *because* (1) we keep his commands, and (2) we "do what pleases him." The phrases are synonymous, stressing the point that confidence in prayer comes from obedience.

22 This verse plays a key role in debates over the "health and wealth gospel" on the one hand and the "problem of evil" on the other. On the surface, John seems to suggest that believers can demand anything they wish from God and expect to receive it. Some modern Western Christians take this to mean that God will grant any material luxury they desire. From this perspective, unanswered prayer indicates that the supplicant is not truly obedient to God, perhaps concealing some secret sin or lack of faith. At the same time, this verse can present a serious obstacle to Christian apologetics, for it makes it difficult to explain why God does not answer the legitimate prayers of those who are suffering and oppressed. It is also hard to reconcile

John's confident assertions here with passages such as John 15:18–16:4, which suggest that alienation and pain are the norm of Christian experience and that God does not plan to answer prayers for relief.

The raw facts of life suggest that v.22 cannot be correct. How, then, can this verse be reconciled with "our humdrum and often disappointing experience" (Marshall, 199)? To understand John's perspective, we must recognize that v.22 builds on the same complex of ideas that underlies several passages in the fourth gospel. On three occasions during the farewell address (Jn 13–17), Jesus states that the disciples, as they pray by the authority of Jesus and in the confidence that this produces, will receive anything they ask for in his name (Jn 14:13–14; 15:7; 16:23–24). In these passages John clearly connects answered prayer with (1) obedience and faith (cf. 14:15; 15:5–6) and (2) the glorification of Jesus and/or the Father (cf. 15:8).

It seems, then, that at 1 John 3:22 John is thinking specifically of prayers for divine power and strength to proclaim the gospel. True believers "receive from him anything we ask," the power and strength to overcome the world and the Antichrists, "*because we obey* his commands." Similarly, John assures "you who believe in the name of the Son of God" (5:13) that "if we ask anything according to his will, he hears us" (5:14). Presumably the only concern of the true disciple is that God will be glorified, so that true disciples offer prayers in accordance with God's will. This condition automatically excludes prayers for material luxury or expectations that God will relieve suffering. In fact, since God commands us not to "love the world or anything in the world" (2:15), those who pray for fulfillment of their worldly desires automatically remove themselves from the provisions of these verses. They may, of course, receive the wealth they seek, but the source of such wealth is the world, not God (see comments at 1Jn 3:16, 17).

23 This verse epitomizes Johannine Christianity. John has insisted throughout this section that true Christians do not sin because they keep God's commands, and here he specifies the two commands he has in mind. The first relates to one's ideology: "believe in the name of his Son, Jesus Christ." True Christians, unlike the Antichrists, accept that the human Jesus was also the divine Son of God. While it may seem unusual to portray faith as an act of obedience, the same idea underlies John 6:29. There the Jews, after the miraculous feeding, ask Jesus to tell them what they must do to fulfill God's desires. His reply replaces works of faith with faith itself: "The work of God is this: to believe in the one he has sent." John's second command relates to one's lifestyle: "love one another as he commanded us" (cf. Jn 13:34; 15:12). Although not stated as a test, these two characteristics distinguish true believers from the world (those who reject Jesus altogether) and from the Antichrists (those who claim to be believers but remain outside the community because they do not love [i.e., do not accept John's teaching and authority]).

24 John concludes the present section and transitions toward the next (4:1–6). Up to this point, the discussion has focused heavily on what the individual must do to establish her status as a true child of God. John has emphasized sinlessness, correct beliefs, and expressions of love—all personal achievements—as the marks of a Christian. Verse 24 highlights the spiritual dimension of genuine Christian experience. Those who obey enjoy the mystical, mutual indwelling with the Father that Jesus requested for his disciples at John 17:20–23. To stress this point, John introduces a community slogan with the formula *ginōskomen hoti* ("we know"): "He remains [*menō*] in us" (NIV, "we know that he lives in us"). This proposition is validated by the Christian experience of the Spirit. John closely associates Jesus with the Spirit, so much so that Jesus will come to the disciples in the form of the Paraclete (Jn 14:15–18). The fact, then, that true believers have the Spirit proves that God is with them and that they have passed the tests. John's implication that the Antichrists do not possess God's Spirit suggests that belief, ethics, and union with God go hand in hand. Those who do not hold to a proper belief and do not live under Jesus' commands cannot legitimately claim that God's Spirit dwells in them. Rensberger, 107, notes that "although the possession of the Spirit and mutual abiding with God are interior events, they are validated by means that are . . . thoroughly public."

NOTES

3:9 Contra the majority view of ἐν αὐτῷ, *en autō*, as meaning "in the believer," the Moffatt translation takes this to mean "in God," with the idea that God's "seed," his children, "remain in Him," making it impossible for those who are truly born of God to sin. Moffatt's interpretation is supported by the fact that the fourth gospel uses σπέρμα, *sperma*, on several occasions to refer to physical descent (Jn 7:42; 8:33– 37). Some commentators seek a compromise position, arguing that God's σπέρμα, *sperma*, is "a divine principle of life which abides in the believer" and includes the influence of both the Spirit and the Word (so Marshall, 186–87; Brown, 409–11; Smalley, 173–74).

17 Scholars are divided on the implications of the genitive θεοῦ, *theou*. Some suggest it has ablative force, meaning that the love that comes "from God" does not flow through the person who does not love her brother. Brown, 450, for example, concludes that "the person described in 17abc is blocking the movement of divine love, which would lead him to treat his brother as Christ treated us, so divine love does not function in such a person" (cf. Bultmann, 56; Culpepper, 71; Stott, 144; Rensberger, 101). Others conclude, based on the analogy with Jesus' self-sacrifice, that John means "the type of love shown by God," a qualitative use of the genitive that is reflected in the NRSV rendering (so Smalley, 197; Johnson, 85).

REFLECTIONS

First John 2:28–3:24 opens on an eschatological note, but the tests in this section place Christian life squarely in the present. The eternal aspects of Christian experience are lived out now, in this world, and the future will only reveal what God and true believers have known all along. For John, "being a Christian" means believing in Jesus as the Christ and showing love to other Christians by remaining in the community. The benefits for those who pass these tests are available *now*, not just in a vague eschatological future: true life, confidence in prayer, and God's presence through the Spirit. Likewise, the Antichrists reap the rewards of their wickedness in this life. By leaving John's fellowship, they prove that they have not seen God or known him, that they are children of the devil, and that they do not have eternal life in themselves.

First John 3:23 introduces two hallmarks of genuine Christianity that John will explore in the next two sections: 4:1–6 explains what it means to "believe in the name of his Son, Jesus Christ," while 4:7–21 clarifies what it means to "love one another."

C. Test #7: The True Spirit (4:1–6)

OVERVIEW

John has just reminded believers that the Spirit's presence confirms their relationship with God. While this assertion should give Christians confidence, it also touches on a key problem in John's struggle with the Antichrists (see Introduction). Since both true and false teachers could claim to speak by the Spirit's guidance, and since Johannine tradition could be taken to suggest that the Spirit may lead the church beyond the boundaries of established belief (Jn 16:12–13), how can one tell which teachers are telling the truth? In this section John affirms the spiritual dimension of all teaching, while offering a test to distinguish God's Spirit from the Antichrists. In the process he clarifies that "believing in the name of his Son, Jesus Christ" (1Jn 3:23) has both subjective (spiritual) and objective (doctrinal) dimensions.

---

¹Dear friends, do not believe every spirit, but test the spirits to see whether they are from God, because many false prophets have gone out into the world. ²This is how you can recognize the Spirit of God: Every spirit that acknowledges that Jesus Christ has come in the flesh is from God, ³but every spirit that does not acknowledge Jesus is not from God. This is the spirit of the antichrist, which you have heard is coming and even now is already in the world.

⁴You, dear children, are from God and have overcome them, because the one who is in you is greater than the one who is in the world. ⁵They are from the world and therefore speak from the viewpoint of the world, and the world listens to them. ⁶We are from God, and whoever knows God listens to us; but whoever is not from God does not listen to us. This is how we recognize the Spirit of truth and the spirit of falsehood.

COMMENTARY

1 John immediately introduces what will become the key term in this section, *pneuma* ("spirit," GK *4460*). Some believers have been led astray by those who falsely claim to speak by God's Spirit, and John wishes to protect those who remain in his fellowship. Today such claims might be countered by denying that *any* teaching is "inspired" and by accusing those who make such claims of spiritualizing a natural process. John, however, clearly believes that the Spirit plays a key role in Christian instruction (cf. Jn 16:12–15), which leads him to insist that true orthodox teaching (such as his own) is inspired by God's Spirit, while the Antichrists' doctrines are not. Again, a modern approach would insist that the Antichrists have generated these false teachings from their own minds. John, however, consistent with his dualistic worldview, subscribes to the notion that *all* teaching, true or false, has a spiritual dimension. He can therefore acknowledge that both true teachers and Antichrists are inspired by spirits, but he warns his audience that they must not "believe every spirit." The term "believe" (NIV) renders the Greek *pisteuō* (GK *4409*), which here means "trust." Not all teachers can be trusted, because some of them are driven by spirits that do not come from God.

To stress the danger of the situation, John tells his audience that "many false prophets have gone out into the world." The NIV is probably correct in translating the *hoti* that introduces this phrase with causal force ("because many false prophets . . ."), as the presence of false prophets states the reason why Christians must exercise caution. At the same time, John may be introducing a slogan or a traditional saying with an eschatological flavor. Although no similar saying appears in the fourth gospel, the reference to false prophets going out into the world resembles Mark 13:22, where Jesus warns the disciples that false prophets will appear with the purpose of "deceiving the elect." At 1 John 4:6, John associates the Antichrists with the "spirit of falsehood," and his use of *exerchomai* ("go out") in v.1 suggests that his opponents are on a mission to deceive (see comment at 1Jn 2:19). This again portrays the Antichrists as allied with the cosmic forces of evil; their teachings are inspired by the end-times spirit of false prophecy, which seeks to lead people astray (cf. 1Ti 4:1).

2–3 John says believers must "test the spirits" (v.1) to distinguish between true teachers and Antichrists. Strangely, this statement is sometimes taken to refer to a mystical power of discernment or, in extreme cases, a technique of exorcism, despite the fact that John has very little to say about demons or spiritual gifts. The Greek *dokimazō* ("test," GK *1507*) suggests a more objective inquiry, and vv.2–3 offer the criteria for such an investigation. The positive version of the test (v.2) is introduced clearly with the statement "in this you know the Spirit of God" (NIV, "this is how you can recognize the

Spirit of God"). "Know" (*ginōskō*) has a wide range of meanings in 1 John (see comment at 2:3), but here it refers to an objective conclusion based on empirical data. The NIV thus correctly translates the term "recognize." "Of God" (*tou theou*) is genitive of source or ablative: the test will distinguish whether or not a person's teaching comes from the Spirit that proceeds from God, the Paraclete.

The test itself is introduced by *homologeō* ("confess"; the NIV's "acknowledge" is too weak here), which suggests that John is citing a creed most Johannine Christians would accept. Everyone who speaks by God's spirit will assert that "Jesus Christ has come in the flesh." This confession is clearly important to the background of 1–2–3 John because it distinguishes John's belief from that of the Antichrists, but regrettably the sentence is obscure in the Greek. The word translated "has come" (NIV) is actually a perfect tense participle ("having come") that characterizes Jesus, and no other verb appears in the sentence. It is therefore unclear exactly what John thinks the Spirit will confess. Some scholars suggest that the words "Jesus" and "Christ" are used together here as a compound proper name. This can lead to one of two conclusions: (1) one must confess "Jesus Christ [the divine person] as having come in the flesh," i.e., must accept that "there was a true union of the divine Word, the Son of God, with a human personality in Jesus Christ" (Marshall, 204–5); or (2) one must accept the confession "Jesus Christ come in the flesh," i.e., one must accept the whole of Johannine Christology, which is summarized by this statement (so Brown, 492–93; Smalley, 222–23). As a third possibility, it may be that the word "Jesus" is the subject of the sentence. From this perspective, true teachers must confess two things about Jesus: that Jesus is "the Christ," the divine Son of God, and that Jesus also "came in the flesh," that he had a true physical body (so Dodd, 96–99; Houlden, 107).

All three readings are reasonable within the broader context of Johannine theology. The first two are supported by the fact that John occasionally uses the compound name "Jesus Christ" (e.g., 1:3; 2:1; 3:16, 23; 5:6) to refer to the incarnate Son. Stronger parallels, however, may be adduced in support of the third reading. On four other occasions in 1 John, John presents absolute creeds that require true believers to confess that the human Jesus was also the divine Christ: 2:22, where the "liar" and "Antichrist" is the person who "denies [*arneomai*, the opposite of *homologeō*] that Jesus is the Christ" (*Iēsous estin ho Christos*); 4:15, where John says that anyone who confesses "Jesus is the Son of God" (acknowledging that the human Jesus and the divine Son are one) remains in God; 5:1, where the one who believes that "Jesus is the Christ" has been born of God; and 5:5, where the one who believes that "Jesus is the Son of God" has victory over the world.

It seems, then, that Johannine creeds tend to follow a formula in which the human Jesus is associated with the Christ who has come from God. From this perspective, 4:2 means that one must confess that Jesus was both a human being with physical flesh and the divine Christ. This conclusion is supported by the fact that the negative version of the test at v.3 mentions those who do not acknowledge "Jesus" rather than those who do not acknowledge "Jesus Christ." True Christians must acknowledge Jesus as the Christ. If they do not, their teaching is not from God.

3 For John, then, the Spirit's revelatory ministry does not go beyond accepted tradition. The negative version of the test follows from this principle: *If* any teacher/"spirit" does not confess Jesus (i.e., does not accept John's Christology), *then* one must conclude that such teaching does not originate with God. This is a logical extension of John 16:13–15, where Jesus says that the Paraclete will "speak only

what he hears" from Jesus and will "take from what is mine and make it known to you." Since the Johannine Jesus clearly presents himself as the human Son of God, the Spirit must do the same. John thus makes personal religious experience subservient to doctrinal norms. The creed sets the boundaries for the Spirit's work.

If the message of the true teachers comes from the Paraclete, where do those who disagree with John get their teaching? John might logically say Satan, but, continuing the eschatological motif, he concludes that such people are inspired by the Antichrist, the ultimate opponent of God. As at 1 John 2:18 (see comment), John cites the slogan "Antichrist is coming" but specifies that the power of the Antichrist is already at work in the world in the form of those who spread false notions about Jesus. Here again, in John's application the "Antichrist" is not a person opposed to God, the Messiah, or the forces of good in general but rather one who specifically denies the Jesus proclaimed by orthodox Christians and opposes those who bear this witness.

4 Whether or not the Antichrists harbored hard feelings toward John (see comment at 2:19), John cannot allow a peaceful coexistence. In his view, the struggle between true believers and Antichrists is the visible expression of a cosmic, eschatological conflict between good and evil. Those who remain in John's fellowship may rest assured of victory. In fact, the perfect tense of *nikaō* indicates that believers "have overcome" the Antichrists already. The next phrase is introduced by *hoti*, which most translations interpret causally ("because the one who is in you . . .") to indicate the reason or means by which victory has been secured (NIV, NASB, NRSV, NEB, NKJV). More likely, John is introducing a saying or community slogan that affirms his claim to conquest. Breaking from a pure dualism, the slogan asserts that real believers must inevitably defeat the

Antichrists because the Spirit that drives them is inherently stronger than the spirit of Antichrist.

5 This verse attempts to account for the inconsistency between John's claim to victory in v.4 and the real-life experiences of those in his fellowship. If God is truly stronger than the devil, and if God's people have already conquered, why are the Johannine Christians suffering pain and humiliation at the hands of nonbelievers and Antichrists (see Introduction)? John explains that, while the cosmic battle takes place in this world, the fruits of victory cannot be enjoyed here. The same tension pervades the farewell address in the fourth gospel, where Jesus promises God's strength and presence but also the world's hatred and abuse (Jn 15:1–16:4). From a human perspective, it seems that the spirit of Antichrist is winning, but truth *will* triumph in the end.

The Antichrists have fared better than John's party because they are "from the world." Since John has earlier revealed that they were actually once members of his group (2:19), the genitive here must be qualitative: the Antichrists are "worldly" and are therefore able to speak the language of the world—and the world listens to them. John's suffering results from the fact that he does not speak this language.

The dualistic idea that there are two languages, one of the world and one of true believers, derives from two episodes in the fourth gospel. In the first, Jesus, while arguing with the Jews at the Feast of Tabernacles, insists that his language is not clear to them because they are of the devil, making it impossible for them to understand the words of God. Confirming his analysis, the Jews conclude that Jesus is "a Samaritan and demon-possessed," and shortly after that they attempt to kill him (Jn 8:42–48, 59). The reverse concept appears in John 10:1–21. There Jesus asserts that his true sheep will understand him and follow his voice, while refusing to follow the voice of the stranger or thief. Just as those in the world cannot understand God's language, those who

are "of God" cannot understand the world's language. The fact that the Antichrists not only understand the world's language but actually speak it would only confirm John's belief that they were never true Christians in the first place (1Jn 2:19); those who truly "know God," however, heed the true message proclaimed by John (4:6).

Since the Antichrists speak the language of the world, it is no surprise that "the world listens to them." Most scholars believe that this phrase is a comment on the Antichrists' evangelistic efforts. Rensberger, 113–14, for example, suggests that the Antichrists "were engaged in a successful mission to non-Christians" and winning more converts than John. Lest his followers interpret this as a sign of divine approval, John insists they are successful only because they compromise the truth (cf. Marshall, 209; Johnson, 98). But what aspect of the Antichrists' message would make them so popular? Why would people prefer their version of Christianity over John's? Some have suggested that the Antichrists promoted a less rigorous ethic than John, which made it possible for people to accept the message of Christ without adopting the Johannine lifestyle. Brown, 508, feels that the Antichrists' message was more acceptable because it eliminated "all that is scandalous in the earthly career of Jesus" by avoiding problematic philosophical issues such as the incarnation and resurrection. While such theories are reasonable, it seems more likely John is referring to the *quality* of the Antichrists' audience rather than its *quantity*, the *nature* of those who subscribe to their teaching rather than the *number*. In John's view, any person who listens to the Antichrists shows by this positive response that she is "of the world." "World" is thus used here in a way similar to "pagans" at 3 John 7 as a label for all who do not accept John's teaching. Consistent with John's dualistic perspective, those who are "of God" seek teachers who are "of God," while those who seek teachers who are not of God must be "of the world." This would serve as a warning to believers who were attracted to the Antichrists' teachings but had not yet accepted them.

6 John offers a second test to help believers distinguish the "Spirit of truth," God's Spirit (Jn 14:16–17), from "the spirit of deceit" (*planē*, GK *4415*; NIV, "error"). The opening phrase here indicates that John himself is the basis for this test. "We are from God" establishes John's faith and practice, which proceed from the Spirit's power, as the measure of all spiritual experience. This being the case, *if* someone "listens to us," *then* that person "knows God." On the other hand, *if* someone "does not listen to us," *then* that person is "not from God." The referent of the term *ho* ("whoever") is important here. Most scholars believe that John is categorizing all individuals on the basis of their response to his message—"whoever is of God" versus "whoever is not of God" (so Marshall, 209–10; Brown, 499–500; Smalley, 229–30; Culpepper, 82). While John has, indeed, just stated that those who listen to the Antichrists are "from the world," the general concern of 4:1–6 is to distinguish true teachers from false teachers. It is therefore more likely that this test, like that in vv.2–3, is aimed specifically at the Antichrists and is not making a general statement. John uses *akouō* ("listens, "GK *201*) with the genitive here in the sense of obeying a command. Those teachers who do not obey John's commands, who have "gone out from us" (2:19) and who do not remain within the confines of John's doctrine, thereby prove that they are actually inspired by "the spirit of falsehood." True Christians should therefore avoid them, recognizing that they do not speak with John's authorization.

This test, along with the one in vv.2–3, uses orthodox doctrine to set the boundary for the Spirit's activity. While John cannot prove that the Antichrists' teaching does not have a spiritual origin, he can point out that what they say is inconsistent with received tradition. This being the case, either the Antichrists or the tradition must be wrong, and since John knows that the tradition is based on a genuine witness (1:1–3), the tradition must be preserved. Verse 6 thus portrays the conflict between John and the Antichrists as a struggle between established belief and personal religious experience.

NOTES

2 Reading this verse to mean that one must confess Jesus Christ as having come in the flesh treats the perfect participle ἐληλυθότα, *elēlythota*, as an infinitive ("to have come") and for all practical purposes makes "Jesus Christ" here the name of the preexistent member of the Godhead (cf. Culpepper, 79; Johnson, 94–95; Rensberger, 111–12).

2–3 The terms χριστὸς, *christos* ("Christ"), and υἱὸς τοῦ θεοῦ , *huios tou theou* ("Son of God"), are synonymous in the Johannine literature when referring to Jesus' deity (cf. Jn 20:30–31; 1Jn 2:22–23).

3 Paul, who has much more to say about the prophetic aspect of Christian teaching than John, uses the same rhetorical strategy at 1 Corinthians 12:3, telling the Corinthians they can distinguish true teachers from false in that "no one who is speaking by the Spirit of God says, 'Jesus be cursed,' and no one can say, 'Jesus is Lord,' except by the Holy Spirit." Notably, this remark immediately precedes a discussion on revelatory gifts that consumes the next three chapters. Both John and Paul may be basing this restriction of the Spirit's activity on Deuteronomy 13:1–5, where Moses says that any prophet who advises people to worship foreign gods in violation of the commandments must be put to death.

4–6 "The world" is clearly used in vv.4–6 to refer to those who reject Christ and who, in John's experience, are hostile to Christians (see Introduction). Verse 4 implies that this opposition derives from "the one who is in the world," presumably Satan. While John does not highlight the devil's role in human affairs as much as other NT authors, he does refer to Satan as "the prince of this world" on several occasions (Jn 12:31; 14:30; 16:11; cf. 2Co 4:4; Eph 2:2; Col 1:12–13). The relationship between Satan and the Antichrist in this context is not clear, and perhaps John did not distinguish them carefully. Both represent evil and opposition to God, so that either can be identified as the spiritual force that leads the world and the Antichrists away from truth.

REFLECTIONS

The message of 4:1–6 is particularly relevant to the modern church. Contemporary spirituality is characterized by a heavy emphasis on personal experience, often supported by claims that one's beliefs and actions are guided, and therefore validated, by the Holy Spirit. Texts such as John 14:26 and 16:13 have, ironically, contributed to this mindset. But John insists that, while every believer enjoys the comfort and guidance of the Paraclete, the Spirit cannot operate outside the well-defined boundaries of orthodox belief, particularly christological belief. The failure to observe traditional boundaries, or indeed any boundaries, has led to the micro-fragmentation of the modern church. The letters of John were written in response to a similar situation. Without corporate parameters for individual experience, the vision of unity promoted in John 17 can never be realized.

D. Test #8: Perfect Love (4:7–21)

OVERVIEW

This section defines "perfect love" (*teleia agapē*; 4:18), the second pillar of Johannine Christianity mentioned at 3:23. The discussion here is a logical corollary to John's remarks on the Spirit at 4:1–6. While the Antichrists may claim that their teaching is inspired by God, John insists that the Spirit's presence can only be demonstrated by (1) orthodox doctrine and (2) perfect love. Regrettably for the Antichrists, "perfect love" is love that follows the pattern of God's love shown in the incarnation of Jesus, a doctrine they reject. Even if the Antichrists act in a way that from a worldly perspective appears to be loving, *perfect love* can be shown only by those who accept John's witness.

The language of 4:7–21 is strongly reminiscent of John 3. Several of the major themes in this passage seem to build directly on the dialogue between Jesus and Nicodemus. First, Jesus informs Nicodemus that he must be "born again" in order to enter the kingdom of God and then contrasts the person who is "born of Spirit" with the one "born of flesh" (Jn 3:3, 5–6); similarly, 1 John 4:7–8 highlights spiritual "birth," insisting that every person who loves has been "born of God." Second, John 3:16–21 makes spiritual birth conditional on one's acceptance that God sent Jesus into the world to grant salvation—indeed, "whoever believes in him is not condemned, but whoever does not believe stands condemned already" (3:18); similarly, 1 John 4:9 opens with an almost verbatim citation of John 3:16 and then proceeds (vv. 10–21) to make faith in the Son and love of other believers the primary evidence that one has experienced rebirth (and vv. 17–18 explore the consequences of a lack of love in language reminiscent of Jn 3:17). Finally, John's argument at 1 John 4:12–16 depends on the principle that "no one has ever seen God," a maxim that derives from Jesus' contention that "no one has ever gone into heaven except the one who came from heaven—the Son of Man" (Jn 3:13). It seems, then, that 1 John 4:7–21 is an extension and application, in light of the Antichrist conflict, of the traditions that made up John 3.

> ⁷Dear friends, let us love one another, for love comes from God. Everyone who loves has been born of God and knows God. ⁸Whoever does not love does not know God, because God is love. ⁹This is how God showed his love among us: He sent his one and only Son into the world that we might live through him. ¹⁰This is love: not that we loved God, but that he loved us and sent his Son as an atoning sacrifice for our sins. ¹¹Dear friends, since God so loved us, we also ought to love one another. ¹²No one has ever seen God; but if we love one another, God lives in us and his love is made complete in us.
>
> ¹³We know that we live in him and he in us, because he has given us of his Spirit. ¹⁴And we have seen and testify that the Father has sent his Son to be the Savior of the world. ¹⁵If anyone acknowledges that Jesus is the Son of God, God lives in him and he in God. ¹⁶And so we know and rely on the love God has for us.
>
> God is love. Whoever lives in love lives in God, and God in him. ¹⁷In this way, love is made complete among us so that we will have confidence on the day of judgment, because in this world we are like him. ¹⁸There is no fear in love. But perfect love drives out fear, because fear has to do with punishment. The one who fears is not made perfect in love.
>
> ¹⁹We love because he first loved us. ²⁰If anyone says, "I love God," yet hates his brother, he is a liar. For anyone who does not love his brother, whom he has seen, cannot love God, whom he has not seen. ²¹And he has given us this command: Whoever loves God must also love his brother.

COMMENTARY

7 John opens this section by offering two tests (vv. 7–8), one positive and one negative. Following his dualistic perspective, these tests sort people into opposite categories on the basis of love. Perfect love belongs to the "divine sphere" that is opposed to the world. Consequently, those who exhibit this love place themselves in God's realm (Marshall, 211). Appropriate to this topic, John refers to his audience as *agapētoi* ("beloved," GK *28*). While the NIV's "dear friends" treats this as a statement of John's own affection, the latter portion of v. 7 suggests that John is reminding them that they are "beloved *of God*" (cf. Brown, 263–64, 513). The experience of God's love should motivate Christians to love ("let us love one another"), which implies that those who do not love do not know God's love.

To support the admonition to love, John reminds his audience of a familiar slogan that is introduced by *hoti* (NIV, "for"): "love comes from God." It is difficult to tell whether the original slogan ended here or whether it included the phrase that follows, "and everyone who loves has been born of God and knows God." The NIV suggests a break in thought by beginning a new sentence at this point ("Everyone who loves . . ."). But since the theme of rebirth is common in the Johannine tradition, and since knowledge of God is a key element in John's thinking about the Christian experience (see comment at 2:3), it is possible that the entire statement on love in v.7 is based on a familiar community slogan. Combining this creed with the admonition to love makes v.7 a test: *If* we love one another, *then* we are born of God and know God, *because* love is from God. Loving the brothers is a mark of genuine Christianity, one that the world and Antichrists do not bear.

8 The negative version of the test of love appears in v.8. Based on the principle that "God is love"— apparently another community slogan introduced by *hoti* (NIV, "because")—John suggests that *if* someone does not love, *then* that person does not know God. The connection between love, knowledge, and rebirth in vv.7–8 follows the principle "the child resembles the parent." By this reasoning, if God is love, all true children of God will also bear this trait. Therefore, no person can legitimately claim to have a relationship with the God who is love while at the same time withholding love from other believers. Brown, 515, 549, is probably correct to suggest that v.8 is countering the Antichrists' claims to know God, thereby placing the Antichrists in the same category as the world and the Jews. It is not clear, however, that John is attempting to discredit some sort of esoteric theological "knowledge" that the Antichrists may have claimed to possess. *Ginōskō* ("know") seems to be used here in the experiential

sense rather than the cognitive (see comment at 2:2; cf. Schnackenburg, 207). The Antichrists, who do not show love to the brothers (see comments at 3:11–15, 16–17), do not "know" God in the sense that they do not have a relationship with him. The same reasoning underlies John 16:3, which refers to the hostile Jews, who are surely well acquainted with the OT teaching on God, as those who "have not known the Father," and also underlies 1 John 3:1, which says that "the world" does not know God either. "Knowledge" in these contexts is not a recognition of God's existence or special theological insight but rather a relationship with God based on faith in Jesus.

9 John now describes the specific kind of love that proves that God is present in one's life. While the NIV emphasizes the action by which God revealed his love to humanity ("this is how God showed his love"), the genitive *tou theou* ("the love *of God*") has almost attributive force here—"godly love" ("this is how *godly love* was shown"). While John does not deny that the world, the Jews, and the Antichrists do things that appear to be "loving" by some standards, his dualistic worldview distinguishes acts of love by their source or by the nature of the person performing them. Only those acts of love that reflect "godly love" manifest the presence of God in a person's life. This "godly love" is then defined by a traditional slogan introduced by *hoti*: God "sent his one and only Son into the world." The incarnation, then, is the pattern of godly love.

The language of v.9 is clearly reminiscent of John 3:16, and both verses establish the incarnation as the ultimate expression of God's love for humanity. In both contexts the connection between God's love and the incarnation is highlighted by the term *monogenēs* (GK *3666*). This word literally means "only begotten" (NASB, KJV), but it is unlikely that John is thinking of "begotten" in the biological sense of the Christmas story. Rather, the focus is on the special relationship between God and Christ. Marshall, 214, notes that *monogenēs* "is concerned with derivation or kind . . . rather than [physical] birth." Jesus is of the same *kind* as God (*-genēs*, cf. the English "genetic") and is also the *only one* (*mono-*) who is of the same kind as God. The NIV thus captures the true intention of the term with the translation "one and only Son," which highlights Jesus' unique relationship with God.

In the context of v.9, John refers to Jesus as *monogenēs* for two reasons. First, contra the claims of the Antichrists, the term associates Jesus directly with God, uniting the human and divine aspects of his identity. Since Christ alone reveals God to the world, any denial of Jesus' divine origin makes it impossible to receive God's revelation (cf. Schnackenburg, 208). Second, *monogenēs* stresses the depth of God's sacrificial love in sending his *only* heir into a hostile world. The accompanying *hina* clause, "that we might live through him," stresses the salvific dimension of the incarnation. God sent the Son for the purpose of saving us through the Son, so that to deny the Son is to deny salvation.

By citing this familiar slogan, John attempts to rally the faithful around a statement of core beliefs and to connect the Christian social ethic directly to his own witness about the incarnation. While the Antichrists might perform acts that appear to proceed from genuine concern and compassion for others, such works do not prove that they have experienced rebirth. Indeed, even the world loves "its own" (Jn 15:19), but such love is not sufficient because its object is misdirected. The Antichrists' love cannot come from God because they do not accept the ultimate expression of God's love in the incarnation.

10 This verse extends the thought of v.9 by emphasizing the sacrificial dimension of the incarnation. The first phrase, "this is love," would normally introduce a test in 1 John, but here it refers to the two statements that follow about the love of God (as the NIV, "This is love:"; cf. Brown, 518). The second of these two statements, both of which are introduced by *hoti*, is a slogan closely related to v.9 and to John 3:16, while the first statement is a sarcastic play on the true slogan to highlight God's love in sending the Son.

John clues the reader that the first slogan is sarcastic by the introduction *ouch hoti*. John's followers will recall that he did *not* teach them, "we loved God," rather, he taught them, "*God* loved us." The contrast between the two slogans is highlighted in the Greek text by a change in tense. In the first statement, the perfect tense of *agapaō* ("love"), which describes a state of being resulting from a past action, stresses that we did *not* love God *before* he sent his Son. Indeed, since the world hates God and wants nothing to do with God (see Introduction), and since even true believers were members of the world before their rebirth (see comment at 3:11–15), there is no way to argue that believers loved God at any point before their conversion. The sending of the Son was, therefore, an act of purely benevolent love, not motivated by anything believers had done, and not God's requiting of a love they already had for him.

The second statement, however, which cites the true version of the slogan, switches to the aorist tense of *agapaō*, highlighting a specific act of love. The fact that "sent" (*apostellō*, GK *690*) is also aorist suggests that the act of God's love John has in mind is the incarnation. Even though the world did not love God, God showed his love for the world at the moment when he sent his Son into the world. Indeed, the world did not know what "love" was until Jesus came.

11 With this verse, John begins to develop the ethical implications of the incarnation. Those who, unlike the Antichrists, accept God's love as expressed in the sending of the Son ought to love one another (cf. 1Jn 3:16). The logic of this conclusion is similar to that underlying John 13:12–17. After washing the disciples' feet, Jesus instructs them that they should do the same for one another because, if "I, your Lord and Teacher, have washed your feet, you also should wash one another's feet" (13:14). If Jesus served the disciples in a sacrificial way, they should follow his example by serving one another sacrificially. Similarly, if God has defined perfect love by sending his Son as a sacrifice, we should love other believers the way God does.

12 The opening phrase at first seems out of place. John has just cited several slogans about the incarnation, an event other Johannine passages clearly associate with human experience of God. In John 14:9, for example, Jesus tells Philip that "anyone who has seen me has seen the Father." Why, then, does John now suddenly assert that "no one has ever seen God"? Some suggest that John is countering the Antichrists' claim to a special revelation of the Father (so Marshall, 216; Grayston, 126; Schnackenburg, 217–18). It seems more likely that John is simply appealing to the accepted OT principle that "no one may see [God] and live" (Ex 33:20). While the fourth gospel does portray Jesus as the exclusive revealer of God, John is also clear that this revelation is not yet complete. The Johannine Jesus therefore tells a crowd in Jerusalem that they "have never heard [God's] voice nor seen his form" (Jn 5:37), even though he himself has said and done only what the Father commands. Similarly, the prologue to the fourth gospel, the highest extant Christological statement from the primitive church, insists that "no one has ever seen God," even though the Word, which "was God," "became flesh and . . . we have seen his glory" (Jn 1:1, 14, 18). While Jesus reveals everything human beings may know about God, what humans may know is only a small portion of what is yet to be known (1Jn 3:2).

The assertion that God cannot be seen, whether directed to a specific belief of the Antichrists or simply expressing a general theological principle, introduces the second test in this section. Although God cannot be seen directly, his presence is evident in those who love. The condition of the test appears in an *ean* + subjunctive clause, which is followed by two conclusions: *If we love one another, then* (1) God remains in us, and (2) God's love has been perfected (*teleioō*; NIV, "made complete") in us. The logic of this test is similar to the "parent and child" principle at 4:7. Grayston, 126, notes that "like recognizes like": if God loves other believers and we love other believers, we place ourselves in the same category as God. Even though we cannot see God himself, we can be certain that he is in us when we show love, because God is love (v.8). The fact of loving one's brothers thus becomes a second form of objective proof (along with sound doctrine) of the Spirit's presence, against the Antichrists' subjective claims to an individual spiritual experience that cannot be evaluated by others (4:1–6).

13 This verse largely restates the thought of 3:24, which emphasizes that possession of the Spirit is proof that God "remains in us" (NIV, "lives in us"). Marshall, 219, suggests that John is here returning to the thought of 4:1–6 and is thinking of the Spirit's presence as evident in charismatic gifts, which "need to be tested by their fidelity to the apostolic witness" mentioned in v.14. While doctrine and practice are closely intertwined in this section, it seems more likely that John has finished with the confessional issue and is now turning to a behavioral test of God's presence. Having stressed at 4:1–6 that God's Spirit may be distinguished from the spirit of Antichrist on the basis of doctrine, John will now stress that God's Spirit is also distinct in the type of love he produces in true believers.

The opening phrase, "in this we know" (NIV, "we know that"), indicates that John is preparing to offer another test to distinguish real Christians from Antichrists on the basis of love. Two community slogans are cited, one representing the condition of the test and the other the necessary conclusion: *If* he has given us of his Spirit, *then* we remain (NIV, "live") in him and he in us. The latter phrase is highly reminiscent of John 15:4–7, where Jesus exhorts the disciples several times to "remain in me, and I will remain in you." First John 4 may be John's attempt to interpret and clarify the traditional sayings that underlie John 15 in the light of the Antichrist conflict, clarifying the nature of this mutual indwelling. In v.12 John simply asserted that God "remains" in the believer, but now he specifies that this occurs through the presence of the Spirit (cf. Jn 14:17). Presumably, it is the Spirit's presence that motivates believers to exhibit godly love. When believers allow the Spirit to influence them in this way, they in turn "abide/remain" in God in the sense that they obey his commands. Obedient love proves, then, that God's Spirit is present in us, which in turn separates believers from Antichrists.

14 John has just asserted that "no one has seen God"; now he emphasizes what he himself has "seen" and "witnessed." The plural forms of "see" and "witness" probably refer to the total group of people who had physical contact with Jesus, of which John claims to be a member (most scholars believe that "we" here refers to the general "witness" of the community rather than the group of living witnesses to Jesus [so Dodd, 115; Marshall, 220; Brown, 522–23, 557–58; Culpepper, 90–91]; see comment at 1:3). What John has seen has led him to the conclusion summarized by the creedal statement here, which closely parallels John 3:17: "the Father has sent his Son to be the Savior of the world." Marshall, 220, notes that the term "Savior" is a logical extension of "atoning sacrifice" at v.10, for "it is through being the [sacrifice] that Jesus can be the [Savior]." While no one has ever seen God, John has seen the Son in the form of Jesus. Refusal to accept this witness leaves one with no means of salvation, for Jesus is also the Savior.

15 The language here is similar to that of v.12, offering the same conclusion about mutual indwelling but subtly replacing the test of love with a creed ("If we love one another" versus "If anyone acknowledges"). Schnackenburg, 219, therefore concludes that vv.14–15 are a digression from the main theme, shifting from an emphasis on love to an emphasis on orthodox faith. It seems more likely that John is explicitly using the incarnation to tie godly love to the orthodox confession (introduced here by *hoti*) so that life and doctrine cannot be isolated from one another. John has already established that God remains in us if we love other believers, and now he further insists that *if* someone should confess, "Jesus is the Son of God," *then* God remains in her and she in God. God's presence, then, is dependent not only on mutual love among believers but also on the right *kind* of love, specifically, a love based on the premise that God sent his Son as Savior. Schnackenburg, 220, himself acknowledges this point by concluding that "faith and love as conditions and hallmarks of our fellowship with God simply cannot be separated from each other."

16a The language here is subject to different translations with varying exegetical implications. The first difficulty relates to the meaning of the verbs *ginōskō* and *pisteuō*. The NIV's "rely on" for *pisteuō* is strained, for John typically uses *pisteuō* ("I believe") in the more literal sense of Christian faith. The translation "rely on" also implies that *ginōskō* ("I know") refers in this context to a cognitive recognition of God's love. It seems more likely that John is using *ginōskō* in an existential sense to describe the believer's personal experience of God's love and the confidence that arises from that experience. Further, the NIV translation does not reflect the fact that both verbs are in the perfect tense, indicating that a past action has had a continuing result in the present. The use of this tense suggests that John is thinking of the starting point of the believer's present experience, the time when she first accepted "the love God has for us" (cf. Brown, 524). Since John has already specified that God's love was revealed in the incarnation, *pisteuō* probably refers to the moment when the believer accepted John's witness about Jesus, and *ginōskō* refers to the experience of God's presence that followed that recognition. The first portion of v.16 should therefore be translated, "And we have experienced and have accepted the love . . ."—where "love" refers to the coming of Jesus and all its benefits.

A second difficulty relates to the unusual phrase *hēn echei ho theos en hēmin*, "[the love] which God has in us." The NIV's "the love God has *for* us" is possible but would represent an obscure use of the dative case. The more typical meaning of the dative, however, still permits of two possibilities. Although *hēmin* ("us") is plural, John may be using the term to refer to the sum total of individual believers, "God's love *in* each of us." If this is the case, John is focusing on "the personal experience of [God's] love in our hearts created by the Spirit" (Marshall, 221). On the other hand, *hēmin* may have collective force here, referring either to the entire Christian community ("God's love *among* us [= believers]") or even possibly to the entire world (those to whom God sent the Son as Savior; v.14). This reading can be supported by the context, for John has just been speaking of "God's love" specifically as the incarnation, which occurred in the human sphere, "among us" (cf. Rensberger, 121). It seems, however, that the phrase "the love which God has in us" is an awkward restatement of v.9's "the love of God in us," which referred to the presence of God's Spirit in the believer and the effect the Spirit has on one's behavior (see comment). The first reading discussed above, then, is probably correct. "Among us" seems to refer to the universal Christian experience of God's love in each person, which results from believing the incarnation.

16b As the NIV suggests, the latter portion of v.16 seems to introduce a new thought or paragraph. John repeats the creed "God is love" from v.8 and reiterates the points he has made at vv.7 and 12 to elaborate it. The verb *menō* (NIV, "lives") appears three times in this sentence and carries two distinct meanings. In the first phrase, "the one who *remains* in love" (NIV, "whoever lives in love") is the person who holds to the view that God's love was revealed through the sending of the Son. Since John has already established that "love" in this context has explicit Christological implications, *menō* here relates primarily to doctrinal beliefs. In the second and third phrases, John uses *menō* to describe the unique relationship between God and true believers. Those who hold to the truth "remain in God" (NIV, "lives in God") in the sense that they receive his approval while the world and the Antichrists are rejected, and they consequently enjoy the gift of God's Spirit ("God *remains* in her"; cf. Jn 14:17). In this context, divine indwelling takes the form of love for the brothers and the inner witness of the orthodox creed.

17 John now returns to a theme introduced in v.12, the means by which God's love is "perfected" (*teleioō*) in the believer's life. The NIV suggests that the *en toutō* ("in this"; NIV, "in this way") that opens this verse refers to what John has just said in v.16, so that to "live in love" and have "God live" in oneself is the most complete form of love (so Marshall, 223 n. 17; Brown, 526–27, 560; Culpepper, 92). It seems more likely that John is using this phrase to introduce the test that follows the *hoti* later in the verse (so NRSV, NEB; Dodd, 119; Schnackenburg, 222; Rensberger, 121). Those who pass the test that John is about to offer can be assured that love is perfected in them. John uses *teteleiōtai* ("perfected"; NIV, "made complete") here to distinguish orthodox Christian love from other expressions of love that he deems inadequate because they do not proceed from a proper view of Jesus.

Before offering the test of perfect love, however, John introduces a purpose clause that explains why the pursuit of perfect love is desirable: "so that we will have confidence on the day of judgment." As he has done earlier (2:18–19, 28; 3:1–3), John thus situates the conflict between true believers and Antichrists in an eschatological arena. Those who pass the test will have nothing to fear from God in the judgment because they will be complete, lacking nothing (2:28). The Greek *parrēsia* (NIV, "confidence") is used by John elsewhere to represent speech that is bold and direct (Jn 16:25–30; 1Jn 3:21). Those whose love is found adequate have nothing to hide from God and may therefore speak plainly to him about their deeds in the hour of judgment.

The test of perfect love measures the believer's life against the example of the incarnate Jesus. While the NIV takes the *hoti* that introduces the test in a causal sense ("because in this world"), it seems more likely that John is either citing a slogan that summarizes community ethics or simply highlighting what he is about to say. The conclusion of the test is drawn from the preceding note of eschatological confidence. *If* we are like "that one is [*estin*]" in this world, *then* we may have boldness on the day of judgment. "That one" here must be Jesus, the one who was sent "into the world" (4:9; cf. 2:6; 3:3, 7). Why, then, does John use the present tense of *eimi* ("that one *is*") in reference to Jesus? Brown, 529–30, suggests that John is thinking of Christ's complete union with God, a present heavenly reality that believers can also enjoy while on this earth. In the context of the impending judgment, "the logic of the statement is that since we are already like Christ [in our relationship with the Father], we shall not be judged harshly."

It seems more likely that John is using the "historic present," referring to the past actions of Jesus in the present tense, in order to strengthen the analogy between Jesus' life and the believer's life. Johannine ethics typically portray Christ as a model of obedient service (Jn 4:34; 5:19; 6:38; 10:11–13; 12:25–28; 13:12–17), and the use of the present tense would simply stress the continuing validity of Jesus' example. Hence "in this world" refers both to the arena of current Christian behavior and to the arena in which Jesus modeled the ideal Christian behavior (1Jn 4:9–10, 14). Those who accept that Jesus was God in flesh and who follow Jesus' example may be confident of their salvation, because Jesus himself is the model of perfect love.

18 John now explores *phobos* ("fear," GK *5832*), the opposite of the *parrēsia* (NIV, "confidence") enjoyed by those who pass the test of love. Bultmann, 73–74, suggests that "fear" here characterizes the present experience of those who do not have a positive relationship with God. The fact that "fear has to do with punishment" might indeed suggest that fear itself is the punishment unbelievers receive for rejecting God. While this may be an accurate observation of human psychology, John seems to be continuing the eschatological motif he introduced in v.17. "Fear" is not used here in the healthy sense of a respect and awe toward God, but rather in the negative sense of concern over God's impending wrath. "There is no fear in love" in the sense that those who follow Jesus' example need not fear God's future judgment (Marshall, 224; Schnackenburg, 225; Rensberger, 122). Hence, when one experiences *teleia agapē*, "perfect love," all fear is "cast out" because that person has passed the test. John's use of *exō ballō* ("cast out'" NIV, "drive out") follows an exorcism motif, which is somewhat unusual in light of the fourth gospel's lack of interest in exorcism. But since "perfect love" is engendered in the believer by God's Spirit (v.13), John's dualistic perspective would lead to the natural conclusion that the fear resulting from lack of this love also has a spiritual dimension. For this reason, when perfect love enters the believer, the fear that results from imperfect love is naturally eliminated.

The exorcism of fear leads John to reflect on a principle introduced by *hoti*. It is difficult to tell whether this is a community slogan, but in any case the NIV is correct to see a causal relationship between this portion of the verse and what has preceded. "Fear holds punishment, *because* the one who fears has not been perfected in love." It is important to note that John does not make the presence or absence of fear a test of one's love. The fact that one's guilt has caused her to doubt her salvation does not mean such a person is in danger of God's judgment. The focus, rather, is on the status of the person whose love is imperfect. Such people have good reason to fear, although, as John's experiences with the Antichrists would attest, they very rarely demonstrate this feeling. But things will be different in the day of punishment, when such people will experience the terrible fear of realizing that God finds them inadequate. John, then, is thinking of the person whose doctrine is not based on a proper understanding of Jesus and whose love is therefore incomplete because it is not supported by orthodox faith.

19 This verse summarizes vv.7–16 by concisely restating the principle that Christian love is based on the example of God's love. Despite its brevity, the verse is complicated by two translation issues. First, it is unclear whether the verb *agapaō* is indicative ("we love") or a hortatory subjunctive ("let us love") in this context. The NIV suggests the former (cf. Culpepper, 95; Marshall, 225 n. 26). Brown, 532, 562, believes that John is using the indicative to establish a contrast between Antichrists and true believers: while the Antichrists have "fear" (v.18), true believers have "love." Barker, 347, who also

prefers the indicative reading, suggests that the usage here is "descriptive," characterizing true Christian love by analogy with God and Christ (i.e., "we love one another in the way that God and Christ love us"). It seems more likely, however, that *agapaō* is subjunctive, offering an exhortation. This reading creates an inclusio by returning to the parallel injunction at 4:7—"let us love one another" (cf. Schnackenburg, 225; Rensberger, 125).

The second translation issue relates to the object of the verb *agapaō*. What or who are believers told to love? Several ancient manuscripts include the words *ton theon*, or simply *auton*, to specify that John is thinking of the love Christians have for God (Marshall, 225; Rensberger, 125–26). But in the light of v.20 and the inclusio with v.7, it seems that John is returning to his original exhortation to love other believers (Schnackenburg, p. 225). Those manuscripts that supply the word *allēlous* ("one another") are therefore correct in spirit, even if they do not reflect the original reading. Since, as the NIV suggests, the *hoti* that connects the two clauses in v.19 has causal force, the statement is best rendered, "Let us love one another, for [God] first loved us." In other words, the experience of being loved by God should motivate believers to show the same love for one another.

20 Verse 20 closes this section with a final test that focuses on the social rather than the doctrinal dimension of perfect love. This test resembles several tests from the first portion of the book in that it contrasts people's words with their actions to expose "liars" (1:6, 8, 10; 2:4, 6, 9). *If* someone says "I love God," *and if* that person hates her brother, *then* that person is a "liar," i.e., she does not truly love God as she professes and consequently belongs to the realm of Satan (Jn 8:44–45).

To support this test, John offers an argument that again builds on the principle at v.12. The one who does not love a Christian brother whom he has seen cannot love a God whom no one has ever seen. The logic of this statement is unclear, and several explanations of John's thinking have been offered. Brown, 564, suggests that the reference to "seeing" one's brother may echo 3:17, where John condemned those who "see" a brother in need but refuse to help. Perhaps John is targeting the Antichrists, who may have been wealthy members of the community who now refuse to assist those allied to John. If one cannot show love to those who are in such need, how can one love a God she has never seen (cf. Culpepper, 95–96)?

A second solution also highlights the Antichrist context by analogy with the first portion of ch. 4. First John 4:1–6 offered a concrete doctrinal test to help believers determine which teachers are motivated by the Spirit of God. While anyone can claim divine inspiration, only those who hold to John's witness can prove this claim. Similarly, anyone can claim to love God and can claim that her actions are motivated by godly love, because such claims cannot be directly disproved. One's visible actions, however, will make it plain whether she loves other believers. John therefore suggests, on the basis of the rabbinic principle *qal waḥōmer* ("the lesser to the greater"), that love for the brothers is tangible evidence of one's love for God. If one cannot even show love for one's brothers ("the lesser"), how can she achieve the greater work of loving God ("the greater"; cf. Culpepper, 95–96; Schnackenburg, 226; Rensberger, 126)? Dodd, 124, observes that this view does not suggest that loving one's brothers is a simpler and preliminary task to complete love of God, but rather that the absence of concrete proof of one's ability to love in general suggests that a person does not love God. Since godly love does not discriminate among its objects, the person who does not love a brother clearly has no godly love within herself and therefore has no love with which to love God (cf. Brown, 534).

A third and related possibility highlights John's dualistic worldview. In John's view, all people belong in one of two categories—God's realm or the world. Because God is love, all those who love belong in the same category as God. Continuing the principle that "like loves like" (see comment at 4:12), any person who loves God and loves true believers must therefore be a true believer herself. On the other hand, people who do not love true believers are in a different category—"the world"—and therefore inherently hate God (see Introduction). This extends the principle of love from the realm of doctrinal norms and personal experience of God to one's relationship with other members of the faith community. Perfect love is thus dependent both on a proper understanding of Christ and on a proper understanding of one's relationship to other believers.

21 The connection here between love for God and love for one's brothers has led Dodd, 123–24, to conclude that John is referring "clearly to the tradition of the teaching of Jesus, as we have it in Mark xii. 28–31" (cf. Barker, 347; Rensberger, 126–27). While this is an intriguing possibility, it should be noted that elsewhere in 1 John the "commandment" relating to love is John 13:34 (1Jn 2:7–11; 3:23–24). Further, John 13:34 clearly demands that those who love God must also love their brothers—the point John has just stressed. In the context of the Antichrist conflict, the love command means that those who aspire to perfect love must (1) show love toward God by accepting John's true witness about Jesus and (2) stay in good fellowship with other believers who make the same confession. The Antichrists have failed on both counts (see comments at 2:18–27) and therefore have reason to fear God's judgment.

It is important to stress that the "love" which proves our relationship to God in 4:7–21 cannot refer merely to benevolent acts. From time to time, people of the world and the Antichrists act in a way that appears to be "loving," but these acts alone cannot be taken as proof of God's indwelling presence any more than a charismatic facade can prove that one is driven by God's true Spirit (4:1–6). Real "love" proceeds from a belief in God's ultimate act of love in sending the Son. Those who do not believe that the Son came through the human Jesus do not, in John's view, have God dwelling within them, regardless of how they treat other people.

NOTES

8 This verse is often cited as proof that God by nature accepts and tolerates all people, regardless of their behavior, or as proof that anyone who shows love is therefore secure in her relationship with God. Ironically, both conclusions entirely contradict the main thrust of Johannine thought. In the first place, as Marshall, 212, notes, John would insist that even the highest acts of human love "cannot be put into the balance to compensate for the sin of rejecting God." Second, this perspective views "love" as an abstract quality or emotion that God possesses. John, however, is speaking from the ancient Jewish perspective of defining people and things by their actions (cf. Dodd, 107–8). Because "no one has seen God" (4:12), "If we . . . ask what God is, the answer must be given in terms of what He does" (Rensberger, 117). "God is love" in the sense that he acts in a loving way toward his people. Further, it is clear from the following verses that John does *not* mean to suggest that "*all* [God's] activity is loving activity" (Dodd, 110). God's love is revealed exclusively through the incarnation and is therefore accessible only to those who accept John's witness about the incarnate Christ. As a consequence, God's tolerance and acceptance are limited to those who believe and obey him.

9 While v.9 and John 3:16 are clearly drawn from the same traditional unit, John probably did not understand this unit to be a saying of Jesus. Despite the NIV's red-lettering, Jesus' remarks in John 3 seem to end at v.15, with vv.16–21 representing John's own reflections on the christological significance of the Nicodemus episode.

10 John's use of the perfect ἠγαπήκαμεν, *ēgapēkamen* ("love"), rather than the pluperfect, portrays the experience of the world. Members of the world did not love God in the past and continue to hold this sentiment into the present, despite the fact that God loved them and sent his Son. The Christian experience would be represented by the pluperfect, indicating a past action that initiated a continuing state of being which has since ended. Presumably, John would say that Christians did not love God in the past and continued this sentiment up to the point when they believed that God sent his Son, at which point they experienced rebirth (Jn 1:12).

12 Two points of translation warrant special consideration. First, as the NIV indicates, the verb τελειόω, *teleioō*, probably carries the idea of "completion" throughout this section (also 2:5). While the complex of words associated with τέλος, *telos*, can have a broad range of meanings, from "perfect" to "mature," John seems to be stressing that the person who shows godly love lacks nothing in her relationship to God or others. Second, contra the NIV's "his love," the genitive αὐτοῦ, *autou* (love "of him"), probably does not indicate possession but rather source—"God's kind of love," or the love that flows from him to others through us (so Marshall, 217; Schnackenburg, 218; cf. comment on 4:7). When we show love to others, we prove that God is present in us, even though God cannot be seen.

REFLECTIONS

First John 4:14–15 indicates that John's dualistic perspective has not left him entirely pessimistic toward the world. Despite the fact that the world hates Jesus, John does not limit Jesus' salvific work to the faithful. Here, as at John 1:11–12 and 3:16–17, God did not send the Son only to those who believed in him but rather as Savior "of the world." John continues to believe this, even though the world did not recognize or accept Jesus (Jn 1:10). It

seems, then, that John's Christology is both broad and narrow—broad in the sense that God sent the Son to be Savior of everyone, not just those who loved him, and narrow in the sense that one must accept John's witness about the Son in order to enjoy the benefits of this act. Theoretically, then, anyone could accept John's testimony and enjoy rebirth, but experience seems to have taught him that this does not happen very often.

E. Test #9: True Faith (5:1–13)

OVERVIEW

All commentators detect a break in 1 John somewhere near the beginning of ch. 5, but it is difficult to pinpoint where the preceding section ends and the new section begins. It is clear that 4:7–21 emphasizes love and that 5:6–12 emphasizes faith, but at the end of ch. 4 and the beginning of ch. 5 the two topics are closely intertwined. Rensberger, 125, writes, "Without noticing how, we simply find ourselves in the midst of an entirely different topic at the end of the section from the one at the beginning." Several major theories on the outline of 1 John at this point have been advanced.

Some commentators extend the thought of ch. 4 into ch. 5 and end John's discussion of love at 5:4. Marshall, 218–19, for example, believes that 5:1–4 explains John's preceding exhortations (4:19–21) by assuring believers that faith gives them power to keep God's commands. Brown, 543–44, further points out that after 5:4a the theme of "love" disappears altogether, suggesting that John is changing topics.

Some extend the section on love to 5:5. Dodd, 122, 128, argues for this position on the basis that 5:6ff. discusses the theological nuances of the incar-

nation with little concern for "faith" or "love" per se. Rensberger, 124–25, points out that 5:1 and 5:5 both include the phrase "the one who believes that Jesus is the Christ," suggesting a close connection between these verses. Because the logic of 5:1 is parallel to that of 4:21, 5:1–5 seems to be grammatically connected to the preceding discussion.

Others believe that the chapter break follows John's own outline, with 5:1 introducing a new section. This argument is supported by the repetition of the phrase "whoever believes that . . ." at 5:1, 5, 10 (NIV, "Everyone who believes that . . ."). The repetition of this formula unifies John's remarks on faith, indicating that he has finished his discussion of love (Culpepper, 97). Contra Rensberger, Grayston, 132, concludes that the parallelism between 4:21 and 5:1 indicates that John is summarizing his remarks on love and introducing a new topic—faith (cf. Barker, 348).

The variety of opinions points to the most likely solution: John probably did not intend a strong break in thought between 4:7 and 5:13. While the rhetoric of John's presentation moves gradually from love to orthodox faith, the two topics are not sharply distinguished in his thinking (see 3:23–24). The commentary here will follow the chapter break at 5:1 because 5:1–13 focuses on the more technical aspects of Christian doctrine, whereas 4:7–21 is more concerned with love for God and other believers. In modern Christian theology these two topics are generally discussed separately. The reader should keep in mind, however, that love and doctrine go together in Johannine thought.

> [1]Everyone who believes that Jesus is the Christ is born of God, and everyone who loves the father loves his child as well. [2]This is how we know that we love the children of God: by loving God and carrying out his commands. [3]This is love for God: to obey his commands. And his commands are not burdensome, [4]for everyone born of God overcomes the world. This is the victory that has overcome the world, even our faith. [5]Who is it that overcomes the world? Only he who believes that Jesus is the Son of God.
>
> [6]This is the one who came by water and blood—Jesus Christ. He did not come by water only, but by water and blood. And it is the Spirit who testifies, because the Spirit is the truth. [7]For there are three that testify: [8]the Spirit, the water and the blood; and the three are in agreement. [9]We accept man's testimony, but God's testimony is greater because it is the testimony of God, which he has given about his Son. [10]Anyone who believes in the Son of God has this testimony in his heart. Anyone who does not believe God has made him out to be a liar, because he has not believed the testimony God has given about his Son. [11]And this is the testimony: God has given us eternal life, and this life is in his Son. [12]He who has the Son has life; he who does not have the Son of God does not have life.
>
> [13]I write these things to you who believe in the name of the Son of God so that you may know that you have eternal life.

COMMENTARY

1 John opens this section with a doctrinal test: *If* anyone believes "Jesus is the Christ," *then* that person has been born of God. Notably, the phrases *pas ho pisteuōn* ("everyone who believes") and *pas ho agapōn* ("everyone who loves") are parallel: confessing Jesus as the Christ and loving the Father are indistinguishable. The Antichrists' claims to love are therefore inherently deficient.

The latter portion of the verse ties the orthodox confession of Jesus to the discussion of love at 4:7–21. As the NIV indicates, John suggests that "everyone who loves the father loves his child as well."

The Greek text here is open to several interpretations. First, the verb *agapaō* could be indicative ("she loves") or a hortatory subjunctive ("she should love"). The NIV adopts the indicative reading, which makes the statement a proverb: as a rule, those who love the parent love the child (Dodd, 124; Marshall, 227; Schnackenburg, 227). Technically, John is probably thinking of the subjunctive to allow for possible exceptions to this rule. By the nature of things, "everyone who loves the one who gives birth *should love* the one born from him," but some do not love the child and therefore do not truly love the parent either. According to John's dualistic perspective, "like loves like" (see comment at 4:12). A person can only love people and things in the same category as herself and, further, *must* love people in the same category as herself. Following this principle, 4:7–21 established that one's affections reveal one's true nature. Logically, then, anyone who truly loves God will also love the one "born of God."

Who, then, is "the one born from him" (*gegennēmenon ex autou*; NIV, "his child")? One might think of Jesus. This would be consistent with the parallelism between the two phrases in v.1: the one who believes that "Jesus is the Christ" is the same person who loves Jesus, God's "child." Jesus is sometimes called God's "son" in the fourth gospel, most notably in the purpose statement at 20:30–31 (also 3:16; 8:34–36). But it is difficult to see where the word *gegennēmenon* ("the one born," GK *1164*) would fit into Johannine Christology. The fourth gospel has no birth story, which would give the term a literal meaning, and almost suggests that Jesus came directly from heaven (Jn 1:1–4). On the other hand, John typically uses cognates of *gennaō* to describe Christian conversion. It seems more likely that "his child" in this context refers to other believers (Brown, 535–36; Culpepper, 99). While 1 John 4:21 follows the logic of "the lesser to the greater," 5:1 follows the opposite principle—"the greater to the lesser." Because the parent is greater than the child, one who loves the parent should logically love the child as well. In the present context, this means that those who truly love God will *both* accept Jesus as the Christ *and* love other believers.

2 The introduction to v.2, "in this we know" (NIV, "this is how we know"), clearly indicates that John is preparing to offer a second test. The phrase that immediately follows this introduction, however, can be taken one of two ways, depending on the function of *hoti*. It could be that *hoti* simply introduces

indirect discourse here, a summary statement of the conclusion of the test or what "we know." The NIV's "we know *that* we love" follows this reading. The historical context of 1 John, however, suggests that John is using *hoti* to quote a false claim to love, which he intends to satirize. The Antichrists would insist that they "love the children of God," but John seeks to challenge this assertion by showing that they cannot identify God's true children. In either case, the basic test that underlies this verse applies the parent/child principle of v.1 to John's situation: If we love God, *then* we know that we love God's children.

In view of the Antichrists' claims, John feels it necessary to specify exactly what it means to "love God." He achieves this with the last phrase in v.2: we show love for God when we obey his commands. The *kai* that connects love with obedience has the force of the English "even" here, equating two things. "Loving God" and "obeying God's commands" are synonymous, so that obedience is the test of our love for other believers. The test in the first part of v.2 may therefore be restated: *If we do what God commands, then* we know that we love God's children.

The logic of this test seems unusual. John normally appeals to one's love for other believers as proof of one's love for God, but here love for God seems to prove love for other believers. Brown, 537, summarizes the problem concisely: in the light of 4:20, "how can the love for God, which cannot be measured, become the criterion for knowing the much more measurable love for brother?" The test in v.2 is, however, consistent with John's dualistic logic. If we love God, we are in the same category as God, and consequently we will also (1) love other people in the same category and (2) do what God desires. On the other hand, those who do not do what God desires—the Antichrists—are not in God's category and therefore cannot exhibit true, godly love. If John's logic here is not satisfying to modern readers, it is perhaps because modern religious thought carefully distinguishes love for God from love for others in a way John would not accept.

3 Verse 3 further emphasizes the relationship between love and obedience. The genitive *tou theou* ("love *of God*") here is probably objective—"love for God" (NIV, NEB)—rather than "God's love" or "love which comes from God." This verse parallels 2:4, which insists that one cannot "know God" apart from obedience. Since "knowing God" in 1 John describes a relationship with God (see comment at 2:3), and since "God is love" (4:8, 16), love and faith go hand in hand. The NIV suggests that the next phrase in v.3 goes with v.4: God's commands "are not burdensome" because/for (*hoti*) believers have overcome the world (cf. Grayston, 133). It seems more likely that this phrase finishes the thought of vv.2–3. John is stressing that love means obedience, but he tempers this emphasis by insisting that God's commands are easy to obey for any who care to pay attention to them. John may be alluding to Deuteronomy 30:11, where Moses, after rehearsing the stipulations of the Sinaitic covenant to the Israelites, reminds them that "what I am commanding you today is not too difficult for you or beyond your reach." God's commands never surpass human ability to fulfill them.

4 Verse 4 builds on vv.2–3 by describing the benefits of obedience. All those who are born of God "conquer [*nikaō*, GK *3771*] the world" (NIV, "overcome the world"). The conquest metaphor is consistent with John's dualistic perspective, which sees a hostile relationship between the world and God's children. But the precise meaning of *nikaō* here is open to debate, especially since it seems to contrast starkly with the real-life experiences of the Johannine Christians (see Introduction).

Some suggest that *nikaō* is used in an eschatological sense. Schnackenburg, 229–30, for example, sees

here a reference to "the victory that Christ won once for all in salvation history," the victory that is "repeated in the lives of the Christians." By participating in the work of Christ, then, believers experience the future victory over evil in the midst of the pain of this world. Rensberger, 129, takes a somewhat similar view with the suggestion that John is touching on the notion that Satan is "the ruler of this world" (Jn 12:31; 14:30; 16:11). Jesus has conquered the ruler of this world, and all those who believe share the benefits of this victory. Other commentators believe that John is thinking of the moral sphere of human experience. Dodd, 126–27, for example, says that "the world" refers here to "the power of evil inclinations, false standards and bad dispositions." "Victory" is achieved when believers choose to obey God and resist temptation (cf. Marshall, 228–29; Schnackenburg, 229).

While both of these views are reasonable, the most likely reference point for the believer's "victory over the world" is John 16:33. First John 5:4 opens with a *hoti* clause that seems to introduce a traditional slogan or saying, and the phrase that follows is strongly reminiscent of Jesus' words in the upper room. After assuring the disciples that they will be hated by the world, put out of the synagogues, and persecuted for his name (Jn 15:18–16:4), Jesus predicts that they will soon scatter and abandon him. Despite all this, they should not be discouraged, because "I have conquered the world" (NIV, "overcome the world"; 16:33).

Jesus' "conquest" seems to consist of his resolution to obey God's calling and suffer death. By analogy, 1 John 5:4 uses *nikaō* to describe the true believer's willingness to serve God in spite of the world's persecutions. Hence the conquest of the world may be reduced to "our faith"—the fact of holding fast to the orthodox confession in the face of pressure to abandon Christ. The verb *nikaō* is used with the same connotation in Revelation, where the believer's "victory" is gained by overcoming the temptation to abandon the faith in the face of severe suffering and possibly death (Rev 2:7, 11, 17, 26; 3:5, 12, 21). If 1 John and Revelation were produced by the same person or by members of the same community, these references would also support the interpretation adopted here.

5 Verse 5 is a rhetorical question that identifies "the one who conquers the world" as the person who believes in the orthodox confession of Jesus as God's Son. The language of this verse forms an inclusio with 5:1 by common reference to John 20:31. The fourth gospel was written so "that you may believe that Jesus is the Christ, the Son of God." First John 5:1 highlights the first portion of this statement, while 5:5 highlights the second portion in the light of John's discussion of the Christian's identity as a child of God.

6 John now turns from love to proper Christology. Verse 6 opens with the masculine form of *houtos*, "this one," which here refers to "Jesus" in the creed at v.5. The remarks that follow are an attempt to prove John 20:30–31, as restated at 1 John 5:1 and 5, through a series of ad hominem arguments based on the beliefs and traditions of the Johannine community. John's thesis appears in the phrase "[Jesus] came by water and blood." The emphasis that Jesus "did not come *by water only*, but by water *and* blood" suggests that the Antichrists took the position that "Jesus came by water." Unfortunately, the historical background of this conflict is far from clear, and 1 John 5:6 has been one of the more controversial NT verses from the very early days of biblical scholarship. Careful consideration will be given to this issue, as its resolution is essential to one's understanding of 5:6–12.

At least since the days of Ambrose and Augustine (early 4th century AD), some scholars have argued that "water" and "blood" are veiled references to the sacraments of baptism and the Eucharist. From this perspective, *dia* and *en* (both "by" in the NIV) should both be translated "with": Jesus came "with water and blood," bringing these sacraments to the church through his incarnation. Support for this position is garnered from John 3:5 ("born of water") and John 6:56 ("eat my flesh and drink my blood"), both of which are also interpreted as references to the sacraments. This was the dominant interpretation until the 1800s, but very few scholars today find this position convincing. Brown, 575, points out that *dia* and *en* do not normally mean "with," and Culpepper, 101, observes that John uses "water and blood" to "validate the manner of Jesus' coming," not to describe something effected or instituted by his ministry. The traditional view would also suggest that the Antichrists accepted baptism ("water only") but not the Lord's Supper, a position difficult to comprehend. Further, it is hard to see why John would suddenly make a veiled reference to the sacraments in the midst of a discussion of orthodox Christology. For all of these reasons, modern scholars have largely rejected the sacramental reading of 5:6.

As a second possibility, some scholars suggest that "water" and "blood" together represent a single entity. Perhaps John is stressing the physical incarnation of Jesus, so that "water and blood" is synonymous with "flesh" in 1 John 4:2 and 2 John 7. On the other hand, "water and blood" might refer more specifically to Jesus' death, for John 19:34 reports that these fluids flowed from the body of the crucified Jesus. Proponents of both versions of this view would argue that the Antichrists denied the physicality of Jesus' existence, perhaps insisting that his human body was only an apparition.

Most modern commentators resolve the problems of v.6 by highlighting the connection between water, blood, and Jesus' "coming" in the first line of the verse. The identification of Christ as "the one who came" (*ho elthōn*) suggests that "water" and "blood" refer to significant events from the life of the historical Jesus. From this perspective, "water" refers to Jesus' baptism, the moment when he was first revealed to the world as the "Lamb of God" (Jn 1:29–34), and "blood" refers to Jesus' sacrificial death (so Dodd, 130; Barker, 350; Marshall, 231; Brown, 578, 596–97; Schnackenburg, 233; Culpepper, 101–2; Rensberger, 132). This would mean that the Antichrists emphasized Jesus' baptism over his death ("water only"), and a variety of hypotheses have been offered as to how this would fit their theology. Many commentators suggest that the Antichrists subscribed to the doctrines of Cerinthus, a Gnostic teacher who argued that the divine spirit of Christ came on the human Jesus at baptism but abandoned him on the cross (Dodd, 130; Marshall, 232–33; Schnackenburg, 233). The Antichrists, then, would argue that the whole of the incarnation was accomplished at Jesus' baptism and would deny that his death was of any salvific significance. John counters this claim by stressing that Jesus' salvific work was completed "in the blood," i.e., through his death as a sacrifice for sins.

Given John's usage elsewhere of the term "blood" (*haima*) exclusively in reference to the physical aspect of human existence and when discussing Jesus in reference to the human physicality of the incarnate Christ (Jn 1:13; 6:54–56; 19:34; see Notes, 1Jn 5:6), it appears that "blood" is used at 1 John 5:6 to emphasize the physical nature of Jesus, perhaps highlighting his sacrificial death. In John's view, any confession of Jesus as "Christ" that does not understand his death in this way is inadequate. The Antichrists' denial of this principle ("water *only*") probably reflects their view that Jesus' death was of little significance, because salvation is granted through some other aspect of his ministry.

What, then, is implied by the phrase "he did not come *by water only*" (see note)? Could water in the most literal sense be the intended reference here?

This possibility may be supported by John 3:5. There Jesus tells Nicodemus that he cannot enter the kingdom unless he is "born of water and spirit." Birth "of spirit" is apparently equivalent to birth "from above" (*anōthen*; Jn 3:3, NIV footnote). The opposite state is described in 3:6—"born of flesh" (*gegennēmenon ek tēs sarkos*, NIV, "flesh gives birth to flesh; GK *4922*). It may be that John is suggesting that believers experience two "births," one of water/flesh and the other of spirit ("from above"). Similar imagery is used at John 1:12–13 to distinguish normal human birth from rebirth as a child of God. The "water" at John 3:5 could thus refer to the flow of water associated with physical childbirth. If "water" is used in the same way at 1 John 5:6, the notion that Jesus "came by water" would emphasize that Jesus experienced normal physical birth. This reading would support the theory that "water and blood" refers to Jesus' birth and death, the totality of his human incarnation.

While this interpretation is reasonable, it is unlikely for three reasons. First, while there is no doubt that 1 John 5:6 is intended to support John's incarnational Christology, the language of the verse itself suggests that "water" and "blood" are separate entities. The NIV translates the second sentence in v.6 as "he did not come by water only, but by water and blood." The distinction between "water" and "blood" that this reading indicates is even sharper in the Greek text, where John includes the preposition ("in") and the article ("the") before both terms: Jesus came not only *en tō hydati* ("in the water") but also *en tō haimati* ("in the blood"). It seems that the Antichrists accepted the proposition that Christ came "by water," but John finds this confession insufficient. He therefore finds it necessary to distinguish "water" from "blood" in order to highlight the importance of each. Second, John shows very little interest in the birth of Jesus, and the fourth gospel does not include a Christmas story. It seems unlikely, then, that he would allude to Jesus' birth in such a vague way, or even that Jesus' birth would play an important part in his Christology. Third, it is difficult to understand why the Antichrists would accept that Jesus came "by water only," i.e., that he was born a physical human being, while rejecting the notion of his physical death ("by blood").

Most scholars today believe that 1 John 5:6 uses the term "water" to refer to Jesus' baptism by John. While this view is reasonable, its primary weakness is evident in Barker's admission, 350, that "John's Gospel does not describe the water baptism of Jesus." While the fourth gospel does include the Baptist's testimony that the Spirit fell upon Jesus in the form of a dove (Jn 1:29–34), this event is not directly associated with Jesus' baptism. Indeed, the Johannine Jesus is never specifically baptized at all. Of course, one could argue that the gospel of John avoids direct reference to Jesus' baptism in response to the Antichrists' overemphasis on that event or to avoid the implication that John was greater than Jesus. But since there is no clear evidence that baptism was practiced by the Johannine community, it is difficult to conclude that "by water" at 1 John 5:6 refers to Jesus' baptism.

This third use of "water," as a symbol of the Spirit, is the most likely reference point for v.6, for it highlights the essential difference between John and the Antichrists. It has already been observed that the Antichrists apparently claimed that their teachings were inspired by the Spirit (see Introduction; comments at 2:20–21; 4:1–6). These claims were likely based on sayings such as John 14:26 and 16:13, which specifically indicate that the Spirit will lead and guide the church in Jesus' absence. The Spirit is, in fact, Jesus himself, who continues to be present to the community in the form of the Paraclete (Jn 14:17–18). In the light of these doctrines, the Antichrists could argue, via

John 19:34, that the Christ "came through water" to his people in the form of the Spirit after Jesus' death. Since they also apparently denigrated the physical aspect of Jesus' existence (see Introduction), they could further assert that Jesus came "through water *only*," i.e., that everything significant about Jesus is revealed in the present through the Spirit.

Against this background 1 John 5:6–12 would represent a brief summary of and response to the Antichrists' doctrine. Notably, the absence of *hoti* in v.6 suggests that John does not intend to quote the Antichrists or to counter their teaching with a specific creed. While not denying the presence and power of the Spirit, John insists that Jesus also came "in the blood," referring to his human physicality. In John's view, the Spirit only reminds the community of what the human Jesus has already taught, without revealing new information (Jn 14:26; see comment at 1Jn 4:2–3). Throughout the epistle John has pitted himself against the Antichrists on the basis that his teachings are based on an actual observation of Jesus' earthly ministry (see comments at 1:1–3; 4:6, 14–15). John therefore asserts that no teaching can proceed directly from the Spirit ("water") unless it also takes into account the community's Jesus tradition, which supports John's own orthodox views about Jesus' humanity ("blood"). Christ, then, came to the community not only "by water," i.e., not only through individual revelations of the Spirit; Christ also came to the community "by blood," i.e., through the established traditions about Jesus' life and death, which are based on John's "witness."

The reading that "water" represents the Spirit while "blood" represents Jesus' human life and death explains John's sudden introduction of the Spirit in the last phrase of v.6, which the NIV translates, "And it is the Spirit who testifies, because the Spirit is the truth." The NIV is correct to suggest that *pneuma* here refers specifically to the Paraclete and is therefore to be capitalized. At the same time, however, this translation obscures the logic of the phrase by reading *hoti* causally: the Spirit testifies *because* the Spirit is truth. Marshall, 234 n.12, who also supports the causal reading, recognizes this problem and attempts to account for it by explaining that "John must mean that the Spirit is able to bear (true) witness because the Spirit is truth." If this is correct, however, it is more likely that *hoti* should be taken as the introduction to a creed or community slogan about the Paraclete: "The Spirit is the one who witnesses; 'the Spirit is the truth.'" The second phrase thus supports the value of the Spirit's witness by insisting that the Spirit supports the truth, so that the community slogan would serve to strengthen the significance of the Spirit's witness. In John's mind this means that, even if Christ continues to come to the community via the Spirit, the teachings of the Spirit will be in complete harmony with the "truth," the orthodox Jesus tradition that the community has supported all along.

Commentators are divided on the means by which the Spirit gives this "testimony" to the church. Marshall, 234, highlighting John's use of the present tense ("the Spirit *testifies*"), suggests that "the Spirit presently testifies to us, in our inward hearts or through the preaching of the Word." Dodd, 129, extending the theory that "water" refers to Jesus' baptism, suggests that the Spirit's "witness" represents the descent of the Spirit on Jesus at baptism as a "divine sign." This witness continues into the present life of the church, where the activity of the Spirit primarily takes the form of "inspired or prophetic utterance . . . by which the Church proclaimed and confirmed the truth of the Gospel." The Spirit thus "witnesses" to Jesus' sonship by preserving the church's traditions about his life and baptism. Rensberger, 132–33, believes that the

Spirit's "witness" consists of nothing more than the community's tradition about Jesus' death, specifically passages such as John 19:34–35 that stress the "blood." Since "water" seems to represent the Spirit here, and since John generally appeals to community tradition when making Christological points, Rensberger's reading is the most accurate. John has already established that every person speaking by God's Spirit will confess that "Jesus Christ has come in the flesh" (1Jn 4:2), and now he simply reaffirms that assertion in the context of the debate over "water and blood." This counters the Antichrists on their own ground, for the very Spirit they claim as their inspiration supports John's view rather than their own.

7–8 Those readers who are more familiar with the KJV may be surprised by the NIV text here. The KJV includes the "Johannine comma" at v.7: "For there are three that bear record in heaven, the Father, the Word, and the Holy Ghost: and these three are one." These words have been excluded from more recent translations because, as Dodd, 127 n.1, notes, they are "found in no Greek MS [manuscript] earlier than the fourteenth century, in no ancient Greek writer, in no ancient version other than the Latin, and in no early manuscripts of the Old Latin version or of Jerome's Vulgate." It seems most likely that the KJV formula was added to an early Latin version of 1 John as a marginal note, perhaps out of concern that no single NT verse directly supports the doctrine of the Trinity. The statement was gradually incorporated into the text, then translated from Latin to Greek and inserted into several Greek manuscripts in the early sixteenth century (cf. Marshall, 236 n.19). Even though the extended version of v.7 appears in some ancient Latin manuscripts, Brown, 781, notes that "all recent Roman Catholic scholarly discussion has recognized that the Comma is neither genuine nor authentic." In light of the overwhelming evidence that John did not compose this sentence, the NIV is correct to relegate it to a footnote.

Verse 7 opens with a *hoti* that, contrary to the NIV's "for," probably introduces a community slogan about the incarnation. According to this slogan, there are three witnesses to the orthodox creed about Jesus—"the Spirit, the water and the blood." That these three are "in agreement" is not surprising. First, as noted in the comment on v.6 above, "water" probably symbolizes the Spirit in this context, so that the terms are synonymous. Second, the connection between Spirit, water, and blood proceeds naturally from John 19:34–35. In that passage, the Beloved Disciple "witnesses" (NIV, "testifies") that water and blood flowed from the crucified body of Jesus. John probably associated the Spirit's testimony with the community's Jesus tradition, so that the Beloved Disciple's "witness" was preserved by the Spirit (see comment at v.6). The Spirit, then, fully agrees that Jesus came "by water and blood." The Antichrists' attempt to divide this witness by denying that Jesus came "by blood" merely demonstrates, in John's view, that they do not speak under the inspiration of the Paraclete (see comment at 4:3).

9 The Spirit, water, and blood together represent "the testimony of God" himself about Jesus. By nature of this fact, these witnesses are greater than "the witness of men" (NIV, "man's testimony"), an allusion to the worldly notions of the Antichrists (see 4:5–6). It is somewhat surprising, however, that John makes this blanket assertion about human testimony, in light of his constant appeal to his own witness (see comment at 1:1–3) and the fourth gospel's appeal to the witness of the Beloved Disciple. In fact, the community's primary evidence for the "water and blood" comes from the Beloved Disciple's human testimony (Jn 19:34–35). For this reason, v.9 cannot be understood apart from the slogan in v.7. "Water and blood" highlights the human witness at the heart of the community's Jesus tradition. The Beloved Disciple's observation that water and blood flowed from Jesus' side proves that Christ died a physical death and that the Spirit ("water") was given to the church through this death. This testimony is "greater" than the Beloved Disciple's himself, however, because it is confirmed and preserved for the community by the Spirit. The unity of the Spirit's witness with human testimony stresses once again that personal spiritual experience cannot validate doctrine apart from the church's accepted traditions about Jesus (see comments at 4:2; 4:6). On the other hand, these traditions become more than mere history only through the Spirit's influence.

10 This verse summarizes John's remarks on water and blood in a test that demonstrates whether one has the true witness that proceeds from God. *If* anyone believes in the Son of God, *then* that person "has the witness within herself" (NIV, "has this testimony in his heart"). Negatively, one may also conclude that *if* someone does not believe God (i.e., does not accept God's witness about the Son), *then* that person "has made [God] out to be a liar." The similarity of the latter conclusion to 2:4 suggests that those who do not accept the Spirit's witness about Jesus show that they are members of the world, just like those who deny that they have sinned. Since the Spirit, water, and blood represent a unified testimony, God's testimony about Jesus is not distinct from John's testimony, especially since the Spirit is the source of John's testimony (4:6). To "believe in the Son of God," then, means to accept John's word that the human Jesus was God incarnate.

What does it mean for the believer to "have this testimony in his heart"? Many commentators conclude that John is speaking of an inner experience that comes from the Spirit. Those who take this position understand the "testimony" to be "an inward work of the Spirit in the believer which confirms outward kinds of experience. If a person believes in the Son of God, he experiences or develops an inner conviction that what he believes is verified in practice" (Grayston, 140). Barker, 352, believes that the "testimony" is "faith itself" and a subsequent "forgiveness of sins and inward establishment of the love of God," both of which are gifts given by the Spirit in the move from "believing" to "receiving" (cf. Stott, 82). While this view is reasonable, it seems to suggest that John's witness about Jesus requires a special work of God to become credible—the very point John has attempted to refute in vv.7–9 by stressing the harmony of the Spirit, the water, and the blood. Other commentators have sought to explain v.10 in more natural terms. Marshall, 241, argues that this verse simply indicates that "to believe in the Son of God is to accept and keep God's testimony," while rejecting the Son means rejecting God as a liar. "It is inconsistent to profess belief in God, as John's opponents did, and yet to disbelieve what God has said." This reading limits God's "testimony" to the inspired, prophetic preaching of the church, which preserved and propagated the true witness about Jesus.

As a third possibility, v.10 may have both the natural and supernatural dimensions of faith in mind. Perhaps John does not distinguish these aspects of faith to the degree that they are distinguished in modern Christian theology. The most immediate parallel to the thought of v.10 appears in 2:20–21, 27. The "testimony of God" here seems equivalent to the "anointing" mentioned in that passage, and both terms probably refer primarily to the orthodox belief in Jesus' literal, sacrificial death (see comment at 2:20–21). At the same time, John's dualism complicates the process by which this testimony

may be accepted. Dodd, 131–33, points out that 1 John 5:6–12 closely parallels John 5:19–47, both in its language and in its appeal to the same dualistic framework. In John 5 Jesus discusses the value of different types of "testimony" about himself, including John the Baptist's witness, the Scriptures, and the power God has given him to do signs. The Jews cannot accept this overwhelming evidence, however, because God's word does not "dwell in you" (5:38). It would therefore be against their nature to believe in Jesus, no matter how strong the testimony. Similarly, although John's Christology is supported both by God's actions in the life of Jesus and by the Spirit's continuing testimony in the church's prophecy, the Antichrists cannot believe because God's word is not in them. They therefore must belong to the same category as the Jews and the world. Those who do accept John's witness, on the other hand, automatically demonstrate that they have God's testimony in themselves, i.e., that they are in the same category as God (see Jn 6:44; 10:3–4). This would suggest that the initial act of faith, crossing over from the sphere of darkness to the sphere of light, is based on obvious public facts but also has a supernatural dimension. Unfortunately, John does not describe the mechanisms of this transformation as carefully as modern theologians might wish.

11 Verse 11 summarizes the preceding verses by defining the "testimony" of God with a community slogan introduced by *hoti* (note the NIV's colon): "God has given us eternal life, and this life is in his Son." In John's mind, "Son" and "life" are synonymous terms, as indicated by the use of *didōmi* ("has given," GK *1443*). God "gave" life just as he "gave" his Son (Jn 3:16); in fact, John would say that life was given to the world in the form of God's Son (Jn 1:4; 1Jn 4:9). Notably, this slogan furnishes the creedal content of God's witness without defining the means by which God has made this "testimony." As indicated in the comment on v. 10, John probably has in mind both the work of God through the life of Jesus and the continuing proclamation of Jesus in the church under the Spirit's influence.

12 Verse 12 offers a test of "eternal life" based on the preceding discussion of belief and witness. *If* someone "has the Son," *then* that person "has life." To "have life" is a typically Johannine way to describe salvation (see comment at 1:2), and the language of this phrase has influenced the somewhat unusual "has the Son" in the conditional statement of the test. In this context, to "have the Son" means to accept God's witness about Jesus, i.e., to accept John's teaching that Jesus came in both "water and blood." Negatively, *if* someone does not "have the Son," *then* that person "does not have life." The Antichrists, then, do not enjoy salvation, because they do not properly understand Jesus. For John, doctrinal issues are not tangential to Christian experience. One's actions cannot secure salvation apart from correct beliefs about Christ.

13 This verse is frequently referred to as the "purpose statement" of 1 John, summarizing "not just the preceding verses but the entire epistle" (Culpepper, 107). The main verb uses an "epistolary aorist," literally "I wrote these things" (NIV, "I write"). In this usage, the aorist tense represents the perspective of the reader, for whom the writing of the letter is a past event. John is therefore attempting to summarize what he has already written in 1 John. The language of this summary is notably similar to John 20:30–31, which indicates that the fourth gospel was written so that the reader "may believe that Jesus is the Christ, the Son of God, and that by believing you may have life in his name." Unlike the fourth gospel, however, the purpose statement of this letter has a strong note of assurance for those who are already believers. Perhaps the pressures of heresy and persecution have left them uncertain, and John may fear that his rigorous tests of orthodoxy have shaken their confidence. He wants them, therefore, to "know" (*oida*, GK *3857*) that they are in good standing with God, no matter what the world and the Antichrists tell them (cf. Marshall, 243; Brown, 633; Rensberger, 138–39).

John refers to his audience as those who believe "in the *name* of the Son of God." Rensberger, 72, notes that the "name" of Jesus "refers to Jesus' identity as such, his entire being," making it a convenient catchword for John's Christology. Jesus' "name" is frequently used in the Bible as a symbol of his power and authority, especially in contexts relating to salvation (Lk 24:47; Jn 1:12; 20:31; Ac 2:38; 10:43; 22:16). In oral cultures, knowledge of a deity's name often implies a special relationship with that deity, which gives the worshiper special rights, privileges, and powers. To believe in "the name of the Son" is to enjoy a relationship with Christ that grants true believers special privileges, specifically "eternal life."

NOTES

6 The Greek αἷμα, *haima*, ("blood," GK *135*), while not occurring frequently in the fourth gospel, is always used in a literal, biological sense. The first reference to αἷμα, *haima*, appears at John 1:13. John assures the reader that those who receive Jesus are given authority to become children of God (v. 12); to emphasize the security of this new status, John stresses that God's children "have not been born from blood nor from the will of flesh" (NIV, "born not of natural descent, nor of human decision"). "Blood" and "flesh" here are apparently synonyms, both referring to the physical aspect of human conception. The human physicality and resultant pedigree of the natural birth process are irrelevant to one's status as a child of God. Continuing in this vein, v.14 stresses the physicality of Jesus' incarnation by insisting that "the Word became flesh."

The next reference to αἷμα, *haima*, appears at John 6:54–56, a passage that parallels 1 John 4–5 at several points. Jesus tells the crowd, which has just witnessed the feeding of the five thousand, that anyone who "eats my flesh and drinks my blood" has eternal life, because his flesh is "true food" and his blood is "true drink" (NIV, "real drink"). In this context, Jesus' "flesh" is explicitly compared to the manna given to the Israelites in the wilderness; his "blood" may therefore represent the water that Moses provided from the rock. This metaphorical usage, however, does not obscure the fact that "flesh and blood" refers primarily to Jesus' physical body (6:52). In actuality, "eating" is a metaphor for belief, and "flesh" and "blood" are literal references to Jesus' person, with the idea that one must accept Jesus as the incarnate Son of God to receive salvation.

The final reference appears at John 19:34–35. When a soldier pierces Jesus' side to ascertain whether he is dead, "water and blood" flow out. These verses are clearly connected to 1 John 5:6, as both passages mention "water and blood," the "witness," and the need to "believe." John 19:34 is also the apparent background for 1 John 1:7. There John says that all those who "walk in the light" will have their sins cleansed by "the blood of Jesus, his Son," a reference to the sacrificial nature of Jesus' violent death. Like 1 John 5:5–6, 1:7 also connects Jesus' blood with his status as the "Son of God."

6 All usages of the Greek ὕδωρ, *hydōr* ("water," GK *5623*) fall into one of three categories in the Johannine literature. First, John often uses the word "water" in the most literal sense, as the name of the common liquid found in wells and rivers and used for bathing and purification (Jn 2:7–9; 3:23; 4:46; 5:7; 13:5). The second usage is an extension of the first, representing the several occurrences of ὕδωρ, *hydōr*, in the testimony of John the Baptist at John 1:26–33. When asked about his authority to baptize, John explains that he baptizes "in water" but stresses that someone greater is coming after him. In fact, John baptizes "in water" solely for the purpose of revealing Jesus to Israel. This passage suggests that John's water baptism is inferior to Jesus' coming revelation of God (also Jn 3:22–30). A third group of texts indicate that the Johannine community sometimes used "water" as a symbol for the Holy Spirit. In John 4, for example, the Samaritan woman comes to Jacob's well to draw physical water, but Jesus offers her "living water" and promises that those who drink this water will never thirst again (4:10–13). The "living water" will, in fact, form a spring within those who drink it and will grant them "eternal life" (v.14). The most significant passage in this category is John 7:37–39. There Jesus promises that all who are thirsty may come to him and drink from the "living water" that flows from his belly. John immediately clarifies that this "living water" is the Spirit, which would be given to "those who believe in him" after Jesus' "glorification."

13 Many scholars take the epistolary aorist ταῦτα ἔγραψα, *tauta egrapsa*, to indicate a break in the text between v.12 and v.13 (so Barker, 353; Marshall, 242–43; Brown, 602, 630–33; Culpepper, 106; Schnackenburg, 246–47; Rensberger, 137–38). The reference to "eternal life" in this verse, however, clearly continues the thought of vv.10–12, while v.14 clearly shifts to the subject of prayer. The outline here is supported by Dodd, 133, and Grayston, 141–42.

REFLECTIONS

First John 5:1–13 is calculated to correct three erroneous approaches to religion, all popular in contemporary Christianity. Many people would insist that, because "God is love," their own beliefs and behaviors are irrelevant to salvation. Judgment is considered to be foreign to God's character, and tolerance is elevated as the supreme ethical principle. John flatly rejects this notion by insisting that "loving God" means keeping his commands. Failure to obey reveals that one has not been reborn and is therefore a member of the world.

But those modern Christians who would broadly agree with John on this point are often guilty of two other fallacies. Some believers emphasize doctrine over practice, being comfortable with the notion that those who accept the correct creeds find favor with God, whether or not they seriously attempt to obey God and love others; other Christians take the opposite approach and insist that doctrine is irrelevant as long as one follows the love command, making the church primarily an organ for social reform. John rejects both approaches by insisting that true Christianity consists of correct beliefs *and* obedience to God's commands, specifically the command to love. This approach requires a well-reasoned faith mixed with a passion for action—a rare combination in the modern church. Indeed, if John's tests of doctrine and love were rigorously applied, one might have to conclude that most Christians today are Antichrists.

F. Test #10: Sin That Leads to Death (5:14–21)

OVERVIEW

The closing section of 1 John contains two of the most difficult verses in the epistle. John's vague reference to a "sin that leads to death" (5:16) has long been the subject of theological debate, and the closing admonition to avoid idols (5:21) is abrupt and confusing. In fact, vv. 16 and 21 are intertwined, and together they form the backbone of this section. It will therefore be necessary to identify the "sin that leads to death" and to define "idolatry" before commenting on the individual verses.

All commentators agree that 1 John's closing statement, "Dear children, keep yourselves from idols," seems out of place. John has not mentioned idolatry previously in the letter, and it seems unlikely that his followers, who have been believers long enough to become involved in disputes over Christology, would still be tempted to return to paganism. "Idolatry" is therefore probably used in a metaphorical sense in v. 21, but to what beliefs or practices does it refer? Brown, 627–28, outlines no fewer than ten major views on the issue. Three of the most popular will be summarized here.

First, some suggest that "idolatry" at v. 21 refers to a general compromise with paganism. Since Greco-Roman culture was saturated with pagan traditions and practices, even mature Christians might occasionally fail to separate themselves from "idolatry" in the broadest sense. This view is most often associated with Dodd, 141, who paraphrases v. 21 as "avoid any contact with paganism." Idolatry thus includes "not only images of the gods, but all false or counterfeit notions of God." A second major theory suggests, by analogy with the Dead Sea Scrolls, that "idolatry" symbolizes "sin as a satanic power." John thus warns believers to avoid sin so that they can maintain their fellowship with "the true God" mentioned in v.20 (so Schnackenburg, 263–64). Marshall, 255–56, combines these two views, concluding that "John urges his readers to have nothing to do with false ideas of God and the sins that go with them."

While these theories are reasonable, "idolatry" most likely characterizes the teachings and practices of the Antichrists. John has just been discussing "the true God and eternal life" through Jesus (v.20). Because God is revealed through Christ alone, and because the Antichrists deny John's true teaching about Christ, the Antichrist's image of God is distorted. Their doctrines are "idolatrous" in the sense that all false images of God are idols (cf. Barker, 357; Brown, 629, 640–641; Grayston, 147–48; Culpepper, 114–15; Thompson, 148; Rensberger, 144–45). Throughout the latter half of 1 John, the author has offered criteria to distinguish true believers from Antichrists. This final admonition urges them to stay on the right side of these tests and cling to the "true God," the Jesus John preaches, rather than the false notions of God propagated by the Antichrists.

Moving to the second problem, debate has raged for centuries over the "sin that leads to death" mentioned in v.16. Does God actually punish some sinners by killing them? The answer is not obvious, for numerous OT and later Jewish texts prescribe the death penalty for certain sins. Further, several NT passages indicate that some early Christians believed that God punishes sinners in a physical way. Paul, for example, warns the Corinthians that abuses of the Lord's Supper have left many "weak and sick" (1Co 11:30). James 5:13–16 urges believers to pray for those whose sin has led to physical illness. The same type of thinking is evident at John 5:14, where Jesus tells the man just healed of a thirty-eight-year illness, "Stop sinning or something worse may happen to you."

Most modern commentators, however, believe that John is using "death" in a spiritual or metaphorical sense in 1 John 5. Grayston, 144, says that "death" refers to "the world of darkness" from which Christians have escaped to receive "life." Schnackenburg, 250, suggests that John is speaking of "spiritual, eternal death," so that "mortal sin is an act God is bound to punish with exclusion from the divine realm of life." Brown, 614–15, supports these spiritual interpretations on the basis that the Johannine literature has very little to say about physical death and nothing to say about physical death as a punishment for sin. While John's language about a "sin that leads to death" may have a literal reference point, he is probably referring metaphorically to an act that places the sinner outside the realm of salvation ("life").

What type of "sin" leads to the spiritual death John is speaking of? Since the days of Thomas Aquinas, this verse has been used to support the distinction between "mortal" and "venial" sins— "mortal" sins being those that involve a deliberate turning from God and subsequent loss of grace ("leading to death"), while "venial" sins being those that do not deprive the soul of grace and therefore do not require formal confession or penance ("not leading to death"). Many modern commentators have rejected this paradigm in favor of the view that John is speaking not of different kinds of sin but different kinds of *sinners*. Marshall, 247, highlights the OT distinction between willful and accidental sins. Those who sin accidentally have their sins resolved by sacrifices on the Day of Atonement, while conscious sins "could be atoned for only by the death of the sinner." Thompson, 142–44, argues that those whose sin "leads to death" are members of the world, non-Christians, whose sins cannot be forgiven because they do not accept Christ. Those who "sin in the realm of life"—the weak brothers whom John urges other believers to pray for—enjoy forgiveness of sins through confession and repentance. It seems, then, that John may be thinking of a type of person rather than a type of action, specifically the nonbeliever who is not a "brother" (v.16).

Combining these preliminary conclusions, it seems that John's reference to a "sin that leads to death" (v.16) builds on the condemnation of idolatry at v.21. Several OT passages pass the death sentence on those who practice idolatry and witchcraft (Ex 22:18; Lev 26:27–30; Dt 17:2–5; 18:9–13). Since "idolatry" here refers to the teachings of the Antichrists, John simply points out that the OT says that such people deserve death.

Perhaps he is thinking particularly of Deuteronomy 18:20, which asserts that any prophet who speaks against the Law or advocates idolatry must be killed. But since these OT laws could not be literally enforced in John's cultural setting, "death" takes on a primarily spiritual connotation. John has already asserted that the Antichrists "remain in death" because they do not love true believers (1Jn 3:14–15). The "sin that leads to death" is therefore a combination of false doctrine ("idolatry") and the lack of love the Antichrists have shown by leaving the community over doctrinal issues (cf. Rensberger, 140).

---

¹⁴This is the confidence we have in approaching God: that if we ask anything according to his will, he hears us. ¹⁵And if we know that he hears us—whatever we ask—we know that we have what we asked of him.

¹⁶If anyone sees his brother commit a sin that does not lead to death, he should pray and God will give him life. I refer to those whose sin does not lead to death. There is a sin that leads to death. I am not saying that he should pray about that. ¹⁷All wrongdoing is sin, and there is sin that does not lead to death.

¹⁸We know that anyone born of God does not continue to sin; the one who was born of God keeps him safe, and the evil one cannot harm him. ¹⁹We know that we are children of God, and that the whole world is under the control of the evil one. ²⁰We know also that the Son of God has come and has given us understanding, so that we may know him who is true. And we are in him who is true—even in his Son Jesus Christ. He is the true God and eternal life.

²¹Dear children, keep yourselves from idols.

COMMENTARY

14–15 The closing section of 1 John summarizes the privileges enjoyed by true believers. Primary among these privileges is the ability to pray with "confidence" (*parrēsia*). John elsewhere uses *parrēsia* to describe speech that is clear and direct, hiding nothing (Jn 16:25–30). Believers will speak to God with *parrēsia* on the day of judgment because they

have no fear (1Jn 4:17). The reason believers may pray in this way is indicated in v.15: God hears our requests and is ready to grant them. This being the case, we should hold nothing back in our prayers.

Sadly, these two verses have been much abused by advocates of the "health and wealth gospel." This school of thought insists that God wants all believers to be healthy, happy, and prosperous. Christians can therefore expect to receive any material blessing they ask God to grant them. Such thinking can produce two dangerous extremes. On the one hand, it can sanctify materialism and greed by cloaking the objects of worldly desire under a divine blessing; on the other hand, it can engender deep guilt and remorse in those whose prayers are not answered, under the logic that God is not listening because one's faith is insufficient. John would reject both conclusions. Those who believe that God desires for them to have a new car and designer clothes while others starve should recall 1 John 2:16—that such cravings come not from the Father but from the world. The Johannine Jesus promises his followers pain and persecution in this world, not health and wealth (Jn 15:18–16:4). And those who fear that God has rejected them because their whims have not been granted should recall 1 John 3:19–20, which assures believers that all who love and obey God "belong to the truth," regardless of their circumstances.

As though anticipating these misunderstandings, John specifies that God hears us "if we ask anything according to his will" (5:14). A similar condition appears at 3:21–24, which says that believers may receive anything they ask for as long as "we obey his commands and do what pleases him." Marshall, 246, notes that the reference to God's will at v.14 directs the reader's attention to the main point of this section in v.16. John is not offering a general principle about prayer but rather is urging believers to pray for sinning brothers. God's will is that all sinning believers confess and repent so that they may remain in fellowship with him. Barker, 355, is therefore correct to suggest that vv.14–15 have more the force of a command than a promise. While only God can forgive sins, intercessory prayers indicate the community's forgiveness and acceptance of the sinner and are therefore a critical aspect of complete restoration. To "ask according to his will" (v.15), then, means that we should ask for things that God wishes to achieve; it doesn't mean that God wants us to have whatever we ask for.

16–17 John's teaching on intercession here is remarkable in its historical context. Both paganism and ancient Judaism insisted that mediation for sinners is limited to priests, patriarchs, prophets, or other "holy men." John, however, stresses that *any* person who believes can pray for a fallen brother and can have confidence that God will respond to that prayer. The ability to make petitions for others is a unique benefit of membership in the Christian community.

Notably, John does not command believers to pray for those who commit a "sin that leads to death"—the Antichrists (see Overview above). Does this mean that the doctrinal conflict has left him so bitter that he is no longer concerned for their salvation? Brown, 613–14, thinks so, arguing that v.16 "means that the author does not want prayers for such sins" in order to "quarantine the secessionists so that they cannot further contaminate his audience" (cf. Culpepper, 111; Thompson, p. 143 n.). Scholars who take this position point to John 17:9, where Jesus refuses to pray for the world during his final prayer in the upper room.

Reacting to this sort of reading, Dodd, 137, suggests that John was perhaps "misled by a too rigorous exegesis of the sayings of Jesus [Jn 17:9]," or possibly he "misapplied them under the tension of a situation of extreme peril to the Church." It is therefore necessary, in Dodd's view, to ignore John's teaching on this point. Dodd and Brown have read far too much into John's remarks. While John does specifically urge that believers should pray for sinning brothers, nothing in the language of these verses prohibits prayers for the Antichrists. The NIV captures the neutral spirit of the verse: "I am not saying that he should pray about that [sin]" (v.16).

John's intention is to emphasize the need to pray for brothers, not to forbid prayers for unbelievers.

At the same time, John's persistent dualism limits the scope of such prayers. Christians are to pray for brothers who sin under the presupposition that a true brother will confess and repent. The Antichrists, on the other hand, are persistent idolaters unwilling to accept that Christ died to remove sins (see comment at 5:6). Marshall, 249, observes that "when a person himself refuses to seek salvation and forgiveness, there is not much point in praying for him" to be restored to God, for such a person never enjoyed a relationship with God in the first place. The only prayers a believer could offer on behalf of an Antichrist are prayers for that person's repentance and salvation.

18–20 John closes the letter with three affirmations of what believers "know." Each opens with *oidamen* ("we know") followed by a *hoti* clause, which suggests that John is rallying his audience around established community creeds. The nature of these statements indicates that *oida* is synonymous with *ginōskō* elsewhere in the letter (see comment at 2:3), representing not cognitive information but key aspects of Christian faith. Believers may be confident in their struggles with the Antichrists because they "know" they are on God's side. Each statement also implies that nonbelievers are categorically different from believers, reinforcing John's consistently dualistic presentation.

18 The first reminder of what believers "know" appears here: "anyone born of God does not sin [NIV, continue to sin]; the one who was born of God protects him [NIV, keeps him safe], and the evil one cannot touch [NIV, harm] him." The language of "rebirth" to describe Christian experience is typical of Johannine literature (Jn 1:12–13; 3:3–5; 1Jn 3:9; 4:7; 5:1–4), but three other aspects of this statement are confusing. First, the identity of "the one who was born of God" (*ho gennētheis*, GK *1164*) is

unclear. Is this person identical to the person described in the first phrase? In other words, do those who are "born of God" protect *themselves* in some way, or does someone else protect them? This issue was apparently troublesome to early Christian scribes as well, for some manuscripts read *heauton* ("himself") while others read *auton* ("him"). In the former case "everyone born of God protects *herself*," while in the latter case "the one who was born of God protects *her*," i.e., the one who was born of God protects others who have been born of God. Brown, 620–22, strongly advocates the former reading ("herself"), suggesting that the Christian is either protected from evil by her faith or that God protects her because of her faith. Most commentators, however, accept the latter view ("her"), understanding John to mean that "those who are born of God" (= Christians) are protected by "the one who was born of God" (= Jesus).

The latter reading is preferable for several reasons. First, the first phrase in v.18 describes the believer with a perfect participle of *gennaō*, focusing on the present status that has resulted from past acceptance of the truth: "everyone who *has been born of God*" continues to enjoy that status; the second phrase shifts to an aorist participle of *gennaō*, which suggests that John is now thinking of a person with a specific past experience of divine birth, most likely Jesus. Further, John 17:11–15 suggests that Jesus and God protect believers from "the evil one," and 1 John 3:5–8 states that Jesus came to do away with sin and destroy the works of the devil. First John 5:18 thus stresses the fraternity between true believers and Jesus by reminding the reader that Jesus is able to protect those who believe in him.

A second problem in v.18 relates to John's statement that those born of God "do not sin." The NIV takes "sin" in the conventional sense of violations of God's law and emphasizes the present tense of the verb *hamartanō* to avoid the implication of moral perfection: "anyone born of God does not *continue to sin*." This translation allows that believers may violate specific moral commands as long as their lives are not characterized by sinfulness. While this interpretation is consistent with Christian experience, John is more likely returning to the nuanced meaning of "sin" developed in 1 John 3 (see Overview at 2:28–3:24). For John, the greatest "sin" is to leave the fellowship of the community because one rejects the truth. The fact that the Antichrists have left John's fellowship, i.e., have "sinned," proves that they are not born of God, while those who accept Christ (i.e., who "do not sin") thereby prove that they are God's children.

The third problem in v.18 relates to the verb *tēreō*, "protects" (NIV, "keeps safe"; GK *5498*). If the subject of this verb is Jesus, "the one who was born of God," in what sense does Jesus "protect" believers from the devil? John might be thinking of Jesus' continuing presence in the church as the Paraclete, in which form he teaches believers "all things" and "guides you into all truth" (Jn 14:26; 16:13). This interpretation would be consistent with the fact that 1 John 5:20 mentions a special "understanding" that the Son has given to believers, perhaps suggesting that Jesus protects true Christians from falsehood through the continuing illumination of the Holy Spirit. On the other hand, John's use of the aorist participle to refer to Christ as "the one *who was born of God*" suggests that he is thinking of Jesus as a historical person who lived in the past. In this connection, the Johannine Jesus uses *tēreō* in his final prayer to assert that he has "protected" the disciples in the Father's name (Jn 17:12). First John 5:18 therefore probably means that those who accept John's witness that Jesus the human being was God incarnate are protected from falsehood by this "knowledge."

The last phrase in v.18 describes the benefits of Jesus' protective care. The word *haptō* (GK *721*), translated "harm" in the NIV, literally means "touch" or "grasp." The same word is used at John 20:17 when Jesus urges Mary not to "hold on to" him when he appears to her at the tomb. The NIV understands *haptō* as a description of the injuries the devil might inflict on people. John, however, is probably using *haptō* to contrast the state of believers with the state of the lost. Those who are not born of God are, in John's view, members of the world and therefore in the grasp of the devil, who rules this world (Jn 12:31). Believers escape his clutches by accepting John's witness.

19 John's second statement of what believers "know" uses terms synonymous with those in v.18 to make explicit his earlier implication about "the world." Believers may be certain that they are "from God" (NIV, "children of God"), while "the whole world" lies under the power of the devil.

20 John's third statement of what believers "know" summarizes the two major themes of the epistle: the identity of Jesus and the difference between true believers and the world/Antichrists. Jesus is the Christ, the Son, and the "true God" in contrast to the false "idols" (v.21) promoted by the Antichrists. Jesus "has come" for the purpose of giving those who accept him a true understanding of God. The perfect tense indicates that this understanding was not only for those who witnessed the human Jesus but also extends to those who now accept authentic testimony about him. The same point is made at John 1:18, where it is stressed that no human being, not even Moses, has ever seen God, so that only Christ, "who is at the Father's side," can reveal God to the world. Of course the "understanding" (*dianoia*, GK *1379*) God gives is synonymous with John's witness about Jesus, so that knowing God means accepting John's Christology. As a consequence, anyone who denies Jesus has a distorted view of God.

In what sense has the Son "given us understanding"? If v.20 parallels verses such as John 14:26 and 16:13, one might conclude that John is thinking of a supernatural revelation of religious truth through the work of the Spirit. However, the focus of 1 John 5:18–20 is not on a mystical ascent to knowledge of God but rather on the knowledge of God that came through the descent of Christ to earth. Most likely, then, "the moment of the giving of the *dianoia* (understanding) or revelatory insight is surely the moment when the author's readers became Christians" (Brown, 639). In conjunction with John's teaching on the "anointing" at 2:27, 5:20 suggests that those who accept John's witness already have a complete and full knowledge of God, which the world and the Antichrists cannot enjoy.

NOTES

18 Contra John thinking of "the one who was born of God" as Jesus, Brown, 622, points out that John nowhere else describes Jesus as "begotten by God." While John does not refer to Jesus elsewhere as ὁ γεννηθεὶς, *ho gennētheis* ("born," GK *1164*), he does identify Christ with the cognate term μονογενής, *monogenēs* ("only begotten," GK *3666*; NIV, "one and only"), on several occasions (Jn 1:14, 18; 3:16, 18; 1Jn 4:9).

REFLECTIONS

First John 5:14–21 offers tests to reassure believers that a correct view of Jesus separates them from the world and the Antichrists. While this is the dominant theme of the entire epistle, the closing section stresses the benefits believers enjoy because of this special status. From a worldly perspective, faith has led the Johannine Christians to persecution and doctrinal division (see Introduction), but from John's perspective these disadvantages are far outweighed by the privileges of membership in the covenantal community. True believers enjoy complete confidence when they approach God in prayer, the assurance that they are God's children, and protection from false idols. In turn for their suffering, John offers them the truth and reminds them that a relationship with the true God is worth any price.

2 JOHN

TOM THATCHER

Introduction

1. **Summary**
2. **Bibliography**
3. **Outline of 2 John**

1. SUMMARY

The background and authorship of 2 John have been discussed in the introduction to 1 John. Second John presents warnings and encouragements, while stressing the Elder's desire to maintain fellowship with the recipients.

Unlike 1 John, both 2 and 3 John follow standard conventions for ancient letters. Their introductions and conclusions use common formulae, and their tone and themes would be widely recognized in the ancient world. These epistolary features will be highlighted in the analysis that follows.

2. BIBLIOGRAPHY

See the bibliography listed in 1 John (p. 424).

3. OUTLINE OF 2 JOHN
   I. Greeting (1–3)
  II. Protecting the Truth (4–11)
 III. Farewell (12–13)

Text and Exposition

I. GREETING (1–3)

OVERVIEW

John L. White (*Light from Ancient Letters* [Philadelphia: Fortress, 1986], 198) notes that "the general nature of the relationship between reader and recipient is conveyed by the opening and closing" sections of the ancient letter. For this reason, the introduction and conclusion to ancient letters are particularly important in analyzing the type of relationship that existed between the author and reader(s). Within the generally accepted conventions of style, modifications to the typical elements reveal the author's estimate of herself and her audience. Second and 3 John clearly follow this pattern.

The "opening" of an ancient private letter generally includes a prescript, "health wish," and prayer. The prescript takes the formula "X (in the nominative case) Y (in the dative case) *chairō*" ("greetings," GK *5897*), where "X" is the sender and "Y" the recipient. A typical prescript formula might be translated, "Paul to Timothy: Greetings!" Embellishment of the names or the basic greeting serves to clarify the relationship between the two parties. The "health wish" expresses concern over the reader and/or reports on the writer's condition. The prayer follows naturally from the health wish as a thanksgiving for good health or a request for good health.

Two basic elements appear in the closing section of Greek letters: secondary greetings and a closing word. Greetings, which typically open with the verb *aspazomai* (NIV, "send greetings," GK *832*; 2Jn13), could be from the writer to parties with the reader or to the reader from parties with the writer.

The opening verses of 2 John clearly follow the typical epistolary formula. The author introduces himself in the nominative case as "the Elder" and refers to the reader in the dative case as "the Elect Lady" (NIV, "chosen lady"). Verses 1–2 express the author's warm feelings for the recipients and explain the basis for this affection. Verse 3 is a prayer for the reader's well-being, here with a specifically Johannine flavor. The overall tone of the introduction indicates that John wishes to establish a relationship of common belief, love, and loyalty between himself and the audience.

---

¹The elder,

To the chosen lady and her children, whom I love in the truth—and not I only, but also all who know the truth—²because of the truth, which lives in us and will be with us forever:

³Grace, mercy and peace from God the Father and from Jesus Christ, the Father's Son, will be with us in truth and love.

COMMENTARY

1 Verse 1 raises two significant issues for the background of the Johannine Epistles. While the author's means of identifying himself and his audience complies with typical Greco-Roman epistolary conventions, the names he uses have generated considerable controversy. Before proceeding to exegesis, it will be necessary to discuss the significance of the self-designation "the Elder" and the identity of the "Elect Lady" to whom the letter is addressed.

The Greek word *presbyteros* ("elder," GK *4565*) occurs sixty-five times in the NT but only twice in Johannine literature (2Jn 1; 3Jn 1). *Presbyteros* is elsewhere used as a title for officers who hold the highest level of leadership in the Pauline and Jerusalem churches (Ac 11:30; 14:32; 15:2–6, 22–23; 16:4; 20:12; 21:18; 1Ti 4:14; 5:1, 17–19; Tit 1:5). The "elders" of these congregations, who are distinct from the apostles, seem to have been responsible for the church's vision, mission, and doctrine, as is evident from the synonymous term *episkopos*, "overseer" (GK *2176*). Some scholars have interpreted 2 John 1 in this Pauline sense, understanding the author to mean that he functions as an "elder" in a particular congregation (so Smalley, 317). Because the author of 2 and 3 John claims an authority that extends to several congregations, Houlden, 4, suggests that "'Elder,' in the usage of the Johannine community, signifies one ... who writes and visits and from the setting of his own congregation exercises supervision over a number of others," similar to early bishops such as Ignatius and Polycarp.

A closer examination reveals that the NT authors do not limit the term *presbyteros* to a specific church office. The word seems to have been borrowed from Judaism, for the Gospels and Acts typically refer to the leaders of the Jewish community as "elders." The Jewish elders are to be found in the company of the high priests (Mt 27:12, 20–23; 28:11–12; Lk 22:51;

Ac 4:23; 22:5; 23:14; 24:1; 25:15), scribes (Mt 26:51; Mk 11:27; 14:53; Lk 20:1; Ac 4:5; 6:12), and sometimes both high priests and scribes (Mt 16:21; 27:41; Mk 8:31; 14:43; 15:1; Lk 9:22). In several of these contexts, the "elders" are apparently members of the Sanhedrin, the ruling council of Judaism. When they appear by themselves, they are normally designated *presbyteroi tou laou*, "elders of the people," or *presbyteroi tōn Ioudaiōn*, "elders of the Jews." In Matthew 15:2; Mark 7:3–5; and Hebrews 11:2, however, the "elders" are the forefathers of the Jewish nation, including heroes from the OT and famous rabbis.

In other cases, *presbyteros* is used synonymously with *presbytēs* to refer to someone simply as an "old man." Luke 15:25 refers to the brother of the prodigal son as the "elder" brother, and Acts 2:17 borrows the term from the LXX version of Joel 2 to promise that "old men will dream dreams" in the last days. Notably, the only occurrence of *prebyteros* in the fourth gospel falls into this category. John 8:9 indicates that when Jesus disrupted the plot of those who prosecuted the adulterous woman, the "older men" left the scene first. An interesting interplay between the various nuances of the term may be seen at 1 Peter 5:1–5. The author, presumably the apostle Peter, addresses the leaders of the congregation as "elders" and refers to himself more generally as *sympresbyteros* (GK *5236*), a "fellow elder," despite the fact that he does not hold a specific office in the church to which he writes. Then in v.5, Peter urges young men to show respect "to those who are older" (*presbyteros*). In this context, "elder" refers variously to an apostle, a local church leader, and men of a certain age.

In summary, *presbyteros* is used in at least four distinct ways in the NT: (1) It may refer to those in the upper echelon of religious and political authority in the Jewish community; (2) in a usage adapted by Christians, *presbyteros* also became a technical term for an officer in the Pauline churches; (3) *presbyteros* is sometimes used as a title of respect for the Jewish forefathers; and (4) most generally, *presbyteros* may be synonymous with *presbytēs* to describe an elderly man.

The self-designation "the Elder" in 2 John 1 and 3 John 1 clearly does not fit the first or third categories above. The second option is possible, especially if one assumes that the Johannine churches, being located in the vicinity of Ephesus (see Introduction), had adopted the Pauline model of leadership. If this is the case, however, it seems odd that John does not call on "the elders" specifically to protect the congregation from Antichrists, a responsibility the Pauline elders seem to have held. Further, Titus 1:5 and Acts 14:23 suggest that the authority of Pauline elders was limited to the local congregation, whereas the author of 2 and 3 John feels himself privileged to instruct other churches. The fact that congregational leaders are addressed directly by name or by honorary epithet in 1–2–3 John (2Jn 1; 3Jn 1, 5–7, 9, 12) may indicate that the Johannine churches did not use official titles for their officers. While the familiar Pauline usage is certainly possible, there is not enough evidence to conclude that the author of 2 and 3 John thinks of himself as an "elder" in the Pauline sense.

The fourth possibility, that the author calls himself *presbyteros* as an indication of age, is attractive. First, the only use of the term elsewhere in the Johannine literature (Jn 8:9) carries this implication, although the textual problems surrounding John 7:52–8:11 make the origins of that verse uncertain. Further, 1 John 1:1–3 indicates that the author thinks of himself as a direct witness of Jesus (see comment) and uses this status as the platform of his authority against the Antichrists. If, as most scholars suggest, 1–2–3 John dates from the late first century, any living witness of Jesus would necessarily be "an old man" by this time. Notably, the term "elder" is used in just this sense by the church father Papias to refer to those authorities on Jesus who were still living at the turn of the second century (see Eusebius, *Hist. eccl.* 3.39.4). In the same vein, 1 Peter 5:1 refers to the apostle Peter as both a "witness" (*martys*, GK *3459*) of Jesus and a "fellow elder" (*sympresbyteros*). If the same sense underlies 2 John 1, the title "the Elder" establishes the author as a person old enough to have been an associate of the historical Jesus. Because this claim would form the basis of the author's authority and status in the church, the word "elder" had probably developed unique connotations in the Johannine community. Houlden, 4, therefore suggests that "[the elder's] role may be more personal and charismatic .... Instead of being an embryonic provincial metropolitan [bishop] ... perhaps he was a man valued for qualities in relation to which his age was more significant" than his office. Because the author is an "elder" in this sense, he has taken on a role in the Johannine churches parallel to that of the Jewish forefathers and rabbinic authorities in Jewish life and thought. The Johannine usage would thus represent a unique adaptation of *presbyteros* from the Jewish background parallel to, but not dependent on, the Pauline application.

The name used for the recipients of the letter, "the Elect Lady and her children," is difficult for two reasons. First, it is unclear whether John is referring specifically to an individual or metaphorically to an entire congregation. The Greek *eklektē kyria* (GK *1723* + GK *3257*) could literally mean "to the elect Kyria" or "to the lady Electa," both proper names, or could be an honorary nickname for a Christian woman ("the Elect Lady"). Plummer, 132, advocates this last option, arguing that the reader is a female Christian and the literal mother of the "children" John mentions. In his view, this explains the author's "somewhat informal [self-] designation" as "the Elder" (cf. R. B. Edwards, *The Johannine Epistles* [NTG; Sheffield: Sheffield

Academic Press, 1996], 27–29). In support of this interpretation, one might note Romans 16:13, where Paul refers to his friend Rufus as "elect [NIV, chosen] in the Lord." Most modern commentators, however, conclude that "the Elect Lady" is a general reference to an entire congregation, so that "her children" are the individual members of that congregation (so Houlden, 142; Culpepper, 117; Marshall, 60–61; Stott, 203–4; Rensberger, 148). This reading is supported by the closing verse of 2 John, where the Elder sends greetings from "the children of your elect [NIV, chosen] sister," apparently the congregation of which John is a member (v.13). While it is possible that both congregations were led by individual Christian women, it seems more likely that the terms "lady" and "sister" are used metaphorically to portray a familial relationship between the two churches. Outside the Johannine literature, the NT frequently portrays the church as a woman or bride as the counterpart to Jesus (2Co 11:2; Eph 5:22–32; Rev 19:6–9). Smalley, 318, thus correctly emphasizes the absence of the definite article at 2 John 1 with the translation "to *an* Elect Lady," i.e., the church.

The reference to believers as "elect" (*eklektos*) is more typical of Paul than John (see Ro 8:33; 16:13; Col 3:12; 2Ti 2:10). Revelation 17:14 refers to the faithful as "elect" (NIV, "chosen") and "called" (*klētos*, GK *3105*), but many modern scholars doubt that Revelation and 2 John were written by the same person. In any case, although the terminology is somewhat unusual, the notion that believers are God's chosen people is typically Johannine (Jn 1:12–13; 6:37–39, 43, 65, 70; 10:14–16, 27–29; 13:18; 15:16, 19; 17:6, 9, 24). In all these cases, John uses election language to emphasize that believers are God's unique community in spite of the world's denial of this status. Because they have been chosen by God, even persecuted Christians may be certain that their salvation is secure.

John's affection for his readers is indicated by the epithet "whom I love in the truth." The phrase *en alētheia* ("in truth," GK *237*) could be dative of manner, indicating that the Elder "truly" loves them, that his affection is sincere (NASB; NEB). But the NIV is more likely correct in emphasizing the definite article: "whom I love in *the* truth." Throughout the Johannine literature, "truth" normally refers to Jesus or to John's witness about Jesus as a body of doctrine (Jn 1:14, 17; 8:32; 14:6; 16:13; 1Jn 2:21; 3:19; 2Jn 2, 4; 3Jn 3). "*In* the truth" refers to the mutual faith that binds believers together. For this reason, the readers are also loved by "all who know the truth." "Know" (*ginōskō*, GK *1182*) is used here in the specifically Johannine sense of an experience of God through Christ that transcends cognitive knowledge (see comment at 1Jn 2:3).

2 John now reveals the *reason* for his love for the readers. According to Johannine dualism, "like loves like" (see comments at 1Jn 4:12, 20). Because John and his associates accept the truth, they in turn love all others who accept it. The word translated "lives" in the NIV is *menō* (GK *3531*), the same term Jesus uses to describe the relationship between himself and those who obey him (Jn 15:4–10). Such truth "will be with us forever" because it comes from the "Spirit of Truth" who will "be with you forever" (Jn 14:16) and because its acceptance leads to eternal life.

3 John's prayer for the reader combines Jewish and Greco-Roman customs. Greek letters typically include a "grace" greeting (*charis*, GK *5921*), while "mercy" and "peace" (*eleos*, GK *1799*, and *eirēnē*, GK *1645*) are customary Jewish salutations. In most ancient letters, the prayer formula implies a subjunctive verb ("*should* be . . ."), indicating that the author hopes his wish will be granted for the reader. John, however, uses the future indicative of *eimi*, which represents, as the NIV indicates, a promise that these things "will be" with those who have faith. In light of the experience of the Johannine Christians (see Introduction), it may seem odd that John would promise "peace" as well as "grace" and "mercy." He is probably thinking of "peace" as a positive relationship with God, irrespective of the difficulties presented by the world and the Antichrists. Throughout the Johannine literature, peace with God is the flipside of the world's hatred (Jn 15:18–16:4; 17:14).

The function of the last phrase in v.3, *en alētheia kai agapē* ("in truth and love"), is uncertain. Marshall, 64, suggests that these qualities go along with "grace, mercy and peace" as specifically Johannine benefits of faithfulness. Similarly, Dodd, 147, believes that all five terms describe facets of the same experience, "because the grace of God is shown in that revelation of Himself which is the Truth, and in the divine charity expressed in the work of Christ … and takes effect in the true belief and mutual charity of Christians." The NIV, on the other hand, suggests that the phrase "modifies the way in which grace, mercy, and peace indwell" (Brown, 659), i.e., these blessings "will be with us in truth and love"

(NIV). Brown, 682, believes that the phrase conditions the entire preceding greeting, so that the believer's receipt of grace is contingent on her commitment to the "truth" of John's message and subsequent good fellowship ("love") with the community. Another possibility is suggested by the fact that John has positioned the phrase immediately after the words "the Father's Son." "In truth and love" may refer to the relationship that exists between Jesus and God, for God is referred to as *ho patros* ("the father"), and Jesus is then redundantly called "the Father's Son." The Johannine Jesus uses cognates of *agapē* (GK 27) to describe his relationship with God on several occasions (Jn 3:35; 10:17; 14:31), and John consistently advocates the "truth" of Jesus' claims to this relationship. If this is the case, Jesus is the Son "in love," in the sense that he and God love one another, and "in truth," in the sense that this doctrine is true. In any case, "'truth and love' provide the transition to the next section, where they become the chief topic[s]" (Barker, 362).

II. PROTECTING THE TRUTH (4–11)

[4]It has given me great joy to find some of your children walking in the truth, just as the Father commanded us. [5]And now, dear lady, I am not writing you a new command but one we have had from the beginning. I ask that we love one another. [6]And this is love: that we walk in obedience to his commands. As you have heard from the beginning, his command is that you walk in love.

[7]Many deceivers, who do not acknowledge Jesus Christ as coming in the flesh, have gone out into the world. Any such person is the deceiver and the antichrist. [8]Watch out that you do not lose what you have worked for, but that you may be rewarded fully. [9]Anyone who runs ahead and does not continue in the teaching of Christ does not have God; whoever continues in the teaching has both the Father and the Son. [10]If anyone comes to you and does not bring this teaching, do not take him into your house or welcome him. [11]Anyone who welcomes him shares in his wicked work.

COMMENTARY

4 The verbs in v.4 may reveal something of the background of the letter. The word translated "to find" in the NIV is in the perfect tense (lit., "to have found"), while "it has given me great joy" is aorist. This suggests that John is responding to a positive report he has received about this congregation. Perhaps some of his associates had visited the church and informed him that the Antichrists had not yet infiltrated their ranks.

The exact content of that report is, however, unclear. The word "some" in the NIV does not appear in the Greek but may be reasonably implied from the genitive *ek tōn teknōn sou* ("from your children"). Scholars who support this reading conclude that John has learned that only a portion of the congregation "goes about in truth," while the rest have been drawn away by the Antichrists (so Dodd, 147; Bultmann, 110; Barker, 362–63). It is also possible that John means simply "those from your children," which would imply that all members of the congregation have remained faithful. Marshall, 65, who takes this view, suggests that John had perhaps met with representatives of the congregation and gathered from them that the entire church was healthy (cf. Brown, 661; Culpepper, 119–20). This situation would indeed give John "great joy" and would also explain his warm affirmations.

"Walking" (*peripateō*, GK *4344*) is a common metaphor in Greco-Roman moral rhetoric to describe adherence to a particular lifestyle. Paul frequently uses *peripateō* in discussions of Christian conduct (see Ro 14:15; Gal 5:16; Eph 4:17; 5:2, 15; 1Th 2:12; 4:1), and the same metaphor underlies modern idioms such as "the Christian *walk*" or "*walk the talk*." The phrase that follows, *en alētheia* ("in truth," GK *237*), could be adverbial, indicating that believers go about "truly" (so Bultmann, 110), but the NIV is more likely correct to suggest that "in

truth" refers to orthodox Christian belief (cf. Barker, 363; Marshall, 66; Brown, 662). To go about "in the truth" is, as the next line indicates, to obey the command from the Father.

5 The "command" in question is specified in v.5—"love one another"—which John seems to cite from the same community tradition that underlies John 13:34 and 1 John 4:21. The love command is "from the beginning" in the sense that it originates with Jesus and is therefore foundational to Christian faith. Since John defines "love" as remaining in fellowship with those who accept his witness (see comments at 1Jn 3:11–20), "going about in love" should be seen as an exhortation for believers to stick together in the face of the threat from Antichrists.

6–7 These verses function together as an objective test, similar to those in 1 John, whereby believers can immediately identify any Antichrists who might come into their midst: *If* someone loves [God], *then* that person will "walk in obedience to his commands." Consequently, those who do not obey the commands clearly do not love God. Verse 7 specifies the test by offering a creed that indicates which "command" John has in mind: *If* anyone "does not acknowledge Jesus Christ as coming in the flesh," *then* that person "is the deceiver and the Antichrist." Such clear guidelines will leave the "Elect Lady" with little doubt as to whose doctrine is authentic.

6 Verse 6 is a commentary on the command of Jesus cited in v.5. John uses a circular argument to highlight the close connection between love for God, obedience to God, and love for brothers. Christians are commanded to love others, and to love God is to follow this command. The latter principle is drawn from Jesus' teaching that his "friends," those who love him, will obey his teachings (Jn 14:15; 15:14). As a result, love for God and the command to love others are one and the same, so that a deficiency in one area

516

shows a failure in the other as well. John is probably again thinking specifically of the Antichrists, who have shown that they do not love God by failing to remain in the fellowship of the community.

Verse 6, along with v. 5, takes pains to stress that John's teaching, unlike that of the Antichrists, is not new or innovative. While the Antichrists have led many astray with new doctrines, John grounds his position firmly in the teaching of Jesus and the community's creeds. The things he writes are not "new" (*kainē*, GK *2785*), in the sense that they are not different from what believers have heard all along. (In contrast with *neos* [GK *3742*], *kainē* refers to something that is new in kind, not necessarily in age, as when one buys a used automobile and refers to it as "my new car.") While the Antichrists may teach a new kind of doctrine, John only repeats "*his* [Jesus'] command," which has existed "from the beginning," so that he needs only to remind them of what "you have heard" already. This emphasis is consistent with the conservative tone of 1 John, which strongly prefers traditional truths over new religious experiences (see comments at 1Jn 4:2–3, 6).

7 The *hoti* that opens this verse is omitted by the NIV, perhaps because its significance is unclear (cf. Grayston, 154). It may be that the word has a mild causal force, indicating that believers must hold to the command "*because* many deceivers . . . have gone out" (so Marshall, 69; Brown, 668; Culpepper, 121). It is also possible that *hoti* here introduces an eschatological community slogan used proverbially to stress the danger of the situation. Similar language appears at Matthew 24:24, where Jesus warns that in the last days false christs and false prophets will "deceive [*planaō*, GK *4414*] even the elect [*eklektos*]"—the same term John uses to refer to believers at 2 John 1 and 13. The notion that the Antichrists are "deceivers" who have "gone out" closely parallels Revelation 20:8, which describes Satan leaving the pit as he "goes out to deceive the nations." Revelation 12:9 and 20:10 both refer to the devil as *ho planōn*, "the deceiver." In conjunction with the term "Antichrist," which itself seems to be drawn from a community slogan of unknown origin (see comment at 1Jn 2:18), the phrase "many deceivers have gone out into the world" is probably John's adaptation of a familiar eschatological creed. As with the creed cited at 1 John 2:18, John has shifted the tense of the statement to apply it to the immediate situation, so that the future *exeleusontai* ("deceivers *will go out*") has become the aorist *exēlthon* ("deceivers *have gone out*"; both are forms of *exerchomai*, GK *2002*).

The adaptation of a familiar creed to the Antichrist crisis allows John to portray the danger of the situation in absolute eschatological terms. Just as the believers were clearly warned about the coming of the Antichrist (1Jn 2:18), they have also heard that deceivers will come in the last days. Both prophecies have, in John's view, been partially fulfilled with the appearance of the Antichrists. As in 1 John, an "Antichrist" is a person who promotes a doctrine of Christ that differs from that taught by John (see Introduction), specifically refusing to confess "Jesus Christ as coming in the flesh."

The wording of this christological confession at v.7 differs somewhat from that at 1 John 4:2. In the latter verse, John says that every teacher who truly comes from God will support the confession "Jesus Christ *has come* in the flesh." In the Greek, "has come" is *elēlythota* (GK *2262*), a perfect tense participle. At 2 John 7, however, John shifts to the present tense participle *erchomenon*, which gives the reading indicated by the NIV—"Jesus Christ *as coming* in the flesh." The potential significance of this shift is the topic of considerable debate. Dodd, 149, notes that the most natural implication is that the Antichrists denied that "Christ is coming," i.e., they denied the second coming of Christ. From this perspective, the confession parallels the community slogan about the coming of the Antichrist cited at 1 John 2:18. Some scholars, however, see the present tense as an emphasis on "the timeless character of the event" of the incarnation (so Bultmann, 112; Barker, 364). Stott, 212, notes that Jesus' "two natures, manhood and Godhead, were united already at his birth, never to be divided. The combination of the present and perfect tenses (in 1 Jn. 4:2 and here) emphasizes this permanent union of [two] natures in the one person." Marshall, 70–71, who takes this position, suggests that John may be countering the Gnostic doctrine that the "Christ" was a heavenly power that descended on the human Jesus at baptism, used his body for several years, and then returned to heaven just before Jesus' death on the cross. A third group of scholars regard the shift in tense from 1 John 4:2 to 2 John 7 as insignificant. Since John is generally concerned to demonstrate that the incarnation was a real historical event of the past, the two verses are seen as alternative wordings of the same christological creed (so Brown, 670; Culpepper, 122; Rensberger, 153–54). From this perspective, the two verses are virtually synonymous.

All three positions are reasonable, and it is difficult to ascertain which most accurately represents John's thinking. The first position, that the Antichrists denied the second coming, is supported by the grammar of the verse and by the fact that the parallel slogan about the Antichrist in 1 John 2:18 seems clearly to imply a future event (see comment there). Just as the readers have heard that "Antichrist is coming," they have heard that "Jesus Christ is coming [again] in the flesh." This position is generally rejected for lack of evidence that a denial of the parousia [second coming] presented a problem in the early church or to the readers of John's letters in particular (so Smalley, 329; Stott, 212). Such an argument, however, begs the question, for if v. 7 indeed refers to the Antichrists' denial of the second coming, the verse itself would become evidence for

such a "problem." Further, Paul warns the Thessalonians about those who teach that "the day of the Lord has already come" (2Th 2:1–2), apparently denying a future parousia on the basis that Christ has already returned to the church in the form of some spiritual experience. It is very possible that the Antichrists used a similar line of reasoning to argue that Christ "comes" in the form of the Paraclete, so that the experience of the incarnate Jesus was not radically different from the experience of all Christians (see Introduction; comment at 1Jn 5:6).

The second position—that John wishes to emphasize the continuing reality of the incarnation—would seem to be counterproductive to his argument. The Antichrists have degraded Jesus' humanity by overemphasizing his spiritual nature (see Introduction), and it is this very point that John wishes to counter. It is unclear how he could do this by spiritualizing the human nature of Jesus to the point that "in the flesh" refers to the present state of Christ's existence in heaven. Such a statement would support the position of the Antichrists, who would say that Christ's past earthly state was no different from his present divine state.

The difficulties associated with these first two solutions make the third position most attractive. While the participle *erchomenon* is present tense ("is coming"), its force here is primarily substantive, characterizing Jesus as "the one coming *in flesh*," the very point the Antichrists would deny. Rather than highlighting Jesus' continuing deity, John is stressing his past humanity, the fact that he lived and acted as a real human being in human history. Verse 7 may therefore be paraphrased, "Many deceivers have gone out into the world, who do not confess that Jesus [the human being] is the divine Christ who came to earth in physical flesh." The verse is therefore parallel in thought, if not in wording, to 1 John 4:2.

8 Having portrayed the readers' situation in eschatological terms, John now warns them to stay on the right side of the conflict. The verb translated "lose" in the NIV is *apollymi* (GK *660*), which means "destroy" or "ruin." Those who hold to the truth will receive, as children of God, "grace, mercy and peace" (v.3), while those who do not will have their hopes ruined.

The specific nuances of this verse are complicated by a difficult textual variant. The NIV follows the reading *eirgasasthe*, the aorist second person plural of *ergazomai* (GK *2237*): "do not lose what *you* have worked for." There is strong manuscript evidence, however, for the alternative reading *eirgasametha*, the first person plural, which would render the meaning of the phrase, "do not lose what *we* have worked for" (NASB, NRSV, NEB; cf. Marshall, 72). Barker, 364, assuming that the Elder is John the son of Zebedee, supports this alternative reading on the grounds that "the apostles could not help but feel completely involved in the lives of their charges." If this is the case, John would have a sense that his apostolic mission had failed if the readers fell away—a sense similar to Paul's sentiments at Galatians 4:11; 2 Corinthians 7:5–16; and 1 Thessalonians 2:17–3:9. But even aside from the obvious uncertainty as to whether "the Elder" was an apostle, this argument is inconsistent with John's general feeling toward those who fall away. While the Antichrists themselves were once members of John's fellowship, he nowhere expresses remorse or a sense of failure about their departure. The fact that they and others have fallen away does not reveal that John has failed, but rather that such people "did not belong to us" in the first place (see comment at 1Jn 2:19). Even if the reading "what *we* have worked for" is correct, it is more likely John is speaking collectively of all Christians and attempting to stress his solidarity with the reader (so Brown, 671; Rensberger, 154). All Christians are working toward a common goal; John is confident he personally will receive his reward, and he hopes the same will be true of others. From this perspective, either reading is acceptable, and both would stress that the efforts of John and the readers are wasted if they should leave the true faith.

9 This verse largely summarizes the arguments of 1 John 4–5, which stress the complete unity of the Father and Son. Jesus claims to be one with the Father (Jn 10:30; 14:9), so in John's mind denial of Christ (i.e., denial that the human Jesus was the divine Christ incarnate) amounts to denial of God as well. It is unclear, however, what John means by "the teaching of Christ." If the genitive *tou christou* is objective, John means "the teaching *about* Christ which you heard from me" (so Bultmann, 113; Marshall, 72; Smalley, 332). On the other hand, if the genitive is subjective, John means "the teaching *from* Christ" or "Christ's teaching" (so Brown, 674–75; Stott, 214). Some who take the latter position equate "Christ's teaching" with the love command in v.5 (so Houlden, 146). Both translations are reasonable, and the difficulty is complicated by the fact that *didachē* (GK *1439*) is not a typically Johannine way of referring to a body of doctrine (in Jn 7:16–17, Jesus refers to "my teaching" [*hē emē didachē*] but says this teaching also comes "from God"; the only other Johannine occurrence of *didachē* appears at Jn 18:19, where Annas questions Jesus "about his disciples and his teaching"). In the light of the broader context, 2 John 9 probably refers to Jesus' own teaching about love and God as preserved by John's witness.

The Antichrists have, in John's words, "run ahead" and deviated from the authentic tradition. The origin of the term *proagō* (GK *4575*) is debated. Some believe that "John is almost certainly borrowing from the vocabulary of the heretics" (Stott, 13). If this is the case, the Antichrists would have claimed that their doctrine was more sophisticated or advanced than John's. Whether or not they did so cannot now be determined, and even if the Antichrists did think or speak of themselves this way, it would not necessarily represent hostility toward John. They may have seen their views as a logical and legitimate extension of Johannine tradition (see comment at 1Jn 2:19). In any case, it seems more likely that "run ahead" is John's own term, used here as a complement to the metaphor "walk in obedience to his commands" in the test at v.6. There John asserted that true love for God is evident when one walks within the confines of the orthodox confession. Verse 9 offers the negative version of this test: If "anyone runs ahead and does not continue [to walk] in the teaching of Christ," *then* that person "does not have God" either. On the other hand, *if* someone "continues [to walk] in the teaching," *then* one may conclude that that person "has both the Father and the Son."

Dodd, 150, interprets this verse to mean that John is stigmatizing "any kind of 'advance' as disloyalty to the faith," thereby "condemn[ing] Christian theology to lasting sterility." A number of scholars have reacted strongly to Dodd's position, insisting that John means only that Christian theology must be continually reconstructed within clearly defined parameters (Brown, 687–89; Culpepper, 123–24). Admittedly, the language of v.9 is very narrow. John elsewhere emphasizes that personal experience and new theological ideas are to be judged exclusively in reference to established tradition (see comment at 1Jn 4:6). Dodd's negative interpretation, as well as the attempts of others to soften it, only emphasizes the difference between

John's dualistic perspective and the ecumenical tone of dialogue in the modern church.

10 At this point, John shifts from pastoral exhortations to an explicit command to protect the church from heresy. "You" is plural, suggesting that John envisions a congregation that meets in a member's home, perhaps that of the "Elect Lady" (see comment at v.1). "This teaching" would refer to the "teaching of Christ" in v.9. Those whose doctrine is inconsistent with traditionally accepted beliefs should not be allowed to speak in church meetings. John literally demands of believers, "Do not say 'welcome' [*chairein*] to them." The fact that John elsewhere makes benevolence a mark of Christian love (see comment at 1Jn 3:16–18; 3Jn 5–8) shows that he believes his opponents are not Christians and therefore are unworthy of the church's support.

11 While the language of this verse is guarded, the context makes the tone clear. John fears that open dialogue between believers and Antichrists might lead some of his flock to error, and against this possibility he demands absolute separation. In such a situation, one must be considered guilty by association. The text literally reads, "The one who says 'Welcome' to him [an Antichrist] shares in his wicked work." The leaders of the church should therefore understand that John will hold them responsible if heretics are allowed to infiltrate the congregation.

NOTES

8–9 There is some debate over the implication of the warnings and consequences described in vv.8–9. Barker, 364–65, suggests that John envisions three possible responses to the Antichrist situation: (1) an avoiding of the errors of the Antichrists and thereby securing the full promise of grace (v.3); (2) some being partially deceived and therefore not attaining their full reward (v.8); and (3) "a more radical departure from the faith" leading to a complete "loss . . . of God himself" (v.9).

Barker's reading relies heavily on the terms μισθὸν πλήρη, *misthon plērē*, "full blessing" (GK *655* + GK *4441*; NIV, "rewarded fully"), and προάγων, *proagōn*, "run ahead" (GK *4575*), which he takes to imply varying degrees of apostasy and reward. Such a distinction seems too fine, and Barker's argument entirely overlooks the fact that John's dualistic way of thinking eliminates the possibility of "degrees" of loyalty or reward. Those who do not fully accept John's witness are "liars" (1Jn 2:22; 5:10) who "love darkness" (Jn 3:19). The notion of a partial falling away and partial reward are alien to the main lines of Johannine thought (see Introduction).

REFLECTIONS

John's remarks in vv.10–11 clearly contradict the ecumenical tone of dialogue in the modern church, making it difficult to apply his precedent to contemporary realities. Dodd, 151–52, noting the serious nature of the Antichrist crisis, allows that "if we could imagine ourselves in such a situation, we could better understand [John's] fierce intolerance." Not being in such a situation, however, "we must doubt whether this policy [of segregation] in the end best serves the cause of truth and love," and therefore "we may . . . decline to accept the Presbyter's ruling here as a sufficient guide for Christian conduct." Culpepper, 125, suggests that "emergency regulations make bad laws for less troubled periods," and Brown, 693, warns that "fierce exclusiveness, even in the name of truth, usually backfires on its practitioners."

On the other hand, some commentators applaud John's unwillingness to compromise. Barker, 366, believes that the readers of 2 John were not yet strong enough to defend themselves against the "active and aggressive promotion of perversions of truth and practice" propagated by the Antichrists; modern Christians should realize that "we today are the beneficiaries of the spiritual discernment and moral courage of John and others like him." Similarly, Stott, 216–17, feels that "if John's instruction still seems harsh, it is probably because his concern for the glory of the Son and the good of human souls is greater than ours."

From a purely historical perspective, there is no doubt that Barker and Stott accurately assess John's own feelings. John's dualistic approach to religious truth leaves very little room for "dialogue" in the modern sense of the term. The "truth" of the

orthodox creed is based on his own eyewitness experience of Jesus (see comments at 1Jn 1:1–3), and he thus sets the limits of Christian dialogue at "what you have heard from the beginning." This leaves him unable to tolerate other positions, especially those that depend on subjective or charismatic claims to spiritual insight. Thus, it is difficult to agree with Smalley, 334–35, who states that "the presbyter is pleading simply for a maintenance of the truth, with which tolerance . . . is not incompatible. John's method of maintaining truth by drawing dualistic boundaries is, in fact, radically intolerant.

The real question for the modern church, then, is not John's own meaning but the extent to which his historical precedent can inform theological dialogue in a culture that places a high value on tolerance. Even those who applaud John's response to the Antichrists are cautious in their application of his methods to modern situations. For example, Stott, 216, tempers his general remarks by specifying that "John is referring to teachers of false doctrine about the incarnation, and not to every false teacher," so that 2 John "gives us no warrant to refuse fellowship to those . . . who do not agree with our interpretation . . . in every particular." In this way, scholars attempt to limit John's precedent to modern debates over Christology, thus allowing room for discussion on other theological and ethical issues. But John is notably adept at portraying *all* aspects of Christian faith in terms of the christological conflict and seems unable to conceptualize other doctrinal issues apart from his doctrine of Christ. At 1 John 3:16–20, for example, he connects Christian benevolence with Jesus' self-sacrifice and then makes the

Antichrists' refusal to help his allies evidence of their association with Cain. Similarly, the Spirit's role in the life of the believer is established and authenticated in reference to the confession "Jesus Christ has come in the flesh" (1Jn 4:1–3). John interprets the community's eschatological creeds in terms of the Antichrist conflict (see comments at 1Jn 2:18; 2Jn 7), and the rare direct allusion to Christ's return (1Jn 2:28–3:3) stresses that those who wish to "see him as he is" must "continue in him" and "purify themselves," i.e., must accept John's version of Jesus' nature and ethical teaching. Attempts to limit the implications of 2 John 10–11 to modern christological debates require historical reconstructions of John's situation that seem inconsistent with the broader evidence.

The varying attempts to relate vv.10–11 to modern life betray the different ways of constructing truth claims in ancient and modern churches and between different groups within the modern church. Modern Christian dialogue, both between denominations and between Christians and members of other religions, is informed by a concept of "orthodoxy" much broader than John's. Two reasons (among many) may be noted for this difference. First, John's dualistic worldview has been largely rejected by most mainline Christian groups as archaic and unenlightened. Since John cannot conceptualize a theological "gray area," it is impossible for him to understand the value of entering into dialogue with those who disagree with him (Antichrists) unless the dialogue would result in their complete conversion to his position. In modern ecumenical dialogue, "light and darkness" have been replaced with shades of gray. Second, modern Christians are more open to constructions of truth based on subjective religious experience than John appears to be. Since our experience of Christ is limited to worship, the Holy Spirit, and the traditions of the church and Scriptures, we may be lacking the certainty that comes from the Elder's claim to a firsthand experience of Jesus. It will not do, however, to recognize these differences between John and us and then pretend that John's views are compatible with our own.

Each church and each believer must determine which doctrines and practices are *sine qua non* for those who wish legitimately to call themselves "Christian." The tests of 1 and 2 John are intended to provide a clear limit for this title. In John's view, "Christians" are people who (1) accept John's witness that "Jesus is the Christ who came in the flesh" and (2) accept Jesus' teaching as the foundation of Christian faith and practice. These two beliefs are to be *accepted*, not debated, and the very desire to debate them reveals that one is no longer a true member of the community. Any real application of 2 John to the situation of the modern church must recognize that John would consider dialogue on these two issues to be dangerously illegitimate. A strict application would place grave limitations on dialogue between Christians and members of other religions, and it is doubtful that John would see such restrictions as anything but positive.

III. FAREWELL (12–13)

12I have much to write to you, but I do not want to use paper and ink. Instead, I hope to visit you and talk with you face to face, so that our joy may be complete. 13The children of your chosen sister send their greetings.

COMMENTARY

12 The closing section of 2 John follows common conventions for ancient Christian letters. Verse 12 is a notable example of the "apostolic *parousia*" ("presence"), a rhetorical technique typical of Paul's epistles. At the surface level, the author appears to express a warm desire to visit the readers and enjoy their fellowship, but these anticipated visits interact with the complex social dynamics of physical presence in the Greco-Roman world. In a culture where personal status was based on relationships with one's superiors, public shame or blame from a patron could have significant social implications. The possibility that an angry patron might suddenly appear and catch one doing something wrong was a powerful motivation for good behavior.

Within the early church, the apostles and their associates were seen as spiritual patrons of local congregations and the church at large. In light of this fact, direct public censure from an apostle could bring great disgrace to members of local churches and severely reduce their status in the congregation. Paul often capitalizes on this fact to offer subtle warnings against disobedience, appearing on the surface to express a genuine desire for the fellowship of the readers, but at a deeper level warning that he expects to find that they have followed his instructions (cf. 1Co 16:5–7; 2Co 13:10). Perhaps Paul's most skillful use of the "apostolic *parousia*" appears at Philemon 22, where he instructs a church leader, Philemon, to release a slave, Onesimus, who

had robbed him and fled to Rome. After assuring Philemon that he is confident of his obedience and knows that he will do even more than Paul asks (v.21), Paul goes on to tell him to prepare for an upcoming visit from Paul (v.22). While the news of this pending visit would surely bring joy to Philemon, he could not fail to see this announcement as a veiled threat that Paul intends to determine exactly how "obedient" his friend has been.

Similar to the Pauline usage, at one level the Elder's desire "to visit you and talk with you face to face, so that our joy may be complete" (2Jn 12) "suggests an intimacy which requires personal presence" (Barker, 366). But it is also plain that this "joy" will come only to those who have not fraternized with the Antichrists (vv.8–11); those who have will share their condemnation (v.11), suggesting that they will be excommunicated. While John seems hopeful that his readers will remain loyal to him, he subtly warns them of his intention to come and see just how loyal they are.

13 Second John closes with a typical epistolary farewell. Secondary greetings are sent from "the children of your chosen sister," probably the members of John's own congregation (see comment at v.1). Aside from general courtesy, the greeting reinforces the doctrinal solidarity of two churches that are geographically separated. John wants his readers to remember that they are members of a larger faith community, and he hopes they will remain loyal to that community.

NOTES

12 The motif of public shame from a patron forms the basis of several of Jesus' parables: the wicked servant (Mt 24:45–51), the ten virgins (Mt 25:1–13), the talents (Mt 25:14–30), and the watchful servants (Lk 12:35–38). All of these parables assume that the Christian audience would not want to be found slacking if Jesus should suddenly return.

3 JOHN

TOM THATCHER

Introduction

1. **Summary**
2. **Bibliography**
3. **Outline of 3 John**

1. SUMMARY

The background and authorship of 3 John have been discussed in the introduction to 1 John. Third John presents warnings and encouragements, while stressing the Elder's desire to maintain fellowship with the recipients.

Unlike 1 John, both 2 and 3 John follow standard conventions for ancient letters. Their introductions and conclusions use common formulae, and their tone and themes would be widely recognized in the ancient world. These epistolary features will be highlighted in the analysis that follows.

2. BIBLIOGRAPHY

See the bibliography listed in 1 John (p. 424).

3. OUTLINE OF 3 JOHN

Text and Exposition

OVERVIEW

Third John is an excellent example of a Greco-Roman recommendation letter. Itinerant teachers were a common fixture in the life of the early church, and recommendations were frequently used to indicate a person's doctrinal credentials. At Acts 18:27, for example, the church at Ephesus sends a recommendation to Corinth on behalf of Apollos, a recent convert brought to Christ by Priscilla and Aquila. The entire letter of Philemon is a recommendation on behalf of the runaway slave Onesimus, whom Paul hopes will be forgiven of his crimes. In some cases it seems that the brief recommendation letter was intended to introduce its bearer, who would in turn deliver a longer message to the congregation. The letter sent to the Gentile churches by the Jerusalem Council opens with a brief recommendation for Barnabas, Paul, Judas, and Silas, the men who were sent to deliver it, and then briefly summarizes the Council's decisions with the understanding that these men "will confirm by word of mouth what we are writing" (Ac 15:27). Such recommendations would indicate that a newcomer enjoyed the blessing of his previous congregation, implying that he should be allowed full fellowship with the new church.

Recommendation letters were a widely recognized genre in the ancient world, with established guidelines for proper form and content. One of the best-known discussions of the recommendation appears in *Epistolary Types*, a first-century AD work attributed to Demetrius of Phalerum. Demetrius refers to the *systatikos*, or "commendatory" letter, as one written "on behalf of one person to another, mixing in praise." Demetrius gives the following hypothetical example of a letter of recommendation (cited in Abraham Malherbe, "Ancient Epistolary Theorists," *OJRS* 5 [1977]: 31]:

> So-and-so, who is conveying this letter to you, has been tested by us [the author] and is loved on account of his trustworthiness [*pistis*]. You will do well to deem him worthy of hospitality, both for my sake and his, and indeed for your own. For you will not be sorry if you entrust to him, in any matter you wish, either words or deeds of a confidential nature. Indeed, you, too, will praise him to others when you see how useful he can be in everything.

Several themes from Demetrius's typical recommendation letter appear prominently in 3 John. Like Demetrius's example, 3 John is a private letter written to an individual named Gaius rather than to an entire church (cf. 1 and 2 John). Its purpose is to recommend to Gaius a certain Demetrius (v.12), who appears to be one of John's envoys, in hopes that Gaius will extend hospitality to him. Demetrius is praised as a person of high reputation, and John clearly intimates that Gaius will benefit from the relationship, at least inasmuch as it will keep him on good terms with John (v.11). The need for such a recommendation is apparent when one considers the background of 1–2–3 John (see Introduction). Although Gaius does not seem to know Demetrius, John's primary goal is to establish Demetrius's credentials so that Gaius will allow him to speak to the church. It is possible that John had sent Demetrius to deliver 1 John to the congregation.

The fact that 3 John is written in the form of a recommendation has led many scholars to conclude that it is a purely personal letter with little theological concern (so Rensberger, 161, who notes the preponderance of "non-Johannine and even non-Christian language" in the document. Indeed, 3 John never mentions Jesus or Christ, and it is concerned primarily with praising Gaius, discrediting Diotrephes, and commending "the brothers" and Demetrius. While this may be case from a purely formal perspective, it is doubtful that the Elder would think of the letter and its underlying controversies in these terms. John sees benevolence and hospitality toward his allies as touchstones for loyalty in the Antichrist conflict (see comments at 1Jn 3:11–20). The reasons why Gaius accepted John's envoys and Diotrephes did not were presumably related to doctrine, and John praises Gaius solely on the basis of the fact that he supports orthodox missionaries. While the doctrinal concern is less explicit, 3 John highlights the social implication of the christological debates that were rending the Johannine churches.

I. GREETING (1–4)

¹The elder,

To my dear friend Gaius, whom I love in the truth.

²Dear friend, I pray that you may enjoy good health and that all may go well with you, even as your soul is getting along well. ³It gave me great joy to have some brothers come and tell about your faithfulness to the truth and how you continue to walk in the truth. ⁴I have no greater joy than to hear that my children are walking in the truth.

COMMENTARY

1 Like 2 John, the opening of 3 John follows typical Greco-Roman epistolary conventions (see Overview at 2Jn 1–3). The author first identifies himself as "the Elder" (see comment at 2Jn 1) and addresses the recipient of the letter in the dative case. Demetrius and the brothers (vv.5–8, 12) are recommended to Gaius, probably the leader of a house church or a group of small congregations. Gaius is referred to as *agapētos*, "the beloved" (NIV, "dear friend," GK *28*). This might mean "beloved of God," but the NIV is probably correct to see the term as an expression of John's feelings. The NIV also correctly maintains the Greek dative of the phrase "in the truth," which does not mean that John "truly" loves Gaius (so Bultmann, 96) but rather that the basis of their relationship is a commitment to common beliefs (so Marshall, 82; Brown, 703; see comment at 2Jn 1).

2 Verse 2 is a classic example of the epistolary "health wish." Although John literally refers to "your *psychē* getting along well," the NIV correctly leaves *psychē* (GK *6034*) neutral (cf. Dodd, 157–58; Brown, 704; Grayston, 159). The English "soul" evokes spiritual connotations, but the Greek word refers more generally to the biological force in living things, especially in the Johannine literature where it is the physical counterpart to *zōē* (GK *2437*), spiritual or eternal life (see comment at 1Jn 1:2). Marshall, 82–83, suggests that Gaius had been ill and that John is hoping for a change in his circumstances. There is little evidence for this conclusion, though, and the Greek text actually implies that Gaius has been doing well and that John simply wants his health to continue. John's wish for Gaius's well-being continues the tone of love and concern suggested in the affectionate moniker *agapētos* ("beloved").

3 John quickly reveals the basis of his love for Gaius and the reason he feels confident in writing to him. It appears that a group of believers returned from Gaius's church and reported that they had received a favorable reception. The precise identity of these "brothers" is uncertain. Marshall, 83–84, notes that *adelphoi* (GK *81*) normally refers to "ordinary Christians" in the NT and understands the present tense participle *erchomenōn* (NIV, "*to have some brothers come*") to mean that several different groups of Christians had commended Gaius's

hospitality (cf. Barker, 371–72; Smalley, 346–47). Most scholars, however, accept the conclusion of E. Earle Ellis ("Paul and His Co-Workers," *NTS* 17 [1970/71]: 448) that, by analogy with the Pauline usage, "III John presents the brothers as a circle of traveling workers, probably preachers or teachers associated with or led by the Elder" (cf. Dodd, 159–60; Brown, 704–5). The fact that John refers to these emissaries as "brothers" may suggest that the Johannine congregations used familial titles for their officers or perhaps were not as tightly organized as the Pauline churches. The brothers "testified" (*martyreō*, GK *3455*; NIV, "tell about") that Gaius is "walking in the truth," a phrase that elsewhere in the NT is used to describe an ethical lifestyle but here probably means that Gaius has remained faithful to John's true teaching (see comment at 2Jn 6).

4 Verse 4 closely parallels the thought of 1 John 1:4. In the difficult situation created by the Antichrists, John's primary source of joy and comfort came from the knowledge that some people had remained loyal to him.

II. COMMENDATION OF GAIUS (5–8)

OVERVIEW

In this section, John thanks Gaius for entertaining his envoys ("the brothers") in the past and encourages him to do so again. On the basis of this precedent, and in contrast with the bad example of Diotrephes, John will request that Gaius accept Demetrius into his home.

> [5]Dear friend, you are faithful in what you are doing for the brothers, even though they are strangers to you. [6]They have told the church about your love. You will do well to send them on their way in a manner worthy of God. [7]It was for the sake of the Name that they went out, receiving no help from the pagans. [8]We ought therefore to show hospitality to such men so that we may work together for the truth.

COMMENTARY

5–6 These verses offer a clue to John's strategy in assessing and addressing the Antichrist conflict. The "brothers" seem to have been sent out on a preaching tour to ascertain which churches had fallen into heresy. When they returned, they made a public report of their findings. The NIV's "they have told the church" is somewhat weak here, as John literally says, "they testified . . . before the congregation" (*emartyrēsan enōpion ekklēsias*), implying a more formal meeting to review their findings (cf. Stott, 225).

John summarizes the brothers' report on Gaius by saying that he "sent them on their way in a manner worthy of God." In conjunction with *axiōs* ("worthy," GK *547*), *propempō* ("send on their way," GK *4636*) probably implies both proper respect and financial support (Dodd, 159–61; Rensberger, 161). The principle that Christian teachers should be supported by those to whom they minister was established by Jesus (cf. Mk 6:8–11, where Jesus sends the Twelve on a preaching tour and instructs them to take nothing along; Lk 10:1–16, where Jesus tells the Seventy not to take money or extra clothing but to depend on the hospitality of those to whom they preach). In both cases it is clearly implied that failure to support the missionaries represents a rejection of the message and, in fact, a rejection of Jesus himself ("he who rejects you rejects me," Lk 10:16).

Shortly after the time of 3 John, an early Christian manual known as the *Didache* (lit., "teaching") offers similar instructions. The author of this document urges that "every true prophet who wishes to stay with you is worthy of his food" (13:1), but at the same time he gives careful instructions on how to determine which prophets come from the Lord and which are simply seeking free lodging (11–14).

Third John extends this principle to the conclusion that supporting an orthodox teacher is an indication of godliness, while harboring a heretic reveals that one is of the world.

John is especially pleased with Gaius because the brothers were "strangers" to him. Although hospitality is touted as a key Christian virtue throughout the NT, Gaius's support for the brothers is especially significant because it must have been based solely on their association with John and/or their faithfulness to John's teaching. By receiving and supporting them, Gaius has shown himself to be John's ally.

7–8 These verses paint the backdrop against which Gaius's hospitality becomes significant. "For the sake of the Name" refers to the name of Jesus and, by extension, to John's teaching about Jesus. The brothers, John's envoys, set out on a tour to proclaim the truth, depending solely on the support of people such as Gaius because they received "nothing from the Gentiles" (*apo tōn ethnikōn*; NIV, "no help from the pagans"). The wording of this condemnation is somewhat unusual, for John very rarely refers to anyone as a "Gentile." The only other usages of *ethn–* cognates in the Johannine literature appear at John 11:48–50 and 18:35, and in both cases *ethnos* (GK *1620*) refers to the Jewish people collectively as a "nation."

Further, if the Johannine churches were indeed located in the vicinity of Ephesus, it must be assumed that many of their members would be of non-Jewish heritage, making them "Gentiles" by race. This would certainly include Gaius, Demetrius, and Diotrephes, all of whom have Greek names. It seems most likely, then, that "Gentile" is used here in a nonracial sense as a label for those who are opposed to God, making the word synonymous with "the world" in John's vocabulary (cf. Brown, 713; Culpepper, 131–32). Paul uses *ethnos* in a similar sense to characterize people by their godless lifestyle rather than their race (Eph 4:17 [NIV, "Gentiles"]; 1Th 4:5 ["heathen"]). The NIV is therefore correct to translate *ethnikōn* as "pagans" here at v.7, implying opposition to the "true God" (1Jn 5:20) and true believers.

Who, then, are the "Gentiles" John has in mind? If the term refers to the nonbelieving people of the world, it would seem superfluous for John to note that his evangelists do not receive support from such people. Further, the brothers in question seem to have been sent on a pastoral visit to Christian congregations rather than on an evangelistic mission. The "Gentiles" are therefore probably Christian leaders such as Diotrephes who refuse to support John's envoys. The logic here would be similar to that underlying 1 John 4:5–6. There John argues that those who listen to the Antichrists show themselves to be members of the world by the very fact that they listen to the Antichrists. Similarly, those who reject John's envoys and their teachings thereby demonstrate that they are "pagans," people opposed to the true God and his work.

8 This principle of "identity by association" becomes explicit at v.8. Gaius should continue to support the brothers because in so doing he demonstrates that he is their "fellow worker in truth" (NIV, "work together for the truth"). Since the brothers promote God's truth, anyone who supports them must be on God's side as well. Financial support is a real and legitimate form of participation in Christian missionary activity, making it important for believers to reflect carefully on the missions they support. Those ministries that glorify God and are doctrinally sound will bring a reward to those who support them, while those that promote falsehood will bring judgment on everyone involved with them.

III. A BAD EXAMPLE: DIOTREPHES (9–10)

OVERVIEW

It is doubtful that John hopes to bring Diotrephes to repentance with this brief condemnation. Since 3 John is a personal letter to Gaius, Diotrephes is mentioned only as an example of the bad behavior the Elder wants Gaius to avoid. John does not want Gaius to reject the brothers and probably means to imply that, should he do so, he will get the same treatment Diotrephes is going to receive when John comes to visit.

⁹I wrote to the church, but Diotrephes, who loves to be first, will have nothing to do with us. ¹⁰So if I come, I will call attention to what he is doing, gossiping maliciously about us. Not satisfied with that, he refuses to welcome the brothers. He also stops those who want to do so and puts them out of the church.

COMMENTARY

9-10 These verses are clearly significant to the historical setting of 1–2–3 John, but it is difficult to reconstruct the situation they envision. In contrast to his praise for Gaius, John wishes to condemn a certain Diotrephes for disloyalty, but Diotrephes's identity and specific crimes are unclear. If *ti* in the opening phrase (*egrapsa ti*) is taken to mean "something," v.9 indicates that John "has written something to the church" which Diotrephes has not accepted. But to which church and when? And how are Gaius and Diotrephes related?

A key term here is *egrapsa*, the aorist form of *graphō* ("I write," GK *1211*). It is possible that *egrapsa* ("I wrote") is an epistolary aorist. In this usage, an author refers to the writing of a document from the reader's perspective, making the act of writing a past time event. When *egrapsa* is used as an epistolary aorist, it refers to remarks the author has already made in the same letter and is best translated with the English perfect tense, "I have written" (cf. 1Co 5:9). If this is the case at 3 John 9, "I wrote" refers to the exhortation to support the brothers in vv.7–8. The *alla* ("but") that opens the second phrase in v.9 would then contrast Diotrephes with Gaius, indicating that John does not expect Diotrephes to honor the brothers, because he "loves to be first." Most scholars, however, believe that *egrapsa* refers to a different letter, one that John had previously written to the congregation and that Diotrephes had disregarded (so Culpepper, 133–34; Stott, 228; Rensberger, 161–62). John seems to have sent a previous recommendation on behalf of the brothers, a letter that Diotrephes had ignored, refusing to allow John's envoys to speak to his congregation (cf. Dodd, 161; Marshall, 88).

But by what authority could Diotrephes prevent John's associates from speaking to the church? Considerable debate has been waged on the precise role Diotrephes played in his congregation, particularly whether he functioned as a ruling bishop in a primitive monarchical episcopacy. Countering this reading, some commentators insist that Diotrephes did not hold an appointed office but simply assumed authority within one of the Johannine churches (so Smalley, 356; Culpepper, 133). It seems unlikely, however, that Diotrephes could successfully challenge John's authority solely on the basis of a dominant personality. Further, Diotrephes has clearly taken steps to establish martial law in his congregation, excommunicating those who support John's allies (v.10). His leadership therefore seems to have been more formal, whether or not he is a true example of the emerging bishopric described by Ignatius (cf. Dodd, 162–64; Houlden, 153–54; Marshall, 89–90; Brown, 737–38). The pattern of evolving church polity throughout the second century is consistent with 3 John's presentation, for it appears that monarchical bishops arose in response to the same type of external political pressures and internal doctrinal conflicts that threatened the Johannine community. Diotrephes is therefore probably the official leader of a house church under John's jurisdiction, whether or not a true Pauline "elder" or a "bishop" in the sense described by Ignatius.

This conclusion in turn raises several possibilities about the relationship between Gaius and Diotrephes. Gaius may have been a member of the congregation over which Diotrephes had assumed authority. If this is the case, Gaius perhaps went against Diotrephes's orders and supported John's envoys. Marshall, 88–89, who takes this view, suggests that Gaius lived at some distance from the main meeting place of the congregation and was in poor health, making him unaware of what Diotrephes had done. Perhaps Diotrephes had withheld John's earlier letter from the congregation, and John is now attempting to communicate to the church indirectly via Gaius. In support of this view, it is notable that John refers to "*the* church" in the singular (v.10), suggesting that only one congregation is under consideration.

Other scholars believe that Gaius was not directly involved with Diotrephes's group. Brown, 731–32, suggests that Gaius was a wealthy Christian who was not a member of Diotrephes's house church, but neither was he the head of another house church. As a member of a pro-Johannine congregation, Gaius was using his resources to support John's envoys financially on an informal basis. Brown's reading is supported both by the fact that John deems it necessary to inform Gaius of what Diotrephes has done, as though Gaius is unaware of these developments, and also by the fact that John

literally says Diotrephes "loves to be first *among them*" (*autōn*; see NASB), implying that Gaius is not a member of the same group. Another major view has been promoted by Abraham Malherbe ("The Inhospitability of Diotrephes," in *God's Christ and His People*, ed. Jacob Jervell and Wayne Meeks [Oslo: Universitetsforlaget, 1977], 226–29), who suggests that Gaius, like Diotrephes, was the leader of another house church in the same general area. The letter mentioned in v.9 had been sent to both Gaius and Diotrephes, probably being delivered by the brothers whom Gaius received and Diotrephes rejected. John is now recommending Demetrius to Gaius and informing his friend of the cold reception his people had received from Diotrephes. To allay Gaius's concerns, John promises in v.10 that he will soon come to resolve the situation among the churches in that area. While certainty is impossible, some version of Malherbe's theory seems most likely.

NOTES

9 It is possible that "Diotrephes" is a sarcastic moniker rather than the person's actual name. Brown, 716, notes that the name appears in a few Greek literary works and inscriptions but is somewhat rare. Since it literally means "nurtured by Zeus" (Zeus being the head of the Greco-Roman pantheon of gods), John may have labeled this person "Diotrephes" to portray him as the leader of the ἐθνικῶν, *ethnikōn*, "Gentiles" (NIV, "pagans"), in v.7.

REFLECTIONS

The most difficult puzzle presented by 3 John 9–10 is the nature of the relationship between John and Diotrephes and the Antichrists. Most scholars today conclude that Diotrephes was not directly involved with the Antichrists and that his rejection of John's envoys resulted from political rather than doctrinal concerns. In support of this position is the fact that the christological concerns of 1 and 2 John are

notably absent from 3 John, even to the point that the words "Jesus" and "Christ" never appear in the letter.

Some scholars conclude that Diotrephes's lust for power was the primary cause of the problem. Stott, 229–31, noting John's statement that Diotrephes "loves to be first among them," concludes that "the motives governing the conduct of Diotrephes were neither theological, nor social, nor ecclesiastical, but moral." Marshall, 90, sees in Diotrephes a lesson for Christian leaders, a "standing warning against the danger of confusing personal ambition with zeal for the cause of the Gospel." On the other hand, Brown, 738, believes that Diotrephes's motives were more admirable: in light of the dangers presented by the Antichrists, Diotrephes concluded that the safest course was to forbid any traveling preacher—even those sent by John—from speaking to his congregation. From this perspective, Diotrephes may not have harbored any hostile feelings toward John.

The key to the relationship between John and Diotrephes perhaps lies in the relationship between Diotrephes and the Antichrists. While it is true that John does not explicitly refer to the Antichrists or their doctrines in 3 John, most scholars would agree that the situation described somehow arose from the Antichrist conflict. Within this historical context, and within the context of John's dualistic thinking, one must question the common distinction between "doctrinal" and "ecclesial" disputes. Since John's authority is based on his claim to be a "witness" to key elements of the Johannine tradition (see comments at 1Jn 1:1–4), any challenge to that authority would inherently imply doctrinal deviation. John

tends to portray all social and doctrinal issues in dualistic terms and is inclined to categorize people on the basis of both their beliefs and their actions. Even if Brown is correct that Diotrephes bears no hard feelings toward John, John clearly does not see things that way. In his view, Diotrephes has slandered him with "evil words" (NIV, "gossiping maliciously"). This is not dissimilar to his response to the Antichrists, who may have seen themselves as John's allies (see comment at 1Jn 2:18). Although some modern commentators might want to portray Diotrephes as a person of good intentions but misguided actions, or as a person with sound theology but sinful pride, John's dualistic mind-set offers only two categories in which to place people: dark and light. Since John belongs in the category of light and truth, and since he knows that Diotrephes has made moves to resist complete association with him, he can only conclude that Diotrephes "walks in the darkness." This being the case, it is hard to see that John would see any difference between Diotrephes and the Antichrists, even if they were not formally allied. Indeed, anyone who does not accept the authority of John's witness for any reason is no better than a "pagan" (see comment at vv.7–8).

IV. RECOMMENDATION FOR DEMETRIUS (11–12)

OVERVIEW

John now arrives at the main point of the letter: recommending Demetrius to Gaius's hospitality. Demetrius is a devotee of the Elder who seems to have appeared at Gaius's house bearing 3 John, and perhaps 1 John as well. Later Christian legends associate him with the silversmith named Demetrius (Ac 19:24), and the *Apostolic Constitutions* claim that John later appointed him bishop of

Philadelphia. There is, however, little reason to believe these accounts, and it seems more likely that Demetrius was one of John's otherwise unknown representatives, perhaps functioning in a way parallel to Timothy and Titus in the Pauline circle. John hopes that Gaius will continue to show goodwill by allowing Demetrius to speak before Gaius's congregation.

> [11]Dear friend, do not imitate what is evil but what is good. Anyone who does what is good is from God. Anyone who does what is evil has not seen God. [12]Demetrius is well spoken of by everyone—and even by the truth itself. We also speak well of him, and you know that our testimony is true.

COMMENTARY

11 First John presents a series of tests by which true believers can distinguish themselves from the world and the Antichrists. Following an exhortation to imitate good rather than evil, John now offers a similar test of character: If anyone does good, *then* he is from God. On the other hand, *if* anyone does evil, *then* that person "has not seen God." In this context, "doing evil" clearly means rejecting John's associates, as Diotrephes has done, while "doing good" means to continue supporting orthodox teaching. As in vv.7–8, one's nature is revealed by the people with whom one associates.

12 This verse gives a brief résumé of Demetrius's credentials. He enjoys the recommendation or "witness" (NIV, "is well spoken of") of John and of "everyone," which here must mean everyone allied to John and not people such as Diotrephes. Remarkably, Demetrius even enjoys the recommendation of "the truth itself." Bultmann, 102, suggests that "truth" is used here as a personification for "the divine reality or its revelation," meaning that God and Christ testify for Demetrius. Most scholars, however, accept Brown's suggestion, 723–24, that John is thinking of "the truth that abides in the Christian (2Jn 2) and to which the Christian belongs (1Jn 3:19)"; this would mean that "in Demetrius's case the truth that abides in him finds expression in the holiness of his life and the soundness of his preaching." In other words, Demetrius's doctrine and lifestyle will speak on his behalf (cf. Dodd, 167; Barker, 376; Stott, 233).

V. FAREWELL (13–14)

> [13]I have much to write you, but I do not want to do so with pen and ink. [14]I hope to see you soon, and we will talk face to face.
>
> Peace to you. The friends here send their greetings. Greet the friends there by name.

COMMENTARY

13–14a These verses strongly resemble 2 John 12 in their use of the "apostolic *parousia*" (see comment there). While John's visit would presumably be pleasant to Gaius, his travel plans carry an underlying threat. In v.10 John makes clear that he intends to confront Diotrephes for rejecting his envoys, and Gaius may expect to receive the same treatment if he does not accept Demetrius. The meeting will therefore be joyous only if John discovers that Gaius has followed his instructions.

14b As is typical of Greco-Roman letters, 3 John closes with an *aspazomai* ("greeting") section. Those with John greet Gaius's church, and he asks that Gaius greet the members of his congregation on John's behalf. More distinctive is the brief closing greeting: "Peace to you." The peace wish is a typical feature of Pauline greetings but always appears at the beginning of the letter rather than the end (Ro 1:7; 1Co 1:3; 2Co 1:2; Eph 1:2). Similarly, 2 John opens with an assurance that the reader will receive "grace, mercy and peace" (v.3) but closes only with the general greeting on behalf of other members of the congregation (v.13). As many scholars have noted, *eirēnē* ("peace") is the Greek equivalent of the Hebrew *shalōm* (GK 8934) that was used both as an introductory greeting and a farewell (see 1Pe 5:14). The *shalōm* greeting would have taken on special significance in the Johannine community, for "peace to you" (*eirēnē hymin*, the plural form) is the greeting the resurrected Jesus gives to the disciples when he first appears to them (Jn 20:26). If this is the case, John is reminding Gaius that their fellowship is based on a common belief in Christ.

If, however, "peace to you" was a common Johannine farewell formula, one must ask why the phrase does not appear at the end of 1 and 2 John as well. While it might be argued that 1 John does not include the typical opening and closing conventions of ancient epistles, 2 John clearly betrays a concern with proper style. It is possible that John's inclusion of "peace to you" at the end of 3 John reflects the background of the letter. Since Gaius had apparently never met John or Demetrius, he might be concerned that the recommendation was counterfeit, leading him to unwittingly forbid Demetrius to speak to the church without any hostility toward John. Indeed, some have suggested that Diotrephes had rejected "the brothers" on an earlier occasion for a similar reason (see comment at vv.9–10).

It is possible, then, that "peace to you" is the Elder's autograph. In the ancient world, where no more than 10 percent of the population could read and even fewer could write, most letters were composed orally by dictation. To verify the accuracy of the contents of the document, the author would normally sign the letter at the end, often using a personal moniker. The NT book of Romans, for example, was written down by a scribe named Tertius (Ro 16:22), and Paul closes the epistle to the Galatians with a brief summary in his own large handwriting (Gal 5:11–18). Since 3 John was written in a period of extreme turmoil, it may be that John felt it necessary to sign the letter personally to indicate that its contents were authentic. "Peace to you," the words of the resurrected Lord, would be a fitting signature for John, whose whole purpose was to witness on behalf of Jesus.

JUDE

J. DARYL CHARLES

Introduction

1. **History of Interpretation: Authorship, Dating, and Epistolary Destination**
2. **Canonical Considerations**
3. **Literary Composition**
4. **Literary Relationship of Jude to 2 Peter**
5. **Recent Scholarship on Jude**
6. **Purpose and Prominent Themes**
7. **Structure**
8. **Bibliography**
9. **Outline**

1. HISTORY OF INTERPRETATION: AUTHORSHIP, DATING, AND EPISTOLARY DESTINATION

Scholarship has traditionally considered Jude to be of pseudonymous authorship,[1] a reflection of the sub-apostolic era, and thus assigns a relatively late date to its composition. This dating has ranged from the late first century to mid-second century. Several factors have contributed to this scholarly consensus: Jude's literary relationship to 2 Peter (normally viewed as second century), the lack of historical indicators in the epistle, the strident nature of Jude's warnings against antinomians, and the assumption that Jude exemplifies a second-century response to Gnosticism. The general consensus has been that the adversaries of Jude are Gnostic— and thus are to be located in the second century[2]—or proto-Gnostic in nature, in keeping with the "early Catholic" line of interpretation.[3] The view of Mayor, cxlv (1907), is representative: "The communications of the Apostles had now ceased, either by their death or by their removal from Jerusalem."

In light of the amount of the epistle (vv. 5–19) that focuses on denouncing the unfaithful, some have concluded that Jude reflects a later period, when the church is encountering mature forms of heresy. Plentiful allusions to OT characters and intertestamental Jewish sources, however, such as we find in Jude, would be relatively insignificant in the second century, considering the church's expansion in the Gentile world. In a first-century Palestinian environment, on the other hand, these would be pregnant with meaning.

---

1. The matter of pseudonymity in the NT has been dealt with at length in the commentary on 2 Peter in this volume.
2. Ferdinand Hahn ("Randbemerkungen zum Judasbrief," *TZ* 37 [1981]: 209–10 [my translation]) is convinced of a second-century dating for Jude, since heresy requires a "fixed confession of faith": "Even though the implications might not yet be clearly seen, there is a practical awareness that the apostolic era is surely closed and that the immediate postapostolic period is soon ending. Hence, now the present tradition-material must be preserved in its basic meaning and form."
3. Walter Grundmann (*Der Brief des Judas und der zweite Brief des Petrus* [THKNT 15; Berlin: Evangelische Verlagsanstalt, 1967], 31 [my translation]) is representative: "In the ancient church up through modern exegesis, there have not been enough attempts to correlate the false teachers of the epistle of Jude with a particular Gnostic system. . . . It is with precursors . . . that we have to do in Jude, yet the fundamental nature of this conflict is already apparent."

While an "early Catholic" interpretation of Jude and 2 Peter has been broadly assumed by NT scholars,[4] nothing in Jude requires this sort of reading of the epistle. The character of Jude's dispute with the opponents, thought by many commentators to mirror second-century Gnostic heresy, is more one of *moral obligation* than doctrinal heterodoxy.[5]

For its notable brevity, Jude is theologically rich—particularly due to its lordship Christology (vv.4, 9, 14, 17, 21, 25). The readers are eagerly to await the appearance of Christ's mercy and eternal life (v.21). The hope of the Lord's return (the parousia), as it turns out, is very much alive in Jude, contrary to the supposition of most scholars who read Jude through an "early Catholic" lens. Hence, the language of lordship and the focus on the Lord's return naturally place Jude squarely within a first-century NT environment, alongside writings such as the Corinthian and Thessalonian correspondence.

Correlatively, Kraftchick, 21, correctly notes that the call to "remember what the apostles ... foretold" (v.17) suggests only that Jude's audience was familiar with the early Christian tradition; it does not tell us about when these predictions were made. It neither proves that the apostolic era is past nor that the readers are converts of the apostles.[6] Thus the statement in Jude 17–18 does not provide a basis for a dating, whether early or late.

Finally, all the exhortations in the epistle are addressed to the *hearers*. Not a word is present that indicates the need for ecclesiastical officials to intervene, as one would expect in the second century. It is Jude's readers who are to deal with the problem at hand; *they* are to keep *themselves* in God's love and mercy (v.21). Such stands in notable contrast to the institutionalization of the postapostolic church, which is broadly assumed of 2 Peter and Jude. An "early Catholic" reading of Jude, in the final analysis, has little to commend itself.

At the advent of the Christian era, the name Jude (Gk. *Ioudas*) was commonplace among the Jews. The writer identifies himself as "a brother of James" (v.1). Several Jameses are mentioned in the NT—James son of Zebedee (Mt 10:2); James son of Alphaeus and one of the Twelve (Mt 10:3); James, the brother of Jesus (Mt 13:55); James, the younger and son of Mary (Mk 15:40); James, the father of Judas the apostle (Mt 10:3; Lk 6:16; Ac 1:13); and James, the author of the NT epistle (Jas 1:1). Given the linkage between a James and Jude in Matthew 13:55 ("his brothers James, Joseph, Simon and Judas"), the James of Jude 1 is more than likely the brother of Jesus, who according to tradition (cf. also Ac 12:17; 15:13–21; Gal 2:9; 1Co 15:7) became a leader in the Jerusalem church and was stoned by the Sanhedrin in AD 62 (Josephus, *Ant.* 20.200). If Jude was younger than James, a date of composition falling in the sixties or seventies is not unlikely.

Clement of Alexandria (*Strom.* 3.9) tells us that the author of this epistle is Jude, the brother of James, the Lord's brother. The same claim is made by Origen, Athanasius, Jerome, and Augustine. Given Paul's allusion in Galatians 1:19 to "James, the Lord's brother," it is a reasonable assumption that the Lord's brothers were widely known, particularly in Palestine.

Eusebius relates a story about the grandsons of "Jude the brother of the Lord" who had been accused by the emperor Domitian (AD 81–96) of being revolutionaries (*Hist. eccl.* 3.19–20). The grandsons, according to

---

4. On which, see 2 Peter.
5. The seeds of Gnosticism (which in the second and third centuries developed into sophisticated schools of thought) were already evident by the mid-first century. Ample evidence for this can be found in Paul's first letter to the Corinthians. Furthermore, Jude alludes to what the apostles had *said* (*legō*) and not what they had *written* (*graphō*). Nothing in Jude requires a considerable chronological gap between the apostolic and subapostolic era.
6. Contra Kelly, 281; Krodel, 108; and others.

the narrator Hegesippus, eventually became bishops in the church. Commentators favoring a second-century composition of the letter have used this as evidence to support the claim that Jude, the Lord's brother, would not have lived long enough to be the author. Nevertheless, this tradition related by Eusebius does square with NT chronology. Mayor has showed that Jude could have been in his early seventies at the beginning of Domitian's reign. In the end, the epistle of Jude mirrors no inherent conflict with NT chronology.

The epistle of Jude is an impassioned exhortation to a church that finds itself living in the midst of ethical lapse and doctrinal compromise. The writer's foremost burden, while it has doctrinal implications, is ethical in nature. Posing a threat to the Christian community is a self-indulgent group that spurns spiritual authority, perverts grace into licentiousness, and at the same time arrogantly appropriates its own authority.

The reader finds it impossible to identify with precision who these schismatics might be or who the recipients of the letter were. The markings of the letter, however, indicate that Jude is addressed to a particular situation. Jude grants us some insight into the danger posed by the schismatics. They retain a religious guise while supporting a lifestyle of licentiousness. Jude further assumes among his readers a minimal acquaintance with Jewish apocalyptic tradition that is characteristic of the intertestamental period. For this reason, the fate of the ungodly is spelled out in apocalyptic terms. And to this end the writer employs themes rooted squarely in the OT—election, predestination and divine foreknowledge, apostasy, theophany, judgment by fire, the day of the Lord, and divine kingship. The literary and theological features of the epistle strongly suggest that its readers belong to a Palestinian-Jewish milieu.

2. CANONICAL CONSIDERATIONS

The epistle of Jude is cited by writers as early as Tertullian, Clement of Alexandria, and Origen, with possible traces in Clement of Rome, Polycarp, Barnabas, and the *Didache*. Coupled with its mention in the Muratorian Canon, evidence strongly suggests that Jude was viewed as sacred Scripture in the early church. The fact that Eusebius (*Hist. eccl.* 3.25.3) includes it among the so-called "disputed" books (*antilegomena*) is less an argument against its authenticity than it is a reflection in some parts of the church that apocryphal and pseudepigraphal works were in relatively wide circulation. This of itself would account for the fact that it did not enjoy universal acceptance, especially given the writer's use of apocryphal traditions.[7]

3. LITERARY COMPOSITION

The message and world of Jude are strangely unfamiliar to the modern reader. Whether among laypeople, pastors, teachers, or seminarians, this unfamiliarity is conspicuous. With good reason the letter of Jude has been called "the most neglected book in the NT" (D. J. Rowston, "The Most Neglected Book in the New Testament," *NTS* 21 [1974/75]: 554).[8] Most readers of the Bible, puzzled by cryptic references to Enoch, the archangel Michael, the devil, and a slate of OT characters, are best acquainted with the letter's doxology.

---

7. On patristic witnesses to Jude, see Bigg, 305–8; Mayor, cxv-cxxxiv, cxlvi-clii; Guthrie, 901–2.
8. Whether or not this neglect is "benign," as J. H. Elliott (*I–II Peter/Jude* [ACNT; Minneapolis: Augsburg-Fortress, 1982], 161) suggests, is debatable.

Whereas most of the NT epistles mirror something of the historical situation and pastoral needs lying behind their writing, Jude offers little in the way of clues.

Given these challenges, it is not surprising that the epistle has languished in the backwaters of NT interpretation. Comprehensive neglect extends even to serious students of the NT. In the main, biblical scholarship has bypassed a thorough treatment of the letter. Where it is studied, Jude is usually lumped together with the other "catholic" ("universal") epistles or subsumed under the study of 2 Peter, given the parallel material in the two letters. The assumption typically follows that Jude and 2 Peter reflect nearly identical historical occasions, with the later writing—normally held to be 2 Peter—presumably exhibiting either a considerable lack of literary originality or the need to "smooth out" particular features in Jude.

In its own right, however, Jude is a remarkable piece of literature. Rich and original in style and vocabulary, this short letter, "filled with flowing words of heavenly grace" (Origen, *Comm. Matt.* 17.30), not only displays astounding brevity but a thorough acquaintance with and calculated use of Jewish literary sources. The literary milieu of Jude is very much Palestinian Jewish-Christian. Extracanonical source material— notably, *1 Enoch* (mid-second century BC–AD first century?) and the *Assumption of Moses* (first or second century)—as well as OT figures are marshaled in a concise, well-conceived polemic that simultaneously exhorts the faithful and warns the unfaithful.

Although not a single explicit OT citation is found in Jude, the letter is nonetheless replete with OT prophetic typology. No fewer than nine subjects—unbelieving Israel, the fallen angels, Sodom and Gomorrah, the archangel Michael, Moses, Cain, Balaam, Korah, and Enoch—are employed against ungodly "antitypes" who have "wormed their way in" (Kelly, 248) among the faithful and thus pose a danger to the believing community. It is these unfaithful (vv. 4, 8, 10, 12, 14, 16, 19) who are the focus of Jude's invective.

Not unlike commentary on the OT found in the *pesharim*, or commentaries of the Qumran community (thus Ellis, 226; Bauckham, 4–5, 46–47), the epistle of Jude links types from the past with corollaries in the present in order to confront—prophetically and pastorally—needs within the community. This is achieved logistically by the use of catchwords—e.g., "these," "keep," "godless/ungodly," "judgment," "error," "slander/speak abusively against"—which form the links in Jude's polemical argument.

Equally important as the message of Jude is its literary form. Effective literature embodies meaning in a way that allows the reader to experience it. With passion and great eloquence, Jude engages his audience. He exploits with remarkable effectiveness the imaginative and sensory dimensions of language. His writing style is energetic and vivid, reflecting a high degree of moral tension inherent in the social setting of the recipients. The moral tenor is that of a prophet more than a pastor, though both elements are present. His few words carry intensity and urgency, bearing the inflection of authority. Allusions not only to historical lessons, embodied in the moral typology, but to apostolic, received teaching enforce (and reinforce)— haggadically and authoritatively—moral truth needed in the present situation. Taken together, graphic symbolism, wordplay, frequent alliteration, parallelism, typology, midrash, woe-cry, and the use of triplets all serve to add force to the writer's burden as he seeks to address pastoral needs of the Christian community. The reader, alas, is witness to a literary-rhetorical artist at work[9]—all this within the remarkably brief span

---

9. See D. F. Watson, *Invention, Arrangement, and Style: Rhetorical Criticism of Jude and 2 Peter* (SBLDS 104; Atlanta: Scholars Press, 1988), 29–79; T. Wolthuis, "Jude and the Rhetorician," *CTJ* 24 (1989): 126–34; my "Literary Artifice in the Epistle of Jude," *ZNW* 82/1 (1991): 106–24; my *Literary Strategy in the Epistle of Jude*, 25–48.

of only twenty-five verses—an artist who authoritatively delivers what generically might be classified as a "word of exhortation."[10]

4. LITERARY RELATIONSHIP OF JUDE TO 2 PETER

Commentators have traditionally focused attention on both the notable literary parallels in Jude and 2 Peter and on the order in which these appear, an extensive listing of which appears in the introduction to 2 Peter (p. 372). Since Jude might appear more or less to be an abstract of 2 Peter, most commentators favor the latter's use of the former, rather than vice versa, to explain the parallel material. There are those, however, who hold to third and fourth views, namely, that both epistles employ a common written source and that both stem from one and the same author.[11]

While there is a measure of plausibility to each of these explanations, it is nevertheless important to observe that the tradition-material utilized in Jude functions in a slightly different way from that of 2 Peter. One survey of this literary dependence has shown that, of the total number of words in both epistles, 70 percent of the vocabulary is different (Guthrie, 925). This observation would lend support to the notion that the historical situations behind Jude and 2 Peter and the intent of each writer are unique. Copying a literary source while in the process of editing 70 percent of the material would seem rather unlikely. Furthermore, two different social situations are indicated by the epistles—one Palestinian-Jewish and one pagan Gentile. Evidence of the former includes Jude's reference to "James," his rampant use of the OT and Jewish tradition-material (notably the pseudepigraphal *Assumption of Moses* and *1 Enoch*), his strongly apocalyptic tone, the language of divine foreknowledge and predestination, and his rampant use of triplets. In addition, whereas the message of 2 Peter is both *judgment* and *the assurance of rescue* from amid the cultural furnace, the message of Jude is categorical judgment.[12]

5. RECENT SCHOLARSHIP ON JUDE

Truly it can be said that the last decade of the twentieth century began to rectify the neglect of Jude lamented by Rowston in 1975. Much of the impetus for the beginnings of this reversal can be attributed to an important 1978 essay by E. Earle Ellis, "Prophecy and Hermeneutic in Jude,"[13] and to Richard Bauckham's

---

10. Thus v.3: "I felt I had to write and urge you to contend" (*anankēn eschon grapsai hymin parakalōn epagōnizesthai*). On the word of exhortation (*logos parainētikōs/paraklēseōs*; cf. Ac 13:15), see K. Berger, "Hellenistische Gattungen im Neuen Testament," in *ANRW* II.25.2, ed. H. Temporini and W. Haase (Berlin: W. de Gruyter, 1984), 1049–1148; L. Wills, "The Form of the Sermon in Hellenistic Judaism and Early Christianity," *HTR* 77 (1984): 277–99; C. C. Black, "The Rhetorical Form of the Hellenistic-Jewish and Early Christian Sermon," *HTR* 81 (1988): 155–79.

11. For representatives of the four positions, see the introduction to 2 Peter, p. 371.

12. On which distinction, see my "On Angels and Asses: The Moral Paradigm in 2 Peter 2," *PEGLMBS* 21 (2001): 1–12.

13. Earlier scholarly work that sought to identify the outworking of midrash in the NT serves as something of a precursor to more recent scholarship in the General Epistles, which broadly assumes the presence of *pesher* and midrashic interpretation. See, e.g., W. H. Brownlee, "The Background of Biblical Interpretation at Qumran," in *Qumran: sa piété, sa theologie et son milieu*, ed. M. Delcor (Paris: Duculot, 1978), 183–93; J. Doeve, *Jewish Hermeneutics in the Synoptic Gospels and Acts* (Assen: Van Gorcum, 1954); J. A. Fitzmyer, "The Use of Explicit Old Testament Quotations in Qumran Literature and in the New Testament," *NTS* 7 (1960/61): 297–333; A. G. Wright, "The Literary Genre Midrash," *CBQ* 28 (1966): 105–38, 417–57.

masterful commentary on Jude and 2 Peter, which appeared in 1983.[14] While a significant number of works relating to Jude were published by German NT scholars in the 1970s, virtually all fell into two categories: (1) arguments for pseudepigraphy in the NT and (2) one-volume commentaries that treated all the General Epistles together. Hence the quality of Jude commentary, with some exceptions, was unoriginal, furthering the standard "early Catholic" interpretation of Jude that has reigned for the last century and a half.

Two trends in Jude scholarship spanning the last two decades can be detected. One is the sheer volume of commentaries published since 1990 (see bibliography). Second, a number of monographs on Jude have appeared—a remarkable development in and of itself, since one is hard-pressed to identify a single monograph before 1990 devoted solely to the interpretation of Jude (see the bibliography for works by J. D. Charles, Landon, Reese, and Jones). Significantly, each of these works concerns itself with a particular aspect of the literary-rhetorical character of Jude, which suggests that literature is incarnational in character. A work of literature does not merely impart information to the reader; rather, it embodies meaning, combining precept with paradigm, with the aim of creating in sufficient detail a scenario in such a way that allows the reader to *experience* it. Good writers exploit imagination and the sensory dimensions of discourse. Happily, the much-maligned and "neglected" Jude is beginning to get its due.

6. PURPOSE AND PROMINENT THEMES

The epistle of Jude mirrors a sharp and calculated polemic against certain opponents ("these," *houtoi*; vv. 4, 8, 10, 12, 14, 16, 19) who are posing a threat to the community ("you"; *hymeis*; vv. 3, 5, 12, 17, 18, 20). By means of an unusual verbal economy, apocalyptic force, strategic use of catchwords and wordplay, an ungodly-faithful antithesis, and triadic illustration, the writer associates past paradigms of ungodliness with his opponents of the present. There exists throughout the short epistle a fundamental tension between the ungodly and the faithful. Both poles of this contrast are said to be "kept," or "reserved" for their appointed end—the *houtoi* for divine retribution and the *hymeis* for divine inheritance. Jude's purpose is to underscore the certainty of judgment.

Both triads of moral types in Jude (vv. 5–7, 11) share a common feature. In both there is a movement from privilege to dispossession. As a group, the Israelites of old, the angels who fell, and the cities of the plain were utterly disenfranchised, while the second threesome, united by means of a woe-cry, moves from deception (Cain) to error (Balaam) to destruction (Korah). This is the movement, both past and present, of apostasy. Thus from a reading of Jude we may posit the centrality of "keeping"—or, more precisely, "safekeeping."

This safekeeping, moreover, has multiple sides: it is both past and present, and it applies to both the ungodly and the faithful. The same destiny that applies to ancient paradigms of wickedness, which have been "kept" for judgment on the great day (e.g., the disenfranchised angels), awaits their contemporary counterparts. But more important, the sovereign Lord also "keeps" the faithful. In fact, "safekeeping" forms something of an inclusio in the letter's opening and closing. Those to whom greetings are extended in the introduction are described as "called," "loved," and "kept" (*tēreō*, GK *5498*) by God himself (v. 1). And the writer concludes with doxological praise for the glory and majesty of this God "who is able to keep" (*phylassō*, a strengthened form of

---

14. Also deserving mention are two important 1988 essays by Bauckham: "James, 1 and 2 Peter, and Jude," in *It Is Written: Scripture Citing Scripture*, ed. D. A. Carson and H. G. M. Williamson (Cambridge: Cambridge Univ. Press, 1988), 303–17, which analyzed literary tendencies in these four epistles and built on the interpretive insights of Ellis; and "The Letter of Jude: An Account of Research," in *ANRW* II.25.5, 3791–3826.

keeping, i.e., to safeguard; GK *5875*) the saints (v.24). All told, "keeping" as a verb occurs six times in twenty-five verses of text, confirming the centrality of *preservation* in the writer's theological outlook.

Subordinate themes in Jude that support the writer's argument for "keeping" in addressing the adversaries are all in debt to OT motifs and a Palestinian-Jewish matrix. To be noted in Jude are the conspicuous juxtaposing of the ungodly and the faithful, theophany and the day of the Lord, judgment by fire, divine foreknowledge, and divine glory. The contrast of doom and glory is accentuated in Jude. While the fate of the apostate is clearly and graphically illustrated through types from the past, Jude's readers, in remaining established in the faith, can be assured of future glorious presentation before the Lord.

7. STRUCTURE

In considering the structure of Jude, one is struck by the writer's repeated use of particular catchwords. These terms are not arbitrary; rather, they are rhetorically significant (so Bauckham, 3–6; cf. my *Literary Strategy in the Epistle of Jude*, 30–32). In a mere twenty-five verses, nine terms occur five times or more, with five of these appearing seven or more times. Consider the following survey of vocabulary (based on occurrences in Greek):

godless/ungodly:	vv.4, 15 [3x], 18
you:	vv.3 [3x], 5 [2x], 12, 17, 18, 20 [2x], 24
keep/reserve:	vv.1, 6 [2x], 13, 21, 24
these:	vv.4, 8, 10, 11, 12, 14, 16, 19
Lord:	vv.4, 5, 9, 14, 17, 21, 25
holy/without fault:	vv.3, 14, 20 [2x], 24
love/dear friends:	vv.1, 2, 3, 12, 17, 20, 21
mercy/show mercy:	vv.2, 21, 22, 23
judgment/condemnation:	vv.4, 6, 9, 15

A conspicuous use not only of catchwords but also conjunctions reflects conscious deliberation on the writer's part in the structuring of his material. Consider the logical progression of Jude's argumentation within sections of material as well as between them:

vv.1–2, greeting	
vv.3–4, occasion/purpose	[For] certain men have slipped in
vv.5–19, illustrative paradigms, reminder	[Now] I want to remind you
	[for] the Lord destroyed
	[and] the angels who did not keep
	[but] abandoned
	[just as] Sodom and Gomorrah gave themselves up
	[Yet] in the very same way these dreamers pollute
	[But] Michael did not dare
	[but] said
	[Yet] these men speak abusively
	[for] they walk

	[Indeed] Enoch . . . prophesied
	[but] you, dear friends, remember
	[for] they said
vv.20–23, exhortation	[But] you, dear friends, build
	[and] be merciful
	[and] snatch
	[and] save

8. BIBLIOGRAPHY

See also the bibliographies listed in 1 Peter (p. 294–95) and 2 Peter (p. 380).

The following is a selective list of commentaries and monographs on Jude available in English, confined for the most part to those referred to in the commentary (they will be referred to simply by the author's name [and initials only when necessary to distinguish two authors of the same surname]). References to other resources will carry full bibliographic details at the first mention and thereafter a short title.

Bauckham, R. J. *Jude, 2 Peter.* Word Biblical Commentary 50. Waco, Tex.: Word, 1983.

Bigg, C. *A Critical and Exegetical Commentary on the Epistles of St. Peter and St. Jude.* International Critical Commentary. Edinburgh: T&T Clark, 1901.

Bray, G., ed. *James, 1–2 Peter, 1–3 John, Jude.* Ancient Christian Commentary on Scripture 11. Downers Grove, Ill.: InterVarsity, 2000.

Charles, J. D. *Literary Strategy in the Epistle of Jude.* Scranton: University of Scranton Press, 1993.

Charles, R. H. *The Apocrypha and Pseudepigrapha of the Old Testament.* 2 vols. Oxford: Clarendon, 1913.

Craddock, F. B. *First and Second Peter and Jude.* Westminster Bible Companion. Louisville, Ky.: Westminster John Knox, 1995.

Ellis, E. E. "Prophecy and Hermeneutic in Jude." Pages 221–36 in *Prophecy and Hermeneutic in Early Christianity.* Tübingen: Mohr, 1978.

Goppelt, L. T. *Typos. The Typological Interpretation of the Old Testament in the New.* Translated by D. H. Madvig. Grand Rapids: Eerdmans, 1982.

Guthrie, D. *New Testament Introduction.* 4th ed. Downers Grove, Ill.: InterVarsity, 1990.

Jones, P. R. *The Epistle of Jude as Expounded by the Fathers.* Texts and Studies in Religion 89. Lewiston, N.Y.: Mellen, 2001.

Kelly, J. N. D. *A Commentary on the Epistles of Peter and Jude.* Black's New Testament Commentaries. London: Adam and Charles Black, 1969.

Knight, J. *2 Peter and Jude.* New Testament Guides. Sheffield: Sheffield Academic Press, 1995.

Kraftchick, S. J. *Jude, 2 Peter.* Abingdon New Testament Commentaries. Nashville: Abingdon, 2002.

Krodel, G., ed. *The General Letters: Hebrews, James, 1–2 Peter, Jude, 1–2–3 John.* Rev. ed. Minneapolis: Fortress, 1995.

Landon, C. *A Text-Critical Study of the Epistle of Jude.* The Journal for the Study of the New Testament: Supplement Series 135. Sheffield: Sheffield Academic Press, 1996.

Lucas, D., and C. Green. *The Message of 2 Peter & Jude.* The Bible Speaks Today. Downers Grove, Ill.: InterVarsity, 1995.

Marshall, I. H. *Kept by the Power of God.* Minneapolis: Bethany Fellowship, 1969.

Mayor, J. B. *The Epistle of St. Jude and the Second Epistle of St. Peter.* New York: Macmillan, 1907.

Moo, D. J. *2 Peter and Jude.* NIV Application Commentary. Grand Rapids: Zondervan, 1996.

Neyrey, J. H. *2 Peter, Jude.* Anchor Bible 37C. New York: Doubleday, 1993.

Perkins, P. *First and Second Peter, James, and Jude.* Interpretation. Louisville, Ky.: Westminster John Knox, 1995.

Reese, R. A. *Writing Jude: The Reader, the Text, and the Author in Constructs of Power and Desire.* Biblical Illustrator 51. Leiden: Brill, 2000.

Richard, E. J. *Reading 1 Peter, Jude and 2 Peter: A Literary and Theological Commentary.* Macon, Ga.: Smyth & Helwys, 2000.

Turner, J. D. et al. *Jude—A Structural Commentary.* Lewiston, N.Y.: Mellon Biblical Press, 1996.

Waltner, E., and J.D. Charles. *1–2 Peter, Jude.* Believers Church Bible Commentary. Scottdale, Pa.: Herald, 1999.

9. OUTLINE

Text and Exposition

I. THE AUTHOR, HIS AUDIENCE, HIS PURPOSE FOR WRITING (1–4)

¹Jude, a servant of Jesus Christ and a brother of James,

To those who have been called, who are loved by God the Father and kept by Jesus Christ:

²Mercy, peace and love be yours in abundance.

³Dear friends, although I was very eager to write to you about the salvation we share, I felt I had to write and urge you to contend for the faith that was once for all entrusted to the saints. ⁴For certain men whose condemnation was written about long ago have secretly slipped in among you. They are godless men, who change the grace of our God into a license for immorality and deny Jesus Christ our only Sovereign and Lord.

COMMENTARY

1 A curious ingredient in the opening verse is the choice of descriptions the writer uses to identify himself—"a servant of Jesus Christ and a brother of James." If he is in fact the brother of the Lord and Messiah, why not derive authority by writing "brother of the Lord Jesus"? Yet this confession of humility, remarkable for someone who was a skeptic before the resurrection (Jn 7:5), illustrates the nature of paradox inherent to the Christian faith. Servanthood brings freedom, abandonment yields blessing, humble submission grants authority. Out of humility, neither Jude nor James (cf. Jas 1:1) make any reference to their blood kinship with Jesus.

The three designations given to Jude's audience—"called," "loved by God the Father," and "kept by Jesus Christ"—are not chosen at random. Together they strengthen the believers' confidence in God to fulfill his purpose. Bauckham, 25, suggests that these three derive from the Isaianic "Servant songs," and Jude applies them eschatologically to the church. Two

of the three—"loved" and "kept"—are perfect participles, with the implication that divine love and keeping power, having been once and for all bestowed, remain in force for those who are called. This is especially important if Jude is to counter any element of apostasy at work within the community by reminding his readers of their high privilege.

2 The triad of virtues listed in v.2—mercy, peace, and love—is imparted by divine grace alone. Jude's prayer is that his readers abound in these, that they receive them in abundance. Despite the letter's seemingly harsh tone, both mercy and judgment are highlighted in Jude. While those who choose to depart incur certain judgment, those who choose to be "kept" can anticipate mercy. Both elements reflect God's character and are not antithetical. As noted by Michael Green (*2 Peter and Jude* [TNTC; Grand Rapids: Eerdmans, 1989], 170), one could hardly imagine a more comprehensive greeting than the fullest measure of mercy, peace, and love.

3 The statement "I had to write," which follows his original intention to write on a common theme, suggests that Jude is under constraint to write due to an urgent need. His prior intention to enlarge on a theme of salvation more than likely was eclipsed by news of problems in the Christian community. His imperative has a ring of urgency to it: the readers are to "contend [earnestly]" (*epagōnizesthai*, a strengthened form of "agonize"; GK *2043*) for the faith. Here Jude employs an athletic metaphor—specifically, one from the gymnasium. The image calls to mind a wrestling match. For the believers the implication is that they are presently engaged in an intense moral struggle over truth. With "all the energy and watchfulness of an athlete in the arena" (so A. Plummer, *The General Epistles of St. James and St. Jude* [New York: Armstrong & Son, 1893], 387), they should "agonize" over the Christian faith.

The "faith that was once for all entrusted to the saints" is the Christian teaching handed down to the Christian community by way of apostolic tradition, a teaching that is normative. This apostolic deposit establishes what is authoritative Christian truth, not what is currently theologically fashionable. This "once for all" character is eternally bound up with the nonnegotiables of the historic Christian faith— the self-disclosing, transcendent Creator-God; the incarnation, atonement, resurrection, future judgment, absolute lordship of Christ. Because divine revelation has been historically mediated, apostolic witnesses are central to the unique and *once for all* quality of Christian claims. The test, then, of Christian character is faithfulness to the apostolic witness.

4 The reason Jude's audience must wrestle earnestly for the faith lies in the subtle method of the opponents. Certain individuals have utilized stealth in attaching themselves to the community. They have crept in virtually unnoticed; the sense is that a spy or crook is at work by way of infiltrating action (so Bauckham, 35). The identity of these individuals is not known, although commentators normally attribute to them an itinerant ministry (cf. *Did.* 11–12; Ignatius, *Eph.* 9:1; both are early second-century writings). With three examples of prototypical rebellion following in vv.5–7, the implication is that these are apostate believers.

An intriguing depiction of the ungodly is given: those "whose condemnation was written about long ago." Keeping in mind the Palestinian Jewish-Christian milieu represented by Jude, the reader may best interpret this description along the lines of standard apocalyptic genre. A feature not uncommon to the OT and intertestamental apocalyptic literature is the notion of names written in heavenly books (e.g., Ex 32:32–33; Pss 40:4; 56:8; 69:29; 139:16; Isa 4:3; Jer 22:30; Da 7:10; 12:1; Mal 3:16; *1 En.* 81:1–2; 89:62; 90:14, 17, 20, 22; 104:7; 108:3, 7; *T. Ash.* 7:5; *2 Bar.* 24:1; cf. Rev 3:5; 5:1, 7, 8; 10:8–11; 20:12). These heavenly books reflect a religious self-understanding that is basic to Hebrew thought, namely, that the divine purpose, though hidden from human view, is predestined and revealed in history. They point to the divine foreknowledge by which *the chosen* (of Israel and now the church) have been called as God's own possession.

Casting his opponents as ungodly antitypes for which judgment, long since prescribed, has already been appointed "on the great Day" (v.6), Jude views judgment as fulfilled in his adversaries. Their appointed end, just as that of the past unfaithful, is sure.

NOTES

1–2 Most of the NT letters conform to the pattern normative in ancient letter-writing. The typical threefold introductory formula "A to B . . . grace" was in broad use from the third century BC until the third century AD (so F. X. J. Exler, *The Form of the Ancient Greek Letter* [Washington, D.C.: Catholic University of America, 1923], 61–62). We find this pattern in numerous NT epistles, including Jude: "Jude, . . . to those who have been called, . . . loved . . . and kept . . . , mercy, peace and love be yours in abundance."

1–2 One of the primary stylistic features of the epistle is Jude's propensity for using triplets. Not two but three elements combine to define, illustrate, or underscore truth. The writer's self-designation ("Jude, a servant . . . a brother"), the attributes ascribed to his audience ("called . . . loved . . . kept"), and elements in the greeting ("mercy, peace and love") are but several among the extraordinary *twenty* sets of triplets in a mere twenty-five verses (see my "Literary Artifice in the Epistle of Jude," *ZNW* 82/1 [1991]: 107–9). Stylistically, the writer begins in a thoroughly calculating fashion.

1–2 Verses 1–2 and 24–25 (the doxology) form a literary device of inclusion, which effectively reminds the audience of God's ability to preserve. Although divine action in no way negates the element of human responsibility, the faithful can be encouraged. God preserves them for their appointed end; their inheritance is secure. "Keep" is an important catchword throughout the epistle, occurring six times in twenty-five verses—τηρέω, *tēreō* (GK *5498*), in vv.1, 6 (2x), 13, 21, and φυλάσσω, *phylassō* (a strengthened form of "to guard"; GK *5875*), in v.24.

3 Jude's exhortation against antinomianism and moral laxness finds numerous parallels in the Pauline epistles. The antinomian spirit, which leads to ethical compromise, is a perversion of the Christian gospel. Paul's first letter to the church in Corinth primarily addresses ethical lapse within the Christian community. This lapse is scandalous, for it negates the objective reality of Christ's lordship.

4 The essence of the verb προγράφω (*prographō*; NIV, "was written about"; "to mark out in former times," GK *4592*) in Jude is juridical, as in Malachi 3:16 ("A scroll of remembrance was written . . .") and Jeremiah 22:30 ("This is what the LORD says: 'Record this man . . .'"). It carries a specific penal sense—that of a public accusation against criminals. This verb, προγράφω, *prographō*, also corresponds in tone and meaning to the verbs προεφήτευσεν, *proephēteusen* ("prophesied"), in v.14, and προειρημένων, *proeirēmenōn* ("foretold"), in v.17. The past speaks prophetically to the present, and in Jude it finds fulfillment in the ungodly who are presently threatening the community.

II. PROFILE OF THE APOSTATE (5–19)

A. Tales of Woe—Part 1: An Intolerable Triad (5–7)

OVERVIEW

One of two sets of triplets (vv.5–7 and v.11) is employed here as a paradigm or model of ungodliness leading to destruction. In vv.5–7, unbelieving Israel, the rebellious angels, and the cities of the plain serve to illustrate catastrophic loss through divine judgment. Three examples of disenfranchisement in these verses underscore the fact that wickedness has both human and superhuman antecedents. All three are linked by their rejection of the normative and subsequent loss in the present life.

1. Unbelieving Israel (5)

⁵Though you already know all this, I want to remind you that the Lord delivered his people out of Egypt, but later destroyed those who did not believe.

COMMENTARY

5 Jude's interest in the first of three illustrations of ungodly examples is Israel, God's "chosen." Allusion to the OT covenantal community would suggest that the opponents in view are the formerly "orthodox," who had experienced divine redemption. Note the emphatic terminology. The readers already know "all this"; for this reason Jude wishes to call to mind Israel of old. Accounts of Israel's unbelief in the wilderness, after miraculous deliverance from Egypt, are found in Numbers 11; 14; 26; and 32. Throughout the OT there is a constant prophetic reminder of Israel's deliverance—and severance—from Egypt. Yahweh had delivered Israel "once for all" (*hapax*) in the old covenantal scheme; "later" ("on a second occasion," *to deuteron*) he did not deliver—rather he judged.

By implication Jude is saying that the same applies to those who threaten the community. Those having formerly experienced redemption who have denied the Lord (v.4) will be judged at Jesus' second coming. The contrast before the readers concerns two divine acts—one of mercy and one of judgment. The present need calls for a prophetic reminder: "you already know all this."

NOTES

5 This verse contains the first of a triplet of ungodly examples. Such lists belonged to popular Jewish tradition. Similar catalogs are found in writings of both mainstream and sectarian Judaism. All typically occur in a literary context dealing with hard-heartedness, apostasy, or disregard for the Torah. A few examples of apocryphal and pseudepigraphal writings will illustrate these lists. In Sirach 16:5–15, the writer provides a catalog of historical examples that includes Korah, Assyria, giants, Sodomites, Canaanites, and unbelieving Israel. The context of 3 Maccabees 2:3–7 is a prayer for Israel against a Ptolemaic ruler that lists Pharaoh, Sodomites, and giants. In the *Testaments of the Twelve Patriarchs* (*T. Naph.* 2:8–4:3), the writer draws lessons from the flood, "the Watchers," Sodom, and the Gentiles.

On the text of Jude 5 and variant readings, see C. D. Osburn, "The Text of Jude 5," *Bib* 62 (1981): 107–15; C. Landon, *A Textual-Critical Study of the Epistle of Jude* (JSNTSup 135; Sheffield: Sheffield Academic Press, 1996).

2. The Fallen Angels (6)

⁶And the angels who did not keep their positions of authority but abandoned their own home—these he has kept in darkness, bound with everlasting chains for judgment on the great Day.

COMMENTARY

6 The angels are said to have "abandoned" their heavenly home. (Note the prefix *apo-* in the participle *apolipontas*, denoting movement away.) They fell from a domain of divine liberty and light to imprisonment and darkness. Jude's readers are to be mindful of the lesson of the angels: punishment is proportionate to privilege. In heavenly realms the angels were exposed to great light; now they are consigned to the gloom of darkness. Having chosen not to "keep" their unique and exalted status, they are consequently *being* "kept" in chains of darkness awaiting a fate—"the great Day"—which should cause humans to shudder. Like Israel of old, they departed from their "allotted" place. Apostasy in the Christian community has both earthly and heavenly antecedents.

Neither the OT nor the NT makes any explicit statements as to the fall of the rebellious angels. The NT implies at most that Satan, a fallen angel chief among many (cf. Eph 2:2), was hurled down (Lk 10:18; Jn 12:31; Rev 12:4, 7, 9, 10), yet it gives no clear time or explanation for the fall. Some hold Jesus' words in Luke 10:18 to refer to an original fall; others interpret the statement to be a dramatic way of expressing Satan's certain ruin (so G. Aulen, *Christus Victor* [New York: Macmillan, 1956], 111). Still others view the fall as coinciding with Jesus'

earthly ministry (so G. B. Caird, *Principalities and Powers* [Oxford: Clarendon, 1965], 31).

Virtually all commentary—past and present—has related Jude 6 (and 2Pe 2:4) to Genesis 6:1–4 in some way or another. This interpretation of "the sons of God" (Ge 6:2), following the lead of Clement of Alexandria, is largely due to two reasons: (1) a mistaken linking of the angels in Jude 6 with Sodom and Gomorrah in v.7 and (2) the association of demons with Genesis 6:1–4 that began to emerge in second-century BC Jewish interpretation. In *1 Enoch* (second-first century BC?), for example, we find perhaps the most elaborate expansion of this connection between the angels' fall and sexual promiscuity.

The sin of the angels, though veiled to humans, was very real. The point of Jude's witness, however, is not the precise *nature* of their sin. Rather, the angels of v.6, mentioned parenthetically, share something in common with Israel of v.5 and the cities of the plain in v.7, namely, a radical disobedience and total disenfranchisement. The reader must be careful to note what Jude, in his borrowing of apocalyptic motifs, stresses and what he omits. Contrary to the view of numerous commentators, there is nothing concerning angels in Genesis 6 that is mentioned in Jude; rather, the conceptualization of the angelic realm in Jude is simply an extension of that which emerged during the intertestamental era. The Jewish apocalypticist was inclined to assimilate pagan mythology into his conceptualization of the angelic world. Biblical writers, on the other hand, by nature were nonmythological, i.e., they wrote from a divine revelatory and prophetic posture, even when they utilized the apocalyptic literary mode for their own purposes.

Jude employs apocalyptic motifs without necessarily embracing Jewish apocalyptic theology. The central point of his illustration involving the angels is the *fact* that they were dispossessed, not *how* or specifically *why* they were dispossessed. This basic interpretive premise is confirmed by the grammar and syntax of v.6. The issue at hand is *apostasy*, not fornication (see my *Literary Strategy in the Epistle of Jude*, 108–16). All three examples in Jude 5–7 underscore the fact of *enduring loss*. Any speculation as to the particular nature of the sins of the angels, intriguing as it may be, is of secondary importance. The point of Jude's allusion to the angels is that they exercised their free will wrongly—to their own discredit.

NOTES

6 While angels in the OT figure prominently in certain historical narratives, during and following Israel's exile they acquire increasing importance and a more clearly defined function (e.g., Eze 9:2.; 40:3.; 43:6.; Da 3:28; 4:13; 6:22; 7:16; 8:13; 10:5–6.; 12:1; Zec 1:8; 2:1; 3:1 4:1; 5:5; 6:4). In Jewish intertestamental literature, the depiction of angels becomes far more systematic, with a particular number having their names and functions expressly stated, a prime example being *1 Enoch*.

6 Corresponding typology to the fallen angels of Jude might well be drawn from several prophetic oracles in the OT—oracles serving as graphic illustrations of fall or ruin: Isaiah 14:5–23, a taunt against the king of Babylon; Isa 24:21–22, a symbolic representation of Yahweh's judgment; and Ezekiel 28:1–19, a prophetic funeral dirge against the king of Tyre. The oracles in Isaiah 14 and Ezekiel 28 reflect, as in Jude, utter fall from glory. Significantly, several elements are present in all three sources: (1) there is a conspicuously abrupt transition from the earthly plane to the heavenly; (2) a correlation is made between the earthly and heavenly realms; and (3) the objects of condemnation all tumble from the heavens as "stars" (cf. v.13). Falling from glory, whether it is an arrogant king or those to whom truth has been committed, has an extraordinary antecedent in the heavenly realm.

6 The imprisonment of spirits, undefined in the OT, is a prominent theme in Jewish apocalyptic literature (notably in *1 En.*; *2 Bar.*; *Jub.*) and surfaces in the book of Revelation. Within the apocalyptic tradition, a frequent pattern tends to emerge: (1) war erupts in heaven, often depicted in astral terms; followed by (2) a spilling over of this rebellion to earth; culminating in (3) ultimate vindication and punishment by the king of heaven (see P. D. Hanson, "Rebellion in Heaven, Azazel, and Euhemeristic Heroes in 1 Enoch 6–11," *JBL* 96 [1977]: 208).

3. Sodom and Gomorrah (7)

OVERVIEW

According to the rabbis, there were seven groups that had no portion in the coming world: the generation of the flood, the generation of the Diaspora, the spies who brought back evil reports of the land, the generation in the wilderness, the congregation of Korah, the ten tribes, and the men of Sodom (*m. Sanh.* 10:3). For Jude, Sodom and Gomorrah are the type par excellence for the finality of divine judgment. Three times in Genesis 18–19 there occurs the cry of the anguished oppressed, mandating divine visitation. The Abraham narrative takes great pains to show that God is absolutely just. By Jude's

account, the fate of these cities is continually open to exhibit. In the first century, Philo (*Abraham* 140–41; *Moses* 2.56) and Josephus (*J.W.* 4.483) indicates that later generations are to learn from the example of Sodom and Gomorrah. And even though the sin of Sodom is linked in several apocryphal Jewish sources to the fallen angels, Jude's intention is to link Sodom with both the angels and with Israel.

> ⁷In a similar way, Sodom and Gomorrah and the surrounding towns gave themselves up to sexual immorality and perversion. They serve as an example of those who suffer the punishment of eternal fire.

COMMENTARY

7 Whereas the Jewish apocalypticist was inclined to explain the state of the world in unseen, angelic terms, Jude, in line with the OT prophetic tradition, focuses on the *human* face of evil. Moreover, his qualification "In a similar way" speaks not to the nature of sin but to the same *end* met by Israel, the angels, and Sodom and Gomorrah. A suitable translation for v.7 would be as follows: " . . . just as Sodom and Gomorrah and the surrounding cities in the same manner as these—who have given themselves to utter sexual immorality and perversion—are an ongoing example of those undergoing the punishment of eternal fire." This rendering, it should be stressed, does justice to the context of vv.5–7; all three examples display an *unnatural rebellion*. Taken together, they characterize the opponents of Jude who are despising normal life and perverting the good.

NOTES

7 Consistently throughout OT and Jewish literature the example of the cities of the plain (Ge 19) stands out. Sodom's overthrow is reiterated again and again (e.g., Dt 29:23; 32:32; Isa 1:9–10; 3:9; Jer 23:14; 49:18; 50:40; La 4:6; Eze 16:49–59; Am 4:11; Hos 11:8; Zep 2:9; *Jub.* 16:5, 6, 9; 20:5; 22:22; 36:10; Wis 10:6–7; Sir 16:8; *T.Ash.* 7:1; *T. Naph.* 3:4; 3 Macc 2:5; *Gen. Rab.* 27:3; *m. Sanh.* 10:3; *m.* ʾAbot 5:10). What is most striking about the OT's depiction of Sodom is the city's flaunting of sin, as well as the permanent nature of its judgment. The prophet Jeremiah enunciates that no person would henceforth live there (Jer 49:18; 50:40). In intertestamental Judaism, Sodom remains the classic Jewish example of immorality and a model of certain and consuming divine judgment.

7 Several types from the past appear with regularity in Jewish extrabiblical lists—most notably, Sodom and Gomorrah, the fallen angels or "Watchers," giants, the flood, and unbelieving Israel. In similar fashion, vv.5–7 of Jude represent evidence—exhibits A, B, and C—compounded against the guilty.

B. Marks of the Apostate—Part 1 (8–10)

OVERVIEW

The motif of spiritual warfare, vaguely hinted at in similar OT passages and developed broadly by NT writers, is assumed by Jude in his polemic against the apostate. Jewish traditions that grew out of the OT account of Moses' death are employed by Jude to underscore the corrupt and brutish nature of those he is opposing. Their denial of the lordship of Christ is plainly manifest in their insubordination, rebellion, antinomianism, and despising of spiritual authority. They, too, have a heavenly antecedent.

---

[8]In the very same way, these dreamers pollute their own bodies, reject authority and slander celestial beings. [9]But even the archangel Michael, when he was disputing with the devil about the body of Moses, did not dare to bring a slanderous accusation against him, but said, "The Lord rebuke you!" [10]Yet these men speak abusively against whatever they do not understand; and what things they do understand by instinct, like unreasoning animals—these are the very things that destroy them.

COMMENTARY

8 The contextual flow begins in v.8 with a portrait of Jude's opponents—a portrait drawn from the preceding historical antecedents. The opponents carry three identifying marks: moral defilement, rejection of authority, and shocking irreverence. They resemble Sodom and Gomorrah in their sexual practices, and they bear resemblance to the angels who, astonishingly, chose to rebel against heaven's authority and consequently were disenfranchised. Michael (v.9) is meant to stand in stark contrast to these. Although he who *was* in fact superior could have railed at the prince of darkness, he declined. Contrarily, the unfaithful of v.8, though considering themselves superior, are in actuality *inferior*.

9 The contextual link between Jude 8 and 9 is significant. The writer continues, "But even the archangel Michael . . ." Building on the implied notion of demonic conflict, Jude assumes his readers' acquaintance with an apocryphal tradition concerning angelic dispute over Moses' body. We learn first from Origen (*Princ.* 3.2.1) that this tradition was contained in the apocryphal *Assumption of Moses* (for a fuller treatment of the traditions behind the *Assumption of Moses*, see Bauckham, 65–76). Here, as elsewhere, the traditions surrounding the burial of Moses serve Jude's overall polemic.

9 This verse is framed in the language of legal disputation. In light of the accusation raised by the devil, Michael appeals to the Lord's judgment, not his own authority: "The Lord rebuke you!" The implication of Jude 9, which portrays the devil in an accusatory mode, is consistent with both OT and NT portraits of the prince of darkness. His role is foremost that of an accuser or prosecutor (e.g., Job 1–2; 1Ch 21:1; Zec 3:1; Mt 4:1–11; Mk 1:12–13; Lk 4:1–13; 2Co 2:11; Rev 2:9; 12:10).

NOTES

9 The Moses tradition proliferated within mainstream as well as sectarian Judaism. Philo (*Moses* 2.291) and Josephus (*Ant.* 4.326) both allude to the event; Philo writes that Moses was buried by angels. The OT background for the tradition is found in Deuteronomy 34:5–6 and Numbers 27:12–13. Imagery from Daniel 10:4–21; 12:1; and Zechariah 3 is also incorporated; in Zechariah 3, Joshua the high priest is standing before the angel of the Lord, with Satan rising up to accuse him. While a Targum on Deuteronomy 34 and several rabbinic sources bring the reader a bit closer to the background of Jude's illustration, they do not inform us that Satan and Michael fought over Moses' body.

9 What is striking about the few OT allusions to Satan is that he would seem to fall into the same category as the "sons of God" who are part of the heavenly council (the book of Job offering a prime example). Yet, in several other OT passages the reader finds faint traces of hostility orchestrated against God. The serpent in Genesis 3, for example, is endowed with a peculiar cunning, doing more than merely acting as one of Yahweh's "court lawyers." Indeed, he contradicts God's statements and in the end wages war against the woman's seed (cf. Rev 12:13–17). First Chronicles 21, a slight variation on 2 Samuel 24, finds David tempted to number Israel. According to the chronicler, the influence of this "accuser" is not neutral. Before all is said and done, seventy thousand of Israel's men have died.

C. Tales of Woe—Part 2: An Intractable Triad (11)

OVERVIEW

A second triplet of OT paradigms or deserting types appears here. Cain, Balaam, and Korah are the object of a woe-cry, i.e., a prophetic denunciation. Each of the three, notably, is signified by a formula—"the way of Cain," "Balaam's error," and Korah's rebellion"—giving the appearance of a standardization of type having already been formulated in intertestamental and first-century Judaistic and Christian circles. Having blasphemed and rejected authority (v.8), the opponents have brought themselves under divine curse. Together with vv.5–7, this set of triplets serves to underscore the realities of divine fiat—both to the Christian community and those who pose a threat. These paradigms emphasize the progressive nature of apostasy: first one departs, but eventually one perishes.

> [11]Woe to them! They have taken the way of Cain; they have rushed for profit into Balaam's error; they have been destroyed in Korah's rebellion.

COMMENTARY

11 Genesis 4:3–4 tells us that Cain brought as an offering to the Lord the "fruits" (*pĕrî*, GK 7262) of the earth, while his brother Abel brought "firstfruits" (*bĕkōr*, GK 1147; NIV, "firstborn"). The Lord consequently looked with favor on Abel but not Cain. To the Jewish mind, Cain represents the epitome of wickedness, the ungodly man par excellence. He is the first individual in the Hebrew Scriptures to defy God and despise man; hence he is prototypical. Interestingly, the rabbis, taking note of the wording of Genesis 4:10 ("your brother's blood cries out"), charge Cain with destroying a whole world, for the Scriptures specify "both his blood and the blood of his succeeding generations" (*m. Sanh.* 4:5). In the words of Philo (*Posterity* 38), Cain is type and teacher of ungodliness.

11 Numbers 22–24 is the account of Balaam son of Beor (see 2 Peter commentary). These three chapters offer a mixed review of the Midianite prophet. In several OT passages (Nu 31:16; Dt 23:4–5; Jos 13:22; 24:9; Ne 13:2; Mic 6:5), Balaam is portrayed chiefly as a negative memorial for his role in betraying Israel. While being consumed with greed, he more significantly led Israel into idolatry and immorality at Peor (cf. Nu 31:16). To the rabbis, Balaam constituted the antithesis to Abraham (*m. ʾAbot* 5:22). "Balaam's error" is the error of selfish profit (Kelly, 268). Balaam typically loved the wages of wickedness (2Pe 2:15).

11 The third of this prophetic triad, Korah, is perhaps the most arresting illustration of insubordination in all the OT. It is he who challenged the authority of the man of God (Nu 16). Moreover, siding with him were some 250 men (Nu 16:17, 35) among Israel's leaders. Along with the men of Sodom, Korah and his following, according to the rabbis, would find no place in the world to come (*m. Sanh.* 10:3). In effect, Korah's fate is commensurate with his deed.

Cain, Balaam, and Korah are united in Jude by means of a woe-oracle. The woe-cry in the OT is found in several contexts: a call for attention (e.g., Zec 2:6), mourning for the dead (e.g., 1Ki 13:30; Jer 22:18), a cry of excitement (e.g., Isa 55:1; Zec 2:10), a cry of revenge (e.g., Isa 1:24), and the announcement of doom (e.g., Isa 3:9, 11; Jer 13:27; Eze 13:3, 18; Hos 7:13; Am 6:1; Mic 2:1). The vast majority of incidents fall under the latter heading.

NOTES

11 In the minds of the prophets, to whom the primary use of "woe," *hôy* (GK 2098), is restricted, the promise of judgment was synonymous with judgment itself. Initially derived from a funerary setting (so R. J. Clifford, "The Use of *hôy* in the Prophets," *CBQ* 28 [1966]: 458–64; W. Janzen, *Mourning Cry and Woe Oracle* [BZAW 125; Berlin: W. de Gruyter, 1972], 83–87), the woe-cry came to incorporate a vengeance pattern. For Jude's purposes, the trio of v.11 foreshadows the fate of those who rebel and blaspheme (vv.8, 10). With a cry of condemnation and threat of divine vengeance hanging over their heads, Jude's opponents await the execution of irrevocable judgment.

11 On the variations of the Balaam tradition in Jewish and early Christian exegesis, see M. S. Moore, *The Balaam Traditions: Their Character and Development* (SBLDS 113; Atlanta: Scholars Press, 1990); J. T. Greene, *Balaam and His Interpreters: A Hermeneutical History of the Balaam Tradition* (Atlanta: Scholars Press, 1992).

D. Marks of the Apostate—Part 2 (12–13)

OVERVIEW

In these two verses the writer piles metaphor upon metaphor to express his indignation over the apostates: they are dangerous, self-absorbed, deceptive, and doomed.

> [12]These men are blemishes at your love feasts, eating with you without the slightest qualm—shepherds who feed only themselves. They are clouds without rain, blown along by the wind; autumn trees, without fruit and uprooted—twice dead. [13]They are wild waves of the sea, foaming up their shame; wandering stars, for whom blackest darkness has been reserved forever.

COMMENTARY

12 The double meaning of *spilades*—"spots," or "blemishes," and "rocks" (GK *5070*)—may account for the differences in translations of v.12. Both fit the context. On the one hand, Jude is concerned about pollution and defilement of the faithful in the community (vv.8, 23, 24) by the apostate. On the other hand, the metaphor of shipwreck due to hidden rocks is equally fitting, since Jude's opponents pose unseen dangers to the faithful. Inasmuch as it is impossible for the faithful to avoid the faithless, the former stand in peril.

Describing the adversaries as "clouds without rain" reveals their lack of true substance. They disappoint; they promise but do not deliver (cf. Pr 25:14). Describing them as "late autumn trees, without fruit trees and uprooted—twice dead" has elicited a wide range of interpretations. "Late autumn" has commentators divided: some suggest that this is the very end of the harvest, while others argue that in the Mediterranean region harvest comes well before late autumn, preferably in the late summer. At the very minimum, "late autumn" would suggest diminishing expectation of fruit and the approach of winter. While the appellative "twice dead" also finds no unified interpretation, the metaphor would seem to possess eschatological significance, not unlike

Matthew 7:19; 15:13; John 15:5. It too speaks of barrenness, a chief element in Jesus' preaching. If, in fact, the adversaries of Jude are apostate from the faith, then the imagery is pregnant with meaning. Regeneration is offered once; after that, people await the second death (Rev 21:8). Given the "once for all" (*hapax*) and "second time" (*to deuteron*) language associated with Israel in v.5, this interpretation is consistent with Jude's purpose.

13a Mayor, 43, sees the images here as progressive, depicting the specious profession of the faithless, their true condition, their shamelessness, and their eventual fate. Following the Aphrodite tradition, the apostates are waves that bring to the shore the vile state to which they, in fact, have returned. In pagan mythology, Aphrodite is not merely associated with love. There is a dark side to her as well: wantonness and sexual perversion. In Jewish-Christian apocalyptic terms, the opponents of Jude are "wandering stars, for whom the blackest darkness has been reserved forever." Jude's imagery here, while it raises a host of interpretive questions for the modern reader, is suggestive and meant to conjure up an extremely graphic portrait of the opponents. They have an antecedent—in Israel's past but also in pagan mythology. There can be no doubt as to their true nature.

NOTES

12a Mention of the "love feasts" here (cf. 2Pe 2:12–13) has normally led commentators to conclude that Jude reflects a second-century milieu, since the love feast is first mentioned in subapostolic literature. The meal evidently became independent of the Eucharist, perhaps because of its corruption and dilution, as suggested by Clement of Alexandria (*Strom.* 3.2). In the *Didache* (11.9), a subapostolic writing contemporary with the epistles of Ignatius, the character of a "true prophet" is described in relation to the "meal," somewhat reminiscent of Jude and 2 Peter. Nevertheless, defilement of the Lord's Table as reflected in 1 Corinthians 11:17–34 was a mid-first-century problem.

12b Some commentators (e.g., C. D. Osburn, "1 Enoch 80:2–8 [67:5–7] and Jude 12–13," *CBQ* 47 [1985]: 296–303) see traces of the book of Enoch in Jude at this point; in the former both rain (80:2) and fruit (80:3) are linked together. With explicit reference in Jude 14 to *1 Enoch* 1:9, this connection is well possible.

13 These images are reminiscent of those found in Greek mythology. J. P. Oleson ("An Echo of Hesiod's Theogony vv 190–2 in Jude 13," *NTS* 25 (1978/79): 492–503) has suggested that the "wild waves of the sea, foaming up their shame" constitutes a reference to the grotesque account of Aphrodite's birth in *Theogony*, literature dated 730–700 BC. By this ancient account Kronos, a son of Mother Earth, castrates Uranos (the Sky) using a sickle. The severed genitals are then thrown into the sea, where they are covered with foam (ἀφρος, *aphros*, GK *931*). Out of the foam Aphrodite is nurtured, the protectress of sailors at sea. The foam then washes her ashore.

E. Judgment of the Ungodly (14–15)

> ¹⁴Enoch, the seventh from Adam, prophesied about these men: "See, the Lord is coming with thousands upon thousands of his holy ones ¹⁵to judge everyone, and to convict all the ungodly of all the ungodly acts they have done in the ungodly way, and of all the harsh words ungodly sinners have spoken against him."

COMMENTARY

14 The expression "the seventh from Adam" also occurs in *1 Enoch* 60:8; 93:3 and in rabbinic literature (*Lev. Rab.* 29:11); the OT does not call Enoch "the seventh from Adam," although it can be inferred from a reading of Genesis 5. Thus we seem to be dealing with a Jewish literary convention roughly contemporary with the NT writings.

14–15 These verses—a citation of *1 Enoch* 1:9—use the language of theophany and judgment associated with the Day of the Lord. Patterned after numerous similar statements in the OT (e.g., Dt 33:2; Jdg 5:4; Pss 18:9; 46:8–9; 68:17; 76:9; 96:13; Isa 19:1; 31:4; 40:10; 66:15; Jer 25:31; Da 7:10; Am 1:2; Joel 3:2; Mic 1:3; Hab 3:3; Zep 1:7–9,12; Hag 2:22; Zec 3:8; 9:14; Mal 3:3–5), this prophetic denunciation serves as a reminder to Jude's readers that the Lord comes to judge the ungodly. The fate of the faithless is certain. For more on Jude 14–15 and theophany in *1 Enoch*, see my "Jude's Use of Pseudepigraphal Source-Material as Part of a Literary Strategy," *NTS* 37 (1991): 139–44; my *Literary Strategy in the Epistle of Jude*, 153–62.

NOTES

14–15 The Enoch prediction can be understood as "prophecy" in the same way as a Cretan poet is a "prophet" in Titus 1:12 and "some of your own poets" (Ac 17:28) is cited by Paul authoritatively before the Council of the Areopagus. Viewed as such, Jude 14–15 is a citation of *1 Enoch* not so much based on Jude's veneration of the work as on its potential impact on Jude's audience. Given the Jewish-Christian character of the epistle, it is possible—indeed, most likely—that Jude's readers are products of a distinctly Palestinian religious-cultural milieu. Thus allusion to a popular sectarian Jewish work, while not necessarily viewed by Jude as "inspired," nevertheless is cited strategically for "inspired" usage, i.e., to suit Jude's particular theological/pastoral purpose. Similar circumstances may well stand behind the theophanic statement of *1 Enoch* 1:9 and Jude 14–15: "See, the Lord is coming . . . to judge everyone, and to convict all the ungodly of all the ungodly acts they have done in the ungodly way, and of all the harsh words ungodly sinners have spoken against him." For this reason, the literary strategy and the pastoral agenda of Jude call for vigilance and repentance.

REFLECTIONS

The engaged reader discovers numerous points of contact between Jude and Jewish sectarian literature of the late intertestamental period. The letter's apocalyptic mode, its reinterpreting of Israel's past history for the present, and the use of Jewish tradition are several such examples.

The book of *1 Enoch*, parts of which are dated to the second century BC, requires further discussion. *First Enoch* was Palestinian in origin and in use at Qumran roughly concurrent with the emergence of the Christian church. It is quite plausible that the work was well known in the early Christian community, particularly in the region of Judea. While Jude is the sole NT writer to quote directly from *1 Enoch*, its author and the writers of the NT, broadly speaking, share a common world of thought—even when their theological orientation differs drastically.

Jewish literature of the second century BC, especially that which reflected a Palestinian milieu, was fervently anti-Hellenistic in character and frequently took on the literary form of apocalypses or testaments. At the time of the Maccabean revolt (167/166 BC), we find the "assembly of the pious,"

the "Hasidim," as a clearly defined Jewish sect (cf. 1 Macc 7:13; 2 Macc 14:6). The Hasidim are significant for two reasons: (1) they are thought to be the common root of both the Essenes and the Pharisees and (2) their theological agenda is mirrored in the earliest parts of *1 Enoch*, dated roughly to this time. The deep crisis emerging from Hellenistic reform is explained by the conviction of the pious that this was a period of apostasy. Thus Enoch is depicted in this apocalypse as a messenger of repentance and judgment sent to call God's people back to the faith. Numerous statements to this effect are found in the pseudepigraphal *Testaments of the Twelve Patriarchs*, also dated to around the second century BC.

In similar fashion, Jude passionately exhorts his audience to fiercely "contend" against the apostate, who have perverted the faith "once for all entrusted to the saints" (Jude 3). These "godless men" v.4)—*asebeis* (GK *814*) is an important catchword in the epistle—furnish a notable parallel between *1 Enoch* and Jude. Thus a statement found in *1 Enoch* 1:9, shaped by conditions that helped birth a pre-Christian "repentance" movement, rings prophetically true: "Behold, he comes with myriads of his holy ones in order to execute judgment upon all, and he will destroy all the ungodly and will reprove all flesh on account of all their ungodly works which they have done and for the harsh things which ungodly sinners have spoken against him."

F. Marks of the Apostate—Part 3 (16–19)

> [16]These men are grumblers and faultfinders; they follow their own evil desires; they boast about themselves and flatter others for their own advantage.
>
> [17]But, dear friends, remember what the apostles of our Lord Jesus Christ foretold. [18]They said to you, "In the last times there will be scoffers who will follow their own ungodly desires." [19]These are the men who divide you, who follow mere natural instincts and do not have the Spirit.

COMMENTARY

16–19 Consistent with the Israel and Korah typology, the adversaries are "grumblers" and "fault-finders." Jude seeks to underscore the pernicious nature of sowing discord within the community of faith. The fate of Israel in the wilderness was not ambiguous; they perished. That Jude's opponents are "scoffers" (v.18) strengthens my premise that apostasy is the prime issue at hand.

Furthermore, moral law and self-restraint are for Jude's opponents cast aside. As sensual persons, these libertines hold the constraints of moral law in wholesale contempt. And, though claiming to have the Spirit, they are in truth devoid of it, as evidenced by their carnal state (cf. 1Co 2–3).

17 The exhortation to "remember what the apostles ... foretold" is often assumed by commentators to reflect a distance of several generations between Jude and the apostles of the first century (thus, e.g., Kelly, 281). This assumption, however, does not derive from the text. Attention in Jude is given to what the apostles "say," not what they "write." What is significant here is the reality of *authoritative, prophetic speech* and not a chronological distance. Jude himself is not one of the chief apostles, given his

somewhat late conversion (see Jn 7:5). For him, then, the antidote to faithlessness is the sure anchor of apostolic teaching, just as it was for the apostle Paul (e.g., Ro 16:7; 1Co 12:28; 15:9; 2Co 8:23; Gal 1:17, 19; Eph 2:20; 3:5; 4:11). Remembering what the saints first believed and what the apostles have said is the urgent and ongoing need, for discipleship entails pressing on, while reaffirming the all-important foundations. Spiritual foundations, not earlier generations, are that which is to be recalled.

The opponents are guilty in both word and deed. Most likely, the verbal sins that have accrued—being grumblers and malcontents and engaging in bombasting and selfishly flattering others (v.16)—stand in relation to the opponents' rejection of authority and lustful indulgence (vv.16, 18). In bold contrast to this profane speech stands the word of the apostles, through which the believers were grounded in the faith. The faithful are to remember the foundational teaching given to them. Reminder terminology plays an important role in both 2 Peter and Jude. As with Israel of old (v.5), the tendency toward forgetting God's commands, though typically human, is nevertheless inexcusable.

NOTES

16 Allusion in the *Assumption of Moses* (see esp. 7:7, 9) to the malcontent and to "bombastic speech" further suggests Jude's acquaintance with this work and its appropriateness to the occasion.

REFLECTIONS

The effect of moral typology is to comfort, exhort, and warn. The end, though in some respects hidden and unannounced, is certain. Those who pervert and blaspheme the truth go to their appointed end. In Jude, examples from the past are marshaled chiefly to warn against the cancer of apostasy. The past explains the present and thus can serve as a token for the future.

The pattern found in vv.5–19 is type and explanation and constitutes a form of "midrash" or commentary on the fate of the ungodly (so Ellis, 221–36; Bauckham, 4–5). Jude is skillful in reworking OT and Jewish tradition-material, whereby he makes application of those traditions in relevant ways for his readers. Not unlike Jewish apocalyptic writers (and, similarly, the writer of the book of Revelation), Jude alludes to OT characters or events without formal citation. The relating of OT tradition-material prophetically to the situation at hand, (2) the modifying of the text to suit the peculiar needs of the present, and (3) the use of particular catchwords to form rhetorical links in the polemic are all features of a Jewish-Christian "midrashist." His audience clearly belongs to a distinct cultural milieu—that of Palestinian Jewish-Christianity.

Jude 5–19 marshals evidence against those who, according to the writer, have "secretly slipped in" (v.4) and, consequently, have had a corrosive effect on the community. The opponents are condemned in no uncertain terms; theirs is a fate that is sealed—indeed, a fate foretold (vv.4, 17). Very artfully and with almost breathtaking precision, Jude describes this fate.

Typology is integral to the sometimes knotty question of the NT's use of the OT. Apostolic

preaching reflects the underlying premise that the OT points beyond itself, finding completion in the NT. For the first-century Jew, it was entirely natural to view past episodes in Israel's history as a shadow of the future, to view the significance of the present in terms of the past. By means of typology, the NT writers apply a deeper, often christological sense of present truth. A type presupposes a purpose in the linear movement of history; it bears out a spiritual correspondence and historical connection between people, events, or institutions.

Typological interpretation grows out of the conviction that, contained within Israel's history—history that is inscripturated—are all the principal forms of divine activity pointing to God's ultimate purposes. The theological "center" of this is the life, death, and resurrection of Jesus Christ. In Christ much of what constituted OT institutions, events, and offices is fulfilled. Beyond christological typology, however, lies moral typology. OT characters or events project themselves in ways that allow them to serve as paradigms or models in the Christian moral tradition. It is the abundance of the moral type that makes the General Epistles such a rich and distinct contribution to the NT canon.

The best resources on typology in the NT remain G. W. H. Lampe and K. J. Woollcombe, *Essays on Typology* (Naperville, Ill.: Allenson, 1957), and L. Goppelt, *Typos. The Typological Interpretation of the Old Testament in the New* (Grand Rapids: Eerdmans, 1982). On the moral typology that pervades the epistle of Jude, see my essays "'Those' and 'These': The Use of the Old Testament in the Epistle of Jude," *JSNT* 37 (1990): 109–24; "The Angels under Reserve in 2 Peter and Jude," *BBR* 15 (2005): 39–48.

III. PROFILE OF THE FAITHFUL (20–23)

OVERVIEW

Structurally, the epistle of Jude moves back and forth between the present danger posed to the Christian community and past examples of apostasy. This is achieved, as we have noted, by means of typology. The past models of ungodliness speak forcefully in the present.

3–4	I felt I had to write. . . .
	For certain men . . .
5	But I want to remind you . . .
8	In the very same way, these . . .
9–11	But even the archangel
	Michael. . . . Woe to them!
12	These . . .
14	But Enoch . . .
16	These . . .
17	But you . . .
19	These . . .
20	But you . . .

"But you" begins Jude's final rhetorical response to these individuals who threaten the spiritual vitality of the Christian community. The marks of the faithful stand in bold contrast to those of the unfaithful. Whereas the latter are sensual, divisive, and devoid of the Spirit, the truly Christian community builds itself up in its faith, prays in the Spirit, keeps itself in the love of God, and awaits Christ's mercy. It is by these practical steps that the believer can develop the spiritual life and remain "kept" by God. Not only do the faithful guard themselves; they also have the moral obligation to rescue those who have become morally tainted.

The epistle up to this point has utilized rhetorical flare, graphic imagery, and apocalyptic warnings. Now the writer, reflecting genuine pastoral concern, waxes eminently practical by suggesting in concrete terms what believers can do humanly speaking to be "kept" by God's power. The paradox of divine keeping and human responsibility remains intact. On the one hand, God is ultimately responsible for the care of his people; on the other hand, the believers themselves are obliged to remain actively in that place of divine keeping.

A. Personal Obligations (20–21)

OVERVIEW

Bauckham, 111, rightly observes that these verses are no appendix to the letter, rather a climax. They constitute the strategy for "contending for the faith" as originally announced in v.3. Jude's pastoral burden is felt at this point. The Christian community must grasp not only the sobriety of the moment but the reality of God's sure provision.

> ²⁰But you, dear friends, build yourselves up in your most holy faith and pray in the Holy Spirit. ²¹Keep yourselves in God's love as you wait for the mercy of our Lord Jesus Christ to bring you to eternal life.

COMMENTARY

20–21 How is it that Jude's burden is refracted pastorally? Four admonitions are linked together to underscore the believer's responsibility: (1) building yourselves up in your most holy faith, (2) praying in the Holy Spirit, (3) keep yourselves in God's love, and (4) anticipating the mercy of our Lord Jesus Christ.

Several features of this fourfold admonition—edifying, praying, remaining, and awaiting—strike the reader. One is the involvement of the Trinity. Each person of the Godhead is at work; the Spirit aids the prayer life, God the Father bestows love, and Christ the Lord dispenses mercy. Another notable feature is the recurrence in v.21 of the catchword "keep" (*tēreō*, GK *5498*). Of the four verbs in vv.20–21, three are participial—"building," "praying," "awaiting"—and one is imperative—"keep." The believers are to remain rooted in the love of God. While it is God who calls and initiates (v.1) and in the end preserves (v.24), the emphasis here is clearly on human responsibility. Obedience is the fundamental imperative.

Furthermore, the believer anticipates mercy to be revealed in Jesus Christ. Here again we encounter in Jude the link between eschatology and ethics. And it is by Jesus, through whom mercy was originally extended, that final judgment will be meted out. Jesus is no less than the sovereign Lord; mercy and judgment rest in his hand. In addition, the believer demonstrates the genuine presence of the Holy Spirit, in contrast to Jude's opponents (v.19), by cultivating a rich prayer life. Life in the Spirit is carried out not by inflated claims but by dependence on God and corresponding fruit.

The fourth admonition, listed first in most English translations, draws from a metaphor quite common in early Christian tradition (e.g., Mt 16:18; Ac 15:16; 1Co 3:9–15; 2Co 6:16; Gal 2:9; Eph 2:19–22; Col 2:7; 1Pe 2:5; cf. 2Pe 1:5): "building yourselves up in your most holy faith." This foundation of faith, on which the Christian community is built, is "most holy." The contrast between the faithful and the unfaithful, the holy and the defiled, is painted in the strongest terms. The saints have been *morally* transformed; this is the hallmark of the church in a pagan culture.

REFLECTIONS

Taken together, these four admonitions, far from advocating passivity, are meant to incite the Christian community as it deals with the cancer of apostasy. They represent tangible means of reaffirming the foundation of faith imparted to them at the outset of their spiritual pilgrimage. A fresh commitment to the spiritual "first things" will allow them to deal with those individuals who pose a threat to the life of the Christian community.

B. Obligations toward Others (22–23)

²²Be merciful to those who doubt; ²³snatch others from the fire and save them; to others show mercy, mixed with fear—hating even the clothing stained by corrupted flesh.

COMMENTARY

22–23 The text of vv.22–23 is uncertain and has been the object of several studies. A longer and a shorter text have been proposed by text critics. The longer, consistent with Jude's rampant use of triplets, lists three types of response to the apostate.

Adopting a longer reading, as Marshall, 165, has noted, allows us to extrapolate concerning three groups of people. The first group consists of waverers, those trapped in a state of doubt and spiritual confusion. These are to be extended compassion so that they remain steadfast in the truth. The second group is portrayed as those near the point of being touched by the fire. These, one can assume, have succumbed to the influence of the ungodly and require urgent intervention. The third group would appear to have already become tainted by error. Contact with them, as reflected in the "clothing" imagery, would result in becoming defiled, since they are presumed to be defiled themselves.

Our acceptance of the longer, triadic reading of vv.22–23 leaves us with a problem: how to render both usages of the verb *eleaō* (GK *1790*; "be merciful," "show mercy") appropriately. This is not easily done if the first group is to receive pity and is in need of genuine mercy, while the third group is already corrupted. Mayor, cxci, gets around this by translating the second *eleaō* in the sense of rendering "trembling compassion" in light of the modifier "with fear" (*en phobō*).

Some commentators believe that "snatch others from the fire" borrows from the vision of Zechariah 3:1–5, especially given Jude's prior allusion to the *Assumption of Moses*, which would appear to derive from Zechariah (e.g., Kelly, 268; Bauckham, 114–15). Also of note is Amos 4:11, where both "Sodom and Gomorrah" and the phrase "snatched from the fire" appear together. The fire imagery is a reminder to Jude's readers of the relationship between eschatology and ethics; they are to reflect on the fact of future consequences for present moral decisions. Some in the community presently stand at considerable risk.

The defilement imagery associated with the third group connotes the fear of contamination and is also reminiscent of Zechariah 3. Defilement to the Jewish way of thinking is a picture of one who has passed through ceremonial purification but who, pathetically, has again transgressed the Law. Clearly, Jude's opponents have already been corrupted by their lawless spirit. It is these individuals risking contact with the apostate who are to be rescued, and they are to be rescued in the utter "fear" of God. While evil is to be recognized for what it is—and hated—compassion for its victims is to be demonstrated. As construed by Jude, sympathy that is motivated by holy fear will not deteriorate into sympathy for sin.

NOTES

22–23 The primary objection to this longer reading is that it has the same verb—"have mercy" (ἐλεάω, *eleaō*, GK *1790*)—in both the first and third clauses, thus raising questions as to how to translate the whole exhortation. Two factors, however, suggest that the longer reading is to be preferred: (1) it has the greater number of manuscript witnesses, and (2) it conforms to the pattern of triads that Jude so skillfully employs throughout the letter. One commentator extrapolates by suggesting that the threefold reading is meant to coincide with the three-stage process of church discipline found in Matthew 18 (so Bauckham, 111).

A shorter text, having less manuscript evidence, reads, "Snatch some out of the fire, but have mercy on those who are in doubt with fear, hating even the garment spotted by the flesh." The strength of this reading is that it allows an easier explanation of the longer reading rather than vice versa (thus J. N. Birdsall, "The Text of Jude in 𝔓⁷²," *JTS* 14 [1963]: 394–99).

On the longer or shorter reading, see C. D. Osburn, "The Text of Jude 22–23," *ZNW* 63 (1972): 134–44; S. Kubo, "Jude 22–3: Two-division Form or Three?" in *New Testament Textual Criticism*, ed. E. J. Epp and G. D. Fee (Oxford: Clarendon, 1981), 239–53.

IV. TRIBUTE TO THE ONE WHO "KEEPS" (24–25)

OVERVIEW

Having called forth past examples of divine judgment and exhorted the faithful to realize their part in being a disciplined community, Jude concludes by offering an exalted tribute to the One who preserves them. This is done in the form of a doxology, a "proclaiming of glory." Several basic patterns of speech to God tend to emerge from the OT: petition, praise, and thanksgiving. Hymnic material that offers praise and glorification of God can assume the form of any of these. The origin of doxology is owing to a distinctly Jewish matrix. The early Christian doxology, in style and content, resembled that of the Jewish synagogue and was not infrequently accompanied by an eschatological deliverance call. Normally framed in the third person (as in Jude 24—*to de dynamenō phylaxai . . .*), the doxology functioned to proclaim God's praise ("To him who is able . . .") as well as to affirm his eternality ("before all ages, now and forevermore."

²⁴To him who is able to keep you from falling and to present you before his glorious presence without fault and with great joy—²⁵to the only God our Savior be glory, majesty, power and authority, through Jesus Christ our Lord, before all ages, now and forevermore! Amen.

COMMENTARY

24 The epistle concludes with a benediction praising God for his attributes that express themselves in his power to preserve the saints. This doxological benediction reiterates in the active voice what the author stated in his salutation through the passive voice: his readers are called, loved, and kept by God. The introduction and conclusion of the letter thus form a rhetorical inclusio by opening and closing with the same theme: the saints are kept by the power of God. The conclusion follows a series of eight exhortations to the faithful that are to serve as antidotes to apostasy in the light of the previous condemnations (so Marshall, 166). The saints are to remember, build themselves up, pray, keep themselves, anticipate, convince, save, and have mercy (vv.17–23).

The rhetorical effect of the doxology, following the rather brief but rapid-fire hortatory section, is deliberate. After all has been humanly done to safeguard against the cancer of apostasy, it is the power of Almighty God our Savior mediated through Jesus Christ that is "able to keep you from falling." Exploiting a prominent catchword in the epistle, the author uses a strengthened form of "preserve"—*phylassō* (GK *5875*)—to describe divine action: God is able, literally, to "guard [safely] as a prison." More-

over, he is able not only to safeguard the saints against falling but even cause them to stand "before [God's] glorious presence without fault and with great joy." In the end, then, it is not mere persistence or the great investment of human energy that is ultimately responsible for the saints' salvation; rather, it is the saving and keeping power of God.

25 It is to this God our Savior alone that the following attributes are ascribed—glory, majesty, power, and authority. The cumulative force of these resources is the surpassing might of the one who called us (cf. v.1). With precise calculation, Jude employs the language of sovereignty. The saints need not be shaken by the sobering instances of God's judgment in history if, in fact, they have a genuine desire to be established in the faith.

Finally, praise is due this Almighty Savior "before all ages, now and forevermore." Although throughout the epistle Jude draws on the language and imagery of Jewish apocalyptic familiar to intertestamental literature, in his concluding doxology he aligns himself with a decidedly OT prophetic view of history, i.e., the past, the present, and the future are all seen as working toward the consummation of the divine purpose.

NOTES

24–25 Structurally, the doxology is normally positioned at the conclusion of kerygmatic or hymnic material and consists of three parts: the person named; an expression of praise often comprised of two or more elements, including the term δόξα, *doxa* (GK *1518*); and a formula for time. Jude conforms to this standard pattern. The Jewish doxology typically concluded with the affirmation ἀμήν, *amēn* ("indeed, it is so"; "so be it"; GK *297*). Equally common to the OT and rabbinic milieu, ἀμήν, *amēn*, reinforces that declarations, confessions, or oaths are valid. At times ending a prayer (e.g., Ne 8:6; 1Ch 16:36) and frequently a psalm (e.g., Pss 41:14; 72:19; 89:53; 106:48), ἀμήν, *amēn*, can also be doubled in the OT for emphasis (e.g., Nu 5:22; Ne 8:6). In extracanonical apocalyptic literature, ἀμήν, *amēn*, often appears with eschatological statements. In the synagogue it constituted the most common benediction pronounced by the rabbis. It is only natural that the ἀμήν, *amēn*, found its way into the liturgy of the early church.

REVELATION

ALAN F. JOHNSON

Introduction

1. GENERAL NATURE AND HISTORICAL BACKGROUND

The book of Revelation fascinates and also perplexes the modern reader. For the present generation, it is the most obscure and controversial book in the Bible. It has suffered from both neglect and speculative excesses. Yet those who study it with care agree that it is a unique source of Christian teaching and one of timeless relevance. Accordingly, Swete, viii, says, "The Apocalypse offers to the pastors of the church an unrivaled store of materials for Christian teaching, if only the book is approached with an assurance of its prophetic character, chastened by a frank acceptance of the light which the growth of knowledge has cast and will continue to cast upon it." Indeed, it may well be that, with the exception of the Gospels, the Apocalypse is the most profound and moving teaching on Christian doctrine and discipleship found anywhere in Holy Scripture. Neither the fanaticism of some who have fixed their attention on prophecy but not on Christ, nor the diversity of interpretative viewpoints should discourage us from pursuing Christian truth in this marvelous book.

The title of the last book of the NT sheds light on its character. Revelation differs in kind from most other NT writings. The difference is not in doctrine but in literary genre and subject matter. It is a book of prophecy (1:3; 22:7, 18–19) that involves both warning and consolation—announcements of future judgment and blessing. For communicating its message, John uses symbol and vision.

Why did John use a method that seemingly makes his message so obscure? The answer is twofold. First, the language and imagery were not as strange to first-century readers as they are to many today. Faced with the apocalyptic style of the book, the modern reader who knows little about biblical literature and its parallels is like a person who, though unfamiliar with stocks and bonds, tries to understand the Dow-Jones reports. Therefore, familiarity with the prophetic books of the OT (especially Daniel and Ezekiel), apocalyptic literature current during the first century, the Dead Sea Scrolls, and the Targums (paraphrases of the OT into Aramaic and Greek) will help the reader grasp the message of the Apocalypse. (See the commentary for references to these cognate materials.)

Second, the subject matter, with its glimpses into the future and even into heaven itself, required the kind of language John used. Only through symbolism and imagery can we gain some understanding of the things the Lord was unveiling through the writer John. Moreover, while the symbolic and visionary mode of presentation creates ambiguity and frustration for many of us, it actually conduces to evocative description of unseen realities with a poignancy and clarity unattainable by any other method. For example, "evil" is an abstract term, but a prostitute "drunk with the blood of the saints" graphically sets forth the concrete and more terrible aspect of this reality. Such language can trigger all sorts of ideas, associations, existential involvement, and mystical responses that the straight prose found in much of the NT cannot attain.

The letters to the seven churches in the Roman province of Asia (modern Turkey) specifically locate the recipients of the book and give some broad indication of the historical situation. Some of the churches were experiencing a form of persecution (2:10, 13). From this it has been customary since the early part of the twentieth century to assume not only that persecution was quite intense and widespread but that the persecution in particular that the book spoke of was what William Ramsay in 1904 called the "Flavian" persecution, including but not limited to that perpetrated by the emperor Domitian (AD 81–96). Revelation was then viewed as a "tract for the times," a crisis document warning Christians against emperor worship and encouraging them to be faithful to Christ even to death. However, since the mid-twentieth century the trend in historical scholarship has changed. Most scholars today doubt how intense, widespread, or sustained Christian persecution was in the first century, even under Domitian.[1] Thus the primary occasion for the writing of the book must be sought elsewhere than in some widespread real persecution of that later first-century time.

Four strategies have emerged to deal with this doubt about the widespread persecution of Christians. First, John A. T. Robinson (*Redating the New Testament* [Philadelphia: Westminster, 1976]) has argued that the previous dating of the book (in fact of the whole NT) is mistaken. Revelation was written immediately after and as a result of the author's real experience of sufferings not under Domitian but under Nero (late AD 68 or early 70). While Robinson's views have not won wide acceptance, he has raised some valid questions about the late dating of the book.

A second strategy is to keep the Domitian dating of the book (AD 81–96) but to see not a "Flavian persecution" of Christians involving widespread governmental searches and executions but a more limited, albeit real, harassment and occasional death and imprisonment in certain localities (so Elisabeth Schüssler Fiorenza, *The Book of Revelation—Justice and Judgment* [Philadelphia: Fortress, 1985]).

---

1. Cf. F. F. Bruce, *New Testament History* (New York: Doubleday, 1972), 412–13; Barclay Newman, "The Fallacy of the Domitian Hypothesis," *NTS* 10 (1963): 133–39; G. Edmundson, *The Church in Rome in the First Century* (London: Longmans, Green, 1913); Leonard L. Thompson, *The Book of Revelation: Apocalypse and Empire* (New York: Oxford Univ. Press, 1990), 15–17; Paul Duff, *Who Rides the Beast?* (Oxford: Oxford Univ. Press, 2001), 3–16; Jonathan Knight, *Revelation: Readings: A New Biblical Commentary* (Sheffield: Sheffield Academic Press, 1999), 21–24.

A third solution has come from Adela Yarbro Collins (*Crisis and Catharsis: The Power of the Apocalypse* [Philadelphia: Westminster, 1984]). While she dates the book traditionally (mid-90s), she claims there was no actual widespread persecution of Christians, but instead John feels as though such is the case and he vents his emotions in a kind of psychological catharsis that other Christians might also experience.

A fourth strategy is proposed by Leonard L. Thompson (*The Book of Revelation: Apocalypse and Empire* [New York: Oxford Univ. Press, 1990]). He, like Collins, believes there was no real crisis of persecution when John wrote, but in addition he believes there was no *perceived* persecution either. Instead the persecution theme is part of the genre of apocalypse that John chose to use for his book and has no relationship to the actual sociopolitical situation of the Christian churches at the end of the first century. (Thompson, 201–10, has an excellent overview of recent theories about the social setting of Revelation in an appendix at the back of his book.)

The most recent attempt to solve this puzzle disagrees with all four of the above solutions. David E. Aune (*Revelation 1–5*, 98–117) proposes that the entire book was written in the late 60s (except for the passages 1:1–6; 12b–3:22; and 22:6–21, which were added by the author in a second edition around the time of Domitian or even Trajan). Prigent, 20–21, had earlier advocated a similar two-edition hypothesis and now expresses agreement with Aune. The main weakness of this theory is that key elements of chs. 1–3 permeate the rest of the book and seem essential to the meaning of chs. 4–22 (cf. Duff, 11).

Finally, it may be noted that all of these current reconstruction theories of the date and social setting of the book are based on the assumption that the book is explicitly describing throughout the fate of Christians at the hand of Rome (the preterist view). I will raise questions about this scholarly consensus in the following pages.

The letters to the churches imply that five of the seven had serious problems. The major problem seemed to be disloyalty to Christ. Persecution is only mentioned briefly in two of the churches. This may indicate that the major thrust of Revelation is not sociopolitical but *theological*. John is more concerned with countering the heresy that was creeping into the churches toward the close of the first century than in addressing the political situation. Barclay Newman suggests that this heresy could well have been some form of incipient Gnosticism, an idea he derives from a critical study of Irenaeus's statements in the second century about the book of Revelation.[2]

Revelation is also commonly viewed as belonging to the body of nonbiblical Jewish writings known as *apocalyptic* literature. The name for this type of literature (some nineteen books) is derived from the word "revelation" (*apokalypsis*, GK 637) in Revelation 1:1. The extrabiblical apocalyptic books were written in the period from 200 BC to AD 200. Usually scholars stress the similarities of the Apocalypse of John to these noncanonical books—similarities such as the use of symbolism and vision, the mention of angelic mediators of the revelation, the bizarre images, the expectation of divine judgment, the emphasis on the kingdom of God, the new heavens and earth, and the dualism of this age and the age to come. Although

---

2. See Newman, "Fallacy of the Domitian Hypothesis," 133–39; also his "A Consideration of the Apocalypse as an Anti-Gnostic Document" (Th.D. diss., Southern Baptist Theological Seminary, 1959) and *Rediscovering the Book of Revelation* (Valley Forge, Pa.: Judson, 1968); cf. Minear, 250–56. See also the discussion in the Overview, pp. 701–4.

numerous similarities exist, John's writing also has some clear differences from these writings, and these differences must not be overlooked.[3]

Unlike the Jewish and Jewish-Christian apocalyptic books, the Apocalypse of John clearly claims to be a book of prophecy (1:3; 22:7, 10, 18–19), the effect of which is to identify the message, as in the OT prophetic tradition, with the Word of God (1:2; 19:9). The Jewish apocalyptists used the literary form of *ex eventu* prophecy to trace the course of history from ancient times down to their own day but under the guise of an ancient writer prophesying that this would happen in the future. John does not follow this method. He clearly places himself in the contemporary world of the first century and speaks of the future eschatological consummation in much the same way as Ezekiel and Jeremiah did. While extrabiblical apocalypses are clearly pseudonymous (e.g., *Enoch, Abraham, Ezra, Baruch*), the last book of the NT is plainly attributed to John. It does not, however, explicitly identify him as being well known or an apostle. Surely a pseudonymous author would have made it much clearer that the John he ascribes authorship to was in fact the well-known apostle by that name. Further, many of the noncanonical apocalyptic works are ethically passive: they blame the immediate plight of God's people, not on their unfaithfulness, but on the pervasive presence of evil in the world. While Revelation is not lacking in words of encouragement to the faithful, it also strongly urges the churches to repent.

Finally, and importantly, these apocalypses are pessimistic concerning the outcome of God's present activity in the world, and for hope they look wholly to the eschatological end, when God will once again intervene and defeat the evil in the world. Though Revelation is often read in this manner, there are great differences between it and the noncanonical apocalypses. In the latter, the turning point of history is the future event

---

3. The literature on apocalyptic discussion is extensive. See, e.g., D. S. Russell, *The Method and Message of Jewish Apocalyptic* (Philadelphia: Westminster, 1964); Russell, *Apocalyptic Ancient and Modern* (Philadelphia: Fortress, 1978); Paul D. Hanson, *The Dawn of Apocalyptic* (Philadelphia: Fortress, 1975); John J. Collins (who believes that the differences between Revelation and the Jewish apocalyptic writings are superficial, except in the former's reference to the earthly Jesus), "Pseudonymity, Historical Reviews and the Genre of the Revelation of John," *CBQ* 39 (1977): 329–43; J. H. Charlesworth, *The Pseudepigrapha in Modern Research* (Missoula, Mont.: Scholars Press, 1976). For the primary documents, see R. H. Charles, ed., *The Apocrypha and Pseudepigrapha of the Old Testament* (New York: Oxford Univ. Press, 1913; J. H. Charlesworth, ed., *The Pseudepigrapha of the Old Testament* (Garden City, N.Y.: Doubleday, 1980).

Among those who point out the difference between the Apocalypse of John and other apocalyptic literature are G. E. Ladd, "The Revelation and Jewish Apocalyptic," *EvQ* 29 (1957): 95–100; Ladd, "Apocalyptic and NT Theology," in *Reconciliation and Hope*, ed. Robert Banks (Grand Rapids: Eerdmans, 1974), 285–96; James Kallas, "The Apocalypse— An Apocalyptic Book?" *JBL* 86 (1967): 69–80. See esp. Elisabeth Schüssler Fiorenza (*The Apocalypse* [Chicago: Franciscan Herald, 1976], 14–26), who emphasizes that the book is a "Christian prophetic-Apocalyptic Circular letter"; see also Fiorenza, "Composition and Structure of the Book of Revelation," *CBQ* 39 (1977): 344–66. For a survey of Roman Catholic views on Revelation, see John J. Pilch, *What Are They Saying About the Book of Revelation?* (New York: Paulist, 1978). More recently on the ongoing discussion, see Mazzaferri, *The Genre of the Book of Revelation from a Source-Critical Perspective*; Fiorenza, *The Book of Revelation—Justice and Judgment*; Fiorenza, "Reading the Apocalypse Theologically," in *The Old Testament in the Book of Revelation*, ed. Steve Moyise (JSNTSup 115; Sheffield: Sheffield Academic Press, 1995), 1–16; John J. Collins, "From Prophecy to Apocalypticism," in *The Encyclopedia of Apocalypticism*, ed. J. J. Collins (London: Continuum, 2000), 129–61.

of the Messiah's coming as a conquering warrior-king. In Revelation, the climactic event has already occurred in the victory of the slain Lamb (ch. 5). Now, however, the Lamb's victory is being worked out in history in the obedient suffering of his followers (12:11; 15:2). Their deaths are seen in Revelation as a part of the victory over evil that God is already effecting in the world. This partial victory through the suffering of the saints is combined with the hope of the final unambiguous victory of God at the end of history.

By viewing history in this way, the book makes clear that the source of Christian hope is not immanent in history itself but relates to a transcendent future. For John, there is no evolutionary progress of righteousness in history; thus any identification of the Apocalypse with the writings of the extrabiblical apocalyptists must be severely qualified. Indeed, the reader would do well to reexamine every method of interpreting Revelation that rests on this assumed similarity. For example, is it truly a "tract for the times," as other apocalyptic books, or should this supposed connection be questioned and the book freed to speak its own message about realities that are far more determinative of world events than immediate political powers?

John was undoubtedly quite familiar with the Jewish apocalyptists of the intertestamental period, and in some instances there seems to be a direct allusion to them (cf. comments at 2:7). But the relation is, in general, superficial. Only twice is an interpreting angel involved in the explanation of a vision (Rev 7; 17), a feature constantly present in the other kind of apocalyptic writing. In no case can it be demonstrated that John depends on the assumed knowledge among his readers of the Jewish apocalyptists for clarity of meaning.[4] On the other hand, he is everywhere dependent on the OT canonical books, especially those where symbol and vision play a dominant role, such as portions of Isaiah, Ezekiel, Daniel, and Zechariah.[5] Mazzaferri, 258, draws this conclusion:

> The title, apocalyptic, certainly derives from Revelation, but this is irrelevant. *Apokalypsis* is not a technical term in John's day, although he employs it prophetically. In terms of actual generic definition, Revelation cannot be equated with apocalyptic in form. It lacks essential pseudonymity, while its written form is circumstantial. Neither does it qualify in contents. Its eschatology is Christian, with a modified temporal dualism and an optimistic view of the present. Its imminence is explicit and personal, not pseudo-prophetic, and conditional, not deterministic. . . . Despite certain superficial similarities, Revelation completely fails to qualify as a genuine apocalypse.

Ladd's suggestion that we create a new category called "Prophetic-Apocalyptic" to distinguish canonical materials from the late Jewish apocalyptics, if not so much in form, certainly in worldview, has much merit.[6] Thus Ladd, 14, notes that the beast of chs. 13 and 17 is historical Rome, but it is far larger than the ancient city and is also the future Antichrist. The references to the persecution of Christians likewise go far beyond the known historical situation of John's day. Evil at the hands of Rome is realized eschatology. Recently this view has also been held by others (e.g., Morris, 24; Mounce, 30). The commentary

---

4. J. Julius Scott Jr. ("Paul and Late-Jewish Eschatology—A Case Study, 1 Thess 4:13–18 and 2 Thess 2:1–12," *JETS* 15 [1972]: 3:133–43) arrives at the same conclusion with regard to the connection between Paul and the apocalyptists. See also Mounce, 1–7; Prigent, 5–9.

5. Although throughout the following pages I make frequent references to noncanonical apocalyptic literature, they are given as aids in understanding the background of John's writing and should not be taken as sources of his thought or method in the same way that the inspired canonical Scriptures influenced him.

6. See G. E. Ladd, "Apocalyptic," in *Evangelical Dictionary of Theology*, ed. W. Elwell (Grand Rapids: Baker, 1984), 65.

on chs. 13 and 17 will reveal sympathy for Ladd's break with the dominant, purely preterist interpretation while at the same time arguing that the preterist-futurist viewpoint, like that of the preterist, rests on the questionable assumption that John's Apocalypse is basically describing contemporary historical-political entities rather than theological archetypes (see "Interpretative Schemes," pp. 584–87; Overviews at chs. 13 and 17).

In a critique of Gregory Beale's massive commentary (see bibliography), Paul Duff ("Reading the Apocalypse at the Millennium," *RelSRev* 26 [2000], 219) criticizes Beale for not giving greater attention to the debt of John to the "larger Greco-Roman milieu, exhibiting a familiarity with pagan mythology, Roman political gossip, and magic, among other things." This is an overstatement. Better is Prigent's assessment that there are good reasons for believing that John was *not* appealing to these pagan traditions, except rarely (ch. 12), and that instead such parallels are literarily anachronistic and quite unlikely, given John's fanatical aversion to idolatry in any form and the writings of the prophets, which offer very impressive parallels.

Much more important than the late Jewish apocalyptic or magic or mythology sources is the debt John owes to the eschatological teaching of Jesus, such as the Olivet Discourse (Mt 24–25; Mk 13; Lk 21). The parallelism is striking and certainly not accidental. In the commentary these connections are dealt with in more detail (cf. Overview at 6:1–17). In short, we believe that the ultimate source of John's understanding of the future, as well as his interpretation of the OT, lies not in his own inventive imagination but definitely in Jesus of Nazareth.[7]

Recent study has emphasized that understanding the literary genre of John's Revelation must take into consideration three factors: (1) A critical awareness of its similarities to the Jewish apocalyptic style, (2) the epistolary nature of the book, and (3) its emphasis on prophetic revelation (see Aune, *Revelation 1–5,* lxx–xc).

2. UNITY

The question of the unity of Revelation is a relative one. Even R. H. Charles, 1:lxxxvii, who consistently advances a fragmentary approach to the book, recognizes the pervading unity of thought in the majority of the material. Ford, 46, who views the book as originating from three different authors, nevertheless insists that it displays an amazing and masterly literary unity that she ascribes to the work of still another person—an editor.

The evidence that allegedly argues against a single author revolves around a number of internal difficulties, which fall into four categories: (1) the presence of doublets—the same scene or vision described twice; (2) sequence problems—persons or things introduced seemingly for the first time when, in fact, they had already been mentioned; (3) seemingly misplaced verses and larger sections; and (4) distinctive content within certain sections that does not fit the rest of the book. In each case, however, there are satisfying alternative explanations. In fact, the difficulties just named stem more from the reader's presuppositions than from the text itself. Dissection of the text has been notoriously unfruitful in shedding further light on the book

---

7. The development of this parallelism with the Olivet Discourse has been noted by Austin Farrer (*The Revelation of St. John the Divine* [Oxford: Clarendon, 1964], 31–32); Swete, cli–clii; Beckwith, 139–40; Louis A. Vos, *The Synoptic Traditions in the Apocalypse* (Kampen: J. H. Kok, 1965).

itself. We are more likely to discover the author's original intent if we approach Revelation with the assumption of its literary integrity than if we attempt at every turn to judge it by a modern Western mentality.[8]

There is also a certain artificiality about interpolation theories that claim unity for the book until a passage is encountered that does not fit with preconceived views by which, without the slightest evidence, "interpolation" is cited to alleviate the embarrassment. Some of the best interpreters have succumbed to this temptation.[9]

Yet without belaboring the argument we may affirm that the book everywhere displays both the literary and conceptual unity to be expected from a single author. This does not eliminate certain difficult hermeneutical problems or preclude the presence of omissions or interpolations encountered in the extant MSS of the book. Nor does the view of single authorship preclude that John, in expressing in written form the revelation given to him by Christ, used various sources, whether oral or written (cf. comments at 1:2). Yet under the guidance of the Holy Spirit, who is of course the primary author, John has everywhere made these materials his own and invested them with a thoroughly Christian orientation and content.

3. AUTHORSHIP AND CANONICITY

The question of the authorship of Revelation is the same as that of the authorship of the other Johannine writings (John's gospel and epistles). The earliest witnesses ascribe Revelation to John the apostle, the son of Zebedee (Justin Martyr [d. ca. 165]; Irenaeus [d. ca. 200]; Clement of Alexandria [d. ca. 220]; Hippolytus [d. ca. 236]; Origen [d. ca. 254]; cf. Swete, clxxi). Not until Dionysius (d. ca. 264), the distinguished bishop of Alexandria and student of Origen, was any voice raised within the church against its apostolic authorship.[10] Dionysius questioned the apostolic origin of Revelation because the advocates of an earthly eschatological hope ("Chiliasts"), whom he opposed, appealed to Revelation 20. He based his arguments on four main comparisons between the first epistle of John and the gospel of John at points where these differ from Revelation: (1) the gospel and first epistle do not name their author, but Revelation does; (2)

---

8. This is precisely the point of three studies that look critically but fairly at the general trends of form and redaction criticism of NT documents: Northrop Frye, *Anatomy of Criticism: Four Essays* (Princeton, N.J.: Princeton Univ. Press, 1957); Walter Wink, *The Bible in Human Transformation* (Philadelphia: Fortress, 1973); Leland Ryken, "Literary Criticism of the Bible: Some Fallacies," in *Literary Interpretations of Biblical Narratives*, ed. Kenneth R. R. Gros Louis (Nashville: Abingdon, 1974). G. Mussies, 351, has done detailed work on the language of the Apocalypse that has reaffirmed the unity of the entire book, as has Vos (*Synoptic Traditions*). Most recently the massive work of Aune (*Revelation 1–5*, cxxiii) has affirmed the single authorship of the book, albeit two editions.

9. Thus Eller, 159, 165–66, following Mathias Rissi ("The Kerygma of the Revelation to John," *Int* 22 [1968]: 4), chooses to dismiss John's number "666" as an interpolation mainly because it is unlike John to be a "calenderizer," which is contrary to his overall view of the Apocalypse. The issue, however, is not whether interpolations have crept into the text but the method of approach to determining interpolations. If there is no evidence to support such a view, there is no way of distinguishing whether an actual interpolation has occurred anywhere except in the mind of the commentator.

10. Feine and Behm, 330, mention certain heretical parties ("Alogoi") who opposed the Montanists as tracing the authorship of the book to the Gnostic Cerinthus. Gaius, the Roman anti-Montanist, held such a view as well. Dionysius (*ANF* 6:82) refers to these earlier views in his treatise against the apostolic authorship of the Apocalypse. For the most extensive treatment of the canonical evidence, see Ned B. Stonehouse, *The Apocalypse in the Ancient Church* (Grand Rapids: Eerdmans, 1929).

the gospel and first epistle contain parallels to each other but not to Revelation; (3) no reference to Revelation appears in the gospel or first epistle, and no reference to the gospel or first epistle is found in Revelation; and (4) the Greek in which Revelation is written is faulty and entirely different from that of the gospel and first epistle.

From the time of Dionysius, the apostolic origin of the book was disputed in the East until Athanasius of Alexandria (d. ca. 373) turned the tide toward its acceptance. In the West, the story was different. From at least the middle of the second century, the book held its own, being widely accepted and listed in all the principal canonical enumerations. The Reformation period witnessed a renewal of the earlier questions concerning the apostolic authorship and canonical status of Revelation. Thus Martin Luther, offended by the contents of the book (especially its millennial references in ch. 20), declared that he regarded it as "neither apostolic nor prophetic."[11]

Typical of current views is that of C. F. D. Moule, who claims that "few can now believe that the John of the Apocalypse is the same as the author (or authors) of what are commonly called the Johannine writings—the Gospel and the three epistles."[12] The chief obstacle is the allegedly barbarous Greek style of Revelation as compared to that of the other Johannine writings. Of course, there is no good reason why the John of the Apocalypse could not have been the apostle John, while another John wrote the gospel and the epistles. Some have defended this position (e.g., Beasley-Murray, *Book of Revelation*, 33; J. H. Bernard [cited in Aune, *Revelation 1–5*, lii]).

However, despite the linguistic problem, a number of scholars have been convinced of the similarities between Revelation and the other Johannine books. So a group of dissenting scholars attribute the Apocalypse to the apostle, the son of Zebedee, or lean in that direction (e.g., most of the Roman Catholic scholars, Alford, Swete, Feine/Behm, Zahn, Mounce). Others leave the question open but do not deny apostolic authorship (Beasley-Murray, Beckwith, Bruce, Morris). Ford's view, 28–40, that the book was not

---

11. Cited in Feine and Behm, 330.
12. C. F. D. Moule, *An Idiom Book of New Testament Greek* (2d ed.; Cambridge: Cambridge Univ. Press, 1960), 3. Mussies, 352, notes, "The linguistic and stylistic divergence of the Apoc. on the one hand and the Gospel and Letters of St. John on the other, proves beyond any reasonable doubt that all these works as we have them before us were not phrased by one and the same man." While Mounce, 13–15, probably understates the negative linguistic evidence against a common authorship of the gospel and Apocalypse, he does cite an early Gnostic text, the *Apocryphon of John* (ca. AD 150), as crediting the passage in Revelation 1:19 to "John, the brother of James, these who are the two sons of Zebedee" (see my review of Mounce, "A New Standard on the Apocalypse," *ChrT* [January 5, 1979]: 36–37). Aune (*Revelation 1–5*, lii–liii), however, points out correctly that "the widespread use of the past-present-future prophetic formula makes it difficult to prove that *Ap. John* is in fact dependent on Rev. 1:19." Elisabeth Schüssler Fiorenza ("The Quest for the Johannine School," *NTS* 23 [1977]: 402–27) argues for a Johannine school as the explanation of the origin of both the gospel and Revelation. Thus, recent NT scholarship is tilting toward the view that the writing of NT books was more located in "schools" or "communities" of disciples in various locations. Thus a school of Matthew or a school of John, Paul, or Peter may account for the diversity in style and emphasis among the NT writings attributed to the same author. See E. Earl Ellis, "Further Reflections on John A. T. Robinson and the Dating of the New Testament," *NTS* 26 (1980): 487–502; K. Stendahl, *The School of St. Matthew and Its Use of the Old Testament* (Philadelphia: Fortress, 1968); Raymond E. Brown, *The Community of the Beloved Disciple* (New York: Paulist, 1979); Stephen S. Smalley, "John's Revelation and John's Community," *BJRL* 69 (1987): 549–71. However, this approach has been challenged recently by a group of British scholars (see Richard Bauckham, ed., *The Gospel for All Christians: Rethinking the Gospel Audiences* [Grand Rapids: Eerdmans, 1998]).

written by the apostle but was a composite writing by John the Baptist (chs. 4–11), a disciple of John the Baptist (chs. 12–22), and a later unknown Christian author (chs. 1–3), rests on conjectural evidence and has little to commend it to serious scholarly acceptance. Her arguments, instead, could be used to support the traditional view that the apostle, the son of Zebedee, who was a disciple of John the Baptist, was the author.

From the internal evidence, the following assertions about the author can be made with some confidence: First, he calls himself John (1:4, 9; 22:8). This is likely not a pseudonym but instead the name of a well-known person among the Asian churches. Other than the apostle, John the Baptist, and John Mark, the only other John we know about is the disputed "John, the presbyter [elder]" that Papias spoke of (Eusebius, *Hist. eccl.* 3.39.1–7). (The John mentioned in Ac 4:6 would obviously not be a serious candidate.)

Second, this John of the Apocalypse identifies himself not as an apostle but as a prophet (1:3; 22:6–10, 18–19) who was in exile because of his prophetic witness (1:9). As such, he speaks with great authority to the churches of Roman Asia. That an apostle could also be a prophet is mentioned at least once in the NT (Ac 13:1). Third, his use of the OT and Targums make it virtually certain he was a Palestinian Jew steeped in the temple and synagogue ritual.[13] He may also have been a priest.[14] Fourth and finally, the author uses a modified literary form—apocalypse—that is unknown outside Palestine (cf. Aune, *Revelation 1–5*, l).

In sum, it must be admitted that the question of the authorship of Revelation is problematic. On the one hand, the language and grammatical style are allegedly incompatible with the gospel and the epistles; on the other hand, in imagery, literary forms, liturgical framework, and symbolism, there are notable similarities to the gospel and the epistles. Early and widespread testimony attributes the book to the apostle John, and no convincing evidence has been advanced against this view. Perhaps we must be satisfied at present with a judgment for this book similar to what Origen suggested for the authorship of Hebrews: "Who wrote the letter, God really knows."[15] Regardless of the problem of authorship, the church universal has come to acknowledge the Apocalypse as divinely authoritative, inspired Scripture.

4. DATE

Only two suggested dates for Revelation have received serious support. An early date, shortly after the reign of Nero (AD 54–68), is supported by references in the book to the persecution of Christians, the "Nero *redivivus*" myth (a revived Nero would be the reincarnation of the evil genius of the whole Roman Empire), the imperial cult (ch. 13), and the temple (ch. 11) that was destroyed in AD 70 (so Westcott, Hort, Ford, Aune). Some external evidence for the early date exists in the Muratorian Fragment (AD 170–90) and the Monarchian Prologues (AD 250–350). These documents claim that Paul wrote to seven

---

13. See L. Paul Trudinger, "Some Observations Concerning the Text of the Old Testament in the Book of Revelation," *JTS* 17 (1966): 82–88; the Jewish authorship of the book has recently been challenged by Robert K. MacKenzie, *The Author of the Apocalypse: A Review of the Prevailing Hypothesis of Jewish-Christian Authorship* (Lewiston, N.Y.: Mellen, 1997).

14. See Ethelbert Stauffer, *New Testament Theology* (London: SCM, 1965), 40–41.

15. Cited in Daniel J. Theron, *Evidence of Tradition* (Grand Rapids: Baker, 1958), 86–87.

churches following the pattern of John's example in Revelation.[16] But this would date the book before the Pauline Epistles!

The alternative and more generally accepted date rests primarily on the early witness of Irenaeus (ca. 185; *Haer.* 5.30.3), who stated that the apostle John "saw the revelation . . . at the close of Domitian's reign" (AD 81–96). Both views appeal to the book's witness to persecution because of refusal to comply with emperor worship. On the other hand, if most of the persecution referred to in the book is anticipatory, and if the exegesis that sees references to the number 666 as Nero (13:18), the succession of the emperors (ch. 17), and the Nero *redivivus* myth and enforced emperor worship (ch. 13) as questionable, then no substantial argument can be advanced for either date in preference to the other. Therefore, though the slender historical evidence on the whole favors the later date (81–96), in the light of present studies the question as to when Revelation was written must still be left open.[17] (See also "General Nature and Historical Background," pp. 573–78.)

5. PURPOSE

Swete, xc, captures the basic thrust of the book when he observes, "In form it is an epistle, containing an apocalyptic prophecy; in spirit and inner purpose, it is a pastoral." As a prophet, John is called to separate true belief from false—to expose the failures of the congregations in Asia. He desires to encourage authentic Christian discipleship by explaining Christian suffering and martyrdom in the light of how Jesus' death brought victory over evil. John is concerned to show that the martyrs (e.g., Antipas [2:13]) would be vindicated. He also discloses the end of evil and of those who follow the beast (19:20–21; 20:10, 15), and

---

16. See ibid., 59, 111; cf. K. Stendahl, "The Apocalypse of John and the Epistles of Paul in the Muratorian Fragment," in *Current Issues in New Testament Interpretation*, ed. W. Klassen and G. F. Snyder (New York: Harper, 1962), 239–45. Stendahl argues that, in addition to apostolic inspiration, a canonical book needed to be universal in nature, i.e., written for the whole church. Apparently the Apocalypse served as a standard for including other books in the NT canon. Thus the canon of Mommsell (ca. early fourth century) states, "But as it is said in the Apocalypse of John, 'I saw twenty-four elders presenting their crowns before the throne,' so our fathers approved that these books are canonical and that the men of old have said this" (Theron, *Evidence of Tradition*, 121).

17. See chs. 13 and 17, where the dating schemes are discussed in more detail and questioned. Feine and Behm, 329, suggest that since the congregation of Smyrna had undergone trials for a long time (2:8–11) and that according to Polycarp (*Phil.* 11) the church did not exist in Paul's day; and since 3:17 describes the church at Laodicea as rich, though this city was almost completely destroyed by an earthquake in AD 60–61, the later date for the book is to be preferred. However, Robinson (*Redating the New Testament*, 229–30) has recently challenged the above objection to the early date and favors a date prior to AD 70. He has effectively shown that this evidence is misinterpreted by some scholars. Robinson's early date for the Apocalypse is conceded by D. Moody Smith ("A Review of John A. T. Robinson's *Redating the New Testament*," *DukeDivR* 42 [1977]: 193–205). Morris, 39, correctly concludes that "the date of John is far from certain and there are some grounds for holding that it is to be dated before the destruction of Jerusalem in AD 70." Albert A. Bell Jr. ("The Date of John's Apocalypse: The Evidence of Some Roman Historians Reconsidered," *NTS* 25 [1978]: 93–102) has argued that the Domitian dating is not credible since the only direct evidence comes from Irenaeus. Bell says, "Second-century traditions about the apostles are demonstrably unreliable, and Irenaeus's testimony is not without difficulties." He argues against the persecution theory as a backdrop to Revelation by refuting the evidence of the Roman historian Cassius Dio (d. ca. 250), and Bell places the date of Revelation between June 68 and January 69!

he describes the ultimate issue of the Lamb's victory and the end of those who follow him. John himself is centrally concerned with God's saving purpose and its implementation by Jesus. John writes to the church universal in every age so that they too might join him in confirming this witness of Jesus (1:9; 22:16).[18] Sadly, because of the occasional overemphasis on either the symbolic or the literal, and because of the theological problems (see next section), the church has often been deprived of the valuable practical thrust of this book, as through it God seeks to lead us into authentic Christian discipleship.

6. THEOLOGICAL PROBLEMS

From earliest times, certain theological emphases in Revelation are cited as objections to the whole book or to parts considered unworthy and sub-Christian. Among these are (1) its eschatological view of history, which includes an earthly millennium (ch. 20); (2) the cry for vengeance in 6:10; (3) its "weakly Christianized Judaism";[19] and (4) its overuse of visions and symbols, according to Martin Luther, who said that Christ is neither taught nor accepted in this book and who considered it neither apostolic nor prophetic; most recently the ethical humanists condemn Revelation for its desire for violence and its misogyny (see Greg Carey, "The Apocalypse and its Ambiguous Ethos," in Moyise, 163–80).

In sum, Revelation is alleged to be sub-Christian in its Christology, eschatology, doctrine of God, and morality, all four of which are thought to obscure or to contradict outright the central message of the NT.[20] While none of the above problems should be glossed over, it is becoming apparent that prior commitment to a certain viewpoint on these four areas, rather than the intrinsic incompatibility of John's ideas with the central NT message, often determines the negative judgments that some scholars pass on Revelation. A helpful study by Beasley-Murray points out the basic difference in John's views from standard Jewish apocalyptic thought and wisely argues for the necessity to read Revelation in conjunction with the NT books that preceded it, not as contradictory but as complementary to them.[21]

7. TEXT

The MSS of Revelation are few compared to those of other NT literature. Of the important early witnesses, only seven papyri and fewer than a dozen uncials of the Apocalypse are extant. While there are

---

18. See Minear, 213–17, for an excellent discussion of the prophet's motives in writing the book.
19. Rudolph Bultmann, *Theology of the New Testament* (New York: Scribner, 1951), 2:175.
20. Cf. Feine and Behm, 331–32. Even the conservative Morris (*Apocalyptic* [Grand Rapids: Eerdmans, 1972], 86) complains that apocalyptic is not a good medium for expressing the "cruciality of the cross," and he believes it does not express it: "Apocalyptic fails us at the heart of the faith." Yet the book of Revelation seems to capture splendidly this cruciality of the cross in its own unique way (cf. chs. 5 and 12) and provides a needed complement to the other NT descriptions of the cross (see G. R. Beasley-Murray, "How Christian Is the Book of Revelation?" in *Reconciliation and Hope: New Testament Essays on Atonement and Eschatology*, ed. Robert Banks [Grand Rapids: Eerdmans, 1974], 275–84).
21. Beasley-Murray, "How Christian Is the Book of Revelation?" 275–84. See also Carl E. Braaten, *Apocalyptic Themes in Theology and Culture: Christ and Counter-Christ* (Philadelphia: Fortress, 1972), esp. ch. 1; G. E. Ladd, "The Theology of the Apocalypse," *GR* 7 (1963–64): 73–86; Richard Bauckham, *The Theology of the Book of Revelation* (NTT; Cambridge: Cambridge Univ. Press, 1993); Smalley, "John's Revelation and John's Community," 549–71.

over a thousand minuscule MSS for each of most of the other NT books, Revelation has a total of only about 293.[22] Thus we have $\mathfrak{P}^{18}$ (third–fourth century), $\mathfrak{P}^{24}$ (fourth century), $\mathfrak{P}^{43}$ (sixth–seventh century), $\mathfrak{P}^{47}$ (late third century), $\mathfrak{P}^{85}$ (fourth–fifth century), $\mathfrak{P}^{98}$ (second century), $\mathfrak{P}^{115}$ (third–fourth century), ℵ (fourth century), A (fifth century?), C (fifth century), P (ninth century), and a few minuscules cited in Metzger's apparatus and commentary. In the Notes sections throughout this commentary, only those textual variants are discussed where, in my opinion, the sense of the passage is affected. I have also followed the practice of not citing all the textual evidence, since those who understand such technicalities have ready access to the standard critical editions of the Greek NT and works such as Metzger's textual commentary and Hoskier's collations (see n. 22). In general, MSS A, ℵ, C, and $\mathfrak{P}^{47}$ weigh heavily in the external evidence, especially where they agree. A alone is sometimes the preferred reading. Most of the cases must be settled on intrinsic probability and context. I have given Metzger's conclusions throughout but have occasionally dissented when the internal evidence seems to warrant it. The Greek text used is the UBS *Greek New Testament* (4th ed.).

8. INTERPRETATIVE SCHEMES

Four traditional ways of understanding Revelation 4–22 emerged in the history of the church. In our day, additional mixed views have been developed by combining elements from these four main traditions.

Futurist

This view holds that, with the exception of chs. 1–3, all the visions in Revelation relate to a period immediately preceding and following the second advent of Christ at the end of the age; therefore, the seals, trumpets, and bowls refer to events still in the future. The beasts of chs. 13 and 17 are identified with the future Antichrist, who will appear at the last moment in world history and will be defeated by Christ in his second coming to judge the world and to establish his earthly millennial kingdom.

Variations of this view were held by the earliest expositors, such as Justin Martyr (d. ca. 165), Irenaeus (d. ca. 195), Hippolytus (d. ca. 236), and Victorinus (d. ca. 303). After nearly a ten-century eclipse, during which time the allegorical method prevailed, the futurist view was revived in the late sixteenth century by Franciscus Ribeira, a Spanish Jesuit. He held that the beast was the Antichrist of the end-time and that Babylon was not Rome under papal rule but a degenerate Rome of a future age. Unlike many modern futurists, Ribeira founded his views on a thorough appreciation of the historical backgrounds of Revelation and its language. Thus he understood the first five seals to depict various elements of early Christianity. The white horse was the apostolic age; the red, the early persecutors; the black, heresies; the pale, the violent persecutions by Trajan. But when Ribeira came to the sixth seal, he took this to indicate the signs that would precede the return of Christ; he also understood the seven trumpets and seven bowls to follow the three and a half years.

---

22. H. C. Hoskier's monumental work (*Concerning the Text of the Apocalypse* [2 vols.; London: Bernard Quaritch, 1929]) has collated afresh all the uncial and minuscule witnesses to the book and is the best source for variants; additionally, the extensive examination of manuscripts by Joseph Schmid (1955) is described in Aune (*Revelation* 1–5, cxxxiv–clx), along with a complete listing and discussion of all manuscript evidence.

This futurist approach to the book has enjoyed a revival of no small proportion since the nineteenth century and is widely held among evangelicals today. The chief problem with it is that it seems to make all but the first three chapters of Revelation not directly but only indirectly relevant to the contemporary church. This objection is pressed more strongly when adherents of the futurist view affirm, as many do today, that the church will be removed from the earth before the events described in 6:1ff. occur.[23] This "dispensational" variety of futurist interpretation that arose in the nineteenth-century teaching of the Plymouth Brethren leader, John Nelson Darby, has recently enjoyed unprecedented popularity in the best-selling Left Behind series of novels by Tim LaHaye and Jerry B. Jenkins. The present commentary demurs from this position while at the same time recognizing elements in it of the historic futurist position that go back to a number of early church fathers. (See "My Position," p. 587, and comments throughout, starting at 3:10 and 4:1.)

Historicist

As the word implies, this view centers on history and its continuity as seen in Revelation. This approach began with Joachim of Floris (d. ca. 1202), a monastic who claimed to have received on Easter night a special vision that revealed to him God's plan for the ages. He assigned a day/year value to the 1,260 days of the Apocalypse. In his scheme, the book was a prophecy of the events of Western history from the times of the apostles (in some varieties, from the creation) until Joachim's own time. Shortly after his death, the Franciscans considered themselves to be the true Christians of his vision. They interpreted Babylon not only as pagan Rome but also as papal Rome.

In the various schemes that developed as this method was applied to history, one element became common: the Antichrist and Babylon were connected with Rome and the papacy. Later, Luther, Calvin, and other Reformers came to adopt this view. That this approach does not enjoy much favor today is largely because of the lack of consensus as to the historical identifications it entails. The distinguished exegete Henry Alford (1810–71) held a guarded version of this view.

Preterist

According to this view, Revelation describes what was happening in the time of the author; it is a contemporary and imminent historical document dealing with the evil Roman Empire. So the main contents of chs. 4–22 are viewed as describing events wholly limited to John's own time. This approach identifies the book with the Jewish apocalyptic method of producing "tracts for the times" to encourage faithfulness during intense persecution. One version of this view sees the fall of "Babylon the Great" as God's judgment on an apostate Israel in the fall of Jerusalem in AD 70. Yet the same interpreters see the beasts of chs. 13 and 17 as the pagan nation of Rome (so K. L. Gentry, *Before Jerusalem Fell: Dating the Book of Revelation* [Tyler, Tex.: Institute for Christian Economics, 1989]). However, as Beale, 44–45, points out, it would be strange that unbelieving Israel is the primary object of judgment and not all the

---

23. Some good sources for the history of interpretation are the works by Beckwith, Elliott, Wainwright, and Swete (see bibliography).

nations including Israel, and that the book does not refer to a final *universal* judgment as anticipated in Daniel 2 and 7.

A second type of preterist interpretation sees the fall of "Babylon the Great" as the fall of the Roman Empire. The two beasts of ch. 13 are identified respectively as imperial Rome and the imperial priesthood. This is the view held by a majority of contemporary NT scholars of various theological persuasions. It did not appear as a system till 1614, when a Spanish Jesuit named Alcasar developed its main lines. Today some commentators argue that the events were imminent but not yet realized when John wrote; hence, they suggest an imminent historical view (so Caird). While they do not ignore the importance of the historical setting, those who accept Revelation as a book of genuine prophecy concerning events extending beyond the first six centuries are little attracted by this view. Therefore, a number of evangelical, conservative commentators have developed a variation known as the preterist-futurist interpretation (e.g., Ladd, Beasley-Murray, Mounce, Morris, Osborne). The beasts and Babylon refer to Rome, but they are pregnant with a larger meaning that also describes the future Antichrist and the final judgment of all peoples at Christ's second coming.

Further, a new spate of conservative books, influenced by James Stuart Russell's *The Parousia* (1878; repr. Bradford, Pa.: International Preterist Association) and emphasizing the preterist interpretation, has recently appeared. There is a hard view and a soft view among these interpreters. The hard view, or full preterist, sees everything in the book as having been fulfilled during John's day in the destruction of the temple, including the second coming of Jesus, the resurrection, and the judgment of the world (so Don K. Preston, *Who Is This Babylon?* [self-published, 1999]); the soft, or partial preterist, view is held by those who cannot bring themselves to accept that the second coming and the resurrection have already occurred (so R. C. Sproul, *The Last Days According to Jesus* [Grand Rapids: Baker, 2000]).

Idealist-Symbolical

This method of interpreting Revelation sees the book as being basically poetic, symbolic, and spiritual in nature. Indeed, it is sometimes called the spiritualist view—not, of course, in reference to the cult of spiritualism but because it "spiritualizes" everything in the book. Thus Revelation does not predict any specific historical events at all (with the possible exception of the second coming of Christ and the resurrection); on the contrary, it sets forth timeless truths concerning the battle between good and evil, which continues throughout the church age. As a system of interpretation, it is more recent than the three other schools and somewhat more difficult to distinguish from the earlier allegorizing approaches of the Alexandrians (Clement and Origen). In general, the idealist view is marked by its refusal to identify any of the images with specific future events, whether in the history of the church or with regard to the end of all things.[24] Undoubtedly, the book does reflect the great timeless realities of the battle between God and Satan and of divine judgment; undoubtedly, it sees history as being ultimately in the hand of the Creator. But it also depicts the consummation of this battle and the triumph of Christ in history through his coming in glory.

---

24. For other interpreters who favor this view, see the bibliography.

Mixed Views and Postmodern Approaches

In addition to the preterist-futurist view mentioned in the preterist section, there are other attempts to combine desirable features of different interpretive schemes. So the preterist-symbolical emphasis may be found (e.g., Caird, Boring), as well as the futurist-symbolical (e.g., Beale, Osborne, this commentary). Furthermore, modern narrative emphasis has produced different readings of Revelation as story and drama (e.g., Barr, Prigent, Resseguie).

Which view is the right one? Since there have been evangelicals and conservatives who have held to each of the four views, as well as certain mixed views, the issue is not that of orthodoxy but of interpretation. In recent years, many expositors have combined the stronger elements of the different views. The history of the interpretation of Revelation should teach us to be open to fresh approaches, even when this attitude goes contrary to the prevailing interpretations. Nothing short of the careful exegesis of the text, uninhibited by prior dogmatic conclusions, is required for the fullest understanding of the Apocalypse.

My Position

This commentary will pay close attention to the historical situation of first-century Christianity in its Judeo-Greco-Roman world setting. I do not take the position, however, that this emphasis necessarily leads to the conclusion that John's language and visions describe specifically the political entities of imperial Rome or the imperial priesthood (though I do see these entities included in a more general way in what he does actually describe). I believe that the preterist's view, and to a lesser extent the preterist-futurist's view, is misled.[25] On the other hand, I hold that John is describing the final judgment; the physical, bodily return of Christ to the world; and the future resurrection of believers. This means that, in every age, Revelation continues to both encourage the church in persecution and warn the church of the beast's satanically energized, multifaceted deception. Its language describes the deeper realities of the conflict of Christ's sovereignty with satanic power rather than mere temporary historical-political entities, whether past (such as Rome) or future.

Revelation may then be viewed, on the one hand, as an extended commentary on Paul's statement, "For our struggle is not against flesh and blood, but against the rulers, against the authorities, against the powers of the dark world and against the spiritual forces of evil in the heavenly realms" (Eph 6:12). On the other hand, it also reveals the final judgment on evil and the consummation of God's kingdom in time and eternity. It is encouraging to see other commentators coming to a similar conclusion (e.g., Beale, Osborne, Mazzaferri).

---

25. Beasley-Murray, Bruce, Ladd, Morris, and Mounce, among others, are recent evangelical interpreters who have endeavored to combine the preterist and futurist schools. The key question seems to be this: To what extent does the Apocalypse fit the literary genre of apocalyptic at the point of its view of history? The Jewish apocalyptists related their messages to the immediate historical-political entities; but does John do this? I believe he does not. His language about the beast and Babylon describes more a theological than a political entity (see Overviews at chs. 13 and 17). While the preterist-futurist view is a big step in the right direction away from the purely preterist or nonhistorical futurist views, in my opinion it falls short of the actual sense of the language throughout the book.

9. USE OF THE OLD TESTAMENT

While Revelation does not have a single direct quotation, there are hundreds of places where John alludes in one way or another to the OT Scriptures. Swete, cxxxv, notes that of the 404 verses of the Apocalypse, 278 contain references to the Jewish Scriptures. UBS's Greek NT (pp. 891–901) cites well over five hundred OT passages as possible allusions or verbal parallels in the book. But just what counts for an allusion? This question has received more careful scrutiny in certain recent studies. Jon Paulien ("Criteria and the Assessment of Allusions to the Old Testament in the Book of Revelation," in Moyise, 126), commenting on the validity of Beale's work on OT allusions, concludes from a sample study of his commentary that projecting from the sample to whole book would suggest some *twelve hundred* allusions overall. In any case, the author's use of the OT is unique (e.g., Paul's epistles contain ninety-five direct quotations and possibly an additional one hundred allusions to the OT).

The OT used by John is primarily Semitic rather than Greek, agreeing often with the Aramaic Targums and occasionally reflecting midrashic background materials to the OT passages; and it can be shown that he used a text other than the Masoretic that has a close affinity with the Hebrew text of the Qumran MSS.[26] From the Prophets, John refers quite frequently to Isaiah and Jeremiah, and especially Ezekiel and Daniel. John also refers repeatedly to Psalms, Exodus, and Deuteronomy. Especially important are John's christological reinterpretations of OT passages he alludes to. He does not simply use the OT in its pre-Christian sense but often recasts the images and visions of the OT. While there is an unmistakable continuity in Revelation with the older revelation, the new emerges from the old as a distinct entity.[27] Yet scholarly studies are tending to agree that there is a reciprocal relationship between John's OT allusions and his NT message. Beale, 97, observes, "The New Testament interprets the Old and the Old interprets the New."

10. STRUCTURE

The main contents of Revelation are given in terms of a series of sevens—some explicit, some implied: seven churches (chs. 2–3); seven seals (chs. 6–7); seven trumpets (chs. 8–11); seven signs (chs. 12–15); seven bowls (chs. 16–18); seven last things (chs. 19–22). It is also possible to divide the contents around four key visions: (1) the vision of the Son of Man among the seven churches (chs. 1–3); (2) the vision of the seven-sealed scroll, the seven trumpets, the seven signs, and the seven bowls (4:1–19:10); (3) the vision of the return of Christ and the consummation of this age (19:11–20:15); and (4) the vision of the new heaven and new earth (chs. 21–22). Commendable attempts have also been made to show that the literary structure of the Apocalypse is patterned after the Easter liturgy of the early church.[28]

---

26. The Dead Sea Scrolls have shown that there were many text types in the first century, including a Masoretic-like text. John's use of the OT reflects some of the Qumran text types rather than the MT. See Trudinger, "Some Observations Concerning the Text," 83–88; cf. D. Moody Smith Jr., "The Use of the Old Testament in the New," in *The Use of the Old Testament in the New and Other Essays*, ed. James M. Efird (Durham, N.C.: Duke Univ. Press, 1972), 58–63. See also Vos's excellent chapter "The Apocalyptist's Manner of Using Pre-Existent Material As Illustrated from His Employment of the Old Testament," in *Synoptic Traditions*, 16–53.

27. Austin Farrer (*A Rebirth of Images*) has opened my eyes to this dimension of the Apocalypse. The chief difficulty with Farrer is that many find his own book more difficult to understand than Revelation itself.

28. See, e.g., Massey H. Shepherd Jr., *The Paschal Liturgy and the Apocalypse* (Richmond, Va.: John Knox, 1960).

Most recently, David Barr (*Tales of the End*) has similarly argued that the purpose of the book is to bind the community together in a participatory worship service around a shared vision of the cosmic struggle against evil. As such, he sees three separate narratives. The first is the appearance to John of the Son of Man with messages to the seven churches (chs. 1–3). The second story is about John's invitation to visit the heavenly throne room (chs. 4–11). The third story tells of a cosmic war (chs. 12–22). In the final analysis, however, all such literary schemes must be compatible with the exegesis of the book.

11. BIBLIOGRAPHY

The following is a selective list of commentaries and monographs on the book of Revelation available in English, confined for the most part to those referred to in the commentary (they will be referred to simply by the author's name [and initials only when necessary to distinguish two authors of the same surname]). References to other resources will carry full bibliographic details at the first mention and thereafter a short title.

Limited space allows for the mention of only a few major representative books in each interpretative category. Some defy exact categories, and it may be unfair to classify them. I have used the interpretation of the beast (ch. 13) and Babylon (ch. 17) as the chief indicators of the nature of the books listed.

Futurist

A. Dispensational

Smith, J. B. *A Revelation of Jesus Christ*. Scottdale, Pa.: Herald, 1961.
Tenney, Merrill C. *Interpreting Revelation*. Grand Rapids: Eerdmans, 1957.
Thomas, Robert L. *Revelation: An Exegetical Commentary*. Two Volumes. Chicago: Moody Press, 1992–95.
Walvoord, John F. *The Revelation of Jesus Christ*. Chicago: Moody Press, 1966.

B. Purely Eschatological

Eller, Vernard. *The Most Revealing Book of the Bible: Making Sense Out of Revelation*. Grand Rapids: Eerdmans, 1974.
Lilje, Hanns. *The Last Book of the Bible: The Meaning of the Revelation of St. John*. Philadelphia: Muhlenberg, 1955.

C. Preterist-Futurist

Beasley-Murray, G. R. "The Revelation." New Bible Commentary. Revised Edition. Edited by D. Guthrie et al. Grand Rapids: Eerdmans, 1970.
Beckwith, Isbon T. *The Apocalypse of John*. New York: Macmillan, 1922.
Bruce, F. F. "The Revelation to John." In *A New Testament Commentary*. Edited by G. C. D. Howley, F. F. Bruce, and H. L. Ellison. Grand Rapids: Zondervan, 1969.
Ladd, George E. *A Commentary on the Revelation of John*. Grand Rapids: Eerdmans, 1972.
Morris, Leon. *The Revelation of St. John*. Revised Edition. Grand Rapids: Eerdmans, 1987.
Mounce, Robert H. *The Book of Revelation*. New International Commentary on the New Testament. Revised Edition. Grand Rapids: Eerdmans, 1998.

Historicist

Alford, Henry. *The Revelation*. London: Cambridge, 1884.
Elliott, E. B. *Horae Apocalypticae*. Four Volumes. Third Edition. London: Seeley, Burnside, and Seeley, 1828.

Preterist

Aune, David E. *Revelation 1–5*. Word Biblical Commentary 52A. Dallas: Word, 1997.
———. *Revelation 6–16*. Word Biblical Commentary 52B. Nashville: Thomas Nelson, 1998.

———. *Revelation 17–22.* Word Biblical Commentary 52C. Nashville: Thomas Nelson, 1998.

Barclay, William. *The Revelation of John.* 2 vols. The Daily Study Bible Series. Philadelphia: Westminster, 1959.

Bauckham, Richard. *The Climax of Prophecy: Studies on the Book of Revelation.* Edinburgh: T&T Clark, 1993.

Charles, R. H. *A Critical and Exegetical Commentary on the Revelation of St. John.* 2 vols. International Critical Commentary. Edinburgh: T&T Clark, 1920.

Ford, J. Massyngberde. *Revelation.* Anchor Bible. New York: Doubleday, 1975.

Glasson, T. F. *The Revelation of John.* The Cambridge Bible Commentary on the New English Bible. New York: Cambridge at the University, 1965.

Swete, Henry Barclay. *The Apocalypse of St. John.* New York: Macmillan, 1906.

Idealist-Symbolical

Kiddle, Martin. *The Revelation of St. John.* Harper New Testament Commentary. New York: Harper, 1940.

Kistemaker, Simon J. *Exposition of the Book of Revelation.* New Testament Commentary 20. Grand Rapids: Baker, 2001.

Michaels, J. Ramsey. *Revelation.* IVP New Testament Commentary Series 20. Downers Grove, Ill.: InterVarsity, 1997.

Minear, Paul S. *I Saw a New Earth: An Introduction to the Visions of the Apocalypse.* Cleveland: Corpus, 1968.

Rissi, Mathias. *Time and History.* Richmond, Va.: John Knox, 1966.

Mixed and Postmodern Narrative

Barr, David L. *Tales of the End: A Narrative Commentary on the Book of Revelation.* The Storyteller's Bible 1. Santa Rosa: Polebridge, 1998. (A postmodern narrative treatment)

Beale, Gregory K. *The Book of Revelation: A Commentary on the Greek Text.* New International Greek Testament Commentary. Grand Rapids: Eerdmans, 1999. (Modified symbolical-futurist)

Caird, G. B. *The Revelation of St. John the Divine.* Harper's New Testament Commentaries. New York: Harper, 1966. (Preterist-Symbolical)

Chevalier, Jacques M. *A Postmodern Revelation, Signs of Astrology and the Apocalypse.* Toronto: University of Toronto, 1997. (Postmodern)

Osborne, Grant R. *Revelation.* Baker Exegetical Commentary on the New Testament. Grand Rapids: Baker, 2002. (Futurist-symbolical-modified preterist view)

Prigent, Pierre. *Commentary on the Apocalypse of St John.* Tübingen: Mohr, 2001. (Narrative approach)

Resseguie, James L. *Revelation Unsealed: A Narrative Critical Approach to John's Apocalypse.* Biblical Interpretation Series 32. Leiden: Brill, 1998. (Narrative approach)

Further Works Cited in This Commentary

Bauckham, Richard. *The Theology of the Book of Revelation.* New Testament Theology. Cambridge: Cambridge Univ. Press, 1993.

Beasley-Murray, G. R. *The Book of Revelation.* Revised Edition. New Century Biblical Commentary. Grand Rapids: Eerdmans, 1978.

Berkouwer, G. C. *The Return of Christ.* Grand Rapids: Eerdmans, 1972.

Boring, M. Eugene. *Revelation.* Interpretation: A Bible Commentary for Teaching and Preaching. Louisville, Ky.: John Knox, 1989.

Charles, R. H. *The Apocrypha and Pseudepigrapha of the Old Testament.* Two Volumes. New York: Oxford Univ. Press, 1913.

Duff, Paul B. *Who Rides the Beast? Prophetic Rivalry and the Rhetoric of Crisis in the Churches of the Apocalypse.* Oxford: Oxford Univ. Press, 2001.

Farrer, Austin. *A Rebirth of Images: the Making of St. John's Apocalypse.* London: Darce, 1949.

Feine, Paul, and Johannes Behm. *Introduction to the New Testament.* Edited by W. Kümmel. New York: Abingdon, 1966.

France, R. T. *Jesus and the Old Testament.* Downers Grove, Ill.: InterVarsity, 1971.

Gaebelein, A. C. *The Revelation.* New York: Our Hope, 1915.

Gundry, Robert H. *The Church and the Tribulation*. Grand Rapids: Zondervan, 1973.

Mazzaferri, Frederick David. *The Genre of the Book of Revelation from a Source-Critical Perspective*. Beihefte zur Zeitschrift für die neutestamentliche Wissenschaft 54. Berlin: de Gruyter, 1989.

Metzger, Bruce M. *A Textual Commentary on the Greek New Testament*. Revised Edition. Stuttgart: German Bible Society, 1994.

Moyise, Steve, ed. *Studies in the Book of Revelation*. Edinburgh: T&T Clark, 2001.

Mussies, G. *The Morphology of Koinē Greek as Used in the Apocalypse of St. John*. Leiden: Brill, 1971.

Rowland, Christopher. *Revelation*. Epworth Commentaries. London: Epworth, 1993.

Seiss, J. A. *The Apocalypse*. Grand Rapids: Zondervan, 1957.

Shepherd, Massey H. Jr. *The Paschal Liturgy and the Apocalypse*. Richmond, Va.: John Knox, 1960.

Wainwright, Arthur W. *Mysterious Apocalypse. Interpreting the Book of Revelation*. Nashville: Abingdon, 1993.

Zahn, Theodor, *Introduction to the New Testament*. Volume 3. Grand Rapids: Kregel, 1953.

12. OUTLINE

Text and Exposition

I. INTRODUCTION (1:1–8)

A. Prologue (1:1–3)

OVERVIEW

The prologue contains a description of the nature of the book, a reference to the author, and a statement that the book was meant for congregational reading. Probably vv.1–3 were written last.

> ¹The revelation of Jesus Christ, which God gave him to show his servants what must soon take place. He made it known by sending his angel to his servant John, ²who testifies to everything he saw—that is, the word of God and the testimony of Jesus Christ. ³Blessed is the one who reads the words of this prophecy, and blessed are those who hear it and take to heart what is written in it, because the time is near.

COMMENTARY

1 The disclosure is called the "revelation of Jesus Christ." "Revelation" (*apokalypsis*, GK 637) means to expose in full view what was formerly hidden, veiled, or secret. In the NT, the word occurs exclusively in the religious sense of a divine disclosure. "Revelation" may refer to either some present or future aspect of God's will (Lk 2:32; Ro 16:25; Eph 3:5) or to persons (Ro 8:19) or especially to the future unveiling of Jesus Christ at his return in glory (2Th 1:7; 1Pe 1:7, 13). In this single occurrence of *apokalypsis* in the Johannine writings, the meaning is not primarily the appearing or revealing of Christ—though certainly the book does this—but rather, as the following words show, the disclosure of "what must soon take place." The *apokalypsis* may, then, not refer to the whole book but only to that portion that "must soon take place" (see comments at 5:1).

The content of the revelation comes from its author, Jesus Christ. Yet even Christ is not the final author but a mediator, for he receives the revelation from God the Father ("which God gave him to show"). John is the human instrument for communicating what he has seen by the agency of Christ's messenger or angel (cf. 22:6, 8, 16). Through John, the revelation is to be made known to the servants of God who comprise the churches (cf. 22:16).

"What must soon take place" implies that the revelation concerns events that are future to John's present (cf. Da 2:28–29, 45; Mk 13:7; Rev 4:1; 22:6). But in what sense can we understand that the events will arise "soon" (*en tachei*)? From the preterist point of view (i.e., the events are seen to be imminent to the time of the author; cf. Introduction), the sense is plain: all will "soon" take place—i.e., in John's day (including, according to some today, the second coming and the resurrection). Others translate *en tachei* as "quickly" (a grammatically acceptable translation) and understand the author to describe events that will rapidly run their course once they begin. However, it is better to translate *en tachei* as "soon" in light of the words "the time is near" in v.3 (cf. 22:10).

Yet, if we adopt this sense, it is not necessary to follow the preterist interpretation of the book. In eschatology and apocalyptic, the future is always viewed as imminent without the necessity of intervening time (cf. Lk 18:8). That *en tachei* does not preclude delay or intervening events is evident from the book of Revelation itself. In ch. 6 we hear the cry of the martyred saints, "How long, Sovereign Lord, holy and true, until you . . . avenge our blood?" They are told to "wait a little longer" (vv.10–11). Therefore, "soonness" means imminency in eschatological terms. The church in every age has always lived with the expectancy of the consummation of all things in its day. Imminency describes an event possible any day, impossible no day. If this sense is followed, we are forced to accept neither a "mistaken apocalyptic" view, as Albert Schweitzer (*The Quest of the Historical Jesus* [New York: Macmillan, 1968]) advocated, nor a preterist interpretation.

Two more focal points are introduced by the words "by sending his angel to his servant John." The first is "angel" (*angelos*, GK *34*); here we are introduced to the significance of angels in the worship of God, in the revelation of God's Word, and in the execution of his judgments on the earth. Angels are referred to sixty-seven times in Revelation. The second focal point is "servant" (*doulos*, GK *1528*). All God's people are known in Revelation as his servants. No fewer than eleven times in the book are they so described (e.g., 2:20; 7:3; 22:3). John is one servant selected to receive this revelation and communicate it to other servants of God. "Servant," used throughout the NT to describe those who are so

designated as the special representatives of the Lord Christ himself, becomes a beautiful title of honor for God's people. Here, then, in the prologue are five links in the chain of authorship: God, Christ, his angel, his servant John, and those servants to whom John addressed his book.

2 Two elements in the book are of chief importance: "the word of God and the testimony of Jesus Christ." In referring to his visions as the "word of God," John emphasizes his continuity with both the prophets in the OT and the apostles in the NT. The following passages show us John's concept of the Word of God: 1:9; 3:8, 10; 6:9; 12:11; 17:17; 19:9; 20:4. In 19:13, Jesus is himself identified with the name "the Word of God." Here in ch. 1 the reference is not directly to Christ but to the promises and acts of God revealed in this book that are realized through Jesus, the Word of God incarnate (cf. Jn 1:1–2; 1Jn 1:1). The church needs to be reminded that the neglected book of Revelation is the very Word of God to us. While John's literary activity is evident throughout, he claims that what he presents he actually "saw" in divinely disclosed visions. And in the book, God himself bears witness to the readers that these things are not the product of John's own mind (1:1–2; 21:5; 22:6; cf. 2Pe 1:21).

"Testimony" translates the Greek *martyria* (GK *3456*), another important term for the author. It is variously rendered as "witness," "attestation," "validation," and "verification." "The testimony of Jesus" grammatically could be the testimony "to" Jesus—i.e., John's own testimony about Jesus (objective genitive). However, the alternative grammatical sense—the testimony or validation "from" Jesus (subjective genitive)—is to be preferred. John testifies both to the Word of God received in the visions and also to the validation of his message from Jesus himself. The important range of possible implications of the term in the following references is worthy of study: 1:9; 6:9; 12:11, 17; 19:10; 20:4; 22:16–20.

3 "The one who reads" reflects the early form of worship where a reader read the Scriptures aloud on the Lord's Day. "Those who hear" are the people of the congregation who listen to the reading. "This prophecy" is John's way of describing his writing and refers to the entire book of Revelation (10:11; 19:10; 22:7, 9–10, 18). Prophecy involves not only future events but also the ethical and spiritual exhortations and warnings and the words of comfort and hope contained in the whole writing. Thus John immediately sets off his writing from the late Jewish apocalyptic literature (which did not issue from the prophets) and at the same time puts himself on a par with the OT prophets (cf. 10:8–11; see David Hill, "Prophecy and Prophets in the Revelation of St. John," *NTS* 18 [1971–72]: 401–18).

The twofold benediction "blessed" (*makarios*, GK *3421*) pronounced on the reader and the congregation emphasizes the importance of the message in that they will be hearing not only the word of John the prophet but, in actuality, the inspired word of Christ (Revelation contains six more beatitudes: 14:13; 16:15; 19:9; 20:6; 22:7, 14). John wrote in anticipation of the full and immediate recognition of his message as worthy to be read in the churches as the Word of God coming from Christ himself. In the ancient Jewish synagogue tradition in which

John was raised, no such blessing was promised on anyone who recited a mere human teaching, even if from a rabbi, while one who read a biblical text (Scripture) performed a *mitzvah* (commanded act) and was worthy to receive a divine blessing.

All must listen carefully and "take to heart what is written" (*tēreō*, "observe, watch, keep," GK *5498*) because "the time is near"—the time or season (*kairos*, GK *2789*) for the fulfillment of the return of Christ (v.7; cf. Lk 11:28; 21:8) and for all that is written in this book (cf. 22:10). The season (*kairos*) for Christ's return is always imminent—today just as it has been from the days of his ascension (Jn 21:22; Ac 1:11).

A comparison of the prologue (1:1–3) with the epilogue (22:7–21) shows that John has followed a deliberate literary pattern throughout Revelation. This should alert us to the possibility that the entire book was designed to be heard as a single unit in the public worship service. Minear, 5, observes, "The student should not be content with his interpretation of any passage unless and until it fits into the message of the book as a whole." This should not in any way detract from the fact that John claims to have seen real visions ("saw," v.2), which we may assume were arranged by John in their particular literary form for purposes of communication.

NOTES

1 Ἀποκάλυψις Ἰησοῦ Χριστοῦ, *apokalypsis Iēsou Christou* ("the revelation of Jesus Christ"), raises three questions: (1) What is the relation of this book to the late Jewish apocalyptic literature (*1 Enoch*; *Testaments of the Twelve Patriarchs*; etc.)? "Apocalyptic" as applied to this body of literature comes from the Greek title of the Revelation (*apokalypsis*) of John. (2) Is "Jesus Christ" an objective or subjective genitive? If the latter, as most commentators suggest, the sense is the "revelation from Jesus Christ"; if the former, the meaning would be the "revelation about Jesus Christ." Grammatically, either is possible. The sense of from Jesus Christ is preferred. For a recent case for the sense "the revelation *about* Jesus Christ," see Barr, *Tales of the End*. (3) Does the "revelation" refer to the whole book (most commentators), to the contents of the little scroll of ch.10 (i.e., how the nations are converted by the suffering of the saints; so Bauckham, 243–337), or to the contents

of the scroll in ch. 5 (i.e., "the outcome of the final tribulation of God's people"). "What must take place soon" as shown to John by an angel are the judgment of the prostitute Babylon and the exaltation of the Bride the new Jerusalem (so Marko Jauhiainen, Ἀποκάλυψις Ἰησοῦ Χριστοῦ (Rev. 1:1): The Climax of John's Prophecy?" *TynBul* 54 [2003]: 99–117). Bauckham's thesis is the least attractive.

2 The Greek τὴν μαρτυρίαν Ἰησοῦ Χριστοῦ, *tēn martyrian Iēsou Christou* ("the testimony of Jesus Christ"), involves the same question as above—whether "Jesus Christ" is an objective or subjective genitive in relation to "witness." If the former, the sense is "the witness to Jesus Christ"; if the latter, it is "the witness received from Jesus Christ," i.e., attested by him.

3 This is the first place in the book where synoptic parallels to the Apocalypse can be noted (cf. Lk 11:28; 21:8). No fewer than twenty-five direct and indirect uses of the sayings of Jesus can be identified in the Apocalypse. See the excellent work by Vos, *Synoptic Traditions*.

B. Greetings and Doxology (1:4–8)

OVERVIEW

John proceeds to address the recipients of his book: "To the seven churches in the province of Asia" (cf. 1:11; 2:1–3:22). Almost immediately he introduces an expanded form of the Christian Trinitarian greeting that merges into a doxology to Christ (vv.5b–6) and is followed by a staccato exclamation calling attention to the return of Christ to the world (v.7). The Father concludes the greeting with assurances of his divine sovereignty.

⁴John,

To the seven churches in the province of Asia:

Grace and peace to you from him who is, and who was, and who is to come, and from the seven spirits before his throne, ⁵and from Jesus Christ, who is the faithful witness, the firstborn from the dead, and the ruler of the kings of the earth.

To him who loves us and has freed us from our sins by his blood, ⁶and has made us to be a kingdom and priests to serve his God and Father—to him be glory and power for ever and ever! Amen.

⁷Look, he is coming with the clouds,
    and every eye will see him,
even those who pierced him;
    and all the peoples of the earth will mourn because of him.
                        So shall it be! Amen.

⁸"I am the Alpha and the Omega," says the Lord God, "who is, and who was, and who is to come, the Almighty."

COMMENTARY

4 The epistolary form of address immediately distinguishes this book from all other Jewish apocalyptic works (see Introduction). None of the pseudepigraphical works contain such epistolary addresses. John writes to real, historical churches, addressing them in the same way the NT epistles are addressed. The churches to which he writes actually existed in the Roman province of Asia (the western part of present-day Turkey), as the details in chs. 2 and 3 indicate. But the question is this: Why did John address these churches and *only* these seven churches? There were other churches in Asia at the close of the first century. The NT itself refers to congregations at Troas (Ac 20:5–12), Colossae (Col 1:2), and Hierapolis (Col 4:13). There might also have been churches at Magnesia and Tralles, since Ignatius wrote to them fewer than twenty years later.

It is difficult to say why the Lord selected these seven churches. Some, especially dispensationalists, have suggested that the churches chosen were prophetic of the church ages throughout history (so Seiss, 64; the Scofield Reference Bible adopts this view in its notes). For example, Ephesus would represent prophetically the apostolic period until the Decian persecution (AD 250) followed by Smyrna, which represents the church of martyrdom extending until the time of Constantine (AD 316). After this initial agreement, however, identifications become more difficult—except for the last church. All agree that Laodicea is the final period of lukewarm apostasy. Yet there is no reason arising from the text itself to hold this prophetic view. The churches are typical of churches found in every age. If the churches were genuinely prophetic of the course of church history rather than representative in every age, those who hold to the imminent or soon return of Christ would surely have been quickly disillusioned once they realized this.

The reason seven churches were chosen and then placed in this order seems to be that seven was simply the number of completeness, and here it rounds out the literary pattern of the other sevens in the book (cf. "Structure," p. 588–89). These seven churches contained typical or representative qualities of both obedience and disobedience that are a constant reminder to all churches throughout every age (cf. 2:7, 11, 17, 29; 3:6, 13, 22; esp. 2:23). Mounce, 45, suggests that the seven may have been chosen because of some special relationship to emperor worship. But this is speculative and tends to support Mounce's preterist thesis. As for the order of their mention (1:11), it is the natural ancient travel circuit, beginning at Ephesus and arriving finally at Laodicea (see map of the area, p. 611).

"Grace and peace" are the usual epistolary greetings that represent the bicultural background of the NT—Greek ("grace," *charis*, GK *5921*) and Hebrew ("peace," *šalôm*, GK 8934; in v.4 the Greek *eirēnē*, GK *1645*). The source of blessing is described by employing an elaborate triadic formula for the Trinity:

- "from him who is, and who was, and who is to come," i.e., the Father;
- "from the seven spirits before his throne," i.e., the Holy Spirit;
- "from Jesus Christ," i.e., the Son (v.5).

Similarly there follows a threefold reference to the identity and function of Christ—"the faithful witness, the firstborn from the dead, and the ruler of the kings of the earth"—and three indications of his saving work: "who loves us and has freed us from our sins . . . , and has made us to be a kingdom and priests."

The descriptive name of the Father is "him who is [*ho ōn*], and who was [*ho ēn*], and who is to come *[ho erchomenos].*" Each name of God in the Bible is replete with revelatory significance. This particular title occurs nowhere else except in Revelation (4:8; cf. 11:17; 16:5). It is generally understood as a paraphrase for the divine name represented throughout the OT by the Hebrew tetragrammaton, YHWH. In Exodus 3:14, the LXX has *ho ōn* for the Hebrew tetragrammaton; in the LXX of Isaiah 41:4, the Lord is described as the one "who is to come." The complete combination of the three tenses does not occur elsewhere in our Bibles but can be found in a Palestinian Targum on Deuteronomy 32:39. A case can be made that John has made a literal translation here of this Aramaic Targum (cf. Trudinger, "Some Observations Concerning the Text," 87). The force of the name has been widely discussed. In 1:8 and 4:8, it is parallel with the divine name "Lord God Almighty." The tenses indicate that the same God is eternally present with his covenant people to sustain and encourage them through all the experiences of their lives.

"And from the seven spirits before his throne" seems clearly to focus symbolically on the Holy Spirit, not on angels (NASB, "Spirits"). But why "seven spirits"? Some understand John to mean the "sevenfold Spirit" in his fullness (NIV footnote; see Ladd, 24). Borrowing from the imagery of Zechariah 4, where the ancient prophet sees a lampstand with seven bowls supplied with oil from two nearby olive trees, John seems to connect the church ("lampstands," v.20) to the ministry of the Holy Spirit (3:1; 4:5; 5:6). The "seven spirits" represent the activity of the risen Christ through the Holy Spirit in and to the seven churches. This figure brings great encouragement to the churches, for it is "'not by might nor by power, but by my Spirit,' says the LORD Almighty" (Zec 4:6) that the churches serve God. Yet the figure is also a sobering one because the history of each church (chs. 2–3) is an unfolding of that church's response to the Holy Spirit—

"he who has an ear, let him hear what the Spirit says to the churches" (e.g., 2:7; so Beale, 189–90).

Mounce and Aune opt for the view that the seven spirits are perhaps "part of the heavenly entourage that has a special ministry in connection with the Lamb" (Mounce, 46–48; cf. Aune, *Revelation 1–5*, 33–34). However, to identify the seven spirits with angels is highly unlikely because (1) such reference to angels would break the symmetry of the Trinitarian address in 1:4–5 by the intrusion of an angelic greeting, and (2) "spirit(s)" in the book of Revelation refers only to the Spirit of God or to demons, with the exception of 11:11 and 13:15, neither of which refers to angels. (For further objections to Mounce's view, see F. F. Bruce, "The Spirit in the Apocalypse," in *Christ and the Spirit in the New Testament*, ed. B. Lindars and S. Smalley [Cambridge: Cambridge Univ. Press, 1973], 333–37.)

5 Finally, greetings come from the Son—"from Jesus Christ." John immediately adds three descriptive epithets about Christ and a burst of doxology to him. He is first the "faithful witness." His credibility is proved by his past earthly life of obedience; his present witness to the true condition of the churches; and the future consummation of all things in him. In the past, he was loyal to the point of death (cf. Jn 7:7; 18:37; 1Ti 6:13), as was his servant Antipas (Rev 2:13). That Christ was a reliable witness to God's kingdom and salvation—even to the point of suffering death at the hands of the religious-political establishment of his day—is an encouragement to his servants, who also are expected to be loyal to him—even to their death (2:10).

The fact that he is "the firstborn from the dead" brings further encouragement. As Christ has given his life in faithfulness to the Father's calling, so the Father has raised Christ from the dead, pledging him as the first of a great company who will follow (cf. 7:13–14). John nowhere else refers to Christ as the "firstborn" (*prōtotokos*, GK *4758*), though Paul uses the term in Romans 8:29 and Colossians 1:15, 18 (it also occurs in Heb 1:6). In Colossians 1:18, the same expression is found; it is associated with words of supreme authority or origin such as "head," "beginning" (*archē*, GK *794*; cf. Rev 3:14), and "supremacy." In Colossians 1:15, Paul refers to Christ as the "firstborn over all creation." This cannot mean that Christ was the first-created being but rather that he is the source, ruler, or origin of all creation. So for Christ to be the "firstborn" of the dead signifies not merely that he was first in time to be raised from the dead but also that he was first in importance, having supreme authority over the dead (cf. v.18). In the LXX of Psalm 89:27, the same word is used of the Davidic monarch: "I will also appoint him my firstborn, the most exalted of the kings of the earth." Rabbinic tradition believed that this reference was messianic.

The further title for Jesus, "the ruler of the kings of the earth," virtually connects John's thought with the psalm just quoted. Christ's rulership of the world is a key theme of Revelation (11:15; 17:15; 19:16). Jesus Christ is the supreme ruler of the kings of the earth. But who are the "kings of the earth" over whom he rules? John could mean emperors such as Nero and Domitian, territorial rulers such as Pilate and Herod, and their successors. In that case, John was affirming that even though Jesus is not physically present and the earthly monarchs appear to rule, in reality it is he, not they, who rules over all (6:15; 17:2). Another approach holds that Jesus rules over the defeated foes of believers, e.g., Satan, the dragon, sin, and death (1:18). A third possibility sees believers as the kings of the earth (2:26–27; 3:21; cf. 11:6). Support for this view comes from the reference both to Christ's redeeming activity in the immediate context and to believers in v.6 as a "kingdom." All three ideas are true, so it is difficult to decide which was uppermost in John's mind. We should be careful, however, not to read into

the term "king" our own concepts of power but to allow the biblical images to predominate.

The mention of the person and offices of Christ leads John to a burst of praise to his Savior: "To him who loves us . . . be glory and power." In the present, Christ is loving us. Through all the immediate distresses, persecutions, and even banishment, John is convinced that believers are experiencing Christ's continual care. Moreover, in the past Christ's love was unmistakably revealed in his atoning death, by which he purchased our release from the captivity of sin. Christ's kingly power is chiefly revealed in his ability to transform individual lives through his "blood" (i.e., his death; cf. 5:9; 7:14). Through his death on the cross, he defeated the devil, and those who follow Christ in the battle against the devil share this victory: "They overcame [the devil] by the blood of the Lamb and by the word of their testimony" (12:11).

6 This transformation simultaneously involves the induction of blood-freed sinners into Christ's "kingdom" and priesthood. Of Israel it was said that they would be a "kingdom of priests and a holy nation" (Ex 19:6; cf. Isa 61:6). The OT references and John's probably point to both a "kingdom" and "priests" rather than a "kingdom of priests" (RSV). As Israel of old was redeemed through the Red Sea and was called to be a kingdom under God and a nation of priests to serve him, so John sees the Christian community as the continuation of the OT people of God redeemed by Christ's blood and made heirs of his future kingly rule on the earth (5:10; 20:6). Furthermore, all believers are called to be priests in the sense of offering spiritual sacrifices and praise to God (Heb 13:15; 1Pe 2:5). While John sees the church as a kingdom, this does not mean it is identical with the kingdom of God. Neither do the new people of God replace the ancient Jewish people in the purpose of God (cf. Ro 11:28–29).

7 What Christ will do in the future is summed up in the dramatic cry "look, he is coming." This is a clear reference to the return of Christ (22:7, 12, 20). The preceding affirmation of Christ's rulership over the earth's kings and the Christians' share in the messianic kingdom leads to tension between the believers' actual present condition of oppression and suffering and what seems to be implied in their royal and priestly status. So the divine promise of Christ's return is given by the Father, and the response of the prophet and congregation follows in the words "so shall it be! Amen." Or we might think of Christ as saying "so shall it be!" and the prophet and the congregation as responding with "Amen" (cf. 22:20). The promise combines Daniel 7:13 and Zechariah 12:10 (taken from the Hebrew text rather than LXX, as in Jn 19:37; cf. Mt 24:30, which also refers to the coming of Christ). Daniel 7 provides a key focus for John throughout the whole book (there are no fewer than thirty-one allusions to it).

Christ's coming will be supernatural ("with the clouds") and in some manner open and known to all ("every eye"), even to those who "pierced" him, i.e., put him to death. "Those who pierced him" might be those historically responsible for his death—such as Pilate, Annas, and Caiaphas—and those Jewish leaders of the Sanhedrin who pronounced him guilty. And yet, when he comes, there will be mourning among "all the peoples of the earth." From the NT point of view, Pilate, Annas, Caiaphas, and the others were acting as representatives of all humanity in crucifying Jesus. While it is possible to see this mourning as a lament of repentance and sorrow for putting the Son of God to death, it is more likely that the mourning results from the judgment Christ brings on the world. The expression "peoples of the earth" (*phylai*, lit., "tribes"; GK *5876*) is normally used throughout the LXX and NT of the tribes of Israel (7:4–9; 21:12; cf. Mt 19:28; 24:30). John, however, uses *phylai* in a number of places to refer more broadly to the peoples of all the nations (5:9; 7:9; 11:9; 13:7; 14:6)—a usage that also seems natural here.

8 Such a stupendous promise requires more than the prophet's own signature or even Christ's "Amen." God himself speaks and, with his own signature, vouches for the truthfulness of the coming of Christ. Of the many names of God that reveal his character and memorialize his deeds, there are four strong ones in this verse: "Alpha and Omega"; "Lord God"; "who is, and who was, and who is to come"; and "the Almighty" (cf. v.4 for comments on the second title). Alpha and omega are the first and last letters of the Greek alphabet. Their mention here is similar to the "First" and "Last" in v.17 and is further heightened by the "Beginning" and the "End" in 21:6 and 22:13. Only the book of Revelation refers to God as the "Alpha and the Omega." God is the absolute source of all creation and history; nothing lies outside of him. Therefore, he is the "Lord God" of all and is continually present to his people as the "Almighty" (*pantokratōr*, lit., "the one who has his hand on everything"; GK *4120*; cf. 4:8; 11:17; 15:3; 16:7, 14; 19:6, 15; 21:22; 2Co 6:18).

NOTES

4 ᾽από (*apo*, "from") plus the nominative in the divine name presents a problem. Mussies, 93, takes the nominative as an appositional nominative and not as an instance of ᾽από with the nominative case.

5 Textual problems exist as to whether λύσαντι (*lysanti*, "freed") or λούσαντι (*lousanti*, "washed") is correct and whether ἀγαπῶντι (*agapōnti*, present tense, "loves") or ἀγαπήσαντι (*agapēsanti*, aorist tense, "loved") is the correct reading. In both cases the evidence is divided, but more diverse witnesses favor the adoption of the readings "freed" and "loves."

II. VISION OF THE SON OF MAN AMONG THE SEVEN CHURCHES OF ASIA (1:9–3:22)

A. The Son of Man among the Lampstands (1:9–20)

1. Introduction and Voice (1:9–11)

OVERVIEW

This section begins a third introduction in which the author again identifies himself as John and adds significant information about where and when the visions took place, together with their divinely appointed destination. John stresses his intimate identification with the Asian Christians and the reason for his presence on Patmos.

One of the Sporades Islands, Patmos lies about thirty-seven miles west-southwest of Miletus in the Icarian Sea. Consisting mainly of volcanic hills and rocky ground, Patmos is about ten miles long and six miles wide at the north end. It was an island used for Roman penal purposes. Tacitus (*Ann.* 3.68; 4.30; 15.71) refers to the use of such small islands for political banishment. Eusebius (*Hist. eccl.* 3.20.8–9) mentions that John was banished to the island by the emperor Domitian in AD 95 and released eighteen months later by Nerva.

> [9]I, John, your brother and companion in the suffering and kingdom and patient endurance that are ours in Jesus, was on the island of Patmos because of the word of God and the testimony of Jesus. [10]On the Lord's Day I was in the Spirit, and I heard behind me a loud voice like a trumpet, [11]which said: "Write on a scroll what you see and send it to the seven churches: to Ephesus, Smyrna, Pergamum, Thyatira, Sardis, Philadelphia and Laodicea."

COMMENTARY

9 John indicates that it was "because of the word of God and the testimony of Jesus" that he was formerly on Patmos (cf. 1:2; 6:9; 20:4). He was not there to preach that Word but because of religious-political opposition to his faithfulness to it. John sees his plight as part of God's design and says he is a partner with Christians in three things: "suffering" (ordeal, tribulation, distress, agony), "kingdom," and "patient [or faithful] endurance." John and the Asian believers share with Christ and one another the suffering or agony that comes because of faithfulness to Christ as the only true Lord and God (Jn 16:33; Ac 14:22; Col 1:24; 2Ti 3:12). Also, they share with Christ in his "kingdom" (power and rule). In one sense, they already reign (v.6), though through suffering. Yet, in another sense, they will reign with Christ in the eschatological manifestation of his kingdom (20:4, 6; 22:5). Finally, John sees the present hidden rule of Christ and his followers manifested through "patient endurance." As believers look beyond their immediate distresses and put their full confidence in Christ, they share now in his royal dignity and power. Even in the face of imprisonment, ostracism, slander, poverty, economic discrimination, hostility (both violent and nonviolent in synagogue or marketplace), disruption of the churches by false prophets, and the constant threat of death from mob violence or judicial action, the Asian believers could realize their present kingship with Christ in their faithful endurance.

Endurance is "the spiritual alchemy which transmutes suffering into royal dignity" (R. H. Charles, 1:21). It is the Christians' witness and their radical love in all spheres of life. It produces the conflict with the powers of the world, and it calls for long-suffering as the mark of Christ's kingship in their lives (2:2, 19; 3:10; 13:10; 14:12; cf., e.g., Lk 8:15; 21:19; Ro 2:7; 1Co 13:7; Col 1:11). Christ's royal power does not now crush opposition but uses suffering to test and purify the loyalty of his servants. His strength is revealed in their weakness (2Co 12:9). Christians are called, as was John, to reign now with Christ by willingly entering into the suffering resulting from conflict with the powers of this age.

10 "I was in the Spirit" describes John's experience on Patmos. The words imply being transported into the world of prophetic visions by the Spirit of God (4:2; 17:3; 21:10; cf. Eze 3:12, 14; 37:1; Ac 22:17). At least the first vision—if not the whole book of Revelation—was revealed on "the Lord's Day" (*kyriakē hēmera*). Since this is the only place in the NT where this expression is used, its identification is difficult. Paul uses *kyriakē* (GK *3258*) as an adjective in 1 Corinthians 11:20 in reference to the Lord's Supper (*kyriakon deipnon*). Some feel that John was transported into the future day of the Lord—the prophetic day of God's great judgment and the return of Christ. The major objection to this is that John does not use the common expression for the eschatological "day of the Lord" (*hēmera kyriou*). Others find a reference here to Easter Sunday and base it on the tradition reported in Jerome's commentary on Matthew 24 that Christ would return on Easter Eve.

A convincing attempt has been made to link the literary form of Revelation with the paschal (Easter) liturgy of the ancient church (cf. Shepherd, *Paschal Liturgy and the Apocalypse*). Most commentators, both ancient and modern, have, however, taken the expression to mean Sunday, the first day of the week (so W. Stott, "A Note on *kyriakē* in Rev 1:10," *NTS* 12 [1965]: 70–75). This usage occurs early in the apostolic fathers (*Did.* 14; Ignatius, *Magn.* 9). Tendencies toward recognizing Sunday as a day designated by Christ to celebrate his redemption occur even in the earlier parts of the NT (Ac 20:7; 1Co 16:2). Such a reference would bind the exiled apostle to the worshiping churches in Asia through his longing to be with them on Sunday. It is not impossible, however, that the day referred to here was an Easter Sunday.

11 The "voice" John heard could be Christ's or, more likely, that of the angel who appears frequently to John (4:1; 5:2). What John sees (visions and words) he is to write down in a papyrus scroll and send to the seven Asian churches (v.4). This writing would include the substance of the whole book, not just the first vision. (For a map of the seven churches, see p. 611.)

NOTES

9 Newman (*Rediscovering the Book of Revelation*, 15), in defending his thesis that Revelation is an anti-Gnostic document, proposes that 1:9 should be repunctuated as follows: "I John, . . . was on the island called

Patmos. On account of the Word of God and the testimony of Jesus, I was in the Spirit on the Lord's day." John's words would then "indicate that the revelation which he received was given to him while he was *in the Spirit*. This revelation would be a direct rebuttal against his Gnostic opponents, who claimed to possess revelations which came to them while they were under the influence of the Spirit" (italics his).

11 The words "I am the Alpha and Omega, the first and the last," found in the KJV, have very little MS support, though the expression is represented in vv.8, 11.

2. The Sight of the Vision (1:12–20)

OVERVIEW

Certain important literary features of John's first vision are noted:

1. Beginning with v.12, the vision extends as a unit through ch. 3. The quotation that begins in v.17 is not closed until the end of ch. 3.

2. The introductory section (1:12–20) can be divided into two parts—(1) the sevenfold features in the description of the glorified Christ (vv.12–16) and (2) the address to John (vv.17–20).

3. In this symbolic picture, the glorified Lord is seen in his inner reality that transcends his outward appearance. The sword coming out of his mouth (v.16) alerts us to this. In words drawn almost entirely from imagery used in Daniel, Ezekiel, and Isaiah of God's majesty and power, John uses hyperbole to describe the indescribable reality of the glorified Christ. These same poetic phrases reappear in the letters to the churches in chs. 2 and 3, as well as throughout the rest of the book (14:2; 19:6, 12, 15).

4. The words of Christ give his absolute authority to address the churches. And the vision (vv.12–16) leads to John's transformed understanding of Jesus as the Lord of all through his death and resurrection (vv.17–18).

[12]I turned around to see the voice that was speaking to me. And when I turned I saw seven golden lampstands, [13]and among the lampstands was someone "like a son of man," dressed in a robe reaching down to his feet and with a golden sash around his chest. [14]His head and hair were white like wool, as white as snow, and his eyes were like blazing fire. [15]His feet were like bronze glowing in a furnace, and his voice was like the sound of rushing waters. [16]In his right hand he held seven stars, and out of his mouth came a sharp double-edged sword. His face was like the sun shining in all its brilliance.

[17]When I saw him, I fell at his feet as though dead. Then he placed his right hand on me and said: "Do not be afraid. I am the First and the Last. [18]I am the Living One; I was dead, and behold I am alive for ever and ever! And I hold the keys of death and Hades.

[19]"Write, therefore, what you have seen, what is now and what will take place later. [20]The mystery of the seven stars that you saw in my right hand and of the seven golden lampstands is this: The seven stars are the angels of the seven churches, and the seven lampstands are the seven churches."

COMMENTARY

12 For the OT tabernacle, Moses constructed a seven-branched lampstand (Ex 25:31–40). Subsequently this lampstand symbolized Israel. Zechariah 4:10 records the vision of a seven-branched golden lampstand fed by seven pipes—explained to him as the "eyes of the LORD, which range throughout the earth." Thus the lampstand relates directly to the Lord himself. Since other allusions to Zechariah's vision of the lampstand appear in Revelation—e. g., "seven eyes, which are the seven spirits of God" (5:6) and the "two witnesses" that are "the two olive trees" (11:3–4)—it is logical to assume here a connection with that vision as well.

But there are problems in any strict identification. In v.20 Christ tells John that the "seven lampstands are the seven churches," and in 2:5 that it is possible to lose one's place as a lampstand through a failure to repent. Therefore, the imagery represents the individual churches scattered among the nations—churches that bear the light of the divine revelation of the gospel of Christ to the world (Mt 5:14). If Zechariah's imagery was in John's mind, it might mean that the churches, which correspond to the people of God today, are light-bearers only because of their intimate connection with Christ, the source of the light, through the power of the Holy Spirit (1:4b; 3:1; 4:5; 5:6).

13 Evidently the words "someone 'like a son of man'" are to be understood in connection with Daniel 7:13 as a reference to the heavenly Messiah, who is also human. Jesus preferred the title "Son of Man" for himself throughout his earthly ministry, though he did not deny on occasion the appropriate use of "Son of God" as well (Jn 10:36; cf. Mk 14:61). Both titles are nearly identical terms for the Messiah. The early church, however,

refrained from using "Son of Man" for Jesus except in rare instances, such as when there was some special connection between the suffering of believers and Christ's suffering and glory (e.g., Ac 7:56; Rev 14:14; cf. Richard N. Longenecker, *The Christology of Early Jewish Christianity* [London: SCM, 1970], 92).

"Dressed in a robe" begins the sevenfold description of the Son of Man. The vision creates an impression of the whole rather than of particular abstract concepts. John saw Christ as the divine Son of God in the fullest sense of that term. He also saw him as fulfilling the OT descriptions of the coming Messiah by using terms drawn from the OT imagery of divine wisdom, power, steadfastness, and penetrating vision. The long robe and golden sash were worn by the priests in the OT (Ex 28:4) and may here signify Christ as the great High Priest to the churches in fulfillment of the OT Aaronic priesthood or, less specifically, may indicate his dignity and divine authority (Eze 9:2, 11). In Sirach 45:8, Aaron is mentioned as having the symbols of authority: "the linen breeches, the long robe, and the ephod."

14 In an apparent allusion to Daniel, Christ's head and hair are described as "white like wool, as white as snow" (Da 7:9; cf. 10:5). For John, the same functions of ruler and judge ascribed to the "Ancient of Days" in Daniel's vision relate to Jesus. In Eastern countries, white hair commands respect and indicates the wisdom of years. This part of the vision may have shown John something of the deity and wisdom of Christ (cf. Col 2:3). Christ's eyes were like a "blazing fire," a detail not found in Daniel's vision of the Son of Man (Da 7) but occurring in Daniel 10:6. This simile is repeated in the letter to Thyatira (Rev 2:18) and in the vision of Christ's triumphant return and defeat of his enemies

(19:12). It may portray either his penetrating scrutiny or fierce judgment.

15 The Greek of "his feet were like bronze glowing in a furnace" (cf. 2:18) is difficult (see Notes). Christ's feet appeared like shining bronze fired to white heat in a kiln. A similar figure of glowing metal is found in Ezekiel 1:13, 27; 8:2; and Daniel 10:6. In both Ezekiel and Daniel, the fiery brightness of shining metal is one of the symbols connected with the appearance of the glory of God. Revelation 2:18–29 might imply that the simile of feet "like burnished bronze" represents triumphant judgment (i.e., treading or trampling down) of those who are unbelieving and unfaithful to the truth of Christ.

"His voice was like the sound of rushing [lit., many] waters" describes the glory and majesty of God in a way similar to that in Ezekiel (1:24; 43:2). Anyone who has heard the awe-inspiring sound of Niagara or Victoria Falls cannot but appreciate this image of God's power and sovereignty (Ps 93:4). The same figure occurs in 14:2 and 19:6 (cf. also the *Apocalypse of Ezra*, a Jewish book written about the same time or slightly earlier than Revelation; it similarly refers to the voice of God [*4 Ezra* 6:17]).

16 In the phrase "in his right hand he held seven stars," the right hand is the place of power and safety, and the "seven stars" Christ held in it are identified with the seven angels of the seven churches in Asia (v.20). This is the only detail in the vision that is identified. Why the symbolism of stars? This probably relates to the use of "angels" as those to whom the letters to the seven churches are addressed (chs. 2–3). Stars are associated in the OT and in Revelation with angels (Job 38:7; Rev 9:1) or faithful witnesses to God (Da 12:3). The first letter (that to Ephesus) includes in its introduction a reference to the seven stars (2:1), and in 3:1 they are associated closely with the "seven spirits of God."

John sees a "sharp double-edged sword" going forth from the mouth of Christ. The metaphor of a sword coming from the mouth is important for three reasons: (1) John refers to this characteristic of Christ several times (1:16; 2:12, 16; 19:15, 21); (2) he uses a rare word for sword (*rhomphaia*, GK *4855*), found only once outside Revelation (Lk 2:35); and (3) there is no scriptural parallel to the expression except in Isaiah, where it is said that the Messiah will "strike the earth with the rod of his mouth; with the breath of his lips he will slay the wicked" (Isa 11:4) and "his lips are full of wrath, and his tongue is a consuming fire" (Isa 30:27). The sword is both a weapon and a symbol of war, oppression, anguish, and political authority. But John seems to intend a startling difference in the function of this sword, since it proceeds from the mouth of Christ rather than being wielded in his hand. Christ will overtake the Nicolaitans at Pergamum and make war with them by the sword of his mouth (2:12, 16). He strikes down the rebellious at his coming with such a mouth sword (19:15, 21). The figure points definitely to divine judgment but not to the type of power wielded by the nations. Christ conquers the world through his death and resurrection, and the sword is his faithful witness to God's saving purposes. The weapons of his followers are loyalty, truthfulness, and righteousness (19:8, 14).

Finally, the face of Christ is likened to "the sun shining in all its brilliance." This is a simile of Christ's divine glory, preeminence, and victory (Mt 13:43; 17:2; cf. Rev 10:1; *1 En.* 14:21).

17–18 These verses identify Christ to John and connect the vision of the glorified Christ (vv.13–16) with his existence in history. The vision is seen in the light of the Eternal One, who identifies himself in these verses. "I fell at his feet as though dead" indicates that in the vision John actually saw a supernatural being and was stricken with trembling and fear, as had the prophets before him (Eze 1:28; Da 8:17; 10:9). Immediately Christ placed his hand on John and assured him that he would not die: "Do not be afraid" (cf. 2:10; 19:10; 22:8; Mt 17:6–7). The title "the First and the Last," which belongs to God in Isaiah 44:6 and 48:12 (where it means that he alone is God, the absolute Lord of history and the Creator), shows that in John's Christology Christ is identified with the Deity.

18 Christ is also "the Living One" in that he, like God, never changes. Probably this expression is a further elaboration of what it means to be "the First and the Last," i.e., he alone of all the gods can speak and act in the world (Jos 3:10; 1Sa 17:26; Ps 42:2; Rev 7:2). These divine qualities of his person are now linked to his earthly existence in first-century Palestine—"I was dead, and behold I am alive for ever and ever!" This passage is sufficient to counter the claim that John's view of Christ does not revolve around atonement theology. On the contrary, his whole view of Jesus and his kingdom revolves around the cross and resurrection—an interpretation that should serve to set the tone for all the visions that follow.

It was through Jesus' suffering, death, and resurrection that he won the right to have the "keys of death and Hades." Keys grant the holder access to interiors and their contents, and in ancient times the wearing of large keys was a mark of status in the community (cf. 3:7; 9:1; 20:1; 21:25). "Hades" translates the Hebrew term *šěʾôl* ("death, grave") almost everywhere in the LXX. In the NT, the word has a twofold usage: in some cases, it denotes the place of all the departed dead (Ac 2:27, 31); in others, it refers to the place of the departed wicked (Lk 16:23; Rev 20:13–14). Since Christ alone has conquered death and has himself come out of Hades, he alone can determine who will enter death and Hades and who will come out of these. He has the

"keys." For the Christian, death can only be seen as the servant of Christ.

19 John is told to "write, therefore, what you have seen." This verse presents us with an important exegetical problem concerning the sense of the words and the relationship of the three clauses: "what you have seen, what is now and what will take place later." Does Christ give John a chronological outline as a key to the visions in the book? Many think he does. If so, are there three divisions: "seen," "now," and "later"? Or are there two: "seen," i.e., "now," and "later"? In the latter case, where does the chronological break take place in the book? For others, v.19 simply gives a general statement of the contents of all the visions throughout the book as containing a mixture of the "now" and the "later" (so Caird, 26).

While no general agreement prevails, the key may lie in the middle term, "what is now." The Greek simply reads "which [things] are" (*ha eisin*). There are two possibilities. First, the verb can be taken temporally ("now"), as the NIV has done. This would refer to things that were present in John's day, e.g., matters discussed in the letters to the churches (chs. 2–3). Or second, the verb can be taken in the sense of "what they mean" (so Alford, 4:559). This later explanation agrees with John's usage of the verb *eisin* throughout the book (cf. 1:20; 4:5; 5:6, 8; 7:14; 17:12, 15). "What they are [i.e., mean]" would immediately be given in the next verse, i.e., the explanation of the mystery of the lamps and stars. The change from the plural verb *eisin* in the second term to the singular *mellei* ("will") in the third tends to distinguish the last two expressions from both being time references.

Most commentators understand the phrase "what you have seen" as referring to the first vision (1:12–16); but it may refer to the whole book, as the expression "what you see" in v.11 does. In this case, the translation could be either "what you saw, both the things that are and the things that will occur afterwards," or "what you saw, both what it means and what will occur afterwards." "What will take place later" clearly refers to the future, but to the future of what? Some have taken the similar but not identical phrase in 4:1 to mean the same as here and have rendered it, "what shall take place after these present things," i.e., after the things relating to the seven churches (chs. 2–3). This results in either the historicist view or the futurist view of chs. 4–22. But if the future is simply the future visions given to John after this initial vision, then the statement has little significance in indicating chronological sequence in the book. While v.19 may provide a helpful key to the book's plan, it by no means gives us a clear key to it (see Notes).

John is told to write down a description of the vision of Christ he has just seen, what it means, and what he will see afterward, i.e., not the end-time things but the things revealed later to him; whether they are wholly future, wholly present, or both future and present depends on the content of the vision. This leaves the question open concerning the structure of the book and its chronological progression, as John may have intended.

20 The first vision is called a "mystery" (*mystē-rion*, GK *3696*). In the NT, a "mystery" is something formerly secret but now revealed or identified. Thus John identifies the "mystery" of the harlot in ch. 17 by indicating she is the "great city" that rules over the kings of the earth (vv.7, 18; cf. 10:7). The seven stars represent the "angels of the seven churches." Who are the angels? There is no totally satisfactory answer to this question. The Greek word for angels (*angeloi*, GK *34*) occurs sixty-seven times in Revelation and in every other instance refers to heavenly messengers, though occasionally in the NT it can mean a human messenger (Lk 7:24; 9:52; Jas 2:25 [NIV, "spies"]).

A strong objection to the human messenger sense here is the fact that the word is not used this way anywhere else in apocalyptic literature. Furthermore, in early noncanonical Christian literature no historical person connected with the church is ever called an *angelos*. Mounce, 82, and others (Beckwith, Morris) identify the angels as a "way of personifying the prevailing spirit of the church" (following Swete, 22, who claims the idea comes from the Spanish Benedictine Beatus of Liebana [ca. 785]). Though this is an attractive approach to our Western way of thinking, it lacks any supporting evidence in the NT's use of the word *angelos* and especially of its use in Revelation. Therefore, this rare and difficult reference should be understood to refer to the heavenly messengers who have been entrusted by Christ with responsibility over the churches and yet who are so closely identified with them that the letters are addressed at the same time to these "messengers" and to the congregation (cf. the plural form in 2:10, 13, 23–24).

The "stars" are clearly linked in 3:1 with the seven spirits of God. Whatever may be the correct identification of the angels, the emphasis rests on Christ's immediate presence and communication through the Spirit to the churches. There is no warrant for connecting the seven stars with the seven planets or with images on Domitian's coins, as some have done. In some sense, the reference to angels in the churches shows that the churches are more than a gathering of mere individuals or a social institution; they have a corporate and heavenly character (cf. 1Co 11:10; Eph 3:10; Heb 1:14). (See H. Berkhof, *Christ and the Powers* [Scottdale, Pa.: Herald, 1962] for further insight on the angelic ministries.) That the "seven lampstands are the seven churches" not only shows that the churches are the earthly counterpart of the stars but links the vision of Christ with his authority to rule and judge his churches.

NOTES

13 C. Rowland ("The Vision of the Risen Christ in Rev. 1:13ff.: The Debt of an Early Christology to an Aspect of Jewish Angelology," *JTS* 31 [1980]: 1–11) argues that the elements in this vision are not only taken from the angelophany of Daniel 10:5–11:1 and the "son of man" image in Daniel 7:15–28, but that these texts also can be traced to a theological history within Judaism that stretches back to the call vision of the prophet Ezekiel (1:4–28). Apparently a trend developed in Jewish angelology that separated the human figure from the throne chariot in Ezekiel 8:2. Rowland suggests that Revelation 1:13–20 reflects this history and attempts to develop a Christology based on the "angel of the Lord" figure in the Old Testament.

15 While πεπυρωμένης, *pepyrōmenēs* ("glowing"), is supported by only A and C, Metzger, 663, favors the reading. This ending would modify καμίνω, *kaminō* ("furnace"), which is feminine, but Mussies, 98, says it could just as well go with χαλκολιβάνω, *chalkolibanō* ("brass").

19 W. C. vanUnnik ("A Formula Describing Prophecy," *NovT* 9 [1962–63]: 86–94) argues from early Christian and Gnostic literature, especially from the *Apocryphon of John*, that this threefold expression was a standing formula to identify the true Christian prophet. Beale, 154, has recently argued that the threefold structure is not chronological at all but instead is related to the fulfillment of Daniel 2:29, 45 and indicates that Daniel's "the latter days" (2:28, 29a, 45a NASB) and his "what must take place after these things" (2:29b, 45b NASB) are alluded to by John in 1:19 as the fulfillment of Daniel's prophecy: "John views the death and resurrection of Christ as inaugurating the long-awaited kingdom of the end times predicted in Daniel 2." However, the parallel expression ("after this") found in 4:1 seems to point more in the direction of some sequential relation to what has preceded (at least the vision sequence) and not merely to constitute a reference to the eschatological end.

B. The Letters to the Seven Churches (2:1–3:22)

OVERVIEW

The letters are more in the nature of messages than letters. Each message to an individual church was apparently also intended for the other six churches (2:7, 11, 17, etc.; esp. 2:23). By reading and comparing each similar component of all the letters, one may gain a fuller insight into the messages. Each message generally follows a common literary plan consisting of seven parts:

1. The addressee is first given. This pattern occurs in the same way at the beginning of each letter (e.g., "To the angel of the church in Ephesus write").

2. Then the speaker is mentioned. In each case, some part of the great vision of Christ and of his self-identification (1:12–20) is repeated as the speaker identifies himself (e.g., "him who holds the seven stars in his right hand and walks among the seven golden lampstands" [2:1; cf. 1:13, 16]). This identification is preceded in each case with the significant declaration "these are the words of him"—a declaration strongly reminiscent of the OT formula for introducing the words of God to the congregation of Israel.

3. Next the knowledge of the speaker is given. His is a divine knowledge. He knows intimately the works of the churches and the reality of their loyalty to him despite outward appearances. Each congregation's total life is measured against the standard of Christ's life and the works they have embraced. In two cases this assessment proves totally negative (Sardis and Laodicea). In the message to Philadelphia, the speaker designates himself as "holy and true" (3:7); to the Laodiceans he is "the faithful and true witness" (3:14). The enemy of Christ's churches is the deceiver, Satan, who seeks to undermine the churches' loyalty to Christ (2:10, 24).

4. Following his assessment of the churches' accomplishments, the speaker pronounces his verdict on their condition in such words as, "You have forsaken your first love" (2:4), or, "You are dead" (3:1). While two letters contain no unfavorable verdict (those to Smyrna and Philadelphia) and two no word of commendation (those to Sardis and Laodicea), yet since all seven letters would be sent to each church along with the entire book of Revelation (cf. 1:11), we may assume Christ intended that all the churches hear words of both commendation and blame. In the letters, all derelictions are viewed as forms of inner betrayals of a prior relation to Christ. Each congregation is responsible as a congregation for its individual members and for its leaders; each leader and each individual believer is at the same time fully responsible for himself and for the congregation. This responsibility especially involves the problem of self-deception concerning good and evil, the true and the false, in situations where they are easily confused. The evil appears under the cloak of good; the good appears as apparent evil. Christ's verdict sets before each church the true criteria for leading it out of self-deception into the truth.

5. To correct or alert each congregation Jesus issues a penetrating command. These commands further expose the exact nature of the self-deception involved. We are mistaken if we believe that the churches readily identified the heretics and heresies involved in Christ's descriptions. Because they were deceptions, they would not easily be identified; thus there is the use of OT figures such as Balaam, Jezebel, etc., to alert the churches to the deceptiveness of the error. The greater the evil, the more deceptive the cloak. In the exposition of the letters, the commands must be carefully considered so as to determine precisely the particular nature of the various errors. The thrust of the commands is not in the direction of consolation for persecuted churches. It is rather the opposite, namely, that John, like Jesus, was concerned to bring not peace but a sword.

6. Each letter contains the general exhortation "he who has an ear, let him hear what the Spirit says to the churches" (2:7, 11, etc.). Seven exactly identical exhortations occur with only the position in the letter as a variable. The words of the Spirit are the words of Christ (cf. 19:10). Actually, the commands of Christ in the letters are somewhat ambiguous and therefore require the individual and the congregation to listen also to the Spirit's voice, which accompanies the words of Jesus, if they are truly to realize the victory he considers appropriate for them. The exhortations provide both warnings about apathy and words of challenge and encouragement. Even though the words of Christ refer initially to the first-century churches located in particular places, by the Spirit's continual relevance they transcend this time limitation and speak to all the churches in every generation.

7. Finally, each letter contains a victor's promise of reward. These promises are often the most metaphorical and symbolic portions of the letters and thus in some cases present interpretative difficulties. Each is eschatological and is correlated with the last two chapters of the book. For example, "the right to eat from the tree of life, which is in the

paradise of God" (2:7) is parallel to "the tree of life" in 22:2; protection from "the second death" (2:11) finds its counterpart in 21:4: "There will be no more death," etc. Furthermore, the promises are echoes of Genesis 2–3: what was lost originally by Adam in Eden is more than regained in Christ. The expression "I will give" or "I will make" identifies Christ as the absolute source and donor of every gift. Probably we are to understand the multiple promises as different facets that combine to make up one great promise to believers, namely, that wherever Christ is, there will the overcomers be. Who are the "overcomers"? Certainly it is those who are fully loyal to Christ as his true disciples, those who are identified with him in his suffering and death (1Jn 5:4–5). Compare those who do not overcome in 21:8 with those referred to in the letters, e.g., the "cowardly" (2:10, 13), the "sexually immoral" (2:14, 20), the "idolaters" (2:14, 20), and the "liars" (2:2, 9, 20; 3:9).

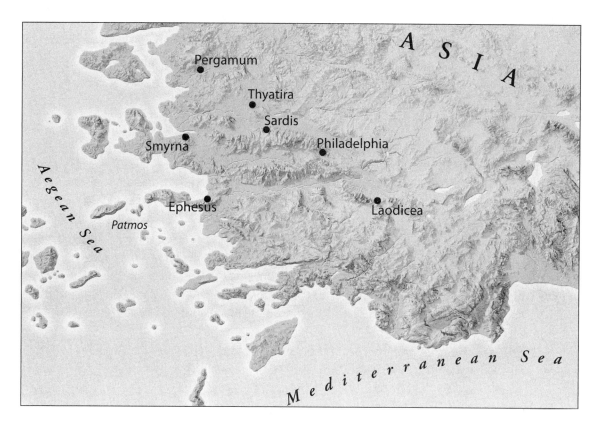

1. To Ephesus (2:1–7)

OVERVIEW

The church at Ephesus is addressed in the first letter. Ephesus was a crossroads of civilization. Politically it had become the de facto capital of the province, known as Asia's Supreme Metropolis. The Roman governor resided there. It was a "free" city, i.e., self-governed. Located on the western coast of

Asia Minor at the convergence of three great highways from north, east, and south, Ephesus was the trade center of the area. It has been called "The Vanity Fair of the Ancient World" (William Barclay, *Letters to the Seven Churches* [New York: Abingdon, 1957], 12).

Religiously, Ephesus was the center for the worship of the fertility "bee" goddess, known in Greek as "Artemis," or Romanized as "Diana" (Ac 19:24). The temple with its statue of Artemis was one of the wonders of the ancient world. Thousands of priests and priestesses were involved in her service. Many of the priestesses were dedicated to cult prostitution. (This may be related to the "practices of the Nicolaitans" in v.6.) The temple also served as a great bank for kings and merchants, as well as an asylum for fleeing criminals. To what extent the temple phenomena contributed to the general moral deterioration of the population cannot be assessed, but one of Ephesus's own citizens, the weeping philosopher Heraclitus, said that the inhabitants of the city were "fit only to be drowned and that the reason why he could never laugh or smile was because he lived amidst such terrible uncleanness" (Barclay, *Letters to the Seven Churches*, 17). The church at Ephesus was probably founded jointly by Aquila, Priscilla, and (later) Paul (Ac 18:18–19; 19:1–10). The Ephesians were cosmopolitan and transient, and their city had a history of cultural-political change; these factors may have influenced the apostasy of the congregation at Ephesus from its first love (cf. 2:4).

---

[1]"To the angel of the church in Ephesus write:

These are the words of him who holds the seven stars in his right hand and walks among the seven golden lampstands: [2]I know your deeds, your hard work and your perseverance. I know that you cannot tolerate wicked men, that you have tested those who claim to be apostles but are not, and have found them false. [3]You have persevered and have endured hardships for my name, and have not grown weary.

[4]Yet I hold this against you: You have forsaken your first love. [5]Remember the height from which you have fallen! Repent and do the things you did at first. If you do not repent, I will come to you and remove your lampstand from its place. [6]But you have this in your favor: You hate the practices of the Nicolaitans, which I also hate.

[7]He who has an ear, let him hear what the Spirit says to the churches. To him who overcomes, I will give the right to eat from the tree of life, which is in the paradise of God."

COMMENTARY

1 The speaker identifies himself by a reference to the vision of ch. 1: "him who holds the seven stars in his right hand" (cf. 1:16). These words strike both a note of reassurance, signaling Christ's strong protection and control of the church, and his vital concern. On the other hand, there is a note of warning in the description of Christ as the one who "walks [travels] among the seven golden lampstands," since he may journey to Ephesus to remove their lampstand (v.5).

2–3 The speaker's knowledge includes awareness of their activity, their discernment of evil, and their patient suffering. Their "deeds," their "hard work" (*kopos*, "wearisome toil," GK *3160*), and their "perseverance" are underlined by the phrase "you have . . . endured hardships for my name, and have not grown weary" (v.3). The Ephesian Christians did not lack serious and sustained activity, even to the point of suffering for Christ's name. Paul attributes the same threefold activity to the Thessalonians and there adds to each quality its motivating source: "faith," "love," and "hope" (1Th 1:3).

Christ also knows that doctrinal discrimination accompanies the toil and patience of the Ephesians. They "cannot tolerate wicked men." These were not the pagans in Ephesus but false brothers who "claim to be apostles but are not." It is not easy to determine precisely who these people were, what they taught, or how the church tested them. An "apostle" is one who is sent as a representative of another and bears the full authority of the sender. The word is applied first in the NT to the original circle of the Twelve (Mk 3:14; Ac 1:2, 26), who had a special place historically in the foundation of the church (Eph 2:20; Rev 21:14). But the NT further broadens this circle to include others such as Paul (Gal 1:1), Barnabas (Ac 14:14), James the brother of Jesus (Gal 1:19), and still others (cf. Ro 16:7). The name was applied to those who were authentically and specially called by Christ to be his authoritative spokesmen.

Miracles were the signs of apostolic authority (2Co 12:12; Heb 2:4), but miracles may also accompany false prophets (Mk 13:22; 2Th 2:9; 2Ti 3:8; Rev 13:13–14). Thus it was necessary to "test the spirits to see whether they are from God, because many false prophets have gone out into the world" (1Jn 4:1). Beyond their denial of Jesus as Lord, these self-proclaimed apostles also sought selfish advantage through their claims (2Co 11:5, 13; 12:11).

As to whether the authoritative function of apostles continued after the first century, the apostolic fathers are instructive. In no case do the many references to apostles in the writings of Clement of Rome, Ignatius, Barnabas, and the Shepherd of Hermas relate to any recognized apostles other than those associated with the NT. The Fathers apparently understood the special apostolic function to have ceased with the end of the apostolic era.

About fifteen years after John's writing of Revelation, Ignatius (*Eph.* 6, 7, 9, 16) wrote to the church of Ephesus and commended them for refusing to give a "home" to any heresy. Thyatira had failed (2:20), but the Ephesians had won the victory over false teachers. They had heeded Paul's earlier warning (Ac 20:28–30).

4 The speaker's verdict shows that, however much had been gained at Ephesus by resisting the false apostles, not all was well there. They had "forsaken," or "let go" (*aphiēmi*, GK *918*), their "first love." This was a serious defect. If uncorrected it would result in their loss of light bearing (v.5). The majority of commentators take the first love to refer to the original Christian love the Ephesians had for one another. Paul's exhortation to the Ephesian elders to "help the weak" (Ac 20:35) and the warm commendation he gives them in their early years for their fervent love for one another (Eph 1:15) may lend support to this view.

Other commentators see the "first love" as a reference to the inner devotion to Christ that characterized their earlier commitment, like the love of a newly wedded bride for her husband (John R. W. Stott, *What Christ Thinks of the Church* [Grand Rapids: Eerdmans, 1958], 27; Alford, 4:563). This interpretation is supported by the fact that the letters to the other churches reveal problems of inner betrayal to Christ. Neither view necessarily eliminates the other. Loving devotion to Christ can be lost in the midst of active service, and certainly no amount of orthodoxy can make up for a failure to love one another. "First" (*prōtos*, GK *4755*) love would suggest that they still loved, but with a quality and intensity unlike that of their initial love.

5 The speaker's command further exposes the problem and offers a way to correct the fault. The imperatives are instructive: "Remember"; "Repent and do." The Ephesians are called to reflect on their earlier works of fervent love (as are the Sardians in 3:3), to look in comparison at the present situation, to ponder how far they have fallen from their former devotion and enthusiasm, to humbly "repent" (totally change) before God, and to do the former works motivated by love. These imperatives are all part of a single action designed to keep the Ephesians from the judgment of Christ, which would effectively remove them as his representatives in the world.

How many churches today stand at this same crossroad? Do we sense the importance to Christ of not only honoring his name by our true confession but also reflecting his life by our loving relationship to others? This threat of loss of light bearing (or witness) likely applies equally to the other four churches, to whom a similar exhortation to repent is given (Pergamum, Thyatira, Sardis, and Laodicea).

6 Christ adds a further commendation concerning the Ephesians' hatred of the practices of the Nicolaitans (cf. 2:15)—a hatred directed at the practices of the Nicolaitans, not the people themselves (cf. Ps 139:21). It is difficult to determine exactly who the Nicolaitans were and what they taught. Etymologically the name means "to conquer [or consume, *nikaō*, GK *3771*] the people [*laos*, GK *3295*]." Did they call themselves by this name, or is it a derogatory title Christ applied to them? The close association of the name with the Balaamites in 2:14–15 may suggest either identity with this group or similarity to their teachings (see comments at 2:14–15).

Information about the Nicolaitans is limited, ambiguous, and based on John's references here in Revelation. Irenaeus (*Haer.* 3.11.7) claims that John wrote the gospel to thwart the teaching of the Gnostic Cerinthus, whose error was similar to the earlier offshoot of the same kind of teaching known as Nicolaitanism (cited in Theron, *Evidence of Tradition*, 73). Eusebius (*Hist. eccl.* 3.29.1) mentions that the Nicolaitans lasted only a short time. Seeing the sect as a heresy would agree with the reference in 2:14 and 2:20, which warns against mixing Christian faith with idolatry and cult prostitution. Elisabeth Schüssler Fiorenza ("Apocalyptic and Gnosis in the Book of Revelation," *JBL* 92 [1973]: 570) identifies the group as Gnostics and summarizes the problem well: "The Nicolaitans are according to Revelation a Christian group within the churches of Asia Minor and have their adherents even among the itinerant missionaries and the prophetic teachers of the community. They claim to have insight into the divine or, more probably, into the demonic. They express their freedom in libertine behavior, which allows them to become part of their syncretistic pagan society and to participate in the Roman civil religion" (see also Newman, *Rediscovering the Book of Revelation*, 11–30, who sees the entire book of Revelation as an anti-Gnostic polemic rather than a political-religious persecution document). Others understand the Nicolaitans as Christians who still showed devotion to the emperor by burning incense to his statue or image (so William M. Ramsay, *The Letters to the Seven Churches of Asia* [London: Hodder & Stoughton, 1904], 300–301; cf. Aune, *Revelation 1–5*, 148–49). See also the letters to Pergamum and Thyatira.

7 On the general exhortation and the meaning of "overcomes," see the Overview to this section. The overcomer is promised access to the "tree of life, which is in the paradise of God." The "tree of life" is first mentioned in Genesis 2:9 as one of the many trees given to Adam and Eve for food; it became off-limits after their fall into sin (Ge 3:22, 24). It is last mentioned in Revelation 22:19.

Rabbinic and Jewish apocalyptic works mention that the glorious age of the Messiah would be a restoration to Edenic conditions before the fall (see also Isa 51:3; Eze 36:35; cf. Eze 28:13; 31:8–9). Jewish thought joined the concepts of the renewed city of God, the tree of life, and the paradise of God. The apocalyptic book the *Testament of Levi* (18:10–11) contains a promise that God (or Messiah) "shall open the gates of Paradise, and shall remove the threatening sword against Adam, and he shall give the saints to eat from the tree of life, and the spirit of holiness shall be on them."

"Paradise" (*paradeisos*, GK *4137*) is a Persian loanword meaning "park" or "garden." The LXX uses it to translate the Hebrew expression the "garden" of Eden (Ge 2:8–10). John seems to reinterpret the Jewish idea of paradise. First, Jesus Christ is the restorer of the lost paradise (22:1–4, 14). He gives access to the tree of life. Paradise means to be with him in fellowship rather than the idea of a hidden paradise with its fantastic sensual delights (*TDNT* 6:772). The tree of life conveys symbolically the truth of eternal life or the banishment of death and suffering (22:2). Those at Ephesus who truly follow Christ in deep devotion and thus experience the real victory of Christ will share the gift of eternal life that he alone gives.

NOTES

1 Of all the apocalyptic literature (Jewish and Christian), only Revelation is framed as a letter (Aune, *Revelation 1–5*, 40). In addition to Ramsay's and Barclay's work on the seven churches, see also Otto E. A. Meinardus, *St. John of Patmos and the Seven Churches of the Apocalypse* (Athens, Greece: Lyeabettus, 1974); Meinardus, "The Christian Remains of the Seven Churches of the Apocalypse," *BA* 37 (1974): 69–82; Minear, *I Saw a New Earth*; R. C. Trench, *Commentary on the Epistles to the Seven Churches in Asia: Revelation II and III* (New York: Scribner's, 1862); Stott, *What Christ Thinks of the Church*. Two very detailed and accurate treatments of the historical interpretation and archaeological research regarding the cities of the seven churches, with extensive bibliographies, are Edwin Yamauchi's *Archaeology of New Testament Cities in Western Asia Minor* (Grand Rapids: Baker, 1980) and especially Colin Hemer's *The Letters to the Seven Churches of Asia in Their Local Setting* (JSNTSup 11; Sheffield: JSOT Press, 1986). The two recent volumes of Roland H. Worth are excellent sources (*The Seven Cities of the Apocalypse and Greco-Asian Culture* [New York: Paulist, 1999] and *The Seven Cities of the Apocalypse and Roman Culture* [New York: Paulist, 1999]).

2. To Smyrna (2:8–11)

OVERVIEW

Smyrna (modern Izmir) lay almost due north of Ephesus at a distance of about forty miles. The city was exceptionally beautiful and large (population ca. 200,000) and ranked with Ephesus and Pergamum as "First of Asia." Known as the birthplace of Homer, it was also an important seaport that commanded the mouth of the Hermus River valley. Smyrna was a wealthy city where learning, especially in the sciences and medicine, flourished. An old city (dating as far back as the third millennium BC) allegedly founded by a mythical Amazon who gave her name to it, Smyrna repeatedly sided with Rome in different periods of her history and thus earned special privileges as a free city and assize (self-governed) town under Tiberius and successive emperors. Among the beautiful paved streets traversing it from east to west was the "Golden Street," with the temples to Cybele and Zeus at either end and along which were temples to Apollo, Asclepius, and Aphrodite.

Smyrna was also a center of emperor worship, having won the privilege (over eleven other cities) from the Roman Senate in AD 23 of building the first temple in honor of Tiberius. Under Domitian (AD 81–96) emperor worship became compulsory for every Roman citizen on threat of death. Once each year a citizen had to burn incense on the altar to the godhead of Caesar, after which he was issued a certificate. Barclay (*Seven Churches*, 29] quotes a request for such a certificate, and the certificate itself:

> To those who have been appointed to preside over the sacrifices, from Inares Akeus, from the village of Theoxenis, together with his children Aias and Hera, who reside in the village of Theadelphia, we have always sacrificed to the gods, and now, in your presence, according to the regulations, we have sacrificed and offered libations, and tasted the sacred things, and we ask you to give us a certification that we have done so. May you fare well.
>
> We, the representatives of the Emperor, Serenos and Hermas, have seen you sacrificing.

Such an act was probably considered more an expression of political loyalty than religious worship, and the only thing a citizen had to do was burn a pinch of incense and say, "Caesar is Lord [*kyrios*, GK 3261]." Yet most Christians refused to do this. Perhaps nowhere was life for a Christian more perilous than in this city of zealous emperor worship. About sixty years later (ca. 156), Polycarp was burned alive at the age of eighty-six as the "twelfth martyr in Smyrna" (*IDB* 4:393). His words have echoed through the ages: "Eighty-six years have I served Christ, and he has never done me wrong. How can I blaspheme my King who saved me?" (cited in Eusebius, *Hist. eccl.* 4.15.25). A large and hostile Jewish community at Smyrna was prominent in Polycarp's death and no doubt troubled the church also in John's day (2:9; cf. Barclay, *Seven Churches*, 31). A modern-day parallel to the predicament of Christians under Roman emperor worship is seen in the Japanese occupation of Korea in 1937–40, when Christians were ordered to worship at the Shinto shrines. Many refused and were imprisoned and tortured (see Han Woo Keun, *History of Korea*, ed. G. K. Muntz [Seoul: Eul-Woo, 1970], 496).

Concerning the founding of the church in Smyrna, we have no information other than this letter.

8"To the angel of the church in Smyrna write:
These are the words of him who is the First and the Last, who died and came to life again. 9I know your afflictions and your poverty—yet you are rich! I know the slander of those who say they are Jews and are not, but are a synagogue of Satan. 10Do not be afraid of what you are about to suffer. I tell you, the devil will put some of you in prison to test you, and you will suffer persecution for ten days. Be faithful, even to the point of death, and I will give you the crown of life.
11He who has an ear, let him hear what the Spirit says to the churches. He who overcomes will not be hurt at all by the second death."

COMMENTARY

8 The speaker identifies himself as "him who is the First and the Last, who died and came to life again" (see comments at 1:17–18). The "First and Last" might remind those suffering persecution and rejection from their countrymen (vv.9–10) that the one they belong to is the Creator and the Lord of history. He is in control, regardless of appearances of evil. Ramsay (*Seven Churches*, 269–70) suggests that the term may allude by contrast to Smyrna's claim to be the "first" of Asia in beauty and loyalty to the emperor. But Christians at Smyrna were concerned with him who was truly first in everything.

He who is "the First and the Last" is also the one "who died" (lit., "became a corpse") and "came to life again." To a congregation where imprisonment and death impend, the prisoner who died and came back to life again can offer the crown of life to other executed prisoners and protect them from the second death (vv.8, 10–11). There might also be an allusion here to the history of the city of Smyrna, which had been destroyed in the seventh century BC and rebuilt in the third century BC (see Ramsay, *Seven Churches*, 269; C. J. Cadoux, *Ancient Smyrna* [Oxford: Blackwell, 1938], esp. 228–366).

9 The speaker's knowledge is threefold. First, he knows their "afflictions" (*thlipsis*, GK *2568*)—a word later translated "persecution" (v.10). Second, he knows their "poverty"—which can only mean material poverty because the speaker (Christ) immediately adds, "Yet you are rich" (toward God). Why was this church so poor in such a prosperous city? We do not know. Perhaps the high esteem of emperor worship in the city produced economic sanctions against Christians who refused to participate. In Smyrna, economic pressure may have been the first step toward persecution. Even today, for Christians to be loyal to their Lord can sometimes

entail economic loss (cf. 3:17). Third, the risen Lord knows "the slander of those who say they are Jews and are not, but are a synagogue of Satan" (cf. 3:9).

So who are these Jews? One view is that this group involved non-messianic Jews who opposed Christians. From this perspective, certain Jews used malicious untruths (NASB, "slander") to incite persecution against the impoverished saints in Smyrna. They "say they are Jews but are not" shows that even though these persons claimed descent from Abraham, they were not his true descendants because they did not have faith in Christ, the "Seed" of Abraham (Gal 3:16, 29). These unbelieving and hostile Jews probably viewed the Jewish Christians at Smyrna as heretics of the worst sort, deserving ridicule and rejection. Here the question of whether Christians in general were now the "true" Jews or whether it is those Jews in Smyrna who became Christians who are the "true" Jews is debatable (see comments at 7:4).

Another understanding is to see these Jews as professing Christians who by following the teaching of the Nicolaitans ate the sacrificed food to idols and were guilty of giving worship to pagan gods. As such they were really not true Jews but apostate Jews (cf. John W. Marshall, *Parables of War: Reading John's Jewish Apocalypse* [ESCJ 10; Waterloo, Ont.: Wilfrid Laurier Univ. Press, 2001], 132–34). The opposition is then not between Jews and Christians but between true Jews (i.e., Christians) and false Jews (i.e., Christians such as Jezebel [2:20], who worshiped pagan gods by eating food sacrificed to idols). I find this view more persuasive than the traditional understanding.

"But are of the synagogue of Satan" reveals for the first time in Revelation the ultimate source of the persecution of Christians, namely, Satan. Many further references to the archenemy of the followers of Christ are found throughout the book (2:13; 3:9; 9:11; 12:9–10, 12; 13:4; 20:2, 7, 10). In fact, he is one of the principal actors in the apocalyptic drama. While Satan is the author of persecution, and wicked persons are his instruments, God remains sovereign in that he will give "the crown of life" to those who are "faithful, even to the point of death" (v.10).

10 The speaker's command immediately follows, since no word of verdict or fault is spoken of. The prospect of further and imminent suffering may have made the believers at Smyrna fearful: "Do not be afraid of what you are about to suffer" (lit., "Stop being afraid . . ."). The risen Christ reveals that some of them will be imprisoned by the devil in order to test them, and they will have ten days of persecution. Who will do this—whether Jew or pagan—is not stated. The testing will show where their true loyalty lies. For a faithful and suffering church, Christ offers further trial and suffering, even "to the point of death." "Ten days" may denote ten actual days or constitute a Semitism for an indeterminate but comparatively short period of time (cf. Ne 4:12; Da 1:12). In the first-century Roman world, prison was usually not punitive but the prelude to trial and execution; hence the words "be faithful, even to the point of death."

For those who would face martyrdom out of loyalty to Christ, there was to be a "crown of life" given by Christ himself. Those at Smyrna would be familiar with the term "the crown of Smyrna," which no doubt alluded to the beautiful skyline formed around the city by the "hill Pagos, with the stately public buildings on its rounded sloping sides" (Ramsay, *Seven*

Churches, 256). The "crown" usually referred to a garland of flowers worn chiefly in the worship of pagan gods such as Cybele or Bacchus, who was pictured on coins with a crown of battlements. Faithful servants of the city appeared on coins with laurel wreaths on their heads (Barclay, *Seven Churches*, 39). As the patriots of Smyrna were faithful to Rome and to their crown city, so Christ's people are to be faithful unto death to him who will give them the imperishable crown of life (Jas 1:12; 1Pe 5:4).

11 The general exhortation to all the churches is identical to the parallel passages in the other letters ("he who has an ear . . ."). For those who overcome, the promise is that they "will not be hurt at all by the second death." Death was a real possibility for these believers. But greater than the fear of physical death should be the fear of God's eternal judgment (Lk 12:4–5). The "second death" is a well-known targumic expression, but it does not occur elsewhere in Jewish literature. Moses prays, "Let Reuben live in this world, and not die in the second death, in which death the wicked die in the world to come" (paraphrase of Dt 33:6 found in the Paris MS 110; cited by M. McNamara, *Targum and Testament* [Grand Rapids: Eerdmans, 1962], 148). Even though death was the outcome of Adam's sin, in Christ there is a complete reversal for humankind (Ge 2:16–17; Ro 5:15–19). Since the messianic believers at Smyrna were under attack by some in the Jewish community, it was reassuring indeed to hear the Lord himself say that his followers would not be harmed by the second death, i.e., the lake of fire (20:14; 21:8).

3. To Pergamum (2:12–17)

OVERVIEW

The inland city of Pergamum lay about sixty-five miles north of Smyrna along the fertile valley of the Caicus River. Pergamum held the official honor of being the provincial capital of Roman Asia, though this honor was also claimed by Ephesus and Smyrna. Among its notable features were its beauty and wealth, its library of nearly 200,000 volumes (second only to the library of Alexandria); its famous sculpture; its temples to Dionysus, Athena, Asclepius, and Demeter, along with the three temples to the emperor cult; its great altar to Soter Zeus; and its many palaces. The two main religions seem to have been the worship of Dionysus, the god of the royal kings symbolized by the bull, and Asclepius, the savior god of healing, represented by the snake (Ramsay, *Seven Churches*, 284). This latter feature made Pergamum the "Lourdes of the ancient world" (Charles, 1:60). Tradition also records that in Perga-

mum, King Eumenes II (197–159 BC) planned to build a library to rival the one in Alexandria. Ptolemy Epiphanes of Egypt (205–182 BC) took action to stop this venture by cutting off the export of papyrus sections—an embargo that forced Eumenes to develop vellum or parchment (*pergamēnē*, "from Pergamum"), a writing material made from animal skins. Josephus (*Ant.* 14.247 [10.22]) mentions a Jewish community at Pergamum. Recent excavations at Pergamum are reported in Helmut Koester, ed. *Pergamon, Citadel of the Gods* (HTS 46; Harrisburg, Pa.: Trinity, 1998).

¹²"To the angel of the church in Pergamum write:

These are the words of him who has the sharp, double-edged sword. ¹³I know where you live—where Satan has his throne. Yet you remain true to my name. You did not renounce your faith in me, even in the days of Antipas, my faithful witness, who was put to death in your city—where Satan lives.

¹⁴Nevertheless, I have a few things against you: You have people there who hold to the teaching of Balaam, who taught Balak to entice the Israelites to sin by eating food sacrificed to idols and by committing sexual immorality. ¹⁵Likewise you also have those who hold to the teaching of the Nicolaitans. ¹⁶Repent therefore! Otherwise, I will soon come to you and will fight against them with the sword of my mouth.

¹⁷He who has an ear, let him hear what the Spirit says to the churches. To him who overcomes, I will give some of the hidden manna. I will also give him a white stone with a new name written on it, known only to him who receives it."

COMMENTARY

12 The speaker identifies himself as "him who has the sharp, double-edged sword" (see comments at 1:16; cf. Isa 49:2). In dealing with the congregation at Pergamum, divided by deceptive teaching, the risen Lord will use this sword to fight against the Balaamites and the Nicolaitans (v.16). It is interesting to note that Pergamum was a city to which Rome had given the rare power of capital punishment (*ius gladii*), which was symbolized by the

sword. The Christians in Pergamum were thus reminded that, though they lived under the rule of an almost unlimited *imperium*, they were citizens of another kingdom—that of him who needs no other sword than that of his mouth (cf. Caird, 38).

13 The speaker's knowledge is searching. He knows they live in a hostile and difficult place "where Satan has his throne." This certainly refers to the fact that Pergamum was a center for worship of the pagan gods, especially the emperor cult. The first temple in the empire was established in honor of Augustus in AD 29 at Pergamum because it was the administrative capital of Asia. In succeeding years the city boasted of being the official *neōkoros* ("temple sweeper") of the "temple where Caesar was worshiped" (Barclay, *Seven Churches*, 45). Others see the reference to the altar of savior Zeus or the center of worship of Asclepius, the snake god of healing. Pergamum was a center of idolatry; and to declare oneself a Christian who worships the one true God and Savior Jesus Christ would certainly provoke hostility.

Furthermore, the risen Lord knew their loyalty to him in all that he is revealed to be ("my name"), even when "Antipas, my faithful witness ... was put to death in [their] city." Nothing further is known about Antipas than the meaning of his name—"against all." The proximity of the name "Satan" before and after Antipas in v.13 makes it virtually certain that his death was instigated by the enmity of pagans in Pergamum. He may have been the first or most notable of martyrs. Christ pays this hero of the faith a noble tribute: "faithful witness"—words that John applies to Christ himself in 1:5. Satan tries to undermine loyalty to Christ by persecution; Christ strengthens this loyalty by commending those who are true to him and by exposing those who are deceitful.

14–15 The speaker's verdict reveals that the church in Pergamum was divided. Some had followed Antipas and did not deny Christ's name or his faith (v.13). Others held to the teaching and practice of the Balaamites and Nicolaitans that Christ hates (v.6). Since the name "Balaam" can mean "master of the people" (Heb. *baʿalʿam*), which is equivalent in meaning to "Nicolaitans," and since they are mentioned together in this letter, both groups may be closely related (see Notes, v.15). In fact, the error in the church at Thyatira through the teaching of the woman Jezebel may also be similar to this one. In that letter and this one, the more deadly effects of the error are described as "eating food sacrificed to idols and by committing sexual immorality" (2:14, 20).

The OT names "Balaam" and "Jezebel" serve to alert the church community to the insidious nature of the teaching that was not until now recognized as overtly evil. Since Satan's chief method is deception, his devices are not known until they are clearly pointed out. Christ exposes error here by identifying the false teaching in Pergamum with clear-cut evil such as that of Balaam and Jezebel. Balak, king of Moab, could not succeed in getting the venial prophet Balaam to curse Israel directly. But Balaam devised a plan whereby the daughters of the Moabites would seduce the Israelite men and lead them to sacrifice to their god Baal and worship him (Nu 25:1–5; 31:16; cf. 2Pe 2:15; Jude 11). So God's judgment fell on Israel because of fornication and idolatry. What Balak was not able to accomplish directly, he did through Balaam's deception. While the Ephesians recognized the Nicolaitan error (v.6), apparently Pergamum and Thyatira were deceived by it; it was an unconscious subversion. What Satan could not accomplish at Smyrna or Pergamum through intimidation, suffering, and death from outside the church, he achieved from within.

The combination of "food sacrificed to idols" with "sexual immorality" may refer to the common practice of participating in the sacrificial meal of the pagan gods (cf. 1Co 10:19–22) and indulging in sexual intercourse with temple priestesses in cult prostitution. This is the more normal way to understand the term "sexual immorality" in the context of the pagan gods. Some feel, however, that the term refers to spiritual unfaithfulness and apostasy from Christ (cf. Isa 1:21; Eze 23:37). But the prevalence of sexual immorality in first-century pagan society makes it entirely possible that some Christians at Pergamum were still participating in the holiday festivities and saw nothing wrong in indulging in the "harmless" table in the temples by eating known sacrificial food, and the sexual excitement everyone else was enjoying (cf. 1Jn 5:21). Will Durant (*The Story of Civilization: Life of Greece* [New York: Simon and Schuster, 1939], 75, 185) made the following observation on the pagan festivities:

> At the center and summit of [each Greek] city was the shrine of the city god; participation in the worship of the god was the sign, the privilege, and the requisite of citizenship. In the spring, the Greek cities celebrated the Athesterion, or feast of flowers, a three-day festival to Dionysus [a chief deity at Pergamum] in which wine flowed freely and everybody was more or less drunk. At the end of March came the great Dyonysia, a widely observed series of processional and plays accompanied by general revelry. At the beginning of April, various cities in Greece celebrated [Aphrodite's] great festival, the Aphrodisia; and on that occasion, for those who cared to take part, sexual freedom was the order of the day.

16 The speaker's command includes both a call to the whole congregation to repent and a special threat to the heretical members if they do not repent. Since those who did not indulge in these things tolerated their practice by some of the church's members, they along with the guilty needed to repent. If those at Pergamum will not heed the word of Christ's warning, that word from his mouth will become a "sword" to fight against the disloyal. (Curiously, Balaam himself was slain by the "sword" [Nu 31:8].) The idolatry of Ephraim was to be punished similarly: "Therefore I cut you in pieces with my prophets, I killed you with the words of my mouth" (Hos 6:5). The words "I will soon come to you" should be understood as a coming "against" the congregation in judgment, as in v.5, and not as a reference to Christ's second coming.

17 The promise to the overcomer includes three difficult symbols: "hidden manna," "a white stone," and "a new name." The "hidden manna" is reminiscent of the manna hidden in the ark of the covenant by Moses (Ex 16:33–34; Heb 9:4). Since Moses' pot of manna was designed to remind the Israelites of God's grace and faithfulness in the wilderness (Ps 78:24), there may be a similar thought here. In apocalyptic Jewish teaching, however, the messianic era will see the restoration of the hidden wilderness manna: "And it shall come to pass at that self-same time (in the days when the Messiah comes) that the treasury of manna shall again descend from on high, and they will eat of it in those years" (*2 Bar.* 29:8; *Sib Or.* 7:149). To those at Pergamum who refused the banquets of the pagan gods, Christ will give the manna of his great banquet of eternal life in the kingdom (Jn 6:47–58).

The "white stone" is a puzzle. It has been thought of in relation to voting pebbles, an inscribed invitation to a banquet, a victory symbol, an amulet, or a counting pebble. It seems best to link the stone to the thought of the manna and see it as an allusion to an invitation that entitled its bearer to attend one of the pagan banquets.

The "new name . . . known only to him who receives it" is either the name of Christ himself, now hidden from the world but to be revealed in the future as the most powerful of names (3:12; 14:1), or the believer's new name or changed character through redemption (Isa 62:2; 65:15). J. B. Pritchard (*Ancient Near Eastern Texts* [3d ed.; Princeton, N.J.: Princeton Univ. Press, 1969], 12) cites an Egyptian text concerning the goddess Isis, who was plotting to learn the secret name of the supreme god Re to gain his hidden power for herself. The one who knew the hidden name received the power and status of the god who revealed it. Hence the name was jealously guarded by the god. This background would fit the context here in Revelation; to Christians tempted to compromise their loyalty to Christ to gain the favor of the pagan gods, Christ generously offers himself and the power of his name so that those who have faith in him may overcome.

NOTES

13 The reading καὶ ὅπου ὁ θρόνος τοῦ Σατανᾶ, *kai hopou ho thronos tou Satana* ("even the throne of Satan"), in the TR and reflected by the KJV seems warranted on good MS evidence (046 plus many late MSS). Καὶ (*kai*, "even") modifies the sense slightly by broadening the faithfulness of those in Pergamum beyond Antipas's time. Copyists probably omitted the word, not recognizing its ascensive use in the sentence (Metzger [1971 ed.], 733).

Peter Wood ("Local Knowledge in the Letters of the Apocalypse," *ExpTim* 73 [1962]: 264) has argued that the reference to Satan's throne may be "topographical" rather than merely religious: "The actual shape of the city-hill towered, as it still does, like a giant throne above the plain."

15 The TR has ὅ μισῶ, *ho misō* ("which I hate"), instead of ὁμοίως, *homoiōs* ("likewise"). However, *homoiōs* agrees with οὕτως, *houtōs* ("also, in this way"), to call attention to the strong similarity of the two teachings—possibly to imply their identity. The sentence might then read, "In fact, you have people there who similarly hold the teaching of the Nicolaitans."

4. To Thyatira (2:18–29)

OVERVIEW

On the inland route about forty-five miles due east of Pergamum was the city of Thyatira. Although not a great city, it was nevertheless important because of commerce in wool, linen, apparel, dyed stuffs, leatherwork, tanning, and excellent bronzework. Associated with its commerce was an extensive trade guild or labor union network, which must have played a prominent role in the social, political, economic, and religious life of the city. Each guild had its own patron deity, feasts, and seasonal festivities that included sexual revelries. Religiously the city was unimportant, though worship of Apollo and Artemis (Diana) was prominent. Acts 16:14 mentions that Lydia came from the Jewish settlement at Thyatira. She was a distributor of garments made of the purple dye substance known as "Turkey red" and no doubt a member of the dyers' guild. It has been suggested that some of Paul's converts at Ephesus went out and evangelized Thyatira (Ac 19:10).

18"To the angel of the church in Thyatira write:

These are the words of the Son of God, whose eyes are like blazing fire and whose feet are like burnished bronze. 19I know your deeds, your love and faith, your service and perseverance, and that you are now doing more than you did at first.

20Nevertheless, I have this against you: You tolerate that woman Jezebel, who calls herself a prophetess. By her teaching she misleads my servants into sexual immorality and the eating of food sacrificed to idols. 21I have given her time to repent of her immorality, but she is unwilling. 22So I will cast her on a bed of suffering, and I will make those who commit adultery with her suffer intensely, unless they repent of her ways. ²³I will strike her children dead. Then all the churches will know that I am he who searches hearts and minds, and I will repay each of you according to your deeds. ²⁴Now I say to the rest of you in Thyatira, to you who do not hold to her teaching and have not learned Satan's so-called deep secrets (I will not impose any other burden on you): ²⁵Only hold on to what you have until I come.

²⁶To him who overcomes and does my will to the end, I will give authority over the nations—

²⁷'He will rule them with an iron scepter;
　　he will dash them to pieces like pottery'—

just as I have received authority from my Father. ²⁸I will also give him the morning star. ²⁹He who has an ear, let him hear what the Spirit says to the churches."

COMMENTARY

18 The speaker of this fourth letter—the longest of the seven—identifies himself as "the Son of God, whose eyes are like blazing fire and whose feet are like burnished bronze" (see comments at 1:14–15). The expression "Son of God" appears only here in the book. It is a designation for the Messiah and is almost equivalent to the more frequently used title "Son of Man"; it probably anticipates the quotation from the messianic Psalm 2 in v.27, which implies the term. But the name might also have captured the attention of those who were enticed by the emperor cult into calling Caesar the Son of God. That Christ's eyes are here described as blazing fire might be an allusion to the sun god, Apollo, worshiped at Thyatira. More likely, however, it refers to his penetrating discernment of the false prophetess Jezebel (v.23). The feet of Christ, which are like burnished bronze, would no doubt have special significance to the bronze-workers at Thyatira.

19 The speaker's knowledge of the Thyatirans' works is essentially twofold: he knows (1) their love and (2) their faithfulness. Their love manifests itself in "service," and their faithfulness in "perseverance"

during trial. Their present state reflects outstanding progress, but there is a perilous flaw in the church there.

20 The speaker's verdict reveals that the congregation had allowed a woman prophetess (a false one, according to Christ's assessment) to remain in the church and to continue to teach the saints to indulge in "sexual immorality" and to "eat food sacrificed to idols." The genuine gift of prophecy was highly respected in the early church. Along with apostles, teachers, and elders, prophets were often elevated to leadership (1Co 12:28; Eph 4:11). Women also received the genuine gift of prophecy (Lk 2:36; Ac 21:9; 1Co 11:5). Prophets generally brought direct revelation from God in the form of teaching, as well as occasional predictions of the future (Ac 11:27). Tests for a true prophet, as for the true apostle (Rev 2:2), were available but often difficult to apply.

This supposedly Christian woman at Thyatira had claimed to be a "prophetess," gifted as such by the Holy Spirit. She must have been elevated to prominence in the church because of her unusual gifts. But only a small minority saw through her pious deception (v.24); the rest either followed her or ignored her views without objecting to her presence in the church. In order to expose her true character, she is labeled "Jezebel"—the name of the Canaanite wife of Israel's King Ahab. Jezebel had not only led Ahab to worship Baal but through Ahab had promulgated her teachings of idolatry throughout all Israel (1Ki 16:31–33; 2Ki 9:22).

We must not, however, press the similarity too far. As this wicked and deceptive OT woman led Israel astray and persecuted the true prophets of God, so this woman at Thyatira was enticing the servants of God to abandon their exclusive loyalty to Christ. Her teaching was no doubt similar to that of the Nicolaitans and Balaamites at Ephesus and Pergamum. While most commentators prefer to see the "sexual immorality" as spiritual adultery (i.e., idolatry), the possibility of cultic fornication should not be ruled out for reasons cited above (v.14). The distinction between the woman and those who follow her (v.22) may argue against the view that she is symbolic of a group in the church, unless the "woman" represents the false prophets and her "children" are those who follow the teaching. In 2 John the "chosen lady" is probably a reference to the faithful congregation, while "her children" refers to individuals in the congregation who represent her.

21–22 Christ's verdict continues with his strongest accusation directed against not Jezebel's perversion, serious as that is, or even against her successful deception of fellow Christians, but against her refusal to repent. Although Christ has dealt with her over a period of time, she will not change her ways or her thinking. The Lord, therefore, will judge Jezebel by two swift acts. She will be "hurled" (NIV, "cast") into a bed, and her children will be put to death. The "bed," or "couch" (*klinē*, GK *3109*), can mean a bed used for resting, for guild banqueting, or for sickness. Ramsay (*Seven Churches*, 352) adopts the banqueting sense and relates it to the idol-feast

couches. Others suggest a bed of sickness or suffering, seen as an act of God's visitation or judgment. On a bed she sinned, on a bed she will suffer; and those who committed adultery with her will also suffer intensely.

As in the case of Jezebel, Christ's strongest threat to the offenders is not in regard to their sin, serious as that is, but to their reluctance to repent. The Lord is walking among his churches. He judges evil, but he also offers deliverance to those who have fallen, if they repent and stop doing Jezebel's deeds.

23 For those who follow Jezebel ("her children") and refuse to repent, a fatal judgment will be meted out by the Lord Christ: "I will strike her children dead" (lit., "I will kill her children with death"—perhaps a Hebrew idiom denoting "pestilence" [6:8]). Some understand "her children" to refer to her actual children, born of the sexual sins, rather than to her followers (so Beckwith, 467). This cannot be decided with certainty. Whatever the exact nature of the judgment, it is announced beforehand by Christ so that when it occurs, not just Thyatira, but "all the churches will know that I am he who searches hearts and minds," since they, too, will read the same letter and will later hear of the historical outcome. OT references ascribe omniscience to God alone (Ps 7:9; Pr 24:12; Jer 17:10). "Heart" is literally "kidneys" (Heb. *kĕlayot*, GK *4000*; Gk. *nephroi*, GK *3752*), which in Semitic thought represented the moral and spiritual center of the life, while "mind" is literally "heart" (Heb. *lēb*, GK *4213*; Gk. *kardia*, GK *2840*), which represents the totality of the feelings, thoughts, and desires traced back to one's deepest inner life. There is nothing in our thoughts or desires that is hidden from Christ's penetrating gaze (Heb 4:12–13). Our only safety from judgment is in repentance. The risen Lord does not stop with his searching of hearts and minds but brings recompense according to deeds—for faithfulness, reward; for unfaithfulness, judgment.

24–25 Christ's only command to the church at Thyatira was probably for the minority who had sufficient insight to penetrate Jezebel's deception. They are simply to "hold on to what you have" (i.e., their insight into Jezebel's teaching and evil deeds) until Christ returns (v.25). This small group may have been nearer his standard than any other group mentioned in Revelation because they could discriminate between authentic and spurious worship.

The reference to "Satan's so-called deep secrets" is ambiguous (cf. "the deep things of God" [1Co 2:10]). It may mean the "deep things," i.e., the secret knowledge of God reserved only for the initiates into the heretical teaching. This would suggest a form of Christian Gnosticism, an early heretical teaching. The words "so-called" would then be John's mocking remark—"the so-called deep things of God, which are in fact of Satan" (Bruce, 639). This view rests on the doubtful thesis of a developed Christian Gnosticism in the first century (cf. Edwin Yamauchi, *Pre-Christian Gnosticism* [Grand Rapids: Eerdmans, 1973], 55, 185) and strains the normal sense of the Greek. Therefore, another sense is preferable, namely, that Satan's "deep secrets" is the actual phrase Jezebel used. But could she lure Christians by using such a term? The reasoning of some in the early church (the Nicolaitans) might have gone something like this: The only effective way to confront Satan was to enter into his strongholds; the real nature of sin could only be learned by experience, and therefore only those who had really experienced sin could truly appreciate grace. So by experiencing the depths of paganism (the "deep secrets" of Satan), one would better be equipped to serve Christ or be an example of freedom to his brothers (cf. 1Co 8:9–11). Thus the sin of Jezebel was deadly serious because of the depths of its deception. Only a few perceived where the teaching was leading.

"Until I come" is the first of several references to the second coming of Christ in these letters (cf. 1:7).

26–27 The promise to the overcomers is twofold: (1) "authority over the nations" and (2) the gift of "the morning star." It contains one important modification of the regular overcomer's formula. Added to the words "to him who overcomes" is "and does my will to the end" (lit., "who keeps my works until the end"). It reminds us of Jesus' statement in his great eschatological discourse that "he who stands firm to the end will be saved" (Mt 24:13) and of Paul's words to the Colossians about continuing in the faith "established and firm" (Col 1:23). The proof of authentic trust in Jesus is steadfastness of belief and continuance in God's will until Christ returns or death comes.

The first promise is a fulfillment of Psalm 2, which is messianic and tells how the Father gave to Messiah the rule over the nations of the world. This psalm plays an important part in thinking about Christ (11:18; 12:5; 19:15). The coming reign of the Messiah over the world is to be shared with his disciples (1:6; 3:21; 20:6; 1Co 6:2). In the pre-Christian apocryphal *Psalms of Solomon* (17:23–24), the same psalm is used with reference to the Messiah and the Jews who will reign with him. Here in vv.26–27 its use seems to indicate that the overcomers will participate with Christ in fulfilling the promise of Psalm 2:9. There is a paradox in the combination of the mild word "rule" (*poimainō*, lit., "to shepherd"; GK *4477*) with the harsh words "with an iron scepter; he will dash them to pieces like pottery" (see comments at 19:11–21). The prospect of such a reversal of their present experience of oppression and persecution would be a constant encouragement for suffering Christians.

28 The overcomers in Thyatira are promised "the morning star" (*astera ton prōinon*). Some link this expression to Christ himself, as in 22:16. Believers would then receive Christ as their very life. Or it may refer to the resurrection in the sense that the morning star rises over the darkness of this world's persecution and offers victory over it. Perhaps a combination of the two thoughts may be intended. The promise of Christ's return is like the "morning star [*phōsphoros*, GK *5892*]" (2Pe 1:19; see 22:16, where Jesus calls himself "the bright Morning Star"

[*ho astēr ho lampros ho prōinos*], in apparent reference to his return).

29 In this fourth letter and in the three that follow it, the general exhortation comes at the very end; in the first three letters, however, it precedes the promise (cf. comments at Overview, p. 610).

NOTES

20 Alexandrinus (A), generally a good witness in Revelation, and a number of other witnesses include the word σοῦ, *sou* ("your"), after γυναῖκα, *gynaika* ("woman"), giving the sense "your wife." This implies taking "angel" in 1:18 and elsewhere in chs. 2–3 as the bishop or overseer of the church. This inferior reading probably arose through scribal confusion with other frequent references to σοῦ, *sou*, in the letters.

The TR has ὀλίγα, *oliga* ("a few things"), included in the verdict words, thus reading, "I have a few things against you." The NIV and NASB rightly follow the numerous and varied witnesses that omit ὀλίγα, *oliga*.

27 According to Trudinger's analysis ("Some Observations Concerning the Text," 84–85), the text John follows in the OT quotation from Psalm 2:9 is closer to a Semitic original than to the LXX, from which it is generally thought to be derived. He finds at least thirty-nine direct quotations and as many allusions in Revelation that go against the LXX in favor of a Semitic text. For a different view, see Robert K. McKensie, *The Author of the Apocalypse* (Lewiston, N.Y.: Mellen, 1997).

5. To Sardis (3:1–6)

OVERVIEW

Sardis was about thirty miles south of Thyatira. Its location commanded the trade of the Aegean Islands and the military road through the important Hermus River valley. Sardis enjoyed prominence as a commercially prosperous and militarily strategic city throughout its history. The city's topography was notable for the acropolis; the temple of Artemis (possibly Cybele), which, though never finished, equaled in size the famous temple of Artemis in Ephesus; and the impressive necropolis, or cemetery, of "a thousand hills" (modern Bin Tepe), so named because of the hundreds of burial mounds visible on the skyline some seven miles from Sardis.

The acropolis rose about eight hundred feet above the north section of Sardis and was virtually impregnable because of its rock walls, which were nearly vertical, except on the south side. Formerly the site of the original city, the acropolis became a refuge for the inhabitants in time of siege. Only twice in the history of Sardis was its fortress ever captured, though attacks on it were frequent. When Cyrus attacked it in the sixth century BC, a shrewd Persian soldier observed a Sardian descending the southern winding path to retrieve his fallen helmet. Unknown to the soldier, the Persians followed his path back up to the summit and captured the whole city, taking them quite by surprise. There was a similar occurrence when Antiochus attacked Sardis about two hundred years later.

Sardis retained its wealth into the first two centuries of the Christian era. But its political brilliance as the capital city of Asia for Persia lay in the past. Ramsay (*Seven Churches*, 375) aptly remarks, "No city of Asia at that time showed such a melancholy contrast between past splendor and present decay as Sardis." In AD 26, Sardis begged the Roman Senate to grant it the coveted honor of building a temple to Caesar. The distinction, however, went to Smyrna. The luxurious living of the Sardians led to moral decadence. Herodotus (fifth century BC) wrote despairingly of Sardis and its people as "the tender-footed Lydians, who can only play on the cithara, strike the guitar, and sell by retail" (cited in Barclay, *Seven Churches*, 71). Sardis was a city of peace—not the peace won through battle but "the peace of the man whose dreams are dead and whose mind is asleep, the peace of lethargy and evasion" (Barclay, *Seven Churches*, 72). A great wool industry flourished at Sardis, and this may account for Christ's reference to clothing (v.4).

---

¹"To the angel of the church in Sardis write:

These are the words of him who holds the seven spirits of God and the seven stars. I know your deeds; you have a reputation of being alive, but you are dead. ²Wake up! Strengthen what remains and is about to die, for I have not found your deeds complete in the sight of my God. ³Remember, therefore, what you have received and heard; obey it, and repent. But if you do not wake up, I will come like a thief, and you will not know at what time I will come to you.

⁴Yet you have a few people in Sardis who have not soiled their clothes. They will walk with me, dressed in white, for they are worthy. ⁵He who overcomes will, like them, be dressed in white. I will never blot out his name from the book of life, but will acknowledge his name before my Father and his angels. ⁶He who has an ear, let him hear what the Spirit says to the churches."

COMMENTARY

1 The speaker identifies himself as "him who holds the seven spirits of God and the seven stars" (see comments at 1:4, 16, 20; 2:1). To the Sardians, Christ reveals himself as the one who controls the seven spirits of God. If the Sardian church is strong, it is because Christ has sent his Spirit to encourage and quicken the Sardian believers; if they are dead like Sardis, it is because in judgment he has withdrawn his Spirit from them. Yet the faithful minority at Sardis (v.4) can count on that divine power of Christ to sustain, give life, and mobilize them to do his will, even though the majority are dead. (On the "seven stars," see comments at 2:1.)

The speaker's knowledge of the church in Sardis reveals their true condition. He knows their "deeds." It is not clear whether this alludes to their past accomplishments, which gave them their reputation of being alive, or whether the reference is to their present deeds, which were not those Christ sought from them. This latter view is supported by v.2, where he mentions their deeds again and says they are incomplete. He also knows that, though they claim to be a healthy Christian church, in reality they are "dead."

How does a church die? Why does Christ use this expression for Sardis even though the churches in Thyatira and Laodicea also had serious problems? Sardis had had significant fame as a royal city, but now it was nothing. The citizens were living off past fame. Apparently the same spirit had affected the church. Their loyalty and service to Christ was in the past. Now they were nothing. It may be that they had so made peace with the surrounding society that the offense of the cross had ceased, and they were no longer in jeopardy of life or vulnerable to suffering. Further facts emerge when we consider the series of commands in vv.2–3. Death was a special preoccupation of the Sardians, as witnessed by the impressive necropolis seven miles from the city. What had been a part of the pagan rites had also crept into the church. But again this work of the enemy came through deception. The Sardian church was, for the most part, a duped church.

2 The command "wake up!" or "be watchful" (present tense, "be constantly alert") is a call to reverse their attitudes radically. The congregation must be alerted to the seriousness of the situation. Their complacency led them to give up their identification with Christ and their mission for him. The situation was dire but not totally hopeless. Immediate steps were to be taken to "strengthen what remains." Some persons and things were salvageable if quick and decisive action was taken. Otherwise, death would follow.

The Sardians' deeds are in danger of judgment because Christ has not found them "complete [*peplērōmena*, 'full, fulfilled, filled up to measure,' GK 4444] in the sight of my God." Though this could refer to incompleteness in the number of their deeds, more likely it describes the quality of their

deeds—they do not measure up to the standard Christ sets. In the other letters, works acceptable to Christ are love, faithfulness, perseverance, keeping Christ's words, and not denying his name.

3 Like those in Ephesus, the Sardians must remember what they "have received and heard." What they "received" was the apostolic tradition of the gospel; what they "heard" probably were the teachings of the apostles and prophets who brought the gospel to them. Unlike the church at Philadelphia (v.8), the Sardians were not holding to the word of Christ. For them, repentance was the only way out of certain and final death. So they were to repent by restoring the gospel and the apostolic doctrine to its authority over their lives. This would mean they would once more start obeying (*tēreō*, "keep, watch," GK 5498) the truth of Christ's word. Today's church needs to hear this challenge to take the word of Christ seriously. Unless the church at Sardis repents, Christ says he will come to them in judgment "as a thief"—i.e., by surprise—just as Sardis had been attacked and defeated by Cyrus long before. "As a thief" should probably not be taken as referring to the second coming but to Christ's coming against them (opposing them) in judgment (cf. his threat to the church in Ephesus in 2:5).

4 While the majority had departed from faithful obedience to Christ, a few at Sardis remained true. Here an allusion to the wool industry at Sardis intensifies the image of soiled and defiled garments. Those with soiled garments were removed from the public lists of citizens in Sardis. In the pagan religions, it was forbidden to approach the gods in garments that were soiled or stained (Barclay, *Seven Churches*, 77). Soiling seems to be a symbol for mingling with pagan life and thus defiling the purity of one's relation to Christ (14:4; 1Co 8:7; 2Co 7:1; 11:2; Jude 23). To "walk with Christ" symbolizes salvation and fellowship with him—something the others at Sardis had forfeited through their sin (1Jn 1:6–7). "White" garments are symbolic of the righteousness, victory, and glory of God (3:18; 6:11; 7:9, 13f.; 19:14). As Caird, 49, observes, this passage shows that not all faithful Christians were martyrs, nor can we make emperor worship the sole source of the problems of the early Christians. Ironically, the Sardians were occupied with their outward appearance, but they were not concerned with inner purity toward Christ and their outward moral life in a pagan society.

5 The overcomer's promise is threefold and grows out of the reference to white clothing. First, "like" the faithful Sardian Christians who would receive white clothes from Christ, the others there who overcame the stains of pagan society would similarly be dressed in white.

Second, the pure relationship to Christ is permanently guaranteed: "I will never blot out his name from the book of life." In ancient cities the names of citizens were recorded in a register till their death; then their names were erased or marked out of the book of the living. This same idea appears in the OT (Ex 32:32–33; Ps 69:28; Isa 4:3). From the idea of being recorded in God's book of the living (or the righteous) comes the sense of belonging to God's eternal kingdom or possessing eternal life (Da 12:1; Lk 10:20; Php 4:3; Heb 12:23; Rev 13:8; 17:8; 20:15; 21:27). For Christ to say that he will never erase the overcomer's name from the book of

life is the strongest affirmation that death can never separate us from Christ and his life (Ro 8:38–39). A person enrolled in the book of life by faith remains in it by faithfulness and can be erased only by disloyalty. There is some evidence that a person's name could be removed from the city register before death if he were convicted of a crime. In the first century, Christians who were loyal to Christ were under constant threat of being branded political and social rebels and then stripped of their citizenship. But Christ offers them eternally safe citizenship in his everlasting kingdom if they only remain loyal to him.

Third and finally, to the overcomer Christ promised to "acknowledge his name before [the] Father and his angels." "Acknowledge" (*homologeō*, GK *3933*) is a strong word for confession before the courts. It is Christ's confession of our name before the Father and his angels (implying our fellowship with him) that assures our heavenly citizenship (Mt 10:32; Lk 12:8).

What ultimately counts, then, is not our acceptance by this world's societies but that our relationship to Christ is genuine and hence will merit his approbation in the coming kingdom.

6 Again the general exhortation comes last, as in the previous letter (cf. comments at Overview, p. 610).

NOTES

1 See John G. Pedley, *Ancient Literary Sources on Sardis* (Cambridge, Mass.: Harvard Univ. Press, 1972).

2 The imperfect tense in ἃ ἔμελλον ἀποθανεῖν, *ha emellon apothanein* ("what is about to die"), probably looks back from the reader's point of view to the time when John saw the vision. At the same time, it expresses the conviction of the writer that the worst would soon be past (Swete, 48; Ernest Burton, *Syntax of the Moods and Tenses of New Testament Greek* [3d ed.; Edinburgh: T&T Clark, 1898], paragraph 73).

4 S. David Garber ("Symbolism of Heavenly Robes in the New Testament in Comparison with Gnostic Thought" [PhD diss., Princeton Theological Seminary, 1974], 307–14) argues that the white robes mentioned throughout the book of Revelation refer to the divine gift of salvation that can be preserved only through continued discipleship. He also sees a possible allusion to the idea of a heavenly or spiritual body of glory that accompanies the resurrection—an idea that occurs frequently in the Jewish apocalyptic literature but that is different from the white-clothing imagery found among the Gnostic religions.

5 The reading οὕτως, *houtōs* ("like them") over οὗτος, *houtos* ("this one"), is by no means certain. While Metzger, 664, argues for the first reading on superior MS evidence, Alford and Beckwith have a point in suggesting that the author would have used ὁμοίως, *homoiōs* ("likewise"), not οὕτως, *houtōs*, to express similarity.

6. To Philadelphia (3:7-13)

OVERVIEW

About twenty-five miles southeast of Sardis, along the Hermus River valley, lay the important high-plateau city of Philadelphia (modern Alasehir). A main highway that ran through the city connected Smyrna (about a hundred miles due west) to northwest Asia, Phrygia, and the east. Furthermore, the imperial post road of the first century AD, which came from Rome via Troas, Adramyttium, Pergamum, and Sardis, passed through this valley and Philadelphia on the way to the east. So situated, Philadelphia became a strong fortress city. To the northeast was a great vine-growing district, which, along with textile and leather industries, contributed greatly to the city's prosperity.

Philadelphia was established by the Pergamenian king Attalus II (159–138 BC), who had been given the epithet "Philadelphus" ("brother lover") because of his love for his brother. The city was to be a mission city for disseminating Greco-Asiatic culture and language in the eastern part of Lydia and in Phrygia. Its success is attested by the fact that the Lydian language ceased to be spoken in Lydia by AD 19 and the Greek language took over (Ramsay, *Seven Churches*, 391). But beyond this language achievement, Philadelphia had not been successful in converting the Phrygians (Barclay, *Seven Churches*, 80).

According to Strabo (*Geogr.* 12.579; 13.628), the whole region was earthquake prone. In AD 17, an earthquake that destroyed Sardis and ten other cities also destroyed Philadelphia. Consequently, many

people preferred to live in the rural area surrounding the city. The fear of earthquakes caused those who continued to live in the city to leave it at the slightest sign of a tremor.

After the devastating earthquake, Tiberius had the city rebuilt. In gratitude the citizens renamed it Neocaesarea ("New Caesar"). Later the name was changed to Flavia (AD 70–79), and this, along with Philadelphia, continued to be its name through the second and third centuries AD. Later, the establishment of the emperor cult in the city earned it the title "Neokoros," or "Temple Warden" (ca. 211–17). In the fifth century it was nicknamed "Little Athens" because of its proliferation of festivals and pagan cults. Whether this indicates something of its early period is uncertain. Since wine was one of the city's important industries, some have assumed that the worship of Dionysus was a chief pagan cult there (Swete, 52).

Although nothing is known about the origin of the Philadelphian church, in AD 100–160 the church prospered under the ministry of a prophetess named Ammia, who was universally recognized as ranking with Agabus and the four daughters of Philip in her possession of the gift of prophecy (Eusebius, *Hist. eccl.* 5.17.2). Long after all the surrounding country had succumbed to Muslim control under Turkey, Philadelphia held out as a Christian populace till 1392. Even the noted historian Edward Gibbon admired its fortitude (Ramsay, *Seven Churches*, 400).

7"To the angel of the church in Philadelphia write:

These are the words of him who is holy and true, who holds the key of David. What he opens no one can shut, and what he shuts no one can open. 8I know your deeds. See, I have placed before you an open door that no one can shut. I know that you have little strength, yet you have kept my word and have not denied my name. 9I will make those who are of the synagogue of Satan, who claim to be Jews though they are not, but are liars—I will make them come and fall down at your feet and acknowledge that I have loved you. 10Since you have kept my command to endure patiently, I will also keep you from the hour of trial that is going to come upon the whole world to test those who live on the earth.

11I am coming soon. Hold on to what you have, so that no one will take your crown. 12Him who overcomes I will make a pillar in the temple of my God. Never again will he leave it. I will write on him the name of my God and the name of the city of my God, the new Jerusalem, which is coming down out of heaven from my God; and I will also write on him my new name. 13He who has an ear, let him hear what the Spirit says to the churches."

COMMENTARY

7 The letter to the church in Philadelphia begins with the speaker's identifying himself as "him who is holy and true, who holds the key of David. What he opens no one can shut, and what he shuts no one can open." Each of these identifications calls attention to Jesus as the true Messiah. "Holy and true" relates to God himself and describes aspects of his presence among us (cf. 6:10). Holiness is the attribute of God whereby we sense the presence of the "Wholly Other," the one who says, "I am God, and not man—the Holy One among you" (Hos 11:9). He is the "True One" in that he is wholly trustworthy and reliable in his words and actions. For this congregation for whom Christ has only commendation, these titles would bring encouragement, despite their "little strength" (v.8) to go on in their faithfulness, in contrast to those described in v.9.

The reference to the "key of David" alludes to Isaiah 22:20–25 and the incident of transferring the post of secretary of state in Judah from the unfaithful Shebna to the faithful Eliakim. The "key" signifies the power of the keys normally held by the king himself, unless delegated to another. The use of the name "David" points to Christ as the Messiah, who alone determines who will participate in his kingdom and who will be turned away: "what he opens no one can shut, and what he shuts no one can open." This may allude to the false claims of certain Jews at Philadelphia who argued that they, not the heretical Nazarenes, would inherit the kingdom of David (v.9) and thus excluded the followers of Jesus. But the true Messiah, Jesus, will exclude them!

8 Here the knowledge of the speaker and his verdict blend together in untarnished praise, as in the letter to Smyrna. Between the declaration "I know your deeds" and the words "you have little strength, yet you have kept my word and have not denied my name" is the somewhat awkward interjection "see, I have placed before you an open door that no one can shut."

Since Christ has absolute authority from the Father, he has opened a door for the Philadelphians that even their enemies cannot close. But an open door to what? Swete sees an inference here to Philadelphia as a missionary city. As the easternmost of the seven cities and an outpost on the high tableland of upper Asia, it was effective in evangelizing the area with Hellenism. So the witness of the church in Philadelphia will be effective, despite its small strength (1Co 16:9; Col 4:3). Others believe that v.8 refers to Christ's opening the door to his kingdom for those who love him and thus reinforces the statement in v.7 about opening and shutting.

Beckwith, 430, protests against the first view: "Such a reference to future missionary activity of the church is singularly out of place, thrust in as a parenthesis between the parts of a sentence concerned with commendation of the church for its steadfastness in the past." The context strongly favors the second view (so Ladd). What became a serious problem at Sardis (v.3) was not the case with the Philadelphian congregation, to whom the risen Christ said, "You have kept my word." They had been faithful to the gospel and the apostles' teaching, even during the trial of their faith alluded to in the words "and have not denied my name" (cf. 2:13).

9 Here those opposing the witness of the congregation are characterized as "those who are of the synagogue of Satan, who claim to be Jews though they are not, but are liars." The words are like those spoken to the church in Smyrna (see comments at 2:9). Perhaps the words "have not denied my name" in v.8 relate to this same issue of idolatry. But Christ will make those who have compromised their loyalty to Christ through the teachings of the Nicolaitans (= Jezebel) acknowledge that God is indeed with the faithful church in Philadelphia and that they are God's true people and worthy of the name "Jews."

10 This is another promise given to the church in Philadelphia. Though not part of the promise to the overcomers in Philadelphia (v.12), as with the special promises to Smyrna and Sardis (2:10; 3:4), it may be taken as a promise to all the churches. The words "since you have kept my command to endure patiently" (lit., "kept the word of my patience") refer to the condition under which the promise is valid. Some translate the phrase as in the NIV, inferring that the "word of my patience" means the command of Christ to endure suffering, or to endure until he returns (Lk 21:19; cf. Heb 10:36). Others translate it as "the word enjoining Christ's patient endurance" (Ladd, 61). In that case, it would refer to an apostolic teaching (such as Paul's) encouraging Christians to endure the contrariness of a sinful world after the pattern of Christ's own endurance (2Th 3:5; Heb 12:3). The Greek text slightly favors the latter translation, though the former is also possible.

Related to the promise "I will also keep you from the hour of trial that is going to come upon the whole world to test those who live on the earth" are two problems: (1) the identification of the "hour of trial" and (2) the precise sense of the phrase "keep you from the hour of trial." Both involve the ongoing debate among evangelical eschatologists over the tribulation/rapture question.

We can dismiss the view that the "hour of trial" refers to some general or personal distress that will come upon the Philadelphian community and from which the church will be delivered (so J. Barton Payne, *The Imminent Appearing of Christ* [Grand Rapids: Eerdmans, 1962], 78–79). Though the universality of the expression "the whole world" is reason enough to refute Payne's view, the phrase "those who live on the earth" is repeated in Revelation a number of times and refers not to believers but to unbelievers who are the objects of God's wrath—i.e., the "beast-worshipers" (6:10; 8:13; 11:10; 12:12; 13:8, 12, 14; cf. Isa 24; Jer 13:12–14; cf. 1QH 16.19–36).

According to some interpreters (Ladd, Mounce, Walvoord, Thomas), the "hour of trial" (*hōras tou peirasmou,* "time of temptation," GK *6052, 4280*) is better understood as the time known to the Jews as the "messianic woes," a time of intense trouble to fall on the world before the coming of Christ and known as the eschatological "day of the Lord," or the "great tribulation" (Da 12:1; Joel 2:31; Mk 13:14; 2Th 2:1–12; Rev 14:7). This "hour of trial," then, will be the one described in such detail in the following chapters of the book. In that case, what, then, is the effect of the promise, "I will also keep you from the hour of trial"? There are two possibilities. Some argue, with reference to the same Greek expression (*tēreō ek,* "keep from") in John 17:15, that the sense is preservation while in the trial, since to be kept from evil or the evil one does not mean to be removed from his presence but simply to be kept from his harmful power. Therefore, the church universal will experience preservation from harm in the trial of persecution and suffering and will not be raptured until the end of the period (so Ladd; cf. 1Th 4:13–5:11).

On the other hand, some writers offer objections to this exegesis: (1) The "hour of trial" John describes is a judgment from God on the unbelieving inhabitants of the world, not a form of evil such as John 17:15 describes (cf. Thomas, 1:284–85). (2) It is not true that the saints of the tribulation period are exempt from harm during this period; a great group of them will be martyred (6:9–11; 7:9–14; etc.). (3) In the gospel of John, preservation is from the devil; in Revelation, from a time period—the "hour" of trial (cf. Smith, 88–89).

Ladd, 62, offsets some of this criticism by advocating that the hour of trial has two aspects—(1) the fierce persecution of believers by the beast and (2) the outpouring of divine judgments on a rebellious world represented in the trumpet and bowl plagues. Believers are kept from the harm of the latter but not the former. The difficulty in this view lies in Ladd's failure to identify clearly the hour of trial in this verse. It cannot refer to both the great tribulation (7:14) on believers and the wrath of God.

In my opinion, this confusion may be avoided by clearly identifying "the hour of trial" as the wrath of God, deliverance from which is promised to every one of Christ's overcomers. As a matter of fact, the expression *tēreō ek* ("keep out of") cannot be proved exegetically to be different from *tēreō apo* ("keep from"). In the LXX of Proverbs 7:5, the sense of this latter expression is to deliver the man from contact with or the presence of the adulteress. In James 1:27, the same expression means to be kept from the pollution of the world. In both instances the sense is that of exemption from something. Can one, then, be exempt from the "hour of trial" that will try the whole world by famines, earthquakes, wars, floods, etc., and still be present on the earth? Yes, but removal is still a possible method of protection.

The above discussion shows that v.10 does not settle the question of the time of the rapture in relation to the tribulation. Rather, it remains ambiguous. One might be on the earth and yet be exempt from the "hour of trial" if (1) the "hour of trial" is an equivalent derived from the briefer term "trial," and (2) this "trial" is directed only at the unbelievers in the world, while the believers are divinely immune not from trial or persecution in general but from a specific type of trial (God's wrath) aimed at the rebellious on the earth. To this writer, the most natural way to understand the expression to be "kept from the hour" of something that is universal in the world is not to be preserved through it but to be kept from being present when it happens. In any event, we have here a marvelous promise of Christ's protection (*tēreō,* "keep") for those who have protected (*tēreō*) his word by their loving obedience.

11 Here the words of Christ "I am coming soon" (cf. 22:7, 12, 20) are not a threat of judgment but a promise of Christ's second coming, such as the promise the faithful Christians in Thyatira received (2:25).

The testing that faced the Philadelphians was not the same as that facing the unbelieving earth-dwellers (v.10). Loyal disciples must face one type of conflict, the world with its earth-dwellers quite another (cf. Minear). Some such conflict is envisioned when Christ says, "Hold on to what you have, so that no one will take your crown." They had kept his word and had not denied his name in the face of persecution. Either Satan or men could rob them of their crown by diverting them from exclusive loyalty to Jesus (on "crown," see comments at 2:10).

12 The promise to the overcomer is again twofold and related to the experience and memory of the inhabitants of the city. First, Christ will make the overcomer a "pillar in the temple of my God." As already noted, the city was constantly threatened with earthquakes. Often the only parts of a city left standing after a severe quake were the huge stone temple columns. Christ promises to set believers in his temple (the future kingdom?) in such a secure fashion that no disturbance can ever force them out.

Moreover, a faithful municipal servant or a distinguished priest was sometimes honored by having a special pillar added to one of the temples and inscribed with his name (Barclay, *Seven Churches,* 89). This may well be the sense of the second promise, "I will write on him the name of my God and the name of the city of my God, the new Jerusalem, ... and ... my new name." The inscribed name signifies identification and ownership. To those who have "little strength" (little influence) because of being ostracized, Christ promises recognition in his kingdom worthy of the most noble hero of any society.

Remembering the changes of name their city received in days past (e.g., Neocaesarea; see comments at v.7), the Philadelphians would be impressed that God himself (not the emperor) had chosen to identify himself with them and to ensure their citizenship in the new Jerusalem (cf. 21:2–4; Eze 48:35). Christ's "new name" could be either the name that he alone knows, signifying his absolute power over all other powers (19:12), or the new name of Christ given to the believer, i.e., his possession by Christ through redemption (Isa 62:2;65:15).

13 The general exhortation follows the promise. (See comments at Overview, p. 610.)

NOTES

10 Cf. Gundry, 53–61. Gundry follows closely Ladd's views on this question, yet with much more elaborate weaponry. Thomas (1:284–90) argues against Gundry and Ladd.

Commenting on Revelation 15:1, Victorinus says, "For the wrath of God always strikes the obstinate people with seven plagues, that is, perfectly, as it is said in Leviticus; and these shall be in the last time, *when the Church shall have gone out of the midst*" (italics mine; cited in *ANF* 7:357).

7. To Laodicea (3:14–22)

OVERVIEW

Laodicea was about forty-five miles southeast of Philadelphia and about one hundred miles due east of Ephesus. Along with Colossae and Hierapolis, it was one of the cities in the fertile Lycus Valley. The great Roman road stretching to the inland of Asia from the coast at Ephesus ran straight through its center, making Laodicea an important center of trade and communication. In addition, its wealth came from the production of a fine quality of famous glossy black wool—whether dyed or natural in color is not known. That the city's banking assets were noteworthy is evidenced by the fact that Cicero cashed huge bank drafts in Laodicea. So wealthy was Laodicea that after the great earthquake of AD 17, which destroyed it, the people refused imperial help in rebuilding the city, choosing rather to do it entirely by themselves.

Laodicea had a famous school of medicine; and a special ointment known as "Phrygian powder," famous for its cure of eye defects, was either manufactured or distributed there, as were ear ointments. Near the temple of the special god associated with healing, Men Karou (who later became identified with Asclepius), there was a

market for trading all sorts of goods (Ramsay, *Seven Churches*, 417). Zeus, the supreme god, was also worshiped in the city.

Ramsay, 423, notes that Laodicea is difficult to describe because no one thing about it stands out. There were no excesses or notable achievements to distinguish this city, whose people had learned to compromise and accommodate themselves to the needs and wishes of others. They did not zealously stand for anything. A six-mile-long aqueduct brought Laodicea its supply of water from the south. The water came either from hot springs and was cooled to lukewarm or came from a cooler source and warmed up in the aqueduct on the way. For all its wealth, the city had poor water. A large and influential Jewish population resided there. As for the church in Laodicea, it may have been founded by Epaphras (cf. Col 4:12–13).

14"To the angel of the church in Laodicea write:

These are the words of the Amen, the faithful and true witness, the ruler of God's creation. 15I know your deeds, that you are neither cold nor hot. I wish you were either one or the other! 16So, because you are lukewarm—neither hot nor cold—I am about to spit you out of my mouth. 17You say, 'I am rich; I have acquired wealth and do not need a thing.' But you do not realize that you are wretched, pitiful, poor, blind and naked. 18I counsel you to buy from me gold refined in the fire, so you can become rich; and white clothes to wear, so you can cover your shameful nakedness; and salve to put on your eyes, so you can see.

19Those whom I love I rebuke and discipline. So be earnest, and repent. 20Here I am! I stand at the door and knock. If anyone hears my voice and opens the door, I will come in and eat with him, and he with me.

21To him who overcomes, I will give the right to sit with me on my throne, just as I overcame and sat down with my Father on his throne. 22He who has an ear, let him hear what the Spirit says to the churches."

COMMENTARY

14 The speaker identifies himself by a threefold affirmation: "the Amen, the faithful and true witness,

the ruler of God's creation." The normal Hebrew adverb rendered by the Greek *amēn* (GK *297*) means the acknowledgment of that which is sure and valid. It is a word of human response to the divine verity or action. Jesus is the "Amen" in the sense that he is the perfect human, obedient response to the divine promises (cf. Isa 65:16). Jesus' response to God's will was the perfect response of obedience and suffering: he is the "faithful and true witness" (cf. comments at 1:5, 9; 2:13). The same thought is expressed by Paul in 2 Corinthians 1:20: "For no matter how many promises God has made, they are 'Yes' in Christ. And so through him the 'Amen' is spoken by us to the glory of God." In one sense, all Christians are called to be "little amens" after the example of Christ.

The "ruler" (*archē*, "source, origin," GK 794) further amplifies the "Amen" statement. Paul used *archē* in Colossians 1:18 to describe Christ as the source or origin of all creation (not the first created; cf. Pr 8:22; Jn 1:3), no doubt to correct a heresy. Since Colossae was a neighboring city of Laodicea, it is not improbable that the same heresy was also affecting the sister church at Laodicea. But this is not explicit. What is plain is this: When Christ addresses a church that is failing in loyalty and obedience, he is to them the "Amen" of God in faithfulness and in true witness, the only one who has absolute power over the world because he is the source and origin of all creation (1:17; 2:8; 22:13).

15–16 Sadly, the speaker's knowledge reveals an unqualified condemnation of the Laodicean church. The verdict is the exact opposite of the church's own evaluation and expectations. Their deeds were "neither cold nor hot." The expression "cold nor hot" may refer to their lack of zeal (v.19) or their uselessness, for Christ says, "I wish you were either one or the other!" (lit., "either cold or hot"). There is good reason why we should not try to take both of these words as though Christ meant, "I wish you were either spiritually cold [i.e., unsaved or hostile] or spiritually hot [i.e., alive and fervent]!" In the first

place, it is inconceivable that Christ would wish that people were spiritually cold, or unsaved and hostile. Furthermore, the application of "hot" and "cold" to spiritual temperature, though familiar to us, would have been completely foreign to first-century Christians. The two adjectives in "neither hot nor cold" should be understood together as equivalent to "lukewarmness" (v.16)—i.e., they were useless to Christ because they were complacent, self satisfied, and indifferent to the real issues of faith in him and of discipleship.

Since the city of Hierapolis, seven miles north of Laodicea, had famous "hot springs," it may be that similar springs were located south of Laodicea and affected the temperature of the water supply. "I am about to spit [*emesai*, vomit, GK 1840] you out of my mouth" seems to allude to the lukewarm water. "Cold" could refer to the useful cool water located at Colossae, fewer than ten miles away. "Hot" would remind the Laodiceans of the beneficial "hot springs" to the north of Hierapolis. Yet Laodicea, for all its wealth, had an insipid water supply—one that induced vomiting! Christ detests a Laodicean attitude of compromise, one that seeks easy accommodation and peace at any cost. With such a condition, he must deal harshly. To be a Christian means to be useful to Christ.

17 The deeper problem in the Laodicean church was not simply their indifference—it was their ignorance of their real condition: "You say, 'I am rich; I have acquired wealth and do not need a thing.'" Observe the way this indictment is related to the general condition of the populace at large— rich in material possessions and self-sufficient. The spirit of the surrounding culture had crept into the congregation and had paralyzed their spiritual life. But did they actually claim to be materially rich, or spiritually rich? Since it is difficult to see how a Christian community would boast of material wealth, many prefer the latter interpretation. Yet the

Laodiceans may have interpreted their material wealth as a blessing from God and thus have been self-deceived as to their true spiritual state. In any case, they had misread their true condition.

Christ's revelation of the Laodiceans' actual situation shatters their illusions and calls them to repentance: "But you do not realize that you are wretched, pitiful, poor, blind and naked." Probably the first two characteristics—"wretched" and "pitiful"—are to be linked together, while the latter three explain this twofold condition in more detail (cf. v.18). They are not, as they thought, rich and without need; they are pitifully wretched and in great need, being "poor, blind and naked." Conversely, Jesus said to the church at Smyrna, "I know . . . your poverty—yet you are rich!" (2:9).

To be "wretched" physically describes life when everything one owns has been destroyed or plundered by war (LXX Ps 137:8). Here it refers to the Laodiceans' spiritual destitution and pitiableness before God. "Poor, blind and naked" refers to the three sources of their miserable condition. "Lukewarmness," then, does not refer to the laxity of Christians but the condition of not really knowing Christ as Savior and Lord and thus being useless to him. Origen (*Princ.* 3.4.3) likewise understood the passage to refer not to lapsed Christians but to the unregenerate.

18 The commands of Christ correspond exactly to the self-deceptions of the Laodiceans. Gold—a source of the wealth for the city—was to be bought from Christ and to become the true wealth of the spiritually poverty-stricken. Their shameful nakedness was to be clothed, not by purchasing the sleek, black wool of Laodicea, but by buying from Christ the white clothing that alone can cover shameful nakedness (16:15). For those who were blind to their true condition, the "Phrygian powder" was useless (cf. comments at v.14). They needed to buy salve from Christ so that they could truly see. The reference to buying would recall the famous market near the temple of Men Karou, where the commodities manufactured at Laodicea could be bought, along with imports from other areas. But to what do gold, white clothes, and salve symbolically refer? Minear, 57, suggests the following:

> The only cure for poverty-stricken disciples was to purchase from Christ gold which is refined in the agonies of the shared passion. For their nakedness (did Hans Christian Andersen find here the theme of "The Emperor's New Clothes"?) the only recourse was to buy such clothes as the naked Christ had worn on the cross. The blindness of self-deception could be cured only by understanding the correlation between Christ's love and his discipline. These three purchases constitute a substantial definition of the kind of zeal and repentance which was the burden of all John's prophecies. The thrust of these commands moves in the direction of rigorous warning. They are tantamount to saying "Open your eyes" and "Carry your cross." This letter argues against the widespread assertion of many interpreters to the effect that John's chief concern was to provide consolation to a persecuted church. Nearer the mark would be the opposite assertion; that John, like Jesus, was concerned to bring not peace but a sword.

The three figures all point to the Laodiceans' need of authentic salvation through Christ.

19 Even though the state of a church such as the Laodicean one verges on disaster, not all is lost if there are those in it who will receive Christ's loving rebuke and come back to him. "I love" is the Greek *phileō* ("to have affection for," GK *5797*). This verb does not necessarily connote a lower level of love than *agapaō* (GK *26*). Sometimes it has the force of *agapaō* (e.g., Jn 5:20; 16:27; 20:22; cf. BDAG, s.v.). Christ's statement "I rebuke and discipline" speaks of his love (Pr 3:12; 1Co 11:32; Heb 12:6). He spits out those he does not love and "rebukes" (*elenchō*, "reproves, convicts," GK *1794*) and disciplines those who hear his voice. The difference between the expelled and the disciplined lies in their response: "So be earnest [*zēleuō*, zealous, enthusiastic, GK *2418*], and repent." The Laodiceans' repentance would come from a rekindling of their loyalty to Christ.

20 To those who hear the words of rebuke, Christ extends an invitation to dine with him. Some older commentators find the reference to the "door" as parallel to the new age that will dawn at the advent of Christ (so Swete, Beckwith; cf. Mt 24:33; Jas 5:9). So the challenge is to be ready to enter the banquet of Christ at his return. This view, however, does not seem to fit the immediate context, nor does it agree with other NT teaching on the Lord's return.

Others hold that the figure represents Christ standing at the door to the hearts of the members of the congregation at Laodicea. Christ will come and have fellowship with anyone who hears his voice of rebuke and thus proves himself Christ's friend by zeal and repentance. The "eating" (*deipneō*, GK *1268*) refers to the main meal of the day, which in Oriental fashion was a significant occasion for having intimate fellowship with the closest of friends. It is through the Holy Spirit that Christ and the Father come to have fellowship with us (Jn 14:23). There may be an allusion to Song of Songs 5:2: "Listen! My lover is knocking: Open to me, my sister, my darling, my dove, my flawless one."

While most commentators have taken this invitation as addressed to lapsed, halfhearted Christians, the terminology and context (v.18) suggest that these Laodiceans were, for the most part, merely professing Christians who lacked authentic conversion to Christ, which is the essential prerequisite for true discipleship. Verse 20 is, therefore, more evangelistic than admonitory. Those who find in it an allusion to the Lord's Supper may be right. Oscar Cullmann (*Early Christian Worship* [London: SCM, 1953]) sees v.20 as a response to the old eucharistic prayer, "Maranatha" (*marana tha*, "Our Lord, come!" GK *3448*).

21 The promise to the overcomers concerns the sharing in Christ's future reign in the eschatological kingdom: "I will give the right to sit with me on my throne." Such a joint reign with Christ has already been referred to earlier in the book (1:6, 9; 2:26–27) and also appears later (5:10; 20:4–6). The kingdom reign is also a theme in other NT writings (Lk 22:28–30; Ro 8:17; 2Ti 2:12). As Christ overcame through his suffering and death (Jn 16:33) and entered into the highest honor God could bestow—that of being seated at his "right hand" of sovereignty (Mk 16:19; Ac 2:22–36; Rev 22:1)—so believers who suffer with Christ, even to the point of death, will share in the honor of Christ's exalted position. The distinction between the Father's throne and Christ's throne is no mere rhetoric. On the contrary, it differentiates aspects of God's program in history (1Co 15:24–28). Christ is reigning now, for there is a sense in which the eschatological or messianic kingdom of God was inaugurated in Christ's earthly ministry, death, and resurrection. But the promise here, as elsewhere in the NT, foresees a final earthly consummation of the kingdom that awaits Christ's return.

22 The general exhortation closes the seventh letter (cf. comments at Overview, p. 610).

NOTES

15–16 On the meaning of "hot," "cold," and "lukewarm" as related to the city water supply and the consequent reinterpretation this suggests, see the helpful articles by M. J. S. Rudwick and E. M. B. Green, "The Laodicean Lukewarmness," *ExpTim* 69 (1958): 176–78; and Stanley Porter, "Why the Laodiceans Received Lukewarm Water," *TynBul* 38 (1987): 143–49.

III. VISION OF THE SEVEN-SEALED SCROLL, THE SEVEN TRUMPETS, THE SEVEN SIGNS, AND THE SEVEN BOWLS (4:1–19:10)

A. The Seven-Sealed Scroll (4:1–8:1)

1. Preparatory: The Throne, the Scroll, and the Lamb (4:1–5:14)

a. The throne (4:1–11)

OVERVIEW

In view of the elaborate use of imagery and visions from 4:1 through the end of Revelation and the question of how this material relates to chs. 1–3, it is not surprising that commentators differ widely regarding them. One problem is that of interpretation: What do the imagery and visions mean? Another problem involves chronology: When do the things spoken of occur? Furthermore, how does John use his frequent OT images? Does he interpret them in exact accordance with their OT sources, or does he freely reinterpret these images and figures? What is symbolic and what is literal? Answers to such questions will determine the interpreter's approach. Since few of these questions can be answered dogmatically, there is a need for tolerance of divergent approaches in the hope that the Spirit may use open-minded discussion to bring us further into the meaning of the Apocalypse.

Chapters 4–5 form one vision of two parts—the throne (ch. 4) and the Lamb and the scroll (ch. 5). In actuality, the breaking of all seven seals (chs. 6–8:1) together with the throne vision (chs. 4–5) form a single, continuous vision and should not be separated. Indeed, the throne pictures (chs. 4–5) should be viewed as dominating the entire seven-seal vision (4:1–8:1). In the tradition of the former prophets, John is given an authenticating vision of heaven that confirms that he is called by God as a genuine prophet and that he speaks with divine authority (cf. Isa 6:1–13; Jer 1:4–19; Eze 1:1–28).

¹After this I looked, and there before me was a door standing open in heaven. And the voice I had first heard speaking to me like a trumpet said, "Come up here, and I will show you what must take place after this." ²At once I was in the Spirit, and there before me was a throne in heaven with someone sitting on it. ³And the one who sat there had the appearance of jasper and carnelian. A rainbow, resembling an emerald, encircled the throne. ⁴Surrounding the throne were twenty-four other thrones, and seated on them were twenty-four elders. They were dressed in white and had crowns of gold on their heads. ⁵From the throne came flashes of lightning, rumblings and peals of thunder. Before the throne, seven lamps were blazing. These are the seven spirits of God. ⁶Also before the throne there was what looked like a sea of glass, clear as crystal.

In the center, around the throne, were four living creatures, and they were covered with eyes, in front and in back. ⁷The first living creature was like a lion, the second was like an ox, the third had a face like a man, the fourth was like a flying eagle. ⁸Each of the four living creatures had six wings and was covered with eyes all around, even under his wings. Day and night they never stop saying:

"Holy, holy, holy
is the Lord God Almighty,
who was, and is, and is to come."

⁹Whenever the living creatures give glory, honor and thanks to him who sits on the throne and who lives for ever and ever, ¹⁰the twenty-four elders fall down before him who sits on the throne, and worship him who lives for ever and ever. They lay their crowns before the throne and say:

¹¹ "You are worthy, our Lord and God,
    to receive glory and honor and power,
  for you created all things,
    and by your will they were created
    and have their being."

COMMENTARY

1 Seeing a "door standing open in heaven," John is told to "come up here" (cf. Eze 1:1, where the prophet says he saw the heavens opened). A new view of God's majesty and power (throne) is disclosed to John so that he can understand the events on earth that relate to the seven-seal vision (cf. 1Ki 22:19). For the first time in Revelation, the reader is introduced to the frequent interchange between heaven and earth found in the remainder of the book. What happens on earth has its inseparable heavenly counterpart.

Chapter 4 focuses on the throne vision that provides the setting for the dramatic action of the slain Lamb in ch. 5. There is a connection between this throne vision and the vision of the glorified Christ in 1:10–16. Here we are told that John heard the same voice speaking to him that he "had first heard speaking . . . like a trumpet" (cf. 1:10). The words of this messenger (not Christ) relate to what has just transpired: "I will show you what must take place after this" (*meta tauta*, "after this, next," i.e., after the time of the historical churches in Asia [cf. 1:19]).

There is *no* good reason for seeing the invitation for John to come up into the opened heaven as a symbol of the rapture of the church. Some have so interpreted it and have inferred that the absence of the word "church" (*ekklēsia*, GK *1711*) from Revelation 4:1 until 22:16 and the continued references to the "saints" indicate that at this point the church departs from the earth. But the word "church" or "churches" always stands in Revelation for the historic seven churches in Asia and not just for the universal body of Christ. Since 4:1–22:15 concerns the believing community as a whole, it would be inappropriate, at least for John's usage, to find the narrower term "church" in this section (cf. 3Jn 6, 9–10).

Finally, it is significant that in the visions that continue to the end of the book there are references to the throne, the book, the crowns, the four living creatures, the twenty-four elders, and the victory of the Lamb. In all this, the central focus appears to be the five hymns of praise that begin in 4:8 and continue through ch. 5.

2–3 Chapter 4 is above all a vision of the royal throne of God. The prophet ascends "in the Spirit" to see the source of all that will happen on earth (cf. 1:10). It will all be an expression of the throne's purpose; nothing happens, nothing exists—in the past, present, or future—apart from God's intention. Whatever authority is given to an angel or to a horseman is given by God. The throne symbolizes God's majesty and power. Yet his majestic transcendence is fully safeguarded—John does not attempt to describe the "someone sitting on" the throne (cf. 1Ki 22:19; 2Ch 18:18; Ps 47:8; Isa 6:1–5; Eze 1:26–28; Sir 1:8).

The minerals "jasper" and "carnelian" portray the supernatural splendor of God, while the "rainbow, resembling an emerald" conveys the impression of God's encircling brilliance (cf. Eze 1:27–28). But we need not find symbolism in each element of the vision; it is enough to allow the archetypical imagery to create the impression of transcendent glory. Whether John intends God's judgment to be part of the symbolism of the throne vision (cf. Ps 9:4, 7) is not clear. What is unmistakably clear is that all—whether elders, angels, lamps, sea of glass, or living creatures—centers on the throne and the One who sits on it, the One "who lives for ever and ever" (v.9).

It is significant that the earliest Jewish mysticism is throne mysticism (Merkabah mysticism). Its essence is not absorbed contemplation of God's true nature but perception of his appearance on the throne, as described by Ezekiel, and cognition of the mysteries of the celestial throne world (cf. Gershom G. Scholem, *Major Trends in Jewish Mysticism* [New York: Schocken, 1961], esp. ch. 2).

4 John also sees "twenty-four elders." It would be helpful if we could ask an interpreting angel, "Who are the elders?" There are at least thirteen different views of their identity, ranging from the twenty-four ruling stars (or judges) in the heavens to the simple figure of wholeness and fullness (cf. Minear, 83; Aune, *Revelation 1–5*, 287–92). Part of the discussion hinges on the correct text in 5:10 (cf. Notes). The following passages are pertinent to the elders' identification: 4:9–11; 5:5–14; 7:11–17; 11:16–18; 12:10–12; 14:3; 19:4.

The elders are always associated with the "four living creatures" (v.6) and engage in acts of worship of God and the Lamb. While not entirely ruling out the elders' possible representative or symbolic significance (a view held by many good expositors), the arguments of Ned B. Stonehouse (*Paul Before the Areopagus* [Grand Rapids: Eerdmans, 1957], 88–108), Mounce, 121–22, and others who have argued that the elders are a class of heavenly spirit-beings belonging to the general class of angels and living creatures seem more compelling. From this viewpoint, the "angels," the "twenty-four elders," and "the four living creatures" all designate actual supernatural beings involved with the purpose of God on earth and his worship in heaven. They are always distinguished from the "saints" (5:8; 11:17–18; 19:1–4), and the text of 5:10 is uncertain.

In the Bible, the number twelve appears to be the number of divine government—twelve months in a lunar year, twelve tribes of Israel, twelve apostles, twelve gates in the new Jerusalem, twelve angels at each gate, twelve foundations, twelve thousand sealed from each tribe, twelve thousand stadia (the length of the new Jerusalem), etc. Multiples of twelve—such as twenty-four—probably have a similar significance. Thrones are related to the heavenly powers in Colossians 1:16. In Revelation, "white" clothing generally belongs to the saints but relates to angelic beings elsewhere in the NT (e.g., Jn 20:12). While the "crowns of gold" are likewise usually related to the redeemed, here they refer to the royal dignity of those so closely associated with the throne of God (cf. 1Ki 22:19; Ps 89:7). Golden crowns are referred to in 4:4, 10; 9:7; 14:14.

5 "Flashes of lightning, rumblings and peals of thunder" coming from the throne are symbolic of God's awesome presence and the vindication of the saints and occur with slight variation four times in Revelation (4:5; 8:5; 11:19; 16:18; cf. Ex 19:16; Ps 18:13–15; Eze 1:13). On the expression "seven blazing lamps," see comments at 1:4 (cf. Eze 1:13).

6–8 "A sea of glass, clear as crystal" simply adds to the magnificence of the scene (cf. 15:2). Caird, 65, considers the "sea of glass" as identical to the "sea" in 13:1 and 21:1 and identifies it as "a reservoir of evil." But a sea of "glass" may be an intentional reversal of this sea imagery (cf. Ex 24:10; Eze 1:22, 26). The mirrorlike reflecting quality could symbolize the fact that before the sight of God all is revealed, i.e., "Everything is uncovered and laid bare before the eyes of him to whom we must give account" (Heb 4:13).

The "four living creatures" should be linked with Isaiah's seraphim and Ezekiel's cherubim (cf. Isa 6:3; Eze 1:5–25; 10:1–22). They, like the elders and angels, are heavenly creatures of the highest order involved with the worship and government of God. "Covered with eyes" may give the impression of their exceeding knowledge of God, while the faces of a "lion," "ox," "man," and "flying eagle" suggest

qualities that belong to God, such as royal power, strength, spirituality, and swiftness of action. Each of the creatures mentioned is the chief of its species. Together they embody the reflection of God's nature as the fullness of life and power. Their six wings (cf. Isa 6:2) give the impression of unlimited mobility in fulfilling God's commands. Their position "in the center, around the throne" suggests that one might be before and one behind the throne with one on either side (so Beckwith). The four living creatures appear throughout Revelation (cf. 5:6, 8, 14; 6:1–7; 7:11; 14:3; 15:7; 19:4).

The four living creatures ceaselessly proclaim the holiness of God: "Holy, holy, holy" (cf. Isa 6:3). In Hebrew, the double repetition of a word adds emphasis, while the rare threefold repetition designates the superlative and calls attention to the infinite holiness of God—the quality of God felt by creatures in his presence as awesomeness or fearfulness (cf. Ps 111:9: "Holy and awesome is his name"). The living creatures celebrate God's holiness and power as manifested in his past, present, and future activity. Such holiness cannot tolerate the presence of evil (21:27). (On these titles of God, see comments at 1:4, 8.) The trisagion ("holy, holy, holy") is a liturgical expression used in both ancient Jewish and Christian worship. Its use does not, however, reach back to the first century.

This hymn is the first not only of the five sung by the heavenly choirs in chs. 4–5 but also of a number of others in Revelation (4:8, 11; 5:9–10, 12, 13; 7:12, 15–17; 11:15, 17–18; 12:10–12; 15:3–4; 16:5–7; 18:2–8; 19:2–6). These hymns relate to the interpretation of the visions and provide a clue to the literary structure of Revelation. In these two chapters, the sequence of hymns shows that the first two are addressed to God, the next two to the Lamb, and the last one to both. There is also a gradual enlargement in the size of the choirs. The internal movement also builds as the last hymn is sung by "every creature in heaven and on earth and under the earth and on the sea" to "him who sits on the throne and to the Lamb" (5:13).

9–11 The second hymn is sung by the twenty-four elders. When the living creatures confess the truth of God's holy deeds, the response of the highest order of God's heavenly creatures is to relinquish their crowns of honor before the feet of him who alone is "worthy" of "glory and honor and power" because he alone (no man, not even the emperor) is the source and stay of every created thing (Pss 33:6–9; 102:25; 136:5–9). The expression "by your will they were created and have their being" (v.11), presents a translation difficulty because the Greek text has two different tenses—imperfect (ēsan, "they were" [NIV, "have their being"]) and aorist (ektisthēsan, "they were created"). Although a number of possible explanations have been advanced, Alford, 4:602–3, gives the best one: the imperfect tense describes the *fact* of their existence while the aorist captures the sense of the *beginning* of their existence. Consequently, the phrase might be translated thus: "Because of [not by] your will they continually exist and have come into being."

NOTES

1 The expression ἃ δεῖ γενέσθαι μετὰ ταῦτα, *ha dei genesthai meta tauta* ("what must take place after this"), is found in the LXX of Daniel 2:29, 45, where it has the sense of "next" in historical sequence from the time of the writer or next in the sequence of his visions (i.e., next, after the *vision* of Christ and the seven churches in chs. 2–3). Keil and Delitzsch (*Daniel*, 111) note that "after this" does not mean "at some future time" but refers to what is after that which is at present. Alternatively, Beale, 152–70, argues that the term refers to the time of the eschatological fulfillment that began with the coming, death, and resurrection of Christ and the outpouring of the Spirit and continues in this age of the "latter days."

8 John's Greek text of this verse agrees with 1QIsa at Isaiah 6:2 against both the MT and the LXX (cf. Trudinger, "Some Observations Concerning the Text," 88).

b. The Scroll and the Lamb (5:1–14)

OVERVIEW

This chapter is part of the vision that begins at ch. 4 and continues through the opening of the seven seals (6:1–8:1; cf. comments at Overview, ch. 4). Its center of gravity lies in the three hymns (vv.9, 12, 13), all addressed to the Lamb. They beautifully combine the worship of the Lamb (hymns one and two) with the worship of the One who sits on the throne (hymn three, which is addressed to both God and the Lamb). The movement of the whole scene focuses on the slain Lamb as he takes the scroll from the hand of the One on the throne. The actions of all other participants are described in terms of worship directed to the Lamb and the One on the throne. The culminating emphasis is on the worthiness of the Lamb to receive worship because of his death.

¹Then I saw in the right hand of him who sat on the throne a scroll with writing on both sides and sealed with seven seals. ²And I saw a mighty angel proclaiming in a loud voice, "Who is worthy to break the seals and open the scroll?" ³But no one in heaven or on earth or under the earth could open the scroll or even look inside it. ⁴I wept and wept because no one was found who was worthy to open the scroll or look inside. ⁵Then one of the elders said to me, "Do not weep! See, the Lion of the tribe of Judah, the Root of David, has triumphed. He is able to open the scroll and its seven seals."

⁶Then I saw a Lamb, looking as if it had been slain, standing in the center of the throne, encircled by the four living creatures and the elders. He had seven horns and seven eyes, which are the seven spirits of God sent out into all the earth. ⁷He came and took the scroll from the right hand of him who sat on the throne. ⁸And when he had taken it, the four living creatures and the twenty-four elders fell down before the Lamb. Each one had a harp and they were holding golden bowls full of incense, which are the prayers of the saints. ⁹And they sang a new song:

> "You are worthy to take the scroll
>   and to open its seals,
> because you were slain,
>   and with your blood you purchased men for God
>   from every tribe and language and people and nation.
> ¹⁰ You have made them to be a kingdom and priests to serve our God,
>   and they will reign on the earth."

¹¹Then I looked and heard the voice of many angels, numbering thousands upon thousands, and ten thousand times ten thousand. They encircled the throne and the living creatures and the elders. ¹²In a loud voice they sang:

> "Worthy is the Lamb, who was slain,
> to receive power and wealth and wisdom and strength
> and honor and glory and praise!"

¹³Then I heard every creature in heaven and on earth and under the earth and on the sea, and all that is in them, singing:

> "To him who sits on the throne and to the Lamb
> be praise and honor and glory and power,
>   for ever and ever!"

¹⁴The four living creatures said, "Amen," and the elders fell down and worshiped.

COMMENTARY

1 John sees "in the right hand of him who sat on the throne a scroll with writing on both sides and sealed with seven seals." This raises a problem involving the phrase "with writing on both sides." Papyrus codices (which were like books as we know them) did not originate until the second century AD, or perhaps the late first century (cf. Bruce M. Metzger, *The Text of the New Testament* [2d ed.; Oxford: Clarendon, 1964], 6). In ancient times, papyrus rolls were used for public and private documents. Usually the writing was on one side only—the inside part—arranged in successive vertical columns. Occasionally a scroll was written on both sides; in that case, it was called an "opisthograph." Such double-sided writing was for private, non-salable use in contrast to the usual scrolls written on only one side, which were sold (cf. Edward Maunde Thompson, *An Introduction to Greek and Latin Paleography* [Oxford: Clarendon, 1912], 49–50). In the context of ch. 5, an opisthograph would signify a scroll full of words. The importance of establishing the scroll rather than codex character of the document lies in the interpretation of the opening of the seals. If the book were a codex, the seals could have been opened one at a time and portions of the book disclosed; a scroll, however, could be opened only after *all* the seals were broken.

Scrolls, or folded sheets, were sealed with wax blobs impressed with a signet ring to protect the contents or guarantee the integrity of the writing. Only the owner could open the seals and disclose the contents. Original documents were usually sealed; copies were not. Sealed documents were kept hidden, while unsealed copies were made public (22:10; cf. *TDNT* 7:941–42).

The phrase "with writing on both sides" (*gegrammenon esōthen kai opisthen*) is literally "written inside and on the back side," where "on the back side"

(*opisthen*, GK *3957*) is generally understood as going with "written" (*gegrammenon*, GK *1211*). Theodor Zahn (*Introduction to the New Testament* [Grand Rapids: Kregel, 1953], 3:405–6), however, argues that "back side" should go with the verb "sealed" (*katesphragismenon*, GK *2958*) and not with "written." While tempting and grammatically possible, his view has not found acceptance among exegetes; and the adverbial use of *opisthen* in the rest of Revelation and the NT favors always taking it with a preceding rather than a following verb.

As to the identity and significance of the scroll, there are a number of different views:

1. Ancient Roman wills or "testaments" were sealed with six seals, each of which bore a different name of the sealer and could only be opened by him (*TDNT* 7:941). This has led some to identify the scroll as the testament of God concerning the promise of the inheritance of his future kingdom (so Zahn, 3:395–96). A slight variation of this view refers the scene to the Roman law of *mancipatio*. Under this law an heir received either an inheritance at the death of the testator or the use of *mancipatio* in connection with transference of the inheritance to an executor, known as the *familiae empto*. The executor could use the property until the death of the testator, at which time he was obligated to distribute the possessions in accordance with the instructions of the testator (cf. Emmet Russell, "A Roman Law Parallel to Revelation Five," *BSac* 115 [1958]: 258–64).

2. Others see the scroll containing, like Ezekiel's scroll, "words of lament and mourning and woe" (Eze 2:9–10) and depicting the future judgment of the world (so Walvoord, 113; Thomas, 1:378–79). In Isaiah 29:11, a sealed scroll is likened to the inability of the Jewish people to know the divine vision Isaiah is proclaiming.

3. Still others find the significance to be the progressive unfolding of the history of the world. As each successive seal is opened, the further contents of the book are revealed. Seiss, 112, connects the scroll with a "title-deed" (Jer 32:10–14). It is the "title-deed" to creation that was forfeited by sin in Genesis. By his redeeming death, Christ has won the authority to reclaim the earth.

4. Another study equates the scroll with the OT Torah (so Lucetta Mowry, "Revelation 4–5 and Early Christian Liturgical Usage," *JBL* 71 [1952]: 75–84).

Each of these views has merit and may provide elements of truth for the background of the striking imagery in these chapters. Yet each view is vulnerable to criticism. Only from Revelation itself can the content and nature of the scroll be determined. Since the seals hinder the opening of the scroll until they are all broken, we may assume that the seals are preparatory to the opening of the scroll and the disclosure of its contents. This means that the seals have the effect of hiding the contents of the scroll (i.e., the "revelation," 1:1) until they are broken (Isa 29:11).

The following internal evidence relating to the contents of the scroll may be noted:

1. Just prior to the opening of the seventh seal, in connection with the events under the sixth seal, we read, "For the great day of their [i.e., the One sitting on the throne and the Lamb] wrath has come, and who can stand?" (6:17).

2. When the seventh seal is opened (8:1–5), no immediate events as such follow on earth—except for the earthquake—as in the first six seals, unless the opening of the seventh seal includes among its events the blowing of the seven trumpets of judgment (8:6–11:15). This appears to me to be precisely the case.

3. The seventh trumpet likewise is not immediately followed by any specific events on earth (11:15–19), except for an earthquake and a hailstorm (v.19). However, just before the seventh

trumpet is sounded, we read, "The second woe has passed; the third woe is coming soon" (v.14). When the seven angels prepare to pour out "the seven last plagues," symbolized by the bowls, we read that with these bowls God's wrath is completed (15:1, 7–8). Thus it seems reasonable to identify the contents of the seventh trumpet with the seven bowls of judgment (chs. 16–19).

Furthermore, frequent references to the events of the seals, trumpets, and bowls appear throughout the remaining visions in Revelation (cf. 19:19–21; 20:4; 21:9), indicating that the content of the seven-sealed scroll ultimately includes the unfolding of the consummation of the mystery of all things, the goal or end of all history, for both the conquerors and the worshipers of the beast. In 10:7, we are told that in the days of the sounding of the seventh trumpet "the mystery of God will be accomplished, just as he announced to his servants the prophets." From this it may be concluded that the scroll contains the unveiling of "the mystery of God" that OT prophets foretold (cf. comments at 10:7). Thus the "seals" conceal the mystery, which only Christ can now disclose (Da 12:9; Rev 10:4), of how God's judgment and his kingdom will come. In 11:15, when the final trumpet sounds, heavenly voices say, "The kingdom of the world has become the kingdom of our Lord and of his Christ," indicating that the scroll also contains the announcement of the inheritance of Christ and the saints who will reign with him (5:10).

The scroll, then, is not only about judgment or about the inheritance of the kingdom. Rather, it contains the divine announcement of the consummation of all history—how things will ultimately end for all people: judgment for the world and the final reward of the saints (11:18). Christ alone, as the Messiah, is the revealer and executor of the purposes of God and the heir of the inheritance of the world. He obtained this by his substitutionary and propitiatory death on the cross (5:9).

2–4 A mighty angel shouts out a challenge for anyone to come forth who is "worthy" to open the great scroll and its seals. All creation in heaven and earth and under the earth stood motionless and speechless. No one was worthy to open the scroll, i.e., no one had the authority and virtue for such a task. If the scroll contains both the revelation and the carrying out of the final drama of history, then John's despair can be appreciated. In this vision, the execution of events on earth is ascribed to the Lamb. As the seals are broken and the roll opened, salvation history unfolds until history culminates in the kingdom reign of the Messiah over the whole earth. History, then, has its center in Jesus Christ and its goal in his triumphant reign over all the powers of the world.

5 John's sorrow is assuaged. One of the elders announces that there is one who has "triumphed" (*nikaō*, "overcome, conquer, win a victory," GK *3771*—the same word as in 2:7; 3:21; etc.). He has triumphed because of his death (v.9). Two figurative titles are used of the one who is worthy—"the Lion of the tribe of Judah" and "the Root of David." Both are familiar OT messianic titles (Ge 49:9–10; cf. Isa 11:1, 10; Jer 23:5; 33:5; Rev 22:16). But they are linked together only here and in the Qumran literature (cf. 4Q252; Trudinger, "Some Observations Concerning the Text," 88). In Jewish apocalyptic literature contemporary with John, the figure of a lion was used to designate the conquering Messiah who would destroy Rome (*4 Ezra* 11:58). Close attention should be paid to John's understanding of the role and function of the Messiah, observing where it is similar to the Jewish understanding of the Messiah and where it differs.

6 As John looked to see the mighty Lion (the conquering warrior-Messiah from the Root of David), he saw instead the striking figure of a "Lamb" (*arnion*, "a young sheep," GK *768*) that had the appearance of being slaughtered, standing in the center of the throne court. This new figure portrays

sacrificial death and links the Messiah to the OT Passover lamb (Ex 12:5–6; Isa 53:7; Jn 1:29, 36; Ac 8:32; 1Pe 1:19). Here John joins the OT royal Davidic Messiah with the Suffering Servant of Isaiah (Isa 42–53). Both prophetic themes come together in Jesus of Nazareth, the true Messiah. "As if it had been slain" (*esphagmenon*, "with its throat cut," GK *5377*) could refer to the "marks of death" the living Lamb still bore or to his appearance "as if being led to the slaughter," i.e., "marked out for death" (so Minear). The "lamb" metaphor dominates John's thought in the rest of the book (e.g., 6:1–14; 7:9–17; 12:11; 13:8; 21:9).

The Lamb is said to be "standing in the center of the throne, encircled by the four living creatures and the elders" (NIV); or is he "between the throne (with the four living creatures) and the elders" (NASB)? The NIV is the preferred translation and agrees with 3:21 and 22:3. The first phrase, "standing in the center of the throne," means that the Lamb shares the throne with God. The second, "encircled by the four living creatures," means that they surround the throne; and the final phrase, "and the elders," refers to another circle around the throne but farther away than the living creatures. The christological implications of this are immense. Christ shares the throne with God as his divine equal. Not two thrones but a single throne with two equal figures on it. Paul can see Jesus as exalted to the right hand of God (Ro 8:34), but John sees him as in the center of the throne with God. The "eyes" are more explicitly identified as the "seven spirits of God sent out into all the earth"—probably a symbolic reference to the divine Holy Spirit who is sent forth by Christ into the world (1:4; 4:5). The teaching of the fourth gospel is similar, where the Spirit is sent forth to exalt Christ and convict the world of sin (Jn 14:26; 15:26; 16:7–15).

This image of the Lamb with "seven horns and seven eyes, which are the seven spirits of God ..." sees God, the Lamb, and the Spirit together on the single throne. This is the visionary testimony to the tripartite nature of the divine being (cf. Jonathan Knight, "The Enthroned Christ of Revelation 5:6 and the Development of Christian Theology," in Moyise, 43–50).

John notices that the Lamb who bears the marks of death is also the ruler who bears the signs of the fullness of divine omnipotence, dominion, and omniscience ("seven horns and seven eyes"). Following R. H. Charles, Mounce, 132–33, suggests that the figure of a lamb with seven horns is undoubtedly drawn from the apocalyptic tradition, citing *1 Enoch* 90:9 (the Maccabees are symbolized by "horned lambs") and the *Testament of Joseph* (19:8–9—a lamb destroys the enemies of Israel). However, the passage in *1 Enoch* bears little relationship to the messianic Lamb as portrayed in Revelation, and the *Testament of Joseph* is notorious for Christian interpolations. Since the lamb image is used in the fourth gospel to depict the Suffering Messiah in passages where apocalyptic connections would be quite remote, it may still be better to connect the lamb vocabulary to the OT Passover motif and Isaiah's Suffering Servant (Isa 53:7), especially in light of the author's interest in the Passover theme elsewhere in the book (e.g., ch. 19). Bauckham, 183, likewise sees "no evidence that the Lamb was already established as a symbol of the messianic conqueror in pre-Christian Judaism."

7 Next the Lamb acts: "He came and took the scroll." The Greek conveys a dramatic action in the tense of the verb "took" (perhaps a dramatic perfect?): "He went up and took it, and now he has it!" Symbolically, the one on the throne thus authorizes the slain messianic King to execute his plan for the redemption of the world, because in and through the Lamb God is at work in history for the salvation of humanity. Observe that this dramatic act of seizing the scroll is not itself the act of victory referred to in v.6 and later in v.9. Christ's victorious death on the cross is the basis of his authority to redeem the world by taking and opening the seven-sealed scroll.

8 The Lamb's act calls forth three hymns of praise (vv.9, 12, 13) from the living creatures and elders. John sees them fall down in worship before the Lamb, as they had earlier done before the One on the throne (4:10), thus acknowledging the deity of the Lamb. They have "harps," which are the "lyres" used for the older psalmody (cf., e.g., Pss 33:2; 98:5) but will now be used for the "new song" of praise to the Lamb (v.9; 15:2–3).

The "bowls full of incense" represent the "prayers of the saints" (8:3–4). Prayer (*proseuchē*, GK 4666) in this scene is not praise but petition. Why would John mention the saints on earth as petitioning God? In 6:10 the martyrs are seen as calling to God for his judgment on those who killed them, and in 8:3–4 the prayers of the saints are immediately connected with the trumpets of God's judgment. These prayers, then, are evidently for God's vindication of the martyred saints. And since v.10 refers to the coming kingdom, it may be that the prayers are petitions for God to judge the world and to extend his kingdom throughout the earth (Lk 18:7–8). "Saints" here, as elsewhere in the NT and the rest of Revelation, is simply the normal term for the rank and file of Christians, i.e., those set apart for God's purposes (2Co 1:1; Php 1:1; Rev 11:18; 13:7, 19; 19:8; 22:21).

9 The three hymns interpret the symbolism of the scroll and the Lamb. The number of singers increases from twenty-eight in v.8 to every creature in all creation in v.13. The first two hymns are songs of praise to the Lamb, whereas the last is praise to both the One on the throne and the Lamb (v.13). The first hymn (vv.9–10) is called a "new" song because there was never any like it before in heaven (see comments at 14:3).

"You are worthy" (*axios*, "comparable, equal to, deserving"; GK 545) refers to the qualifications of this person who alone has won the right to take the scroll and open its seals. His worthiness for this task was won by his loving sacrifice on the cross—"because you were slain." This must be understood as a direct reference to the earthly death of the human Jesus of Nazareth—an understanding supported by the Greek aorist tense used here. It is no mythological death or salvation. Like other NT writers, John views the death of Jesus as a redeeming death—"and with your blood [or by the price of your blood] you purchased [or redeemed, *agorazō*, GK 60] men for God."

The death of Jesus broke the stranglehold of the "powers and authorities" over the creation and produced a great victory of liberation for humankind (Col 2:15). It is this victory, obtained through suffering and death, that entitles Christ to execute the unfolding of the mystery of God's consummation of history. The centrality of the cross and its meaning as a redemptive act comes repeatedly to the fore and should dominate our understanding throughout Revelation (1:5; 5:12; 7:14; 12:11; 13:8; 14:4; 15:3; 19:7; 21:9, 23; 22:3; etc.). Jesus' death secured a salvation universally applied to all classes and peoples of the earth—"every tribe and language and people and nation" (cf. 7:9). Handel's great closing chorus, "Worthy is the Lamb," of his masterful oratorio *Messiah* has immortalized this text for the concert hall and the church since its first presentation in Dublin on April 13, 1742.

10 The Lamb's right to open the scroll rests also on the fact that he has made the ransomed into a "kingdom" and made them "priests" (to serve God in praise; cf. Heb 13:15–16). Christians "will reign on the earth" with Christ because they have been given kingly authority through his death (1:6; 20:4–6). While not excluding the present reign of believers, "the earth" is best taken to refer to the future eschatological kingdom reign of Christ (see Notes for various problems in this verse).

11–12 Now John sees a new feature in the vision: "thousands upon thousands, and ten thousand times ten thousand" angels surrounding the throne. The vision is similar to Daniel's vision of the countless multitude before the Ancient of Days (Da 7:10). The imagery suggests the infinite honor and power of the One who is at the center of it all. The angels shout out their song of praise to the Lamb who was slain (cf. Heb 1:6). Their sevenfold shout rings out like the sound from a huge bell—"power . . . wealth . . . wisdom . . . strength . . . honor . . . glory . . . praise." All of these are intrinsic qualities of Christ except the last, which is the expression of the creatures' worship—"praise" (lit., "blessing"). Elsewhere the same qualities are ascribed to God himself (5:13; 7:12). The sevenfold multiplication of these attributes by angelic choirs is a Qumranic liturgical method for creating the feeling of God's majesty and glory (7:12; cf. 4Q400).

13–14 Finally, far beyond the precincts of the throne there arises an expression of praise and worth from the whole created universe to the One on the throne and to the Lamb. John beautifully blends the worship of the Father (ch. 4) and the worship of the Son (5:8–12). In appropriate response, the living beings utter their "amen" (see comments at 3:14), and the elders fall down in worship.

NOTES

1 The difficult expression ὄπισθεν, *opisthen* ("behind, back of"), has textual variants here. A strongly supported tradition in the versions and Fathers has the reading ἔξωθεν, *exōthen* ("outside"), which probably arose when codices replaced scrolls in the Christian community, making the expression "back side" sound strange (Metzger, [1971 ed.], 737).

5 While evidence supporting a pre-Christian Jewish understanding of a suffering Messiah is meager, there do exist some traces of it. Alfred Edersheim (*The Life and Times of Jesus the Messiah* [Grand Rapids: Eerdmans, 1965], 2:727) points out that Isaiah 53 was applied to the Messiah in the Targum and in the Midrash on Samuel, "where it is said that all sufferings are divided into three parts, one of which the Messiah bore."

6 The word for "lamb" or young sheep used in Revelation some twenty-eight times is ἀρνίον (*arnion*, GK *768*), which occurs only once elsewhere in John 21:15 (in the plural). The alternative word is ἀμνὸς (*amnos*, GK *303*), which occurs only four times and is used of Christ (Jn 1:29, 36; Ac 8:32; 1Pe 1:19). Both words occur in the LXX and are used in Exodus 12 to refer to the sacrificial Passover lamb. No distinction between ἀρνίον, *arnion*, and ἀμνὸς, *amnos*, should be pressed; their use merely reflects the author's preference. The diminutive ending ιον (*ion*) has lost its diminutive force (cf. Mussies, 109).

9 Here the chief problem is whether the text should read "redeemed us [ἡμᾶς, *hēmas*] to God" or simply "redeemed to God," omitting ἡμᾶς, *hēmas* (NIV, "purchased men"). The reading is crucial to the identification of the elders. If ἡμᾶς, *hēmas*, is original, it would be difficult to argue that the elders are angelic beings. The evidence for the shorter reading consists of one Greek MS (A) and one version (Ethiopic), while all other versional and Greek evidence has the word ἡμᾶς, *hēmas*. Unless unusual weight is given to A (it is considered the best witness), the most reasonable conclusion is to charge A at this point with an omission. On the other hand, Metzger, 666, argues that the reading of A best accounts for the origin of the longer variations, since scribes were unsatisfied with a less direct object for ἠγόρασας (*ēgorasas*, "redeemed"; NIV, "purchased") and supplied the awkward ἡμᾶς, *hēmas*, which does not fit the αὐτοὺς (*autous*, "them") of v.10. It is a difficult question to settle with certainty, but this commentary follows the shorter reading (as with the NIV) and views the elders as a class of supernatural beings.

10 More difficult are the readings βασιλεύουσιν, *basileuousin* ("they reign" [present tense]), or βασιλεύσουσιν, *basileusousin* ("they will reign" [future tense]). Both have nearly equal MS support. Although the NIV has the future tense here, it would seem better to adopt—with reservation—the present-tense reading and understand it as a "future present," in keeping with John's other references to the future reign of the saints (20:4). Mounce, 136 n. 36, concurs. For a helpful inductive discussion of the whole chapter, see also Robert H. Mounce, "Worthy is the Lamb," ch. 5, in *Scripture, Tradition, and Interpretation*, ed. W. Ward Gasque and William Sanford LaSor (Grand Rapids: Eerdmans, 1978).

John's expression "a kingdom and priests" is a combination of the LXX rendering of Exodus 19:6 and that of the Targum (cf. McNamara, *Targum and Testament*, 156). The source of this idea of the saints' reign could well be Daniel 7:10, though no direct verbal allusion appears in Revelation (cf. France, 204).

2. Opening of the First Six Seals (6:1–17)

OVERVIEW

The opening of the seals continues the vision begun in chs. 4 and 5. Now the scene shifts to events on earth. Before expositing each of the seals, it will be helpful to consider their overall meaning. As we have already seen (see comments at 5:1), the scroll itself involves the rest of Revelation and has to do with the consummation of the mystery of all things, the goal or end of history for both the overcomers and the worshipers of the beast. But what relationship do the seals have to this mystery? Are the events of the seals representative and simultaneous world happenings that occur throughout the church age (so Minear)? Do they occur sequentially? Are they part of the final drama (so Bruce) or merely preparatory to it (so Ladd)? One thing is certain: the Lamb has the scroll and he himself opens the seals (6:1, 3, 5, etc.).

With the opening of the fifth seal, the martyrs cry out, "How long, ... until you judge the inhabitants of the earth?" and they are told to wait "a little longer" (vv.10–11). And when the sixth seal is opened, the judgment appears to be imminent (v.17)—a seeming indication that there is a time progression in the seals. I tentatively suggest that the seals represent events preparatory to the final consummation. Whether these events come immediately before the end or whether they represent general conditions that will prevail throughout the period preceding the end is a more difficult question.

The seals closely parallel the signs of the approaching end times spoken of in Jesus' Olivet Discourse (Mt 24:1–35; Mk 13:1–37; Lk 21:5–33). In these passages, the events of the last days fall into three periods: (1) the period of false christs, wars, famines, pestilences, earthquakes, and death called "the beginning of birth pains" (Mt 24:8); (2) the period of the great tribulation (Mt 24:21; NIV, "great distress"); and finally, (3) the period "immediately after the distress

of those days," when the sun, moon, and stars will be affected and Christ will return (Mt 24:29–30). This parallel to major parts of Revelation is too striking to be ignored. Thus the seals would correspond to the "beginning of birth pains" found in the Olivet Discourse. The events are similar to those occurring under the trumpets (8:2–11:19) and bowls (15:1–16:21), but they should not be confused with those later and more severe judgments. In Jewish apocalyptic literature (cf. *2 Bar.* 25–30), the great tribulation precedes the age to come and is divided into twelve parts of various trials lasting possibly one week of seven weeks, or forty-nine years (cf. C. K. Barrett, *The New Testament Background* [New York: Harper and Row, 1961], 245–48). Moreover, in the eschatological reckoning of time (see comments at 1:1), the events immediately preceding the end can stretch out over the whole age of the church, from John's time until now, and can still be viewed as "next" (4:1) in the sense that the "last days" began in the first century and are still continuing (cf. 1Jn 2:18).

The first four seals are distinct from the last two in that they describe four horses of different colors with four riders who are given different powers over the earth. We find the background for the imagery of these four seals in Zechariah 1:8–10 and 6:1–8. In Zechariah's visions, the horsemen and chariots are divine instruments of judgment on the enemies of God's people, while the colors represent geographical points of the compass. This may also be the best interpretation of the horses and their riders in Revelation 6, where each is sent by Christ through the instrumentality of the living creatures.

[1]I watched as the Lamb opened the first of the seven seals. Then I heard one of the four living creatures say in a voice like thunder, "Come!" [2]I looked, and there before me was a white horse! Its rider held a bow, and he was given a crown, and he rode out as a conqueror bent on conquest.

³When the Lamb opened the second seal, I heard the second living creature say, "Come!" ⁴Then another horse came out, a fiery red one. Its rider was given power to take peace from the earth and to make men slay each other. To him was given a large sword.

⁵When the Lamb opened the third seal, I heard the third living creature say, "Come!" I looked, and there before me was a black horse! Its rider was holding a pair of scales in his hand. ⁶Then I heard what sounded like a voice among the four living creatures, saying, "A quart of wheat for a day's wages, and three quarts of barley for a day's wages, and do not damage the oil and the wine!"

⁷When the Lamb opened the fourth seal, I heard the voice of the fourth living creature say, "Come!" ⁸I looked, and there before me was a pale horse! Its rider was named Death, and Hades was following close behind him. They were given power over a fourth of the earth to kill by sword, famine and plague, and by the wild beasts of the earth.

⁹When he opened the fifth seal, I saw under the altar the souls of those who had been slain because of the word of God and the testimony they had maintained. ¹⁰They called out in a loud voice, "How long, Sovereign Lord, holy and true, until you judge the inhabitants of the earth and avenge our blood?" ¹¹Then each of them was given a white robe, and they were told to wait a little longer, until the number of their fellow servants and brothers who were to be killed as they had been was completed.

¹²I watched as he opened the sixth seal. There was a great earthquake. The sun turned black like sackcloth made of goat hair, the whole moon turned blood red, ¹³and the stars in the sky fell to earth, as late figs drop from a fig tree when shaken by a strong wind. ¹⁴The sky receded like a scroll, rolling up, and every mountain and island was removed from its place.

¹⁵Then the kings of the earth, the princes, the generals, the rich, the mighty, and every slave and every free man hid in caves and among the rocks of the mountains. ¹⁶They called to the mountains and the rocks, "Fall on us and hide us from the face of him who sits on the throne and from the wrath of the Lamb! ¹⁷For the great day of their wrath has come, and who can stand?"

COMMENTARY

1 The emphatic call "come!" (vv. 1, 3, 5, 7) should not be viewed as addressed either to John (as with some ancient Greek MSS and many commentators; cf. Notes, v. 1) or to Christ (as with Alford, Swete), but rather to the horsemen in each case. An analogy may be a first-century amphitheater or circus, with various charioteers being summoned into the arena of the world by the call "come!" or "go forth!"

2 The identification of the first rider seated on a white horse has been difficult for interpreters. Essentially, the difficulty is whether the rider on the white horse represents Christ and the victory of the gospel (so Alford, Ladd) or whether he represents the Antichrist and the forces of evil (so Beckwith, Bruce, Caird, Mounce, Swete, Walvoord). In favor of the first identification is (1) the striking similarity of this rider to the portrayal of Christ in 19:11–16, (2) the symbolism of white throughout Revelation always being associated with righteousness and Christ (e.g., 1:14; 2:17; 3:4–5, 18; 4:4; 7:9, 13–14; 20:11), and (3) the references in the Olivet Discourse to the preaching of the gospel throughout the world before the end.

Support for the identification of the white horse with the Antichrist and his forces is the parallelism with the other three horses, which are instruments of judgment. The references in 19:11–16 to the rider on the white horse as "Faithful and True" and of whom it is said that "with justice he judges and makes war" may stand in contrast to the rider in 6:2, who is not faithful or true and who wages war for unjust conquest. As for the Lamb, he opens the seals and would not be one of the riders. Moreover, it would be inappropriate to have an angelic being call forth Christ or his servants. Again the "bow" would most naturally be connected with the enemy of God's people (Eze 39:3; cf. Rev 20:7–8). Finally, the parallelism to the Olivet Discourse shows that the first events mentioned are the rise of "false Christs and false prophets" (Mt 24:24).

It must be admitted that the problem of the identity of this rider may be solved either way, depending on the presuppositions one brings to the passage. The evidence, however, seems to favor slightly the second solution—identifying the white horse with the Antichrist and his forces, which seek to conquer the followers of Christ. John sensed that these persecutions were already present in his day and that they would culminate in a final, more severe form (1Jn 2:18; Rev 13:7).

Each of the first four seals, then, represents conflict directed at Christians to test them and to sift out false disciples (6:10). This interpretation need not preclude the fact that the seals may also refer to judgments on humanity in general. Yet since the fifth seal stresses the cry of the martyred Christians,

probably the thought of Christian persecution also belongs in the first four seals (Minear, 78, 266–69). Each of them unleashes events that separate false belief from true. The destruction of Jerusalem is a case in point (Lk 21:20–24). The white horse is released to conquer. As he goes forth, judgment falls on unbelieving Israel (21:22–23), while at the same time there is a testing of believers to separate the chaff from the wheat (cf. 21:12–19).

Although the bow could be a symbol of either the Parthian or Cretan invaders bent on the conquest of Rome, in this context it suggests forces opposed to Christians (cf. Mt 24:5). A "crown" refers to victorious conquest in 19:12, where Christ wears "many crowns." "He was given" is the formula for the sovereign permission to carry out acts that, from a human viewpoint, seem contrary to God's character but nevertheless accomplish his will (cf. 13:5, 7, 15). Thus the rider on the white horse may also point to the attacks of the false Jews (2:9; 3:9), the affront to Christians from pagan religionists, and the persecutions from Rome, as well as all future, limited victories over the church by Satan (cf. 2:13; 12:17).

While v.2 would be sobering for first-century believers, at the same time it would encourage them, provided they understood that the Lamb had, for his own beneficent ends, permitted their testing and suffering. So they could trust that, in the midst of seeming defeat from their enemies, he would ultimately be the victor (17:14).

3–4 The second horseman is war and bloodshed. He rides on a "fiery red" steed, whose color symbolizes slaughter (2Ki 3:22–23); he is given the "large sword" because the number of those he kills is so great (cf. 13:10, 14). John might have thought of Nero's slaughter of Christians, the martyrdom of Antipas (2:13), or perhaps those slain under Domitian's persecutions (cf. Mt 10:34; 24:9).

5–6 The third horseman is poverty and famine. He rides on a "black horse" and symbolizes the effects of war and bloodshed: sorrow, mourning, and desolation (Isa 50:3; Jer 4:28; La 5:10 KJV). In the rider's hand there is a "pair of scales." A voice is heard interpreting its significance in economic terms: "a quart of wheat . . . and three quarts of barley for a day's wage" (lit., "for a denarius," a Greek coin). This amount suggests food prices about twelve times higher than normal (Beckwith, 520) and implies inflation and conditions of famine (Mt 24:7). A quart of wheat would supply an average person with one day's sustenance. Barley was used by the poor to mix with the wheat. The expression "do not damage the oil and wine" is less clear. Some view oil and wine as luxuries not necessary for bare survival, and the rich would have them while the poor were starving (cf. Pr 21:17). Others take oil and wine as showing the extent of the famine, since a drought affecting the grain may not be severe enough to hurt the vines and olive trees (so Beckwith, 521). Moreover, oil and wine are staple foods in the East, both in dearth and in prosperity (e.g., Dt 7:13; Hos 2:8, 22). So in this view the third seal brings poverty and partial, though not severe, famine. Mounce, 144, notes, "This interpretation is in harmony with the increasing intensity of the three cycles of judgment. The fourth seal affects 'the fourth part of the earth' (6:8), the trumpets destroy a third (8:7, 8, 10, 12), and the destruction by the bowls is complete and final (16:1ff.)."

7–8 The fourth seal reveals a rider on a "pale horse." "Pale" (*chlōros*, GK *5952*) denotes a yellowish green, the light green of a plant, or the paleness of a sick person in contrast to a healthy appearance (cf. BDAG, 1085). This cadaverous color blends well with the name of the rider—"Death" (*thanatos*, GK *2505*). This probably refers to the death brought by pestilence or plague, which often follows famine (cf. Jer 14:12; Eze 5:17; 14:21; Lk 21:11). "Hades was following close behind [Death]." But how? On foot? On the back of the same horse? On a separate

horse? Scripture does not say. (On "Hades," see comments at 1:18.) There seems to be a growth of intensity in the judgments as they are carried out by various agencies—the sword (human violence), famine, plague, and now the wild beasts of the earth.

9–11 The fifth seal changes the metaphor of horsemen and discloses a scene of martyred saints under the altar crying out for justice against those who killed them. They are told to wait a little longer until their fellow servants are also killed. Who are these martyrs? They are referred to again in 18:24 as "all who have been killed on the earth" and in 20:4 as "those who had been beheaded." In 13:15 they are referred to as those who refused to worship the image of the beast and were "killed." Others also take the group seen in 7:9 as martyred saints in heaven. At any rate, the question arises as to why the martyrs alone receive so much attention rather than all suffering or persecuted Christians. One solution understands John to be referring to all those who so faithfully follow Christ as to form a group that may be characterized as the slain of the Lord. They may or may not actually suffer physical death for Christ, but they have (like John) so identified themselves with the slain Lamb that they have in effect already offered up their lives ("because of the word of God and the testimony they had maintained" [cf. 1:2, 9]); and they are seen as a group (cf. Ro 8:36).

9 John says that he saw the "souls" (*psychas*, GK *6034*) of those slain. This is generally understood to mean the disembodied souls of these saints. However, the Greek *psyche* has various meanings and probably stands here for the actual "lives" or "persons" who were killed rather than for their "souls." They are seen by John as persons who are very much alive, though they have been killed by the beast. "Under the altar" sets the scene as occurring in the temple of heaven. Depending on which altar is meant, one of two different ideas is connoted. In 8:3, 5 and 9:13, the altar is the golden altar of incense that stood in the tabernacle either in or before the Most Holy Place (Ex 30:1–10; Heb 9:4). Likewise, the other references in Revelation to "altar" can also be understood as referring to this altar of incense (11:1; 14:18; 16:7). In accord with this sense, the prayers of the saints would be for God's vindication of the martyrs of Christ (cf. Lk 18:7–8). On the other hand, some understand this as the bronze altar of sacrifice and see in the imagery the blood of the martyrs at the base or "under the altar" (so Ladd). But if the symbolism is sacrificial, it would be more natural to read "on" the altar, not "under" it.

10 The martyred address God as "Sovereign Lord" (*despotēs*, GK *1305*). This term implies "ownership" (*TDNT* 2:44) and is used elsewhere in the NT to denote slave masters (1Ti 6:1; 1Pe 2:18), God (Lk 2:29; Ac 4:24), and Jesus Christ (2Pe 2:1; Jude 4). (On the phrase "holy and true," see comments at 3:7.) The martyrs cry out for God's vengeance on the evildoers. The word "avenge" (*ekdikeō*, GK *1688*) relates everywhere in the OT (LXX) and in the NT to the idea of punishment or retribution (*TDNT* 2:442–44). These saints are following the teaching of Paul in Romans 12:19: "Do not take revenge, my friends, but leave room for God's wrath, for it is written: 'It is mine to avenge; I will repay,' says the Lord." Though believers are forbidden to take revenge, God will vindicate his elect by punishing those who killed them (Lk 18:7–8; 2Th 1:8).

11 The martyrs were each given a "white robe" as evidence of their righteousness and victory before the Judge of all the earth, who will speedily avenge their deaths. The wait of a "little longer" is in God's estimate but a fleeting moment, though for us it may stretch out for ages (cf. 12:12; 20:3). The Dead Sea Scrolls refer to the final reward of the righteous as "the garment of honor in everlasting light" (1QS 4.8). The expression "until the number of their fellow servants . . . was completed" presents a slight

exegetical difficulty (cf. Notes). It is usually taken to mean that the number of either the martyred or their companions on earth who will be killed will be completed (so the NIV). However, another sense may be possible. The verb "completed" (*plēroō*, GK *4444*) may mean "until their fellow servants complete their course" or "fulfill their Christian calling," which will also involve martyrdom. In any event, what constitutes the essence of Christian discipleship in John's eyes should not be overlooked. As Lilje, 130, says, "Every believer in Christ ought to be prepared for martyrdom; for Christians . . . cannot express their priestly communion with their Lord more perfectly than when they accept the suffering and the glory of martyrdom."

12–14 The sixth seal is broken by the Lamb, and John witnesses certain eschatological signs heralding the imminent, final day of the Lord so often described in Scripture (e.g., Isa 2:10, 19, 21; 13:10; 34:4; Jer 4:29; Eze 32:7–8; Joel 2:31; 3:15; Zep 1:14–18; Mt 24:29; Lk 21:11, 25–26). The signs are threefold: (1) the great earthquake and its storm, affecting the sun and moon; (2) the falling of the stars; and (3) the terror on earth (vv.15–17). It is difficult to know how literally the whole description should be taken. Some of the events are described from the standpoint of ancient cosmology—e.g., the falling of the stars to earth like figs from a shaken tree, or the sky rolling up like a scroll. The firmament suspended like a roof over the earth is shaken by the great earthquake.

The scene, whether taken literally or figuratively, is one of catastrophe and distress for earth's inhabitants. As later biblical authors seized on the earlier imagery of the theophany on Sinai to describe appearances of God to man (e.g., Hab 3:3–6), so John uses the archetypal imagery of the OT to describe this terrible visitation of God's final judgment on the earth. In much the same manner as we would describe a chaotic situation by saying "all hell broke loose" (though not intending it to be taken in a strictly literal sense), so the biblical writers use the language of cosmic turmoil to describe the condition of the world when God comes to judge the earth (v.17). "Earthquakes" are mentioned in Revelation 8:5; 11:13, 19; 16:18, and sun, moon, and/or stellar disturbances in 8:12; 9:2; 16:8. Of course, actual physical phenomena may also accompany the final judgment (see Notes).

15 Here we see the terror of all classes of people at these events and at the wrath of God and the Lamb. "The kings of the earth, the princes [dignitaries], the generals" describes the powerful; "the rich, the mighty" describes the affluent and the heroes. Finally, political distinctions of the widest kind—"every slave and every free man"—are referred to. Since all kinds of people are included, we cannot say that God's wrath is directed only at the powerful, at the rich, or at false Christians. His judgment will fall on all who refuse to repent and instead worship demons and idols and persecute Christ's followers (9:20–21; 16:6, 9).

16 The plea of people for the rocks and mountains to fall on them occurs in OT contexts of God's judgment (Isa 2:19, 21; Hos 10:8). It expresses the desire to be buried under the falling mountains and hills so as to escape the pains and terrors of the judgment. Jesus said that in this way the inhabitants of Jerusalem would cry out when God's judgment fell on the city (Lk 23:30; recall the Roman devastation of Jerusalem in AD 70).

16–17 The "wrath" (*orgē*, "anger," GK *3973*) of the Lamb is not only a new metaphor but also a paradoxical one. Lambs are usually gentle. But this Lamb shows "wrath" against those who have refused his grace (cf. Jn 5:27). Henceforth in Revelation the wrath of God and of the Lamb is a continuing theme and is described under the figures of the trumpets and bowls (11:18; 14:7, 10, 19; 15:1, 7; 16:1, 19; 19:15). Moreover, God's wrath is a present historical reality as well as an eschatological judgment (cf. Ro 1:18–32; 2:5). So great is the day of destruction that "who can stand?" (cf. Joel 2:11; Na 1:6; Mal 3:2).

NOTES

1 The verb ἔρχου (*erchou*, GK *2262*) can mean "go forth" rather than "come," thus clearly showing that the horseman rather than John is being addressed. In 16:1, however, John uses a different word, ὑπάγετε (*hypagete*, GK *5632*), for "go forth." ℵ understands ἔρχου, *erchou*, as addressed to John and adds καὶ ἴδε (*kai ide*, "and see") here and also in vv.3, 5, 7 (as does the TR). "Come and see" could be understood as a rabbinic invitation to enlightenment (cf. Jn 1:46). There is, however, stronger MS support for the abbreviated readings that also agrees with the sense given in the exposition. When John himself is addressed, another word is used—δεῦρο (*deuro*, "come," GK *1306*; 17:1; 21:9).

On the problem of the identification of the white horse and its rider, Mathias Rissi ("The Rider on the White Horse," *Int* 18 [1964]: 407–18) argues for antichristic forces; Zane Hodges ("The First Horseman of the Apocalypse," *BSac* 119 [1962]: 324–34) argues for the Christ identification following the early father Irenaeus.

11 The verb πληρωθῶσιν, *plērōthōsin* ("was completed"), an aorist passive subjunctive, is supported by A C, et al., and is followed by the NIV. An alternative reading, πληρώσωσιν, *plērōsōsin* ("was complete"), the plain aorist subjunctive, is supported by ℵ P, et al. The passive would mean that the "number" was complete, while the plain aorist subjunctive reading favors either the sense that the fellow servants will be complete (a rare intransitive sense for the verb; cf. BDAG, 829) or that they will complete their course.

12–14 The cosmic language of these and other verses has recently led N. T. Wright (*Jesus and the Victory of God* [Minneapolis: Fortress, 1996], 360–67), following the earlier lead of R. T. France, to propose that this language is to be understood as sociopolitical upheaval, not physical or cosmological. For an excellent critique of this view and many other current trends in eschatology, see Craig Blomberg, "Eschatology and the Church: Some New Testament Perspectives," *Them* 23.3 (1998): 3–26. Wright probably goes too far in socializing the cosmic language of the Apocalypse and demythologizing the second coming of Christ into some supposed coming of Jesus in judgment on Jerusalem and the temple in the first century.

3. First Interlude (7:1–17)

OVERVIEW

Indications that ch. 7 is a true interlude are the change in tone from the subject matter referred to in the sixth seal and the delay until 8:1 in opening the seventh seal. Two main subjects may be distinguished here. John first sees the angels who will unleash destruction on the earth restrained until the 144,000 servants of God from every tribe of Israel are sealed (vv.1–8). Then he sees an innumerable multitude clothed in white, standing before the throne of God, and identified as those who have come out of the "great tribulation" (vv.9–17). R. H. Charles, 1:189, remarks that this chapter is in many respects one of the most difficult and yet most important in the book. Lilje calls the whole picture one of the most glorious in the entire Apocalypse. It very likely functions both prospectively and retrospectively.

The principal exegetical difficulty in ch. 7 centers around the identification of the 144,000 (vv.1–8) and of the innumerable multitude (vv.9–17). Is the reference to the tribes of Israel symbolic, representative, or literal? What is the "great tribulation" (v.14)? Are those described in vv.9–17 martyrs? There is considerable divergence of opinion about these questions, and the dialogue can be traced only briefly here.

a. The 144,000 Israelites (7:1–8)

¹After this I saw four angels standing at the four corners of the earth, holding back the four winds of the earth to prevent any wind from blowing on the land or on the sea or on any tree. ²Then I saw another angel coming up from the east, having the seal of the living God. He called out in a loud voice to the four angels who had been given power to harm the land and the sea: ³"Do not harm the land or the sea or the trees until we put a seal on the foreheads of the servants of our God." ⁴Then I heard the number of those who were sealed: 144,000 from all the tribes of Israel.

⁵From the tribe of Judah 12,000 were sealed,
from the tribe of Reuben 12,000,
from the tribe of Gad 12,000,

⁶from the tribe of Asher 12,000,
from the tribe of Naphtali 12,000,
from the tribe of Manasseh 12,000,
⁷from the tribe of Simeon 12,000,
from the tribe of Levi 12,000,
from the tribe of Issachar 12,000,
⁸from the tribe of Zebulun 12,000,
from the tribe of Joseph 12,000,
from the tribe of Benjamin 12,000.

COMMENTARY

1 The "four angels" at "the four corners of the earth" hold back "the four winds of the earth" from blowing on the earth until the servants of God are sealed on their foreheads. The expression "the four corners of the earth" was used in antiquity among the Near Eastern nations much as we use "the four points of the compass." Since nowhere in Revelation do we read of the four winds actually blowing, they may be taken as representing the earthly catastrophes that occur under the trumpets and bowls.

2–3 Another angel comes from the "east" (possibly from Jerusalem or Zion—to emphasize its mission of salvation?) and calls to the four others not to release their destruction until the servants of God have a "seal" on their foreheads. Such a seal surely indicates ownership by God and the Lamb (14:1). Furthermore, a seal may offer protection or security for the bearers. Such seems to be the emphasis in 9:4, where the demonic forces are told to harm "only those people who did not have the seal [*sphragis*] of God on their foreheads." R. H. Charles (*Studies in the Apocalypse* [Edinburgh: T&T Clark, 1913], 124–25) believes that only protection from demonic forces is involved in the sealing rather than escape from physical harm from the plagues, the Antichrist, or spiritual apostasy.

By examining references to events that happened to those who, by contrast, have the "mark" (*charagma*, GK *5916*) of the beast (13:16–17), Charles's view may be evaluated. In 13:16–17, those who do not have the mark of the beast face severe socioeconomic sanctions. Those who have the mark of the beast are not only identified as beast-worshipers but become the objects of the irreversible wrath of God (14:9, 11). This implies, by contrast, that those who have "the seal [*sphragis*] of the living God" are God-worshipers and will be the objects of his abiding grace. In 16:2, the bowl of God's wrath appears to be directed exclusively toward those who have the mark of the beast, thus excluding those with the seal of God (cf. 16:6). Those having the mark of the beast are deluded by the beast (13:20), implying that the sealed of God are not thus deceived. Finally, a martyred group is seen just prior to their resurrection and thousand-year reign with Christ and are described as not having the mark of the beast or worshiping him (20:4).

In the light of these passages, we may say that the "sealed" are the people of God and that their sealing must be related to their salvation, as in the comparable figure used by Paul (2Co 1:22; Eph 1:13; 4:30; cf. *4 Ezra* 6:5). This is also evident in 14:3–4, where the sealed are described as those who were redeemed from the earth as firstfruits to God (cf. Ro 8:23; Jas 1:18). In fact, "baptism" was considered a "seal" of salvation in the early church (cf. BDAG, 980–81).

Furthermore, while the seal may not protect the sealed against harm inflicted by human agency (13:7; 20:4), they are protected from the divine plagues (16:2). It is clear that the protection from famine, pestilence, and sword afforded the sealed in the apocryphal *Psalms of Solomon* (15:6, 9) cannot also apply to John's sealed, since they are beheaded (20:4). As for OT background for the problem, Ezekiel 9:4–7 may well be primary. In this passage, a divine messenger with stylus in hand was to go throughout the apostate Jerusalem of Ezekiel's day and put a mark on the foreheads of those who deplored the faithless idolatry of the Israelites. Those so marked were the faithful and true servants of God, in contrast to the professed but false servants who had abandoned him. The sealed would be spared the divine slaughtering of the rebellious inhabitants of the city. Interestingly, the "mark" (*taw*) in the Phoenician script looked like a cross and was later adopted by early Jewish Christians as a symbol of their faith in Jesus (cf. Matthew Black, "The Chi-Rho-Sign-Christogram and/or Staurogram," in *Apostolic History and the Gospel*, ed. W. Gasque and R. P. Martin [Grand Rapids: Eerdmans, 1970], 319–27).

The sealing language would have the effect of assuring God's people of his special concern and plan for them. Even when facing persecution and martyrdom at the hand of the beast, they can be certain that no plague from God will touch them but that they will be in his presence forever because they are his very own possession. Therefore, the seal on the forehead is equivalent to the divine mark of ownership on them that elsewhere in the NT is referred to as the presence of the Holy Spirit (2Co 1:22; Eph 1:13; 4:30). This act of God will fulfill the promise to the Philadelphian church: "Since you

have kept my command to endure patiently, I will also keep you from the hour of trial that is going to come upon the whole world to test those who live on the earth" (Rev 3:10). Consequently, those thus sealed must be Christians and not unconverted Jews or Gentiles (contra Gundry, 83).

4 John next gives the number of those sealed—144,000—and their identification: "from all the tribes of Israel." There are two principal views regarding the identification of this group: (1) the number and the tribal identifications are taken literally and refer to 144,000 Jewish Christians who are sealed (to protect them from destruction) during the time of the great tribulation (so Seiss, Walvoord, Gundry, Glasson, Thomas); alternatively, (2) John is understood to use the language of the new Israel and thus refers to the completed church composed of Jew and Gentile (so Alford, Beckwith, Caird, Swete, Mounce, Beasley-Murray, Aune, Beale, Osborne, Bauckham).

In support of the first view is the normal usage of "Israel" in the NT as referring to the physical descendants of Jacob. Galatians 6:16 is no exception, as Peter Richardson (*Israel in the Apostolic Church* [Cambridge: Cambridge Univ. Press, 1969], 74–84) observes: "Strong confirmation of this position [i.e., that 'Israel' refers to the Jews in the NT] comes from the total absence of an identification of the church with Israel until AD 160; and also from the total absence, even then, of the term 'Israel of God' to characterize the church." Reference to the twelve tribes (vv. 5–8) would most naturally be understood to refer to the ancient historic Israel and not to the church. The view that the ten tribes were "lost" in the first century, though it is popular, hardly needs refuting (cf. F. F. Bruce, *The Book of Acts* [NICNT; Grand Rapids: Eerdmans, 1954], 489 n. 13). Thus in this first view, John would symbolically be describing the beginning of what Paul foretold in Romans 11:25–29 as the salvation of "all Israel."

In support of the second view, which identifies Israel with the church, is the fact that the NT identifies the followers of Christ as "Abraham's seed" (Gal 3:29), "the true circumcision" (Php 3:3), and the "Israel of God" (Gal 6:16; though disputed, cf. above). Furthermore, John himself earlier in Revelation makes a distinction between the true Jew and the false (cf. 2:9; 3:9), possibly implying that here in ch. 7 he intends also to designate the true Israel, or the church (Ladd, 116). Additional support for this view is found if there is a unity between the first and second groups in ch. 7—groups that otherwise must be treated as different and unconnected.

Without discussing at length the disputed issue of the Jews as Israel versus the church as Israel (though it obviously bears on the interpretation of this passage), we may agree with Walvoord, 143, who says, "The decision as to who are included in the term 'Israel' should be reached on the basis of exegesis and usage." Those who argue that the term "Israel" in other NT books refers exclusively to Jews are in our opinion correct (so Richardson). Strict exegesis, however, must also ask whether the author of Revelation wishes the term to have this same, more restricted usage or whether he uses it differently. It is possible that the usage of the term "Jew" among Christians had undergone a historic change from the earlier days when Paul wrote Romans (AD 56) until Revelation was written toward the close of the century.

By the middle of the first century, Paul made a distinction between the true, spiritual Jew and the physical descendants of Abraham (Ro 2:28–29; 9:8). Only those Jews who recognized Jesus as Messiah could rightly be called "Israel" in the strictest sense (Ro 9:6), though the term might be used with qualifications to refer to the historic descendants of Jacob ("Israel 'after the flesh'" [1Co 10:18, in Gk.]). Peter likewise described the church (Jewish and Gentile) in terms drawn from the OT that historically describe the true people of God among the Jewish descendants ("holy priesthood . . . chosen people . . . royal priesthood . . . holy nation" [1Pe 2:4, 9]). Moreover, even Gentiles who received Jesus as the Messiah and Lord were considered "Abraham's seed" (Gal 3:29) and the true "circumcision" (Php 3:3).

Already in Revelation there has been the distinction between Jews who were Jews in name only and those who were not true Jews because they did not acknowledge Jesus as Lord (2:9; 3:9). Also, the OT image of the people of Israel as a kingdom and priests to God is used by John of the followers of Jesus (1:6). Similarly, many of the promises to the victors in the churches of Asia (chs. 2–3) are fulfillments of OT promises given to the true people of Israel. In Christ's rebuke to the churches, we have the OT imagery of "Balaam" and "Jezebel," describing error that had influenced not OT Israel but the NT church. In ch. 12, it is again difficult to distinguish whether the "woman" represents the ancient Jewish people of the covenant or the NT followers of Jesus. In 21:9–12, the church is called the "bride, the wife of the Lamb"; she is identified with the new Jerusalem, and on its twelve gates are inscribed the "names of the twelve tribes of Israel." Even in the gospel of John (assuming the apostle wrote it as well as Revelation), Jesus is the "true vine," which many commentators understand to be an allusion to the vine that decorated the temple entrance and stood as a symbol for Israel (cf. Isa 5:1–7 with Jn 15:1–17). Jesus is claiming to be the true Israel and his followers, the branches, would then be related to the true Israel (cf. Ro 11:17–24).

The usage seems evident in the NT itself; the only question is whether John takes the final step in Revelation and, in the context of a largely Gentile church, uses the OT terminology to speak of the church. Richardson's summary (*Apostolic Church*, 204) is provocative: "As long as the church was viewed as a community gathered from Gentiles and

Jews, it could not readily call itself 'Israel.' But when it was sharply separated from both, and when it had a theory that Judaism no longer stood in continuity with Israel *ante Christum*, and when Gentiles not only could take over other titles but in some cases could claim exclusive rights to them, then the church as an organizational entity could appropriate 'Israel.'"

All this simply suggests the possibility that in John's mind the followers of Jesus (14:4) are the true servants of God, the Israel of God (cf. Jn 11:51–52). Richardson, 217, also observes that in Qumranic and late Jewish apocalyptic literature the term "Israel" was jealously and exclusively restricted to members of certain Jewish groups who even denied its use to other Jews and claimed that only they were the true Israel of God.

The identification of the 144,000 with all the elect people of God, including both Jews and Gentiles, does not negate Paul's teaching to the effect that the majority of the Jews themselves will one day be brought back into a relationship of salvation before God. At this point in Revelation, John simply is not dealing with Paul's emphasis (but cf. at 11:2–3).

Mounce, 154, has a further suggestion on the identity of the two groups in the chapter: "In both visions it is the church that is in view, but from two vantage points. Prior to the trumpet judgments the last generation of believers is sealed so as to be saved from the destruction coming upon the earth and to be brought safely into the heavenly kingdom. The second vision is anticipatory of the eternal blessedness of all believers when in the presence of God they realize the rewards of faithful endurance." But he later identifies the "great tribulation" (7:14) through which the second group passes as "that final series of woes which will immediately precede the end." This seems to contradict the earlier statement that the second group represents "all believers." Confessedly

this is a difficult chapter. Perhaps the confusion revolves around our inability to understand John's precise perspective on "the great tribulation."

The number 144,000 is obviously obtained by combining 12,000 for each of the twelve tribes of Israel (vv.5–8). Earlier in Revelation (cf. 4:4), twenty-four (a multiple of twelve) serves as a symbolic number. The "thousand" multiple appears again—this time in relation to the size of the Holy City:"He measured the city with the rod and found it to be 12,000 stadia in length, and as wide and high as it is long" (21:16). Thus 12,000 is symbolic of completeness and perfection. Even the wall is "144 cubits" (twelve times twelve; 21:17). The tree of life bearing "twelve crops of fruit, yielding its fruit every month" (i.e., twelve months; 22:2) further supports the view that John intends the number twelve to be taken symbolically and not literally. By 144,000 he signifies the sealing of *all* or the *total* number of God's servants who will face the great tribulation.

Those who are sealed come from "all the tribes of Israel," and this emphasizes even more the universality and comprehensiveness of the Christian gospel. Whereas in first-century Judaism there were many sects with exclusive tribal claims to being the true Israel, for the followers of Jesus all such sectarianism is broken down, and all groups, regardless of race, culture, religious background, or geographical location, are accepted before God (7:9; 14:4). There is an exclusivism in Revelation, but it is based on loyalty to Christ, not on historical or liturgical continuity.

5–8 John goes even further. He enumerates each of the twelve tribes and their number: "From the tribe of Judah 12,000 were sealed," etc. Why was it necessary to provide this detailed enumeration? And why the particular tribal selection? In answering these difficult questions, some facts about the list should be noted. John places Judah first, evidently to emphasize the priority of the messianic King who came from the tribe of Judah (5:5; Heb 7:13–14). Nowhere in the tribal listings of the OT, except in the space arrangement of the wilderness camp (Nu 2:3–9), does Judah come first. This exception may itself be linked with the messianic expectation through Judah (Ge 49:10; 1Ch 5:2). The priority John gives to Judah is comparable to the emphasis placed in late Judaism on the tribe of Levi (the priestly tribe). It is significant that John includes Levi among the other tribes, and thus gives no special place to the Levitical order, and that he also places Levi in the comparatively unimportant eighth place.

The particular order and names of the tribes as given here by John is unique. The OT has no fewer than twenty variant lists of the tribes, and these lists include anywhere from ten to thirteen tribes, though the number twelve is predominant (cf. Ge 49; Dt 33; Eze 48). The grouping of twelve may be a way of expressing the corporate identity of the elect people of God as a whole and may be maintained—even artificially at times—to preserve this identity (cf. the need to make up the "twelfth" apostle when Judas fell [Ac 1:25–26]). John omits Dan (which elsewhere is always included) and Ephraim. In order to maintain the ideal number twelve with these omissions, he must list both Joseph and Manasseh as tribes. This is peculiar because the tribe of Joseph is always mentioned in the other lists by either including Joseph and excluding his two sons, Ephraim and Manasseh (Ge 49), or by omitting Joseph and counting the two sons as one tribe each (Eze 48). It is not until the Levitical priesthood gains more prominence that the tribe of Levi is omitted from the lists and is replaced by the two sons of Joseph.

Various efforts have been made to solve the enigma of John's list and especially to explain the absence of the tribe of Dan. As yet we have no completely satisfactory solution. Ladd's proposal, 115, is interesting: "John intends to say [by the irregular list]

that the twelve tribes of Israel are not really literal Israel, but the true, spiritual Israel—the church." While this may be true, whether the mere irregularity of the list is intended to convey it is questionable. It might be more helpful to seek some satisfactory reason why John specifically omitted Dan and Ephraim.

The early church held that the Antichrist would arise from the tribe of Dan. R. H. Charles (*Apocrypha and Pseudepigrapha*, 2:334) has argued that this belief is pre-Christian Jewish tradition, first mentioned in Christian sources in Irenaeus (d. second century AD). Furthermore, Dan was associated in the OT with idolatry (Jdg 18:18–19; 1Ki 12:29–30). This may be the clue. If John sought to expose Christian idolatry and beast worship in his day by excluding Dan from the list of those sealed, it may also be possible to explain on the same basis why Manasseh and Joseph were chosen to fill up the sacred number rather than Manasseh and Ephraim. In the OT, Ephraim was also explicitly identified with idolatry (Hos 4:17). Qumran literature is of little help because in it both Ephraim and Manasseh are apostate tribes (4QpNa 7; 4Qp Ps 37:3—cited by Richardson, *Apostolic Church*, 227, cf. A. Dupont-Sommer, *The Essene Writings from Qumran* [Cleveland, Ohio: World, 1962], 269 n. 2; 273 n. 2).

If idolatry, then, seems to be the reason for omitting both Dan and Ephraim, the readjustment of the list to include Joseph and Manasseh to complete the twelve can be understood. Since Dan will be reckoned first in the tribal listing of the restored eschatological Jewish community (Eze 48) and John's list puts Judah first, it may be that John's listing describes the church rather than ethnic Israel.

It is important to note that John does not equate the 144,000 with all in the tribes. Rather, his repeated use of the preposition *ek* ("from") in vv.4–8 implies that the sealed were an elect group chosen out of the tribes: "144,000 from all the tribes of Israel. . . . From the tribe of Judah 12,000 were sealed," etc. If John had the actual Jewish Israel in view, this use of "from" would indicate an election from the whole nation. On the other hand, if he intended to imply something about the church, his language might indicate God's selecting the true church out "from" the professing church. This thought, mentioned earlier (cf. 2:14–15; 2:20; 3:16), is supported by Ezekiel 9:4–7, where the seal identified the true servants of God from the false ones among the professing people of God (see above under vv.2–3). Paul stated the same thought when he wrote, "Nevertheless, God's solid foundation stands firm, sealed with this inscription: 'The Lord knows those who are his,' and, 'Everyone who confesses the name of the Lord must turn away from wickedness'" (2Ti 2:19).

The description of the judgments under the sixth seal (6:12–17) ends with the question, "The great day of their wrath has come, and who can stand?" Chapter 7 answers this question by implying that only the true servants of God, who are divinely sealed, can be protected from the wrath of God and the Lamb.

NOTES

4–8 For a more thorough discussion of the various views on the identification of the 144,000, see Gundry, 81ff.; Charles, *Studies in the Apocalypse*, 114–15; Elliott, 1:226ff.; Aune, *Revelation 6–16*, 440–45.

b. The great white-robed multitude (7:9–17)

OVERVIEW

John now sees a great multitude from every nation and cultural background standing before the throne of God and clothed in white robes. They are identified by the angel as those "who have come out of the great tribulation" (v.14). Again the question is that of identity. Are they the Gentiles who are saved in the tribulation in contrast to the Jews in vv.1–8? Beckwith, 539, answers no because they are described as coming from every nation, tribe, people, and language, and this would mean both Jews and Gentiles. Are they, then, martyrs who have given their lives in the great tribulation and have been slain by the beast? If martyrs, are they the remainder of those to be killed, referred to when the fifth seal is opened (6:11)? Are they the complete group of martyrs? Or do they represent the whole company of the redeemed in Christ as seen in glory?

Although there is no direct evidence that the great multitude are martyrs, there are some indications that they are: (1) they are seen in heaven "before the throne" (v.9) and "in his temple" (v.15); (2) they are described as those "who have come out of the great tribulation" (v.14), and thus it is assumed that, since they have died in the great tribulation, they have most likely been martyred, because the tribulation will be a time of great killing of the saints (17:6; 18:24; 19:2; 20:4; etc.).

The multitude would not be the whole company of the martyred throughout history but only those who were victims of the beast's persecution during the great tribulation. The group is probably those future martyrs referred to under the fifth seal as those "who were to be killed as they had been" (6:11). Neither, then, would they be the whole redeemed church (so Beckwith, Eller), unless all Christians are to be identified with the martyrs.

The identification of this second group is related to the identification of the first one (vv.1–8). Some argue that the two groups must be different because the first is numbered, the second innumerable; the first is limited to Jews, the second refers to every nation (so Gundry, 81). These objections are not serious if we recall the exposition of vv.1–8, where it was noted that (1) the number of the sealed was symbolic and not literal, and (2) the delineation of the twelve tribes was seen as John's deliberate attempt to universalize the election of God. Thus what some have seen as contrasts may actually be designed as complementarity and show the continuity of the first group with the second. Furthermore, we should bear in mind that John does not see any group at all in vv.1–8 but merely hears the number of the sealed, whereas in vv.9–17 he actually sees a group and describes what he sees and hears; therefore, the unity of both groups can be maintained and vv.9–17 understood as the interpretative key to the 144,000. John's vision then leaps ahead to a scene in heaven after the great tribulation has run its course and views the glorified saints of the tribulation as being in God's presence, at rest from their trial and serving him continually.

Two slightly different variations of the more literal Jewish identity of those in vv.1–8 and the relationship of this first group to the second are quite popular today. Some see the 144,000 as a select group of Jews who will be converted to Jesus shortly after the rapture of the church to heaven. These Jewish evangelists will preach the gospel to the world during the tribulation. As a result of their preaching, a great multitude of Gentiles will be converted to Christ (so Gaebelein, 58–59). Others, accepting a posttribulational view of the church's rapture, understand the 144,000 as a literal Jewish remnant preserved physically through the tribulation and converted immediately after the rapture. They will be the people who will constitute the beginning of the restored Jewish Davidic kingdom

at the inception of the millennial reign of Christ on the earth (so Gundry, 82–83).

The Bible speaks of three different types of tribulation or distress, and it is important to distinguish among them:

1. There is tribulation that is inseparable from Christian life in the world (Jn 16:33; Ac 14:22; Ro 5:3; 2Ti 2:11–12; 1Pe 4:12; Rev 1:9; 2:10). All Christians during all ages participate in tribulation. Thus they share in the continuing sufferings of Christ (Col 1:24).

2. The Bible also speaks of an intense tribulation that will come on the final generation of Christians and climax all previous persecutions. Daniel 12:1 refers to such a time: "There will be a time of distress [*thlipseōs*, LXX] such as has not happened from the beginning of nations until then." Likewise Jesus predicts such an unprecedented persecution: "For then there will be great distress [*thlipsis*, GK *2568*], unequaled from the beginning of the world until now—and never to be equaled again" (Mt 24:21). Paul's mention of "the rebellion" (*apostasia*, GK *686*) and "the man of lawlessness" (2Th 2:3) surely refers to this same period. In Revelation, this more intense persecution is mentioned in 7:14; 11:7–10; 13:7; 16:6, and possibly the events under the fifth seal should be included here (6:9–11; so J. Barton Payne, *The Imminent Appearing of Christ* [Grand Rapids: Eerdmans, 1962], 115). This future tribulation is distinguished from previous persecutions of the church in its intensity, in its immediate connection with Christ's second coming, and in the presence of Antichrist during it.

3. Scripture also speaks of a future time of God's intense wrath on unbelievers. Revelation refers to this as "the great day of their wrath" (6:17) and "the hour of trial that is going to come upon the whole world to test those who live on the earth" (3:10). Such wrath from God comes especially under the trumpets and bowls (8:2; 16:1). Probably drawing

on the teaching of Jesus in the Olivet Discourse (Mt 24), Paul refers to this punitive action of God in 2 Thessalonians 1:6–10 and even uses the word *thlipsis* ("trouble"). While for Christians the great tribulation may be concurrent with a portion of the period of God's wrath on the rebellious, the final and more intense judgment of God seems to *follow* the great tribulation itself and is directly connected with the coming of Christ (Mt 24:29; Rev 6:12–17; 19:11–21).

⁹After this I looked and there before me was a great multitude that no one could count, from every nation, tribe, people and language, standing before the throne and in front of the Lamb. They were wearing white robes and were holding palm branches in their hands. ¹⁰And they cried out in a loud voice:

"Salvation belongs to our God,
who sits on the throne,
and to the Lamb."

¹¹All the angels were standing around the throne and around the elders and the four living creatures. They fell down on their faces before the throne and worshiped God, ¹²saying:

"Amen!
Praise and glory
and wisdom and thanks and honor
and power and strength
be to our God for ever and ever.
Amen!"

¹³Then one of the elders asked me, "These in white robes—who are they, and where did they come from?"

¹⁴I answered, "Sir, you know."

And he said, "These are they who have come out of the great tribulation; they have washed their robes and made them white in the blood of the Lamb. ¹⁵Therefore,

"they are before the throne of God
    and serve him day and night in his temple;
and he who sits on the throne will spread his tent over them.
¹⁶Never again will they hunger;
    never again will they thirst.
The sun will not beat upon them,
    nor any scorching heat.
¹⁷For the Lamb at the center of the throne will be their shepherd;
    he will lead them to springs of living water.
And God will wipe away every tear from their eyes."

COMMENTARY

9 "A great multitude . . . from every nation, tribe, people and language" pictures what Swete, 97, calls a "polyglot cosmopolitan crowd." The words might well describe the crowds common to the agora or the quay of a seaport in first-century Asia. (Similar fourfold descriptions of the members of the Christian community or of the inhabitants of the world also occur in Revelation 5:9; 11:9; 13:7; 14:6; 17:15.) "Standing before the throne and in front of the Lamb" signifies their position of acceptance and honor as God's true servants (cf. v.15) and reminds us of the continuity of this vision with the earlier vision of the throne and the Lamb (chs. 4–5). This group seems to complete the full circle of participants before the throne begun in ch. 4.

Their "white robes" impress John and are an important feature of the vision (vv.9, 13–14). We cannot fail to connect them with the white robes given to the martyrs under the fifth seal (6:11). The white robes symbolize salvation and victory (v.10), and their possessors obtained them by "[washing] their robes and [making] them white in the blood of the Lamb" (v.14). This implies that they were true recipients of Christ's redemption in contrast to others who, though professing belief in Christ, were not genuine overcomers (cf. 3:5–6, 18).

"Palm branches" are referred to only one other time in the NT (Jn 12:13), where they are connected with the Passover celebration. Moses provided that palms should be used at the Feast of Tabernacles (Lev 23:40). Later they were used on other festal occasions (1 Macc 13:51; 2 Macc 10:7). Jewish coins of the period 140 BC–AD 70 frequently contain palms and some have the inscription "the redemption of Zion" (*IDB* 3:646). Palms were emblems of victory; in John 12 they denote the triumph of Christ, while here in Revelation the reference is to the victory of the servants of Christ.

10 In accord with the literary symmetry of chs. 4–7, this group also expresses their worship of the King and the Lamb. Their praise to God is for his "salvation" (*sōtēria*, GK *5401*), not their own accomplishments. Since the same word is associated with the final manifestation of God's power and kingdom (12:10; 19:1), here it may also denote God's final victory over sin and the principalities of this world that crucified Christ and that kill his true disciples (cf. Isa 49:8; 2Co 6:2).

11–12 The angelic hosts respond to the cry of the redeemed (v.10) with "Amen" and voice their praise and worship of God for the salvation given to humanity (cf. Lk 15:10). Compare this doxology with 5:12–13.

13 After the manner of the OT apocalyptic passages, the interpreting angel asks concerning the white-robed throng, "Who are they, and where did they come from?" (cf. Da 7:15–16; Zec 1:9, 19; 4:1–6). Here and in 5:5 are the only references in Revelation to an elder speaking individually— a fact that supports the view that the elders in Revelation are angels and not a symbolic group representing the church.

14 The reference to the washed robes should be viewed in relation to 3:4, where soiled clothes represent defection from Christ through unbelief and worship of false gods (cf. 21:8). On the "great tribulation," see Overview, pp. 663–65.

"The blood of the Lamb" connotes here more even than the profound reference to the sacrificial death of Jesus (5:9); it also suggests faithful witness in following Jesus in his death (2:13; 12:11).

15 This and the following verses describe the activity and condition of the true servants of God in their future and eternal relation to the Lamb. The scene is one of the most beautiful in the Bible. In it, those who have washed their robes in the blood of the Lamb are described as being before the throne of God without fear or tremor, fully accepted by the divine Majesty. What are they doing? Theirs is no state of passivity but of continual service to God in praise and worship.

The reference to the "temple" of God raises the question of whether the scene describes the final state of the saints or an intermediate state, as 21:22 tells us that the new Jerusalem has no temple. However, the language used in vv.15–17 (esp. v.17) seems to depict the same condition as that of the saints in chs. 21–22 (cf. 21:3–4, 6; 22:1). Since 7:15 relates to worship, it would be appropriate to refer to the presence of God and the Lamb as "in" the temple. In chs. 21–22, however, the future existence of the people of God is described as a city; and in that glorious city, unlike the pagan cities of the present world, there will be no special temple in which to worship God because God himself and the Lamb will be present everywhere.

To "spread his tent [*skēnoō*, GK *5012*] over them," or to "reside permanently" (*TDNT* 7:385), calls to mind the *shekinah* presence in the OT tabernacle or temple (Ex 40:34–38; 1Ki 8:10–11; cf. Eze 10:4, 18–19) and later in Jesus (Jn 1:14) and also the idea of a permanent residence (Rev 21:3). Never again will these people endure torment. They have the supreme protection of the living God himself.

16 The condition described here contrasts to the earthly experience of those who suffered much for their faith (cf. Heb 11:37–38). For them, starvation, thirst, and the burning desert are forever past. There may be allusion here to Isaiah 49:10, which places the time of relief from such distresses in the days of Messiah's kingdom. There may also be an allusion to what the four horsemen bring (6:1–8; cf. Mt 24:7).

17 We now have a beautiful pastoral figure—that of the Lamb shepherding his people (cf. Jn 10:1–8; Heb 13:20; 1Pe 2:25). It is not through some perfect environment but through the presence and continual ministry of the Lamb that their sufferings are forever assuaged. Whereas on earth their enemies may have tormented them, now the Lamb guides them: "He will lead [*hodēgēsei*, GK *3842*— the same verb used of the Holy Spirit in Jn 16:13] them to springs of living water." In contrast to the burning thirst experienced in their tribulation, now they will enjoy the refreshing waters of life. Thus in the future life the saints will not know stagnation, boredom, or satiation (Ps 23:1–3; Jer 2:13; Eze 47:1–12; Zec 14:8).

Finally, even the sorrowful memory of the pain and suffering of the former days will be mercifully removed by the Father: "God will wipe away every tear from their eyes" (cf. 21:4). Tribulation produces tears. Like a tenderhearted, devoted mother, God will wipe each tear from their eyes with the eternal consolation of glory itself. Never again will they cry out because of pain or suffering. Only through the resurrection can all this become real (Isa 25:8; 1Co 15:54).

NOTES

14 The correct translation of the nominative participle οἱ ἐρχόμενοι (*hoi erchomenoi*, "they who have come out of"; GK *2262*) is a problem. Grammatically, present participles depend on the main verb for their time of action and are generally coincident in time with it. But is the time of action here the time of John's writing or, for John, some future time? If it is present time for John, the translation would be, "they who are coming out of the great tribulation"—if future, two possibilities arise: (1) The time is in the future when the vision is to be fulfilled. In this case, the description looks back to the earthly scene that preceded the heavenly bliss: "They who have come [or were coming] out of the great tribulation" (NIV). (2) The time is in the present of John's writing. In this case, the words predict what will happen: "They who will come out of the great tribulation" (cf. 1Th 1:10). Charles, 1:213, understands the construction as a Semitism and favors the idea of an imperfect participle—"were coming." One's theology and general exegesis of Revelation will determine which rendering is preferred.

4. Opening of the Seventh Seal (8:1)

¹When he opened the seventh seal, there was silence in heaven for about half an hour.

COMMENTARY

1 After the long interlude of ch. 7, the sequence of the opening of the seals is resumed by the opening of the final or seventh seal. This action provides both a conclusion to the seals and a preparation for the seven trumpets. The praises ordinarily heard uninterruptedly in heaven (4:8) now cease in order to allow the prayers of the suffering saints on earth to be heard: "There was silence in heaven for about half an hour." Even heaven's choirs are subdued to show God's concern for his persecuted people in the great tribulation (8:4; cf. Lk 18:2–8). A Jewish teacher states, "In the fifth heaven are companies of angels of service who sing praises by night, but are silent by day because of the glory of Israel," i.e., that the praises of Israel may be heard in heaven (cited in Charles, 1:223). But in John's view, heaven is quieted not to hear praises but to hear the cries for deliverance and justice of God's persecuted servants (6:10). Most interpreters, however, understand the silence to refer to the awesome silence before the great storm of God's wrath on the earth (cf. Hab 2:20). A kind of Sabbath pause might be thought of here. (The relation between the seals, trumpets, and bowls is discussed at 8:6.)

B. The Seven Trumpets (8:2–11:19)

1. Preparatory: The Angel and the Golden Censer (8:2–5)

²And I saw the seven angels who stand before God, and to them were given seven trumpets.

³Another angel, who had a golden censer, came and stood at the altar. He was given much incense to offer, with the prayers of all the saints, on the golden altar before the throne. ⁴The smoke of the incense, together with the prayers of the saints, went up before God from the angel's hand. ⁵Then the angel took the censer, filled it with fire from the altar, and hurled it on the earth; and there came peals of thunder, rumblings, flashes of lightning and an earthquake.

COMMENTARY

2 While the seven seals are opened by the Lamb himself, the judgments of the seven trumpets and the seven bowls (15:1) are executed by seven angels. In *1 Enoch* 20:2–8, reference is made to seven angels who stand before God and are named Uriel, Raphael, Raguel, Michael, Saraqael, Gabriel (cf. Lk 1:19), and Remiel. John may not have these in mind, but the offering up of the prayers of the saints was in Jewish thought connected with archangels (Tob 12:15; *T. Levi* 3:7).

3–4 Before the trumpet judgments are executed, another angel enacts a symbolic scene in heaven. He takes a golden censer filled with incense and offers the incense on the altar in behalf of the prayers of all God's people. Earlier, in connection with the martyred saints (6:9), John mentioned the altar that was near God's presence. Likewise, a strong

assurance is here given to the suffering followers of Christ that their prayers for vindication are not forgotten, because God will speedily vindicate them from their enemies' assaults. So close is the altar to God that the incense cloud of the saints' prayers rises into his presence and cannot escape his notice (cf. Ps 141:2).

5 The censer, or firepan, is now used to take some of the burning coals from the altar and cast them to the earth. Symbolically, this represents the answer to the prayers of the saints through the visitation on earth of God's righteous judgments. God next appears on earth in a theophany. The language, reminiscent of Sinai with its thunder, lightning, and earthquake, indicates that God has come to vindicate his saints with his presence and rule (Ex 19:16–19; Rev 4:5; 11:19; 16:18).

2. Sounding of the First Six Trumpets (8:6–9:21)

OVERVIEW

Two questions confront the interpreter at this point: (1) What is the relationship of the trumpets to the preceding seals and the following bowls? and (2) Are the events described symbolic or more literal?

In answer to the first question, there are two basic options: either the series are parallel and simultaneous, or they are sequential or successive. It is not possible to decide with certainty for either of these views. Each contains elements of truth. Both sequential factors and parallel ingredients are evident. This commentary has already argued for the chronological priority of the first five seals to the events of the trumpets and bowls (see comments at 6:1). But the sixth seal seems to take us into the period of the outpouring of God's wrath enacted in the trumpet and bowl judgments (6:12–17).

The sequential factors are as follows: (1) There is a rise in the intensity of the judgments—only a part of earth and humans are affected in the trumpets, but all are affected under the bowls. (2) There is a difference in sequence and content of events described in each series. (3) The reference to those not sealed in 9:4 (fifth trumpet) presupposes the sealing of 7:1–8. (4) The explicit statement in 8:1–2 implies a sequence between seals and trumpets—"When he opened the seventh seal . . . And I saw the seven angels . . . to them were given seven trumpets"—on which Tenney, 71, remarks, "The vision of the angels with the trumpets follows the seals directly, and conveys the impression that the seals and the trumpets are successive." (5) The bowl judgments are directly called the "last plagues" because "with them God's wrath is completed" (15:1), indicating the prior trumpet judgments. When the seventh bowl is poured out, the words "it is done!" are spoken (16:17).

On the other hand, there are parallels. The sixth-seventh seal, the seventh trumpet (11:15–19), and the seventh bowl (16:17–21) all seem to depict events associated with the second coming of Christ. This last-event parallelism may indicate that all of these series (seals, trumpets, bowls) are parallel in their entirety or that there is a partial recapitulation or overlap in the three series. This is especially evident in connection with the sixth-seventh seal (6:12–8:1), the seventh trumpet (11:15–19), and the seventh bowl (16:17–21). The text seems to demand some type of sequential understanding and hence rules out a complete parallelism.

The main issue here is whether the parallelism indicates that the events described under the sixth-seventh seal, seventh trumpet, and seventh bowl are identical, or merely similar and hence really sequential and not exactly parallel. The following points are relevant: (1) The sixth seal brings us into the period of God's wrath on the beast-worshipers but does not actually advance beyond that event to refer to the coming of Christ (6:12–17). (2) The seventh seal introduces the trumpet judgments, which run their course, and the seventh trumpet seems to bring us into the kingdom of Christ (11:15–18). (3) The seventh bowl likewise brings us to the consummation and return of Christ—if we keep in mind that the incident of Babylon's destruction is an elaboration of events under the seventh bowl (16:17–21; 19:11–21).

But are all three series parallel in their last events (for the affirmative, see Dale Ralph Davis, "The Relationship Between the Seals, Trumpets, and Bowls in the Book of Revelation," *JETS* 16 [1973]: 149–58), or only parallel in the last trumpet and last bowl (so Ladd and Mounce)? Ladd and Mounce, following Beckwith, have correctly noted that the

"third woe" (9:12; 11:14) is never fulfilled by the seventh trumpet—unless the content of the seventh trumpet is the seven bowls, which is also the "third woe." This is another way of saying that there is some limited recapitulation or overlap with the seventh seal and the first trumpets and in the seventh trumpet with the first bowls. This might be called a telescopic view of the seals, bowls, and trumpets. Further support for this view is also found in observing that interludes come between the sixth and seventh seals and between the sixth and seventh trumpets but not between the sixth and seventh bowls, which would be expected if the trumpets were strictly parallel to the bowls. Bauckham (8–9, 15–18, 250) and Thomas (2:5, 525–43) also seem to espouse this view.

The second question concerns the literalness of the events described under each trumpet. The important but hard question is not literal versus nonliteral but *what did John intend?* Some things may need to be understood more literally and others quite symbolically. For example, the reference to the army of two hundred million (9:16–19) can hardly be literal (see comments at 9:16). Either the number is figurative or the army refers to demonic powers rather than human soldiers. It is also difficult to handle literally the reference to the eagle that speaks human words (8:13). While there is no way to settle this problem finally, the exposition will attempt to steer between a literal approach and a totally symbolic one.

As in the seals, there is a discernible literary pattern in the unfolding of the trumpets. The first four trumpets are separated from the last three, which are called "woes" (8:13; 9:12; 11:14), and are generally reminiscent of the plagues in Exodus. While John refers in 15:3 to the song of Moses (Ex 15:1–18), he does not follow out the plague parallelism precisely, and the connections should not always be pressed.

Shofar trumpets (usually made of a ram's horn) were used in Jewish life as signaling instruments.

They sounded alarms for war or danger as well as for peace and announced the new moon, the beginning of the Sabbath, or the death of a notable. Trumpets were also used to throw enemies into panic (Jdg 7:19–20). Their use as eschatological signals of the day of the Lord or the return of Christ is well established in the OT and NT (Isa 27:13; Joel 2:1; Zep 1:16; Mt 24:31; 1Co 15:52; 1Th 4:16). The Dead Sea community had an elaborate trumpet signal system patterned after Joshua 6 (cf. 1QM).

⁶Then the seven angels who had the seven trumpets prepared to sound them.

⁷The first angel sounded his trumpet, and there came hail and fire mixed with blood, and it was hurled down upon the earth. A third of the earth was burned up, a third of the trees were burned up, and all the green grass was burned up.

⁸The second angel sounded his trumpet, and something like a huge mountain, all ablaze, was thrown into the sea. A third of the sea turned into blood, ⁹a third of the living creatures in the sea died, and a third of the ships were destroyed.

¹⁰The third angel sounded his trumpet, and a great star, blazing like a torch, fell from the sky on a third of the rivers and on the springs of water—¹¹the name of the star is Wormwood. A third of the waters turned bitter, and many people died from the waters that had become bitter.

¹²The fourth angel sounded his trumpet, and a third of the sun was struck, a third of the moon, and a third of the stars, so that a third of them turned dark. A third of the day was without light, and also a third of the night.

¹³As I watched, I heard an eagle that was flying in midair call out in a loud voice: "Woe! Woe! Woe to the inhabitants of the earth, because of the trumpet blasts about to be sounded by the other three angels!"

⁹:¹The fifth angel sounded his trumpet, and I saw a star that had fallen from the sky to the earth. The star was given the key to the shaft of the Abyss. ²When he opened the Abyss, smoke rose from it like the smoke from a gigantic furnace. The sun and sky were darkened by the smoke from the Abyss. ³And out of the smoke locusts came down upon the earth and were given power like that of scorpions of the earth. ⁴They were told not to harm the grass of the earth or any plant or tree, but only those people who did not have the seal of God on their foreheads. ⁵They were not given power to kill them, but only to torture them for five months. And the agony they suffered was like that of the sting of a scorpion when it strikes a man. ⁶During those days men will seek death, but will not find it; they will long to die, but death will elude them.

⁷The locusts looked like horses prepared for battle. On their heads they wore something like crowns of gold, and their faces resembled human faces. ⁸Their hair was like women's hair, and their teeth were like lions' teeth. ⁹They had breastplates like breastplates of iron, and the sound of their wings was like the thundering of many horses and chariots rushing into battle. ¹⁰They had tails and stings like scorpions, and in their tails they had power to

torment people for five months. ¹¹They had as king over them the angel of the Abyss, whose name in Hebrew is Abaddon, and in Greek, Apollyon.

¹²The first woe is past; two other woes are yet to come.

¹³The sixth angel sounded his trumpet, and I heard a voice coming from the horns of the golden altar that is before God. ¹⁴It said to the sixth angel who had the trumpet, "Release the four angels who are bound at the great river Euphrates." ¹⁵And the four angels who had been kept ready for this very hour and day and month and year were released to kill a third of mankind. ¹⁶The number of the mounted troops was two hundred million. I heard their number.

¹⁷The horses and riders I saw in my vision looked like this: Their breastplates were fiery red, dark blue, and yellow as sulfur. The heads of the horses resembled the heads of lions, and out of their mouths came fire, smoke and sulfur. ¹⁸A third of mankind was killed by the three plagues of fire, smoke and sulfur that came out of their mouths. ¹⁹The power of the horses was in their mouths and in their tails; for their tails were like snakes, having heads with which they inflict injury.

²⁰The rest of mankind that were not killed by these plagues still did not repent of the work of their hands; they did not stop worshiping demons, and idols of gold, silver, bronze, stone and wood—idols that cannot see or hear or walk. ²¹Nor did they repent of their murders, their magic arts, their sexual immorality or their thefts.

COMMENTARY

8:7 *The first trumpet*. Hail and fire are reminiscent of the fourth Egyptian plague of the exodus (Ex 9:23–26), with added intensity suggested by the reference to hail and fire mixed with blood (cf. Eze 38:22). A "third" refers to a relative fraction of the total and should not be construed as a specific amount (cf. Eze 5:2; Zec 13:8–9).

8–9 *The second trumpet*. A huge blazing mass like a mountain is thrown into the sea and turns part of the sea into blood. This suggests the first plague, when the Nile was turned bloodred and the fish were destroyed (Ex 7:20–21; cf. Zep 1:3). Reference to the destruction of ships shows the intense turbulence of the sea.

10–11 *The third trumpet*. John next sees a huge fiery star fall on the rivers and springs of water and turn a part of these freshwater supplies into very bit-ter water. The star's name is "Wormwood," which refers to the quite bitter herb *Artemisia absinthium* found in the Near East and mentioned elsewhere in the Bible (Jer 9:15; 23:15; La 3:15, 19; Am 5:7). It is not clear whether John intended the star to be understood as an angel, as in 9:1 and in 1:20. Here is the first reference in the plagues to the loss of human life (cf. 9:15, 20). This plague, aimed at the fresh water, is a counterpart of the preceding one, which was aimed at the sea.

12 *The fourth trumpet*. The heavens are struck with partial darkness, reminiscent of the ninth plague (Ex 10:21–23). The designations of "a third of . . ." refer to a partial impairment of the ordinary light from these bodies. In the OT, the darkening of the heavens appears in connection with the theophany of God in judgment (cf. Isa 13:10; Eze 32:7–8; Joel

2:10; 3:15; cf. Mt 24:29). An unusual darkness also attended the crucifixion of Christ (Mt 27:45).

13 Before the last three trumpets sound, John hears a flying eagle call out "woe" three times. His cry announces the especially grievous nature of the last three plagues, which kill a third part of the population of the earth (9:18). Two of the woes are identified with the fifth and sixth trumpets (9:12; 11:14; see the comments at 8:6, which argue that the third woe should be seen as the seven bowl judgments of ch. 16). The "inhabitants of the earth" distinguishes the Christ-rejecters of the world from the true, faithful followers of the Lamb (cf. comments at 3:10). A flying "eagle" announces these words. This must be taken symbolically. In Revelation there are two other references to eagles (4:7; 12:14). Since 4:7 relates to the description of one of the four living beings, it may be that John intends the eagle mentioned here to have the same significance.

9:1–11 *The fifth trumpet*. John now focuses attention on the fifth and sixth trumpets (first and second woes) by giving more than twice the space to their description than he gives the previous four trumpets together. The fifth trumpet releases locusts from the Abyss. For five months these locusts torment the inhabitants of the earth who do not have the seal of God. John sees a "star" that has fallen to the earth. Since this star is given a key to open the Abyss, it is reasonable to understand it as being a symbolic reference to an angel. This is supported by v.11, where "the angel of the Abyss" is mentioned and named "Abaddon," as well as by 20:1, where reference is also made to "an angel coming down" (i.e., stars "fall") and having the key to the Abyss, into which Satan is thrown.

2 The Abyss is also referred to in 11:7 and 17:8 as the place from which the beast arises. The word *abyssos* ("Abyss," GK *12*) refers to the underworld as (1) a prison for certain demons (Lk 8:31; cf. 2Pe 2:4; Jude 6) and (2) the realm of the dead (Ro 10:7;

cf. *TDNT* 1:9). When the Abyss is opened, huge billows of smoke pour out, darken the sky, and release horselike locusts on the earth.

3–4 Locust plagues are one of the severest plagues affecting human beings. The imagery of locusts appearing like armies, advancing like a cloud, darkening the heavens, and sounding like the rattle of chariots goes back to Joel's vision of the army of locusts that came on Israel as a judgment from God (Joel 1:6; 2:4–10). But the locusts of the Apocalypse inflict agony like the sting of scorpions (vv.3, 5, 10). This and the fact that they do not eat grass show that these locusts are something other than ordinary earthly insects. Indeed, they have the special task of inflicting a nonfatal injury only on the beast-worshipers, who do not have the seal of God on their foreheads (see comments at 7:3). This may imply that these locustlike creatures are not simply instruments of a physical plague, such as that in Moses' or Joel's day or under the first four trumpets, but are demonic forces out of the Abyss from whom the true people of God are protected (cf. John's use of frogs to represent demonic powers in 16:13).

5–6 The five months of agony (vv.5, 10) may refer to the lifespan of the locust (i.e., through spring and summer [cf. Charles, 1:243]). So severe is the torment they inflict that their victims will seek death (cf. Job 3:21; Jer 8:3; Hos 10:8).

7–10 John describes the locusts as an army of mounted troops ready for the attack. The heads of the locusts resemble horses' heads. John does not say that the locusts had crowns of gold on their heads but that they wore "something like crowns of gold" on their heads. Charles, 1:244, suggests this might refer to the yellow-green of their breasts. This combined with their humanlike faces suggests something unnatural, hence demonic. The comparison of their "hair" with that of women may refer (as in other ancient texts) to the locusts' long antennae, while their lionlike teeth suggest the terrible devastation they can bring (cf. Joel 1:6–7). The "breastplates of iron" refer to their scales, which appeared as a cuirass of metal plates across the chest and long flexible bonds of steel over the shoulders. Their sound was like the rushing of war chariots into battle (cf. Joel 2:5).

11 This description creates an image of the fearful onslaught of demonic powers in the last days. Thus their leader is called "Abaddon" in Hebrew and "Apollyon" in Greek. The Hebrew *ʾabaddôn* (GK 11) means "destruction" or "ruin" (as in Job 26:6; Pr 27:20), and more often "the place of ruin" in Sheol (as in Job 26:6; Pr 15:11; 27:20), "death" (as in Job 28:22), or "the grave" (as in Ps 88:11). In late Jewish apocalyptic texts and Qumran literature, it refers to the personification of death (1QH 3.16, 19, 32; 1QapGen 12:17).

The Greek *apollyōn* (GK *661*) means "exterminator" or "destroyer" and does not occur elsewhere in the Bible, though it can be readily understood as John's way of personifying in Greek what is personified in the Hebrew word *ʾabaddôn* (*apōleia*, LXX). Some understand Apollyon as a separate angel entrusted with authority over the Abyss. Attempts to identify Apollyon with the Greek god Apollo, who in some Greek texts of Revelation is connected with the locusts, or another Greco-Roman deity have not met with much success. The creature, his name, and his responsibility seem to be original with the author of the Apocalypse.

Why John names the king of the Abyss in both Hebrew and Greek is open to question. Perhaps his readers' background in Hebrew, on which John's names and thoughts seem to turn (cf. 16:16), was so slender that an additional help here and there was necessary. This stylistic trait of giving information in bilingual terms is peculiar to Revelation and the fourth gospel (Jn 6:1; 19:13, 17, 20; 20:16). It may also reveal a mind steeped in the targumic tradition of the ancient synagogue, where it was customary to render Scripture in Hebrew and then in either Aramaic or Greek for those who did not understand Hebrew.

12 This seems to be a transitional verse, indicating that the "first woe" (fifth trumpet) is finished and two woes are yet to come (presumably the sixth and seventh trumpets; cf. 8:13 with 11:14). There may be in this verse a resumption of the eagle's words (cf. 8:13).

13–19 *The sixth trumpet: the second woe.* Here we find a description of disasters that reach to the death of a third of humanity (vv.15, 18; cf. 8:7). "Four angels," the instruments of God's judgment, are held at the river Euphrates, from where traditionally the enemies of God's ancient people often advanced on the land of Israel (Jer 2:18; 13:4–5; 51:63; Rev 16:12) and which was recognized as its eastern extremity (Ge 15:18). John here makes use of the ancient geographical terms to depict the fearful character of God's approaching judgment on a rebellious world. While the language is drawn from historical-political events of the OT, it describes realities that far transcend a local geographical event. God's dealings are not accidental but planned and precise in time as to a definite hour of a definite day of a definite month of a definite year. By a reference to the "golden altar" of incense, the release of these angels is again connected with the prayers of God's saints for vindication (6:9; 8:3).

At v.16, a mounted army of some two hundred million horses and riders is rather abruptly introduced. While some (e.g., Walvoord) argue for a literal human army here, several factors point to their identity as demonic forces. First, the horsemen are not in themselves important but wear brightly colored breastplates of fiery red, dark blue, and sulfurous yellow, more suggestive of supernatural than natural riders. More important are the horses, which not only have heads resembling lions but are, rather than their riders, the instruments of death by the three plagues of fire, smoke, and sulfur that come from their mouths. Furthermore, these horses have tails like snakes that are able to kill (vv.17–19), unlike the locusts' scorpionlike tails that do not inflict death but only injury (v.5). Finally, according to General William K. Harrison (an expert in military logistics), an army of two hundred million could not be conscripted, supported, and moved to the Middle East without totally disrupting all societal needs and capabilities ("The War of Armageddon," photocopy of unpublished, undated article). As Harrison brings to mind, God has made human beings with certain limitations; and the actual raising and transporting of an army of the size spoken of in v.16 completely transcend human capability. All the Allied and Axis forces at their peak in World War II were only about 70 million, according to the 1971 *World Almanac*.

Thus it seems better to understand the vast numbers and description of the horses as indicating demonic hordes. Such large numbers do occasionally indicate angelic hosts elsewhere in Scripture (Ps 68:17; Rev 5:11; cf. 2Ki 2:11–12; 6:17). This would not preclude the possibility of human armies of a manageable size from also being involved. But the emphasis here (vv.16–19) is on their fully demonic character as utterly cruel and determined and without mercy toward man, woman, or child. These demons might also be manifest in pestilences, epidemic diseases, or misfortunes. Such would explain the use of "plagues" to describe these hordes (vv.18, 20; cf. 11:6; 16:9, 21).

20–21 God's purpose for the plagues is first of all a judgment on humanity for the willful choice of idolatry and the corrupt practices that go with it. John had earlier called the churches to "repent" of their faithless tendencies, lest they also share in God's judgment (2:5, 16, 21–22; 3:19). In these verses we see the end result of refusing to turn to God. This stubbornness leads to both the worship of demons and of cultic objects made by human hands (gold, silver, bronze, stone, and wood; cf. Pss 115:4–7; 135:17; Jer 10:1–16; Da 5:23). "Demons" may mean either pagan deities (Dt 32:17; Ps 106:37) or malign spirits (1Co 10:20–21; 1Ti 4:1). But since the Greek here in Revelation distinguishes the cultic objects from the demons, John no doubt shared Paul's concept of demons as evil spirits (16:14; 18:2). Hence there is a twofold evil in idol worship: (1) it robs the true God of his glory (Ro 1:23), and (2) it leads to consorting with corrupting evil spirits.

21 This demonic corruption is manifest in the inhuman acts of those who have given up God for idols—acts of murder, sexual immorality, and thefts (cf. Ro 1:24, 28–32). In general, these are violations of the Ten Commandments. "Magic arts" (*pharmakon*, GK *5760*) means the practice of sorceries or "witchcraft" (LXX Ex 7:11; 9:11; Gal 5:20; Rev 21:8; 22:15). Drugs were usually involved in these arts. Sometimes the word *pharmakon* means "to poison," as in a Jewish prayer from the first century BC: "I call upon and pray the Most High, the Lord of the spirits and of all flesh, against those who with guile murdered or poisoned [*pharmakon*] the wretched, untimely lost Heraclea, shedding her innocent blood wickedly" (cited in MM, 664).

The second purpose of God revealed in the agonizing plagues described in chs. 8 and 9 is to bring societies to repentance (cf. 16:9, 11). God is not willing that any person should suffer his judgment but that all should repent and turn to him (Lk 13:3, 5; 2Pe 3:9). But when God's works and words are persistently rejected, only judgment remains (Eph 5:6; Heb 10:26–31).

NOTES

8:13 In place of ἀετός, *aetos* ("eagle"), read by ℵ A B and most MSS and versions, other texts read ἄγγελος, *angelos* ("angel"; P and some minuscules). Metzger (1971 ed., 743) comments, "The substitution may have been accidental . . . but more likely was deliberate, since the function ascribed to the eagle seems more appropriate to an angel (cf. 14:6)."

9:1 The noun ἄβυσσος (*abyssos*, "Abyss"; from Heb. *tehōm*, "the deep," GK 9333) is referred to in *1 Enoch* in the sense of both an intermediate and a final abode for fallen angels, Satan, demons, and fallen humans (*1 En.* 18:12–16; 21:7–10; 108:3–6; cf. Charles, 1:240–41).

11 Ἑβραϊστὶ (*Hebraisti*, GK *1580*) has generally been understood here and elsewhere in the NT to mean "Aramaic," but some studies question this identification and argue for the sense "in Hebrew" rather than "in Aramaic" (cf. Philip Edgcumbe Hughes, "The Language Spoken by Jesus," in *New Dimensions in New Testament Study*, ed. R. N. Longenecker and M. C. Tenney [Grand Rapids: Zondervan, 1974], 127–28).

16 The words δισμυριάδες μυριάδων (*dismyriades myriadōn*, "two hundred million") are Hebrew and not Aramaic in background (cf. Mussies, 353).

3. Second Interlude (10:1–11:14)

a. The little book (10:1–11)

OVERVIEW

As in the seals, the sequences of the sixth and seventh trumpets are interrupted to provide additional information bearing on the previous events and to prepare the reader for further developments.

¹Then I saw another mighty angel coming down from heaven. He was robed in a cloud, with a rainbow above his head; his face was like the sun, and his legs were like fiery pillars. ²He was holding a little scroll, which lay open in his hand. He planted his right foot on the sea and his left foot on the land, ³and he gave a loud shout like the roar of a lion. When he shouted, the voices of the seven thunders spoke. ⁴And when the seven thunders spoke, I was about to write; but I heard a voice from heaven say, "Seal up what the seven thunders have said and do not write it down."

⁵Then the angel I had seen standing on the sea and on the land raised his right hand to heaven. ⁶And he swore by him who lives for ever and ever, who created the heavens and all that is in them, the earth and all that is in it, and the sea and all that is in it, and said, "There will be no more delay! ⁷But in the days when the seventh angel is about to sound his trumpet, the mystery of God will be accomplished, just as he announced to his servants the prophets."

⁸Then the voice that I had heard from heaven spoke to me once more: "Go, take the scroll that lies open in the hand of the angel who is standing on the sea and on the land."

⁹So I went to the angel and asked him to give me the little scroll. He said to me, "Take it and eat it. It will turn your stomach sour, but in your mouth it will be as sweet as honey."

> [10]I took the little scroll from the angel's hand and ate it. It tasted as sweet as honey in my mouth, but when I had eaten it, my stomach turned sour. [11]Then I was told, "You must prophesy again about many peoples, nations, languages and kings."

1 The author sees a mighty angel (possibly Michael, "the great prince" [Da 12:1]), whom he describes in such dazzling terms (cloud, rainbow, sun, fiery pillars) that some have identified him with Christ. But angels are always angels in the Apocalypse, as well as in the rest of the NT, and should not be identified with Christ. The *voice* that speaks in vv.4, 8 could, however, be that of Jesus.

2 The angel has in his hand a small scroll (v.2). This scroll should not be confused with the Lamb's scroll of chs. 5–7 (contra Bauckham, 238–66; cf. Notes) but should be connected with the symbolic scroll of Ezekiel (Eze 2:9–3:3; cf. Jer 15:15–17). This prophet was told to "eat" the scroll, just as John was told to eat the scroll given to him (vv.9–10). Such an action symbolized the reception of the Word of God into the innermost being as a necessary prerequisite to proclaim it with confidence. John could see the words on the scroll because it "lay open" in the angel's hand. The angel standing on both land and sea symbolizes that the prophetic message is for the whole world.

3–4 When the angel shouted, seven thunders spoke, and John proceeded to write down their words. But he is interrupted and is commanded, "Seal up what the seven thunders have said and do not write it down" (v.4). Conceivably, this might have been another series of sevens. Either the seven thunders were intended for John's own illumination and were not essential to the main vision of the seven trumpets or the reference is designed to strike a note of mystery with reference to God's revelatory activities (cf. 2Co 12:4). As the visible portion of an iceberg is only a small part of the iceberg, most of which is hidden from man's sight, so God's disclosures reveal only part of his total being and purposes.

5–7 The angel's action of raising his right hand to heaven undoubtedly alludes to the Jewish oath-swearing procedure (Dt 32:40; Da 12:7). He swears that "there will be no more delay" (v.6). Clearly there is some type of progression in the seals, trumpets, and bowls that nears its conclusion as the seventh trumpet is about to sound (v.7). When the seventh trumpet is finally sounded, there is an announcement that "the kingdom of the world has become the kingdom of our Lord and of his Christ" and that the time has come to judge the dead, reward the saints, and destroy the destroyers of the earth (11:15, 18). These events are recorded in the remaining chapters of the book, which include descriptions of the seven bowl judgments and the new heavens and new earth. Thus here in v.7 it is announced that "the mystery of God" is accomplished. "The mystery of God" is his purposes for humanity and the world as revealed to both OT and NT prophets.

The way the NIV translates v.7 suggests that the consummation comes before the blowing of the seventh trumpet: "when the seventh angel is about to sound his trumpet . . ." (also NASB). While this is grammatically possible, it is also possible to render the expression "about to sound" as "when he shall sound." Thus understood, the meaning is that "in the days of" (i.e., during the period of) the sound of the seventh trumpet, when the angel sounds, the final purposes of God will be completed. This rendering clarifies the statement in 11:14, "The second woe has passed: the third woe is coming soon"—a statement made just before the seventh trumpet sounds. Hence the seventh trumpet will reveal the final judgments of the bowls and the final establishment of God's rule on the earth.

This final trumpet could possibly be the content of the little scroll (cf. Notes).

8–11 John, like Ezekiel, is now commanded to take the prophetic scroll and eat it. The scroll tasted "as sweet as honey" but was bitter to the stomach. Receiving the Word of God is a great joy; but since the Word is an oracle of judgment, it results in the unpleasant experience of proclaiming a message of wrath and woe (cf. Jer 15:16, 19). The symbolic act of eating the scroll might also mean that the prophetic message was mixed with joy and comfort as well as gloom. Mounce, 216, following Bruce, argues that the content of the scroll is "a message for the believing church and is to be found in the following verses (11:1–13). . . . It is *after* the eating of the book that John is told he must prophesy again, this time concerning many peoples, nations, tongues, and kings (Rev 10:11). This begins with chapter 12. The sweet scroll that turns the stomach bitter is a message for the church. Before the final

triumph believers are going to pass through a formidable ordeal. . . . So the little scroll unveils the lot of the faithful in those last days of fierce Satanic opposition." This may be too narrow—the scroll may contain the whole of chs. 11–14. In any case, the sweetness should not be taken to refer to the joy of proclaiming a message of wrath, for to all God's prophets this was a sorrowful, bitter task (Jer 9:1).

11 The chief import of ch. 10 seems to be a further confirmation of John's prophetic call, as this verse indicates: "You must prophesy again about many peoples, nations, languages and kings." This prophesying should not be understood as merely a recapitulation in greater detail of the previous visions but a further progression of the events connected with the end as revealed in the little scroll. Notice the use of the word "kings" instead of "tribes" (as in 5:9; 7:9; 13:7; 14:6). This may anticipate the emphasis on the kings of the earth found in 17:9–12 and elsewhere.

NOTES

2 Bauckham's thesis, 238–66, is that the "little scroll" (1) is the same as the scroll in ch. 5; (2) is also the content of the "revelation" of Jesus Christ in 1:1 (the conversion of the nations), and (3) is expounded more fully in 11:1–22:5. Jauhiainen (Ἀποκάλυψις Ἰησοῦ Χριστοῦ [Rev. 1:1]') recently raised important objections to this thesis. He proposes instead that the focus of the little scroll is the struggle and suffering of the saints at the hand of the beast (chs. 12–14), while the sealed scroll (ch. 5) is the hitherto unrevealed final outcome of this conflict and suffering—the "revelation of Jesus Christ" (1:1), namely, "what must take place soon" (the final end of the two cities, Babylon and the Bride, found in chs.17–22), which was hidden from Daniel ("closed up and sealed," Da 12:9).

6 The Greek word χρόνος (*chronos*, GK *5989*; NIV, "delay") can refer to time in a number of aspects. Other verses where χρόνος, *chronos*, means "delay" are Matthew 25:5 and Hebrews 10:37.

7 There are two possibilities for rendering μέλλω (*mellō*, GK *3516*) plus the infinitive: (1) imminence ("about to," NIV), or (2) strong future certainty ("shall"). I have opted for the second sense to throw the action into the time of the blowing of the seventh trumpet and not to the time *before* its sounding.

11 The preposition ἐπί, *epi*, translated correctly as "about" in the NIV, may with the dative also mean "upon, over, against, near, to, with." The KJV rendering "before" would not be accurate unless the genitive were used (BDAG, 363).

b. The two witnesses (11:1–14)

OVERVIEW

Some have considered this chapter as one of the most difficult to interpret in the book of Revelation (so Lilje, 159). Alford, 4:655, agrees: "This passage may well be called . . . the *crux interpretum*, as it is undoubtedly one of the most difficult in the whole Apocalypse." In it, John refers to the temple, the holy city, and the two prophets who are killed by the beast and after three and a half days are resurrected and ascend to heaven. Does John intend all this to be understood simply as it is given—the literal temple in Jerusalem; two people who, after prophesying for 1,260 days, are killed by the Antichrist, raised from the dead, and ascend to heaven; a great earthquake that kills seven thousand people and the survivors of which glorify God? Or does he intend all or part of these as representative symbols? Most commentators take at least part of these things as symbolic. Furthermore, how does this section (vv.1–13) relate to the total context (10:1–11:19)?

While details of interpretation vary, there are two main approaches to the chapter: (1) the temple, altar, worshipers, and holy city have something to do with the Jewish people and their place in the plan of God; or (2) John is here referring to the Christian church. As in ch. 7, John's references to particular Jewish entities create the chief source of the problem. Does he use these references in a plain, one-to-one sense, or does he use them representatively or symbolically?

At the outset, it may be helpful to state why the Jewish view is less preferable. This approach actually has two slightly different tracks. One school of commentators, generally dispensational, understands the "temple" and the "city" to refer to a rebuilt Jewish temple in Jerusalem (still future). While in this view, elements in the description may be symbolic, the main import of the passage is seen as depicting a future protection of the nation of Israel prior to her spiritual regeneration. The Antichrist (beast) will permit the rebuilding of the temple in Jerusalem, as well as the restoration of Jewish worship for three and a half years, but then he will break his covenant and trample down a part of the temple and the holy city until Christ returns to deliver the Jewish people (cf. Da 9:27; so Smith, Seiss, Walvoord, Thomas).

Ladd, 150, following Beckwith and Zahn, has argued for a modified Jewish view. He contends that John is prophetically predicting the "preservation and ultimate salvation of the Jewish people," much in the manner of Paul in Romans 11:26 ("and so all Israel will be saved"). Unlike those who hold the strict dispensational view, Ladd believes that the temple and the city of Jerusalem are not the literal Jewish restored temple or the city located in Palestine. Rather, they represent on the one hand the believing Jewish remnant (temple, altar, and worshipers), and on the other hand the Jewish people or nation as a whole who are currently under Gentile oppression (outer court and city). Both Jewish views suffer from their inability to relate this chapter to the context of ch. 10, the parallelism in the seal interlude (ch. 7), the ministry and significance of the two witnesses, or the further chapters in Revelation (esp. chs. 12–13). Therefore, it is better to understand John as referring in ch. 11 to the entire Christian community (so Beale, Aune, Osborne, Bauckham, Mounce, Kistemaker, Boring, Beasley-Murray). This is the view followed in this commentary.

¹I was given a reed like a measuring rod and was told, "Go and measure the temple of God and the altar, and count the worshipers there. ²But exclude the outer court; do not measure it, because it has been given to the Gentiles. They will trample on the holy city for 42 months. ³And I will give power to my two witnesses, and they will prophesy for 1,260 days, clothed in sackcloth." ⁴These are the two olive trees and the two lampstands that stand before the Lord of the earth. ⁵If anyone tries to harm them, fire comes from their mouths and devours their enemies. This is how anyone who wants to harm them must die. ⁶These men have power to shut up the sky so that it will not rain during the time they are prophesying; and they have power to turn the waters into blood and to strike the earth with every kind of plague as often as they want.

⁷Now when they have finished their testimony, the beast that comes up from the Abyss will attack them, and overpower and kill them. ⁸Their bodies will lie in the street of the great city, which is figuratively called Sodom and Egypt, where also their Lord was crucified. ⁹For three and a half days men from every people, tribe, language and nation will gaze on their bodies and refuse them burial. ¹⁰The inhabitants of the earth will gloat over them and will celebrate by sending each other gifts, because these two prophets had tormented those who live on the earth.

¹¹But after the three and a half days a breath of life from God entered them, and they stood on their feet, and terror struck those who saw them. ¹²Then they heard a loud voice from heaven saying to them, "Come up here." And they went up to heaven in a cloud, while their enemies looked on.

¹³At that very hour there was a severe earthquake and a tenth of the city collapsed. Seven thousand people were killed in the earthquake, and the survivors were terrified and gave glory to the God of heaven.

¹⁴The second woe has passed; the third woe is coming soon.

COMMENTARY

1 John is given a "reed" (*kalamos*, GK *2812*), or "cane," long and straight like a "rod" and thus suitable for measuring a large building or area. (The measuring rod referred to in Eze 40:5 was about ten feet long.) The purpose of the reed is to "measure the temple of God and the altar." Most agree that the principal OT passage in John's mind was Ezekiel's lengthy description of the measuring of the future kingdom temple (Eze 40:3–48:35). Since interpreters are confused about what Ezekiel's vision

means, the ambiguity extends also to John's description. In the ancient world, measuring was accomplished for shorter lengths by the reed cane (Eze 40:3) and for longer distances by a rope line (1Ki 7:23; Isa 44:13). Measuring with a line may have various metaphorical meanings. It may refer to the promise of restoration and rebuilding, with emphasis on extension or enlargement (Jer 31:39; Zec 1:16). Measuring may also be done to mark out something for destruction (2Sa 8:2; 2Ki 21:13; Isa

28:17; La 2:8; Am 7:7–9). In Ezekiel 40–48 this latter sense would be inappropriate. But what does John's measuring mean?

Since John is told in v.2 not to measure the outer court but to leave it for the nations to overrun, it may be that in ch. 11 the measuring means that the temple of God, the altar, and the worshipers (who are to be counted) are to be secured for blessing and preserved from spiritual harm or defilement. So in 21:15–17 John similarly depicts the angel's measuring of the heavenly city (with a golden rod), apparently to mark off the city and its inhabitants from harm and defilement (21:24, 27). As a parallel to the sealing of 7:1–8, the measuring does not symbolize preservation from physical harm but the prophetic guarantee that none of the faithful worshipers of Jesus as Messiah will perish, even though they suffer physical destruction at the hand of the beast (13:7). Such seems also to be the sense of the measuring passage in *1 Enoch* 62:1–5 (cf. Charles, 1:276).

In Ezekiel 43:10 the prophet is told to "describe the temple to the people of Israel, that they may be ashamed of their sins." The purpose of the elaborate description and temple measurement in Ezekiel is to indicate the glory and holiness of God in Israel's midst and to convict them of their defilement of his sanctuary. Likewise, John's prophetic ministry calls for a clear separation between those who are holy and those who have defiled themselves with the idolatry of the beast.

John is to measure "the temple of God." There are two Greek words used in the NT for temple. One of them (*hieron*, GK *2639*) is a broad term that refers to the whole structure of Herod's temple, including courts, colonnades, etc. (e.g., Mt 4:5; Jn 2:14). The other (*naos*, GK *3724*) is narrower and refers to the sanctuary or inner house where only the priests were allowed (Mt 23:35; 27:51; always in Rev). While the distinction between the two words is not always maintained (*TDNT* 4:884), in this context (11:1) it may be appropriate since the next verse mentions the outer precinct as a separate entity.

Does John mean the heavenly temple often mentioned in Revelation (cf. 11:19; 15:5, 8; 16:17), or does he refer to the Christian community, as in 3:12: "Him who overcomes I will make a pillar in the temple of my God"? In the postapostolic *Epistle of Barnabas* (16:1ff.), the temple is the individual Christian, or alternatively the community of Christians—as it is in Paul (1Co 3:16; 6:19; 2Co 6:16). Since John refers to the "outer court" in v.2, which is trampled by the nations, it is quite likely he has in mind not the heavenly temple of God but an earthly one—either the (rebuilt?) temple in Jerusalem or, symbolically, the covenant people.

The word for temple (*naos*) always refers to the Jerusalem temple in the Gospels, with the single exception of John's gospel, where it refers to Jesus' own body (Jn 2:19–21; cf. Rev 21:22). Outside the Gospels it refers either to pagan shrines (Ac 17:24; 19:24) or, in Paul's letters, metaphorically to the physical bodies of Christians or the church of God (1Co 3:16; 6:19; 2Co 6:16; Eph 2:21). In only one case is it debatable whether Paul means the literal Jerusalem temple or the church (2Th 2:4).

While to take the temple in 11:1 as representing the church in the great tribulation is not without problems, this seems the best view. Other NT usage outside the Gospels, the figurative use of temple in John 2:19–21, and his use in Revelation all point to the image of the temple as representing the messianic community of both Jews and Gentiles, comparable to his symbol of the woman in ch. 12 (so Alford, 4:657).

The "altar" would then refer to the huge stone altar of sacrifice in the court of the priests, and the expression "the worshipers" would most naturally indicate the priests and others in the three inner courts (the court of the priests, the court of Israel, the court of the women). These represent symbolically the true servants of God, and the measuring symbolizes their recognition and acceptance by God in the same manner as the numbering in ch. 7. The writer of Hebrews likewise speaks of an "altar" from which Christians eat but from which Jewish priests who serve in the temple are not qualified to eat (Heb 13:10). By this language he speaks of the once-for-all sacrifice of Christ on the cross, utilizing the background of the temple images, as does John.

2 As the "outer court" in the Jerusalem temple was frequented by a mixed group including Gentiles and unbelievers, so in John's mind the earthly temple or community of God may involve a part where those who are impure or unfaithful will be (21:8–22:15). The effect of not measuring this part of the temple is to exclude it and those in it from spiritual security and God's blessing, in contrast to the way the measuring secured these things for the true community. So in measuring the temple, Ezekiel is instructed to exclude from the sanctuary "the foreigners uncircumcised in heart and flesh" (Eze 44:5–9)—i.e., pagans who do not worship the true God and whose presence would desecrate the sanctuary. Previously John has shown concern about those who were associated with the local churches but were not true worshipers of Christ (cf. 2:14–16, 20–25; 3:1–5, 16). When the great test comes, they will join the ranks of the beast and reveal their true colors.

On the other hand, while Swete suggests that the outer court is perhaps the rejected synagogue (cf. 2:9; 3:9), it may be better to understand the desecration of the outer court as a symbolic reference to the victory of the beast over the saints that is described in v.7. Thus by using two slightly different images—the "temple-altar-worshipers" and the "outer court-holy city"—John is viewing the church under different aspects. Though the Gentiles (pagans) are permitted to touch the "outer court"

and to trample on the "holy city" for a limited time ("42 months"), they are not able to destroy the church, because the "inner sanctuary" is measured or protected in keeping with Christ's earlier words, "And the gates of Hades will not overcome it" (Mt 16:18; so Morris, 146; Mounce, 214).

Since John says the outer court will be "given to the Gentiles," it is important to establish the best translation of *ethnē* ("Gentiles," GK *1620*). In the NT, *ethnē* may have the more general sense of "nations," describing the various ethnic or national groups among humankind (e.g., Mt 24:9, 14; Lk 24:47; Ro 1:5; 15:11). In other contexts it may be used as a narrower technical term to denote "Gentiles" in contrast to the Jewish people (e.g., Mt 4:15; 10:5; Lk 2:32; Ac 10:45; Ro 11:11). In many cases, the broader sense may fade into the narrower, producing ambiguity.

But there is another use of *ethnē*. Just as the Jews referred to all other peoples outside the covenant as "Gentiles," so there gradually developed a similar Christian use of the term that saw all peoples who were outside Christ as *ethnē*, including unbelieving Jews (1Co 5:1; 12:2; 1Th 4:5; 1Pe 2:12; 3Jn 7). Our word "heathen" may parallel this use of the word (*TDNT* 2:370 n. 19). When the sixteen cases of the plural form in Revelation are examined, not once is the sense "Gentiles" appropriate. Everywhere the *ethnē* are the peoples of the earth, either in rebellion against God (11:18; 14:8; 19:15; 20:3) or redeemed and under the rule of Christ (2:26; 21:24, 26; 22:2). There is no good reason why John does not intend the same sense here. Nevertheless, the versions reflect the uncertainty of the translators: Gentiles (KJV, REB, NIV) or nations (NRSV, NASB, NLT).

In summary, John's words "given to the Gentiles" refer to the defiling agencies that will trample down the outer court of the church, leading either to defection from Christ or physical destruction, though all the while the inner sanctuary, i.e., the community of the true believers, will not be defiled by idolatry. This spiritual preservation of the true believers will be accomplished by John's prophetic ministry, which distinguishes true loyalty to Christ from the deception of the beast.

The nations will "trample on the holy city for 42 months." Opinion varies between the literal and the symbolic significance of the designation "the holy city." The more literal viewpoint sees "the holy city" as the earthly city of Jerusalem. Support for this is found in (1) the OT's use (Ne 11:1; Isa 48:2; 52:1; Da 9:24) and Matthew's use (Mt 4:5; 27:53) of "holy city" for Jerusalem; (2) the proximity of "the holy city" to the temple reference (v.1); and (3) the mention in v.8 of the "great city," "where also their Lord was crucified."

Since Jerusalem was destroyed in AD 70, and since Revelation was presumably written about AD 95 (cf. Introduction), the more literalist interpreters hold two views about the meaning of this reference to the city. Some believe it to refer to the rebuilt city and temple during the future period of the tribulation (Walvoord, 177; Thomas, 2:84). Others see the city as merely a representative or symbolic reference to the Jewish people without any special implication of a literal city or temple (Beckwith, 588; Ladd, 152–53; Rissi, 96–97). But if John does in fact differentiate here between believing Jews (inner court) and the nation as a whole (outer court), it would be the only place in the book where he does so. Furthermore, such a reference at this point in the context of chs. 10 and 11 would be abrupt and unconnected with the main themes in these chapters, the subject of which is the nature of the prophetic ministry and the great trial awaiting Christians.

Far more in keeping with the emphasis of the whole book and of these chapters in particular is the view that, in the mind of John, "the holy city," like the temple, refers to the church on earth. The consistent use in the book of the expression "holy city" means the community of those faithful to Jesus Christ, composed of believing Jews and Gentiles (21:2, 10; 22:19; cf. 3:12; 20:9). It should also be noted that the name "Jerusalem" nowhere appears in ch. 11 but that there is a circumlocution for it in v.8—"where also their Lord was crucified"—which is prefaced with the word "figuratively" (*pneumatikōs*, lit., "spiritually"; GK *4461*). While the vision of the future Holy City (chs. 21–22) describes the condition of the city when she has completed her great ordeal and is finally delivered from the great deceiver, the present reference is to the people as they must first endure the trampling of the pagan nations for "42 months."

Does the trampling (*pateō*, GK *4251*) indicate defilement and apostasy, or does it instead mean persecution? The word "trample" can metaphorically mean either of these (BDAG, 786). Two factors favor the latter sense. The time of the trampling is "42 months," which is the exact time John attributes to the reign of the beast (13:5–7). Furthermore, in Daniel's prophecy the trampling of the sanctuary and host of God's people by Antiochus Epiphanes (Da 8:10, 13; 2 Macc 8:2, *katapateō*, LXX) is clearly a persecution of the people of God. The apocryphal *Psalms of Solomon* (17:24, 42–47) relates that the trampling of Jerusalem by the pagans will be reversed by the Messiah.

But what of the designation "42 months"? This exact expression occurs in the Bible only here and in 13:5, where it refers to the time of the authority of the beast. Mention is also made of a period of 1,260 days (i.e., 42 months of 30 days each) in 11:3 and 12:6. In 12:14, a similar length of time is referred to as "a time, times [i.e., two times] and half a time." All these expressions equal a three-and-one-half-year period.

In the various uses of the terms, "42 months" refers to the period of oppression of the holy city and the time of the authority of the beast (11:2; 13:5). As for the "1,260 days," this is the period the two witnesses prophesy and the time the woman is protected from the dragon's reach (11:3; 12:6). "Time, times and half a time" seems to be used synonymously for the 1,260 days during which the woman will be protected in the desert (12:14). We cannot assume that because these periods are equal they are identical. On the other hand, the three different expressions may well be literary variations for the same period.

Daniel is generally taken to be the origin of the terms. In Daniel 9:27, a week is spoken of ("seven," NIV), and the context makes it clear that this is a week of years, i.e., seven years (cf. Glasson, 67). Further, the week is divided in half—i.e., three and a half years for each division. These half weeks of years are spoken of in Daniel 7:25 as "a time [one year], times [two years] and half a time [half a year]." Early Jewish and general patristic interpretation followed by the early Protestant commentators referred to this period as the reign of the Antichrist (James A. Montgomery, *A Critical and Exegetical Commentary on the Book of Daniel* [ICC; Edinburgh: T&T Clark, 1964], 314).

In Daniel 12:7, the identical expression refers to the period "when the power of the holy people has been finally broken"; in 12:11 the equivalent period expressed in days (1,290) refers to the time of the "abomination" and defilement of the temple. Whether or not these designations refer to the second-century BC activities of Antiochus Epiphanes must be left to the exegetes of Daniel; but it is known that the Jews and later the Christians believed that these events at least foreshadow, if not predict, the last years of world history under the Antichrist (cf. Glasson, 68). Thus John would have a ready tool to use in this imagery for setting forth his revelation of the last days.

Glasson, 70, following Victorinus, Hippolytus, and Augustine, suggests that the first three and a half years is the period of the preaching of the two witnesses, while the second half of the week is the time of bitter trial when Antichrist reigns supreme. Others believe the expressions are synchronous and thus refer to the identical period (so Swete, 131). With some reservations, the view of Glasson may be followed. The 1,260-day period of protected prophesying by the two witnesses (11:3–6) synchronizes with the period of the woman in the desert (12:6, 14). When the death of the witnesses occurs (11:7), there follows the forty-two-month murderous reign of the beast (13:5, 7, 15), which synchronizes with the trampling down of the holy city (11:2). This twofold division seems also to be supported by Jesus' Olivet Discourse, where he speaks of the "beginning of birth pains" (Mt 24:8) and then of the period of "great distress" shortly before his return (Mt 24:21).

Finally, are the two periods of three and a half years symbolic, or do they indicate calendar years? Not all will agree, but a symbolic sense that involves a real period but understands the numbers to describe the kind of period rather than its length is in keeping with John's use of numbers elsewhere (cf. 2:10; 4:4; 7:4). Hence, if we follow the twofold division of Daniel's seventieth week of seven years, the preaching of the two witnesses occupies the first half, while the second half is the time of bitter trial when the beast reigns supreme, and during which time the fearful events of chs. 13–19 take place. Since these time references are by no means clear, any explanation must be tentative.

3 Perhaps more diversity of interpretation surrounds these two personages than surrounds even the temple in the previous verses. They are called "two witnesses" here, "two prophets" (v.10), and, more figuratively, "two olive trees and the two lampstands that stand before the Lord of the earth" (v.4). Identifications range all the way from two historic figures raised to life, to two groups, to two principles, such as the Law and the Prophets.

Tertullian (d. ca. 220) identified the two with Enoch and Elijah.

On the other hand, Jewish tradition taught that Moses and Elijah would return, and this view is followed by a number of Christian interpreters. According to Jochanan ben Zakkai (first century AD) God said to Moses, "If I send the prophet Elijah, you must both come together" (Charles, 1:281; also Seiss, Smith, Gundry, Thomas; cf. Mk 9:11–13). Beckwith, 595, believes they are two prophets of the future who will perform the functions of Moses and Elijah. Others understand the figures to represent the church (so Primasius [d. ca. 552]). Swete, 132, observes, "The witness of the church, borne by her martyrs and confessors, her saints and doctors, and by the words and lives of all in whom Christ lives and speaks, is one continual prophecy" (cf. also Beasley-Murray). Ladd, 154, cannot make up his mind between the witnessing church to Israel and two historical eschatological prophets. Bruce, 649, believes they are symbolic of the church in its royal and priestly functions. Others identify them as representative of the martyrs (so Morris, 147; Caird, 134).

More recently, Johannes Munck has identified them with the Christian prophets Peter and Paul (cited in Bruce, 649). Rissi ("Kerygma of the Revelation to John," 16) sees them as representative of the Jewish and Gentile believers in the church. Minear, 99, understands the two to represent all the prophets.

Since opinion varies so greatly at this point, it may be wise not to be dogmatic about any one view. Minear's arguments, however, seem to me more persuasive than the others. The two witnesses represent those in the church who, like John, are specially called to bear a prophetic witness to Christ during the whole age of the church (cf. Beale, Osborne). They also represent those prophets who will be martyred by the beast. Indications that they are representative of many individuals and not just two are that (1) they are never seen as individuals

but do everything together—they prophesy together, suffer together, are killed together, are raised together, and ascend together—and all this is hardly possible for two individuals; (2) the beast makes war on them (v.7), which is strange if they are merely two individuals; (3) people throughout the whole world view their ignominious deaths (v.9)—something quite unlikely if only two individuals are involved; (4) they are described as two "lamps" (v.4), a figure applied in chs. 1 and 2 to local churches comprised of many individuals. They are "clothed in sackcloth" because they are prophets (cf. Isa 20:2; Zec 13:4) who call for repentance and humility (Jer 6:26; 49:3; Mt 11:21); it was the most suitable garb for times of distress, grief, danger, crisis, and humility. That God himself will appoint or "give power to" them would encourage the church to persevere, even in the face of strong opposition.

4 The reference to the "two olive trees and the two lampstands" is an allusion to Joshua and Zerubbabel in Zechariah's vision, who were also said "to serve the Lord of all the earth" (Zec 4:1–6a, 10b–14). The whole import of Zechariah's vision was to strengthen the two leaders by reminding them of God's resources and to vindicate them in the eyes of the community as they pursued their God-given tasks. Thus John's message would be that the witnesses to Christ who cause the church to fulfill her mission to burn as bright lights to the world will not be quenched (cf. Rev 1:20; 2:5).

Why there should be two olive trees and two lampstands has been variously answered. Some suggest that "two" is the number of required legal witnesses (Nu 35:30; Dt 19:15; cf. Mt 18:16; Lk 10:1–24); others suggest that "two" represents the priestly and kingly aspects of the church or the Jewish and Gentile components. Perhaps the dualism was suggested to John by the two olive trees from Zechariah and the two great prophets of the OT who were connected with the coming of the

Messiah in Jewish thought, i.e., Moses and Elijah (v.6; cf. Mt 17:3–4). What Joshua (the high priest) and Zerubbabel (the prince) were to the older community and temple, Jesus Christ is to the new community. He is both anointed Priest and King, and his church reflects this character especially in its Christian prophets (1:6; 5:10; 20:6).

5 Here the prophets' divine protection from their enemies is described in terms reminiscent of the former prophets' protection by God (2Ki 1:10; Jer 5:14). Fire is understood symbolically as judgment from God; and since it proceeds from the witnesses' mouths, we understand that their message of judgment will eventually be fulfilled by God's power (Ge 19:23–24; 2Sa 22:9; Ps 97:3). Their Lord gives them immunity from destruction until they complete their confirmation of God's saving deed in Christ. This assures the people of God that, no matter how many of its chosen saints are oppressed and killed, God's witness to Christ will continue until his purposes are fulfilled.

6 The words "power to shut up the sky" and "power to turn the waters into blood" clearly allude to the ministries of the prophets Elijah and Moses (1Ki 17:1; Ex 7:17–21). There is, however, no need for the literal reappearing of these two if it is understood that the two witnesses come in the same spirit and function as their predecessors. Thus Luke interprets the significance of John the Baptist as a ministry "in the spirit and power of Elijah" (Lk 1:17). The author of Revelation is simply describing the vocation of certain Christian prophets, indicating that some follow in the same tradition as the former prophets of Israel. According to Luke 4:25 and James 5:17, Elijah's prophecy shut up the heavens for "three and a half years," a curious foreshadowing, perhaps, of the span of time that these prophets witness (1,260 days [v.3]).

7 When the witnesses finish their witnessing, they are killed by the beast from the Abyss. This is the first reference to the beast in the book. The abruptness with which it is introduced seems not only to presuppose some knowledge of the beast but also to anticipate what is said of him in chs. 13 and 17. Only here and in 17:8 is the beast described as coming "up from the Abyss" (cf. 9:1), showing his demonic origin. He attacks the prophets (lit., "makes war with them," *polemos*, GK *4483*; cf. 9:7; 12:7, 17; 13:7; 16:14; 19:19; 20:8). This possibly reflects Daniel 7:21: "As I watched, this horn was waging war [*polemos*, LXX] against the saints and defeating them." This attack is again described in 12:17 and 13:7: "Then the dragon was enraged at the woman and went off to make war against the rest of her offspring. . . . [The beast] was given power to make war against the saints and to conquer them." This is the second and final phase of the dragon's (Satan's) persecution of the Christian prophets and saints.

8 Here we have the place of the attack on the witnesses and the place of their death: "the street of the great city, which is figuratively called Sodom and Egypt, where also their Lord was crucified." Verse 8 is both full of meaning and difficult to interpret. At first glance it seems apparent that John is referring to the actual city of Jerusalem where Christ died (Thomas, 2:94). This allusion seems obvious. Charles Maitland (*The Apostles' School of Prophetic Interpretation* [London: Longman, Brown, Green and Longmans, 1849], 16) claims that this was the universal view of the ancient church. Yet John's terminology also implies more than this. The city is called the "great city," a designation referring to Babylon throughout the rest of the book (16:19; 17:18; 18:10, 16, 18–19, 21). Moreover, John's use of the word "city" is symbolic from its very first occurrence in 3:12. In fact, there are really only two cities in the book: the city of God and the city of Satan, later referred to as Babylon. A city may be also a metaphor for the total life of a community of people (Heb 11:10; 12:22; 13:14; see Notes).

Here the "great city" is clearly more than merely Jerusalem, for John says it is "figuratively called Sodom and Egypt." "Figuratively" renders the Greek *pneumatikōs* (GK *4461*), which BDAG, 837 says means "spiritually, in a spiritual manner, in a manner caused by or filled with the divine Spirit." Elsewhere in the NT the word characterizes that which pertains to the Spirit in contrast to the flesh (1Co 2:14–15; Eph 1:3; 5:19; Col 3:16; 1Pe 2:5; etc.). The RSV and NEB translate it as "allegorically," which is questionable since there is a Greek word—*allēgoreō* (GK *251*)—meaning precisely that (cf. Gal 4:24); and nowhere else does *pneumatikōs* have this sense. The NASB has "mystically." Closer may be Knox, who renders *pneumatikōs* "in the language of prophecy," or NRSV's and Paul Minear's ("Ontology and Ecclesiology in the Apocalypse," *NTS* 12 [1966], 94 n. 1) "prophetically," or Phillips' "is called by those with spiritual understanding."

The spiritually discerning will catch the significance of the threefold designation of this city. It is called "Sodom," which connotes rebellion against God, the rejection of God's servants, moral degradation, and the awfulness of divine judgment (cf. Eze 16:49). In Isaiah's day, the rebellious rulers of Jerusalem were called the "rulers of Sodom" (Isa 1:10; cf. Eze 16:46). The second designation is "Egypt." Egypt, however, is a country, not a city. It is virtually certain that by John's day Egypt had become a symbolic name for antitheocratic world kingdoms that enslaved Israel (cf. Rabbi Jose ben Chalaphta, "All kingdoms are called by the name of Egypt because they enslave Israel" [cited in Str-B 3:812]). The third designation is "the great city, . . . where also their Lord was crucified" (cf. Mt 23:28–31, 37–38; Lk 13:33; 21:20–24).

If, as most commentators believe, John also has Rome in mind in mentioning the "great city," then there are at least five places all seen by John as one—Babylon, Sodom, Egypt, Jerusalem, and Rome. (This one city has become, in the eyes of the spiritually discerning, all places opposed to God and the witness of his servants—Sodom, Tyre, Egypt, Babylon, Nineveh, Rome, et al.) Wherever God is opposed and his servants are harassed and killed, there is the "great city," the transhistorical city of Satan, the great mother of prostitutes (cf. 17:1). What can happen to God's witnesses in any place is what has already happened to their Lord in Jerusalem. (John Bunyan's city "Vanity Fair" approaches this idea, though not precisely, since John uses actual historical places where this great transhistorical city found its manifestation.) Mounce, 221, suggests that "the great city in which the martyred church lies dead is the world under the wicked and oppressive sway of Antichrist"; yet he and others continue to insist that the "great city" is nevertheless Rome. It is curious that in the Greek the singular noun *ptōma* ("body," GK *4773*) is used for both witnesses in vv.8–9a, but the plural *ptōmata* ("bodies") is used in v.9b. Their dead bodies lie undignified in full public view "in the street."

9–10 People from every nation—Jew and Gentile—will "gloat over" their corpses and refuse them the dignity of burial. For a person to have his or her corpse lie in view of everyone was the worst humiliation by an enemy that one could suffer (Ps 79:3–4; Tob 1:18–20). Furthermore, the pagan world will celebrate the destruction of the witnesses and the victory over them by exchanging gifts, a common custom in the Near East (Ne 8:10, 12; Est 9:19, 22). Thus the beast will silence the witness of the church to the glee of the beast-worshiping world. The time of their silence corresponds in days to the time of their witness in years; it denotes only a brief time of triumph for the beast.

11–12 The witnesses now experience a resurrection and an ascension to heaven following their three-and-one-half-day death. In regard to this puzzling passage, it is generally held that Ezekiel's vision of the restoration of the dry bones was in

John's mind (Eze 37:5, 10–12). Just as interpretations of Ezekiel's vision vary, so interpretations of these verses also vary. Some hold that the vision of the dry bones refers to the spiritual quickening of the nation of Israel (so Keil and Delitzsch); others, following rabbinic interpretation and some church fathers, understand the descriptions to refer to the physical resurrection of the dead. If the two witnesses represent the witness of the church, then physical resurrection and ascension could be in mind. (The summons "come up here," followed by "they went up to heaven in a cloud," perhaps points to the rapture [1 Th 4:16–17].)

On the other hand, John may be using the figure of physical resurrection to represent the church's victory over the deathblow of the beast. In Romans 11:15 Paul uses the figure of resurrection symbolically to depict a great spiritual revival among the Jews in a future day. Here in Revelation 11:12 the reference to the "cloud" may be significant. The "cloud" depicts the divine power, presence, and glory, and yet this is the only instance in the book where strictly human figures are associated with a cloud. This must be significant. The two witnesses share in Christ's resurrection. The cloud is a sign of heaven's acceptance of their earthly career. Even their enemies see them, as they will see Christ when he returns with the clouds (1:7). The events of Christ's return and the ascension of the witnesses seem to be simultaneous. Thus in the two witnesses John has symbolized the model of all true prophets, taking as a central clue the story of Jesus' appearance in Jerusalem and describing the common vocation of appearing in the holy city (or temple) in such a

way that reaction to their work would separate the worshipers of God from the unbelievers in language drawn from the stories of many prophets (cf. Minear, 103).

13 The earthquake is God's further sign of the vindication of his servants (cf. 6:12). But unlike the earthquake under the sixth seal, this one produces what appears to be repentance: "the survivors . . . gave glory to the God of heaven." The opposite response in 16:9—"they refused to repent and glorify him"—seems to confirm that 11:13 speaks of genuine repentance (cf. 14:7; 15:4). Although Ladd, 159, understands the entire chapter as a reference to the conversion of the Jews, since the death, resurrection, and ascension of the two witnesses is more worldwide in scope (vv.9–10), we may infer that the earthquake is also symbolic of a worldwide event. Verse 13 shows that even in the midst of judgment God is active in the world to save those who repent. If there is such hope in the terrible time of final judgment, how much more so now! God has not abandoned the human race, regardless of the recurring waves of unbelief. Neither should we!

14 All the events from 9:13 to 11:14 fall under the sixth trumpet and are called the second woe (see comments at 8:13; 9:12). Since there are further judgments (woes) mentioned in this chapter, it is natural to see at the sounding of the seventh trumpet (vv.15–19) the third woe as taking place. Its nature is described in the bowl judgments (ch. 16). Apparently the third woe will come without further delay. Indeed, the seventh trumpet (v.15) brings us to the final scenes of God's unfolding mystery (10:7).

NOTES

1–14 A. McNicol ("Revelation 11:1–14 and the Structure of the Apocalypse," *ResQ* 22 [1979]: 193–202) has argued that these verses represent a Christian response to the fall of Jerusalem. He sees the section as reflecting the post-AD 70 conflict between Christians and Jews. Michaels, 136, believes the temple (as elsewhere in the book) is the *heavenly* temple, and the outer court (not measured) is some part or the whole of the *earth*. This is unlikely because of the term "the holy city" that immediately follows, which is in turn identified as "where also their Lord was crucified" (v.8), i.e., Jerusalem.

3 Hill ("Prophecy and Prophets in the Revelation," 401–18) argues that the two prophets represent the messianic remnant which survives the destruction of unbelieving Israel and bears within its life the continuing testimony of the Law and the Prophets: "In its readiness to proclaim the truth of God in the face of Jewish unbelief, and even to die for that truth, the entire church is being symbolized." Hill also argues that John, the author of Revelation, while identifying himself with the prophets, sees himself as "unique in his community and as standing closer to the tradition of the Old Testament prophets than the function of the New." Michaels, 138–39, following Mazzaferri, 325, believes on the other hand that the two prophets symbolize John himself in his prophetic ministry—a view that has not yet received wide acceptance.

8 Recently articulated into a fourfold parallelism between four women (Jezebel, 2:20–23; woman clothed with the sun, 12:1–6; whore astride beast, 17:1–6; bride, 19:6–9a; 21:9–10) and four cities (seven church-cities, 2:1–3:22; Jerusalem, 11:1–13; Babylon, 14:8; 18:1–24; new Jerusalem, 21:1–22:6). Gordon Campbell ("Antithetical Feminine-Urban Imagery and a Tale of Two Women-Cities in the Book of Revelation," *TynBul* 55 [2004]: 81) notes that their "fullest development is an elaborate literary contrast between two women-cities—Babylon-the-whore and new Jerusalem-the-bride."

4. Sounding of the Seventh Trumpet (11:15–19)

OVERVIEW

The seventh trumpet sounds, and in heaven loud voices proclaim the final triumph of God and Christ over the world. The theme is the kingdom of God and of Christ—a dual kingdom eternal in its duration. The kingdom is certainly a main theme of the entire book of Revelation (1:6, 9; 5:10; 11:17; 12:10; 19:6; 20:4; 22:5). This kingdom involves the millennial kingdom and its blending into the eternal kingdom (chs. 20–22). The image suggests the transference of the world empire once dominated by a usurping power that has now at length passed into the hands of its true owner and king. The present rulers are Satan, the beast, and the false prophet. The announcement of the reign of the king occurs here, but the final breaking of the enemies' hold over the world does not occur until the return of Christ (19:11–21).

> [15]The seventh angel sounded his trumpet, and there were loud voices in heaven, which said:
>
> "The kingdom of the world has become the kingdom of our Lord and of his Christ,
> and he will reign for ever and ever."
>
> [16]And the twenty-four elders, who were seated on their thrones before God, fell on their faces and worshiped God, [17]saying:
>
> "We give thanks to you, Lord God Almighty,
> the One who is and who was,

> because you have taken your great power
> and have begun to reign.
> [18]The nations were angry;
> and your wrath has come.
> The time has come for judging the dead,
> and for rewarding your servants the prophets
> and your saints and those who reverence your name,
> both small and great—
> and for destroying those who destroy the earth."
>
> [19]Then God's temple in heaven was opened, and within his temple was seen the ark of his covenant. And there came flashes of lightning, rumblings, peals of thunder, an earthquake and a great hailstorm.

COMMENTARY

15–18 Verses 15–18 are reminiscent of Psalm 2. The opening portion of this psalm describes the pagan nations and kings set in opposition to God and his Messiah (Anointed One). Then there follows the establishment of the Son in Zion as the Sovereign of the world and an appeal to the world rulers to put their trust in the Son before his wrath burns. John does not distinguish between the millennial kingdom of Christ and the eternal kingdom of the Father (but cf. 3:21), as Paul does (1Co 15:24–28). This should be viewed as a difference merely of detail and emphasis, not of basic theology. Furthermore, in John's view this world becomes the arena for the manifestation of God's kingdom. While at this point the emphasis is on the future, visible establishment of God's kingdom, in John's mind that same kingdom is in some real sense now present, and he is participating in it (1:9).

16–17 As the other features in these verses are anticipatory, so the expression "have begun to reign" looks forward to the millennial reign depicted in ch. 20. Significantly, the title of God found earlier in the book ("who is, and who was, and who is to come"; 1:8; 4:8) is now, "who is and who was." He has now

come! God has taken over the power of the world from Satan (Lk 4:6).

18 This passage contains a synopsis of the remaining chapters of Revelation. The nations opposed to God and incited by the fury of the dragon (12:12) have brought wrath on God's people (Ps 2:1–3). For this, God has brought his wrath upon the nations (14:7; 16:1–21; 18:20; 19:19b; 20:11–15). The time (*kairos*, "season," GK *2789*) has now come for three further events: the judgment of the dead (20:11–15); the final rewarding of the righteous (21:1–4; 22:3–5); and the final destruction of the destroyers of the earth (Babylon, the beast, the false prophet, and the dragon; 19:2, 11; 20:10).

In Revelation there are three groups of people who receive rewards: (1) God's "servants the prophets" (cf. 18:20; 22:9); (2) the "saints" (perhaps the martyrs [cf. 5:8; 8:3–4; 13:7, 10; 16:6; 18:20, 24] or simply believers in every age [cf. 19:8; 20:9]); and (3) "those who reverence [God's] name" (cf. 14:7; 15:4). In whatever way these groups are defined, it is important to note that in Revelation the prophets are specially singled out (16:6; 18:20, 24; 22:6, 9).

19 In the heavenly temple, John sees the ark of God's covenant. In the OT, the ark of the covenant was the chest God directed Moses to have made and placed within the holiest room of the tabernacle sanctuary (Ex 25:10–22). He was directed to put in the ark the two tables of the Decalogue—the documentary basis of God's redemptive covenant with Israel (Ex 34:28–29). It is presumed that the ark was destroyed when Nebuchadnezzar burned the temple in 586 BC; there was no ark in the second temple (Josephus, *J.W.* 5.219).

A Jewish legend reported in 2 Maccabees 2:4–8 indicates that Jeremiah hid the ark in a cave on Mount Sinai until the final restoration of Israel. There is no reason, however, to believe that John is alluding here to this Jewish tradition, since he is clearly referring to a heavenly temple and ark, which is symbolic of the new covenant established by the death of Christ. As the way into the holiest place was, under the old covenant, barred to all except the high priest, now full and immediate access for all, as well as perfect redemption, has been secured by Christ's death (Heb 9:11–12; 10:19–22).

In v.19 the kingdom of God is seen retrospectively as having fully come. Yet its coming will be elaborated in chs. 20–22. Prospectively, this sight of the ark of the covenant also prepares us for the following chapters, which concern God's faithfulness to his covenant people. As the ark of the covenant was the sign to Israel of God's loyal love throughout their wilderness journeys and battles, so this sign of the new covenant will assure the followers of Christ of his loyal love through their severe trial and the attack by the beast. "Flashes of lightning, rumblings, peals of thunder" call our attention to God's presence and vindication of his people (see comments at 6:12; 8:5).

NOTES

15–19 Elisabeth Schüssler Fiorenza ("The Eschatology and Composition of the Apocalypse," *CBQ* 30 [1968]: 537–69) has argued that the author of Revelation does not seek to comfort the persecuted Christian community with reference to past and future history (as in the Jewish apocalyptic literature) but with reference to the eschatological reality of God's kingdom. She sees this main theme briefly but precisely expressed in the hymn in 11:15–19 and presents an outline for structuring the whole book around this concept.

C. The Seven Signs (12:1–14:20)

OVERVIEW

In this section there is what might be called a "Book of Signs." While no signs (*sēmeia*, GK *4956*; see comments at 12:1) appear in chs. 1–11, at least seven signs are mentioned in chs. 12–19 (cf. the seven signs in Jn 1–11). Three are in heaven (12:1, 3; 15:1), and four are on earth (13:13–14; 16:14; 19:20). Only one is a sign of good (12:1); the others are omens of evil or judgment from God. These signs explain and amplify previous material (e.g., the beast in 11:7 is more fully described in ch. 13) and also advance the drama to its final acts. More specifically, chs. 12–14 contain seven further images, though only two are directly identified as signs.

This intermediate section (chs. 12–14) preceding the final bowl judgments (15:1–16:21) picks up and develops the theme of the persecution of God's people, which has already appeared (3:10; 6:9–11; 7:14; 11:7–10). Chapter 12 gives us a glimpse into the dynamics of the persecution of God's people under the symbolism of the dragon, who wages war on the woman and her children (v.17). Chapter 13 continues the same theme by telling of the persecution of the saints by the dragon-energized beasts. Finally, the section closes with (1) the scene of the redeemed 144,000 on Mount Zion who are triumphant over the beast (14:1–5) and (2) looks at the final hour of judgment on the beast-worshipers (14:6–20).

1. The Woman and the Dragon (12:1–17)

OVERVIEW

In this chapter there are three main figures: the woman, the child, and the dragon. There are also three scenes here: the birth of the child (vv.1–6), the expulsion of the dragon (vv.7–12), and the dragon's attack on the woman and her children (vv.13–17).

[1]A great and wondrous sign appeared in heaven: a woman clothed with the sun, with the moon under her feet and a crown of twelve stars on her head. [2]She was pregnant and cried out in pain as she was about to give birth. [3]Then another sign appeared in heaven: an enormous red dragon with seven heads and ten horns and seven crowns on his heads. [4]His tail swept a third of the stars out of the sky and flung them to the earth. The dragon stood in front of the woman who was about to give birth, so that he might devour her child the moment it was born. [5]She gave birth to a son, a male child, who will rule all the nations with an iron scepter. And her child was snatched up to God and to his throne. [6]The woman fled into the desert to a place prepared for her by God, where she might be taken care of for 1,260 days.

[7]And there was war in heaven. Michael and his angels fought against the dragon, and the dragon and his angels fought back. [8]But he was not strong enough, and they lost their place in heaven. [9]The great dragon was hurled down—that ancient serpent called the devil, or Satan, who leads the whole world astray. He was hurled to the earth, and his angels with him.

[10]Then I heard a loud voice in heaven say:

"Now have come the salvation and the power and the kingdom of our God,
    and the authority of his Christ.
For the accuser of our brothers,
    who accuses them before our God day and night,
    has been hurled down.
[11]They overcame him
    by the blood of the Lamb
    and by the word of their testimony;

they did not love their lives so much
    as to shrink from death.
¹²Therefore rejoice, you heavens
    and you who dwell in them!
But woe to the earth and the sea,
    because the devil has gone down to you!
He is filled with fury,
    because he knows that his time is short."

¹³When the dragon saw that he had been hurled to the earth, he pursued the woman who had given birth to the male child. ¹⁴The woman was given the two wings of a great eagle, so that she might fly to the place prepared for her in the desert, where she would be taken care of for a time, times and half a time, out of the serpent's reach. ¹⁵Then from his mouth the serpent spewed water like a river, to overtake the woman and sweep her away with the torrent. ¹⁶But the earth helped the woman by opening its mouth and swallowing the river that the dragon had spewed out of his mouth. ¹⁷Then the dragon was enraged at the woman and went off to make war against the rest of her offspring—those who obey God's commandments and hold to the testimony of Jesus.

COMMENTARY

1 John sees a dazzling sight—a pregnant woman "clothed with the sun, with the moon under her feet" and wearing a victor's crown (*stephanos*, GK *5109*; cf. 2:10; 3:11; 4:4–10; 6:2; 9:7; 14:14) of twelve stars. John calls the sight a "great sign" (*mega sēmeion*). This shows that the woman is more than a mere woman. She signifies something. Generally John uses *sēmeion* ("sign," GK *4956*) to refer to a miraculous sign that points to some deeper spiritual significance in connection with the event or object (Jn 2:11, 18, etc.; Rev 12:1, 3; 13:13–14; 15:1; 16:14; 19:20). In classical Greek the word referred especially to the constellations as signs or omens (LSJ, 1593).

The basic plot of the story was familiar in the ancient world. A usurper doomed to be killed by a yet unborn prince plots to succeed to the throne by killing the royal seed at birth. The prince is miraculously snatched from his clutches and hidden away until he is old enough to kill the usurper and claim his kingdom. In the Greek myth of the birth of Apollo, when the child's mother—the goddess Leto—reached the time of her delivery, she was pursued by the dragon Python, who sought to kill both her and her unborn child. Only the tiny island of Delos welcomed the mother, where she gave birth to the god Apollo. Four days after his birth, Apollo found Python at Parnassus and killed him in his Delphic cave. In Egypt it is the red dragon Set who pursues Isis, the pregnant mother of Horus. When the child is grown, he too kills the dragon. These stories were living myths in the first century and were probably known to both John and his Asian readers.

While it is easy to point to parallels between these earlier myths and Revelation 12, the differences are striking enough to eliminate the possibility that John merely borrowed pagan myths. As Mounce, 230, points out, "Would a writer who elsewhere in the book displays such a definite antagonism toward paganism draw extensively at this point upon its mythology? As always, John is a creative apocalyptist who, although gathering his imagery from many sources, nevertheless constructs a scenario distinctly his own." To this argument could be added the evidence of the patristic testimony of the first eight centuries. Not a single voice was raised in favor of interpreting the woman as the embodiment of a mythological figure (cf. Bernard J. LeFrois, *The Woman Clothed With the Sun* [Roma: Orbis Catholicus, 1954], 210). Did he, then, draw more directly on OT parallels? Some cite Genesis 37:9–11, where the heavenly bodies of sun, moon, and eleven stars are associated together in Joseph's vision. Joseph's father, Jacob (the sun), and his mother, Rachel (the moon), together with Joseph's eleven brothers (the stars), bow down before Joseph. Yet while the sun, moon, and stars are parallel in both accounts, the other details are quite different. For example, the woman and the child who are central to John's account are totally absent from the dream of Joseph. It thus seems highly unlikely that John intended his readers to interpret this chapter in the light of the Genesis material.

Others see a more conscious parallelism between the story and the activities of the emperor Domitian around AD 83. After the death of his ten-year-old son, Domitian immediately proclaimed the boy a god and his mother, the mother of god. Coinage of this period shows the mother Domitia as the mother of the gods (Cerea, Demeter, Cybele), or seated on the divine throne, or standing with the scepter and diadem of the queen of heaven with the inscription "Mother of the Divine Caesar." Another coin shows the mother with the child before her. In his left hand is the scepter of world dominions, and with his right hand he is blessing the world. Still another coin shows the dead child sitting on the globe of heaven and playing with seven stars, which represent the seven planets, symbolic of his heavenly dominion over the world. A recently discovered coin of the same period shows on the obverse, like the others, the head of Domitia; instead of the child on the reverse, it has the moon and the other six planets, emblematic of the golden age. Ethelbert Stauffer (*Christ and the Caesars* [London: SCM, 1965], 151–52) interprets this coin's imagery as representing the imperial Zeus-child, who has been exalted to be lord of the stars and who will usher in the age of universal salvation that is to come.

Whereas the coinage of Domitian glorifies the son of Domitia as the lord of heaven and savior of the world, Revelation 12 presents Jesus Christ, the Lord of heaven and earth, as he who will rule all nations with a scepter of iron (v.5). Merrill Tenney (*New Testament Times* [Grand Rapids: Eerdmans, 1955], 337) says, "The parallel imagery seems almost too similar to be accidental." From this viewpoint, what John does is to demythologize the contemporary Domitian myth by presenting Christ as the true and ascended Lord of heaven, the coming Ruler and Savior of the world.

Another approach to the source problem here is to compare the chapter with a passage in the Dead Sea Scrolls. The Hymn scroll (1QH 11:9–10) contains this disputed passage:

> She who is big with the Man of distress is in her pains. For she shall give birth to a man-child in the billows of Death, and in the bonds of Sheol there shall spring from the crucible of the pregnant one a Marvellous Counsellor with his might; and he shall deliver every man from the billows because of Her who is big with him.

In notes explaining the above translation, Andre Dupont-Sommer (*The Essene Writings from Qumran* [Cleveland: World, 1962], 208 nn. 1–5) indicates that not only is the man-child (also called Marvelous Counselor and firstborn) a reference to the Messiah based on Isaiah 9:5–6, but that the "crucible" refers to the suffering of the Messiah. The woman symbolizes the "congregation of the just, the Church of the Saints, victim of the persecution of the wicked," and is also associated with the redeeming work of the Messiah. Dupont-Sommer also notices that in the verses of the hymn that immediately follow there is a reference to another pregnant woman, who represents the community of the wicked. She gives birth to the "Asp" or serpent (from Ge 3), which refers to Satan.

Other OT references to the birth of the Messiah through the messianic community (Isa 9:6–7; Mic 5:2) and to the travailing messianic community (Isa 26:17; 66:7) should also be noted. In the OT, the image of a woman is frequently associated with Israel, Zion, or Jerusalem (Isa 54:1–6; Jer 3:20; Eze 16:8–14; Hos 2:19–20). If the main thrust of Dupont-Sommer's interpretation can be accepted (see Notes, v.1), this background seems to provide a much closer link to the intended significance of ch. 12 than the other proposed parallels. In any case, there seems to be in ch. 12 a blending of elements from OT concepts, Jewish materials, ancient mythical stories, and possibly the Domitian child myth. Regardless of the sources or allusions, John reinterprets the older stories and presents a distinctively Christian view of history in the imagery of the woman and her children.

Who, then, is the woman? While it is not impossible that she is an actual woman, such as Mary, the evidence clearly shows that she, like the woman in ch. 17, has symbolic significance. At the center of ch. 12 is the persecution of the woman by the dragon, who is definitely identified as Satan (v.9). This central theme, as well as the reference to the persecution of the "rest of her offspring" (v.17), renders it virtually certain that the woman could not refer to a single individual. Thus, even some recent Roman Catholic interpreters have departed from

this view (e.g., Ford, 207; but for a strong case for Mary as the woman, see LeFrois, *Woman Clothed With the Sun*, esp. 211–35).

Some identify the woman exclusively with the Jewish people, the nation of Israel (so Walvoord, 188; Thomas, 2:120). This view seems to be supported by the reference to the woman's giving birth to the Messiah or "male child" (v.5); the stars would refer to the twelve tribes (Ge 37:9–11). The twelve signs of the zodiac were thought by the Jews to represent the twelve tribes; their tribal standards corresponded to the zodiacal names (*b. Ber.* 32; cf. Ford, 343). (On the floor of the ancient sixth-century synagogue of Beth Alpha [near Gilboa in Israel] lies a mosaic with the crescent moon and the sun and the twelve signs of the zodiac with twenty-three stars scattered around a figure representing the sun god.) While these factors must be taken seriously, there are internal problems with this view. The dragon's persecution of the woman after the Messiah's birth could hardly refer to the devil's attack on the nation as a whole but could apply only to the believing segment of the people. The entire intent of the passage is to explain the persecution of the believing community, not the persecution of the nation of Israel as a whole.

Since the context indicates that the woman under attack represents a continuous entity from the birth of Christ until at least John's day or later, her identity in the author's mind must be the believing covenantal-messianic community. This group would include the early messianic community, which under John the Baptist's ministry was separated from the larger Jewish community to be the people prepared for the Lord (Mk 1:2–3). Later this group merged into the new community of Christ's disciples called the church or, less appropriately, the new Israel, composed of both Jews and Gentiles. John does not at this point seem to distinguish between the earlier, almost totally Jewish community and the one present in his day. Their continuity in identity is so strong that whatever ethnic or other differences they have do not affect his single image as representing one entity.

The woman's dazzling appearance like the sun relates her to the glory and brilliance of her Lord (Rev 1:16), as well as to her own light-bearing quality (1:20). With the moon under her feet signifying her permanence (Pss 72:5; 89:37; cf. Mt 16:18) and a crown of twelve stars on her head indicating her elect identity (cf. comments at 7:4; 7:5–8), she appears in her true heavenly and glorious character despite her seemingly fragile and uncertain earthly history (vv.13–16). A possible allusion to her priestly nature may be suggested by the cosmic imagery of stars, sun, and moon—figures that Josephus (*Ant.* 3:179–87) uses in describing the high priestly vestments (cf. 1:6; 5:10; see Ford, 197). Peter likewise refers to the priestly function of the church (1Pe 2:5, 9). The church viewed as a woman is found elsewhere in the NT, as well as in early Christian literature (2Co 11:2; Eph 5:25–27, 32; cf. 2Jn 1, 5 with 3Jn 9; Shepherd of Hermas, *Vis.* 2.4).

2 The woman is in the throes of childbirth. The emphasis is on her pain and suffering, both physical and spiritual. The meaning of her anguish is that the faithful messianic community has been suffering as a prelude to the coming of the Messiah himself and the new age (Isa 26:17; 66:7–8; Mic 4:10; 5:3). The "birth" (*tiktō*, GK *5503*) itself does not necessarily refer to the actual physical birth of Christ but denotes the travail of the community from which the Messiah has arisen (see same word in Heb 6:7 and Jas 1:15).

3 The second "sign" now appears. It likewise is a heavenly sign and introduces us to the second character, the ultimate antagonist of the woman. The dragon is clearly identified with the "ancient serpent called the devil, or Satan" (v.9; cf. 20:2–3). The description of him as an "enormous red dragon"

symbolically suggests his fierce power and murderous nature. He is further described as having "seven heads and ten horns and seven crowns on his heads." Except for the exchange of the crowns from the heads to the horns, the same description is used for the beast from the sea in ch. 13 and the beast of ch. 17. There is no way of understanding how the horns fit on the heads. While some have tried to find specific meaning for each of the heads and horns, John probably intends to give no more than a symbolic sense of the whole impression rather than of its parts. It is a picture of the fullness of evil in all its hideous strength. (Cf. here the OT references to Rahab and Leviathan: Ps 74:13–14; Isa 27:1; 51:9–10; Da 7:7; 8:10.) There is more than a coincidental similarity in these descriptions and John's image. The diadem crowns on the heads may indicate fullness of royal power (13:1; 19:12).

4 So great is the dragon's power that his tail can even sweep away a large number of the stars and cast them down to the ground (for "a third," see comments at 8:7). This should probably be understood simply as a figure representing the dragon's power and not as a reference to Satan's victory over some of the angels. In any event, the stars cast down would, after the analogy of Daniel 8:10, 24, refer to the saints of God who were trampled by Satan and not to fallen angels. Satan has placed himself before the woman, thus expecting certain victory over the messianic child. It is through this figure that the church shows her awareness that Satan is always threatening the purposes of God within history (so Lilje). Although the attack of Herod against the children of Bethlehem, as well as many incidents during the life of Jesus—such as the attempt of the crowd at Nazareth to throw him over the cliff (Lk 4:28–39)—must also be included, the greatest attempt to "devour" the child must certainly be the crucifixion.

5 This verse records the last element of the story. The messianic child comes, finishes his mission, is delivered from the dragon, and is enthroned in heaven. John again refers to the destiny of the child as he alludes to Psalm 2:9: "You will rule [all the nations] with an iron scepter" (Rev 2:27; 19:15). It is not clear whether John also intends a collective identity in the birth of the male child. Daniel 7:13–14, 27 seems to fuse the individual Son of Man with the people of God. Likewise in Revelation John seems to alternate between the rule of Christ (1:5; 11:15) and the rule of the saints (1:6; 2:26–27). It is, however, difficult to see how the child, as well as the woman, could be a group of believers. Nevertheless, many early interpreters such as Tyconius (d. ca. 390), Pseudo-Augustine (d. ca. 542), Primasius (d. ca. 552), Quodvultdeus (d. ca. 453), and others understood the male child to be simultaneously Christ and the members of Christ; and even a few (e.g., Methodius [d. ca. 312]; Venerable Bede [d. ca. 735]) saw the child as a reference only to the church (LeFrois, *Woman Clothed With the Sun*, 58–61). Through Christ's resurrection and ascension, the dragon's attempt to destroy God's purposes through the Messiah has been decisively defeated.

6 What is this flight into the desert? Is it a symbolic or an actual historic event? Among those who take it literally, some have understood the reference as the escape of the early Christians of Jerusalem to Pella (modern Tabaqat Fahil, about twenty miles south of the Sea of Galilee) in AD 66 to escape the Roman destruction of Jerusalem. Pella continued to be an important Christian center, even after a large portion of the community returned to Jerusalem in AD 135. Others refer the event to the future, when a portion of the Jewish people will be preserved through the tribulation period to await Christ's return (so Walvoord, Thomas). Other approaches view the desert as a symbol for the hiddenness of the church in the world because of persecution (so Swete) or as a symbol of its pure condition (so Lilje).

Most commentators, however, understand the wilderness to mean the place of safety, discipline, and testing (so Caird, Farrar, Ford). This view is preferable because of the highly symbolic nature of the whole chapter, the symbolic use of "desert" in 17:3, and the parallelism to the exodus where the children of Israel fled from Pharaoh. All are agreed that the reference here to the flight of the woman is anticipatory of vv.13–17. The intervening verses show why the dragon is persecuting the woman (vv.7–12).

For a discussion of the 1,260 days, see comments at 11:2.

7–12 All agree that the section beginning with this verse, which describes the battle in heaven between Michael and the dragon (vv.7–12), provides the explanation as to why the dragon has turned on the woman and caused her to flee to the desert for protection (vv.6, 13–17). The account is in two parts: (1) the battle in heaven between Michael and his angels and the dragon and his angels, which results in the ejection of Satan from heaven to the earth (vv.7–9), and (2) the heavenly hymn of victory (vv.10–12).

As elsewhere in the book, the narrative material can be interpreted only in the light of the hymns. This principle is especially important in vv.7–9, where the victory takes place in heaven as the result of Michael's defeat of the dragon. Were this the only thing told us about the "war in heaven," it might be concluded that the dragon's defeat was unrelated to Jesus Christ. But the interpretative hymn (vv.10–12) says that it was in fact the blood of Christ that dealt the actual deathblow to the dragon and enabled the saints to triumph (v.8; cf. 5:9). Does this not suggest that Christ's redeeming work is here depicted by the cosmic battle of Michael and the dragon, as it is elsewhere seen, as a loosing from sin (1:5), a washing of our garments (7:14), and a purchasing to God (5:9)? The time of the dragon's defeat and ejection from heaven must therefore be connected with the incarnation, ministry, death, and resurrection of Jesus (v.13: Lk 10:18; Jn 12:31). Christ has appeared in order that he may destroy the works of the devil (Mt 12:28–29; Ac 10:38; 2Ti 1:10; 1Jn 3:8).

Early Jewish belief held the view that Michael would cast Satan from heaven as the first of the end-time struggles to establish the kingdom of God on earth. John, in contrast, sees this event as already having taken place through Jesus Christ's appearance and work. Only the final, permanent blow of Satan's ejection from earth remains (Rev 20:10; cf. Charles, 1:324). The fact that the battle first takes place in heaven between Michael, the guardian of God's people (Da 10:13, 21; 12:1; Jude 9), and the dragon shows that evil is cosmic in dimension (not limited merely to this world) and also that events on earth are first decided in heaven. By way of contrast, in the Dead Sea Scrolls the decisive final battle takes place on earth, not in heaven (1QM 9.16; 17.6–7). The single intent of the passage is to assure those who meet satanic evil on earth that it is really a defeated power, however contrary it might seem to human experience (cf. Ladd, 171).

8–9 The triumph of the archangel results in the ejection of the dragon and his angels from heaven to earth. Apparently, prior to this event Satan had access to the heavens and continually assailed the loyalty of the saints (Job 1:9–11; Zec 3:1), but now, together with his angels, he has been cast out (cf. Lk 10:18). Whatever appears to be the earthly situation for God's people now, the victory has already been won. When the battle grows fiercer and darker for the church, it is but the sign of the last futile attempt of the dragon to exercise his power before the kingdom of Christ comes (v.12). The "ancient serpent" who tempted Eve with lies about God (Ge 3:1–5) is in John's mind the same individual as the "devil" and "Satan." Farrer, 142, notes that "it is precisely when Satan has lost the battle for the souls of the

saints in heaven that he begins the fruitless persecution of their bodies." Satan is also the one who "leads the whole world astray." His power lies in deception, and by his lies the whole world is deceived about God (2:20; 13:14; 18:23; 19:20; 20:3, 8, 10; cf. Ro 1:25; 2Jn 7).

10–12 This anonymous hymn, which interprets the great battle of the preceding verses, has three stanzas: the first (v.10) focuses on the victorious inauguration of God's kingdom and Christ's kingly authority; the second (v.11) calls attention to the earthly victory of the saints as they confirm Christ's victory by their own identification with him in his witness and death; the third (v.12) announces the martyrs' victory and the final woe to the earth because of the devil's ejection and impending demise.

10 In the first stanza, the triumph of Christ is described as the arrival of three divine realities in history: God's "salvation" or victory (7:10; 19:1), God's "power," and God's "kingdom." This latter reality is further identified as Christ's assumption of his "authority." The historic event of Christ's life, death, and resurrection has challenged the dominion of Satan and provoked the crisis of history. At the time of Christ's death on earth, Satan was being defeated in heaven by Michael. As Caird, 154, has said, "Michael . . . is not the field officer who does the actual fighting, but the staff officer in the heavenly room, who is able to remove Satan's flag from the heavenly map because the real victory has been won on Calvary."

In times past, Satan's chief role as adversary was directed toward accusing God's people of disobedience to God. The justice of these accusations was recognized by God, and therefore Satan's presence in heaven was tolerated. But now the presence of the crucified Savior in God's presence provides the required satisfaction of God's justice with reference to our sins (1Jn 2:1–2; 4:10); therefore, Satan's accusations are no longer valid, and he is cast out. What strong consolation this provides for God's faltering people!

11 This stanza is both a statement and an appeal. It announces that the followers of the Lamb also become victors over the dragon because they participate in the "blood of the Lamb," the weapon that defeated Satan, and because they have confirmed their loyalty to the Lamb by their witness, even to death. The blood of the martyrs, rather than signaling the triumph of Satan, shows instead that they have gained the victory over the dragon by their acceptance of Jesus' cross and by their obedient suffering with him. This is one of John's chief themes (1:9; 6:9; 14:12; 20:4).

Verses 12 and 17 lead to the conclusion that only a portion of the martyrs are in view (cf. 6:11). Thus this hymn of victory also becomes an appeal to the rest of the saints to do likewise and confirm their testimony to Christ, even if doing so means death. This seems to suggest that, in some mysterious sense, the sufferings of God's people are linked to the sufferings of Jesus in his triumph over Satan and evil (Jn 12:31; Ro 16:20; Col 1:24). Since the martyrs have won the victory over the dragon because of the cross of Jesus (i.e., they can no longer be accused of damnable sin, since Jesus has paid sin's penalty [1:5b]), they are now free even to give up their lives in loyalty to their Redeemer (Jn 12:25; Rev 15:2).

12 Satan has failed; therefore, the heavens and all who are in them should be glad. But Satan does not accept defeat without a bitter struggle. His final death throes are directed exclusively toward "the earth and the sea." Therefore their inhabitants will mourn, for the devil will now redouble his wrathful effort in one last futile attempt to make the most of an opportunity he knows will be brief (three and a half years; cf. vv.6, 14).

13–14 The narrative is resumed after the flight of the woman into the desert (v.6). Why? Because she is under attack from the defeated but still vicious dragon (vv.7–12). Banned from heaven and no longer able to attack the male child who is in heaven or to accuse the saints because of the victory of Jesus on the cross, the devil now pursues the woman, who flees to the desert. The word "pursue" was no doubt carefully chosen by John because it is also the NT word for "persecute" (*diōkō*, GK *1503*; Mt 5:10; etc.). Since the woman has already given birth to the child, the time of the pursuit by the dragon follows the earthly career of Jesus.

The reference to an eagle's wings once again introduces imagery borrowed from the exodus account, where Israel was pursued by the dragon in the person of Pharaoh: "You yourselves have seen what I did to Egypt, and how I carried you on eagles' wings and brought you to myself" (Ex 19:4). As God's people were delivered from the enemy by their journey into the Sinai desert, so God's present people will be preserved miraculously from destruction (cf. Dt 32:10–12; Isa 40:31).

15–16 The serpent spews a floodlike river of water out of his mouth to engulf and drown the woman. The water imagery seems clear enough. It symbolizes destruction by an enemy (Pss 32:6; 69:1–2; 124:2–5; Na 1:8) or calamity (Ps 18:4). As the desert earth absorbs the torrent, so the covenant people will be helped by God and preserved from utter destruction (Isa 26:20; 42:15; 43:2; 50:2). The dragon-inspired Egyptians of old were swallowed by the earth: "You stretched out your right hand and the earth swallowed them" (Ex 15:12). In similar fashion, the messianic community will be delivered by God's power. Whatever specific events were happening to Christians in Asia in John's day would not exhaust the continuing significance of the passage.

17 This attack of Satan against "the rest" of the woman's offspring seems to involve the final attempt to destroy the messianic people of God. Having failed in previous attempts to eliminate them as a whole, the dragon now strikes at individuals who "obey God's commandments and hold to the testimony of Jesus." To "make war" (*poiēsai polemon*) is the identical expression used of the beast's attack on the two witnesses in 11:7 and on the saints in 13:7. Could this possibly correlate the three groups and indicate their common identity under different figures?

Those attacked are called "the rest of her [the woman's] offspring." Some identify this group as Gentile Christians in distinction from the Jewish mother church (so Glasson). Others who identify the mother as the nation of Israel see the "rest" as the believing remnant in the Jewish nation (the 144,000) who turn to Christ (so Walvoord, Thomas)—a view that depends on the prior identification of the woman with the whole nation of Israel. Others have suggested that the woman represents the believing community as a whole—the universal or ideal church composed of both Jews and Gentiles—whereas the "offspring" of the woman represent individuals of the community (Jews and Gentiles) who suffer persecution and martyrdom from the dragon in the pattern of Christ (so Swete, Caird, Kiddle, Beale, Aune, Minear). The close identification of the seed of the woman as first of all Jesus and then also those who have become his brothers through faith agrees with other NT teaching (Mt 25:40; Heb 2:11–12). While Satan cannot prevail against the Christian community itself, he can wage war on certain of its members who are called on to witness to their Lord by obedience even unto death, i.e., "those who obey God's commandments and hold to the testimony of Jesus" (Mt 16:18; Rev 11:7; 13:7, 15). The church, then, is paradoxically both invulnerable (the woman) and vulnerable (her children; cf. Lk 21:16–18).

NOTES

1 On whether the Qumran Hymn (1QH 11 [formerly 1QH 3]) bears a direct relation to John's image of the woman as the Christian community, see Dupont-Sommer, *Essene Writings from Qumran*, 207–8 nn. 1–5 (pro); Ford, 204–5 (pro); William LaSor, *The Dead Sea Scrolls and the New Testament* (Grand Rapids: Eerdmans, 1972), 208–9 (contra).

5 A recent attempt to defend the "male child as the church alone" view, first advocated by Methodius and later by Venerable Bede, is found in Michael J. Svigel, "The Apocalypse of John and the Rapture of the Church: A Reevaluation," *TJ* 22NS (2001): 23–74. He believes that the male child is a reference to the church only and that 12:5 is the only reference to the rapture of the church in the book of Revelation.

6 The third person plural τρέφωσιν (*trephōsin*, GK *5555*) may be a Semitism for the simple singular passive, meaning "she might be taken care of." No plural antecedent fits, and the sense is passive. Such occurrences are found in the OT and possibly also in Revelation 11:2 ("they will trample," meaning "the holy city shall be trampled"). For this idiom, see Ronald J. Williams, *Hebrew Syntax* (Toronto: Univ. of Toronto Press, 1967), 32 paragraph 160.

7 The infinitive construction τοῦ πολεμῆσαι (*tou polemēsai*; NIV, "fought") has been discussed by Charles, 1:322, and Mussies, 96, who both conclude this is a pure Semitism and should be translated "Michael and his angels had to fight with the dragon." Almost all translations fail to catch this nuance, so illuminating to the context.

On the dragon myths of the ancient world, see Bruce Waltke, "The Creation Account in Genesis 1:1–3," *BSac* 132 (Jan.–March 1975): 32.

11 The NIV does not translate the connective particle καὶ (*kai*, normally "and") that begins this verse in the Greek text. The particle could be translated "for"; if so rendered, it would give an additional connection between the defeat of Satan and the death of the martyrs.

15–16 Paul S. Minear ("Far as the Curse Is Found: The Point of Revelation 12:15–16," *NovT* 33 [1991]: 71–77) has argued that the river issued by the dragon is a river of deceit: "Just as Genesis traced the world's evil to a lie and to the curses that followed that lie, so John traced victory over that evil to a refusal to lie under threat of death. . . . We should detect subtle allusions to Genesis 4:1–16. . . . In both Genesis and the Apocalypse the earth is treated as 'an actor in the drama'. . . . It is from all such lies that the earth protects the woman by drinking those lies." Minear wants us to see the reversal of the curse on the ground given in Genesis because of sin, as well as the redemption of the earth's curse through the shed blood of Christ and those who refuse to follow the lie of the beast by pouring out their blood into the earth to redeem it from the curse. These two verses, notes Minear, "celebrate the end of the curse on the earth, and with it the end of the curse on the woman and on the woman's seed. This is in line with Eugene Boring's conclusion: 'If Revelation teaches us anything, it is that the power by which God brings the kingdom is the power of suffering love revealed in the cross.' We may find echoes of the same curse and the same rescue in one of Isaac Watts' hymns: 'No more let sins and sorrows grow, Nor thorns infest the ground (the earth of Ge 3:18); He comes to make his blessings flow, Far as the curse is found.'"

2. The Two Beasts (13:1–18)

OVERVIEW

This chapter forms part of the theme of the persecution of God's people that John began to develop in ch. 12. Turning from the inner dynamics of the struggle, ch. 13 shifts to the actual earthly instruments of this assault—the two dragon-energized beasts. In accord with the discussion in ch. 12, we may assume that the beast-related activities constitute the way the dragon carries out his final attempts to wage war on the offspring of the woman (12:17). A contest is going on to seduce the whole world—even the followers of Jesus—to worship the beast. As Minear, 118, shows, John seeks to emphasize three things about the first beast: he shows (1) the conspiracy of the dragon with the beast (vv.3–4); (2) the universal success of this partnership in deceiving the whole world to worship them (vv.3–4, 8); and (3) that the partnership will succeed in a temporary defeat of

the saints of God, thus accomplishing the greatest blasphemy of God (vv.6–7a).

Finally, not being able to seduce all the earth alone, the conspirators summon yet a third figure to their aids—the beast from the earth. He must remain loyal to his associates and at the same time be sufficiently similar to the Lamb to entice even the followers of Jesus. He must be able to perform miraculous signs (*sēmeia*) much as the two witnesses did (vv.11–17; cf. v.13 with 11:5). As the battle progresses, the dragon's deception becomes more and more subtle. Thus the readers are called to discern the criteria that will enable them to separate the lamblike beast from the Lamb himself (cf. v.11 with 14:1).

Two basic interpretative problems confront the reader. These have led students of the book to different understandings of this chapter: (1) The identification of the beast and his associate—are they personal or some other entity? (2) The time of the beast's rule—is it past, continuous, or still future? In seeking some satisfactory answers to these questions, it may be helpful first to present the facts about the beast. He (1) rises from the sea (v.1); (2) resembles the dragon (v.1); (3) has composite animal features (v.2); (4) is empowered by the dragon (v.2); (5) has one head wounded to death but healed (vv.3–4, 7b–8); (6) blasphemes God and God's people for forty-two months (vv.5–6); (7) makes war against the saints and kills them (vv.7a, 15); and (8) gives to those who follow him his "mark," that is either his name or his number—"666" (vv.16–18).

In addition, there are no fewer than a dozen further references in Revelation to the beast (11:7; 14:9, 11; 15:2; 16:2, 10, 13; 19:19–20; 20:4, 10), excluding the nine references to the scarlet-colored beast in ch. 17, which should probably be included. These further references contain no new information, but 11:7 indicates that the beast rises from the Abyss. Also, 19:19 refers to a coalition of the beast with the "kings of the earth," and 19:20 describes his final end in the lake of fire.

The history of the interpretation of ch. 13 is far too extensive for this commentary to cover. As early as the second century, two different understandings of the Antichrist appeared. Some early interpreters take the position that the Antichrist will be a person, a world deceiver who will reign for the last half of Daniel's seventieth week (Da 7:25). The *Epistle of Barnabas* (4:3–6, 9–10) warns believers to be alert to the imminent appearing of "the final stumbling-block," who is identified with the "little horn" of Daniel 7:24. The *Didache* (16.4) refers to a "world deceiver [who] will appear in the guise of God's Son. He will work 'signs and wonders' and the earth will fall into his hands and he will commit outrages such as have never occurred before." Justin Martyr (*Dial.* 32) likewise looked for the appearance in his lifetime of the Antichrist prophesied by Daniel, who

according to Daniel 7:25 would reign for three and a half years.

Irenaeus (*Haer.* 5.25.1–5; 5.28.2; 5.30.2; d. ca. 202) gives the first extensive discussion of the Antichrist. He is to be an unrighteous king from the tribe of Dan, the little horn of Daniel 7:8, who will reign over the earth during the last three and a half years of Daniel's seventieth "week" (Da 9:27). Irenaeus identifies the Antichrist with the first beast of Revelation 13 and the "man of sin" ("lawlessness," NIV) of 2 Thessalonians 2:3–4, who will exalt himself in the (rebuilt) Jerusalem temple. This view, with modifications, is followed by Irenaeus's student Hippolytus (d. ca. 235), by Tertullian (d. ca. 220) and Victorinus (d. ca. 303), and in recent times by many commentators, including Barnhouse, Bruce, A. C. Gaebelein, Ladd, Morris, Mounce, Scofield, Walvoord, and Thomas. In its favor is the more literal reading of 2 Thessalonians 2:1–10 and the natural understanding of the Antichrist as being the personal counterpart to the personal Christ.

On the other hand, from the earliest times some interpreters have understood the Antichrist as a present threat of heresy, depending more on the concept found in the Johannine Epistles (1Jn 2:18, 22; 4:3; 2Jn 7). Thus Polycarp (*Phil.* 7.1), said to be a disciple of the apostle John, understands the Antichrist to be revealed in the docetic heresies of his time. Likewise Tertullian (*Marc.* 5.16) identifies the many false prophets of Docetism with the Antichrist but sees these teachers as the forerunners of the future Antichrist, who as the archdeceiver will come "in all kinds of counterfeit miracles, signs and wonders" to mislead those who "have not believed the truth but have delighted in wickedness" (2Th 2:9–12).

Martin Luther, John Calvin, and other Reformers adopting this general view identified the beast with the papacy of the Roman Catholic Church. Only one nineteenth-century interpreter, Henry

Alford, seems to follow the Reformers in their view. However, other modern commentators adopt the "theological heresy" interpretation of the Antichrist (so Berkouwer, Minear, Newman). In its favor are the references to the Antichrist in the Johannine Epistles and the advantage of seeing the beast not as a past but as a present threat to the church and not merely as an eschatological figure of the last times. This view also argues that the passage in 2 Thessalonians 2 need not be understood as referring to a single, future individual (cf. Berkouwer, 268–71). The issue is difficult to settle with any finality. However, I will develop chapter 13 in accord with the "theological heresy" view, while at the same time recognizing that Tertullian's position as stated above is consistent with my position and that the personal future Antichrist view has strong support. (See also comments at v. 11.)

In modern interpretation, as Minear, 248–49, points out, there is almost complete agreement that the "wounded head" (v. 3) refers to the Nero *redivivus* legend. It will be helpful to have Minear's summary of the legend before us:

> Let us look first, then, at the Neronic legend itself. Toward the end of his reign Nero's unpopularity among Roman citizens had assumed high proportions. In 67 and 68 open revolts had broken out against his authority in Gaul and Spain. At length he had been repudiated by the praetorian guard and by the Senate. Fleeing from the city, he had taken refuge in a friend's suburban villa, where he had received word that the Senate had proclaimed him a public enemy and had approved Galba as his successor. Having been warned that pursuing soldiers were approaching his hideout, he had cut his own throat with a sword (June 9, 68). After his death a rumor spread abroad that he had not actually died but had escaped to Parthia, whence he would soon return to regain his throne. This rumor circulated most quickly in the eastern provinces, and assumed strange forms. At one stage, popular expectation envisaged the return of Nero from Parthia, with a huge army subduing all opposition:

> And to the west shall come the strife of gathering war and the exile from Rome, brandishing a mighty sword, crossing the Euphrates with many myriads.

> On the basis of this rumor, impostors arose in the East who assumed the name of Nero in an effort to exploit the legend. There are records of at least two such claimants. There seems to have been a later stage in the legend in which Nero's figure has become invested with supernatural status. Now his return from the Abyss with hordes of demons is anticipated as an omen of the "last days." Among the oracles of the Sibyl [*Sib. Or.* 5.361–69] we find an extensive reference to this expectation:

> There shall be at the last time about the waning of the moon, a world-convulsing war, deceitful in guilefulness. And there shall come from the ends of the earth a matricide fleeing and devising sharp-edged plans. He shall ruin all the earth, and gain all power, and surpass all men in cunning. That for which he perished he shall seize at once. And he shall destroy many men and great tyrants, and shall burn all men as none other ever did.

This Neronic interpretation presupposes an identification in John's mind between the sea beast and the Roman Empire, a view espoused in our day by both preterist and not a few preterist-futurist interpreters of Revelation (cf. Mounce, 246, who, it should be noted, denies the "Nero" part of the Roman Empire theory). Actually this view begins with the assumption that Revelation 17 identifies the seven heads of the beast as the successive emperors of the Roman Empire. This in turn is read back into the beast of ch. 13. Yet a question concerning the reliability of this whole Neronic approach must be raised. Minear, 228–60, argues convincingly that the Nero *redivivus* view will fit neither the facts of history nor the text of chs. 13 and 17 (see comments at 17:8–9).

Newman ("Fallacy of the Domitian Hypothesis," 133–39) also impressively calls the Nero myth into question. He argues that Irenaeus, the best source for the Domitian dating of the book, never refers either to a Domitian persecution as the background for John's thought or to any "Nero myth" interpretation, even though he is attempting to refute the identification of the number 666 with any Roman emperor. Newman concludes that Revelation could just as well be viewed as a theological polemic against some form of Gnosticism than, as popularly held, a political polemic. He also challenges the widely held assumption that all apocalyptic literature—and especially the book of Revelation—must be understood as arising out of some contemporary political crisis for the saints. Little evidence can be cited for more than a selective and local persecution of Christians under Domitian's rule (cf. E. T. Merrill, *Essays in Early Christian History* [London: Macmillan, 1924], 157–73; F. F. Bruce, *New Testament History*, 412–14; G. Edmundson, *The Church in Rome*

in the First Century [London: Longmans, Green, 1913]; see "General Nature and Historical Background," pp. 574–75).

Likewise rejecting the "beast equals Rome" hypothesis is W. Foerster (*TDNT* 3:134–35, esp. n. 11), who points out that rabbinic exegesis up to the first century AD identified the fourth beast of Daniel 7 as "Edom equals Rome." Since the beast of Revelation 13 is a composite that unites all the features of the four beasts of Daniel 7, it therefore cannot be identified with Rome. I will attempt in this exposition to demonstrate that the Rome hypothesis is debatable. This leaves the question open as to whether John sees the Antichrist (or beast) as a person or some more encompassing entity. Other interpreters now raising similar objections to the dominant "beast equals Rome [Nero]" view are Rowland, Michaels, Resseguie, and Beale.

[1]And the dragon stood on the shore of the sea.

And I saw a beast coming out of the sea. He had ten horns and seven heads, with ten crowns on his horns, and on each head a blasphemous name. [2]The beast I saw resembled a leopard, but had feet like those of a bear and a mouth like that of a lion. The dragon gave the beast his power and his throne and great authority. [3]One of the heads of the beast seemed to have had a fatal wound, but the fatal wound had been healed. The whole world was astonished and followed the beast. [4]Men worshiped the dragon because he had given authority to the beast, and they also worshiped the beast and asked, "Who is like the beast? Who can make war against him?"

[5]The beast was given a mouth to utter proud words and blasphemies and to exercise his authority for forty-two months. [6]He opened his mouth to blaspheme God, and to slander his name and his dwelling place and those who live in heaven. [7]He was given power to make war against the saints and to conquer them. And he was given authority over every tribe, people, language and nation. [8]All inhabitants of the earth will worship the beast—all whose names have not been written in the book of life belonging to the Lamb that was slain from the creation of the world.

[9]He who has an ear, let him hear.

[10]If anyone is to go into captivity,
   into captivity he will go.

> If anyone is to be killed with the sword,
> with the sword he will be killed.

This calls for patient endurance and faithfulness on the part of the saints.

[11]Then I saw another beast, coming out of the earth. He had two horns like a lamb, but he spoke like a dragon. [12]He exercised all the authority of the first beast on his behalf, and made the earth and its inhabitants worship the first beast, whose fatal wound had been healed. [13]And he performed great and miraculous signs, even causing fire to come down from heaven to earth in full view of men. [14]Because of the signs he was given power to do on behalf of the first beast, he deceived the inhabitants of the earth. He ordered them to set up an image in honor of the beast who was wounded by the sword and yet lived. [15]He was given power to give breath to the image of the first beast, so that it could speak and cause all who refused to worship the image to be killed. [16]He also forced everyone, small and great, rich and poor, free and slave, to receive a mark on his right hand or on his forehead, [17]so that no one could buy or sell unless he had the mark, which is the name of the beast or the number of his name.

[18]This calls for wisdom. If anyone has insight, let him calculate the number of the beast, for it is man's number. His number is 666.

COMMENTARY

1a The NIV and most other modern translations include v.1a as the concluding verse of ch. 12 because a variant Greek reading changes the KJV text "I stood" to "he stood" (i.e., the dragon). The latter reading is favored by a majority of textual scholars, though the KJV text may be the original (see Notes). If "he stood" is the correct reading, the sense would be that the dragon, who has now turned his rage on the children of the woman (12:17), stands on the seashore to summon his next instrument, the beast from the sea. But if the text reads "I stood," the sense is that John receives a new vision (cf. 10:1) as he gazes out over the sea in the same manner as Daniel (Da 7:2).

1b–2 The beast (*thērion*, "wild beast," GK *2563*) has already been described in 11:7 as rising from the

"Abyss" (cf. 17:8). Thus the sea may symbolize the Abyss, the source of demonic powers that are opposed to God (cf. 9:1; 20:1–3), rather than "the agitated surface of unregenerate humanity (cf. Isa 57:20), and especially of the seething cauldron of national and social life" (Swete, 158). This view agrees with the OT images of the sea as the origin of the satanic sea monsters—the dragon (Tannin), Leviathan ("Coiled One"), and Rahab ("Rager"; Job 26:12–13; Pss 74:13–14; 87:4; 89:10; Isa 27:1; 51:9; cf. also Eze 32:6–8). The ancient Hebrews demythologized the sea-monster myths to depict the victory of the Lord of Israel over the demonic forces of evil that in various manifestations had sought to destroy God's people. Thus John later foresees the final day of Christ's victory when there will "no longer [be] any sea" or source of demonic opposition to God and his people (21:1).

John describes the beast in words similar to those he used in 12:3 of the dragon: "He had ten horns and seven heads, with ten crowns on his horns." There is a slight difference here in the matter of the crowns, which may represent some change in the dragon's authority. As previously indicated (see comments at 12:3), any attempt to identify the heads or horns as separate kings, kingdoms, etc., should be resisted.

The image of the seven-headed monster is well attested in ancient Sumerian, Babylonian, and Egyptian texts. A cylinder seal coming from Tel Asmar (ancient Eshnunna some fifty miles northeast of modern Baghdad) and dating back to about 2500 BC shows two divine figures killing a seven-headed monster that had flames arising from its back. Four of its heads are drooping as though already dead. A spear is in the hand of a figure who is striking the

fourth head (see Alexander Heidel, *The Babylonian Genesis* [Chicago: Univ. of Chicago Press, 1942], 107–14 and figs. 15, 16; E. A. Wallis Budge, *The Gods of the Egyptians* [New York: Dover, 1969], 1:278–79).

It may be argued that John's beast from the sea is to be connected with Leviathan in the OT. Psalm 74:14 specifically mentions the "heads" of the monster: "It was you who crushed the heads of Leviathan." The seven heads and ten horns, regardless of the imagery used in Daniel or elsewhere, are not to be identified separately. It is true that Leviathan, Rahab, and the dragon (serpent) in the cited OT texts have a reference to political powers such as Egypt and Assyria that were threatening Israel. In the minds of the OT writers, however, the national entities were inseparably identified with the archetypal reality of the satanic, idolatrous systems represented by the seven-headed monster (Leviathan, Rahab, and the dragon) so that the beast represented, not the political power, but the system of evil that found expression in the

▼ THE CHAOS MONSTER. *Courtesy of the Oriental Institute, University of Chicago.*

political entity (cf. Budge, *Gods of the Egyptians*, 1:278). The reason this point is so important is that it helps us see that the beast itself is not to be identified in its description with any one historical form of its expression or with any one institutional aspect of its manifestation. In other words, the beast may appear now as Sodom, Egypt, Rome, or even Jerusalem and may manifest itself as a political power, an economic power, a religious power, or a heresy (1Jn 2:18, 22; 4:3).

In John's mind, the chief enemy is diabolical deception; his description, therefore, has theological overtones, not political ones. This interpretation does not exclude the possibility that there will be a final climactic appearance of the beast in history as a person, in a political, religious, or economic system; or in a final totalitarian culture combining all of these. The point is that the beast cannot be limited to either the past or the future.

John further states that this beast had "on each head a blasphemous name." This prominent feature is repeated in 17:3 (cf. 13:5–6). Arrogance and blasphemy also characterize the "little horn" of Daniel's fourth beast (Da 7:8, 11, 20, 25) and the willful king of Daniel 11:36. John alludes to the vision of Daniel but completely transforms it.

In keeping with the Rome hypothesis, many have tried to identify the blasphemous names with the titles of the emperor: "Augustus" ("reverend, to be worshiped"); *divus* ("deified"); "Savior"; *dominus* ("Lord"). But was this all that was in John's mind? In 2:9, he refers to the blasphemy "of those who say they are Jews and are not," a reference that seems to highlight the fact that some at Smyrna had spoken against the lawful messianic claims of Jesus. They may also have charged the Christians with disloyalty to the empire and thus sided with the pagan officials in persecuting them. Could these persons also be part of the blasphemous names (cf. comments at 2:9)? In 13:6, the blasphemies are directed against God and

are further defined: "to blaspheme God by blaspheming his name, his temple, and those who dwell in heaven" (my translation). Thus the beast challenges the sovereignty and majesty of God by denying the first commandment: "You shall have no other gods before me" (Ex 20:3). Therefore, whatever person or system (whether political, social, economic, or religious) cooperates with Satan—by exalting itself against God's sovereignty and by setting itself up to destroy the followers of Jesus or entice them to become followers of Satan through deception, idolatry, blasphemy, and spiritual adultery—embodies the beast of Revelation 13. Oliver O'Donovan (*The Desire of the Nations* [Cambridge: Cambridge Univ. Press, 1996], 274) observes, "When believers find themselves confronted with an order that, implicitly or explicitly, offers itself as the sufficient and necessary condition of human welfare, they will recognize the beast."

The description John gives of the beast from the sea does not describe a merely human political entity such as Rome, though what he does describe includes Rome. Rather, it describes in archetypal language the hideous, Satan-backed system of deception and idolatry that may at any time express itself in human systems of various kinds, such as Rome. Yet at the same time, John also seems to be saying that this blasphemous, blaspheming, and blasphemy-producing reality will have a final, intense, and, for the saints, utterly devastating manifestation.

3 The beast has a fatal wound, but the wound is healed. This results in great worldwide influence, acceptance, and worship for both the beast and the dragon. Verse 3 is important and requires careful exegesis because of the widespread Nero *redivivus* viewpoint read into the wounded head (see Overview, pp. 703–4). There are a number of features of John's description that are inconsistent with both the Nero *redivivus* and the Roman Empire interpretations. I am indebted for the following arguments to Newman ("Fallacy of the Domitian Hypothesis," 133–39); Minear, ch. 5; Resseguie, 54–57; and J. Ramsey Michaels (*Interpreting the Book of Revelation* [Grand Rapids: Baker, 1992], 157–58, 197–98).

1. It should be observed that the wounded "head" of v.3 is elsewhere in the chapter a wound of the whole beast (vv.12, 14). A wound inflicted in a former and rejected emperor is not a wound inflicted on the whole empire. If the reference is to Nero, it is difficult to see how his self-inflicted wound could have wounded the whole empire or how the legendary healing of his throat enhanced the authority of the beast or the dragon's war against the saints.

2. The "wound" unto death, or fatal wound, must be carefully examined. The Greek word for "wound" is *plēgē* (GK *4435*), which everywhere in Revelation means "plague"—in fact, a divinely inflicted judgment (9:18, 20; 11:6; 15:1–8; 16:9, 21; 18:4, 8; 21:9; 22:18). Elsewhere in the NT the word is used of "beatings" or official "floggings" (Lk 10:30; 12:48; Ac 16:23, 33; 2Co 6:5; 11:23). In 13:14, we find that the beast has the plague of the "sword" (*machaira*, GK *3479*), which supposedly refers to Nero's dagger. Elsewhere in Revelation the "sword" (*machaira* or *rhomphaia* [GK *4855*]) (1) symbolically refers to divine judgment by the Messiah (1:16; 2:12, 16; 19:15, 21); (2) is the sword of the rider on the red horse and equals divine judgment (6:4, 8); and (3) is a sword used as a weapon against the saints of God (13:10). We are, then, nearer to John's mind if we see the sword, not as referring to an emperor's death, but as the symbol of God's wrath that in some event had struck a deathblow to the authority of the beast (and the dragon), yet which had been deceptively covered up or restored. (For a probable antecedent, see Isa 27:1.)

3. The correct identification, therefore, of the beast's enemy will enable us to understand what event John had in mind in the deathblow. Everywhere in the book the only sufficient conqueror of the beast and the dragon is the slain Lamb, together with his faithful saints (12:11; 19:19–21). Furthermore, it is the event of the life and especially the crucifixion, resurrection, and exaltation of Jesus that dealt this deathblow to the dragon and the beast (1:5; 5:9; 12:11). This same thought is paralleled by other NT teaching (Lk 10:17–24; 11:14–22; Jn 12:31–33; Col 2:15). Irenaeus (*Haer.* 5.25–34) suggests that the wound, so central to the Apocalypse, must be understood as an appeal to Genesis 3:13–19. What possible connection could Nero have with the death of Christ? How could he be wounded by Christ, the woman's seed according to Genesis 3:15?

Yet the same paradox found in ch. 12 also appears here in ch. 13. While the dragon (ch. 12) is on the one hand defeated and cast out of heaven, on the other hand he still has the time and ability to wage a relentless war against the people of God. Likewise the beast (ch. 13) has been dealt a fatal blow by the cross of Christ and yet still has the time and ability to wage war against the saints. He appears to be alive and in full command of the scene; his blasphemies increase. What the sea beast cannot accomplish, he commissions the earth beast to do (vv.11–17). All three—the dragon, the sea beast, and the earth beast—though distinguishable, are nevertheless in collusion to effect the same end: the deception that led the world to worship the dragon and the sea beast, and the destruction of all who oppose them.

It is this description that leads to the fourth reason why identifying the beast exclusively with any one historical personage or empire is probably incorrect. In John's description of the beast, there are numerous parallels with Jesus that should alert the reader to the fact that John is seeking to establish not a historical identification but a theological characterization (though in this there is no implication against the historicity of Jesus): both wielded swords; both had followers on whose foreheads were inscribed their names (13:16–14:1); both had horns (5:6; 13:1); both were slain, the same Greek word being used to describe their deaths (*sphazō*, GK *5377*; 13:3, 8); both had arisen to new life and authority; and both were given (by different authorities) power over every nation, tribe, people, and language, as well as over the kings of the earth (1:5; 7:9; with 13:7; 17:12). The beast described here is the great theological counterpart to all that Christ represents and not the mere Roman Empire or any of its emperors. So it is easy to understand why many in the history of the church have identified the beast with a future, personal Antichrist.

It is curious that Ford, 220, refers to Minear's "most challenging argument against this [Nero] theory" without offering any refutation. She then proceeds, contrary to Minear's whole thesis, to try her own hand at another *historical* identification that is even less convincing than the long succession of previous ones (see comments at v.11).

While the references in the Johannine literature may be taken as supporting the view that the Antichrist is manifested in multiple persons and was a reality present in John's day (1Jn 2:18, 22; 4:3; 2Jn 7), Paul's description in such personal terms of the coming "man of lawlessness" (2Th 2:3–4, 8–9) has led the majority of ancient and modern interpreters to adopt the viewpoint that it is a personal Antichrist. Bavinck (cited in Berkouwer, 265) believes that the solution to the conflict between Paul and John lies in seeing John as describing the forerunners (anti-Christian powers in history), while Paul talks about the day when these powers will be embodied in one king(dom) of the world, the epitome of apostasy. John, however, says that in the false teachers "the antichrist" was actually present (2Jn 7). Berkouwer, 270, shows that it is not necessary to understand Paul's apocalyptic language as describing a personal Antichrist.

But the question must remain open as to whether John in the Apocalypse points to a *single* archenemy of the church, whether past or future, or to a transhistorical reality with many human manifestations in history. Thus the imagery would function similarly with regard to the image of the woman of ch. 12 or the prostitute of ch. 17. If such is the case, this does not mean that John would have denied the earthly historical manifestations of this satanic reality, but it would prevent us from limiting the imagery merely to the Roman Empire or to any other single future political entity.

4 The goal of the dragon and the beast in their conspiracy is to promote the idolatrous worship of themselves. This perversion is further enhanced by the earth beast (vv.12, 15). The means of deception varies because not all human beings are deceived in the same way. People follow and worship the beast because he is apparently invincible: "Who can make war against him?" His only real enemies seem to be the saints of Jesus, whom he effectively destroys (2:10, 13; 12:11; 13:15). But little does he realize that in the death of the saints the triumph of God appears. As they die, they do so in identification with the slain Lamb, who through the cross has decisively conquered the dragon by inflicting on him a truly fatal wound. "Who is like the beast?" echoes in parody similar references to God himself (Ex 15:11; Mic 7:18).

5–6 (See comments at v.1.) The period of the beast's authority is given as "forty-two months," the same period already referred to in 11:2–3; 12:6, 13 (see comments at 11:2).

7 Here as elsewhere in the Apocalypse, to "make war" does not mean to wage a military campaign but refers to hostility to and destruction of the people of God in whatever manner and through whatever means the beast may choose. (Study carefully 2:16;

11:7; 12:7, 17; 16:14; 17:14; 19:11, 19; 20:8; cf. 2Co 10:4.) "To conquer them" refers not to the subversion of their faith but to the destruction of their physical lives (cf. Mt 10:28). As in T. S. Eliot's *Murder in the Cathedral* (New York: Harcourt, Brace & Co., 1935), their apparent defeat by the beast and his victory turns out in reality to be the victory of the saints and the defeat of the beast (15:2). Messiahlike universal dominion was given to the beast by the dragon (Lk 4:4–7; 1Jn 5:19).

8 John further identifies the worshipers of the beast as "all whose names have not been written in the book of life belonging to the Lamb." (For a discussion of the meaning of the "book of life," see comments at 3:5; also 17:8; 20:12, 15; 21:27.) This contrast further emphasizes the theological nature of the description of the beast. The beast from the earth represents the idolatrous system of worship instigated by the dragon to deceive human beings into breaking the first commandment.

It has been debated whether the words "from the creation of the world" (also 17:8) belong grammatically with "have not been written" or with "that was slain." In other words, is it the Lamb who was slain from the creation of the world, or is it the names that were not recorded in the book of life from the creation of the world? In Greek, either interpretation is grammatically acceptable. But the reference in 17:8 implies that the word order in the Greek (not the grammar) favors the latter view and suggests that John is deliberately providing a complementary thought to 17:8. In the former instance, the emphasis would rest on the decree in eternity to elect the Son as the redeeming agent for humanity's salvation (13:8; 1Pe 1:20); in the latter, stress lies on God's eternal foreknowledge of a company of people who would participate in the elect Son's redeeming work (17:8). In any event, the words "from the creation of the world" cannot be pressed to prove eternal individual election to salvation or

damnation, since 3:5 implies that failure of appropriate human response may remove one's name from the book of life. Therefore, we must allow John's understanding of predestination to qualify earlier rabbinic and Qumranic as well as later Christian views. This verse strikes a sharp note of distinction between the followers of the beast and those of the slain Lamb. It also calls for faithful commitment and clear discernment of error on the part of the Lamb's people.

9–10 These verses are both important and difficult. This is the only occurrence in Revelation of the words "he who has an ear, let him hear" apart from their use in each of the messages to the seven churches (chs. 2–3). Here they call special attention to the need for obedience to the exhortation in v.10b. Kiddle, 248, believes v.10 is the focal point of the whole chapter, as it calls on the Christian to display faith and patience in the face of the divinely permitted predominance of evil. Most agree that the language of v.10 alludes to Jeremiah 15:2 and 43:11 (LXX 50:11), where the prophet describes the certainty of divine judgment that will come upon the rebels in Israel—they will suffer captivity, famine, disease, and death from the sword. Yet it is difficult to see how Jeremiah's words are appropriate here in this context of an exhortation for believers to be faithful. John's meaning must be different, namely, that as the rebels in Jeremiah's day would certainly encounter the divine judgment, so the faithful to Christ are assured that their captivity and martyrdom are in God's will. John Yoder (*The Christian Witness to the State* [Newton, Kan.: Faith and Life, 1964], 76) rejects the popular contrasting of Romans 13 (where Christians are to be subject to a presumably more or less just state) with Revelation 13 (where the state has become diabolical and can be resisted and even overthrown by Christians); instead the subject of Revelation 13 is apostasy: "The task of Christians in Revelation 13 is not to rebel in any politically relevant way; it is suffering submission, 'the patience and faithfulness of the saints.'" For the textual problem in v.10, see Notes.

No completely satisfying resolution of the problems in v.10 is available. Since the difficult part (10a) is both preceded by (v.9) and followed by (v.10b) appeals to obedience and loyalty, it seems best to stay with the sense of obedient faithfulness and follow the textual readings that support it. Charles, 1:355, puts it this way: "The day of persecution is at hand: the Christians must suffer captivity, exile or death: in calmly facing and undergoing this final tribulation they are to manifest their endurance and faithfulness." Paul's statement is similar: "I will know that you stand firm in one spirit, . . . without being frightened in any way by those who oppose you. This is a sign to them that they will be destroyed, but that you will be saved—and that by God" (Php 1:27–28). While the Dead Sea Scrolls reveal that the Essenes held to an active, violent participation in the final eschatological battle for the elect, and while the then current Zealot holy-war doctrine advocated violent revolution, John seems to call believers here to passive resistance against their enemies. Yet this resistance, which may result in captivity and even martyrdom, seems to contribute to the eventual defeat of evil (cf. Adela Yarbro Collins, "The Political Perspective of the Revelation to John," *JBL* 96 [1977]: 241–56).

11 John sees another (*allo*, "one of a similar kind") beast rising from the earth. This second beast completes the triumvirate of evil—the dragon, the sea beast, and the land beast. The land beast is subservient to the beast from the sea and seems utterly dedicated to promoting not himself but the wounded beast from the sea. Elsewhere the land beast is called the "false prophet" (16:13; 19:20; 20:10). As with the first beast, identification is a problem. That this beast comes from the land rather than the sea may simply indicate his diversity from the first, while other references stress their collusion.

A survey of the history of interpretation reveals, as with the first beast, two main lines: the beast either represents a power or movement or describes a human being allied with the Antichrist at the close of the age (cf. Berkouwer, 260–61). Early Christian interpreters, such as Irenaeus (*Haer.* 5.28.2; second century), who identify the first beast not with Rome but with a personal Antichrist find in the second beast the "armor-bearer" of the first, who employs the demonic forces to work magic and deceive the inhabitants of the earth. Hippolytus (*Christ and Antichrist*; third century) identified the second beast as "the kingdom of Antichrist." Victorinus (*Apocalypse* 13:11–13; late third century) speaks of this beast as the false prophet who will work magic before the Antichrist (he then blurs the identification of the second beast with the first in further remarks). Andreas (sixth century) reports that in his day "some say this [second] beast is the Antichrist, but it seems to others that he is Satan, and his two horns are the Antichrist and the false prophet" (cited in Swete, 166).

Calvin, Luther, and other Reformers drawing on earlier traditions were led to identify this beast with the papacy or specific popes. Berkouwer, 262–63, notes that, while the Reformers may have been mistaken as to their actual identifications, they were right in seeing the beast as a present threat and not some entity awaiting a yet future manifestation. Most modern commentators, following the Nero *redivivus* view of the first beast, identify this beast as the priesthood of the imperial cultus (Charles, 1:357). Alford, 4:679, and others would extend the symbolism to all ages and see in the second beast "the sacerdotal persecuting power, pagan or Christian," and would call special attention to the Roman papacy, though by no means limiting it to this priesthood.

While recognizing that no view is without problems, the following discussion takes the position that the land beast is John's way of describing the false prophets of the Olivet Discourse (Mt 24:24; Mk 13:22). This identification is consistent with the previously stated view of the sea beast as describing not merely a specific political reality but the worldwide anti-God system of Satan and its manifestation in periodic, historical human antichrists. The land beast is the antithesis to the true prophets of Christ symbolized by the two witnesses in ch. 11. (See Berkouwer, ch. 9, for a full and helpful discussion of the whole Antichrist issue.) If the thought of a nonpersonal Antichrist and false prophet seems to contradict the verse that describes them as being cast alive into the lake of fire (19:20), consider that "death" and "Hades" (nonpersons) are also thrown into the lake of fire (20:14).

The reference to the "two horns like a lamb" can be understood as highlighting the beast's imitative role with respect to the true Lamb in the rest of the book (e.g., 5:6; 13:8; 14:1). Could the two horns be in contrast to the two witnesses in ch. 11? Since one of the primary characteristics of this second beast consists in his deceptive activities (v.14; 19:20), his appearance as a lamb would contribute to the confusion over the beast's true identity. If the land beast represents satanic false teaching and false prophets, their evil is intensified because of the deceptive similarity to the truth. Even though the beast is like the Lamb, in reality he is evil because "he [speaks] like a dragon," i.e., he teaches heresy. Jesus gave such a twofold description of false prophets in the Sermon on the Mount: "Watch out for false prophets. They come to you in sheep's clothing, but inwardly they are ferocious wolves" (Mt 7:15). On the other hand, the "lamblikeness" may simply be a reference to the beast's gentle outward manner in contrast to his true identity as a fierce dragon.

12 The activity of the land beast is repeatedly described as that of promoting the worship of the first beast (v.14). Could this be the kind of activity represented in the reference to the false prophets in Pergamum and Thyatira seducing the servants of God to idolatry (2:14–15, 20, 24)? The NIV misses a nuance by rendering the Greek *enōpion* ("in behalf of") as though the second beast exercised all the authority of the first beast merely as the latter's representative. The preposition *enōpion* occurs no fewer than thirty-four times in Revelation and in every instance means "in the presence of" or "before." The same word is used of the two witnesses in 11:4: "These are the two olive trees and the two lampstands that stand before [*enōpion*] the Lord of the earth." Kiddle, 255, points out how this word in such a context indicates "prophetic readiness to do the bidding of God, and with the authority inalienable from divine communion." As the antitheses of the two witnesses, the false prophets derive their authority and ministry from the first beast.

13 One of the strategies the land beast uses to deceive people into following the first beast is the performance of "miraculous signs" (*sēmeion*; see discussion at 12:1). The ability of the Satan-inspired prophets to perform deceiving miracles is attested elsewhere in Revelation and in other parts of the Bible (16:14; 19:20; Dt 13:1–5; Mt 7:22; 24:24; Mk 13:22; 2Th 2:9). Distinguishing between the true and false prophets has always been difficult but not impossible. The followers of Jesus must be constantly alert to discern the spirits (1Jn 4:1–3).

The reference to "fire . . . from heaven" deserves brief comment. It could refer to the fire the prophet Elijah called down from heaven (1Ki 18:38) or to the fire coming out of the mouths of the two witnesses (Rev 11:5). Either reference is preferable to the attempt to see here some indication of the imperial cult priests of Rome. John may intend a deliberate contrast between the true witnesses' use of fire and its use by the false prophets (11:5; cf. Lk 9:54).

An elaborate theory was worked out by E. Watson and B. Hamilton (cited in Minear, 124–27) that connects the fire of God with the true word of God and the Holy Spirit's witness (such as at Pentecost [Ac 2:3]). The false fire would then be a reference to pseudocharismatic gifts that create a counterfeit church community whose allegiance is to the Antichrist. Regarding the fire from heaven, remember the priests Nadab and Abihu, who offered "unauthorized fire" before the Lord, apparently by their own will, and received God's judgment in the form of "fire" that "consumed them" (Lev 10:1–2). In any case, the reference to fire from heaven indicates that no mighty deed is too hard for these false prophets, because they derive their power from the Antichrist and the dragon. Christ's true servants are not to be deceived by even spectacular miracles the false prophets may perform. Such miracles in themselves are no evidence of the Holy Spirit.

14a Here more must be involved than the deceptions of the imperial priesthood. The quality of the miracles deceives those who follow the beast—"the inhabitants of the earth." "Deceive" (*planaō*, GK *4414*) is John's term for the activity of false teachers who lead people to worship gods other than the true and living God (2:20; 12:9; 18:23; 19:20; 20:3, 8, 10; cf. 1Jn 2:26; 3:7; 4:6; also Mt 24:11, 24).

14b–15 The second beast orders the setting up of an "image" (*eikōn*, GK *1635*) of the first beast. Elsewhere, the worship of the first beast, his "image," and his "mark" are inseparable (14:9, 11; 15:2; 16:2; 19:20; 20:4). The *eikōn* of something is not a mere copy but partakes in its reality and in fact constitutes its reality (cf. *TDNT* 2:389). Most interpreters, following the Roman-emperor exegesis, readily identify the image with the statue of Caesar and refer the "breath" and speaking of the image to the magic and ventriloquism of the imperial priests. But as has been argued earlier (see comments at vv. 1, 11), serious questions can be raised against such an exegesis

of John's language, which is much more theologically descriptive than the Roman hypothesis allows. This is not to deny that the imperial worship could be included as one form of worshiping the beast. But the reality described is much larger and far more transhistorical than the mere worship of a bust of Caesar. John, however, would not deny that these realities have their historical manifestations, for in every age the beast kills those who will not worship his image. In terms reminiscent of the great golden image Nebuchadnezzar made and commanded every person to worship on the threat of death (Da 3:1–11), John describes the worldwide system of idolatry represented by the first beast and the false prophet(s) who promotes it, and he describes this reality as a blasphemous and idolatrous system that produces a breach of the first two commandments (Ex 20:3–5).

In speaking about giving "breath" (*pneuma*, GK *4460*) to the image, John implies the activity of the false prophets in reviving idolatrous worship, giving it the appearance of vitality, reality, and power (cf. Jer 10:14). Curiously, the two witnesses were also said to receive "breath" (11:11). The idolatrous satanic system has the power of death over those who worship the true God and the Lamb. The same "image" tried to kill Daniel and his friends, killed many of the prophets of God, crucified the Lord Jesus, and put to death Stephen (Ac 7:60), James the apostle (Ac 12:1–2), and Antipas (Rev 2:13). Thus the sea beast demonstrated to his followers the apparent healing of his wounded head. To limit the image to the bust of Caesar or to some future statue or ventriloquistic device constricts John's deeper meaning and eliminates the present significance of his language.

The phenomenon of the Korean religious leader Sun Myung Moon may provide a modern-day example of what seems to be John's teaching about antichrists and false prophets (cf. Young Oon Kim, *Divine Principle and Its Application* [Washington, D.C.:

The Holy Spirit Association for the Unification of World Christianity, 1969]). Moon is being heralded as the "Lord of the Second Advent" by Kim and others. His whole stance clearly embodies heresy and blasphemy, and many have been deceived into following him and his teaching. Moon has advertised in American newspapers, proclaiming that Jesus, Muhammad, the Buddha, and God had told him he is "the Savior, Messiah and King of Kings of all humanity!" (*Washington Times*, July 4, 2002). His idolatrous image receives continual breath by worship from his followers. Other characteristics of the beast, such as its violence against the true church, are not found in Moon.

16 The immediate effect of the worship of the beast involves receiving a mark on the right hand or forehead. By comparing the other passages where the beast, image, mark, and name of the beast are mentioned, it seems clear that the "mark" (*charagma*, GK *5916*) is an equivalent expression to the "name of the beast" (v.17; 14:11; also 14:9; 15:2; 16:2; 19:20; 20:4), which is also the "number of his name" (v.17; 15:2).

In Greek, *charagma* may refer to a work of art such as a carved image of a god (Ac 17:29), any written inscription or document, the "bite" of a snake, a red "seal" (an impress) of the emperor and other official attestors of documents, or a "brand" on camels indicating ownership (cf. *TDNT* 9:416; MM, 683; G. A. Deissmann, *Bible Studies* [Edinburgh: T&T Clark, 1903], 240–47). No evidence, however, can be cited from the ancient world where a *charagma* is placed on a *person*, let alone on the "right hand" or on the "forehead," though a seal (*sphragis*) was customarily put on slaves and soldiers. This lack of concrete evidence has led Swete, 170, who is committed to the Roman emperor view, to reject any connection between the *charagma* and a literal mark of the emperor. He argues that as the servants of God receive on their foreheads the

impress of the divine seal (7:3; 14:1), so the servants of the beast are marked with the stamp of the beast. In other words, the *charagma* is not a literal impress seal, certificate, or similar mark of identification, but it is John's way of symbolically describing authentic ownership and loyalty. Those who worship the beast have his *charagma* or brand of ownership on them, as the followers of Jesus have the brand of God's possession on them.

17 Those having the *charagma* ("mark") can "buy or sell"; those without it cannot. This statement apparently refers to some sort of socioeconomic sanctions that would, of course, affect the social and economic condition of Christians in the world. Earlier John alluded to certain such conditions. Smyrna was a greatly persecuted church and was "poor" (2:9). Philadelphia was of "little strength" (3:8). Those faithful to Christ in the great tribulation are seen in heaven as never again hungering (7:16), while the great harlot grows rich and wallows in luxury (18:3). Other NT writers also apparently refer to socioeconomic sanctions practiced against Christians (Ro 15:26; Heb 10:34). Such a sanction was more social than political, imposed not by the government but by the communities. When governmental Rome took official notice of an illegal religion, it was always by criminal charges in the courts, not by economic sanctions (cf. Caird, 173).

18 In v.17 John indicates that the *charagma* ("mark") is the name of the beast or the number of his name. He now reveals the number of the beast: "His number is 666." The list of conjectures concerning the meaning of the number (or its alternates—see Notes) is almost as long as the list of commentators on the book. Taking their cue from the words "let him calculate the number of the beast," most of these interpreters have tried to play the ancient Hebrew game of *gematria* or, as it is called by the Greeks, *isopsephia*. Ancient languages, including Hebrew and Greek, use standard letters from their alphabets as numerical signs. For example, α (*alpha*) in Greek can represent the number one, β (*bēta*) the number two, ιβ (*iōta bēta*) twelve, etc. A series of letters could form a word and at the same time indicate a number. *Gematria* took many forms and consisted in trying to guess the word from the number or trying to connect one word with another that has the same numerical value. On the walls of Pompeii there are some graffiti, dated no later than AD 79, that illuminate the practice. One reads, "Amerimnus thought upon his lady Harmonia for good. The number of her honorable name is 45 (*me [mu epsilon]*)." The key to the puzzle seems to be in the word "Harmonia"—probably not the girl's actual name but a reference to the nine Muses (the goddesses of song and poetry); and forty-five is the sum of all the digits from one to nine (cited in E. M. Blaiklock, *The Archaeology of the New Testament* [Grand Rapids: Zondervan, 1970], 131). Another runs, "I love her whose number is 545 (*phme [phi mu epsilon]*)" (cited in G. A. Deissmann, *Light from the Ancient East* [London: Hodder & Stoughton, 1910], 277). In these cases, the number conceals a name, and the mystery is perhaps known for certain only by the two lovers themselves. Another mentioning Nero runs, "Nero, Orestes, Alemeon their mothers slew. A calculation new, Nero his mother slew" (Suetonius, *The Lives of the Caesars: Nero* [LCL, 6.39]). The sum of the Greek letters in the phrase "his mother slew" is 1,005; "Nero" also adds up to 1,005.

Similarly the Jews (esp. the Hasidim) used Hebrew alphabetical numbers to indicate concealed names and mysterious connections with other words of the same numerical value. For example, the Hebrew word *naḥaš* ("serpent") has the same numerical value as the Hebrew word *mašiaḥ* ("Messiah"), namely, 358. From this it was argued that oné of the names of the Messiah was "serpent." Some suggest this may relate to Moses' lifting up the "serpent" in the wilderness

(cf. Nu 21; Jn 3:14). For these and many other examples, see William Barclay, "Great Themes of the New Testament: Part V, Revelation xiii (continued)," *ExpTim* 70 (1959): 292–96.

Thus it is not difficult to understand why most commentators have understood John's words "let him calculate the number. . . . His number is 666" to be an invitation to the reader to play *gematria* and discover the identity of the beast. This interpretation is not new. Irenaeus (*Haer.* 29.30) mentions that many names of contemporary persons and entities were being offered in his day as solutions to this number mystery. Yet he cautioned against the practice and believed that the name of the Antichrist was deliberately concealed because he did not exist in John's day. The name would be secret until the time of his future appearance in the world (cf. Thomas, 2:185). Irenaeus expressly refutes the attempt of many to identify the name with any of the Roman emperors. He feels, however, that the *gematria* approach is John's intended meaning but warns the church against endless speculations. Curiously neither he nor any other early church interpreter suggested Nero!

Irenaeus's fear was not misplaced. Endless speculation is just what has happened in the history of the interpretation of v.18, as Barclay ("Great Themes," 295–96) has well documented. Barclay himself (perhaps following Charles) is quite certain that the only possible solution is to use Hebrew letters, and so he comes up with "Neron Caesar," which equals 666. This identification is linked with the view that the Antichrist would be Nero *redivivus* (see Overview at 13:1). Yet this use of Hebrew letters requires a spelling for "caesar" that is not normal for the word (*qsr* instead of *qysr*). However, in a publication of an Aramaic document from the Dead Sea cave at Murabbaat, dated to the second year of the emperor Nero, the name is spelled *nrwn qsr*, as required by the theory (cf. D. R. Hillers, "Revelation 13:13 and a

Scroll from Murabba'at," *BASOR* 170 [1963]: 65). But this evidence has problems (see Notes). The whole line of Nero *redivivus* interpretation has been seriously challenged by Minear, ch. 5, and others (cf. Overview at 13:1). In the first place, none of the keywords of v.18—name, number, man, 666—require the effort to find an emperor (or future political dictator) with a name whose letters will add up to 666. The sheer disagreement and confusion created through the years by the *gematria* method should have long ago warned the church that it was on the wrong track. Rühle (*TDNT* 1:464), after surveying all the evidence, observes, "It may be said that all the solutions proposed are unsatisfactory." If John was seeking to illumine believers so they could penetrate the deception of the beast as well as to contrast the beast and his followers with the Lamb and his followers (14:1–5), he has clearly failed—i.e., if he intends for us to play the *gematria* game. How Nero could fit these requirements is, on closer examination, difficult to see. If some Christians of John's time did succumb to Caesar worship, it was due less to their being deceived than to their fear of death.

Moreover, several exegetical factors argue strongly for another sense of John's words. In the first place, nowhere does John use *gematria* as a method. Everywhere, however, he gives symbolic significance to numbers (e.g., seven churches, seals, trumpets, and bowls; twenty-four elders; 144,000 sealed; 144 cubits for the new Jerusalem, etc.). Furthermore, in 15:2 the victors have triumphed over three enemies: the beast, his image, and *the number of his name*, which suggests a symbolic significance connected with idolatry and blasphemy rather than victory in solving the puzzle of correctly identifying someone's name.

John seeks to give "wisdom" (*sophia*, GK *5053*) and "insight" (*nous*, GK *3808*) to believers as to the true identity of their enemy. A similar use of *nous* and *sophia* occurs in 17:9, where John calls attention to the identity of the beast ridden by the harlot. What John seems to be asking for in both cases is divine discernment and not mathematical ingenuity! Believers need to penetrate the deception of the beast. John's reference to his number will help them to recognize his true character and identity.

The statement "it is man's number" (*arithmos ... anthrōpou*) further identifies the kind of number the beast represents. Does John mean that the beast is a person (NRSV), that he has a human name? In 21:17, John uses similar words for the angel: "by man's measurement, which the angel was using." The statement is difficult. How can the measure be both "man's" and at the same time that of an "angel"? Sensing the peculiarity of the statement in 21:17, Kiddle suggests that John is attempting to call attention to some inner meaning in the number measuring the height of the wall with respect to the size of the city. The meaning perhaps is a mild polemic against first-century tendencies to venerate angels unduly by stating that both men and angels can understand and enter the future city (see comments at 21:15–21). In any case the statement "it is man's number" alerts the reader to some hidden meaning in 666. From this we may conclude that the number of the beast is linked to humanity. Why would it be necessary for John to emphasize this relationship unless he assumed his readers might have understood the beast to be otherworldly without any connection to humanity. Might it be, then, that the statement signifies that the satanic beast, which is the great enemy of the church, manifests itself in human form? Thus as the similar phrase in 21:17 linked the angelic and the human, so here it joins the satanic with the human.

Finally, how are we to understand 666? The best way is to follow Minear, ch. 5, and Newman ("Fallacy of the Domitian Hypothesis," 133–39) and return to one of the most ancient interpretations, that of Irenaeus (second century). Irenaeus (*Haer.* 5.29.30), while still holding to a personal

Antichrist, held that the number indicates that the beast is the sum of "all apostate power," a concentrate of six thousand years of unrighteousness, wickedness, deception, and false prophecy. He states that "the digit six, being adhered to throughout, indicates the recapitulations of that prophecy, taken in its full extent, which occurred at the beginning, during the intermediate periods, and which shall take place at the end." He also held that the wound of the beast has reference to Genesis 3:13–19. The Messiah has freed men from this wound by wounding Satan and by giving them the power to inflict wounds on the beast by overcoming his blasphemy.

The significance of the name of the beast is abundantly clear in Revelation (12:3; 13:1–6; 14:9–12; 17:3). Wherever there is blasphemy, there the beast's name is found. The number 666 is the heaping up of the number 6. Minear, 258, adds, "Because of its contrast with 7 we may be content with an interpretation which sees in 666 an allusion to incompleteness, to the demonic parody in the perfection of 7, to the deceptiveness of the almost-perfect, to the idolatrous blasphemy exemplified by false worshipers, or to the dramatic moment between the sixth and the seventh items in a vision cycle (cf. seals, trumpets, bowls, and kings 17:10)." This interpretation of 666 as a symbolic number referring to the unholy trinity of evil or to the humanly imperfect imitation of God rather than a cipher of a name is not restricted to Minear; it has been held also by a long line of conservative commentators—e.g., A. C. Gaebelein, J. A. Seiss, J. F. Walvoord, L. Morris—and more recently by Beale, Michaels, Kistemaker, and others.

NOTES

1 In many critical editions of the Greek text, the sentence "And the dragon stood on the shore of the sea" is included in v.18 of ch. 12 rather than v.1 of ch. 13, following the reading ἐστάθη, *estathē* ("he stood"), instead of ἐστάθην, *estathēn* ("I stood"). The third person reading is well supported and may be correct, though the first person yields good sense, and the MS evidence is not such as to eliminate it from consideration. A single letter in the Greek text makes the difference.

10 A major textual problem in the last half of this verse presents a difficulty to understanding its meaning. The problem involves whether the first reference to the verb ἀποκτείνω (*apokteinō*, "kill") should be read with the majority as ἀποκτενεῖ (*apoktenei*, "will kill," a future indicative) or with A as ἀποκτανθῆναι (*apoktanthēnai*, "be killed," an aorist passive infinitive). The KJV, RSV, NRSV, and NASB all follow the first reading and render it, "If anyone kills with the sword." Combining this with the last phrase, the latter part of the verse yields either a warning directed toward Christians for them not to turn to violence and killing to vindicate themselves or a promise of requital to believers that their persecutors will be judged by God.

If, on the other hand, we follow the reading of A (preferred by Metzger, 674–75, and Charles, 1:355), the translation will be as in the NIV (cf. NEB, TEV, TNIV). This yields the sense that Christians who are destined by God for death must submit to his will and not resist the oppressor. It is an appeal to loyalty. In adopting this reading and sense, Charles points out that the construction in A is the same idiomatic Hebrew as that in 12:7 (see Notes) and yields this sense: "If anyone must be killed with the sword, with the sword he must be killed." Metzger argues that the majority-text reading reflects an altered text influenced by the retribution idea found in Matthew 26:52: "For all who draw the sword will die by the sword." No entirely satisfactory solution is available, but the NIV/TNIV rendering is preferred.

11 A curious interpretation of the first and second beasts is offered by Ford, 227–30. She holds that the first beast is the emperor Vespasian and peculiarly identifies the second beast tentatively with Flavius Josephus, the renegade Jew and historian. While Ford's attempt is not without interesting parallels, it founders chiefly on the fact that she should be the first to suggest it. On such a premise, how could we explain the fact that Josephus's writings were not preserved by Jews but by Christians if he were, in fact, recognized as one of their great enemies?

16 The apocryphal *Psalms of Solomon* (15.8) refers to the "mark of God" on the righteous and the "mark of destruction" on the wicked.

17 When John says "the name of the beast or the number of his name," the "or" (ἤ, *ē*) may signify mere interchangeability so that the name and/or the mark are equivalent (BDAG, 432).

18 Beale, 717, comments on the document from the Dead Sea cave at Murabbaat: "But in the scroll fragment the part of the word that would include the [Hebrew] *yodh* is missing. . . . We have only the initial *qoph*. . . . But if the broken word was *qsr*, which is possible, there does not appear to be enough space for it to include the *yodh*. . . . Indeed, a concordance check of the Talmuds, the Mishnah, the Tosephta, and the Tannaitic Midrashim finds only a spelling with the *yodh*." He goes on to offer a number of reasons for rejecting the Nero and the *gematria* explanation. However, numerous commentators have failed to take this evidence seriously (e.g., Beasley-Murray, Bauckham, Aune, Osborne, Duff).

Some have suggested that 666 is a triangular number of 36 (i.e., the sum of the integers of 1 through 36 is 666), and 36 is itself the triangular number of 8 (the sum of the integers 1 through 8), which is the number of the beast in 17:11 ("the eighth"). Bauckham, 391–404, has attempted an elaborate (putting it mildly) triangular, square, and rectangular number scheme he thinks John has used to link the identity of chs. 13 and 17. But beyond the objection that this is more complicated than the text of the 666 itself, such an explanation is tautological: The number of the beast (666) is converted into another number (36) that in turn is identified with another number (8), both of which represent the beast but neither of which identify who the beast is. Why should the "wisdom" (not mathematical intelligence) of the reader be required (v. 18a; so Aune, *Revelation 6–16*, 772)?

Instead of 666, which is strongly supported, one good MS and a few lesser witnesses have 616, which is explained as either a scribal slip or a deliberate alteration to give the numbers necessary for the Greek "Caesar god" (Deissmann, *Light from the Ancient Near East*, 278 n. 3), or "Gaios Caesar" (Barclay, "Great Themes," 296), or the Latin form of Nero Caesar (Metzger, 676). Irenaeus (*Haer.* 5.30) strongly deplored this 616 reading as heretical and deceptive. A few MSS read 646 or 747, according to H. C. Hoskier (*Concerning the Text of the Apocalypse* [London: Bernard Quaritch, 1929], 2:364).

3. The Lamb and the 144,000 (14:1–5)

OVERVIEW

The two previous chapters have prepared Christians for the reality that as the end draws near, they will be harassed and sacrificed like sheep. This section shows that their sacrifice is not meaningless. A glance back at ch. 7 reminds us that there the 144,000 were merely sealed; here, however, they are seen as already delivered. When the floods have passed, Mount Zion appears high above the waters; the Lamb is on the throne of glory surrounded by the triumphant songs of his own, and the gracious presence of God fills the universe.

Chapter 14 briefly answers two pressing questions: (1) What becomes of those who refuse to receive the mark of the beast and are killed (vv.1–5)? and (2) What happens to the beast and his servants (vv.6–20)?

¹Then I looked, and there before me was the Lamb, standing on Mount Zion, and with him 144,000 who had his name and his Father's name written on their foreheads. ²And I heard a sound from heaven like the roar of rushing waters and like a loud peal of thunder. The sound I heard was like that of harpists playing their harps. ³And they sang a new song before the throne and before the four living creatures and the elders. No one could learn the song except the 144,000 who had been redeemed from the earth. ⁴These are those who did not defile themselves with women, for they kept themselves pure. They follow the Lamb wherever he goes. They were purchased from among men and offered as firstfruits to God and the Lamb. ⁵No lie was found in their mouths; they are blameless.

COMMENTARY

1 The Lamb standing on Mount Zion is contrasted to the dragon standing on the shifting sands of the seashore (13:1). Although the mood of rapid movement in the previous chapters gives way to one of victorious rest (vv.1–5, 13), activity continues because the battle between the dragon and the woman (cf. 12:11) is still going on. Immediately the question arises as to whether the 144,000 here are the same as those in ch. 7. The only reason for viewing the 144,000 in ch. 7 differently is that here they are described as "firstfruits" and "pure" who "did not defile themselves with women" (v.4). The two-group viewpoint has been defended especially by some Roman Catholic exegetes but has been effectively refuted by other Roman Catholic exegetes (see comments at v.4; cf. W. G. Heidt, *The Book of the Apocalypse* [Collegeville, Minn.: Liturgical Press, 1962], 94–95; Ford, 234).

The problem of the location of this group of 144,000 is more complex. Mount Zion may refer to the hilly area in southeast Jerusalem, the Temple Mount, the whole city of Jerusalem, or, as in postexilic days, the whole land of Judah and the whole Israelite nation. In the prophetic tradition, Zion came to symbolize the place where the Messiah would gather to himself a great company of the redeemed (Ps 48; Isa 24:23; Joel 2:32; Ob 17, 21; Mic 4:1, 7; Zec 14:10). Likewise in late Jewish apocalyptic literature there is a similar idea: "But he shall stand upon the summit of Mount Zion. . . . And whereas thou didst see that he summoned and gathered to himself another multitude which was peaceable, these are the ten tribes" (*4 Ezra* 13:35, 39–40; *4 Ezra* 2:42 is similar). Zion may here symbolize the strength and security that belong to the people of God.

In the seven NT references to Zion, five occur in OT quotations. Of the other two, one is here in Revelation and the remaining reference (Heb 12:22–23) implies a connection between Mount

Zion and the church: "But you have come to Mount Zion, to the heavenly Jerusalem, the city of the living God . . . to the church of the firstborn." Some, connecting the reference in Hebrews to the one here in v.1, have argued for the heavenly location of the 144,000 (so Kiddle). By contrast, Beckwith's view, 647, is significant: "The 'mount Zion, the city of the living God, the heavenly Jerusalem' in Heb 12:22, the 'Jerusalem that is above' in Gal 4:26, denote the perfect archetype or pattern of the earthly, which in Hebrew thought now exists in heaven and in the end is to descend in full realization: they are not designations of heaven, the place of God and his hosts." For Beckwith and others, Mount Zion refers to the earthly seat of the messianic or millennial kingdom (also Beasley-Murray, Charles, Walvoord). Whether this Mount Zion has any connection (as to locality) with ancient and historical Zion, John does not say. At any rate, that the 144,000 are singing "before the throne" (v.3) is not an objection to seeing them as the earthly Zion; it is not the redeemed who are singing but the angelic harpists (cf. Alford, 4:684).

The 144,000 have on their foreheads the names of the Father and the Lamb, showing that they belong to God, not the beast. In 7:3–8 the elect group have the seal of God on their foreheads, linking them to this group in ch. 14, while the further description that "they follow the Lamb" (v.4) may show their connection with the second group in 7:9–17 (see esp. 7:17: "lead them"). One of the most beautiful and assuring promises in the whole book is that God's servants will have his name on their foreheads (cf. 3:12; 22:4).

Chapter 14 advances the drama a step further than ch. 7. While the members of the multitude are the same, the circumstances in which they are seen have changed. In ch. 7 the whole company of God's people are sealed (7:1–8), thus readied for the satanic onslaught, and then a company (a martyred portion?) are seen in heaven serving before the throne of God (7:9–17), whereas in ch. 14 the whole body of the redeemed is seen (resurrected?) with the Lamb in the earthly eschatological kingdom. The repetition of the reference to the 144,000 may also be a liturgical phenomenon, a chief characteristic of the book—either the repetition of the introit or of antiphons.

The background of the scene (vv.1–5) may reflect John's reinterpretation of Psalm 2, to which he had alluded elsewhere and which describes the battle between the rebellious nations and God, with God suppressing the revolt by enthroning his Son on Mount Zion (so Caird). John, however, does not see the warrior-king hoped for by the writer of Psalm 2, but he sees the Lamb and those who repeated his victory over the enemy by their submission (his name on their foreheads). Psalm 76 may also be part of the background, where Zion is the symbol of the defeat of God's enemies and the salvation of his people.

2 The "sound" John hears is probably a "voice" (*phōnē*, GK *5889*), as in 1:15. It is important to recognize that this voice is not that of the redeemed; it is a loud angelic chorus (cf. 5:11), sounding like "the roar of rushing waters," like "a loud peal of thunder," and like "harpists playing their harps" (1:15; 5:8; 6:1; 19:1, 6; see comments at 5:8; Notes, 5:9–10). Charles indicates that grammatically the sentence is Hebraistic. Again the scene is liturgical, emphasizing the connection between the earthly victory and the heavenly throne.

3 This "new song" should be related to the "new song" in 5:9, also sung by the angelic choirs. It is the song of redemption and vindication. What was seen in ch. 5 as secured for the redeemed by Christ's death (i.e., that "they will reign on the earth" [v.10]) has now been realized on Mount Zion. In the one further reference to a song in Revelation, the redeemed "victors" now sing "the song [*ōdē*, GK

6046] of Moses . . . and the song of the Lamb" (15:3), which may also relate to the new song of chs. 5 and 14 (see comments at 15:3). This heavenly example of worship may help us understand and appreciate Paul's references to songs inspired by the Spirit (*ōdais pneumatikais*) and sung in the first-century congregations (Eph 5:19; Col 3:16). Also instructive are the OT references to a new song (Pss 33:3; 40:3; 96:1; 144:9; 149:1; Isa 42:10). A "new song," in consequence of some mighty deed of God, comes from a fresh impulse of gratitude and joy in the heart (so Keil and Delitzsch, *Psalms*, 1:402). The angels sing a new song because now the victors themselves have become victorious. We are reminded again of the Passover motif (Ex 15).

While the angels sing, only the 144,000 can "learn" the new song, for they alone of the earth's inhabitants have experienced God's mighty deed of victory over the beast through their ordeal of suffering and death. Possibly the word "learn" (*manthanō*, GK *3443*) in this context may mean to "hear deeply" (cf. *TDNT* 4:407). In the gospel of John the word is used in the sense of a deep listening to divine revelation that results in learning: "Everyone who listens to the Father and learns from him comes to me" (Jn 6:45).

The 144,000 who were "redeemed" or "purchased" (*agorazō*, GK *60*) from "the earth" or "from among men" (v.4) must be the same as those "purchased" (*agorazō*) from all the earth's peoples in 5:9 and those sealed in 7:4–8, who have washed their garments in the blood of the Lamb (7:14–17).

4 John's most difficult statement about this group is that they did "not defile themselves with women." Does he mean that this group consists only of men who had never married? Or should it be understood as referring to spiritual apostasy or cult prostitution? It is unlikely that "defiled" (*molynō*, GK *3662*) refers merely to sexual intercourse, since nowhere in Scripture does intercourse within

marriage constitute sinful defilement (cf. Heb 13:4). On the other hand, the word "defiled" is found in the *Letter of Aristeas* (15.2) in connection with the promiscuous intercourse practiced by the Gentiles that defiled them but from which the Jews have been separated by the commandments of God (cf. Charles, *Apocrypha and Pseudepigrapha*, 2:109). Therefore the words can refer only to adultery or fornication; and this fact, in turn, establishes "pure" as the meaning of *parthenoi* ("virgins") in this context. (The NIV is paraphrastic here, but accurately so.) In fact, *parthenos* (GK *4221*) can be used of formerly married persons in this figurative way and is so used of widows by Ignatius (*Smyrn.* 13). The same masculine plural word (*parthenous*) is used in the LXX of Lamentations 2:10, which Ford, 242, suggests may be in parallel with "the elders of the daughter of Zion."

Kiddle, 268, thinks the reference is to actual celibacy, which alone could fit a man to be a sacrificial lamb for God. Caird connects the purity reference with holy-war regulations for soldiers who were ceremonially unclean because of sexual reasons (Dt 23:9–10; 1Sa 21:5; 2Sa 11:11). Each of these views founders because of the assumption that "uncleanness" (*akathartos*, GK *176*) is the equivalent of "defile" (*molynō*). Such an assumption not only fails on linguistic grounds but also involves us in a scriptural contradiction, i.e., that the marriage bed is defiling and sinful. It is better, then, to relate the reference to purity to the defilement of idolatry. In fact, John seems to use *molynō* this way elsewhere of cult prostitution (3:4; cf. 2:14, 20, 22).

The group as a whole has remained faithful to Christ: "They follow the Lamb wherever he goes" in obedient discipleship. They are purchased by Christ's blood and offered to God as a holy and pure sacrifice of firstfruits. Surely this symbolically implies that the bride of Christ must be pure from idolatry. Paul, likewise, uses this figure: "I promised you to one husband, to Christ, so that I might present you as a pure virgin to him" (2Co 11:2).

Those spoken of in v.3 are "firstfruits" (*aparchē*, GK *569*; v.4) presented to God. The word can have two meanings. It may designate the initial ingathering of the farmer, after which others come; so it may mean a pledge or down payment, with more to follow. Though it is difficult to find this sense of the word in the OT, it seems to be its meaning in several NT references (Ro 8:23; 11:16?; cf. 1Co 15:20; 16:15). On the other hand, in the usual OT sense and alternate NT usage, *aparchē* means simply an offering to God in the sense of being separated to him and sanctified (wholly consecrated), where no later addition is made, because the firstfruits constitute the whole (Nu 5:9 [NIV, "sacred contributions"]; Dt 18:4; 26:2; Jer 2:3; Jas 1:18). That this is John's intended sense is evident from the expression "offered as firstfruits to God."

5 The "lie" that would bring blame refers to the blasphemy of the beast-worshipers who deny the Father and the Son and ascribe vitality to the beast by believing his heresies and worshiping his image (21:27; 22:15; cf. Jn 8:44–45; Ro 1:25; 2Th 2:9–11; 1Jn 2:4, 21–22, 27).

NOTES

4 Beckwith, 646ff., has an especially helpful discussion of this verse in his commentary.

4. The Harvest of the Earth (14:6–20)

OVERVIEW

This section forms a transition from the scene of the saints' final triumph (14:1–5) to the seven bowls (ch. 16), which depict the final judgments on the enemies of the Lamb. As such, it forms a consoling counterpart to the first vision as it assures the 144,000 that God will judge the beast, his followers, and his worldwide system—Babylon.

> [6]Then I saw another angel flying in midair, and he had the eternal gospel to proclaim to those who live on the earth—to every nation, tribe, language and people. [7]He said in a loud voice, "Fear God and give him glory, because the hour of his judgment has come. Worship him who made the heavens, the earth, the sea and the springs of water."
>
> [8]A second angel followed and said, "Fallen! Fallen is Babylon the Great, which made all the nations drink the maddening wine of her adulteries."
>
> [9]A third angel followed them and said in a loud voice: "If anyone worships the beast and his image and receives his mark on the forehead or on the hand, [10]he, too, will drink of the wine of God's fury, which has been poured full strength into the cup of his wrath. He will be tormented with burning sulfur in the presence of the holy angels and of the Lamb. [11]And the smoke of their torment rises for ever and ever. There is no rest day or night for

those who worship the beast and his image, or for anyone who receives the mark of his name." 12This calls for patient endurance on the part of the saints who obey God's commandments and remain faithful to Jesus.

13Then I heard a voice from heaven say, "Write: Blessed are the dead who die in the Lord from now on."

"Yes," says the Spirit, "they will rest from their labor, for their deeds will follow them."

14I looked, and there before me was a white cloud, and seated on the cloud was one "like a son of man" with a crown of gold on his head and a sharp sickle in his hand. 15Then another angel came out of the temple and called in a loud voice to him who was sitting on the cloud, "Take your sickle and reap, because the time to reap has come, for the harvest of the earth is ripe." 16So he who was seated on the cloud swung his sickle over the earth, and the earth was harvested.

17Another angel came out of the temple in heaven, and he too had a sharp sickle. 18Still another angel, who had charge of the fire, came from the altar and called in a loud voice to him who had the sharp sickle, "Take your sharp sickle and gather the clusters of grapes from the earth's vine, because its grapes are ripe." 19The angel swung his sickle on the earth, gathered its grapes and threw them into the great winepress of God's wrath. 20They were trampled in the winepress outside the city, and blood flowed out of the press, rising as high as the horses 'bridles for a distance of 1,600 stadia.

COMMENTARY

6–7 The first angel announces that there is still hope, for even at this crucial moment in history God is seeking to reclaim the beast's followers by issuing a message appealing to the people of the world to "fear God and . . . worship him." That this appeal is called a "gospel" (*euangelion*, GK *2295*) has raised a question. How can it be good news? Yet is not the intent of the gospel message that men should fear God and worship him? Is it not the "eternal" gospel because it announces eternal life (Jn 3:16)? Could this be John's way of showing the final fulfillment of Mark 13:10? Let us not fail to see how in the NT the announcement of divine judgment is never separated from the proclamation of God's mercy.

The reference to the coming of the hour of judgment (v.7) supports the view that there is

chronological progression in Revelation and that not everything described by John is simultaneous (see comments at 15:1). This is the first reference in the book to the "judgment [*krisis*, GK *3213*] of God" (16:7; 18:10; 19:2), though the "wrath" (*thymos* [GK *2596*] or *orgē* [GK *3973*]) of God, which appears to be synonymous with judgment (v.19), has been mentioned earlier (6:16–17; 11:18; 14:8, 10; 15:1; cf. 16:1, 19; 18:3; 19:15).

8 In anticipation of a more extended description in chs. 17–18, the fall of Babylon—the great anti-God system of idolatry—is announced. The actual fall does not occur until the final bowl judgment (16:19). There may be in 11:8 a previous allusion to Babylon as the "great city" (cf. 17:18).

9–12 The explicit reference to the certain judgment of the beast-worshipers ties this section to ch. 13. Through an OT figure of eschatological judgment—unmixed wine (not diluted with water) in the cup of God's wrath (Ps 75:8; Jer 25:15) and "burning sulfur" (Isa 30:33; 34:8–10; cf. Ge 19:24; Rev 19:20; 20:10; 21:8)—John describes God's judgment inflicted on those who refused his truth and worshiped a lie (Ro 1:18, 25). To those who drink Babylon's cup (v.8), the Lord will give his own cup of wrath.

10 The reference to "torment" (*basanizō*, GK *989*; cf. 9:5; 11:10; 12:2; 20:10) has troubled some commentators, since the torment takes place "in the presence . . . of the Lamb" (so Ford, 237). Thus Glasson, 86, calls the passage "sub-Christian," while Caird only concedes a momentary final "extinction," the force mitigated by the further statement that "the smoke of their torment rises for ever and ever" (v.11), which is more appropriate to cities than individuals. While the view that some recalcitrant individuals will suffer eternal deprivation seems repugnant to Christian sensitivities, it is clear that it is not only John's understanding but that of Jesus and other NT writers as well (Mt 25:46; Ro 2:3–9; 2Th 1:6–9).

John's imagery conveys a sense of finality and sober reality. It is not clear whether the imagery points only to the permanency and irreversibility of God's punitive justice, or whether it also includes the consciousness of eternal deprivation (cf. Rev 20:10; Jn 5:28–29). Berkouwer, 417–23, wisely says that preaching about hell should never be used as a terror tactic by the church but should always be presented in such a way as to show that God's mercy is the final goal. C. S. Lewis (*The Problem of Pain* [New York: Macmillan, 1954], ch. 8) acknowledges that hell is a detestable doctrine that he would willingly remove from Christianity if it were in his power. But, as he points out, the question is not whether it is detestable but whether it is true. We must recognize that the reality of hell has the full support of

Scripture and of our Lord's own teaching. Indeed, it has always been held by Christians and has the support of reason.

11 The worshipers of the beast will be unable to rest day or night. Notice the contrast with the saints who will "rest" from their labor (v.13). While the beast-worshipers have their time of rest, and while the saints are persecuted and martyred, in the final time of judgment God will reverse their roles (7:15–17; cf. 2Th 1:6–7).

12 The great test for Christians is whether through patient endurance they will remain loyal to Jesus and not fall prey to the deception of the beasts (see comments at 13:10). They do this by their serious attention to God's Word and their faithfulness to Christ Jesus (1:3; 2:26; 3:8, 10; 22:7, 9; cf. Php 1:28–30).

13 A fourth voice comes from heaven (an angel's or Christ's?), pronounces a beatitude, and evokes the Spirit's response. This is the second beatitude in Revelation (cf. comments at 1:3). Its general import is clear, but how are the words "from now on" to be understood? Do they mean that from the time of the vision's fulfillment onward (i.e., the judgment of idolaters and the 144,000 with the Lord on Mount Zion), the dead will be blessed in a more complete manner (so Alford)? Or do they refer to the time of John's writing onward (so Beckwith)? If the latter, why from *that* time? While either interpretation is grammatically possible, the preceding verse, which implies an exhortation to Christians in John's day, favors the latter view. John expects the imminent intensification of persecution associated with the beast, and the beatitude indicates that those who remain loyal to Jesus when this occurs will be blessed indeed.

Apart from 22:17, this is the only place in Revelation where the Spirit speaks directly (cf. Ac 13:2; Heb 3:7; 10:15). The beatitude is no doubt intended to emphasize the reality of the martyrs' future. Their blessedness consists in "rest" from the onslaught of the dragon and his beasts and the assurance that their own toil (*kopos*, GK *3160*; cf. 2:2) for Christ's name will not be in vain but will be remembered by the Lord himself after their death (Heb 6:10; cf. 1Ti 5:24–25).

14–20 After a brief pause to encourage the faithfulness of the saints, John returns to the theme of divine judgment on the world. He does this by first describing the judgment in terms of a harvest (vv.14–20) and then by the seven bowl plagues (chs. 15–16). John sees a white cloud and seated on it one resembling a human being ("a son of man"). He has a crown of gold and a sharp sickle, the main instrument of harvest. John clearly wishes to highlight this exalted human figure and his role in the eschatological judgment. The question of the identity of the "son of man" is not unlike the problem of the identity of the rider of the white horse (6:1). The same words, *homoion huion anthrōpou* ("like a son of man"), are used of Jesus in 1:13, in both places without the definite article. Some have noted the close association of the one "seated on the cloud" with the words "another angel" in v.15 and the similar implications in v.17, that another angel "too" had a sharp sickle, implying that the former figure with the sickle was likewise an angel. Further, if the figure on the cloud is Jesus, how can we account for an angel giving a command to him to reap the earth (v.15)?

Though there are difficulties, Charles, 2:19, is no doubt right when he says, "There can be no question as to the identity of the divine figure seated on the cloud. He is described as 'One like a Son of Man.'" Charles shows how Daniel 7 comes to be associated with the person of the Messiah under the title "a son of man." Indeed it is quite appropriate for John to use the term "son of man," since in the Gospels that term is most frequently associated with the Messiah's suffering and the glory of the second

advent, as well as with his right to judge the world (Mt 26:64; Jn 5:27). Both themes are present in the context of Revelation. The imagery of Daniel 7, frequently used in the Apocalypse, links the suffering people of God ("the saints") to the Son of Man who sits in judgment over the kingdoms of the world (cf. Longenecker, *Christology of Early Jewish Christianity*, 82–93; France, *Jesus and the Old Testament*, 202–5). It should, of course, be remembered that this is a highly symbolic description of the final judgment.

The harvest is an OT figure used for divine judgment (Hos 6:11; Joel 3:13), especially on Babylon (Jer 51:33). Jesus also likens the final judgment to the harvest of the earth (Mt 13:30, 39). He may use the instrumentality of angels or men, but it is his prerogative to put in the sickle. While this reaping may be the gathering of his elect from the earth (so Caird, citing Mt 9:37–38; Jn 4:35–38; et al.), the context favors taking the harvest to be a reference not to salvation but to judgment.

17–20 "Another" angel here has no more necessary connection with the Son of Man than the angel designated "another" in v.15; it may simply mean another of the same kind of angel mentioned in the succession of personages in the book. (Cf. 14:6, where no other angel is involved except the one mentioned.) The angel here will gather the vintage of the earth. He is associated with the angel from the altar who has authority over its fire (v.18). Though opinion about the identification of the altar is divided, it is the incense altar; and the fire is symbolic of God's vindication of his martyred people (cf. 8:3–5; comments at 6:9–11).

The divine eschatological judgment is presented in a threefold image: the unmixed wine in the cup (v.10), the grain harvest (vv.14–16), and the vintage harvest (vv.17–20). These are best understood as three metaphors describing different views of the same reality, i.e., the divine judgment. Again the OT provides the background for this imagery of divine judgment (Isa 63:1–6; La 1:15; Joel 3:13; cf. Rev 19:13, 15). Caird, 192, certainly strains the text when he argues that the vintage overflowing with blood does not refer to the enemies of Christ but, connecting the "earth's vine" (v.18) with the new Israel, that it must refer to the death of the martyrs of Jesus. The reference to the "great winepress of God's wrath" (v.19) should clarify the imagery and leave no doubt that it denotes God's judgment on the rebellious world and not the wrath of the beast on the followers of the Lamb.

20 This verse is gruesome: blood flows up to the horses' bridles for a distance of about two hundred miles (sixteen hundred stadia). Again the source of the imagery is Isaiah 63:1–6, heightened by John's hyperbole. A similar apocalyptic image for the final judgment on idolaters occurs in the pre-Christian book of *1 Enoch*, where the righteous will slay the wicked: "And the horse shall walk up to the breast in the blood of sinners, and the chariot shall be submerged to its height" (*1 En.* 100:1, 3). Here in Revelation the judgment is not the task of human vengeance but belongs exclusively to the Son of Man and his angelic reapers (cf. Ro 12:19–21). The symbolism is that of a head-on battle, a great defeat of the enemy, a sea of spilled blood. To go beyond and attempt to find a symbolic meaning in the sixteen hundred stadia or to link the scene to some geographic location (cf. 16:4–6) is pure speculation.

The designation "outside the city" requires explanation. It may refer merely to ancient warfare when a besieging army was slaughtered at the city walls and the blood flowed outside the city. Some think John may have had an actual city in mind and have suggested Jerusalem because of the OT predictions of a final battle to be fought near the city (Da 11:45; Joel 3:12; Zec 14:4; but cf. Rev 16:16—"Armageddon" is not near Jerusalem; so Beckwith, Ford, Mounce, Swete). On the other hand, John's symbolic use of "city" in every other reference favors taking the word symbolically in this verse. In Revelation there are only two cities (the "cities" of the seven churches in chs. 2–3 are not called cities): the city of God, which is the camp of the saints, and the city of Satan (Babylon), which is made up of the followers of the beast (cf. Beasley-Murray, Kiddle). There is no way to be certain of the identity of the city, nor is its identity important. It is sufficient to take it as the same city that was persecuted by the pagans (11:2) and is seen in 20:9, i.e., the community of the saints (so Charles).

NOTES

14 A few of the many who identify the figure on the cloud as Christ are Beckwith, Bruce, Caird, Charles, Ford, France, Ladd, Lilje, Morris, Mounce, Walvoord, Beale, and I. H. Marshall ("Martyrdom and the Parousia in the Revelation of John," *SE* 4 [1968]: 337). Others identify the figure with an angel (Glasson, Kiddle, Beasley-Murray, Aune). However, as Beale, 771, points out, "Even calling Christ himself an angel is not necessarily problematic theologically, since the 'strong angel' of 10:1 appears to be Christ as the equivalent of the OT 'angel of the Lord' (the angel in 10:1 could also be Christ's representative). In the OT God alone comes in heaven or to earth in a cloud. . . . This reinforces the conclusion that the figure here is the divine Christ" (contra Aune, *Revelation 6–16*, 841).

18 The "sickle" is a δρέπανον (*drepanon*, GK *1535*), which is a "reaping hook" used both for reaping grain and for pruning the vine and cutting off clusters at vintage (Beckwith, 664).

20 Some commentators have seen in the number sixteen hundred stadia the approximate length of Palestine from Dan to Beersheba (so Ladd, 202). Taking four as a universal number and the multiplier forty times four, Victorinus suggested that the number was symbolic, i.e., "throughout all the four parts of the world" (cited in *ANF*, 7:357).

D. The Seven Bowls (15:1–19:10)

OVERVIEW

It is difficult to know where the divisions should fall in these further visions. Since the last series of sevens in Revelation includes the fall of Babylon under the seventh bowl (16:19), it has seemed appropriate to include the extensive description of the city's fall under the bowl-series division.

Chapter 15, a sort of celestial interlude before the final judgment, is preparatory to the execution of the bowl series described in ch. 16, while chs. 17 and 18 elaborate the fall of Babylon. What has already been anticipated under the three figures of the divine eschatological judgment—the cup of wine (14:10), the harvest of the earth (14:14–16), and the vintage (14:17–20)—is now further described under the symbolism of the seven bowls. In typical Hebrew fashion, each cycle repeats in new ways the former events and also adds fresh details not found in the former series.

It is clear that in these final judgments only the unbelieving world is involved; therefore, they are punitive plagues (16:2). Yet even in these last plagues God is concerned with effecting repentance, though none abandon their idolatry (16:9, 11). But are the faithful still on the earth? Verse 2 of ch. 15 locates the whole company of conquerors not on earth but before the throne. So intense are these final judgments that Victorinus argues, "For the wrath of God always strikes the obstinate people with seven plagues, that is, perfectly, as it is said in Leviticus; and these shall be in the last time, when the church shall have gone out of the midst" (cited in *ANF*, 7:357). It is difficult to support or refute such a view. Farrer, 155, also argues that the saints are now gone.

My position is that the inclusive series of bowl judgments constitutes the "third woe" announced in 11:14 as "coming soon" (so Alford, Beckwith, Ladd—see comments at 11:14). Since the first two woes occur under the fifth and sixth trumpets, it is reasonable to see the third woe, which involved seven plagues, as unfolding during the sounding of the seventh trumpet, when the mystery of God will be finished (10:7). The actual woe events were delayed until John could give important background material not only concerning the inhabitants of the earth but also the church herself—her glory and shame, her faithfulness and apostasy (12:1–14:20). These last plagues take place "immediately after the distress of those days" referred to by Jesus in the Olivet Discourse and may well be the fulfillment of his apocalyptic words, "The sun will be darkened, and the moon will not give its light; the stars will fall from the sky, and the heavenly bodies will be shaken" (Mt 24:29). Significantly, the next event that follows this judgment—the coming of the Son of Man in the clouds—is the same event John describes following the bowl judgments (19:11).

1. Preparatory: The Seven Angels with the Seven Last Plagues (15:1-8)

OVERVIEW

Chapter 15 is tied closely to ch. 16. Both deal with the seven last plagues of God's wrath. One is preparatory and interpretative, the other descriptive. Chapter 15 is largely oriented to the OT account of the exodus event and is strongly suggestive of the liturgical tradition of the ancient synagogue. The chapter has two main visions: the first portrays the victors who have emerged as triumphant from the great ordeal (vv.2–4); the second relates the appearance from the heavenly temple of seven angels clothed in white and gold who hold the seven bowls of the last plagues (vv.5–8).

[1]I saw in heaven another great and marvelous sign: seven angels with the seven last plagues—last, because with them God's wrath is completed. [2]And I saw what looked like a sea of glass mixed with fire and, standing beside the sea, those who had been victorious over the beast and his image and over the number of his name. They held harps given them by God [3]and sang the song of Moses the servant of God and the song of the Lamb:

"Great and marvelous are your deeds,
　Lord God Almighty.
Just and true are your ways,
　King of the ages.
[4]Who will not fear you, O Lord,
　and bring glory to your name?
For you alone are holy.
All nations will come
　and worship before you,
for your righteous acts have been revealed."

[5]After this I looked and in heaven the temple, that is, the tabernacle of the Testimony, was opened. [6]Out of the temple came the seven angels with the seven plagues. They were dressed in clean, shining linen and wore golden sashes around their chests. [7]Then one of the four living creatures gave to the seven angels seven golden bowls filled with the wrath of God, who lives for ever and ever. [8]And the temple was filled with smoke from the glory of God and from his power, and no one could enter the temple until the seven plagues of the seven angels were completed.

COMMENTARY

1 This verse forms a superscription to chs. 15 and 16. The final manifestation of the wrath of God takes the form of seven angels of judgment and is called a "sign" (sēmeion, GK 4956). This is the third explicitly identified heavenly "sign" (cf. the woman and dragon at 12:1, 3). The qualifying adjective "marvelous" (*thaumaston*, GK *2515*; cf. v.3) is apparently added because John understood the seven angels to represent the completion of God's wrath, namely, the last plagues. They are awesome as well as final in character. The word *teleō* (GK *5464*) means "to finish, bring to an end, accomplish, perform" (BDAG, 997; cf. Rev 10:7; 11:7; 15:8; 17:17; 20:3, 5, 7). While these plagues may be the finale to the whole historical panorama of God's judgments, it would be exegetically preferable to find a connection with events related in Revelation itself. As has already been argued, the first reference to the eschatological judgments is found in 6:17: "For the great day of their wrath has come, and who can stand?" After the interlude of the sealing of the saints from spiritual harm (ch. 7) the seven trumpets are sounded (8:6–9:21; 11:15–19). The sixth one involves three plagues that kill a third of mankind (9:18). The third woe (11:14) includes the bowl judgments that are called the "last" plagues. From this we may conclude that the trumpets begin the eschatological wrath of God that is finished in the seven bowls.

2 As in 14:1–5, John again focuses his attention on a scene that contrasts sharply with the coming judgment—an indication of his pastoral concern. He sees before the throne the likeness of a sea of glass shot through with fire (cf. 4:69). It is a scene of worship, and its imagery is suitable for depicting God's majesty and brilliance, which the sea of glass is reflecting in a virtual symphony of color. No further symbolic significance needs to be sought here. Firmly planted on (*epi* can also mean "beside," NIV) the sea are those who were "victorious over the beast." They are the same ones who are seen throughout Revelation as having won out over the idolatrous beasts through their faithful testimony to Christ, even to the extent of martyrdom (e.g., 2:7,

11, 26; 12:11; 21:7; cf. 3:21; 5:5). They are the 144,000, the elect of God (7:4; 14:1), the completed company of martyrs (6:11). Note the absence of "received his mark," since mention is made of the equivalent expression "the number of his name" (see comments at 13:17–18). Suddenly in this dazzling scene the sound of harps and singing is heard.

3–4 The song sung by the redeemed is the "song of Moses, the servant of God and the song of the Lamb"—a single song, as these verses show. The Song of Moses is recorded in Exodus 15:1–18. It celebrates the victory of the Lord in the defeat of the Egyptians at the Red Sea. In the ancient synagogue, it was sung in the afternoon service each Sabbath to celebrate God's sovereign rule over the universe, of which the redemption from Egypt reminds the Jew (cf. Joseph Hertz, *The Authorized Daily Prayer Book* [rev. ed.: New York: Block, 1948], 100). Such is the emphasis in the liturgical collection of psalms and prophets John quotes from (e.g., "King of the ages"). As the deliverance from Egypt, with its divine plagues of judgment on Israel's enemies, became for the Jew a signpost of God's just rule over the world, so God's eschatological judgment and the deliverance of the followers of the Lamb bring forth from the victors over the beast exuberant songs of praise to God for his righteous acts in history.

Each line in vv.3–4 picks up phrases from the Psalms and Prophets. Compare the following OT words with vv.3–4: "Then Moses and the Israelites sang this song" (Ex 15:1); "your works are wonderful" (Ps 139:14); "LORD God Almighty" (Am 4:13); "all his ways are just. A faithful God . . . , upright and just is he" (Dt 32:4); "who shall not revere you, O King of the nations" (Jer 10:7); "they will bring glory to your name" (Ps 86:9). John may or may not have heard the victors over the beast singing these actual words, but it was revealed to him that they were praising God for his mighty deliverance and judgment on their enemies. His rendering of the song may be drawn from the liturgy of the synagogue and no doubt from the early Christian church. In fact, it is precisely in connection with the ancient Easter liturgy that the church's dependence on the synagogue Passover liturgy is most easily recognizable (cf. Shepherd, 96; comments at 1:10). The Exodus background is quite obvious throughout both chs. 15 and 16 (cf. Rev 8:7–9:21). On the possible theme of resurrection in the hymn, see Notes.

5–7 A second and still more impressive scene follows. The door to the temple in heaven is again opened (cf. 11:19), and the seven angels dressed in white and gold come out of the temple. In a dignified manner, one of the living creatures gives a bowl to each of the seven messengers. The bowls (*phialē*, GK *5786*) are the vessels used in the temple ministry especially for offerings and incense (5:8). *Phialē*

translates the Hebrew *mizrāq* (a bowl for throwing liquids) in most instances in the LXX. This might have been a large banquet bowl for wine (Am 6:6), but more often it was a ritual bowl used for collecting the blood of the sacrifices (Ex 27:3). Golden bowls seem to be always associated with the temple (e.g., 1Ki 7:50; 2Ki 12:13; 25:15). *Phialē* in the Greco-Roman world was a broad, flat bowl or saucer used ritually for drinking or for pouring libations (LSJ, 1930).

8 The "smoke" that filled the temple refers to the *shekinah* cloud first associated with the tabernacle and then with the temple. It symbolizes God's special presence and the fact that he is the source of the judgments (Ex 40:34–38; 1Ki 8:10–11; Eze 11:23; 44:4). His awesome presence in the temple until the plagues are finished (16:17) prohibits even angels from entering it (cf. Isa 6:4; Hab 2:20).

NOTES

3 K. Boronicz ("'*Canticum Moysi et agni*'—Apoc. 15:3," *Ruch Biblit* 17 [1964]: 81–87) argues that according to Jewish tradition the doctrine of resurrection is implicitly contained in the Law and is exemplified by the Canticle (Song) of Moses (Ex 15:1–18). Revelation 15:3–4 has a prophetic and messianic sense and points to resurrection. In their prophetic symbolism, the Song of Moses and the Song of the Lamb are identical. Could this also be the reason why all the early church liturgies included the Song of Moses somewhere in the Easter commemoration and some also included it on other Sundays (cf. Eric Werner, *The Sacred Bridge: Liturgical Parallels in Synagogue and Early Church* [New York: Schocken, 1970], 142)?

In the ancient synagogue, the *Haftorah* (prophetic reading) accompanying the Seder on Exodus 15:1–21 was Isaiah 26:1: "In that day this song will be sung in the land of Judah. We have a strong city; God makes salvation its walls and ramparts"; and Isaiah 65:24: "Before they call I will answer; while they are still speaking I will hear." Both prophetic portions are part of the texts called "Consolation of Israel" and emphasize the strengthening of the faith of Israel (cf. Jacob Mann, *The Bible as Read and Preached in the Old Synagogue* [New York: Ktav, 1971], 1:431–32). The Song of Moses was apparently not so frequently used in the synagogue but principally in the temple services (cf. Werner, *Sacred Bridge*, 141).

6 There is good MS evidence for reading that angels were dressed in λίθον, *lithon* ("stone"), instead of λίνον, *linon* ("linen"). But the sense of "stone" is strained, and thus both Metzger, 680, and Swete argue for λίνον, *linon*, as the preferred reading.

2. Pouring Out of the Seven Bowls (16:1–21)

OVERVIEW

This chapter describes the "third woe" (see comments at Overview, ch. 15) in the form of the outpouring of seven bowl judgments. They occur in rapid succession, with only a brief pause for a dialogue between the third angel and the altar, accentuating the justice of God's punishments (vv.5–7). This rapid succession is probably due to John's desire to give a telescopic view of the first six bowls and then hasten on to the seventh, where occurs the far more interesting judgment on Babylon, of which the author will give a detailed account. Again seven symbolizes fullness—this time fullness of judgment (cf. Lev 26:21). The striking parallelism between the order of these plagues and those of the trumpets (8:2–9:21), though clearly not identical in every detail, has led many to conclude that the two series are the same. The similarity, however, may be merely literary.

Each plague in both series (the trumpets and the bowls) is reminiscent of the plagues on Egypt before the exodus. The first four in both series cover the traditional divisions of nature: earth, sea, rivers, sky. But in each of the bowls, unlike the trumpets, the plague on nature is related to the suffering of humanity. Furthermore, each bowl plague seems to be total in its effect ("every living thing ... died" [v.3]), whereas under the trumpets only a part is affected ("a third of the living creatures ... died" [8:9]). Therefore, it seems better to understand the trumpets and bowls as separate judgments, yet both are described in language drawn from the pattern of God's judgment on Egypt under Moses (see comments at 8:7–9:21). The final three plagues are social and spiritual in their effect and shift from nature to humanity.

The question arises as to whether these descriptions should be taken more or less literally. The answer is probably less literally. But the important point is that they depict God's sure and righteous judgment that will one day be literally and actually done in this world.

¹Then I heard a loud voice from the temple saying to the seven angels, "Go, pour out the seven bowls of God's wrath on the earth." ²The first angel went and poured out his bowl on the land, and ugly and painful sores broke out on the people who had the mark of the beast and worshiped his image.

³The second angel poured out his bowl on the sea, and it turned into blood like that of a dead man, and every living thing in the sea died.

⁴The third angel poured out his bowl on the rivers and springs of water, and they became blood. ⁵Then I heard the angel in charge of the waters say:

"You are just in these judgments,
    you who are and who were, the Holy One,
    because you have so judged;
⁶for they have shed the blood of your saints and prophets,
    and you have given them blood to drink as they deserve."

7And I heard the altar respond:

"Yes, Lord God Almighty,
   true and just are your judgments."

8The fourth angel poured out his bowl on the sun, and the sun was given power to scorch people with fire. 9They were seared by the intense heat and they cursed the name of God, who had control over these plagues, but they refused to repent and glorify him. 10The fifth angel poured out his bowl on the throne of the beast, and his kingdom was plunged into darkness. Men gnawed their tongues in agony 11and cursed the God of heaven because of their pains and their sores, but they refused to repent of what they had done.

12The sixth angel poured out his bowl on the great river Euphrates, and its water was dried up to prepare the way for the kings from the East. 13Then I saw three evil spirits that looked like frogs; they came out of the mouth of the dragon, out of the mouth of the beast and out of the mouth of the false prophet. 14They are spirits of demons performing miraculous signs, and they go out to the kings of the whole world, to gather them for the battle on the great day of God Almighty.

15"Behold, I come like a thief! Blessed is he who stays awake and keeps his clothes with him, so that he may not go naked and be shamefully exposed."

16Then they gathered the kings together to the place that in Hebrew is called Armageddon.

17The seventh angel poured out his bowl into the air, and out of the temple came a loud voice from the throne, saying, "It is done!" 18Then there came flashes of lightning, rumblings, peals of thunder and a severe earthquake. No earthquake like it has ever occurred since man has been on earth, so tremendous was the quake. 19The great city split into three parts, and the cities of the nations collapsed. God remembered Babylon the Great and gave her the cup filled with the wine of the fury of his wrath. 20Every island fled away and the mountains could not be found. 21From the sky huge hailstones of about a hundred pounds each fell upon men. And they cursed God on account of the plague of hail, because the plague was so terrible.

COMMENTARY

2 The first bowl has no strict counterpart in the trumpets but recalls the sixth plague (that of boils) under Moses (Ex 9:10–11). As the antagonists of Moses were affected by the boils, so the enemies of Christ who worship the beast will be struck by this plague. Perhaps "painful" sores might be translated "malignant" sores (so Swete).

3 The second bowl turns the sea into polluted blood (see comments at 8:8). Genesis 1:21 is reversed; all marine life dies (cf. Ex 7:17–21).

4 The third bowl affects the fresh waters of the earth, which are essential to human life. They too become polluted as blood (cf. Ex 7:17–21).

5–7 Here the reference to blood calls forth the dialogue between the angel and the altar concerning the logic of the plagues. The blood that sinners drink, which is poured out on them, is just requital for their shedding of the blood of the saints (15:1a) and prophets (11:3–13; cf. 17:6; 18:20). With blood God vindicates the blood of the martyrs for Jesus. God's wrath is exercised in recognition of their love. People must choose whether to drink the blood of saints or to wear robes dipped in the blood of the Lamb.

8–9 The fourth bowl increases the intensity of the sun's heat; it is the exact opposite of the fourth trumpet, which produced a plague of darkness (cf. 8:12). The earth-dwellers, instead of repenting of their deeds and acknowledging the Creator—the only act that could even now turn away God's wrath—curse (*blasphēmeō*, "slander, blaspheme," GK *1059*) God for sending them agonizing pain (vv.11, 21). Yet their problem goes beyond the awful physical pain and is moral and spiritual (cf. Isa 52:5; Ro 1:25; 2:24).

10–11 The fifth bowl plunges the kingdom of the beast into darkness. This is not a reference to the fall of the Roman Empire or Caesar worship, though John's words would include this level of meaning. In 2:13, John used the word "throne" (*thronos*, GK *2585*) to designate the stronghold of Satan at Pergamum. Thus "the throne of the beast" symbolizes the seat of worldwide dominion for the great satanic system of idolatry (the Abyss? cf. 20:1). This system is plunged into spiritual darkness or disruption, bringing chaos on all who sought life and meaning in it. Charles seeks to connect this darkness to the darkness and pain caused by the demon-locusts of the fifth trumpet (9:1–11). But in the trumpet plague the locust-demons are the direct cause of the pain, while the darkness is incidental. This bowl plague, however, though similar to the fifth trumpet, strikes at the very seat of satanic

authority over the world, and the darkness is probably moral and spiritual rather than physical (cf. 21:25; 22:5; Jn 8:12; 12:35–36, 46; 1Jn 1:5–7; 2:8–10; Wis 17:21). Again the terrible refrain is repeated: "but they refused to repent of what they had done."

12–16 The sixth bowl is specifically aimed at drying up the Euphrates River and so will allow the demonically inspired kings from the East to gather at Armageddon, where God himself will enter into battle with them. The reference to the Euphrates in the sixth trumpet is a striking parallel to the sixth bowl plague (9:14). Thus many identify the two series as different aspects of the same plagues. But while the sixth trumpet releases demonic hordes to inflict death on the earth-dwellers, the sixth bowl effects the assembling of the rulers (kings) from the East to meet the Lord God Almighty in battle.

The Euphrates marked not only the location of Babylon, the great anti-God throne, but also the place from which the evil hordes would invade Israel (see comments at 9:14). Thus in mentioning the Euphrates by name, John is suggesting that the unseen rulers of this world are being prepared to enter into a final and fatal battle with the Sovereign of the universe. It is a warfare that can be conceived of only in terms that describe realities of a primordial and eschatological order, an order that is more descriptive of contemporary actualities than political history (so Minear). Thus John does not, in my opinion, describe the invasion of the Parthian hordes advancing on Rome or any future political invasion of Israel (contra Mounce, 12). How could such political groups be involved in the battle of the great day of God Almighty? Instead, in terms reminiscent of the ancient battles of Israel, John describes the eschatological defeat of the forces of evil, the kings from the East.

13 Further confirmation that these Eastern kings represent the combined forces of evil in the world is John's reference to the three froglike evil (*akathartos*, "unclean," GK *176*) spirits that proceed out of the mouths of the dragon, the beast, and the false prophet. Frogs were considered unclean animals by the Jews (Lev 11:10, 41). The background for this figure is not clear but probably relates more to pagan metaphors for evil than to any specific OT references. To the Persians, the frog was the double of Ahriman, god of evil and agent of plagues.

To the Egyptians the frog was not loathsome, as some suggest, but the symbol of the goddess Heqt, a goddess of resurrection and fertility. In the Jewish mind, however, such gods were demons (*daimonīon*, GK *1228*; v.14), Satan's emissaries, and inseparable from idolatry (Rev 9:20; 18:2; 1Co 10:20–21). These demons produce miraculous signs, as the false prophet does (13:13–14), and this connects their activity to the deception of the earth's kings. Since these demons come from the "mouths" of the figures, lying and deceptive words are implied (cf. the sword from Christ's mouth that is equal to his word of truth). These kings are summoned to the battle of the great day of God Almighty. It is not necessary to limit John's language to the imperial emperor cult or to the Nero *redivivus* myth (see Overview, ch. 13). Under the sixth bowl the kings are only gathered; not until the seventh bowl do the confrontation and defeat actually occur (19:19–21).

15 Somewhat abruptly, but not inappropriately so, a warning is issued. Those who worship and serve the Lamb must be constantly vigilant lest their loyalty to him be diverted through the satanic deception (cf. Mt 24:43–44; 1Th 5:2, 4). The parousia (coming) of Christ is here connected with the judgment of Armageddon and the fall of Babylon. After John has described the latter in more detail (chs. 17–18), he describes the vision of the return of Jesus (19:11–16). Here in v.15 the third of the seven beatitudes is pronounced (cf. 1:3; 14:13; 19:9; 20:6; 22:7, 14).

Similar to the exhortation given to those in the churches at Sardis (3:2–4) and Laodicea (3:18), the warning about Jesus' coming "like a thief" implies a need for alertness to the deception of idolatry and disloyalty to Jesus. Like a guard who watches by night, the true Christian will remain steadfast and prepared. It is not necessary to relate this warning only to the end-time, since the appeal for the steadfast loyalty of Christians is relevant at any time. Such appeals, however, are associated in the Gospels with the return of Christ (Mk 13:32–37). There is no evidence that John is here reinterpreting the second coming of Christ, seeing that event in the crises of history, as Caird, 208, suggests. Since John's description does not refer to the Roman Empire but to the eschatological judgment, there is no need to resort to any reinterpretation hypothesis.

16 Many modern interpreters identify Armageddon with the Galilean fortified city of Megiddo and believe that a literal military battle will be fought in the latter days in that vicinity (cf. Seiss, Smith, Walvoord, Thomas; see also notes at Jdg 5:19 and Rev 16:16 in the New Scofield Reference Bible). While this sense is not impossible, it is better to take the name as being symbolic. In Hebrew, *har* means hill or mountain, while *megiddon* (Gk. *magedōn*) could mean Megiddo, a Canaanite stronghold in the Jezreel Plain later captured by the Israelites (Jos 12:21; Jdg 5:19). Megiddo, however, was a tell (artificial mound) only seventy feet high in John's day, according to Mounce, 301, not a hill or mountain—and is never designated as such, though the fact that over two hundred battles have been fought in this vicinity makes the site an appropriate symbol for the eschatological battle (so Swete). Neither can it mean Mount Carmel near Megiddo, for such a designation is never used and would be totally obscure to the residents of Asia to whom John writes and who probably were, for the most part, ignorant of Hebrew. Therefore it is better to understand the term symbolically, in the same manner as "in Hebrew" in 9:11 alerts us to the symbolic significance of the name of the angel of the Abyss.

Several other possibilities for the meaning of *har megiddon* have been suggested. Rissi, 84–85, derives the word from *har moēd* ("mount of the assembly") and connects it with Isaiah 14:12–15, where the king of Babylon, lifted up in pride, tries to ascend to the "mount of the assembly," i.e., the throne of God. While the theory is interesting, it rests on a conjectural emendation of the Greek text without any MS evidence and has no direct support from the immediate context (vv. 12–16). Another suggestion derives from the Hebrew *har megiddō* the phrase "his fruitful mountain," i.e., Jerusalem, and connects the reference to the final battle to be fought near Jerusalem (Joel 3:2; Zec 14:2–11; cited by Charles, 2:50). Caird, 207, mentions a view where *magedōn* (from *Armagedon*, "Armageddon") is related to the Hebrew *gādad*, which means "to cut, attack, maraud"; as such, with *har* ("mountain") it would mean "marauding mountain" and would be John's variation on Jeremiah's "destroying mountain" (Jer 51:25).

It is surprising that no one has suggested taking *magedōn* as deriving from the secondary sense of the Hebrew *gādad*, meaning "to gather in troops or bands" (BDB, 151). The simple way in Hebrew to make a noun from a verb is to prefix a *ma* to the verbal form. Thus we have *maged*, "a place of gathering in troops," and the suffix *ō*, meaning "his," yielding "his place of gathering in troops." This is almost equivalent to the expressions in vv. 14, 16— "to gather them [the kings] for the battle on the great day of God Almighty"—and would allude to the prophetic expectation of the gathering of the nations for judgment (Joel 3:2, 12).

In any case, the name is symbolic and probably does not refer to any geographical location we can now identify, whether in Palestine or elsewhere; but it describes the eschatological confrontation where God will meet the forces of evil in their final defeat. As Mounce, 302, states, "Har-Magedon is symbolic of the final overthrow of all the forces of evil by the might and power of God. The great conflict between God and Satan, Christ and Antichrist, good and evil, which lies behind the perplexing course of history will in the end issue in a final struggle in which God will emerge victorious and take with him all who placed their faith in him. This is Har-Magedon." Nevertheless, the name refers to a real point in history and to real persons who will encounter God's just sentence.

17–21 The seventh bowl is poured into the air. Nothing further is said about the "air"; rather, John is concerned with the loud voice that cries out, "It is done" (*gegonen*, GK *1181*), or, "It has come to pass." With this seventh bowl, the eschatological wrath of God is completed (cf. 6:17; 21:6; Jn 19:30). Flashes of lightning, peals of thunder, and a severe earthquake occur (cf. 4:5; 8:5; 11:19). These eschatological signs symbolize the destruction of the anti-God forces throughout the world (cf. Heb 12:27). So great is the earthquake of God's judgment that it reaches the strongholds of organized evil represented by the cities of the pagans (*ethnē*, "nations," GK *1620*). Even the great city Babylon, which seduced all the earth's kings and inhabitants (17:2), now comes under final sentence (see comments at 11:8).

The judgment of Babylon will occupy John's attention in chs. 17 and 18. While the catastrophe continues to be described in geophysical terms (islands and mountains disappearing, huge hailstones accompanying a gigantic storm), there is a question whether John intends the destruction to be merely natural or even of politico-historical entities, or to be exclusively of the unseen powers of evil. Like the Egyptian plague of hail that further hardened Pharaoh's heart, this plague of hail falls on the unrepentant to no avail; they curse God for sending his judgment on them (cf. Ex 9:24). By such language, John describes the rising pitch of God's wrath on the rebellious powers of the earth. His words should not be politicized as though he spoke merely of Rome or of some impending historical crisis for the church. He is speaking of the great realities of the end, when God has put down all his enemies.

3. The Woman and the Beast (17:1–18)

OVERVIEW

In an important sense, the interpretation of this chapter controls the interpretation of the whole book of Revelation. For a majority of exegetes, Babylon represents the city of Rome. The beast stands for the Roman Empire as a whole, with its subject provinces and peoples. The seven hills (v.9) are the seven selected dynasties of Roman emperors from Augustus to Domitian. The ten kings are heads of lesser and restless states eager to escape their enslavement to the colonizing power. John's prediction of the fall of Babylon is his announcement of the impending dissolution of the Roman Empire in all its aspects. For such a view there is considerable evidence. Babylon was a term used by both Jews and Christians for Rome (2 Bar. 11:1; Sib. Or. 5:143, 158; 1Pe 5:13; Hippolytus, Christ and Antichrist 36; TDNT 1:516). Rome was a great city (v.18), a city set on seven hills (v.9); by the time of Domitian (AD 85) it was notorious for persecuting and killing the saints (v.6). Thus the argument goes. Many scholars of unquestioned competence have been fully convinced of the certainty of these equations.

Yet there is evidence that casts doubt on this exegesis and impels us to look for a more adequate, if also more subtle, understanding of John's intention. It is simply not sufficient to identify Rome and Babylon. For that matter, Babylon cannot be confined to any one historical manifestation, past or future. Babylon has multiple equivalents (cf. 11:8). The details of John's description do not neatly fit any past city, whether literal Babylon, Sodom, Egypt, Rome, or even Jerusalem. Babylon is found wherever there is satanic deception. It is defined more by dominant idolatries than geographic or temporal boundaries. The ancient Babylon is better understood here as the archetypal head of all entrenched worldly resistance to God. Babylon is a transhistorical reality that includes idolatrous kingdoms as diverse as Sodom, Gomorrah, Egypt, Babylon, Tyre, Nineveh, and Rome. Babylon is an eschatological symbol of satanic deception and power; it is a divine mystery that can never be wholly reducible to empirical earthly institutions. It may be said that Babylon represents the total culture of the world apart from God, while the divine system is depicted by the new Jerusalem. Rome is simply one manifestation of the total system.

Chapters 17 and 18 form one continuous unit dealing with the judgment on Babylon. The woman is identified as the great city (17:18) whose fall is described in ch. 18. From internal evidence, the identification of Babylon the woman (ch. 17) as Babylon the great city (ch. 18) is so unmistakable that it would be inappropriate to make them different entities. Neither should ch. 17 be viewed as an interpolation, as some have suggested (so Rissi, "Kerygma of the Revelation to John," 4), simply on the grounds that it seems to be politically specific in the manner of ordinary Jewish apocalyptics (see Introduction: "General Nature and Historical Background"). While the Roman Empire theory leads more readily to this conclusion, if we reject it, the contents of chs. 17 and 18 are wholly compatible with John's emphasis elsewhere. These two chapters form an extended appendix to the seventh bowl, where the judgment on Babylon was mentioned

(16:19). They also expand the earlier references to this city (11:8; 14:8) and look forward by way of contrast to the eternal Holy City (chs. 21–22).

Chapter 17 may be divided as follows: the vision of the great harlot (vv.1–6) and the interpretation of the vision (vv.7–18). In suspenseful literary fashion, John first describes the nature of the harlot and the beast she rides (ch. 17); he then describes her momentous fall in terms drawn from the OT descriptions of the fall of great cities (ch. 18).

¹One of the seven angels who had the seven bowls came and said to me, "Come, I will show you the punishment of the great prostitute, who sits on many waters. ²With her the kings of the earth committed adultery and the inhabitants of the earth were intoxicated with the wine of her adulteries."

³Then the angel carried me away in the Spirit into a desert. There I saw a woman sitting on a scarlet beast that was covered with blasphemous names and had seven heads and ten horns. ⁴The woman was dressed in purple and scarlet, and was glittering with gold, precious stones and pearls. She held a golden cup in her hand, filled with abominable things and the filth of her adulteries. ⁵This title was written on her forehead:

MYSTERY
BABYLON THE GREAT
THE MOTHER OF PROSTITUTES
AND OF THE ABOMINATIONS OF THE EARTH.

⁶I saw that the woman was drunk with the blood of the saints, the blood of those who bore testimony to Jesus.

When I saw her, I was greatly astonished. ⁷Then the angel said to me: "Why are you astonished? I will explain to you the mystery of the woman and of the beast she rides, which has the seven heads and ten horns. ⁸The beast, which you saw, once was, now is not, and will come up out of the Abyss and go to his destruction. The inhabitants of the earth whose names have not been written in the book of life from the creation of the world will be astonished when they see the beast, because he once was, now is not, and yet will come.

⁹"This calls for a mind with wisdom. The seven heads are seven hills on which the woman sits. ¹⁰They are also seven kings. Five have fallen, one is, the other has not yet come; but when he does come, he must remain for a little while. ¹¹The beast who once was, and now is not, is an eighth king. He belongs to the seven and is going to his destruction.

¹²"The ten horns you saw are ten kings who have not yet received a kingdom, but who for one hour will receive authority as kings along with the beast. ¹³They have one purpose and will give their power and authority to the beast. ¹⁴They will make war against the Lamb, but the Lamb will overcome them because he is Lord of lords and King of kings— and with him will be his called, chosen and faithful followers."

¹⁵Then the angel said to me, "The waters you saw, where the prostitute sits, are peoples, multitudes, nations and languages. ¹⁶The beast and the ten horns you saw will hate the

prostitute. They will bring her to ruin and leave her naked; they will eat her flesh and burn her with fire. [17] For God has put it into their hearts to accomplish his purpose by agreeing to give the beast their power to rule, until God's words are fulfilled. [18] The woman you saw is the great city that rules over the kings of the earth."

COMMENTARY

1 "One of the seven angels" connects this vision with the preceding bowl judgments, showing that it is a further expansion or appendix of the final bowl action and not an additional event.

John sees a great prostitute (*pornē*, GK *4520*) established on many waters. The verse forms a superscription for the chapter. The relationship between prostitution (*porneia*) and idolatry has already been discussed (see comments at 2:14, 20). The prevalence of cult prostitution throughout the ancient world makes this figure appropriate for idolatrous worship. The expressions "abominable things" (17:4) and "magic spell" (18:23) confirm this connection. In the OT, the same figure of a harlot city is used of Nineveh (Na 3:4), of Tyre (Isa 23:16–17), and frequently of idolatrous Jerusalem (Eze 16:15–42). The best background for understanding the language of the chapter is not the history of the Roman Empire or pagan god parallels but the descriptions of Jerusalem the harlot in Ezekiel 16 and 23 and Babylon the harlot in Jeremiah 51. A quick reading of these chapters will confirm the many parallels to John's language.

But the great prostitute (*pornē*) Babylon described in Revelation is not any mere historical city with its inhabitants, whether in John's past, present, or future. Rather, this city is the mother of all these historical prostitutes, the archetypal source of every idolatrous manifestation in time and space. Therefore, it is as much a mistake to identify Babylon with Rome (though most scholars do [recently Mounce, 310]) as with Jerusalem (so Ford, 285). Babylon could equally well be seen in any of these classic manifestations from the past or in modern times—Nazi Germany, Idi Amin's Ugandan regime, Stalin's Soviet Russia, Mao's China, British colonialism, Saddam Hussein's Iraq, or even in aspects of American life (so William Stringfellow, *An Ethic for Christians and Other Aliens in a Strange Land* [Waco, Tex.: Word, 1973]).

Amazingly, all the harlot-city societies mentioned in Scripture have certain common characteristics also reflected in John's description of the great Babylon, in which he merges the descriptions of ancient Babylon, Tyre, and Jerusalem into one great composite. Royal dignity and splendor, combined with prosperity, overabundance, and luxury (Jer 51:13; Eze 16:13, 49; Na 2:9; cf. Rev 18:3, 7, 16–17); self-trust or boastfulness (Isa 14:12–14; Jer 50:31; Eze 16:15, 50, 56; 27:3; 28:5; cf. Rev 18:7); power and violence, especially against God's people (Jer 51:35, 49; Eze 23:37; Na 3:1–3; cf. Rev 18:10, 24); oppression and injustice (Isa 14:4; Eze 16:49; 28:18; cf. Rev 18:5, 20); and idolatry (Jer 51:47; Eze 16:17, 36; 23:7, 30, 49; Na 1:14; cf. Rev 17:4–5; 18:3; 19:2)—they are all here. Wherever and whenever these characteristics have been manifested historically, *there* is the appearance of Babylon.

The great prostitute "sits on many waters." This goes back to Jeremiah's oracle against historical Babylon, situated along the waterways of the Euphrates, with many canals around the city greatly multiplying its wealth by trade (Jer 51:13). While the description alludes to ancient Babylon, it also has a deeper significance, explained in v.15 as "peoples, multitudes, nations and languages"—figurative for the vast influence of the prostitute on the peoples of the world.

2 Earth's kings and inhabitants committed fornication with the prostitute. This language goes back to references to the harlot cities of the past (e.g., Jer 51:7) and means that the peoples of the world have become drunk with abundance, power, pride, violence, and especially false worship. The expression "kings of the earth" may be in poetic synonymous parallelism (i.e., an equivalent term) with "inhabitants of the earth." If this were so, the exegesis of the former term would be enriched. The evidence for this is not conclusive, however (cf. 14:8; 17:4–5; 18:3, 9). "The kings of the earth" may simply describe the rulers in contrast to the hoi polloi.

3 John is carried in the Spirit (see comments at 1:10 and cf. 4:2; 21:10) into a "desert." Again the allusion is to ancient Babylon (Isa 14:23; 21:1; cf. Rev 18:2; see comments at 12:6). Caird, 213, following the imagery of 12:6, thinks that John was taken to the desert to be free from the charms and attractions of the whore so that he could understand her exact nature. Yet it is in the desert that he sees the prostitute seated on "a scarlet beast"—scarlet, presumably, because the color symbolizes the beast's blasphemy in contrast to the white-horse rider and those dressed in white, who are faithful and true (19:8, 11, 14). Since this beast is a seven-headed monster, there is no cogent reason against identifying it with the first beast in ch. 13, which is also inseparable from the seven-headed dragon of ch. 12.

4 Dressed in queenly attire (Eze 16:13; cf. Rev 18:7) the woman rides the beast, swinging in her hand a golden cup full of her idolatrous abominations and wickedness. Note the contrast—beauty and gross wickedness. Her costly and comely attire suggests the prostitute's outward beauty and attractiveness (Jer 4:30). The golden cup filled with wine alludes to Jeremiah's description of Babylon's worldwide influence in idolatry (Jer 51:7). Her cup is filled with "abominable things" (*bdelygmatōn*, GK *1007*). The *bdelygmatōn* are most frequently associated with idolatry, which was abhorrent to Jews and Christians alike (Rev 21:27). It is the same word Jesus used in referring to Daniel's "abomination that causes desolation" standing in the temple (Mk 13:14; cf. Da 9:27; 11:31; 12:11). Babylon is the archetype of all idolatrous obscenities in the earth (v.5). "Filth" (*akathartos*, "uncleannesses") is a word frequently associated in the NT with evil (unclean) spirits (e.g., Mt 10:1; 12:43) and also with idolatry (2Co 6:17) and perhaps cult prostitution (Eph 5:5).

5 The woman has a title written on her forehead, showing that in spite of all her royal glamour she is nothing but a prostitute. From the writings of Seneca and Juvenal, we know that it was the custom for Roman prostitutes to wear their names in the fillet that encircled their brows (cf. Swete, 214). The OT also refers to the peculiar brow of the prostitute (Jer 3:3, "a harlot's brow," NEB).

The first word in the woman's title is MYSTERY (*mystērion*, GK *3696*; cf. 1:20; 10:7; 17:7). But does the word belong to the name "MYSTERY BABYLON" itself, or is it a prefix before the actual name—"She has a name written on her forehead, which is a mystery, 'Babylon . . .'"? Scholars disagree, but the latter explanation fits better with John's use of *mystērion* as a word denoting a divine mystery or allegory that is now revealed. Furthermore, his use of *pneumatikōs* ("figuratively," GK *4462*) before the words "Sodom and Egypt" in 11:8, by which the reader is alerted to a special symbolic significance in what follows, likewise supports this.

No doubt, as Lilje, 223, suggests, the specific part of the title that is a divine mystery is that this prostitute is the *mother* of all the earth's idolatrous prostitutes. She is the fountainhead, the reservoir, the womb that bears all the individual cases of historical resistance to God's will on earth; she is the unholy antithesis to the woman who weds the Lamb (19:7–8) and to the new Jerusalem (21:2–3). Therefore, she cannot be merely ancient Babylon, Rome, or Jerusalem, because these are only her children—*she* is the mother of them all. While at its beginning Babel was associated with resisting and defying God (Ge 11:1–11), it is probably the epoch of the Babylonian captivity of Israel that indelibly etched the proud, idolatrous, and repressive nature of Babylon on the memories of God's people and thus provided for succeeding generations the symbolic image that could be applied to the further manifestations of the mother prostitute.

6 This mother prostitute is also the source of the shed blood of the followers of Jesus, the martyrs referred to throughout the book (6:9; 7:9–17; 13:8; 18:24). The same mother harlot who had killed the saints of old throughout salvation history is now also responsible for the deaths of the Christians (cf. 2:13). Though there is no direct reference here to Rome or Jerusalem, early Christian readers would understand that whenever they were threatened with death by any temporal power—whether political, religious, or both—they were in reality facing the bloodthirsty mother prostitute God was about to judge and destroy once for all. To be drunk with blood was a familiar figure in the ancient world for the lust for violence (Charles, 2:66; cf. Isa 34:7; 49:26).

7–18 These verses contain an extended interpretation of the vision that parallels the method used in apocalyptic sections in OT prophecy (cf. the prophetic visions in Zec 1:7–6:8). First the beast is described and identified (vv.7–8), then the seven heads (vv.9–11), the ten horns (vv.12–14), the waters (v.15), and finally the woman (v.18). John's astonishment over the arresting figure of the woman on the beast is quickly subdued by the interpreting angel's announcement that to John will be revealed the divine mystery of the symbolic imagery of woman and beast.

Much difficulty in interpreting this section has resulted from incorrectly applying John's words either to the succession of Roman emperors (the seven heads), to the Nero *redivivus* myth ("once was, now is not, and will come up out of the Abyss" [v.8; see comments at Overview, ch. 13]), or to a succession of world empires. None of these views are satisfactory for reasons that will be stated below. John's description is theological, not political. He describes a reality behind earth's sovereigns, not the successive manifestations in history. When this is seen to be the case, it is unnecessary to revert to source theories (contra Beasley-Murray, "The Revelation," 1300), interpolation theories (Charles, 2:67; Eller, 165–67), or other theories in an attempt to relate John's descriptive language to past events.

8 The beast is the monster from the Abyss, i.e., the satanic incarnation of idolatrous power, described in 13:1–10, mentioned earlier in 11:7, and whose destruction is seen in 19:19–20. John is told that the beast "once was, now is not, and will come up out of the Abyss." This seems clearly to be a paraphrase of the idea in 13:3, 14 of the sword-wounded beast who was healed; the language is similar, the astonishment of the world's inhabitants identical, and the threefold emphasis on this spectacular feature repeated in both contexts (13:3, 12, 14; 17:8, 11).

The play here on the tenses, "was, . . . is not, . . . will come," refers to a three-stage history of the beast that requires a mind with wisdom to understand its mystery. Isaiah refers to the chaos monster as "Rahab the Do-Nothing," i.e., the monster thought to energize Egypt is in reality inactive, rendered impotent by the hand of the Lord (Isa 30:7). That John's beast "is not" refers to his defeat by the Lamb on Calvary. To those who worship only the Father and Son, all other gods are nothing or nonexistent (1Co 8:4–6). Satan once had unchallenged power over the earth ("was," cf. Lk 4:6; Heb 2:14–15).

Now he is a defeated sovereign ("is not"; cf. Jn 12:31–32); yet he is given a "little time" to oppose God and his people (12:12c; 13:5; 20:3b) before his final sentencing to destruction (*apōleia,* GK *724;* v.11; cf. Mt 7:13; Jn 17:12; Ro 9:22; 2Th 2:3). It is this apparent revival of Satan's power and authority over the world after his mortal wound (Ge 3:15) that causes the deceived of earth to follow him.

Note the subtle change in perspective from the way the first reference to the beast is stated (v.8a) to that of the second (v.8b). Whereas the first instance refers to his satanic origin ("out of the Abyss") and his final destruction (a divine revelation to believers), the second simply states how that he was, is not, and yet comes (an unbeliever's view). This twofold viewpoint is paralleled in vv.9–11 where one of the kings "is" (v.10) and an eighth king "is" (v.11), yet the beast "is not" (v.11). There seems to be an intentional doubletalk whereby the author seeks to identify theologically the nature of the power that supports the profligate woman.

John's use of the present tense for the beast's coming up out of the Abyss (*anabainein,* GK *326;* cf. 11:7) may suggest a continuing aspect of his character, similar to the use of the present tense to describe the new Jerusalem descending from heaven (*katabainousa,* GK *2849;* cf. 3:12; 21:2, 10). That the beast goes to perdition (present tense) may likewise indicate one of his continuing characteristics. There is also a possible parallelism in the expression "once was, now is not, and will come" with the divine attributes described in the phrase "who is, and who was, and who is to come" (1:8). On the meaning of the book of life, see comments at 3:5 (cf. 13:8).

9 This and the following verses form the heart of the Roman emperor view of the Apocalypse. The woman not only sits on many waters (vv.1, 15) and on the beast (v.3), but she also sits on seven hills. As previously stated, most scholars have no doubt that the seven hills refer to the seven hills of Rome, and

the seven kings to seven successive emperors of that nation. Mounce, 315, states, "There is little doubt that a first-century reader would understand this reference in any way other than as a reference to Rome, the city built upon seven hills."

Yet there is very good reason to doubt that this interpretation in its various forms is the meaning John intended. The following dissenting view is drawn largely from Minear, 237. In the first place, the seven hills belong to the monster, not the woman. It is the woman (i.e., the city [v.18]) who sits on (i.e., has mastery over) the seven heads (or seven hills) of the monster. If the woman is the city of Rome, it is obvious that she did not exercise mastery over seven successive Roman emperors that are also seven traditional hills of Rome. This introduces an unwarranted twisting of the symbolism to fit a preconceived interpretation. Also, how could the seven hills of Rome have any real importance to the diabolical nature of the beast or the woman? Nor does it help to make the prostitute the Roman Empire and the hills the city of Rome (so Kiddle), since the woman is explicitly identified in v.18 not as the empire but as the city. In fact, nowhere in the NT is Rome described as the enemy of the church.

If it is argued that what is really important in the mention of the seven hills is the identification with Rome, how then does this require any special divine wisdom ("this calls for a mind with wisdom" [v.9])? Caird notes that any Roman soldier who knew Greek could figure out that the seven hills referred to Rome. But whenever divine wisdom is called for, the description requires theological and symbolical discernment, not mere geographical or numerical insight (cf. comments at 13:18). Those who follow Charles and argue for a fusing of sources or images to explain the dual reference to the hills and kings simply evade the implications of the incongruity they have created.

In the seven other instances of the word *orē* in Revelation, it is always rendered "mountain," except here in 17:9, where it is translated "hills" (see Notes). Is this a case where previous exegesis has influenced even the best translations (KJV has "mountains")? On the other hand, in the Prophets mountains allegorically refer to world powers (Isa 2:2; Jer 51:25; Da 2:35; Zec 4:7). It seems better, then, to interpret the seven mountains as a reference to the seven heads or kings, which describe not the city but the beast. The expression "they are also seven kings" (v.10) seems to require strict identification of the seven mountains with seven kings rather than with a geographic location.

John's use of numbers elsewhere in the book likewise argues against the Roman Empire identification. He has already shown a strong disposition for their symbolic significance (e.g., seven churches, seals, trumpets, bowls, and thunders; twenty-four elders; 144,000 sealed, etc.). By his use of seven he indicates completeness or wholeness. The seven heads of the beast symbolize fullness of blasphemy and evil. It is much like our English idiom "the seven seas," i.e., all the seas of the world. Caird, 218–19, recognizes the patent absurdity of trying to take the symbolic number seven and make it refer to exactly seven Roman emperors; yet he goes on to explain the seven kings as a reference to an indefinite number of emperors, including Nero *redivivus*. While Caird's view is much more in keeping with John's symbolism, it still labors under the unacceptable assumption that John is identifying the beast with Rome and alludes to the Nero *redivivus* myth.

10 If the seven heads symbolically represent the complete or full source of evil power and blasphemy, why does John talk about five fallen heads or kings, one existing head or king, and one yet to come? Does this not most readily fit the view of dynastic successions to the imperial throne? To be sure, there have been many attempts to fit the date

of Revelation (the then contemporary king would be he who "is") into the emperor lists of the first century (for detailed discussions, see Caird, 217–18; Ford, 289–91). But immediately there are problems. Where do we begin—with Julius Caesar or Caesar Augustus? Are we to count all the emperors, or just those who fostered emperor worship? Are we to exclude Galba, Otho, and Vitellius, who had short, rival reigns? If so, how can they be excluded, except on a completely arbitrary basis? A careful examination of the historic materials yields no satisfactory solution. If Revelation were written under Nero, there would be too few emperors; if under Domitian, too many. The original readers would have had no more information on these emperor successions than we do, and possibly even less. How many Americans can immediately name the last seven presidents? Furthermore, how could the eighth emperor, who is identified as the beast, also be one of the seven (v.11)?

Recognizing these problems, others have sought different solutions to John's five-one-one succession of kings. Since the word "king" may also represent kingdoms, Seiss, 393 (followed by Ladd, Walvoord, Thomas), has suggested an interpretation that takes the five-one-one to refer to successive world kingdoms that have oppressed God's people: Egypt, Assyria, Babylon, Persia, Greece (five fallen), Rome (one is), and a future world kingdom. While this solves some of the emperor succession problems and fits nicely, it too must admit arbitrary omissions, such as the devastating persecution of the people of God under the Seleucids of Syria—especially Antiochus IV Epiphanes. This view also suffers in failing to respect the symbolic significance of John's use of seven throughout the book. Also, how can these kings (kingdoms) survive the destruction of the harlot and be pictured as mourning over her demise (18:9)? And what logical sense can be made of the fact that the seventh king (kingdom), usually identified with Antichrist, is separate from the eighth king (kingdom), which is clearly identified with the beast (vv.10b–11)?

A convincing interpretation of the seven kings must do justice to three considerations: (1) Since the heads belong to the beast, the interpretation must relate their significance to the beast, not to Babylon. (2) Since the primary imagery of kingship in Revelation is a feature of the power conflict between the Lamb and the beast and between those who share the rule of these two enemies (cf. 17:14–19:19), the kind of sovereignty expressed in 17:10 must be the true antithesis to the kind of sovereignty exercised by Christ and his followers. (3) Since the kings are closely related to the seven mountains and to the prostitute, the nature of the relationship between these must be clarified by the interpretation (cf. Minear, 240).

If we can see that the seven heads do not represent a quantitative measure but show qualitatively the fullness of evil power residing in the beast, then the falling of five heads conveys the message of a significant victory over the beast. The image of a falling sovereignty is better related to God's judgment on a power than to a succession of kings/kingdoms (cf. Jer 50:32; 51:8, 49; Rev 14:8; 18:2).

The imagery of the seven heads presented in 12:3 and 13:1 must be restudied. The ancient seal showing the seven-headed chaos monster being slain (see comments at 13:1b) well illustrates John's imagery here. In that ancient scene, the seven-headed monster is being slain by a progressive killing of its seven heads. Four of the heads are dead, killed apparently by the spear of a divine figure attacking the monster. His defeat seems imminent. Yet the chaos monster is still active because three heads still live. Similarly, John's message is that five of the monster's seven heads are already defeated by the power of the Lamb's death and by the identification in that death of the martyrs of Jesus (12:11).

One head is now active, thus showing the reality of the beast's contemporary agents who afflict the saints; and one head remains, indicating that the battle will soon be over but not with the defeat of the contemporary evil agents. This last manifestation of the beast's blasphemous power will be short—"he must remain for a little while." This statement seems to go with the function of the ten horns (kings) who for "one hour" (v.12) will rule with the beast. The seventh king (head) represents the final short display of satanic evil before the divine blow falls on the beast (cf. 12:12c; 20:3c).

11 This verse presents interpreters with a real difficulty. One common interpretation refers the language to the Nero *redivivus* myth (see comments at Overview, ch. 13)—i.e., a revived Nero will be the reincarnation of the evil genius of the whole Roman Empire (Beasley-Murray, "The Revelation," 1300). Furthermore, among futurist interpreters there is no agreement as to whether the seventh or the eighth king is the Antichrist. It must be admitted that any king(dom) succession hypothesis founders on v.11. On the other hand, if John has in mind qualitative identification, not quantitative (i.e., a theological rather than historical or political sense), the passage may yield further insight into the mystery of the beast.

First, we note the strange (to us) manner in which the sequence of seven kings gives way to the eighth, which is really the whole beast. This pattern of "seven to eight equals one" was familiar to the early church. It is a concept those raised in the great liturgical traditions can grasp. The eighth day was the day of the resurrection of Christ—Sunday. It was also the beginning of a new week. The seventh day, the Jewish Sabbath, is held over to be replaced by the first of a new series, namely, Sunday. Austin Farrer, 70–71, has noted how even the whole theme of the Apocalypse is integrally related to this idea. "Sunday is the day of Resurrection. The 'week' with which the Apocalypse deals extends from the Resurrection of Christ to the General Resurrection, when death has been destroyed." He further states the relation between the seventh and eighth: "God rests from his completed work, but in so resting he initiates a new act which is the eighth-and-first day. We may compare the Gospel once more. On the sixth day Christ conquered, and achieved his rest from the labours of his flesh. But the sabbath-day which follows is in itself nothing, it has no content: it is simply the restful sepulchre out of which, with the eighth and first day, the resurrection springs."

Each of the series of sevens in the book, except for the seven churches, follows a pattern of the seventh in the series becoming the first of a new series; thus seven to eight equals one. The eighth was the day of the Messiah, the day of the new age and the sign of the victory over the forces of evil (cf. Alexander Schmemann, *Introduction to Liturgical Theology* [London: Faith, 1966], 60–64). Shepherd, 20–21, 80, also calls attention to this phenomenon in Revelation. But does this provide a key to interpreting the symbolism of the chaos monster?

Of the three stages of the beast—was, is not, will come—only the last is related to his coming "up out of the Abyss" (v.8). These words appear to be the equivalent of the beast's healed wound (plague) mentioned in 13:3, 14. While on the one hand Christ has killed the monster by his death (Ge 3:15; Rev 12:7–9)—and for believers the monster "is not" (has no power)—yet on the other hand the beast still has life ("one is" [v.10]) and will attempt one final battle against the Lamb and his followers ("the other has not yet come; . . . he must remain for a little while"). In order to recruit as many as possible for his side of the war, the beast will imitate the resurrection of Christ (he "is an eighth king" [v.11]) and will give the appearance that he is alive and in control of the world (cf. Lk 4:5–7). But for

the pastoral comfort of God's people, John quickly adds that the beast belongs to the seven, i.e., qualitatively, not numerically (as though he were a former king revived); he is in reality (to the eyes of the saints) not a new beginning of life but a part of the seven-headed monster that has been slain by Christ, and therefore he goes "to his destruction." While this imagery may seem to us unnecessarily obscure, it reveals the true mystery of the beast in a fashion that exposes the dynamics of satanic deception so that every Christian may be forearmed.

12–14 Here John seems to allude to Daniel 7:7, 24. The ten horns are usually understood as either native rulers of Roman provinces serving under the emperors or native rulers of satellite states, or governors of Palestine. Others see in them a ten-nation confederacy of the future revived Roman Empire (so Walvoord, 254–55). There are good reasons for abandoning these explanations. In the first place, the number ten should—like most of John's numbers—be understood symbolically. Ten symbolizes a repeated number of times or an indefinite number. It is perhaps another number like seven, indicating fullness (Ne 4:12; Da 1:12; Rev 2:10). Thus the number should not be understood as referring specifically to ten kings (kingdoms) but as indicating the multiplicity of sovereignties in confederacy that enhance the power of the beast.

Second, since these kings enter into a power conflict with the Lamb and his followers (v.14), the kind of sovereignty they exercise must be the true antithesis of the kind of sovereignty the Lamb and his followers exercise. These rulers and the beast with which they will be allied can be no other than the principalities and powers, the rulers of the darkness of this world, the spiritual forces of evil in the heavenly realms that Paul describes as the true enemies of Jesus' followers (Eph 6:12). To be sure, they use earthly instruments, but their reality is far greater than any specific historical equivalents (see Notes). These "kings" embody the fullness of Satan's attack against the Lamb in the great eschatological showdown. They are the "kings from the East" (16:12–14, 16), and they are also the "kings of the earth" who ally themselves with the beast in the final confrontation with the Lamb (19:19–21).

Finally, there is a link between v.12 and v.11. The ten kings are said to receive authority for "one hour" along with the beast. This corresponds to the "little while" of the seventh king. From the viewpoint of the saints, who will be greatly persecuted, this promise of brevity brings comfort.

13 These kings have "one purpose" (*gnōmē*, GK *1191*); they agree to oppose the Lamb. But the Lamb will overcome them because he is Lord of lords and King of kings (cf. Dt 10:17; Da 2:47; Rev 19:16). He conquers by his death, and those who are with him also aid in the defeat of the beast by their loyalty to the Lamb, even to death (cf. 5:5, 9; 12:11)—a sobering thought.

15 On first reading, this verse appears to be out of place. However, closer examination shows that v.16 also refers to the prostitute and the horns. Verse 15 teaches that the influence of the idolatrous satanic system of Babylon is universal (cf. vv.1–2) and embraces all peoples, from the humblest to the kings of the earth.

16–17 On these verses the Roman hypothesis (empire and city) breaks down. For in that view, the emperors (the beast and its heads) will turn against the city or empire and destroy her. Swete, 222, tries to locate this event in Rome's history and argues that there is some supporting evidence for it. But the attempt is unconvincing. Rather, the attack on the prostitute indicates that in the final judgment the kingdom of Satan, by divine purpose, will be divided against itself. The references

to the prostitute being hated by her former lovers, stripped naked, and burned with fire are reminiscent of the OT prophets' descriptions of the divine judgment falling on the harlot cities of Jerusalem and Tyre (e.g., Eze 16:39–40; 23:25–27; 28:18). The description of the punishment of convicted prostitutes who are priests' daughters (cf. Lev 21:9; the burning with fire is explained by Ford, 55, as "a pouring of molten lead down their throats") is combined with the picture of judgment against rebellious cities (18:8). Caird, 221, aptly captures the meaning of John's imagery in v.16: "The ravaging of the whore by the monster and its horns is John's most vivid symbol for the self-destroying power of evil."

17 In the declaration "God has put it into their hearts to accomplish his purpose," there is another indication of God's use of the forces of evil as instruments of his own purposes of judgment (Jer 25:9–14; cf. Lk 20:18). Nothing will distract them from their united effort to destroy the prostitute till God's purposes given through the prophets are fulfilled (cf. 10:7; 11:18).

18 The "woman" and "the great city" are one. Yet this city is not just a historical one; it is the *great* city, the *mother* city, the archetype of every evil system opposed to God in history—a billing that Rome cannot fit (see comments at Overview, ch. 17). Her kingdom holds sway over the powers of the earth. John's concept of the city in Revelation entails much more than a specific historical city, even in its political and sociological aspects. The cities in Revelation are communities; they are twofold: the city of God, the new Jerusalem (3:12; 21:2, 10; 22:2–5), and the city of Satan, Babylon the Great (11:8; 14:8; 16:19; 18:4, 20). The meaning cannot be confined to Sodom or Egypt or Jerusalem or Rome or any future city. Instead, John describes the real trans-historical system of satanic evil that infuses them all.

NOTES

1–18 For Minear's general view, see *I Saw a New Earth*, 228–46; Minear, "Babylon in the New Testament," *IDB* 1:338. While Ford, 216, presents five good reasons why Babylon cannot be the city of Rome, she falls into a similar error by identifying the city as Jerusalem. But Jerusalem, like Rome, is only one of the multiple manifestations of Babylon in history. Josephus (*Ant.* 15.97) refers to Cleopatra in language very similar to that of the Apocalypse, but as a historical type Jezebel would probably come closer to John's imagery (cf. comments at 2:20).

The Greek πόρνη (*pornē*, "prostitute") may be either male or female, married or unmarried. The word is generally used of unmarried sexual relationships (μοιχεία, *moicheia*, GK *3657*, is used for extramarital relations, i.e., adultery and cult prostitution), but it can denote sexual perversions in general, whether among married or unmarried persons (*TDNT* 6:579–95).

8 Ladd, 230–31, following Zahn, interprets the play on tenses in a more literal manner, understanding the reference to the beast as the beast that "was" and as pointing to the Syrian king Antiochus Epiphanes IV, the great persecutor of God's people in the days of the Maccabees (ca. 167 BC). There is some support for this view in Daniel 8:9, 21. But the beast that "was" could just as well have been the emperor Vespasian, who ordered Jerusalem destroyed in AD 70 by Titus. Or it could also refer to Nero, who undertook an attack on Christians in the city of Rome a short time earlier.

9 Translations that render ὄρος (*oros*, GK *4001*) as "hills" include the RSV, NEB, TEV, NLT, NIV, TNIV; those translating the word as "mountains" include the KJV, ASV, NASB, NRSV. Places in Revelation where ὄρος, *oros*, occurs and is translated "mountain(s)" in almost all versions are 6:14–16; 8:8; 14:1; 16:20; 21:10. The Shepherd of Hermas (*Sim.* 9.17) refers to a vision of "twelve mountains" that are interpreted symbolically as the twelve tribes of Israel. The coinage of Vespasian depicts the goddess of the city, Roma, enthroned on the seven hills, with the Tiber and the she-wolf (Stauffer, *Christ and the Caesars*, 154). One could, however, count at least eight hills in Rome: the Capitol, the Palatine, the Aventine, the Caelian, the Oppian, the Esquiline, the Viminal, and the Quirinal—the Vatican would make a ninth (*ZPEB* 5:162). Beale, 869–70, objects by pointing out that Rome was popularly referred to in the ancient world as "the city of seven hills" and lists a number of Latin texts (e.g., Virgil, Martial, Cicero). John may have been influenced by this to choose the "seven hills" as a reference to the contemporary embodiment of the beast in Rome. However, seven for John is ultimately symbolic of the "full complement of evil set against Christ and his people." Aune (*Revelation 17–22*, 944, 948) indicates that the seven hills as a designation for Rome is uncontestable and was probably invented by Varro (116–27 BC); yet he feels there are good reasons to see the number seven as symbolical and not historical. Kistemaker, 471–72, also helpfully reminds us that the seven hills/mountains in OT biblical usage is well established and regularly refers to political powers (Isa 2:2; Jer 51:25; Da 2:35b); but he then, incorrectly in my view, adopts an historical identification of seven empires that opposed God.

10 Caird, 218–19, refers to the symbolic significance of the seven heads as indicating not seven specific emperors but a whole line of emperors. Why the emperors should then be limited to Rome, Caird does not tell us. He also refers to the well-known "eagle vision" of *4 Ezra* 11–12 as support for the emperor succession interpretation of Revelation 17:10. However appropriate this interpretation is to Jewish apocalyptic writing, it remains to be demonstrated that John had such an intent in mind. The Jewish visions are more allegorical (language with a specific historical counterpart in mind), while Revelation is symbolical (language of universal reality having many historical counterparts).

11 In the early church there was an interpretation that took the seven mountains as referring to the seven millennia of world history, a theme current in that period. Thus after asserting that the Sabbath is a type of the millennial reign of Christ, Hippolytus (*Comm. Dan.* 4.23) says, "Since, then, in six days God made all things, it follows that six thousand years must be fulfilled. And they are not yet fulfilled, as John says: five are fallen, one is, the other is not yet come (Rev 17:10). Moreover, in speaking of the other he specifies the seventh, in which there shall be rest."

14 For an enlightening and thorough discussion of the relationship between the angelic powers who rule and their earthly agents, see Oscar Cullmann, *The State in the New Testament* (New York: Scribner's, 1956), 95–114.

4. The Fall of Babylon the Great (18:1–24)

OVERVIEW

Chapter 18 contains the description of the previously announced "judgment" (*krima*, GK *3210*; NIV, "punishment") of the prostitute (17:1). It is important not to separate this chapter from the portrayal of the prostitute in ch. 17, for there is no warrant for making the prostitute in ch. 17 different from the city in ch. 18 (cf. 17:18). Under the imagery of the destruction of the great commercial city, John describes the final overthrow of the great prostitute, Babylon. He is not writing a literal description, even in poetic or figurative language, of the fall of an earthly city, such as Rome or Jerusalem; but in portraying the destruction of a city he describes God's judgment on the great satanic system of evil that has corrupted the earth's history. Drawing especially from the OT accounts of the destruction of the ancient harlot cities of Babylon (Isa 13:21; 47:7–9; Jer 50–51) and Tyre (Eze 26–27), John composes a great threnody that might well be the basis of a mighty oratorio. Here in chs. 17–18

is some of the most beautifully cadenced language in the whole book. John combines the song of triumph and the wailing strains of lamentation into a noble funeral dirge (cf. 2Sa 1:17–27; Isa 14:4–21; La 1–5).

First, there is a kind of prelude in which the whole judgment is proclaimed (vv.1–3). Then comes a call for God's people to separate themselves from the city because the divine plagues are about to descend on her in recompense for her crimes (vv.4–8). The main movement that expresses the laments for the city's fall is divided into three parts: (1) the lament of the kings of the earth (vv.9–10), then (2) the lament of the merchants who traded with her (vv.11–17), and (3) the lament of the sea captains who became rich from the cargoes they took to the city (vv.18–20). Lastly, the finale sounds the death knell of the life of the city for her deception of the nations and killing of God's people (vv.21–24).

¹After this I saw another angel coming down from heaven. He had great authority, and the earth was illuminated by his splendor. ²With a mighty voice he shouted:

"Fallen! Fallen is Babylon the Great!
    She has become a home for demons
and a haunt for every evil spirit,
    a haunt for every unclean and detestable bird.
³ For all the nations have drunk
    the maddening wine of her adulteries.
The kings of the earth committed adultery with her,
    and the merchants of the earth grew rich from her excessive luxuries."

⁴Then I heard another voice from heaven say:

"Come out of her, my people,
    so that you will not share in her sins,
    so that you will not receive any of her plagues;
⁵ for her sins are piled up to heaven,
    and God has remembered her crimes.
⁶ Give back to her as she has given;
    pay her back double for what she has done.
    Mix her a double portion from her own cup.
⁷ Give her as much torture and grief
    as the glory and luxury she gave herself.
In her heart she boasts,
    'I sit as queen; I am not a widow,
    and I will never mourn.'
⁸ Therefore in one day her plagues will overtake her:
    death, mourning and famine.
She will be consumed by fire,
    for mighty is the Lord God who judges her.

⁹"When the kings of the earth who committed adultery with her and shared her luxury see the smoke of her burning, they will weep and mourn over her. ¹⁰Terrified at her torment, they will stand far off and cry:

"'Woe! Woe, O great city,
    O Babylon, city of power!
In one hour your doom has come!'

¹¹"The merchants of the earth will weep and mourn over her because no one buys their cargoes any more— ¹²cargoes of gold, silver, precious stones and pearls; fine linen, purple,

silk and scarlet cloth; every sort of citron wood, and articles of every kind made of ivory, costly wood, bronze, iron and marble; [13]cargoes of cinnamon and spice, of incense, myrrh and frankincense, of wine and olive oil, of fine flour and wheat; cattle and sheep; horses and carriages; and bodies and souls of men.

[14]"They will say, 'The fruit you longed for is gone from you. All your riches and splendor have vanished, never to be recovered.' [15]The merchants who sold these things and gained their wealth from her will stand far off, terrified at her torment. They will weep and mourn [16]and cry out:

> "'Woe! Woe, O great city,
>> dressed in fine linen, purple and scarlet,
>> and glittering with gold, precious stones and pearls!
> [17]In one hour such great wealth has been brought to ruin!'

"Every sea captain, and all who travel by ship, the sailors, and all who earn their living from the sea, will stand far off. [18]When they see the smoke of her burning, they will exclaim, 'Was there ever a city like this great city? [19]They will throw dust on their heads, and with weeping and mourning cry out:

> "'Woe! Woe, O great city,
>> where all who had ships on the sea
> became rich through her wealth!
> In one hour she has been brought to ruin!
> [20]Rejoice over her, O heaven!
>> Rejoice, saints and apostles and prophets!
> God has judged her for the way she treated you.'"

[21]Then a mighty angel picked up a boulder the size of a large millstone and threw it into the sea, and said:

> "With such violence
>> the great city of Babylon will be thrown down,
>> never to be found again.
> [22]The music of harpists and musicians, flute players and trumpeters,
>> will never be heard in you again.
> No workman of any trade
>> will ever be found in you again.
> The sound of a millstone
>> will never be heard in you again.
> [23]The light of a lamp
>> will never shine in you again.

> The voice of bridegroom and bride
>   will never be heard in you again.
> Your merchants were the world's great men.
>   By your magic spell all the nations were led astray.
> ²⁴ In her was found the blood of prophets and of the saints,
>   and of all who have been killed on the earth."

COMMENTARY

1 So magnificent is the event about to be enacted that a dazzling angel of glory bears the divine news. Some interpreters have associated this glory with the *shekinah* glory that in Ezekiel's vision departed from the temple because of the harlotry of the Israelites (Eze 11:23) but later returned to the restored temple (Eze 43:2).

2 In words very similar to those of the prophets who encouraged God's people as they faced ancient Babylon, the angel announces that Babylon the Great, mother of all the earthly prostitute cities, has fallen (cf. Isa 21:9; Jer 51:8 with Rev 14:8; 18:2). Again, in words reminiscent of the judgment announced against ancient Babylon, forewarning the city's habitation only by detestable creatures and evil spirits (Isa 13:19–22; 34:11; Jer 50:39), John hears the same fate announced for this urban mother of prostitutes. "Demons" (*daimoniōn*, GK *1228*) are associated elsewhere with idolatry (see comments at 9:20; 16:14). The "haunt" (*phylakē*, GK *5871*) is a watchtower; the evil spirits, watching over fallen Babylon like night birds or harpies waiting for their prey, build their nests in the broken towers that rise from the ashes of the city (cf. Swete). She who was a great city has become a wilderness.

3 The prostitute city will be judged because of her surfeit of fornication. Here the same thought of 17:2 is expanded as we hear echoes of the judg-ments on ancient Tyre and Babylon (Isa 23:17; Jer 51:7; Rev 14:8). One of the great sins of Babylon was her luxury (*strēnos*, GK *5140*; cf. at 18:7, 9). Because wealth may lead to pride, the prophets and John view surfeit as a manifestation of Babylon (18:7; cf. Eze 28:4–5, 16–18). The close proximity of fornication with luxury may suggest that with Babylon there is a fornication that not only involves idolatry (cult prostitution) but that may display pride in excessive wealth.

4 "Come out of her, my people" forms the burden of Jeremiah's refrain concerning Babylon (Jer 50:8; 51:6–9; cf. Isa 48:20; 52:11; 2Co 6:17). Even in its OT setting, this was no mere warning to leave the actual city of Babylon, much less here in Revelation. John is burdened to exhort the churches to shun the charms and ensnarements of the queen prostitute (v.7) as her qualities are manifest in the world they live in. Wherever there are idolatry, prostitution, self-glorification, self-sufficiency, pride, complacency, reliance on luxury and wealth, avoidance of suffering, and violence against life (v.24), there is Babylon. Christians are to separate themselves ideologically and, if necessary, physically from all the forms of Babylon. Already John has warned the churches of her deceit and snares (chs. 2–3). If they refuse to separate themselves, they will "share in her sins" and also in the divine judgments (NIV, "plagues"). It is not necessary to see this as one last call to repentance addressed to the beast-worshipers (so Caird). Rather, like the warnings in the letters to the churches (chs. 2–3), it is addressed to professing Christians who, through the wiles of the queen prostitute, were being seduced by Satan to abandon their loyalty to Jesus. If this occurred, Christ would be forced by their own decision to blot out their names from the book of life and to include them in the plagues designed for Babylon when she is judged (cf. 3:5; so Farrer, 155 n. 2).

5–6 God will not forget her crimes (*adikēmata*, GK *93*), which are multiplied to the height of heaven (cf. Ge 18:20–21; Jer 51:9). Her punishment will fit her crimes (v.6; cf. Ps 137:8; Jer 50:15, 29; Mt 7:2). This OT principle of *lex talionis* is never enjoined on God's people in the NT but, as here, is reserved for God alone (Mt 5:38–42; Ro 12:17–21). "Mix her a double portion from her own cup" (cf. Ex 22:4, 7, 9; Isa 40:2) reflects both the ideas of the severity of God's judgment on those who persistently refuse to repent and the truth that God's wrath is related to the outworking of sin (cf. Ro 1:24–32). Verse 7 illustrates the latter point.

7–8 Babylon's threefold web of sin is described as satiety ("luxury"), pride ("boasts, . . . sit as queen"), and avoidance of suffering ("I will never mourn"). The three may be interrelated. Luxury leads to boastful self-sufficiency (Eze 28:5), while the desire to avoid suffering may lead to the dishonest pursuit of luxury (Eze 28:18). "I sit as queen" echoes Isaiah's description of judgment on Babylon (Isa 47:7–11) and Ezekiel's description of Tyre (Eze 27:3). As she avoided grief through her satiety, her punishment therefore is grief (*penthos*, "mourning, sorrow, misfortune," GK *4292*). Suddenly, "in one day," she will experience what she has avoided by her luxury: "death, mourning and famine." Like ancient Babylon, this queen of prostitutes will become unloved

and barren (Isa 47:9). In spite of her many charms (v.23c), she will be powerless to avert her destruction. The words "consumed by fire" (cf. 17:16) may refer to the destruction of a city (cf. vv.9, 18) or to the OT punishment for prostitution if the woman is a priest's daughter (Lev 21:9). As strong as "Babylon the Great" is, the Lord God is stronger and will judge her.

9–19 Even a quick reading of Ezekiel 27 shows that here in these verses John had in the back of his mind Ezekiel's lamentation over the fall of ancient Tyre. Those who entered into fornication with the great mother prostitute wail over her destruction. In terms drawn from the fall of harlot cities in the past, John describes the end of the great reality of evil, Babylon the Great. While allusions to Rome seem to appear, it is only because Rome—like Tyre, Babylon, or Jerusalem—is herself a prostitute city; the characteristics of all of these cities are found in the queen mother of prostitutes.

9–10 First, the kings of the earth cry out their dirge (vv.9–10). There is a connection between their adultery with Babylon and their sharing of her luxury, as though sharing her luxury was part of their adultery (cf. Eze 26:16; 27:30–35). So great is the heat and smoke of her burning that they must stand "far off" (v.10). Though ultimately the kings are all the heavenly powers that rule in the affairs of earthly kings and kingdoms (see comments at 17:10, 14; cf. 1Co 2:6, 8), in this extended poetic allegory they are the merchant princes who bewail the collapse of the last great city of man under Satan's rule. The lament "Woe! Woe" (cf. 8:13; 9:12; 11:14; 12:12) is repeated three times in this part of the threnody over Babylon and reflects pain at the suddenness of her downfall ("in one hour," cf. vv.8, 17) and the emptiness of their own existences apart from her.

11 The merchants wail (vv.11–17a). They have the most to lose because Babylon the Great was built on luxury. The lists that follow are inventories of exotic items reminiscent of the great Oriental *souks* (marketplaces). Swete, 230–31, has an excellent discussion of the more important items.

13 "Bodies and souls of men" require special mention. "Bodies" (*sōmata*, GK *5393*) is a Greek idiom for slaves (cf. LXX of Ge 36:6), while "souls of men" (*psychas*, GK *6034*) means essentially the same as bodies (slaves). Thus the whole expression means "slaves, that is, human beings."

16 The refrain also shows the blending of the prostitute image of ch. 17 (dressed in fine linen, etc.; cf. 17:4) and the city image of ch. 18 ("O great city"). The wares are less suitable for Rome than for Asia Minor (cf. Lilje, 236).

17b–19 The sea captains and sailors add their lament, for they too suffer irreparable loss because of the city's burning (cf. Eze 27:28). This language is more appropriate to Tyre as a great port city than to Rome, which was inland and had the not-too-distant Ostia as its port. But in any case, it is not John's intent to describe any single city but the great harlot city, the archetype of the earth's evil cities.

20 The threefold lament is balanced by a song of heavenly jubilation. Babylon has also persecuted the church of Jesus (saints, apostles, prophets). Except for the mention of false apostles earlier in the book (2:2), this is the only reference to apostles in Revelation (cf. 21:14). If it is correct to see in v.20 a reference to their being killed (cf. v.24), perhaps John had in mind Herod's martyring of James (Ac 12:1–2) or Rome's killing of Peter and Paul. The picture of Babylon cannot, however, be confined to the political activity of Rome; therefore, John attributes the deaths of the martyrs to Babylon the Great. It is she who has killed Jesus (11:7–8), Stephen by the hands of unbelieving Jews (Ac 7:57–60), and the martyr Antipas by the hands of pagan cultists (2:13; cf. Mt 23:34–37).

21 The final lament over the fall of Babylon, spoken by an angel, is poignant and beautiful. A mighty angel picks up a huge stone like a giant millstone (four to five feet in diameter, one foot thick, and weighing thousands of pounds) and flings it into the sea. One quick gesture becomes a parable of the whole judgment on Babylon the Great! Suddenly she is gone forever (cf. Jer 51:64; Eze 26:21). The melancholy recollection of the pulsing life that once filled this great city with the joy of life sounds through vv.21–24 "like footsteps dying away in the distance in a desolate city which lies in ruins" (Lilje).

23 All nations were deceived (*planaō*, "led astray," GK *4414*) by her "magic spell" (*pharmakeia*, "sorcery," GK *5758*). John has previously used *pharmakeia* in conjunction with "murders," "fornicators," and "thefts" (see comments at 9:21). An element of drugging is involved that results in fatal poisoning (MM, 664). With her deceit, Babylon charmed the nations. Compare the similar charge against the harlot city Nineveh for her lies to other nations (Na 3:4).

24 In the final verse, the great sin of Babylon is cited. She has martyred the prophets and followers of Jesus. John has already mentioned this blood-guiltiness (17:6; 18:12; cf. 19:2). Elsewhere the death of martyrs is attributed to "the inhabitants of the earth" (6:10), the "beast that comes up from the Abyss" (11:7, 13:7), and the "beast, coming out of the earth" (13:15). In the OT, the cities of Jerusalem (Eze 24:6, 9; cf. Mt 23:37) and Babylon (Jer 51:35) are called cities of bloodshed. Here "the blood . . . of all who have been killed on the earth" refers to all those who in history have been martyred because of their loyalty to the true God. John's word for kill (*sphazō*, GK *5377*) is consistently used for martyrs (5:6, 9, 12; 6:4, 9; 13:8). In John's mind, Babylon the Great (v.2) is much more comprehensive than ancient Babylon, Nineveh, Jerusalem, or Rome. She encompasses all the persecution against God's servants until the words of God are fulfilled (cf. 17:17).

5. Thanksgiving for the Destruction of Babylon (19:1–5)

OVERVIEW

In stark contrast to the laments of Babylon's consorts, the heavenly choirs burst forth in a great liturgy of celebration to God. In these verses we hear four shouts of praise for the fall of Babylon. First, there is the sound of a great multitude praising God for his condemnation of the prostitute (vv.1–2). Then they shout out in celebration of the city's eternal destruction (v.3). Following this, we hear in antiphonal response the voices of the twenty-four elders and the four living creatures (v.4). Finally, a voice from the throne calls on all the servants of God to praise him (v.5).

¹After this I heard what sounded like the roar of a great multitude in heaven shouting:

"Hallelujah!
Salvation and glory and power belong to our God,
2   for true and just are his judgments.
He has condemned the great prostitute
   who corrupted the earth by her adulteries.
He has avenged on her the blood of his servants."

³And again they shouted:

"Hallelujah!
The smoke from her goes up for ever and ever."

⁴The twenty-four elders and the four living creatures fell down and worshiped God, who was seated on the throne. And they cried:

"Amen, Hallelujah!"

⁵Then a voice came from the throne, saying:

"Praise our God,
   all you his servants,
you who fear him,
   both small and great!"

1–2 The word "Hallelujah" (*hallēlouia*) transliterates the Greek, which in turn transliterates the Hebrew *hallĕluyah*, meaning "Praise the LORD!" (In v.5, "Praise our God" [*Aineite to theo hēmon*] is equivalent to "Hallelujah.") The Hebrew transliteration occurs only in this chapter in the NT (vv.1, 3, 4, 6), but in the LXX it is a frequent title for certain of the psalms (e.g., Pss 111:1; 112:1; 113:1). This phenomenon clearly illustrates the connection of the early church's liturgical worship with the synagogue and temple worship of the first century. These praise psalms formed an important part of the Jewish festival celebrations: "Hallel is the Jewish song of jubilation that has accompanied our wanderings of thousands of years, keeping awake within us the consciousness of our world-historical mission, strengthening us in times of sorrow and suffering, and filling our mouths with song of rejoicing in days of deliverance and triumph. To this day, it revives on each Festival season the memory of Divine Redemption, and our confidence in future greatness" (S. R. Hirsch, quoted in Hertz, *Daily Prayer Book*, 756).

The Hallel is the name especially applied to Psalms 113–118. These psalms are also called "the Hallel of Egypt" because of the references in them to the exodus. They thus have a special role in the Feast of Passover (*m. Pesaḥ*. 10:9). The midrashic sources also unanimously associate the Hallel with the destruction of the wicked, exactly as this passage in Revelation does (cf. Werner, *Sacred Bridge*, 151, 158, 302–3).

The Hallel was most certainly what Jesus and the disciples sang after the Passover-Eucharist celebration before going out to the Mount of Olives the night before his death (Mt 26:30). This close connection between the Hallel, Passover, and death of Jesus no doubt explains why all the early church liturgies incorporated the Hallel into the propers for Easter and Easter Week (cf. Shepherd, 96). This Easter liturgy is the Christian experience of the gospel of redemption from sin, Satan, and death in the victorious triumph of Christ, our Passover. The Paschal liturgy concludes with the celebration of the eucharistic banquet of Christ as he holds intimate communion with his church, giving it light and life.

Shepherd links the great banquet of vv.7–9 to the eucharistic celebration in the early church. The psalms in the great Hallel (Pss 113:1; 115:13) are unmistakably cited in 19:5. One can hardly read this Hallel section of Revelation without thinking of the "Hallelujah Chorus" in Handel's *Messiah*.

The theme of "salvation" (*sōtēria*, GK *5401*) has already been sounded in Revelation in connection with victory or divine justice (7:10; 12:10). God has indeed vindicated the injustice visited on his servants by meting out true justice on the great prostitute, Babylon. She deserves the sentence because she corrupted the earth (cf. 11:18; Jer 51:25) and killed the saints of God (cf. 18:24).

3 The second Hallel supplements the first one. Babylon's permanent end is celebrated in words reminiscent of ancient Babylon's judgment (Isa 34:10).

4 In response to the heavenly Hallels, the twenty-four elders cry out, "Amen, Hallelujah!" (cf. comments at 1:7 on "Amen"; at 4:4 on the elders).

5 This final praise is spoken by a single voice from the throne (cf. 16:17). The voice is probably neither that of God nor Christ because of the words "*our* Lord God Almighty reigns" (v.6). Here is a clear reference to the great Hallel psalms 113 and 115. "Praise our God, all you his servants" reflects Psalm 113:1, while "you who fear him, both small and great!" reflects Psalm 115:13 (cf. Ps 135:1, 20). All socioeconomic distinctions are transcended in the united worship of the church ("both small and great"; cf. 11:18; 13:16; 19:18; 20:12).

6. *Thanksgiving for the Marriage of the Lamb (19:6–10)*

6Then I heard what sounded like a great multitude, like the roar of rushing waters and like loud peals of thunder, shouting:

"Hallelujah!
For our Lord God Almighty reigns.

> ⁷Let us rejoice and be glad
>   and give him glory!
>   For the wedding of the Lamb has come,
>   and his bride has made herself ready.
>   ⁸Fine linen, bright and clean,
>   was given her to wear."
> (Fine linen stands for the righteous acts of the saints.)
>
>   ⁹Then the angel said to me, "Write: 'Blessed are those who are invited to the wedding supper of the Lamb!'" And he added, "These are the true words of God."
>   ¹⁰At this I fell at his feet to worship him. But he said to me, "Do not do it! I am a fellow servant with you and with your brothers who hold to the testimony of Jesus. Worship God! For the testimony of Jesus is the spirit of prophecy."

6 Finally the cycle of praise is completed with the reverberating sounds of another great multitude. If the multitude in v.1 was angelic, then this one would most certainly be the great redeemed throngs (cf. 7:9). They utter the final Hallel in words reminiscent of the great kingship psalms (93:1; 97:1; 99:1). The first of these psalms is used in the synagogue in Sabbath morning and evening services and also in the Armenian church liturgy for Easter Sunday (Werner, *Sacred Bridge*, 153). It is also the prelude to the messianic Psalms 95–99 and has as its theme the eternal sovereignty of God, who will conquer all his enemies (cf. Hertz, *Daily Prayer Book*, 362). The Greek verb *ebasileusen* ("reigns"), an ingressive aorist, may better be rendered, "has begun to reign."

7 There is also rejoicing because the "wedding of the Lamb has come, and his bride has made herself ready." It is John's way of giving us a glimmer of the next great vision at the close of the former one (cf. 21:2, 9). Contrast the prostitute and her lovers in the preceding chapters with the Lamb and his chaste bride (v.8, "fine linen, bright and clean").

The bride is the heavenly city, the new Jerusalem (21:2, 9), which is the symbol of the church, the bride of Christ, the community of those redeemed by Christ's blood. The wedding imagery, including the wedding supper, was for the Jews a familiar image of the kingdom of God. Jesus used wedding and banquet imagery in his parables of the kingdom (Mt 22:2–14; 25:1–13; Lk 14:15–24). The OT used the figure for the bride of Israel (Eze 16:8; Hos 2:19), and NT writers have applied it to the church (2Co 11:2; Eph 5:25–33). Heaven's rejoicing has signaled the defeat of all the enemies of God. The time of betrothal has ended. Now it is the time for the church, prepared by loyalty and suffering, to enter into her full experience of salvation and glory with her beloved spouse, Christ. The fuller revelation of the realization of this union is described in chs. 21 and 22.

8 The church's garments are white linen—in marked contrast to the purple and scarlet clothing of the great mother of prostitutes (17:4; 18:16). Linen was an expensive cloth used to make the garments worn by priests and royalty. It has two qualities: brightness and cleanness (cf. 16:6). Bright (*lampros*, GK *3287*) is the color of radiant whiteness that depicts glorification (*TDNT* 4:27; cf. Mt 13:43). Clean (*katharos*, GK *2754*) reflects purity, loyalty, and faithfulness, the character of the new Jerusalem (21:18, 21).

An explanatory interjection, probably added by John, states that "fine linen stands for the righteous acts of the saints." In 15:4, *dikaiōmata* ("righteous acts," GK *1468*) describes the manifest deeds of God that relate to truth and justice. The *dikaiōmata* do not imply any kind of meritorious works that would bring salvation. Rather, there is a delicate balance between grace and obedient response to it. The bride is "given" the garments, but she "has made herself ready" (v.7) for the wedding by faithfulness and loyalty to Christ (cf. 3:4–5, 18). In the parable of the man without a wedding garment, the garment he lacked was probably a clean one supplied by the host but either refused or soiled through carelessness by the rejected guest. The meaning of the clean garment is probably repentance and obedient response to Christ, both of which the Pharisees lacked (Mt 22:11–12.; cf. J. Jeremias, *The Parables of Jesus* [rev. ed.; New York: Scribner's, 1963], 188–89). Thus John contrasts the faithful disciples of Jesus, who have been true to God, with those who were seduced by the beast and the prostitute. The bride prepared herself, then, by her obedient discipleship (see comments at 12:11).

9 This beatitude is the fourth of seven (1:3; 14:13; 16:15; 20:6; 22:7, 14) in Revelation. In each beatitude there is a subtle contrast to those who are not loyal and faithful followers of the Lamb. The word translated "invited" is *keklēmenoi* ("called"), a form of the verb *kaleō* ("call," GK *2813*), which is used in the NT of the call to salvation (e.g., Mt 9:13; Ro 8:30; 9:24; 1Co 1:9; 2Th 2:14). However, the word may also mean "invited," with no connotation of election (cf. Mt 22:3, 8; Lk 14:16; Jn 2:2).

The wedding supper began toward evening on the wedding day, lasted for many days, and was a time of great jubilation. Here in Revelation the wedding is the beginning of the earthly kingdom of God, the bride is the church in all her purity, and the invited guests are both the bride and people who have committed themselves to Jesus.

To assure John and his readers of the certainty of the end of the great prostitute and the announcement of the wedding supper of the Lamb, the angel adds, "These are the true words of God" (cf. 1:2; 17:17; 21:5). A similar sentence later seems to give the same assurance for the whole book (22:6).

10 John, who was himself a prophet and who had received such a clear revelation about idolatry, now falls prey to this temptation. After the final vision, he again slips into idolatry (22:8). Whether John included these references to his own failure because he knew of the tendency toward angel worship in the churches of Asia is not clear. Be that as it may, we need to recognize how easy it is to fall into idolatry. Whenever Christians give control of their lives to anyone or anything other than God, they have broken the first commandment. The "testimony of Jesus" is Jesus' own testimony that he bore in his life and teaching and especially in his death (cf. comments at 1:2, 9; also the same expression in 6:9; 12:11; 14:12; 20:4). Those who hold to or proclaim this testimony are Christian prophets. Thus "the testimony of Jesus is the spirit of prophecy." The words spoken by the Christian prophets come from the Spirit of God, who is the Spirit of the risen Jesus; they are the very words of God.

NOTES

10 See commentary at 1:2 for arguments supporting the identification of Ἰησοῦ (*Iēsou*, "Jesus") in this verse as a subjective genitive and rendering it as "Jesus' witness" (so Caird, Minear).

IV. VISION OF THE RETURN OF CHRIST AND THE CONSUMMATION OF THIS AGE (19:11–20:15)

A. The Rider on the White Horse and the Destruction of the Beast (19:11–21)

OVERVIEW

The great vision that begins here reminds us of the first vision of the book (1:12–20), though its function is entirely different from that of the earlier vision. The whole scene looks alternately to the OT and to the previous references in Revelation to Christ, especially the seven letters (chs. 2–3). So strong are the parallels with chs. 1–3 that Mathias Rissi (*The Future of the World: An Exegetical Study of Revelation 19:11–22:15* [Naperville, Ill.: Allenson, 1972], 19) believes that the first section (vv. 11–13) of this vision deals with the judgment on the church and the second section (vv. 14–16) with the world.

This new vision is introduced by the words "I saw heaven standing open." Earlier John had seen a door standing open in heaven (4:1) and the temple in heaven standing open (11:19); now, in preparation for a great revelation of God's sovereignty, he sees heaven itself flung wide open to his gaze (cf. Eze 1:1). In one sense this vision, which depicts the return of Christ and the final overthrow of the beast, may be viewed as the climax of the previous section (vv. 1–10) or as the first of a final series of seven last things—the return of Christ; the defeat of Satan; the binding of Satan; the millennium; the final end of Satan; the last judgment; and the new heaven, the new earth, and the new Jerusalem.

Early as well as modern interpretation has for the most part seen in vv. 11–16 a description of the second coming of Christ—an event to which the NT bears a frequent and unified witness. As for the features of this event, they are variously understood by interpreters.

---

¹¹I saw heaven standing open and there before me was a white horse, whose rider is called Faithful and True. With justice he judges and makes war. ¹²His eyes are like blazing fire, and on his head are many crowns. He has a name written on him that no one knows but he himself. ¹³He is dressed in a robe dipped in blood, and his name is the Word of God. ¹⁴The armies of heaven were following him, riding on white horses and dressed in fine linen, white and clean. ¹⁵Out of his mouth comes a sharp sword with which to strike down the nations. "He will rule them with an iron scepter." He treads the winepress of the fury of the wrath of God Almighty. ¹⁶On his robe and on his thigh he has this name written:

KING OF KINGS AND LORD OF LORDS.

¹⁷And I saw an angel standing in the sun, who cried in a loud voice to all the birds flying in midair, "Come, gather together for the great supper of God, ¹⁸so that you may eat the

flesh of kings, generals, and mighty men, of horses and their riders, and the flesh of all people, free and slave, small and great." [19]Then I saw the beast and the kings of the earth and their armies gathered together to make war against the rider on the horse and his army. [20]But the beast was captured, and with him the false prophet who had performed the miraculous signs on his behalf. With these signs he had deluded those who had received the mark of the beast and worshiped his image. The two of them were thrown alive into the fiery lake of burning sulfur. [21]The rest of them were killed with the sword that came out of the mouth of the rider on the horse, and all the birds gorged themselves on their flesh.

COMMENTARY

11 A white horse with a rider has appeared at 6:1 (cf. discussion in loc.). Both white horses represent conquest or victory, but with that the similarity changes to total contrast: The rider here in ch. 19 is "Faithful and True" (cf. 1:5; 3:7, 14) in contrast to the forces of Antichrist with their empty promises and lies. Christ will keep his word to the churches. In contrast to those who pervert justice and wage unjust war, John says of Christ, "With justice [righteousness] he judges and makes war," an allusion to the messianic character described in Isaiah 11:3b–5. In only one other place (2:16) is Christ described as making war (*polemeō*, GK *4482*), and there the reference is to his judgment of the church. Furthermore, the questions in 13:4, "Who is like the beast? Who can make war against him?" anticipate the answer that *Christ alone* can do this, while in 17:14 the beast and the ten kings wage war against the Lamb.

Though John uses OT language descriptive of a warrior-Messiah, he does not depict Christ as a great *military* warrior battling against earth's sovereigns. John reinterprets this OT imagery, while at the same time inseparably linking Christ to its fulfillment. The close proximity in v.11 of justice and war shows us that the kind of warfare Christ engages in is more the execution of justice than a military conflict. He who is the faithful and true witness will judge the rebellious nations.

12 The reference to the blazing eyes definitely connects this vision with that of ch. 1 (cf. 1:14; 2:18). On his head are not just seven crowns (12:3), or ten (13:1), but many crowns of royalty (*diadēmata*, GK *1343*). Perhaps they signify that the royal power to rule the world has now passed to Christ by virtue of the victory of his followers (11:15). All the diadems of their newly won empire meet on his brow (cf. Caird).

So great is Christ's power that his name is known only by himself. Knowledge of the name is in antiquity associated with the power of the god. When a name becomes known, then the power is shared with those to whom the disclosure is made (cf. comments at 2:17). But since two names of Christ are revealed in this vision—"the Word of God" (v.13) and "KING OF KINGS AND LORD OF LORDS" (v.16)—we may conclude that the exclusive power of Christ over all creation is now to be shared with his faithful followers (3:21; 5:10; 22:5). On the other hand, the secret name may be one that will not be revealed till Christ's return.

13 The imagery in this verse has traditionally been related to Isaiah 63:14, a passage understood messianically by the Jews and one that John has used in portraying God's wrath in 14:9–11, 17–19. Isaiah pictures a mighty warrior-Messiah who slaughters his enemies. Their lifeblood splashes on his clothing as he tramples them down in his anger, as the juice of the grapes splashes on the treader in the winepress. But is Christ's blood-dipped robe red from his enemies' blood or from his own blood? There are good reasons for accepting the latter (contra Mounce, 353–54). If the blood is that of his enemies, how is it that Christ comes from heaven with his robe already dipped in blood before any battle is mentioned? Furthermore, the blood that is always mentioned in connection with Christ in the Apocalypse is his own lifeblood (1:5; 5:6, 9; 7:14; 12:11). However, Caird, 242–43, has no difficulty identifying the blood as that of the saints, which Christ turns into victory over his enemies; but he has understood the vintage passage (14:7–20) as a reference to the death of the saints. Perhaps both are in mind: "Before the 'last battle' ever begins, [Christ's] garments are already bloody with his sacrifice of himself (1:5; 5:9). In contrast to the divine warrior of Isaiah 63:1–3, the source for this imagery, this blood is not the blood of his enemies but his own martyr blood in union with the martyr blood of his followers who, like him, have suffered/testified at the hands of Rome" (Boring, 196).

Admittedly, there is a close connection between the discolored clothing of Christ, the Word of God (to whom the saints bear witness and give their lives), and "the armies of heaven"—i.e., the saints (v.14). Moreover, the word "dipped" (*bebammenon*, from *baptō*, GK 970) does not fit the imagery of Isaiah 63:2, but it does fit that used in Revelation of believers' garments being washed thoroughly in Christ's blood (7:14; 22:14). The interpretation of the blood as Christ's own is an early one (so Hippolytus, Origen, Andreas; cf. Swete, 249). Finally, the sword with which Christ strikes down the nations comes from his mouth and is not in his hand (v.15);

and this too is incompatible with battle imagery. In any case, there is sufficient warrant not to press the allusion to Isaiah 63:1–6 too literally.

Applying the expression "the Word of God" (*ho logos tou theou*) to Jesus in a personal sense is peculiar to the Johannine writings (Jn 1:1, 14; cf. 1Jn 1:1). In Revelation, "the Word of God" refers to the revelation of God's purpose (1:2; 17:17; 19:9). It is also the message and lifestyle for which the saints suffer oppression and even death (1:9; 6:9; 20:4). The adjectives "true" and "faithful," which are applied to Christ, are likewise identified with the Word of God (19:9; 21:5; 22:6; cf. 1:5; 3:14; 19:11). Thus Jesus in his earthly life had borne reliable and consistent witness in all his words and actions to the purposes of God and had been completely obedient in doing this. In him God's will finds full expression. The Word of God and the person of Christ are one.

14 This verse seems somewhat parenthetical because it does not refer directly to Christ's person or actions. The armies of heaven mounted on white horses are understood by most to be angelic hosts, since passages in the OT and NT speak of the armies or soldiers of heaven as angels, though infrequently (Pss 103:21; 148:2; Lk 2:13; Ac 7:42). Moreover, elsewhere in the NT the coming of Christ is associated with angels (e.g., Mt 13:41; 16:27; 24:30–31). Yet this may not be John's meaning. These soldiers, like their leader, are riding white horses of victory—something hardly true of angels. Their clothing of bright and clean linen is identical to the bride's attire (cf. v.8). Thus it is probably the victors who accompany Christ—either all of them (resurrected and raptured [1Th 4:16–17]) or the company of the martyrs. Revelation 17:14 confirms this: "They [the beast and the ten kings] will make war against the Lamb, but the Lamb will overcome them because he is Lord of lords and King of kings—*and with him will be his called, chosen and faithful followers*" (italics added; cf. 15:1–2).

15 There are three OT allusions to the warrior-Messiah in this verse: he strikes down the nations (Isa 11:3b–5); he rules them with an iron scepter (Ps 2:9); he tramples the winepress of God's wrath (Isa 63:1–6; for the last metaphor, see comments at v.13). In the first OT allusion, there are significant changes in the imagery: in Revelation, the Lamb-Messiah does not wield a sword in his hand; rather, his sword comes from his mouth (cf. comments at 1:16 and 2:16). This has no exact OT parallel and cannot be accidental, since John emphasizes it so much in Revelation (1:16; 2:12, 16; 19:15, 21). Christ conquers by the power of his word. Yet it is not necessary to see the reference to the sword coming from Christ's mouth as pointing to the expansion of Christianity and the conquest of the nations by their conversion to Christ (so Swete). The scene here is the eschatological return of Christ and his judgment of the nations, not the whole intervening age. Besides, Christ's words are also the instruments of his judgment as well as his salvation (Mt 12:37; Jn 12:48). On "the iron scepter" and the relationship between "rule" and "shepherd," see comments at 2:27. For the winepress figure, see 14:17–20.

16 This third name of Christ, which all can read, is displayed on that most exposed part of his cloak, the part that covers the thigh, where it cannot escape notice (cf. Swete). The name has already appeared attached to the Lamb (17:14). He is the absolute Lord and King, full of the divine power and authority.

17–18 This section finally brings us to the second last thing (cf. comments at Overview, 19:11–21): the anticipated great confrontation between the beast and his soldiers and the Lamb (cf. 16:12–16; 17:14). First, there is the summons to the vultures to come to God's great supper and gorge themselves on the slain corpses of the battlefield—a horrible picture of human carnage. The language is borrowed from Ezekiel 39:17–20, which describes the eschatological overthrow by God. It may be unnecessary to press the literalness of the description. This battlefield language is designed to indicate that a great victory is about to occur.

19–21 The contrast between the assembling of the beast's might with his kings and their soldiers and the ease by which he is overthrown and captured highlight the beast's powerlessness before his mighty conqueror. The "kings of the earth" refers to the ten horns (kings) of the beast, which is another way of describing the beast's power (see comments at 17:12–14). Both the beast and the false prophet (ch. 13) are simply seized and thrown into the lake of fire (v.20; see comments at 20:14). Their followers fall before the sword (word) of Christ (v.21). No battle is actually fought. Only the arrangement of the foes and the defeat of the beast is described. Is this accidental? Is John indicating that the battle has already been fought and this is simply the final realization of that previous victory? In ch. 5 the Lamb had overcome (won the victory) by his death (5:5, 9). Further, we are told that there was a battle in heaven, and Satan was cast out and defeated by the blood of the Lamb and the word of his followers' testimony (12:7–9, 11).

There seems to be only one actual battle described in Revelation. Thus these further scenes may be understood as more judicial in character than as literal battlefield descriptions. Because of John's christological reinterpretation, no great eschatological military battle, such as that envisaged in the Qumran War Scroll, will actually be fought. The decisive battle has already been won at the cross. These armies and the beast are the destroyers of the earth (11:18), who ultimately are the satanic principalities of the world that ally themselves with human puppets for their idolatrous ends. These have been positionally defeated at the cross (Col 2:15), but they will finally be stripped of all power at Christ's return.

Certainly John would not have denied that Satan and his evil powers are active in the world and that they use historical persons such as a Nero or a Hitler and oppose and harass Christians today.

NOTES

11 The divine warrior motif of the OT is certainly present in the book of Revelation. What is often unappreciated is the way John's understanding of Christ and his cross reverses the OT concept. As Tremper Longman III ("The Divine Warrior: The New Testament Use of the Old Testament Motif," *WTJ* 44 [1982]: 303–5) points out, "Jesus' Holy War is different from the Holy War of Israel. While the latter, at the Lord's command, directed their warfare against earthly enemies, Jesus struggled with the forces, the powers and the principalities, which stand behind sinful mankind (cf. his miracles and healings). . . . His command is not to slay but to convert (Mt 28:16ff.). . . . Note the reversal—Christ the Divine Warrior wins the war by being killed, not by killing. . . . The Christian is called upon to wage war. Once again, the warfare is not directed toward human adversaries but toward the evil powers which stand behind evil men . . . (Eph 6:10–20)."

13 For references to the messianic interpretation of Isaiah 63:1–6 by the rabbis, see Edersheim, *Life and Times of Jesus*, 2:730; Swete, 248–49. The Targum on Genesis 49:10–12 has a reference to the warring Messiah, whose clothes are discolored with the blood of his enemies (McNamara, *Targum and Testament*, 141). While this seems to add further evidence to support the view that the blood is from the enemies of Christ, it must still be asked whether John has reinterpreted the figure.

14 For angels accompanying the Messiah in his return, cf. *Ascension of Isaiah* 4.14–17. This is probably a Christian document of the first century AD.

15 While there are no other references in our literature to a sword from the Messiah's mouth, there are references to the destruction of the godless by the mouth of the Messiah, no doubt deriving from Isaiah 11:4: "He will strike the earth with the rod of his mouth, with the breath of his lips he will slay the wicked." Thus *4 Ezra* 13:6, 19 and *Psalms of Solomon* 17:10, 45, 49 mention the Messiah in words such as, "He shall destroy the godless nations with the word of his mouth."

19–21 An eschatological military battle is described in both Jewish apocalyptic and Qumran literature (cf. *1 En.* 90:13–19; *4 Ezra* 13:1–13; *As. Mos.* 10; *Pss. Sol.* 17:23–51; 1QM; 1QH 14:25–26). In these references, the war is to be fought in the future. It involves actual earthly rulers of the godless, and according to Qumran documents it will require the military assistance of the godly to effect the defeat of the ungodly. However, this does not seem to be John's view, since Christ alone executes the wrath, and the decisive victory has already been won before the actual eschatological end. Christ *will* really defeat evil once and for all, but not in the literal military sense envisaged by the Jewish apocalyptists.

REFLECTIONS

Although Satan has been dealt a deathblow at the cross (cf. Jn 12:31; 16:11), he nevertheless continues to promulgate great evil and deception during this present age (cf. Eph 2:2; 1Th 3:5; 1Pe 5:8–9; Rev 2:10). Yet he is a deposed ruler who is now under the sovereign authority of Christ but who for a "little while" (17:10) is allowed to continue his evil until God's purposes are finished. In this scene of the overthrow of the beast and his kings and their armies, John is showing us the ultimate and swift downfall of these evil powers at the hands of the King of kings and Lord of lords. They have met their Master in this final and utterly real confrontation.

B. Binding of Satan and the Millennium (20:1–6)

OVERVIEW

Charles has described this passage as a constant source of insurmountable difficulty for the exegete. Berkouwer, 291, has called the millennium one of the most controversial and intriguing questions of eschatology. He believes that one's view of ch. 20 is internally connected with the rest of one's eschatology. While the OT and later Jewish literature point forward to a time when the kingdom of God will be manifest in the world, nowhere in Jewish literature is the time of the reign of the Messiah stated to be a thousand years.

The exegesis of the passage leads me to an historic, nondispensational premillennial interpretation. It should be recognized, however, that there are problems with this view of 20:1–6, just as there are problems with other views of this difficult portion of the book, and that responsible Christian scholars vary in its interpretation according to their convictions and presuppositions.

For the moment, the question of the duration of the reign of Christ (which is equal to the duration of the binding of Satan) may be delayed. The main problem concerns whether the reference to a millennium indicates an *earthly* historical reign of peace that will manifest itself at the close of this present age, or whether the whole passage is completely symbolic (e.g., the triumph of the saints over the beast) of some present experience of Christians or some future nonhistorical reality.

In the first place, we may note that, with only minor exceptions, the ancient church down to the time of Augustine (AD 354–430) unquestionably held to the teaching of an earthly, historical reign of peace that was to follow the defeat of Antichrist and the physical resurrection of the saints but precede both the judgment and the new creation (cf. Jean Daniélou, *The Theology of Jewish Christianity* [Philadelphia: Westminster, 1964]). To be sure, in the ancient church there were various positions as to the material nature of the millennium (see comments at v.4), but the true conception of the thousand years was a balance between the worldly aspects of the kingdom and its spiritual aspects as a reign with Christ.

It is well known that the break with this earlier position came with the views of the fourth-century interpreter and African Donatist Tyconius, who, partly dependent on the Alexandrian allegorizing of Origen, developed a view of the millennium based on a recapitulation method of interpretation. In applying this principle, Tyconius viewed Revelation as containing a number of different visions that repeated basic themes throughout the book. Though Tyconius's original work is not available, his exegesis of the Apocalypse can be largely reconstructed through his prime benefactor, Augustine, and his many Roman Catholic followers. He interpreted the thousand years of ch. 20 in nonliteral terms and understood the period as referring to the church age, the time between the first and second advents of Christ. Tyconius interpreted the first resurrection as the resurrection of the soul from spiritual death to the new life, while the second resurrection was the resurrection of the body at the end of history. The binding of Satan had already taken place in that the devil cannot seduce the church during the present age. Moreover, the reign of the saints and their "thrones of judgment" had already begun in the church and its rulers. Augustine, following Tyconius, "cast the die against the expectation of a millennial kingdom for centuries to come" (H. Berkhof, *Christ the Meaning of History* [Grand Rapids: Baker, 1979], 161). The recapitulation method adopted by Augustine continued through the centuries and is not without its modern exponents in both the Protestant and Roman Catholic branches of the church. This is the first main option in modern nonmillennial (or amillennial) interpretations of ch. 20.

Augustine's approach, however, was not to remain unchallenged. Joachim of Floris (ca. 1135–1202) saw in the Apocalypse a prophecy of the events of Western history from the time of Christ till the end. He thought the millennium was still future in his time but soon to begin. The Franciscans, who followed Joachim, identified Babylon with ecclesiastical Rome and the Antichrist with the papacy. The Reformers followed suit. In the nineteenth century, Henry Alford (1810–71) adopted this view.

During Reformation times still another type of interpretation developed, expounded by a Jesuit scholar named Ribeira (1537–91). He held that almost all the events described in the Apocalypse are future and apply to the end-time rather than to the history of the world or contemporary Rome and the papacy. However, he still held to Augustine's view of the millennium as the period between the first and second advents of Christ. But at one important point he changed Augustine's view. Instead of the millennium's taking place on earth between the advents, Ribeira saw it as taking place

in heaven. It is a reward for faithfulness. When the saints at any time in history are martyred, they do not perish but live and reign with Christ in heaven in the intermediate state before the final resurrection. This is the second main option today for nonmillennialists. According to this viewpoint, John's basic message in ch. 20 is pastoral. If Christians face the prospect of suffering death for Jesus, they should be encouraged because if they are killed, they will go to reign with him in heaven. This seems to be the drift of Berkouwer's conclusions, 314, and earlier those of B. B. Warfield ("The Millennium and the Apocalypse," *PTR* 2 [1904]: 599–617) and most recently defended by Beale, 998–99.

The Augustinian view of Revelation 20 and its variant espoused by Joachim in my view cannot be harmonized with a serious exegesis of ch. 20 on two important counts: (1) it founders on the statements concerning the binding of Satan (vv. 1–3), and (2) it must handle in an absurd fashion the statements about the coming to life of the martyrs, which cannot be exegetically understood as anything other than physical resurrection without seriously tampering with the sense of the words. While it is popular among certain nonmillennialists to view vv. 1–4 as a symbolic description of the reward to be granted the martyrs on their entrance into heaven (so Beckwith, Berkouwer, Boer, Beale), this variation of the Augustinian exegesis, while removing the criticism that the passage refers to the present rule of Christ in the church age, fails to deal seriously with the binding of Satan and other details of the text.

There is yet another view that, though not free of problems, does more justice to the book of Revelation as a whole and to the exegesis of ch. 20 in particular. This view rejects both the Augustinian interpretation that the millennium is the rule of Christ during this dispensation and the variant of Joachim that locates the resurrection and the reign of the martyrs in heaven for an interim period before their bodily resurrection and Christ's return. It likewise rejects the variation of Augustine's view known as postmillennialism or evolutionary chiliasm, which teaches that the forces of Antichrist will gradually be put down and the gospel will permeate and transform the world into an interim of the reign of peace before the return of Christ (see Notes, v. 1, for representatives of this view). Berkouwer, 208–9, justly criticizes this postmillennial view as exegetically and theologically weak. He then goes on to espouse a totally mystical viewpoint of ch. 20 that fails to grapple exegetically with the text. For him, the millennial language is purely a figure of speech to depict the reality of the hidden triumph of Christ (see also Bauckham, *Theology of the Book of Revelation*, 106–8). Such a view, however, fails to account for how the reality of the divine kingdom of God has actually invaded history in Jesus Christ.

If eschatological realities are simply mystical, figurative, and pastoral in intent and never impinge on the empirical world, then the Christ-event as an eschatological event must likewise be abandoned. Instead, the view espoused in this commentary argues that the millennium is in history and on the earth as an eschatological reality. Much in the same manner as the kingdom of God was eschatologically present in the life and ministry of Jesus—present, yet still future—so the millennium is at once the final historical event of this age and the beginning of the eschatological kingdom of Christ in eternity. Oscar Cullmann (*The Christology of the New Testament* [Philadelphia: Westminster, 1959], 226), one of the principal advocates of this view, states, "The millennium is future and is, so to speak, the very last part of Christ's lordship, which at the same time extends into the new aeon. Consequently, the thousand-year kingdom should be identified neither with the whole chronological extent of Christ's lordship nor with the present Church. That lordship is the larger concept; it has already begun and continues in the aeon for an undefined length of time. The thousand-year reign, on the other hand, belongs temporally to the final act of Christ's lordship, the act which begins with his return and thus already invades the new aeon."

This view is called the "end-historical" view. It follows the same chronological sequence as the early church's position, i.e., parousia—defeat of Antichrist—binding of Satan—resurrection—millennium—release of Satan—final judgment—new heaven and new earth. It differs slightly from earlier chiliasm in viewing the millennium as an end-historical event that at the same time is the beginning of the eternal reign of Christ and the saints.

The problem as to the limits of the description of the millennium in chs. 20–22 is a more difficult question. A group of expositors of varying theological thought (Beasley-Murray, R. H. Charles, Ford, A. C. Gaebelein, Zahn) believe that 21:9–22:5, 14–15 belongs with 20:1–10 as a further description of the millennial reign, whereas 21:1–5 refers to the eternal state, which follows the final judgment of the dead. This approach is an attempt to harmonize a more literal understanding of certain statements in 21:9–22:5, 14–15 with the assumed conditions during the eternal state. For example, according to Beasley-Murray ("The Revelation," 1305) the references to nations and kings seem to describe an earthly kingdom better than they describe the eternal condition (21:24, 26); references to leaves'"healing" the nations" (22:2) seems to describe an imperfect condition better than they describe the perfected eternal state; and finally, the blessing pronounced on those who eat from the tree of life while a curse rests on all those outside the city (22:14–15) seems to relate better to the thousand years than to the eternal state when the wicked are in the lake of fire.

Admittedly, this is a possible solution that has the advantage of giving more descriptive content to the millennial reign. This approach, however, suffers from two serious criticisms. First, though it rightly assigns 21:1–5 to the postmillennial new Jerusalem in the context of the new heaven and new earth, it arbitrarily assigns 21:9–22:5, 14–15 to the millennial new Jerusalem without the slightest hint from the text that this is a recapitulation of 20:1–10. Thus there is an eternal new Jerusalem, followed immediately by a millennial new Jerusalem, both bearing the same title. This is hardly plausible. Second, this view strongly argues for historical progression in 19:11–21:5 (see above) and then it argues for recapitulation in 21:9–22:5, 14–15.

Therefore, despite some problems, it seems best to regard the sequence begun at 19:11 as running chronologically through 22:6, thus placing all the material in 21:1ff. after the millennium. At this point, a suggestion might be offered for further study. If—like the person, ministry, and resurrection of Jesus—the millennium is a true eschatological, historical event, may not 21:1ff. be viewed as the full manifestation of the kingdom of God, a partial manifestation of which will be realized in the thousand-year reign of Christ and the saints, during which Christ will defeat all of his enemies, including death (1Co 15:23–28)? Some of the same conditions described in 21:1ff. would then, at least in part, characterize the millennium.

A final question: Why the millennium? There are at least four answers:

1. During the millennium, Christ will openly manifest his kingdom in world history; the millennium will provide an actual demonstration of the truthfulness of the divine witness borne by Christ and his followers during their life on earth. It will be a time of the fulfillment of all God's covenant promises to his people.

2. The millennium will reveal that humanity's rebellion against God lies deep in the human heart, not in the devil's deception. Even when Satan is bound and righteousness prevails in the world, some people will still rebel against God. The final release of Satan will openly draw out this hidden evil.

3. The release of Satan after the millennium shows the invulnerability of the city of God and the extent of the authority of Christ, since the devil is immediately defeated and thrown into the lake of fire forever.

4. The millennium will serve as a long period required to do the general "housecleaning" needed after the preceding ages of sin, during which sin was prevalent.

¹And I saw an angel coming down out of heaven, having the key to the Abyss and holding in his hand a great chain. ²He seized the dragon, that ancient serpent, who is the devil, or Satan, and bound him for a thousand years. ³He threw him into the Abyss, and locked and sealed it over him, to keep him from deceiving the nations anymore until the thousand years were ended. After that, he must be set free for a short time.

⁴I saw thrones on which were seated those who had been given authority to judge. And I saw the souls of those who had been beheaded because of their testimony for Jesus and because of the word of God. They had not worshiped the beast or his image and had not received his mark on their foreheads or their hands. They came to life and reigned with Christ a thousand years. ⁵(The rest of the dead did not come to life until the thousand years were ended.) This is the first resurrection. ⁶Blessed and holy are those who have part in the first resurrection. The second death has no power over them, but they will be priests of God and of Christ and will reign with him for a thousand years.

COMMENTARY

1–3 These verses are integrally related to 19:20–21. After the destruction of the beast and his followers and of the false prophet, Satan (the dragon, the ancient serpent) is dealt with. He is thrown into the Abyss to be imprisoned there for a thousand years, which is the third last thing (see comments at Overview, 19:11–21). The Abyss is the demonic abode (see comments at 9:1; cf. 11:7). The angel's mission is to restrain Satan from deceiving the nations—thus the key, the chain, and the violent casting into the Abyss. That this whole action is not a recapitulation of earlier descriptions of Satan is evident from a number of points. In 12:9 (note the same titles for Satan), Satan is "hurled" out of heaven "to the earth," where he goes forth with great fury to work his deception and persecute God's people (13:14; 18:23c). But in 20:1–3, the situation is completely different. Here Satan is cast *out of the earth* into a place where he is kept from "deceiving the nations." The former period of Satan's restriction to earth is described as a "short time" (12:9, 12), while the time here (20:1–3) of his binding is a thousand years. In the earlier references to Satan, he is very active on the earth (2:10, 13; 12:17; 16:13, cf. 1Pe 5:8); here he is tightly sealed in "prison" (*phylakē*, GK 5871; v.7). The binding of Satan removes his deceptive activity among "the nations" (*ta ethnē*, GK 1620), a term never used to describe the redeemed community (until ch. 21, after Satan's permanent end).

From at least the time of Victorinus (d. ca. 303), some have interpreted the binding of Satan as the work of Christ in the lives of believers. Thus Satan is "bound" for believers since he no longer deceives them, but he is still "loose" for unbelievers who are deceived (Victorinus, *Apocalypse* 20; cf. Minear, 162). This explanation, however, does not take seriously the language of the Abyss and the prison in which Satan is confined, nor does it account for the releasing of

Satan after the thousand years. The binding of spirits or angels is mentioned in Isaiah 24:21–23; Jude 6 (cf. Tob 8:3; *1 En.* 10:4, 11–12; 88:1–3; *Jub.* 23:29; *T. Levi* 18:12). In all of these references there is no question of the spirits' being bound in some respects and not in others; it signifies a complete removal as to a prison, usually in the depths of the underworld (cf. Beasley-Murray, "The Revelation," 1305). Mounce's observation, 362, is well taken: "The elaborate measures taken to insure his custody are most easily understood as implying the complete cessation of his influence on earth (rather than a curbing of his activities)."

In only one NT reference is there a question as to the limited binding of Satan. In Mark 3:27, Jesus refers in his parable to the strong man's first being bound before his goods can be plundered. The reference is to Satan's being bound by Christ and according to Jeremias (*Parables of Jesus*, 122–23) specifically relates to the temptation of Jesus, or according to others to Jesus' exorcisms mentioned in the immediate context. In any case, the binding of Satan by the ministry of Jesus did not totally immobilize the devil but did strike him a vital blow. But does the reference in Mark provide a true analogy for the binding of Satan in 20:1–3, as Augustine claimed? A careful examination of Mark 3:27 and Revelation 20:1–3 leads to the conclusion that the two passages are not teaching the same truth. There is a sense in which, according to the gospel account, Satan is in the process of being bound by the activity of Christ and the kingdom of God; but this is clearly an event different from the total consigning of Satan to the Abyss as taught in Revelation 20:1–3.

Finally, it may be noted that the thousand-year binding of Satan is concurrent with and inseparable from the thousand-year reign of the resurrected martyrs. For the span of a thousand years on this earth, within history, the activity of Satan in leading humanity into false worship and active rebellion against God and his people will be totally curbed under the authority of Christ in his kingdom. If that reign is yet future, the binding is future. If the binding refers to an earthly situation—which it clearly does—the thousand-year reign most naturally refers to an earthly situation.

4 The fourth last thing (see comments at Overview, 19:11–21) is the thousand-year reign of Christ on the earth. John gives us no picture of life in the millennium in these verses; they contain only a statement about who will participate in it. He sees thrones, and judges sitting on them. The scene is usually connected with Daniel's vision of the Son of Man (Da 7:9, 22, 27). In Daniel, justice was done for the saints by the Ancient of Days, and they began their kingdom reign. The thought may be similar here. If this is the case, those who sit on the thrones are the angelic court. However, those on the thrones may be the resurrected martyrs, who exercise judgmental and ruling functions during the millennium. This possible reinterpretation of Daniel seems preferable in the light of other NT teaching as well as of Revelation itself (cf. Lk 22:30; 1Co 6:2; Rev 2:26). They who were once judged by earth's courts to be worthy of death are now the judges of the earth under Christ.

A more difficult question concerns the identity of those who will rule with Christ. They are the "beheaded" (with an ax [*pelekizō*, GK *4284*]; elsewhere *sphazō*, "slaughter," GK *5377*; cf. 6:9) martyrs who have previously occupied John's attention. The cause of their death is attributed to their faithful witness to Jesus and the word of God (on these terms, see comments at 1:9; cf. 6:9; 12:11). The reference to "souls" (*psychas*, GK *6034*) immediately recalls 6:9, where the same expression is used of the slain witnesses under the altar. The word describes those who have lost their bodily lives but are nevertheless still alive in God's sight. This term prepares

us for their coming to (bodily) life again at the first resurrection. It is a mistake to take *psychas* to imply a later spiritual resurrection or rebirth of the soul, as did Augustine and many since (contra Swete, Beale).

These martyrs are also those who did not worship the beast or his image or receive his mark on them (cf. 13:1–17; 15:2); in a word, they are the followers of the Lamb. At this point, the NIV omits a very important term. Between the description of those beheaded and the description concerning the beast worship in v.4 are the two words *kai hoitines* ("and who"). This construction can bear two different meanings. It could simply introduce a further qualifying phrase to the identification of the martyrs (so NIV, TEV). But it may also be understood as introducing a second group. There are (1) those who were beheaded for their witness and (2) "also those who" did not worship the beast (so Rissi, Swete; see JB; MLB, "and of these also"; NASB, "and those who"). This immediately alleviates a thorny problem, i.e., why only the martyrs should live and reign with Christ. Usually in Revelation the relative pronoun *hoitines* ("who") simply refers to the preceding group and adds some further detail (2:24, 9:4; 17:12); however, in one other reference that alone has the identical introductory terms (*kai hoitines*), the phrase so introduced singles out a special class or group from the more general group in the preceding statement (1:7). Thus the *kai hoitines* clause introduces a special class of the beheaded, i.e., those who were so beheaded because they did not worship the beast, etc. In any case it seems that John has only the beheaded in mind (cf. 14:13).

But this presents a problem, because John has elsewhere indicated that the kingdom reign will be shared by every believer who overcomes (2:26–28; 3:12, 21) and is purchased by Christ's blood (5:10). Also, in 1 Corinthians 6:2–3 Paul clearly speaks of all believers—not just martyrs—exercising judgment in the future. Revelation 5:10 indicates that the kingdom will be a "reign on the earth." Unless only those beheaded by the beast and resurrected will reign in the millennium (so Mounce), another explanation is demanded. The pastoral approach would explain John's reference to the martyrs only as a piece of special encouragement to them, while not implying that others would be left out (so Beasley-Murray).

I feel somewhat more comfortable with the view expressed earlier (see comments at 6:9)—that the martyrs represent the whole church that is faithful to Jesus, whether or not they have actually been killed (cf. G. A. Krodel, *Revelation* [Minneapolis: Augsburg, 1989], 333–34; Boring, 204; Osborne, 705). They constitute a group that can in truth be described as those who "did not love their lives so much as to shrink from death" (12:11). As such, the term is a synonym for overcomers (chs. 2–3). Thus John could count himself in this group, though he may never have suffered death by the ax of the beast. In 2:11, those who during persecution are faithful to Christ even to the point of death are promised escape from the second death, which in 20:6 is promised to those who share in the first resurrection, i.e., the beheaded (v.4). In fact, a number of the other promises to overcomers in the letters to the seven churches also find their fulfillment in ch. 20 (cf. 2:11 with 20:6; 2:26–27 with 20:4; 3:5 with 20:12, 15; 3:21 with 20:4).

The martyrs "came to life." The interpretation of these words is crucial to the whole passage. Since Augustine, the majority of interpreters have taken the words to refer to a spiritual resurrection or new birth, or to the triumph of the church. For example, Caird, 255, sees the parallel to Christ's resurrection (2:8) but seems to spiritualize Jesus' resurrection and concludes that resurrection for the martyrs "means that they have been let loose into the world." This substitutes some symbolic sense of

physical resurrection for the historical event. Others, rightly chastened by a more serious exegesis of the text, hold that the language teaches bodily resurrection but that the whole section (vv.1–10) is not to be taken as predicting events within history but is apocalyptic language, figurative of the consolation and reward promised the martyrs (so Beckwith, 737). Berkouwer's position, 307, typifies the mystical and vague language used by nonmillennialists to explain what the passage means: "We may not tamper with the real, graphic nature of the vision of Revelation 20, nor may we spiritualize the first resurrection. But one question is still decisive: does this vision intend to sketch for us a particular phase of *history* [italics his]? If one does interpret it this way, it seems to me that he must include the first (bodily) resurrection in his concept of a future millennium.... This vision is not a narrative account of a future earthly reign of peace at all, but is the apocalyptic unveiling of the reality of salvation in Christ as a backdrop to the reality of the suffering and martyrdom that still continue as long as the dominion of Christ remains hidden." While alleviating the criticism of a spiritual resurrection, Berkouwer's position fails to take with equal seriousness the language of the thousand-year reign, which is everywhere in the Apocalypse a reign on the *earth* within *history*.

The verb *ezēsan* ("came to life," from *zaō*, GK *2409*) is used in v.4 of the martyrs and also in v.5 of the "rest of the dead" who did not come to life until the thousand years were completed. When the context is that of bodily death, *ezēsan* is used in the NT to connote physical resurrection (Jn 11:25; Ac 1:3; 9:41), though the normal word is *egeirō* ("raise up," GK *1586*). More importantly, Revelation clearly uses *zaō* ("live") for the resurrection of Christ (1:18; 2:8) and also curiously for the sea beast (13:14). John 5:25 is sometimes cited as evidence that *zaō* refers to spiritual life, not physical resurrection. But a careful reading of the context clearly shows that while 5:25 does indeed use *zaō* in the sense of spiritual life (as do other NT passages), John 5:29 is definitely referring to physical resurrection and uses the phrase "rise to live" (*anastasin zoēs*, from *zaō*). John plainly says in Revelation 20:5 that "this is the first resurrection" (*anastasis prōtē*). The word *anastasis* (GK *414*), which occurs over forty times in the NT, is used almost exclusively of physical resurrection (Lk 2:34 is the only exception). There is no indication that John has departed from this usage in these verses.

5–6 Why does John call this the "first" resurrection? The term *prōtē* (GK *4755*) clearly implies the first in a series of two or more. John does not directly refer to a second resurrection; a second resurrection is, however, correctly inferred, both from the use of *prōtē* and also from the expression "the rest of the dead did not come to life until the thousand years were ended." Irenaeus (*Haer.* 39.3–10) clearly connects John's first resurrection with the "resurrection of the just" (cf. Lk 14:14). Likewise, Justin Martyr (*Dial.* 80–81) held to a physical resurrection before the millennium and a general physical resurrection after the thousand years, though he does not explain whether believers will also participate in the latter. From at least the time of Augustine, the first resurrection was understood as a regeneration of the soul and the second resurrection as the general bodily resurrection of just and unjust. It must, however, be insisted that it is quite weak exegesis to make the first resurrection spiritual and the second one physical unless the text itself clearly indicates this change, which it does not.

Another way to understand "the rest of the dead" who didn't come to life until the close of the thousand years is to see them as all the faithful except the martyrs, plus the entire body of unbelievers (so Mounce, 370). This view, in our opinion, runs aground on the fact that John clearly seems to

tie exclusion from the second death with those who are part of the first resurrection, thus strongly implying that those who participate in the second resurrection are destined for the second death.

Therefore, following the lead of the earlier exegesis of Irenaeus, we may understand the first resurrection as being the raising to physical life of all the dead in Christ (cf. 1Co 15:12–28; 1Th 4:13–18); this is the resurrection to life of John 5:29 (NIV, "rise to live"). For those who participate in this resurrection, "the second death [the lake of fire (Rev 20:14)] has no power over them" (v.6). Therefore, they are "blessed and holy" (the fifth beatitude in Revelation; see comments at 1:3) and shall be priests of God and of Christ for the thousand years. On the other hand, those over whom the second death will have power must be "the rest of the dead" (v.5), who will be participants in the second resurrection but will "rise to be condemned" (Jn 5:29; cf.Ac 24:15).

In the only place other than Revelation 2:11 and 20:6 where the second death is mentioned, it refers to exclusion from physical resurrection (v.14). Likewise in the Palestinian Targum on Deuteronomy 33:6—the OT *locus theologicus* in rabbinic Judaism for proving the resurrection from the dead—the Targum reads, "Let Reuben live in this world and not die in the second death in which death the wicked die in the world to come." In the Targum, the second death means exclusion from the resurrection. Not to die the second death, then, means to rise again to eternal life (cf. McNamara, *Targum and Testament*, 123).

What now may be said as to the *length* of the kingdom reign? Nowhere in other literature is the kingdom reign of the Messiah specified as one thousand years (on *2 En.* 33, see Notes, vv.4–6), though estimates of 400, 40, 70, 365, or an indefinite period (*b. Sanh.* 99*a*) are found. Thus parallels to John's use of a thousand years must be sought elsewhere. According to Daniélou (*Theology* *of Jewish Christianity*, 377–404), the most primitive traditions in Asia relate the thousand years to Adam's paradisiacal time span. According to the book of *Jubilees*, Adam's sin caused him to die at 930 years of age (Ge 5:5), "seventy years before attaining a thousand years, for one thousand years are as one day [Ps 90:4] in heaven. . . . For this reason [because he ate from the tree of knowledge] he died before completing the years of this day" (*Jub.* 4:29–30). Here the thousand years are based on an exegesis of Genesis 2:17 in terms of Psalm 90:4—Adam dies on the day when he eats the forbidden fruit; but according to Psalm 90:4, a day means one thousand years, and therefore Adam dies before reaching one thousand years. Daniélou believes this is the origin of John's use of the thousand years.

Later the thousand years began to be associated with the Jewish cosmic-week framework, in which the history of the world is viewed as lasting a week of millennia, or seven thousand years. The last-day millennium is the Sabbath-rest millennium, followed by the eighth day of the age to come. This idea was then linked interpretatively but inappropriately to 2 Peter 3:8. While early Christian writings such as the *Epistle of Barnabas* reflect this reasoning, it was not, according to Daniélou, the most primitive tradition.

Is the thousand years, then, symbolic of a perfect human life span or some ideal kingdom environment on the earth? In the first place, the number symbolisms of John in Revelation should not be used to argue against an *earthly* kingdom. It might be said that the number is symbolic of a perfect period of time of whatever length (so Craig Koester, *Revelation and the End of All Things* [Grand Rapids: Eerdmans, 2001]). The essence of premillennialism is in its insistence that the reign will be on earth, not in heaven, for a period of time before the final judgment and the new heaven and new earth. For example, we may rightly understand the 1,260 days (forty-two months) of earlier chapters as a symbolic number, but it still refers to an actual historical period of whatever length during which the beast will destroy the saints. If we look at the time of suffering of the Christians of Smyrna, it is "ten days" (2:10)—a relatively short time in comparison to a thousand years of victorious reign with Christ. In any case, it is not of primary importance whether the years are actual 365-day years or symbolic of a shorter or longer period of bliss enjoyed by believers as they reign with Christ on earth (cf. 5:10 with 11:15; 22:5).

NOTES

1–6 Some selected bibliographic references on the millennial question may be helpful:

Premillennial—*Historic, Nondispensational:* Henry Alford, *The Revelation"* (1884); G. R. Beasley-Murray, "The Revelation" (1970) and *The Book of Revelation* (1978); George Ladd, *A Commentary on the Revelation of John* (1972); Merrill Tenney, *Interpreting Revelation* (1957); Oscar Cullmann, *The Christology of the New Testament* (1959); Mathias Rissi, *Time and History* (1966) and *The Future of the World: An Exegetical Study of Revelation 19:11–22:15* (1972); ***Dispensational:*** John Walvoord, *The Revelation of Jesus Christ* (1966); Robert Thomas, *Revelation* (1992–95).

Amillennial: Augustine, *The City of God* 20.6–15; G. B. Caird, *The Revelation of St. John the Divine* (1966); Rudolf Schnackenburg, *Present and Future: Modern Aspects of New Testament Theology* (South Bend,

Ind.: Univ. of Notre Dame Press, 1966); G. C. Berkouwer, *The Return of Christ* (1972); Harry Boer, "What About the Millennium?" *RefJ* 25 (Jan. 1975): 26–30, and "The Reward of Martyrs," *RefJ* 25 (Feb. 1975): 7–9, 28; Gregory Beale, *The Book of Revelation* (1999).

Postmillennial: Lorraine Boettner, *The Millennium* (Philadelphia: Presbyterian & Reformed, 1958); Rousas J. Rushdoony, *The Institutes of Biblical Law* (Nutley, N.J.: Craig, 1973); H. Berkhof, *Christ the Meaning of History* (1979). For background material, see G. R. Beasley-Murray, H. Hobbs, and R. Robbins, *Revelation: Three Viewpoints* (Nashville: Broadman, 1977); Robert G. Clouse, ed., *The Meaning of the Millennium: Four Views* (Downers Grove, Ill.: InterVarsity, 1977); Millard J. Erickson, *Contemporary Options in Eschatology: A Study of the Millennium* (Grand Rapids: Baker, 1977); John Jefferson Davis, *Christ's Victorious Kingdom: Postmillennialism Reconsidered* (Grand Rapids: Baker, 1986).

For helpful **historical surveys** of the origins of millennial thought, see Jean Daniélou, *Theology of Jewish Christianity*; R. J. McKelvey, *The Millennium and the Book of Revelation* (Cambridge: Lutterworth, 1999); Marcellus J. Kik, *The Eschatology of Victory* (Nutley, N.J.: Presbyterian & Reformed, 1975), 229–33; D. H. Kromminga, *The Millennium in the Church* (Grand Rapids: Eerdmans, 1945); Charles Maitland, *The Apostle's School of Prophetic Interpretation* (London: Longman, Brown, Green, and Longmans, 1849).

4 The plural ἐκάθισαν (*ekathisan*, GK 2767; lit., "they sat"; NIV, "were seated") may be another instance of the Semitic idiom where the plural is used for the passive idea (cf. note on 12:6). In this case, the NIV's rendering is perfectly justified.

4–6 An interesting comment on Gregory Beale's treatment of 20:1–7 (*John's Use of the Old Testament in Revelation* [JSNTSup 166. Sheffield: Sheffield Academic Press, 1998], ch. 6) is Aune's assessment (*RelSRev* 27 [2001], 174) that Beale uses "exegetical legerdemain to produce a figurative interpretation acceptable to Reformed theology."

Second Enoch 33:1ff. (of doubtful age) is sometimes cited as evidence that the Jews believed in a thousand-year messianic age. However, the Jewish cosmic-week explanation for the history of the world did not explicitly connect the Messiah's reign to the seventh-day millennium. Thus there arose a multitude of different-year periods assigned to the messianic age that would precede the eternal period or age to come.

On the possibility that the first resurrection refers to the intermediate state, see M. Kline, "The First Resurrection," *WTJ* 37 (1974–75): 366–75; J. R. Michaels, "The First Resurrection: A Response," *WTJ* 39 (1976): 100–109; P. E. Hughes, "The First Resurrection: Another Interpretation," *WTJ* 39 (1977): 315–18; see also J. S. Deere, "Premillennialism in Revelation 20:4–6," *BSac* 135 (1978): 58–73.

Following Beckwith, Mounce (369–70), Bauckham (*Theology of the Book of Revelation*, 107–8), and recently Dave Mathewson ("A Re-examination of the Millennium in Rev 20:1–6: Consummation and Recapitulation," *JETS* 44 [2001]: 237–52) have argued that there is a difference between essential truth of prophecy and its form. Mounce, 369, notes that "John taught a literal millennium [form], but its essential meaning may be realized in something other than a temporal fulfillment." So John teaches a literal era or period for the millennium, but we may understand it as merely a theme of the martyr's reward for faithfulness. This whole approach seems arbitrary at best and problematic at worst. What if we were to apply this to Paul's eschatological teaching in 1 Corinthians 15 about the resurrection of Christ and of believers? Is this not a form of demythologization?

C. The Release and End of Satan (20:7–10)

OVERVIEW

The fifth last thing (see comments at Overview, 19:11–21) is the defeat of Satan. In v.3 the release of Satan after the millennium was anticipated: "He must [*dei*] be set free for a short time [*mikron chronon*]" (cf. 12:12, *oligon kairon*). Why must he once again be released? The answer is so that he can "deceive the nations" (v.8) throughout the world and lead them into conflict against "God's people" (v.9). But why should God allow this? Certainly if humans alone were prophetically writing the history of the world they would not bring the archdeceiver back after the glorious reign of Christ (vv.4–6). But God's thoughts and ways are not humankind's (Isa 55:8).

Ezekiel's vision of Gog brought out of the land of Magog (Eze 38–39) seems to be clearly in John's mind. Ezekiel also saw an attack on God's people, who had been restored for some time ("after many days" [Eze 38:8])—i.e., after the commencement of the kingdom age. In Ezekiel 38–39, Gog refers to the prince of a host of pagan invaders from the North, especially the Scythian hordes from the distant land of Magog. In Revelation, however, the names are symbolic of the final enemies of Christ duped by Satan into attacking the community of the saints. The change in meaning has occurred historically through the frequent use in rabbinic circles of the expression "Gog and Magog" to refer symbolically to the nations spoken of in Psalm 2 that are in rebellion against God and his Messiah (cf. Caird, 256, for talmudic references).

---

⁷When the thousand years are over, Satan will be released from his prison ⁸and will go out to deceive the nations in the four corners of the earth—Gog and Magog—to gather them for battle. In number they are like the sand on the seashore. ⁹They marched across the breadth of the earth and surrounded the camp of God's people, the city he loves. But fire came down from heaven and devoured them. ¹⁰And the devil, who deceived them, was thrown into the lake of burning sulfur, where the beast and the false prophet had been thrown. They will be tormented day and night for ever and ever.

COMMENTARY

8 If the beast and his armies are already destroyed (19:19–21), who are these rebellious nations? It may be that the beast and his armies in the earlier context refer to the demonic powers and those in 20:7–10 to human nations in rebellion—not an unlikely solution (see comments at 19:19–21)—or it may be that not all the people in the world will participate in the beast's armies, and thus those mentioned here in v.8 refer to other people who during the millennial reign defected in their hearts from the Messiah. In any case, this section shows something of the deep, complex nature of evil. The source of rebellion against God does not lie in humanity's environment or fundamentally with the devil but springs up from deep within the human heart. The return of Satan will demonstrate this in the most dramatic manner once for all. The temporal reign of Christ will not be fulfilled till this final challenge to his kingdom occurs and he demonstrates the power of his victory at the cross by putting down all his enemies (1Co 15:25).

9 The gathered army, which is extensive and worldwide, advances and in siegelike fashion encircles the "camp [*parembolē*, GK *4213*] of God's people, the city he loves." Most commentators take the terms "camp" and "city" as different metaphors for God's people. The word *parembolē* in the NT refers to either a military camp or the camp of Israel (Ac 21:34, 37; 22:24; Heb 11:34; 13:11, 13). It is a word that reminds us of the pilgrim character of the people of God even at the end of the millennium, as long as evil is active in God's creation.

The "city he loves" presents more difficulty. According to standard Jewish eschatology, this should refer to the restored and spiritually renewed city of Jerusalem in Palestine (Pss 78:6–8; 87:2; cf. Beckwith, 746). A number of modern commentators of various theological opinions have taken this Jewish identification as a clue and have so understood the passage (Berkhof, *Christ the Meaning of History*, 153; Ladd, 270; Charles, 2:145). On the other hand, John may have intended to refer merely to the community of the redeemed without any specific geographical location in mind. This would be in harmony with his previous references to the city elsewhere in the book (cf. comments at 3:12; 11:2, 8). There are only two cities or kingdoms in the Apocalypse—the city of Satan, where the beast

and harlot are central, and the city of God, where God and the Lamb are central. The city, then, is the kingdom of God in its millennial manifestation; it is the same city that appears in its final, most glorious form in the last chapters (21–22). Wherever God dwells among his people, there the city of God is (21:2–3). Following this understanding of the beloved city in no way weakens the validity of an earthly reign of Christ and the saints.

The swiftness and finality of the divine judgment emphasizes the reality of the victory of Christ at the cross. The fire imagery may reflect Ezekiel's vision of the destruction of Gog (Eze 38:22; 39:6). Note that unlike the Qumran and Jewish apocalyptic literature it is God, not the saints, who destroys the enemy (cf. comments at 19:19).

10 The devil is now dealt the long-awaited final and fatal blow (Ge 3:15; Jn 12:31). The "lake of fire" imagery is probably related to the teaching of Jesus about hell (*geenna*, GK *1147*; Mt 5:22; 7:19; 10:28; 13:49–50; Mk 9:48). The lake image may be related to certain Jewish descriptions of eternal judgment (cf. *2 En.* 10:2: "a gloomy fire is always burning, and a fiery river goes forth"). The figure may intensify the idea of the permanency of the judgment (cf. comments at 14:11; also 19:20; 20:14–15; 21:8). That the beast and false prophet are already there does not argue for their individuality (contra Beasley-Murray, "The Revelation," 1308), since later in the chapter "death" and "Hades"—nonpersonal entities that for the sake of the imagery are personified—are cast into the same lake of fire (20:14).

NOTES

8 On "Gog," see *TDNT* 1:789–91; Ralph Alexander, "A Fresh Look at Ezekiel 38 and 39," *JETS* 17 (1974): 157–69. Alexander argues for multiple manifestations of Gog in history and the close parallelism between Ezekiel 38–39 and Revelation 20:7–10.

The Palestinian Targum on Exodus 40 refers to the Messiah of Ephraim "by whose hand the house of Israel is to vanquish Gog and his confederates at the end of days" (cited by Ford, 356).

D. Great White Throne Judgment (20:11–15)

OVERVIEW

John describes in vivid pictures the sixth last thing (see comments at Overview, 19:11–21)—the final judgment of humankind. Unlike many of the vivid, imaginative paintings based on this vision, here John describes a strange, unearthly scene. Heaven and earth flee from the unidentified figure who sits on the majestic white throne. The language of poetic imagery captures the fading character of everything of the world (1Jn 2:17). Now the only reality is God seated on the throne of judgment, the One before whom all must appear (Heb 9:27). His verdict alone is holy and righteous (white symbolism). It is possible that in Revelation the earth and sky refer more to the religio-political order than to the cosmological one (cf. Caird). Since vv.11–12 make use of the theophany of Daniel 7:9–10, the One seated on the throne is presumably God himself; but since 22:1, 3 mentions the throne of God *and of the Lamb*, it may well be that here Jesus shares in the judgment (Jn 5:27; cf. France, 203). God has kept the last judgment in his own hands. This vision declares that even though it may have seemed that earth's course of history ran contrary to his holy will, no single day or hour in the world's drama has ever detracted from the absolute sovereignty of God (cf. Lilje).

¹¹Then I saw a great white throne and him who was seated on it. Earth and sky fled from his presence, and there was no place for them. ¹²And I saw the dead, great and small, standing before the throne, and books were opened. Another book was opened, which is the book of life. The dead were judged according to what they had done as recorded in the books. ¹³The sea gave up the dead that were in it, and death and Hades gave up the dead that were in them, and each person was judged according to what he had done. ¹⁴Then death and Hades were thrown into the lake of fire. The lake of fire is the second death. ¹⁵If anyone's name was not found written in the book of life, he was thrown into the lake of fire.

COMMENTARY

12 But who are "the dead"? Earlier in the chapter, John has mentioned the "rest of the dead" who are not resurrected until the thousand years are completed (v.5). As Mounce, 365, observes, "If the first resurrection is limited to actual martyrs, then the judgment of verses 11–15 involves both believer and impenitent. If the second resurrection is of the wicked only, then the judgment is of those who will in fact be consigned to the lake of fire." While no resurrection is mentioned in vv.11–15, the dead may well be those who did not participate in the first resurrection. Since the second death has no power over those who were raised in the first resurrection (v.6), it may be argued that only those who are the enemies of God—i.e., the wicked dead—stand before this throne (Jn 5:24). This is by no means a necessary inference, though it is the most satisfying exegesis.

A moment of tension arrives. The books are opened. It is sobering to ponder that in God's sight nothing is forgotten; all will give an account of their actions (v.13). Judgment always proceeds on the basis of works (Mt 25:41–46; Ro 2:6; 2Co 5:10; Heb 4:12–13). The "books" are the records of human deeds. While in Jewish thought there are references to books of good and evil deeds as being kept before God (*4 Ezra* 6:20; *1 En.* 47:3), John is probably alluding to Daniel 7:10: "The court was seated, and the books were opened." We are not told whether these books contain both good and evil works, or only the latter. John is more concerned about another book, the book of life, which alone seems to be decisive (vv.12, 15; cf. at 3:5; also 13:8; 17:8; 21:27). How can these two pictures be harmonized? In reality there is no conflict. Works are unmistakable evidence of the loyalty of the heart; they express either belief or unbelief, faithfulness or unfaithfulness. The judgment will reveal through the records whether or not the loyalties were with God and the Lamb or with God's enemies. John's theology of faith and its inseparable relation to works is the same as Jesus' and Paul's (Jn 5:29; Ro 2:6–16). This judgment is not a balancing of good works over bad works. Those who have their names in the Lamb's book of life will also have records of righteous deeds. The opposite will be true as well. The imagery reflects the delicate balance between grace and obedience (cf. comments at 19:6–8).

13 Three broad places are mentioned as containing the dead: the sea, death, and Hades. The sea represents the place of unburied bodies, while death and Hades represent the reality of dying and the condition entered on at death (cf. 1:18; 6:8). The imagery suggests release of the bodies and persons from their places of confinement following death; i.e., it portrays resurrection. They rise to receive sentence (Jn 5:29b). Death and Hades are personified (cf. 6:8) and in a vivid image are cast into the lake of fire to be permanently destroyed (cf. 19:20; 20:10). This not only fulfills Paul's cry concerning the last enemy, death, which will be defeated by the victorious kingdom of Christ (1Co 15:26), but also signals the earth's new condition: "There will be no more death" (21:4).

15 The final scene in this dark and fearful passage is found here. From the English rendering it might be inferred that John is doubtful whether anyone will be thrown into the lake of fire. The Greek construction, however, is not so indefinite. John uses a first-class condition, which assumes the reality of the first clause and shows the consequences in the second clause. Thus we might paraphrase the verse this way: "If anyone's name was not found written in the book of life, and I assume there were such, he was thrown into the lake of fire." When taken seriously this final note evaporates all theories of universalism or *apokatastasis* (GK *640*; cf. Berkouwer's excellent discussion, 387–423).

NOTES

15 The "second death" terminology does not occur in rabbinic teaching in this period, but it is found in the Targum to the Prophets on Isaiah 65:6, where it is said that the bodies (resurrected) of the wicked are delivered to the second death. This supports the idea of a second resurrection of the unjust that precedes the casting into the second death (cf. Israel Abrahams, *Studies in Pharisaism and the Gospels* [New York: Ktav, 1967], 41–49).

V. VISION OF THE NEW HEAVEN AND THE NEW EARTH AND THE NEW JERUSALEM (21:1–22:5)

A. The New Jerusalem (21:1–27)

OVERVIEW

The seventh last thing (see comments at Overview, 19:11–21) is the vision of the new heaven, the new earth, and the new Jerusalem. J. Moffatt's striking remark (EGT, 5:477), which captures something of the freshness of this moment in the book, is worth remembering at the outset of the exposition of this incredibly beautiful finale: "From the smoke and pain and heat [of the preceding scenes] it is a relief to pass into the clear, clean atmosphere of the eternal morning where the breath of heaven is sweet and the vast city of God sparkles like a diamond in the radiance of his presence."

Countless productions of art and music have through the ages been inspired by this vision. Cathedral architecture has been influenced by its imagery. John discloses a theology in stone and gold as pure as glass and color. Archetypal images abound. The church is called the bride (21:2). God gives the thirsty "to drink without cost from the spring of the water of life" (21:6). Completeness is implied in the number twelve and its multiples (21:12–14, 16–17, 21), and fullness in the cubical dimension of the city (21:16). Colorful jewels abound, as do references to light and the glory of God (21:11, 18–21, 23, 25; 22:5). There is the "river of the water of life" (22:1) and the "tree of life" (22:2). The "sea" is gone (21:1).

Allusions to the OT abound. Most of John's imagery in this chapter reflects especially Isaiah 60 and 65 and Ezekiel 40–48. John weaves the new Jerusalem vision of Isaiah together with the new temple vision of Ezekiel. The multiple OT promises converging in John's mind seem to indicate that he

viewed the new Jerusalem as the fulfillment of all of these strands of prophecy. There are also allusions to Genesis 1–3—the absence of death and suffering, the dwelling of God with men as in Eden, the tree of life, the removal of the curse, etc. Creation is restored to its pristine character (cf. Claus Westermann, *Beginning and End in the Bible* [Philadelphia: Fortress, 1972]).

The connection of this vision with the promises to the overcomers in the letters to the seven churches (chs. 2–3) is significant. For example, to the overcomers at Ephesus was granted the right to the tree of life (2:7; cf. 22:2); to those at Thyatira, the right to rule the nations (2:26; cf. 22:5); to those at Philadelphia, the name of the city of my God, the new Jerusalem (3:12 and 21:2, 9–27). In a sense, a strand from every major section of the Apocalypse appears in chs. 21–22. Moreover, almost every major theme and image found in these chapters can be duplicated from Jewish literature (cf. Rissi, *Future of the World*, 46–51). But there is in the totality of John's vision a dimension clearly lacking in Jewish parallels. Furthermore, his theology of the Lamb's centrality in the city and the absence of a temple in the new Jerusalem is unique.

In other NT passages, the vision of the heavenly city is described as having the character of eschatological promise. The kingdom reality of the age to come has already appeared in history in the life of Jesus and also in the presence of the Holy Spirit in the church. But the reality is now present only in a promissory way, not in actual fulfillment. Therefore, while the Jerusalem that is above has present implications for believers (Gal 4:25–31), they are nevertheless, like Abraham, "looking forward to the city with foundations" (Heb 11:10; 13:14). In this sense the medieval synthesis that made the church on earth and the kingdom synonymous and built its cathedrals to depict that notion was misdirected. John's vision in chs. 21–22 is one of eschatological promise, future in its realization, and totally depen-

dent on God's power to create it, yet having present implications for the life of the church in this age.

Outlines of the chapters are necessarily arbitrary because of the familiar Semitic style of doubling back and elaborating previous subjects. Perhaps 21:1–8 may be seen as a preface or introduction to the vision of the new Jerusalem (21:9–22:6), and this in turn may be seen as followed by the conclusion in 22:7–21.

[1]Then I saw a new heaven and a new earth, for the first heaven and the first earth had passed away, and there was no longer any sea. [2]I saw the Holy City, the new Jerusalem, coming down out of heaven from God, prepared as a bride beautifully dressed for her husband. [3]And I heard a loud voice from the throne saying, "Now the dwelling of God is with men, and he will live with them. They will be his people, and God himself will be with them and be their God. [4]He will wipe every tear from their eyes. There will be no more death or mourning or crying or pain, for the old order of things has passed away."

[5]He who was seated on the throne said, "I am making everything new!" Then he said, "Write this down, for these words are trustworthy and true."

[6]He said to me: "It is done. I am the Alpha and the Omega, the Beginning and the End. To him who is thirsty I will give to drink without cost from the spring of the water of life. [7]He who overcomes will inherit all this, and I will be his God and he will be my son. [8]But the cowardly, the unbelieving, the vile, the murderers, the sexually immoral, those who practice magic arts, the idolaters and all liars—their place will be in the fiery lake of burning sulfur. This is the second death."

[9]One of the seven angels who had the seven bowls full of the seven last plagues came and said to me, "Come, I will show you the bride, the wife of the Lamb." [10]And he carried me away in the Spirit to a mountain great and high, and showed me the Holy City, Jerusalem, coming down out of heaven from God. [11]It shone with the glory of God, and its brilliance was like that of a very precious jewel, like a jasper, clear as crystal. [12]It had a great, high wall with twelve gates, and with twelve angels at the gates. On the gates were written the names of the twelve tribes of Israel. [13]There were three gates on the east, three on the north, three on the south and three on the west. [14]The wall of the city had twelve foundations, and on them were the names of the twelve apostles of the Lamb.

[15]The angel who talked with me had a measuring rod of gold to measure the city, its gates and its walls. [16]The city was laid out like a square, as long as it was wide. He measured the city with the rod and found it to be 12,000 stadia in length, and as wide and high as it is long. [17]He measured its wall and it was 144 cubits thick, by man's measurement, which the angel was using. [18]The wall was made of jasper, and the city of pure gold, as pure as glass. [19]The foundations of the city walls were decorated with every

kind of precious stone. The first foundation was jasper, the second sapphire, the third chalcedony, the fourth emerald, [20]the fifth sardonyx, the sixth carnelian, the seventh chrysolite, the eighth beryl, the ninth topaz, the tenth chrysoprase, the eleventh jacinth, and the twelfth amethyst. [21]The twelve gates were twelve pearls, each gate made of a single pearl. The great street of the city was of pure gold, like transparent glass.

[22]I did not see a temple in the city, because the Lord God Almighty and the Lamb are its temple. [23]The city does not need the sun or the moon to shine on it, for the glory of God gives it light, and the Lamb is its lamp. [24]The nations will walk by its light, and the kings of the earth will bring their splendor into it. [25]On no day will its gates ever be shut, for there will be no night there. [26]The glory and honor of the nations will be brought into it. [27]Nothing impure will ever enter it, nor will anyone who does what is shameful or deceitful, but only those whose names are written in the Lamb's book of life.

COMMENTARY

1 The new heaven and new earth were foreseen by Isaiah (65:17) as a part of his vision of the renewed Jerusalem. It is remarkable that John's picture of the final age to come focuses not on a platonic, ideal heaven or a distant paradise but on the reality of a new earth and a new heaven. God originally created the earth and heaven to be the permanent home of human beings. But sin and death entered the world and transformed the earth into a place of rebellion and alienation; it became enemy-occupied territory. But God has been working in salvation history to effect a total reversal of this evil consequence and to liberate earth and heaven from bondage to sin and corruption (Ro 8:21). "The first heaven and the first earth" refers to the whole order of life in the world—an order tainted by sin, death, suffering, and idolatry (cf. v.4: "the old order of things [death, mourning, crying, pain] . . . has passed away"). John's emphasis on heaven and earth is not primarily cosmological but moral and spiritual. So Peter also speaks of the new heaven and the new earth, "the home of righteousness" (2Pe 3:13).

The Greek word for "new" (*kainē*, GK *2785*) means new in quality, fresh—rather than recent or

new in time (*neos*, GK *3742*; *TDNT* 3:447). That it is a *kainē* heaven and earth and not a second heaven and earth suggests something of an endless succession of a new heaven and earth. It is the newness of the endless eschatological age (2:17; 3:12; 5:9; cf. Eph 2:7). What makes the new heaven and earth "new" is above all else the reality that now "the dwelling of God is with men. . . . They will be his people, and God himself will be with them and be their God" (v.3). The heaven and earth are new because of the presence of a new community of people who are loyal to God and the Lamb, in contrast to the former earth in which a community of idolaters lived.

The sea—the source of the satanic beast (13:1) and the place of the dead (20:13)—will be gone. Again the emphasis is not geographic but moral and spiritual. Most see the sea as an archetype with connotations of evil (cf. comments at 13:1); therefore, no trace of evil in any form will be present in the new creation. Others detect an exodus motif: "One could say the sea was no more when the Israelites walked on dry land through the Red Sea" (Ford, 361). Most recently this exodus motif has been linked to the new creation emphasis: "More than signifying some change in the cosmological landscape, the removal of the sea expresses the hope of God's people in the final removal of all things that threaten and hinder them from the full experience of salvation. Even as God's people await their eschatological inheritance, the declaration that 'the sea was no more' provides a stark reminder that all the evils which threaten God's people already stand within the sphere of God's power" (Dave Mathewson, "New Exodus as a Background for 'The Sea Was No More' in Revelation 21:1c," *TJ* 24 NS [2003]: 258).

2 The Holy City, the new Jerusalem, occupies John's vision for the remainder of the book. How different is this concept of heaven from that of Hinduism, for example. Here heaven is depicted as a city with life, activity, interest, and people, as opposed to the Hindu ideal of heaven as a sea into which human life returns like a raindrop to the ocean. John first sees the city "coming down out of heaven from God"— a phrase he uses three times (3:12; 21:2, 10) in an apparent spatial reference. But the city never seems to come down; it is always seen as a "descending-from-heaven kind of city" (Caird, 257). Therefore, the expression stresses the idea that the city is a gift of God, forever bearing the marks of his creation.

Second, John calls the city a "bride" (*nymphē*, GK *3811*; cf. 21:9; 22:17). Earlier he referred to the bride of the Lamb (19:7–8) by a different word (*gynē*, GK *1222*), though the reality is the same. The multiple imagery is needed to portray the tremendous reality of the city. A bride-city captures something of God's personal relationship to his people (the bride), as well as something of their life in communion with him and one another (a city, with its social connotations). The purity and devotedness of the bride are reflected in her attire.

The subtitle of the Holy City—"the new Jerusalem"—raises a question. The "old" Jerusalem was also called the "holy city" and a "bride" (Isa 52:1; 61:10). Since the Jerusalem from above is the "new" (*kainē*) Jerusalem, we may suppose that it is connected in some manner with the old one, so that the new is the old one renewed. The old Jerusalem was marred by sin and disobedience. In it was the blood of prophets and apostles. Still worse, it became a manifestation of Babylon the Great when it crucified the Lord of glory (11:8). The old city always involved more than the mere inhabitants and their daily lives. Jerusalem represented the covenantal community of God's people, the hope for the kingdom of God on earth. Thus the OT looked forward to a renewed Jerusalem, rebuilt and transformed into a glorious habitation of God and his people. But the prophets also saw something else. They saw a new heaven and new earth and a Jerusalem connected with this reality. Thus it is not altogether clear precisely what the relationship is between the old and the new—the earthly, restored Jerusalem of the prophets and the Jerusalem associated with the new heaven and earth, the Jerusalem called a heavenly Jerusalem in later Jewish thought (cf. Gal 4:25–31; Heb 11:10; 12:22; 13:14; see Rissi, *Future of the World*, 50).

The key to the puzzle must be understood with due respect for the old city. Any exegesis, therefore, that completely rejects any connection with the old city cannot take seriously the name "new" (*kainē*) Jerusalem, which presupposes the old. To speak of the heavenly Jerusalem does not deny an earthly city, as some suggest, but stresses its superiority to the older Jewish hope and affirms the eschatological nature of that hope (cf. *TDNT* 5:540–41)—a hope that could not be fulfilled by the earthly Jerusalem, a hope John now sees realized in the Holy City of the future. This city is the church in its future glorified existence. It is the final realization of the kingdom of God. The new Jerusalem may indeed be, as Robert Gundry proposes ("The New Jerusalem: People as Place, Not Place for People," *NovT* 29

[1987]: 254–264), a "narrative parable" not of the place where the saints will dwell but of the saints themselves and God's dwelling place in the saints.

3–4 God's dwelling (*skēnē*, GK *5008*) among his people is a fulfillment of Leviticus 26:11–13, a promise given to the old Jerusalem but forfeited because of apostasy. As a backdrop for the scene, consider Genesis 3, when humanity lost fellowship with God (cf. Ex 25:8; Eze 37:26–27). Thus the Holy Jerusalem is not only humanity's eternal home but the city where God will place his own name forever. God's presence will blot out the things of the former creation. In a touching metaphor of motherly love, John says that God "will wipe away every tear from their eyes" (cf. 7:17; cf. Isa 25:8). These tears have come from sin's distortion of God's purposes for humankind. They are produced by death and mourning for the dead, by crying and pain. An enemy has done this to the old order. Now God has defeated the enemy and liberated his people and his creation.

5 Now, for the second time in the book, God himself is the speaker (cf. 1:8). From his throne comes the assurance that the one who created the first heaven and earth will indeed make all things new (*panta kaina*, GK *4246, 2785*). This is a strong confirmation that God's power will be revealed and his redemptive purposes fulfilled. Since these words are, in truth, God's words (cf. 19:9; 22:6), it is of utmost importance that this vision of the new heaven and the new Jerusalem be proclaimed to the churches.

6 With the same word that declared the judgment of the world finished, God proclaims that he has completed his new creation: "It is done" (*gegonan*, GK *1181*; cf. 16:17). The names of God—"the Alpha and the Omega, the Beginning and the End"—emphasize his absolute control over the world and his creatorship of everything (cf. comments at 1:8; see 22:13).

To those who thirst for God, he offers the water of life without cost (cf. 7:17; 22:1, 17; Jn 7:37–39; Ro 3:24). Here salvation is beautifully depicted by the image of drinking at the spring of life. Twice in these last two chapters of Revelation, God offers an invitation to those who sense their need and are drawn toward him. John knows that the visions of God's glory among his people, which he is proclaiming as the Word of God, will create a thirst to participate in the reality of this glory. Nothing is required except to come and drink.

7 Those who come and drink and remain loyal to Christ as overcomers (*nikaō*, GK *3771*; see comments at 2:7, 11, etc.) will inherit all the new things of the city of God. They will be God's children, and he will be their Father. This is the essence of salvation—intimate, personal relationship with God himself, age upon age unending (cf. Jn 17:3). For John, this is really what the heavenly city is all about.

8 Before John shows us the city, however, he must first confront us with a choice. This choice must be made because there are two cities—the city of God, and the city of Babylon. Each has its inhabitants and its destiny. Those who drink from salvation's springs supplied by God himself are true followers of Christ. The "cowardly" (*deilos*, "fearful," GK *1264*) are those who fear persecution arising from faith in Christ. Not having steadfast endurance, they are devoid of faith (Mt 8:26; Mk 4:40; cf. Mt 13:20–21). Thus they are linked by John to the "unbelieving" and "vile" (a participial form of the verb *bdelyssomai*, "detest, abhor" [GK *1009*], which is used of idolatry [Ro 2:22]). They are called "murderers" because they are guilty of the death of the saints (17:6; 18:24). The "sexually immoral" (fornicators), practitioners of "magic arts, the idolaters and all liars" are those associated with idolatrous practices (cf. 9:21; 18:23; 21:27; 22:15; contrast 14:5). By their own choice, Babylon, not the new Jerusalem, is their eternal home (cf. Caird). Thus this passage is not a picture of universal salvation in spite of man's recalcitrance, though it contains a universal invitation for all who thirst to drink the water of life.

9 Beginning here and continuing through 22:5, the vision of the new Jerusalem introduced in vv.1–8 is fully described. (For reasons why this section does not describe the millennial kingdom of ch. 20, see comments at Overview, ch. 20.) Verses 9–14 focus on the description of the gates and the walls of the city. This is followed by the action of the angel who measures the city and John's precise mention of the precious stones in the twelve foundations (vv.15–21). Finally, he describes various aspects of the life of the city (21:22–22:5).

9–10 Here the parallelism with 17:1 is clearly deliberate. The bride, the wife of the Lamb, contrasts with the great prostitute. As the prostitute was found to be John's archetypal image for the great system of satanic evil, so the bride is the true counterpart. She is pure and faithful to God and the Lamb, whereas the prostitute is a mockery. To see the prostitute, John was taken to the desert, but now he is elevated by the Spirit to the highest pinnacle of the earth to witness the exalted new Jerusalem (cf. comments at 1:10; 4:2; 17:3). As his vision will be a reinterpretation of Ezekiel's temple prophecy (Eze 40–48), like the former prophet he is taken to a high mountain (Eze 40:2). For the moment, the author drops the bridal metaphor and in magnificent imagery describes the church in glory as a city with a lofty wall, splendid gates, and jeweled foundations. There is no warrant for thinking of the city as descending like a space platform to the mountain or as hovering over the earth, as some suggest (see comments at v.2).

11 In John's description of the city, precious stones, brilliant colors, and the effulgence of light abound. The problem of the literalness of the city has received much attention. If the city is the bride and the bride is the glorified community of God's people in their eternal life, there is little question that John's descriptions are primarily symbolic of that glorified life. This in no way diminishes the reality behind the imagery. In the most suitable language available to John—much of it drawn from the OT—he shows us something of the reality of the eschatological kingdom of God in its glorified existence.

Its appearance is all glorious, "with the glory of God" (cf. Eze 43:4). The city has a "brilliance" (*phōstēr*, "light-bearer," GK *5891*), given it by God's presence, that appears as crystal-clear jasper (cf. Isa 60:1–2, 19; Rev 21:23). Jasper (*iaspis*, GK *2618*) is mentioned three times in ch. 21 (vv.11, 18–19); earlier in Revelation it refers to the appearance of God (4:3). Jasper is an opaque quartz mineral that occurs in various colors—commonly red, brown, green, and yellow; rarely blue and black, and seldom white. Some suggest it may be an opal (so BDAG, 465); others believe it to be a diamond, which is not quartz but a crystalline carbon. Ford, 335, citing a source who said the stone changes color "even as Benjamin's feelings toward his brothers changed," thinks that the rare and valuable white color is referred to here. Actually, there is no basis for certainty about it.

12–13 The wall is very high, its height symbolizing both the greatness of this city and its impregnability against those described in 21:8, 27. The twelve gates are distributed three on each of the four walls. These may be like the triple gates that can now be seen in the excavated wall of the old Jerusalem. John later describes the gates as single pearls (v.21). What impresses him at this point about the gates is their angelic guards and the inscribed names of the twelve tribes of Israel. The presence of angels proclaims that this is God's city, while the twelve tribes emphasize the complete election of God (cf. comments at 7:4). Here there seems to be a deliberate allusion to Ezekiel's eschatological

Jerusalem on whose gates the names of the twelve tribes appear (Eze 48:30–34). Ezekiel 48:35 says, "The name of the city from that time on will be: THE LORD IS THERE" (cf. Rev 21:3; 22:3–4).

14 Like the gates, the twelve foundations of the wall have twelve names written on them—in this case, the names of the twelve apostles of the Lamb. Foundations of ancient cities usually consisted of extensions down to bedrock of the rows of huge stones that made up the wall. Jerusalem's first-century walls and foundation stones have been excavated in recent years. Huge stones—some of which are about five feet wide, four feet high, and thirty feet long, weighing eighty to one hundred tons each and going down some fourteen to nineteen layers below the present ground level—have been found.

In vv.19–21, John turns to the precious stones that make up the foundations. Here, however, he stresses the names of the twelve apostles. Theologically, it is significant that he brings together the twelve tribes and the twelve apostles of the Lamb and yet differentiates them. This is not unlike what Matthew and Luke tell us that Jesus said (Mt 19:28; Lk 22:30). The earlier symbolic use of twelve (see comments at 7:4), representing in Revelation completeness, implies that it is unnecessary for us to know precisely which twelve will be there. Judas fell and was replaced by Matthias (Ac 1:21–26), but Paul also was a prominent apostle. Furthermore, the number "twelve" is sometimes used to refer to the elect *group* when all twelve are not in view. (Jn 20:24 has ten; 1Co 15:5 has eleven; cf. Lk 9:12.) The group of apostles represents the church, the elect community built on the foundation of the gospel of Jesus Christ, the slain Lamb. The dual election here depicted admittedly entails some difficulty in identifying the twelve tribes in 7:4–8 with the church, as this writer and other commentators have done (see comments at 7:4, 5–8). Thus some commentators have insisted

that "twelve tribes" refers to an eschatological purpose for the elect Jewish people (so Rissi, *Future of the World*, 73; Walvoord, 322–23; Thomas, 464–65; Osborne, 751–52). It is a puzzling problem.

15–17 The angel measures the city with a golden measuring rod. (The significance of measuring was discussed at 11:1.) The act of measuring signifies securing something for blessing so as to preserve it from spiritual harm or defilement. Ezekiel's elaborate description of the future temple and its measuring was to show the glory and holiness of God in Israel's midst (Eze 43:12). The measuring reveals the perfection, fulfillment, or completion of all God's purposes for his elect bride. Thus the city is revealed as a perfect cube of twelve thousand stadia (12 x 1,000 [about 1,400 miles]). The wall is 144 cubits (about 200 feet) thick (12 x 12). These dimensions should not be interpreted as providing architectural information about the city; rather, we should think of them as theologically symbolic of the fulfillment of all God's promises. The new Jerusalem symbolizes the paradox of the completeness of infinity in God. The cube reminds us of the dimensions of the Most Holy Place in the tabernacle (10 x 10 cubits [15 x 15 feet]) and in the temple (20 x 20 cubits [30 x 30 feet]). John adds that the measurement was both human and angelic (divine): "by man's measurement, which the angel was using." This statement is not unimportant. In some sense, it shows that both the human and the divine will intersect in the Holy City. Others take v.17 to be John's way of making the reader realize the "disparity" between the city and the size of the wall, thus forcing us to seek a deeper meaning in the angel's measurements (so Kiddle).

18–21 In these verses, John describes in more detail the priceless materials of which the city, with its foundations and gates, is made (cf. Isa 54:11–15). The symbolism is not meant to give the impression of wealth and luxury but to point to the glory and holiness of God. The wall of jasper points to the glory of God (4:2–3; see comments at 21:11), while the fabric of the city is pure gold—as clear as glass (v.21). Such imagery portrays the purity of the bride and her splendor in mirroring the glory of God (cf. Eph 5:27).

19–20 The foundation stones are made of twelve precious stones. Here the imagery may reflect three possible sources: (1) the high priest's breastplate (Ex 28:17–20); (2) the jewels on the dress of the king of Tyre (Eze 28:13); or (3) the signs of the zodiac. The second one, though referring to only nine stones, suggests the splendor of ancient royalty and might be appropriate as a symbol for the glorious kingdom reign in the Holy City. Yet, regardless of how one feels about the way some have identified the king of Tyre (Eze 28:11–19) with Satan (cf. Feinberg, A. C. Gaebelein, New Scofield Reference Bible), there is something inappropriate about taking this pagan king as symbolic of the future kingdom. Swete and Ford prefer the first option—that of the high priest's breastplate. But while the twelve stones are perhaps the same, the order of their mention is different. This leaves the third option. According to Philo and Josephus, Israel associated these same stones with the signs of the zodiac, and their tribal standards each bore a sign of the zodiac (cf. Caird, 276). If we begin with Judah, the tribe of Christ (Rev 7:5), the sign is Aries, the ram, which has the amethyst as its stone. The last sign is Pisces, the fish, which has jasper as its stone (cf. Charles, 2:167). So the first zodiacal sign agrees with the twelfth foundation, and the last zodiacal sign with the first foundation. In fact, the whole list agrees with John's, though in reverse order. This may be a significant device to show John's disapproval of pagan cults. But these matters are uncertain.

21 The gates are twelve great pearls. Though pearls are not mentioned in the OT, some rabbinic texts refer to gates for Jerusalem hewn out of jewels about forty-five feet square (*b. Sanh.* 100*a*).

As for the one main street of the Holy City, it is like the fabric of the city itself—of pure gold, clear as glass (see comments at v.18).

22 John turns from this beautiful description of the city to the life within it. In antiquity, every notable city had at least one central temple. The new Jerusalem not only differs in this respect from ancient cities but also from all Jewish speculation about the age to come. Illuminated by the overflowing radiance of the presence of the glory of God, the Holy City no longer needs a temple (*naos*, GK *3724*). Yet paradoxically it has a temple, for the Lord God Almighty and the Lamb are its temple. And in another sense, the whole city is a temple, since it is patterned after the Most Holy Place (v.16). Jewish expectation was centered on a rebuilt temple and the restoration of the ark of the covenant. In his glorious vision, John sees the fulfillment of these hopes in the total presence of God with his purified people, while the Lamb, the sign of the new covenant, is the fulfillment of the restoration of the ark of the covenant (see comments at 11:19; cf. Jn 4:21, 23). As long as there is uncleanness in the world, there is need for a temple where God's presence and truth are in contrast to the uncleanness. But in the new city, no such symbol is needed any longer.

23 In fulfillment of Isaiah 60:19–20, there will be no further need, as in ancient temples, for any natural or artificial lighting because the glory of God will dim the most powerful earthly light into paleness (cf. Zec 14:7). In the earthly tabernacle and temple, there was, to be sure, artificial lighting (the seven-branched lampstand in the OT tabernacle and the temple); yet the Most Holy Place had no such lighting because of the *shekinah*, the light of God's own presence.

24 Here we see a remarkable picture of "the nations" and "the kings of the earth" entering the city and bringing into it their splendor (*doxa*, "glory, honor, magnificence," GK *1518*). John sees a vision of social life bustling with activity. Elsewhere in Revelation, the nations (*ethnē*, GK *1620*) are the pagan, rebellious peoples of the world who trample the Holy City (cf. comments at 11:2; 11:18), who have become drunk with the wine of Babylon, the mother of prostitutes (18:3, 23), and who will also be destroyed at the second coming of Christ (19:15). The same description applies to the kings of the earth. But there is another use of these terms in Revelation. They stand for the peoples of earth who are the servants of Christ, the redeemed nations who follow the Lamb and have resisted the beast and Babylon (1:5; 2:26; 5:9; 7:9; 12:5; 15:3; 19:16). It is this latter group that John describes figuratively as having part in the activity in the Holy City, the kingdom of God. What this may involve regarding the relation of this life to the future kingdom is not stated.

25−26 Life in the age to come will certainly involve continuing activities and relationships that will contribute to the glory of the Holy City throughout eternity. Instead of the nations bringing their precious possessions to Babylon, the harlot city, the redeemed nations will bring these offerings to the throne of God (cf. Isa 60:3−7). So certain is its perpetual light and security that the gates will never be shut for fear of evil by night (cf. Isa 60:11). This imagery should not, however, be allegorized as indicating some sort of perpetual invitation to salvation.

27 One thing is absolutely certain: "Nothing impure" (*koinos*, "common, profane," GK *3123*) will ever enter the city's gates. By *koinos* John means ceremonial impurity (cf. comments at v.8; 22:15). No idolatrous person may enter. Only those can enter whose names are in "the Lamb's book of life" and who thus belong to him through redemption (cf. 3:5; 20:12, 15). This should not be taken as implying that in the new Jerusalem there will still be unsaved people roaming around outside the city who may now and then enter it by repenting (contra Caird). Instead, the exhortation warns present readers that the only way to participate in the future city is to turn one's total loyalties to the Lamb now (cf. v.7).

NOTES

16, 21 Many see a possible allusion to ancient Babylon, which was described in antiquity in language similar to John's. According to Herodotus, Babylon was foursquare, magnificent beyond all other cities. As John does in Revelation, Herodotus (*Hist.* 1.178) gives the dimensions of the city in stadia and those of the wall in royal cubits. Ancient Babylon also had a great street down its center. While these allusions are no more than hypothetical, the similarities are striking.

19−21 Glasson, 118, argues that the jewels fulfill the allusion to Isaiah 54:11−12, which in turn is based on the high priestly breastplate. The city itself is as sacred as the Most Holy Place, and all the inhabitants are named priests of the Lord (Isa 61:6; cf. Rev 1:6; see also Glasson, "The Order of Jewels in Revelation 21:19−20: A Theory Eliminated," *JTS* 26 [1975]: 95−99).

B. The River of Life and the Tree of Life (22:1−5)

OVERVIEW

This section continues the description of the Holy City begun in 21:9 but now with the emphasis on its inner life. John returns to his archetypal images from Genesis (Ge 1–3) and Ezekiel (Eze 40–48). The paradisiacal quality of the future age is briefly but beautifully described. Here Paradise is regained. As in the OT imagery of the age to come, metaphors of water and light abound (cf. Isa 12:3; Zec 14:7–8). The river of the water of life recalls Ezekiel 47:1–12 (cf. Joel 3:18) and the pastoral scene of Revelation 7:17. In both Testaments, water is frequently associated with the salvation of God and the life-imparting and cleansing ministry of the Holy Spirit (Isa 44:3; cf. Jn 3:5; 4:13–14; 7:37–39; 13:10; 19:34; Tit 3:5).

> [1]Then the angel showed me the river of the water of life, as clear as crystal, flowing from the throne of God and of the Lamb [2]down the middle of the great street of the city. On each side of the river stood the tree of life, bearing twelve crops of fruit, yielding its fruit every month. And the leaves of the tree are for the healing of the nations. [3]No longer will there be any curse. The throne of God and of the Lamb will be in the city, and his servants will serve him. [4]They will see his face, and his name will be on their foreheads. [5]There will be no more night. They will not need the light of a lamp or the light of the sun, for the Lord God will give them light. And they will reign for ever and ever.

1 In the new city of God the pure water does not issue from the temple as in Ezekiel but comes from the throne of God, since this whole city is a Most Holy Place with God at its center. Life from God streams unceasingly through the new world.

The scene brings to mind the old hymn by Robert Lowry (1864): "Shall we gather at the river, / Where bright angel feet have trod; / With its crystal tide forever / Flowing by the throne of God?"

2 The tree of life spreads all along the great street of the city. What was once forfeited by our forebears in Eden and denied to their succeeding posterity is now fully restored (cf. Ge 3:22–24). In Ezekiel's vision, these are multiple trees on each side of the river that bear fruit monthly and whose leaves are for healing (Eze 47:12); therefore, the tree (*xylon*, GK *3833*) John speaks of may be a collective word for Ezekiel's trees. So abundant is its vitality that it bears a crop of fruit each month. Its leaves produce healing for the nations. The imagery of abundant fruit and medicinal leaves should be understood as symbolic of the far-reaching effects of the death of Christ in the redeemed community of the Holy City. So powerful is the salvation of God that the effects of sin are completely overcome. The eternal life God gives to the redeemed community will be perpetually available, sustain the well-being of every believer, and cure eternally the memory of every former sin.

3 Thus the curse pronounced in Eden will be removed (cf. Ge 3:17). This may mean, according to Swete, that no one who is cursed because of idolatry will be in the city (v.15). Instead of Babylon and its servants occupying the earth, the throne of God will be central, and his servants will serve him (cf. 2:13). Wherever the throne is in sight, the priestly service of the saints will be perpetual (cf. 1:6). Here our true liturgy is fulfilled (cf. Ro 12:1). Observe John's emphasis on God and the Lamb (21:22–23; 22:1, 3): they share the same glory, the same throne, the same temple significance. The Christology of John's vision is everywhere evident even though stated in functional terms.

4 With no restrictions such as those that pertain to Moses (Ex 33:20, 23) or the high priests (Heb 9:7), the redeemed community will be in Christ's presence perpetually, beholding his glory (cf. Ps 17:15; Mt 5:8; 1Co 13:12; 2Co 3:18; 1Jn 3:2). Eternal life is perfect communion, worship, the vision of God, light, and victory. Since God and the Lamb are always viewed together, there is no point in saying that the redeemed will see Jesus but not the Father. (Concerning the name on their foreheads, see comments at 14:1.)

5 A final burst of light engulfs the whole scene, and an announcement that the saints will reign for ever and ever fulfills the first promise of the book (1:6; cf. 5:10; 20:4–6; see esp. 11:15). The logical sequence and the inner relationship of the words "his servants will serve" (v.3) and "they will reign" (v.5) have deep implications for the whole nature of God's kingdom in contrast to that of the satanic Babylon. Surely it is fitting for such a book of prophecy as Revelation to close around the throne, with God's servants both worshiping and ruling.

VI. CONCLUSION (22:6–21)

OVERVIEW

With consummate art, the notes of the introit (1:1–8) are sounded again in the conclusion. So the book ends with the voices of the angel, Jesus, the Spirit, the bride, and finally John (v.20). The book is a seamless garment. There are three major emphases in the conclusion: (1) confirmation of the genuineness of the prophecy (vv.6–7, 16, 18–19); (2) the imminence of Jesus' coming (vv.7, 12, 20); and (3) the warning against idolatry and the invitation to enter the city (vv.11–12, 15, 17–19).

> [6]The angel said to me, "These words are trustworthy and true. The Lord, the God of the spirits of the prophets, sent his angel to show his servants the things that must soon take place."
>
> [7]"Behold, I am coming soon! Blessed is he who keeps the words of the prophecy in this book."
>
> [8]I, John, am the one who heard and saw these things. And when I had heard and seen them, I fell down to worship at the feet of the angel who had been showing them to me. [9]But he said to me, "Do not do it! I am a fellow servant with you and with your brothers the prophets and of all who keep the words of this book. Worship God!"
>
> [10]Then he told me, "Do not seal up the words of the prophecy of this book, because the time is near. [11]Let him who does wrong continue to do wrong; let him who is vile continue to be vile; let him who does right continue to do right; and let him who is holy continue to be holy."
>
> [12]"Behold, I am coming soon! My reward is with me, and I will give to everyone according to what he has done. [13]I am the Alpha and the Omega, the First and the Last, the Beginning and the End.

¹⁴"Blessed are those who wash their robes, that they may have the right to the tree of life and may go through the gates into the city. ¹⁵Outside are the dogs, those who practice magic arts, the sexually immoral, the murderers, the idolaters and everyone who loves and practices falsehood.

¹⁶"I, Jesus, have sent my angel to give you this testimony for the churches. I am the Root and the Offspring of David, and the bright Morning Star."

¹⁷The Spirit and the bride say, "Come!" And let him who hears say, "Come!" Whoever is thirsty, let him come; and whoever wishes, let him take the free gift of the water of life.

¹⁸I warn everyone who hears the words of the prophecy of this book: If anyone adds anything to them, God will add to him the plagues described in this book. ¹⁹And if anyone takes words away from this book of prophecy, God will take away from him his share in the tree of life and in the holy city, which are described in this book.

²⁰He who testifies to these things says, "Yes, I am coming soon."

Amen. Come, Lord Jesus.

²¹The grace of the Lord Jesus be with God's people. Amen.

COMMENTARY

6 Words of assurance, like those in 19:9 and 21:5, provide the transition from the glorious vision of the Holy City to the final words of the book. An angel declares that it is "the Lord, the God of the spirits of the prophets," the one from whom the prophets such as John receive their messages, that assures the readers of the speedy fulfillment of all that has been revealed (cf. 1:1; 10:6–7). John has been the recipient of divine prophecy that will have its immediate consequences (cf. v.10).

7 This first declaration of the imminent coming of Jesus is his own response to the yearnings of the church (cf. comments at 1:7; 2:25; esp. 3:11). It is the sixth beatitude in Revelation, and like the first one (1:3) it is directed toward those who keep (obey) the words of the prophecy (cf. vv.18–19).

8–9 The "I, John" is reminiscent of 1:4, 9. His confession that he "heard and saw these things" and the repetition of the prohibition (19:10) against John's worshiping of the angel serve a purpose. No believer, not even one of great spiritual stature such as John's, is beyond the subtle temptation to worship what is good itself in place of God, who alone is to be worshiped.

10–11 These verses stand in contrast to the command given to Daniel to seal up his book (Da 8:26; 12:4, 9–10) and in contrast to Jewish apocalypses in general. Could this signal the fulfillment of Daniel's sealed book? John's message cannot be concealed because the contents of the vision are needed immediately by the churches. (On the sealing metaphor, see comments at 7:3.) Verse 11 appears at first reading to be fatalistic. Yet, on further reflection, the exhortation stresses the imminency of the return of Jesus and the necessity for immediate choices. It echoes the aphorism "as now, so always." Far from being an encouragement to remain apathetic, it is evangelistic in spirit. It may also allude to the great ordeal John viewed as imminent. For the unfaithful and wicked, this appeal would be a deep confirmation of their choice; for the faithful, it would alert them to the necessity of guarding themselves against apostasy (cf. Jude 20–21). There is no reason to take this passage as teaching the irreversibility of human choices (contra Swete). Repentance is always a real option as long as a person is living. After death, however, there remains only judgment, not opportunity to repent (Heb 9:27).

12–13 This second of three announcements of the imminent return of Jesus in this chapter (cf. vv. 7, 20) is associated with the truth of rewards and judgment based on deeds (cf. comments at 20:12; also 11:18). On the terms "Alpha" and "Omega," etc., see comments at 1:8, 17.

14 The seventh and last beatitude in Revelation is evangelistic in emphasis (cf. 21:6; 22:11, 17). Strands of the earlier imagery are blended in it. In 7:14, the washing of the robes indicates willing identification with Jesus in his death. It also carries the thought of martyrdom during the great ordeal for the saints (cf. 6:11). Thus it symbolizes a salvation that involves obedience and discipleship, since it is integrally related to the salvation imagery of the tree of life (cf. comments at 22:2) and the gates of the city (cf. 21:25).

15 John has already made it clear that no idolaters can ever enter the city but only those whose names are in the Lamb's book of life (cf. comments at 21:8, 27). Outside the city are "the dogs"—those who practice magical arts, etc.—i.e., those who rebel against the rule of God (cf. Dt 23:18, where a dog signifies a male prostitute; Mt 15:26, where "dogs" refers to Gentiles; Php 3:2–3, where "dogs" refers to the Judaizers). There is no doubt that such people will not be admitted through the gates of the Holy City; they will be in the lake of fire (20:15). But the problem involves what appears to be their present exclusion from the city at the time of John's writing. Are they "outside" now? As has been previously argued in this commentary, the city is future and is not to be identified with the present historical church (see Overview, ch. 21; comments at

21:2). Only in an eschatological sense can it be maintained that the new city exists in the present.

On the other hand, it is not necessary to place the time of v. 15 in the present (contra Caird). There is no verb in the Greek text of the verse, so the time of the action is determined by the context. Since the fulfillment of v. 14 lies in the future, the time of v. 15 is also most naturally future. The word "outside" is simply a figure that agrees with the whole imagery of the Holy City. It means exclusion. To be outside the city means to be in the lake of fire. Thus it is not necessary either to place the Holy City in the present or to place it in a millennial Jerusalem. The Holy City, as we have previously argued, is a symbol for the future realization of the corporate community of God's people (i.e., the eschatological kingdom of God), and as such it does not have a geographical location apart from its being on the new earth.

16 As in 1:8, 17–20, Christ addresses John and the churches directly. The "you" is plural in the Greek text. Christ's words here authenticate the whole book of Revelation ("this testimony") as being a message to the churches. Therefore, any method of interpreting Revelation that blunts the application of this message in its entirety to the present church must disregard these words of Christ. He is the Messiah of Israel, "the Root and the Offspring of David" (cf. Isa 11:1; see comments at Rev 5:5) and the fulfillment of the promise to the overcomers at Thyatira (see comments at 2:28).

17 The first two sentences in this verse are not an evangelistic appeal but express the yearning of the Holy Spirit and the "bride" (the whole church; cf. 21:9) for the return of Christ. In v. 20, John gives us the Lord Jesus' answer: "Yes, I am coming soon." Those who hear ("him who hears")—the members of the local congregations in John's time—join in the invitation for Christ to return. Then, any in the congregations who are not yet followers of

Jesus are invited to come and take the water of life as a free gift (*dōrean*, "freely," GK *1562*; cf. 21:6; Ro 3:24). On the water of life, cf. 21:6; 22:1; also, for the liturgical and eucharistic use of this verse, see comments at v.20.

18–19 These verses should not be taken as a warning against adding anything to the Bible. Early interpreters understood them as a warning to false prophets not to alter the sense of John's prophecy— i.e., Revelation (so Irenaeus, *Haer.* 30.2). Meredith Kline (*Treaty of the Great King* [Grand Rapids: Eerdmans, 1963], 44) has likened the force of these words to the curses pronounced for disobedience in the covenantal law codes of the OT period (cf. Dt 4:2; 12:32). Verses 18–19 are a strong warning against any who would tamper with the contents of "this book" (Revelation), either textually or in its moral and theological teaching (cf. 1Co 16:22). So severe is the danger he is warning against that John says that those who teach contrary to the message of Revelation will not only forfeit any right to salvation in the Holy City but will have visited on them the divine judgments (plagues) inflicted on the beast-worshipers.

20 This is the third affirmation in ch. 22 of Jesus' imminent return and perhaps the response to the longing cry in v.17. John responds to the Lord Jesus' declaration by saying, "Amen. Come, Lord Jesus." These fervent words are part of the liturgy of the early church. They were a prayer used at the close of the meal in the eucharistic liturgy (*Did.* 10.6). Cullmann (*Early Christian Worship*, 13–14) believes that these words are the earliest expression of the recognition that the Lord's Day (Sunday) is the day of the resurrection. As Jesus appeared to his disciples alive on the first day of the week, so he was expected to be present in the Spirit at every first-day eucharistic celebration and to appear again at the end, which is often represented by the picture of a messianic meal. The expression "come, Lord Jesus" (*erchou, kyrie Iēsou*) is equivalent to the Aramaic *marana atah* (Gk. *marana tha*; cf. 1Co 16:22, "come, O Lord" [NIV]). So in closing Revelation, John alludes to ch. 1, with its reference to the Lord's Day (1:10).

21 A conclusion such as this, while quite unsuitable for a Jewish apocalypse, is wholly appropriate for this Christian prophetic message addressed to the ancient church and indeed to the whole church of all times. The benediction is reminiscent of Paul's usual practice (cf. the final verses of Romans, 1 Thessalonians, Colossians, et al.). Whether in this benediction we should accept the textual reading "with all" (so Metzger [1971 ed.], 768–69) or "with all the saints" (so Swete, various MSS) cannot be completely settled. We may, however, agree that nothing less than God's grace is required for us to be overcomers and to triumphantly enter the Holy City of God, where we shall reign with him for ever and ever.

NOTES

14 Here most of the better textual witnesses read πλύνοντες τὰς στολὰς αὐτῶν, *plynontes tas stolas autōn* ("wash their garments"). Following a number of later minuscule MSS, the KJV follows the reading ποιοῦντες τὰς ἐντολὰς αὐτοῦ, *poiountes tas entolas autou* ("those who do his commands"). The former reading is preferred.

19 While only one or two late Greek MSS have βίβλιον τῆς ζωῆς, *biblion tēs zoēs* ("book of life"), instead of ζύλον τῆς ζωῆς, *zylon tēs zoēs* ("tree of life"), the KJV curiously follows this inferior reading, probably because of its presence in the Latin Vulgate.

Share Your Thoughts

With the Author: Your comments will be forwarded to the author when you send them to *zauthor@zondervan.com*.

With Zondervan: Submit your review of this book by writing to *zreview@zondervan.com*.

Free Online Resources at
www.zondervan.com

Zondervan AuthorTracker: Be notified whenever your favorite authors publish new books, go on tour, or post an update about what's happening in their lives at www.zondervan.com/authortracker.

Daily Bible Verses and Devotions: Enrich your life with daily Bible verses or devotions that help you start every morning focused on God. Visit www.zondervan.com/newsletters.

Free Email Publications: Sign up for newsletters on Christian living, academic resources, church ministry, fiction, children's resources, and more. Visit www.zondervan.com/newsletters.

Zondervan Bible Search: Find and compare Bible passages in a variety of translations at www.zondervanbiblesearch.com.

Other Benefits: Register yourself to receive online benefits like coupons and special offers, or to participate in research.

ZONDERVAN.com/